EIGHTH EDITION

A Short History of Western Civilization

RICHARD E. SULLIVAN
Michigan State University

DENNIS SHERMAN
John Jay College of Criminal Justice
City University of New York

JOHN B. HARRISON
Late Professor Emeritus of History
Michigan State University

McGraw-Hill, Inc.

New York   St. Louis   San Francisco   Auckland   Bogotá
Caracas   Lisbon   London   Madrid   Mexico City   Milan
Montreal   New Delhi   San Juan   Singapore   Sydney   Tokyo   Toronto

to Mary, Vivian, and Pat

The present overwhelms our forgotten selves;
but we are what we were,
with only a frosting of changes
—D.S.

A Short History of Western Civilization

Copyright © 1994, 1990, 1985, 1980, 1975, 1971 by McGraw-Hill, Inc. All rights reserved. Copyright © 1966, 1960 by John B. Harrison and Richard E. Sullivan. All rights reserved. Printed in the United States of America. Except as permitted under the United States Copyright Act of 1976, no part of this publication may be reproduced or distributed in any form or by any means, or stored in a data base or retrieval system, without the prior written permission of the publisher.

This book is printed on recycled, acid-free paper containing a minimum of 50% total recycled fiber with 10% postconsumer de-inked fiber.

2 3 4 5 6 7 8 9 0   DOH DOH   9 0 9 8 7 6 5 4

ISBN 0-07-026897-5

This book was set in Palatino by Ruttle, Shaw & Wetherill, Inc.
The editors were Pamela Gordon and Larry Goldberg;
the production supervisor was Richard A. Ausburn.
The cover was designed by Katherine Hulse.
The photo researcher was Elsa Peterson.
R. R. Donnelley & Sons Company was printer and binder.

Credits
COVER: Diego Velázquez, ''The Spinners,'' 1599–1600, © Museo del Prado, Madrid. All rights reserved. *PART OPENING PHOTOS: Part One,* Ralph Mandol/DPI; *Part Two,* National Archaeological Museum, Athens; *Part Three,* Phototheque Armand-Colin; *Part Four,* The Pierpont Morgan Library, New York. M.705, f.38v.; *Part Five,* The Granger Collection; *Part Six,* The Granger Collection; *Part Seven,* NASA. *MAPS: Map 40.1:* From *Civilizations of the West: The Human Adventure* by Richard L. Greaves, Robert Zaller, and Jennifer Tolbert Roberts. Copyright © 1992 by HarperCollins Publishers. Reprinted by permission. *Map 59.1, left:* From Perry, Marvin, Myrna Chase, James R. Jacob, Margaret C. Jacob, and Theodore H. Von Laue, *Western Civilization: Ideas, Politics and Society,* Fourth Edition. Copyright © 1992 by Houghton Mifflin Company. Used with permission. *Map 59.1, top right:* Copyright Carto Ltd. Used by permission of Carpress International Press Agency, Brussels. *Map 59.3:* From *Facts On File.* Copyright © 1992 by Facts On File. Reprinted with permission by Facts On File, Inc., New York.

Library of Congress Cataloging-in-Publication Data

Sullivan, Richard Eugene, (date).
    A short history of Western civilization / Richard E. Sullivan,
Dennis Sherman, John B. Harrison.—8th ed.
     p.   cm.
    Harrison's name appears first on previous editions.
    Includes bibliographical references and index.
    ISBN 0-07-026897-5
    1. Civilization, Western—History.   I. Sherman, Dennis.
II. Harrison, John Baugham.   III. Title.
CB245.S9415   1994
909'.09821-dc20   93-14409

ABOUT THE AUTHORS

Richard E. Sullivan was born and raised near Doniphan, Nebraska. He received a B. A. degree from the University of Nebraska in 1942, and an M.A. degree and a Ph.D. degree from the University of Illinois in 1947 and 1949 respectively. His doctorate was earned in the field of medieval history. He has taught history at Northeast Missouri State Teachers' College (1949–1954) and at Michigan State University (1954 until his retirement in 1989). While at Michigan State University he has served as chairman of the Department of History (1967–1970), Dean of the College of Arts and Letters (1970–1979), and Associate Provost (1984–1987). Professor Sullivan held a Fulbright Research Fellowship and a John Simon Guggenheim Fellowship to Belgium in 1961–1962. He is a Fellow in the Medieval Academy of America. He is the author of *The Coronation of Charlemagne* (1959), *Heirs of the Roman Empire* (1960); *Aix-La-Chapelle in the Age of Charlemagne* (1963), *Speaking for Clio* (1991), and *Christian Missionary Activity in the Early Middle Ages* (forthcoming). His articles have appeared in many scholarly journals.

Dennis Sherman is Professor of History at John Jay College of Criminal Justice, the City University of New York. He received his B.A. (1962) and J.D. (1965) from the University of California at Berkeley and his Ph.D. (1970) from the University of Michigan. He was Visiting Professor at the University of Paris (1978–1979, and 1985). He received the Ford Foundation Prize Fellowship (1968–1969, 1969–1970), a fellowship from the Council for Research on Economic History (1971–1972), and fellowships from the National Endowment for the Humanities (1973–1976). His publications include *Western Civilization: Images and Interpretations* (1991), *World Civilizations: Sources, Images, and Interpretations* (co-author), a series of introductions in the Garland Library of War and Peace, several articles and reviews on nineteenth-century French economic and social history in American and European journals, and short fiction in literary journals.

John B. Harrison was born in Lawrenceville, Virginia, and grew up in Rich Square, North Carolina. He received his B.A. and M.A. at the University of North Carolina, and his Ph.D. at the University of Wisconsin. He also studied at the Sorbonne. He taught history at Lees Junior College, Jackson, Kentucky, the University of Wisconsin extension, Ohio Northern University, and Michigan State University, where he was Professor Emeritus of History. He was Visiting Professor at the University of North Carolina, 1963–1964. Professor Harrison was a member of the American Historical Association and the Society for French Historical Studies. During seven trips to Europe he visited twenty-one countries. He had also traveled in the Far and the Middle East, Africa, and Latin America. He is the author of *This Age of Global Strife* (1952), and of a number of articles and book reviews.

CONTENTS

PREFACE

[Publisher's Note: In order to provide an alternative to the hardcover edition, A Short History of Western Civilization *is being made available in a three-volume paperbound edition. Volume One includes Chapters 1–36; Volume Two, Chapters 31–59; and Renaissance to the Present volume, Chapters 25–59. The page numbering and cross-references in these chapters remain the same as in the hardcover text.]*

In this eighth edition of *A Short History of Western Civilization,* we have attempted to achieve the right mix of continuity and change. Those features that made the seventh and previous editions so successful have been retained. We have kept our account brief enough so it offers readers a realistic opportunity to absorb a meaningful overview of the essentials of the history of Western civilization. The scope of the book is not limited to European history; brief treatments of other parts of the world, such as the United States, and non-Western civilizations as they have come to interact with the Western world, are included to put Western civilization into a broader context. Introductory and retrospective essays at the beginning and end of each of the units of the book provide a broad summarizing perspective on major historical eras. Primary documents introduce readers to the sources historians use to investigate a subject. The interpretative essays featuring points on which historians disagree are designed to encourage readers to develop a healthy skepticism toward accepted generalizations about the past and to learn to ask questions about the meaning of historical investigation. The large number of maps and illustrations highlights and complements the written text. The suggested reading lists offer alternatives for deeper study of topics. The student and instructor's guides are available to assist in making full use of this book.

Several important changes have been made in this edition to improve the quality and appeal of the book. There has been an additional infusion of social history and women's history into the text, continuing the changes already made in this direction in the seventh and sixth editions. The addition of this material reflects a growing consensus in modern scholarship that such matters need greater attention in order to portray past human experience fully and accurately. Several parts of the book have been reorganized to better integrate our understanding of the past. There have been extensive revisions of the text to include the most recent historical scholarship, and in some cases new sections have been written. A number of illustrations are new to this edition. Most of the maps have been revised and clarified. Seven "Historians' Sources" sections have been created for this edition, providing a balance to the "Where Historians Disagree" essays and the introductory "History and the Historian" essay. A new chapter covering the extraordinarily important developments of the past few years has been written. The suggested readings have been completely revised and updated.

As in previous editions, our goal is to produce a high-quality, clearly written, useful, and flexible account of Western civilization. We are indebted to numerous teachers and students who have aided us in this effort. We hope this book can serve as the basis for an effective survey of the history of Western civilization, a subject that remains essential for any understanding of who we are and what of significance is happening in the present.

We would like to thank the following reviewers: Janet Cornelius, Danville Area Community College; Kenneth E. Cutler, Indiana University; John C. Moore, Hofstra University; James Parry, Seattle University; and Carl Pohlhammer, Monterey Peninsula College.

RICHARD E. SULLIVAN
DENNIS SHERMAN

HISTORY AND THE HISTORIAN

This book seeks to expand and enrich our readers' connections with the past. Before each of you becomes engaged in that adventure, we ask you to reflect for a moment on some of the challenges involved in discovering, understanding, and retelling what has already happened.

Why should we turn our faces from the present and the future to explore what has already happened? Despite the inclination of many in our time to take seriously Henry Ford's pronouncement that "History is bunk," most of us find looking backward irresistible, as did our forebears. Many have found and still find the past inherently interesting, chiefly because a venture into that realm offers us an opportunity to relive in our minds all kinds of experiences otherwise closed to us by limitations imposed by the cultural environment in which we live. Others have been and still are convinced that learning about the past has an important social function. It can inform us about who and what we are as human beings. It can shed light on contemporary conditions, either by providing an understanding of how things came to be what they are or by supplying analogies that help us to comprehend our situation and formulate solutions to issues that face our society. Societies have especially prized history as an instrument for socializing their members (particularly their young), that is, for teaching them how and how not to behave and to think in ways that are appropriate to the cultural milieu in which they find themselves. As you begin your venture into the past, we urge each of you to reflect on why you are making the journey. Whatever your answer, it will make a difference in what you find and how you interpret your discoveries.

Also, we urge each of you to be mindful that the past is a unique territory. It involves an infinite number of "happenings," each of which is finished and therefore cannot be experienced directly. We can gain access to these already completed events only by reconstructing them in our minds and putting those constructs into words.

Thus, there is always a distance between what actually happened in the past and what those who try to reconstruct the past can discover and make understandable. As a consequence, the exploration of the past goes on continuously, and its reconstruction incessantly changes as those who explore it discover more information and bring new perspectives to bear on their interpretations of their findings.

Although any person is capable of reconstructing the past and often does so with respect to his or her personal or family past, most societies have entrusted that task of discovering the past to specialists, called historians. Most of them agree that there is a basic methodology suited to the task of reconstructing what happened. A first step involves formulating a question about past happenings. For example, this book was shaped by the question of what happened in the past that made the present world what it is. Or, on a smaller scale, suppose you asked yourself what happened to you between the ages of six and eight that relates to what you are now. The range of such questions is obviously infinite; as a result, historical inquiry is richly and unpredictably varied. In many ways the vitality of inquiry about the past depends on the imagination and ingenuity of historians in formulating problems they wish to study.

Once having defined a "subject," the historian starts searching for empirical, verifiable evidence that might provide an answer to his or her question. In the case of your interest in your earlier years, you might begin to look for letters and diaries, school records, picture albums, old clothing in the attic, toys in the basement, oral accounts of those who knew you then, and anything else possibly connected with your activities during that period in your life. What you would be looking for are "traces" left behind that provide evidence that something happened in the past involving you. These traces are what historians call primary sources, which are pieces of evidence produced by human beings who were directly involved in the past activity under investigation or by those in a position to know what happened. Primary sources exist in many forms. Most important are written documents in which observers of past events recorded what they thought happened; this book contains some examples of primary documents. But other kinds of primary sources can help historians find out what happened, including buildings, artworks, maps, pottery, tools, clothing, and oral traditions. Primary sources seldom speak to the historian in clear terms. Historians must subject them to rigorous criticism in order to assess their value as witnesses to what actually happened and to extract information from them that has a bearing on what the historian wants to know. In addition to primary sources, historians must also take into account and critically evaluate what are called secondary sources, which consist of the works of other historians who have examined the same general subject and the same segment of time. You will find examples of how secondary sources are used in the ''Where Historians Disagree'' sections of this book.

The search for, criticism of, and extraction of data from sources by no means finishes the historian's work. In our hypothetical cases involving your earlier years, when you had gathered and evaluated all the sources you could find, you would still not be able to say what had happened to you; all you would have is a collection of raw data. You, like all historians, would have to put your data together into some form that would approximate the realities in which you were involved then. This is a formidable task. In oversimplified terms it involves a series of choices: what sources deserve the greatest weight; what data are not relevant; how the sources relate to one another; how to organize the data contained in the sources in a way that would convey a meaningful and believable account of what happened; what literary devices to use in order to permit others to experience vicariously and to understand what happened. The process of converting data into history can never be totally objective, for historians inevitably decide these issues in terms of their own perspective and their own values. For this reason, many prefer to call the reconstruction of the past an art rather than a science.

In a rough way historians tend to reflect one of two perspectives in organizing their data to provide a comprehensible reconstruction of past reality. Some, representing a humanistic orientation, see the past in terms of unique actions and events that provide insights into the human situation in a particular setting. These historians tend to present the past as a narrative, telling a story that unfolds in a chronological order with each succeeding episode having its own significance but somehow related to and conditioned by what went before. If you were to choose this model in reconstructing your early life, you would proceed day by day, focusing attention on unique events in your experience that had a particular meaning to you then and something to do with what happened to you the next day or month or year. Other historians, reflecting a social science orientation, look for generalized patterns emerging from the record of the past. They tend to focus on repetitive commonalities rather than on the uniqueness of each happening, on thematic rather than chronological arrangement of evidence, on analysis rather than description, and on causal relationship linking data rather than linear connections. Sometimes they even seek to extract from their reading of the past generalized statements about human behavior that suggest how the future may unfold. Your own history written in this mode might highlight common occurrences in your life, an analysis of the relative weight of different experiences in making you what you are now, and what your experiences tell about what might happen to other children in the future. Quite clearly, each perspective produces a different history. Perhaps a combination of the two allows the fullest and most meaningful reconstruction of the past. We have tried to achieve that end in our reconstruction of the past.

Given the vastness and the complexity of the past, historians have been forced to adopt strategies that allow them to segment the past into manageable entities. One means to this end is to divide the past into discrete segments of time, each of which has common features that allow it to be treated as an entity. Another is to treat the past in terms of major topics around which data can be clustered to create meaning. Still another way of segmenting the past is to focus on geographical areas. As each of you proceeds through this book, you will become aware that we have employed all of these strategies as a means of making the past more understandable. Be aware that these are artificial devices, imposed on the record by historians. Choices have been made in defining periodization schemes, significant topics, and geographical partitions. Obviously, those choices have an important bearing on how the past is reconstructed. We urge each of you to be alert to the uses we have made of these conventions and to think about what the consequences might have been had other periodization systems, topical approaches, and geographical divisions been chosen.

Historical research and writing are decisively affected by judgments made by historians as to what facet of human activity is most important in shaping the destinies of individuals and collectives in the past. For example, in reconstructing your personal history, you might conclude that private reading was more significant to you than formal schooling or that your family's economic status was more important in shaping your life than its political affiliation. Such choices would obviously affect how you reconstructed your past. In viewing the past from a broader perspective, historians are influenced by similar considerations. Some argue that political factors are crucial in forming societies, while others insist that economic conditions are decisive. Such formulations have produced several widely recognized categories or branches of history: political history, economic history, social history, intellectual history, religious history, and cultural history. The marks of this compartmentalization of past events will be evident in this book, calling on each of you to think about what facet of human activity was most crucial in determining the course of events at any particular stage in human development. Perhaps the supreme challenge for historians is achieving a synthesis that will produce a version of the past embracing all aspects of human activity. In presenting our reconstruction of the past we have sought to meet that challenge, and we urge each of you to try to grasp the whole picture that undergirds the diverse activities into which the human experience can be categorized.

Each passing generation brings changes in approaches to the past that provide particular stimulation to the historical consciousness and a special thrust to historical inquiry. In recent years three broad developments have been particularly influential. We have tried to integrate some of the results of these developments into our reconstruction of the past.

First, there has been a broadening of the approach to social history. Social historians increasingly emphasize looking at the past "from the bottom up" by studying the everyday experiences and attitudes of "ordinary" people, including especially subordinated groups, rather than concentrating on political leaders, elite groups, and "high culture" produced by great thinkers, writers, and artists. To recount the history of these heretofore "silent" people and to assess its significance in the total picture of the past, social historians have had to ask new questions and to make innovative use of sources often overlooked by traditional historians. Their efforts have greatly expanded the stage that we call the past, increased the number of actors on that stage, and changed the theme of the drama played out there in ways that have radically altered our understanding of the dynamic forces that gave shape to the past.

The second development has been the emergence of what is often termed "the new history" (although, like many elements of social history, its roots go back several decades). The new history has been shaped by the marriage of history and the social sciences. By applying the techniques and concepts formulated by demographers, psychologists, anthropologists, geographers, physiologists, linguists, and biologists derived from their study of the present, historians have been able to open immense new vistas on the past pertaining to matters of vital importance to the human condition. Just to cite a few examples, we are learning much more about past birth and death rates, marriage patterns, fertility rates, family size, child rearing, sexuality, death, disease, environmental conditions, patterns of popular belief, the impact of technology, ethnic stereotypes, insanity, and criminality. Many historians practicing the new history rely on comparative and statistical analyses of quantitative data to expand their knowledge of what happened in the past, a methodological technique that has been greatly facilitated by the use of computers. The result of the new history is unmistakable: the past looks different than it once did.

A third development has been the growing interest in women's history. Traditionally history was written from a male perspective and was focused primarily on the thoughts and behavior of men. Women's history attempts to correct this neglect of women in history and the distortions that inevitably result. It focuses on women's experiences and on the roles women played in a variety of developments in the past. It seeks to discern and clarify what has been unique and distinctive in the past experiences of women. And it tries to alert us to gender bias in the way historical questions are posed, evidence is evaluated, and history is written. Once again, the past has been enlarged and a different view of what mattered has taken shape.

Perhaps all of these considerations relative to reconstructing the past lead to one final and all-important point: Establishing a relationship with the past presents a real challenge to our intellectual faculties. Access to the past is possible only to those willing to perform a diverse range of mental activities: posing questions about what is essential in human existence; searching out evidence; evaluating the worth of that evidence; making judgments about the relative weight of different kinds of data; establishing causal relationships; organizing information into intelligible patterns; interpreting the meaning of newly acquired knowledge; communicating new knowledge and insight to others in ways that are intelligible and relevant to their situation. All of these are essential mental powers that each of us must exercise if we are to live usefully in the present. It follows, then, that the greatest value to come from the effort to connect with the past stems from the way that enterprise stretches our minds and hones our intellectual powers along lines that equip us to respond more effectively to challenges that face us and our society now and in the future. We hope that your venture into the past that we have reconstructed in the pages that follow turns out to be a great intellectual experience. Indeed, the writing of this book was that for us, not the least because we had to stretch our minds in order to cope with new evidence about what happened, changing views about how to judge things past, and new questions about what really matters in the human experience.

PART ONE
THE ANCIENT NEAR EAST, 4000–300 B.C.

This book will seek to explain the evolution of Western civilization by describing the numerous ingredients that combined over a long period of time to shape its basic features. While the emergence of civilized life on this planet occurred over immense ages, the crucial "roots" from which Western civilization developed began to grow about six thousand years ago in a particular area of the world known as the Near East.

This first section of the book will concentrate on developments occurring in the Near East over a long era strecthing from about 4000 B.C. to 300 B.C. After a few introductory remarks concerning the long era of human history that preceded the emergence of civilization in the Near East, we shall focus on the amazing activity that unfolded in two river valley systems in the Near East: the Tigris-Euphrates in Mesopotamia and the Nile in Egypt. For it was in the challenging environment of these river valleys that human communities developed the first complex patterns of institutions, techniques, and ideas that can be called "civilizations." What was achieved in this setting established the foundations upon which Western civilization was to grow. Beyond characterizing the main features of the early civilizations of Mesopotamia and Egypt, we must consider the beginnings of a process as important to the history of the Western world as was the original creation of civilized life—namely, the beginning of the expansion of the river valley civilizations into a large area of northeast Africa and southwest Asia. Not only did this process permit new peoples to raise the level of their existence, but it also created a cultural setting in which they made their own unique contributions to the broadening stream of civilization. Until at least 500 B.C. the peoples of the Near East were in the forefront of the civilized world. This creative population fashioned a priceless heritage that was later exploited by other peoples participating in the shaping of Western civilization.

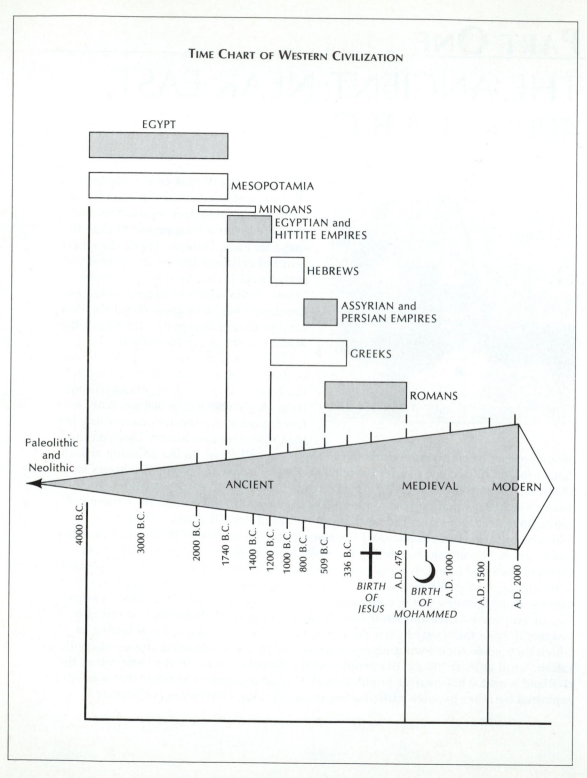

TIME CHART OF WESTERN CIVILIZATION

EGYPT

MESOPOTAMIA

MINOANS
EGYPTIAN and
HITTITE EMPIRES

HEBREWS

ASSYRIAN and
PERSIAN EMPIRES

GREEKS

ROMANS

Paleolithic
and
Neolithic

ANCIENT

MEDIEVAL

MODERN

4000 B.C.

3000 B.C.

2000 B.C.

1740 B.C.

1400 B.C.

1200 B.C.

1000 B.C.

800 B.C.

509 B.C.

336 B.C.

BIRTH
OF
JESUS

A.D. 476

BIRTH
OF
MOHAMMED

A.D. 1000

A.D. 1500

A.D. 2000

CHAPTER 1

The River Valley Civilizations: Mesopotamia and Egypt, 4000–1750 B.C.

FIGURE 1.1 A Divine Ruler The statue of Menkure (an Egyptian pharaoh of the Fourth Dynasty) and his queen conveys the majesty and power that surrounded the rulers of the early river valley societies of the Near East. The ability of such rulers to organize human effort on a large scale was crucial in establishing control over the rich river valleys that provided the material base for the first civilizations. This statue also illustrates the basic characteristics of Egyptian sculpture—rigid posture, stylized clothing, a personal touch revealed in the faces of even the majestic god-kings and their consorts. (Museum of Fine Arts, Boston)

Western civilization had its origins in what is known today as the Near East, a somewhat imprecise area embracing southwest Asia and northeast Africa. There diverse peoples utilized their creative talents and accumulated experiences to exploit a unique physical environment in ways that allowed them to create the first higher civilizations. An understanding of what these people did to achieve this end and how they did it is essential if we are to know anything about western Europe's cultural roots.

1. THE PREHISTORIC BACKGROUND

The emergence of higher civilizations in the Near East was made possible by complex developments during an immensely long prehistoric period of preparation—at least five or six hundred times longer than the time span shown on the chart on page 2. Our knowledge of what happened during this prehistoric period is fragmentary, and there is disagreement on how to interpret what is known. In simple terms these vast ages involved three interrelated processes: geological developments, which created the topography and the climate of the planet earth; biological developments, which produced the human species as well as other creatures and plants; and cultural developments, through which human beings created techniques and practices that allowed them to enhance their capabilities to survive and improve in a constantly changing physical and biological environment.

On the basis of meager skeletal remains found scattered over the earth, it appears that the existence of humanlike creatures (hominids) must be extended back at least 3 million years. It was only about forty thousand years ago that the human species (conventionally designated *homo sapiens*, meaning ''thinking man'') assumed its present physical form, perhaps first in East Africa or southwest Asia. During the long period separating primitive hominids from *homo sapiens*, most of it dominated by conditions created by four successive ice ages, something happened biologically to create unique creatures endowed with special physical traits that prepared them for a unique role in the earth's history. Especially important was the large and complex brain structure that *homo sapiens* possessed.

As a consequence of their superior brain, these evolving human beings developed a special capacity that was crucial in preparing for the emergence of higher civilization. They were able to create and transmit *culture* in the form of objects, techniques, and behavioral patterns that increased their ability to control the environment in ways beneficial to them. The reconstruction of prehistoric cultural development, derived chiefly from artifacts discovered and interpreted by archaeologists, is as complex and as open to debate as is the biological history of the human species. Despite these difficulties, certain broad lines of cultural development are generally agreed upon by specialists in the study of prehistory.

The cultural activity of prehistoric peoples is most fully recorded in the stone tools these creatures left scattered across the face of the earth. For this reason the prehistoric age has been called the Stone Age. Surviving stone tools indicate that during 99 percent of all human prehistory men and women lived as hunters and food gatherers. Although this culture varied in detail from place to place around the globe, it involved certain basic features that permit us to give it a common name—*Paleolithic* (Old Stone Age) culture. Paleolithic peoples lived in small groups dispersed at considerable distances from one another. These packs were made up of several nuclear families, probably related to one another by kinship ties, who cooperated in their quest for sustenance. They were perpetual wanderers, their lives controlled by the movements of animals and the growth patterns of plants upon which survival depended. They sheltered themselves temporarily in caves or fragile tents made of skins and branches. At best their existence was precarious, and improvement in the human condition was slow.

No matter how slowly and painfully, Paleolithic peoples did enrich their culture. They developed increasingly complex and effective techniques for making a greater variety of stone tools, eventually complemented by implements made from bone, horn, and wood. These improved tools made them more efficient killers of even the largest and fiercest animals. They learned how to use fire to warm themselves and prepare their food more easily. They developed spoken languages, a powerful instrument not only in facilitating group action in hunting and food-gathering activities but also in passing on to succeeding generations their cumulative knowledge about animals and plants. Specialized economic and social functions began to emerge within the hunting pack, perhaps based originally on gender. The efforts of male hunters and toolmakers were complemented by equally vital activities carried out by female plant gatherers, fire keepers, garment makers, and child raisers. These specialized functions probably played a prime role in defining the mental attitudes that controlled the relationships between males and females and between parents and children. Scanty bits of evidence indicate the existence of religious life centered on a belief in the existence of spirits in all things that had power to control the destiny of both the living and the dead, but that were also susceptible to human manipulation through the efforts of humans with special powers that allowed them to reach into the spirit world. The cave paintings found at Altamira in Spain and Lascaux in France, as well as crudely shaped human figures, decorated hunting weapons, and jewelry scattered wherever Paleolithic groups passed, suggest both an urge and the capacity to express ideas and feelings about the world and to enhance life by creating beauty.

A culture based on hunting and food gathering had limitations, perhaps too narrow to contain expanding human capabilities. Ultimately, Paleolithic culture gave way to a new pattern of life that changed the human condition in a fundamental way. This great transformation, which marked an essential step toward higher civilization, involved the domestication of plants and animals, which allowed human societies to rely on agriculture to provide the material basis for society. The results of recent archaeological research into human cultural development on a worldwide scale make it almost certain that the change from a hunting and food-gathering to a farming culture first occurred in a relatively limited area of southwest Asia lying along the western, northern, and eastern boundaries of what is called the Fertile Crescent (see Map 1.1). Not too much later, as time is measured on the scale of human prehistory, agricultural life appeared in most other areas of the world, sometimes borrowed from the original inventors and other times "invented" anew.

Archaeological evidence suggests that the "agricultural revolution" came gradually in southwest Asia and was accompanied by much experimentation. The transition period, extending from about 9000 to 6000 B.C. and coinciding in a rough way with the end of the last period of glaciation, has been called the *Mesolithic* (Middle Stone) age. The experimentation occurred in an ecosystem that had a unique combination of features: moderate but regular rainfall; large numbers of wild sheep, goats, cattle, and swine; rich stands of wild cereals, legumes, and plants with oil-bearing seeds; a substantial population sustained by a well-established Paleolithic culture. Perhaps modest changes in the climate and population pressure played a part in the change, but the main impetus most likely came from the capacity of human beings long accustomed to hunting and food gathering to take advantage of the resources offered by the ecosystem. In any case, behavior patterns began to change in Mesolithic times. People stayed longer in one place and gave increasing attention to the control and selective killing of animal herds and to management of wild plants. As these practices continued, certain wild animals—sheep, goats, cattle, and pigs—and certain wild plants—especially wheat and barley—were modified genetically to the point where they flourished best under human care. When that happened, human beings were in a position to abandon hunting and food gathering in favor of agriculture.

The emergence of agriculture as the basis of life opened what is called the *Neolithic* (New Stone) age. Its revolutionary impact is evident in the remains of many settlement sites excavated in recent years, including Jericho in Palestine, Halicar and Catal Hüyük in modern Turkey, and Jarmo and Tepe Gawra in modern Iraq (see Map 1.1). People settled permanently in villages, some of which supported populations of several hundred. They built substantial baked-mud houses featuring not only living quarters but also storage facilities, household shrines, and even burial places. Facilities serving communal functions, such as temples, protective walls, and wells, appeared. Human activity, shared by men and women alike, focused on regular planting and harvesting of wheat, barley, legumes, and fruits and on the care of domesticated animals, valuable not only for meat but also for milk, cheese, hides, and wool. This new mode of life called for a new kit of stone tools, especially hoes and sickles. Before Neolithic culture progressed far, people were beginning to complement stone tools

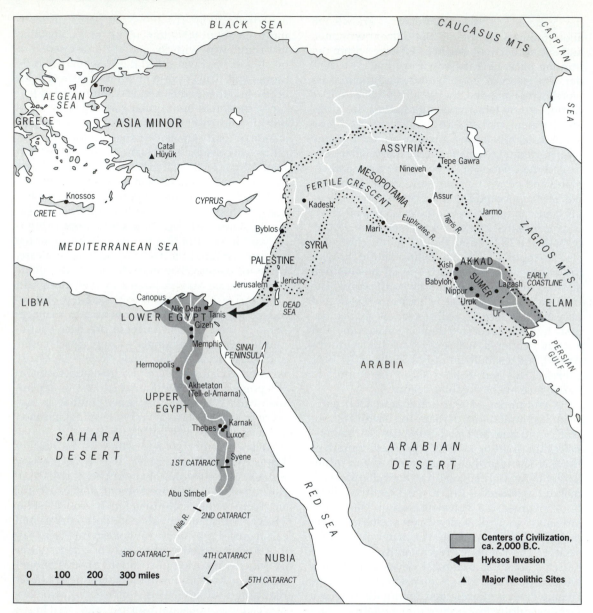

Map 1.1 **CENTERS OF THE FIRST HIGHER CIVILIZATIONS: MESOPOTAMIA AND EGYPT** This map locates the two centers where higher civilization originated. It dramatically highlights the limited geographical areas initially affected by the transition from Neolithic agricultural cultures to urban-based patterns of civilization. The revolutionary changes that occurred in the small areas nourished by the waters of the Tigris-Euphrates and the Nile rivers soon began to assert a powerful influence on the lives of the peoples inhabiting the vast stretches of territory surrounding the river valleys.

with copper instruments, heralding the age of metals that would make stone tools obsolete. Pottery making and basket weaving developed to provide storage for food, and the weaving of fibers emerged to create a new range of clothing.

Besides its new technological features, Neolithic culture had significant new social characteristics. Settled agricultural life demanded greater specialization of labor, which allowed for more highly developed skills and better products and made possible the accumulation of wealth in the form of stored grain and animal herds. This wealth provided the basis of exchange for products that a particular village was unable to provide for itself, thus creating trade; the development of trade is evident in the spread of pottery made in a specific area to widely scattered places across the Near East. Increased wealth also made the successful peasant village the target of outsiders, requiring collective action to defend the village. And wealth based on land and animal ownership generated quarrels that posed a threat to the internal order in the village. A major consequence of problems related to trade, defense, and adjudication of quarrels was the development of a more complex system of village governance. This system usually took the form of a tribal structure in which several kinship groups or clans acting through family heads selected a village chief who joined the family elders in making and carrying out collective decisions to meet common problems.

Neolithic villagers also had to expand their mental skills to cope with their new situation. The demands of farming called for more complex calculations, extended planning, and disciplined behavior than did hunting and food gathering. Different moral standards were required to fit situations arising from closer contacts with larger numbers of people and from ownership of things. Religion, increasingly centered on the worship of the forces of nature believed to control the fertility of plants and animals, challenged Neolithic villagers with concepts far more complex than those associated with animal spirits. The increasing complexities surrounding religion also led villagers to place greater trust in religious experts—priests—and to dedicate more energy and wealth to winning the favor of the spirits who nourished the crops and animal

herds and protected the village. The responsibilities of directing the government of the village and of conducting religious life began to bestow on those involved in these functions a special place of prominence and power in village life, creating the basis for social stratification. Although women continued to play a key role in the economic life of farming villages, the evidence strongly suggests that males monopolized leadership roles as well as family life. Perhaps the emergence of agricultural life created a social system and a set of values that cast women into a position of dependence and inferiority that would be difficult to eradicate. However, it is worth noting that the female figure was a prime symbol used in Neolithic religious cults to represent the regenerative powers of nature. This symbolism suggests a high respect, perhaps even awe, for femininity as a potent force in shaping and controlling human destiny.

2. MESOPOTAMIAN CIVILIZATION: POLITICAL, ECONOMIC, AND SOCIAL LIFE

From a global perspective the emergence of agriculture put the peoples practicing dryland farming on the fringes of the Fertile Crescent in the forefront of human activity by about 6000 B.C. Recent archaeological explorations of the development of some of the area's peasant villages between 6000 and 4000 B.C. suggest a potential for further evolution, but nothing indicates that any of them was capable of developing the complex urban life that marked the advent of higher civilization. Urban civilization was created by farmers who mastered the more demanding environment of a particular region called Mesopotamia (from a Greek term meaning "between the rivers") whose character was defined by the Tigris and Euphrates rivers (see Map 1.1).

From their sources in the Caucasus Mountains these rivers flow southward through the semiarid steppes of northern Mesopotamia, cutting valleys too deep to allow the use of their waters for irrigation of the adjacent lands. Roughly three hundred miles northwest of where they flow into the Persian Gulf, the rivers enter a flat alluvial plain created by the silt deposited by the floodwaters that annually spilled over their low banks. This relatively small territory presented both opportunities and challenges to the Neolithic peoples on its fringes. The silt deposited by the annual floods made the soil immensely fertile. Those same floods provided a dependable water supply to an area almost devoid of rainfall. However, the potential gifts of lower Mesopotamia were not easily possessed. The somewhat irregular floods were destructive unless they were controlled, and the rich soil was useless unless it was cleared of swamp vegetation and properly drained to avoid salination. And even then the soil was nonproductive unless it could be watered during the arid growing season. Most of Mesopotamia was lacking in natural resources, especially stone, timber, and minerals. Unless its occupants could organize trading ventures extending over considerable distances, only the most primitive level of culture could be sustained. Finally, Mesopotamia lacked any natural barriers to restrain the incursions of neighboring peoples.

While agriculture slowly evolved around the fringes of Mesopotamia during the Mesolithic age, lower Mesopotamia remained relatively backward. Eventually, perhaps just before 4000 B.C., small peasant villages did appear that depended on primitive techniques of irrigation for survival in this arid region. Sometime after about 3500 B.C., larger and more complex communities began to develop, fed perhaps by immigrants from the area to the east between the river valleys and the Zagros Mountains, where Neolithic farming villages had existed for a long time. The evolution of these settlements was accompanied by the development of carefully planned artificial irrigation systems that permitted the cultivation of larger areas at greater distances from the riverbeds. Perhaps that achievement was the work of the Sumerians, a people of mysterious origin from whom south Mesopotamia took its name: Sumer. By 3100 B.C. several rich and populous city-states had developed in Sumer, including Ur, Lagash, Uruk, and Umma. Each consisted of a densely populated urban center surrounded by an island of irrigated farmland carved out of the chaotic river valley environment by an elaborate system of dikes, canals, and reservoirs and systematically cultivated under direction from the urban center. The Sumerian

accomplishment soon served as a model for another group of intruders who occupied the area just north of Sumer. These were Semitic-speaking seminomads originally from the northern Arabian Desert, who developed several thriving city-states in an area called Akkad. For at least seven centuries, from about 3100 to 2400 B.C., these city-states, each jealously guarding its independence, enjoyed remarkable stability and prosperity that produced a common pattern of culture marked by brilliant accomplishments in all aspects of life.

Of fundamental importance to the development of urban civilization was the creation of an effective system of government capable of controlling a large population engaged in a variety of mutually supportive activities. From an early date responsibility for decision making in each Sumerian city-state rested in the hands of a single human leader. Perhaps initially that power was held by a high priest, but eventually a secular king (called *lugal* in Sumerian) came to dominate. In either case authority was grounded primarily in religious belief. The Sumerians believed that each city-state had been created originally by a god or goddess who owned the city and its surrounding lands and who required all members to serve the divine will. The earthly ruler was the agent through whom the will of the divine owner was made known and carried out. Each city developed an elaborate temple-palace complex that served as the center of political life. From there flowed divine orders coordinating the numerous activities required to exploit the resources belonging to the patron deity. The efforts of the rulers to control the population were greatly aided by the development of writing, which allowed the keeping of records of what was produced and what was due. Back to the temple-palace came a huge income, much of it in the form of agricultural produce, that was used to sustain the divine city. A key function of government was the distribution of this income. Part of it went as rations to sustain those who tilled the soil and kept the irrigation system in repair. Another part provided for the support of a wide array of specialists who clustered around the temple-palace complex to serve the ruler and the community in a variety of ways: record keepers, scribes, engineers, architects, artists, traders, artisans, soldiers, and tax collectors. The combined efforts of these specialists, whose activities were made possible by the surplus agricultural production, created the essential features that elevated civilized urban life to a plane far beyond life in Neolithic villages. As part of his effort to carry out the will of the city's divine patron, the ruler developed instrumentalities that became permanent features of civilized polity: laws to define the relationships among citizens; courts to adjudicate disputes; a police force to maintain civic order; armies to protect the city-state from hostile outsiders; and public ceremonies to honor and placate the deities.

Although the independent city-state pattern of government dominated Mesopotamia between 3100 and 2400 B.C., tensions emerged that eventually modified its basic forms. Constant attacks from outsiders attracted by the wealth of Mesopotamia's urban centers, conflicts among city-states seeking to expand their territories, and the quest for vital raw materials lacking in Sumer and Akkad increasingly required that effective rulers look beyond the walls of their own city-states. These pressures led them to undertake conquests aimed at creating larger political entities. The establishment and maintenance of these *empires* required new political techniques for keeping peace and order among peoples of diverse backgrounds and loyalties.

The first attempts at shaping empires were made by strong kings from prominent Sumerian cities, but their "empires" were short-lived. Ultimately, the Semitic-speaking peoples from north of Sumer were more successful in uniting Mesopotamia. The first great empire builder was Sargon I (ca. 2370–2315 B.C.) from Akkad. He conducted military campaigns that not only subdued the city-states of Sumer but also extended Akkadian dominance into the foothills of the Zagros Mountains, Assyria, and Syria. Sargon's empire was sustained by his descendants until about 2200 B.C., but then it collapsed under the combined pressure of internal resistance and external attacks. For a brief interval the Sumerian city-states regained their independence, and one of them, Ur, even managed to assert dominance over much of Mesopotamia between about 2100 and 2000 B.C. However, the long history of the independent city-state as the prime political institution in Mesopotamia was drawing to an end in favor of larger political entities. Toward 1800 B.C. a new Semitic-speaking people, the Amo-

rites, began to assert dominance. Their day of glory came with the reign of Hammurabi (ca. 1792–1750 B.C.), who from his city of Babylon organized a series of military campaigns that once again created a large empire stretching in a great arc from the Persian Gulf to the Mediterranean Sea and imposed on diverse peoples a single political order. For all its brilliance, the Amorite Empire was relatively short-lived. Shortly after 1700 B.C., outside attackers began to batter its frontiers, until eventually the Kassites established control over Mesopotamia. As we shall see later (Chapter 2), the power structure prevailing in the Near East had undergone significant changes which redefined Mesopotamia's position in that area.

Hammurabi's career exemplifies the new ideas and practices of government introduced by the empire builders who dominated Mesopotamia between 2400 and 1700 B.C. These contributions, aimed chiefly at using political power to create common bonds among diverse peoples, proved to be among the most important of all Mesopotamian contributions to civilization. One technique used by Hammurabi to unify the peoples over which he ruled was to impress on them their total dependence on the power of their one ruler. This technique called for a conscious effort to exalt the person of the king as the sole source of earthly power. To heighten his visibility, Hammurabi made his court at Babylon the setting for a vast display of wealth toward which his subjects from "the Four Quarters of the World" could turn for their well-being. He sought to create a common religion in his empire, based on the worship of Marduk, once the patron god of the city of Babylon but now presented as the divine lord of all the other deities and of the earth. Hammurabi proclaimed himself as Marduk's sole agent, alone capable of bringing divine favor to his subjects. But his power was more than appearance. He maintained a well-organized army ready to curb threats to peace in the empire, a centralized bureaucracy based at the court in Babylon that was devoted to administration, and a network of governors sent out to the local units into which the empire was divided to collect taxes, raise troops, and administer justice.

One of Hammurabi's most significant measures to solidify and unify his empire was his law code. He claimed it was handed down to him from the deities "to destroy the wicked and the evil, so that the strong may not oppress the weak" (see Figure 1.2). Although a modern reader of Hammurabi's law code is taken aback by the brutal punishments imposed on lawbreakers, the code is better characterized by its commonsense, humane approach to basic human problems: protection for women, children, and slaves; fairness in commercial exchanges; protection of property; standard procedures for adjudicating disputes; debt relief for victims of flood and drought. It reflected an enlightened concept of justice that encouraged people of all kinds to accept the authority of a king trying to provide common rules to govern the behavior of his subjects.

The material base undergirding Mesopotamian civilization remained remarkably stable during the long period from about 3100 to 1750 B.C. Of crucial importance was a carefully organized and controlled agricultural system. Although there were some technological advances in agriculture, especially the introduction of bronze tools and wheeled plows, farming depended chiefly on the traditional crops and animals of Neolithic times. The chief difference was the larger productive capacity of the fertile, irrigated fields of Mesopotamia. The prime agricultural unit was a large farm, usually owned by the king, the temple priests, or a member of the aristocracy and tilled by tenants and slaves working under careful supervision of the owner or his agents. The rulers of each city or empire sought to develop and control extensive trade networks designed to make basic resources available. Every city supported a large number of skilled artisans who made a variety of fine products consumed in the city or distributed across the Near East by enterprising merchants in exchange for raw materials lacking in Mesopotamia. The urban civilization of Mesopotamia both required and permitted the development of a more complex and structured social system than was typical of Neolithic peasant villages. At the summit of society stood an aristocracy made up of priests, landowners, and royal officials who derived their high status from their close association with the ruler and their involvement in the governance of society. This aristocracy benefited most from Mesopotamia's material wealth. Merchants and artisans enjoyed a prosperous

FIGURE 1.2 An Ancient Lawgiver This relief, showing Hammurabi receiving a code of laws from a deity, was carved at the top of a stone cylinder upon which were inscribed the provisions of the law written in cuneiform script. Sumerian artists were especially adept in relief carving, an art form that would have an illustrious history. (Giraudon)

and relatively free life, often closely attached to the court, the temple, or aristocratic households. Each city-state had a large population of urban laborers who performed the menial tasks required to run the city and the households of the powerful. The bulk of the population consisted of farmers living in villages outside the urban center and devoting themselves to agricultural routines from which they derived meager rewards. Slavery existed but was not a dominant feature of Mesopotamian life. The relationships among various social classes, as well as the rights and responsibilities of each, were carefully defined by law.

At all levels of Mesopotamian society the family was a basic institution. Marriages were arranged by family agreements, and the husband and father exercised almost absolute control over his wife and children. As a consequence, women played a limited role in societal decision making. However, the law did recognize that they had certain rights. Surviving records indicate that women often inherited their husbands' property and were engaged in economic ventures of many kinds. Aristocratic women certainly shared in the luxuries that accompanied their husbands' social status. The wives and children of artisans and farmers were actively engaged in the work of the heads of households—and they shared the meager returns for their efforts. As a whole, Mesopotamian society was stable and seldom troubled by social strife and tension.

3. MESOPOTAMIAN BELIEF, THOUGHT, AND EXPRESSION

The advent of higher civilization in Mesopotamia was marked by impressive developments in religion, literature, and the arts which had a major influence on the later history of cultural life in the Western world. By and large, the Sumerians created the basic elements of Mesopotamian culture which Semitic-speaking peoples readily assimilated and sustained. The result of this relationship was a common culture based on Sumerian models that ultimately embraced all of Mesopotamia.

Religion was the prime force shaping all aspects of Mesopotamian life. The Mesopotamian religion was *polytheistic*, based on a worship of many deities who were believed to possess powers that allowed them to control all that happened. Especially awesome were the spirits that controlled the forces of nature: gods and goddesses of the sky, air, water, sun, moon, storms. One or another of these deities was usually accepted as the founder and ruler of each city-state. Particularly appealing to ordinary people who lived close to the soil was the goddess of fertility, called Inanna by the Sumerians and Ishtar by the Semites, whose munificent power renewed nature every spring, usually with the help of a male lover. Sharing the universe with these great gods and goddesses were legions of lesser spirits, each

of whom could bring blessings or misfortunes, great or small, to men and women in all stations of life. The Mesopotamians spent considerable intellectual energy trying to define the powers of these deities, determine their origins, and clarify their relationships to one another and to the human community. The result was a rich and intriguing mythology that had a powerful influence on later religious thinking.

The lot assigned to human beings in the god-dominated universe was not an easy one. They were viewed as slaves of the deities, bound to suffer whatever the angry, vengeful, unpredictable gods and goddesses wished. Especially heavy was the burden of trying to please the deities. To do so required building splendid temples and countless shrines where the deities could live, supporting priests and priestesses who attended to divine needs, offering prayers and gifts, organizing expensive public festivals, and expending endless effort to discover the intentions of the gods and goddesses as these might be revealed in the movement of the stars, dreams, and the shapes of the entrails of animals. In return for their services to the deities, Mesopotamians expected the material gifts the deities had to offer—the safety and material prosperity of the city-state, the family, and the individual. Most men and women were never sure that the all-powerful gods and goddesses would smile on them. A tone of pessimism and fatalism permeated their view of life. Their religion was lacking in any ethical dimensions that taught that good behavior and good deeds were pleasing to the divine powers. Nor did the Mesopotamians entertain any hope for a happy life after death; the dead passed on to a "land of no return" somewhere underground "where dust is their feed, clay their substance; where they see no light and dwell in darkness." Without a chance to please the deities through good behavior or a hope for a happy afterlife, perhaps there was little choice but fear of the deities and pessimism about the human lot.

The urge to know and to please the gods and goddesses inspired an impressive literature, the recording of which was made possible by the development of a writing system—one of the great inventions in history. The Sumerians were the first to develop writing. In its earliest form their writing consisted of pictures (pictograms) used primarily to record what was due to the deities and the rulers. Gradually pictograms evolved into symbols representing sounds that could be combined into words expressing chains of thought of various kinds. To record such thoughts, these symbols were pressed onto soft clay tablets with a wedge-shaped stylus and then the tablets were baked; thus the writing is called *cuneiform* (from a Latin word meaning "wedge"). Eventually the Sumerian system of writing was adapted by Semitic-speaking Akkadians, whose language had by Sargon I's time begun to replace Sumerian in Mesopotamia. However, for centuries learned people continued to study Sumerian texts much as modern scholars learn ancient Greek, Latin, and Hebrew. Thus, much Sumerian literature survived as a model to be followed by peoples speaking and writing in other languages.

While writing in Mesopotamia served a major function in keeping records of a large array of ordinary activities, talented individuals learned to use it for creative purposes. Their most impressive literary productions were religious epics, of which the *Creation Epic* and the *Epic of Gilgamesh* are the most notable examples. The *Creation Epic* describes how Marduk won supremacy over the spirit world and created earth and human beings, a feat that earned him universal worship in the time of Hammurabi. The *Epic of Gilgamesh* recounts the adventures of a semilegendary king of Uruk, Gilgamesh, in his quest to learn from the deities how to gain immortality. The Mesopotamians also wrote hymns glorifying the deities and chronicles recounting the deeds of great rulers. The literary forms, themes, and styles developed by Mesopotamian writers not only enriched their own culture but also had an important influence on the literature of later peoples, as is evident in the ideas and stories of Mesopotamian origin imbedded in the Bible of the Hebrews, put into writing many centuries later.

From the beginning of their civilization, the Mesopotamians showed impressive skills and creativity in the visual arts. The need to provide their deities with suitable dwellings was the prime stimulant to monumental architecture and produced impressive mud brick temple complexes that were the central feature of every city. In its most fully developed form the temple complex featured a tower, called a *ziggurat*, designed as a series of terraces one on top of another, each successive layer smaller than the one below. A sanctuary dedicated to the patron deity of each city was placed atop the final terrace. Around the ziggurat there usually developed an elaborate array of lesser shrines, offices, priestly dwellings, storehouses, and workshops, all comprising a sacred precinct where the deities could be served. Hardly less elaborate were the palaces where the kings and their courts lived. The palace at Mari, an important city in the Amorite Empire, covered six acres and contained more than two hundred fifty rooms. Mesopotamian architects knew how to use columns, domes, arches, and vaults, but the lack of stone as a building material limited their ability to exploit these forms fully.

The Mesopotamians were also skilled sculptors. Most three-dimensional statues portrayed the deities and famous kings. Sculptors took some pains to give a distinctive character to the faces of their subjects but concerned themselves little with a realistic rendering of the human body. Their work, strongly influenced by geometrical forms, is solid, stiff, and motionless (see Color Plate 1). More realistic and animated scenes were created by sculptors working in low relief to depict historic events or divine exploits (see Figure 1.2). The most exquisite carving was done by seal makers, who wrought miniaturized scenes carved in stone that were used to press an identifying mark onto documents written in clay. The same deft skill is illustrated in jewelry, metalwork, and decorated pottery.

Chiefly as a result of their efforts to cope with the divine forces and the rivers, the Mesopotamians produced a body of knowledge that can be called science. They devised a system of time reckoning based on cycles of the sun and the moon. They developed a standard system of weights and measures almost universally used by Hammurabi's time. Their numbering system combined a decimal system with units of sixty. They were able to perform the basic functions of arithmetic and geometry. A body of medical knowledge, mixing observations and religious lore, was developed. As a result of the travels of merchants and soldiers, the Mesopotamians amassed a considerable store of geographical information. Inspired by an urge to foretell the future, the Mesopotamians gathered accurate information about the movement of the stars. Although the Mesopotamians were seldom concerned with gathering knowledge about the physical world for its own sake, the information they did compile in the course of meeting practical problems was stored up for the use of later peoples, particularly the Greeks, as the basis for theoretical science.

4. EGYPTIAN CIVILIZATION: POLITICAL, ECONOMIC, AND SOCIAL LIFE

Not long after urban civilization took shape in Mesopotamia, a similar leap forward occurred in Egypt. Although bits of archaeological evidence found in Egypt suggest the presence of Mesopotamian influences there at the moment of transition to higher civilization, the basic developments in northeast Africa were native and the resultant pattern of civilization was unique.

Just as in Mesopotamia, the advent of higher civilization in Egypt hinged on meeting the challenges posed by a river valley environment. The Nile has its sources in the mountains of equatorial Africa (see Map 1.1). From there it flows northward past a series of rapids (cataracts) to trace a narrow trough through bleak deserts almost devoid of rainfall. As it nears the Mediterranean, the river fans out into a series of channels to create the Delta, a triangle of rich land about one hundred twenty miles on each side. The annual floods of the Nile come with predictable regularity to create what the Egyptians called the "black land" of the narrow valley and the Delta, which they contrasted with the dreaded "red land" of the desert. However, the Nile floods had to be controlled and their waters distributed across the "black land" during the rainless growing season before the productive potential of the valley could be realized.

During many centuries prior to the emergence of higher civilization in the Nile Valley, Neolithic agricultural life existed across much of North Africa. However, only somewhere between 5000 and 4500 B.C. did some of these farmers begin to move from the west and south to establish villages on the fringes of the Nile Valley. During the next thousand years these peoples developed the technical and organizational skills that permitted them to establish irrigation systems capable of controlling the floods and utilizing the immensely rich soil as a basis of village life. By a process that is ill understood, these villages in time were joined together to form small kingdoms.

The era dominated by these small kingdoms, called the Predynastic Age, ended suddenly about 3100 B.C., when Egypt was united under a single ruler, later given the title *pharaoh*. Egyptian tradition ascribed this feat to Menes, who founded the first dynasty of pharaohs (a dynasty was a group of rulers from a single family who followed one another as pharaoh) and opened an era called the Old Kingdom (3100–2200 B.C.). Six dynasties ruled during this long era, the most glorious being the Third and Fourth dynasties. From their capital at Memphis, these pharaohs asserted a beneficial authority that brought prosperity and peace to the valley. Egypt benefited especially from freedom from outside attacks, a boon afforded by the formidable natural barriers guarding the Nile Valley: the cataracts, the deserts, the Mediterranean Sea. The massive pyramids built at Gizeh by the powerful pharaohs of the Fourth Dynasty—Menkure, Kephren, and Khufu (Cheops)—mirror the immense wealth of a society unified in exploiting the Nile and the great power of the rulers who directed this collective effort. During the period of the Old Kingdom basic political, economic, and social structures, religious concepts and practices, and modes of thought and expression were shaped that would dominate Egyptian civilization for the next two millennia.

The key to this remarkable civilization was the political system that had been put into place by the time of the Third Dynasty. Its central feature was the absolute power of the pharaoh, who was considered to be a god. The pharaoh literally owned Egypt and its people. Every person was his servant, subject to his unchallengeable orders. Despite their divine status, most of the pharaohs of the Old Kingdom were active leaders occupied in overseeing the irrigation system, giving justice, directing building programs, and sponsoring trade. They exercised their power through a highly developed administrative system centered at Memphis. Egypt was divided into smaller administrative units, called *nomes*, each controlled by royal officials held closely accountable for carrying out the pharaoh's orders in the villages making up each nome.

During the Sixth Dynasty this highly effective system faltered. Egypt entered a period of disorder called the First Intermediate Period (2200-2050 B.C.), marked by ineffectual pharaohs whose authority was challenged by local potentates. About 2050 B.C. political unity was restored by the princes of Thebes to begin what is known as the Middle Kingdom (2050–1750 B.C.). These rulers of the Eleventh and Twelfth dynasties consciously restored the basic political institutions and practices characteristic of the Old Kingdom—the divine power of the pharaoh, the centralized bureaucracy, the provincial administration—and labored successfully to revive and even to expand the economic system. A major concern of the pharaohs was to ensure that *ma'at* prevailed. In Egyptian thought *ma'at* was the principle of right order, justice, and harmony that should prevail throughout the universe, including the human community. Out of respect for this principle the pharaohs of the Middle Kingdom sought actively to provide justice, protection, and respect for all of their subjects, including the poor and the powerless, who had been badly abused by the powerful during the First Intermediate Period. The concern that *ma'at* should prevail for all society gave the government of the Middle Kingdom a quality not often seen in the history of the ancient Near East.

The Middle Kingdom came to an end about 1750 B.C., chiefly as a consequence of a threat that Egypt had not heretofore faced: outside invasion. A people called the Hyksos who came from Asia succeeded in taking control of part of the Nile Valley. Their presence led to divisions within Egypt and to violence and lawlessness. This interlude, called the Second Intermediate Period (1750–1580 B.C.), set the stage for another recovery and a new era of glory in Egypt to be discussed later (see Chapter 2).

The establishment of a unified political regime by the divine pharaohs was accompanied by the development of a remarkably stable economic and social order. A carefully controlled agricultural system provided the prime source of wealth in Egypt. This system was sustained by a numerous peasant population, living in small villages and devoting their lives to the endless round of labor required to maintain the irrigation system, to plant and harvest the crops of wheat, barley, flax, vegetables, and fruit, and to care for herds of animals. To these responsibilities was added the burden of extra labor on the immense building programs organized by the pharaohs and their agents and friends. The economy was enriched by the efforts of artisans and merchants who produced or acquired by exchange the luxury goods desired by the powerful and rich in society. Both artisans and traders often worked directly for the pharaohs, the rich officials of his court, the numerous priests, and the powerful provincial nobility.

Egyptian society was dominated by a relatively small aristocracy. At its summit stood the pharaoh and his family, who enjoyed command over all elements of society and control over the total wealth of the state. The rest of the aristocracy consisted of those to whom the pharaoh chose to extend high status and reward with wealth. Especially influential were the priests, who managed the religious system, and the officials, who assisted the pharaoh in governing Egypt. Despite the efforts of the good pharaohs the lower classes were sometimes exploited and oppressed; their laments constitute a major theme in literature. Yet the surviving evidence, much of it in the form of pictorial representations of the lower classes adorning the tombs of the pharaohs and their nobles, suggests social harmony. The scenes depicting peasants and artisans at work and play convey a sense of contentment and even joy. Slavery played only a minor role in Egypt during the Old and Middle kingdoms, and although women were subjected to control by fathers and husbands, they enjoyed an important place in society. The consorts of the mighty pharaohs were extended high respect by their divine husbands (see Figure 1.1) and by society in general. Noblewomen shared most aspects of aristocratic life, especially its material wealth. They owned property and played an important role as priestesses serving the chief deities of Egypt. Lower-class women joined their husbands in working in the fields and played a key role in sustaining the economy. In general, Egyptian society was stable and secure. Most people apparently felt that *ma'at* prevailed to reward a happy, confident society.

5. EGYPTIAN BELIEF, THOUGHT, AND EXPRESSION

The cultural achievement of ancient Egypt was an outgrowth of the same powerful religious forces that shaped political and social life. The fifth-century B.C. Greek historian Herodotus concluded that the Egyptians were the most religious of all peoples. From at least some perspectives that seems to be true. Certainly few peoples honored more gods and goddesses; the deities worshiped by the Egyptians numbered in the thousands. These spirits were portrayed in a confusing array of forms—as humans, animals, birds, plants, abstractions, and mixtures of any of these forms. They lived everywhere and were always present wherever and whenever humans were at work or at play. The deities were generally conceived as benevolent toward humans, easy to live with, and not to be feared. Over time the Egyptians did come to agree that certain deities possessed special powers and deserved universal worship. This mythology accorded special prominence to deities associated with pharaohs victorious in earthly wars, such as the falcon god Horus worshiped by Menes, the unifier of Egypt, and Amon, a minor deity at Thebes who became a powerful national god after the princes of Thebes rose to power as pharaohs of the Middle Kingdom. Two deities ultimately emerged as the most powerful divine forces in Egyptian religion: Ra, the sun god, whose worship reflected the power of nature in shaping the good life of the Nile Valley; and Osiris, the god who had the power to grant a happy life after death.

The Egyptians expended enormous energy and resources in an effort to please their deities and win their favor. An elaborate set of ritual practices was established early in Egyptian history and changed little over the centuries. To the pharaoh belonged prime responsibility for bringing the favor of his fellow gods and goddesses upon his land and people; no small part of the activities of a typical pharaoh was devoted to religious worship. He was aided by numerous priests and priestesses, who conducted an elaborate round of rituals to please the deities with food, gifts, song, prayer, and dance. A considerable portion of public income was devoted to these activities. Acts of worship and sacrifice took place not only in great public temples but also in simple shrines in homes and villages. A rich array of magical practices evolved to attract the attention of the deities and to drive away evil spirits.

Much of this religious activity was intended to win the material rewards that the gods and goddesses had to offer—abundant harvests, good health, security, happy times. Besides earthly benefits, the divine powers held another precious gift for deserving Egyptians—a happy life after death. From early times, Egyptians believed that every person had a *ka*, a spiritual double for the material body that lived on after death in close association with the divine spirits. The *ka* had to be supplied with what it needed for a happy afterlife. In early Egyptian history a key to caring for the *ka* centered on mummification of the body and its burial in a tomb where its spirit could continue to live in it. Elaborate arrangements were made to ensure that the spirit would have food, drink, luxuries, company—everything it had enjoyed during life—to make immortal life tolerable. Perhaps initially only the pharaoh could afford such equipment, as evidenced by the pyramids built to house his spirit eternally. But pharaohs were willing to build and provide tombs for their wives, children, officials, and friends so that they could continue to be their companions in the enjoyment of eternal life.

Although the fate of the spirits of ordinary people in early Egypt is not clear, the expectation of gaining immortality was gradually democratized and universalized. The concept of immortality found its focus in the worship of Osiris, which by the Middle Kingdom had assumed a central place in religious life and was embodied in a touching myth. Osiris, a god associated with life forces and the Nile, was murdered by his wicked brother, Seth, who dismembered his body and scattered it over the earth. Isis, the wife of Osiris, patiently gathered the pieces, whereupon Osiris returned to life. Thereafter, Osiris had the power to grant a happy afterlife in a paradise much like the earthly Nile Valley to those who could meet his test for goodness (see Figure 1.3). Implicit in this concept of immortal life was the idea of moral worth attached to each person, a concept that would have a rich history. One must be cautious, however, in assessing the impact of moral concerns on Egyptian society. People continued to provide for the material welfare of the dead, although from the Middle Kingdom onward the emphasis was not so much on the grandeur of the tomb as on its decoration with texts and pictures seeking to convince Osiris that its occupant had lived a "good" life; in time, many busied themselves devising clever formulas to conceal their moral shortcomings.

The immense effort to understand, please, and thank the divine forces produced vigorous literary activity. Egyptian literature proper was preceded by the development of a system of writing, called *hieroglyphic*, which made its appearance about 3200 B.C. Like cuneiform writing, it began as pictograms out of which evolved symbols representing sounds that could be combined into words. The first use of writing was probably in record keeping and letter writing connected with the pharaoh's court, but it was not long before more artistic uses were found. Much early writing has survived on pyramid walls in the form of hymns, prayers, magical incantations, mythology, and accounts of the deeds of the occupant of the pyramid, all intended to send a message to the divine forces. Besides the pyramid texts other forms of literature survive, set down on either stone or papyrus (a writing material made from the pulp of the papyrus plant pressed into flat sheets). The Egyptians apparently enjoyed poetry, collections of maxims and wise sayings, often presented in the form of instructions given by father to son or teacher to pupil, and tales of fancy and romance recounting the adventures of travelers, sailors, and soldiers. On the whole Egyptian literature was confident in mood but perhaps not as profound in content as Mesopotamian literature.

The visual arts reflect the character and quality of the Egyptian genius most clearly. In all its forms, Egyptian art mirrors what may be the keystone of Egyptian civilization: the ability of a creative people to work for long ages with set forms

and subjects without loss of freshness and vitality. Egyptian artists created for eternity with confidence that the existing order was right and worth sustaining.

Architecture was the queen of all the arts, most of the other forms serving to adorn great buildings. Architects worked with bricks, reeds, and timber, but the most monumental work was in stone, of which there was a plentiful supply in Egypt. The first flowering of architecture came early in the Old Kingdom and was devoted chiefly to tomb building, which reached its apogee with the construction of the pyramids. The pyramid of Khufu, built about 2600 B.C., still stands as one of the major construction feats of all time. Built on a cliff overlooking the Nile, it measured 755 feet on each side and was 480 feet high. It contained over 2 million blocks of stone, each of which was precut in quarries many miles away and floated down the Nile to the building site, a procedure that required careful planning, skilled engineering, and a huge expenditure of labor. Surrounding the pyramid was a complex of temples and tombs for Khufu's dead family and friends. A roadway led down to the valley, where there was another building complex intended to house the priests, officials, and laborers who carried on the many services required to care for the spirit living in the pyramid tomb. Pyramid building continued for many centuries, but later architects never equaled those of the Old Kingdom. By the end of the Old Kingdom temples and palaces commanded more attention. The basic temple style, established very early, was the hypostyle hall, consisting of a high-ceilinged central hall flanked by side halls, each covered with a roof set on columns shorter than those of the central hall. Builders achieved splendid artistic effects by modeling their columns after plants—the palm tree, the lotus plant, the papyrus plant, the reed. Within the temple, numerous chambers were grouped to create a sanctuary where the god or goddess to whom the temple was dedicated could live (see Color Plate 2). Before the temple was an open court surrounded by a columned portico and entered by a massive gate. Scanty surviving evidence indicates that the palaces built for pharaohs and nobles were as splendid as the temples and probably utilized the same basic architectural forms.

FIGURE 1.3 Judgment Day This Egyptian funerary papyrus from the tomb of a princess shows some of the steps in the transition to afterlife. In the center, the gods weigh her heart in a balance against the figure of the Goddess of Truth. Any flaw in her life would result in a loss of eternal happiness. (The Metropolitan Museum of Art)

Egypt's sculptors matched architects in skill. At a very early date sculptural styles became fixed and changed little over most of Egypt's history. The chief subjects of three-dimensional sculpture were the deities, the pharaohs, their families, and their companions, most such statues being intended to adorn tombs and temples. Human forms were usually massive, stiff, unemotional portrayals following fixed proportions. But the faces were another matter; here the sculptor tried to project a quality embodied in or exemplified by the subject: the power of a god or goddess, the majesty of a pharaoh, the devotion of a royal servant (see Figure 1.1). Sculptors were also skilled at relief work, most of which was carved on the walls of tombs and temples and intended to record the deeds of those commemorated (see Figures 2.1 and 2.2). As a consequence, Egyptian reliefs contain a remarkably rich record of everyday life at all levels of society. However, sculptors seldom tried to be realistic. They let the space available determine the size and shape of their figures, and they often used conventional designs to represent objects. Human figures are distorted, the feet and faces usually shown in profile while the main trunk of the body faces the viewer. Many of the reliefs were painted to heighten the effect. Painting, most of which also survives in tombs, bears striking similarity to relief work in terms of subject and form.

The Egyptians made advances in technology and science that rivaled the work of the Mesopotamians. They recorded information about the movement of the stars, from which they developed an accurate time-reckoning system and a calendar of twelve thirty-day months plus five days added at the end of each year. They developed a system of numbers that permitted them to perform basic arithmetic functions and to calculate areas and volumes. They accumulated considerable information about the properties of metals and about plant and animal life. In medicine they developed surgical techniques and learned to use a wide range of drugs. Their understanding of anatomy was extensive, undoubtedly a result of observations made in the process of mummifying the dead. However, like the Mesopotamians, the Egyptians had little interest in pursuing knowledge about nature for its own sake. Once they found a practical solution for a problem of engineering, metallurgy, medicine, or discovering the intention of the deities, they sought no further.

SUGGESTED READING

Overview of the Ancient Near East to ca. 330 B.C.

H. W. F. Saggs, *Civilization before Greece and Rome* (1989).
Arthur Bernard Knapp, *The History and Culture of Ancient Western Asia and Egypt* (1988).
Either of these two books will provide an excellent overview.

Prehistory

Frank E. Poirier, *Understanding Human Evolution* (1987).
Richard E. Leakey, *The Making of Mankind* (1981).
John E. Pfeiffer, *The Emergence of Humankind*, 4th ed. (1985).
Robert J. Wenke, *Patterns in Prehistory: Humankind's First Three Million Years* (1990).
Each of these four works provides a provocative treatment of the much-disputed problem of human origins.
Brian M. Fagan, *People of the Earth: An Introduction to World Prehistory*, 4th ed. (1983). An excellent treatment of prehistoric culture.
Margaret Ehrenberg, *Women in Prehistory* (1989). An informative survey.

Mesopotamia

Hans J. Nissen, *The Early History of the Ancient Near East, 9000–2000 B.C.*, trans. Elizabeth Lutzeier and Kenneth J. Northcott (1988). A good survey taking archaeological data into account.
H. W. F. Saggs, *Everyday Life in Babylonia and Assyria*, rev. ed. (1987). Rich in material on how people lived in ancient Mesopotamia.
Thorkild Jacobsen, *The Treasures of Darkness: A History of Mesopotamian Religion* (1976). An excellent introduction.
Anton Moortgat, *The Art of Ancient Mesopotamia: The Classical Art of the Near East*, trans. Judith Filson (1969).

André Parrot, *Sumer: The Dawn of Art*, trans. Stuart Gilbert and James Emmons (1961).
Either of these beautifully illustrated volumes will provide a good introduction to Mesopotamian art.

Egypt

Cyril Aldred, *The Egyptians*, rev. and enl. ed. (1984).
T. G. H. James, *An Introduction to Ancient Egypt* (1990).
Micahel Rice, *Egypt's Making. The Origins of Ancient Egypt, 5000-2000 B.C.* (1990).
Any of these three works will provide an excellent guide to the development of Egyptian civilization.
Barbara Mertz, *Red Land, Black Land: Daily Life in Ancient Egypt*, rev. ed. (1978).
John Romer, *People of the Nile: Everyday Life in Ancient Egypt* (1982).
These two works are rich in details about how people lived in ancient Egypt.
Barbara Watterson, *Women in Ancient Egypt* (1991).
Wolfgang Decker, *Sports and Games in Ancient Egypt*, trans. Allen Guttmann (1992).
Erik Hornung, *Conceptions of the Gods in Ancient Egypt: The One and the Many*, trans. John Baines (1982).
A. Rosalie David, *The Ancient Egyptians: Religious Beliefs and Practices* (1982).
Either of these works will help the reader understand the complexities of ancient Egyptian religion.
Kurt Lange and Max Hirmer, *Egypt: Architecture, Sculpture, Painting in Three Thousand Years*, trans. Judith Filson and Barbara Taylor, 4th ed. (1968).
W. Stevenson Smith and William Kelly Simpson, *Art and Architecture of Ancient Egypt*, 2nd ed. (1981).
Either of these two works, both well illustrated, will provide a sense of the basic characteristics of Egyptian art.

CHAPTER 2
The Diffusion of Near Eastern Civilization, 1750–800 B.C.

FIGURE 2.1 Egyptian Imperialism This scene, from the temple of Karnak, shows the pharaoh Thutmose III (1504–1450 B.C.) grasping Egypt's enemies by the hair prior to striking them to show Egypt's mastery over them. This scene captures the spirit of Egyptian imperialism during the period of the New Kingdom. Such relief carvings occupied a major place in Egyptian artistic activity. (Hirmer Fotoarchiv)

By about 1750 B.C. the history of the Afro-Asian zone of civilization entered a new phase with a new focus. The higher civilizations produced in the unique environment of the river valleys had matured fully. Well before 1750 B.C. the influence of the Mesopotamian and Egyptian civilizations had begun to spread beyond their original settings. During the period 1750-800 B.C. the process of cultural diffusion quickened and became a central theme of Near Eastern history. Not only did new peoples come to share higher civilization, many of them also made important contributions that enriched the basic patterns of civilized life.

1. DIFFUSION AND THE MOVEMENT OF PEOPLES

Cultural diffusion in this period was a complex process. Ideas, products, and techniques were carried out from the established centers of civilization by traders, soldiers, and diplomats. Imitation of the superior ways of the river valley civilizations by people long settled on their fringes was common. As cultural patterns spread, they were adapted and modified to fit new settings and situations. Especially important as a catalytic force was the movement of peoples into and around the civilized zones to create new political entities eager to share the benefits of civilized life.

Two peoples were especially significant in creating conditions that encouraged cultural diffusion. The Semitic-speaking seminomads of the Arabian Desert, with whom we are already familiar as intruders into Mesopotamia, continued their migrations after 1800 B.C. to play a prime role in the history of northern Mesopotamia, Syria, Palestine, and Egypt.

No less important were some newcomers, the Indo-Europeans, so named because they spoke a language that was new to the Near East and from which later evolved Sanskrit, Latin, Greek, Persian, and most modern European languages. Beginning about 2000 B.C., they fanned outward from their ancient homeland, perhaps north of the Caspian Sea, to make their impact felt over a broad area embracing central Europe, Italy, Greece, the Aegean area, the Near East, Iran, and India. At the time of their intrusion into the Near East, the Indo-Europeans had not reached the level of culture prevailing there. However, their superior weapons and military organization allowed them to play an important political role. And they proved adept at assimilating established patterns of civlization, especially the Mesopotamian, which they combined with their native culture to create cultural patterns with unique features.

2. THE EGYPTIAN AND HITTITE EMPIRES, 1750–1200 B.C.

The millennium under review in this chapter began with a series of disturbances that led to a major rearrangement of the power structure across the Near East (see Map 2.1). The Amorite Empire founded by Hammurabi suffered attacks which led to its destruction shortly after 1600 B.C. by the Kassites, immigrants from east of Mesopotamia, who were able to establish political domination over Mesopotamia. They ruled there for nearly four centuries, a period during which Mesopotamia played a secondary role in Near Eastern political life but continued to assert a major cultural influence over many peoples beyond Mesopotamia. To the north of Mesopotamia, Hurrian warlords established dominance over an area embracing the upper Tigris-Euphrates valleys and northern Syria to create the kingdom of the Mitanni, which flourished from about 1550 to 1350 B.C. As we shall see in the next section, a new power, the Indo-European Hittite kingdom, was emerging in Asia Minor. Also about 1750 B.C. the Hyksos, predominantly Semitic wanderers from the Palestine area, intruded into Egypt, contributing to a new era of internal disorder called the Second Intermediate Period (ca. 1750–1580 B.C.).

The Hyksos' presence in Egypt generated a powerful reaction against foreigners that led not only to the restoration of internal order but also to a new role for the Egyptians in the Near East. An effort to expel the Hyksos, led by local princes from Thebes, was finally achieved by Ahmose I (1558–1533 B.C.), the founder of the Eighteenth Dynasty. His victory opened the third period of glory in Egyptian history, the New Kingdom or Empire (1558–1200 B.C.). During the first century of the Eighteenth Dynasty, Egypt

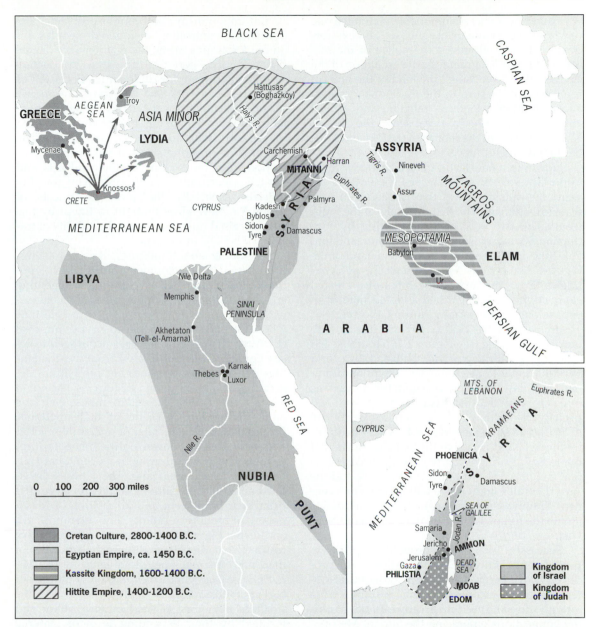

Map 2.1 THE ANCIENT NEAR EAST, CA. 1450 B.C. This map illustrates the main centers of political power during the period 1600–1200 B.C. The ambitions of the rulers of the major states led to considerable conflict, especially in Syria and Palestine, where Egyptian and Hittite interests clashed. The map also indicates how extensively the ways of civilized life had spread beyond the original centers of civilization in the river valleys shown on Map 1.1.

was ruled by a succession of able pharaohs, one of whom was a woman, Hatshepsut. Her extraordinary career epitomized the policy of the restorers of Egyptian greatness: the exaltation of the divine ruler; "cleansing" the land of the taint of foreigners; the return to the traditional order in administration, economy, religion, and artistic and intellectual life. In a real sense, the "New" Kingdom was but the rebirth of the Old and Middle kingdoms.

However, a new factor played an increasingly important role: a more aggressive posture toward the outside world that ripened into full-scale imperialism. The first pharaohs of the Eighteenth Dynasty initiated expansionism by conducting raids against Nubia to the south and into Palestine and Syria, the original homeland of the Hyksos. These raids not only built Egypt's confidence in its military strength but also created elements in society that had a vested interest in expansionism. Eventually, during the reign of Thutmose III (1504–1450 B.C.), raiding turned into outright conquest (see Figure 2.1). Thutmose led a series of campaigns into Nubia, Libya, and Syria-Palestine that established Egyptian dominance. This expansion brought the Egyptians into contact with other Near Eastern powers, especially the Mitanni, who were rivals for control of Syria-Palestine (see Map 2.1). These confrontations resulted in active diplomatic efforts that made Egypt's might felt beyond the areas of actual conquest. The Mitanni, the Kassites, and the Assyrians all sought peace with Egypt. For a century Thutmose's successors pursued his policy and made Egypt the dominant power in the Near East.

Successful imperialism brought Egypt a new period of magnificence. Added to the wealth produced by the carefully managed agricultural system was a vast income from tribute exacted from foreign subjects and from greatly expanded trading connections embracing the Sudan, Mesopotamia, Asia Minor, Crete, and the Aegean world. Artistic life again blossomed, expressing itself with special brilliance in the magnificent temples built at Luxor and Karnak in honor of Amon-Ra, the chief national god (see Color Plate 2). The influences of Egyptian art styles, literary models, pottery and metalworking techniques, and religious practices were felt throughout the Near East with a force unknown prior to the New Kingdom.

But imperialism also brought problems. The burden of controlling conquered peoples required a standing army, the maintenance of garrisons abroad, periodic campaigns to display strength, and complex diplomatic efforts. All of this put a heavy demand on Egypt's resources. Major consequences were an increasing regimentation of Egypt's native populace and a growing reliance on slavery in the service of the state. The concerns of empire distracted the pharaohs' attention from the welfare of their subjects and created opportunities for oppression by grasping officials, especially the powerful priests of Amon-Ra. New ideas brought to Egypt by foreigners raised questions about the validity of traditional beliefs and practices.

Beginning about 1400 B.C., these problems, complicated by developments outside Egypt, put the New Kingdom to a severe test. The emerging crisis found its focus in the increasing rebelliousness of the dependent princes of Syria-Palestine, whose loyalty was a keystone of Egypt's imperial structure. These princes were encouraged to resist Egypt by a formidable external foe, the Hittites. Of Indo-European origins, the Hittites began to settle in central and eastern Asia Minor at least as early as 2000 B.C. and to impose their rule on the natives to form a series of small kingdoms. By about 1600 B.C. the ruler of one of these kingdoms imposed his power on the others to form a single Hittite kingdom with its capital at Hattusas (modern Boghazköy). The Hittites developed an advanced culture, derived in large part from their borrowing and adaptation of Mesopotamian models in politics, law, literature, art, and technology but also marked by distinctive features that displayed the creative powers of this "new" people. Their dominance in Asia Minor marked a significant expansion of the area of higher civilization.

Once firmly established in Asia Minor and fortified by their expanding level of material wealth and culture, the Hittites were able to expand eastward and southward to create their own empire (see Map 2.1). By 1400 B.C. they were actively engaged in encouraging and supporting rebellion among Egypt's client principalities in Syria and Palestine. Hittite power reached its zenith under King Suppiluliumas (1375–1355 B.C.), who threatened to oust Egypt from its Asian holdings.

In the face of the mounting threat to its empire, Egypt was distracted by an internal crisis brought on by a religious reform instituted by Amenhotep IV (1379–1362 B.C.) with the help of his queen, Nefertiti. Although his motives have been much debated, it appears that this enigmatic pharaoh acted for both political and religious reasons: to reestablish the pharaoh's absolute supremacy in the face of threats offered by such powerfully entrenched groups as the military establishment, the royal officials, and especially the priests of Amon-Ra and to revitalize a traditional religious system that had become encrusted with contradictory beliefs and overelaborate rituals based on crude materialism. In any case, Amenhotep IV proclaimed a new religion based on the worship of the god Aton, depicted as the source of all life, who was represented to humanity in the form of the sun disc giving off rays that sustained all existence (see Figure 2.2). To dramatize his break with the old order, Amenhotep IV changed his name to Akhnaton ("It pleases Aton") and abandoned the old capital at Thebes for a new one named Akhetaton (modern Tell el Amarna). Worship of the old deities was forbidden, their temples destroyed, their priests demoted. New rituals and a new art style, fresh and naturalistic, developed to honor and portray Aton. Many uncertainties surround what kind of religious system Akhnaton intended. Some have argued that he sought to establish monotheism, that is, a religion based on the worship of one god, a concept heretofore unknown. However, close scrutiny of the record does not support this view, for Akhnaton continued to present himself as a god. Perhaps he envisaged a religion that would rid Egyptian society of its restrictive traditionalism rooted in the old religious order and equip the Egyptians to take the lead in exploiting the cosmopolitan currents circulating in the Near East in this era of the mixing and mingling of cultures.

However, such questions are moot. Akhnaton's proclamation of a new religion raised a storm of protest, led by the priests of Amon-Ra, which for a decade consumed the energy of society. Even before his death Akhnaton's foes had forced him to abandon his reforms. Under his successor, his son-in-law Tutankhamon, the forces of reaction rapidly restored the cult of Amon-Ra and made a concerted effort to eradicate Aton worship and the memory of its chief proponent. The restoration of the traditional or-

FIGURE 2.2 An Egyptian Religious Reformer This scene shows Akhnaton with his wife, Nefertiti, and one of their daughters making an offering to the new deity, Aton, promoted by Akhnaton. The new deity is represented by the sun disc pouring its fruitful rays on the worshipers, who in turn would bestow such benefits on the pharaoh's subjects. The artistic style reflected in this carving is more naturalistic than the traditional Egyptian artistic canon (compare with Figures 1.1, 1.3, and 2.1). (The Metropolitan Museum of Art)

der is dramatically reflected in the objects found in "King Tut's" tomb; first excavated in 1922, its contents provide one of the most magnificent reflections of traditional Egyptian art and thought that has survived.

The disturbances caused by Akhnaton's attempted reform and the efforts to undo it weakened Egypt's capability to defend its empire. Hittite aggression in Syria and Palestine, accompanied by defections of local princes, temporarily ended Egyptian control in that area. Eventually, under the early rulers of the Nineteenth Dynasty, especially Seti and Rameses II, the Egyptians were able to regroup their military forces and to redress the balance in Syria and Palestine after a bitter and costly struggle with the Hittites which finally ended about 1270 B.C. with a settlement that assigned each a sphere of influence in that embattled area.

For an interval both Egyptians and Hittites regained their former vitality as the leading powers of the era. However, both empires were approaching the end of their greatness. Decisive in determining their fate was a new wave of Indo-European invaders, especially formidable because they possessed iron weapons, who spilled over Asia Minor, the Aegean Sea area, and the waterways of the eastern Mediterranean. The Hittite Empire was completely destroyed about 1200 B.C. Attacks by Nubians, Libyans, and the mysterious "People of the Sea," seafaring marauders probably from Asia Minor, forced the Egyptians back within their old boundaries and for a time established foreigners from Libya and sub-Saharan Africa as pharaohs. These setbacks greatly reduced Egypt's capacity to influence developments in the Asiatic Near East but opened opportunities for cultural interaction between Egypt and large areas of northeast Africa.

3. THE MINOAN WORLD, 2000–1400 B.C.

The age of diffusion witnessed the development of a vital new civilization on the island of Crete, named Minoan by modern historians after Minos, a legendary Cretan king. Although the development of Minoan civilization was affected by borrowings from other civilizations of the Near East, the Cretans demonstrated a capacity to create a pattern of culture that had a unique character. Their accomplishment was especially important because of the influence it asserted over the world to the north and west—especially Greece.

Minoan civilization had its roots in a Neolithic farming culture that took shape on Crete about 6000 B.C. For many centuries thereafter Neolithic farmers shared a simple pattern of culture with other people living in Greece, the Aegean Islands, and Asia Minor. Gradually, the Cretans developed skills in pottery making and metalwork; especially important was the introduction of bronze technology from Asia Minor about 3000 B.C. Moreover, the Cretans learned to sail the seas to establish contacts with the advanced civilizations of Egypt and Asia and to enrich themselves by gaining access to markets and raw materials in the area around the Aegean. By about 2000 B.C. their developing technical skills, increasing wealth, and expanding contacts resulted in the emergence of several full-fledged urban centers, including Knossos, Phaistos, and Mallia. Each was ruled by a king whose magnificent palace was the center of civilized life. Minoan civilization reached its peak between about 1700 and 1450 B.C. During this period Knossos outstripped the other cities of Crete, asserting a cultural leadership that provided a common pattern of life on the island and extending Cretan influences over much of the Aegean world, chiefly through trading ventures. Then, between 1500 and 1450 B.C., a disaster struck the Minoan world, destroying many cities. Perhaps this catastrophe was a consequence of a devastating volcano on the island of Thera, north of Crete. At about the same time Crete suffered at the hands of invaders from Greece called Mycenaeans (see Chapter 4). Knossos continued for an interval as a center from which the invaders ruled the island, but shortly after 1400 B.C. it too was destroyed, perhaps as a result of a revolt against the outsiders. Minoan civilization had run its course.

Our knowledge of the major features of Minoan civilization is derived chiefly from archaeological evidence produced by excavations of palace sites, especially Knossos. The Minoans did develop their own writing system, called Linear A by modern scholars, but it has not yet been deciphered. About 1450 B.C. that system was replaced by another, called Linear B, which has been deciphered and proved to be based on an early form of the Greek language. It probably represents an adaptation of Minoan writing by the Mycenaean invaders from Greece. The surviving documents in Linear B are chiefly economic records and provide only limited information about many facets of Minoan society.

At the height of Minoan civilization Crete was governed by several kings, each controlling a particular city and its surrounding territory. Perhaps the king of Knossos exercised some form of authority over the other kingdoms, but that overlordship was based on consent rather than force. The fact that Minoan cities were unwalled indicates that the kingdoms lived without serious conflict and great expenditure for arms. The power of Minoan kings rested on strong religious sanctions and on wealth derived from control of the agricultural system and from overseas trade. Royal administration was conducted by a highly developed bureaucracy especially skilled at orderly record keeping. A wealthy and influential nobility made up chiefly of landowners grouped itself around the kings to uphold royal authority.

The Minoan economy was based on a productive agricultural system devoted to the cultivation of grain, olives, grapes, and vegetables and to the raising of livestock, especially sheep. But trade and industry produced the additional wealth necessary to support an advanced civilization. Highly skilled artisans laboring in the workshops of the royal palace or in their own shops produced a wide variety of goods that adorned the lives of the rulers, their officials, and the wealthy landowners and merchants. Especially skilled were Minoan potters and metalworkers. Enterprising merchants, sometimes serving the kings and sometimes working on their own, carried Minoan manufactured products over the seas to a wide area around the Mediterranean, including not only the major Near Eastern centers of civilization but also the less developed peoples of the Aegean world. These merchants brought back a variety of raw materials and manufactured goods. The wealth produced by this vigorous economy allowed the Minoan upper class to live in well-furnished houses and enjoy fine clothing and abundant jewelry. Upper-class women shared freely in the social life of the palaces and aristocratic households. Every royal city had a considerable population of laborers who performed all kinds of work needed to sustain city life. The rural population clustered in villages, where they labored under the supervision of royal officials and pow-

FIGURE 2.3 Minoan Sports This bronze figure dating from the sixteenth century B.C. portrays a favorite Minoan sporting activity—vaulting over a charging bull. Both young men and young women participated in this dangerous game. The artist's ability to convey a feeling of movement on the part of both the leaper and the animal is reflective of much of Minoan art. (The British Museum)

erful landowners. There was little slavery in Minoan society.

The Minoans worshiped a variety of gods and goddesses, most of them representing the forces of nature and especially the goddess of fertility, whose life-giving powers were invoked by all classes of people. Religious practices were less elaborate than those of Mesopotamia and Egypt. The Minoans built no great temples; they worshiped at simple shrines in private houses, on hills, in groves and caves, and near springs. Priests and priestesses were maintained at the palace to serve the deities, but they played only a limited role in shaping Minoan life and culture. Prominent place in religious ceremonies was given to animal sacrifice, gift giving, dancing, and athletic events (see Figure 2.3). The pictorial representations of these rituals suggest an outlook that was joyful and lighthearted, little marked by fear or gloom. There was a belief in afterlife, and some attention was given to the care of the dead, but never on the scale that occurred in Egypt.

The spirit of Minoan civilization emerges most forcefully in the visual arts. Minoan architecture, devoted chiefly to building palaces and private dwellings such as those revealed by the ruins of Knossos rather than temples and tombs, reflected a technical mastery of a variety of materials and forms and a fine sense of scale. Many of the multistoried structures were equipped with a piped water supply, skillfully constructed drainage systems, and indoor toilets. Palaces and houses were decorated with paintings and carvings that focused on nature and human activity. Especially skilled were elaborate frescoes portraying processions of young men and women bearing gifts to the gods and goddesses. Animals, fish, and birds were also favorite subjects of carvers and painters. Minoan decorated pottery reflects a fine sense of form and a love of color. In all its forms Minoan art is mobile, free of stylization, intense, and energetic. It reflects a civilization focused on worldly concerns, lacking in fear, open to experimentation, and pleasure loving. In many ways the mentality shaping Minoan civilization contrasts sharply with that of Mesopotamia and Egypt, heralding a world yet to come.

4. THE ERA OF SMALL STATES, 1200–800 B.C.: PHOENICIANS AND ARAMEANS

The collapse of the Hittite and Egyptian empires about 1200 B.C., coupled with the decline of Minoan power, left the Near East without a dominant power center for about four centuries. Several small groups located in Syria and Palestine, the crossroad of the Near East, seized the opportunity to carve a place in and to make their unique contributions to the increasingly homogeneous world of the Near East.

Two peoples stand out especially as creative adapters and disseminators of established cultural patterns: the Phoenicians and the Arameans. Both were Semitic seminomads in origin, the products of the numerous migrations from the Arabian Desert that had been in progress for many centuries. These migrants were repeatedly conquered and strongly influenced by the Mesopotamians, Egyptians, and Hittites. Consequently, by 1200 B.C. they were already highly civilized peoples. The Phoenicians, located in the narrow coastal area between the Mediterranean Sea and the mountains of Lebanon, developed a number of independent city-states, chief of which were Byblos, Tyre, and Sidon. The Arameans were located east of the Lebanon Mountains between the northern fringes of the Arabian Desert and the Euphrates River. They were organized into a number of small kingdoms centered around Damascus, Kadesh, and Palmyra (see Map 2.1). For about four centuries these city-states and kingdoms enjoyed independent existence until they were finally absorbed into the Assyrian Empire (see Chapter 3).

The Phoenicians and the Arameans derived most of their wealth from trade. The Phoenicians took to the seas and established a virtual monopoly on trade in the Mediterranean, chiefly as successors to the Minoan traders. Their merchants carried manufactured goods from the entire Near East to the less developed peoples of Greece, Italy, North Africa, Spain, and southern France and brought back the raw materials of these areas. From these traders many peoples to the west got their first taste of higher civilization. The Phoenicians not only traded but also established colonies, notably the North African city of Carthage, destined to become an important center of civilization after 800 B.C. The Arameans were overland traders, exploiting the trade routes that linked Egypt, Mesopotamia, Asia Minor, and points beyond. Both Phoenicians and Arameans reaped a rich reward from their commerce, which allowed them to live well and to support a wide range of cultural activities. Neither people was particularly creative in learning and the arts. However, the Phoenicians did perfect an alphabet that later served as a model for the written languages of the Mediterranean basin, and the Aramean language was widely adopted in the Near East.

5. THE ERA OF SMALL STATES, 1200–800 B.C.: THE HEBREWS

One people emerging into prominence during the Era of Small States had a particularly enduring impact on the spiritual and moral history of Western civilization. These were the Hebrews, who left a magnificent literary record of their version of their history in their Bible, now generally referred to as the Old Testament. The interpretation of this complex document, composed over many centuries by many authors drawing on a mixture of historical traditions, folklore, legal enactments, moral exhortations, and prophecies, confronts the modern historian with formidable problems. However, the main lines of the story it tells, coupled with supporting evidence from non-Hebrew literary sources and from archaeology, provide a fairly accurate account of the history of the Hebrews during the age of diffusion.

The surviving evidence suggests that the Hebrews were originally nomads searching for a place in which to settle, part of the extensive migration of Semitic-speaking peoples that played a crucial role in the age of diffusion. During what the Hebrew Bible called the age of the patriarchs, tribal groups based on kinship ties left their settlements on the fringes of Mesopotamia and, under the leadership of family heads such as Abraham, Isaac, and Jacob, migrated around the southern fringes of the Fertile Crescent to the area of Palestine. Perhaps this migration began about 1800 B.C., roughly in the time of Hammurabi, and took place over a relatively long period. In the Palestinian region the nomadic Hebrew herders encountered and began to clash with more advanced agricultural societies, especially the Canaanites. As a result of this interaction the Hebrews began a slow transition to settled agricultural life. An important feature of Hebrew tribal life was a religion rooted in a fierce allegiance by tribal members to a deity who gave special protection to the tribe and interacted with it through its patriarch. Among such deities was Yahweh, the god of Abraham.

Not all of the wandering Hebrews remained in the Palestine area. Some made their way to Egypt and settled in the Delta region (the biblical land of Goshen), where they prospered for a time, and some, like Joseph, even found favor at the pharaoh's court, suggesting that the Hebrews accommodated to the higher civilization of the Egyptians. Eventually, however, there arose a pharaoh "who knew not Joseph" and whose mistreatment led to a decisive event in Hebrew history—the Exodus from Egypt, which probably occurred during the reign of Pharaoh Rameses II (1292–1235 B.C.).

During a period of wandering in the desert of the Sinai Peninsula that followed the Exodus, there occurred a religious experience that gave fundamental shape to the religious consciousness of the Hebrews. Under the leadership of Moses, the Hebrews of the Exodus came to believe that they as a people had become special partners of Yahweh, whom at least some had worshiped during the age of the patriarchs. Master of history and of nature, as he had demonstrated through the events of the Exodus, Yahweh made a *covenant*, or mutual contract, with Moses' people: He selected them as his people and promised to care for them. In return, they pledged to honor him as their only god and to follow his law, revealed to Moses as the Ten Commandments, in the conduct of their individual and collective existences. These fundamental concepts, which thereafter remained central to the Hebrew religion, became the basis for the transformation of Moses' "mixed multitude" of tribal groups into "a holy nation," the Israelites, whose identity was rooted in their unique relationship with their god.

Fortified by their pact with Yahweh, Moses' followers joined forces with other Hebrew tribes in search of the Promised Land. Their object became Palestine, an area where considerable instability existed in the wake of the collapse of the Egyptian and Hittite empires (see Map 2.1). The biblical version of this quest presents a relatively simple account of a succession of military triumphs, beginning with Joshua's dramatic capture of Jericho and forged by the collaboration of the twelve tribes into which the Hebrews were organized. In reality, the Hebrew struggle for Palestine was a drawn-out process involving more than military engagements. To be sure, the Canaanites were formidable foes, but they were not the only ones. Repeatedly the Hebrews had to contend with other outsiders equally intent on occupying Palestine, a threat that often necessitated cooperation between Hebrews and Canaanites and led to gradual assimilation of the two peoples in a way that hastened the transformation of the Hebrews into farmers and city dwellers. This process challenged traditional values in ways that caused tensions within Hebrew society. The Hebrew effort was impeded by tribal jealousies, intensified as a result of the attempts of each tribe to establish its identity on the basis of its claim to a particular territory won in the struggle for Palestine. These complex stresses produced crisis after crisis, sometimes dramatically resolved by charismatic figures such as Gideon, Samson, and Samuel, collectively designated in the Bible as "judges," who often employed religious arguments to persuade the Hebrews to act in unity—at least temporarily.

After about a hundred and fifty years of struggle and change, the Hebrews were close to winning the Promised Land. Then they were almost destroyed by the Philistines, warlike newcomers armed with iron weapons who settled along the south Palestine coast after being rebuffed in their attempt to enter Egypt. By about 1050 B.C. the Philistines had made major inroads into Palestine and seemed to be on the verge of overpowering the Hebrews. The threat of disaster led to a momentous step: an agreement among the Hebrew tribes—forged in large part through the efforts of a famous judge, Samuel—to place themselves under a single king, thereby creating a political "nation."

The unified Hebrew nation survived for about a century (1020–930 B.C.), embracing the reigns of Saul, David, and Solomon, who collectively brought the Hebrews to the high point of their history in ancient times. These kings were able to organize military resources that expelled the Philistines from Palestine and then subdued not only the Canaanites but also many small principalities on the borders of Palestine, allowing the unified Hebrew kingdom to assume a place as an important power in the Syria-Palestine area. A centralized government was established at Jerusalem, which, especially under Solomon, took on many characteristics of a typical Near Eastern monarchy. The kingdom was greatly enriched by royal economic policies that helped Hebrew traders take advantage of Palestine's strategic location on international trade routes. Solomon was particularly effective in creating an extensive network of diplomatic ties in the Near East that enhanced the prestige of the kingdom and brought its ruling elements into contact with the increasingly cosmopolitan world of the Near East; evidence of these contacts was provided not only by Solomon's many foreign wives but also by foreign influences on the arts and on lifestyles increasingly prevalent among the Hebrews.

As the Hebrews' political fortunes advanced

between 1200 and 930 B.C., their religion—Judaism—continued to develop. The struggles to occupy Palestine brought constant reminders to the Hebrews, especially from the aforementioned judges, to remain loyal to the covenant with Yahweh. The success under the early monarchs appeared to vindicate Yahweh's concern for his people and thus to keep his worship central to Hebrew life. In fact, the institution of a monarchy, which was believed to be sanctioned by Yahweh in a special way, marked an important step in creating a truly national religion. A prime symbol of this national religion was the establishment by David and Solomon of Jerusalem as the cult center as well as the political capital of the Hebrew people; the city's jewel was the splendid temple built by Solomon to house the Ark of the Convenant, a wooden chest containing sacred objects associated with the worship of Yahweh. The system of law originally set forth in the Ten Commandments was greatly expanded to serve as a common bond among the Hebrews and to relate their new lives as farmers and urban dwellers to basic religious principles rooted in the covenant. A more complex set of religious practices shaped by an emerging priesthood took on increasing importance in the collective lives of the Hebrews. The changes in law and worship involved the absorption into Judaism of elements from non-Hebrew sources, especially Canaanite cult practices associated with the agricultural seasons. This process of assimilation generated constant tension in Hebrew religious life but ultimately resulted in an enriched and flexible common religion attuned to the more advanced level of civilization that the Hebrews had attained by the time of Solomon.

Even while Solomon reigned in all his glory, deep-seated discontents within the Hebrew community threatened the unity of the kingdom. Among the major causes of this discontent were the autocratic methods of the kings, growing economic and social inequality, rural-urban rivalry, and concerns over foreign religious practices in the rituals of the temple and the royal court. Immediately after Solomon's death these discontents resulted in a division of the unified state into two kingdoms: Israel in the north, with its center at Samaria, and Judah in the south, with its capital at Jerusalem ruled by kings descended from the house of David (see Map 2.1). Each of these nations had a stormy internal history, marked by social and religious conflict. Ultimately, neither was able to survive outside aggression. In 722 B.C. Israel was conquered by the Assyrians and many of its people were carried off into captivity, to be enshrined in Hebrew memory as the Ten Lost Tribes. Judah survived until 586 B.C., when the Chaldeans captured Jerusalem, destroyed the Temple, and took large numbers of Hebrews to Babylon as captives. The Persian ruler Cyrus (ca. 560–530 B.C.) allowed those victims of the Babylonian captivity who wished to do so to return to Jerusalem and to rebuild the Temple, which again became the center of a vital religious community. However, the Hebrews remained politically subject to the Persians and then were absorbed into the empire of Alexander the Great when he destroyed the Persian Empire in 330 B.C. An important consequence of this troubled course of events was the beginnings of the Diaspora, the scattering of many Hebrews across the map of the Near East into new settings where their religion would undergo new challenges and where they would assert an important influence on the non-Hebrews among whom they lived.

In these times of almost constant tribulation Judaism took on new dimensions. During the period of the divided kingdoms and foreign conquests, religion became the sole force that sustained a sense of commonality and uniqueness among the Hebrews. Thrust into a position of leadership of a community ruled by foreign potentates, the Hebrew priesthood fashioned a sober, austere cult that cut away much of the magic and superstition surrounding other Near Eastern religions; observance of these practices became a mark of belonging to Yahweh's special community. Much more significant was the reformulation of the traditional concepts of Judaism by a series of powerful religious leaders known as *prophets*. Several of them rank among the world's greatest spiritual leaders: Elijah, Amos, Isaiah, Jeremiah, Ezekiel, the anonymous second Isaiah. And occasionally a female voice sounded among them: Esther, Ruth, and Judith. Although their careers spanned several centuries and each spoke a unique message appropriate to his or her own time, these remarkable figures

collectively explored with deep spiritual insight and articulated with great force many of the elements essential to all religious experience. Usually individuals of modest social status, little concerned with wealth and power or office, they presented themselves as messengers of Yahweh driven by an urge to put back on the right course all who claimed to be followers of Yahweh, including especially the rich and the powerful. The religious message of all of them was rooted in a shared conviction, based on their reading of history and their interpretation of their own times, that the Hebrews were guilty of abandoning their covenant with Yahweh. Their prophetic mission was to call Yahweh's errant and hardhearted people back to that covenant. In the course of reinterpreting the essence of that covenant, they expanded and clarified certain fundamental concepts that became the essence of Judaism and the source of its powerful impact on the future course of Western civilization.

First, the prophets insisted that the Hebrews worship only one god; to give any sign of recognition to any other deity except Yahweh was the greatest of all sacrileges. In fixing this point at the center of religious life, the prophets ensured that Judaism became the first truly monotheistic religion.

Second, the prophets gave ultimate shape to a radically new concept of Yahweh's nature, a concept set forth in terms that demanded that he alone be worshiped. Yahweh, whose name means "he causes to be," was the creator of all things. He was omnipotent, ruling the entire universe and causing everything in the past, present, and future to happen. Unlike other gods worshiped in the Near East, he was not in nature and could not be depicted in any natural form; he created and controlled natural forces which were to be seen as reflections of his divine power but not as objects to be worshiped. Likewise, he was outside time, which was a created dimension of the universe within which would be worked his plan for the universe and for humanity, a plan in which all created things were destined to participate; each event along the trajectory of time was a meaningful manifestation of his unfolding plan. He was a god of justice, acting according to law instead of whim. He was a god of righteousness, pleased by those who did good according to his commands but offended to the point of vengeance by those who did evil. He was a caring god, "merciful and gracious, long-suffering, and abundant in goodness and truth," always watchful over his entire creation.

Third, the prophets projected a new vision of the essence of human nature. As Yahweh's special creatures, human beings were created to play a special role in the working out of the divine plan. This role could be achieved only by the realization by humans of their capacity for moral perfection, which involved a choice by each individual between good and evil. Human beings were basically moral beings, each endowed with the freedom and capacity to choose the good. They were not Yahweh's slaves, for whom he cared not and upon whom he might vent his wrath at his whim; rather, each was his child who could earn divine mercy and love and favor by righteousness. This moral freedom, allowing human beings to determine what they wished to be, imposed an awesome responsibility on each person, but it opened avenues of human aspiration and endeavor largely absent from the other religious systems in the ancient Near East.

Fourth, in what historically was probably their most provocative insight into the human condition, the prophets proclaimed a new basis for defining the behavior of each individual toward others and of a community toward the individuals who were its members. Just as Yahweh treated men and women with righteousness and justice, so also must moral human beings treat all others according to these same principles. Likewise, the community of Yahweh's followers must conduct its collective actions to promote righteousness and justice. The principles of responsible social behavior were set forth in a code of law (Torah, defined in the first five books of the Hebrew Bible) that provided detailed regulations for all aspects of individual and communal life that all were obliged to observe if they were to be counted among those faithful to Yahweh. The Hebraic law was firm in its insistence that every individual was worthy of respect and compassionate treatment. But beyond the letter of the law the prophets projected a vision of individual and collective social responsibility with radical implications for the conduct of human affairs. Their reflections on the relationships which interlinked the divine, society, and the in-

dividual led them to postulate certain fundamental principles that must undergird a righteous social order: an egalitarian social system; the responsibility of those with authority to abide by the law; the obligation of their subjects to challenge them if they do not do so; the right of each to keep what he or she possesses as long as those possessions have not been gained by unjust actions; and above all else the obligation of each individual and of the community to show mercy, charity, and compassion to the weak and unfortunate. To the prophets these principles undergirding the right social order seemed self-evident in terms of their understanding of Yahweh's nature and what he expected of his special creatures.

Finally, the prophets reaffirmed that the Hebrews—the followers of Yahweh—were the people chosen to carry out Yahweh's plan for his creation. No matter what disasters might befall them, they would ultimately serve as the instrument through which the world would come to know and to serve the true god according to his commands. In the face of the disasters that befell the Hebrews after Solomon, the prophets put special emphasis on Yahweh's intention eventually to send a messiah to lead the Hebrews to victory. While awaiting their deliverer, the Hebrews must remain steadfast in their allegiance to Yahweh, maintain their religious ties with one another, abide by the law in their social and individual behavior, and resist the temptation to follow false gods. Their role as the chosen people and their expectation of a messiah instilled in the adherents of Judaism a forward-looking attitude which made every moment in history pregnant with meaning of things to come and rich in challenges to serve Yahweh in ways that would ensure the day of deliverance.

As the last centuries of Near Eastern leadership in shaping the foundations upon which Western civilization would be built unfolded, Yahweh's promise to his chosen people seemed unlikely to be realized. By about 300 B.C. Yahweh's followers were few in number: a small community living around Jerusalem and tiny cells of Jews scattered around the Near East. All were dominated by non-Jewish overlords. Their situation generated disagreement among the faithful over how they should conduct their lives and relate to the foreign cultures of their masters.

The bulk of the population of the Near East remained untouched by the religion shaped by the Hebrews; these people preferred their traditional nature deities, their elaborate mythologies, their powerful priesthoods, and their complex rituals devoted to winning divine favor. Despite their religion's modest impact on the ancient Near East, the Hebrews had shaped one of the great chapters in the spiritual and moral history of humanity. Neither the message of Judaism nor those who proclaimed it would go unnoticed as the history of Western civilization unfolded.

SUGGESTED READING

Egyptian and Hittite Empires

P. H. Newby, *Warrior Pharaohs. The Rise and Fall of the Egyptian Empire* (1980). A full treatment of the history of the New Kingdom.

Donald B. Redford, *Egypt, Canaan, and Israel in Ancient Times* (1992). Helps understand the nature of Egyptian imperialism.

Donald B. Redford, *Akhenaton: The Heretic King* (1984). An excellent study of an enigmatic figure.

T. G. H. James, *Pharaoh's People: Scenes from Life in Imperial Egypt* (1984). An excellent social history of the New Kingdom.

J. P. Mallory, *In Search of the Indo-Europeans: Language, Archaeology and Myth* (1989). A balanced picture of the early Indo-Europeans and their culture.

J. G. Macqueen, *The Hittites and Their Contemporaries in Asia Minor*, rev. and enl. ed. (1986). An excellent survey.

Ekrem Akurgal, *The Art of the Hittites*, trans. Constance McNab (1962). A well-illustrated study.

Minoans and Phoenicians

Arthur Cotterell, *The Minoan World* (1979). A good introduction.

Reynold Higgins, *Minoan and Mycenaean Art*, rev. ed. (1981). A sound study that is well illustrated.

Raymond Weill, *Phoenicia and Western Asia to the Macedonian Conquest*, trans. Ernest F. Row (1980). A clear account of the role of the Phoenicians in the ancient world.

Hebrews

John Bright, *A History of Israel*, 3rd ed. (1981).

J. Maxwell Miller and John H. Hayes, *A History of Ancient Israel and Judah* (1986).

H. Jagersma, *A History of Israel in the Old Testament Period*, trans. John Bowden (1983).

Three fine histories of ancient Israel; the Miller and Hayes book provides the fullest treatment.

Bernhard W. Anderson, *Understanding the Old Testament*, 4th ed. (1986). A well-done attempt to weave together history, literary criticism, archaeology, and biblical theology in order to show how Judaism developed.

G. W. Anderson, *The History and Religion of Israel* (1966). A helpful treatment of the evolution of ancient Judaism.

Irving M. Zeitlin, *Ancient Judaism* (1984). Written from a sociological perspective.

Roland de Vaux, *Ancient Israel: Its Life and Institutions*, 2 vols. (1961). Rich in details about ancient Hebrew society.

CHAPTER 3

The Great Empires: Assyria and Persia, 800–300 B.C.

FIGURE 3.1 A Near Eastern Empire Builder This portrayal of the Assyrian ruler Sargon II (721–705 B.C.) conveys a sense of power—even arrogant power—that was typical of the rulers of the great Near Eastern empires from ca. 800 to 300 B.C. One can well believe that this man was capable of dominating "the four rims of the world," as Assyrian and Persian empire builders claimed to do. (Hirmer Fotoarchiv)

During the ninth century B.C. a new era began in the Near East that featured the formation of vast empires unifying almost the entire area which enjoyed the benefits of higher civilization under a single political regime. The ground for this development had been prepared during the previous millennium, when the diffusion of the river valley cultures had provided diverse peoples with common technologies, religious practices, and literary and art styles. Expanding trade connections had drawn distant communities into economic interdependency. Shared cultural, religious, and economic interests invited attempts at political consolidation, and adventuresome leaders arose to respond to the opportunity.

1. THE ASSYRIAN EMPIRE, 800–612 B.C.

The first people to unify almost the entire Near East were the Assyrians. They were a Semitic-speaking people who as early as 3000 B.C. had established a homeland on the plateau astride the upper Tigris River, a land that lacked natural barriers and was open to repeated attacks. During the ensuing centuries the Assyrians were so powerfully influenced by Mesopotamian civilization that their history is sometimes treated as an extension of Mesopotamian history. Although repeatedly assaulted by Akkadians, Amorites, Kassites, Hittites, Mitanni, nomads from the Arabian desert, and mountaineers from the east and north, the hardy farmers of Assyria maintained their political identity. A major factor in their survival was their success in developing a potent military force, especially after they adopted the new iron weapons and the horse-drawn war chariots introduced into the Near East shortly before 1000 B.C.

Eventually the absence of any major political powers in the Near East during the Era of Small States allowed the Assyrians to assert themselves more aggressively. During the ninth century several surrounding peoples began to feel the force of Assyrian raids. None was able to resist the well-armed Assyrian infantrymen, archers, and charioteers, ably backed by siege equipment and skilled engineers. The effectiveness of the military machine was increased by deliberate terrorism waged against those defeated by the Assyrians. So awesome did the Assyrians become that many people preferred to "embrace the feet" of the attackers rather than resist (see Figure 3.2).

FIGURE 3.2 Embracing the Feet of an Assyrian King This carving from an Assyrian royal palace represents Jehu, King of Israel, bowing before his Assyrian conqueror, King Shalmaneser III. It conveys the awe that Assyrian rulers struck into the victims of their conquest. (The British Museum)

These raids showed the Assyrians that they could enrich themselves by exacting tribute from their victims, a prospect that prompted them to undertake outright conquest and the establishment of permanent control over Assyria's enemies. Under the leadership of Tiglath-Pileser III (745–727 B.C.) and a successor, Sargon II (721–705 B.C.), Assyrian armies launched a series of expeditions that destroyed the chief political powers from Mesopotamia northward and westward to Syria and Palestine. Assyrian governors were imposed on most of the conquered peoples, although a few minor kingdoms, such as Judah, were allowed to exist as tribute-paying clients of Assyria. The central administration of Assyria was enlarged to supervise tribute collection, and effective means of communication were devised to keep the royal court informed of affairs throughout the empire. The army stood ready to crush all signs of resistence; it continued its policy of terrorism, even resorting to the large-scale deportation of conquered peoples, as was the case with a large part of the population of the kingdom of Israel. Once this power base was established, rulers such as Sennacherib (705–681 B.C.), Esarhaddon (681–669 B.C.), and Ashurbanipal (669–626 B.C.) devoted their energies to dealing with outsiders who insisted on interfering with Assyrian rule. Egypt was forced to accept Assyrian overlordship, and Assyrian influence was extended into Asia Minor, the Zagros Mountains region, Iran, the northern Arabian Desert, and the highland region north of the Assyrian homeland. By 650 B.C. almost the entire civilized Near East stood subject to a single master, the great king of Assyria, "ruler of the four rims of the world" (see Map 3.1). The arrogant visages of these conquerors still stare out at us in the remarkable stone busts and reliefs wrought by Assyrian artists to celebrate their deeds (see Figure 3.1); all of them left boastful written accounts of their exploits in building the first ecumenical empire in the Near East.

However, the Assyrian Empire was not as strong as its size and heavy-handed rule suggested. Its brutal treatment of subject peoples aroused their undying hatred, nowhere better reflected than in the writings of some of the Hebrew prophets. Constant warfare depleted Assyria's human resources and eventually forced its rulers to rely on less efficient levies from con-

quered subjects. Internal discontent, often stemming from dissatisfaction over the distribution of tribute, arose. Worst of all, the Assyrians encountered the plague of all empire builders—enemies beyond the frontiers, aroused by the threat of absorption and greed for the riches of the empire. During the reign of Ashurbanipal these problems began to weaken Assyrian power, and troubles mounted rapidly after his death in 626 B.C. The Egyptians successfully revolted and then stirred up trouble among Assyrian subjects in Syria and Palestine. A Semitic group, the Chaldeans, raised the standard of revolt in southern Mesopotamia, a threat so serious that the Assyrians were forced to commit most of their resources to quelling it. Then the Medes, a people living east of the Zagros Mountains who had learned a great deal by imitating Assyrian military techniques, struck out of the east. In 612 B.C. they and the Chaldeans destroyed the Assyrian capital at Nineveh. Assyrian power collapsed almost immediately, leaving the empire to be partitioned by its many foes.

No one in the Near East lamented Assyria's passing. The Hebrew prophet Nahum spoke for all the world: "All who hear the news of you clap their hands at your downfall." However, the Assyrians' bad reputation should not conceal their contributions to history. Their attempt to erect a centralized monarchy was to be imitated by others. They wiped out many artificial political boundaries that kept small groups at sword's point. At least briefly they imposed a beneficial, albeit burdensome, peace on the Near East, protecting it for nearly three centuries against barbarians who might have destroyed its civilization had they not been rebuffed. Even though their regime funneled vast amounts of wealth to the Assyrian homeland at the expense of their subjects, they promoted trade by breaking down barriers impeding the movement of goods, and they encouraged the spread of a common spoken language, Aramaic, across their empire, greatly facilitating the exchange of goods and ideas and the dissemination of technical skills.

The Assyrians also made a notable contribution to cultural history. Although their culture was derived primarily from Mesopotamian models, Assyrian leaders were active patrons of artistic and literary activities, chiefly as a means of glorifying their political accomplishments.

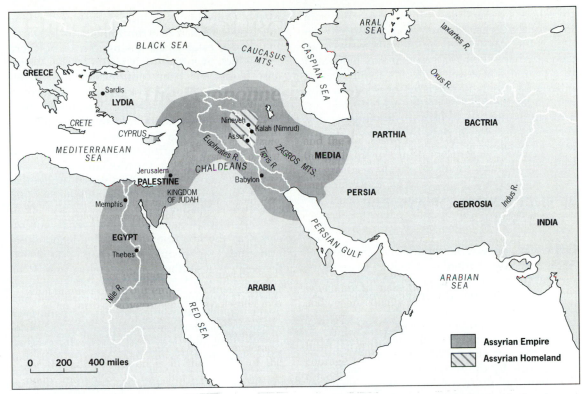

Map 3.1 THE ASSYRIAN EMPIRE, CA. 662 B.C. This map shows the extent of the Assyrian Empire just before its collapse. Some idea of its size is illustrated by the fact that it was more than one thousand miles from its capital at Nineveh to Thebes in Egypt—roughly as far as Washington, D.C., is from Omaha, Nebraska. Its size should be compared with that of the earlier empires of the Egyptians and the Hittites (see Map 2.1). A better appreciation of the Assyrian Empire can be gained by making an effort to account for the different peoples we have studied who were included in it.

Their kings were avid builders, constructing the great cities of Assur, Kalah (modern Nimrud), and Nineveh as monuments of their power and glory. In these cities earlier Mesopotamian architectural styles were followed closely and thus kept alive. Temples and palaces were decorated with massive sculptured pieces and excellent stone reliefs. To the tradition they honored, Assyrian artists often gave a unique quality. Especially impressive were the carved friezes done in relief to decorate the walls of royal palaces. This narrative art put together a succession of carved panels to tell in realistic detail the story of a military campaign or a hunting expedition (see Figure 3.2). The Assyrians were avid collectors and copiers of the literary treasure left behind by the Sumerians and the Akkadians. King Ashurbanipal built a huge library at Nineveh as a repository for thousands of cuneiform tablets containing copies of what was revered as "classical" literary works, especially the religious epics and creation stories so dear to the Mesopotamians. The Assyrians did show some originality in compiling annals vividly recounting the innumerable military campaigns of the kings, thereby making a contribution to the art of historical writing.

Assyrian religion was likewise strongly colored by borrowings from Mesopotamia. The great state god of Assyria, Assur, resembled the Amorite Marduk. Assyrian rituals, prayers, and priesthoods were almost indistinguishable from those of the earlier Mesopotamians. Assyrian religious life was colored by the militarism of society; perhaps their imperialism was motivated by a compulsion to assert Assur's dominion over other gods. In many reliefs Assur is shown hovering over the field of battle, ready to take up arms to assure the victory of the king serving Assur's cause. In all these ways the Assyrians kept alive some of the most precious cultural traditions in the Near East.

2. SUCCESSORS OF ASSYRIA, 612–550 B.C.

In the wake of Assyria's sudden collapse several states entered a spirited competition to carve up the empire. Some of these rivals even aspired to replace the Assyrians as masters of the Near East.

One of the competitors was Egypt. After a long period of weakness following the end of the New Kingdom about 1200 B.C. (see Chapter 2), foreign rule by the Assyrians again goaded the Egyptians to unify under a single pharaoh, Psammetichus (663–609 B.C.), founder of the Twenty-sixth Dynasty. Egypt again enjoyed a brief period of internal order, prosperity, and international prestige, especially in the Syria-Palestine area. But the Egyptians were incapable of sustaining the role of great power. The pharaohs had to rely on foreign mercenaries (chiefly Greeks) to provide a military force; these forces were a constant source of internal trouble. A backward-looking spirit, nourished especially by a reactionary priesthood, dominated thought and expression. Old age had gripped Egyptian society. In 525 B.C. the Persians were able to conquer Egypt without much difficulty.

In Asia Minor the small kingdom of Lydia, which first emerged after the fall of the Hittities, benefited from the fall of Assyria. Its rulers, the most famous of whom was Croesus (560–546 B.C.), fabled by the Greeks for his wealth, were able to establish control over most of Asia Minor, including several important Greet city-states on the Aegean seacost. Despite the considerable prosperity of Lydia, it was no match for the Persians, who conquered the kingdom in 546 B.C.

Another rival for succession to Assyria was Media. Descendants of Indo-European-speaking migrants who had overrun Iran about 1000 B.C., the Medes established a kingdom in northern Iran which eventually fell victim to the Assyrians. Under Assyrian domination the Medes raised their level of life considerably by borrowing from their oppressors. Eventually they played a major military role in destroying Assyria. After Assyria's fall, they laid claim to a vast area extending from Iran westward toward Asia Minor. However, the Median kingdom was badly organized. Eventually a vassal prince, Cyrus of Persia, deposed the Median king and laid claim to the Median realm.

The most spectacular of all Assyria's successors was the kingdom of the Chaldeans, a Semitic-speaking people who had established themselves in southern Mesopotamia prior to its conquest by the Assyrians. After playing a major role in destroying the Assyrian Empire, the Chaldeans established a kingdom based in southern Mesopotamia that consciously sought to restore the glory of old Babylonia. Under its greatest king, Nebuchadnezzar II (605–562 B.C.), Syria and Palestine were conquered. Among the victims of Chaldean expansion was the tiny kingdom of Judah. Jerusalem and its Temple were destroyed, and many Hebrews were deported to Babylon as captives. In their efforts to reclaim Mesopotamia's past glory Nebuchadnezzar and his successors promoted a notable cultural and religious renaissance. The jewel of this revival was the rebuilding of the city of Babylon. Its massive walls, its temples, its towering ziggurat (the legendary Tower of Babel), its royal palace featuring fabulous hanging gardens, its impressive sculpture and painting made it one of the most splendid of ancient cities. Even the redoubtable Hebrew prophet Jeremiah, amid his lamentations over the Babylonian captivity of his people, had to admit that "Babylon was a golden cup in the hands of Yahweh." A religious revival in this period restored the worship of ancient Mesopotamian deities, above all Marduk, and the authority of the traditional priesthood. Chaldean scribes and scholars were renowned for their mastery of ancient literature and their knowledge of astronomy. However, despite its outward brilliance, "New Babylonia" lacked military and economic strength and eventually proved an easy victim of the Persians in 539 B.C.

3. THE PERSIAN EMPIRE, 550–330 B.C.

The final victory in the competition for the Assyrian Emire belonged to the Persians. They were a people of Indo-European origin who about 1000 B.C. settled in the barren southern part of Iran as simple farmers and herders. For centuries they maintained their political independence. However, during this period civilizing influences, especially from Assyria, penetrated Persia, so that the Persians were slowly drawn into the orbit of the higher civilization of the Near East.

They did retain significant aspects of their old Indo-European culture, especially in religion and language. In the late seventh century they were forced to accept the overlordship of the Medes, who were closely akin to them in language and culture. About 560 B.C. a Persian prince, Cyrus, overthrew the Median king and proclaimed himself "king of the Medes and the Persians."

Cyrus (ca. 560–530 B.C.) and his two successors, Cambyses (530–522 B.C.) and Darius I (522–486 B.C.), launched a series of spectacular military campaigns that created one of the largest empires that ever existed (see Map 3.2). Victories over the

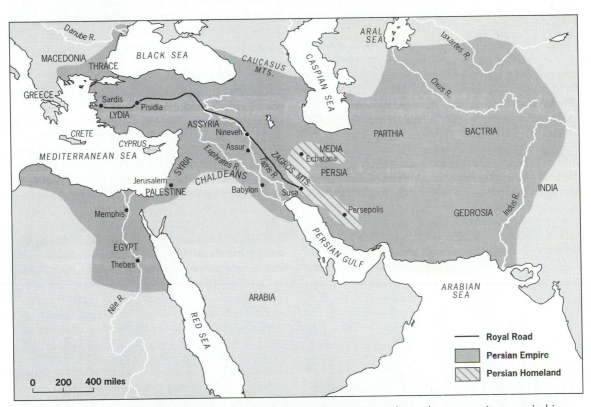

Map 3.2 THE PERSIAN EMPIRE, CA. 500 B.C. At its peak the Persian Empire embraced a vast territory, varied in terrain and climate and occupied by a complex mixture of peoples. In area the Persian Empire was approximately the size of the continental United States. The Persians were able to overcome some of these vast distances by building an excellent road system that fanned out from the capital cities of Susa and Persepolis to key cities across the empire. One of the most famous was the Royal Road, which extended from Susa to Sardis, a distance of about sixteen hundred miles. The Persians developed a system of regular outposts along this road and teams of mounted couriers who, by working in relays, could carry a message from Susa to Sardis in as little as a week.

Median Empire, the Lydian kingdom, the Chaldean kingdom, and Egypt gave them control over the heartland of the Near Eastern civilized world. Persian armies swept across vast stretches east of the Persian homeland to embrace the highly civilized Indian society of the Indus River Valley. Persian forces occupied Thrace to establish a foothold in Europe, but the thrust in that direction met a stubborn obstacle in the Greeks, whose dramatic encounter with the Persians had far-reaching consequences for the history of Western civilization (see Chapter 5).

The first Persian rulers were not only successful conquerors but also skilled, enlightened statesmen whose decisions in the face of the complex problems involved in ruling their huge and diverse empire laid the basis for sound government. Eschewing the brutal policy of the hated Assyrians, they ruled in a spirit of tolerance of and respect for the diverse cultural traditions and values of conquered peoples as long as those people accepted Persian political overlordship peaceably. That policy was dramatically illustrated by Cyrus' treatment of the Hebrews. He freed them from their Babylonian captivity, allowed them to return to Jerusalem, helped them to rebuild the Temple, and encouraged them to reconstitute their religious community. For this generous act the Hebrews hailed Cyrus as Yahweh's "shepherd." Many others enjoyed comparable treatment. Such treatment played a major role in making Persian domination more acceptable.

Committed to maintaining peace within their vast empire, the Persians were highly resourceful in developing effective political institutions fashioned by the creative adaptation of old ideas and practices in statecraft. Reaching its most mature form during the reign of Darius I, "the Great," that system was often imitated by later empire builders. Like his Near Eastern predecessors, Darius claimed absolute power with authority to make laws, to judge, and to command obedience and service from his subjects. Court life at his capital cities of Ecbatana, Susa, and Persepolis involved an elaborate etiquette designed to impress the constant stream of dignitaries who came there from throughout the vast empire and beyond that the ruler was indeed the "King of Kings" (see Figure 3.3). The ruler was served by a highly skilled bureaucracy staffed by officials, usually of Persian or Median origin, who represented an elite fanatically devoted to maintaining Persian power. Royal power was supported by an effective military establishment built around the Immortals, a loyal disciplined corps of about ten thousand professional warriors recruited from the Persians and the Medes. When occasion

FIGURE 3.3 The "King of Kings" at Work This relief from the royal palace at Persepolis shows Darius receiving a commander of the royal guard. Behind the king stands his son, Xerxes. (Oriental Institute, University of Chicago)

demanded, this elite force was reinforced by contingents mobilized in awe-inspiring numbers from the subject population of the empire. The Persians also commanded impressive naval forces, composed largely of Phoenician and Greek ships and crews.

Perhaps the most innovative feature of the Persian governmental system was the techniques devised for extending central authority to the component parts of the vast empire. By Darius' reign the empire was divided into twenty large districts, called *satrapies*, some of which were defined to respect ancient political, ethnic, and cultural entities. Over each the "King of Kings" appointed a governor, called a *satrap*, usually a Persian and often a member of the royal family, who was given sufficient power to control local affairs. The satraps were removable at the will of the king and were held strictly accountable for the effective administration of their districts. Periodically, the king sent out inspectors to investigate local administration and report to the central court. Contingents of the imperial army under trusted commanders were garrisoned in strategic spots both to support the satraps and to curb their ambitions. An excellent road system and a postal service were developed, permitting rapid communications between the satrapies and the central government. Careful records were maintained by the central government as a means of holding each satrap accountable. By these methods the great kings managed to create twenty semi-independent governments, each capable of reacting to situations that were unique to each locality by means that respected local customs and concerns but all guided by common policies shaped by the "King of Kings" and his high officials in an effort to maintain peaceful unity amid diversity.

The political regime fashioned by the Persians created an environment that was beneficial to economic, social, religious, and cultural life throughout the empire. For the most part farmers, artisans, and traders continued their traditional practices to sustain a prosperous economy. Trade and the transfer of technology were promoted by the abolition of restrictive political barriers, an improved system of communication, and the encouragement of the royal government. A rich and powerful nobility continued to dominate the social order. At its summit stood the Persian families who served the great king, but many local nobles gained status by involvement in the affairs of their local satrapy and by exploiting opportunities to serve the imperial regime. The climate of tolerance prevailing in the Persian Empire nurtured the development of a common cosmopolitan lifestyle that defined aristocratic attitudes and behavior throughout the empire. While the Persian government was concerned with protecting and affording justice to all subjects, the nonnoble elements of society remained in a position of social subservience that left them open to exploitation.

Assessing the intellectual and artistic life of the Persian Empire is a difficult task, chiefly because much important activity in these realms occurred in local settings as a result of the tolerant attitude of the Persian regime toward the different cultural traditions long established across the vast expanse of the empire. Preoccupied with administrative, military, and diplomatic affairs, the Persians were not innovators in cultural life. Like the Assyrians, they were primarily borrowers from the rich cultural resources that already existed in their vast empire. But they created an open, tolerant cultural environment that encouraged the synthesizing of the rich treasures of diverse cultures into common patterns of thought and expression that were increasingly meaningful and appealing to a variety of peoples. In this complex process the royal court played a key role. The great kings were active patrons of art and learning, in part as a means of exalting their authority. Their patronage centered primarily on the royal palaces built at Ecbatana, Susa, and Persepolis. These massive complexes reflect an eclectic blending of architectural and sculptural themes and techniques drawn from the artistic traditions of the entire Near Eastern world, perhaps best reflected in the stone reliefs recording royal exploits. Not only the great kings but also their satraps welcomed to their courts individuals from all over the empire who were schooled in the literary, religious, and scientific traditions of the past. As a result, the Persians helped substantially to keep these traditions alive to serve the cause of learning and expression among later peoples, especially the Greeks.

The Persians did make one significant contribution to Near Eastern civilization in the form of a new religion called Zoroastrianism, named for its founder, Zoroaster (Zarathustra in Persian). Although the details of Zoroaster's life are clouded by legend, it appears that he lived about 600 B.C., before the Perians established their empire. During his lifetime he played the role of reformer, seeking to purify the traditional religion of the Persians on the basis of revelations that came to him after long contemplation. The old religion of the Persians centered around the worship of many deities who represented forces of nature, especially a god of the sky and a god of fire. A complicated ritual, including sacrifices, magic, and prayer, developed as a means of winning the favors of the deities. Priests, called magi, played a prominent role in directing religious life among the early Persians.

Zoroaster's exact teachings are as elusive as the details of his life. His message was eventually set forth in a sacred book called *Zend-Avesta*, a work compiled over many centuries that contains a confusing array of interpretations and refinements of Zoroaster's original teachings. As a consequence, it is difficult to reconstruct what Zoroaster thought and said. Aside from his protest against many aspects of the prevailing Persian religious system, especially its polytheism and its ritualistic formalism, Zoroaster set forth a unique concept of the nature of the cosmic order based on a principle of dualism. On the one hand, there is the god Ahura Mazda (Lord of Wisdom), the all-powerful, all-pervading lord of creation. This good and benevolent spirit presides over all creation, emanating and personifying such qualities as justice, pure thought, integrity, good intentions, and virtue. But the good Ahura Mazda is opposed by the diabolical Ahriman, an evil force seeking to blot out justice, light, wisdom, and good. The warfare between Ahura Mazda and Ahriman, good and evil, which has been going on since the beginning of the world, provides the dynamic force in the universe. Eventually, in a final day of judgment, Ahura Mazda will prevail; but in the meantime, the conflict will rage, extending into every soul and demanding that each individual elect whether to serve good or evil. On the final day of reckoning, those who have chosen good will be rewarded with eternal happiness, while those who have elected the way of Ahriman will be condemned to eternal misery.

By postulating the struggle between good and evil as fundamental in the cosmic order, Zoroaster made the basic obligation of each human being clear. Only good conduct would win favor in the eyes of Ahura Mazda. The worship of old deities, magic, sacrifices, and priestly ministrations were irrelevant and even constituted a surrender to evil because they diverted attention from doing good. Zoroaster defined a vigorous moral code for his followers, derived in its particulars from the qualities of goodness surrounding Ahura Mazda. Obversely, he set forth a clear concept of sin, rooted in the evil nature of Ahriman. Certainly none of the religions in the world that the Persians were soon to rule, except Judaism, gave such emphasis to ethical issues— and not even Judaism placed the burden of goodness so squarely on each individual. Zoroaster did not associate goodness and righteousness with the history of a chosen people, adherence to a system of law, or the observance of a set of ritual practices. His message called all humankind to seek moral perfection by thinking and acting according to right.

Although Zoroaster's ideas initially met resistance, they took firm hold after the master's death. Accepted by the Persian rulers, Zoroastrianism became the official religion of the Achaemenid dynasty. However, its acceptance was not universal in the Persian Empire. The general policy of tolerance in the empire permitted other religions to maintain their hold. As time passed, Zoroaster's original message lost its uniqueness. Ritual practices aimed at pleasing Ahura Mazda and warding off Ahriman's evil powers grew increasingly prominent. Polytheistic concepts crept back into Zoroastriansim. Old Persian deities and hosts of angels and devils reappeared as combatants in the eternal war between light and dark. The concept of the struggle between good and evil tended to associate good with purely spiritual forces and evil with material things. This interpretation of dualism had the effect of belittling the practice of virtue in everyday life and of exalting withdrawal from the world. After the collapse of the Persian Empire, Zoroastrianism declined as a major religious force in the Near East. However, it has survived to the present among its modern adherents, called Parsees, who are concentrated chiefly in Iran and India. The Zoroastrian concept of dualism long provided a rich source of spiritual speculation for later religions, especially Christianity.

The generally benevolent regime of the Persians lasted more than two centuries. The imperial administrative and military system maintained internal peace and rebuffed numerous enemies along the empire's immensely long frontiers. The Persians played a major role in the diplomacy of the period, often using their money to build alliances with foreign powers and to manipulate relations among these outsiders; Persian diplomacy was especially significant in the Greek world during the fifth and fourth centuries B.C. Gradually, however, the Persian strength began to erode. Some of the later kings were deficient in political ability. Their courts became corrupt and torn by intrigue involving royal wives and children, officials, and friends. Ambitious satraps constantly attempted to overthrow the rulers, often putting themselves forward as champions of subject peoples and usually generous in their promises of rewards for those who joined them against the great king. A gradual decline in the efficiency and loyalty of the royal bureaucracy and the armed forces impeded the ability of the kings to control the satraps. By the middle of the fourth century B.C. all that was needed to destroy the Persian Empire was a strong attack from the outside. That attack was soon forthcoming from a powerful Greek-Macedonian army led by Alexander the Great, who was driven in part by an urge to destroy the Persian menace that had haunted the Greek world since the time of Darius the Great. After a brief, brilliant military campaign culminating in a decisive victory in 330 B.C., Alexander was able to destroy the Persian power and to claim possession of its territory.

Neither the dramatic end of the Persian Empire nor the negative attitude of its accomplishments bequeathed to the Western consciousness by the anti-Persian bias of the Greeks should detract from the importance of the Persians in history. The enlightened, tolerant rule of the Achaemenids built a universal empire in the ancient Near East in which all kinds of people at many levels of civilization were brought together into a viable community. The cosmopolitan environment in that empire permitted local cultures to persist and grow while providing instruments through which all could mix and fertilize one another. In a sense, the resulting amalgam reflected the best the ancient Near East had produced during the thirty-five centuries in which its people stood in the forefront of civilized life.

SUGGESTED READING

Assyrians

H. W. F. Saggs, *The Might That Was Assyria* (1984).
Georges Roux, *Ancient Iraq*, 2nd ed. (1980).
Two well-written treatments of Assyrian history and civilization.
André Parrot, *Arts of Assyria*, trans. Stuart Gilbert and James Emmons (1961). An excellent introduction to all aspects of Assyrian art.

Persians

J. M. Cook, *The Persian Empire* (1983). An effective treatment of Persian history and institutions.
Richard N. Frye, *The History of Ancient Iran* (1983). Surveys Persian history down to the Moslem conquest in the eighth century A.D.

Richard N. Frye, *The Heritage of Persia* (1963). Excellent survey of Persian cultural influence on the larger world.
Mary Boyce, *Zoroastrians: Their Religious Beliefs and Practices* (1984). A brief treatment covering the entire history of Zoroastrianism.
Mary Boyce, *A History of Zoroastrianism*, 2 vols. (1975-1982). A detailed history of early Zoroastrianism.
Roman Ghirshman, *Persia from the Origins to Alexander the Great*, trans. Stuart Gilbert and James Emmons (1964).
Edith Porada, *The Art of Ancient Iran. Pre-Islamic Cultures* (1965).
This and the preceding work provide a full treatment of all aspects of Persian art.

RETROSPECT

When in 330 B.C. Alexander the Great stood in triumph over the body of Darius III, a chapter in world history had ended. The Persians, symbolizing the old order, had given way to a youthful conqueror who represented a vital new order emerging on the western periphery of the Near East. That old order deserves a brief epitaph that will fix its accomplishments in our minds.

For the purposes of this epitaph, let us view the Persians as the last scions of a great family whose origins were rooted in simple Neolithic villages and whose members included all the peoples from southwestern Asia and northeastern Africa whose histories have been reviewed in the preceding pages. Over several millennia, especially after 4000 B.C., that family had put together a rich and varied patrimony. Its various members had devised effective techniques of agriculture, manufacturing, and trading for extracting sustenance from nature. They had made crucial advances in developing the technology by which humans exploited the world of nature, a leap forward epitomized by the transition from Stone Age technology through the Bronze Age to the Iron Age. They had developed impressive techniques of government and social control that allowed creative interactions among large numbers of people playing a variety of economic and social roles. Their religions provided an integrative, unifying, direction-giving dimension to their collective and individual existences. Their efforts to comprehend the mysterious cosmos generated a rich written literature, magnificent works of art, and a large store of knowledge about the natural world. In all these ways the African-Asian peoples of the ancient Near East created a priceless storehouse from which future peoples could draw without having to invent higher civilization over again. In one sense, Western history—indeed, world history—is a story of the diffusion of ancient Near Eastern achievements to future generations living in different geographical settings.

Yet, for all the splendid achievements of the peoples of the ancient Near East, the patterns of civilization that eventuated in the Persian imperial order ultimately proved incapable of generating additional creative forces capable of advancing the human condition. Historians have advanced various explanations for this seeming irony. Some have argued that the creative capacities of the peoples of the Near East were stifled by the fateful turn of political events which almost continuously from the time of Alexander the Great to the present has imposed foreign political masters on that area. Others have suggested that the physical environment imposed serious constraints, arguing that aside from the river valleys the Near East had limited potential in terms of material resources. Still others have argued that the Near Eastern world was limited by a constrictive political and social order based on control of power, wealth, and thought by numerically small elites who were unable and unwilling to tap wider sources of human talent. A persuasive case has been made that the mentality undergirding Near Eastern civilization became entrapped by one of its most striking creations, the rich array of myths explaining the cosmic order in terms of deified forces of nature. That mythic world view provided limited scope for reflection on human capacities, especially the potential of the human mind to seek, to discover, and to organize knowledge that would empower human beings to new levels of achievement.

Here, then, is the epitaph of the peoples of the ancient Near East: Their wondrous accomplishments created an enduring base—an unfinished pyramid or ziggurat, as it were—upon which new levels of achievement could be built by peoples bold enough to seek and inventive enough to unleash a wider range of human capacities.

PART TWO
GRECO-ROMAN CIVILIZATION, 1200 B.C.–A.D. 500

While the patterns of civilization established in the ancient Near East were assuming their most mature forms, a different pattern of life began to take shape to the west. It is called Greco-Roman civilization after the two peoples who played a central role in its development. Centered first around the Aegean Sea, the fundamental outlines of this civilization were established by the Greeks between about 1200 and 400 B.C. Well before 400 B.C., its institutional patterns and cultural values began to spread both eastward and westward. In the fourth century, the Greek world fell under the political domination of the Macedonians, who immediately combined forces with the Greeks to conquer the Persian Empire. That victory resulted in the spread of Greek civilization over that empire's huge expanse and its enrichment by borrowings from the ancient Near Eastern cultural heritage. In the third century B.C. the Romans began to be drawn into the orb of Hellenic civilization and soon became its prime imitators and disseminators. In addition to enriching what they took from the Greeks, the Romans forged a huge empire which until its collapse in the fifth century A.D. provided the setting for a further extension of the Greco-Roman pattern of life over much of western Europe and North Africa.

Since what the Greeks and Romans wrought has been fundamental in shaping modern Western civilization, it is essential to trace the main stages of the development of Greco-Roman civilization in search of a fuller understanding of what the Western world's debt to the Greeks and the Romans is. That debt is perhaps greatest as regards the Greco-Roman world's vision of the potential of human beings. Much of the Greco-Roman accomplishment focused on an effort to explore the implications of a statement made by the Athenian dramatist Sophocles: "Many are the wonders of the world, and none so wonderful as Man."

CHAPTER 4
The Origins and Development of the Greek City-State Polity

FIGURE 4.1 The Heart of a *Polis* The fact that the rocky promontory shown in this photo features the surviving ruins of one of the great artistic achievements in all history should not hide another important consideration: Such physical settings played a prime role all over ancient Greece as focal points that drew people together to form a unique community—the *polis*. That the Athenians chose to invest their wealth and talent in adorning the Acropolis is a reflection of the role that this modest hill played over many centuries as a center of their collective activities. (Alison Frantz)

Greco-Roman civilization initially took form in a group of small, independent communities located around the Aegean Sea. Their formation was a slow process involving experimentation and creativity. Only by tracing that evolution is it possible to understand what was history-making about these communities.

The development of the early Greek communities was conditioned by the physical environment of the Aegean basin. The area is blessed with a benevolent climate marked by mild winters and long, dry summers which allow comfortable living without great expenditure on clothing and housing. The topography, especially of the Greek mainland, is dominated by mountains, valleys, bays, and peninsulas that cut the land into small pockets of farmland and grazing areas defining settlement patterns that made unified political control extremely difficult. But such is the lay of the land that few communities are far from the sea. The area's resources are not abundant. Tillable soil is limited, poor in quality, subject to erosion, and ill suited to cereal production. Tin, copper, iron, and timber are in short supply. As a Greek historian said, "Greece has always poverty as her companion." But there was an avenue of escape: the sea. The Aegean provides excellent harbors and good sailing winds during the summer. It served as a roadway allowing access by sea to a wider world of raw materials and markets and stimulating contacts with other peoples. The challenges posed by a hard land and far-reaching seaways placed a premium on human resourcefulness.

1. THE MYCENAEAN AND DARK AGES, 2000–800 B.C.: GREEK ORIGINS

Except for fanciful accounts imbedded in Greek mythology, the distant origins of Greek civilization remained a mystery until the advent of systematic archaeological explorations of the Aegean world in the late nineteenth century. The evidence unearthed since then reveals that Neolithic culture was introduced to the Aegean area about 6000 B.C. During many ensuing centuries life centered around simple agricultural villages and typical Neolithic institutions. About 2000 B.C. this primitive order was profoundly affected by the intrusion of Indo-Europeans into the area, part of the same movement that disturbed much of the Near East. The newcomers in Greece imposed their overlordship and their language on the natives, but they adopted from their victims the basic features of agricultural life. For the next four or five centuries, Aegean history centered on the activities of a number of small principalities dominated by aggressive warlords and their armed retainers. The power and wealth of these rulers are reflected in the ruins of their huge fortress-palaces, the most impressive of which was located at Mycenae, which has given its name to this first phase of Greek history. The archaeological finds at Mycenae and other important centers provide clear proof that Mycenaean society was powerfully influenced by expanding contacts with more advanced societies of the Near East, especially the Minoan world. Not only the magnificence of Mycenaean palaces but also the records surviving in a written form of the Greek language, called Linear B, indicate that Mycenaean rulers had devised highly effective ways of asserting political and economic control over the populations living in the areas surrounding their fortress cities.

Mycenaean culture reached its zenith about 1300 B.C. As it matured, its political structures, religious usages, technology, and art increasingly reflected features that suggest that the first Greeks were on the way to being absorbed into the larger pattern of civilization developing across the Near East during the age of cultural diffusion described earlier (see Chapter 2). However, that process was cut short about 1200 B.C. by the decline and then collapse of Mycenaean culture. While the reasons for that collapse are not entirely clear, perhaps the rupture of trade connections accompanying the collapse of Minoan civilization and the disruption of the Hittite and Egyptian empires resulted in economic constraints that caused the warlike Mycenaean kings to turn on each other in search of a means to sustain their expensive way of life. It was during these troubled times, for instance, that warriors from several Mycenaean kingdoms joined hands to destroy Troy in Asia Minor, a venture immortalized in the poetry of Homer. Whatever the cause, between about 1200 and 1100 B.C. most of the mighty Mycenaean citadels, including Mycenae, were violently destroyed, bringing to an end the first chapter in Greek history.

Following the collapse of Mycenaean culture, the Aegean world began an era lasting about four centuries that modern historians have called a "Dark Age." Information about this period depends largely on scarce and enigmatic archaeological remains. The scanty evidence leaves no doubt that many aspects of Mycenaean civilization disappeared: the dominant royal courts, the great palaces, Linear B writing, trading, art, technical expertise. Many settled locations disappeared, suggesting a population decline. Life was simpler than during the Mycenaean Age, depending on simple farming carried on by the inhabitants of small communities with limited contacts with the larger world. But this simple world was not stagnant, as is evident in two literary masterpieces, the *Iliad* and the *Odyssey*, attributed to the poet Homer, who lived during the eighth century B.C. at the end of the Dark Age. Although his epics claim to recount the adventures of heroes living more than four centuries earlier during the Trojan War, Homer describes the feats of his legendary figures in terms that reveal much about the world in which he lived.

Homer's testimony combined with archaeological evidence indicates that during the Dark Age developments fundamental to the future course of Greco-Roman civilization occurred. Although the Greek world remained economically poor, its potential for growth was enhanced by technological advances, especially the adoption of Iron Age technology and advancing skills in pottery making. Between about 1200 and 800 B.C. there was considerable shifting of peoples from mainland Greece to the Aegean Islands and the coast of Asia Minor, where important contacts with the Near Eastern world were again established. The population of this entire area, whose people were linked by common cultural traits, established the demographic base for future Greek development. The peoples occupying the Aegean basin came to share a common Greek language, although that language had several different dialects. A new writing system, based on the adaptation of the Phoenician alphabet to accommodate the Greek spoken language, was developed to a level that made possible the magnificent Homeric epics. A common pattern of religious belief and practice spread among the Greeks, nurturing a unique set of values forcefully delineated by Homer's literary masterpieces and in artistic forms which found expression especially in pottery decoration. Much of the future of Greek intellectual, literary, and artistic history involved working out the implications of these early forms of thought and expression. In a word, the Dark Age was marked by complex processes converging to define a people participating in a common pattern of life; these people would soon call themselves "Hellenes," a term that for them indicated an awareness of shared values that both transcended the localism dictated by political realities and made those who were Hellenes different from those who were not.

As the Homeric poems make clear, the Dark Age was especially important in shaping a form of community life of crucial importance to Greco-Roman civilization. The Greek world of the Dark Age remained politically divided into many petty kingdoms, each identified with a particular territory. Over each presided a chieftain who led his people in war, judged their disputes, and represented them before their deities. In marked contrast to the power enjoyed by kings during the Mycenaean Age, the power of these kings was limited by a politically active nobility whose authority was based on patriarchal family ties, loyal personal retainers, and control of the best lands and herds. The nobles in each kingdom met regularly to share with the king decision making on matters of common interest. The nobles' power was enhanced by the dominant role aristocrats played in warfare, an activity that contributed in an important way to defining the nobles' values. Peasants and artisans were considered to be free and even participated to a degree in political life through attendance at assemblies, where they shouted their approval or disapproval of decisions made by kings and nobles. By the end of the Dark Age each of these small political entities—its members united by kinship and personal ties, shared religious life, and active involvement in political decision making—constituted a base from which would emerge the key institution shaping Greek civilization: the city-state, called the *polis* by the Greeks.

2. THE GREEK ARCHAIC AGE, 800–500 B.C.: DEVELOPMENT OF THE *POLIS*

The crucial steps in the evolution of the *polis* occurred during what modern historians call the Archaic Age, which extended from about 800 to 500 B.C. The shaping of that institution fundamental to Greek civilization involved a complex process, proceeding at a different pace and in different ways from one place to another. However, among the nearly seven hundred city-states that established an independent identity during the Archaic Age (see Map 4.1 for the location of the major city-states) there were certain common patterns of development that provide the key to the basic nature of the *polis*.

Central to the emergence of each *polis* were processes that created powerful bonds linking the inhabitants of a relatively small geographical area into a community and that expanded the involvement of the "citizens" of each community in civic life. These communal bonds found their focus at a physical center, an urban center. Already at the beginning of the Archaic Age the rudiments of such urban centers were emerging in the petty kingdoms that had been established during the Dark Age. At such centers were the king's residence and often a hilltop fortress, called an *acropolis*, where those from the surrounding countryside could find protection. There temples were built where members of the community could gather to honor their shared deities. The same center served as a meeting place for the noble clan leaders when they gathered from their rural estates to counsel with the king; some even established residences there. A market, called an *agora*, developed in connection with the fortress. As the Archaic Age progressed, the range of activities affecting group life expanded in each urban center, and increasingly the members of each community developed a sense of attachment to and dependence on that special place. At the same time there emerged institutional forms that gave structure to the shared experiences of those belonging to the community. Involvement and participation in the political, economic, religious, and cultural activities unfolding at each urban center became the central focus in the lives of those belonging to each *polis*.

A major step in shaping the political and social structure of the typical *polis* occurred in all but a few communities during the eighth century B.C. In a radical departure from the political order typical of both the ancient Near East and early Greece, monarchy was replaced with what the Greeks called *oligarchy*. Ultimate authority was entrusted to a council of nobles whose decisions were executed by elected officials drawn from that same noble class. Noble status, which qualified individuals for a political role, was based on landed wealth, control over the clan structure that undergirded early Greek society, and domination of the legal system. Although they were often greedy and always jealous of their authority, the nobles felt a strong attachment to their *polis* and were willing to take political action to resolve basic problems affecting the entire community.

One such step involved reshaping the military system in a way that broadened the base of participation in this key civic activity. As reflected in the Homeric epics, warfare during the Dark Age had been monopolized by nobles, who alone could afford the horses and equipment needed for cavalry and chariot combat. That system was replaced by a military organization based on the *phalanx*, a massed formation of infantry soldiers, called *hoplites*, armed with shields, breastplates, helmets, swords, and spears. This change brought larger numbers of citizens with modest means into the service of the *polis*, placed a premium on disciplined action in a common cause, and increased the civic importance of the new soldiers upon whom the safety of the *polis* now depended. Before long these *hoplites* were demanding a share in making the decisions that determined the course of affairs in the *polis*.

Even more significant in expanding the bonds that attached people to the *polis* were actions taken by oligarchies to cope with the major economic and social problems that began to afflict much of the Greek world during the Archaic

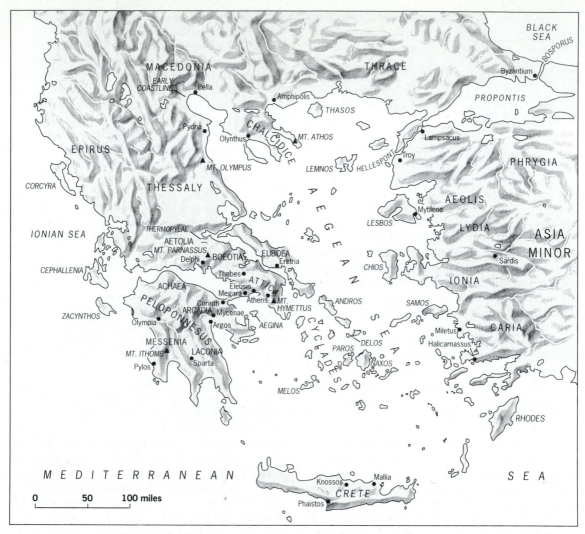

Map 4.1 THE WORLD OF THE GREEKS This map identifies the major geographical regions of the Aegean world and locates the most important Greek city-states—but by no means all of them. It highlights the extent to which the mountainous terrain of the Aegean Basin encouraged political localism in the Greek world and limited the agricultural resources available to most city-states. At the same time, it shows the near proximity of most Greek city-states to seaways that provided access to a larger world.

Age. The nature and impact of the crisis are reflected in a poem entitled *Works and Days*, written about 700 B.C. by Hesiod, a wealthy farmer embittered by the growing poverty and injustice of his time. The causes of the crisis were deepseated: growing population, competition for limited land, and the greediness of what Hesiod called "the land-devouring lords" who controlled each *polis*. The chief victims were small landholders, who were forced into debt, economic dependence on noble landlords, and even slavery, thereby losing their status as citizens of their *polis*.

One response to this crisis was the resettle-

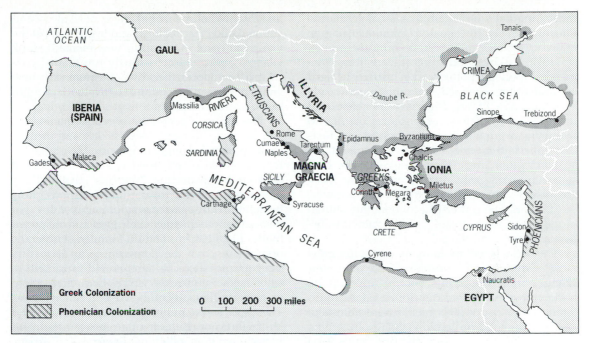

Map 4.2 GREEK COLONIES, CA. 500 B.C. This map shows the major areas colonized by the Greeks during the period 800–500 B.C. By 500 B.C. their major rival for dominance of trade in the Mediterranean Basin was the North African city of Carthage, originally a Phoenician colony but not a major power in control of most of the areas originally colonized by the Phoenicians. Wherever the Greeks colonized, they took with them the main elements of Hellenic civilization; as a result, their geographical expansion marked the spread of the Greek way of life beyond the confines of its Aegean homeland.

ment of Greeks outside Greece. In many city-states oligarchical regimes encouraged or even ordered colonizing ventures, usually led by enterprising nobles who recruited impoverished compatriots to follow them in search of new homes. A prime target for such ventures was southern Italy and Sicily, an area that was eventually so completely Hellenized that it became known as Magna Graecia (Greater Greece). Other Greek settlements were established on the northern shores of the Aegean, around the Black Sea, in southern France, in Spain, in Egypt, and in modern Libya (see Map 4.2). In all of these areas the Greeks carved out territorial enclaves where they established themselves as farmers, traders, and artisans. Although its objective was not usually conquest, successful colonization often allowed the Greeks to assert control over native populations or at least to assert a powerful cul-

tural impact on them. The new communities were not colonies in the modern sense. Rather, each was an independent *polis* with its own government, laws, and civic pride. Many such new city-states maintained contact with the Aegean city-states from which the settlers had originally emigrated. As a consequence, they became prime channels for a massive extension of Hellas—the area dominated by Greeks and their culture.

Economic pressures were also relieved by developments that created a more diverse economy in each *polis*. Especially important was the growth of trade and industry. The increasing number of Greek settlements around the Aegean, Mediterranean, and Black seas provided access to raw materials and markets. Greek traders exploited these opportunities vigorously, and by 500 B.C. they had become the leading traders in the Mediterranean world, rivaled only by Carthage, originally established as a colony by the Phoenicians. Trade spurred manufacturing in many city-states, and Greek artisans proved skillful at making products that were in high demand, especially pottery. The traditional agricultural system changed as a consequence of expanding trade. Enterprising farmers abandoned the raising of grain in favor of grapes, olives, and livestock, from which were derived products that found profitable markets throughout the Mediterranean area. Increasingly, Greek city-states imported grain, especially from the Black Sea area. For merchants, artisans, and commercial farmers, the center of economic life shifted to the urban marketplace, creating new ties between citizens and the *polis*.

The social structure in many city-states grew more diverse and complex amid economic change. Some aristocrats became involved in trade and industry and developed interests different from those of their peers whose status and wealth depended on landownership. Diverging economic interests among the aristocrats bred factionalism and intensified competition for control of public decision making. Enterprising individuals from the lower ranks of society were able to amass sufficient wealth through trade and industry to become rivals of the landowning aristocracy for power. Small farmers, lacking the resources needed to engage in the new forms of agriculture and unwilling to become dependents of great landowners, moved to the urban centers to become traders, artisans, or hired laborers. This change dissolved ancient family ties, weakened the control of aristocratic clan leaders over the populace, and thrust upon public authorities new burdens of providing for and controlling the socially displaced.

In this environment of economic and social change new mental attitudes began to emerge. They were mirrored in new religious concepts, innovative forms of literary and artistic expression, and the beginning of philosophical speculation. We shall return to the particulars of Archaic cultural developments later (see Chapter 6). Suffice it to say here that the new modes of thought and expression revealed increasing concern about the nature of individual human beings and their place in the cosmic order, their potential for independent action, and rational explanations of the natural world. The *polis* increas-

ingly provided a forum where new ideas and values could be articulated and tested against the views of others. And as this new mentality took form, it generated consciously formulated concepts for reshaping the *polis* to accommodate new views of human beings and to deal with changes in the human condition.

The tensions generated by economic, social, and mental changes necessitated and helped shape political change. In general, the oligarchic regimes in each *polis* tried to relieve mounting tensions by instituting "reforms" that did not require surrender of the monopoly of power held by nobles. They enacted written codes of law that defined more precisely the rights and responsibilities of all citizens and that limited aristocratic dominance over the administration of justice. They granted relief to debtors and protection to small farmers. They devised policies that sought to gain trading advantages for their city-state. They sponsored public projects that improved the facilities of the *polis*, often in ways that promoted changing religious, literary, and artistic trends. In these "reforms" the aristocrats were motivated in part by self-interest, but they were also moved by a realization that steps must be taken to retain the allegiance and services of artisans, soldiers, sailors, shopkeepers, farmers, writers, artists, and intellectuals, who increasingly made vital contributions to the welfare of the *polis*.

In many city-states these "reforms" were not sufficient to maintain stability. Continued economic, social, and cultural turmoil coupled with the growing attachment of individuals of all social levels to the city-state generated demands for broader political participation than the aristocratic masters were willing to grant. Usually force was required to break the nobles' monopoly on power. In many city-states the assault on entrenched power was spearheaded by individual leaders called *tyrants* (from a Greek word meaning "those who rule illegally"). Often of noble origin and ambitious for personal power, these charismatic figures seized control over the *polis* by force, sometimes with support from the *hoplites*, who dominated the military establishment in many city-states. The typical tyrant made no effort to change the existing political structure; rather, each sought to dominate it by filling the council and elective offices with loyal followers. Once in power, the tyrant launched policies aimed at currying popular support. Measures were taken to depose wealthy, highborn nobles from power, to tax their wealth, and to deprive them of their land, which was redistributed to small farmers. Policies pleasing to non-aristocratic elements of society were pursued, including measures to increase trade and industry, expenditures on city beautification, and efforts to assure more equitable administration of justice.

The duration of tyranny was relatively brief in most city-states, often little more than the tyrant's lifetime. Since tyrants had seized power illegally, their regimes depended on their individual talents and popularity. Eventually, the aristocrats who had been their chief victims took the lead in unseating them and in restoring "legitimate" government. But these aristocrats were seldom able to reestablish their traditional monopoly based on landownership and kinship ties. In those city-states where oligarchical control continued after the overthrow of tyranny, the ruling element was greatly expanded to include men of wealth but without noble heritage. In some city-states that had avoided tyranny, leaders of the old nobility understood the course of affairs well enough to open noble ranks and political power to a wider circle. In many city-states the end of tyranny led to radical political changes which established a *democracy* that allowed the total citizen body to take control of civic affairs. With all citizens entitled to participate in government, the last knot binding them to the *polis* was tied. For some Greeks as well as many in the modern world, the democratic *polis* represented the ideal form of government.

3. ATHENS

The history of Athens during the Archaic Age provides a case study illustrating the evolution of a democratic *polis*. During the Mycenaean Age, Athens was a prominent fortress center exercising control over the surrounding area, called Attica. The general decline occurring over most of the Aegean world during the Dark Age resulted in the emergence in Attica of a number of small agricultural villages led by local tribal leaders. Sometime early in the Archaic Age, under circumstances still not well understood, these villages coalesced into a single political entity centering on Athens and its *acropolis* to constitute an embryo *polis* (see Figure 4.1) embracing about a thousand square miles—the largest city-state in ancient Greece except for Sparta. The emerging *polis* was ruled by a hereditary king assisted by a council of clan heads called the *Areopagus* and a popular assembly called the *ecclesia*. For political and military purposes, the citizen body was grouped into four tribes, each composed of brotherhoods (called *phratries*, from which is derived our word "fraternity") made up of several clans. Citizenship was established by admission to a brotherhood and depended on an individual's ties to a clan. As a consequence, kinship ties provided the fundamental bond in the social order.

About 700 B.C. the monarchy was abolished and officials called *archons* (eventually nine in number) were elected annually by the *ecclesia* to provide collective leadership of the *polis*. Only wealthy men of noble birth were eligible for this high office. The real power rested in the Areopagus, composed of ex-archons who, upon completion of their terms as elected officials, automatically entered into lifetime membership in the Areopagus. Combining their political position with their control over the clan structure, this narrow circle of aristocrats completely dominated Athenian life for two centuries after 700 B.C. During those centuries Athens experienced mounting tensions, rooted primarily in the deterioration of the economic and social position of free small farmers. Under the pressures of a growing population, competition for limited land, and increasing emphasis on the production of olives, grapes, and livestock, many of them became debtors obligated to turn over a sizable portion of their crops to their noble creditors as debt payment; some were eventually enslaved because they could not pay what they owed. Athens was slow to seek overseas colonies but ultimately directed its efforts toward the grain-rich Hellespont and Black Sea areas, suggesting that the city suffered a serious food shortage. Toward the end of the seventh century B.C. trade and industry began to expand, creating a sector of the populace whose economic interests were not always satisfied with the policies of the dominant aristocrats, whose concerns were primarily agricultural.

Ultimately, the ruling aristocracy responded to these pressures by introducing reforms. During the seventh century Athens developed a *hoplite* army that brought a wider circle of citizens into a key role in society. In 621 B.C. a reformer named Draco drew up the first Athenian written code of law, harsh in its details (whence the modern term "draconian") but significant because it curtailed the power of aristocratic judges and family heads to administer justice in their own interests.

Shortly after, there appeared a more significant reformer, Solon, who was elected archon about 594 B.C. Although an aristocrat, Solon was a man of broad vision and strong patriotism whose concern for injustice in Athens is reflected in surviving fragments of his poetry. Central to Solon's program was his effort to aid the poor and oppressed by a "shaking off of burdens." He struck down the ancient debt laws that permitted landlords to extract exorbitant rents from small farmers who fell into debt and to enslave them. Many who had fallen into bondage were freed. However, while Solon ensured personal freedom to those victimized by debt, he did not return their lost land. He apparently realized that Athens could not remain a city-state totally dependent on an agricultural system devoted to grain growing. Thus, he took steps to promote new forms of agriculture, notably olive oil production, which would provide products for export. He was especially concerned with encouraging the growth of trade and industry as a means of providing new opportunities for displaced farmers. Particularly important was his encouragement of the immigration of foreign artisans with skills that would upgrade the quality of Athenian manufactured goods and the ability to teach those skills to Athenians.

Solon introduced political changes designed to curb the aristocratic abuse of power but not to deprive the oligarchy of control of political life. He reorganized the entire citizen population into four classes, each defined in terms of income derived from land. This classification system greatly diminished the power exercised by aristocratic families through their domination of the brotherhoods that had previously defined the tribal structure. Eligibility for the chief elective offices—from which individuals passed to life membership in the Areopagus—was confined to the two upper wealth groups, but under the new system involvement in the direction of the *polis* was no longer restricted solely to the highborn. Solon extensively revised Draco's law code to broaden public control over the administration of justice. He also sought to curb abuses in the administration of justice by making the *Heliaea* instead of the Areopagus the final court of appeal. The Heliaea was a large panel of citizens drawn by lot from the membership of the *ecclesia* for the specific purpose of hearing judicial appeals. Its operation permitted the citizen body to correct judicial inequities perpetrated in the tribal and brotherhood courts dominated by noble family heads. While Solon was certainly no democrat, taken together, the changes he introduced marked an important step in limiting the aristocratic monopoly of power and expanding the role of the citizen body in public affairs.

Despite Solon's reforms Athens continued to be torn by tensions caused chiefly by the competition among aristocratic factions for dominance of the *polis* and the continued unrest of depressed small farmers. Increasing civic turmoil paved the way for tyranny. Athens' first tyrant was an ambitious nobleman, Pisistratus, who after two unsuccessful attempts finally seized control in 546 B.C. with the help of mercenary troops paid for out of his own wealth and the contributions of foreign city-states hostile toward Athens. He held power until his death in 527 B.C., and his sons continued his regime until 510 B.C. Pisistratus and his sons made no changes in the constitutional structure of Athens. They sustained their power by controlling the election of archons, which in turn gave them a powerful hold on the Areopagus. They used harsh means, including confiscation of property and exile, to cow the powerful aristocratic families. Like most Greek tyrants, their major policy was directed toward building a popular following, chiefly among the small farmers and the emerging merchant and artisan groups. They provided jobs by sponsoring public works projects, promoted Athenian commercial and manufacturing interests through an aggressive foreign policy, tried to ensure an equitable administration of justice, and promoted civic, religious, and cultural life (see Figure 4.2). Their policies increased Athens'

FIGURE 4.2 Greek Civic Religion An important part of Greek civic life involved public religious ceremonies, the chief of which was the sacrifice of animals. This pottery painting shows Athenians sacrificing to Apollo, whose statue is shown on the right. The priest is placing the animal parts due the god on the blood-stained altar, while the good meat from the sacrificial animal is held on a spit by a youth; it will be cooked and enjoyed by the sacrificers. The scene reflects the familiarity felt by the Greeks toward their deities. (Museum für Vor und Frühgeschichte, Frankfurt)

wealth and expanded the number of citizens whose welfare depended on the well-being of the entire *polis*.

Despite its broad appeal and its role in promoting the advance of Athens as a leading city-state, tyranny marked only a temporary chapter in Athenian history. Under Pisistratus' sons the regime grew more arbitrary and oppressive. Finally, a coalition of aristocratic families with the support of Spartan military forces drove Hippias into exile in Persia in 510 B.C. Although some of the noble victors hoped to reestablish an aristocratic monopoly on power, their dreams were dashed by another noble faction, led by Cleisthenes, which turned to the citizenry for support

of reforms aimed at broadening citizen participation in political life as a means of restoring order.

Assuming leadership in 508 B.C., Cleisthenes instituted basic structural changes in the political system that allowed control by the citizen body. He abolished the political functions of the ancient clans, brotherhoods, and tribes, although he left them certain religious and social roles. To replace the kinship-dominated system, he divided Attica into territorial units, called *demes*. All free males living in each *deme* were registered as citizens, a right that passed to their descendants. The *demes*, perhaps totaling about a hundred and fifty, were grouped together to form thirty second-level organizations called *trittyes*. Three *trittyes* were then combined to create a *tribe*, of which there was a total of ten. In arranging this basic structure, Cleisthenes utilized an ingenious tactic aimed at overcoming regionalism and reconciling clashing economic interests. During the sixth century Attica had become divided into three distinct geographical regions, each with special economic and social concerns: the hill or interior country, dominated by poor farmers; the plain, where the land was most fertile and the great noble families were entrenched; and the shore or city, where merchants, artisans, and urban laborers predominated. Cleisthenes created ten *trittyes* in each of these regions. In shaping the ten tribes, he included one *trittyes* from each region in each tribe. As a consequence, each tribe contained a cross section of the entire population, requiring that conflicting interests be conciliated before each tribe could determine its position on major issues affecting the entire polis. Each *deme* and tribe was a political entity in its own right, with elected officials, courts, taxes, and military forces. Each offered wide opportunity for direct participation in local affairs by its citizen members.

Cleisthenes then rearranged the organs of government that controlled the entire *polis* to fit the new tribal organization. A Council of Five Hundred, composed of fifty citizens selected by lot from each tribe for an annual term, was created as a prime agency in shaping the political life of the *polis*. No one could serve on this council more than twice in a lifetime, thus ensuring that many citizens had an opportunity to participate in this all-important body. The Council of Five Hundred was in essence a steering committee for the citizen body, meeting frequently to supervise many aspects of the administration of the city and to prepare agenda of issues to be presented to the *ecclesia*, which had the ultimate authority in the government. Made up of all male citizens over eighteen years of age voting by tribe, this body met at least once a month to hear debate on issues presented by the Council of Five Hundred and to vote on courses of action. The citizens were further involved in governing the city by their participation in the popular court, the Heliaea, which played an increasing role in the administration of justice. Cleisthenes did not change the Areopagus, although it now lacked

the authority to guide crucial decisions, and the elected archons remained the executive officers of the *polis*. These magistrates were elected by the *ecclesia* and were still usually from the wealthy, aristocratic segment of the population, but now aristocratic candidates for high office had to win the support of the entire citizen body. Perhaps it was Cleisthenes who introduced a powerful instrument for controlling elective officials and overly ambitious aristocrats by establishing the practice of *ostracism*, through which a majority of the *ecclesia* could declare an individual dangerous to the state and order that person into exile for ten years.

Although Cleisthenes' reforms created the framework for democratic government in Athens, not until the time of Pericles, the chief political figure from 461 to 429 B.C., did Athenian democracy reach full bloom. During that interval changes were made to encourage greater participation. The chief executive offices were increasingly filled by lot, expanding the chances of ordinary citizens to hold high office. The number of magistrates increased steadily, again allowing a larger number of citizens to take part in public life. Especially significant was the establishment shortly after 500 B.C. of a new elective official, called general (*strategos*), from each tribe to constitute a group of ten military leaders who quickly assumed a key role in directing public affairs. In contrast with the archons, who were eligible for only a one-year term, the generals could be elected year after year if they could command sufficient votes in their tribes. Property qualifications for officeholding tended to disappear. A crucial step in the development of democracy came when Pericles introduced public payment for service in the Council of Five Hundred, the Heliaea, the elected magistracies, and the army and navy. This step enabled ordinary citizens to serve the *polis* without sacrificing their livelihood. Increasingly, Athenian citizens were encouraged to exercise their power by leaders such as Pericles, an aristocrat by birth and wealth who felt no fear in entrusting the final political decisions of Athens to the citizens and who sought to convince them that public life was a dignified, responsible, and rewarding activity owed by all who enjoyed the benefit of living in Athens.

Never before in history had ordinary individuals enjoyed a greater role in determining their own political fate than did the citizens of Periclean Athens. However, Athenian democracy had its limits. Participation in political life was confined to males descended from those enrolled as citizens in the time of Cleisthenes. Women, foreigners (called *metics*), and slaves did not qualify for participation in the political life of the *polis*. In the fifth century B.C. the citizen population of Athens was about forty-five thousand; the total population of Attica was probably about three hundred fifty thousand. Thus, a male minority ruled the democratic Athenian *polis*.

4. SPARTA

The history of another important city-state, Sparta, illustrates a different pattern of development of the *polis* in the Greek world. Sparta emerged as a city-state during the ninth century B.C. as a result of the coalition of several small agricultural villages clustered around the site of the city. After this union the Spartans slowly established control over an area in the southern Peloponnesus known as Laconia, creating a base for future Spartan prominence. Until about 750 B.C. Sparta's development followed a pattern that differed little from most other city-states during the Archaic Age. But then Spartan society diverged from the common pattern. When the Spartans began to feel the economic stresses that gripped most of the Aegean world during the Archaic Age, their solution was to conquer a neighboring territory, Messenia, a fertile agricultural region west of Laconia, and to make the Messenian population servile dependents of Sparta, forced to labor as tillers of the soil to support their conquerors. In about 640 B.C. the Messenians revolted and were suppressed only after a desperate struggle lasting twenty years. That struggle led to a radical restructuring of Spartan society aimed at ensuring sufficient military strength to maintain control of the city-state's subject population. These reforms were attributed to a single lawgiver, Lycurgus, but probably were carried out by several leaders during the decades just before and after 600 B.C.—at roughly the same time that Solon was reshaping Athenian history.

A fundamental feature of the new order was the division of the population into rigidly defined classes, each with specific responsibilities in the service of the *polis*. Most important were the Spartans, a relatively small portion of the total population who alone enjoyed full citizenship. Numbering about ten thousand males considered to be social equals, the Spartans were required to devote their lives to military service in the interest of exerting control over other elements in the population and defending Sparta against outside enemies. The Lycurgan system prescribed a strict regimen for this group. At birth each male child of a Spartan citizen was inspected for physical fitness. If he was defective, the state ordered death by exposure. If allowed to live, the child remained with his mother until he was seven. Then he joined other males in barracks life, where all were subjected to rigorous military training until they were twenty. At twenty the Spartan became a regular soldier. He was assigned a piece of state land along with laborers to farm it as a source of his livelihood, thus freeing him from economic concerns so that he could serve the state. He could marry after the age of twenty, but he was not permitted to establish his own household until the age of thirty, when he became an "equal" with full rights to participate in the political life of the *polis*. During these long formative years the social life of each Spartan found its focus in a mess group, a small circle of military companions who shared barracks life and contributed payments derived from their state-assigned land allocations to provide common meals. The values molded in this environment dominated the life of each male Spartan: loyalty, obedience, devotion to the community, conformity, disdain for wealth and luxury. All Spartans were required to perform military service until they were sixty years of age. Spartan females were likewise rigorously trained to become wives and mothers. Their training emphasized physical fitness and the development of skills in the household arts. As wives, they often played an important role in managing the family economic resources, but there was no place for them in political life.

A second element of the population of Sparta was made of *perioeci* ("those who live around" the city of Sparta), most of whom were descendants of peoples subjected by the Spartans when they asserted mastery over Laconia. Although they were required to render military service and pay taxes, they were not subjected to the training regimen required of full Spartans. They served the state chiefly as artisans and traders. They enjoyed some degree of control over local affairs in the towns they inhabited but were not permitted to take part in the processes of government which made decisions affecting the entire *polis.*

Finally, there were the *helots*, state slaves required to spend their lives as agricultural laborers or household servants toiling to support the full Spartan citizens who had no occupation except soldiering. The *helots* were allowed to maintain family life and were permitted to keep enough of what they produced to maintain a simple level of life. However, they were treated brutally by the Spartans, who were intent on ensuring their service as the mainstay of the Spartan economy. The fear of *helot* revolt remained a constant factor in Spartan life, so much so that the Spartan state declared war on the *helots* every year, permitting the killing of a suspected *helot* troublemaker on the spot. Part of the military training of Spartan youths involved seeking out and murdering allegedly dangerous *helots.*

This rigid social order was held in place by a governmental system that Lycurgus was credited with shaping but that was derived in large part from earlier political institutions. The government was formally headed by two kings, but the actual power of the co-kings was slight unless they were able to distinguish themselves as military leaders. Real power rested with the *gerousia*, a council made up of the two kings and twenty-eight other men over sixty elected to serve for life. This body formulated all legislation, judged the most important cases, and acted as an advisory body in the administration of the state. Its decisions were subject to approval by an assembly made up of all male Spartans over thirty. Theoretically, the assembly could repudiate any proposed policy, but usually its members, trained from childhood to obey orders, were inclined to accept direction from superiors. The execution of laws was entrusted to a board of five *ephors*, elected annually by the assembly, which conducted foreign affairs, supervised military training, policed the *helots*, controlled state finances, and organized military operations. When supported by the *gerousia*, the *ephors* were able to exercise almost complete control over Spartan political life, despite the fact that the male citizens possessed the power to check them. In essence, Sparta was ruled by an oligarchy of military commanders.

Although the Spartan political and social system has often been judged harshly for its restrictive militaristic features, its brutal treatment of its slaves, and its stress on conformity (a later Greek historian, Plutarch, described the Spartans as bees, "every individual an extension of the hive"), it worked. Sparta enjoyed an internal stability that was envied by many other Greeks. The dedication of Spartan citizens to the service of their *polis* was often praised. While the system was not conducive to intellectual and cultural activities, it made Sparta a dominant force in Greek intercity affairs. Proof of the effectiveness of the Spartan system was the ability of Sparta to persuade or compel most of the other city-states in the Peloponnesus to become members of the Peloponnesian League, whose members followed Spartan leadership in foreign affairs. Its control over this League allowed Sparta to play a major role in Greek history in the critical times after 500 B.C.

5. THE CHARACTER OF THE *POLIS*

A complete understanding of the nature of the Greek *polis* would require the study of the institutions of several hundred other city-states that had been formed by 500 B.C., each of which believed its institutions to be as typically "Greek" as those of Athens and Sparta. Such a wide-ranging study would certainly highlight diversity in the structure of Greek city-states, but it would also reveal certain shared characteristics of the *polis.*

Greek city-states were all small entities within which residents could interact intimately. In each *polis* life focused on an urban center, where there were concentrated political, economic, religious, and cultural activities bearing directly on the lives of all. Each city-state made citizenship a distinctive and precious condition of life. In some fashion or other, citizenship involved those who held it—almost exclusively males with the proper family pedigree—directly and actively in civic life. Such involvement was at once a great privilege and a grave responsibility. As Pericles allegedly put it, "We alone regard a man who takes no interest in public affairs, not as harmless, but as a useless character." The giving of one's talent in the service of the *polis* made one a complete human, drawing each out of self, clan, calling, and class into participation in a community enterprise. Active involvement nourished patriotism, a fierce pride in and love for the *polis*. Every *polis* was thus a pressure chamber compelling citizens to discover and exercise their individual capabilities in the interests of something larger, more enduring, and more splendid than themselves. As such, the *polis* nourished an intensity of life that produced a level of achievement seldom witnessed in the historical record.

SUGGESTED READING

General Surveys of Greek History

Michael Grant and Rachel Kitzinger, eds., *Civilization of the Ancient Mediterranean: Greece and Rome*, 3 vols. (1988). A stimulating collection of essays touching on many facets of Greco-Roman civilization.

John V. A. Fine, *The Ancient Greeks: A Critical History* (1983).

M. G. L. Hammond, *A History of Greece to 322 B.C.*, 3rd ed. (1986).

Hermann Bengston, *History of Greece: From the Beginnings to the Byzantine Era*, trans. Edmund F. Bloedow (1988).

Any of these three works will provide a full treatment of Greek history down to the time of the Macedonian conquest.

Early Greece to 500 B.C.

John Chadwick, *The Mycenaean World* (1976). An excellent treatment that reflects the best of recent scholarship.

R. J. Hopper, *The Early Greeks* (1976).

Oswyn Murray, *Early Greece* (1980).

Anthony Snodgrass, *Archaic Greece. The Age of Experiment* (1980).

M. I. Finley, *Early Greece: The Bronze and Archaic Ages*, new ed. (1981).

Any of the above four titles will provide an excellent treatment of a period in Greek history that has received significant new interpretations in recent times.

L. H. Jeffery, *Archaic Greece: The City States c. 700-500* (1976). Valuable for the attention paid to city-states other than Athens and Sparta.

Chester G. Starr, *Individual and Community. The Rise of the Polis 800-500 B.C.* (1986). A masterful treatment of the forces that produced the *polis*.

R. Osborne, *Demos* (1985). A clear discussion of early Athens.

W. G. Forrest, *History of Sparta, 950-192 B.C.*, 2nd ed. (1980).

J. T. Hooker, *The Ancient Spartans* (1980).

Two very perceptive treatments of Spartan history.

Economic and Social History

Chester G. Starr, *The Economic and Social Growth of Early Greece, 800-500 B.C.* (1977).

M. M. Austin and P. Vidal-Naquet, *Economic and Social History of Ancient Greece: An Interpretation* (1977).

Either of these two works will provide invaluable information on all aspects of Greek economy.

John Boardman, *The Greeks Overseas*, rev. ed. (1982). An excellent treatment of a crucial aspect of Greek development.

Sources

Homer, *Iliad* and *Odyssey* (many translations; among the best are those by Richmond Lattimore). Two works that played an essential role in shaping the Greek civic mentality.

Hesiod, *Theogeny and Works and Days*, trans. M. L. West (1988). A picture by a contemporary of the problems that caused stress in the Greek world about 700 B.C.

CHAPTER 5
The Greek Golden Age, 500–336 B.C.: Life, War, and Politics

FIGURE 5.1 Pericles This statue portrays Pericles, under whose leadership the city-state of Athens reached the peak of its power politically, economically and culturally. The key to Pericles' fame rests largely in the faith he had in the Athenian citizen body to decide its own destiny democratically. The artist captures the intelligence, dignity, and political sagacity for which Pericles was honored. (Museo Vaticano/ Alinari)

Driven by the energies unleashed in its many city-states, the Greek world enjoyed a golden age during the fifth and early fourth centuries B.C. Shaped within the framework created by the *polis*, a pattern of daily life prevailed which engaged the energies and satisfied the needs of most Greeks. Central to the Greek way of life were ongoing political engagements, through which the citizen body reached decisions defining the rules governing collective behavior in each *polis*. Those engagements provided powerful stimuli to creative activity in artistic, literary, and intellectual life. However, the Golden Age had a darker side involving another issue that grew ever more critical: the problem of relationships among the fiercely patriotic communities, each struggling to strengthen and enrich itself. At the beginning of the fifth century, a threat from the outside demonstrated the need for cooperation, but progressively the city-states surrendered to their parochialism and became embroiled in destructive intercity struggles whose burdens created increasing instability within each *polis*. Their failure to resolve the dilemma posed by their dedication to self-determination and their need for cooperation left the Greek city-states easy prey for a powerful external foe.

1. DAILY LIFE IN GREECE

The triumphs and tribulations of the Golden Age were shaped by the conditions that surrounded the daily lives of men and women. Rooted in the long history that had produced each *polis*, the economic and social patterns defining life in ancient Greece constituted an essential aspect of Greek civilization.

Most Greeks devoted a part of every day to some kind of work related to Greece's diversified economy. In every *polis* the bulk of the people earned their living in agriculture. Most farms were small, producing barely enough cereal grains and animal products to sustain a household. The most productive agricultural enterprises, devoted to raising olives, grapes, and livestock, took place on larger farms managed by aristocratic owners and tilled by tenants and slaves. In the urban center, which was the focal point of each *polis*, large numbers of people worked as traders, artisans, and hired laborers.

The scale of operations of retail shops and artisan workshops was small, usually involving a family household with the help of a slave or two. Only a few enterprises, such as overseas trading, mining, and arms making, were large-scale, often utilizing slaves as laborers. As illustrated by the cases of Athens and Sparta, in every *polis* a considerable portion of the population lived as public employees or as recipients of state-allocated land. Compared to both earlier and later societies, the Greek economic system did not produce abundant wealth, an important factor in creating economic rivalry among city-states and social tensions within each.

By the fifth century B.C. the social structure in most city-states lacked sharp class distinctions among the citizen population. Leading families enjoying wealth and prestige did exist, but their status depended less on birth and legal sanctions than on their ability to persuade other citizens to follow their leadership in political life and on their willingness to use their wealth to support civic activities. Citizens of lesser means were treated with respect, perhaps because their voices counted in shaping public life. There was a strong tendency in Greek society to afford greater status to those who owned land, even in small amounts, than to those who worked as artisans and traders. This attitude not only bred a disdain for labor but also opened a place in most city-states for foreign noncitizens willing to fill economic roles demanding labor without enjoying the benefits of citizenship. Slavery was pervasive in Greek society and viewed by those who enjoyed freedom, including most political and intellectual leaders, as a necessary part of a viable society. These "man-footed animals"—both male and female—bore a heavy burden on farms, in households, in artisan and trading establishments, in mines, in building projects, and even in public service activities, but they enjoyed minimal legal protection against whatever their masters chose to do to them.

Although most Greeks worked to earn a livelihood, those who considered themselves free placed a high value on leisure. Free time was possible in part because slavery played an important role in the Greek economy. Equally important was the willingness of the Greeks to live simple lives, made easier by Greece's good climate. Their diet was plain: Bread, olive oil, vegetables and fruit, cheese, fish, and wine were the staple items. Even among the wealthy, houses were modest in size and sparsely furnished. Most men and women dressed in rough-spun tunics and sandals, although the more affluent favored linen garments and at least some jewelry. However, this simplicity of tastes and needs was confined chiefly to private life. The Greeks spent lavishly to adorn their city-states with costly temples and public buildings, sculpture, and paintings and to support festivals, games, and dramas at whatever price.

The family was the fundamental unit of Greek society. The nuclear family—husband, wife, children—living in a single household and perhaps served by a slave or two stood at the base of the family structure. But kinship bonds extending to a larger circle of relatives played an important role in determining citizenship, defining social status, controlling property, and deciding associations. Marriage contracts were arranged by families. The bride's father provided a dowry, which was returned to the bride if the marriage ended. Actual cohabitation of the contracted couple, an occasion for much celebration, usually began when the girl was fifteen or sixteen; the husband was usually older. Children were important in marriage, but a constant concern with the problems resulting from too many mouths to feed resulted in modest-sized families. The Greeks practiced various methods of birth control, and they were not averse to exposing unwanted children to death or giving them up for adoption. Husbands could divorce their wives easily, but it was much more difficult for a woman to end a marriage.

Greek women had a limited place in society. Although powerful and active women were enshrined in Greek legends (for example, Helen of Troy and Penelope as portrayed by Homer) and celebrated in poetry and drama (including Clytemnestra, Antigone, and Medea) and although powerful goddesses (such as Athena) figured significantly in Greek religion, the lives of most women were severely restricted. Greek literature and philosophical writing, most of it produced by men, are filled with portrayals of women as inferior in intelligence and self-control. That view found expression in legal terms. Although wives and daughters of male citizens were recognized and protected under the law, they were always subject to a male. Women could not own property (except, ironically, in Sparta) or engage in legal transactions and were excluded from political life. The prime role of respectable women was to direct the household, care for young children, and train their daughters for the same role. Women rarely participated in any aspect of public life, except for religious festivals, and they were usually excluded from the social activities of their husbands. Women of poor households did help their husbands run their farms and shops, thus involving themselves at least to some degree in the affairs of the larger society. But most women were literally out of sight, exerting whatever influence they had within the walls of their home. Some evidence suggests that in that private sphere wives enjoyed the respect and the genuine love of their husbands. A few rare women of beauty, intelligence, and social grace became the sexual companions of important citizens and shared their social lives with them; the most notable example was Aspasia, the sophisticated and widely admired mistress of Pericles. Prostitution was common in the Greek world.

While the household was the center of life for most Greek women, men appear to have spent as little time there as possible. Shortly after the break of day they were out of the house to occupy themselves with their jobs or with the bustling life of the *polis*. Almost from birth males found their lives enmeshed in a variety of social groups whose activities consumed much of their energy. When boys were seven or eight, they went forth daily from their homes to begin their education in reading, writing, speaking, and physical education under the guidance of private teachers. By the fifth century B.C. in a city such as Athens, that education might continue for years, focusing on skills suitable to political activity, especially rhetoric. The sisters of these young men remained at home to be educated in household arts by their mothers or household slaves. At an early age males were enrolled in a *phratry*, a kinship group that sponsored a variety of religious and social activities. As young men grew older, they gravitated to the *gymnasia*, male gathering places devoted to physical education, athletic competition, and endless talk. It was not unusual for a youth to attract the attention of an adult male who served as a role model in introducing young men to the full range of activities of the *polis*. These relationships, forged in a setting that provided little female influence and that often involved homosexuality, played an important role in shaping male values. No less intriguing to the maturing youth were the marketplace, the theater, and the bordello. Often his adult mentor began to involve him in private gatherings, called *symposia*, where males met in private houses to eat, drink, and talk—free from wives and mothers, who withdrew to the special female quarters featured in the typical house. By the time his teenage days were ending, a male entered into the responsibilities of citizenship: military service, participation in the popular assembly, officeholding. For the rest of his life these political activities would command an important part of his time and energies. Perhaps shortly after becoming a full-fledged citizen, the typical Greek male married, but already his life was so involved in the affairs of the *polis* and in the social associations to which he was attached that marriage was incidental to his life. Indeed, involvement in the *polis* was more than a political matter; it defined a broad range of activities that engaged its male members completely. And the Greeks were scornful of any man who did not involve himself in that life.

Even a brief look at the essentials of Greek daily life suggests that Greek citizens enjoyed considerable freedom to do what they wished and that many chose to use that freedom to involve themselves intensely in the varied activities of the *polis*. This environment posed challenges that unleashed powerful creative forces that played a prime role in shaping the political and cultural destiny of the Greek world in the Golden Age. It was especially on the political scene that the challenge to serve the *polis* was posed during the fifth and fourth centuries; the response of the citizens in many city-states was decisive in shaping the course of political history during that period.

2. THE PERSIAN WARS, 490–479 B.C.

The Golden Age began with a defining event in Greek history, a war against the Persians. Its outcome affirmed in the mentality of the Greeks the uniqueness and the superiority of their way of life, an attitude that played an important role in sustaining it in the future. And the threat posed by the Persians demonstrated the need for cooperation among the independent city-states, a lesson the Greeks learned less well.

During the Archaic Age intercity cooperation was not a major issue in the Greek world. No major outside power threatened the city-states, and their not infrequent clashes with one another were on a limited scale. In fact, there were significant developments encouraging interdependence among the Greeks. Their common language promoted a shared culture. Expanding commerce linked the city-states together. Religion was an especially important force promoting pan-Hellenism. It provided a common set of deities, pan-Hellenic festivals—such as the Olympic Games, which drew Greeks together for worship, athletic competitions, and cultural performances honoring their gods and goddesses—and shared shrines, such as the Delphic oracle, to which all Greeks went to seek divine guidance. Some progress had even been made in establishing political federations allowing city-states to collaborate without surrendering their autonomy; a prime example was the already noted Peloponnesian League led by Sparta.

The dramatic expansion of the Persians after about 550 B.C. created a frightening challenge for the Greek world, brought home by the Persian subjugation of Greek city-states along the Aegean coast of Asia Minor and the establishment in 512 B.C. of a Persian outpost in Thrace (see Map 4.1). Although Persian rule over the Ionian city-states was not particularly harsh, their inhabitants hated paying tribute and submitting to "tyrants" imposed on them by that "evil empire" and eventually rebelled in 499 B.C. The rebels appealed to their fellow Greeks on the mainland and received support from Athens and Eritrea. The Persian ruler, Darius the Great, eventually crushed the revolt. Moved probably by fear of future Greek intervention in Persian affairs and by ambition to expand his already huge empire, he apparently decided that Greece must be conquered. Political scheming among factions within many Greek city-states that saw the Persians as potential allies in the struggles for power and the neutrality proclaimed by several key city-states encouraged Darius to think that the Greek world was ready for conquest.

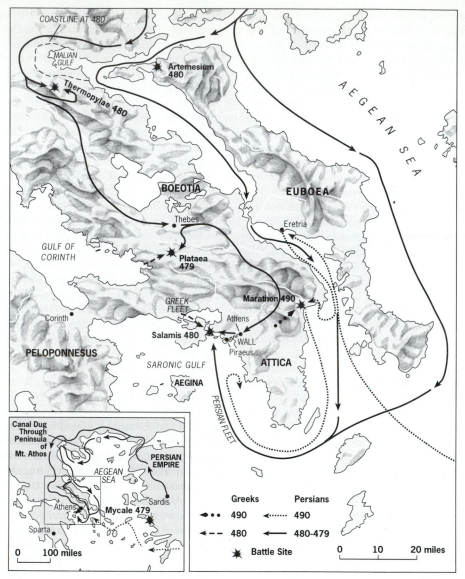

Map 5.1 THE PERSIAN WARS The map shows the location of the crucial engagements between the Greeks and the Persians in the campaigns of 490 B.C. and 480–479 B.C. The inset, showing the long route taken by Xerxes in 480 B.C., may suggest the challenge faced by the Persians in their bid to conquer the Greeks, for they had to engage the Greeks in a constricted setting where the Greeks could make the best use of their resources.

In 490 B.C. Darius made his move (see Map 5.1 for the Persian campaigns). He sent a fleet and a substantial army across the Aegean, ostensibly to punish Athens and Eritrea for their involvement in the rebellion of the Ionians. After destroying Eritrea, the Persian army landed in eastern Attica, near Marathon. The Greek world had made almost no preparations for the Persian onslaught. Standing alone, the Athenians seemed doomed. But they chose to resist, sending an army to challenge the Persians. Although out-numbered, the Athenian *hoplites,* brilliantly led by Miltiades, defeated the Persians and forced the survivors back to their ships. Miltiades then marched his victorious army back to Athens and stood ready to defend the city when the Persian fleet from Marathon appeared there. The Persians elected to return to Asia Minor. Athens celebrated a new breed of heroes whose feats at Marathon rivaled those of the heroes extolled by Homer.

The Persians were not ready to admit defeat, although a new attack was delayed ten years by internal troubles. That interval allowed the Greeks to prepare more adequately. Sparta took the leadership in organizing a Hellenic League made up of thirty-one city-states willing to pool their forces under Spartan commanders. Greek armed strength, based on the superb Spartan army, was greatly enhanced by a crucial decision made by Athens. A farsighted leader named Themistocles persuaded the Athenian citizenry to use the income from silver mines recently discovered in Attica to fund a major increase in the Athenian navy, which the Athenians pledged to the support of the Hellenic League. Despite this show of unity, many city-states remained neutral.

Early in 480 B.C. Xerxes, Darius' successor, launched a new attack spearheaded by a huge army and navy. Xerxes sent his army over a pontoon bridge crossing the Hellespont into Europe. Supplied by a huge fleet, it advanced slowly around the northern Aegean coast and then southward. The Hellenic League made its first stand at Thermopylae. Despite their success in defeating the Persian fleet and the heroic resistance of a Spartan detachment led by King Leonidas, the Greeks suffered a defeat that allowed the Persians to flood into central Greece, capturing Athens and striking terror into the Greek alliance.

At this critical point, Themistocles exercised a decisive influence on the course of the war. Despite strong pressure in the council of the Hellenic League to withdraw the armies to the Peloponnesus and the fleet to the Gulf of Corinth, Themistocles combined persuasion with threats of Athens' withdrawal to convince the League to trust the Greek fate to a naval showdown. In late September 480 B.C., he enticed the Persian fleet

into a disadvantageous position in the narrow waters between Attica and the island of Salamis, where the Athenian fleet delivered a crushing defeat on the Persians. Xerxes was forced to order the surviving remnants of his fleet back to its bases in Asia Minor and the withdrawal of his army to northern Greece.

In 479 B.C. Xerxes again ordered his army southward. The Hellenic League put a major army into the field, anchored by Spartan troops. This force met the Persians at Plataea. Once again the Greeks imposed a major defeat on the larger Persian army. While these events were unfolding, the fleet of the Hellenic League sailed boldly across the Aegean and destroyed the main Persian fleet at Mycale, a victory that triggered a revolt among the Greek city-states of Asia Minor. Xerxes had no choice but to recall his armies from Europe. By their willingness to sacrifice in the service of their city-states, the jubilant Greeks had won a victory that not only saved their independence but also filled them with a sense of superiority.

While the Greeks of the Aegean world were throwing back the Persian threat, their fellow Greeks in the west were winning a victory hardly less significant. The struggle here centered on Sicily, where Carthage, a powerful maritime state, was attempting to expand its commercial empire by subduing the Sicilian Greeks. A coalition of Greek city-states led by Gelon, tyrant of Syracuse, inflicted a decisive defeat on the Carthaginians at the battle of Himera in 480 B.C., ensuring the continued independence of the Greek city-states in Magna Graecia.

3. THE DELIAN LEAGUE AND THE ATHENIAN EMPIRE, 479–431 B.C.

Although the Greeks had won a victory of mythic proportions to them, the Persian Empire remained a major power and a real threat which many felt must be countered by a cooperative offensive against the Persians. Leadership in this undertaking passed from Sparta to Athens, which took the initiative in 478 B.C. in persuading several cities to form the Delian League, so named because its treasury was to be kept on the island of Delos, the site of a temple venerated throughout the Greek world. Dedicated to the continuation of the war against Persia, the League's policy decisions were to be made by an assembly of representatives meeting annually with each member city-state having one vote. Each member pledged to contribute ships and money according to its abilities. Athens was charged with making the initial assessments and with commanding the League's forces. No member city-state would be required to surrender sovereign control over its internal affairs, thus protecting the principle of autonomy.

The League quickly swung into action. An Athenian, Cimon, was placed in command of its joint forces, which enjoyed impressive success. Within fifteen years, all the Greek city-states in Asia Minor were freed of Persian rule, while the Aegean and the Hellespont areas were cleared of Persian naval power. Athens was obviously the most powerful member of the League, but its leaders conducted themselves with marked restraint in dealing with other members and even toward nonmembers, such as Sparta.

This situation was not destined to last, and Athens was largely responsible for the change. As the danger from Persia receded, some members of the Delian League sought to reduce their contributions and even to withdraw. Athens was unwilling to allow the dissolution of the League. Increasingly, Athenian leaders and citizens came to realize that dominance over the League could be turned to commercial ends that would enrich Athens. The emergence of Athenian imperialist ambitions coincided with the final establishment of democracy in Athens under the leadership of Pericles (see Figure 5.1), who from 461 to 429 B.C. was the dominant force in Athenian political affairs. He placed the destiny of the city into the hands of his fellow citizens and constantly urged their support of policies designed to ensure Athenian preeminence in Greece. They responded with enthusiasm, partly because that course enriched the city-state and partly because imperialism fed the Athenians' pride in the greatness of their *polis*, by now the self-acclaimed savior of Hellas.

Emboldened by such support, Pericles launched a two-pronged drive to expand Athenian influence. One was aimed at aggressive actions against "foreign enemies," real or invented. The assault against the Persians, who constantly enhanced their already established reputation as a threat to the Greek world by subversive efforts

aimed at disrupting political life in almost every Greek city-state, was expanded beyond the Aegean into the eastern Mediterranean. On the Greek mainland Pericles employed every device possible to draw more city-states into the Delian League. Athens supported revolts against non-democratic governments, tried to entice the members of the Peloponnesian League to abandon Sparta, and used Athenian sea power to bottle up rival trading powers, such as Corinth. This aggressive policy enjoyed considerable success, but eventually Pericles realized that Athens was overextending its power. In 454 B.C. an unsuccessful Athenian effort to liberate Egypt led to an understanding with the Persians that each would respect the other's sphere of influence: Athens' control of the Aegean and the Greek city-states in Asia Minor and Persia's dominance of the eastern Mediterranean coastal area. In the face of mounting threats of Spartan retaliation against Athenian expansionism on the Greek mainland, Pericles finally agreed to the Thirty Years' Truce of 445 B.C. Athens agreed to halt its aggression against mainland Greek city-states, especially those belonging to the Peloponnesian League, and Sparta promised to recognize Athenian hegemony over the Delian League.

In the years following 445 B.C. Pericles skillfully pursued the second aspect of his imperial policy: imposing control over the nearly three hundred city-states constituting the Delian League. Although the Persian danger no longer existed, Athens continued to collect funds from these cities. This "tribute" was used as Athens wished, chiefly to support the system of pay Pericles introduced for the vastly increased number of citizens who performed public service in Athens and to support the artists and writers who made Athens the "school of Hellas." Athens forced many League members to institute democratic governments. The subject cities were compelled to accept the Athenian money system and Athenian weights and measures, thus ensuring that their economies would be subservient to that of Athens. Athenians were settled on lands confiscated from residents of subject city-states, a policy that relieved Athens of excess population and provided a convenient means of influencing internal affairs in dependent members of what had become an Athenian Empire.

Although the subject city-states benefited from increased commerce and the security re-

Map 5.2 **THE GREEK WORLD, 431 B.C.** This map identifies the members of the two camps into which the Greek world was divided at the beginning of the Peloponnesian War. It highlights why its naval forces were so vital to Athens in the struggle that lasted until 404 B.C. and why an alliance with Persia eventually played a crucial role in the success of Sparta and its allies in dismembering the Athenian Empire.

sulting from enforced peace, their hatred for Athens grew steadily. Athens had usurped their most prized possession, their right to exist as independent city-states. The mighty, enlightened democratic gem of Greek civilization had, in the eyes of most Greeks, become an oppressor. The proud, arrogant Athenians made no attempt to compensate for depriving their subjects of their independence. They were not permitted to become citizens of Athens, and they were denied any representation in the Athenian government. Some Athenians raised concerns about the destruction of the liberty of any *polis*, but the Athenian citizenry, aware that the economic welfare of Athens and its citizens depended on imperial power and proud of Athens' glory, overrode

these voices. Mounting anti-Athenian feeling throughout much of the Greek world caused many to look toward Sparta as the champion of city-state independence. Such sentiments pointed toward a major clash engaging Greek against Greek.

4. THE PELOPONNESIAN WAR, 431–404 B.C.

The conflict pitting two hostile camps—the Spartan-led Peloponnesian League and the Athenian-led Delian League—against each other began in 431 B.C. (see Map 5.2). At the very beginning of the struggle, known as the Peloponnesian War, a Spartan envoy warned the Athenians that "This day will be the beginning of great evil for the Greeks." Implicit in this admonition was the widely shared view, then and now, that responsibility for the war belonged to Athens for threatening the independence of other city-states. That charge had ominous implications; for a generation the clash inflicted a terrible material and psychological cost on the entire Greek world which perhaps doomed the fundamental institution at stake, the independent *polis*.

The first years of the war were indecisive. Confident that the Spartan alliance would crumble, Pericles persuaded the Athenians to avoid land war against the superior Spartan armies; its populace withdrew within Athens' impregnable walls, depending on its superior fleet to hold the empire together and supply the beleaguered city. The Spartans responded by ravaging the Attic countryside, but they were unable to strike a decisive blow. This strategy put too great a burden on the Athenians, who were increasingly impatient as they watched their beloved land ravaged; to their rage was added the suffering caused by a terrible plague which between 430 and 427 B.C. killed at least one-third of the cooped-up population, including Pericles. The cry for bolder military action mounted. A militant democratic and imperialistic leader, Cleon, responded by leading Athenian armies outside Attica, especially into central Greece and western Peloponnesus, in an effort to wean away crucial Spartan allies. A resourceful Spartan leader, Brasidas, persuaded Sparta to send its military forces farther afield to encourage revolt among the subject cities of the Athenian Empire, especially in the northern Aegean area. However, in 422 B.C., before this new phase of the struggle reached a decisive point, both Cleon and Brasidas were killed. Powerful supporters of peace in both camps took advantage of their deaths to end the war. In 421 B.C. Athens and Sparta agreed to a Fifty-Year Truce, which restored the situation to what it had been when the struggle began.

The uneasy peace settlement, which addressed none of the basic issues, lasted only until 415 B.C. Again the Athenians were responsible for the renewal of hostilities. After the death of Pericles, Athenian political life became faction-ridden and unstable. Afflicted by the burdens of war, the citizens were increasingly swayed by ambitious demagogues willing to promise anything in return for power. Such a figure was the flashy, unscrupulous Alcibiades. Playing upon the imperialistic sentiments and the civic pride so strong in Athens, he persuaded the citizenry to undertake a major expedition against the powerful Greek city of Syracuse in Sicily, an important commercial rival of Athens. This ill-conceived venture, badly led by rival politicians, including Alcibiades, who deserted to Sparta to avoid criminal charges brought by his enemies in Athens, ended in a disastrous defeat for Athens in 413 B.C. Worse, the attack on Syracuse provoked Sparta and its allies to renew all-out war against Athens.

After 413 B.C. the fortunes of Athens declined steadily. Internal dissension, pitting prodemocratic forces against a growing faction fearful of the consequences of unbridled democracy, hindered decisive action. The Spartans, brilliantly led by Lysander, mounted a powerful attack on Athenian sea power and a skillful campaign to encourage revolt among the city-states of the Athenian Empire. A decisive step in this campaign was the Spartan success in forming an alliance with Persia which provided Sparta with naval forces sufficient to challenge the Athenian fleet that had so long provided the glue holding the Athenian Empire together. Athens occasionally won an isolated victory, but the net continued to close around the doomed city-state. Finally, in 404 B.C., Athens had to surrender. The victors forced Athens to tear down its walls, destroy all but twelve ships of its once-invincible fleet, and submit to a government of oligarchs backed by a Spartan army stationed in Athens. Although these Thirty Tyrants, as the Athenians called them, were ousted in 403 B.C. and democratic government was restored, Athens would never recover its former power.

Athens was not the only victim of the Peloponnesian War. Its ravages impoverished many Greek city-states, deepened and embittered the rivalries among them, bred internal dissension and violence within many city-states, caused widespread pessimism and disillusionment, and renewed the threat of Persian domination. Its impact unleashed forces that would soon drastically reduce the role of the Greek city-states in shaping the destiny of Greco-Roman civilization.

HISTORIANS' SOURCES

Thucydides: *The Peloponnesian War*

In his Peloponnesian War *the Greek historian Thucydides recorded a speech made by Pericles eulogizing the Athenians who died during the first year of that war. The following passage from that speech provides the historian with an insight into what the Athenians thought of themselves but raises questions about Pericles as an objective reporter of reality.*

"But before I praise the dead, I should like to point out by what principles of action we rose to power, and under what institutions and through what manner of life our empire became great. . . .

"Our form of government does not enter into rivalry with the institutions of others. We do not copy our neighbours, but are an example to them. It is true that we are called a democracy, for the administration is in the hands of the many and not of the few. But while the law secures equal justice to all alike in their private disputes, the claim of excellence is also recognised; and when a citizen is in any way distinguished, he is preferred to the public service, not as a matter of privilege, but as the reward of merit. Neither is poverty a bar, but a man may benefit his country whatever be the obscurity of his condition. There is no exclusiveness in our public life, and in our private intercourse we are not suspicious of one another, nor angry with our neighbour if he does what he likes. . . . While we are thus unconstrained in our private intercourse, a spirit of reverence pervades our public acts; we are prevented from doing wrong by respect for authority and for the laws, having an especial regard to those which are ordained for the protection of the injured as well as to those unwritten laws which bring upon the transgressor of them the reprobation of the general sentiment.

"And we have not forgotten to provide for our weary spirits many relaxations from toil; we have regular games and sacrifices throughout the year; at home the style of our life is refined; and the delight which we daily feel in all these things helps to banish melancholy. Because of the greatness of our city the fruits of the whole earth flow in upon us. . . .

"Then, again, our military training is in many respects superior to that of our adversaries. . . . We rely not upon management or trickery but upon our own hearts and hands. And in the matter of education, whereas they from early youth are always undergoing laborious exercises which are to make them brave, we live at ease, and yet are equally ready to face the perils which they face. . . .

"If then we prefer to meet danger with a light heart but without laborious training, and with a courage which is gained by habit and not enforced by law, are we not greatly the gainers? Since we do not anticipate the pain, although, when the hour comes, we can be as brave as those who never allow themselves to rest; and thus too our city is equally admirable in peace and in war.

"For we are lovers of the beautiful, yet with economy, and we cultivate the mind without loss of manliness. Wealth we employ, not for talk and ostentation, but when there is a real use for it. To avow poverty with us is no disgrace; the true disgrace is in doing nothing to avoid it. An Athenian citizen does not neglect the state because he takes care of his own household; and even those of us who are engaged in business have a very fair idea of politics. We alone regard a man who takes no interest in public affairs, not as a harmless, but as a useless character; and if few of us are originators, we are all sound judges of a policy. . . . For we have a peculiar power of thinking before we act and of acting too, whereas other men are courageous from ignorance but hesitate upon reflection. . . .

"To sum up: I say that Athens is the school of Hellas, and that the individual Athenian in his own person seems to have the power of adapting himself to the most varied forms of action with the utmost versatility and grace."

SOURCE: Francis R. B. Godolphin, ed., *The Greek Historians*, Vol. I (New York: Random House, 1942), pp. 648–650.

5. THE TWILIGHT OF THE WORLD OF THE GREEK CITY-STATES, 404–336 B.C.

Although one Greek historian proclaimed the end of the Peloponnesian War "the beginning of freedom for Greece," in fact the defeat of Athens marked the beginning of even greater trouble in the Greek world. Two interlocking issues dominated the next sixty years: the effort of a succession of leading city-states to establish hegemony over the Greeks and the struggle to sustain internal order and vitality within each *polis*. These issues combined to produce constantly shifting alliances, almost incessant intercity warfare, and bitter civil strife, all of which combined to weaken the Greeks.

At the end of the Peloponnesian War Sparta was the predominant power in the Greek world. For the next thirty years it devoted its energies to asserting its hegemony. The key to Spartan policy was the imposition of an oligarchic government on any city-state that could be bullied into submission, a policy that badly undermined Sparta's claim to be the defender of city-state independence. In fact, Sparta did not have the strength to control the Greek world. Its narrowly restricted citizen body was declining in numbers and in dedication to the Lycurgan regime. Its rigid social system prevented Sparta from replenishing its citizens from the ranks of the *perioeci* and *helots*. Ultimately, Sparta was forced to depend on Persian assistance to maintain its hegemony at the cost of allowing the Persians to reestablish dominance over the Ionian Greeks. Growing fear and resentment against Sparta led to the formation of an alliance led by Thebes. Under the brilliant generalship of Thebes' one great statesman, Epaminandos, this alliance smashed Sparta in a single battle in 371 B.C., a defeat that marked the end of Sparta's long history as a major Greek power. This victory allowed Thebes to play a central role in Greek affairs for a decade, but even with Persian help it was unable to dominate; its power was smashed in a decisive battle in 362 B.C. by an alliance formed by Athens.

In the generation after Thebes' defeat Athens sought to reestablish a dominant position, but its efforts were constantly thwarted by rival city-states and by internal dissension. The result was a succession of petty wars that wasted human and material resources and placed a constant strain on internal affairs in each *polis*. These internal struggles, centered on rivalry between democratic and aristocratic factions for control of political life and on issues pitting poor against rich over the distribution of declining wealth in each city-state, were often marked by a blatant abuse of power by ambitious power seekers and by violence. Increasingly, mercenary forces led by ruthless and adventuresome commanders replaced citizen armies and navies; these professionals much preferred war to peace. Some Greek leaders, aware of the destructive cost of intercity war, formulated a variety of plans aimed at forming some kind of voluntary union among city-states that would provide a peaceful setting in which each *polis* could restore internal stability. However, political pan-Hellenism was a lost cause. No Greek *polis* was willing to surrender any of its sovereignty to a superior organization—even in the interest of peace. Even great philosophers such as Plato and Aristotle, both of whom lived during the fourth century, vigorously insisted that only the traditional self-defining *polis* was fit for the Greeks.

6. THE MACEDONIAN CONQUEST OF GREECE

Incessant warfare and civic strife gradually deprived the Greek city-states of the ability to determine their own destiny. That role was snatched by the kingdom of Macedonia, suddenly elevated from relative obscurity to the rank of a major power under the leadership of King Philip II (359–336 B.C.). A gifted, ambitious ruler, Philip II was able to create a disciplined army and to impose an effective internal organization on his previously diverse, unruly subjects. Assured of a strong power base, Philip II turned his attention toward the turbulent Greek world, driven by an urge to gain access to the Aegean Sea and to bring his backward kingdom into closer contact with the Greek civilization he greatly admired.

Macedonian intrusion into Greece involved a complex play of political forces. The warring Greek city-states and the rival factions within many city-states could not resist seeking Philip's support. Philip encouraged them to do so, often intriguing in Greek affairs to create opportunities for his involvement. His skilled diplomacy and his adroit use of military force increasingly allowed him to manipulate political life over an ever-expanding area of the Aegean world. Although many warned of the Macedonian "menace," the Greeks were seldom able to join forces to resist. In fact, some Greeks favored Macedonian dominance as a solution for incessant warfare. Eventually Athens, moved both by fear of Macedonian power and by dreams of using the Macedonian threat to re-create Athenian hegemony in Greece, became the focal point of resistance. Under the leadership of the eloquent Demosthenes, always ready to use his oratorical skills to warn his fellow Athenian citizens of the Macedonian danger and to damn those in Athens and elsewhere who advocated peace with Macedonia, Athens was able to form a fragile league dedicated to resistance to Macedonian advances. Despite this effort at collective action, the Macedonian advance was irresistible. Philip finally maneuvered the Athenian alliance into committing itself to battle at Chaeronea in 338 B.C., which ended in a crushing defeat that left all of Greece at Philip's mercy.

While treating his vanquished enemies with mildness unusual for the era, Philip quickly demonstrated that he intended to end the old order. Soon after his victory and at his insistence all the Greek city-states except Sparta agreed to join the League of Corinth, dedicated to the establishment of a common peace. Members of the League were theoretically entitled to independence, but crucial restrictions were imposed on their power to make war or change their form of government. Such prohibitions obviously greatly restricted the ancient freedom of the *polis*. The League was to be governed by a council of representatives from each city-state, which would meet regularly and decide League actions to keep peace. Each member was obliged to contribute according to its means to a common military force charged with imposing peace. Macedonia was not a member of the League, but Philip did require that the League sign a treaty of alliance with Macedonia. Philip was also designated as military commander (*hegemon*) of the League, thus putting himself into a position to control its activities. At a meeting of the League council in 337 B.C. Philip proposed that its first undertaking should be joining its forces with Macedonia in a war against Persia; it was difficult for any city-state to protest against such a noble cause. But his assassination in 336 B.C. denied him an opportunity to direct this campaign against an ancient foe of the Greeks. Nevertheless, Philip's statesmanship had achieved a notable end: In the League of Corinth he provided an instrument that would allow the warring city-states to impose peace on themselves while enjoying internal autonomy and the protection of the potent Macedonian army against outsiders. Within this framework the *polis* survived as a key element in Greco-Roman civilization but never again in the same way that that institution had dominated the Greek world during the Golden Age.

SUGGESTED READING

Fifth- and Fourth-Century Greece

Simon Hornblower, *The Greek World, 479–323 B.C.* (1983). A good general survey.
A. R. Burn, *Persia and the Greeks: The Defence of the West, c. 546–478 B.C.*, 2nd ed. (1984). A full treatment of the clash between the Greeks and the Persians.
P. J. Rhodes, *The Athenian Empire* (1985).
Malcolm F. McGregor, *The Athenians and Their Empire* (1987).

Either of these works will help the reader understand Athenian imperialism.
Anton Powell, *Athens and Sparta: Constructing Greek Political and Social History from 478 B.C.* (1988). Helpful in assessing the impact of the Peloponnesian War.
Andrew Lintott, *Violence, Civil Strife, and Revolution in the Classical City, 750–330 B.C.* (1982).
G. E. M. de Ste. Croix, *The Class Struggle in the Ancient Greek World from the Archaic Age to the Arab Conquest* (1981).

Two provocative treatments of a facet of Greek life that was destructive of the *polis*.

J. W. Roberts, *City of Sokrates: An Introduction to Classical Athens* (1984).

R. K. Sinclair, *Democracy and Participation in Athens* (1988).

Josiah Ober, *Mass and Elite in Democratic Athens: Rhetoric, Ideology, and the Power of the People* (1989).

Chester G. Starr, *The Birth of Athenian Democracy: The Assembly in the Fifth Century B.C.* (1990).

These four works are useful in understanding how Athenian democracy worked.

J. R. Ellis, *Phillip II and Macedonian Imperialism* (1976).

George Cawkwell, *Philip of Macedon* (1978).

Two excellent studies explaining the Macedonian victory over the Greeks.

Social Life

In addition to the social and economic histories cited in Chapter 4, the following works treat selected aspects of Greek social life, as indicated by their titles.

R. J. Hopper, *Trade and Industry in Classical Greece* (1979).

Maurice Pope, *The Ancient Greeks. How They Lived and Worked* (1976).

Robert Garland, *The Greek Way of Life from Conception to Old Age* (1990).

M. T. W. Arnheim, *Aristocracy in Greek Society* (1977).

W. K. Lacey, *The Family in Classical Greece* (1984).

Sarah B. Pomeroy, *Goddesses, Whores, Wives, and Slaves: Women in Classical Antiquity* (1975).

Eva Cantarella, *Pandora's Daughters: The Role and Status of Women in Greek and Roman Antiquity*, trans. Maureen B. Fant (1987).

Roger Just, *Women in Athenian Law and Life* (1988).

Mark Golden, *Children and Childhood in Classical Athens* (1990).

Yvon Garlan, *Slavery in Ancient Greece*, trans. Janet Lloyd (1988).

K. J. Dover, *Greek Homosexuality* (1978).

Donald G. Kyle, *Athletics in Ancient Athens* (1987).

Sources

Herodotus, *The Histories*, trans. Aubrey de Selincourt (1955).

Thucydides, *The Peloponnesian War*, trans. Rex Warner (1954).

Most of what we know about the fifth century comes from these two great historians; they are essential reading.

CHAPTER 6
Greek Thought and Expression

FIGURE 6.1 A Greek Goddess This portrayal of the goddess Athena in mourning suggests the capability of the Greek sculptors to render the human form in an idealized fashion while still injecting feeling into an artistic composition. As the divine protector and patron of the city of Athens, Athena was constantly celebrated in art and literature by the city's artists and writers. She and other deities provided a constant source of inspiration for all forms of cultural creativity. (Acropolis Museum, Athens)

From the time of Homer at the beginning of the Archaic Age in the eighth century B.C. until the end of the Golden Age in the middle of the fourth century B.C., the *polis* provided an environment that in a unique way stimulated thought and expression. The result was a cultural achievement that for a thousand years after 500 B.C. provided the dominant force in shaping what people living around the Mediterranean Sea believed and said and thought. No less important, long after that millennium ended the Greek cultural legacy left an indelible mark on the cultural history of much of the world, but especially the western European world. The creations of Greek writers, artists, and thinkers have a quality that still makes them attractive for what they are in their own right—creations to read, to look at, and to think about for the pleasure and mental stimulation they provide. Beyond that these works opened vistas onto the human condition and onto the potential of human beings that have never ceased to challenge anyone concerned with what humanity means. Without coming to grips with the Greek cultural achievement, it is impossible to arrive at a full understanding of the course of Western civilization.

1. RELIGION

Religion played a powerful role in shaping all aspects of Greek life, but it was especially important in providing a seedbed out of which intellectual and artistic life emerged. The foundations of Greek religion were shaped during the earliest stages of Greek history, based on a complex mixture of beliefs and practices drawn from Indo-European, Asian, African, and Minoan sources. By the time the first systematic statements describing Greek religious beliefs were made—in the writings of Homer and Hesiod early in the Archaic Age—a set of beliefs and values expressed in an elaborate mythology and in complex rituals was widely shared in the Greek world. These beliefs and practices provided a framework which gave shape and meaning to individual and collective life and which played an important role in governing the behavioral patterns of the Greeks.

Greek religion was polytheistic. Among the divine agents were certain remote and abstracted forces—such as fate (*nemesis*) and justice—that provided the basic order governing the universe; anyone who defied these forces was sure to suffer. But most Greek deities were conceived of as having human forms and as conducting themselves much as earthly creatures did, except that the gods and goddesses were immortal and more powerful than humans. The most conspicuous and attractive deities were those who made up the tumultuous family of major gods and goddesses living on Mount Olympus under the authority of Zeus, whose position resembled that of an earthly father of a noble household. To each of these Olympian deities was ascribed a special role: Zeus was the father of the divine family, controller of the forces of nature; Hera, his wife, was the protectress of marriage and the family; Athena was the goddess of wisdom; Apollo was the bringer of light and patron of the arts; Ares was the god of war; Aphrodite was the goddess of beauty and love; and so on. One of these deities was often protector of an individual *polis*, so that the worship of the Olympian pantheon provided the basis for civic religion. Aside from the Olympian deities, the Greeks believed that the universe was filled with lesser spirits—nymphs, satyrs, demons, spirits of departed heroes and ancestors—who meddled constantly for good and bad in human affairs. A rich body of mythology developed to recount the activities of the deities and to describe their relationships with the human community. Learning that mythology was a fundamental aspect of the life of every Greek.

At least in the early centuries of their collective history, Greeks believed that the deities controlled human affairs. Therefore, individuals, families, and city-states had to attune their activities to divine will. There were fear-inspiring aspects of Greek religion, especially the inexorable working of fate and the taint of blood pollution that could fall on individuals, families, and even entire communities as divine retribution for such offenses as murder or incest. On the whole, however, the Greeks viewed their deities as benevolent, approachable, and concerned with human well-being. Although the gods and goddesses could be angry and unpredictable, they were too "human" to inflict a burden of terror on human beings. If humans learned the ways of the deities, bent to their will, and refrained from a prideful usurpation of their powers, they could expect divine support in gaining good fortune, long life, honor on earth, and success for their *polis*.

The Greeks devoted considerable energy and talent to pleasing their deities. In general, the gods and goddesses were not much concerned with moral behavior; they expected men and women to approach them in tangible ways. Prayers, sacrifices, and gifts were offered according to carefully defined rituals in shrines maintained in each home and by each clan. More impressive were the splendid civic cults, for which great temples were built and maintained at considerable expense to the city-states. Large numbers of people from all walks of life participated in these civic religious activities (see Figure 4.2). On occasion, the entire Greek world joined in honoring the Olympian pantheon; the Olympic Games, held every four years from 776 B.C. on, represented a pan-Hellenic celebration honoring Zeus. Almost every kind of human activity was acceptable as a way of praising the deities—athletic contests, poetry readings, songs, dances, dramatic presentations, and gift offerings. As a consequence, religious ceremonies were also cultural and social events. There were no elaborate priesthoods in Greece; fathers conducted rituals in households and clan centers, and public officials served as priests for civic ceremonies. Almost everyone depended heavily on the interpretation of dreams, the movement of the stars, and the entrails of animals to provide clues about divine intentions. But most of all, they relied on *oracles*, sacred places where the deities spoke through special agents to deliver responses to requests. The most famous oracle was at Delphi, where innumerable Greeks went to implore Apollo to tell them, usually through the mouth of a simple girl, how to solve problems ranging from personal matters to great political issues.

Alongside the religious life embodied in the cult of the Olympian deities was a more turbulent current involving cults which placed greater emphasis on personal and emotional needs. Rooted in the ancient worship of the regenerative forces of nature and deeply influenced by ideas and practices long familiar to peoples of the ancient Near East, these cults centered on a belief in a god or goddess who died and then came back to life to possess believers in a way that provided a mystical experience. The youthful

wine god Dionysus was the center of such a cult. His worship, based on a belief that he had been torn to pieces by evil gods and then reborn (see pages 15–16 for a comparable concept in the Egyptian religion), involved his devotees in a highly emotional initiation ceremony and in ecstatic rites involving wild dancing, drinking, and the eating of raw flesh. A comparable cult, with its center at Eleusis near Athens, developed around the worship of the fertility goddess Demeter and her daughter Persephone, raised from the dead by her mother's efforts. Over time, the mystery cults became more subdued and respectable, as illustrated by the poorly understood movement called Orphism, which modified Dionysus worship by emphasizing the need for austere, ethical conduct as a way of pleasing Dionysus and winning escape from the material world into a happy hereafter.

In providing answers to many fundamental questions about the universe, religion fulfilled spiritual, psychological, and social functions that powerfully affected the way the Greeks lived. Its basic beliefs and practices asserted a significant influence on the religious history of later ages. Beyond that, religion provided both a framework and a stimulant for intellectual and artistic growth. Religious beliefs and values deeply rooted in the fabric of society constantly needed to be explained and clarified by writers and artists, a process that established a link between Greek daily life and cultural activity. Religion posed questions about the cosmos and about human nature that invited constant rethinking and reformulation of concepts common to all Greeks. Religion supplied writers, artists, and philosophers with themes and motifs that allowed them to communicate with the public in familiar terms. Although Greek thought and expression developed along paths that transcended the worldview defined by Greek religion, Greek culture never completely lost contact with its religious roots.

2. LITERATURE

Greek literature represented a magnificent outburst of creativity emerging from a substratum of religious themes and evolving along lines that reshaped religious consciousness. It was born in glory with two epic poems attributed to Homer, the *Iliad* and the *Odyssey*, probably set down in the eighth century B.C. Behind them lay a long tradition of oral poetry sung by bards for aristocratic audiences who loved to hear of the deeds of Mycenaean heroes. Homer, who remains a shadowy figure, drew these oral threads together into unified compositions of great artistry and dramatic power. The *Iliad* recounts the feats of a circle of heroes during a brief period in the war which the Mycenaean Greeks waged against Troy to avenge the theft of a Greek woman, Helen, by Paris, the prince of Troy. Although filled with an array of striking characters, the poem's central figure is Achilles, whose inflated pride (*hubris*) and misdirected anger cause many warriors to die and threaten to destroy the Greeks before he is brought to his senses and takes his place as a great warrior able to turn the tide of battle. The *Odyssey* is an adventure story celebrating the clever talents of one of the heroes at Troy, Odysseus, who needs ten years to overcome a variety of obstacles preventing his return from Troy to his homeland and his patient, long-suffering wife, Penelope. Not a little of the appeal of these epics lies in their gripping plots; but they have other dimensions. They create a heroic picture of men and women—but particularly men—who assume responsibility for their actions by virtue of their courage, their sense of honor, and their urge to prove their excellence. Homer's heroes served as models for noble character and action for all Greeks and for many people in later ages.

For all its richness, the epic genre could not contain the Greek literary genius. In about 700 B.C. the poet Hesiod wrote *Works and Days*, a guide to the ways of farming into which is woven a bitter lament about injustice heaped on simple farmers by the greed of the rich and powerful, and *Theogony*, a summary of Greek mythology that played an important role in defining the nature and the role of the Greek deities. The forces unleashed in the city-states evolving during the Archaic Age encouraged writers to formulate their individual reactions to life and to give vent to their personal feelings, producing an outburst of lyric poetry that gave new dimensions to literary expression. Among the best lyricists were Archilochus of Paros, Alcaeus of Mytilene, and above all the poetess Sappho of Lesbos. A woman of aristocratic origins who ran a school for young women, Sappho composed lyrics celebrating the beauties of nature and the joys of everyday life and expressing her erotic feelings toward young women placed in her charge (later ages coined a word for female homosexuality—lesbianism—from the name of Sappho's native island). The nobility and force of Greek lyric poetry were perhaps best exemplified by Pindar of Thebes (ca. 518–441 B.C.), most of whose works took the form of choral songs in honor of athletes victorious in the competitions held at religious festivals. His poems set forth the classic view of aristocratic (in the Greek sense of "the best") qualities.

The burgeoning poetic talent reflected in epic and lyric poetry reached full fruition with the development of tragic drama, perhaps the greatest literary achievement of the Greeks. Tragedy originated in the dramatic choruses and hymns developed in connection with the worship of the god Dionysus. By the late sixth century B.C., the dramatic element in these rituals was greatly expanded to allow poets to create parts for actors who retold the deeds of the deities and heroes enshrined in Greek mythology and provided comments on the meaning of these deeds through choral interludes. This developing dramatic art suddenly burst forth in full maturity during the fifth century in the works of three of the world's greatest tragedians, all living in Athens amid the flowering of democracy and the rise and fall of the Athenian Empire. Taken together, their dramas probe deeply into the forces at work in the cosmic order and in human nature to draw human beings into tragic situations and provide profound insights into the resources that human beings possess that allow them to face their tragic fate with courage and determination.

The first was Aeschylus (525–456 B.C.). He wrote about ninety plays, only seven of which survive. His tragedies spell out with great power the consequences that result from prideful human transgressions of the dictates of the divine powers. His most impressive surviving work is a cycle of three plays called the *Orestia*, which employs the well-known legend of the family of Agamemnon to portray the tragic fate resulting from violation of the divine order against spilling the blood of one's own kin. Aeschylus had a genius for making his suffering characters noble and admirable, capable of bearing their burden of punishment with dignity and even with understanding. Implicit in his plays is a warning to his audience to curb pride (*hubris*) and to respect the deities who control the cosmic order.

1) Sophocles (495–405 B.C.), a citizen active in Athenian political life, produced a large number of plays, all but seven now lost. His dramas remained closely bound to the traditional themes provided by religion, but his interest is more human, more intent on searching out the psychological effects of suffering on humans who ran afoul of the gods and goddesses. He portrays suffering as an uplifting and purifying experience. Many would argue that Sophocles' *King Oedipus* is the greatest tragedy ever written. Essentially it is a drama that reveals the measure of the human spirit by showing the response of a heroic individual to a situation not of his making. Oedipus' fateful act was unknowingly killing his father and marrying his own mother (from whence Sigmund Freud's Oedipus complex), vile deeds that violated nature's order and for which he had to atone. In presenting Oedipus' discovery of his crime and his acceptance of his fate, Sophocles evokes a powerful celebration of the greatness of human beings. No less noble is the heroine of *Antigone*, a woman destroyed because she obeyed divine law in the face of the demands of human authority.

2) Euripides (480–406 B.C.) was a dramatist profoundly touched by the growing disillusionment, skepticism, and pessimism of the later fifth century—the generation of the Peloponnesian War. He utilized tragedy as a vehicle for posing profound questions about human values and problems in a way that arouses the suspicion that human powers are limited. His plays represent a search for some understanding of the dark and frightening passions that overpower reason with tragic consequences. That theme is explored with special force in his *Medea*, which portrays the ordeal of a woman whose desertion by her husband so fills her with rage and a desire for vengeance that she kills her children. Again and again Euripides casts doubt on conventional moral values and accepted religious beliefs. But from his incessant probing emerges a picture of humanity that is fuller and subtler—if not nobler—than the portraits drawn by Aeschylus and Sophocles.

Rivaling tragedy in public appeal was comic drama. Like tragedy, it developed out of religious ceremony, especially the ribald songs associated with the worship of Dionysus. By the fifth century, comedy had evolved into a distinct art form intended to inform and entertain audiences by satirical treatment of current politics and social affairs. The master of this form was Aristophanes (ca. 445–385 B.C.), a conservative Athenian whose comedies held up for scorn democratic politicians and institutions, artists and philosophers, and Athenian social mores. Typical is his play *Lysistrata*, in which Aristophanes voiced his own strong feeling about the folly of the Peloponnesian War by describing the plan of Athenian women to deny their husbands any sexual pleasures until they end the war; the audience is told, "We'll soon get Peace, be sure of that."

Prose literature long lingered in the shadow of poetry, but during the fifth century B.C. two historians produced works that demonstrated the Greek genius in that mode of expression. The first was Herodotus (ca. 484–425 B.C.), who wrote a history of the wars between the Greeks and Persians. His work is based on information he gathered through his travels and his search of written records. The result is a dramatic, colorful account of the events tracing the struggle between Greeks and Persians that Herodotus believed not only decided the fate of the Greek world but also revealed the superiority of the Greek way of life. The second major Greek historian was Thucydides (ca. 460–400 B.C.), whose *History of the Peloponnesian War* is one of the great works of historical literature. With unflagging energy he searched out information related to the details of the military campaigns and the political maneuvers associated with the war in which he was personally involved. On the basis of that evidence he compiled a moving narrative account that not only described the course of the war but also provided a critical analysis of the human motives and social forces that stoked that destructive struggle. His study lays bare a compelling picture of the folly, nobility, chicanery, and bravery of which human beings under stress are capable. His astute analysis of the evidence leads one to the conclusion that the Athenians caused that terrible struggle because of their *hubris* and lost it because of their contempt for moral principles and their cynical pursuit of power. Not only did Herodotus and Thucydides produce great literary works; they also pioneered a method of rational inquiry about past human activity based on the objective search for and verification of evidence about what had happened upon which could be based a rational reconstruction and explanation of the past in human terms free of the mythical elements that had governed the approach to the past up to their time. To this day their histories represent an ideal toward which all historians strive: to find the truth about the past and to let it enrich the understanding of the present.

3. ART

The fundamental characteristics of the Greek visual arts were shaped during the Archaic Age through a complex process involving adaptation of Near Eastern models and experimentation with new ideas and techniques. During that period pottery painters established basic themes and conventions for representing humans and animals in action. Sculptors slowly perfected a unique style of portraying the nude male and draped female figures. Although drawing heavily on mythology for their subject matter, these artists increasingly relied on what they saw in their own world to shape their treatment of mythological figures and themes. Out of these observations emerged concepts defining proportion, balance, and movement in new and unique ways. Also during the Archaic Age, architects developed a basic style for temples and other public buildings, which were increasingly built in stone: a rectangular ground plan whose elevation featured columns surrounding an inner temple chamber and low-pitched roofs. In all these art forms artists showed an increasing concern with proportion and balance, reflecting the impact of rational thought on artistic expression. Painters, sculptors, and architects received increasing support from the city-state, whose leaders and citizens were interested in beautifying their *polis* and in elaborating civic religions.

By the beginning of the fifth century, the long apprenticeship was over; a burst of creativity produced a golden age in art. Athens became the focal point of artistic excellence. The city's crowning glory was the complex of buildings constructed on the Acropolis, the hill dominating the *polis*. Under the sponsorship of Pericles and with funds derived from gifts by wealthy citizens and increasingly from tribute paid by the subject city-states of the Athenian Empire, three major temples were built there during the fifth century: the Parthenon, the Erectheum, and the temple to Victorious Athena. A splendid stairway and gate called the Propylaea gave access to the Acropolis, now the center of Athenian civic religion (see Figure 4.1). The Parthenon, portions of which still stand, embodied the basic features of classical Greek architecture (see Figure 6.2). Built in honor of Athena, it is modest in size (228 by 101 feet). Its two inner chambers, serving as shrines, are surrounded by simple, unadorned columns (in a style called Doric), seventeen on each side and eight on each end, which support the roof and create covered colonnades and entry vestibules. Its majesty stems chiefly from its simplicity, its proportions, its unity, and its balance. The total effect derives not only from the logic of its conception but also from subtle technical touches. For example, the middle of every long horizontal line is slightly higher than the ends to avoid the impression of sagging. The other Acropolis temples and the Propylaea incorporate the same features as the Parthenon, all adjusted to the size of each structure. The only basic departure was the utilization of slightly more slender and ornate columns (in the Ionic style), which add grace and lightness. The same basic principles were applied to a variety of other public buildings—theaters, gymnasia, marketplaces, meeting halls—constructed in Athens and other city-states.

The Greek style of architecture provided ample spaces for sculptors and painters to lend their talents in beautifying buildings. Their response brought Greek sculpture to its culmination, exemplified by the works of Phidias (ca. 500–432 B.C.), Polyclitus (ca. 452–412 B.C.), and Praxiteles (ca. 400–320 B.C.). Phidias was in charge of designing the sculptural program adorning the Parthenon. Unfortunately, his statues in the round, especially the famed statue of Athena in the inner chamber of the Parthenon, have been lost and are known only through copies and literary texts; that evidence suggests his skill in portraying divine figures in terms that captured both their majesty and their human qualities. His talents

FIGURE 6.2 The Parthenon This magnificent example of Greek architecture was the chief structure among a complex of temples adorning the Athenian Acropolis (see Figure 4.1). Begun in the Golden Age of Pericles and dedicated to Athena, its distinctive horizontal lines, stately Doric columns, and measured proportions typify the classical Greek architectural style. The pediments above the columns and the triangular space created by the roof were filled with sculpture celebrating Greek deities and portraying themes from Greek mythology. (Marburg)

are also reflected in the surviving remnants of a continuous frieze of carved reliefs extending around the walls of that same inner chamber to depict a procession in honor of Athena. These scenes, which portray ordinary people engaged in various pursuits relating to everyday life, reflect the power of Greek artists to represent the human scene in realistic terms. The external entablature (that part of the structure built atop the columns to support the roof) and pediments (the triangular structures filling the spaces created by the roof gables at each end of the temple) were covered with powerful representations of divine activities drawn from mythology. Polyclitus devoted his talents chiefly to shaping bronze statues of young men (see Color Plate 3—left). Praxiteles created splendid versions of gods and goddesses in human form (see Figure 6.3 and Color Plate 3—right). All of this sculpture fo-

cuses on the portrayal of the idealized human body; the figures are dignified, restrained, beautifully proportioned, filled with the potential for action. The effect of viewing them is to catch a vision of the nobility and the power of human beings extracted from the real world in which human beings lived and acted (see Figure 6.1). Little has survived of Greek painting, except for pottery painting (see Figure 4.2). There is evidence, however, from literary sources that large-scale paintings decorated temples and public buildings. For example, Polygnotus (mid–fifth century B.C.) decorated a colonnade in the Athenian *agora*, the area where political meetings and market activities took place, with painted scenes depicting episodes from the Trojan War. It is highly likely that Greek painting reflected the same traits as the sculpture: idealization of the human figure, balance, restraint, and dignity.

FIGURE 6.3 Hermes with the Infant Dionysus Most likely the work of the famed sculptor Praxiteles, this statue is an excellent example of Greek artistic canons; the gods are taken as subject matter and portrayed in an idealized human form that emphasizes physical perfection rather than spiritual qualities. (Alinari/Art Resource)

4. PHILOSOPHY AND SCIENCE

The feature that most sharply distinguished Greek thought from that of earlier civilizations found expression in philosophy and science, areas of inquiry the Greeks considered to be interdependent. Thinkers in these realms explored a new way of describing and explaining the cosmic order, the natural world, and human society that depended on rational interpretation of phenomena open to human observation. This rationalistic approach eventually touched almost every sphere of Greek political, social, and cultural life in some way and became one of the most enduring bequests left by the Greeks to later history.

Why the Greeks made this revolutionary intellectual leap escapes easy explanation. Until the sixth century B.C., most Greeks, like their Near Eastern predecessors, were content to accept the explanations provided by mythology to describe the nature of the universe and the place of human beings in it. Then, during the sixth century, some thinkers began to move beyond the mythological world view in search of rational explanations of the cosmos. Perhaps such inquiries were prompted by the ferment surrounding the efforts in the late Archaic Age to reshape the structure of many city-states to cope with pressing economic and social problems. The first speculative thinkers came from Greek city-states in Asia Minor and southern Italy, suggesting that perhaps interactions with foreign ways of looking at the universe posed questions to which only reason could provide answers.

The prime concern of these early speculative thinkers was to find a simple, unifying principle that would describe and explain rationally what constituted the universe and what made it work. This quest gave rise to diverse, contradictory answers, often based on imaginative interpretations of physical evidence but also marked by bold insights that have long fascinated those concerned with *cosmology*, that is, inquiry into the origins and nature of the universe. In general terms, the speculations of the Greek cosmologists fell into two broad schools of thought. One such school, originally centered in Ionia, developed a materialistic explanation that argued that some form of matter, such as air or water or fire, was the basic substance out of which all other things emerged through processes inherent in the nature of that substance. This materialistic approach reached its culmination with Democritus (ca. 460–370 B.C.), who propounded an atomic theory according to which the universe is composed of indivisible particles floating at random in empty space; by mere chance these atoms combined into beings and objects and by the same chance decomposed to end existing things. Another school of thought rejected materialism and sought the key to the universe in some nonmaterial force. Perhaps the source of this approach was the sixth-century B.C. thinker Pythagoras, whose career combined scientific interest with a strong religious bent. He argued that the basis of cosmic order lay in a numerical relationship among its many parts. Equally influential in shaping this school was Heraclitus (flourished ca. 500 B.C.), who insisted that change was the essence of the material world and therefore no simplistic physical explanation of the universe could have meaning. This whole school of thinkers ultimately concluded that a nonmaterial, changeless being, endowed with perfect intelligence, supplied the creative force of order in the universe. Despite their divergent views, the early thinkers shared one thing: Their explanations of the universe challenged the traditional mythological explanations based on arbitrary, irrational divine powers. Their thinking posited an ordered universe which could be understood through the power of human reason.

Although Greek thinkers continued to seek an explanation of the fundamental nature of the universe, about the middle of the fifth century B.C. rational inquiry increasingly focused on the human condition. A diverse group of thinkers, collectively called the Sophists, led the way into this new realm. The Sophists were primarily professional teachers interested in preparing their pupils for roles in public life. They rejected speculative philosophy on the grounds that objective truth was nonexistent, as demonstrated by the contradictory schemes put forward by prior thinkers. In the words of one of the chief Sophists, Protagoras (485–410 B.C.), a famous teacher in Periclean Athens, men and women were the measure of all things. Human reason should be dedicated to a search for the kind of knowledge that would be useful to humans in their quest for happy, useful lives. Since most Sophists believed that institutions and standards of behavior were human creations, not the results of an unchangeable natural order, they felt justified in criticizing traditional religious ideas, moral values, and laws and in urging their disciples to seek rules of life that were workable and beneficial. Their attacks led to widespread condemnation of the Sophists as skeptics and destroyers of morality and order. But their arguments deepened the awareness of fundamental ethical issues and encouraged their disciples to trust the power of reason, honed by rigorous training, as an instrument for improving the human condition. The intellectual ferment resulting from their philosophical relativism led to a new search for absolute truth that produced the greatest Greek philosophers.

One of these was Socrates (ca. 469–399 B.C.), an Athenian famous in his own time as a provocative teacher. He left no writings; he set forth his ideas orally in the Athenian *agora*, where he engaged all comers in debate about philosophical issues. From what his pupils remembered about his teaching, it appears that Socrates sought to counter the relativism of the Sophists by insisting on the existence of universal truths which provide objective standards defining moral excellence. Human beings were prevented from discovering these truths by their own ignorance. That ignorance could be dispelled only by active mental endeavor involving rigorous, logical self-examination of beliefs. The Socratic method consisted of asking questions until the error of someone who claimed to know something was exposed and then leading the mind through further questioning to the truth by way of precise definition and exact logic. Socrates' goal was to get people to understand themselves and to conduct their lives by the light of their reason. Although he attracted an eager following for many years, his gadfly tactics eventually led to trouble. In 399 B.C., amid the bitterness surrounding the Athenian defeat in the Peloponnesian War, he was accused of corrupting youth and sentenced to die. Refusing to compromise his principles in order to gain a lighter sentence from the jury of his fellow citizens, he accepted their verdict of guilt and drank the fatal poison.

Plato (427–347 B.C.) carried on the work of Socrates, his master. He spent most of his career as a teacher in a school which he founded in

Athens called the Academy. His voluminous works, elegantly written in dialogue form, provide a sometimes confusing but always challenging record of his thought. Plato was a philosophical idealist; his work brought to full maturity the nonmaterialist philosophical tradition dating back to the sixth century B.C.. He argued that the fundamental realities in the universe are ideas, or abstract forms, which define eternal and absolute standards of good, truth, and justice. The so-called realities that humans perceive with their senses are but imperfect reflections of the perfect universal forms. He likened sense perceptions gained from the material world to shadows cast on the wall of a cave by those moving about in front of a fire; neither is more than a dim, fuzzy, constantly changing image of ultimate reality. For example, the justice practiced in Athens was only a shadowy reflection of perfect justice; a man or a woman is but a pale image of a higher reality, humanity. Plato argued that by pure reasoning the human mind could reach beyond the level of comprehension provided by the senses to an understanding of the higher reality of forms. Only such wisdom could define truth and provide the basis for the good life.

Plato's dialogues center on an attempt to define by rational means the ideas or forms that constitute ultimate reality and to make that wisdom applicable to the problems of human existence. His best-known dialogue, *The Republic*, illustrates his idealism, his method, and his earnest concern for the human condition. This work, undoubtedly shaped in part by Plato's disillusionment with political life in fourth-century B.C. Athens, seeks to define the model *polis* that would provide the ideal setting in which the social nature of human beings could be realized. Plato assumes that the purpose of the state is to achieve justice, the ideal state being an earthly embodiment of the perfect idea of justice. Arguing that justice consists of each individual doing that for which he or she is best fitted, Plato defined the ideal state as one in which every person holds that station and does that job for which he or she is best qualified by nature. Since Plato defined human nature in terms of a hierarchy of capacities, his ideal state would be hierarchically structured. Most humans are suited to work; a lesser number are endowed with qualities that suit them for defending the community; and a very few have the rational power that enables them to grasp truth and act with virtue. To these philosopher-kings must be entrusted the power to rule. Capable of shunning power and wealth by virtue of their wisdom, they alone have the capacity to formulate the laws that would establish a harmonious order in which everyone else would serve the community by doing what each is best qualified to do. Philosopher-kings alone have the ability to convince their subjects to accept what is best for them, even if that sometimes requires a "noble lie." In short, for Plato the perfect society requires an authoritarian political order in which those who are wise by virtue of their rational powers have the obligation to direct the lives of their less-well-endowed subjects in the interest of achieving ideal justice.

In his other dialogues Plato conducts a comparable search for an understanding of the nature of love, friendship, courage, the soul—in fact, virtually the whole range of those elements that constitute the ultimate reality lying behind the appearance of things. In distinguishing between the realm of pure ideas and the material world of the senses, Plato posed issues about what reality is and how it can be comprehended that since his time have been a major stimulant to philosophical inquiry.

The challenge of the Platonic system was central to the career of Aristotle (384–322 B.C.), Plato's most brilliant and productive pupil. As a youth, he came to Athens from northern Greece to study at the Academy. After Plato's death, he spent some time in Macedonia, perhaps as tutor to young Alexander the Great. He then returned to Athens and founded his own school, the Lyceum. His followers were called the Peripatetics (from the Greek for "to walk up and down") because Aristotle often walked about while lecturing. Aristotle produced a massive body of philosophical work dealing with such diverse topics as the physical sciences, political theory, psychology, ethics, and literary theory. Perhaps typical of effective teachers in all ages, he had a passion for systematizing and organizing knowledge, so that his works constitute a kind of encyclopedia of the total learning of the ancient world.

Aristotle's thought was undergirded by an original concept of ultimate being. Although influenced by Platonic idealism, Aristotle arrived at a different position. In his seminal *Metaphysics*, he argues that reality consists of a combination of matter and form (or idea). The form gives each object its shape, but it has no reality separate from the matter in which it exists and can be discerned only by studying things existing and happening in the material world. Every object has some purpose in a larger universal order; its perfection consists in serving that purpose. Behind the wilderness of individual objects lies an ultimate "cause," a higher force that animates everything. The philosopher's path is from the study of material objects toward an understanding of that higher force; such a quest would result in the formulation of concepts that would allow a comprehension of the nature of the entire universe and its operation.

In most of his works Aristotle pursued the course laid down in his *Metaphysics*. His *Politics* provides an illustration of his method. Starting with the assumption that human beings are political animals who cannot fulfill their true nature unless they are members of a state devoted to the promotion of virtue, he seeks to define possible political systems. On the basis of a study of the history and organization of more than a hundred and fifty Greek city-states, he concludes that the state as a "form" manifests itself in three basic systems: monarchy, aristocracy, and limited democracy, each of which is legitimate if it serves the general welfare. However, each form can be perverted when the ruling element—king, aristocrats, or people—seeks power to serve its own ends; monarchy becomes tyranny, aristocracy becomes oligarchy, and limited democracy becomes anarchy (the worst of all governments). Aristotle's analysis of these forms clarifies the unique consequences for human beings of each type of state, thus providing the rational basis for selecting the type of government best suited to the particular situation in which any community finds itself. In his *Ethics* Aristotle asks how men and women should conduct their individual lives and argues that happiness is the proper goal of every human action. Men and women can be happy and good only if they use reason to control the passionate elements in their nature and if they behave with moderation, seeking always to avoid doing anything in excess.

Aristotle's writings made an important contribution to epistemology, that branch of philosophy which seeks to define how human knowledge is acquired. In some cases, such as in his *Politics*, his method of seeking truth was inductive—that is, formulating generalizations on the basis of particular pieces of evidence gained by observing phenomena occurring in the world. Inductive thinking would play a crucial role in the advancement of science. However, he also used deduction, a mode of thinking that employs the rules of formal logic to extract the truth about particular things from premises defining general truths. Aristotle's treatment of the rules of formal logic provided a tool that shaped philosophical inquiry for centuries to come.

Aristotle's works dealing with the physical and biological sciences mark the culmination and provide a summary of what had been accomplished by a sustained interest in natural science among the Greeks extending back at least two centuries before his time. That interest resulted in significant work in astronomy, physics, botany, zoology, physiology, and geography. Although Greek scientists relied heavily on data about the natural world compiled by Mesopotamians and Egyptians, they made significant additions to scientific knowledge by their own observations of natural phenomena. Illustrative of this approach is the work of Hippocrates (460–377 B.C.), a practicing physician to whom is attributed the famous oath still used today to define the responsibilities of a physician. He insisted that nothing could be known about sickness except through observation of sick people and through a search for the natural causes of illness. He repudiated the traditional belief that sickness was due to evil spirits; it was a result of natural causes, and the cure for sickness was a natural process that could be controlled. He collected information about the curative power of drugs and about the effects of diet on health. The collective efforts of Greek scientists allow us to credit the Greeks with the invention of the scientific method, which relies on observation as the source of knowledge about nature. Lacking precision instruments, their observations were often imprecise and their interpretations of data erroneous. Moreover, few were interested in using their knowledge for practical purposes. Scientific knowledge was employed chiefly by philosophers seeking to explain the workings of the universe.

5. THE GREEK SPIRIT

In reflecting on the whole range of Greek achievements in literature, art, philosophy, and science, some common themes emerge that, taken together, give Greek culture its distinctive quality. Greek thought was intensely *humanistic*, concerned with defining the position of humans in the cosmic order, measuring human potential, and finding ways to enlarge human capabilities. Greek culture was *rationalistic;* its creators placed trust in the ability of human beings to understand nature and themselves through human intelligence and to act on the basis of rational decisions to resolve human problems. Rationalism emphasized the need to seek *order* and *symmetry* in all things and to act with *restraint* and *balance* in individual and collective life. Greek culture was animated by a *spirit of inquiry* that constantly pushed thinkers and artists toward new knowledge and new ways of expressing themselves. Greek thought began to map out a realm of *freedom*, where human beings could make responsible decisions shaping their political and moral destinies. These values combined to constitute a cultural ideal that asserted a powerful formative influence on later societies; we shall encounter these ideas again and again in tracing Western history.

It is difficult to ascertain the extent to which these basic values impacted on the lives of ordinary Greeks. Probably most Greeks, engaged in the routine of daily life, seldom paused to think about what their cultural values were or meant, just as most modern men and women seldom dwell on this question. But one thing does seem certain: An ordinary Greek would have had trouble escaping contact with the cultural achievements just described. The best of Greek thought on the human condition was made available to all citizens as an intimate dimension of civic life. Poetry readings accompanied religious ceremonies and athletic contests. The best drama was played out in public theaters. Philosophers wrangled in the streets, joined their fellow citizens in *symposia*, and taught in schools. Architects and sculptors devoted their best efforts to civic art. It seems inconceivable that any citizen could have escaped being touched by some of the values reflected in the most notable cultural artifacts created in the Greek world.

However, we must be cautious in assuming that all Greeks prized the values that modern historians have discerned as setting Greek culture apart from that of their predecessors. There were other facets of Greek cultural life that defined alternative and conflicting values. Many cultured Greeks, including leading intellectuals, were not prepared to ascribe to *all* humans the qualities noted above—among lesser creatures were women, slaves, ''barbarians'' (defined as those who did not speak Greek), and even some citizens. Greek culture was elitist, aristocratic in spirit, exclusive. Those who articulated the values so much admired by later generations were openly challenged by their intellectual peers and repudiated by public opinion; the fate of Socrates is a case in point. Anyone who follows Greek political history in detail or reads Greek drama or grapples with the discourse of Greek philosophers soon becomes aware of powerful currents shaping the Greek mentality other than those noted above. Political issues were often decided by oracles and omens sought out by ''enlightened'' leaders rather than by reasoned deliberation and votes. Belief in the power of some transcendental force—be it the Olympian deities or fate or supreme reason—to control human destiny remained a central feature of the worldview not only of common citizens but also of dramatists and philosophers. The mythical heroes that philosophers sought to debunk remained as models for human behavior. Traditional mores defined standards of individual and social behavior despite the efforts of moralists and social critics to point out their irrational features. The Greek spirit was multifaceted, not monolithic. Perhaps those aspects of Greek culture singled out above made a greater difference in the history of Western civilization than others did, but they by no means define the Greek spirit in its entirety.

SUGGESTED READING

General Cultural History

François Chamoux, *The Civilization of Greece*, trans. W. S. Maguinness (1965). A perceptive overview, well illustrated.

John Boardman et al., eds., *The Oxford History of the Classical World* (1986). Excellent studies of varied aspects of Greek civilization.

Religion

Robert Graves, *The Greek Myths* (1955; illustrated edition, 1981). A full description of the myths undergirding Greek religion.

Walter Burkert, *Greek Religion: Archaic and Classical*, trans. John Raffan (1985). A masterful treatment.

Walter Burkert, *Ancient Mystery Cults* (1987). A well-done guide.

Literature

Jacqueline de Romilly, *A Short History of Greek Literature*, trans. Lillian Doherty (1985).

Peter Levi, *A History of Greek Literature* (1985).

Either of these recent works will provide invaluable guides to the main currents of Greek literary history.

Charles Rowan Beye, *Ancient Greek Literature and Society*, 2nd rev. ed. (1988). A stimulating effort to put Greek literature into its social context.

Art

John Boardman, *Greek Art*, new and rev. ed. (1985). An excellent brief treatment.

Richard Brilliant, *Arts of Ancient Greece* (1973).

Jean Charbonneaux et al., *Classical Greek Art (480–330 B.C.)*, trans. James Emmons (1972).

These longer treatments, both illustrated, provide a rich appreciation of the Greek artistic accomplishment.

J. J. Pollitt, *Art and Experience in Classical Greece* (1972).

Jeffrey M. Hurwit, *The Art and Culture of Early Greece, 1100–400 B.C.* (1985).

Two challenging treatments of the social and intellectual foundations of Greek art.

Philosophy and Science

Rex Warner, *Greek Philosophers* (1958).

W. K. C. Guthrie, *Greek Philosophers: From Thales to Aristotle* (1960).

Although old, either of these two works will provide a good introduction to the Greek accomplishment in philosophy.

Jean-Pierre Vernant, *The Origins of Greek Thought* (1982). A challenging study stressing the uniqueness of Greek thought.

H. D. Rankin, *Sophists, Socratics, and Cynics* (1983). A balanced treatment of the major schools of philosophy in Greece.

G. B. Kerferd, *The Sophistic Movement* (1981). A full treatment.

G. E. R. Lloyd, *Early Greek Science: Thales to Aristotle* (1970). A thorough assessment of the Greek accomplishments in science.

K. D. White, *Greek and Roman Technology* (1984). A well-done assessment of Greek accomplishments in technology.

Sources

Michael Grant, ed., *Greek Literature: An Anthology in Translation* (1973). A rich sampling that will tempt a reader to read Greek writers in their entirety. Good translations of the works of all the authors mentioned in this chapter are easily available.

CHAPTER 7
Greek Imperialism: The Hellenistic World, 336–31 B.C.

FIGURE 7.1 Alexander the Great
This Roman copy of an original bust of Alexander the Great (perhaps done by the fourth-century B.C. sculptor Lycippus) attempts to capture the strength and idealism of a great hero of the ancient world. (Giraudon/Art Resource)

Although many Greeks feared that the coming of the "barbarian" Macedonians spelled doom for Hellenism, the Macedonian conquest set the stage for a new chapter in the history of the Greeks. Under Macedonian leadership, they exploded out of their Aegean-centered world to establish mastery over a wide area of Asia and Africa. Their genius and their traditions began to mix with those of the Near Eastern civilizations to produce a new culture that historians have called "Hellenistic."

1. ALEXANDER THE GREAT

The Greek-Macedonian world was launched into this new phase in its history under the charismatic leadership of Alexander the Great (see Figure 7.1). Imbued with a deep admiration for Greek culture absorbed at the court of his father, Philip II, Alexander drew on his towering ambition, restless energy, iron will, and military genius to achieve feats in the cause of Hellenism that have never ceased to fascinate students of history.

Only twenty when his father died in 336 B.C., Alexander turned to a project that Philip had already planned, the crusade against the hated enemy of the Greeks, the Persians (see Map 7.1). Although Persia possessed a huge empire, a rich treasury, and a large army and navy, Alexander was victorious from the beginning. His initial campaigns, begun in 334 B.C., were aimed at depriving the Persians of control of the coastal cities of Asia Minor and Phoenicia, the chief source of Persian naval power. Shortly after entering Asia Minor, Alexander overpowered a major Persian force at a battle on the Granicus River; this victory ensured control of the Greek cities along the east coast of the Aegean Sea. From there he moved into Syria and in 333 B.C. won a brilliant victory at Issus. This victory solidified Alexander's control of Asia Minor and opened the way for his conquest of Syria, Palestine, and Egypt. Then he marched on the center of Persian power in Mesopotamia and in the spring of 331 B.C. destroyed the last major military strength of the Persians at the battle of Gaugamela (Arbela). Following this victory, he occupied the major centers of Persian political power and hunted down the fugitive King Darius III, who was finally murdered in 330 B.C. by his own officials as Alexander closed in on him.

The conquest of the Persian Empire did not satisfy Alexander's ambition. During the next five years he drove on eastward. Battling vast distances, native resistance, and defection among his own troops, he relentlessly destroyed pockets of resistance led by Persian satraps in the regions of Parthia and Bactria. Then he pushed across the Hindu Kush Mountains into the Indus River Valley, a venture that brought the Greeks into direct contact with Indian civilization. Beyond the Indus Valley his troops refused to go. Alexander therefore turned back westward through southern Persia and into Mesopotamia, where he fell ill and died in June 323 B.C. at the age of thirty-three.

A career so short and so completely occupied with military campaigns left Alexander little time to face the problems of ruling his vast conquests. Probably he had no definite plans when he launched his campaign, but before he died he had made decisions establishing certain broad policies that guided his successors. He moved toward creating a style of rulership that cast him in the role of divinely sanctioned autocrat, a kind of rulership foreign to both Greeks and Macedonians. He at least toyed with the idea of combining the talents of conquered peoples, especially Persians, with those of the conquerors to create a cosmopolitan elite to control his empire. However, his followers found this policy unacceptable, forcing him to take steps to ensure that Greeks and Macedonians would dominate his empire. This plan required their migration to Asia and Africa, a move that Alexander sought to make attractive by establishing city-states in which the newcomers would have a special place. However, aside from his conquests, Alexander's accomplishments were few. His main influence on the course of history lay in his legend: what later generations believed he was trying to do.

2. HELLENISTIC POLITICAL DEVELOPMENTS

In the three centuries following his death, the political history of the vast area that Alexander conquered was not a simple one. Its complexity

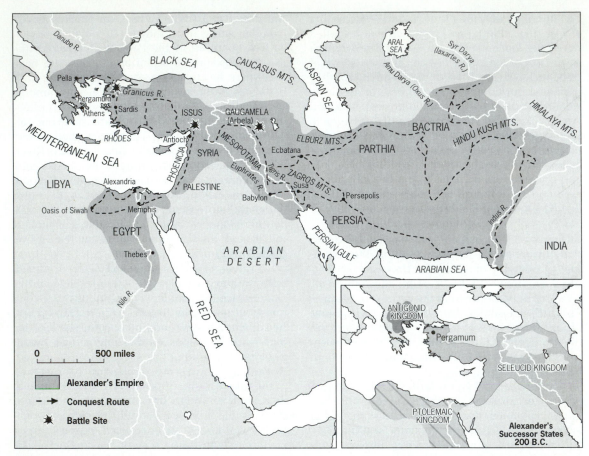

Map 7.1 **ALEXANDER'S EMPIRE AND ITS SUCCESSOR KINGDOMS** This map dramatically depicts the magnitude of Alexander the Great's military accomplishment between 336 and 323 B.C. to create an empire even larger than those of the Assyrians and Persians. His success shaped a vast realm over which Greeks and Macedonians established their political, economic, and cultural mastery in a way that decisively changed the history of the entire area. The most intensive Hellenization occurred around the eastern end of the Mediterranean from Egypt through Palestine, Phoenicia, and Syria into Asia Minor. But the powerful force of Greek culture was also felt in Mesopotamia and still farther east.

stemmed primarily from the division of the empire. Immediately after Alexander's death a council of his generals tried to maintain a united empire ruled jointly by Alexander's son and half brother, but that plan failed amid mounting rivalry among the generals. Within a generation their rivalry had produced a hodgepodge of political entities of various sizes, strengths, and internal structures. By far the most prominent were the major kingdoms established by three of Al-

exander's companions: Antigonus in Macedonia and the Aegean world; Ptolemy in Egypt; and Seleucus in the vast area stretching from Asia Minor to India (see Map 7.1).

Only the briefest summary of the complex histories of these kingdoms can be undertaken here. The Macedonian kings sustained a fairly effective government during most of the third century B.C. Although the Antigonid dynasty always had ambitions to play a major role in the larger Hellenistic world, Macedonian political history centered chiefly on the efforts of the rulers to maintain hegemony over the Greek city-states and to hold back the attackers who were constantly pressing on the northern frontier of Macedonia. These were major burdens, testing the limited human and material resources of Macedonia. Control of the Greek city-states was particularly difficult. Claiming to act in the name of "freedom" for the *polis*, the Greeks constantly intrigued against their masters, often seeking help from outsiders. Macedonian efforts to defuse this resistance by interfering in local city-state political processes and establishing military garrisons in Greece only sharpened the resistance. Ultimately, the Macedonian kingdom was incapable of bearing the burden. Shortly before 200 B.C. some of the Greek city-states appealed to Rome for help against what they claimed was Macedonian interference with their freedom. In the ensuing wars, Roman armies conquered both Macedonia and Greece and absorbed them into Rome's expanding empire.

The kingdom established in Egypt by Ptolemy was the most stable Hellenistic state. The Ptolemaic dynasty quickly organized an autocratic regime modeled on the ancient Egyptian system of the pharaohs. The key to Ptolemaic power was a bureaucracy and a military force dominated by Greek-Macedonian immigrants. This regime skillfully exploited the native population and the agricultural and commercial resources of Egypt to sustain its power. Internal stability and wealth permitted the Ptolemies to play an active role in the larger Hellenistic world. They concentrated chiefly on extending their sphere of influence in Syria-Palestine, Asia Minor, and the Aegean world. These ambitions involved them in almost constant conflict, especially the Seleucid kingdom. By the second century B.C. the grip of the Ptolemies on Egypt began to weaken, chiefly because they were forced to rely increasingly on native Egyptians in the army and the bureaucracy and to make concessions limiting their own royal income. Growing internal unrest ultimately forced the rulers to seek support from the Romans. Eventually, in 30 B.C., Rome annexed Egypt to its empire.

The Seleucid kingdom had the most troubled history. Its huge size and mixed population provided little basis for unity except what its kings and their Greek-Macedonian followers could impose. Rather quickly the Seleucid rulers lost control over the area east of the Tigris-Euphrates Valley, where kingdoms of considerable importance to the future, including Bactria and Parthia, went their separate ways. In northern and western Asia Minor local rulers established small but virile kingdoms. Most of the Seleucid political energy was devoted to creating a viable state embracing Mesopotamia, Syria-Palestine, and southeastern Asia Minor. Royal authority was based chiefly on the military service provided by Greeks and Macedonians established in cities from which they dominated the native population. Attacks by outsiders, especially the Ptolemies, and internal native uprisings constantly threatened the Seleucids. Ultimately, the Seleucid kingdom was torn to pieces by internal strife and squeezed to death by Parthian pressure from the east and Roman intrusions from the west.

Numerous smaller states shared the political scene with the three major kingdoms. Chief among them were many old Greek city-states that remained independent and sought to continue their traditional pattern of governance. A good deal of the political energies of these city-states was devoted to internal affairs, which were often marked by bitter partisanship and class rivalry. But each also had to concern itself with the ambitions of other city-states and the threat of the great powers, especially Macedonia. Their fragile independence encouraged many city-states to develop techniques aimed at reducing intercity rivalry and strengthening the religious and cultural ties shared by all Greeks. Especially innovative was the development of effective leagues or federations based on some compromise of total autonomy in the interest of common action decided upon through shared political processes. Two particularly important leagues were the Aetolian League, which embraced several city-states in central Greece, and the Achaean League in northern Peloponnesus. Despite their continued existence, the old Greek city-states lost much of their power of self-determination during the Hellenistic Age. Among the smaller states of the era, the most successful were the Kingdom of Pergamum in western Asia Minor and the Republic of Rhodes, both of which fared well by capitalizing on commercial activity.

In this world of competing "successor" states into which Alexander's empire was divided, the conduct of interstate relations took on new intensity and sophistication. Great and small states developed techniques designed to ensure safety and to gain advantage over others: military force, diplomacy, psychological warfare, internal subversion, economic penetration, arrangements extending privileges to citizens of other states. In a general way, these techniques tended to promote a balance of power in the Hellenistic world. While that balance was constantly in the process of readjustment, it provided a degree of stability and security until the machinations sustaining it began to draw an emerging external power, Rome, into the scene.

The Hellenistic Age witnessed significant developments in terms of political ideology and institutions that had an important impact on the future, especially in providing models for the Romans. Despite their long enchantment with the small, autonomous *polis* as the ideal political entity, the Greeks' political vision expanded after Alexander. The experiences of the Hellenistic Age put into the Greek vocabulary and mentality a vision of a world state in which peoples of many kinds would share a common citizenship and a common destiny—a concept long familiar to the peoples they had conquered and most effectively manifested in the Persian Empire. Even more significant was the Greek acceptance of the concept of monarchy—an institution that had disappeared from the world of the *polis* as early as the eighth century B.C. During the Hellenistic Age monarchy became the standard form of government among the most successful Greek rulers who succeeded Alexander.

The system of monarchy practiced by the Greeks was shaped by the traditions of the Near East, but it reflected uniquely Greek qualities. In the Hellenistic monarchies the king's power was personal, deriving from his feats at arms, his intelligence, his will, and his favor with the deities. By virtue of his personal abilities, he could bestow blessings on his subjects. No constitution, entrenched nobility, or popular vote acted to limit his power. No law other than what he decreed was recognized. Such a concept of royal power clearly reflected the Greek confidence in human ability. To exercise his vast powers effectively, the king of each Hellenistic kingdom relied on the advice of a circle of "friends" selected because of the king's confidence in their talents and loyalty. Each ruler developed a well-organized central government featuring a strong army, an elaborate bureaucracy, and an efficient taxation system. Greeks and Macedonians filled the chief positions in royal governments and controlled the old structures of local government, which were usually left intact.

Yet in this world tending toward larger political groupings, the idea and the reality of the *polis* lived on. We have already noted the survival of many of the old city-states in the Aegean basin during the Hellenistic Age. The large numbers of Greek and Macedonians who migrated across the Near East to serve Hellenistic kings congregated in cities—some ancient and many newly founded. Into their new settings the newcomers brought political institutions and practices from their native city-states. Assemblies, councils, popular courts, and elected magistrates were established to give the elite outsiders considerable control over local affairs. The Greeks and Macedonians in the Near East thus retained their ancient allegiance to the ideal of the small, intimate *polis*, as did their compatriots still living in old Greece. This continued attachment to the ideal of the *polis* detracted from a complete commitment to monarchy. Generally, the Hellenistic kings encouraged and supported the development of such nearly autonomous communities, chiefly because royal power depended on support from Greeks and Macedonians. At the same time concerns about retaining their ethnic identity and their elite position in political, social, and cultural life forced all Greeks in the Hellenistic world to seek the support of monarchs. As a result, strong, mutually beneficial bonds developed between the monarchs and the city-states of the Near East dominated by Greeks and Macedonians. The kings could usually count on the support of the local communities and, given their superior resources, were able to impose their will on these communities. Slowly but surely, monarchy overshadowed the *polis* as the decisive political force in the Hellenistic world. But the idea of the semiautonomous *polis* as a key component of a larger political entity took deep roots across a wide sweep of the eastern Mediterranean world.

3. HELLENISTIC ECONOMIC AND SOCIAL LIFE

Although the Hellenistic era brought prosperity to some areas and to particular groups, on the whole the economic impact of Greek-Macedonian expansion was modest, chiefly because it was not accompanied by changes in the basic structures of production. Agriculture remained the basic source of wealth in the Hellenistic world, but the new masters did not fundamentally change the established system. The conquerors claimed possession of a considerable portion of the agricultural land in their vast empire and imposed on native tenants and slaves the obligation to till the soil for their benefit. Some Greek owners, including especially the kings seeking revenue, undertook land clearance, new irrigation projects, crop rotation, and the introduction of new crops and equipment; but the resultant increase in production was modest and beneficial to only a few.

An increase in trading activity, promoted by the Hellenistic kings, provided a significant element of prosperity in some areas of the Hellenistic world, especially in a zone embracing the great cities of Egypt, Syria, and Asia Minor. Greek entrepreneurs played a significant role in exploiting the commercial potential of this area and in extending trade connections toward old Greece, Mesopotamia, India, China, the western Mediterranean, and sub-Saharan Africa. Extensive new capital was made available to these entrepreneurs when Alexander confiscated and put into circulation the vast treasury of the Persian kings and the wealth controlled by the Persian aristocracy. At least some of this wealth was invested in activities beneficial to commerce: harbors, roads, market facilities, ships, coinage systems, credit and banking operations. A variety of luxury items, often originating outside the Hellenistic world, as well as foodstuffs, metals, and timber products, moved through the commercial network crisscrossing the Hellenistic world. Industrial activity, carried on chiefly by

native artisans operating small establishments devoted to products needed by the populace of each city, constituted a significant element of the Hellenistic economy. The surviving evidence suggests that there was no great increase in industrial production and no fundamental change in the organization of manufacturing. Especially noteworthy was the lack of technical progress. Despite some remarkable advances in the level of scientific knowledge, almost no effort was made in applying that knowledge to manufacturing, probably because of the vast supply of cheap native labor and slavery.

Whatever economic expansion there was during the Hellenistic period benefited only a few in society—chiefly the newly established Greek-Macedonian rulers and the immigrants who followed them. With the exception of a few natives who adopted Greek ways, most natives were economically exploited. As the Hellenistic era progressed, the gap between the wealthy "foreign" masters and the poor native farmers, city laborers, and slaves widened. Moreover, economic prosperity was not evenly distributed geographically; its effects were felt chiefly in the belt extending from Egypt around the eastern end of the Mediterranean into Asia Minor. Increasingly impoverished were the old Greek city-states in the Aegean area, where depopulation and even starvation were not uncommon.

In both the old Greek world and the vast area conquered by Alexander, established social patterns persisted during the Hellenistic period. In the old Greek city-states family structures and social practices governing daily life remained much as they had been in the fifth century. The chief change involved growing disparities in wealth, which hardened class lines, and social tensions, which bred conflict and even violence. In "new Hellas" native life was little disturbed by the coming of the Greeks; for most people Greek masters merely replaced Persians. Perhaps the chief new social phenomenon of the period was the implantation amid the native population of colonies of Greeks and Macedonians who sought to re-create and perpetuate the social order they brought from their native city-states. But that proved impossible. Wherever Greek migrants settled, they found themselves living among other Greeks from many different cities and were constantly confronted by uprooted Greek intellectuals, athletes, soldiers, merchants, and assorted adventurers seeking their fortunes, a situation that eroded commitment to local customs based on place of origin. All kinds of opportunities existed to abandon old social ties in order to take advantage of new ways of winning wealth, favor, and high status. Despite their commitment to "Greekness," the newcomers could not avoid interactions with the natives of the Near East, an encounter which modified their traditional patterns of behavior and social values. All of these factors combined to nurture individualism, social mobility, and cosmopolitan values within the elite group that dominated the Hellenistic world. One aspect of social life so affected involved the status of women. Although still surrounded by legal constraints, many women in the Hellenistic cities of the Near East enjoyed greatly expanded opportunities for education, involvement in cultural and economic life, and even political life—opportunities not available to their ancestors in old Greece.

As the Hellenistic era progressed, some of these social and economic trends produced increasing instability in Hellenistic society. Deepening differences in wealth, native resentment against Greek exploitation, retreat of the members of the ruling elite from civic-mindedness toward individualistic concerns, and an abiding sense of Greek superiority generated explosive tensions. Unlike their predecessors in the Archaic Age, the Greek leaders of the Hellenistic world were unable to shed their role as exploiters in order to come to grips with economic and social problems in ways that would strengthen the entire fabric of society. That failure, repeated by the Romans, would have serious consequences for the fate of Greco-Roman civilization.

4. HELLENISTIC THOUGHT AND EXPRESSION

The three centuries following Alexander's death marked a highly significant era in cultural history distinguished by two interdependent developments: the spread of the classical Greek culture into an immense area theretofore little touched by it and the recasting of that culture in ways that enriched it. The spread of Greek culture across much of Alexander's empire was a consequence of the migration of numerous Greeks who left their old city-states to serve Alexander and his successors as a ruling elite in the Hellenistic world. Unable to imagine a civilized existence without their accustomed cultural life, these migrants consciously implanted and sought to sustain Greek literary, artistic, philosophical, and scientific concepts and forms wherever they settled. But sustaining classical Greek culture in a foreign setting was not simple. The culturally dominant Greeks found themselves in a political, economic and social milieu in which some aspects of their old culture, originally shaped in the intimate, tightly knit environment of the *polis*, appeared to have little relevance. Moreover, the Greeks soon discovered that the "barbarian" Egyptians, Syrians, Mesopotamians, Persians, and Indians possessed knowledge, techniques, and ideas that were both new and attractive to the conquerors. Inevitably, these conditions set into motion processes that transformed the old modes of thought and expression in ways that broadened and enriched the classical Hellenic culture. The result was the shaping of a distinctive culture deserving its own name: Hellenistic culture.

While many of the old city-states of the Aegean area, particularly Athens, remained important cultural centers, the most intense cultural activity of the Hellenistic Age was generated in the new Greek centers in the Near East, especially Alexandria, Antioch, and Pergamum. The population of these cities was cosmopolitan, mixing Greeks from throughout the Hellenistic world with the native peoples. The royal governments that controlled these cities and the affluent Greeks who dominated social and economic life were generous patrons, anxious to attract artists, writers, and thinkers in order to enhance the prestige of their city and to sustain the main features of civilized life. In Alexandria, for example, the Ptolemaic kings built a large library that contained about seven hundred thousand books (actually handwritten papyrus scrolls) and created a research center, called the Museum, where scholars were supported so that they could pursue scientific studies. The best talent flocked to these centers and devoted their skills to satisfying the cultural interests of those who patronized them. The cultural activities generated in these "new" cities addressed a much broader world, a different set of interests, and a new range of problems than had the Greek cultural efforts within the small, independent *polis* of the Aegean world.

The Hellenistic Age witnessed a massive outpouring of literature written in Greek. This literary activity was due in part to an expanded patronage system supported by wealthy monarchs, their officials, and private individuals, all eager to fortify their status in a world where individual recognition was prized over collective identity. More significantly, there was an increased demand for literature by a growing number of literate people, a demand fostered by the emergence of a simplified version of Greek (*koine* Greek) that became the common tongue of government, commerce, and learning. Many natives learned the language and became readers of Greek literature. While the writers of the Hellenistic Age were prolific, they were not especially inventive. Mainly they devoted their energies to imitations of the epic and lyric poems, the tragedies and comedies, and the histories of classical Greece. Most writers, especially poets, were chiefly concerned with style, often reworking old subject matter in an attempt to achieve stylistic perfection. There were some authors, however, who produced literature that dealt with current situations and appealed to broader audiences than did the "classics"; such literature included digests of scientific and philosophical knowledge, romantic and adventure novels, histories, and biographies.

During the Hellenistic Age creative writers had to share the literary scene with literary critics, scholars concerned with reconstructing earlier Greek literary masterpieces, writing commentaries on their meaning, analyzing their grammar, and discussing their stylistic features. Their scholarly labor played an important role in establishing and preserving the texts of the Greek classics and in elaborating the rules that governed grammar, rhetoric, and literary form. Their work was important in defining an expanding educational system whose substance was increasingly literary. Education played a major role in preparing the Greek ruling elite to discharge its duties and to sustain the cultural brand that was its mark of superiority.

The artists of the Hellenistic period were no less active than the literary figures. Again classical Greek models exerted a powerful influence, almost completely overshadowing the artistic traditions of the Near East. Architecture enjoyed a great boom because of the numerous new cities built by the Greeks and filled with the traditional Greek buildings—temples, *gymnasia*, theaters, and halls for the conduct of public business. Although the basic forms remained classic, there was a tendency to stress size and ornateness in these buildings. Most Hellenistic cities were much better planned than the older Greek cities, with emphasis on a rectangular grid layout, wide streets, adequate water supplies, commercial conveniences, and parks.

Hellenistic sculpture likewise sought to imitate the masters of the Classical Age; in fact, most sculptors did little more than copy classical models, often for sale to private collectors. They remained fascinated by mythological subjects and the human figure. Sometimes they were able to capture the full spirit of classical style, as is illustrated by the well-known *Winged Victory of Samothrace*, with its idealized, well-proportioned portrayal of the human form. Hellenistic sculptors showed a greater interest in the nude female than had sculptors of classical Greece; their best work in this respect reflected a pleasing combination of idealization of the body and sensuousness, as is evident in the famous *Aphrodite of Melos* (more commonly known as the *Venus de Milo*). Hellenistic sculptors produced impressive relief carvings as a part of temple decoration. Although little evidence has survived, it is clear that the classical tradition in painting was continued during the Hellenistic period. Despite the powerful appeal of classical Greek subjects and models in the visual arts, Hellenistic art did develop its own unique characteristics. Perhaps the most striking development was the increasing realism and emotionalism reflected in sculpture and painting. In place of the classic quest to create idealized perfection, Hellenistic sculptors often came down into the streets—the world of children, old people, laborers, barbarians—for their subjects. In portraying these figures they sought to capture the passions, sorrow, suffering, and emotions that are part of real life (see Figure 7.2).

The most original cultural contributions of the Hellenistic Age were made in science and philosophy, where investigators and thinkers often moved beyond their Hellenic predecessors. The moment was especially ripe for scientific advance. Earlier Greek philosophers had postulated challenging theories about the natural world and had argued that nature could best be understood by observing its workings. These concerns continued during the Hellenistic Age and were stimulated when the Greeks gained access to a huge body of data about the natural world compiled over many centuries by learned individuals in the Near East. Hellenistic kings and wealthy Greeks were eager to patronize scientists and to provide facilities to make research possible. The result was active scientific inquiry, centered especially at Alexandria, which led to a more systematic, rational organization of inherited scientific data, an impressive accumulation of new knowledge, and fresh interpretations of its meaning.

Introduced to a much larger world by Alexander's conquests and by commercial expansion, Hellenistic scientists made noteworthy progress in compiling and organizing geographical information. From this data emerged challenging geographical speculation, illustrated by the work of Eratosthenes (ca. 275–200 B.C.). He calculated the circumference of the earth to be 24,662 miles, about 200 miles less than the actual figure. On the basis of his study of tides, he insisted that the Atlantic and Indian oceans were joined and that India could be reached from Spain by sailing south around Africa or directly west. He made maps using lines of longitude and latitude and divided the earth into climatic zones still used by geographers. Seleucus (second century B.C.), along with others, studied the tides and came close to relating them to the gravitational force of the moon.

Two names reflect the widespread interest in astronomy: Aristarchus (ca. 310–230 B.C.) and Hipparchus (ca. 185–120 B.C.). On the basis of geometrical calculations Aristarchus put forward a heliocentric theory of the universe which argued that the earth and the planets rotated around the sun. Hipparchus denied this theory, working out a geocentric version of the cosmos

FIGURE 7.2 An Old Woman of the Hellenistic Age
This portrayal of an old market woman of the third or second century B.C. reflects the concern of Hellenistic artists with portraying the real world about them. The work suggests a world that had its share of suffering and hardship. The contrast with the serene, idealized figures portrayed in the sculpture of the Classical Age in Greece is striking. (The Metropolitan Museum of Art, Rogers Fund, 1909)

that involved an intricate pattern of movements of the sun, moon, and stars around the earth. His system, which took into account what astronomers were then able to observe, won the day and would survive for centuries. He compiled an extensive atlas of the stars and from observation of their movements arrived at an extremely accurate calculation of the solar year. Both these great astronomers tried to calculate the size of the sun and its distance from the earth, but with little success.

Much was also done to advance mathematics. Euclid (323–285 B.C.) compiled a textbook containing hundreds of rationally demonstrated proofs of propositions pertaining to flat surfaces that remained the standard work on plane geometry until the twentieth century. Archimedes (287–212 B.C.) calculated the value of *pi* (the ratio between the circumference and the diameter of a circle), devised a system for expressing large numbers, solved the problem of the relative volumes of a cylinder and a sphere, and laid the foundations for calculus. Trigonometry was developed by Hipparchus, and a fundamental work on conic sections was done by Apollonius of Perga (third century B.C.).

Medicine was of great interest to the scholars of this period. Following the lead of Hippocrates, Hellenistic physicians made important progress in anatomy and physiology, chiefly on the basis of careful and systematic observation. Surgery advanced considerably; so did the use of medicines. Alexandria was especially prominent as a center of medical study, an activity that the Ptolemaic rulers supported even to the extent of supplying physicians with the cadavers of prisoners for dissection.

Hellenistic scientists were also interested in physics, zoology, chemistry, and botany, devoting most of their energies to collecting and classifying data in these areas. Illustrative was the work of Theophrastus (ca. 372–287 B.C.), who compiled descriptive works on botany based on his own observations of plants and their habits. New advances in these fields were limited. However, Archimedes did discover the laws governing floating bodies and developed the theory of the lever.

Although the evidence is scanty, it is clear that the Hellenistic era witnessed noteworthy advances in technology. Archimedes developed the windlass, the double pulley, the endless screw for pumping water, and a variety of devices useful in the defense of besieged cities. Other less famous engineers devised machines operated by water, air pressure, and weights, cranes capable of moving huge weights, surgical instruments, and water clocks. However, Hellenistic scientists, like their Hellenic predecessors, had little interest in the practical applications of scientific knowledge. In fact, virtually the only area where applied technology developed was in the military field. As a consequence, daily life during the Hellenistic era was little affected by the notable advances in science.

Hellenistic philosophy rivaled science in vigor and creativity. The old philosophical interests lived on, as evidenced by the continued activity of Plato's Academy and Aristotle's Lyceum in Athens. However, Hellenistic philosophy was primarily concerned with problems of human conduct and individual destiny, interests that had already attracted the Sophists of the fifth century B.C.. This emphasis reflected the stresses felt by Greeks living in a cosmopolitan, impersonal, changing world, which left them seeking escape from alienation, reassurance against uncertainty, personal identity, and peace of mind.

The search for individual identity and peace of mind produced several schools of thought that competed vigorously for public attention. Some attracted popular fancy and aroused ire for their eccentricity and excess. A school called Skeptics called into question all systems of truth, arguing that peace of mind could come only when people accepted their inability to discover truth by rational means and lived on the basis of practical experience. The Cynics were more spectacular; they advocated that individuals should reject the conventions and material trappings of civilized society in order to gain individual freedom. These disciples of a counterculture refused gainful employment, abandoned family life, took to the streets in filthy rags to deliver diatribes against the establishment, and generally conducted themselves in ways offensive to civilized society.

More appealing was the teaching of Epicurus (ca. 341–270 B.C.), who founded a school at Athens which developed a set of ethical concepts derived from the atomic theory propounded by Democritus. Epicurus argued that the universe consisted of atoms, which by chance formed themselves into beings and things. Given this materialistic cosmos, human beings could put aside troubling fears of the deities, who, if they existed, had nothing to do with the processes that controlled all being, as well as concerns about death, which was nothing more than the dissolution of atoms that had come together by accident to bring living creatures into being. Rather, humans should occupy themselves only with happiness and pleasure. Contrary to some of his disciples, Epicurus argued that happiness did not result from mere physical pleasure but rather from pursuits that avoid physical pain and promote a peaceful mind undisturbed by any anxiety. He urged his disciples to withdraw into a small circle of intimate friends and to avoid excessive wealth, political involvement, and too great contact with the world; "to live in hiding" would shield one from much that could disturb the mind. Many educated and refined Greeks found in Epicureanism justification to escape the uncertainties of a hostile world, but in doing so they turned their backs on the active, involved life that had once been the ideal for the Greek citizen.

The most powerful movement shaping the moral atmosphere of the Hellenistic Age was Stoicism, whose founder, Zeno (336–264 B.C.), taught in Athens while Epicurus was there. Stoicism was based on Zeno's conviction that the universe was governed by an unchanging law of nature ordained by a Divine Reason to establish harmony and order in the universe. By nature every individual, regardless of status or place of origin, shared in the universal order established by the Divine Reason, making them members of the common community of humankind. The course of human beings emerged clearly from such a universal order: They must use their reason to define a pattern of behavior that would attune their lives to the laws of nature. Such a course would compel all humans to accept the inevitable dictates of the natural order. They must bear all misfortunes with patience and accept good fortune without pride, since everything that happens has been ordained by an all-knowing providence. Such harmony with the natural order brings tranquillity and peace of mind. It ends concern for material things and allows the soul to reach the ideal state—*apatheia* (apathy, or absence of feeling). Although in its

early stage Stoicism was primarily an individualistic philosophy, it did in time develop a larger dimension that stressed the community of all humans under one law, the need for involvement in public life in order to sustain order and civility, and concern for other members of the single human community.

As the second century B.C. progressed, Hellenistic cultural activity began to lose momentum, chiefly in the face of ideas and values embodied in religious systems that had roots in the traditions of the ancient Near East. But by that time Hellenic-Hellenistic culture had won the admiration of the conquering Romans, who would continue the diffusion and enrichment of the Greek way that had progressed so remarkably during the Hellenistic Age.

5. HELLENISTIC RELIGION

Religious developments during the Hellenistic Age took an unexpected turn destined to be of major importance for the future. In contrast to Greek dominance in most aspects of life, the religions of the conquered peoples gradually asserted a powerful influence in shaping Hellenistic thought and values. As the Greeks migrated across the Near East, they took with them and sought to sustain their old civic religions as a part of their "superior" culture. Although this effort put the trappings of Greek religion into place everywhere across the Hellenistic world, the old deities and the rites in their honor increasingly ceased to answer the basic spiritual needs generated by the changed environment of the Hellenistic world and consequently suffered eclipse.

In the face of the insecurity and alienation of the Hellenistic world, more and more Greeks found spiritual satisfaction in what are called *mystery religions*. Although pre-Hellenistic Greeks were familiar with such religions in the form of the cults of Dionysus and Demeter, they encountered among their Near Eastern subjects a variety of flourishing mystery cults of diverse origins centering on the worship of different deities: Serapis, Isis, Mithra, the Earth Mother. All shared certain fundamental ideas with wide appeal. They centered around the worship of a savior deity, usually identified with the forces of renewal in nature, whose death and resurrection provided eternal life for each individual believer. Those yearning for assurance drew close to that deity by trusting in the deity's saving power, by submitting to a special initiation ceremony, and by participating in emotional rituals, often involving a reenactment of the deity's death and rebirth. Favor with the saving god or goddess depended heavily on the moral conduct of each believer. Since faith in a savior deity, ritual participation, and upright behavior were tests everyone could meet, the mystery religions appealed to men and women of all classes, all levels of wealth, and all ethnic groups. In the cosmopolitan, mobile environment of the Hellenistic world, ideas from various mystery religions constantly mingled. This process, called *syncretism* (see Figure 7.3), pointed toward the emergence of a common faith that not only tended to link Hellenes and native Near Easterners but also created a seedbed out of which would emerge such universal religions as Christianity and Islam.

As the Hellenistic period unfolded, the religious attitudes exemplified by the mystery religions increasingly asserted a powerful influence over literary and artistic expression and philosophical and scientific thought. This "religionizing" of thought and expression initiated a subtle redirection of Hellenistic cultural life that highlighted a dimension of Hellenistic civilization that was destined to be an important heritage. The Hellenistic mentality was marked by an inner tension. On the one hand, there was a thrust, most evident in science, art, and creative writing, to know and to understand rationally the world of people and nature. On the other, there was an equally powerful impetus, reflected best by philosophers and priests, to retreat from the material world into the spirit world, to abandon thinking in favor of quietude of mind sustained by faith in an all-powerful deity. Perhaps the emergence of this polarity was the most potent consequence of the encounter between the civilizations of the ancient Near East and the Greeks. In any case, the juxtaposition of reason and faith, realism and mysticism, activism and withdrawal that was at the heart of Hellenistic culture would recur in later chapters of the history of Western civilization as a stimulant to creativity.

Even as the Hellenistic world was swept along a course pointing to a common religion, note must be taken of one religion that stood apart from, although not untouched by, the ma-

FIGURE 7.3 Religious Syncretism This Hellenistic relief illustrates the mixing of religions that was an important aspect of Hellenistic civilization. The seated deity reflects a mixture of Greek and Near Eastern concepts of deity. The priest burning incense in honor of the god is Near Eastern, while the garment of the figure on the right crowning the god is clearly Greek/Macedonian. (Yale University Art Gallery, Duro-Europas Collection)

jor religious currents: Judaism. The political status of the adherents of Judaism remained much the same under Hellenistic rule as it had been under the Persians; Jews were subjects of Hellenistic monarchs who granted them special privileges that allowed them to observe their religion and to control many aspects of life in their own community. At the center of the people of Israel was the community in Palestine centered around the Temple in Jerusalem, a community held together and set apart not by nationhood but by adherence to Judaic law as set forth in the Torah and by time-sanctioned cult practices in honor of Yahweh. In addition to the Jerusalem community there were Yahweh's followers dispersed widely across the Hellenistic world, where they were allowed to maintain quasi-autonomous communities in which they too could live and worship according to Judaic law. In this general setting Judaism continued to mature along the basic lines defined prior to the Hellenistic Age (see Chapter 3). The Hebrew Bible assumed the basic form in which it is now known, scribes studied the law and taught its letter and its spirit to the faithful in synogogues, teachers of wisdom scrutinized and refined the ethical dimensions of Judaism, and speculative minds injected concepts of such matters as sin, the afterlife, and divine providence into traditional Judaism. Although sometimes at odds over such issues as the meaning of the law, the standards of right living, the appropriateness of new theological concepts, and the future of Yahweh's chosen people, the adherents of Judaism remained a remarkably coherent group.

As the Hellenistic Age progressed, perhaps the most disruptive force in the Jewish community was the question of Hellenization. Many Jews, especially those dispersed in the great cities of the Hellenistic world, were deeply attracted to and influenced by Greek thought and lifestyle; for example, so many Jews living in Egypt spoke Greek that it was necessary to prepare a Greek translation of the Bible, called the Septuagint, to serve their religious needs. This intrusion of Hellenistic ideas and values seemed to other Jews to be a grave threat to Judaism. That issue was at the heart of the most dramatic event in Jewish history during the Hellenistic Age, the Maccabean revolt, which began in 167 B.C. It was provoked by the efforts of the Seleucid ruler, Antiochus IV, abetted by Hellenizing Jews in Palestine, to force Hellenization on the community in Palestine as a means of unifying the shaky Seleucid kingdom against the threat of Rome. Antiochus' policy led to persecution of the Jews, a suspension of Jewish religious worship, and the desecration of the Temple with a pagan altar. Outraged Jews, led by Judas Maccabaeus, took up arms to wage a successful guerrilla war that culminated with the recapture of Jerusalem, the purification of the Temple (the first Hanukkah), the cessation of Seleucid persecution, and the establishment of a virtually independent Jewish state under Roman auspices. However, the issue surrounding the problem of Hellenization—the relationship of the community made up of adherents of Judaism to the larger world—was by no means settled. It would continue to agitate Judaism and lead to consequences of decisive importance in shaping the future not only of Judaism but also of the non-Jewish world.

SUGGESTED READING

Political History

Peter Green, *Alexander to Actium. The Historical Evolution of the Hellenistic Age* (1990).

F. W. Walbank, *The Hellenistic World* (1982).

Two syntheses covering all aspects of Hellenistic life.

Peter Green, *Alexander of Macedon, 356-323. A Historical Biography* (1991).

Robin Lane Fox, *Alexander the Great* (1973).

Either of these biographies will help understand Alexander.

Cultural Life

John Ferguson, *The Heritage of Hellenism. The Greek World from 323 B.C. to 31 B.C.* (1973). An excellent overview of the main features of Hellenistic culture.

G. E. R. Lloyd, *Greek Science after Aristotle* (1973). A balanced description of the accomplishments of Hellenistic science.

A. A. Long, *Hellenistic Philosophers: Stoics, Epicureans, Sceptics* (1986). A clear presentation of the teachings of the major Hellenistic schools of philosophy.

Jean Charbonneaux et al., *Hellenistic Art (330–50 B.C.)*, trans. Peter Green (1973).

J. J. Pollitt, *Art in the Hellenistic Age* (1986).

Two excellent treatments with good illustrations.

John Onions, *Art and Thought in the Hellenistic Age: The Greek World View, 350–50 B.C.* (1979). A challenging effort to interrelate art and thought.

Arnaldo Momigliano, *Alien Wisdom: The Limits of Hellenization* (1975). Discusses how the Greeks dealt with other cultures, especially during the Hellenistic period.

Walter Burkert, *Ancient Mystery Cults* (1987). A good picture of the most powerful religious forces in the Hellenistic world.

Sources

M. M. Austin, *The Hellenistic World from Alexander to the Roman Conquest. A Selection of Ancient Sources in Translation* (1981). A well-selected collection of documents that will help the reader understand many aspects of Hellenistic life as seen and felt by those who lived in that world.

CHAPTER 8

The Rise of Rome to Domination of the Mediterranean World, 800 B.C.–133 B.C.

FIGURE 8.1 A Roman Patrician Honoring His Ancestors This portrayal of a Roman patrician bearing busts of his ancestors conveys the sobriety, seriousness, and respect for family that characterized the aristocratic citizens who acted through the Senate to lead the Roman Republic to ascendancy in the Mediterranean world. (Art Resource)

The powerful impulse toward the establishment of a common culture in the Mediterranean basin, initiated by the Greek city-states and continued by the Hellenistic kingdoms, was continued toward the end of the third century B.C. by a new power emerging from the West: Rome. The major accomplishment of the Romans was to create a universal political order which allowed the major features of Hellenic civilization to spread over a much larger geographical area, where it affected peoples to whom higher civilization had heretofore been unknown, especially the peoples inhabiting the area around the western Mediterranean. But Rome's political achievement was not done in a day; the shaping of the Roman imperial order required several centuries.

1. THE ORIGINS OF ROME TO 509 B.C.

The emergence of Rome as the dominant force in the Mediterranean world owed much to a combination of geographical factors and the human resources of the Italian peninsula. Aside from its strategic location in the Mediterranean basin, Italy had considerable productive farmland, important mineral deposits, and good timber. Its climate was generally mild and conducive to agricultural production. The Italian population was formed over a long period out of several different elements whose diverse patterns of culture fragmented the peninsula into a bewildering array of political entities and institutional systems. Perhaps as early as 4000 B.C., a native population developed a Neolithic farming culture. Beginning about 2000 B.C., Italy experienced successive waves of Indo-European invaders, who established political dominance over the long-established native Neolithic farmers. Their language eventually prevailed over much of Italy, creating the base from which classical Latin emerged.

The still-backward Italian population was decisively influenced after about 800 B.C. by the settlement in Italy of two outside peoples bringing with them the more advanced civilization of the eastern Mediterranean world. As we have already seen, the Greeks founded numerous city-states in southern Italy and Sicily from which flowed powerful cultural forces affecting the entire Italian population. Even more important

were the Etruscans, probably immigrants from Asia Minor, who established a series of cities along the western coast of Italy in a region called Etruria (see Map 8.1). Although each of these cities remained politically independent, between about 700 and 500 B.C. they collectively dominated western Italy from the Po Valley to Naples. They transmitted to the native population technical skills, agricultural and commercial practices, political techniques, religious usages, and art forms that provided many Italians with their first taste of advanced urban civilization.

Among the most precocious pupils of the Etruscans were the inhabitants of several tiny villages built on a cluster of seven hills lying on the south bank of the Tiber River about fifteen miles from the sea. These first "Romans" later created a colorful legend recounting the founding of their city in 753 B.C. by Romulus and Remus, allegedly descendants of a hero of the Trojan Wars, Aeneas. Legend aside, the evidence suggests that Rome began as a settling place for herder-farmers from an area just south of the Tiber known as Latium, who perhaps were attracted to the site by an important ford which controlled traffic across the Tiber.

Shortly after 600 B.C., these villages coalesced into a single city-state, a unification probably forced on them by Etruscan warlords. Within a century Rome was transformed into a thriving urban center focused around a marketplace called the Forum. Etruscan techniques of trade and industry were adopted, greatly strengthening the city's primitive economy. An alphabet was derived from Etruscan models, resulting in the rapid development of written Latin. Etruscan architecture and decoration served as models for the temples and public buildings in the burgeoning city. Primitive Latin religious practices took on more sophisticated patterns reflecting Etruscan usages.

In this urban setting political and social structures emerged that would exercise a powerful influence over Roman society for centuries. The unified city was ruled by a king who was advised by a council, called the Senate, composed of about three hundred men of wealth who drew their authority from their headship of families. Freemen, who constituted the bulk of the citizen body, were given a limited voice in political affairs by membership in two assemblies, the most

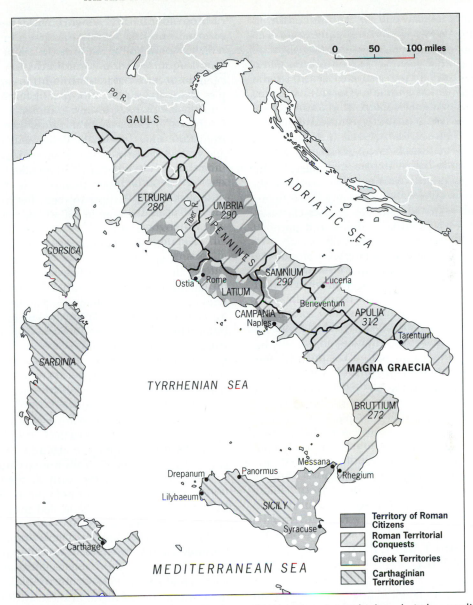

Map 8.1 ITALY, 265 B.C. This map shows the main geographical regions into which early Italy was divided and indicates the date at which each was brought under Roman domination. As noted in the text, Roman domination did not mean total loss of independence for the peoples of Italy. Many in central Italy became citizens, as is indicated on the map; most of the rest were allies who retained considerable rights of local control as long as they supported Rome's foreign policy and kept the peace.

important of which was the Assembly of Centuries. This body emerged from a military reorganization, probably instituted during the sixth century B.C., that grouped the population on the basis of wealth into miliary units called *centuries*. The centuries were composed in such a way as to give predominant voice to Rome's wealthiest citizens. The city-state populace was divided into two distinct classes, *patricians* and *plebeians*. The patricians, consisting of a small number of landowning families each rigidly controlled by the father of the family (*pater familias*), exercised the predominant influence over society. Custom prohibited intermarriage between the two classes. A powerful force of social stability and patrician domination was the institution of *clientage*. Under this system many plebeians were closely tied to patrician families as *clients*, with their noble *patrons* providing legal protection and material assistance in return for various services, including following political orders.

Despite their debt to the Etruscans, the Romans chafed under their domination. Shortly before 500 B.C., Etruscan power began to be contested by the dependent subjects everywhere in western Italy. In Rome the patricians took the lead in a revolution that dethroned the Etruscan king and established in his place two *consuls* elected annually from patrician ranks to wield the *imperium*, that is, the highest executive authority of the state. This revolution of 509 B.C. marked the beginning of the Roman Republic, an episode long celebrated by the Romans as the greatest event in their history.

2. THE EARLY REPUBLIC, 509–265 B.C.

Two themes dominate the first two and one-half centuries of the history of the Roman Republic: Roman conquest of the Italian peninsula (see Map 8.1) and the shaping of an effective political and social order. Given the fact that in 509 B.C. Rome was only a tiny city-state lost among many other political entities, Roman expansion in Italy represented a remarkable feat. In a larger sense, Roman success created the human and material resources that would soon permit Rome to become a world power.

For a century after the expulsion of the Etrus-

cans in 509 B.C., Rome's survival depended on cooperation with neighboring cities in Latium, which joined Rome to form the Latin League. This league fought a long succession of wars against the Etruscans, the tough mountain peoples trying to gain a foothold in the rich agricultural lands of Latium and Campania, and the Gauls, a Celtic people who raided central Italy from their base in the Po Valley and captured and sacked Rome in 390 B.C. Rome survived these threats with sufficient strength to take the offensive against the other members of the Latin League, whose attempts to resist led to the dissolution of the League in 338 B.C., leaving Rome in control of Latium.

From this base, the Romans proceeded to expand their sphere of influence. Between 326 and 290 B.C. they subdued the Samnites, a formidable mountain people living south and east of Rome, who provoked the Romans by challenging them for control of Campania. While engaged in the bitter Samnite Wars, the Romans were attacked from the north by Gauls, Etruscans, and other mountain peoples from north-central Italy, but these attacks were thrown back and Roman dominance was gradually established over most of northern Italy lying south of the Po Valley. Hardly had the Samnite Wars ended than Rome was drawn into the affairs of the Greek city-states of southern Italy, chiefly to arbitrate their quarrels. Despite assistance from military adventurers from "old" Greece, the badly divided Italian-Greek city-states could not hold off the Romans. By 265 B.C. Rome had established mastery over all of Italy south of the Po Valley.

Many forces combined to explain Rome's triumph. Later Romans constantly retold the stories of these wars as proof of their superior civic virtues and divine favor. Beneath these legends there was a core of truth: In these arduous wars the Roman citizens demonstrated bravery, persistence, and self-sacrifice. However, other, more tangible factors also played a decisive part in Roman success.

First, the Romans developed a superior military organization based upon a citizen army in which most of the city's male population served at each soldier's own expense. The effectiveness of this army was greatly enhanced by the development of the *legion* as the basic military formation. The legion was essentially a massed formation of well-armed infantry soldiers, not unlike the Greek phalanx. During the long wars against mountain peoples, the legion formation developed greater flexibility by the creation within it of small subunits capable of independent action.

A second, more important factor contributing to Rome's victory in Italy was the innovative policy devised for the treatment of conquered peoples. In essence this system encouraged conquered peoples to identify their well-being with Roman success. Rome achieved this end through a series of treaties with conquered subjects which provided a flexible definition of "belonging" to Rome's spreading network of power. To some conquered peoples, especially those in Latium, Rome extended full rights of citizenship. The residents of other communities became "citizens without vote." These people could not participate in the Roman political process, but they were permitted to trade in Rome and to intermarry with Romans. These cities continued to govern themselves in most matters except foreign affairs, but their half citizens owed to the Roman state the same financial and military obligations as Roman citizens did. Still other communities were made "allies" (*socii*) of Rome, each enjoying independence in local affairs but required to provide military contingents to serve in Rome's wars. Implicit in these arrangements was the possibility that partial citizenship and ally status would eventually result in full citizenship, especially for those who became Romanized. In many communities that were granted powers of local self-government, the Romans gave strong support to ruling aristocracies who found it in their best interests to support Rome. Roman colonists were settled across Italy to become important agents in the Romanization of the peninsula. This complex set of arrangements, contrasting so sharply with the way in which other conquerors treated their victims, meant that by 265 B.C. Rome ruled over a loose confederation of Italians, most of whom enjoyed a considerable degree of independence but all of whom were tied to Rome by virtue of an obligation to serve in its armies, by the hope of achieving full citizenship, and by an increasing identification with Roman culture in all its facets. From the Roman point of view this system provided a pool of military resources that ensured

the security of Italy and made possible further expansion.

A third element contributing to Rome's success was the ability of its leaders to reshape internal political and social structures in a way that promoted loyalty among its citizens. Those adjustments were painfully worked out during a protracted internal conflict, called the "struggle of the orders," which went on almost continually for over two centuries after the founding of the republic in 509 B.C. On one side stood the patricians, who were determined to maintain their monopoly on power and their exclusive social position. Challenging them were the plebeians, a diverse group ranging from affluent, ambitious figures eager for a share in political decision making to poor, humble farmers and artisans concerned chiefly with escaping economic oppression, gaining more equitable treatment under the law, and finding more land. Aside from the sometimes brilliant tactics of plebeian leaders, occasionally supported by individual patricians, perhaps the decisive factor in the struggle was the fear of the ruling patricians that the plebeian soldiers would refuse to serve the state unless their demands were met. In fact, at certain critical moments in the struggles the plebeians did secede from the state to make their point.

Whatever the motives and however bitter the struggle, the significant fact was that the dominant patricians did give sufficient ground to prevent civil strife and to avoid alienation of any major segment of the citizen body. Certain of their concessions mark crucial stages in shaping the republican constitution. As early as 494 B.C., the plebeians gained the right to elect special plebeian officials, called *tribunes*, who were given the power to veto any act of the regularly elected officials that threatened plebeian interests. A new plebeian assembly, originally called the Council of the Plebs and later the Assembly of Tribes, was instituted to provide a forum where the plebeians could enact resolutions (called *plebiscites*) indicating their will to the tribunes. In about 450 B.C. plebeian pressure led to a written codification of ancient legal customs, called the Twelve Tables, that protected citizens from arbitrary decisions by patrician judges. A succession of laws approved by the Senate and the Assembly of Centuries gave protection to debtors, permitted marriage between patricians and plebeians, limited patrician monopoly on the use of public lands, and provided land grants to poor plebeians. One by one the major elective offices were opened to plebeians; particularly important was a law of 367 B.C. that required that one consul be a plebeian. Since election to the consulship automatically qualified a Roman citizen for membership in the Senate, plebeians had finally gained access to that powerful body. Finally, in 287 B.C., plebiscites enacted by the Assembly of Tribes were recognized as the ultimate law binding on the entire state, a concession that gave the citizen body final authority.

On the surface the struggle of the orders had created a constitution for the republic that placed the control of the state in the hands of Rome's citizen body—the Senate and the people, as the Romans put it. By 265 B.C. the citizen body, acting through the Assembly of Centuries and the Assembly of Tribes, theoretically had the final power to decide public policy. Aside from the power to enact laws binding on all, the citizens elected the various magistrates who executed the decisions of the citizens enacted in the assemblies. The Roman executive system was collegiate in form. With minor exceptions, every administrative function was carried out by a board of at least two members of equal rank, each of whom had the power to veto the acts of his colleagues, a system that both constrained rash action by elected officials and led to intricate bargaining in order to achieve any results. The highest executive authority in the state—the *imperium*—was exercised by two consuls charged with the joint management of all civil and military affairs. Below them were the *praetors*, who were elected primarily to administer justice but under special circumstances were capable of exercising the *imperium*. In time other administrative offices with specialized functions were created to assist in running the increasingly complicated affairs of the expanding republic. Most elective officials were elected for one-year terms. An important exception was the *censor*, chosen every five years to classify citizens for military service and to judge their moral fitness public functions, particularly membership in the Senate. In times of grave crisis, a *dictator* with unlimited power to run the state could be elected for a term of six months. By law any citizen was

eligible for election to these offices, but since there was no pay for service and since electioneering was expensive, few men of humble means aspired to high office and even fewer gained it.

Especially potent in the republican system of government was the Senate. It was composed of about three hundred men who qualified for membership by virtue of service as consul or praetor, a selection process that ensured that the Senate was dominated by the wealthy and the socially prominent. In theory the Senate was an advisory body, counseling the magistrates and the assemblies in making decisions that best served the interests of the state. In fact, its decisions were almost invariably accepted by the assemblies and the magistrates because of the prestige, wealth, and experience of the senators.

Despite appearances, at the conclusion of the struggle of the orders real power in the Roman Republic remained in the hands of a small circle of wealthy landowners, descendants of a few ancient families. The members of this circle were convinced that right order in society depended on their collective political wisdom, and thus they acted consciously to control the machinery of government; involvement in the governance of Rome was their career. From the ranks of this circle came most of the elected magistrates, who passed from elected office into the Senate. That body, with its extensive role in decision making, was the bastion of aristocratic control. The power wielders worked as a group to manage the election process and to control the assemblies. Especially effective in achieving these ends was their ability to maintain and manage their plebeian clients, whose support was usually forthcoming in return for public policies that provided economic concessions and protection from oppression under the law. The chief threat to the political power of the patrician families came from enterprising, increasingly wealthy plebeians who sought a share in power. The patricians met this challenge by absorbing these "new men" into their circle, chiefly by opening public offices and Senate membership to them and by linking them to patrician families through marriage. This process in no way weakened the control over political life by a small circle of wealthy families, which the Romans increasingly called the *nobiles*, the ruling nobility (see Figure 8.1). Most Romans were content to entrust the destiny of the city to these *nobiles*. That trust was based on the deep-seated respect on the part of the Roman citizen body for traditional ways of doing things (what the Romans called "customs of our forefathers"), on a sense that the leadership of the *nobiles* had been effective in enhancing Rome's power and wealth, and on the assurance that citizens had the means to curb abuses of power. By 265 B.C. this oligarchic system was so powerfully entrenched and so widely accepted that it seemed to many Romans that the ideal form of government had been fashioned. Perhaps the only issues for the future were whether the ruling *nobiles* could remain united in their collective exercise of power and whether they would remain sensitive and responsive to the needs of the citizen body as a whole.

The experiences surrounding expansion in Italy and the struggle of the orders played a decisive role in shaping a collective mentality among the Romans that was destined to cast a long shadow over Roman political, social, and cultural life. During the first centuries of the republic the Romans were basically a simple people whose outlook on life was shaped by four major forces—family life, an agricultural economy, warfare, and religion. The family structure was predominantly patriarchal. The authority of the male head of a household (*pater familias*) over his wife and children was total and absolute. Fathers impressed on the other members of their tightly knit families a sense of discipline, obedience, and respect for authority and tradition. Farm life made the early Romans a practical, realistic people, content to live simply and frugally. Constant warfare in defense of hearth and city deepened the sense of duty owed to the larger community and strengthened societal discipline.

Religion had an especially profound effect on early Roman life and thought. Romans believed that all things in existence were animated by powerful spirits, a view that instilled in them a deep awe of the unseen; the Romans called such awe "piety" and lauded it as a prime virtue. In the early stages of Rome's history the chief objects of this piety were household and agricultural deities: Janus, the protective god of the doorway of each household; Vesta, the goddess of the hearth; the *lares* and *penates*, spirits guarding the productive powers of the family and its lands and flocks. As the city grew, it too devel-

oped its divine protectors. Roman civic religion centered especially on a trio of deities, perhaps derived from Etruscan models: Jupiter, the god of lightning, thunder and power; Juno, the goddess of women, family, and procreation; and Minerva, the goddess of arts, sciences, and wisdom. In time, other deities, derived chiefly from the Greek pantheon, were added to this trio as major civic deities. Eventually this divine circle protecting the expanding city became the object of an elaborate mythology, much of it borrowed from the Greeks, that accounted for the behavior of each of its members. The approach to all the gods and goddesses, whether civic or household, was highly formal and unemotional. From very early times the Romans developed set patterns for offering sacrifices and prayers to their many deities. They also had well-defined expectations of what the gods and goddesses would return to families and the city. Close observance of these customary rituals became a part of responsible citizenship; any deviation threatened to earn the wrath of the deities and misfortune for men and women. Responsibility for proper worship rested with the heads of families and with priests elected to represent the city-state community before the civic gods.

The values defined by home, farm, battlefield, and altar combined to exalt sobriety, industry, discipline, piety, civic responsibility, respect for tradition, and honor of the family. Less prized were originality, creativity, and individuality. As time passed, the Roman mentality tended to idealize the values of these early times and to project them onto political and cultural life as norms governing political and social behavior and shaping thought and expression. As a result, the traits ingrained in Roman society during its early history cast a long shadow over all facets of Roman history.

3. OVERSEAS EXPANSION: THE PUNIC WARS, 264–201 B.C.

By 265 B.C. the Romans had completed the unification of Italy and had put into place an effective system of government. Perhaps without yet knowing it, Rome had become a major power because of these developments. During the next

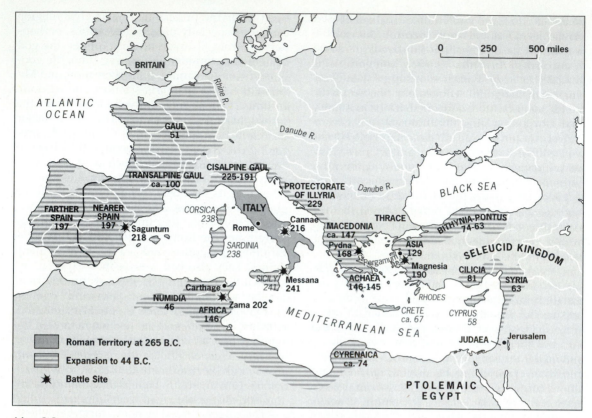

Map 8.2 THE ROMAN EMPIRE, 265–44 B.C. As this map shows, Rome's expansion around the Mediterranean came a bit at a time. By the beginning of the second century B.C. the Romans had established their supremacy in the western Mediterranean, chiefly as a consequence of territory annexed following the Punic Wars. Between about 200 and 125 B.C., the Romans established dominance over Macedonia, Greece, and the west coast of Asia Minor. With that power base it was only a matter of time until further expansion occurred in both the east and west. The circumstances surrounding Rome's expansion after 133 B.C. will be discussed in later chapters.

century and a half, Roman history was shaped by an expanding involvement in the complex affairs of the entire Mediterranean world, which resulted in a series of victories that made the Romans the rulers of a large empire spanning three continents (see Map 8.2).

Rome's first encounter with a major Mediterranean power was with Carthage. Originally a Phoenician colony, Carthage had established its independence about 800 B.C. In the succeeding centuries, the Carthaginians built a thriving commercial empire based on colonies located at stra-

tegic places around the western Mediterranean. During much of this period, their main rivals for commercial supremacy were the Greek city-states of Sicily and southern Italy. Carthaginian relationships with Rome during this period were generally friendly. Eventually their interests clashed over control of Sicily. In 265 B.C. the Carthaginians, who had established a foothold in western Sicily, took steps to protect the Greek city-state of Messana against the aggression of another Greek city-state, Syracuse. After some hesitation, the Romans decided to intervene, perhaps persuaded by fears that Carthaginian control of Messana would result in intervention by a major power in the affairs of Rome's recently conquered allies in southern Italy. The prospect of booty made the choice easier. Rome's decision meant war with Carthage.

The First Punic War (264–241 B.C.) was a struggle for Sicily. The Romans soon realized that they would need a navy to dislodge the Carthaginians from their seaport strongholds. With great resolve coupled with help from their Greek allies, they soon achieved that end. There then ensued a long series of engagements for control of the waters around Sicily. Although the fledgling Roman navy suffered several defeats and an army sent to attack Carthage in Africa was crushed, the Romans persevered until Carthage sued for peace in 241 B.C. By the treaty ending the war, Rome gained Sicily as its first tribute-paying overseas province as well as a sizable monetary payment to cover war expenses.

However, the issue between the two powers was far from settled. In the years following the peace of 241 B.C., the Carthaginians turned their attention to rebuilding their strength, which had been seriously threatened by the loss of Sicily and the Roman challenge to their sea power. Under the leadership of Hamilcar Barca and his son Hannibal Carthage undertook to create a new power base in Spain by subduing the native population, recruiting and training a potent army of Spaniards, and collecting a huge war chest derived from Spain's rich mines. The Romans were much too involved in other matters to pay attention to Carthage's recovery: organizing Corsica and Sardinia, which had been treacherously seized from Carthage; extending Roman control into the Po Valley; coping with plebeian agitation for fairer distribution of public land; and curbing piracy in the Adriatic Sea. When they did finally turn their attention to the rising power of Carthage in Spain, their efforts to intervene there soon led to a new war with Carthage.

The Second Punic War (218–201 B.C.) was Rome's sternest military test, due in large part to the genius of Hannibal. Rome's initial plan to attack the Carthaginians in Spain and Africa was totally negated by Hannibal's bold counterstroke: the dispatch of a major army on a thousand-mile march from Spain to invade Italy. His strategy centered on depriving Rome of the manpower provided by its Italian allies, who, Hannibal presumed, would be glad to rid themselves of the Roman yoke. On three different occasions between 218 and 216 B.C. the Romans challenged him with large armies, only to be crushed each time. The last and most disastrous of these battles, at Cannae, convinced the Romans that they could not match Hannibal in open battle. They adopted a policy of harassing his army, otherwise leaving him free to do as he pleased in Italy. Until 203 B.C.—a total of fifteen years—Hannibal maintained an army in Italy and spread destruction up and down the peninsula; this was a remarkable feat in view of the fact that he received almost no reinforcements or supplies from Carthage or Spain. But he failed to achieve what he had counted on to defeat Rome: He never persuaded a decisive number of Rome's Italian allies to desert.

While holding Hannibal at bay in Italy, Rome mounted an offensive on many fronts and actually won the war outside Italy. Large armies sent to Spain slowly crushed Carthaginian power and cut off Hannibal's reinforcements. Another Roman force was dispatched to Sicily to choke off a rebellion of Greek city-states led by Syracuse in support of Carthage. Roman naval forces patrolled the western Mediterranean and the Adriatic, preventing Hannibal from getting help from Carthage or its chief ally, the kingdom of Macedon. The Romans encouraged African peoples to attack Carthaginian territories. Rome's counteroffensive culminated in 205 B.C., when a large army under Scipio Africanus was sent to Africa. In him, Rome had found a military talent equal to that of Hannibal, who was recalled from Italy in 203 B.C. to save Carthage. But even he could no longer stem the tide: He met Scipio in a battle in 202 B.C. at Zama and suffered a complete defeat.

After Zama, the Carthaginians sued for peace. They were forced to surrender Spain to Rome, to destroy their navy, to accept a heavy fine to be paid over the next fifty years, and to agree never again to wage war outside Africa and within Africa only with Rome's permission. Part of Carthage's African territory was turned over to Numidia, a state Rome hoped would balance Carthaginian power in Africa. Carthage was reduced to a minor power; victorious Rome was dominant in the western Mediterranean.

4. OVERSEAS EXPANSION: THE EASTERN MEDITERRANEAN, 200–133 B.C.

Even before the victory over Carthage had been sealed, Rome was being drawn into the turbulent world of the eastern Mediterranean (see Map 8.2). Although Roman leaders stoutly protested that Rome's engagement there was a "just" cause undertaken to ensure Rome's safety and to protect Roman allies, powerful forces were at work to generate an expansionist policy in the east. As we shall see later, aristocratic Roman society was increasingly enchanted by Greek culture, causing many to feel deeply the need to protect the Greek city-states in which it had originated. The Punic Wars had demonstrated to Roman politicians that leadership in victorious wars was an assurance of fame and power, as illustrated by the career of the immensely popular Scipio Africanus. Equally obvious to all Romans was the fact that successful warfare brought vast riches to Rome in the form of indemnities, tribute, and booty. Developments in the east encouraged many there to turn to "the rising cloud in the west" for help. By 200 B.C. the fragile balance of power that had existed in the Hellenistic world since the partition of Alexander's empire in the early third century was breaking down. Aggressive leaders, such as Philip V of Macedon and Antiochus III of the Seleucid Empire, sought to capitalize on the progressively unstable situation by enlarging their spheres of influence. To many in the east Rome's intervention seemed the only hope for safety against these aggresssors.

Rome's first involvement in the east came during the trying times of the Second Punic War. Seeking to deny the Carthaginians access to the Adriatic Sea, the Romans took steps that challenged the interests of the Illyrians, who controlled the eastern Adriatic coast. Led by an able and ambitious queen, Teuta, the Illyrians resisted and forced Rome to establish a protectorate over the coastal areas. A little later, a new threat arose when Philip V of Macedon formed an alliance with Carthage. As a counterbalance, Rome entered into alliances of friendship with several Greek city-states, especially the Aetolian League. These ventures increased the Roman awareness of possible dangers from the East and led to more serious involvement. In 201 B.C. Pergamum, Rhodes, and several Greek city-states appealed to Rome for help against what they argued was Philip V's threat to their freedom. Although the war-weary Roman populace opposed involvement, the ruling oligarchy, led by the pro-Greek Scipio Africanus, declared war on Philip V in 200 B.C. and within three years defeated his forces. Philip was then required to refrain from further involvement in Greek affairs. Amid considerable fanfare and with understandable praise from the Greeks, the Romans reaffirmed the autonomy of each Greek city-state, which henceforth would be a Roman ally. The "liberators" of Greece then withdrew without annexing any territory or demanding any tribute.

Peace in the east was brief. In 192 B.C. Antiochus III invaded the Greek peninsula at the urging of the Aetolian League, the members of which were angry at their Roman ally for not rewarding them sufficiently for their assistance in the recent war against Philip V. Rome again sent its armies east, moved in part by the fact that Hannibal was serving as military adviser to the Seleucid army. The Roman legions drove Antiochus out of Greece and in 189 B.C. inflicted a crushing defeat on him at the battle of Magnesia in Asia Minor. He was required to keep out of Asia Minor, his fleet was destroyed, and a staggering indemnity was imposed. Rome turned over large areas of Asia Minor to Pergamum and Rhodes and sanctioned them as Roman-backed peacekeepers. Most of the Greek city-states were restored to independence, although those that had aided Antiochus were fined and forced to surrender some territory to Greek city-states that had remained loyal to Rome. Again the victors annexed no lands.

Rome's peacekeeping efforts in the east led only to further frustration. The reduction of the kingdom of Macedon and the Seleucid state to secondary importance finally destroyed the balance of power in the east and opened the way to rivalry, intrigue, and strife among the petty states of the area. Even the Greeks, whom the Romans had "saved," proved treacherous and unreliable. As the chaos mounted, so did the appeals to Rome for intervention. The lure of imperialistic ventures coupled with growing impatience with their fickle allies in the east slowly pushed the Romans toward a more drastic solution: direct Roman rule in the east.

The Kingdom of Macedon was the first to experience the new policy. Macedonian efforts to curry favor among the Greek city-states led to another Macedonian war from 171–167 B.C. In the settlement following Rome's victory the Macedonian monarchy was abolished and the kingdom divided into four weak republics. A few years later a minor disturbance in Macedon led the Romans to annex the entire territory as a tribute-paying province under a Roman governor. Persistent intrigue and disturbances among the Greek city-states resulted in increasingly stern Roman reprisals, culminating in 146 B.C. with the savage destruction of Corinth as an example to all Greeks. By that date Rome had forced pro-Roman governments on most of the Greek city-states. Now the governor of the Macedonian province was charged with supervising the affairs of the Greek city-states, thus ending their freedom. Rome's chief allies in Asia Minor, Pergamum and Rhodes, proved equally unreliable and troublesome, resulting in harsh measures against them by Rome that greatly weakened them. Finally, in 133 B.C., the king of Pergamum willed his weakened kingdom to the Romans, who accepted it as a province. Once established in Asia, rich prizes tempted Rome: Ptolemaic Egypt and the Seleucid kingom, both too weak to offer effective resistance to the Romans.

While concentrating its attention chiefly on the east between 200 and 133 B.C., Rome continued to solidify its power in the west. The occupation of Spain and its organization into two provinces required a long and testing struggle against native resistance. The area of northern Italy between the Alps and the Apennines, called Cisalpine Gaul, was organized into a province. And the Romans finally settled the score with their ancient enemy, Carthage. Although Carthage was no longer a serious threat, fear of it continued to haunt Rome and prompted actions to humiliate what was now a minor state. The final step occurred in 149 B.C., when Rome declared war on Carthage on the pretext that the Carthaginians had violated the terms of the treaty ending the Second Punic War; Carthage's crime was taking up arms to protect itself against incessant harassment by the Kingdom of Numidia, a North African ally of Rome. After a heroic defense Carthage was captured and destroyed in 146 B.C., and its territory was annexed as a Roman province. The destruction of Carthage was a fitting symbol of Rome's position in the Mediterranean world as the second century B.C. drew to a close. With provinces on three continents and with unbeatable military forces, the city-state on the Tiber could speak of the Mediterranean as "our sea." The fate of civilization was now in Roman hands.

SUGGESTED READING

Overview of Roman History

Karl Christ, *The Romans: An Introduction to Their History and Civilization*, trans. Christopher Holme (1984). A fine survey.

Early Italy

Jorgen C. Meyer, *Pre-Republican Rome: An Analysis of the Cultural and Chronological Relations, 1000–500 B.C.* (1983). Relying on archaeological evidence, this challenging work throws important light on the origins of Rome.

Massimo Pallotino, *A History of Earliest Italy* (1991). A good up-to-date synthesis.

R. M. Ogilivie, *Early Rome and the Etruscans* (1976).

Michael Grant, *The Etruscans* (1980).

Ellen MacNamara, *The Etruscans* (1991).

Maja Sprenger, *The Etruscans: Their History, Art, and Architecture* (1983).

Any of the above works will provide a clear picture of Etruscan society and its impact on Rome.

The Republic to 133 B.C.

H. H. Scullard, *History of the Roman World from 753 B.C. to 146 B.C.*, 4th ed. (1980). A detailed account.

Michael Crawford, *The Roman Republic* (1978). A challenging account of political developments with interesting interpretations.

Arthur Keaveney, *Rome and the Unification of Italy* (1987). Treats how Italy was forged into a single community.

R. Develin, *The Practice of Politics at Rome, 366–167 B.C.* (1985).

Richard E. Mitchell, *Patricians and Plebeians: The Origin of the Roman State* (1990).

These two works treat the formation of the republican regime.

R. M. Errington, *The Dawn of Empire: Rome's Rise to World Power* (1972).

William V. Harris, *War and Imperialism in Republican Rome, 327–70 B.C.* (1979).

These two titles deal with the forces that led to Roman expansion and with its effects on Roman society.

Erich S. Gruen, *The Hellenistic World and the Coming of Rome*, 2 vols. (1984). A detailed study explaining how and why the Hellenistic world came under Roman sway.

B. H. Warmington, *Carthage*, 2nd rev. ed. (1969). A fine treatment of the history of Rome's greatest foe.

Nigel Bagnall, *The Punic Wars* (1990). An excellent treatment of the military history of the Punic Wars.

Biographies

Ernle Bradford, *Hannibal* (1981).

H. H. Scullard, *Scipio Africanus: Soldier and Politician* (1970).

CHAPTER 9

The Failure of the Roman Republic, 133–31 B.C.

FIGURE 9.1 A Roman Warship Warships such as the one shown in this relief, created to celebrate Octavian's victory over Antony and Cleopatra at Actium in 31 B.C., played a major role in establishing Roman dominance over the Mediterranean world during the era of the republic. Control over fleets of such ships and the soldiers they carried was also a prime factor in the rise of the military strongmen—such as Sulla, Pompey, Julius Caesar, and Octavian—to positions that allowed them to end the republic. (Alinari/Art Resource)

Rome's rise to dominance in the Mediterranean world during the period 265–133 B.C. had understandably generated confidence among the Roman citizenry, especially the ruling oligarchy, that the political and social system of the republic was not only successful but also capable of meeting any situation. Developments after 133 B.C. proved that such confidence was misplaced. During the next century a series of crises tested that system beyond its capabilities and ultimately left the long-established system of the Roman Republic in ruins.

1. THE BURDENS OF A WORLD POWER

At the root of the crises that afflicted Rome after 133 B.C. were complex problems, some rooted in the nature of the republican order but most a result of Rome's expansion from a small city-state to a large empire. Many of them were neglected during the heady era of triumphant expansion prior to 133 B.C., but eventually they surfaced to create a succession of crises that dominated the history of the last century of the republic.

First, Rome's conquests had by 133 B.C. created a long and ill-defined frontier which faced out toward potentially dangerous enemies, as well as inviting territories still open for conquest (see Map 8.2). While a part-time army composed of Roman citizens and Italian allies had conquered this vast empire, the problem of establishing a military system to defend the empire's boundaries had not been faced.

Second, there was the problem of how the several million conquered subjects would be governed and treated. In contrast to the enlightened policy originally applied to the Italian population, the Romans increasingly viewed conquered non-Italians as subjects to be exploited. Annexed territories were organized into provinces. Control over each province was entrusted to a Roman governor invested with absolute military and civil power; little attention was given to holding these governors accountable. The residents of each province were subject to heavy tribute, the collection of which was entrusted to tax farmers (called *publicans*) who paid the Roman government what it expected from each province and then extorted all they could from the provincials, often in collusion with the governors. The voiceless victims had virtually no way of protecting themselves against their masters. This abusive system disrupted order among the provincials and bred discontent, resistance, and hatred.

Third, Rome's Italian allies, whose military service played a key role in Rome's conquests, were increasingly disregarded. Not only did they benefit little from the fruits of conquest, but the prospect of citizenship implicit in Rome's earlier arrangements also grew increasingly remote. As a consequence, the allies became restless and rebellious.

Fourth, ominous trends began to emerge during the third and second centuries B.C. that pointed toward a significant transformation of the traditional economic system. Rome was greatly enriched by the influx of tribute exacted from conquered peoples. Most of that wealth fell into the hands of a small segment of the population. The beneficiaries not only developed a taste for luxurious living but also sought new opportunities for investment. Trade and manufacturing investments absorbed some of this wealth, but not enough to expand manufacturing production in Italy significantly. Although Roman aristocrats generally disdained trading as unworthy of their status, other Romans began to involve themselves in the extensive commercial activity existing in territories conquered by Rome. Their involvement slowly began to reveal that Rome's continuing prosperity was becoming dependent on the economic well-being of the entire Mediterranean world. Little mindful of this development, most rich aristocrats preferred to invest their new wealth in land and money lending.

Changes affecting agriculture offered them ample opportunity. The traditional Italian agricultural system, based on the small, independent farm tilled by a freeholder and his family and devoted to cereal crops, was eroding. Competition from cheaper grain imported as tribute from more productive provinces debased the income of cereal farmers. Many small farms were ruined as a result of the devastation caused by Hannibal's wars in Italy and the long absence of their owners in military service in far-off places. Often these citizen-soldiers borrowed to save their land, only to find themselves dispossessed for failure to repay their loans. Enterprising Romans with capital began to create large estates (called *latifundia*) by buying or seizing the land of impoverished small farmers and by using political influence to lay claim to public land. These new agricultural units concentrated on the production of cash crops such as grapes, olives, and livestock. Increasingly the labor supply on the *latifundia* was provided by slaves, most of whom were victims of Rome's wars of conquest, or by formerly independent farmers forced to become tenant farmers or hired laborers. The real victims of this transformation of agricultural life were Roman citizens and Roman allies whose loyal service as soldiers had won Rome's empire.

These trends, which heralded a fundamental transformation of the economic system of the Roman Republic, contributed to a fifth set of problems of a social nature. Down to the mid–third century B.C. the Roman social order had been relatively simple. Atop the social structure stood a small circle of nobles of both patrician and plebeian origin whose authority was based on family connections, control of political life, and landed wealth. Below them was the rest of the citizen body, chiefly freeholding farmers, whose economic and social status made them equals. But changing times slowly introduced complexity and tensions into that simple order. As already noted, the aristocrats became richer; their wealth allowed a style of life that distanced them from the rest of the population. Their virtually unchallenged monopoly over political life tended to focus their attention on competition with other members of their group for power and prestige and to dull their concern for the fate of the bulk of the population. Although these *nobiles* were firmly entrenched at the top of society, they were increasingly challenged by a new group known as *equites*. The members of this group were wealthy entrepreneurs who grew rich as military suppliers, organizers of large-scale trading ventures, building contractors, bankers, and provincial tax collectors. Their economic interests were intimately linked to public policies with respect to war, provincial administration, public works, and taxation. Consequently, the *equites* were increasingly anxious for a share of political power and for social recognition.

Changing economic conditions began to cre-ate social distinctions within the ranks of the plebeian population, once a fairly homogeneous group. Many rural plebeians survived as independent farmers but benefited little from Italy's growing prosperity. The inexorable changes affecting agriculture forced increasing numbers of the rural populace to become tenants or hired laborers, with a consequent lowering of their social status. Others in growing numbers left their farms for the cities, especially Rome, to seek a livelihood as artisans, shopkeepers, and laborers; their new condition changed their economic and social needs and concerns. Many citizens who flocked to Rome became members of what the Romans called the proletariat, a rootless, restless population endowed with rights of citizenship but victims of an unstable economic life and an uncertain social status. This volatile "mob," its members ever more dependent on the state or rich patrons for their livelihood, offered a tantalizing power base for ambitious political leaders. At the bottom of the social scale was an expanding slave population; its presence not only helped depress the economic condition of free citizen-farmers but also put a stigma on the menial labor required to sustain Roman society. The stresses building up in this increasingly complex social structure had the potential to disrupt the internal order of the Roman Republic.

Finally, by 133 B.C., there were significant signs that a transformation of the collective mentality of the Roman citizenry was in progress, pointing toward an erosion of confidence in ancient values and an opening of minds to the need for change. The expanding awareness of a world larger and more diverse than Rome not only undermined but even made ridiculous and senseless a narrow dedication to the traditions of a single city-state. As we shall see later in discussing Roman cultural life (Chapter 11), a significant segment of aristocratic society began to experience a broadening of their intellectual horizons as a result of their growing familiarity with Hellenistic culture and the style of life their new wealth permitted. Especially potent in reshaping their values was their encounter with classical Greek literature and Hellenistic philosophical systems such as Epicureanism and Stoicism. Many Romans were captivated by the emotional, individualistic mystery religions from the east. With good reason many groups—the peasantry, the urban population, the *equites*—began to lose faith in the ability of the republican political order to further their interests. Incessant military involvement engendered a disturbing tolerance for violence and arrogance. These currents made the Roman populace less willing to abide by traditional values and moral standards, the "customs of their forefathers" associated with the simpler, more rustic world of the early republic.

These problems created a dangerous situation that required innovative political action. The burden of meeting that challenge rested in the hands of a narrow oligarchy, which by 133 B.C. had established an unchallenged control over Roman political life. There were, however, ominous signs that the traditional consensus within the ranks of the *nobiles* was in danger of dissolving. Ambitious members of that group sought wealth, political and military honors, and cultural distinctions that would exalt them over their aristocratic peers. Although the ruling oligarchy sought to curb such tendencies, there remained the danger that rivalries among the *nobiles* would become another disruptive force. Could that caste utilize political institutions and processes originally shaped to govern a small city-state to find solutions to complex problems rooted in the realities dictated by Rome's rule over an extensive empire? The search for an answer led to a political upheaval that ultimately destroyed the Roman Republic.

2. ATTEMPTED REFORMS AND FACTIONAL STRUGGLES, 133–79 B.C.

The ordeal of the republic opened with an effort to institute reforms aimed at resolving some of the critical problems facing Rome. That effort quickly devolved into a struggle between two factions over how the political process should work in reaching decisions about critical issues. On one side was a group known as the *optimates* (the "best"), who represented the established ruling oligarchy and whose members believed that decision making should remain where it had always been—in the hands of the Senate and the elected magistrates drawn from the *nobiles*. Opposed was a faction known as the *populares* (the "people"), who sought to involve a broader

range of the citizen body in political decisions, utilizing for that purpose the ancient political tools of the "people"—the tribunes and the Assembly of Tribes. The *populares* were usually led by men of noble origin, who often were motivated by a mixture of genuine concern for Rome and ambitions to advance their careers. To achieve these ends, they appealed to the plebeian citizens, especially those living in Rome, and the *equites* to use their votes to shape political decisions.

The initial engagement in the struggle for reform and power occurred between 133 and 121 B.C., when the brothers Tiberius and Gaius Gracchus took up the cause of the *populares*. Aristocratic, well educated, and ambitious, the Gracchi were deeply troubled by the threat posed to Rome's military resources and to the safety of the state by the declining numbers of citizen-farmers who could afford to perform military service. Elected tribune for 133 B.C., Tiberius proposed a land law aimed at enforcing an older law that limited the amount of public land any citizen could hold. Land recovered by the application of this law would be redistributed to landless citizens. Although Tiberius' measure had some support in the Senate, it threatened the wealth of many *nobiles,* who over many generations had blatantly disregarded the existing law to take possession of most of the public lands. In order to pass his proposal, Tiberius resorted to political tactics that were not unconstitutional but that ran counter to the way in which decisions were customarily made. He used his power as tribune to put the land law before the Assembly of Tribes, which approved the measure without senatorial approval. When Tiberius tried to apply his land law, the Senate attempted to thwart him by withholding funding. Tiberius responded by threatening to divert revenues from the provinces for this purpose, a measure that challenged the Senate's traditional control over public finances and foreign affairs. Finally, Tiberius sought reelection as tribune in order to complete his reform. Since such reelection ran contrary to the custom that forbade elected officials to hold office in successive years, the Senate raised the charge that Tiberius was seeking to become a dictator. This inflammatory accusation led to violence and the murder of Tiberius at the hands of those calling themselves "the best." After Tiberius' death the application of his land law went forward, suggesting that the substance of the law was not the real issue. Instead, at the heart of the struggle was the threat to the Senate's monopoly on political power posed by Tiberius' political tactics, especially his appeal to the "people" for support.

A decade after Tiberius' death the reform issue was raised again by his brother Gaius. Elected tribune for 122 B.C., Gaius put forward a much more comprehensive program than that of Tiberius. He persuaded the Assembly of Tribes to pass legislation providing for new land laws, cheap grain at public expense for Rome's urban populace, the establishment of colonies for the resettlement of poor Romans, expanded political privileges for the Italian allies, and greater control by the *equites* over provincial tax collection. These measures, which were aimed at creating broad popular support for Gaius, aroused bitter opposition from the *optimates*, who again resorted to violence, which this time claimed the lives of Gaius and three thousand of his followers.

Although the death of Gaius Gracchus left the *populares* leaderless for more than a decade, the Gracchi had formulated a broad reform program that in the future would provide ambitious leaders with a wide range of issues upon which to build popular support. A leader capable of exploiting this situation soon appeared: Marius (ca. 155–86 B.C.). A wealthy man of nonnoble origin with small prospects of a major political role, Marius took advantage of a military crisis to gain power. The occasion was a badly managed war undertaken by Rome against Jugurtha, a claimant to the throne of Numidia, a client kingdom of Rome in North Africa. Growing impatience with the failure of Roman armies to defeat Jugurtha and charges that this clever, unscrupulous king was holding his own through bribery of Roman officials generated widespread unrest in Rome. Playing upon suspicions of corruption in the Senate and proclaiming his support for *populares* reforms, Marius succeeded in winning the consulship for 107 B.C. He then persuaded the Assembly of Tribes to vote him command of the army in Numidia. In recruiting troops for his campaign, Marius took a bold and fateful step. Disregarding the traditional property qualifications for military service, he enlisted large numbers of propertyless volunteers attracted by promises of rewards from their general. The first step had been taken in the creation of private armies as a political tool.

Marius quickly justified the trust placed in him by defeating Jugurtha in 105 B.C. Then he was annually reelected as consul during the years between 104 and 101 B.C. to conduct campaigns against Germanic tribes threatening northern Italy and southern Gaul. Again Marius was successful, in no small part because of his skill in professionalizing his volunteer army; his efforts marked an important step toward resolving the problem of defending Rome's frontiers. While he earned fame as a general, Marius' *populares* allies asserted pressure on the Roman government to provide land allocations for his veterans. However, in 100 B.C., during his sixth term as consul, Marius was maneuvered by the Senate into using armed force to curb the increasingly violent actions of his own political allies. This action temporarily ended his grip on power.

The decade of the nineties was relatively quiet, perhaps because moderate elements in the Senate took measures to respond to critical problems. However, two issues defied these efforts and provided fuel for the next crisis. One was the festering problem of the Italian allies, long discontented over Rome's failure to expand their rights in recognition of their contribution to military conquests and increasingly impoverished by the decline of small-farm agriculture. To relieve their situation, the allies demanded full citizenship. Although Roman leaders from Gaius Gracchus onward had often proposed such a step, the Romans repeatedly refused to share the rewards of citizenship with their allies. When one more such proposal was voted down in 91 B.C., the allies joined in a great rebellion, sometimes called the Social War, which threatened Rome's very existence. Sulla (138–78 B.C.), a noble who had established a reputation while serving under Marius in the war against Jugurtha, was chosen to lead the army raised to suppress the uprising. By 89 B.C. Sulla defeated the rebels, whose cause was undermined when the Romans finally granted citizenship to the allies. For his success Sulla was elected consul for 88 B.C.

While the Social War was in progress, Rome faced another threat caused by the corruption-ridden, oppressive system of provincial administration. In 89 B.C. Mithradates VI, king of Pontus in Asia Minor, played on this discontent to launch a war of liberation in Asia Minor and Greece. Faced with the threat of loss of its empire in the east, the Senate charged Sulla with leading a campaign against Mithradates. However, a faction of *populares* leaders defied the Senate to vote the command to Marius. Sulla responded by marching his army to Rome, crushing the *populares*, and securing the command by force. His actions left little doubt where the real power lay.

Once in control, Sulla led his army to the east. He forced Mithradates to return to his old kingdom and reestablished Roman control over the eastern provinces. But he made no decisive settlement in the east; his eyes were on Rome, where developments threatening his career were unfolding. Immediately after his departure for the east, the *populares* under Marius forced their way back into power and imposed a reign of terror on the Senate. They dominated until 83 B.C., when Sulla returned to Italy, greatly enriched by booty seized in the east. His battle-tested soldiers routed the *populares*, whose leader had died in 86 B.C. To seal his victory, Sulla ordered the murder of thousands of citizens from all over Italy identified with the *populares* cause and the confiscation of their property, much of which was used to reward his soldiers and political supporters.

Having established dominance by force of arms, Sulla had himself appointed as dictator. Intent on restoring control of the republic to the Senate, he enacted legislation that severely limited the power of the tribunes and the Assembly of Tribes to initiate legislation. The size of the Senate was doubled, many of the new seats being granted to *equites* and upper-class Italians. Steps were taken to regularize the election procedures for the magistracies, to improve the administration of justice, and to organize provincial government more efficiently—all sources of political agitation. Confident that he had restored the ancient constitution with the Senate in control, Sulla retired from public life in 79 B.C. In fact, the Senate was in power only because a powerful military leader had decreed so. The bitter clash between *optimates* and *populares* had resolved few of Rome's basic problems. Rather, the struggle had created a situation that encouraged bold, ambitious individuals to exploit those problems to gain control of the real source of power: military forces and political followings. The republican form of government had suffered a mortal blow.

3. THE ERA OF MILITARY STRONGMEN, 79–31 B.C.

The Senate proved itself unable to bear the burden thrust upon it by Sulla. Its failures created successive opportunities for "strongmen" to control Roman political life during the half century following Sulla. The decade between 79 and 70 B.C. witnessed several serious crises: a revolt in Italy led by a disaffected consul seeking to undo Sulla's reforms; a rebellion in Spain organized by a disillusioned Roman governor who enjoyed widespread native support; a slave uprising in Italy led by a professional gladiator named Spartacus; a mounting threat from pirates to the grain supply for Rome; and a new war with Mithradates VI of Pontus. The Senate responded to these challenges with a singular lack of political imagination: It granted extraordinary powers to ambitious individuals in a fashion that left the Senate little opportunity to control their actions. A protégé of Sulla, Pompey (106–48 B.C.), was given command of forces to deal first with the Italian revolt and then with the insurrection in Spain (see Figure 9.2). Crassus (ca. 115–53 B.C.), a rich moneylender and real estate speculator ambitious for a political career, was charged with suppressing the slave revolt. Both were successful, and although neither was constitutionally eligible for office, they used their military followings to secure election to the consulship for 70 B.C.

During their co-consulship, Pompey and Crassus negated most of Sulla's settlement; their enactments, applauded by the remnants of the *populares*, restored the opportunity for ambitious leaders to exploit popular support as a path to power. But after their term ended neither Pompey nor Crassus was satisfied. Pompey was the first to move toward greater power. By manipulating Rome's political factions, he persuaded the Senate and the people to vote him two important military commands: In 67 B.C. he was granted sweeping powers to clear the Mediterranean of pirates, a task he completed in a matter of months. Then, in 66 B.C., he was voted com-

FIGURE 9.2 Pompey and Julius Caesar These two men, Pompey (left) and Julius Caesar (right), virtually controlled the destiny of the Roman Republic and the Mediterranean world between 79 and 44 B.C. Their busts reflect the talent of Roman sculptors in portraiture. (Pompey, Culver Pictures; Julius Caesar, Alinari/Art Resource)

mand of the army fighting against Mithradates, who since 74 B.C. had again challenged Rome's rule in Asia Minor. Pompey quickly defeated Mithradates. He then took it upon himself to reorganize Rome's position in the east. The territories that formerly had comprised the kingdoms of Bithynia and Pontus were annexed to Rome and combined to create a new province. Still another new province was established in Syria (see Map 8.2), a step that in effect ended the Seleucid kingdom. To protect the eastern provinces, he worked out a series of agreements with small kingdoms beyond Rome's new eastern frontier, making each a client of Rome charged with protecting the frontier in return for Roman support in maintaining each king's power over his subjects. One group cast roughly in that role was the

Jewish community in Judea, the governance of which was entrusted to a high priest expected to support Roman interests. Pompey also regulated tribute collecting in the east so as to greatly increase the return to the Roman government. His efforts represented a major step in solidifying provincial administration; they also won Pompey important support from Romans who had interests in the east, especially *equites* engaged in provincial tax collection and in trade in the east.

Pompey's success, reminiscent of Sulla's rise to power, drove other ambitious politicians to maneuver to check him. A key figure in this endeavor was Crassus, who found a skilled ally in Julius Caesar (100–44 B.C.), a man of patrician origins but with family connections that linked him with Marius and the *populares* cause (see

Figure 9.2). Crassus and Caesar promoted laws to attract popular support and spent huge sums in an attempt to secure extraordinary military commands such as those held by Pompey. Their maneuvers were resisted by the Senate, supported in its effort by Cicero (106–43 B.C.), a "new" man who clawed his way to the consulship for 63 B.C. by utilizing his skills as an orator and lawyer. His finest hour as consul came when he earned public acclaim for foiling an alleged conspiracy by Cataline, a frustrated power seeker and sometime agent of Crassus, to overthrow the system. While Cicero shared the ambition for power with most other political leaders of his time, he disdained one-man rule in favor of a "concord of orders" that would link the talents of the old aristocracy and the *equites* into a new ruling force capable of curbing demogogic rabble-rousers and strong-armed generals.

Finally, in 62 B.C., Pompey returned from the east. Contrary to expectations, his first act was to disband his army and request that the Senate reward his veterans and legalize the settlement he had made in the east. Under the leadership of intractable conservatives, the Senate chose a course that drove Pompey, Crassus, and Caesar into a political alliance. It not only refused to meet Pompey's requests but also acted to curb a major source of Crassus' wealth by restricting the activities of provincial tax farmers and to discredit Caesar by blocking his election to the consulship. Equally frustrated, the three joined in an informal secret agreement, called the First Triumvirate, designed to ensure that each obtained what he wished. Exploiting his growing popular appeal and with the support of Pompey and Crassus, Caesar won the consulship for 59 B.C. Once in office, he forced through measures that satisfied his fellow triumvirs. His reward was a five-year military command to look after Roman interests on its northern frontier in Gaul and Illyria.

During the decade after 59 B.C. Rome's political destiny hinged on the actions of the triumvirs. During the first years of the decade the triumvirate held together uneasily. It was renewed in 56 B.C. with the understanding that Pompey and Crassus would be consuls for 55 B.C. and then be granted governorships of important provinces under terms that would provide them command over armies. Caesar's com-

mand in Gaul was also extended for five years. But the arrangement was increasingly shaky. Caesar proved to be a brilliant military leader, exploiting local political conditions in Gaul to create opportunities for military campaigns that added Gaul as a Roman province and took Roman armies into Germany and Britain. Not only did these highly publicized victories enhance Caesar's reputation, they also allowed him to create a disciplined personal army totally devoted to his cause. Crassus' long search for fame came to an end in 53 B.C., when he was killed leading an unsuccessful campaign against a Roman foe in the east, the Parthians. An important link between Caesar and Pompey was broken in 54 B.C. with the death of Pompey's wife, Julia, the daughter of Caesar. Caesar's growing fame fed a familiar fear in Rome—that of a victorious general returning to impose his will. Pompey increasingly won the favor of the Senate as its protector against such an eventuality and was voted powers that made him virtual dictator. Amid the heightening tension fed by the fear of Caesar and by the violent mob actions fomented in Rome by his agents seeking to protect his interests, Pompey and the Senate moved to ruin Caesar. As his command in Gaul approached its legal end, Caesar sought to run in absentia for the consulship for 49 B.C. so that he could remain in public office and avoid prosecution for alleged illegal acts which his foes claimed he had committed during his service in Gaul. Early in 49 B.C. the Senate decreed that he must surrender his command in Gaul, and Pompey was empowered to take necessary action to protect the state. Rather than face political ruin, Caesar chose to defy the state. He led his legions across the Rubicon River separating Gaul from Italy and plunged Rome into a civil war.

Caesar quickly demonstrated his military genius in guiding his seasoned veterans against the larger forces of Pompey. In a succession of campaigns in Italy, Spain, and finally Greece, he battered Pompey's forces. The defeated Pompey finally fled to Egypt, where he was murdered. Caesar used this crime against a Roman citizen as a pretext to intervene in Egypt, where a struggle for control of the crown was in progress among members of the Ptolemaic family. Caesar supported the claims of Cleopatra against her brother-husband, Ptolemy XIV. Perhaps his decision was prompted by the fact that he had become Cleopatra's lover; but more likely he hoped that by putting the young princess on the throne, he could dominate the last independent Hellenistic kingdom and tap Egypt's fabulous wealth for Rome's benefit. His position secured in Egypt, Caesar continued his triumphant march through the empire—Asia, Africa, Spain—hunting down Pompey's allies and showing his own power. Finally, in 45 B.C., he returned to Rome as undisputed master of the Roman world.

Although Caesar's real power rested on his loyal army, he made an effort to legalize his authority. Despite being elected consul several times, he relied chiefly on the office of dictator as the basis for his actions. He allowed the traditional elective offices to be filled, but with men willing to bend to his command. The Senate was greatly enlarged, the new places being filled with Caesar's supporters. As a consequence, that venerable institution became little more than an advisory council to the dictator. On the basis of his dictatorial power, Caesar assumed control of crucial areas of government previously dominated by the Senate: public finances, provincial administration, command over the military forces. A grateful citizenry heaped a wide range of honors on him, creating around him the aura of superiority over other citizens. In many ways Caesar's position in Rome resembled that of a Hellenistic king; indeed, some of Caesar's contemporaries insisted that it was his intention to establish a monarchy in Rome.

In using these powers, Caesar demonstrated qualities of statesmanship to match his military genius. During his brief rule over Rome, he began shaping a reform program that addressed some of the major problems plaguing Rome: reduction of the number of citizens dependent on the dole by resettling them in the provinces; debt regulation; suppression of mob violence in Rome; aid to Italian farmers; improvement of provincial administration; extension of citizenship to some provincials; reorganization of local government in Italy to allow greater local autonomy. It is not clear, however, whether he planned to reshape the structure of the political system to meet Rome's responsibilities as ruler of the Mediterranean world. Perhaps given more time, Caesar would have faced this issue, but that was not to be. A hard core of conservatives, including

such former supporters of Caesar as Cassius and Brutus, formed a conspiracy to end what they saw as a threat to the traditional order. These guardians of "right" order struck their blow for liberty on the Ides of March (March 15), 44 B.C., stabbing Caesar to death while he was attending a Senate meeting just prior to his departure for a major campaign against the Parthians.

Death caused war

Caesar's murder did not lead to the restoration of the old order; rather, it produced a new civil war among rivals seeking to replace Caesar. Two candidates emerged as the main contenders. One was Mark Antony (ca. 83–30 B.C.), an experienced politician who had served Caesar as a military commander. The other was eighteen-year-old Octavian, a distant relative whom Caesar had adopted as his son. Faced with efforts by the Senate to eliminate them from power, Antony and Octavian, along with another supporter of Caesar named Lepidus, joined forces in 43 B.C. to form the Second Triumvirate and to force the Senate and people to grant them joint absolute power in the state. Within a year the triumvirs brutally murdered most of the anti-Caesar senatorial forces, including Cicero, and conducted a military campaign in Greece that destroyed the armies raised by Caesar's assassins, two of whom—Cassius and Brutus—died at the decisive battle of Philippi in 42 B.C.

After 42 B.C. Antony, Octavian, and Lepidus continued to rule Rome jointly under the powers voted them in the legislation that had established the Second Triumvirate. Actually, each was making preparations to destroy the others. Antony spent most of these years in the east, seeking to strengthen Roman control there and to mount a war against the Parthians. Although he made some progress in these endeavors, his standing in the Roman world was increasingly tainted by his involvement with Cleopatra, for whom he eventually repudiated his Roman wife—none other than Octavian's sister—and by whom he had two sons. This liaison was cleverly exploited by Octavian to portray Antony as a mad traitor and the pitiful victim of a crafty eastern harlot intent on robbing Rome of its territories to advance her own power and reward her children.

Octavian uses affair

Octavian proved more adept at building a power base. Under the arrangement agreed upon by the triumvirs, he was charged with the heavy responsibilities of providing land for the veterans from the large army that had defeated the forces of Caesar's assassins, of rooting out the powerful remnants of anti-Caesar forces in the west, and of coping with the official government still operating in Rome. He worked patiently to meet these challenges, doing so in a way that gave him a solid hold over Italy and the west. Along the way, he forced Lepidus to retire from the triumvirate. Gradually, Octavian came to be looked upon as the protector of Roman interests against Antony, increasingly portrayed by Octavian's clever propaganda as an enemy of Rome. By 32 B.C. Octavian felt strong enough to refuse to rule jointly with Antony and declared war on Cleopatra. The decisive engagement between the huge armies and navies of the protagonists was fought in 31 B.C. at Actium in Greece (see Figure 9.1). Octavian's forces won an easy victory. The triumphant leader pursued Antony and Cleopatra to Egypt, where Cleopatra made one final effort to entice a Roman to support her cause. When Octavian would have none of her favors, she committed suicide, as Antony had already done. Her kingdom was annexed as a Roman province. Again the Roman world had an undisputed ruler whose sword had raised him to a position comparable to that Caesar had enjoyed in 46 B.C. Rome's future depended on what victorious Octavian would decide to do.

4. THE FRUITS OF CIVIC STRIFE

In many ways the events transpiring between the attempted reforms by the Gracchi begun in 133 B.C. and Octavian's victory in 31 B.C. marked a terrible chapter in human history. Civil strife, fomented by ruthless power seekers and abetted by factions seeking to serve self-interests, cost countless lives, loss of property, disruption of livelihoods, dissolution of traditional social bonds, and constant insecurity in every rank of society and across the vast territory that Rome controlled. Nor did Octavian's victory offer his contemporaries any assurance that the ordeal was over. It had often happened earlier that the ascendancy of a strong man was merely a prelude to the emergence of challengers who sparked a new—and usually more destructive—round of civil strife.

One consequence of the long struggle that had wracked the late republic provided a major source of uncertainty. The republican political system shaped prior to 133 B.C. and much revered by many Roman citizens lay in shambles by 31 B.C. Although still in existence, the key institutions marking the republican constitution—citizen assemblies, elected magistrates, the Senate—and the processes by which decisions were reached under the republican system had become totally ineffective. Power lay in the hands of a military dictator whose constitutional position lacked any clear definition beyond the fact that he possessed the brute force to impose his will. Rome's very survival hinged on fashioning a new political system to replace the discredited republican order.

Another ominous result of the turmoil marking the final century of the Roman Republic was the failure to resolve most of the basic problems that had been the cause of civil strife. The frontiers of Rome's empire remained fluid and ill defended. Between 133 and 31 B.C. new provinces were added in Asia, Africa, and Europe (see Map 8.1), chiefly as a result of conquests prompted by ambitious leaders seeking a means of advancing their political fortunes, but little attention had been given to the defense of Rome's ever-lengthening frontiers. Rome's conquered subjects continued to be exploited mercilessly by Roman armies, corrupt governors, and rapacious tax collectors. The economic and social lot of Italy's citizen-farmers deteriorated still further as more of them were deprived of their land, forcing them to become dependents serving noble owners of large estates (*latifundia*) or migrants to urban centers, especially Rome. Rome's population, by now approaching a million residents made up of a polyglot mixture of citizens, foreigners, slaves, and freedmen living in crowded tenements, spawned increasing numbers of impoverished, rootless citizens with little stake in the existing order. Increasingly manipulated by demagogues willing to utilize public resources to provide "bread and circuses" in return for votes and for service in gangs willing to commit acts of political violence, this undisciplined mob was a constant threat to order. And slavery grew apace during the last century of the republic, enlarging the number of people in the Roman world who were exploited mercilessly, breeding a false sense of superiority in the nonslave pop-

FIGURE 9.3 Aspects of Life During the Late Republic These two scenes reflect important aspects of life in the late republic. On the left laborers unload grain brought by ship from African provinces to feed Rome's growing numbers of unemployed citizens. On the right a Roman aristocrat and his wife are instructed by a Greek slave; to be educated in Greek ways was critical to social respectability in first-century B.C. Rome. (Alinari/Art Resource)

ulation, and demeaning many kinds of labor needed to sustain the economy of the Roman world. Unless solutions could be found for this whole range of problems, the prospects for a better future remained uncertain.

However, the political, social, and economic landscape created by a century of turmoil was not completely bleak. Amid the mounting chaos there were factors at work pointing toward recovery, some of them products of the civil strife. Despite the havoc wrought by political and social upheaval, the Roman citizen body still represented a potent human resource. At its center stood the old noble families, who showed a remarkable ability to survive political proscription, confiscation of their wealth, and political humiliation at the hands of military dictators and *populares* demagogues. Although insistent on its social superiority and little averse to accumulating an ever greater share of the wealth, this class became more aware of the wider world now embraced by Rome and more open to new ideas and values. Even aristocratic women, long completely under the domination of male heads of households, began to break the shackles of custom to become property owners, active participants in cultural and social life, and even political forces as key partners in political marriages (see Figure 9.3). The ranks of the old aristocracy were imperceptibly expanded, especially by the

addition to its ranks of the Italian aristocracy, which exercised an important role in shaping local affairs. This noble class represented a considerable political talent and social influence that could be tapped to reconstruct the Roman political order. While taking advantage of the disorder accompanying civil struggle to reap enormous rewards as provincial tax collectors, suppliers of private armies, moneylenders, and speculators in confiscated property, the *equites* gained experience related to provincial administration, military organization, and trade that could be invaluable in reshaping society. Especially significant was the potential of the plebeian citizens as a military resource. Although a source of massive disorder during the last century of the republic, the private armies recruited by Marius, Sulla, Pompey, Julius Caesar, and Octavian chiefly from the ranks of landless plebeians laid the foundation for a professional citizen army capable of defending Rome's huge empire.

In the outwardly destructive course of events unfolding between 133 and 31 B.C., there was some evidence that new directions in the shaping of Rome's public policy were being plotted. Alliances began to take shape that established a network of client states as a stabilizing force along Rome's extensive frontiers. Leaders such as Pompey and Caesar enacted measures pointing toward a regularization of provincial administration that took into account the needs and interests of Rome's huge subject population. Among other things, such arrangements often allowed local authorities in the provinces considerable control over local affairs. In a few instances provincial subjects, especially local aristocrats, were granted rights of citizenship as a reward for their willingness to support Roman interests. Some Romans began to show an awareness that Rome's material welfare depended not only on the exaction of tribute but also on expanding commercial relations that gave Rome access to grain, raw materials, and manufactured goods produced in the provinces (see Figure 9.3). Efforts were made to come to grips with Rome's urban problems, especially by resettling citizens in Italy and the provinces, where they became agents promoting Romanization; by initiating public works projects to provide employment; and by developing regularized administrative personnel to deal with such matters as law enforcement and food supply. Although such actions were usually taken by strongmen seeking to serve their quest for power, they suggested that, despite the violence and the abuse of power so prevalent during the last years of the republic, Roman leadership was not completely bankrupt politically.

Particularly notable about the tumultuous era marking the end of the Roman Republic was a quickening of intellectual and artistic life that heralded the assumption of cultural leadership by Latin-speaking Romans. As we shall see in greater detail later (see Chapter 11), the literary activities of such figures as Cicero, Lucretius, and Julius Caesar and the works of anonymous architects and sculptors signaled the dawn of a golden age in Roman cultural life. Although heavily influenced by Greek models, these figures produced works with a distinctive and unique Roman stamp that established Rome's claim to supremacy in the Mediterranean world beyond the realm of politics and military force. Cultural leadership provided a new focus around which Roman creative energies could rally and opened avenues through which Roman values could be reformulated and propagated to counter the moral confusion brought on by the disturbances accompanying the fall of the Roman Republic.

Viewed in its entirety, the century extending from 133 to 31 B.C. marked a decisive transition period in the history of Western civilization. It witnessed the dramatic, painful collapse of a time-sanctioned order that had permitted the residents of a small city-state to establish domination over an extensive empire surrounding the Mediterranean Sea. But even while that darker side of the era ran its course, there were signs of a regrouping of resources and talents heralding a new day for Rome.

SUGGESTED READING

Political Developments

H. H. Scullard, *From the Gracchi to Nero: A History of Rome from 133 B.C. to A.D. 68*, 5th ed. (1982). A detailed history.

Ronald Syme, *The Roman Revolution* (1952).

Richard E. Smith, *The Failure of the Roman Republic* (1955).

Erich S. Gruen, *The Last Generation of the Roman Republic* (1974).

Mary Beard and Michael Crawford, *Rome in the Late Republic: Problems and Interpretations* (1985).

These four works present significant but differing interpretations of the causes of the failure of the Roman Republic.

Claude Nicolet, *The World of the Citizen in Republican Rome*, trans. P. S. Falla (1980). A reconstruction of the civic life of the average citizen.

A. W. Lintott, *Violence in the Roman Republic* (1968).

Paul J. J. Vanderbroeck, *Popular Leadership and Collective Behavior in the Late Roman Republic (ca. 80–50 B.C.)* (1987).

A. M. Eckstein, *Senate and Generals* (1987).

David F. Epstein, *Personal Enmity and Roman Politics (218–43 B.C.)* (1987).

Keith R. Bradley, *Slavery and Rebellion in the Roman World, 140 B.C.–70 B.C.* (1989).

The preceding five titles all deal with aspects of political life that had a bearing on the decline of the republic.

A. N. Sherwin-White, *Roman Foreign Policy in the East, 168 B.C. to 1 A.D.* (1984). An excellent study.

Economic and Social Developments

Géza Alföldy, *The Social History of Rome*, trans. David Braund and Frank Pollock (1985). A challenging introduction.

P. A. Brunt, *Social Conflicts in the Roman Republic* (1971). A good description of social tensions affecting late republican society.

K. D. White, *Roman Farming* (1970). Clarifies the problems of Roman agriculture during the republican period.

Biographies

A. H. Bernstein, *Tiberius Sempronius Gracchus. Tradition and Apostasy* (1978).

Arthur Keaveney, *Sulla: The Last Republican* (1982).

Peter Greenhalgh, *Pompey: The Roman Alexander* (1980) and *Pompey: The Republican Prince* (1981).

B. A. Marshall, *Crassus: A Political Biography* (1976).

Elizabeth Rawson, *Cicero: A Portrait*, rev. ed. (1983).

Christian Habicht, *Cicero the Politician* (1990).

Matthias Gelzer, *Caesar: Politician and Statesman* (1968).

Arthur D. Kahn, *The Education of Julius Caesar: A Biography, a Reconstruction* (1986).

Sources

Cicero, *Selected Works*, trans. Michael Grant (1971).

War Commentaries of Caesar, trans. Rex Warner (1960). Contains two of Caesar's political works, *The Gallic Wars* and *The Civil Wars*.

CHAPTER 10

The Roman Empire and the *Pax Romana,* 31 B.C.–A.D. 180

FIGURE 10.1 Augustus, First Citizen of Rome This majestic statue of Octavian, or Augustus, as he came to be known soon after he seized power, was intended to idealize and exalt the man who had restored peace to the Roman world after the troubled times of the late republic. (Alinari/Art Resource)

The year 31 B.C. marked a critical point in the history of the Mediterranean world. After suffering a profound internal crisis that ended with the collapse of their traditional political order, its Roman masters faced the challenge of restoring order in their own house if their dominance of the Mediterranean world was to continue in a fruitful way. During the following two centuries the Romans met that challenge by fashioning their most notable contribution to civilization—a system of government known as the Roman Empire. This system became a powerful force promoting peace, order, and cultural diffusion among millions of people living in a vast territory surrounding what the Romans called "our sea."

1. OCTAVIAN'S NEW POLITICAL ORDER, 31 B.C.–A.D. 14

The establishment of a new order was the work of Octavian (see Figure 10.1). His victory at Actium in 31 B.C. made him master of the Roman world by virtue of conquest. With an uncanny grasp of the mentality of his times, Octavian sensed that naked power would not suffice to restore order. In the minds of the Roman citizenry any form of military dictatorship or monarchy was unacceptable because it flaunted a five-century-old tradition that held that Rome's destiny could be determined only by the decisions of the Senate and the people acting through the institutions of the Roman Republic. Yet the experience of the previous century had shown that the only hope for the management of the vast, problem-ridden Roman world lay in the concentration of power in the hands of a single individual. Octavian's challenge was to reconcile the collective mind-set rooted in tradition with existing reality. His solution was masterful: He sought to preserve the outward forms of the republican constitution while obtaining, by legal means, sufficient power to permit him to rule the Roman world. Lacking the charisma of a Julius Caesar, Octavian proved to be a patient, realistic, cautious, pragmatic statesman who understood the deeper currents at work in his world and who was amazingly flexible in devising means to achieve his program. His forty-five-year rule gave him time to experiment and shift direction as the occasion demanded.

As early as 27 B.C., Octavian made a decisive move toward defining his position when he proclaimed before the Senate "the transfer of the state to the free disposal of the Senate and the people." This apparent surrender of all the powers he then held was interpreted as a restoration of the republic. Impressed by this noble gesture, fearful of the recurrence of civil war, and skillfully guided by Octavian, the Senate and the people quickly took legal action to bestow on him a wide array of powers. Included were the power of tribune for life, full consular authority without need to hold that office, authority over most of the provinces, command of the armies, and the highest priestly office. To these legal powers the grateful citizenry added several honors: first senator; *augustus* ("most revered one"); *imperator* ("victorious general"); and *pater patriae* ("father of the country"). This array of legal powers and tradition-laden honors surrounded Octavian with an aura of authority so great that he began to be seen as *princeps*, the first citizen of Rome, trusted to do what he wished to rule the Roman world without a hint of illegal abuse of power or of violating tradition. What was crucial in Octavian's position was that he did not have to share the authority legally granted him and that his power need not be renewed regularly. Buttressing his position as *princeps* were his immense personal fortune and his wide circle of political dependents, both created during the period of his rise to power after Julius Caesar's death.

Octavian—or Augustus, as he came to be known by virtue of the title that vaguely suggested a semidivine status—sought to use his vast authority to resolve the major problems that had so long plagued Roman society. One concern was the revitalization of the citizen body—basically the population of Italy—on whose shoulders rested the responsibility for ruling the vast empire. Adhering to the ancient and widely held conviction that only a class-structured society could ensure right order, Augustus tried to redefine class divisions and to assign civic responsibilities to each group. Rigid standards of birth, wealth, and conduct were established to define senatorial ranking, resulting in a considerable reduction of those eligible for this rank. This elite was assigned a major role in political life. The

Senate, the traditional focus of political life for the *nobiles*, retained important powers in selecting magistrates, judging cases, enacting laws, and governing selected provinces. Members of the senatorial class were expected to fill the traditional elective offices, to serve as provincial governors, and to command armies. Augustus counted on the equestrian order (*equites*) to serve the state in critical administrative positions in the army, the tax system, and the judicial system. To the plebeians, Augustus offered order and economic security in return for their votes in support of his regime and service as citizen-soldiers in the army. While this arrangement was sensitive to traditional class roles, it effectively defined the responsibility of citizenship in terms of service to the state at the direction of the *princeps* rather than in terms of citizen formulation of basic policy.

Concerned by what many perceived to be low morale among the citizens, Augustus initiated sweeping measures to rebuild a sense of community and to revive a feeling of pride in Rome, ends he hoped to achieve by playing on tradition. He made a major effort to revive ancient civic religious practices as a central part of public life. He patronized writers such as Vergil, Horace, and Livy and artists (see Chapter 11) who were willing to celebrate Rome's ancient glory and present blessings. Laws were enacted to curb what Augustus believed to be vices that sapped civic virtue—luxury, sexual irregularities, divorce, childless marriages, gambling, drinking, idleness. Immense sums were spent to beautify Rome and provide better public services in the hope of eliciting pride in what was now "head of the world."

Aware of the need to protect Rome's extended frontiers and mindful of the disruptive role played by private armies during the last century of the republic, Augustus was particularly concerned with the military system. His response was the creation of a professional army consisting of twenty-five legions (about one hundred fifty thousand troops) made up chiefly of Roman citizens serving twenty-year terms. Each legion was complemented by an equal-sized auxiliary unit composed of noncitizens recruited in the provinces and granted citizenship upon completion of service. A command structure, employing carefully selected members of the senatorial and

equestrian orders but always subordinate to the *princeps*, was developed. Steps were taken to provide training, discipline, systematic provisioning, regular pay, and pensions to the soldiers. The bulk of this force was stationed in frontier provinces facing potential enemies. Only the Praetorian Guard, a select contingent of about nine thousand troops acting as a bodyguard for the *princeps*, was garrisoned in the vicinity of Rome. During Augustus' reign the army was used both to secure control over existing provinces and to attack external foes. The most important campaigns were waged in an effort to strengthen the empire's European frontier. As a result, the Roman hold on Illyricum was made secure and the new provinces of Raetia, Pannonia, and Moesia were added along the Danube frontier (see Map 10.1). An effort to expand into the Germanic world east of the Rhine ended in a crushing defeat in A.D. 9. Thereafter, Augustus gave up expansion, seeking instead to establish a fixed frontier between Romans and foreigners to be defended by the imperial army.

Aware of the disarray produced in the provinces by Rome's predatory conduct during the republican period, Augustus made a major effort to improve provincial governance. Provinces needing the presence of armed forces were administered directly by the *princeps*. He was represented in each by a *legate*, usually a senator, who directed provincial administration, and by a *procurator*, usually an equestrian, who was charged with collecting taxes. The provinces not needing armed forces were left under the jurisdiction of the Senate, which annually selected *proconsuls* to act as governors; their selection and conduct were carefully monitored by the *princeps*. This arrangement put an end to the rapacious governors and tax farmers who had for so long preyed on the helpless provincials. To complement this administrative system, Augustus encouraged the city-states scattered across the empire to take responsibility for many matters relating to life in each city-state and its dependent countryside: police regulation, justice, public works, charity, religion. Most city-states had or were encouraged to develop a working system of government based on elected magistrates, a local senate, and assemblies—a system similar to Rome's old republican order. Local aristocracies whose interests were served by cooperating with

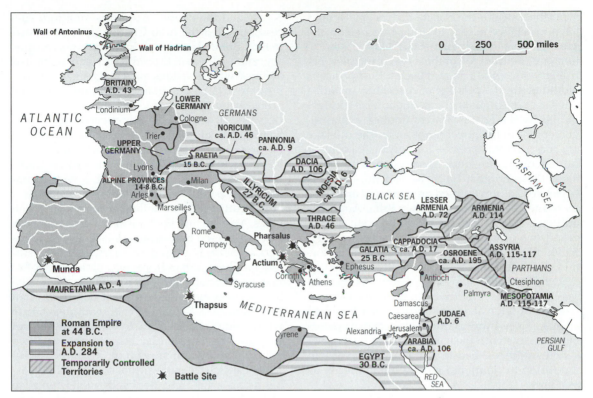

Map 10.1 **THE ROMAN EMPIRE, 44 B.C.–A.D. 284** This map shows the expansion of the Roman Empire between the death of Julius Caesar in 44 B.C. and the accession of Emperor Diocletian in A.D. 284. The territories annexed during these three centuries brought the empire to its greatest size; all the peoples living within its vast expanse felt the influence of Greco-Roman civilization. However, by the beginning of the third century A.D. Roman domination of this territory was being threatened by increasing pressure along the frontiers facing the Germans and the Parthians.

the Roman government tended to dominate these governments. This new system, based on political authority shared by the central government and local authorities, almost immediately brought order and more equitable treatment to the provincials.

The expanding range of functions associated with the office of *princeps* generated the need for permanent civil servants skilled in administration. Although Augustus and a small circle of confidants managed to handle a huge range of administrative detail, there slowly emerged around the *princeps* a corps of helpers, composed chiefly of freed slaves, whose only political attachments were to the *princeps*. In Augustus' time one of the prime accomplishments of this embry-

onic bureaucracy was the establishment of a sound fiscal system to support the imperial regime, especially its army. The key element of that system was a land tax and a head tax equitably imposed on noncitizens on the basis of regular census taking. Roman citizens contributed to support of the state chiefly through a form of sales tax and an inheritance tax.

Concerned with perpetuating his system, Augustus was forced during most of his long reign to wrestle with the issue of succession to his position as *princeps*, a problem complicated by his perennial ill health. Aware that only the Senate and the people could legally bestow the powers upon which his veiled system of one-man rule depended, he sought to establish a successor in a position where the Senate and people would have no choice except to grant that person the same powers that Augustus wielded. To achieve that end, he tried to combine two principles: hereditary succession so that each future princeps would enjoy the prestige of descent from Julius Caesar and Augustus; and public visibility acquired by the future *princeps* through actual involvement in the governance under the tutelage of the present *princeps*. Augustus' problem turned out to be finding someone who could meet these criteria. Since he had no sons, his search for an heir focused on a series of arranged marriages of his only daughter, Julia. Augustus outlived two of her husbands as well as two grandsons considered as possible successors. Finally, chiefly through the connivance of his formidable wife, Livia, Augustus settled on her son (and his adopted stepson), Tiberius, as his successor. Tiberius was forced to divorce a beloved wife in order to become Julia's third husband and after A.D. 4 was granted ever-greater powers by Augustus with the concurrence of the Senate. When Augustus died in A.D. 14, Tiberius was in a position to claim and receive full authority as *princeps*.

2. TESTING THE AUGUSTAN ESTABLISHMENT, A.D. 14–96

During the century following Augustus' death, the Augustan system was severely tested but ultimately proved its viability. The testing took place primarily in a relatively narrow political circle involving each *princeps*, his family, his chief political agents, the senatorial class, and sometimes the army. Their activities, set forth in lurid detail by the historians Tacitus and Suetonius (see Chapter 11), leave the impression that this era was marked by monumental misrule and perpetual crisis. But more constructive developments beyond this circle provide indisputable evidence of the success of the Augustan principate.

A constant source of tension stemmed from the succession problem. The office of *princeps* as defined by Augustus required a leader descended from his family who had the ability to direct a vast empire while remaining respectful of the authority entrusted by Augustus to the Senate and the people. Augustus' first four successors, called the Julio-Claudians, were related to him. But their selection bred intrigue, conspiracy, and violence and produced rulers of limited abilities whose actions provoked incessant opposition and obstructionism from the senatorial order. Augustus' handpicked successor, Tiberius (A.D. 14–37), was an able, experienced leader, but he was also cold, suspicious, distrustful, and easily provoked to brutal retaliation against those he suspected of undermining his power. Gaius (A.D. 37–41), nicknamed Caligula, a term meaning "little boots," given to him when he was a boy strutting about military camps in small boots, was an indolent pleasure seeker whose excesses earned him an assassin's knife. Claudius (A.D. 41–54) was a timid, scholarly man who suffered a physical handicap, was ill at ease in Roman high society, and was constantly victimized by his wives and advisers. Most notorious of all was Nero (A.D. 54–68), a cruel, vain degenerate who avoided assassination by killing himself, but only after he had murdered his mother and two wives, disposed of numerous senators, persecuted Christians, made a fool of himself by posing as an artist, and depleted public funds to satisfy his expensive whims. It is indeed easy to conclude that none of the Julio-Claudians was worthy of respect and trust as "first citizen."

Even during the era of the Julio-Claudians, there occurred a development with ominous implications for the future: the intervention of the army in the choice of the *princeps*. In a single year following Nero's death four different men were thrust into office by the Praetorian Guard in a climate of violence reminiscent of the late republic. Finally, a general named Vespasian seized the office and put an end to the bloody military competition for control of the political system. Between A.D. 69 and 96 he and his sons, Titus and Domitian, known as the Flavian dynasty, ruled effectively but in the face of repeated charges of tyranny. These charges were rooted in a constitutional problem implicit in the Augustan principate: the lack of precise definition of the powers belonging to the *princeps* and those belonging to the Senate and the people. While the Julio-Claudian and Flavian rulers tried to honor the role of the Senate and the people in directing the state, the fuzzy line between the two spheres prompted senators to charge repeatedly that the rulers were usurping authority and destroying the liberties of citizens. The rulers sometimes reacted by silencing their critics; more often, they simply did what had to be done, disregarding the alleged rights of the Senate and people. Either course led to a climate of mistrust so acute that it seemed at times that civil war would again erupt to ruin the Augustan settlement.

In reality, all this strife was little more than an intriguing sideshow detracting from the substantive advances made in achieving the peaceful order envisaged by Augustus. Several of the much-maligned rulers of this era—Tiberius, Claudius, Vespasian, Domitian—were able statesmen who worked patiently and effectively to resolve the problems facing the imperial regime. They maintained Rome's military capability and utilized it to defend the frontiers and to extend Rome's domain: Claudius conquered Britain and annexed Noricum to strengthen the Danube frontier, and Domitian won territory along the upper Rhine frontier that was crucial to the containment of the Germanic threat (see Map 10.1). They worked hard to sustain and improve equitable administration of the provinces, to develop a proficient professional bureaucracy, to sponsor public works in Rome, Italy, and the provinces, and to encourage trade, industry, and agriculture. For the most part, the Senate and people demonstrated little interest and less competence in dealing with these crucial matters. Despite their recurrent laments that their liberties were being usurped by rulers unworthy of such honor in terms of ancient standards, by the end of the first century A.D. most people had reached the conclusion that rule by a powerful *princeps* was the only guarantee of peace, security, and prosperity. The Augustan system had prevailed.

3. *PAX ROMANA:* THE "GOOD EMPERORS," A.D. 96–180

With the end of the Flavian dynasty in A.D. 96 much of the conflict that had marked the testing of the Augustan system ended. During the next century, the empire enjoyed a golden age, a time of *Pax Romana*—the Roman peace. Seldom has an era produced leaders more highly praised than the five "good emperors" who ruled from A.D. 96 to 180. Nerva (A.D. 96–98) was a respected aristocrat whose conciliatory actions calmed fears of military dictatorship. Trajan (A.D. 98–117), a native of Spain and the first emperor from the provinces, won the admiration of the entire Roman world by his respect for the Roman aristocracy, his brilliant military exploits, and his honest administration. Hadrian (A.D. 117–138), also of Spanish origin, was a cultured humanitarian who spent most of his reign traveling throughout the empire promoting the cause of peace, lawful administration, and material well-being. Antoninus (A.D. 138–161), by the excellence of his character and his humane legislation, earned the title "Pius" ("devoted to duty") from a grateful Senate. Most illustrious of all was Marcus Aurelius (A.D. 161–180), a noted Stoic philosopher who exemplified a sense of duty, a willingness to work, and a nobility of purpose in the service of the state.

The regime of the "good emperors" was one that produced little history of a conventional kind—battles, intrigues, scandals. These emperors were sometimes engaged in warfare, chiefly in defense of Rome's sprawling, lightly defended frontiers. Trajan pursued an aggressive policy that resulted in the annexation of a crucial area north of the Danube called Dacia and of extensive territories east of the Euphrates River at the expense of Parthia (see Map 10.1). However, Trajan's conquests in the east were soon abandoned. Hadrian replaced expansionism with a policy emphasizing strong defense of a fixed frontier and diplomacy. The problem of defense remained crucial, as was clear from the fact that peace-loving Marcus Aurelius had to spend most of his reign defending the northern frontier against Germans.

Less spectacular were other activities of the "good emperors" related to internal peace and stability. They resolved the succession problem by utilizing an adoptive system whereby each emperor early in his reign adopted as his son a man of ability who was then involved in imperial governance and vested with increasing legal powers to the point where he was able to take over when his "father" died. All these rulers were tactful and respectful toward the senators, who filled most of the high offices, were regularly consulted, and increasingly became staunch supporters of the imperial system. Citizenship was granted to ever-larger numbers of provincials, some of whom were elevated to senatorial rank; this policy facilitated the Romanization of the provincial population. The administrative system was steadily expanded and regularized. The rulers encouraged the development of a unified body of law for the whole empire. They championed humanitarian projects to aid the downtrodden. Every encouragement was given to city-states to determine their own course as long as that freedom did not threaten the imperial peace. The rulers worked tirelessly to establish a sound financial system to support the imperial structure. All these efforts slowly bound the diverse peoples of the empire—numbering perhaps 70 million—into a secure, peaceful commonwealth guided from Rome. By A.D. 180 a vision expressed nearly two centuries earlier by the poet Vergil in his *Aeneid* seemed fulfilled: "You, Roman, remember—these are your arts: To rule nations, and to impose the ways of peace."

4. THE NATURE OF THE IMPERIAL POLITICAL ORDER

In its mature form in the second century A.D. the imperial government was remarkably effective, but its operation is not easy to describe. One is tempted to oversimplify by stressing form without giving sufficient attention to process. The structure of the imperial government can be described in fairly simple terms. At the head of the Roman state stood a single figure, the *princeps* or *imperator*, who was vested with extensive executive, legislative, and judicial powers and with a variety of honors by the vote of the Senate and the people. Theoretically, the emperor exercised these powers by making decisions that were executed through a bureaucracy consisting of paid "civil servants" appointed by the ruler to serve the central government and of agents dispatched across the empire to carry out imperial orders. Backing the authority of the *princeps* was the army, a highly professionalized body of about three hundred thousand soldiers commanded by officers appointed by the emperor and capable of enforcing imperial orders if the need arose. The emperor's authority was represented in each of the forty-five provinces into which the empire was divided by a governor (usually called a *le-*

gatus) vested with authority to keep order and administer justice and a *procurator* charged with collecting taxes. An efficient tax system supported this complex apparatus and allowed the imperial government to provide a wide range of public services. Complementing the imperial government everywhere in the empire were active city-state governments that played a major role in directing local affairs; however, these local regimes were always open to intervention by agents of the emperor's government. When described in structural terms the imperial government seems best characterized as a highly centralized, bureaucratized regime capable of imposing on a vast population a uniform policy decided upon by one man.

However, an examination of the processes through which the Roman government impacted on the governed peoples in specific situations presents a more subtle, complex picture. The person of the *princeps* or emperor, elevated to semidivine status by a sustained and skillful propaganda effort, commanded a reverence from imperial subjects that inclined them toward obedience. That very reverence led to a widely shared expectation that the emperor could "do" all things. Since Greco-Roman political thought and practice made little allowance for delegation of power, the result was that second-century emperors were personally swamped with detailed administrative work: conducting military campaigns, arbitrating disputes, responding to petitions for favors, receiving embassies, making constant public appearances, and seeing to it that public property was properly exploited. Because the Roman record-keeping system was limited, all this detail had to be handled without much knowledge of specific situations. To assist in meeting this burden, the emperors relied more often on their household servants than on professional civil servants; members of the imperial household became real power wielders without holding official positions or being constrained by rules defining their conduct of public business. The emperors often entrusted public business to private contractors who acted according to their own lights once commissioned to perform a service for the state. Perhaps the only area in which there was anything like a regularized, empirewide administrative system was in revenue collecting, and even in this vital activity the procedures were haphazard and arbitrary.

Beyond the emperor and his circle, the political process was even less systematic and uniform. It is almost unbelievable to a modern observer to realize how few public officials in the Roman system actually had the *imperium*—the legal power to make final decisions. Those who did—army commanders, governors, procurators—held sway over extensive jurisdictions; as a result, they too were swamped with administrative details. Like the emperor, they too relied on their personal servants to assist with these details, and they too depended heavily on private contractors to get things done. All too often, things did not get done; like the famous case involving the Roman official Pontius Pilate, authorities simply "washed their hands" of problems confronting them. Far from being a mechanism through which uniform decisions were imposed upon the population through uniform procedures, the Roman imperial government operated through enclaves of power in which officials vested with the authority of Rome did what they wished in the way they wished.

The lives of most residents of the Roman empire were seldom touched directly by the imperial government—except in the pocketbook. For them the most important political force was the local city-state government, whose far-ranging activities were encouraged by the imperial government. Each urban center with its surrounding territory was ruled by a body of local aristocrats (called *decurions*) who formed a local senate (called a *curia*). These senates elected local magistrates, collected local taxes, administered justice, and assumed responsibility for keeping order and providing public facilities. Although the imperial government sometimes intervened in their activities, especially in fiscal matters, the city-state regimes were allowed wide latitude to govern those in their jurisdiction as they wished.

In view of these aspects of political reality, it is obviously impossible to think of the Roman imperial regime as one headed by a wise emperor who established general policies on the basis of extensive knowledge of conditions and with the advice of informed councilors and then issued orders that were enacted by a hierarchy of public officials capable of ensuring universal conformance to the emperor's law. Instead, governance depended on the decisions and actions of a wide array of individuals, some officeholders and some private parties, acting within a framework of overlapping jurisdictions where pragmatic concerns and individual judgment were more important than rules. To run a vast empire in such a manner would seem to be a formula for chaos. Yet during the second century A.D. the system worked.

One wonders how! The explanation may seem strange in terms of modern conceptions of statecraft. Rome was governed by a narrow, tightly knit elite. Reflecting an attitude deeply ingrained in the Greco-Roman mentality, that elite viewed public life as the highest form of human activity, to be taken seriously by those involved in the political sphere. The members of this elite also shared economic interests, social status, and cultural values that led them to think in a common pattern about the means through which power was exercised and the ends it was to serve. Whether they were public officials, senators, local decurions, army officers, or equestrian contractors, their shared perceptions of the right political order prompted each of them to decide on a course of action in a particular political situation in a way similar to the way all other power wielders would act in that same situation. Thus, without the guidance of clearly formulated policies or rigid rules regulating political behavior, the ruling elite quite unconsciously guided the Roman world in a common direction that especially prized peace and order. Perhaps the tone for this remarkable consensus was set by the "good emperors," whose conduct was shaped by a conviction that power imposed on its holders the duty to unite their subjects in a community where behavior was defined by the law of nature dictated by divine reason—a political philosophy based on Stoic ideas. Certainly from Augustus onward successive emperors acted to sanction the position of this elite and to replenish its ranks, especially by extending citizenship to provincials in a position to exercise power. But in the final analysis it was the political activism of this elite bound together by shared social values and a common culture that ruled the empire in its golden days. In a real sense the future of the empire depended on the continuation of this consensus among the members of this elite.

5. ECONOMIC AND SOCIAL LIFE IN THE ROMAN EMPIRE

A major consequence of the establishment of the imperial regime was a general improvement of material life in the Roman world to a level higher than ever before and not to be equaled again for many centuries. Not all shared that affluence equally; in fact, fewer and fewer of the population of the empire tended to enjoy more and more, a prime factor in making the imperial regime acceptable to the powerful in society. This prosperity was not the consequence of any basic change in the system of production or of a conscious economic policy fostered by the state. Rather, it stemmed from the favorable environment created by peace and order, from the security of property (including slaves) afforded by the imperial regime, from the closer integration of formerly isolated areas into the total economy, from the stimulus supplied by the expanding activities of the imperial political system, and from the entrepreneurial activities of nobles and equestrians eager to expand their family fortunes.

The Roman imperial economy remained basically agricultural. Although the organization of agricultural production varied from region to region, small farms cultivated by freeholders or renters flourished over wide reaches of the empire. The large estate system (*latifundia*), based on the labor of sharecroppers, hired workers, and slaves and devoted to the production of cash crops such as grapes, olives, and livestock, continued to spread in Italy and in the highly Romanized areas of southern Gaul, Spain, and North Africa. For the most part, these diverse forms of agricultural production provided sufficient returns to feed those who labored on them and a modest surplus to supply the needs of local urban centers. However, some areas, such as Egypt and North Africa, produced large surpluses of grain for export to the empire's great cities, especially Rome. Farming methods and technology changed little during the imperial era. Increased agricultural production resulted from better management and from the expansion of land under cultivation, notably in Spain, Gaul, and along the Danube frontier, where urban growth and the presence of Roman army camps stimulated the demand for agricultural products and where retired army veterans provided a steady supply of new settlers.

An important key to prosperity during the first two centuries A.D. was the expansion of trade and industry. Most of the commercial activity involved the exchange of agricultural products and simple manufactured goods on a local level. However, there was a significant movement of luxury goods, raw materials, and foodstuffs on a scale embracing the whole empire and even extending beyond to Parthia, India, China, Africa, and the Germanic world. The Mediterranean became a busy commercial roadway linking its bordering lands into an interdependent economic community. The famed Roman road system encouraged the movement of goods inland to urban centers and army camps. Most manufactured goods were produced by artisans working in their own small shops; often they also marketed their products. In some cases such enterprises were financed by nobles or equestrians, whose slaves and freedmen produced goods and shared the returns with their masters. Large-scale industrial activity was rare, confined chiefly to ceramics, glassware, bricks, and mining. One of the most significant developments of this era was the remarkable expansion of industrial activity in Spain and Gaul as a result of the incorporation of these previously "backward" areas into the mainstream of Mediterranean life. A powerful stimulant to trade and industry was provided by a massive building boom that occurred throughout the empire. Funded by both public and private sources, this outburst filled numerous cities, Rome above all, with forums, basilicas for the conduct of public business, temples, theaters, stadiums, palaces, baths, and private dwellings. Across the countryside were built roads, bridges, aqueducts, villas, and army camps. This vast enterprise required capital, labor, the skilled services of artisans and suppliers, and managerial skills.

Most economic life in the first and second centuries was conducted by private individuals with little interference from the imperial government, which demonstrated a limited interest in economic matters except in tapping the system through taxation. However, what we would today call the public sector played an increasing role in the economy. Through its taxation system the Roman government drained off a portion of the wealth of the entire empire. That wealth was redistributed to pay officials' salaries, support the jobless in Rome, beautify the capital city, and maintain the army. As a consequence, most public expenditures tended to be concentrated in Rome and in frontier areas where the army was stationed. Such distribution of public funds stimulated nonproductive economic activity in these areas while depriving the most productive areas of the financial resources needed to sustain and expand economic activity. Moreover, the expanding role of the Roman government in distributing the wealth of the empire made the economy increasingly sensitive to public policy decisions involving taxation, the size of the army and the bureaucracy, and the frequency of war. This development introduced an element of instability into the economic system.

The basic social order prevailing in the Roman Empire was little changed from that of the late republican period. The distinction between citizens and noncitizens remained an important social fact; citizens had rights and privileges denied noncitizens. However, that division was increasingly blurred by the granting of citizenship to ever-larger numbers of provincials. The citizen population was divided into classes defined by law: *nobiles*, *equites*, plebeians, and slaves. Although the social status of the noncitizen population of the empire varied greatly, over most of the empire there prevailed a social structure roughly equivalent to that of the Roman citizenry.

At the summit of the social order stood the senatorial order, headed by the *princeps* and his family. Aside from its basis in law, the social status of this class was buttressed and enhanced by various factors: family origin, marriage connections, wealth based on land, education, involvement in the highest levels of political life, control over a circle of clients, and lifestyle. While small and keenly conscious of its status, the nobility was never totally exclusive. Its ranks were constantly replenished by those who could meet the standards for noble status; most often those who ascended socially were drawn from rich equestrians who served the state and provincial nobles who gained citizenship.

Although their wealth was based largely on landownership, Roman nobles were creatures of the city. Rome, of course, was the most attractive center for the *nobiles* of senatorial rank, but many other cities across the empire had their noble circles. In this urban setting noble life centered in the family household, where the *pater familias* (father of the family) ruled as he wished over his wife, children, slaves, and clients. He did not "work," as did the lower classes, but "managed" his estates, his investments, and often some segment of public life entrusted to him through selection for an office. Always uppermost in his mind were increasing the family patrimony and enhancing family prestige. These concerns prompted a keen interest in the education, careers, and marriages of his children, especially sons. Roman nobles participated in a constant round of social activities—banquets, festivals, races, gladiatorial contests, cultural events. Worthy nobles were expected to provide the major source of funding for many of these activities.

Although their lives were surrounded by constraints imposed by law and tradition that subjugated them first to their fathers and then to their husbands, women still played a prominent role in aristocratic life (see Figure 10.2). A long succession of talented wives of first- and second-century emperors helped shape decisions on such crucial matters as political patronage, succession, and the selection of advisers to each *princeps*. Noblewomen managed family households, an operation that involved large expenditures and the direction of numerous slaves (see Figure 10.3). They owned and managed property, defended their interests in court, and took part in many social activities. Not a few of them took lovers, just as their husbands did. Some evidence suggests that by the second century male nobles increasingly viewed wives as equal partners in marriage, worthy of respect and considerate treatment. This changing attitude was reflected in new marriage practices that allowed a bride to retain control over property she brought to the marriage and made divorce easier for a wife.

Although Roman moralists often painted the lives of noblemen and women in terms of gluttony, drunkenness, sexual excess, and frivolity, other evidence suggests that noble life was guided by a moral code that placed a high value

FIGURE 10.2 A Roman Lady This painting portrays a noble Roman lady of the imperial period. It suggests that Roman women were respected for their dignity, sobriety, and strength of character. Women such as this one played an important role in managing the affairs of aristocratic households and sometimes in promoting the political careers of their husbands and sons. (Courtesy of the Detroit Institute of Arts)

on sober, ordered, restrained conduct and required concern with and involvement in public affairs in the cause of creating a civilized order. The *equites* imitated the noble lifestyle, often with success, in terms of wealth, sumptuous living, and education; however, members of this order were not accepted as being real nobles and thus were excluded from the summit of the social order unless the nobles chose to co-opt them into the ranks of the real elite.

Rome and most other cities had a teeming lower-class population: shopkeepers, artisans, day laborers, the idle poor, slaves. In Rome and Italy the bulk of these people—slaves excepted—were plebeian citizens; in provincial cities they had some status as members of the community.

The political power of plebeian citizens, traditionally expressed through votes in assemblies, steadily eroded during the first and second centuries, leaving plebeians with few means of influencing their destiny. Tightly knit family units remained at the center of urban life. Most urban residents devoted their time and energy to ignoble "work" through which they earned a living, an enterprise that often occupied not only the heads of lower-class households but also their wives and children. Some shopkeepers and artisans enjoyed comfortable lives, but most urban dwellers lived near subsistence level in crowded tenements. Large numbers of poor people were dependent on the state or noble patrons for the bare essentials; it has been estimated, for instance, that an average of two hundred thousand Roman residents (perhaps a fourth of the city's population) lived off the public grain dole. The Roman imperial government as well as local city-state administrations in the provinces made serious efforts to provide police and fire protection, an adequate water supply, sanitary facilities, and cheap food. Nevertheless, life in the city was for many marred by poverty, violence, and insecurity. There were some avenues of escape from these conditions. Many residents of Rome were resettled in the provinces on their own farms. Especially attractive was service in the army, which provided regular pay, promotion opportunities, adequate pensions, and honor.

Despite its difficulties, city life had its compensations, even for the lowliest. Magnificent public buildings and parks provided an impressive setting for one's life. Holidays were numerous—perhaps as many as a hundred fifty a year by the second century A.D. Each was the occasion for splendid religious festivals featuring animal sacrifices that provided free meals, for the triumphs of victorious emperors, and for chariot races, gladiatorial contests, and bloody combats between wild animals and between animals and human beings. Numerous and sumptuous public baths provided attractive gathering places for everyone. Social clubs (called *collegia*), usually made up of individuals sharing a common occupation, provided opportunities for banqueting and help to members in time of need. Taverns abounded like oases where one could escape from the urban desert.

Those who received the least benefit from the

FIGURE 10.3 Scenes from a Roman Household These two panels done in relief illustrate some of the activities associated with household life in the Roman world: storing, preparing, and cooking food. The scenes suggest that such households were the setting for a secure and comfortable life. (Alinari)

Pax Romana were the peasants and the slaves. Isolated from city life, the rural population seldom felt the impact of the forces that gave the Roman world its vitality. Their existence centered around the family, hard work, and the simple social activities of the rural village. At best, the material return for their labor was small. Powerful trends were at work in the empire pushing many farmers into dependency on powerful absentee landlords; these dependent agricultural workers (called *coloni*) were increasingly victimized by heavy rents, an ever-heavier share of the tax burden, and loss of social status. To its discredit, the imperial government did little to check the exploitation of the peasantry; in fact, the aristocratic landowners who dominated the political process were quite happy to allow this drift toward peasant exploitation.

Slavery, an institution absolutely essential to the economy, remained a basic element of Roman imperial society. Slaves constituted a considerable portion of the population throughout the empire. It has been estimated that in the first century A.D. perhaps one-third of Italy's population of 7 to 8 million inhabitants were slaves. They served as household servants, agricultural laborers, workers in urban workshops and merchant stalls, teachers, miners, rowers, and gladiators; and their reward was minimal. The record is full of instances of brutal treatment by masters, whose rights over slaves were complete. There is some evidence that the condition of slaves improved. Many were freed by their masters, in some cases out of gratitude for faithful service. Funerary inscriptions and literary sources suggest amicable associations between masters and slaves. Slaves were allowed to marry and maintain families. Imperial legislation sought to curb physical abuse of slaves. However, no one—not even the most enlightened of the "good emperors"—thought of ending slavery. That institution continued to debase the lives of the victimized slaves and to poison the minds of their social superiors at all levels of society.

Our description of the Roman world in the second century A.D. points to a remarkable political achievement that established peace, order, and security for a huge population; undoubtedly these were blessings to all. However, the economic and social conditions suggest that the main beneficiaries of the *Pax Romana* were the members of a narrow, proud, self-satisfied circle with limited concern for millions of people less well positioned economically and socially. Many beyond the circle of the favored few—probably more than in earlier societies—appear to have managed fairly well. But it is clear that many suffered from poverty, injustice, and oppression. How these people perceived their existence is almost impossible to ascertain. Implicit in the structure of the Roman Empire at its height were economic and social conditions that meant that many of its members had only a limited stake in its existence. That situation would eventually test the empire's strength.

SUGGESTED READING

Political Developments

Chester G. Starr, *The Roman Empire, 27 B.C.–A.D. 476* (1982).
Colin Wells, *The Roman Empire* (1984).
J. S. Wacher, *The Roman Empire* (1987).
Any of these three works will provide an excellent survey.
Kurt A. Raaflaub and Mark Toher, *Between Republic and Empire: Interpretations of Augustus and His Principate* (1990). Helpful in assessing Augustus' accomplishments.
Fergus Millar, *The Emperor in the Roman World: 31 B.C.–A.D. 337* (1977). Although massive, this study is vital to understanding how the imperial political system worked.
Ronald Syme, *The Augustan Aristocracy* (1986). Rich in insights into how Augustus related to a key social group.
Graham Webster, *The Roman Imperial Army*, 3rd ed. (1986). A thorough treatment.

Economic and Social History

Peter Garnsey and Richard Saller, *The Roman Empire. Economy, Society, and Culture* (1987). An excellent survey.
Ramsay MacMullen, *Roman Social Relations, 50 B.C. to A.D. 284* (1974). Attempts to capture attitudes of major social groups.
Joan Liversidge, *Everyday Life in the Roman Empire* (1976). Excellent treatment of how the Romans lived.
The general picture of social conditions presented in the preceding titles can be supplemented by the following works.
Judith P. Hallett, *Fathers and Daughters in Roman Society: Women and the Elite Family* (1984).

Jane F. Gardner, *Women in Roman Law and Society* (1986).
John K. Evans, *War, Women and Children in Ancient Rome* (1991).
Suzanne Dixon, *The Roman Family* (1992).
Beryl Rawson, ed., *The Family in Ancient Rome: New Perspectives* (1986).
Suzanne Dixon, *The Roman Mother* (1988).
Thomas Wiedemann, *Adults and Children in the Roman Empire* (1989).
K. R. Bradley, *Slaves and Masters in the Roman Empire: A Study in Social Control* (1984).
L. A. Thompson, *Romans and Blacks* (1989).

Biographies

A. H. M. Jones, *Augustus* (1970).
Barbara Levick, *Tiberius the Politician* (1976).
Barbara Levick, *Claudius* (1990).
Miriam T. Griffin, *Nero: End of a Dynasty* (1984).
Steward Perowne, *Hadrian* (1960).
Anthony Birley, *Marcus Aurelius: A Biography*, rev. ed. (1987).

Sources

Moses Hadas, ed., *Complete Works of Tacitus* (1942).
Suetonius, *The Twelve Caesars*, trans. Robert Graves (1957).
Two lively treatments of the history of the first century A.D.

CHAPTER 11
Roman Thought and Expression

FIGURE 11.1 **The Fruits of Peace** This relief is from a larger composition decorating the Ara Pacis (Altar of Peace) built in Rome during the first century A.D. It glorifies the benefits bestowed by Augustus. The serene goddess of fertility and her happy children are surrounded by symbols of well-being. The work reflects how art was used to promote the greatness of Augustus. (Alinari)

While Roman statesmen and their citizen supporters were conquering and organizing a vast empire, writers, thinkers, and artists combined their creative efforts to make a major contribution to cultural history. Rome's prime cultural role was its assimilation and dissemination of Greek culture. But in the course of adapting the basic elements of Greek culture, the Romans put their distinctive mark onto its thought and expression, thereby creating a Latin cultural heritage destined to influence the future decisively, especially in western Europe.

1. ROME AND THE RECEPTION OF GREEK CULTURE

Before the third century B.C. the Romans displayed little interest in cultural pursuits. Although Etruscan cultural models, especially building techniques and religion, influenced early Roman society, the Romans long remained a simple people occupied chiefly with politics, war, and earning a living. As we have seen (see Chapter 8, Section 2), their early experiences in these pursuits ingrained in them deep-rooted values that influenced their cultural life throughout their history.

Beginning in the third century B.C., the simple mentality of the early republic experienced a cultural revolution, brought on largely by Roman expansion. As their armies absorbed first southern Italy and Sicily and then the Hellenistic Near East, Roman aristocrats became aware of Greek culture, especially in its Hellenistic forms. They were so impressed that they were, as the first-century poet Horace put it, taken captive by those they conquered. This encounter, which placed a high social value on becoming culturally Hellenized, was critical in determining Rome's role in the total stream of cultural history.

One of the major consequences of the "discovery" of Greek culture was the introduction into Rome of a new educational system. Down to the end of the third century B.C. young Romans were usually educated at home: males by their fathers, who taught them family customs, the principles of Roman law, civic duties, and religion; females by their mothers, who taught them the household arts. By the second century B.C. that traditional system began to be replaced by the Hellenistic pattern of education. In many aristocratic Roman households Greek slaves were employed to complement basic instruction in reading and writing Latin with instruction in the Greek language and the Greek "classics" of literature and philosophy. Bilingualism became a mark of social distinction, but those not able to master Greek could still gain access to Greek masterpieces through translations into Latin. Not only were young men introduced to this new education, young women were also often involved (see Figure 9.3). Private schools emerged to provide young men with an opportunity to extend their formal education over a longer period of time. They often went to the east, especially to Athens, to finish their education. Grammar (the study of language and literature) and rhetoric (the study of effective expression and argumentation) became the touchstones of the new education, providing invaluable skills for successful public careers and for acceptance into the ranks of the *nobiles* and the *equites*.

Their fascination with Greek culture soon spurred the Romans to imitate it. Borrowing heavily from the content and forms provided by Greek models, Latin writers produced epic poems, dramas, histories, and philosophical tracts. As a result, the Latin language was enriched as a vehicle of independent literary expression. Romans were equally captivated by Greek and Hellenistic art. During the wars in the east, numerous art pieces were "liberated" to decorate Roman residences, and eastern artists were imported to produce copies of Greek statues and paintings. The Greek style of architecture was employed for civic and private buildings so often that Rome began to resemble a Greek or Hellenistic city.

Even the Roman masses felt the impact of Greek influences, but they were touched chiefly through religion. The wars of conquest and the resultant economic and social dislocations left many people intellectually and emotionally lost. Traditional Roman religion offered little to meet these needs. The eastern religions did. New deities, myths, and rituals taken from the Greek civic religions were added to public religion in Rome, but even these additions did not satisfy many. From eastern slaves they learned about more exciting Hellenistic mystery religions such as the worship of Dionysus or Cybele or Isis.

These emotional, personal cults increasingly challenged the traditional religion for the allegiance of the Italian population and began to reshape the value system of the Roman populace.

This cultural revolution was fought by some conservative Romans, most notably Cato the Elder (234–149 B.C.), a prominent statesman who saw foreign culture as a threat to Rome's traditional values. He spent much of his public career railing against the Greek way, bemusing his contemporaries with dramatic exposures of cultural "subversives," and seeking to induce public authorities to curb their activities. But he was fighting a lost cause. Rome was destined by circumstance and choice to be heir to the magnificent patrimony of the Greeks. Many of Cato's contemporaries saw the perpetuation of Greek culture as a Roman responsibility and acted eagerly to fulfill that mission. For example, no less a person than the powerful Scipio Africanus, along with many of his descendants (including the Gracchi brothers), championed the Hellenization of Roman thought and expression.

By the first century B.C. the stimulus provided by the encounter with Greek culture had readied Roman writers, artists, and thinkers to put their own stamp on what they had borrowed. The result was a burst of creativity launching Rome's cultural "golden age"; the Augustan age marked its high point. After a brief slackening in the first century A.D., there followed a second period of considerable activity during the era of the "good emperors," often called the "silver age."

2. ROMAN LITERATURE

The Roman cultural genius is perhaps best reflected in literature. After a long apprenticeship under Greek influence during the third and second centuries B.C., a succession of writers living between about 100 B.C. and A.D. 150 produced a rich and varied body of Latin literature. Almost without exception, these works reflect strong Greek influences in content and form. But their authors demonstrated remarkable talent in adapting Greek modes to produce works in the Latin language that were marked by stylistic grace and force, depth of personal conviction, a powerful grasp of social reality, and a passion for instructing readers. That literature was es-

pecially important to the intellectual history of western Europe because it served as the main vehicle through which Greek literary forms, ideas, and values were transmitted to the West.

Outstanding among all Roman writers was Vergil (70–19 B.C.). Born in rural Italy, he grew to manhood during the last years of the civil wars that ruined the republic, and he personally suffered their ravages. Eventually he attracted the attention of Augustus, whose patronage permitted him to devote the last years of his life to writing. Although much of his great talent was poured out in the service of the new Augustan order, it would be erroneous to overemphasize Vergil's role as a propagandist; he wrote in support of the Augustan system out of deep conviction and enthusiasm. His *Georgics* express a strong feeling for nature and for what involvement in pastoral life can mean—especially to those corrupted by the violence and greed surrounding the last days of the republic. Vergil's masterpiece was his *Aeneid*. An epic modeled after Homer's and filled with material drawn from Greek legend, this majestic work sought to show that Rome's rise to mastery of the world was divinely ordained. The plot centers on the adventures of a mythical Trojan hero, Aeneas, who after the fall of Troy was ordered by the gods to establish, in Italy, a new city destined to rule the world. Aeneas is portrayed as an ideal Roman whose virtue is constantly tested by such challenges as the spiteful behavior of the deities, a heartrending love affair with Dido, queen of Carthage, and a horror-filled journey to the underworld. But he persists in his mission to found a city whose decisive role in shaping the civilized world came to fruition with the accession of Augustus. Never was the Roman ideal of the dedicated patriot portrayed with more intensity and dignity; and never was the theme of Rome's predestination to shape a good world more dramatically stated.

Two other poets, Catullus and Horace, illustrate a more personal, internalized facet of the Roman literary genius. Catullus (ca. 85–54 B.C.) was a product of high society in the late republican period, living his life amid a dissolute, pleasure-seeking crowd of young nobles. Among his many adventures was a love affair with a noble lady who was already married and who eventually jilted him. The experience inspired him to pour forth powerful lyric poetry portraying with great intensity his feelings of love and of the pain and hatred caused by lost love. Horace (65–8 B.C.), a son of a freed slave, enjoyed the patronage of Augustus and was second in influence only to Vergil. His best work, the *Odes*, capture with telling effect his personal reactions to hundreds of situations he met in his lifetime; he was particularly eloquent in his praise of the Augustan peace. Although he lacked the fire of Catullus, Horace spoke to a wider circle, his lyric poems reflecting the reasoned, thoughtful reactions of an educated, humane Roman to life as a whole—a great spirit looking at the world about him with sanity, intelligence, and wit. He was and remains the ideal of a civilized person.

Lucretius (ca. 95–55 B.C.) demonstrated still another aspect of Roman poetic genius: moral seriousness. A contemporary of Catullus, he too was profoundly moved by events of the civil war era. He found his personal salvation in Epicurean philosophy, which he undertook to explain to his Latin-speaking contemporaries in a long poem called *On the Nature of Things*. With almost missionary zeal Lucretius put poetry to the service of instruction. He made a noble plea to educated Romans to seek in philosophy the bases of moral regeneration and personal fulfillment. Seldom has a poet shown greater moral earnestness.

Other notable Latin poets were Ovid, Martial, and Juvenal. Ovid (43 B.C.–A.D. 17) entertained Augustan high society with his *Art of Love*, a frivolous but amusing poem on the art of seduction, and his *Metamorphoses*, an entertaining, lively rendering of Greek mythological stories into Latin. Martial (ca. A.D. 38–102) and Juvenal (ca. A.D. 55–140) exercised their poetic talents as satirists painting in vivid colors the shortcomings of Roman aristocratic society during the post-Augustan age.

The talents of the Latin poets were matched by those of the prose writers. Perhaps Rome's most accomplished prose writer was Cicero (106–43 B.C.). Although an active lawyer and statesman, he produced a wide variety of writing in many forms. His masterful speeches, shaped by the Greek rhetorical tradition, his intimate knowledge of political life, and his personal ambitions, raised political argumentation to the level of art. Among his numerous tracts on various subjects were two important essays on po-

litical theory, *The Republic* and *The Laws*, which defended Roman republican institutions but pleaded for the establishment of a first citizen to guide the state. In other tracts he sought to make abstract Greek philosophical thought understandable to Roman readers and relative to their lives. His numerous *Letters* supply a brilliant picture of Roman politics and society in the first century B.C. Taken together, the works of this eloquent, learned Roman set a model for Latin prose writing that would be imitated for centuries.

The Romans also excelled in historical writing. Interest in the past was promoted by the deep respect for tradition ingrained in the Roman mentality from almost the beginning of Roman history and by the need to explain and justify Rome's rise to supremacy in the Mediterranean world. Those concerns were exemplified by the most influential Roman historian, Livy (59 B.C.–A.D. 17), another of those inspired to creative activity under the Augustan regime. His masterpiece, the immense *Roman History*, sought to treat developments extending from the foundation of Rome by the mythical Aeneas to the time of Augustus. Although a large part of the work has been lost, it is clear from what is left that Livy believed Rome had a great historical mission about which he wished to instruct his readers. To achieve that end, Livy put together in an artful fashion a mixture of truth and legend intended to teach a lesson. The work presented with great dramatic impact the people and events that made Rome great and highlighted the traditional virtues—in Livy's view now restored by Augustus—undergirding that success.

Less monumental but equally artistic was the work of Tacitus (ca. A.D. 55–117), who wrote about Roman history during the century after Augustus. Together his two major works, *Histories* and *Annals*, cover the period A.D. 14–96. Although Tacitus was a man of senatorial and republic sentiments prejudiced against the successors of Augustus, he described the activities of Rome's ruling circle with brilliance and deep moral sense. Another of his works, *Germania*, gives important information about the Germanic peoples, who were soon to play a major part in Roman life. Suetonius (ca. A.D. 75–150) also treated the rulers from Julius Caesar to Domitian in his *Lives of the Twelve Caesars*, a spicy account mixing fact with gossip and especially stressing scandal and sexual excesses. Several Romans produced personal memoirs that were historical in character. Probably the best examples were Julius Caesar's *Commentaries on the Gallic Wars* and Marcus Aurelius' *Meditations*. Emperors

In their initial encounters with Hellenic culture, some Latin writers sought to imitate the magnificent dramatic art of the Greeks. The most notable Roman dramatists were Plautus (ca. 254–184 B.C.) and Terence (ca. 195–159 B.C.), both writers of comedies. But drama failed to take root among the Romans. Moreover, only occasionally did a fiction writer grace the Roman literary scene. These gaps in the repertory of genres cultivated by Roman writers suggest that the creation of highly imaginative literature was foreign to the Romans, whose concerns focused on reality—on history, current moral problems, personal experience.

While our concern here is primarily with assessing the achievements of Latin writers, it is important to note that throughout the golden and silver ages of Latin literature (that is, from about 100 B.C. to A.D. 150) Greek writers continued to produce a significant body of literature in a variety of genres. For example, one of the greatest historians of antiquity was a Greek, Polybius (ca. 200–118 B.C.). While living in Rome from 167 to 151 B.C. as a hostage, he became an intimate of the pro-Hellenic Scipionic circle and produced a superb work chronicling Rome's rise to world power. Another Greek author, Plutarch (ca. A.D. 46–120), wrote of a series of biographies of illustrious Greeks and Romans entitled *Parallel Lives* that sought to provide readers with a guide to moral excellence. But these are only a few of the many Greek authors whose efforts enriched the cultural scene under Roman rule. That Greek literature continued to flourish is an indication of the cosmopolitan, tolerant cultural environment resulting from the *Pax Romana*.

3. ROMAN ART

Like literature, the visual arts developed slowly in the Roman world. After an initial impetus derived from Etruscan models, artistic tastes among the Romans were decisively affected after about 250 B.C. by their growing familiarity with Greek forms, motifs, and techniques. Not until the first century B.C. did the unique artistic genius of the Romans begin to manifest itself; it reached its full maturity during the first two centuries A.D. During that "golden age" the imperial government provided a powerful impetus to artistic creativity, partly as a means of glorifying the imperial regime and its rulers but also because members of the ruling elite in Rome enjoyed beauty and refinement. This imperial art never lost its Greek imprint, but it had qualities that gave it a distinctive character.

Rome's most impressive artistic achievements were in architecture, where important elements were added to what was borrowed. The Romans invented concrete, which provided a cheap, durable, adaptable building material. This material allowed architects to exploit the arch, the dome, and various forms of vaulting more effectively than had been done before and to create imaginative exteriors by the use of marble and brick facings over concrete. These technical advances permitted larger structures and innovative variations on the rectangular ground plans and predominantly horizontal elevation lines characteristic of the typical Greek structure.

Although they were avid temple builders, the Romans were generally content to imitate the Greek temple style, as is illustrated by the famous Maison Carrée still standing in Nîmes, France. However, they were capable of innovation. The Pantheon, built in Rome in the second century A.D., is one of the most imposing round temples ever built. Its domed roof, 142 feet in diameter and supported by niche-filled concrete walls, covers a vast internal space that evokes a sense of awe. A rectangular porch, its gabled roof supported by Greek columns, leads into this inner sanctum, supplying a pleasing mixture of Greek and Roman architectural ideas.

Much more distinctly Roman in style, technique, and spirit were the public buildings: forums, baths, amphitheaters, aqueducts, bridges, meeting halls (basilicas), and palaces, built in abundance not only in Rome but also in provincial cities throughout the empire (see Figures 11.2 and 11.3). The Roman Forum, a huge complex of meeting halls, market facilities, and shrines laid out on an axial plan, reflects the Roman genius for planning and adapting architectural forms to

FIGURE 11.2 A Roman Aqueduct The Pont du Gard, built across the River Gard to bring water to the Gallo-Roman city of Nîmes, is an impressive monument to Roman engineering skill. The structure rises 160 feet above the river bed and is about 900 feet in length; each of the large arches is about 80 feet across at its base. Roman architects and engineers have seldom been matched in the application of the arch to utilitarian ends. (Art Resource)

a variety of uses. The Colosseum, a massive sports facility begun during Vespasian's reign, accommodated fifty thousand spectators and provided special boxes for the emperors and other dignitaries. It featured an elliptical ground plan above which were elevated four levels of arch-covered passageways giving access to the seats looking down on the arena where the bloody gladiatorial combats so beloved by the Romans occurred. The most common Roman building was the basilica, essentially a long hall flanked by side aisles and often featuring a rounded apse at one end. The walls of the main hall extended above the roofs of the side aisles, allowing windows to be cut high in the walls. Arches and columns were skillfully used to permit access from the side aisles into the main hall and to support its roof; in the Basilica of Maxentius (early fourth century A.D.) a concrete roof was put over a main aisle eighty feet wide. Roman baths, which consisted of a great central court surrounded by numerous smaller rooms, demonstrated the Roman talents for organizing interior space for utilitarian purposes and creat-

ing internal plumbing and heating systems. The Romans also built huge imperial palaces (the most famous are those of Nero and Domitian) and rural villas characterized by multistoried layouts featuring different-sized and -shaped rooms and sumptuous internal decor (see Color Plate 4). Not the least accomplishment of Roman architects was the development of living quarters suited to the needs of crowded cities: multistoried concrete structures containing standardized small apartment units suited to the needs of low-income residents.

Roman sculptors were less innovative than the architects were. Greek and Hellenistic models were constantly and even slavishly imitated. The best Roman sculpture was devoted to portraiture and to relief work treating historical incidents, both art forms especially useful in serving the purposes of patrons who wished to keep their images before the public for political and social reasons or to commemorate their deeds for posterity. The artists who rendered portrait sculptures were remarkably adept at realistic portrayal, but always their work accentuated the

FIGURE 11.3 Roman Architecture
This photo of an arena and a theater built in Arles in southern France near the end of the first century B.C. illustrates the Roman talent for constructing impressive public buildings to serve as the focus of civic life. Arenas provided the settings for such popular activities as races, gladiatorial combats, and wild animal hunts. The close proximity of a spacious theater suited for drama, dance, song, and poetry reading suggests a wide range of interests among the citizens of a Roman provincial city. (French Government Tourist Office, New York)

dignity of their subjects (see Figures 8.1, 9.2, and 10.1). Roman relief carvings—featured especially on the walls of public buildings, arches and columns celebrating the deeds of emperors, and coffins honoring the dead—were remarkably effective in capturing scenes from everyday life in a way that conveyed a powerful message lauding the feats of those honored and reinforcing the virtues exemplified by their careers (see Figures 9.1, 9.3, 10.3, 11.1, and 12.2). Perhaps the most remarkable example of Roman relief work is the freestanding column erected to celebrate Trajan's military triumph in Dacia. Around the column spirals a continuous scene seven hundred feet long that depicts in almost photographic detail the activities of about twenty-five hundred figures engaged in various activities associated with a military campaign. Surviving examples of Roman painting (see Figure 10.2 and Color Plate 5) and mosaic work (Color Plate 6) are rare; examples found in the ruins of Pompeii and Her-

culaneum, two cities buried by an eruption of Mt. Vesuvius in A.D. 79., suggest that Greek and Hellenistic influences remained strong and that these arts played an important role in decorating interiors, thus being strongly shaped by architectural plans. Painters and their patrons were especially fond of mythological subjects and portrayals of nature.

4. ROMAN PHILOSOPHY, SCIENCE, AND RELIGION

Philosophical interests in the Roman world were shaped by patterns of thought established during the Hellenistic period, focusing chiefly on applying classical Greek philosophical principles to ethical issues facing individuals and society. While many of the most significant philosophers in the Roman world were Greek speakers, educated Romans absorbed their ideas and sought to utilize those ideas to formulate answers to problems facing the Roman world. The most significant accomplishment of these Roman thinkers lay not in advancing philosophical speculation but in recasting Greek philosophy into a Roman idiom and transmitting that wisdom in the Latin language to later western European society.

Six individuals will illustrate the main currents of philosophical development during the period of Roman domination; most of them were not philosophers in the strict sense but writers, statesmen, or educated citizens seeking personal and social guidance from philosophy. The extensive writings of Cicero (106–43 B.C.) are filled with philosophical reflections which illustrate a powerful tendency in Roman philosophical thought to intermingle the viewpoints of various schools into an eclectic response to moral issues. However, the major Roman philosophers usually became advocates of one or another of the Hellenistic schools of thought. In his *On the Nature of Things* the poet Lucretius (ca. 95–55 B.C.) used his talent to entreat his Roman readers to follow the Epicurean ideal of seeking pleasure and peace of mind in a materialistic universe through contemplation and withdrawal from the world. Particularly attractive to many Romans was the sober philosophy of Stoicism, certainly the most influential philosophical movement of the first two centuries A.D. Three individuals were its noted advocates: Seneca (ca. 4 B.C.–A.D. 65), an essayist who served Nero; Epictetus (ca. A.D. 55–135), a freedman who, after being exiled from Rome, spent most of his life teaching his ideas to ordinary people; and Emperor Marcus Aurelius (A.D. 121–180), whose famous *Meditations* summarized the Roman version of the Stoic worldview, emphasizing acceptance of duty and resignation to whatever fate brings. The Roman Stoics did not neglect the emphasis of Hellenistic Stoicism on personal peace of mind, but they gave greater attention to social responsibility and public morality. Especially influential was their expansion of the idea of an all-pervading, unchangeable law of nature governing the universe to provide a justification for a single human community governed by a system of law that conformed to the law of nature. Perhaps the thinker most important for the future was Plotinus (A.D. 204–270), an Egyptian who spent much of his

career in Rome teaching a system called Neoplatonism. Derived from Plato's thought, Plotinus' system, as set forth in his *Enneads,* posited the superiority of the spiritual world over the material, the existence of a perfect being at the summit of spiritual reality, and the possibility of human participation in spiritual reality through a mystical experience that involved the penetration of the supreme spiritual being into the human spirit properly prepared by contemplation. Neoplatonism represented a fundamental aspect of the development of thought during the Roman period: the merging of philosophy and religion, a trend that perhaps best met the needs of people in what was increasingly becoming an "age of anxiety" who were seeking some higher order of truth beyond the worldly realm.

The Roman period was not marked by significant advances in science. Romans were little interested in speculation about the natural world or in systematic investigation of natural phenomena. Perhaps the most significant scientific achievement resulted from the effort of scholars to compile great encyclopedias intended to summarize in systematic fashion all the scientific knowledge contained in Greek and Hellenistic sources. Notable examples included Strabo (ca. 63 B.C.–A.D. 21) in geography, Pliny the Elder (ca. A.D. 23–79) in natural history, Ptolemy (ca. A.D. 121–151) in astronomy, and Galen (A.D. 131–201) in medicine. These compilations would long remain the chief guides to understanding nature. The Romans excelled in practical science: the engineering of monumental structures; the construction of roads, bridges, aqueducts; more effective farming techniques. The technical skills developed by engineers, artisans, and farmers formed a precious heritage perhaps as important to the West as the literary, artistic, and philosophical tradition nurtured and transmitted by Rome.

While a relatively narrow circle of the educated upper class of the Roman world absorbed Greek and Hellenistic philosophy and science and derived from it new values and patterns of behavior, religion remained a powerful force shaping the basic outlook of the great bulk of society, including many nobles. The ancient Roman family and civic religious beliefs and practices continued to play a prominent role in private and public life. In fact, traditional Roman religion took on new vigor during the first and second centuries A.D. as a result of efforts by rulers from Augustus onward to utilize religion as an official instrument for the renewal of Roman civic life. An important consequence of this overt linkage of imperial politics and religion was the gradual emergence of emperor worship, especially in the eastern provinces of the empire, as a powerful dimension of imperial government. Perhaps the most momentous religious development between about 100 B.C. and A.D. 180 was the spread of Hellenistic mystery religions over the entire world ruled by the Romans. Their diffusion was facilitated by Roman tolerance of any religion that did not threaten to disturb public order or challenge imperial authority. Particularly appealing were the cults of the Great Mother goddess associated with Cybele, of the Egyptian goddess Isis, and above all of the Persian deity Mithra, which took deep root in the Roman army. The ideas and practices associated with these religions emphasized personal identification with a deity through highly emotional rituals and life after death earned for good behavior. Such concepts tended to weaken the appeal of traditional Roman religions, which stressed highly formalized rituals performed by groups in return for material rewards. The trend already under way during the Hellenistic Age toward religious syncretism—the mingling of beliefs and practices—continued everywhere in the Roman world. The ground was being prepared for the acceptance of a common religion. The advocates of the religion that eventually filled that role—Christianity—were already spreading their "good news" during the Golden Age of the Roman Empire (see Chapter 12).

5. ROMAN LAW

One of Rome's most enduring cultural monuments was its law, which was vital not only as a force promoting orderly life throughout Rome's history but also as a legacy handed on to later societies to guide them in establishing effective societal relations. As early as about 450 B.C., the principle was set forth in the famous Twelve Tables that citizens had rights that could be claimed and defended in courts. From then on these rights of citizens, which collectively constituted the law of citizens (*ius civile*), were explored, tested, and expanded in the context of changing times. During the republican period the enactments of assemblies enriched the substance of the law. Even more important, the magistrates charged with administering the law, the *praetors*, were allowed to pronounce their interpretation of the law at the beginning of their term; this practice resulted in a constant reinterpretation of the law within a framework that highlighted principles that should govern the *ius civile*. During this same period, the decisions of the judges who actually conducted cases in court shaped an ever-growing body of precedent that had the weight of law. In reaching their decision judges were advised by *jurisconsults*, specialists whose study of the law allowed them to assert a significant role in shaping the precedents that were applied in court as law. Roman expansion across the Mediterranean world not only witnessed the spread of Roman civil law to new geographical areas but also presented judicial officials with the problem of settling cases involving noncitizens. The result was the development of a law of nations (*ius gentium*), which represented a mixture of the laws of subject peoples, Roman practices, and the commonsense decisions of judges. With the institution of the Roman Empire the content of the law was further expanded by a vast outpouring of decrees and instructions issued by each *princeps* in an attempt to ensure that the huge empire would be ruled uniformly and equitably.

As the body of the law expanded and the society to which it was applied grew more complex, there was increasing pressure to codify the law into a single, systematic body. This concern had become central to the study of law by the second century A.D., when a series of brilliant *jurisconsults*, working under the patronage of the emperors, focused their attention on defining the principles undergirding sound law and its application. Their efforts were spurred by their realization of the importance of unified law as a tool for governing the empire and by their awareness that the distinction between citizens and noncitizens was disappearing. In addition, their thinking was decisively influenced by Stoic philosophy, which argued that there existed a law of nature (*ius naturale*) governing the universe to which human law must conform. The concept of natural law was a fruitful source of principles according to which all aspects of human law could be arranged and interrelated into a consistent, logical body. The codification of Roman law was not completed until the reign of Emperor Justinian (A.D. 527–565) (see Chapter 14). But as imperial legislators, judges, and students of law moved toward that end, their efforts shaped an immense body of law that became a storehouse to which many people would turn in the future for guidance in the humane, equitable conduct of human affairs.

6. THE ROMANS AND CULTURAL DIFFUSION

When assessing the role of the Romans in cultural history, one must give them due credit for raising the level of culture in large areas previously little affected by higher civilization. Since the main ingredients of Roman culture were derived from Greece and the Hellenistic east, the Roman's role as disseminators of culture in that part of the empire was limited. However, it must be noted that the establishment of the *Pax Romana* in that area encouraged the continued maturing of Greek cultural life and promoted the Hellenization of non-Greek natives of the eastern provinces. The case was different in the west, where the impact of Roman culture was widespread and of decisive importance in the lives of non-Romans. The Romans were much less exclusive in their attitude toward non-Romans than the classical Greeks were, chiefly because they understood from early in their history the importance of Romanization in establishing and maintaining their domination over their culturally diverse subjects. The marks of their success as disseminators of culture are still visible. For example, modern "Romance" languages—Ital-ian, French, and Spanish—are direct descendants of the Latin spread into those areas when the Romans conquered them. A modern traveler in Western Europe and North Africa will repeatedly encounter the remains of Roman baths, aqueducts, temples, theaters, and roads—all evidence of the presence of the Romans as a creative force in enriching life in these areas.

The processes through which Romanization was achieved were complex. Roman soldiers, officials, merchants, and colonizers were important agents in carrying Roman culture outward across the empire. The Roman government actively promoted the creation of cities and encouraged those settling in them to imitate Roman ways. Provincial aristocracies were encouraged to become Romanized as a test of their eligibility for citizenship and for Roman approval of their leadership of local government. In these provincial urban centers, schools were established to teach Latin and Greek grammar and rhetoric and to promote the study of literature and philosophy; as a result, a common store of ideas and set of tastes spread to the far corners of the empire. The imperial government promoted extensive building activities, which led to the spread of a common style in architecture, sculpture, and painting. Scholars, religious missionaries, philosophers, artists, and teachers circulated freely throughout the empire to spread a common culture. From the third century B.C. onward, the government and aristocracy of the city of Rome welcomed artistic and intellectual talent from all over the empire, making the capital of the empire the center of a cosmopolitan culture from which flowed influences affecting life throughout the empire. All of these factors combined to bring large numbers of people under the sway of a common culture that would decisively affect their histories for many centuries to come.

SUGGESTED READING

General Overviews

Pierre Grimal, *The Civilization of Rome*, trans. W. S. Maquinness (1963).

John Boardman et al., eds., *The Oxford History of the Classical World* (1986).
Two insightful surveys of Roman cultural life.

Religion

Margaret Lyttelton and Werner Forman, *The Romans: Their Gods and Their Beliefs* (1984).

John Ferguson, *The Religions of the Roman Empire* (1970).

Either of these two titles will provide rich material on religious life in the Roman world.

Stewart Perowne, *Roman Mythology*, new rev. ed. (1984). A splendidly illustrated description of Roman myths.

Alan Wardman, *Religion and Statecraft among the Romans* (1982).

Alan Watson, *The State, Law, and Religion: Pagan Rome* (1992).

These two works explore the role of religion in political life.

Thought and Expression

Stanley F. Bonner, *Education in Ancient Rome: From Cato the Elder to the Younger Pliny* (1977). A full treatment.

Elizabeth Rawson, *Intellectual Life in the Late Roman Republic* (1985). A landmark study dispelling stereotypes about the lack of Roman intellectual creativity.

E. J. Kennedy, ed., *Cambridge History of Classical Literature*, Vol. 2 (1982). A thorough, scholarly survey.

R. M. Ogilivie, *Roman Literature and Society* (1980). Seeks to relate literature to social conditions.

F. H. Sandbach, *The Stoics* (1975). Describes the basic ideas of the Stoics.

H. F. Jolowicz and Barry Nicholas, *Historical Introduction to the Study of Roman Law*, 3rd ed. (1972). A massive survey.

Nancy H. Ramage and Andrew Ramage, *Roman Art: Romulus to Constantine* (1991).

Susan Walker, *Roman Art* (1991).

Two excellent surveys touching all phases of artistic life.

Niels Hannestad, *Roman Art and Imperial Policy* (1986). Relates art and political life.

Sources

Kevin Guinagh and Alfred P. Darjahn, eds., *Latin Literature in Translation*, 2nd ed. (1952). A good sample of Latin literature. Better still would be to read the complete works of the major Latin authors mentioned in this chapter; their works are readily available in good translations.

CHAPTER 12

Crisis in the Roman World, A.D. 180–284: Conflict, Change, and Christianity

FIGURE 12.1 The Ascension of Christ This ivory carving from about A.D. 400 portrays Christ's ascension into the hand of God while an angel speaks to the three Marys and soldiers cower in terror. It illustrates how Christian artists adapted classical art styles to Christian purposes; note especially the pagan sarcophagus, which certainly had no part in the scriptural account of this crucial event in Christian history. (Marburg/Art Resource)

As the second century A.D. progressed, many contemporaries—and many later historians—were persuaded that Greco-Roman civilization as embodied in the Roman Empire marked a high point in human history. A vast, peaceful community of diverse peoples had been joined together by powerful forces: an enlightened system of government fashioned by the Romans; a common culture derived chiefly from the Greeks that fostered a common basis of discourse and shared values; and expanding economic ties linking the far corners of the Roman Empire. However, like any human order, the *Pax Romana* was not immune to the forces of change. During the third century Roman society began to experience stresses which set in motion forces of disintegration so powerful that Greco-Roman civilization was unable to survive. In order to understand the long succession of events leading to the "fall" of Greco-Roman civilization, it is necessary to identify the sources of these tensions, many of which were rooted in the basic structures of the Roman imperial order.

1. CONSTITUTIONAL PROBLEMS

Although it proved remarkably effective during the two centuries after its foundation by Augustus, the governance system known as the principate had inherent limitations that came to the forefront during the third century. The result was a prolonged period of disorder that brought about subtle changes heralding a major transformation of the Roman governmental system.

One important problem centered on an old issue: the choice of a successor to the office of *princeps*. The adoptive principle utilized so successfully by the "good emperors" had been abandoned by Marcus Aurelius, who returned to hereditary succession by designating his incapable son Commodus (A.D. 180–192) as his successor. Commodus' misrule ended with his assassination and a savage struggle among segments of the army to decide on a successor. The victor was Septimus Severus (A.D. 192–211), a career army officer of African origin, whose dynasty controlled the imperial office by right of inheritance until A.D. 235. Following the advice of Septimus to favor the troops and forget the rest of the population, the Severi encouraged the soldi-

ery to think that the state should be run to reward the army, a policy given impetus by the dangers mounting along Rome's frontier. The result was almost constant civil war from the end of the Severan dynasty until A.D. 284, bloody struggles instigated by army units that took up arms to elevate their generals to the imperial office in expectation of special favors. Successful leaders of these uprisings—often called "barracks emperors"—barely had time to eliminate the followers of their predecessor and reward their troops before new rebels violently removed them from office. Amid this civil strife the *Pax Romana* increasingly seemed a distant memory.

The army's involvement in the succession issue was not entirely due to ambition and greed. It stemmed from another unresolved problem: the defense of the frontier. After a long period of successful expansion extending from the third century B.C. to the early second century A.D. (see Maps 8.2 and 10.1), the Romans sought to establish a fixed frontier defended by a professional army of citizen-soldiers. Although temporarily effective, that defense system was insufficient to cope with a massive change destined to affect the geopolitical balance around the Mediterranean world for many centuries to come: For the first time since the Persian attack on the Greeks in the fifth century B.C., forces beyond the empire's control were taking shape that set into motion a massive movement of peoples toward the Mediterranean basin. During the third century the initial thrust of this movement brought a threat to Roman security that reached crisis levels. A new dynasty, the Sassanians, seized power in Parthia in A.D. 224. Its aggressive rulers, dedicated to the restoration of Persia's ancient glory and the repossession of its ancient territory—which included most of Rome's Asiatic provinces—began to assert constant pressure on Rome's eastern frontier. Along the European frontier the Germans became ever more threatening, chiefly because of developments within the Germanic world that prompted the migration of Germans southward under circumstances that led to the formation of larger groupings of tribes into warrior-led "nations" capable of more effective military actions. During the third century Parthian and German intrusions into Roman territory not only disrupted the peace but also posed the need for a stronger Roman military establishment.

The uncertainties surrounding succession and defense were complicated by continued confusion about the exact nature of the office of *princeps* or emperor. Although from its original establishment by Augustus that office had contained the seeds of one-man rule, that potential had been veiled for two centuries by conscious efforts to involve the aristocracy in the political process and by the style of leadership practiced by the "good emperors." That fiction began to dissolve during the third century. The Severan dynasty and the "barracks emperors" were a different breed from earlier rulers. Most were provincials whose entire careers had been spent in the army. They had little experience with the problems of civil administration, sensitivity to the needs of the civilian population, or understanding of the principles undergirding the Augustan principate. Their concern was the acquisition of power and its unrestrained exercise. Rule by a *princeps*, a first citizen on the model of Augustus or Trajan or Hadrian, was being replaced with rule by a *dominus*, an absolute lord over all citizens, who increasingly were viewed as mere subjects.

The emergence of autocratic leadership based on military power led to the dislocation of other basic elements of the imperial political order. To meet the threat to Rome's frontier, the army was steadily enlarged, its ranks increasingly filled by noncitizen recruits, a process that diminished the importance of citizen-soldiers. Increasingly, the chief administrative posts were filled from the army, reducing the crucial role of the senatorial aristocracy in political life. The emperors intruded more decisively into the affairs of local city-state governments to limit local self-determination and to threaten the delicate relationships that had long given local authorities a vital share in the governance of the empire. The thrust of public policy shifted toward administrative centralization and the regimentation of society pursued in the interests of buttressing the power of military autocrats and serving the needs of defense.

Taken together, this array of political problems not only disturbed the internal order to which the Roman populace had grown accustomed but also pointed up the need for a restructuring of the political system.

2. ECONOMIC, SOCIAL, AND CULTURAL STRESSES

During the third century stress and transformation were not confined to the political realm. Faced with the need for greater resources for defense, the Roman world was unable to expand its economic bases; in fact, economic production decreased during the third century. In part this decline was due to the ravages caused by civil strife and invasions, but more ominous were the structural limitations inherent in the traditional economic system.

Most serious was a decline in agricultural production. The Roman world began to be plagued by a shortage of agricultural labor resulting from a variety of factors: a population decline in the entire Mediterranean world caused by a serious plague in the late second century; the ongoing flight of farmers to urban centers; and a decline in the number of slaves. Farmland was increasingly abandoned despite efforts of the state to encourage resettlement. Agricultural technology did not advance to offset soil depletion and erosion. The spread of the large estate system (*latifundia*) continued, displacing independent small farmers with dependent *coloni* and slaves whose status provided little incentive for them to increase production. In the face of political and economic instability the owners of large estates sought economic security in self-sufficiency rather than production for a market.

Trade and industry were also depressed. The disturbances accompanying civil strife impeded the movement of goods. In their search for funds to reward the army the emperors of the third century not only confiscated urban wealth but regularly debased the currency, leading to massive inflation. Increasing regimentation of the economy in the interest of supplying the enlarged army impeded new commercial and industrial ventures. New investment capital was scarce because the directive elements in Roman society continued to invest their wealth in land and luxurious living and because wealth was diverted into nonproductive military expenditures. The aristocratic ethos dominating society continued to preclude any thought of generating economic growth by elevating the standard of living of lower-class members of society. All of these signs pointed toward an impending, perhaps irreversible decline in the real wealth of the Roman world, a development with ominous implications for the poor and the powerless and for the sense of well-being that had prevailed among the elite in the times of the "good emperors."

The highly stratified social structure put into place by Augustus and nurtured by the imperial government during the first and second centuries A.D. began to unravel during the third century. The long-standing and socially important distinction between citizens and noncitizens was finally obliterated in A.D. 212, when Emperor Caracalla decreed that all free residents of the empire were citizens. The ascending military autocrats systematically diminished the role of the old senatorial aristocracy in political life, thereby depriving that group of involvement in an activity that had long been a mark of its social preeminence. In cities throughout the empire local aristocracies had new burdens heaped on them to provide money and supplies for the armies and were deprived of control over local affairs by the bureaucrats representing the central authority; this treatment persuaded many of them to seek escape from what had once been a privileged status. Ever-larger numbers of the equestrian order gave their allegiance to the military emperors in return for opportunities to profit from supplying the expanding military establishment. This realignment of social positions began to undermine the shared values and interests that had once allowed the upper stratum of Roman society to play a vital role in controlling the social order. Artisans and merchants were increasingly forced into compulsory associations (*collegia*) through which their wages and production were controlled in the interests of the state. The peasants were steadily being driven toward hereditary tenancy and dependency on landowners, conditions that made their already depressed condition even worse. Sporadic peasant revolts, usually brutally suppressed, suggested a growing discontent in the peasant ranks.

Two elements in this changing social scene were advantaged by the social flux of the era: great landowners and soldiers. The owners of large estates were able to tighten their control over agricultural production and the labor force. The imperial government, interested chiefly in

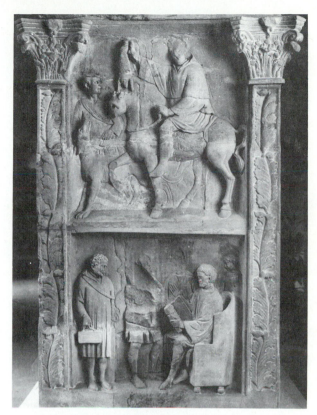

FIGURE 12.2 Roman Aristocratic Life This scene decorating a third-century A.D. mausoleum reflects important aspects of the daily life of a typical Roman noble—returning from the hunt (top) and settling accounts with his tenants and his financial agent (bottom). (Landesmuseum, Trier)

securing revenue and produce from the land to support the army and the bureaucracy, gave the landowners greater freedom to exploit the peasantry and to pass the burden of taxation on to them. As their control over the *coloni* expanded, the great estateholders moved inexorably toward independence of action and the satisfaction of their own self-interest (see Figure 12.2). At the same time, soldiers enjoyed ever-greater status. Men of ability from nonnoble elements of society found the army the chief avenue for social advancement; many rose to key positions in public life—even to the emperorship—to challenge the old aristocracy for social dominance. Even the lowest ranks of the army enjoyed favors not open to other citizens. Because the army was increasingly composed of recruits from the least developed areas of the empire or from "barbarian" outsiders, people little acquainted with or committed to traditional Roman ideas and institutions now moved to leadership roles in society. Perhaps already in the third century the foundations of a future social order dominated by landowners and warriors were being laid.

These transformations of the social order combined to disrupt the traditional patterns of social relationships, to cause widespread discontent and alienation, and to drive many to seek new social ties that would give them moorings in a hostile world. All of these factors pointed toward a restructuring of the social order and a redefinition of social values along lines not yet clear.

In the face of the crisis of the third century the Roman world seemed paralyzed intellectually. Culturally, the third century was one of the least productive periods of the entire classical era. Writers, artists, thinkers seemed to have lost their ability to address the problems of their time creatively and their faith in the humanistic, rationalistic values of the Greco-Roman tradition. The vaunted powers once attributed to human beings to control their own destinies at last seemed inadequate in the face of the realities of a troubled world.

In fact, the troubled society of the third century increasingly sought and found refuge in another realm—religion. The era was alive with powerful religious currents that seriously threatened the classical worldview and undermined allegiance to the state in favor of trust in the divine. Although the ancient civic deities of Greece and Rome still had their adherents, the eastern mystery religions, with their personal deities, emotional rituals, and promises of eternal salvation, won increasing numbers of adherents at all levels of society. There was a vast resurgence of interest in astrology and magic. Even philosophy was permeated by mystical elements. Everyone seemed in search of escape from a meaningless world through mystical contact with the divine. In this quest many Greco-Roman values, including confidence in human reason, seemed irrelevant.

3. CHRISTIANITY: ORIGINS

Among the diverse spiritual movements contending for attention during the third century was Christianity, soon to play a decisive role in transforming Greco-Roman civilization. That role was conditioned in part by what had happened to Christianity since its origin at almost the same moment that Augustus had laid the foundations of the Roman imperial order.

Christianity originated early in the first century A.D. as a splinter movement within the world of Judaism, a world charged with tensions deeply rooted in two fundamental and interconnected elements of Judaism: the hope of recovering lost national independence and the expectation of the moral redemption of all humanity that God had promised to realize through his Chosen People. Particularly incendiary was the political situation of the Jewish community in Palestine following the Maccabean revolt in 168 B.C. against the Seleucid regime (see Chapter 7). That revolt, ending with the establishment of an independent Jewish kingdom, raised high hopes of Jewish independence. However, those hopes were increasingly frustrated both by the misrule by the kingdom's rulers and by the intrusion of Roman power into Asia, which ended in 63 B.C. with Rome's annexation of Palestine. The Romans were willing to concede special privileges allowing the Jews to practice their religion, but they were suspicious of Jewish visions of independence. At first the Romans established a client king in Judea to keep the peace in Rome's name. The autocratic conduct of these kings, typified by the hated Herod (40–4 B.C.), and the burdens imposed by Roman taxation goaded the Jews to constant agitation. In response Augustus abolished the client kingdom and imposed direct Roman rule exercised by a prefect charged with keeping order and collecting tribute.

Faced with an aggressive alien power on its own sacred soil, the unity of the Jewish community was severely tested. Although still joined by the fundamental beliefs defined earlier in their history, the Jews increasingly disagreed on how to act in the immediate historic setting in order to realize what they all agreed was their collective mission. Some of their differences were reflected in various sects prominent at the beginning of the Christian era. The Saducees, an aristocratic group who as high priests controlled the Temple operation, were primarily concerned with shaping community life and cult practices in strict accord with the letter of the written law. Since their position cast them as the intermediaries between the Jewish community and the Roman authorities, they were anxious to maintain a good relationship with the Romans. The Pharisees, along with the learned *scribes,* were lay interpreters of Jewish law (Torah) who asserted a powerful influence on most Jews as a result of their teaching activities in the synagogues where most Jews met for prayer and scripture reading. Convinced that adherence to the law was the key to fulfillment of the promise established by the Covenant, the Pharisees sought to exercise prudence in political affairs so as to avoid measures that would disrupt life according to the law. Interpreting the law in the light of oral tradition rather than according to its strict letter, they introduced a certain flexibility into Judaism that allowed not only for adjustment of the law to fit changing conditions but also for an enrichment of the moral and social values guiding spiritual life. Their position lay at the roots of rabbinic Judaism that by the end of the first century A.D. began to assert a decisive influence on Jewish history. More inflammatory were the Zealots, who followed the Maccabean tradition by urging their compatriots to take up arms in the cause of political independence and who showed their militancy by repeated acts of terrorism against the Romans and against fellow Jews who made any accommodation with foreign culture. The Essenes, whose views have become better known since the discovery nearly a half century ago of a collection of documents known as the Dead Sea Scrolls, represented a community which withdrew from association with other Jews to pursue a collective life of prayer and asceticism in preparation for the deliverance promised by God. Added to these diverse groups were numerous individuals uttering prophecies that the hour of decision for the Jews was at hand and advocating various courses of action. Complicating the situation surrounding the Palestinian Jewish community were the Jews of the Diaspora—those dispersed by accident or choice across the entire Mediterranean world. Pursuing their traditional religion primarily in numerous synagogues while living their daily lives in a setting dominated by "Gentiles" (a term designating non-Jews), these Jews were strongly influenced by Greco-Roman ideas and practices, which they tended to incorporate into their version of Judaism, a process that raised suspicions of compromise in the minds of Palestinian Jews but that also created links between the Jewish and non-Jewish worlds that raised prospects of conversions to Judaism.

To the turmoil created by these diverse responses to what was widely perceived as a crisis in Judaism must be added another ingredient that asserted a powerful influence on Jewish thought and practice during the two centuries following the Maccabean revolt. The times were alive with revelations about the approaching end that touched almost all segments of Judaism to a greater or lesser degree. Rooted firmly in Jews' interpretation of their own history and in the pattern of discerning God's intentions shaped by the ancient prophets, this line of thought focused on a central point: The time was at hand when God would intervene dramatically and decisively in history through a messiah to institute the promised kingdom where oppression, sin, injustice, and idolatry would end and all humanity would be embraced in the true Israel where justice under God's true law would prevail. This apocalyptic vision of the impending end of time raised questions of terrible urgency that agitated and divided the entire Jewish community: How, when, where, by whom, with what consequences would the new age come? Jews who heard the mounting chorus of revelations in this vein were led to act in strange ways that unsettled collective Jewish life. No less important, these apocalyptic prophecies heightened Roman suspicions of political subversion and potential rebellion. They reacted with savage reprisals against suspected insurrectionists, a policy that many Jews interpreted as evidence that Rome epitomized the force of evil impeding the fulfillment of God's promise. The growing climate of hatred and distrust, exacerbated by a succession of incompetent Roman governors little sensitive to the nuances of Judaism, finally provoked a major Jewish rebellion in A.D. 66 that ended four years later with Rome's capture of Jerusalem and the destruction of the Temple. With the end of the temple state at Jerusalem, religious leadership of the Jews passed into the hands of rabbis who sought to rally the faithful to observance of the Torah as the basis for Judaism.

Into this complex and highly charged scene came Jesus, probably born about 6 B.C. at almost that fateful moment when Augustus was taking steps to bring the Jews under direct Roman rule. Any reconstruction of his career upon which everyone can agree presents almost insurmountable obstacles that from Jesus' own time to the present have led to disagreements about his life and teachings. The problem lies in the nature of the evidence relating to his career. The earliest surviving written evidence, the writings of Paul, was recorded a generation after Jesus' death by a writer who admitted that he had not known Jesus in person. The other major sources, the gospels of Mark, Matthew, Luke, and John and the Acts of the Apostles, were all set down later, during the last half of the first century. All of these accounts were written in Greek on the basis of oral memories originally recounted in Aramaic, the language Jesus spoke; how their authors understood and interpreted this material was understandably influenced by their awareness of what had happened to the Christian movement after Jesus' time. But perhaps a few points can be ventured about the historical Jesus.

Jesus was born into a modest Jewish household and raised as a member of the Jewish community. When he was about thirty, he began a public ministry, perhaps influenced by John the Baptist, one of many proclaiming the apocalyptic message that the Kingdom of God was at hand and calling all who would listen to demonstrate repentance by accepting a washing by water symbolizing their cleansing of sin. Jesus' public ministry, lasting about three years, focused primarily on a fervent call to those who would listen to prepare themselves for the imminent coming of God's kingdom. Although some of the later gospel accounts gave a central place in Jesus' teaching to his repudiation of the empty formalism of contemporary observance of Judaic law and cult practices advocated by "the scribes and the Pharisees," there is little to support an interpretation of his ministry as a protest against the

establishment, be it Jewish or Roman. As best it can be reconstructed, his message was firmly anchored in the Judaic religious tradition, reflecting acceptance of a wide range of fundamental beliefs shared by most Jews. Jesus himself observed the Jewish law and taught his followers that they must do likewise. His vision of the new order that was close at hand—as reflected, for example, in his Sermon on the Mount—echoed themes central to the Jewish prophetic tradition, especially the idea that the poor, the weak, the humble, and the peacemakers would receive justice while the rich, the powerful, and the prideful would be brought low. Perhaps the key element in his message was his insistence that fitness for membership in the coming kingdom required a radical spiritual transformation of all who would be children of God. By a self-willed conversion, each must go beyond observance of the law and performance of accustomed rituals to live a life defined by love, forgiveness, turning the other cheek to violence, abandonment of concerns for property and even family. Acceptance of these values would purge from the inner self of every person the demonic forces that were the source of all evil offensive to God and humanity. Repentance cast in these terms meant preparation for a radically different world; in that "kingdom come" such things as rendering unto Caesar what was Caesar's or departure from strict observance of the Judaic law lost all relevance.

Any assessment of how Jesus was viewed by his contemporaries and how his message was interpreted is likewise fraught with immense difficulties. It seems certain that he gained some kind of status as an authority figure. In contrast with John the Baptist, who cried out in the desert to draw those who had repented to come to him, Jesus actively went into the villages and towns of Palestine to seek out and convert sinners. His preaching attracted a diverse, enthsiastic following, including many women to whom he gave a place of equality seldom accorded them in other contemporary religions. Early in his ministry, he gathered around him a small circle of disciples who assisted him in proclaiming his message, a step that suggests the emergence of a distinct sect. Later tradition portrayed his role in many ways: miracle worker, prophet, messiah, Son of God. While it is possible that tradition reflects elements of truth concerning how Jesus' followers viewed him while he was still in their midst, there is no way to speak with absolute certainty on that matter. During his ministry Jesus also made enemies. Again, tradition singled out certain opposition forces: the power establishment in the Jewish community, especially the Sadducees, who were frightened by his appeal to the poor and oppressed; "the scribes and the Pharisees," who were disturbed by his alleged attacks on their formalistic interpretation of the law; political radicals, who were disappointed by his disavowal of a messianic role seeking to restore an earthly Jewish state. But it is no easier to make a definitive statement on how his opponents saw Jesus than it is to establish how his followers viewed him.

However one resolves these uncertainties surrounding Jesus' career, the end of his ministry was decisive. Probably in A.D. 27 during the reign of Tiberius, Jesus and some of his followers went to Jerusalem to fulfill the traditional religious obligations associated with Passover. His appearance and subsequent activities created a situation in which many of the sources of discontent and expectation rife in the Jewish community came into play in a fashion that threatened to produce violence. Faced with the possibility of an insurrection, Pontius Pilate, the Roman prefect representing imperial authority, took action, perhaps encouraged by Jewish leaders anxious to avert Roman reprisal against all Jews. Jesus was arrested by Roman soldiers, tried before Pontius Pilate, convicted of a crime against Rome, and crucified—a form of punishment reserved by the Romans for rebels and slaves. This sequence of events profoundly shocked his followers and created disarray in their ranks, perhaps symbolized by his disciples' denial that they knew him at the decisive moment in his life.

However, the story was not finished. Jesus' death triggered a crucial development. Some of his followers were convinced that he had arisen from the dead, proving to them that he was the Christ ("the anointed"), the Messiah, the Savior sacrificed in accordance with divine plan to bring about the salvation of all humanity. This belief set the little band apart; in the words of Paul, "We preach Christ crucified, a stumbling block to Jews and folly to the Gentiles . . ." (I Cor. 1:23).

The cornerstone of a new religion was put into place.

4. THE SPREAD OF CHRISTIANITY

During the first generation after Jesus' death his followers carried on in Palestine as a sect of Judaism. While observing Judaic law and cult practices, these "Jewish Christians" were sustained by their expectation of the imminent return of the crucified Christ to establish the Kingdom of God. Guided in their community life by Jesus' disciples, they sought to live in a manner that would conform to Jesus' teaching concerning preparation for membership in the kingdom. Among other things, this preparation involved sharing wealth, acts of charity, group prayer, and partaking of a common meal of bread and wine in Jesus' memory. Although the larger Jewish community continued to regard the members of the Christian community with suspicion and sometimes hostility, the flock did grow, not only in Palestine but beyond. Followers of Jesus, called apostles, carried Christian ideas to many cities, particularly in Syria and Asia Minor, where they attracted the attention of Diaspora Jews and of non-Jews, or Gentiles. Before long many Gentiles were asking to join the new community and were being received. This development posed a grave question for the foundling movement: whether or not new converts were to be held to strict observance of Judaic law and practices. There were those in the primitive Christian community who took a conservative position, but others, typified by Peter, leader of the disciples, increasingly insisted on universalizing Jesus' message so that it would be acceptable to Jew and Gentile alike.

A major figure in shaping the Christian mission to the Gentiles was Saul of Tarsus. Saul (soon renamed Paul) was a representative of the Jews of the Diaspora—an ardent adherent of orthodox Judaism in the tradition of the Pharisees but also a Roman citizen who was familiar with the Greco-Roman cultural life. Early in his adult life he took an active part in resisting the spread of Christianity in the Jewish community, even to the point of persecuting Christians. But then he underwent a powerful personal experience that

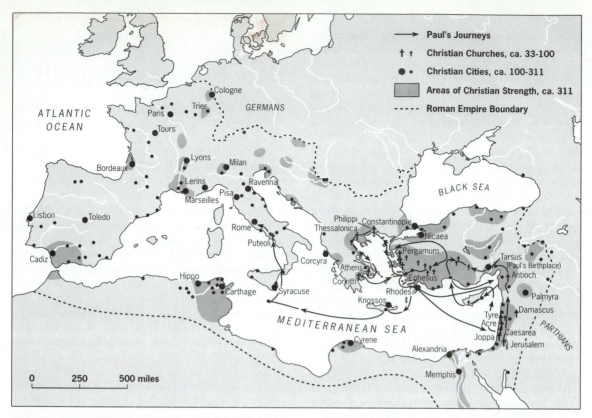

Map 12.1 **THE SPREAD OF CHRISTIANITY TO A.D. 311** This map shows how extensively Christianity had spread across the Roman empire during the first three centuries A.D. In an important way the journeys of Paul provided a crucial beginning step in this expansion. In general, Christian life was still confined largely to cities by A.D. 311. The heavier concentration of Christians in the east is worth noting; it is perhaps understandable why the newly converted emperor, Constantine, chose to move the capital of the empire from Rome to Constantinople.

convinced him that salvation hinged on faith in Christ. Then followed a long missionary career, extending from about A.D. 46 until his martyrdom during the reign of Nero in about A.D. 67, which took him to many cities in Asia Minor, Greece, Macedonia, Palestine, and eventually Rome (see Map 12.1). Central to his missionary effort was his determination to win non-Jews to Christianity. As set forth in letters written to sustain or correct the faith of those he had converted, his message emphasized what he understood to be the precepts of Jesus that were applicable to all humanity: Jesus as the messiah sent to fulfill God's promise; the redemption of sinners ef-

fected by the Son of God through his death; the need for moral regeneration through faith and love of God and humanity; salvation as a reward for belief in Christ and acceptance of God's grace; purity of moral life. These teachings, soon to be elaborated by the Gentile authors of the synoptic Gospels and the Acts of the Apostles, marked a crucial step in establishing the basic formal doctrines of Christianity as a religion distinct from Judaism.

Forces other than the demands of the Gentile mission hastened the separation of the Christian and Jewish communities. The delay in the coming of the kingdom proclaimed by Jesus led

Christians to reformulate traditional Jewish concepts concerning the Covenant, the Chosen People, the messiah, the nature of God's ultimate kingdom, the validity of Judaic law, and the meaning of history in ways that were unacceptable to many Jews. Often these emerging Christian views were validated by interpretations of Jewish scripture that violated Jewish understanding of these sacred text. Quite understandably, such views made Jews increasingly reluctant to recognize Christianity as a sect of Judaism and led them to resist the progress of Christianity, which prompted Christians to portray Jews as enemies of God's truth. The defeat of the Jewish revolt of A.D. 66–70 not only encouraged the Christians to distance themselves from the Jews out of fear of bringing Roman wrath onto themselves but also reinforced the growing conviction in Christian circles that the Jews were not God's Chosen People. Under the guidance of the rabbinical leadership that emerged in the wake of the blasted hopes for a restored Jewish nation after the destruction of the Temple by the Romans in A.D. 70, Judaism sustained a proselytizing effort that put it into competition with Christianity for converts. All of these developments deepened Jewish antipathy toward Christians and imbedded in Christianity a vein of anti-Semitism that would bear evil fruits in the future.

Once launched in the Pauline direction, Christianity spread slowly but steadily over most parts of the Roman world; the pace of conversion quickened, especially in the third century, a development certainly linked with the crisis gripping the Roman world. That expansion was facilitated by the atmosphere of religious toleration prevailing in the Roman Empire, the increasingly intense search for individual spiritual satisfaction in the Greco-Roman world, and the powerful forces of religious syncretism at work in Hellenistic and Roman society that were preparing the ground for a common religious life. Of critical importance to Christian expansion was the existence of the Hellenized Jewish communities of the Diaspora and their synagogues, which often provided the setting for the initial planting of the seeds of the new faith and which served as a model for adapting a religion rooted in Judaism to the needs of the Greco-Roman world. During at least the first century after Jesus' death, a series of dedicated missionary preachers working under all kinds of conditions were the chief agents of expansion. They concentrated their efforts in the major cities of the empire, so that early Christianity developed chiefly as an urban religion. The efforts of these missionary preachers usually won a small group of adherents who formed themselves into self-sustaining cells. The members of these "churches," who increasingly came from the ranks of the Gentiles, then took up the burden of spreading the faith, working in local communities to increase the flock through methods that are not easily discerned in the surviving historical record.

But the results are clear enough. By the end of the third century, vigorous and expanding Christian communities existed in urban centers everywhere in the empire (see Map 12.1). The heaviest Christian population was in the cities of Egypt, Syria, Palestine, Asia Minor, Greece, and Italy. Christians certainly formed only a small minority of the total population by A.D. 300, but they had become a potent factor in the Roman world, far exceeding what might have been expected in view of Christianity's inauspicious beginning and early struggles.

The progress of Christianity was not, however, unopposed. From time to time the Roman government persecuted Christians because of their refusal to discharge any civic responsibility—including military service—that involved recognition of the Roman deities. The Christians who suffered were viewed by their fellow believers as martyrs whose heroic example strengthened the resolve of most Christians to remain steadfast. Anti-Christian feelings developed in many elements of the Roman populace. Among the masses of people there circulated rumors about strange beliefs and immoral, bestial practices of this "third race," rumors fed by the Christian refusal to participate in public religious rites and by their private worship services. Roman intellectuals scorned Christianity, holding up for ridicule its simplistic, illogical beliefs derived from faith in a crucified criminal. The leaders of the state religion and of the Jewish synagogues sometimes charged the Christians with false beliefs and debased practices. Not only Judaism but also several mystery religions featuring ideas and practices similar to those of Christianity proved worthy rivals in the competition for souls.

The Christians made difficulties for themselves as well. From the very beginning there were divisions in their ranks as to what constituted right belief and proper usage. The early communities disagreed on the nature of the relationship between Christianity and Judaism. The proper moral posture for a Christian was often a subject for debate, especially because some insisted on a puritanical denial of the world and its pleasures. By the second century and increasingly in the third, Christians disagreed violently on certain fundamental doctrines, especially those relating to the nature of Jesus' relationship to God, thus generating what may be called the first heresies. These conflicts inevitably set Christian against Christian, diverted the faithful from proselytizing, and discredited the movement in the eyes of nonbelievers.

5. THE TRANSFORMATION OF EARLY CHRISTIANITY

It is not sufficient to discuss the growth of early Christianity simply in terms of geographical and numerical expansion. Christianity proved to be a movement rich in inner resources which allowed it to grow in substance and structure in ways that increased its impact on the Greco-Roman world. That capacity for constant transformation goes far to account for its increasing appeal to the Roman world.

Of central importance in early Christian history was the ongoing reexamination and rearticulation of the new religion's fundamental beliefs. A crucial stage in that process occurred during the first century after Jesus' death, called the Apostolic Age, which produced a collection of writings that came to be called the New Testament, accepted as the divinely inspired "good news" proclaimed by Jesus. Concerned primarily with explaining the meaning of Jesus' career, the authors of the New Testament texts appropriated the Jewish Bible, which became for them the Old Testament, interpreted chiefly as a sacred text prefiguring the coming of Jesus and the new kingdom. Although rich in its many levels of meaning, the New Testament set forth dramatically and simply certain key concepts defining the essence of the new religion: a single, almighty, merciful, loving God; a universe given order and purpose by God's plan for its ultimate destiny; an explantion of the evil and suffering in the world rooted in human sin; a divine savior, made man in the person of Jesus, son of God, sacrificed by his loving father to atone for the sins of all humans; a new covenant established by the coming of Jesus the messiah that assured eternal salvation to all men and women who earned God's grace through faith in Jesus the savior; a hope for a peaceful, just earthly community made up of the faithful who awaited the Kingdom of God by living according to the precepts of Jesus counseling love, forgiveness, nonviolence, and mutual concern for one another.

Originally shaped by believers seeking to explain Jesus' life and ministry within the framework of the Judaic tradition, Christian religious teachings soon began to take on new dimensions as a result of borrowings from Greco-Roman culture. This development marked a rather dramatic departure from primitive Christianity. Jesus had preached in Aramaic to followers who were largely apart from the mainstream of Greco-Roman intellectual and literary life. The early leaders of the new religion were quite open in their rejection of this culture, which would have no place in the new kingdom; for example, Paul could ask: "Has not God made foolish the wisdom of the world?" (I Cor. 1:20). Although there long remained a strain of antipathy toward Greco-Roman culture in Christian thought, another view began to take precedence. As is clearly evident even in Paul's writings and in the rest of the New Testament, as soon as the Christians began their effort to convert Gentiles, they had to employ the Greek and Latin languages and the modes of thought and expression prevailing in the Roman Empire in order to speak intelligibly to those they sought to convert.

During the second and third centuries two additional forces spurred the Christians to borrow increasingly from Greco-Roman culture to explain what they believed: the need to answer charges by non-Christian intellectuals that the new religion was irrational and the problem of resolving differences within Christian ranks on the meaning of basic doctrines. Both the "apologists" answering the critics of Christianity and the theologians defining the exact meaning of the faith relied heavily on various aspects of Greco-Roman intellectual life: the rational mode of

FIGURE 12.3 **Honoring the Christian Dead** Following an ancient Roman custom, early Christians sought to perpetuate the memory of the dead by decorating their sarcophagi with scenes from the life of the deceased. This third-century A.D. sarcophagus, which clearly reflects pagan art styles, shows the dead man (reading in the center while being prayed for) surrounded by representations of Christian history: the good shepherd, John baptizing Jesus (as a child), Jonah being washed ashore. (Alinari/Art Resource)

thought defined by logic; argumentation based on rhetoric; the content of philosophy, especially the Platonic tradition. The most influential figures in this movement wedding Christian religion and Greco-Roman culture were two scholars from Alexandria, Clement (ca. A.D. 150–216) and Origen (ca. A.D. 185–254). Their efforts not only expounded fundamental Christian ideas in rational, systematic terms but also increasingly persuaded Christians that classical learning, like Judaism, had been a preparation for the true revelation and was therefore useful in illuminating the meaning of God's word. The result of what has been called the Hellenization of Christianity was a more systematic, reasoned articulation of Christian beliefs that appealed especially to educated circles. In the process many fundamental Christian teachings, such as the nature of divinity, grace, sin, redemption, the relationship of God the Father to God the Son, and morality took on greater depth, new shades of meaning, and new complexity. Viewed in its entirety, the evolution of Christian belief provided the Christian community with an ever more persuasive armory of teachings that offered a resolution of the spiritual concerns troubling a wide range of people from all levels of society in the Greco-Roman world.

The early Christians strengthened the appeal of their religion by developing ritual practices that were attractive in a world accustomed to public pageantry, spectacles, and the highly charged rites associated with the mystery religions. Originally, Christian worship was simple. The faithful gathered in private houses to share a common meal, called the Eucharist, in commemoration of Jesus, to pray and sing, and to be instructed in Jesus' teachings. As time passed, this ritual life became more complex, marked by the adaptation of Jewish and pagan practices to Christian uses. Special places for worship were built and adorned with art inspired by Christian motifs but increasingly enriched by the adaptation of Greco-Roman art forms to Christian purposes (see Figures 12.1 and 12.3). The eucharistic ceremony became more elaborate, constituting what came to be called the Mass. Ceremonies were established for such events as baptism, marriage, and burial. Special holidays—"holy days" to the Christians—developed to commemorate highlights in Jesus' career and the death of the early martyrs. The end result was a Christian cult life that gave a religious dimension to almost any event in the life cycle of believers and that added an emotional dimension to every encounter with the Divine.

Of decisive importance to the spread of Christianity during the first three centuries of its history was the development of an organization unrivaled by any other religious movement. The first Christian communities consisted of small groups of converts lost in the non-Christian population of the cities of the Roman world. Leaders emerged in these cells to direct worship services, teach, and oversee charitable activities; women often played an important role in these functions. Eventually, these leaders were given titles: bishop (*episcopus*), elder (*presbyter*, later translated as priest), and deacon (*diaconus*). With the passage of time problems emerged that called for firmer organization: larger numbers of Christians, expanding relationships with non-Christians, increasing wealth available to the community, disagreement over what constituted right beliefs and practices. Authority over all the affairs of the entire Christian community in each city began to settle on the bishop. In cases where the number of Christians required additional places of worship within any given city or its surrounding countryside, direction of each new establishment was entrusted to a priest. However, the bishop of the city retained final authority over these new priests and their flocks. The authority of the episcopal office was given ideological justification by the concept of *apostolic succession*, which argued that every bishop was a successor to the original apostles and heir to the spiritual authority that Jesus bestowed on those apostles to proclaim the faith and to forgive sinners. The evolution of the episcopal system resulted in tightly knit, self-governing local units that closely resembled a basic entity of the ancient world—the city-state.

While many congregations were being fashioned from city to city, the Christians never lost sight of their universal spiritual kinship, rooted in their belief in the one God who had given his son to ensure salvation for all his children. From this sense of kinship emerged efforts to forge bonds of unity that would link the many "churches" into one "Church." Jesus' disciples and the early missionaries such as Paul tried to keep in touch with as many Christian communities as possible by means of extensive travel and letter writing. By the second century, bishops met together on a regional basis in *councils* to discuss common problems and decide on common solutions that each could apply in his own church. Bishops of great cities such as Jerusalem, Antioch, Alexandria, and Rome exerted considerable influence over lesser bishops in the regions surrounding these centers. These influential bishops began to be called "patriarchs" to indicate their preeminence.

Eventually some Christians became concerned with vesting ultimate authority over all Christians in the hands of one of these great bishops. A prime candidate was the bishop of Rome, who gained special prestige not only from the fact that Rome was the capital of the world but also from an important doctrine, the *Petrine theory*. According to this doctrine, rooted in a particular scriptural passage (Matt. 16:18–19), Jesus had granted Peter a special place as his vicar on earth; Peter had chosen Rome as the seat of that power; and those who followed him as bishops of Rome after his martyrdom were believed to have succeeded to Peter's authority as head of the total Christian community. By the end of the third century Peter's successors as bishops of Rome, increasingly referred to as *popes* (a title derived from the late Latin word *papa*, meaning "father"), were turning this claim to spiritual supremacy into active leadership in defining doctrine and prescribing discipline for Christian communities over much of the Roman Empire. And many of these communities were seeking the pope's guidance, especially in doctrinal matters. In terms of organization the Christian community was assuming a shape that replicated the structure of the Roman Empire—an expanding structure subdivided into well-governed local units and headed by a spiritual "emperor."

As the Christian movement evolved during the first three centuries, one of its most notable achievements was its success in creating among its followers a sense of community, a feeling of belonging to a tangible, intimate collectivity that provided secure moorings in a world increasingly impersonal and insecure. That sense of community, initially rooted in the Jewish tradition of community and given shape by shared beliefs and cult practices and by organizational structures, was fortified by a strong social consciousness among the early Christians that impinged on the lives of those in each Christian congregation in tangible ways. The teachings and the example of Jesus concerning love for others, charity, and kindness received concrete expression in Christian practice almost from the beginning. Christians poured out their resources to help the sick, the poor, criminals, slaves, orphans, widows, and other unfortunates in society. They devoted their time and energy to actions that sought to console the mourning, counsel the troubled, help the disillusioned and alienated, and seek out the outcasts of society. Such social interactions gave substance to what it meant to be a brother or a sister in a way that forged bonds within each community that transcended wealth, status, education, and power. In a real sense, membership in a Christian community diminished the need for membership in any other community. Many were drawn to the new religion by an urge to share in a bonding that gave them a meaningful place in society.

6. CHRISTIANITY AND THE CRISIS IN THE ROMAN WORLD

Historians have long debated what the advance of Christianity had to do with the crisis that gripped the Roman Empire in the third century A.D. The evidence offers no clear answer. The record provides little evidence that the early Christians were subversives. They earned their living in much the same ways as did all other Romans. They performed their civic duties as long as they were not required to deny their god. They paid their taxes and obeyed the emperor. They tried their best to help the unfortunate members of Roman society. Their minds were not completely closed to what was best in Greco-Roman intellectual, literary, and artistic life, from which they constantly borrowed to sustain their cause.

However, in other important ways, the early Christians were strangers in their world; as one critic put it, they were a people who "wall themselves off and break away from the rest of humanity." They served a god who would tolerate no rivals, including Roman emperors who claimed divinity. Believing that their god disapproved of the ways of non-Christians, they tended to avoid involvement in worldly affairs and to keep apart from social life outside their intimate communities. Their concept of sin led them to regard the world, including the Roman Empire, as a perpetual source of evil, hardly worth saving. Their beliefs in the omnipotence of God and human frailty caused them to distrust human reason and to put little faith in human ability to build a paradise on earth; the kingdom they expected to come with the return of their messiah would bear little resemblance to the powers and dominions of the past and present. They thus found little that appealed to them in the basic premise of Greco-Roman civilization: the conviction that enlightened human activity could create a perfect society on earth. The Christians were committed members of an organization that acted independently of the Roman state to focus attention on social issues defined in the interests of that organization. Through its evolving religious ceremonies, the Christian movement kept before its members a series of symbols that made them feel their separateness and uniqueness.

Perhaps in the final analysis, the growth of Christianity can best be understood as one more facet of a complex of political, economic, social, and cultural forces welling up within Roman imperial society that by the end of the third century A.D. had brought the Roman Empire to a critical juncture. Christianity's prime symbol, the sign of the cross, was an urgent reminder that at least to some there was good news amid all the bad, albeit a different kind of good news than what was usually associated with Greco-Roman civilization. The future of the empire and the entire civilization it sustained depended on what responses would be made to that sign—as well as many other signs—that an old order was passing.

SUGGESTED READING

The Decline of the Empire

Peter Brown, *The World of Late Antiquity from Marcus Aurelius to Muhammad* (1971). A thought-provoking overview.

The following works provide diverse interpretations of Rome's decline.

Joseph Vogt, *The Decline of Rome: The Metamorphosis of Ancient Civilization*, trans. Janet Sondheimer (1969).

Stewart Perowne, *The End of the Ancient World* (1966).

F. W. Walbank, *The Awful Revolution: The Decline of the Roman Empire in the West* (1969).

Michael Grant, *The Fall of the Roman Empire: A Reappraisal*, 2nd ed. (1990).

A. Ferrill, *The Fall of the Roman Empire: The Military Explanation* (1986).

Ramsay MacMullen, *Corruption and the Decline of Rome* (1988).

The Rise of Christianity

R. A. Markus, *Christianity in the Roman World* (1974). An excellent brief account of the rise of Christianity.

H. C. Frend, *The Rise of Christianity* (1984).

Robin Lane Fox, *Pagans and Christians* (1987).

Two masterful, detailed accounts of the rise of Christianity.

E. Mary Smallwood, *The Jews under Roman Rule* (1981).

Shaye J. D. Cohen, *From the Maccabees to the Mishnah* (1987).

These two works present a clear picture of Judaism at the beginning of the Christian era.

Richard A. Horsley and John S. Hanson, *Bandits, Prophets, and Messiahs: Popular Movements in the Time of Jesus* (1985). Provides a sense of the tensions in Jesus' world.

Paula Fredrikson, *From Jesus to Christ: The Origins of the New Testament Images of Jesus* (1988). A brilliant treatment of the problem of the historical Jesus.

Alan F. Segal, *Rebecca's Children: Judaism and Christianity in the Roman World* (1986). A challenging treatment of the interactions between the two religions.

Francis Watson, *Paul, Judaism, and the Gentiles* (1986). Good on the issues involved in Paul's Gentile mission.

John G. Gager, *Kingdom and Community: The Social World of Early Christianity* (1975). Excellent on the formation of the early Christian community.

Wayne A. Meeks, *The First Urban Christians: The Social World of the Apostle Paul* (1983). Excellent social history.

Ben Witherington III, *Women and the Genesis of Christianity* (1990). A provocative study.

Ramsay MacMullen, *Christianizing the Roman Empire*, A.D. 100–400 (1984).

Steven Benko, *Pagan Rome and the Early Christians* (1984).

Marta Sordi, *The Christians and the Roman Empire*, trans. Annabel Bedini (1986).

These three works throw light on the spread of Christianity.

Jocelyn W. Godwin, *Mystery Religions in the Ancient World* (1981). A good treatment of religions competing with Christianity.

CHAPTER 13

Late Antiquity, A.D. 284–500: The End of Greco-Roman Civilization

FIGURE 13.1 **Constantine the Great** This photo shows the surviving pieces of a huge statue, nearly forty feet in height, that Constantine had placed in a magnificent basilica he built in the Roman Forum. The massive head retains some features of earlier Roman portrait sculpture (see Figure 9.2); however, its creator was more intent in conveying Constantine's lordship than in producing a realistic portrayal of the emperor. (Art Resource)

The mounting crisis that gripped the Roman world during the third century finally prompted action aimed at addressing its basic problems. Major reforms were instituted that restored the vitality of the Roman Empire during the fourth century. However, the respite was temporary. During the fifth century the empire was unable to contain Germanic invaders who seized control of the western part of the empire and ruptured the unity of the Mediterranean world. The sequence of events that disrupted the Roman Empire destroyed the framework within which Greco-Roman civilization had developed, thereby ending a distinctive era in history.

1. THE REFORMS OF DIOCLETIAN AND CONSTANTINE

The architect of the reforms that sought to end the third-century crisis was a general named Diocletian, who in A.D. 284 seized the imperial throne by force. Like so many third-century emperors, he was a man of provincial origin who worked his way to prominence in the military service and acquired many of the autocratic ways associated with military life. However, he did have a clear insight into the basic problems facing the Roman world and the will to take action which addressed these problems. The result was a restructuring of the imperial regime into a form that would prevail through late antiquity and even beyond.

Conscious of the chaos resulting from the rivalry within the army for control of the succession and of the impossible burden imposed on a single ruler by the mounting problems of the empire, Diocletian instituted a system of shared authority to ensure orderly succession and a division of administrative responsibility. He and an associate each assumed the title *augustus,* and to each was assigned a subordinate entitled *caesar.* When an augustus died, his caesar would succeed him as augustus and appoint another caesar. In theory the four co-rulers would jointly share the *imperium,* that is, the supreme power to command; in practice each was responsible for administering one of four newly established territorial units, called *prefectures,* into which the empire was divided. Although Diocletian intended that co-rulers would follow a common policy, the ground was being laid for political division of the empire.

Diocletian sought to solidify and exalt the authority of the four co-rulers. Their pronouncements constituted the final law; no pretense was made of consulting with the Senate and the people. The official activities of each ruler were surrounded by elaborate symbols and rituals designed to exalt his position and associate him with divine powers. Few could escape the obvious: Rome was now ruled by an autocratic lord (*dominus*) whose position resembled that of a Persian or Hellenistic ruler more than it did the office of *princeps.*

A significant expansion and restructuring of the bureaucracy was undertaken to ensure that the autocratic rulers were able to exercise their power. At each imperial court greater numbers of professional civil servants were organized under a chief official, called the *praetorian prefect.* The number of provinces was nearly doubled by dividing old ones, and imperial officials were installed in each to carry out the orders of the central government. An intermediate level of administration was interposed between the provinces and imperial court in each prefecture by the grouping of provinces into thirteen administrative units called *dioceses;* each had its own bureaucratic apparatus responsible to the augustus or caesar or to his praetorian prefect. This elaborate hierarchy gave the central government the means to act directly in local affairs and effectively ended the independent political role of the once-active local city-state governments. Perhaps more significantly, the bureaucratic structure opened positions of power and status and opportunities for acquiring wealth to large numbers of people from all levels of life and from all over the empire who had previously been excluded from active political life by the dominance of a narrow circle of *nobiles.*

Administrative centralization was given urgency by the threat of external foes. One of Diocletian's major concerns was increasing the effectiveness of the army. Following initiatives introduced by his immediate predecessors, Diocletian sought to strengthen and regularize the permanent frontier garrisons and to develop a mobile strike force, strong in cavalry and capable of responding quickly to contain crises arising when the frontier forces were unable to cope with outside attackers. This reorganization increased the size of the army considerably—to about six hundred thousand troops—and raised monumental problems of recruitment and support.

The expansion of the bureaucracy and the army placed a massive financial burden on the imperial government. Diocletian tried to meet this challenge in various ways. The taxation system was restructured to provide for a regular census aimed at identifying units of land and human heads upon which uniform levies could be imposed. At the same time, the government imposed upon the key productive elements of society a requisition system aimed at extracting crucial produce in kind and services required to sustain the courts, the army, and the bureaucracy. To assure the labor force required to sustain production in these areas of the economy, steps were taken to freeze those in key occupations and their descendants in their positions. In an effort to stabilize the economy and curb inflation, decrees were issued to fix prices for a wide range of commodities and services. Taken together, these measures created the parameters of a regimented economy in which the state had first claim on all resources and all citizens were required to give first priority to service to the state.

Beyond claiming his subjects' labor and wealth for the service of the state, Diocletian insisted on ideological conformity. Even before his reign, the imperial government initiated steps to rally the citizenry around the worship of the traditional state deities and their agent, the semi-divine emperor. This policy led to conflict with the Christian community, many of whose members steadfastly refused to honor the pagan deities or to obey the state when it commanded them to do so. As had his immediate predecessors, Diocletian responded to Christian resistance with a series of punitive decrees in A.D. 303 and 304 that were aimed at destroying Christianity. His assault, the most serious ever mounted by the Roman state against Christians, took a heavy toll but failed in its prime objective and was soon abandoned. It did, however, demonstrate the close connection between religious conformity and political autocracy.

When Diocletian decided to abdicate in A.D. 305, his reforms had gone far to restore order in the empire. Only one of his initiatives was a signal failure—his elaborate plan for regulating the succession. Although lip service was temporarily given to its provisions, eventually there occurred a new round of armed conflict pitting various contenders and segments of the army against one another for control of the imperial office. The ultimate victor was Constantine (A.D. 306–337), who by force of arms finally won sole control of the entire empire. Constantine (see Figure 13.1) was a worthy successor of Diocletian. He vigorously pursued the main elements of Diocletian's reform program: strengthening the army; expanding and tightening bureaucratic control over imperial affairs; improving the fiscal machinery; enlarging the emperor's power; and imposing tighter control over the imperial population. Under his guidance the autocratic regime took permanent form.

Constantine added important elements to the new order. Most significant was a new religious policy officially proclaimed in A.D. 313, when he and his co-emperor issued the Edict of Milan, which granted religious freedom to all in the empire, including Christians. On the surface the state appeared to take a position of neutrality in religious affairs, but such was not the case. Associated with the grant of toleration was another event of immense psychological impact. According to the somewhat muddled surviving record, Constantine attributed victory in a battle won in A.D. 312 that was decisive in his rise to power to the intervention of the Christian God, who revealed to him in a vision prior to the battle that victory would be his if he displayed the cross as his battle emblem. To many contemporaries this event marked Constantine's conversion to Christianity. Although Constantine was not baptized until just before his death in A.D. 337 and although he took few overt actions against other religions, after the Edict of Milan he gave increasing indications that he favored the Christian cause. He poured out money to build churches, drew Christian clergymen into the councils of state, and extended them a variety of special privileges. His legislation affecting many social issues increasingly reflected Christian teachings. Every sign pointed in one direction: The empire was becoming a Christian state.

Many contemporary Christians hailed Constantine's conversion as a crucial step in the fulfillment of God's plan; in their enthusiasm they soon hailed him as Constantine "the Great," a divinely ordained agent who removed the final barrier to Christian victory. What motivated his decision has long been the subject of debate. Some evidence suggests that he was a man of his age who was powerfully drawn to religion and especially to Christianity, not the least as a result of the influence exercised over him by his Christian mother, Helen. And like so many of his contemporaries of various religious persuasions, he was convinced that the fate of the renewed empire depended on divine favor and on a people united in devotion and service to the imperial community. Perhaps his religious inclinations and political ideology led him to sense that by committing the state to the service of Christian ends, he could create a reliable nucleus of supporters whose obedience to a ruler who was God's agent would sustain a unified empire. Whatever his motives, Constantine's religious policy linked the destinies of the late Roman Empire and Christianity in ways decisive to both and to the history of the future.

Hardly less momentous was Constantine's decision to build a new capital at the ancient Greek city of Byzantium, located on the strait of Bosporus, now renamed Constantinople and officially dedicated in A.D. 330. The building of the "new" Rome was more than an autocratic whim. From the second century onward it was clear that "old" Rome was not the most advantageous physical center for the empire. With increasing frequency, emperors were chosen whose roots were outside Rome. The whole thrust of political development during the third century diminished the role of the *nobiles* of Rome and Italy as prime factors of political life. Because Rome was badly located strategically in terms of frontier defenses, the reorganization of the defense system resulted in the emergence of new political centers: Nicomedia in Asia Minor, Milan in Italy, Sirmium in the Balkans, and Trier in the Rhineland. Prompted by such considerations, Constantine's choice of a capital was well advised. The site was nearly impregnable against attacks by land or sea. It offered ready access to the most vulnerable frontiers—the lower Danube and Euphrates river frontiers. The new city was close to the great centers of wealth in the east, and it was situated where Christian strength was greatest.

It also offered its founder and his successors freedom from the restrictive traditions of republicanism and Roman civic religion, both deeply entrenched in old Rome. Although the full impact of the founding of Constantinople was not immediately obvious, the new city soon became the center of a wide range of activities that pointed toward a shift in the center of gravity of political, economic, religious, intellectual, and artistic life from Rome and Italy to the east. In fact, Constantine had created a bastion that in the not too distant future would serve as the center of a different but long-lasting Roman Empire (see Chapter 14).

2. AN UNEASY PEACE

For a time it appeared that the autocratic, bureaucratized, militarized regime shaped by Diocletian and Constantine had saved the empire. By contrast with the third century, the fourth century was one of relative stability. Succession to the imperial office was usually peaceful, there was little civil strife, the frontier defenses seemed secure, and in some places there was even a semblance of economic recovery. The era witnessed vigorous literary and artistic activity, much of it in the service of Christianity but some of it engendered by enthusiasm for traditional Greco-Roman culture. The eastern part of the empire, with its tradition of autocratic government, superior economic resources, more vital urban centers, and heavier concentration of Christian population, adjusted more easily to the new regime than did the western part with its more primitive economy and the strong commitment to traditional Roman values that was deeply entrenched in the mentality of its upper class. But everywhere there was a sense that the civilized world had been saved, a sentiment voiced by frequent references to "eternal Rome."

Despite the appearance of a restored order, there were ominous signs that the reforms of Diocletian and Constantine had not only failed to resolve but had also deepened the empire's problems. The new regime affected different parts of the empire in different ways, thereby accentuating regional differences that weakened the bonds of imperial unity. The adverse effects were especially apparent in the western part of the empire, while the east reaped greater benefits. The basic factors already present in the third century to cause declining economic production were not resolved; they were worsened by economic regimentation and by the diversion of an ever-greater proportion of wealth to support the army and the bureaucracy. The burden of taxation, requisition in kind, and compulsory labor fell chiefly on groups vital to economic well-being: peasants, artisans, merchants, and local urban aristocrats. The gap between the few rich and the many poor grew ever wider, leading to deepening social discontent. The autocratic imperial government itself became an instrument of economic and social oppression. The costly, ever-growing bureaucracy, unchecked by exalted emperors remote from practical affairs, became intrusive, corrupt, and arbitrary to the point where it was universally detested. The adequacy of the defense system remained uncertain, but the antipathy between the army and the civilian population deepened as a result of brutal, arbitrary actions by military leaders seeking to lay hands on needed supplies.

To manifest their discontent, many citizens from all walks of life sought to escape from civic responsibilities. The traditional senatorial class, once the pillar of civic virtue but now largely replaced in positions of power by nonsenatorial bureaucrats, turned its attention to accumulating land, creating self-sustaining estates, and living in luxury. Ensconced in their rural strongholds and often openly disdainful of "nonnoble" emperors and their lowly agents and army officers, these powerful figures defied the government's efforts to compel them to bear their share of the public burden. In ever-larger numbers peasants sought to escape taxation, compulsory labor service, and military duty by accepting dependent status under these landlords in return for protection and an assured livelihood. In city after city across the empire, members of local aristocracies fled to the countryside, took service in the imperial bureaucracy, or joined the clergy in order to escape the responsibilities thrust on them by the government to deliver the money and the services due from their localities. Such widespread disaffection boded ill for the future of the "new" empire.

Nor did Constantine's religious policy strengthen the bonds of unity. Christianity did continue its march to dominance during the fourth century, culminating when Emperor Theodosius (A.D. 379–395) made it the state religion and outlawed all others. The imperial policy of favoring Christianity alienated many Romans, especially aristocrats, who still placed trust in the ancient civic religions. That resentment surfaced with particular vigor during the reign of Julian (A.D. 361–363), called "the Apostate" by the Christians because he repudiated Christianity and sought to replace it with a restored pagan "church." His effort failed, but it kept alive a fundamental schism in imperial society. The Christian community itself was badly divided by a succession of bitter doctrinal disputes. Often partisans in these quarrels resisted the efforts of the imperial government and the Christian leaders who supported it to impose doctrinal unity, producing "heresies" that divided Christians and made many of them enemies of the state. Some Christian leaders even challenged the right of the imperial government to interfere in religious affairs, claiming that the Christian community constituted an independent authority when religious issues were at stake. In short, Christianity failed to supply a unifying force in the service of the "new" empire; it was a movement with its own ends and strengths, not easily bent to other purposes.

Taken together, these trends suggest that the renewal of the Roman world envisaged by Diocletian and Constantine was flawed. Faithful to a tradition deeply ingrained in the Greco-Roman mentality, they had sought to counter disarray by political means. They had taken action to create a political regime that would compel "citizens" to commit themselves to the service of the state in both body and mind. For reasons deeply imbedded in the very structure of Roman imperial society, the response was far from unanimous. Instead of heightened unity in action and purpose, society was increasingly afflicted by fundamental divisions that frustrated the state's ability to muster its material and human resources in the face of a major crisis that began to emerge at the end of the fourth century in the form of a decisive encounter between the Romans and the Germanic peoples facing each other across the Rhine-Danube frontier.

3. THE GERMANS

In describing the encounter between the Romans and the Germans during the fourth and fifth centuries, historians have traditionally referred to the Germans as "barbarians." The term is appropriate only if used to signify that the Germans differed from the Romans in terms of the basic features of the culture under which they lived. The Germans' pattern of life had been formed in their original homeland in north-central Europe and southern Scandinavia during many centuries before their first encounters with the Roman world in the late republican period. In reconstructing its main features modern historians must rely on limited information, coming chiefly from archaeological remains, the testimony of a few Roman authors, especially Tacitus' *Germania*, and Germanic law codes that were not written down until the sixth century A.D. or later under circumstances that resulted in their coloration by Roman and Christian influences. In its entirety that evidence suggests that there is a danger in assuming that the early Germans shared a uniform culture or any sense of ethnic identity. However, the record does reveal certain fundamental Germanic institutions that set them apart from the Greco-Roman world and that were destined to play a part in shaping life in western Europe in future centuries.

The basic Germanic political institution was the *tribe*, headed by a tribal chief who was chosen primarily because of his ability as a war leader. Each tribe was composed of a number of kinship groups, or *clans*. The elders of these clans, acting as a council, played a decisive role in shaping tribal decisions, but all free males capable of bearing arms were allowed to have some voice in determining collective action. Tribal government concerned itself with a limited range of affairs, chiefly war and religion. Other matters relating to group life were left largely in the hands of kinship groups; especially crucial was the responsibility of each kinship group to protect its members against injury from others. Each tribe had a body of customary law to regulate such relationships that was transmitted orally from one generation to another. Although it has survived only in written versions colored by Roman and Christian concepts, it is clear that in its substance Germanic law was primarily concerned with damages against persons. The law prescribed how much compensation could be demanded for various kinds of damage done to a person. That price, called *wergeld*, varied not only according to the nature of the crime but also according to the rank of the person in the kinship group. For example, any damage to a warrior commanded a higher *wergeld* than did the same offense against a woman of childbearing age; in turn, damage done to such a woman called for a higher *wergeld* than did a comparable crime against an aged person. It was the responsibility of those suffering damage or their kin group, not public authority, to initiate judicial processes to collect the *wergeld* defined by law. Customary law provided complex procedures for resolving disputes involving damages to persons. One such procedure, called *compurgation*, involved finding a certain number of individuals, depending on the nature of the crime and the status of the accused, who would swear under oath that the accused was innocent. Another, called *ordeal*, involved putting the accused to a test, such as holding a hot iron or being thrown into water, the results of which could be interpreted as a divine message indicating guilt or innocence. If the individual judged guilty of damage to another agreed to pay the *wergeld* prescribed by custom, the issue was settled. If not, the aggrieved kinship group often sought vengeance on the clan of the alleged criminal; the resultant feuds were a common feature of Germanic life.

By the first centuries of the Christian era the Germans practiced a mixed economy combining animal husbandry, foraging for natural products, and farming. Exchange activity played a limited role in economic life, and manufacturing focused chiefly on weapons, tools, and items for personal adornment. The basic unit of economic and social life was the family household, controlled by a male who usually but not always had a single wife. Although dependent on males in many ways, women enjoyed considerable status in Germanic society. Kinship ties within clans were established through both male and female lines. Women possessed wealth in their own right, derived chiefly from gifts conveyed to them at the time of marriage. They also played an important part in the economic pursuits that supported family life. In many ways all free males were considered to be equals. However, social gradations existed, evidenced not only by differing *wergelds* but also by a unique Germanic custom of gift exchange through which gift givers who were able to be generous earned prestige and placed recipients who were unable to reciprocate with gifts of equal value into a position of inferiority.

Germanic religion was polytheistic, based on the worship of personfied deities who embodied the forces of nature dominating the skies and the forests. An orally transmitted mythology existed to explain the nature and powers of these deities, who were usually portrayed as remote, terrible forces that must be placated constantly through prayer and offerings. Although the Germans did not develop writing until the fourth century A.D., they did possess a well-developed oral poetic tradition that dealt with the adventures of their deities and with the feats of warrior heroes. The early Germans produced no monumental architecture; their artistic talent expressed itself chiefly in skilled metalwork featuring animal forms and geometric patterns.

Although their pattern of culture differed from that of the Romans, the Germans were not locked into a pattern of "backwardness." By the fourth century their society was changing. Small tribal groups were being unified, often by force, into nations ruled over by elected kings enjoying considerable powers. Within Germanic society a warrior aristocracy was forming around a unique institution—the war band (*comitatus*), composed of individuals united by pledges made under oath to follow a military chief in return for a share of booty. The bonds linking these warriors increasingly took precedence over kinship and tribal ties to create a dominant caste in society that exalted a warrior ethos. The emergence of nations and of skilled war bands greatly increased the military capabilities of the Germans. As already noted, Germanic society was moving toward an agricultural economy that encouraged the development of an aristocracy of landowners at the expense of the older, more egalitarian social structure. These changing conditions made Germanic society dynamic, mobile, adaptable, and open to foreign influences.

Having faced each other across a more or less fixed frontier for nearly four centuries before A.D. 400, the Greco-Roman and Germanic worlds were by no means strangers to each other, divided by irreconcilable cultural and psychological barriers. The Germans had often demonstrated a desire to share the fruits of Greco-Roman civilization, especially its material wealth. Although the Romans saw the Germans as "barbarians," they often expressed admiration for their physical prowess, fighting skills, and moral excellence. They permitted and even encouraged large numbers of Germans to cross the frontier as soldiers and farmers; many even rose to high places in Roman society. Roman products, techniques, and ideas crossed the frontiers to affect many aspects of Germanic society. Such interactions suggested that the Germans might be absorbed into the mainstream of Greco-Roman civilization without causing any great disruption of its development. But that possibility depended on the ability of the Romans to control the interactions between themselves and the Germans, a matter that hinged on maintaining the frontier defenses.

4. THE GERMANIC MIGRATIONS: THE DISRUPTION OF THE ROMAN EMPIRE

Throughout the third and fourth centuries Germanic pressure on the Rhine-Danube frontier mounted steadily due to massive migrations of land-hungry Germans southward and westward and to the coalescence of Germanic tribes into nations led by warrior kings and their war bands. Beginning about A.D. 370, a sequence of events unfolded which resulted in Rome's losing control of the frontier. The crisis was triggered by a horde of nomads, the Huns, who swept out of central Asia westward toward the Germanic world. As they advanced, they encountered two Germanic nations settled along the north shores of the Black Sea: the Ostrogoths, who were overpowered, and the Visigoths, whom the Romans allowed to resettle as a nation within the empire in the area south of the Danube in return for military service. When the imperial government failed to provide for their needs, the Visigoths revolted and inflicted a crushing defeat on the Romans at the battle of Adrianople in A.D. 378. The Romans now had a hostile Germanic nation within their borders. For a time Theodosius (A.D. 379–395), the last ruler of a unified empire, was able to contain the Visigoths in the Balkan area by establishing them as allies (*foederati*) to whom lands were assigned in return for military service. Theodosius was succeeded by two sons, one ruling the west and the other the east. Almost immediately, the two courts became involved in a series of power struggles fomented by ambitious generals seeking not only personal advantage but also resources to support their Germanic soldiers. These struggles distracted attention from the defense of the frontiers, setting the stage for a political disaster.

As the fifth century opened, the Visigoths, led by a capable king named Alaric, skillfully manipulated the conflict between the two imperial courts to win permission from the eastern emperor to migrate from the Balkans to the west (see Map 13.1 for the movements of the Germans). The result was an attack on Italy that led to the capture and sack of Rome in A.D. 410, an event that deeply shocked the Roman world. In an effort to fend off the Visigothic attacks, the imperial court in the west recalled troops from the Rhine and Danube frontiers and from Britain. Other Germanic nations immediately broke through the weakened frontier defenses and overran most of the western provinces. The imperial government in the west sought desperately to control the Germans by assigning them areas where they could settle as allies, nominally subject to Roman authority, and by allocating them a share of public revenues. In fact, wherever the Germans settled and whatever the terms, their kings and warriors soon became the real rulers. As a consequence, during the fifth century a series of independent Germanic kingdoms emerged on Roman soil in the west to create a new political geography of major importance for the future.

After a brief stay in Italy the Visigoths moved on to southern Gaul, where they established a kingdom that soon began to extend into Spain. Already other Germanic nations that had broken across the Rhine—Vandals, Sueves, Alains—had made their destructive way across Gaul and into Spain. The Vandals, under the leadership of their one great king, Gaiseric, crossed into Africa in A.D. 429 and carved out a large kingdom that deprived Rome of access to its main grain supply. The Vandals then developed sufficient sea power to allow them to pillage Rome in A.D. 455.

The Burgundians created a kingdom in southeastern Gaul in the Rhône Valley, effectively blocking the routes linking Italy to Gaul and Spain. Beginning about A.D. 425, Angles, Saxons, and Jutes went by sea to wipe out the badly weakened Roman outposts in Britain and to establish several petty kingdoms; in the process the newcomers drove the native Celtic population into Wales and across the English Channel into Brittany.

Without abandoning their original homelands, Franks and Alemanni began the occupation of northern Gaul and the middle Rhine Valley. Late in the fifth century the Franks, led by a ruthless warrior king named Clovis (A.D. 481–511), seized most of Gaul as their base of power; in the process they drove the Gallic Visigoths into Spain and absorbed the Burgundian kingdom as well as much of the territory of the Alemanni. In A.D. 493 the Ostrogoths, led by King Theoderic, acting as an agent of the eastern emperor, established control over Italy. The confusion caused by the movements of these Germanic peoples was compounded by the presence of a powerful Hunnic kingdom established north of the Danube. Under their feared king, Attila, the Huns harassed the East and then, in A.D. 451–452, invaded Gaul and Italy, which were successfully defended by a coalition of Roman and Germanic troops. After Attila's death in 453, the Hunnic kingdom quickly broke up, leaving central Europe in a chaotic state.

While the boundaries of these new kingdoms remained fluid and their political institutions unstable, there could be no doubt that by A.D. 500 the Germans had won the West. The fate of the empire in the east during the critical fifth century was quite different. Although German forces repeatedly ravaged imperial territory in the Balkans and sought entry into the eastern provinces, their assaults were turned away. The imperial government in Constantinople mustered the superior resources of the East to sustain an effective defense system and mounted a diplomatic effort that successfully diverted Germanic attacks toward the west. The consequence was of immense significance: the Roman imperial regime as structured by Diocletian and Constantine survived virtually intact in the east.

By contrast, in the west the imperial political system slowly disintegrated under the impact of

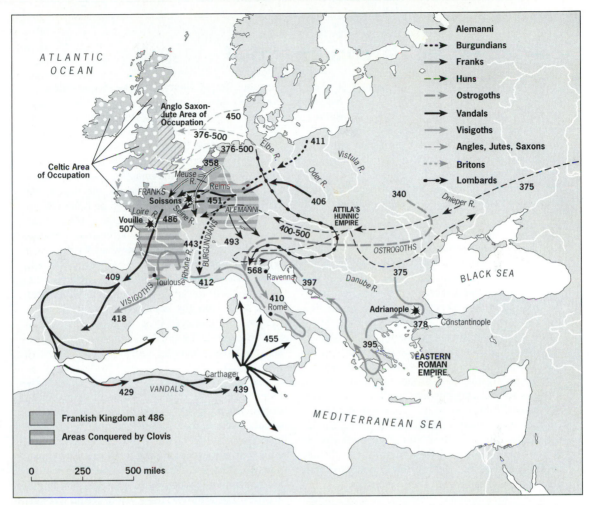

Map 13.1 GERMANIC INVASIONS, FIFTH CENTURY The map shows the movements of the various Germanic nations in the course of their migrations into the Roman Empire in the fifth century. Most of them ended their wandering by establishing a kingdom on Roman soil. Especially important for the future was the kingdom established by the Franks in Gaul.

the Germanic migrations. Despite the efforts of some military leaders to stem the tide, the imperial government was unable to muster the resources required to contain the Germans militarily. The bulk of the Roman population showed little zeal for defending themselves; some even welcomed the Germans as liberators who ended the oppressive policies of the late empire (see Historians' Sources, p. 170). Although the Germans were settled under terms that gave the Roman government nominal lordship over them,

in fact they took over real power. As the settlement process advanced, the Roman bureaucracy broke down, imperial income dwindled, the imperial armies melted away, and the authority of the successors of Augustus vanished. By A.D. 476 the political realities in the west were officially recognized. A German general, Odoacer, deposed the last western emperor and turned the insignia of the imperial office over to the emperor in Constantinople. In theory, this act reunited the empire under a single ruler. In reality, the em-

Salvian: *On the Governance of God*

In a work entitled On the Governance of God, *written just before 450, the Christian priest Salvian set forth a catalogue of the evils of his day resulting from human sin. His observations about the lot of the poor perhaps give the historian an insight into why the Roman government failed to maintain the allegiance of its subjects, why the victory of Christianity did not solve all problems, and why the rule of the "barbarian" Germans was acceptable to many.*

But what else can these wretched people wish for, they who suffer the incessant and even continuous destruction of public tax levies. To them there is always imminent a heavy and relentless proscription. They desert their homes, lest they be tortured in their very homes. They seek exile, lest they suffer torture. The enemy is more lenient to them than the tax collectors. . . . This very tax levying, although hard and inhuman, would nevertheless be less heavy and harsh if all would bear it equally and in common. Taxation is made more shameful and burdensome because all do not bear the burden of all. They extort tribute from the poor man for the taxes of the rich, and the weaker carry the load for the stronger. There is no other reason that they cannot bear all the taxation except that the burden imposed on the wretched is greater than their resources. . . .

If you look at what they pay, you will think them abundant in riches, but if you look at what they actually possess, you will find them poverty stricken. Who can judge an affair of this wretchedness? They bear the payment of the rich and endure the poverty of beggars. . . .

Indeed, the most wretched poor thus pay all that I have mentioned, but for what cause or for what reason they pay, they are completely ignorant. For, to whom is it lawful to discuss why they pay; to whom is permitted to find out what is owed? . . .

But, surely, those who are wicked in one way are found moderate and just in another, and compensate for their baseness in one thing by goodness in another. For, just as they weigh down the poor with the burden of new tax levies, so they sustain them by the assistance of new tax reliefs; just as the lower classes are oppressed by new taxes, so they are equally relieved by tax mitigations. Indeed, the injustice is equal in taxes and reliefs, for, as the poor are the first to be burdened, so they are the last to be relieved.

For when, as has happened lately, the highest powers thought it would be advisable that taxation should be lessened somewhat for the cities which were in arrears in their payments, the rich alone instantly divided among themselves the remedy given for all. Who, then, remembers the poor? Who calls the poor and needy to share in the common benefit? Who permits him who is first in bearing the burden even to stand in the last place for receiving redress? What more is there to say? . . .

Do we think we are unworthy of the punishment of divine severity, when we thus constantly punish the poor? Do we think, when we are constantly wicked, that God should not exercise His justice against all of us? Where or in whom are evils so great, except among the Romans? Whose injustice is so great except our own? The Franks are ignorant of this crime of injustice. The Huns are immune to these crimes. There are no wrongs among the Vandals and none among the Goths. So far are the barbarians from tolerating these injustices among the Goths, that not even the Romans who live among them suffer them.

Therefore, in the districts taken over by the barbarians, there is one desire among all the Romans, that they should never again find it necessary to pass under Roman jurisdiction. In those regions, it is the one and general prayer of the Roman people that they be allowed to carry on the life they lead with the barbarians. And we wonder why the Goths are not conquered by our portion of the population, when the Romans prefer to live among them rather than with us. Our brothers, therefore, are not only altogether unwilling to flee to us from them, but they even cast us aside in order to flee to them.

SOURCE: *The Writings of Salvian, the Presbyter*, trans. Jeremiah F. O'Sullivan (New York: Cima Publishing Co., Inc., 1947), pp. 138–141.

peror in the east had virtually no control over the west, where the Germans ruled by virtue of conquest but without the benefits of the splendid political system created by the Romans. The end of that system marked a turning point in the history of the Mediterranean world.

Beyond the disruption of the imperial political system in the west, the immediate impact of the Germanic migrations must not be overstated. The destruction of life and property was not excessive, and in most cases Germans and Romans soon settled side by side on peaceful terms. Except in Britain and along a thin stretch of the old empire facing the Rhine, the intruders were not sufficiently numerous to affect the ethnic composition or language of the native Roman population. Many aspects of Roman civilization survived the shock of the Germanic intrusion and continued to play a decisive role in the way people in the west lived and thought.

Of more fundamental significance was the fact that the migration of the Germans into the west helped to create a general environment that accelerated and made irreversible certain trends in economic and cultural life which had begun to undermine the fabric of Greco-Roman civilization long before the Germans arrived. The trend toward a predominantly agricultural economy continued during and beyond the fifth century, accentuated by the decline of trade and industry and by political instability. The result was a continued decline in the general level of material wealth. Agricultural life increasingly focused on self-contained large estates tilled by a peasantry dependent on their owners. Of both Roman and German descent, these landowners constituted a new ruling force whose interests were narrowly focused on family welfare, economic self-sufficiency, acquisition of land, and local political power. Most cities in the west shrank to a fraction of their former size and ceased to be active commercial, administrative, and cultural centers. Their decline meant the end of the urban aristocracy that had long sustained Greco-Roman civilization in the west. Deprived of an urban setting and the patronage of the Roman imperial government, Greco-Roman cultural activity stagnated despite the efforts of some rural aristocrats, both Roman and German, to support education, literature, and art. The growing irrelevance of many aspects of classical culture to the realities of a changing world made their efforts ineffectual and opened the way for a different culture defined in Christian terms. All of these aspects of change point to one conclusion: Greco-Roman civilization did not "fall" because of "barbarian" invasions; the arrival of the Germans simply reinforced the powerful forces already at work transforming long-standing patterns of civilization into a different kind of order to which the Germans would contribute in important ways.

5. CHRISTIANITY IN LATE ANTIQUITY

Christianity was inevitably involved in the events of the fourth and fifth centuries that transformed the Roman Empire; that involvement changed the nature of the Christian movement. From one perspective the fourth century was a time of triumph for Christians. Massive numbers of converts from all levels of society swelled the ranks of the Christian community to the point where Christians were the dominant religious force in the empire. Christian clergymen increasingly advanced to prominent leadership positions in society, using the organizational structures and the increasing wealth they commanded as instruments to shape life in imperial society. The imperial government gave powerful support to these developments, thereby intertwining the Christian establishment and the secular authority ever more closely. By about A.D. 400 the Roman Empire had become a Christian Roman Empire, a fact recognized by Theodosius when he proclaimed Christianity as the state religion. That action instilled into many Christians a triumphal, even arrogant sense that the kingdom promised by God had come.

However, success brought problems that troubled the souls of many Christians and prompted still further adaptations of their religion. The avalanche of converts diluted the spiritual fervor of pre-Constantinian Christianity and opened the way for an intrusion of pagan ideas and practices that threatened to obliterate the distinctiveness of Christianity. The massive influx of educated Romans into the Christian community accelerated the efforts to reformulate the essential Christian message in terms that reflected the Greco-Roman philosophical and literary tradition. Wealth and power turned the heads of Christian leaders from pastoral functions toward worldly pursuits. The insistence of Christian emperors on using Christianity to advance political ends that had little to do with the "good news" that Jesus had taught threatened the independence of the Christian community. Large numbers of people, from powerful aristocrats to lowly peasants, still adhered to their traditional religions; what to do with these "pagans" posed troublesome issues.

At the heart of all of these issues was a profound intellectual, moral, and even emotional dilemma posed by the very success of Christianity: How could a movement that had historically been distrustful of the powerful and of worldly things, committed to peace and justice, and expectant of the coming of a kingdom in which the corrupt ways of the world would be overturned suddenly become a willing handmaiden of an oppressive regime upon whose hands was the blood of Christian martyrs? How could a community that had been exclusive, highly selective of its membership, animated by deep moral fervor, and concerned with human interactions based on love and charity suddenly become a corporate entity flooded with members whose moral purity was untested, whose motives for "conversion" were unexamined, and whose subsequent behavior was little changed? These profound contradictions, which touched every aspect of Christianity during the fourth century, led to responses that hastened what one modern scholar has called "the conversion of Christianity." Some of those responses put a mark on the Christian movement that had an immense impact on the future.

One response, aimed primarily at resolving the disciplinary problems brought on by the huge increase in the number of Christians, involved steps to strengthen the organization of the Christian community. The distinctions between religious leaders, the clergy, and ordinary Christians, the laity, were drawn more sharply. The powers of the clergy, especially bishops, were expanded to allow them to define Christian behavior and modes of worship more precisely and to compel the laity to obey the evolving "law" of the Christian establishment, called *canon law*. Bishops were vested with judicial

powers, usually with the support of the imperial government, to punish those violating canon law, including the power of *excommunication*, that is, cutting offenders off from participation in the religious life through which salvation was gained. While the strengthening of a hierarchical system of governance promoted order in the Christian world, it also introduced an element of compulsion and authoritarianism into religious life that contrasted sharply with the voluntarism and self-discipline that had marked earlier Christian community life.

Another response to the new situation in which the Christian movement found itself was a search for new ways of finding and living a holy life, a quest most dramatically illustrated by the rise of monasticism. Although the movement involved elements of protest against political and economic oppression and against an increasingly formalized, legalistic, intellectualized religious establishment, monasticism in its essence represented a radical new way of seeking God defined by individuals lacking the qualifications generally required for positions of authority: wealth, family connections, office, education. This new breed of Christian, calling themselves "athletes of Christ," sought to follow Jesus' command to leave all worldly things behind by physically separating themselves from the civilized world to live in a setting apart where through prayer and mortification of the flesh they sought to purge themselves of temptation and sin. The monastic movement began in the late third and early fourth centuries in Egypt, where individuals of modest circumstances left everything behind to live in the desert. The first desert fathers, exemplified by Anthony, who soon became a hero as the father of monasticism, were hermits who sought perfection through individual ascetic actions; Anthony's model of individual (*eremetic*) spiritual quest was widely imitated outside of Egypt, especially in Syria and Palestine. In time hermits seeking guidance in their quest for perfection began to cluster around a father (*abba*) who had gained renown for his spiritual feats. This led to the formation of monasteries, groups of individuals living in isolated physical compounds where the pursuit of spiritual perfection was governed by rules that defined patterns of communal behavior for achieving perfection. Especially important in establishing models for communal (*cenobitic*) monastic life were the rules of the Egyptian monk Pachomius and the Greek monk and bishop Basil of Caesarea. Spread by word of mouth and by written biographical sketches and collections of sayings of the desert fathers, the spiritual heroics of the early monks soon electrified the Christian world. By A.D. 400 monasticism, especially in its cenobitic form, had spread across most of the Roman world. While the monastic ethos was excessive in its denial of worldly affairs and its obsession with the danger of sexuality as a source of sin, it did remind Christians of the need for inner struggle in order to win salvation. The monastic movement created a new type of hero to replace the martyrs of old and a new type of authority figure to challenge the official clergy. In the eyes of many ordinary Christians, the holy men and women forged in the austere, world-denying environment of the monastery became a special breed able to serve as agents through whom divine favors could flow to relieve the heavy burdens imposed by a troubled, uncaring world.

While some chose to flee the world, other Christians, especially ecclesiastical leaders, chose to become more closely identified with it, a response that likewise had momentous consequences. Operating within a long tradition of viewing religion as an instrument of political control, the religious hierarchy was put into a new position once the Roman imperial order accepted Christianity as the official religion. It came under strong pressure to use its expanding authority to define religious behavior in terms that supported political policy and to use its powers of enforcement in ways that promoted political conformity. For a variety of reasons ranging from pastoral concerns to an urge for power, most Christian officials of the fourth century were quite willing to cooperate fully with the state in the promotion of a Christian empire. That willingness hastened the intermingling of secular and religious affairs to a point where it was virtually impossible to distinguish between the two realms. Equally important, it led to the sacralization of the state and its rulers, whose office bestowed on them a divinely ordained right and duty to promote Christian welfare and to whom obedience became a Christian obligation. Nowhere was this process more dramati-

cally demonstrated than in the case of Constantine. Although his actual conduct as emperor was far from exemplary by any standards, let alone Christian, even during his lifetime he came to be viewed as one touched by divinity, a new David upon whom God had bestowed powers that made him an agent in working out the divine plan for humankind and that allowed him to command Christians as he wished for their own good. A new dimension had been added to Christianity which gave a different meaning to rendering unto Caesar that which was his.

However, to some who were mindful of the earlier Christian tradition of hostility and suspicion toward the world and its ways, that development posed grave dangers. They began to articulate a case for limitation of state control over religion. Of particular importance for the future was the contention that Christian ends were different from and more important than secular ends and therefore must take precedence. That view was given dramatic visibility by the powerful bishop of Milan, Ambrose (ca. A.D. 340–397), who excommunicated Emperor Theodosius for massacring some of his subjects under circumstances that some thought exceeded the authority of worldly rulers. Ambrose justified his sentence on the grounds that the Christian community constituted a corporate body—a Church—which possessed a separate realm of jurisdiction that must take precedence over the state when spiritual issues were at stake. Implicit in this argument were fundamental issues involving the nature of the Christian community and how it should be governed that would long pose a challenge. As the concept of the separateness and independence of the "Church" took shape, it spurred discussion of where the locus of ultimate authority in the Christian community was. As the fourth century proceeded, more and more Christians agreed that the bishop of Rome, Peter's successor, was the spiritual head of the Christian community. The ascendancy of the bishop of Rome was promoted by the imperial government, which relied on the successors of Peter to formulate and lend support to definitions of dogma and discipline that would serve to unify the empire. The popes responded by expanding their claims to authority and by asserting that authority more vigorously over the Christian community, steps that gave added impetus to the evolving hierarchical structure of Christian organization. But not all were happy with the rising star of the bishop of Rome, least of all the patriarchs of the venerable Christian communities in Antioch, Alexandria, and Jerusalem, to which was added a newcomer, the patriarch of Constantinople, who was closely linked to the emperor of Constantinople. The stage was being set for a long, bitter, and sometimes unholy struggle for supremacy within the Christian community.

Fourth-century Christianity was given special shape by a growing concern with doctrinal uniformity. Although doctrinal disagreement had been present in the pre-Constantinian Christian community, the intensified urge to define and enforce "orthodoxy" and to suppress dissident "heresy" represented another response to Christian victory. The basic dilemmas posed by the sudden favorable turn of events for the Christians evoked diverse views that had doctrinal implications and that revealed the possibility of irreconcilable divisions that would make folly of Jesus' "good news" and the whole idea of a single Christian community. The complexity of the issues raised by divergent doctrinal positions is illustrated by two particular "heresies."

One was Donatism, a movement originating in North Africa, which centered on the fate of clergymen who had compromised their faith in the face of Diocletian's persecution but subsequently sought restoration to their offices. A party of zealous Christians, led by Bishop Donatus of Carthage, denied them this privilege, arguing that their apostasy barred them forever from Christian fellowship and that their impurity rendered invalid all the sacred rites they had performed—baptisms, marriages, ordinations, forgiveness of sins. Implicit in the Donatist position was a concept of the true Christian community as a small, elite, pure group led by bishops and priests untouched by sin. When theological arguments failed to dissuade these purists, Constantine used the power of the state to suppress them, but to no avail. Backed by popular support in North Africa which linked religious dissent with resistance to the Roman imperial regime, the Donatist movement survived for over a century, constituting what amounted to a separate Christian establishment that served to keep alive the issue of who qualified as a true Christian.

Even more disruptive was Arianism, a movement that emerged from the teachings of a priest from Alexandria named Arius concerning the Trinity. Disturbed with the blurring of monotheism that had resulted from the absorption of Greco-Roman religious and philosophical ideas into Christian teaching, Arius argued that God the Son was subordinate to God the Father, thereby denying the absolute divinity of Jesus. His position raised a storm of protest from bishops and theologians who supported a trinitarian position maintaining that the Son was coequal with the Father and that, together with the Holy Spirit, these three "persons" constituted a single deity. In an attempt to settle this dispute Constantine summoned bishops from all over the empire to the ecumenical Council of Nicaea in A.D. 325. This assemblage, presided over by the emperor in person, agreed upon the Nicene Creed, which defined "orthodox" teaching on several issues, included a strong affirmation of the trinitarian position. Despite official condemnation and punitive measures taken by the state against its adherents, Arianism survived for generations to divide Christendom. In later efforts to resolve the trinitarian issue, emperors and their supporting theologians demonstrated a tendency to cut doctrinal cloth in ways that would appeal to political factions and regional ecclesiastical rivalries, thereby politicizing the quest for doctrinal unity.

The upshot of the quest for orthodoxy was the hardening of doctrine into an official creed, deviation from which earned the charge of heresy and brought political and religious sanctions down on dissenters. The implications of this development toward a monolithic ideology in terms of personal religious experience were ominous. On the obverse side of this development were increasingly harsh sanctions against paganism and more strident assaults on Judaism; these manifestations of the narrowing of the limits of tolerance had widespread support at all levels of Christian society.

Still another response to the situation in which the Christian community found itself in the fourth century was a more aggressive involvement of Christians in intellectual and artistic life. The result was an outburst of cultural activity that resulted in their assumption of cultural leadership in late antiquity. That leadership was clearly demonstrated in the arts. Church building provided one of the chief outlets for the talents of architects, sculptors, and painters. They developed new modes of conveying the Christian message by creatively adapting the classical artistic tradition to Christian purposes (see Figures 12.1, 12.3, and 13.2). Some of the most inspired poetry of the age flowed from the pens of Christian writers seeking to express their thoughts and feelings about their faith. Christian writers such as Bishop Eusebius of Caesarea (ca. A.D. 260–340) recast the writing of history to incorporate the past of the non-Christian world into the Judeo-Christian version of sacred history as delineated in Scripture; in the process the Roman Empire and its rulers emerged as integral, preordained elements in the working out of God's plan for the cosmos. Inspired chiefly by the feats of the monks, Christian writers developed a new literary genre, hagiography, devoted to the lives of the saints.

But the most important intellectual achievement of the period was the theological writings of a remarkable group of intellectuals, known collectively as the *Church Fathers*. Among the most prominent were the Greeks Athanasius, Basil, Gregory of Nyssa, and Gregory Nazianus and the Latins Augustine, Jerome, and Ambrose. Although each was an individual intellectual in his own right, this potent group of thinkers collectively reshaped the basic thrust of intellectual life. The fruit of their labor was a massive body of literature destined to guide intellectual life for centuries to come. Their intellectual posture was rooted in their deep Christian faith as informed by the Old and New testaments, but they also borrowed boldly and creatively from the content

FIGURE 13.2 A Sixth-Century Christian Church This magnificent church was built in Ravenna in honor of S. Apollinare. Its architectural form represents an adaptation of the Roman basilica style (see p. 140) for Christian purposes. The central hall (the nave) served as a gathering place for the faithful. An altar often stood in the semicircular apse at the far end of the nave. Aisles flanked the nave on either side, set off by columns and arches supporting the walls of the nave. These walls rose above the roof over each side aisle. At their upper levels the walls were pierced by windows that lighted the structure's interior. This style of architecture was destined to assert a powerful influence on religious architecture in later western European history. (G. E. Kidder-Smith)

and methods of the Greco-Roman literary, philosophical, and scientific tradition to formulate a consistent, logical, persuasive statement of the Christian interpretation of the universe. In the process they not only provided reasoned and enduring positions on key elements of Christian doctrine but also literally redefined human values and the purpose of human existence in terms of a quest for salvation in another world, thereby overpowering the classical Greco-Roman worldview, which stressed the reasoned search for excellence in this world. In working out this transformation of values the church fathers selectively appropriated the Greco-Roman intellectual achievement as an indispensable tool for understanding what they perceived to be ultimate Christian wisdom, but in the process they reshaped that achievement in ways that deprived it of much of its original meaning.

As the Church Fathers progressed in formulating a Christian worldview, subtle differences began to emerge that distinguished the Greek Fathers from the Latin Fathers in terms of their basic religious concerns and their interpretation of classical culture. These differences marked an initial step in the emergence of distinctive eastern and western Christian establishments. Of particular importance in shaping the western intellectual tradition was Augustine (A.D. 354–430). Born in North Africa, the son of a pagan father and a Christian mother, Augustine received a good Latin education to prepare him as a teacher of rhetoric. As his education progressed, his searching mind experimented with a variety of pagan philosophical and religious systems, none of which satisfied his yearning for spiritual security. Neither did the mistress he took as a young man nor the child born to that union. Eventually he converted to Christianity and was chosen bishop of Hippo in Africa. As a bishop, Augustine's major concern was to be an effective pastor. In that role he worked tirelessly to guide his flock toward sound belief and spiritual perfection and ended his life trying to protect his city from the Germanic Vandals. But he also turned out a prodigious body of writing on a variety of theological and moral issues, much of it prompted by his efforts to combat heresy, especially Donatism and Arianism. In his own time his writings served many as guides to a fuller understanding of the faith; for centuries to come his thought provided the basis for the major positions adopted in the West on most doctrinal and moral issues.

Two of his many works were particularly significant. His *Confessions* recounts his own spiritual pilgrimage as an educated Roman through most of the philosophical and religious systems of the ancient world to his final realization that only Christianity could satisfy his spiritual hunger. The work presents not only a forceful critique revealing the failure of Greco-Roman philosophy and religion to satisfy many thinking people but also a compelling argument in support of the Christian faith as the only adequate response to life's problems. Even more influential was his *City of God*, written to answer charges that the Visigothic sack of Rome in A.D. 410 was a punishment imposed on the Romans by their ancient deities, who were angry at them for becoming Christians. Augustine sought to demonstrate that this "catastrophe" was only a step in the unfolding of God's plan for the universe. God, he argued, had ordained two cities, that of God and that of the world. The true City of God exists only in the other world; membership will be awarded to true believers who have been predestined for salvation by God. The worldly city, presently embodied in the Roman Empire, is tarnished by sin and due eventually to pass. The coming of Christ had established an earthly embodiment of the City of God in the form of the Christian community, into whose body all must now be enfolded. Not despair but joy should greet the passing of Rome, since that event was a preordained step toward a more perfect world planned by God from the beginning. Members of the human community, both those who are sinners and those destined for salvation, must accept their lot in this world, including submission to worldly government, whose function is restraining the forces of evil by whatever means possible. Augustine justified warfare, slavery, persecution of heretics, social inequality, and suffering as inevitable consequences of flawed human nature, for which there was no cure except God's grace, which would not be bestowed to perfect this world. In offering an explanation for the misery and evil of this world and a vision of redemption in another world that did not hinge on human accomplishment, Augustine's interpretation of both the cosmos and history provided an appealing answer to basic human concerns that had not been supplied by classical philosophy. In this sense, his intellectual achievement marked a watershed between the Classical Age and the future.

Other Christian intellectuals helped to ensure the victory of a Christian culture in the west. One was Ambrose (ca. A.D. 340–397), bishop of Milan and a key figure in guiding Augustine to his conversion. In his writings Ambrose not only helped to shape the rationale for the independence of the Church but also persuasively articulated the basic principles of Christian morality. He drew heavily on the moral principles developed by classical thinkers, but he skillfully recast their moral values to fit within the framework of Christian doctrine. Another influential figure was Jerome (A.D. 340–419), a man of immense learning and a formidable linguist who was drawn to monastic life despite the great appeal that classical literature had for him. His voluminous letters played a significant role in guiding the spiritual life of an important circle of Roman nobles, including many women. He employed his linguistic talents to produce a Latin translation of the Old and New testaments, basing his translation on both Hebrew and Greek versions of Scripture. Jerome's Bible, called the Vulgate, became the standard Latin Bible for centuries. Its existence ensured that Latin would survive as the language of the Christian religion in the West and that its readers would retain an ability to read the literature of classical Latin antiquity. Jerome's extensive commentaries on the Bible also guided later generations in their efforts to interpret the meaning of the Bible.

The traumatic events that befell the Roman Empire during the fifth century posed new problems for Christianity. The collapse of the Roman political system in the west deprived the Christian community there of a major protector and a prime source of material support. Churches were destroyed and Christians were killed by the Germans. Although the Germans converted to Christianity, almost all of them became adherents of Arian Christianity, which resulted in clashes with the main body of the Christian population in the west, which accepted the orthodox trinitarian position; this doctrinal schism impeded the assimilation of Romans and Germans. Moreover, the Germanic nations were usually con-

verted from the top down, their kings decreeing that their followers accept baptism but not having much concern for their instruction in their new faith. As a result, a large residue of Germanic religious ideas and practices continued to flourish in the Germanic population, often reinforcing the paganism still flourishing among non-Germans living in the rural areas of the west. Powerful theological disagreements still divided the Christian population, especially in the east, where heresy often became associated with regional political discontent to form separatist movements threatening the already fragile unity of the empire.

However, firmly in possession of its early traditions and fortified by the new organizational, intellectual, and spiritual vitality shaped during the fourth century, the Christian community survived the ordeal of the fifth century and became a more potent directive force in society. In the east a significant segment of Christian leaders rallied to the support of the imperial government and utilized their position and resources to solidify public acceptance of the imperial policy seeking to perpetuate a Christian Roman Empire as envisaged by Constantine. In many parts of the west, bishops replaced local aristocracies and bureaucrats as keepers of order, administrators of justice, and caretakers of the unfortunate. Pope Leo I (A.D. 440–461), for example, served as virtual governor of the city of Rome and as a forceful diplomat who defended the city against attacks by the Vandals and Huns. Many other bishops played a similar role in cities across the entire west. By A.D. 500 there were clear signs that the Arianism of the Germans was giving way to orthodoxy and that Germans and Romans were finding a common basis in a single faith. A key event in ensuring the victory of orthodoxy was the conversion of the pagan Frankish king Clovis to orthodoxy. Most Germanic kings, whatever their particular religious persuasion, began to lend their support to the Christian establishment and to draw on its personnel for assistance in ruling their kingdoms. As the focus of life shifted from the city to a rural setting, bishops began incorporating the neglected peasantry into the mainstream of Christian life. A sign of its concern with rural life was the emergence of a new organizational structure, the rural parish, which provided a local center from which to convert the nobles and peasants increasingly bound to a rural environment and guide their spiritual formation. As cultural life in the declining cities collapsed, monasteries increasingly provided havens for education and the preservation of culture. By A.D. 500 the Christian clergy had become a pillar of order and stability in all aspects of life in the west. It members had inherited the leadership role once held by the Roman imperial officials, a role that its earliest adherents would probably never have dreamed possible or perhaps even desirable. That leadership provided a clear indication that the old order was giving way to a new one.

SUGGESTED READING

Political, Economic, and Social Developments

The general history of the period covered in this chapter is treated in the works cited in Chapter 12 on the decline of the Roman Empire. The following works cover more specialized aspects of the period, as indicated by their titles.

Ramsay MacMullen, *The Roman Government's Response to Crisis, A.D.. 235–337* (1976).

Diana Bowder, *The Age of Constantine and Julian* (1978).

A. H. M. Jones, *Constantine and the Conversion of Europe* (1948; reprinted 1978).

History of Christianity

The developments in religious history are treated in the works of Markus, Frend, and Fox cited in Chapter 12. The following works treat particular aspects of religious history.

Jaroslav Pelikan, *The Christian Tradition: A History of the Development of Doctrine*, Vol. 1: *The Emergence of the Catholic Tradition (100–600)* (1971). A masterful treatment of the shaping of Christian doctrine.

Derwas J. Chitty, *The Desert a City* (1966).

Philip Rousseau, *Pachomius: The Making of a Community in Fourth-Century Egypt* (1985).

Two excellent studies on monastic origins.

Peter Brown, *Society and the Holy in Late Antiquity* (1982). A brilliant portrayal of the spiritual forces that transformed the late Roman world.

Peter Brown, *The Body and Society: Men, Women, and Sexual Renunciation in Early Christianity* (1988). A masterful treatment of Christian attitudes about sexuality.

John Holland Smith, *The Death of Classical Paganism* (1976). A good account of another side of religious life in the late empire—that of the losers.

The Germans and Their Migrations

Malcolm Todd, *The Northern Barbarians, 100 B.C.–A.D. 300* (1987).

E. A. Thompson, *The Early Germans* (1965).

Either of these works will help the reader understand the nature of early Germanic society.

Hans-Joachim Diesner, *The Great Migrations: The Movements of Peoples Across Europe, A.D. 300–700*, trans. C. S. V. Salt (1982). A brief account, beautifully illustrated.

Lucien Musset, *The Germanic Invasions: The Making of Europe, A.D. 400–600*, trans. Edward and Columba James (1975). A more detailed account of the Germanic migrations.

Justine D. Randers-Pehrson, *Barbarians and Romans: The Birth Struggle of Europe, A.D. 400–700* (1983). Especially good on the efforts of the Germans to establish themselves in the empire.

Biographies

Stephen Williams, *Diocletian and the Roman Recovery* (1985).

Ramsay MacMullen, *Constantine* (1988).

Peter Brown, *Augustine of Hippo: A Biography* (1967).

RETROSPECT

Few epochs in all history witnessed greater achievements than that extending from the Golden Age of Greece in the fifth century B.C. to the generation that saw the Roman imperial system reach its full maturity about A.D. 180—the epoch from Pericles to Marcus Aurelius. The

Greco-Roman accomplishment was driven by one fundamental idea—confidence in the ability of human beings to shape their own destiny by utilizing powers inherent in their own human nature. Trust in those powers, especially the power to reason, prompted a many-faceted search for more knowledge about the physical world in which human beings lived and a fuller understanding of the human condition. The fruits of that inquiry found expression in a rich literature, philosophy, science, and art. Viewed in its entirety, the Greco-Roman cultural achievement provided persuasive evidence that there was order in the universe, that men and women could know themselves, and that they could define and live by ethical standards capable of producing a good and full life. Out of this quest emerged a shared set of values which supplied intellectual, aesthetic, and emotional bonds that drew a wide circle of peoples into a cultural community that persisted across many centuries. The same trust in the human power to shape human destiny generated efforts to shape and reshape political communities in quest of a social environment that would foster the good life and the pursuit of human excellence, an effort that proceeded along a continuous trajectory from the Greek city-state polity to the Roman Empire. These developments not only greatly expanded the human vision but also brought to many—including those who had not heretofore tasted the fruits of higher civilization—peace, security, and even a better material life.

Yet the Greco-Roman achievement was somehow flawed. Not even its creators were completely convinced that their vision of humanity was true. They suspected that in human beings lurked an elusive element of the demonic and that beyond them existed forces they were powerless to control. Moreover, the kind of society that emerged from the centuries-long effort to create a world fit for reasonable, good, enlightened people had some features that were disturbing. The confidence that political action could achieve perfection had given the state a dangerous dominance over its peoples at the expense of other dimensions of existence. The majestic assumptions about human rationality and capacity for good had given undue power to those who managed to acquire the symbols of rationality and good: an education, offices, wealth, and manners. These aristocrats tended to be oblivious to those who had not been enlightened or blessed with power and prestige: women, slaves, even lower-class citizens. The politicized and intellectualized flavor of classical civilization bred in the elitists who wielded power and participated in the mainstream of cultural life a disdain for other kinds of activity and feelings. The rationalizing of human conduct and nature bred an intellectual posture that saw things in terms of absolute, fixed forms and found it difficult to accept or to initiate change.

This darker side of Greco-Roman civilization became more prominent from the third century A.D. onward. In an effort to control the forces threatening to destroy the traditional order, the Roman world was turned into a prison for the human spirit marked by autocratic government, regimented economic life, militarized society, and callous social elitism. Traditional Greco-Roman institutions and values increasingly became empty forms from which flowed no inspiration capable of mitigating what had become the burden of civilization. Into this troubled setting came the first of many "new" peoples—the Germans—who would intrude into the Mediterranean world to become doers, learners, and experimenters and a powerful religious movement—Christianity—that proclaimed a new vision of humanity which provided a new sense of direction. Working within the fabric of a declining civilization, these new forces began a transformation of Greco-Roman civilization that marked its "fall."

However, to speak of the fall of Greco-Roman civilization is to utter only a partial truth. That civilization left behind models of civilized existence that have served to shape human activity over a wide sweep of terrritory around the Mediterranean Sea since A.D. 500. Whatever its limitations, that civilization changed the course of history. Its legacy must occupy the attention of all who would understand the development of civilization during the next millennium and a half.

PART THREE

THE EARLY MIDDLE AGES, 500–1000: TOWARD A NEW ORDER

The dissolution of Greco-Roman civilization posed a challenge for the peoples living around the Mediterranean Sea: how to replace the old order with a new civilizational pattern. Despite false starts and confusion, they met the challenge with remarkable creativity. Between 500 and 1000, an era called the early Middle Ages by modern historians, three new cultural communities were defined, each based partly on old Roman soil but each extending into "new" territory. One was the Byzantine cultural world with its center in Constantinople, its heartland in Asia Minor and the Balkans south of the Danube, and its frontier in Slavic Europe. The second was the Islamic cultural world with its heartland in the ancient Fertile Crescent stretching from Mesopotamia to Egypt and its frontiers eastward to India and Central Asia, westward across North Africa to Spain, and southward toward sub-Saharan Africa. The third new civilization was created by the Germanic invaders of the western Roman Empire. Gaul and Italy formed its center; its frontiers included England, Germany, Scandinavia, Spain, and the western portions of the Slavic world in central Europe.

In each of these societies there were seminal forces at work generating new institutions and new ideas. In all three societies powerful vestiges of Greco-Roman civilization persisted to shape the essential features of each new civilization. In two of them—the Moslem and western European worlds—new peoples, Arabs and Germans, supplied a leavening agent. But perhaps it was religion that furnished the major animating force in this period. Two universal religions dominated the history of the period. Christianity, finally achieving its full power in the fifth century, provided that force in the Byzantine and western European cultural worlds. Islam, a new religion, asserted a powerful formative force over its Arab followers, called Moslems, as they established the foundations of Islamic civilization.

Modern historians have often dismissed this age as a "dark age." Before accepting that characterization, we must try to assess the creative aspects of the period.

CHAPTER 14

Heirs to the Roman Empire: The Byzantine and Moslem Empires

FIGURE 14.1 Moslem Mosque This view of the interior of the magnificent mosque built at Cordoba, Spain, in the eighth century illustrates key features of Moslem architecture, especially the skillful use of arches and pillars to create spaces for private worship and the employment of geometric decorative designs. Many features of Moslem art represent a creative synthesis of artistic traditions borrowed from earlier cultures embraced in the Moslem world. A comparison of this mosque with a typical Christian basilica (see Figure 13.2) will suggest differences between Moslem and Christian religious practices. (Georg Gerster/Comstock)

Two of the new civilizations emerging from the Greco-Roman world—Byzantine and Islamic—had their centers in the eastern territories of the old Roman Empire. These areas, comprising the most affluent and culturally sophisticated part of the Roman Empire, provided a richer seedbed for development than existed in the west. As a consequence, during the early Middle Ages the Byzantine and Islamic cultures were more precocious and vigorous than that of western Europe. Their very success in the early Middle Ages established their own special place in history, separate from the development of western European civilization. Given our focus on the western world, we can give them only limited attention—far less than their accomplishments deserve.

1. BYZANTINE CIVILIZATION: ORIGINS AND HISTORY, 395–1100

Byzantine civilization, so named by modern historians after the ancient Greek city-state of Byzantium where Constantine built his capital, began as a direct continuation of the old Roman Empire. After the division of the empire following the death of Theodosius in 395, a succession of rulers in Constantinople successfully resisted Germanic attacks and maintained the basic features of late imperial society. Their claim to be the heirs to old Rome was validated in 476, when the imperial title in the west was transferred to Constantinople and the eastern emperors assumed themselves to be legitimate rulers over the entire Roman world, including those parts seized by Germans. But that sequence of events aimed at maintaining the fiction of Rome's survival was marked by developments in the east that by the sixth century pointed toward the shaping of a new society.

The watershed between the old and new Rome can perhaps be placed in the reign of Justinian (527–565), often called the last Roman and the first Byzantine emperor. Justinian's talents and accomplishments have been variously judged across the ages, but few would dispute the fact that he made decisions of immense importance in redirecting the course of history. He

was given invaluable assistance by Empress Theodora, one of the most gifted women in history (see Figure 14.2). The daughter of a circus bear trainer, she was an actress and courtesan before Justinian took her as his wife. Intelligent, beautiful, and courageous, she was instrumental in helping her often-indecisive husband make critical decisions. She was especially astute in reading the temper of the complex imperial court circle and the factious populace of Constantinople.

Justinian's claim to be called the last Roman stems from the central focus of his policy: a major effort to restore the unity of the old empire. To this end, he set out to reestablish imperial authority over the western provinces held by Germanic rulers. Although his effort was brilliant, his success was partial. The best his armies could do was to recapture North Africa from the Vandals, Italy from the Ostrogoths, and a small strip of southeastern Spain from the Visigoths. Gaul, most of Spain, England, and the upper Danube provinces remained in German hands. More significantly, the price for these limited conquests was great, for Justinian's western policy left the eastern frontiers exposed to the Sassanian Persians, who continued their efforts to recapture the territory held by the ancient Persians. By the end of his reign, it was clear that imperial resources must be concentrated in the east if areas crucial to the survival of the empire were to be held. The western part of the old Roman Empire would have to be abandoned to its German masters.

Justinian's reign was also significant in shaping a unique governmental system. He saw himself as the direct descendant of the Roman emperors, and he worked actively to perfect the system of absolute, sacred monarchy originated by Diocletian and Constantine. An important part of this effort led him to commission a corps of legal experts to organize into a single, consistent code the complex tradition of Roman law, which dated back at least a thousand years. That commission produced the *Corpus juris civilis*, which not only summarized the substance of Roman law as it had been defined in a long series of legislative acts and imperial edicts but also collected legal opinions that defined the principles on which the law rested. While the Code of Justinian was destined to influence the develop-

FIGURE 14.2 **Justinian and Theodora** These mosaic representations of Emperor Justinian and Empress Theodora were created as part of the decoration of the church of San Vitale in Ravenna (built about 574). They reflect the sense of sacred and solemn majesty that increasingly surrounded the Byzantine imperial office. Byzantine artists were highly skilled in creating mosaics to convey a message while adding color to interior spaces. (Justinian, The Granger Collection; Theodora, Scala/Art Resource)

ment of law considerably in the future, it served Justinian's age to legitimatize a highly centralized, absolutist government that became a distinctive feature of Byzantine civilization.

Justinian's reign was also marked by important religious developments. Following the pattern already established by Constantine and his successors, Justinian claimed as part of his imperial authority the right to play a major role as leader of the Christian religious establishment in his empire. Particularly troublesome in his time were several violent disputes over dogmatic issues concerning the relationship between Christ's human and divine nature. The emperor

sought repeatedly to settle these quarrels by imperial edicts, often worked out after extensive discussions with prelates and theologians, which he hoped would curb the violence generated by religious passion and restore religious unity. His involvement did implant the idea of a Byzantine church whose organization and doctrines were dependent on the authority of the autocratic, semisacred emperor. But his actions also alienated large numbers of his subjects.

Justinian's reign witnessed the birth of a distinctive Byzantine culture. That culture assimilated the ancient Hellenic component of classical culture with Christian ideology. Into that basic mix were incorporated cultural influences from the Near East, especially from Persia. The symbol of this new culture was the church of Santa Sophia built by Justinian, a visible tribute to an earthly empire favored by God and to its exalted ruler.

Byzantine political history from the reign of Justinian until the First Crusade (1095) was dominated by one theme: the constant struggle to fend off attacks from aggressive outsiders, pressing in especially from the east and north. In a sense, the movement of peoples toward the Mediterranean basin left new Rome facing the same type of challenge that had been fatal to old Rome. These assaults reduced the Byzantine state in size, changed its ethnic composition, and caused modifications in its internal structure that accentuated its uniquenesss (see Map 14.1, p. 192).

Hardly was Justinian dead when the first blow was struck. In 568 the Lombards, a Germanic nation, invaded Italy and seized a considerable portion of the peninsula, leaving only Venice, a corridor of land from Rome to Ravenna, and southern Italy under Byzantine control. The partition of Italy was significant for two reasons: It left Rome, the seat of the papacy, in Byzantine hands, and it provided a setting in which the Byzantine and western European worlds would interact. Little could be done to stop the Lombard assault because the Byzantine Empire was facing a greater menace elsewhere. Late in the sixth century the Sassanid rulers of Persia mounted their greatest offensive on the Byzantine eastern frontier, seizing Syria, Palestine, and Egypt and advancing through Asia Minor to Constantinople. At the same time the Avars, an Asiatic nomadic people who established a state composed largely of Slavs north of the Danube, moved into the Balkans and toward Constantinople. In the first decades of the seventh century it appeared that the empire would perish in the Persian-Avar pincer. But a savior appeared in the person of Emperor Heraclius (610–641), who regrouped Byzantine resources and flung back the enemies in a war of liberation that permanently weakened both Persians and Avars.

The dynasty of Heraclius soon had to face an even greater challenge from another "new" people, the Arabs, who suddenly burst out of their homeland in the Arabian peninsula to become a major power in the Mediterranean world, as we shall see later. Within little more than a half century in the middle of the seventh century, Arab armies wrested Syria, Palestine, Egypt, and North Africa from Byzantine control. By the early 700s they occupied most of Asia Minor and in 717 placed Constantinople under siege. Again a savior appeared: Emperor Leo III, the Isaurian (717–741), who rescued the capital and eventually reclaimed Asia Minor. However, the eastern provinces were permanently lost, and the Byzantine Empire was reduced to a state comprising Asia Minor and the Balkan peninsula. This was a far cry from the Mediterranean-wide realm that Justinian claimed or even the eastern Roman Empire that he actually controlled. But it was defensible as a territorial state and would survive nearly intact until the middle of the fifteenth century.

Despite Leo III's remarkable success in rescuing the Byzantine Empire from what seemed certain destruction, his successors suffered renewed trials that plagued the empire for a century after his death. In part their difficulties stemmed from the internal strife brought on by their religious policy (see the next section). But outsiders again contributed to their problems. The Franks seriously undermined the Byzantine position in Italy (see Chapter 16). Even more dangerous was the emergence of a powerful state in the Balkans shaped by the Bulgars, another Asiatic migrant people who established dominance over Slavic peoples north of the Danube. The Bulgar threat eventually produced another series of strong rulers, the Macedonian dynasty (867–1057), under whose rule Byzantine society reached its high point. The greatest Macedonian emperor, Basil II, the Bulgar Slayer (976–1025), finally destroyed the Bulgar state and extended Byzantine influence deep into the Slavic world of central Europe and Russia. Byzantine power was also expanded in the east at the expense of the Moslem world, laying the groundwork for a Christian counterattack against Islam.

By the late eleventh century the Byzantine state began to decline, due in part to internal problems and in part to new assaults from the east by the Seljuk Turks and from the west by Italian cities seeking commercial advantages and Norman princes seeking territorial expansion (see Chapter 20). To save the empire from these threats, the emperors appealed to the West for help, an act that was instrumental in launching the crusading movement. But this policy also meant that the fate of the long self-reliant Byzantine Empire was increasingly dependent on outsiders.

2. BYZANTINE CIVILIZATION: INSTITUTIONAL AND CULTURAL PATTERNS

In response to the pressures caused by incessant attacks, the Byzantine world slowly evolved institutional and cultural patterns that not only permitted its survival but also made its civilization unique and distinctive.

A major source of Byzantine strength was its government, based on the absolute authority of the emperor. That authority was defined in terms that combined traditions drawn from the Roman imperial system and from Christian concepts of governance; Constantine served as the model. To the Byzantine populace the emperor was an agent ordained by God to ensure the material and spiritual well-being of God's people—the "Romans," as the Byzantines called themselves. As an intermediary between God and his holy people, the emperor must be obeyed and served loyally. Without the imperial presence at the center of Byzantine life, God's favors would not be forthcoming and chaos would ensue. Although Byzantine court life was often filled with intrigues and violence and conspiracies and revolts deprived many emperors of their diadems and their lives, still the divinely sanctioned imperial office provided the prime directive force in Byzantine society.

The Byzantine emperors were served by a large, carefully structured bureaucracy. Each civil servant was assigned a specialized function, a rank, and a salary. Well educated and loyal, these bureaucrats efficiently kept the fundamental activities of the state in operation. The empire was divided into districts, called *themes*, where officials representing the emperor recruited troops, collected taxes, maintained order, judged cases, and enforced the emperor's edicts. The emperor's power was buttressed by a well-organized army and navy and an efficient system of taxation. Of crucial importance was the army.

During the crises brought on by Persian and then Arab attacks during the seventh and eighth centuries, the government developed an army recruited from the free small farmers of Asia Minor and Thrace, who were granted plots of land in return for their military service. The peasant contingents were organized by *themes*, each under the command of a local military governor. For centuries these loyal soldiers, their freedom and land carefully protected by the imperial government, provided the key to Byzantium's survival in the face of incessant attacks.

Byzantine society rested on a diversified economic system that produced a high level of prosperity. Agriculture formed the backbone of the Byzantine economy. Large estates, farmed by tenants, existed, but the key component of the agricultural system was the small farm operated by free landowners. The state took a vital interest in keeping agricultural production high so that taxes could be collected from the farmers, whether large or small. The empire also enjoyed tremendous commercial activity; for many centuries Constantinople was the world's chief trading and industrial center. Byzantium's resourceful traders were supplied with many valuable products by the numerous skilled artisans who practiced their crafts in Constantinople and other imperial cities. The imperial government exercised a powerful influence over economic activity through wage and price controls, supervision of the guilds into which merchants and artisans were organized, and a stable money system.

Christianity provided another fundamental force in shaping every aspect of Byzantine society. In terms of beliefs and practices the Christians of the Byzantine Empire were like Christians everywhere. However, with the passage of time Byzantine Christianity underwent changes that gave rise to a separate religious establishment, later called the Greek Orthodox church.

One area of distinctiveness in Byzantine religious life was the close alliance between the state and the religious establishment shaped along lines defined in the fourth-century Roman Empire. In contrast with the situation in the west, where the collapse of the Roman political order forced religious leaders to act independently, the Byzantine emperor claimed to be and was accepted as the divinely ordained director of both spiritual and secular life; in fact, any distinction between those two realms had little meaning in Byzantine society. This system, called *caesaropapism* by modern historians, allowed the emperor to play a decisive role in appointing church officials, defining dogma, settling theological disputes, imposing discipline on both clergy and laity, and using the wealth and the persuasive authority of the religious establishment to serve the state. In its pastoral role the episcopal establishment in Byzantium, headed by the patriarch of Constantinople, served as a crucial force in carrying out imperial policy and in shaping a powerful bond linking the populace to the imperial regime that created a strong and lasting loyalty among imperial subjects.

Byzantine religious life was given a distinctive quality by a widespread, intense interest in questions of dogma. Diverse opinions on such matters as the Trinity and the relationship between Christ's divine and human nature aroused strong feelings and fierce partisanship that produced serious political crises on many occasions, especially when the emperors tried to resolve such quarrels in the interests of unity. Greek Orthodoxy placed a strong emphasis on ritual practice as a key element of religious life, and over the centuries a rich liturgy featuring elaborate symbolism and unique musical forms evolved as a distinctive feature of piety. On occasion both emperors and religious leaders thought this emphasis on ritual life needed to be curbed. The chief such effort led to the bitter iconoclastic struggle that raged from 725 to 843. This quarrel began when Emperor Leo III, backed by part of the clergy, attempted to remove all visual representations of the deity (called icons) from churches and rites, insisting that Christians were worshiping the statues instead of God and thus were guilty of idolatry. But these iconoclasts (icon smashers) ultimately failed, and in 843 the use of icons was restored to ritual practices. Byzantine religious life gave a prominent place to mysticism—religious practices by which believers sought direct communion with God through prayer and contemplation. A powerful, resourceful monastic establishment played an important role in encouraging and shaping a popular spirituality based on ritual and mysticism.

These unique characteristics of the Byzantine religious establishment, coupled with equally unique developments shaping Christian life else-where, led to a separation of the Byzantine Christian community from the rest of Christendom. During the fifth and sixth centuries quarrels over dogma and the claims of the patriarch of Constantinople to precedence over the ancient patriarchs of Alexandria, Jerusalem, and Antioch encouraged the Christians of Egypt, Palestine, and Syria to separate themselves from the imperial religious establishment. The Moslem conquest of these areas severed religious contacts with Christians in the Byzantine Empire and the west. The result was the emergence of separate eastern churches, such as the Coptic church in Egypt and the Jacobite church in Syria. Differences also began to separate the Byzantine church from Christians in the west. Dogmatic disagreements (particularly iconoclasm), different ritual practices, and divergent disciplinary usages played a role in creating the rift. Especially divisive was the ever-deepening quarrel over whether the pope in Rome was superior to or coequal with the patriarch of Constantinople in defining dogma and exercising disciplinary jurisdiction over the entire Christian community. Although the Byzantine emperors often turned to the bishops of Rome to seek sanction for their religious policies, they more often supported the claims of their patriarch to authority equal to that of Rome. The slow drift toward separation between Rome and Constantinople finally culminated in 1054, when pope and patriarch excommunicated each other, creating a schism that to the present has proved irreparable.

The separation between Rome and Constantinople was promoted by rivalry in the missionary field. Early in Byzantine history, Greek missionaries began to penetrate the Slavic world of central and eastern Europe, where missionaries from the west were also active. Supported by the diplomatic, military, and material resources of the imperial government and willing to make concessions to local cultures, such as allowing rituals to be performed in native languages, Byzantine missionaries eventually converted most of the Slavs in the Balkan peninsula and Russia and attached them to the Greek Orthodox church. Not only did they give their converts a new religion, they also spread significant aspects of Byzantine political, economic, literary, and artistic life. As a consequence, at a crucial point in the development of Slavic institutions and culture, a large part of the Slavic world was permanently oriented toward Byzantium and set apart from western Europe.

The Byzantine world gradually developed its own cultural life, maintaining in its essence the thrust established in late antiquity toward turning classical thought and expression to the service of the Christian worldview. Within a short time after Justinian's death the use of Latin virtually ceased in the Byzantine world; as a consequence, Byzantine culture centered on the Greek tradition. A vigorous educational system flourished in the Byzantine world, especially in Constantinople, where imperial, episcopal, and monastic schools offered a curriculum based on the study of classical Greek literature and philosophy. In at least some aristocratic circles, women were often provided a literary education in their homes. The system produced not only a literate clergy but also an educated laity conversant with the literary, scientific, and philosophical masterpieces of ancient Greece and the Hellenistic world. This educated group, which was often associated with the imperial court, the prime patron of cultural life, also collected copies of the Greek classics, commented on them, and wrote in imitation of them. Their efforts ensured the survival of the Greek classics and their eventual dissemination to the Islamic and western European worlds to serve as the basis for cultural renaissances.

The all-pervasive influence of Greek models, however, tended to make Byzantine literature and thought imitative. Probably the most creative figures in Byzantine intellectual circles were the theologians, whose incessant quarrels over dogma produced a huge volume of writing in which philosophical concepts from the classical tradition were applied to Christian teachings. Byzantine historians, influenced by the models of Herodotus, Thucydides, and Polybius, also produced excellent works: Procopius (sixth century) described Justinian's wars and wrote a spicy *Secret History* describing court life; Michael Psellus (1018–1079), a high official in the imperial regime, chronicled the exploits of the Macedonian emperors; and Anna Comnenus (1083-1148), the daughter of Emperor Alexius I, celebrated the career of her father in *Alexiad*. Byzantine poets expressed themselves most originally

in hymns, some of which can still be heard in the Greek Orthodox liturgy.

Byzantine art is perhaps the best mirror of the spirit of the culture. Architecture was the preeminent art. It represents a skillful fusion of classical Greek and Near Eastern traditions. The style was formed during the fourth and fifth centuries in Egypt, Syria, and Asia Minor. It was elevated to official status by Justinian's building program in sixth-century Constantinople. The great church of Santa Sophia was based on a floor plan derived from the Greco-Roman rectangular basilica upon which was imposed a great central dome after the Persian manner. The glory of this combination lies in the internal spaciousness it permits. The dome of Santa Sophia is more than one hundred feet across and rises about one hundred eighty feet above the floor of the church. Although it rests on four great arches springing from four massive pillars that form the central square of the nave, the dome indeed seems "to hang by a golden chain from heaven," as a contemporary put it. Justinian, upon viewing the completed church, exclaimed: "I have outdone you, O Solomon!"

The architectural style represented by Santa Sophia was widely imitated, and in the course of time a variation gained considerable popularity: A ground plan was based on the Greek cross with its four equal arms; each arm was crowned by a dome, as was the space where the arms cross. The famous church of St. Mark in Venice is an example of this five-domed structure. Byzantine architects also built huge and splendid palaces, most of which have unfortunately disappeared.

Byzantine architecture, for all its technical ingenuity, is incomplete without its decor. The churches and palaces were immense frames for sumptuous decoration. Santa Sophia's interior, for instance, blazed with precious metals, mosaics, paintings, jewels, and fine stone. Byzantine mosaics and frescoes centered primarily on portraying the great episodes of the Christian epic; the best surviving examples are seen in the churches built in Ravenna during the sixth century (see Figures 13.2 and 14.2). Byzantine artists made an immense contribution to the development and enrichment of Christian iconography, that is, the visual symbols through which religious ideas and feelings are expressed. They were never basically concerned with portraying the world realistically; rather, they sought to use human, natural, and abstract forms to evoke spiritual understanding. Color, created by glowing combinations of stones, metals, jewels, and paints, played a crucial role in enhancing the impact of every artistic creation (see Color Plate 7). Byzantine artists were also noted as skillful jewelers, goldsmiths, silversmiths, and manuscript illuminators. In every medium the same features predominated—the fusion of Greco-Roman and oriental motifs and styles, the love of elaborate decoration and color, and the preoccupation with symbolism.

3. ISLAMIC CIVILIZATION: ORIGINS AND EARLY HISTORY

A second new civilization emerged in the eastern Mediterranean world during the early Middle Ages to rival Byzantium as an heir of the Greco-Roman world: Islamic civilization, which originated among the nomadic inhabitants of the Arabian Desert. Although peoples from that desolate area had powerfully influenced the course of history in the ancient past (for example, the Akkadians, the Assyrians, and the Hebrews), no one living about 600 would have guessed that the desert-dwelling Bedouins would soon have a major impact on the course of history. Although Arabia's inhabitants shared a sense of ethnic community rooted in a common language, Arabic, and common historical experiences, the Bedouins were badly divided into numerous competing tribes led by warrior chieftains, called *sheiks*. The desert dwellers lived a poverty-stricken life that depended chiefly on the pasturage of animals—particularly camels—around oases. Raids on other tribes were common, so that Bedouin life was dominated by a warrior ethos. Tribal life was bound by rigid customs that governed most social relationships. Especially powerful were kinship ties, which created fierce family loyalties and prompted violent family feuds. Bedouin life was deeply influenced by a polytheistic religious system based on the worship of deities representing the forces of nature.

For the most part the Bedouins had been little influenced by the advanced civilizations lying in a great arc around the northern end of the vast desert. However, they were not completely isolated, which was a significant factor in the changes that thrust the Arabs into a new historical role during the seventh century. In the long struggle between the Romans (and their Byzantine successors) and the Persians, both parties had tried to win allies among the Bedouin tribes of northern Arabia; as a result, Roman-Byzantine and Persian influences touched the lives of some Arabs in that area. Southern Arabia felt significant cultural influences from Ethiopia. The major religions of these civilizations—Christianity, Judaism, Zoroastrianism—had made modest inroads into the Arab world. Much more significant in bringing outside influences into the world of the Arabs were the caravan routes along the western side of Arabia that linked the cities of Egypt, Syria, and Asia Minor to the Indian Ocean and the Far East. During the sixth century these routes became much more important because Byzantine-Persian rivalry disrupted the trade routes running from the eastern Mediterranean area through Persia to the Far East. Increased trade stimulated the growth and expanded the wealth of the Arabian cities along the caravan routes. Mecca, in particular, became a flourishing cosmopolitan center. Merchants from many places mingled with an ever-growing Arab population attracted to Mecca from the desert by the growing economic opportunities created by trade. Many Bedouin tribes came annually to Mecca to worship at a temple called the *Kaaba*, which contained a black stone that was a cult object for most Arabs. The sharp contrast between the affluent, cosmopolitan life in Mecca and the impoverished, tradition-bound Bedouin desert life began to pose disturbing questions about traditional Arabic values and the potential dangers of new ways.

The forces of change were suddenly unleashed in the Arab world early in the seventh century. The catalyst was a religious prophet, Muhammad, who galvanized the Arab world into unity and jolted it out of its isolation. Muhammad was born in Mecca about 570. Orphaned in his youth, he was brought up by an uncle as a trader. Eventually he entered the service of a rich widow, whom he married, thus ensuring himself a respectable and leisured career. As a trader, Muhammad came into contact with foreign merchants passing through Mecca. But there is reason to suspect that the decisive aspects of his life were shaped less by these extraneous conditions than by his own introspective, brooding, ascetic spirit, which caused him to spend much of his time in prayer and meditation, often in the solitude of the desert. While the question of his own salvation may have been central to his spiritual searching, it is likely that he was also troubled about the breakdown of traditional communal values and the moral laxity evident in Mecca.

When Muhammad was about forty, he suddenly claimed that God—*Allah* in Arabic—had spoken directly to him and named him his prophet. Throughout the rest of his life these revelations continued, gradually providing the key elements for a new religion. And they gave Muhammad his mission: He dedicated himself to convincing others that Allah had revealed through his prophet the way to righteousness, truth, and salvation.

What did Allah reveal to his prophet? The answer is contained in the Koran (*Qur'an* in Arabic), the sacred book of Islam, which was compiled shortly after the Prophet's death by his associates as a record of Allah's message delivered through his prophet. The central tenet of Muhammed's teaching was a rigorous monotheism: there is but one god, Allah, whose power is infinite and whose wrath against those who worship other deities is terrible. Muhammad taught that Allah had revealed himself bit by bit down through the ages, the Jewish prophets and Jesus all being accepted as his messengers. However, Muhammad was the last and greatest prophet, superseding all others, and his revelation—Allah's final message—was destined to conquer the world. Muhammad insisted that almighty Allah requires complete submission to his will; the religion is thus called *Islam*, which means "submission to God." Every true adherent of Islam, called a *Moslem*, must regulate his or her life so as to abide completely by the will of Allah as revealed to the Prophet and set down in the Koran. Those who believe in Allah and submit to his law will gain a happy life after death in a sensuous heaven; nonbelievers and the disobedient will be damned to eternal suffering in hell.

It is obvious that many of these fundamental teachings were closely akin to beliefs long held by Jews, Christians, Zoroastrians, and pre-Moslem Arabs, a fact that has led some to the conclusion that Muhammad was little more than a borrower of the religious ideas of others. However true this claim may be, it neglects the essential fact: The Prophet brought to the Arab world in which he lived a religious vision that not only was new to the Arabs but also gave them a historic mission of spreading the true religion revealed in God's final revelation. To the Arab world this message was as radical as early Judaism and primitive Christianity were to their worlds.

To these simple articles of faith Muhammad added a list of duties required of all believers. All must proclaim daily their belief that there is but one God, Allah, pray five times daily while facing Mecca, give of their wealth to support the poor, fast during the holy month of Ramadan, and, if possible, make a pilgrimage to Mecca once in a lifetime. Muhammad also laid down the foundations of a law code regulating diet and marriage, prohibiting drinking and gambling, and demanding honesty, fair play, and respect for others. This code of conduct, strongly reminiscent of that defined in the Jewish Bible, injected a strong ethical vein into the new religion. Each individual was personally responsible to Allah; there were no churches, no clergy, no sacraments to assist in gaining Allah's favor.

For several years, Muhammad's preaching netted only a few converts in Mecca; in fact, Muhammad won many more enemies than followers. By 622 these foes forced him to flee to Yathrib (later renamed Medina, which means "city of the Prophet"), north of Mecca. This flight, called the *Hegira*, marked a turning point in the history of the new religion, which the Moslems recognized by making 622 the first year of their calendar. At Mecca Muhammad—always speaking as Allah's prophet—gave increasing attention to the shaping of a religious-political community, a "people of Allah" dedicated to the advance of Allah's cause by force of arms and to the enforcement of right living on the faithful. Into this community were drawn increasing numbers of Arab converts who subordinated their ancient tribal allegiances to a new, egalitarian companionship based on total submission to Allah and obedience to his prophet. The focus of the new community was the mosque, the meeting place where the faithful gathered as equals to affirm their faith in Allah, pray, and demonstrate their unity in serving his cause. Reflecting the warrior ethos of the Arabic world, this holy community felt justified in living off the booty its warriors seized from nonbelievers, including the considerable Jewish community at Medina and especially the caravans of the rich Meccans. By 630 Muhammad's following was strong enough to recapture Mecca, a feat that persuaded many Arabs of the validity of his message and led them to join his community. During his last years the Prophet used his forces to compel other Arab tribes to accept his leadership, so that when he died in 632 he was the leader of a large and dedicated religious following.

Muhammad's success in uniting the Arab world was impressive enough, but even more astonishing developments were to come. Almost immediately the newly formed "people of Allah" burst out of Arabia and began a series of military conquests that affected most of the civilized world (see Map 14.1). Between 632 and 656, the Arabs destroyed the Persian Empire; wrested the prize provinces of Syria, Palestine, and Egypt from the Byzantine Empire; were probing toward India; and were challenging Byzantine sea power for control of the Mediterranean. After a brief interlude to settle internal problems over Moslem leadership, the advance resumed in the late seventh century. All of North Africa was conquered, and Arab forces pushed into the Indus Valley and the outer reaches of China. An offensive was mounted in Asia Minor that moved closer and closer to Constantinople. Before 700 Moslem naval forces were in virtual control of the Mediterranean. In 711 a Moslem army crossed from Africa into Europe and quickly overran the Visigothic kingdom in Spain. From there the Moslems began to raid Gaul to threaten the Frankish kingdom. But Arab expansion was weakening: In 718 Arab forces besieging Constantinople were defeated by Leo III and soon after were driven out of Asia Minor. The Byzantine victory, which was decisive in checking the Moslem advance into Europe, was complemented in 732 when the Frankish leader Charles Martel defeated a Moslem force at the battle of Tours in Gaul.

The conquest of this vast empire within a century after the Prophet's death represents one of the great military feats in all history. Several factors played a part in Arab expansion. The Arabs' opponents were weak. Both the Sassanid and the Byzantine empires were exhausted from their long struggle. Religious disaffection among the Christians in the eastern Byzantine provinces caused the residents to welcome the Arabs as liberators from religious tyranny and burdensome fiscal exactions. The conquerors interfered little with local affairs, making their overlordship easy to accept. They demonstrated great military prowess, especially in desert warfare, in siege tactics, and in adapting to naval warfare. Their enthusiasm for their cause was also a factor. Muhammad had said, "Fight and fear not; the gates of Paradise are under the shade of the swords." Their wars were thus holy wars (*jihad* in Arabic).

4. ISLAMIC CIVILIZATION: INSTITUTIONAL AND CULTURAL PATTERNS

The amazing victories of the Arabs presented the conquerors with a wide range of challenges: how to rule a huge empire inhabited by diverse peoples; how to support themselves in a strange environment; how to sustain their faith in a world where other religions dominated; how to interact with different cultures. Their responses and the reactions of their subjects to their dominance produced a new, uniquely Islamic pattern of civilization that would be of immense importance to the future of a large part of the world.

A major problem facing the victorious Arabs was establishing a political system that would permit them to control their numerous and diverse subjects. While Muhammad had established the basis for a primitive Islamic state, no one could succeed to his special place as Prophet. From his death in 632 down to 661, his close associates picked one from among themselves to serve as *caliph*—an Arabic term meaning "deputy"—to interpret and apply the law as revealed in the Koran. This office, bestowing on its holder a vast range of powers sanctioned by religion, became the key element in the Moslem political system. Whoever controlled it and used the authority surrounding it effectively could claim ab-

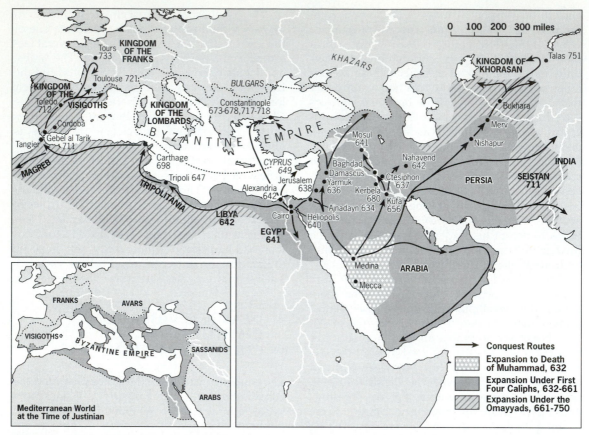

Map 14.1 **THE EXPANSION OF ISLAM TO 750** This map shows the amazing success of the Arabs as conquerors during the first century after Muhammad's death in 632; the dates indicate when each major conquest was completed. It indicates clearly that the Persian Sassanian Empire and the Byzantine Empire were the major victims of Arab expansionism. By 750 large numbers of peoples in the lands conquered by the Arabs had accepted Islam as their religion.

solute lordship over all Moslems and all who were their subjects. But a major problem of Moslem political life centered on deciding who had a legitimate claim to the caliphate.

As long as Muhammad's personal associates were available, they could legitimately claim the office. But with their passing, a struggle developed for succession. Finally, in 661, a military leader seized control and made the office of caliph hereditary. The dynasty he founded, known as the Omayyads, held power until 750. Its legitimacy was challenged from the beginning by Muhammad's nephew and son-in-law, Ali, and Ali's son Hussein, who claimed authority to in-

terpret the Prophet's word on the basis of their kinship with him. Their claims resulted in their assassinations, but their followers formed a powerful and dedicated religious-political faction called the Shiites, which for centuries challenged the authority of successive caliphs.

The Omayyads established their center of power at Damascus. Although totally committed to Arab supremacy in the expanding empire, they realized that ruling the lands and peoples conquered by the Arab armies of Allah demanded more complex political institutions than those that had characterized Muhammad's first Moslem community. Strongly influenced by Byzantine models, the Omayyads created a central-ized court, a bureaucracy, and an efficient tax system. The authority of the Omayyad caliphs was exercised primarily through garrisons of Arab troops established at strategic spots across the vast empire. Bound to the caliph by ethnic and religious ties, the commanders of these gar-risons controlled local affairs; often they did so by utilizing already established native political structures. These garrisons were supported by allocations from the caliph's treasury, which was supplied by booty and by taxes paid by the con-quered non-Moslem population. This system meant that the Moslem world was dominated by an Arab elite whose religious convictions legiti-matized for its members their right to possess and exploit what they had won by the sword. For almost a century, this system worked. Arab military supremacy gave conquered subjects lit-tle choice. Generally, the isolated, exclusivist Arab garrisons interfered little in local affairs ex-cept to enforce peace and to collect the tribute that supported them.

But eventually the Omayyad regime faltered. The strength of the Arab elite was diluted by its dispersion over the huge empire. More impor-tant, as the number of non-Arab converts to Is-lam increased, resentment against Arab domi-nation grew. Non-Arab Moslems could see no reason why their faith should not make them equal to Arab Moslems in the sight of Allah. That sentiment led to the overthrow of the Omayyads in 750—except in Spain—and the seizure of the caliphate by the Abbasid dynasty, a family of Persian origin claiming distant kinship with Mu-hammad. Abbasid rule meant the end of Arab domination. The capital was shifted from Da-mascus to Baghdad, and the political system was reshaped on the model of ancient Persia. The Abbasid caliphs reclaimed the absolute authority to interpret Allah's word for all the faithful, whatever their ethnic origin. Around their court there developed a professional bureaucracy made up of educated Moslems representing many ethnic groups. The caliph's authority was extended across the empire through an elaborate system of governorships over which officials rep-resenting the caliph administered justice and col-lected taxes. In this new political environment Arab militancy was greatly diminished and ex-pansionism by force came to an end.

During the eighth and ninth centuries the Ab-basid caliphs enjoyed immense power, exempli-fied by rulers like Harun al-Rashid (786–809), immortalized in the *Arabian Nights*. But by the end of the ninth century Abbasid power began to decline. Rival caliphs, challenging the legiti-macy of the Abbasids to interpret Allah's will, were established in Spain, North Africa, Egypt, Syria, and India and began to compete with one another for dominance in the Moslem world. Seeking to protect themselves against these ri-vals, the Abbasids increasingly placed their trust in Seljuk Turkish mercenaries, nomads from Central Asia who by 1055 made the Abbasids their puppets. By that time, Moslem political unity had vanished forever. Disunity invited at-tacks from outsiders, especially Byzantine and western European Christians, whose memory of Arabic militarism and hostility toward the Is-lamic religion generated a crusading mentality against the Moslems.

More enduring than the unified Moslem po-litical empire were the economic benefits that flowed from the Arabic conquests. Agriculture remained the basic element of economic life across the Moslem world. The early Arab con-querors were little interested in farming except as a source of tribute to support the military elite. As a consequence, the traditional village-farming structure of the Roman-Byzantine and Persian worlds persisted. Later, under Abbasid rule, fis-cal policies were introduced that stimulated land clearance, production for urban markets, and the introduction of new crops and farming tech-niques, all of which combined to increase agri-cultural production. Economic growth was most marked in commerce and manufacturing. The emergence of Moslem civilization gave new im-petus to urban life. Cities—new and old, large and small—became centers of life for the ruling elite and their dependents. Their needs, ranging from food to luxury items, stimulated trade and industry, which in turn filled cities with mer-chants and artisans. While much commerce and manufacturing filled local needs, long-distance trade routes stretching from Spain to India and from central Asia to sub-Saharan Africa devel-oped, promoted by the removal of artificial trade barriers, a sound money system, and specialized manufacturing developing in many cities (for ex-ample, the steel weapons and textiles of Damascus and the leather goods of Córdoba in Spain). The Moslem political regime allowed merchants and artisans much greater freedom than had been the case in the Byzantine and Persian empires; as a consequence, these groups exercised their entrepreneurial talents to increase their wealth. On the whole, during the early Middle Ages, the Moslem economy was the most advanced and resourceful in the world.

The social structure of the Moslem world was immensely complex. Arab tradition and the teaching of the Koran emphasized the equality of all male Moslems. In fact, important social distinctions existed, initially between Arabs and non-Arabs and then between Moslems and non-Moslems. As time passed, a social elite emerged that was defined by officeholding, wealth, education, and lifestyle. This elite congregated in urban centers, where its ranks were constantly replenished by those whose talents as administrators, merchants, artisans, and scholars permitted them to accumulate the wealth and acquire the social graces required for elite status. The bulk of the agricultural population and urban laborers remained outside this elite circle and were considered to be inferior. Non-Moslems, although tolerated, were also treated as inferiors, subjected to special taxes and excluded from public life. The stratification of Moslem society was countered to some extent by the force of Moslem law, which considered all of Allah's followers to be equal and which sought to define a common standard of conduct binding on all Moslems.

The family was a basic institution in the regulation of social life. But it was an institution dominated by males. Severe restrictions were placed on women, forcing them into a secluded existence and isolating them from many aspects of social and economic life. Polygamy was legally recognized and widely practiced among the affluent, putting women in a position of competing with one another for a place in the family structure and control over children. Husbands were able to divorce their wives easily and exercised considerable control over the destinies of their children. However, Moslem law did permit women to share in inheritances and sought to protect their interests in their possessions.

The most important forces giving Moslem civilization cohesion and unity were religion and culture. The Islamic religion demonstrated an amazing power to win converts. Although there was forced conversion and although many accepted the faith to escape the special taxes imposed on non-Moslems and to gain access to the mainstream of Moslem political and social life, still Islam appealed to many. Christians and Jews were extended special privileges because they were, as Moslems put it, "people of the Book" who had received at least a portion of God's revelation. As the years passed, however, devotees of many religions—Christians, Jews, Zoroastrians, and Hindus—were converted in massive numbers, and the vast Moslem Empire became predominantly Islamic. Islam also expanded beyond the boundaries of the empire to win converts in southern Asia and sub-Saharan Africa. Important non-Moslem communities always remained in the empire, including Christian churches in Egypt, Syria, and Armenia and significant Jewish communities, especially in Spain.

Islam tended to grow more complex as the centuries passed. This enrichment resulted chiefly from the efforts of a long succession of theologians, philosophers, and lawyers, all of whom reflected on the nature of their religion and reinterpreted its meaning from different perspectives. The theologians developed a rich body of literature in the form of commentaries (called *sunnas*) on the Koran and on pronouncements attributed to Muhammad but not recorded in the Koran (called *hadiths*). The philosophers incorporated concepts derived from Greek thought into Islam in an effort to illuminate the meaning of the Koran. The lawyers constantly elaborated the body of law that governed Moslem life, seeking to make it consistent, complete, and relevant to the varied conditions of life among the faithful. The collective efforts of theologians, philosophers, and lawyers resulted in an orthodox faith that was much more complex than the message first proclaimed by the Prophet; yet Islam always remained firmly rooted in the basic doctrines set forth in the Koran. The adherents of this orthodox religion, called Sunnite Moslems, constituted the vast majority in the Islamic world. But there were dissenters, the chief of which were the Shiite Moslems, who insisted that the true faith was preserved by Muhammad's blood descendants. They rejected many of the ideas about Islam proclaimed by the Sunnites and often did battle with Sunnites on many issues—a conflict that still divides the Moslem world.

The Islamic world also sustained a long tradition of seeking to deepen spirituality. The quest was carried on primarily by *sufis*, religious mystics who, through contemplation and ascetic practices, sought to establish a direct communion with the Divine that would deepen their spiritual life as well as that of their followers. Despite these diverse movements, Islam as a common faith provided the prime basis of unity in the Moslem world.

The advent and expansion of Islam generated a tremendous cultural revival that brought together into a rich synthesis nearly all the world's great cultural traditions: Greco-Roman, Persian, Mesopotamian, Egyptian, Germanic, Jewish, Indian, and Arabic. Synthesis remained a central feature of Moslem culture throughout the Middle Ages. Religion provided the matrix and the inspiration for synthesis. Since Muhammad had forbidden the translation of the Koran into any other language, all Moslems had to learn Arabic and all foreign literature had to be translated into Arabic; and since the Koran contained the final truth, all facets of other cultures had to be reconciled with Islamic teachings. The response to these challenges was a brilliant outburst of scholarship that allowed the Moslems to claim with some justification to be the cultural heirs of the ages.

Many historians would agree that the greatest Moslem achievements were in philosophy and science. Moslem philosophers devoted their efforts chiefly to absorbing Greek philosophy and reconciling it with the teachings of the Koran. At the same time, they wrestled with the contradictions inherent in the Greek tradition, especially those separating Platonic and Aristotelian thought. The result was a huge body of philosophical literature that played an important role in sustaining Islam and in giving Moslem intellectual life a high level of sophistication. The efforts of Moslem philosophers are closely akin to those of the scholastic philosophers of medieval western Europe (see Chapter 22). In fact, the speculations of the greatest Moslem thinkers, Ibn Sina (980–1037) and the Spanish Ibn Rushd (1126–1198), known in the West as Avicenna and Averroës, exercised a direct influence on Western scholasticism.

In science the Moslem achievements were spectacular. The efforts of Moslem scholars as collectors resulted in a huge body of scientific information from Greek, Indian, Persian, Mesopotamian, and Egyptian sources—more than scientists anywhere in the world would possess until modern times. To this they added knowledge derived from their own investigations of the natural world, all of which became available to a large circle of people because it was recorded in a common language, Arabic. In mathematics, Moslems adopted the Indian numerical system, to which they added the use of the zero to create the Arabic system of numbers used almost universally today. A Moslem, al-Khwarizmi (ca. 780–850), combined Greek and Indian concepts to create algebra. By combining Greek, Persian, and Mesopotamian data on the movements of heavenly bodies, Moslem scientists made notable advances in astronomy. The works of medical writers such as al-Razi (865–925) and Avicenna represent compilations from numerous sources. Moslem doctors studied diseases, dissected bodies, and experimented with drugs, adding significantly to the existing body of medical knowledge. Geographers and physicists also made significant advances.

Moslem literature demonstrated great vigor and variety. Its poetry, familiar to Western readers chiefly through the works of Omar Khayyám, is marked by brilliant imagery and highly complex verse forms. Perhaps the most characteristic feature of Moslem literature was the ability of writers to recast subject matter borrowed from various non-Arabic sources into masterpieces attuned to the spirit of Moslem religion and the values of Moslem society. Nothing illustrates this feature better than the *Arabian Nights*; the adventures of Sinbad the Sailor and the feats of Aladdin are stories gleaned from the literary traditions of many non-Moslem peoples, but they are given a unique coloration by the genius of Arabic authors, who retell them in a mode reflecting the spirit and tastes of their own culture.

Like most of Moslem culture, Moslem art reflects a creative synthesis of many traditions. Architectural talents were devoted chiefly to building mosques and palaces. The mosques, primarily places for individual prayer rather than community worship, are simple structures whose inner space is often divided by rows of graceful columns creating aisles covered by arches. As a rule, the mosques are covered by domes similar to those of Byzantine churches; above them rise graceful towers (*minarets*) from which the call to prayer is issued. Before each mosque is an open court containing a purification fountain and surrounded by a covered passageway. The greatest mosques, such as those at Damascus and Córdoba, are beautiful structures marked by delicacy and grace (see Figure 14.1). Surviving palaces, such as the Alcazar at Seville and the Alhambra at Granada, reflect the same architectural style but are much more elaborate.

Most Moslem buildings are rather bare on the outside but brilliantly decorated inside, especially with paintings and mosaics in splendid colors. The representation of human and animal forms was discouraged lest the faithful be tempted to compromise their monotheism by worshiping graven images. Instead, the decorations accentuated floral designs and geometric patterns (*arabesques*). Exquisite artistry also manifested itself in the crafts; Moslem fabrics, tapestries, carpets, leatherwork, metalwork, weapons, and jewelry were the most prized articles in the medieval world.

The vitality and achievements of the early Byzantine and Islamic civilizations far excelled that emerging in western Europe, which lagged far behind them for centuries. As we shall see, during the medieval centuries no aspect of western European civilization escaped the subtle influences of the Byzantine and Moslem worlds. That immense debt was often forgotten in the West in later centuries—but not by the heirs of those who created the Byzantine and Islamic civilizations.

SUGGESTED READING

Overview of the Early Middle Ages

Robert Fossier et al., *The Cambridge History of the Middle Ages*, Vol. 1: *350–950*, trans. Janet Sondheimer (1989). Rich in insights, especially into social history.

Byzantine Civilization

Robert Browning, *The Byzantine Empire* (1980).
Cyril Mango, *Byzantium, the Empire of New Rome* (1980). Either of these works will provide a good general treatment of all aspects of Byzantine civilization.
J. J. Norwich, *Byzantium: The Early Centuries* (1989).
Warren Treadgold, *The Byzantine Renewal, 780–842* (1988).
Robert Browning, *Justinian and Theodora*, 2nd ed. (1987). These three works will provide fuller treatment of the period of Byzantine history covered in this chapter.
J. M. Hussey, *The Orthodox Church in the Byzantine Empire* (1986). An excellent treatment.
Jaroslav Pelikan, *The Christian Tradition: A History of the Development of Doctrine*, Vol. 2: *The Spirit of Eastern Christendom* (1974). A masterful but demanding treatment.
D. Talbot Rice, *Byzantine Art*, rev. ed. (1968). A brief treatment, effectively illustrated.
Tamara Talbot Rice, *Everyday Life in Byzantium* (1967). Provides a good feel for how people lived in the Byzantine world.

Moslem Civilization

M. A. Shaban, *Islamic History: A New Interpretation*, 2 vols. (1971–1976).

Hugh Kennedy, *The Prophet and the Age of the Caliphates: The Islamic Near East from the Sixth to the Eleventh Century* (1986).
Ira M. Lapidus, *A History of Islamic Societies* (1988).
Any of these three works provides a challenging introduction to early Islamic history and civilization.
Patricia Crone and Martin Hinds, *God's Caliph: Religious Authority in the First Centuries of Islam* (1986). Good treatment of the way the caliphate worked.
Maurice Lombard, *The Golden Age of Islam*, trans. Joan Spencer (1975). Will help the reader to understand economic and social history.
Alfred Guillaume, *Islam*, 2nd rev. ed. (1956). A clear description of the major features of Islamic religion.
Dominique Sourdel, *Medieval Islam*, trans. J. Montgomery Watt (1983). Especially good on the role of religion in shaping Moslem society.
Martin Lings, *Muhammad: His Life Based on the Earliest Sources* (1983). A sound biography.
W. Montgomery Watt, *The Formative Period in Islamic Thought* (1973). A good introduction to early Moslem intellectual history.
C. A. Qadir, *Philosophy and Science in the Islamic World* (1988). An excellent assessment.
David T. Rice, *Islamic Art*, rev. ed. (1975). A well-illustrated treatment.

CHAPTER 15

Heirs to the Roman Empire: Latin Western Europe

FIGURE 15.1 Life in a Medieval Monastery This scene from an illuminated manuscript reflects the essential elements of the daily routine in a Benedictine monastery: the tolling of bells to summon the monks to worship services; studying and copying manuscripts; manual labor. The combination of these activities into a disciplined routine permitted monastic communities to make a major contribution to the shaping of all aspects of medieval civilization, despite the fact that monks sought to escape the world within the confines of their monasteries. (The Pierpont Morgan Library)

The third heir to the Roman Empire emerged in Latin western Europe. In contrast to developments in the Byzantine and Islamic worlds, western European civilization took shape amid the instability and disorder resulting from the collapse of the Roman political system in the West. Not until about 750 were the first dim outlines of a new order becoming evident in the form of new institutions and ideas destined to be crucial to the future of western Europe.

1. THE POLITICAL ORDER: GERMANIC KINGSHIP

A prime factor in the history of the Latin West between 500 and 750 was political instability stemming from two interrelated factors existing in 500. First, the boundaries of the various Germanic kingdoms established on Roman soil during the fifth century had not been fixed; as a result, there was fierce competition among these kingdoms—Visigothic, Vandal, Ostrogothic, Burgundian, Frankish, Anglo-Saxon—for territory. Second, all of these kingdoms lacked well-defined internal political structures capable of maintaining public order.

Between 500 and 750 there was considerable rearrangement of the fragile boundaries of the Germanic kingdoms (see Maps 13.1 and 14.1). Of prime importance was the emergence of the Franks as a major power. During the fifth century the Franks slowly penetrated northern Gaul but played only a minor role in partitioning the Roman Empire. Then suddenly, led by their first able king, Clovis (481–511), the Franks exploded into prominence. A ruthless warrior, Clovis unified the Franks and unleashed their military potential. He and his immediate successors wiped out the last remnants of Roman power in northern Gaul, absorbed the Burgundian kingdom, drove the Visigoths out of southern Gaul, and established dominance over Germanic peoples living immediately east of the Rhine in territories that had not been part of the Roman Empire. The Frankish cause was aided by the conversion of Clovis and his followers to Orthodox Christianity, which made their domination more acceptable to the population of Gaul than that of the Arian and pagan rulers they had defeated.

Byzantine and Moslem pressures also played a role in shaping the political map of the West. As already noted, Justinian's attempt to reconquer the West led to the destruction of the Vandal kingdom in North Africa and the Ostrogothic kingdom in Italy. However, his successors lost northern and central Italy to the Germanic Lombards; the Byzantines retained a band of land extending across central Italy from Ravenna to Rome, southern Italy, and Sicily. In 711 Moslem forces overran the Visigothic kingdom and established control over the Iberian peninsula except for small Christian enclaves in extreme northern Spain.

Meanwhile, other political entities began to take shape in the West. In England, where several competing petty kingdoms had been formed by Anglo-Saxon intruders, forces pointing in the direction of unification were at work. In central Europe Slavic groups moved westward and southward into lands vacated by the Germans and began to develop territorial principalities. In the Scandinavian world, new political groupings were taking shape, preparing the people of the north for an important role in western European history in the future.

Thus, by 750 the political map of the West had assumed a more settled shape (see Map 14.1). The heartland of western Europe—northern Italy, Gaul, western Germany, and England—was occupied by kingdoms shaped by three Germanic peoples: the Lombards, the Franks, and the Anglo-Saxons. Facing this German-dominated world on the south were the Byzantines in southern Italy and Sicily and the Moslems in Spain, North Africa, and the western Mediterranean. To the east and the north were the Slavs and the Scandinavians.

While the political boundaries of the West took shape, constant experimentation went on as the rulers of each Germanic kingdom searched for a workable system of government to replace the Roman imperial regime. That experimentation varied from kingdom to kingdom. As a result, significant regional differences in political institutions emerged in the West during the early Middle Ages, quite in contrast to the unitary political orders characteristic of the Byzantine and Moslem worlds. Out of this experimentation emerged two systems that would be especially important for the future: those of the Franks and

WHERE HISTORIANS DISAGREE

The Division of Times Past

In order to provide a framework into which random data can be arranged, historians divide past time into segments, each treated as a discrete unit that has its unique characteristics. Although necessary, attempts at *periodization* lead to basic disagreement among historians. Nowhere have such disagreements been more apparent than in the attempt to define the division between classical Greco-Roman civilization and what came after in western Europe.

The first widely accepted periodization system relating to the transition from the classical age to a new era was formulated in the early modern period. It was shaped by Renaissance humanists, Protestant religious reformers, and Enlightenment philosophers, whose various interests led them to agree that a major break occurred in the fifth century A.D. This break took the form of a "disaster" marked by the failure of the Roman political system, the triumph of Christianity, and the victory of the barbarian Germans. What followed was a "dark age." This interpretation found particularly persuasive expression in Edward Gibbon's classic *The History of the Decline and Fall of the Roman Empire* (1776), which argued that in the fifth century a new age began with the victory of "religion and barbarism" over the rational, enlightened civilization of classical Greece and Rome.

The periodization scheme defining a decisive break in the fifth century that separated the ancient world from a prolonged "dark age" dominated historical thinking well into the twentieth century. Then a new approach was developed, chiefly as a result of the work of the Belgian historian Henri Pirenne. In his seminal work, *Mohammed and Charlemagne* (1939), he argued that in western Europe the end of the classical world came not in the fifth but in the eighth century when Moslem expansion finally interrupted the economic unity of the Mediterranean basin. In Pirenne's words, "It is . . . strictly correct to say that without Mohammed Charlemagne would have been inconceivable." Thus, it is to the Carolingian era (ca. 750–900) that one must look for the shaping of the essential features of western European civilization, for the "first" Europe. All developments prior to 750 must be annexed to classical history.

Despite heated criticism from many quarters, the Pirenne "thesis" has enjoyed wide acceptance among historians for the past half century. However, there are signs that a new periodization scheme is emerging. It is being shaped by advocates of what is sometimes called the "new social history." They are convinced that the determinant forces shaping the historical process are basic social structures that dictate the activities and thoughts of common people, the "silent," neglected actors on the human stage. Their investigations of the medieval world have led them to conclude that somewhere around 1000 there occurred changes in the basic structure of western European society so fundamental that a new age was born. These changes had to do not with politics, war, and high culture but with demography, family structures, technology, social groupings, and popular religious mentalities. Compared with these changes, the Carolingian "revival" was a mere episode with little consequence. Before 1000 western Europe was a moribund society, dependent on remnants of the classical world. Only after 1000 did a unique and vibrantly creative civilization emerge in western Europe.

These brief remarks lead to two conclusions. Historians divide time past in terms of what interests them most deeply. And their periodization schemes make a difference in how historical data are organized and interpreted.

Anglo-Saxons. We shall return to the Anglo-Saxons (see Chapter 16); here we shall concentrate on the Frankish political system to illustrate the major features of the new political order in the West.

The Frankish kings sought to create a government based on strong monarchy. Clovis claimed a broad range of royal powers on the basis of his position as elected leader of his Germanic followers and as ruler over former Roman subjects by right of conquest. From these sources derived his right to command (the *bannum*) all his subjects to do the royal will. Although Frankish kingship had been elective, Clovis succeeded in establishing the concept that the power to command belonged to a single family whose royal blood was believed to be sacred, thus ensuring hereditary succession in Clovis' dynasty, called the Merovingians, down to 751. To execute the powers they claimed, Clovis and his successors created a central court of royal officials and established local units of government based on the old Roman administrative system. The kingdom was divided into territorial units, called *counties*, where *counts* appointed by the king were charged with collecting taxes, rendering justice, maintaining order, and mustering freemen to military duty.

However, the Merovingian kings were unable to exercise the power they claimed in a fashion leading to uniform administration and internal order. In fact, royal power steadily declined to the point where the last Merovingians were justifiably dubbed "do-nothing" kings. At the heart of their failure was a simple fact: They sought to build a political order on the Roman model without understanding it or having the political skills to direct it. Repeatedly they fell back on the tactics of Germanic warrior kings, resorting to force as the basis of authority. They had a very limited sense of the public good, so that their policies seldom served little more than the interests of the dynasty and their warrior followers. Most kings had little managerial ability; as a result, their administrative machinery degenerated into a household officialdom serving only to meet the king's personal needs. The Merovingians were unable to sustain an effective system of taxation; increasingly they were forced to depend on their own lands and on booty they could extract by force from their subjects. Following Germanic practice, they allowed each of their subjects to be judged by the law under which he or she was born, be it Frankish, Roman, Burgundian, or Visigothic; the result was chaos in the administration of justice. The Merovingians compounded their problems by treating the kingdom as private property, which in accord with Germanic custom was divided among all male heirs at the death of each king. By the early eighth century this practice had split the unified kingdom once ruled by Clovis into three distinct subkingdoms (Neustria, Austrasia, and Burgundy), each ruled by a branch of the Merovingian dynasty and each often at war with the others for control of territory. Disorder was compounded by constant private feuding among powerful Frankish families who followed Germanic custom in seeking to avenge wrongs to members of their families by other families.

Unable to maintain effective centralized government, the Merovingian kings were gradually forced to share power with lay and ecclesiastical landowners. The emergence of the landed nobility as possessors of political power was one of the major developments of the early Middle Ages. The strength of these nobles was rooted in possession of land, family connections, and control over dependents; some noble families could trace their exalted status back to late antiquity. Increasingly important in establishing their position were royal favors. In part those favors stemmed from Germanic custom, which demanded that warrior kings generously reward their loyal warrior followers. More significantly, they resulted from the kings' dependence on the nobles for vital political services. Lacking regular income and a professional bureaucracy, rulers were forced to rely on subjects who could and would serve the royal government at their own expense. Only the great noble families and high ecclesiastical officials could afford such services. In return they exacted from the kings grants of land and the right to govern those who lived on their possessions. A system of private government thus evolved with great nobles and religious officials controlling affairs in their localities as they wished. This trend was accentuated by the increasing willingness of the weak in an unstable society to seek the protection of the strong. Through a process known as *commendation* individuals from all levels of society pledged under oath to serve others willing to offer protection and material support. Although the specific terms of these arrangements varied considerably, the result was to allow the strong to build up private followings of dependents, often called *vassals*, over whom they exercised control and upon whose services they depended to extend their power. The expanding power of the nobles was a source of incessant strife, for the demarcation between royal authority and noble privilege was imprecise and the rules governing the relationship of one noble to another were chaotic.

Thus by 750 a unique political order had begun to take shape in western Europe. It involved several coexisting kingdoms, each ruled by a king. Surrounded by religious and military sanctions, the royal office was accepted as necessary to right order. Although kings claimed extensive powers, they were incapable of exercising them effectively. As a consequence, many public functions fell into the hands of private individuals. This diminution of the power of the state greatly reduced the role of government in society in western Europe, as is obvious when the West is compared to contemporary Byzantine and Moslem societies. What the role of government should be would become a major issue in western European society in the future, an issue that had seldom arisen in earlier civilizations.

2. ECONOMIC AND SOCIAL PATTERNS

When compared with the Byzantine and Moslem worlds, economic life in western Europe during the early Middle Ages was almost primitive. In many ways the low level of economic production was a consequence of recessionary trends that had begun in late antiquity and that were given impetus by the chaotic conditions surrounding the collapse of the Roman imperial order. However, changes did begin to take place in the organization of economic activity which provided a basis for future economic growth.

The western European economy was almost totally agricultural. Agricultural production was organized in a variety of ways. In some areas, especially around the Mediterranean, where Roman survivals were strongest, the *latifundia* system continued. These large estates, increasingly called *villas*, were owned by lay nobles or church

officials who reserved part of the land for their own support. Although slavery persisted, the villas were tilled chiefly by tenants, each allotted a piece of land sufficient to maintain a household in return for which they performed labor on the soil reserved by the owner of the villa and rendered dues. Their status tended to become hereditary, but such status also assured them permanent use of a plot of land. The villa system offered certain advantages. It provided landowners with a permanent labor force, encouraged cooperative effort, and gave peasants not only security but some freedom of choice in how they exploited their tenancy. In other areas, farming was organized around village communities of free landowners; in such communities each family owned and cultivated its own land but also shared common rights in forest and pasture land. Also scattered across the landscape were numerous individual farms cultivated by free peasants. Tilled land was used chiefly for cereal grains and vegetables. Peasants showed considerable ingenuity in linking the exploitation of tilled land with the exploitation of forests, streams, and animal herds. In gross terms, this agricultural system produced barely enough to provide the basic needs of the population.

The shift of the center of economic life to a rural setting was accompanied by the decline of urban-based commerce and industry, again continuing a trend that had begun in late Roman times. Although urban centers survived, cities served chiefly as political and religious centers rather than centers of economic production. Near the Mediterranean in southern Gaul, Italy, Spain, and North Africa, some commercial activity did continue, and contacts with the rich East were maintained. But on the whole the West experienced a diminishing exchange of goods, a declining flow of money, and the virtual disappearance of active merchants and artisans, except as they were supported by owners of large estates to provide for local consumption. What little long-distance trade did survive was increasingly conducted by foreigners, especially Syrians and Jews.

Amid this grim picture there were signs pointing toward a restructuring of economic life into patterns that promised greater productivity. The end of the voracious Roman taxation system opened opportunities for channeling surplus wealth toward productive ends. The formation of villas and villages created disciplined productive cells encouraging cooperation between landowners and peasants. The emergence of the family household permanently in possession of a piece of land provided a solid foundation for agricultural production. The resourcefulness of peasants in linking field and forest gave flexibility and variety to the agricultural system. Modest technological advances, especially the development of ox-drawn plows capable of turning over heavy soils, allowed full exploitation of the rich land north of the Alps for the first time. Isolated efforts at land clearance held out the promise of bringing forest and wasteland under the plow. Trading activity began to quicken in the North and Baltic seas and along the rivers flowing into them, opening new opportunities for commercial exchange.

The social structure in the West changed in response to new conditions. The direction of change was toward a simpler system than had been characteristic of the Roman world of late antiquity. The old Roman *nobiles*, whose status and social role were intimately linked to the Roman imperial regime and Greco-Roman culture, faded away. A new aristocracy emerged, composed of resourceful, aggressive, self-made individuals of both Roman and German descent who were capable of acquiring land, exercising private political power, and gathering dependents around them. As this new aristocracy (often referred to as the *potentes*, the powerful) took shape, the rest of the population, almost all peasants, tended to be grouped into a single lower class (often called *pauperes*, those without power). While many in this class retained legal status as free persons, increasingly peasants saw their freedom erode as a result of constraints placed on them by landowners that bound them to the soil of a large estate and imposed obligations on them in exchange for use of a piece of land. Slavery continued to exist, especially as a means of supplying household servants, but there was a tendency to attach slaves to the land in the same fashion as other peasant workers.

Social behavior and attitudes among the powerful increasingly reflected Germanic values and habits at the expense of the more refined standards of conduct of the old Roman world. Generally illiterate and often short-lived, aristocratic males were creatures of violence and passion, their lives centered on fighting, hunting, gaming, and sexual exploits. They loved ostentatious display, particularly in the form of personal adornments made of gold and jewels. Especially important to them were family connections, chiefly because the family circle offered security in an uncertain environment. It was not unusual for aristocrats to collect wives and concubines so as to assure themselves of many children who could be advantageously married to promote family interests. Feuds among competing noble families were a common feature of life. Although male heads of families exercised extensive power over females, aristocratic women played a significant role in society. Dowries and gifts associated with marriage gave them control over considerable property. High respect was paid and special protection was extended to them because of their procreative power, the key to family survival. Kinship ties established through female lines provided a basic link in constituting extended families. The social importance of women is illustrated by the prominent role played in public life by several Merovingian queens and by the influence asserted by several gifted leaders of Merovingian monasteries for women. Peasant life, anchored in the nuclear family and confined to a tiny rural community, was marked by poverty, drudgery, and ill-treatment.

3. RELIGIOUS LIFE

Of decisive importance in shaping western European life during the early Middle Ages was the Christian religious establishment, one of the main components of the world of late antiquity that carried over into the new age almost intact. Although Christians in the West shared a vague sense of belonging to a universal body, in reality the religious establishment was embodied in hundreds of individual "churches" led by bishops and priests whose offices bestowed on them considerable authority to direct the lives of their flocks.

Between 500 and 750 these Christian communities were sorely tested by a variety of disruptive forces. The replacement of the unified Roman imperial regime by several Germanic kingdoms meant the end of any agency concerned with Christendom as a whole. The new Germanic kingdoms lacked the material resources to support churches on the scale the Roman government had. Powerful forces were at work diverting the attention of religious leaders from spiritual concerns. Like all other power wielders in the West, influential ecclesiastical officials, especially bishops, paid increasing attention to gaining land and dependents. Not only did this quest detract them from their pastoral duties, it also made their offices a focus of wealth and power. These offices became the object of competition in which the worldly usually triumphed over the pious. Ecclesiastical offices were prizes that kings used to reward their followers and that self-seeking noble families sought to fill as a means of increasing their wealth and power. Discipline among the lower clergy suffered from the lack of spiritual concern among higher church officials; the result was increasing numbers of unlettered priests who were ignorant of basic Christian teaching and morally lax. Powerful nobles often controlled the appointments of local priests, especially those serving the increasing numbers of private churches established on local estates by nobles who viewed such churches as private property. Although the early Middle Ages was a period of intense religious fervor among all people, religious life in general reflected inferior spiritual direction. Pagan and Christian ideas and practices mingled to produce a religious mentality focused on gaining material ends and avoiding evil spirits through magic and the intervention of the saints rather than on learning basic Christian doctrines and practicing Christian morality.

The disruptive forces in spiritual life producing disunity, worldliness in leadership, debased religious consciousness, and moral laxness were still rampant in 750. However, the Christian establishment had begun to devise means of counteracting them in ways that gave western Christianity a distinctive quality.

Of particular significance was the expanded involvement of the Christian establishment in activities that were not strictly religious, filling an important social role to which the weak Germanic monarchs were unable to respond. Bishops played an important role in the councils of kings and royal administrations, allowing them to inject Christian ideas of justice and mercy into the harsh law codes of the era. Ecclesiastical leaders took on the burden of caring for the poor, maintaining schools and hospitals, and protecting the weak. Resources to support such activities were drawn from income derived from church lands and gifts from the faithful, who were prompted to give at least in part by some sense that charity was a Christian responsibility. Each time the religious establishment intervened in such matters, its prestige as a social agency and its influence over the social order increased. No less important, such actions added a social dimension to religious consciousness.

A major source of vitality in religious life was the quest to win new converts. We have already noted that most of the Germanic invaders accepted Christianity as soon as they entered the Roman Empire. In succeeding centuries the Christian frontier continued to advance. During the fifth century missionary forces, spearheaded by St. Patrick, converted Ireland. Missionaries from the Frankish kingdom, itself Christianized late in the fifth century under Clovis, pushed the Christian frontier to the Rhine and beyond during the sixth and seventh centuries. Beginning late in the sixth century, the Anglo-Saxons were converted by missionaries from Rome and Ireland. During the late seventh and eighth centuries, English and Irish missionaries crossed to the Continent to win new converts on the northern and eastern frontiers of the Frankish kingdom. Meanwhile, the work of converting the rural population of the West went forward. As new converts were won, a network of bishoprics, monasteries, rural churches, and private chapels was developed to ensure pastoral care for new Christians. In some cases conversions were imposed from the top down; as a result, acceptance of the new religion had only a superficial impact on most converts. However, the missionary establishment was often especially intent on imposing a high level of religious life, thus serving as a model of pastoral care and a source of reforming zeal.

Another significant development involved the emergence of religious agencies capable of attacking weaknesses within the body of the Christian establishment—corruptness and worldliness of the clergy, moral laxness, ignorance of religious precepts, lack of discipline.

Two agencies, neither new, were especially important: the papacy and the monastic establishment.

During late antiquity the papacy had utilized the Petrine theory (see Chapters 12 and 13) to establish its position as the guardian of true doctrine and right practice. That position was reinforced during the troubled fifth century. With the collapse of the Roman imperial government, the bishops of Rome assumed a larger role in governing the city of Rome, as was dramatically illustrated by the role played by Pope Leo I (440–461) in protecting St. Peter's city from the Huns and the Vandals and in fiercely defending the papal right to define Orthodox doctrine, especially against the claims of the emperors and the patriarchs of Constantinople. The expanding sense of papal authority was reflected by Pope Gelasius I (492–496), who argued that God had established two independent and separate realms of authority, the spiritual and the secular, to achieve different aspects of the divine plan, but when the two powers clashed, spiritual authority must prevail. However, many factors limited the ability of the popes to exert their claimed authority. The Arian Ostrogoths who ruled Italy from 493 to 554 were little inclined to respect papal authority. When Justinian reincorporated Rome into the Byzantine Empire, he treated its bishop as one of his religious agents whose authority was no greater than that of the patriarch of Constantinople. The installation of the hostile, aggressive Arian Lombards as rulers of northern Italy after 568 left the popes with no choice but to accept Byzantine protection and to acquiesce to imperial religious policy as defined by the emperor.

It was Pope Gregory I, the Great (590–604), who began to rechart the papal course (see Figure 15.2). A Roman noble by birth and education and a monk by personal choice, he accepted the papal office with reluctance, but once in control he moved in decisive directions. Convinced that the papacy must command material resources to survive on the troubled Italian scene, Gregory spent considerable energy in the management of the patrimony of St. Peter—that is, the property belonging to the papacy in Italy. He used the large income derived from this property chiefly to expand papal control over Rome, often with little consideration of the officials of the emperor

FIGURE 15.2 Pope Gregory the Great Gregory was one of the most influential figures of the formative period of medieval western European society. His varied activities as bishop of Rome put an important imprint on the office of the papacy as the leader of the Christian community in the West. Throughout the Middle Ages his successors looked back to his career as a model of Christian leadership and as a precedent for their actions. (Alinari/Art Resource)

in Constantinople, who claimed legal authority to rule the Eternal City. His increasingly powerful position in Rome allowed him to play the Lombards against the Byzantines in a way that not only prevented Lombard conquest of Rome but also undermined Byzantine power in the city. This effort marked an important step in laying the groundwork for a future papal state in Italy.

But Gregory was more than a hardheaded administrator and wily diplomat. He never forgot the pastoral responsibilities that tradition assigned to the successor of St. Peter and to all bishops. In this capacity he took significant steps toward reshaping the Christian message to fit the unique needs of the Germanic West and toward drawing the western Christian community to

Rome for spiritual guidance. He wrote important books on theology and ecclesiastical administration that circulated widely to guide the clergy in explaining the faith and shaping the moral lives of their flocks. His powerful sermons became models for preaching as a means of improving spiritual life. He sought to provide a model of liturgical practice that would be useful in all churches; tradition credited him with a role in developing Gregorian chant as an element of the liturgy. He wrote innumerable letters to kings and clergy throughout the West, offering them advice on religious matters and reminding them of Rome's authority in the religious sphere. His influence was crucial in converting the Lombards and Visigoths from Arianism to orthodoxy, thus ending a major cause of religious division in the West. He initiated the missionary effort that played a major role in converting the Anglo-Saxons of England, and he guided the religious organization of the new converts in a way that attached them to Rome. In short, Gregory enlarged the role of the papacy in the religious life of the West and began to direct papal efforts toward the resolution of religious problems unique to the West, thereby setting a model of papal leadership that would serve for centuries.

A second force crucial in shaping religious life in the early medieval West was monasticism. Monasticism had been imported from the east in the fourth century, but early western monasticism failed to sustain its initial vitality, perhaps because it was too imitative of eastern models to address the unique conditions in the West. Only when the West found its own style of monastic life did that instituition begin to assert a decisive force on religious life.

One distinctive form of western monasticism developed in Ireland, where the severe ascetic practices of the east took deep hold as the standard for monastic life. However, Irish monastic communities became thoroughly enmeshed in Irish tribal society, placing monks in a position to shape popular religious life. An example of this engagement was the unique system of penance developed in Irish monastic circles, involving private confession and the use of penitential books that—much like Germanic law codes—cataloged sins and instructed confessors on the appropriate punishment for each. Irish monasticism placed a strong emphasis on learning as a dimension of piety; as a result Irish monasteries became active centers of education and of the study of sacred literature. Finally, Irish monasteries generated a powerful missionary movement that spread Irish monks over England and the Continent, bringing with them deep piety, skill in uplifting the level of religious life, and great learning.

Another unique form of monastic life was introduced by Benedict of Nursia (ca. 480–543). Like Gregory I, he was an Italian of noble origin who abandoned the world to follow a monastic life. After experimenting with the hermit life, he eventually founded a monastic community at Monte Cassino and formulated a rule to guide the lives of its members. The *Benedictine Rule*, which combined features from several earlier rules, emphasized that a community of dedicated individuals could serve God and each other better than the individual hermit isolated from interaction with other humans could. However, such a "school for the service of God" must be made up of selected individuals willing to make a commitment to perfection. After a rigorous testing period, each new member was required to take vows to renounce all personal wealth, to remain chaste, to obey his superiors, and to remain permanently in the community he had entered. The rule entrusted absolute authority over the community to an abbot who was responsible before God to direct each monk toward holiness; thus discipline was a key feature of Benedictine communities. A major aspect of the rule was its provision for an orderly daily routine for all members of the community, consisting of specified periods of prayer, manual labor, contemplation, and reading (see Figure 15.1). This regimen ensured that each community would be self-sufficient economically and that its members would be engaged in varied activities rather than in endless ascetic practices aimed at suppressing the urges of the body and awareness of the world. Although Benedict had no intention of devising a rule for all monasteries, his rule—given powerful endorsement by Pope Gregory I in his popular biography of Benedict—was adopted by both male and female communities across western Europe.

By 750 monasteries, especially Benedictine and Irish houses, were asserting a powerful influence in society. Monks and nuns were the new holy people, "athletes of Christ" serving as models of piety and moral excellence for all elements of society. They were able to teach bewildered Christians the basic elements of the faith and the proper way to perform Christian worship. They were the chief preservers and transmitters of learning. They performed numerous acts of charity and goaded the rich and powerful to emulate them. As a result of their disciplined labors in the service of God, monks carved new estates out of Europe's wilderness and made them the best-managed economic institutions in the West, from which all could learn about farm management and artisanry. As a bulwark against both the Devil and barbarism, many found the monks and nuns worthy of emulation.

4. CULTURAL LIFE

Although the chaotic conditions prevailing in western Europe from 500 to 750 were hardly conducive to cultural activity, certain developments were significant in shaping a new culture. Of prime importance was the preservation of significant elements of classical and patristic literature and learning in Latin (the use of Greek virtually disappeared in the West). During the sixth century both secular society and the religious establishment played a role in this enterprise. In Italy, southern Gaul, and Spain lay aristocrats and bishops of Roman descent continued to read classical and patristic Latin authors, to write works imitating them, and to support schools where the young could study rhetoric and grammar. Germanic courts, especially that of the Ostrogoths, actively patronized learning and art.

As the sixth century progressed, the role of secular society in sustaining cultural life virtually ceased; the burden fell to the Christian establishment, especially the monasteries. Irish and Benedictine monasteries established schools to teach new members to read and write Latin, encouraged the copying of the works of classical and patristic authors, and promoted the writing of commentaries on old texts to make them understandable. Especially active in these enterprises were the Benedictine monasteries of England, where Irish and Continental influences merged to generate an important outburst of literary and scholarly activity in the early eighth century. Monastic intellectual life placed an especially strong emphasis on mastery of the Bible as the prime source of wisdom. The concerns of monks tended to be narrow, governed by a passion to know God, to understand his revealed word, and to pray well. Thus, the monks were selective in their approach to the classical tradition. And they felt no compunction about turning the classical heritage to Christian purposes, sometimes distorting classical thought almost beyond recognition.

In a world dominated by the effort to maintain a tenuous contact with the Latin literary and theological heritage of classical Roman writers and the Church Fathers of late antiquity, there was little room for charting new directions in cultural life. However, a few figures were able to transcend mere preservation to produce works that revealed creative talent. One was Boethius (ca. 475–525), a luminary at the Ostrogothic court who set out to translate the works of Aristotle and Plato into Latin; although he made limited progress in that project, for centuries his translations provided the West with virtually its only access to the Greek philosophical tradition. His famous *Consolation of Philosophy*, written while he was in prison awaiting execution for treason, was a moving defense of philosophy as a guide to inner peace and happiness. In *Etymologies* a Visigothic bishop, Isidore of Seville (ca. 560–636), provided an encyclopedia of information about many subjects derived from ancient sources that encouraged the systematic organization of knowledge. Gregory the Great's writings set forth basic theological concepts in terms more suited to the intellectual capabilities of his age than were the sophisticated works of the Latin Fathers from whom he borrowed most of his ideas. Especially important in shaping western European intellectual life was Gregory's mode of interpreting Scripture, which sought to discover the hidden meaning behind the literal words of the Bible. A Frankish bishop, Gregory of Tours (ca. 538–594), in his *History of the Franks*, demonstrated skill at compiling historical material. The most outstanding intellectual figure of the age was the English monk Bede (673–735), whose theological, historical, and biographical writings set high standards of learning and style. His *Ec-*

clesiastical History of the English People is one of the best pieces of history written during the entire Middle Ages. The age was also rich in saints' lives celebrating the feats of holy men and women who had surrendered themselves to the service of God.

As a few struggled to preserve Latin education and learning, the lay world sank into illiteracy. That world was not without culture; its members kept alive the oral tradition of the Germanic world, as is evidenced by the magnificent epic entitled *Beowulf*, put into writing in about 800 in the Anglo-Saxon language to record oral tradition concerning the heroic struggles of warriors against the forces of evil. The illiteracy of the laity created a situation of immense importance for western European cultural history: The languages men and women spoke in their daily lives were different from the language of learning and literature. For centuries learning would remain the monopoly of an elite especially trained to use Latin, the language of the religious establishment. Under such circumstances, it remained a constant challenge to prevent the world of learning from becoming remote from and irrelevant to the realities of life.

The art of the early Middle Ages reflects a mixture of old and new. Greco-Roman forms and themes persisted in architecture, sculpture, and painting, but they were constantly modified to serve Christian ends. Many of the churches of the era followed the basilica plan characteristic of Roman structures. However, Byzantine architectural forms, shaped by Justinian's building program, asserted a strong influence on sixth-century Italy, especially in Ravenna (see Figure 13.2), and persisted there to affect building styles in other areas of the West. In sculpture and painting, classical and Byzantine influences merged to create a pictorial art emphasizing symbolical representation of religious motifs at the expense of realistic portrayal of humans and the world of nature (see Figures 12.1 and 15.3). Germanic and Celtic influences, especially their decorative style, which used animal and geometric forms to create abstract designs, asserted their effects on the pictorial arts. The vigor of this composite early medieval art is especially evident in the designs created to illustrate handwritten manuscripts; prime examples include the Irish Book of

FIGURE 15.3 Two Thieves Awaiting the Crucifixion This sculpture from the mausoleum of a seventh-century abbot from the Frankish city of Poitiers shows two unhappy thieves bound to crosses while awaiting their end with Christ. While classical art styles persist (e.g., the representation of a building), the portrayal of the human figures indicates that new influences were penetrating artistic expression in the German-dominated world. (Marburg/Art Resource)

Durrow (late seventh century), the English Lindisfarne Gospels (eighth century), and the Irish Book of Kells (early ninth century) (see Color Plate 8).

By 750 the western European world had by no means emerged from the time of troubles that followed the collapse of the Roman imperial regime. Habits of violence, ignorance, poverty, and moral laxness had been ingrained into people's lives and would long affect the western European world. However, out of the experiences of the early Middle Ages had emerged innovative institutions and patterns of life: a form of limited monarchy, a new nobility, a stabilized peasantry, an involved ecclesiastical organization, the papacy, monasticism, a store of Greco-Roman literature and learning, a new art style. Their potential had not yet been realized, but their existence pointed toward the emergence of a vigorous and unique civilization in the West that might in the future equal the level of civilized life already flourishing in the Byzantine and Moslem worlds.

SUGGESTED READING

Political, Economic, and Social History

J. M. Wallace-Haddrill, *The Barbarian West, 400–1000*, 5th rev. ed. (1988).

Roger Collins, *Early Medieval Europe, 300–1000* (1991).

Two excellent general surveys of the early Middle Ages.

Henri Pirenne, *Mohammed and Charlemagne*, trans. Bernard Maill (1939). A classic expounding the thesis that the Islamic invasions of the eighth century brought a break with the classical world.

Patrick Geary, *Before France and Germany: The Creation and Transformation of the Merovingian World* (1988).

Edward James, *The Origins of France: From Clovis to the Capetians, 500–1000* (1982).

Katharine Scherman, *The Birth of France: Warriors, Bishops, and Long-Haired Kings* (1987).

Chris Wickham, *Early Medieval Italy: Central Power and Local Society, 400–1000* (1981).

Roger Collins, *Early Medieval Spain: Unity in Diversity, 400–1000* (1983).

Martyn J. Wittock, *The Origins of England 400–600* (1986).

These six titles provide excellent treatments of the major Germanic kingdoms of the early Middle Ages.

Georges Duby, *The Early Growth of the European Economy: Warriors and Peasants from the Seventh to the Twelfth Century*, trans. Howard B. Clarke (1974).

Renée Doehaerd, *The Early Middle Ages in the West: Economy and Society*, trans. W. G. Deakin (1978).

Two comprehensive treatments of economic and social history.

Richard Hodges, *Dark Age Economies: The Origins of Towns and Trade, A.D. 600–1000* (1982). Uses archaeological evidence to revise views about the low level of trade and urban life.

Philippe Ariès and Georges Duby, *A History of Private Life*, Vol. 1: *From Pagan Rome to Byzantium*, ed. Paul Veyne, trans. Arthur Goldhammer (1987). The appropriate chapter in this study is rich in details about social life.

Suzanne Fonay Wemple, *Women in Frankish Society: Marriage and the Cloister, 500 to 900* (1981). A balanced treatment.

Religious and Cultural History

Judith Herrin, *The Formation of Christendom* (1987). Stresses the role of religion as a prime force in shaping the new civilizations of the early Middle Ages.

Hubert Jedin and John Dolan, eds., *Handbook of Church History*, Vol. 2: *The Imperial Church to the Early Middle Ages*, trans. Anselm Biggs (1980). Deals with all aspects of religious life.

J. M. Wallace-Hadrill, *The Frankish Church* (1983). A topical approach, rich in interpretations.

Jeffrey Richards, *The Popes and the Papacy in the Early Middle Ages, 476–752* (1979). An excellent treatment.

James C. Russell, *The Germanization of Early Medieval Christianity: A Sociohistorical Approach to Religious Transformation* (1992). New views on changes affecting Christianity during the early Middle Ages.

Pierre Riché, *Education and Culture in the Barbarian West: Sixth through Eighth Century*, trans. John J. Contreni (1976). A work rich in insights into the nature of early medieval culture.

Ludwig Bieler, *Ireland: Harbinger of the Middle Ages* (1963). A brilliant treatment of Ireland's contribution to cultural life.

J. Hubert et al., *Europe of the Invasions*, trans. Stuart Gilbert and James Emmons (1969). An excellent treatment of artistic development during the early Middle Ages.

Sources

Rule of Monasteries, trans. L. J. Boyle (1949). Benedict's rule.

Gregory of Tours, *The History of the Franks*, trans. Lewis Thorpe (1974).

Bede, *The History of the English Church and People*, rev. ed., trans. L. Sherley-Price (1968).

Beowulf, trans. D. Wright (1957).

CHAPTER 16

The First Europe: The Carolingian Age, 750–900

FIGURE 16.1 Dispensing Justice in the Carolingian Age This drawing from a ninth-century manuscript shows Emperor Charlemagne and his son, Pépin, king of Italy, presiding over a court of law while a clerk is ready to record their judgment. Concern for justice was an important aspect of the Carolingian effort to provide better government. (Modena Cathedral Archives)

The pace of the slow, troubled struggle to create a new basis for society in western Europe suddenly quickened in the eighth century. Between about 750 and 900 a narrow but energetic segment of society, spearheaded by kings and clergy, devoted its talents to an effort to "renew" society both on the Continent and in England. Although their ambitions were by no means realized, their limited success had two important results: It made the West visible in the larger world as a coherent culture. And it gave the West an expanded awareness of its unique identity. In a sense, this renewal created the first "Europe."

1. THE RISE OF THE CAROLINGIANS

The central force promoting revival on the Continent was a new Frankish royal dynasty, the Carolingians, so named after its most famous king, Carolus, or Charles. The Carolingians originated as one of the many ambitious noble families whose power and wealth grew steadily under the Merovingians. In the middle of the seventh century, the family utilized its extensive landed possessions and its connections with the religious establishment to gain hereditary control over the office of mayor of the palace in the subkingdom of Austrasia, where the family wealth was concentrated (see Map 16.1). This key office allowed the family to control the weak Merovingian kings of Austrasia and to utilize royal lands to increase its wealth and its circle of dependents. As their family power expanded, the Carolingians sought to extend their influence to the other Merovingian subkingdoms—Neustria and Burgundy. That effort culminated in 687, when Pépin of Herstal, the Carolingian mayor of the palace of Austrasia, defeated the Neustrian mayor and claimed the mayoralty of the entire Frankish realm.

Once established as sole mayor of the palace, Pépin of Herstal and his son and grandson, Charles Martel (714–741) and Pépin the Short (741–751), became the most powerful men in the Frankish state, far overshadowing the "do-nothing" Merovingian kings they served. Their efforts were aimed chiefly at checking the forces of disintegration within the kingdom and defending its frontiers. Charles Martel gained undying fame by defeating a Moslem army at the battle of Tours in 732. Their military success was due in part to their ability to take advantage of a significant military innovation that began to spread in the eighth century: the heavily armored mounted warrior. This innovation was perhaps made possible by the invention of the stirrup, which permitted a mounted warrior to keep his mount while striking or receiving blows from sword or spear. The equipping and support of a force of mounted warriors involved costs beyond the means of the impoverished royal government; increasingly it was necessary to rely on men of wealth willing to arm themselves at their own expense. Charles Martel and Pépin rewarded such service by grants of land, called *benefices*, the income from which the recipients used on the condition that they would provide military service at their own expense. Although some of these benefices were derived from royal lands, Charles Martel and Pépin made a regular practice of utilizing ecclesiastical lands to provide military benefices.

Although condemned by some clergymen as pillagers of religious property, Charles Martel and Pépin used other means to court and win the ecclesiastical support that was vital to their growing power. Their support of missionary activity and religious reform was particularly welcome among many bishops and monks. A key figure in shaping their religious policy was Boniface, an Anglo-Saxon Benedictine monk who went to the Continent in 719 to convert the pagans living beyond the eastern frontier of the kingdom. Until his martyrdom by pagan Frisians in 755, Boniface not only won many converts but also organized bishoprics and monasteries in newly converted territories and guided the mayors of the palace in shaping a program to reform Frankish religious life. Soon after his arrival in Francia, Boniface sought and received the blessing of the papacy for his varied activities. As a result, papal influence expanded among the Franks, and the mayors of the palace gained increasing recognition as supporters of the successors of St. Peter.

Although the Carolingian mayors of the palace clearly exercised control over the Frankish kingdom, they legally remained agents of the powerless Merovingian kings. Finally, Pépin took the logical step to end this incongruous situation by transferring the crown to his own fam-

Map 16.1 **THE EMPIRE OF CHARLEMAGNE** One of Charlemagne's great achievements was his military victories, which greatly expanded the Frankish kingdom. This map shows his major conquests. The extent of his holdings indicates that he came close to dominating western Europe, an ambition that would spark the dreams of many later western European rulers. Not long after Charlemagne's death, his empire would suffer savage attacks on all its frontiers and would be divided by his heirs.

ily. Concerned about the potential hostility that might arise among the Franks by a forced deposition of the ancient dynasty, whose sacred blood was held in deep respect, Pépin sought to

sanction his action in an unprecedented way. He sent an envoy to Rome to ask Pope Zachary whether the "right ordering of things" did not demand that he who held actual power should wear the crown. On the basis of the pope's affirmative answer, Pépin in 751 deposed the reigning Merovingian and had himself elected king by the Frankish nobles. On the occasion of his coronation, a clergyman (perhaps Boniface) gave him a special anointment never before bestowed on a Frankish king. This sequence of events indicated to many that Pépin's royal office was different from that held by his Merovingian predecessors. Although duly elected by the Franks according to Germanic tradition, papal consent to the dynastic change and anointment by a clergyman made Pépin an agent of God charged with caring for the material and spiritual needs of the Christian community according to God's will.

The papacy was especially anxious to strengthen its bonds with the Franks because of the significant changes taking place in Italy. Since Justinian's reconquest of Italy in the middle of the sixth century, the city of Rome had been under the jurisdiction of the emperor in Constantinople, and the popes had relied—sometimes reluctantly—on imperial protection. During the first half of the eighth century, however, the Moslem assault on Byzantium left the emperors increasingly unable to defend their position in Italy. Moreover, the iconoclastic policy of emperors Leo III and Constantine V had been condemned as heretical by the papacy. The decline of Byzantine power in Italy encouraged its longtime rivals, the Lombards, to expand their sphere of influence. Beginning early in the eighth century, a succession of able Lombard kings undertook military campaigns that increasingly threatened to engulf Rome and to impose a new master on the papacy. Bereft of help from the Byzantine emperors, now both weak and heretical, the popes desperately needed a new protector.

In the face of the mounting Lombard threat, Pope Stephen II (752–757) undertook a journey to Pépin's kingdom in 754, perhaps emboldened by the fact that his predecessor had extended an important favor to the new king. After long negotiations and despite resistance by some Frankish nobles, the king agreed to protect the pope from the Lombards. In return, the pope reanointed Pépin king of the Franks and bestowed on him the somewhat ambiguous title of "*patricius* of the Romans,*" implying Pépin's role as

protector of the people of Rome, including the papacy. Pépin undertook campaigns into Italy in 754 and 756 and forced the Lombards to surrender territories in central Italy that they had recently annexed. In a grant known as the Donation of Pépin, he bestowed these lands on the papacy, thereby establishing the basis for the papacy's claim to an independent state. Although the lands involved legally belonged to the Byzantine emperor, Pépin's action clearly recognized what was reality: Since the time of Pope Gregory I the bishops of Rome had established de facto control over Rome and its environs. There is some evidence that a document known as the Donation of Constantine may have played a part in these transactions. This document, which seems to have been composed in Rome at about this time, claimed to date from the time of Constantine and stated that the first Christian emperor, out of gratitude for being cured of leprosy, had granted Pope Sylvester I (314–335) the rights to the western empire, especially Rome and Italy. Pepin's donation was therefore only a confirmation of an earlier legal grant made by a universally renowned ruler whose mantle the contemporary emperor in Constantinople had inherited.

2. THE REIGN OF CHARLEMAGNE, 768–814

The foundations established by Pépin of Herstal, Charles Martel, and Pépin the Short were brilliantly exploited by Charlemagne. In the eyes of his contemporaries he possessed many qualities of greatness: imposing physical stature, prowess as a warrior, piety, generosity, intelligence, devotion to family and friends, joy for life. His actions made him a hero not only in his own time but for many future generations of Europeans.

As befitted a Frankish king, Charlemagne was above all else a successful warlord. Few years passed during his long reign without a military campaign; the cumulative result was a considerable expansion of his kingdom (see Map 16.1). His most severe test came from the pagan Saxons along the northeastern frontier of his kingdom; only after many campaigns extending over thirty years was he able to conquer and convert them. The northeast frontier was also advanced by the conquest of Frisia. In 774 he crushed the troublesome Lombards, assumed the title of king of the Lombards, and laid claim to all of Italy except the Byzantine territories in the south and the Papal State, over which he continued the protectorship assumed by Pépin. His armies drove down the Danube and annexed territories held by the Avars and Slavs. His attack on Moslem Spain resulted initially in a defeat at Roncesvalles, later immortalized in an epic poem called *The Song of Roland*. But persistent pressure in that direction led to the creation of the Spanish March, a Frankish bridgehead south of the Pyrenees that threatened Moslem power. Frankish military might also curbed the separatist aspirations of the people of Aquitaine, Bavaria, and Brittany. Beyond the new frontiers established by conquest, and especially in central Europe and Denmark, Charlemagne combined force and diplomacy to compel various Slavic and Scandinavian peoples into a tributary status observing respect for Frankish territory and interests. He was even able to assert military pressure on Byzantine holdings in southern Italy and the northern Adriatic.

A tribute to Charlemagne's skill as a military organizer, these victories yielded a rich harvest of booty, which Charlemagne dispersed liberally to sustain the services and the allegiance of the warriors who fought the many battles and to win the favor of the nobles and church officials upon whose support royal power depended. But Charlemagne succeeded in surrounding his military ventures with an aura transcending mere material considerations. They were struggles against barbarians, pagans, and infidels, fought to save the Christian world and to win converts for the true religion. For his efforts he won the plaudits of popes, poets, and nobles, who hailed him as "the strong right arm of God." And he caught the attention of the larger world, as is demonstrated by his diplomatic exchanges with the emperors of Constantinople, the caliphs of Baghdad, the emirs of Moslem Spain, and the kings of England.

Charlemagne's military successes were accompanied by a strenuous effort to expand royal authority and improve the effectiveness of the central government within his growing realm. Charlemagne's concept of kingship was rooted firmly in the Germanic concept of the *bannum*,

which entitled a ruler to command his subjects to serve him and to punish those who disobeyed. That Germanic basis of royal authority was elevated and enriched by ideas drawn from Christian concepts of royal authority and responsibility and of the public well-being. The Christian view of the state, rooted in Old Testament precedents and especially in Augustine's *City of God*, which was Charlemagne's favorite book, envisioned the state as a society of Christians linked together by a common faith for the purpose of realizing God's plan for humanity, including the salvation of each individual soul. To achieve that end, society must strive for right order, harmony, and justice, each defined in Christian terms. The key to achieving the good Christian society was the king. Like the biblical David, the Christian king was God's anointed agent, who was charged with commanding his subjects to do good and restraining them from evil. He was, in effect, God's minister in the cause of righteousness. This concept of royal power, sometimes called ministerial kingship, provided norms for defining governmental action and political behavior that were much broader than those that had prevailed in the Frankish state during the Merovingian period.

In applying his expanded concept of royal authority, Charlemagne utilized the basic political structures inherited from the Merovingians. What especially marked his reign was his own vigorous action aimed at making those structures work more effectively to realize Christian right order. He was a tireless worker, traveling constantly across his realm, checking incessantly on the performance of his officials, administering justice (see Figure 16.1), and consulting frequently with those upon whom he depended to sustain political order. At the heart of his government was the royal court (called the *palatium*), made up of trusted clergy and lay nobles. Collectively, the court circle advised the king in shaping policies. In addition, each member of the court was assigned a political function as practical needs demanded: guarding the royal treasury, judging cases, keeping records, conducting diplomatic missions, commanding armies, providing for the material needs of the royal family. The royal court was supported chiefly by the products collected from royal lands; additional support, never very predictable, came from war booty, tolls on trade, fines, and gifts offered the king in return for favors. The court moved constantly, chiefly to expedite military campaigns and to gain access to the produce from royal estates. Only near the end of his reign did Charlemagne establish a semipermanent residence at Aachen.

To assert his authority on the local level, Charlemagne relied on the traditional system of counties, of which there were about three hundred. In each county the king was represented by a count who administered justice, enforced order, and mustered the freemen of the county to military service. The counts were rewarded by grants of land from which they could derive income as long as they held office. The counts were served by a small group of subofficials, most of them concerned with administering justice. Bishops and abbots were also assigned important responsibilities in local affairs. Charlemagne tried hard to select capable men for these offices and to supervise their activities. He developed a system of sending out special agents (*missi*) to investigate what was going on, to instruct local officials on what the king expected, and to report back to the court on local conditions. He issued a constant stream of royal orders (*capitularies*) to inform local officials of royal intent and to direct their actions on a wide range of matters relating to public order. Almost every year, Charlemagne also called his officials and other great men of the realm to an assembly at his court, where he heard their concerns and proclaimed new regulations designed to govern their actions.

The operation of this modest political apparatus, which involved only a few thousand officials, depended heavily on the loyalty not only of royal officials but also of all of the king's subjects, especially the *potentes*, the powerful ones. Charlemagne was constantly concerned with expanding the bonds of loyalty. His own feats as a warrior played an important role in this respect. On several occasions he required all of his free subjects to swear an oath of fidelity, binding them to refrain from activities contrary to public order. He regularly bestowed gifts, derived chiefly from war booty, on those whose loyalty he especially prized. Most important of all, he greatly expanded the use of commendation and benefices to bind royal officials, nobles, and churchmen to him. Those who were willing to commend themselves under oath to become royal vassals were granted benefices, usually in the form of land grants or offices, to be enjoyed as long as the recipients served the king faithfully. Unfaithfulness to these oaths was considered a major offense.

In defining the royal office in terms that assigned to the king a God-given duty to sustain the Christian establishment in its mission of saving souls, Charlemagne assumed a major responsibility for religious life in his realm. Religious reform became a prime focus of his program, a policy pursued in a way that made the royal government the directive force in religious affairs and left to the clergy a subordinate role in the service of the ministerial king. Charlemagne assumed a lead role in the spread of Christianity, even using force to compel reluctant pagans, such as the Saxons, to receive baptism. He strengthened church organization by issuing legislation aimed at reestablishing the authority of bishops and subordinating parish priests to them. He sought to improve the quality of the clergy by imposing higher moral and educational standards on those who assumed ecclesiastical office. Monastic establishments were encouraged to adopt the Benedictine rule as a means of upgrading discipline and spiritual life. Royal authority was used to protect ecclesiastical property and to provide material support for the religious establishment; especially important was the imposition of a tax of 10 percent of income, called the *tithe*, on all Christians to support religious life. Charlemagne made a major effort to establish uniform doctrines and ritual practices as a way of eliminating the diverse practices and bizarre beliefs that passed as Christianity. In formulating his religious program, Charlemagne relied heavily on guidance from the papacy; especially close was his relationship with Pope Hadrian I (772–795). As a result, a distinctly Roman stamp was imposed on religious life in his realm. Charlemagne must be counted as a major architect of the Roman Catholic church and as a major force in enhancing the authority of the papacy in the West.

All of these achievements played a part in shaping the culminating event of Charlemagne's career: his coronation as emperor. The stage was set for this event when a disturbance in Rome in 799 led to charges of misconduct against Pope

Leo III (795–816), who was forced to flee to Charlemagne's court. In his role as protector of the pope and the Romans, Charlemagne went to Rome in 800 and acted directly to exonerate the pope and restore him to full authority. Then, on Christmas Day in the year 800, while the king was attending Mass in St. Peter's Basilica, the pope placed a crown on his head, and the clergy and people in attendance hailed the king of the Franks as "Augustus, crowned by God, the great and peace-bringing Emperor of the Romans." For the first time since 476 a ruler from the West was emperor.

Ever since that momentous occasion, there has been a debate about who instigated the renewal of the imperial office and what it signified. Perhaps responsibility for the event was shared by the pope, Charlemagne, and his advisers as a means of realizing different aspirations. For Leo III the bestowal of the crown offered a way to restore papal prestige, recently tainted by Leo's need to depend on Charlemagne merely to hold his office. For Charlemagne the new title was a suitable recognition for his accomplishments as conqueror and protector of the Christian world. Some of Charlemagne's ecclesiastical advisers felt that such a title would exalt their ruler's authority as a new David and a new Constantine seeking to perfect Christian society. Almost everyone in the West shared the opinion that the emperors of the East had failed to serve the Christian cause, especially in view of the fact that a woman, Empress Irene, held the crown at the moment. It is probably also true that Charlemagne's assumption of the imperial title meant different things to different people. The Byzantine rulers saw it as an outrageous usurpation. The popes, at least in the long run, interpreted the event as a precedent for their right to designate the ruler of the Christian world; in the short run, it was now clear beyond doubt who had the legal power to rule Rome. For many church leaders the event was a signal to intensify the effort to create the ideal Christian commonwealth.

What Charlemagne thought of his new title is likewise an enigma. He ruled as emperor for fourteen years. Some of his actions suggest that he took the title seriously. He conducted a skillful military and diplomatic campaign that finally compelled the Byzantine emperor to recognize him as emperor. He pursued his religious reforms with renewed vigor, suggesting a responsiveness to the political Augustinianism of those advisers who had encouraged him to become emperor. However, he disdained the trappings of the imperial office, and he insisted on being called king of the Franks. Contrary to all that the imperial title implied about the unity of his realm, he made plans to divide his empire in order to provide a "kingdom" for each of his three sons; such a division was avoided because only a single son, Louis, outlived him. In 813 Charlemagne personally crowned Louis emperor without papal involvement. These actions suggest that Charlemagne viewed the imperial title as a personal honor that he had earned by his achievements and that he could dispose of as he pleased. Whatever the case, the event of 800, which translated an ancient title rich in political symbolism into a Germanic and Christian context, was of major significance in creating a western European political consciousness.

3. THE CAROLINGIAN RENAISSANCE

Perhaps the most enduring facet of the Carolingian Age was a reinvigoration of cultural life that owed much to the personal interest and effort of the indefatigable Charlemagne. This revival was based on pragmatic motives. Charlemagne was convinced that political and religious reform could be achieved only through the efforts of better-educated leaders, especially the clergy, who were equipped to extract from the learned tradition of the past what the Carolingians called the "norms of rectitude" that would provide guidance in shaping a Christian renewal of the present world. Because of its focus on the past, especially the Roman and patristic worlds, modern historians often speak of a Carolingian "renaissance." Whatever it is called, the movement represented a radical idea in a society that had almost lost sight of the connection between learning and public order.

A major factor in generating cultural revival was Charlemagne's ability to utilize the intellectual leadership produced by the modest cultural revivals that had occurred earlier in several parts of the West—Italy, Spain, Ireland, and especially England. The setting for the interaction of these leaders was what has been called the palace "school," which the king began to form in the 780s and which took on special vigor in the 790s, after Aachen was established as the permanent royal residence. To this somewhat informal circle came some of the most learned individuals from all over Christian Europe, often with Charlemagne's personal encouragement. The palace school served as a setting where individuals of varying cultural perspectives met to study, write, and reflect on intellectual issues. Because Charlemagne himself was an active and enthusiastic participant, the palace school became a highly visible symbol of the dedication of his regime to revitalizing cultural life; some even spoke grandly of Aachen as the "new Athens."

More significantly, the palace school became a kind of laboratory, generating ideas and techniques out of which emerged an educational system that was crucial to the Carolingian renaissance. A key figure in shaping this educational program was Alcuin (735–804), an English monk reared in the monastic cultural environment that had produced Bede and Boniface. Alcuin served at the royal court from 782 to 796 and then became abbot of an important monastery at Tours, where he continued to assert leadership in cultural life until his death in 804. His concepts of education decisively shaped the thinking and practices of cultural leaders across the entire ninth century and even beyond.

Alcuin, and with him most Carolingian cultural figures, saw education as a preparation for understanding the holy literature that contained God's message, from which must be drawn the norms of rectitude that alone could guide the revitalization of Christian life: the Bible, the writings of the Church Fathers, the liturgical books, canon law texts, saints' lives. To comprehend the message of salvation contained in these texts, people must master Latin and acquire a body of knowledge and intellectual skills that would allow them to grasp their meaning. These objectives could best be achieved by organizing education around the old Roman system of the seven liberal arts, which consisted of two basic groupings of "disciplines": the *trivium*, embracing grammar, rhetoric, and dialectic (logic); and the *quadrivium*, comprising arithmetic, geometry, astronomy, and music.

The realization of these educational goals in their culturally impoverished world confronted Carolingian leaders with major challenges. They needed to provide textbooks for each of the seven arts, but especially for the *trivium*, which emphasized language study, effective writing, and logical thinking. The material for such textbooks was to be drawn from classical Latin literature, but textbook compilers had to adapt such material to Christian purposes. Once learners had mastered the skills and knowledge embraced in the seven liberal arts, then they needed to apply their minds to the texts containing true wisdom. This objective raised the problem of the quality and availability of books. A major effort was devoted to establishing authentic versions of Scripture, liturgical books, texts defining ecclesiastical and secular laws, writings of the Church Fathers, and even pagan Latin texts and Germanic legends. Once scholars had established sound texts, accurate copies had to be made. This need encouraged the development of workshops, called *scriptoria*, where book copying was systematically pursued; such work was particularly appropriate for Benedictine monks and nuns seeking to meet their obligation to serve God by working. Concerned with making reading easier, Carolingian copyists developed a simple but effective system of handwriting called Carolingian *minuscule*, which replaced the almost illegible Merovingian cursive writing with separately formed lowercase letters. The formation of libraries was also encouraged so that good texts would be widely available.

As the tools of education were forged, Charlemagne and his successors employed royal authority to universalize their use. Bishops and abbots were commanded to organize schools and to adopt authentic texts as a basis of teaching. This effort resulted in a significant increase in the number of schools and a heightened concern for the quality of teaching. Many bishops and abbots became active collectors of libraries and organizers of *scriptoria*. Although the palace school had declined in importance by the end of Charlemagne's reign, his successors remained active patrons of culture. However, during the ninth century cultural leadership passed to new centers, especially monastic schools, which effectively sustained the thrust of cultural revival even in the face of political decline.

Although Carolingian educational reform

had only a limited impact on the massive illiteracy afflicting all levels of society, it did have significant consequences in shaping an environment more favorable to learning than had existed since late Roman imperial times. The concern with language instruction led to the development of a simplified, flexible form of Latin that became the standard means of literary expression over much of the West. The effort to establish authentic versions of a wide variety of texts created a substantial base of knowledge on which a common intellectual life could be erected. That effort also reestablished contacts with the learning and literature of classical Rome and the patristic age; almost all surviving versions of classical Latin literary works date from the Carolingian period. The capacity for clear thinking and effective writing was considerably improved. Taken together, these developments established the base on which a creative, independent western European intellectual and literary life would eventually develop.

A measure of the impact of the Carolingian renaissance can be found in the literary works produced by leading Carolingian writers and scholars. One court luminary and longtime confidant of Charlemagne, Einhard (ca. 770–840), produced an excellent biography of his master; many other writers tried their hands at biography, especially saints' lives. An Italian, Paul the Deacon (ca. 720–799), wrote a *History of the Lombards* which reflected the capacity of Carolingian writers to produce historical works. Alcuin, Bishop Hincmar of Reims (ca. 806–882), and many others produced lively letters reflecting the major concerns of the age. Theodulf (ca. 750–821), a Spaniard, was but one among many who composed poetry. Several clerics, including Bishop Jonas of Orléans (ca. 780–843), composed books intended to guide princes which reflect considerable sophistication in political thought. A succession of theologians prepared impressive commentaries on Scripture and compiled significant tracts on specific doctrinal points; especially notable as theologians were Hrabanus Maurus (ca. 780–856), abbot of Fulda, and John Scotus Erigena (ca. 810–877), an Irishman who lived in Francia from 850 to 875. Even lay society was affected by the cultural revival to the point where some nonclerics were able to produce literary works of some distinction; not the least was the noble lady Dhuoda, whose handbook prepared to provide moral guidance for her son reflects her good education, her considerable literary talent, and her excellent grasp of Christian precepts. Although most Carolingian scholarly work was derived from earlier works, it did reflect an ability to interpret tradition in terms applicable to contemporary issues. That dimension of Carolingian learning can be grasped only when one observes in detail how the light of learning played on and shaped the efforts of kings, bishops, abbots, scholars, and even lay nobles to cope with a myriad of problems facing the age.

The forces unleashed by the effort to renew Christian life and culture stimulated artistic activity. Carolingian art borrowed from diverse traditions: classical, Byzantine, Germanic, Celtic. The age produced several impressive churches; the most unique was the one built by Charlemagne at Aachen. That octagonal structure, strongly influenced by Byzantine churches in Ravenna, reflects an effort to make architecture a link between religion and the ideology of royalty. The mosaics and frescoes created to decorate churches and the miniature paintings used to illustrate manuscripts reflect skill in producing narrative art, especially in visually reconstructing episodes from sacred history. Carolingian artists produced fine ivory carvings, metalwork, and jewelry, much of which was employed for liturgical purposes. Underlying most Carolingian art was a powerful urge to deepen religious understanding and promote piety. In this respect, art shared the basic urge that sustained the entire Carolingian renaissance.

4. THE DISINTEGRATION OF THE CAROLINGIAN EMPIRE

The religious revival and the cultural renewal initiated by Charlemagne retained their momentum for most of the century after his death. However, his political achievements were less permanent, leaving many unresolved issues for his successors. His son, Louis the Pious (814–840), continued his father's policies with some success. His chief energies were devoted to realizing the ideal of a unified Christian society governed according to Christian principles. In pursuit of this end he formed a close alliance with powerful churchmen that was dedicated to solidifying the unity of the realm, extending religious reform, and deepening cultural renewal. But Louis's course, basically aimed at perfecting ministerial kingship in a direction that magnified the role of the clergy and the centrality of religious values in shaping political life, met resistance from important elements in society which saw political life primarily in terms of advancing the interests of the powerful. Consequent tensions laid bare the basic weaknesses of the Carolingian system.

The most disruptive problem during Louis's reign involved the question of succession. As we have already noted, ancient Frankish custom demanded that a ruler divide his realm among his surviving sons. With minor exceptions—which were resolved without major disturbances—the Carolingian rulers did not have to face the issue of multiple heirs until the reign of Louis. In the face of this problem, Louis's intention, expressed clearly in a document issued in 817, was to preserve the unity of the empire by entrusting the imperial title and authority over the entire empire to his eldest son, with the younger heirs receiving subkingdoms. Throughout the rest of his reign Louis was forced to compromise his plan in the face of intrigue, factionalism, and even civil war fomented by his younger sons, by their noble supporters, and especially by his second wife, Judith, who was anxious to protect the interests of her son by Louis against the claims of his half brothers. On Louis's death his oldest son, Lothair, did succeed to the imperial title but with only a very vague authority over his two younger brothers, each of whom received a kingdom. The pretext of imperial unity lasted only briefly. Shortly after Louis's death, the younger sons declared war on Emperor Lothair and in 843 forced him to sign the Treaty of Verdun. This document legalized the division of the empire into three independent entitites: the kingdom of the West Franks (roughly modern France), to be ruled by Charles the Bald; the kingdom of the East Franks (roughly modern Germany), assigned to Louis the German; and the kingdom of Lotharingia (Lothair's realm), a narrow band lying between the western and eastern kingdoms and stretching from the North Sea to Italy (see Map 16.2). The Treaty of Verdun provided that the ruler of the middle kingdom would hold the imperial title, but his authority over the other

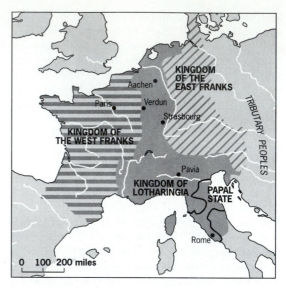

Map 16.2 PARTITION OF THE CAROLINGIAN EMPIRE, 843 This map shows the divisions of the unified Carolingian Empire arranged by the sons of Louis the Pious at the Treaty of Verdun in 843. The kingdom of Louis the German (the Kingdom of the East Franks) and the kingdom of Charles the Bald (Kingdom of the West Franks) became the bases from which Germany and France would evolve. Lothar I's kingdom was later divided into three small kingdoms, the most important of which was the Kingdom of Italy.

kings was only nominal. Later in the ninth century the middle kingdom was further divided to create three kingdoms: Italy, Burgundy, and Lotharingia. With the passing of time the imperial office lost all meaning except to the papacy, which used it to reward anyone willing to protect papal interests in Rome.

The struggles surrounding the succession issue revealed another threat to imperial authority. Louis found many of his royal vassals ready to desert him and to align themselves with one or another of his sons in return for additional benefices. This situation revealed that Charlemagne's widespread use of vassalage and benefice to create bonds of loyalty to the ruler had its dangers. The granting of land and offices to vassals as a means of winning or holding their political support began to diminish royal property, the basic source of support for the government, and to weaken royal control over public admin-

FIGURE 16.2 The Viking Terror This representation of Viking ships filled with fierce warriors illustrates why they struck terror into those who witnessed the vessels approaching their undefended shores. One senses that the artist had witnessed such a scene. (Culver Pictures)

istration. Such benefices became the basis upon which recipients expanded their independence without concern for the obligations they owed. Their growing power allowed them to demand new grants in return for service, thus creating a vicious cycle that undermined royal authority and expanded the power of the landed nobility.

During Louis's reign another ominous danger emerged: mounting attacks from external foes. From bases in North Africa came assaults by sea by aggressive Moslems called Saracens, who ravaged the coasts of Italy and southern France. From the east the empire was attacked by still another wave of invaders from Asia, the Magyars or Hungarians, skilled at hit-and-run attacks by mounted warriors. Most formidable were the Vikings or Norsemen (Danes, Swedes, and Norwegians). Still barbarians and pagans,

the Vikings lived along the wild coasts of Scandinavia, surviving chiefly by fishing and piracy. Late in the eighth century, for reasons not entirely clear, they began to expand. Traveling by sea in small groups, they raided an immense area, touching Ireland, England, the Atlantic coast of Europe, the southern shores of the North and Baltic seas, Russia, Iceland, Greenland, and even North America (see Figure 16.2). Wherever they went, they pillaged for booty and struck terror into their victims. Gradually some of them began to settle permanently in the lands they had been raiding, especially Ireland, northern England, Iceland, a region in northwestern France called Normandy after them, and the area in Russia around Novgorod and Kiev. Slowly their piracy gave way to trade and they adopted the religion and culture of western Europeans. But that was too late to spare the Carolingian Empire from the destructive fury of this last wave of Germanic invaders.

The Carolingian military establishment, organized primarily for attack warfare on land and completely lacking in naval forces, was helpless against these highly mobile marauders. The only effective way to deal with them was to organize local defenses under local leaders willing to assume that responsibility and capable of acting on their own. By assuming this burden, nobles greatly expanded their control over local political affairs. From Louis the Pious onward, kings had no choice but to reward these individuals for their military role with additional grants of land and authority, a process that further undermined royal power.

During the last half of the ninth century royal authority in each of the Carolingian kingdoms steadily declined. The energies of their rulers were absorbed in rivalries aimed at snatching territory from one another. They had no choice but to continue seeking the support of the powerful in society by granting new lands and conceding political power. As a consequence, the landed nobles tightened their control over local territories, creating increasing numbers of independent principalities and forcing the peasantry into dependence. Invaders continued to pillage western Europe almost at will. The most persistent defenders of royal power were ecclesiastical officials, but in the long run even ecclesiastical support worked against the interests of the Carolingian monarchs. Constantly mindful of the important role Charlemagne had attributed to religious leaders in creating Christian order, later Carolingian churchmen became bolder and bolder in their attempts to control the shape of public policy. Frankish bishops repeatedly challenged royal authority and criticized royal conduct. By the middle of the ninth century the pope was openly claiming superior authority over all Christians, including kings and emperors. Pope Nicholas I (858–867) actually tried to assert such claims by interfering in the private lives of Carolingian kings, negotiating to halt civil strife, legislating for the entire Church in the West, taking the lead in spreading Christianity, and doing battle with Byzantine emperors over dogma and jurisdiction—all activities that Charlemagne had claimed to control as ministerial king and em-

peror. And even while expressing lofty sentiments about their role as protectors of Christian order, high church officials joined lay nobles in increasing their landholdings and political power over local affairs at the expense of the royal government.

By 900 the Carolingian rulers had been reduced to impotence. The effort to create, in western Europe, a single Christian state where concord and justice prevailed had foundered. However, this failure must not hide the deeper significance of the Carolingian era. The redefinition of the nature of the state and of the role of the Christian ruler, the religious reform, the cultural renaissance, the revival of empire, the expanded role defined for the papacy, and the expansion of personal bonds as an element of public order would all affect the future shape of western European society. Much of later medieval history consisted of working out the concepts about civilized life given embryonic form in the "first" Europe shaped in Carolingian times.

5. ANGLO-SAXON ENGLAND

While the Carolingians were attempting to renew society on the Continent, active rulers and their followers were pursuing comparable ends in England. The Anglo-Saxon invasions of England in the fifth century had virtually wiped out Roman civilization. Latin culture, including the language, had been replaced by Germanic culture and religion. The newcomers established several small kingdoms whose political institutions were almost completely Germanic. These kingdoms constantly warred with one another to create a condition almost as chaotic as that prevailing on the Continent between 500 and 750.

The introduction of Christianity into this divided society provided an important impetus to the development of a common culture. Late in the sixth century missionaries from Ireland and Rome went to England and within a century had converted most of the land. For a brief period in the seventh century, Roman and Irish forces clashed over the right to dominate England. The Roman forces won, chiefly because of the support offered by the Anglo-Saxon kings. This victory ensured uniformity in ecclesiastical organization, ritual, and doctrine and put England into touch with the mainstream of Continental religious life. The encounter of Irish monasticism and Roman Benedictine monasticism generated a vigorous cultural revival in England, that reached its zenith in the age of Bede in the early eighth century. As already noted, that revival also produced leaders such as Boniface and Alcuin, who helped shape the Carolingian revival and who strengthened the ties between England and the Carolingian world.

During the eighth and ninth centuries, England suffered devastating blows from the Vikings. Some of these raiders occupied a large area in northeastern England known as the Danelaw (see Map 16.1). The Viking raids also destroyed several of the old Anglo-Saxon kingdoms. The kingdom of Wessex became the center of resistance and eventually of counterattack against the Vikings. The reign of Alfred the Great (871–899) was the decisive moment. He not only stopped Viking expansion but also laid the groundwork for the reconquest of the Danelaw. Under his leadership religious and cultural life was revitalized. During the tenth century, Alfred's successors rewon the Danelaw and in the process created a unified kingdom for England.

The unification of England led to a single political system that was heavily influenced by ancient Anglo-Saxon institutions. A king, claiming to be supreme judge, army leader, head of the religious establishment, and lawgiver, ruled over the kingdom. Royal authority was supported by the household officials who constituted the royal court. The king supported himself and his court chiefly from the income from royal estates. However, he could levy direct taxes on his subjects; for example, several kings collected the Danegeld, a tax first levied in 991 to buy off Viking raiders. The monarch retained the authority to summon all freemen to serve in the army (called the *fyrd*). He could also depend on the military services of his noble retainers, called *thegns*, whose support was won by grants of land. He

was advised on matters of public interest by the *Witan*, an assembly of great nobles and churchmen that was held to represent all freemen. However, a strong king could act without this body's approval. This complex of institutions surrounding the king made the central government of England a significant force in public life, much more so than the late Carolingian monarchs were.

A crucial factor in the political order was the system of local government that had developed over a long period. The kingdom was divided into territorial units called *shires*, of which there were about forty in the tenth century. In each shire the king's interests were represented by three officials—the earl, the sheriff, and the bishop. The earl was the most notable in rank and prestige, but the sheriff conducted most of the royal business. A court was held in each shire twice a year, and all free individuals were expected to attend. Royal orders were proclaimed and all civil and criminal cases were adjudicated at this court. Although Anglo-Saxon kings could and did enact laws binding on their subjects, the law administered was primarily customary law, dating from far back in Anglo-Saxon history and "remembered" by the influential members of each shire. Each shire was subdivided into *hundreds*, where courts presided over by a royal official met monthly to settle minor cases; the hundreds also provided the basis for recruiting military forces for the *fyrd*. Agricultural villages also had their own courts, usually conducted by landowners. This network of local institutions, providing a means by which royal authority could be applied at the local level, acted as a buffer against the emergence of private political power and political fragmentation so characteristic of the Continent in the tenth century.

Although by the eleventh century the Anglo-Saxon political order began to falter, the pattern of institutions created in the ninth and tenth centuries provided a heritage that would play a major role in shaping a unique English constitutional system in the future.

SUGGESTED READING

The Carolingian World

The works of Wallace-Hadrill, James, Duby, Doehaerd, Hodges, and Herrin listed in Chapter 15 provide material on Carolingian history. The following titles treat special aspects.

Donald Bullough, *The Age of Charlemagne*, 2nd ed. (1973). An excellent general overview of Carolingian civilization.

Pierre Riché, *The Carolingians: A Family Who Forged Europe*, trans. Michael I. Allen (1993). A good political history.

Rosamond McKitterick, *The Frankish Kingdom under the Carolingians, 751–987* (1983). Especially helpful on the later Carolingians.

Pierre Riché, *Daily Life in the World of Charlemagne*, trans. Jo Ann McNamara (1978). Rich in details on Carolingian life.

Robert Folz, *The Coronation of Charlemagne: 25 December 800*, trans. J. E. Anderson (1974). A balanced treatment of a disputed subject.

Hubert Jedin and John Dolan, eds., *Handbook of Church History*, Vol. 3: *The Church in the Age of Feudalism*, trans. Anselm Biggs (1969). A detailed treatment of religious life.

Rosamond McKitterick, *The Frankish Church and the Carolingian Reforms, 789–895* (1977). A good assessment of Carolingian religious reform.

John Marenbon, *Early Medieval Philosophy (400–1150). An Introduction* (1983). Places the Carolingian intellectual achievement in a larger historical context.

J. Hubert et al., *The Carolingian Renaissance* (1970). A magnificent treatment of Carolingian art.

The Vikings

Gwyn Jones, *A History of the Vikings*, rev. ed. (1984).

P. H. Sawyer, *Kings and Vikings: Scandinavia and Europe, A.D. 700–1000* (1982).

Two excellent treatments of Viking history and the Viking impact on the European world.

Anglo-Saxon England

Peter Hunter Blair, *An Introduction to Anglo-Saxon England*, 2nd ed. (1977).

P. H. Sawyer, *From Roman Britain to Norman England* (1978).

Two concise, clearly written surveys of Anglo-Saxon history.

H. R. Loyn, *The Governance of Anglo-Saxon England, 500–1087* (1984). Excellent on Anglo-Saxon political institutions.

Sources

Two Lives of Charlemagne, trans. Lewis Thorpe (1969). Contains the famous biography by Einhard.

P. D. King, *Charlemagne: Translated Sources* (1987). A good sampling of the Carolingian cultural achievement.

CHAPTER 17
Lordship and Dependency: Feudalism and Manorialism

FIGURE 17.1 The Bastion of Local Lordship: The Medieval Castle Castles such as this one were built over much of western Europe during the eleventh and twelfth centuries as centers from which local potentates and their armed vassals could assert lordship over the surrounding countryside and its inhabitants. This castle, Château Gaillard, built in the late twelfth century on a cliff above the Seine River by King Richard of England to protect his Norman fiefdom from his feudal overlord, the king of France, was virtually impregnable. Outer walls (whose ruins are still visible) and a moat protected the inner fortress and its keep. Living quarters, a great meeting hall, and a chapel were built in the inner courtyard of this structure. (Roger-Viollet)

Chiefly as a result of the failure of the late Carolingians to sustain a strong central government and of the devastations caused by the Saracen, Magyar, and Viking assaults, western European society underwent a new era of instability during the late ninth, tenth, and early eleventh centuries. However, amid these difficulties new institutional patterns began to move to the forefront. This new order was the fruit of a complex process which since the end of the Roman imperial order had been transforming the basic relationships that defined political, social, and economic life. The result of this process became manifest about 1000 in the form of new human communities. The restructuring of society took a variety of forms across western Europe, thus making any attempt at generalization difficult and even misleading. But everywhere certain key patterns emerged that together would provide the basis for a remarkable revival of western European society after 1000.

1. LORDSHIP AND DEPENDENCY

As we have seen, one of the notable features of the western European world during the early Middle Ages was the inability of political leaders to establish effective central governments capable of exercising authority over large numbers of subjects in the interest of the public welfare. A major consequence of this failure was a slow drift toward the privatization of power in the hands of landholders. This trend was given final impetus in the late Carolingian period by the failure of the successors of Charlemagne to sustain his effort to create a strong state. The partition of the Carolingian Empire after 843 resulted in a diminution of royal resources in each of the Carolingian kingdoms. In their attempts to muster support, the late Carolingian kings slowly granted away their royal holdings to powerful nobles and great ecclesiastical officials; technically such grants were made in return for loyalty and service, but the recipients increasingly disregarded their obligations. The inability of the kings to defend their realms against invaders eroded their prestige and necessitated an increasing reliance for security on local power wielders. Although kingdoms and kingship survived this ordeal, by the tenth century public authority had

become a limited force in the lives of most people in the West.

As public authority disintegrated, a new force emerged as the dominant feature of political life. *Private lordships* controlled by individual landholders replaced the state as the effective directive force in society. These lordships were formed in various ways. In some cases, Carolingian public officials, such as dukes, counts, and viscounts, simply arrogated to private use the public authority associated with their offices as well as the territory embraced in their jurisdictions. In other instances, aggressive landowners, with the support of armed followers, forcefully seized control of a territory and imposed their private rule on its inhabitants. Often the key to the success of such lords was their control of castles as the focal points of their military power (see Figure 17.1); thus, they are often referred to as *castellans*. In still other cases, enterprising nobles fashioned lordships out of lands they owned or gained through marriage alliances or received as benefices for services rendered to others under the terms of the feudal contract, which will be examined later. But whatever the means, the results were the same: the fragmentation of kingdoms into a mosaic of private lordships in which powerful individuals exercised control over those who lived within their principalities. Some of these lords occasionally paid a shadowy allegiance to the impotent kings within whose kingdoms their lordships lay, but in reality each was "king" in his own principality.

The development of lordship was accompanied by the spread of *dependency* in various forms. Since late Roman times a variety of forces had been at work to encourage or compel individuals to place themselves in a position of dependence on other individuals under conditions that regulated their political, economic, and social interactions on a private basis beyond the sphere of public authority. By the tenth century almost everyone, including many who exercised some kind of lordship, was a dependent in some form. The conditions of dependency varied enormously from place to place and from person to person. However, two broad categories existed to determine the status of most dependents.

First, some lived in a condition of noble dependency. A prime requirement for those who succeeded in creating and then sustaining independent lordships was military force. To provide this force, lords gathered around themselves armed followers who were willing to provide military service in return for material considerations sufficient to allow them to live a life befitting their warrior status. In some cases, lords supported their retainers as a part of their households, but more often military followers were given grants of land from which a living could be derived. As we shall see, the conditions governing the relationships between lords and followers came to be institutionalized in forms that defined a unique way of life for those involved. Although armed retainers were originally drawn from all levels of life, by the tenth century they along with their lords had come to claim a special status for themselves as nobles.

Second, the bulk of the population lived in a condition of servile dependency. In a world where almost everyone from the most powerful to the lowliest depended on agriculture for a livelihood, those who exercised lordship and their noble dependents required a peasant labor force to till the soil from which power and wealth were derived. They gained it by asserting their jurisdiction over the peasant population in a way that compelled peasants to perform a range of menial services related to agricultural production and to render dues to the lord. The reduction of the peasantry to dependency had been evolving over many centuries, powerfully abetted by the unsettled political conditions that had forced the peasants to seek security at whatever cost. By the tenth century the dominance of the powerful had become nearly complete, subject to almost no controls by public authority. In the process of establishing domination over their servile dependents, lords had in many cases congregated their peasants into village communities to expedite effective management of their labor and the exaction of dues. As was the case with noble dependency, by the tenth century the conditions governing servile dependency had assumed institutional forms that gave stability and permanence to the system.

2. THE COMMUNITY OF THE POWERFUL: THE FEUDAL ORDER

By the tenth century the relationships among the powerful—the lords and their noble dependents—were defined and controlled by a variety of interlocking forces whose impact varied from place to place and time to time. On rare occasions, the community of the powerful might be influenced by the commands of the king in whose realm they lived. Some whose lordships were derived from possession of a former royal office sought to employ the powers inherent in those public offices to define their authority over their noble dependents. All members of the community of the powerful shared the Christian religion, which set forth certain precepts about social behavior. Powerful kinship ties shaped the concerns and actions of all members of the community of the powerful. In short, by 1000 the community of the powerful drew its solidarity from a variety of forces.

In many places in western Europe—although not everywhere—relationships among the members of the dominant warrior class were given a special configuration by a set of institutions called *feudalism*. Over the centuries this term has been given so many ambiguous meanings that some historians question its usefulness in describing the medieval sociopolitical order. However, certain practices associated with it can serve to highlight certain concepts of fundamental importance to the order prevailing in the community of the powerful.

The essential practices associated with tenth-century feudalism grew out of the merger, over the course of many centuries, of two practices with roots in both the Roman and the Germanic worlds: personal dependence and shared rights in land tenure. The confusion and chaos in western Europe following the Germanic migrations encouraged the spread of these ancient institutions. In search of strong protectors, many were willing to enter a *commendation* agreement, which established a personal bond linking the two individuals—often called *lord* and *vassal*—to each other in a way that was mutually useful. Likewise, those in search of a livelihood or a way to enlarge their holdings were willing to accept the use of another's land in return for some kind of service. The lands involved in such grants, called *benefices*, remained the property of the grantor and could thus be made without diminishing one's basic holdings. The Carolingian rulers relied heavily on commendation and benefices to solidify control over their subjects and to support their military forces, thereby expanding these practices across a much broader spectrum of society and giving them status in public law. In many cases, kings also granted their vassals *immunities*, which forbade royal officials to interfere in the governance of their benefices, increasingly called *fiefs*. With the breakdown of royal power after about 850, those seeking to establish private lordships utilized these practices as a means of creating military followings. They gathered around them a circle of followers who agreed to serve as vassals in return for fiefs that gave to each vassal the use of land and a labor force that would provide the basis for status, wealth, and security. Feudal usages took deepest root in the heartland of the Carolingian empire—the land between the Loire and Rhine rivers; from there these practices spread in modified forms to southern France, England, Germany, Spain, southern Italy, and the Holy Land.

Central to the arrangements creating the lord-vassal bond was the establishment of a mutually binding contract between two free persons. The ritual that evolved to mark entrance into such a contract provides a convenient key to the nature of the feudal bond (see Figure 17.2). By a voluntary act called *homage* (after the Latin world *homo*, "man"), one man knelt before another, placed his hands between the other's, and declared himself willing to become his "man," that is, his vassal. Whereupon the second lifted up the first and gave him a kiss signifying that he as lord accepted the other as his man. To solidify the lord-vassal relationship thus established, the vassal then swore an oath of *fealty*, binding himself in the sight of God to be faithful to his lord. The lord then gave his new vassal a token material object symbolizing *investiture* with a fief, that is, something of value in the form of a piece of land, an office, or a money stipend which the vassal could use to support himself. By the acts of homage, fealty, and investiture, two individuals bound themselves together in a way that gave each rights and imposed on each obligations through which their political and social interactions were controlled. By the tenth century the lord-vassal relationship had become hereditary, ensuring that the bonds would continue within the same families for generations.

The specific rights and obligations of lords and vassals were slowly elaborated over time in a special legal system called feudal law. Although feudal law varied widely across western

FIGURE 17.2 The Feudal Contract: The Act of Homage This scene pictures the basic act creating the feudal contract—the act of homage by which the kneeling men became vassals of the seated lord. (Archive of the Crown of Aragon, Barcelona/MAS)

Europe, certain rights and obligations binding on each party in the contract were fairly standard.

The feudal contract established the lord's right to command his vassal's services and to expect obedience from his vassal; in this sense, the lord exercised authority over his vassal. He retained important rights over the fief he had granted to his vassal for the latter's use. The lord was obligated to protect his vassal and to provide him justice—to use his army to defend his vassal against attacks and to maintain a court where the vassal could receive a hearing for any grievances. Put briefly, the lord had the grave responsibility of running a small-scale government to serve the mutual needs of himself and his vassals.

The vassal also had important rights and obligations. He was entitled to the use of the fief and the respect of the lord. In return, he was expected to conduct himself honorably and loyally toward his lord. More specifically, a vassal owed his lord four basic obligations: first, *military service*, which required the vassal to serve at his own expense as an armed knight for a specified length of time each year, usually forty days; second, giving *counsel*, usually defined as compulsory attendance at the lord's court; third, payment of *aids* in the form of money payments in certain specific situations (ransoming the lord, the knighting of the lord's eldest son, the marriage dowry of the lord's eldest daughter); and fourth, *hospitality*, which involved entertainment of the lord and his entourage when the lord visited the fief that the vassal had received. In addition, the vassal was obliged to respect certain usages, called feudal *incidents*, reflecting the lord's rights in the fief and its transmission to the vassal's heirs.

The enforcement of the terms of these private contracts posed constant problems, especially in a society lacking effective public authority. In fact, lords and vassals had to settle disputes surrounding rights and obligations themselves. The chief instrument was the lord's court, where the custom governing the feudal contract was applied as law. A lord could summon to his court any of his vassals accused of infidelity to be judged by the vassal's "peers"—other vassals of the lord—and, if found guilty, to be punished as custom dictated. To this same court every vassal could bring complaints against his lord or his fellow vassals; again, his peers decided whether he had redress. Despite this machinery, force was always the final recourse, with the result that feudal society was plagued by constant petty wars fought to force fulfillment of obligations and to gain redress for violation of rights. It would be wrong, however, to picture lords and vassals as seeking any opportunity to start a brawl. In a society lacking effective means of keeping order, both lords and vassals were often willing and even anxious to observe the terms of the contract that served their mutual interests.

The elements involved in the feudal contract provided the basis for the formation of communities among the powerful. An individual with land at his disposal was able to form a circle of vassals made up of individuals willing to provide specified services to their common lord in return for fiefs that allowed them to meet their material needs on a basis befitting their status. By fulfilling the obligations implicit in the contract binding the lord and his vassals, all of the members of such groupings were able to provide defense and justice for themselves and security for their property and those who tilled it.

How large could such circles be? In theory, an entire kingdom might constitute a single feudal community. At the top of such a theoretical community stood the king as supreme lord, who could divide his kingdom into large fiefs he would then grant to nobles, who became royal vassals in return for services commensurate with the size of the fief. By a process known as *subinfeudation*, each royal vassal could then subdivide his fief to create a second layer of vassals, who in turn could repeat the process until the entire kingdom was subdivided into fiefs just large enough to support a single warrior vassal. From such a process would emerge an orderly hierarchy in which each successive layer of vassals owed allegiance and service to a lord standing one step higher in the hierarchy.

In reality, there were limits on how large communities based on feudal bonds could be. In trying to provide fiefs for too many vassals, a lord ran the danger of depleting his landed resources to the point where he deprived himself of the means of compelling his vassals to render the services they owed. The larger a community based on feudal usages, the more vulnerable it became to disruption by individual vassals who by attaching themselves to several lords acquired sufficient fiefs to create a resource base large enough to permit them to defy all of their lords. Communities of the powerful based on feudal ties were most effective when they involved limited numbers of mutually interdependent warrior nobles concentrated within a small geographical area and directed by competent lords who knew how to compel or persuade their vassals to meet their obligations. Historians are still engaged in trying to reconstruct the relationships governing the working of such communities. Their inquiries leave no doubt that the bonds of lordship and noble dependence did provide a basis for order among limited circles of powerful figures and their servile dependents that restored some semblance of stability to western European society.

Beyond shaping the compact circles of lords and vassals within which order could be maintained, the practices and concepts undergirding feudal arrangements brought into sharp focus a special ethos and style of life that gave distinction to the lords and their noble dependents as a social class. Although the evolution of the western European nobility involved factors reaching back to the Roman and Germanic worlds, the conditions that surrounded lordship and noble dependence finally brought into focus the functions that defined noble status. That group consisted of those capable of engaging in warfare at their own expense using the resources derived from land under their control. Collectively, that group claimed responsibility for protecting and governing society. Although those who enjoyed this distinctive status constitutued a small portion of the total population, the nobility was by no means a closed caste during the tenth and eleventh centuries. In their eagerness to build followings to support their power, lords were willing to accept as vassals free individuals from the lower levels of society who were willing and able to perform miltiary service; such individuals were even attractive as sons-in-law. Since vassalage brought material rewards and status, such individuals were eager to accept it.

The values associated with nobility, reflected with special force in medieval vernacular literature (see Chapter 22), stemmed chiefly from what was vital to sustaining the bonds of lordship and vassalage: loyalty, bravery, faithfulness, generosity. Above all else stood prowess—the ability to excel in warfare. The life of a noble centered on a career of fighting for his lord, his lands, his family, his dependent peasants—and his God. In early youth, he began to learn his craft as an apprentice in the service of someone who already knew the art of warfare, often his father's lord. The culmination of his education was his knighting, an elaborate ceremony surrounded by religious symbolism that climaxed with his receiving the tools of war; these were used often during his adult life. Of course, he had to sustain himself as a warrior, so the management of the lands received as a fief constituted a part of his vocation. And he had a political function stemming

from his position as the vassal of another and probably as lord over still others.

The life of the tenth-century nobility was crude and rough, in part because of the primitive level of economic life and in part because of the habits and mentality of its members. The typical noble residence was a wooden fortress designed for defense rather than comfort. The living quarters were crowded, sparsely furnished, cold, without sanitary facilities, and lacking in privacy. The routine of life featured pursuits typical of male warriors: heavy eating, drinking, gambling, hunting, dancing, wenching, and warfare. Nobles were usually illiterate, "reading" by listening to tales of war sung by bards and to the simple preachings of the priests. Marriage was arranged with an eye toward gaining new lands, more vassals, and stronger lords; seldom was it marred by considerations of sentiment. But the family was another matter, for a household rich in strong sons and nubile daughters was a great asset in a world of war, land acquisition, and personal relationships. Most families shared inheritance with all members of the nuclear family and placed emphasis on maintaining ties with an extended kinship group. Nobles were religious in a simple way: They trusted God to take care of them if they met their obligations as warrior lords and vassals. Their way of expressing their faith was active, impelling them to do something visible to show their piety—build a church, give land to a monastery to ensure prayers for their souls, go on a pilgrimage, or fight for God.

The community of the powerful was dominated by males. Women were accorded inferior legal standing. They were usually excluded from the ranks of lords and vassals; their social status reflected that of their fathers and husbands. Their marriage, the crucial event in determining on whom they would be dependent most of their lives, was controlled by males seeking to enhance family status in a world dominated by warrior landholders. Unless they betook themselves to a convent, unmarried women were a liability to their families. Noble daughters were married young, often to men much older. This situation, coupled with the dangers of warfare, often resulted in widowhood and the burdens of protecting the interests of minor children. But despite their general subservience, women played important roles in sustaining noble society. In a world where concubinage was common, it was the legal wife of a noble male who bestowed legitimacy on those eligible to share the family wealth. Women took an active part in directing the household servants, who produced most of what was needed to sustain the noble household. On occasion, women managed fiefs when their husbands were absent and adjudicated disputes involving their husbands' vassals. Their dowries—over which they maintained control—were often crucially important in expanding the landholdings their husbands could exploit. Women were frequently called upon to witness legal transactions involving land transfers, suggesting an involvement in sustaining the family fortune and a knowledge of the substance of that fortune.

3. THE COMMUNITY OF THE SERVILE: MANORIALISM

The community of the powerful concerned chiefly with warfare and governance rested on an agricultural base. Members of the nobility exercised control over parcels of land of varying sizes that each noble had to exploit in order to sustain himself and his family and to fulfill the complex obligations implicit in noble status. To exploit those lands, the nobility imposed another order of dependency on the peasantry of western Europe. This system, sometimes called the *seigneurial* system, was shaped over a long period out of elements rooted in Germanic and Roman economic and social institutions. By the tenth century the essential features of the system were in place: Each noble had imposed on the peasant inhabitants of the land he controlled an organizational structure that allowed him to command their labor, take a portion of their produce, and govern them. Although agricultural structures varied from place to place, many lords, especially those living in the highly productive area stretching from southern England across northern France and western Germany into northern Italy, organized their land into one or more large estates called *manors*.

The manor was an economic unit organized to produce everything needed by its seigneur and his dependent peasants (see Map 17.1). It was also a political and social unit that provided for the governance of the peasants living there and defined their relationships with their seigneur and with one another. The typical manor's size was determined by the requirements of self-sufficiency. A workable manor required a balanced combination of arable land for raising cereal crops, meadowland for animal support, and woodland for fuel and building material. The seigneur usually reserved one-third to one-half of the arable land as his *demesne*, from which he took all of the produce for his own support. The rest was divided into tenancies, called *mansi* or *hides*, each large enough to support a peasant household. The products of meadows, pastures, wastelands, and woods were shared in common by the manorial community. Under the widely used *open-field* system, the tillable land was divided into large, unfenced plots whose cultivation required extensive cooperation among the peasants. Each open field was subdivided into strips. The seigneur reserved a third to a half of these strips in each large field as his demesne; the tenancy of each peasant was made up of strips located in each open field. To protect the fertility of the soil, part of the land was left idle each year. During the tenth century a *two-field system* of rotation was widely used, with half of the manor's tillable land seeded each year while the other half was left idle. Most peasants supplemented the return from their tenancies with vegetables grown in small, well-fertilized gardens near the huts in which they lived. Yields on most manors were small, discouraging the keeping of animals that could lighten human labor, such as horses and oxen, which were heavy consumers of grain and hay. However, pigs, poultry, and goats, which could live by scavenging in the woods and wastelands, were common.

Since there was little trade in the tenth century, most manufactured goods were made on the manor. Although specialized artisans such as blacksmiths and carpenters plied their trades on some manors, ordinary peasants generally made and repaired equipment, buildings, and furnishings. Women, including noble ladies, made clothing, preserved food, and concocted medicines. Only a few crucial items, such as metals, salt, and wine, came to most manors from out-

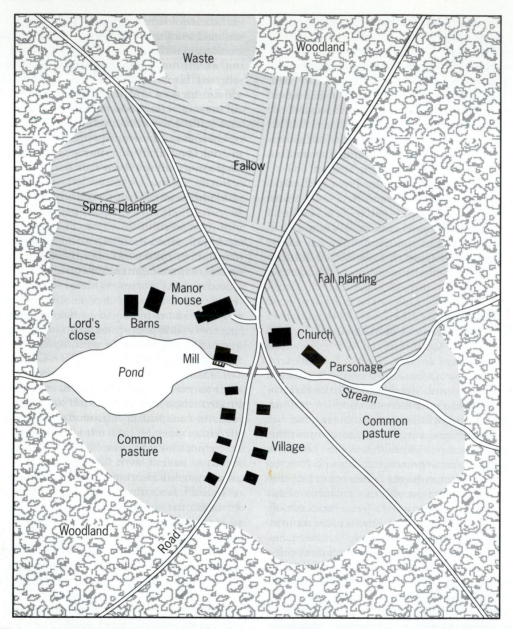

Map 17.1 A HYPOTHETICAL MEDIEVAL MANOR This drawing shows how a medieval manor might have been laid out. It will help identify the major components of a medieval manor as described in the text: the seigneur's manor house, the church, the village settlement, the three-field and strip systems, the commons, the woods, and wasteland. All of these components were required to make the manor self-sufficient.

side. Perhaps from time to time an itinerant merchant arrived offering to sell the seigneur or his lady such luxuries as spices, jewels, or fine cloth; so also did a peddler with trinkets for peasants and their wives.

The center of the manor was a village containing the seigneur's manor house, peasant huts, a church and cemetery, granaries, a mill, a bakery, and a brewery. Each village was more than a collection of buildings; it was a vital human community with a governing system and a social order. Its governor was the seigneur, who exercised the power to command, judge, and punish his dependent peasants with virtually no interference from any authority beyond the manor. If he lived on the manor, the seigneur exercised his lordship in person. If he lived elsewhere—as many nobles with numerous manors did—he entrusted control of the manor to *stewards* and *baillifs*, usually recruited from the peasantry. Although force provided the means of control of last resort, seigneurial overlordship was exercised chiefly through the manorial court. In this court the law of the manor, consisting of a body of custom defining every aspect of the relationships among those involved in manorial life, was applied to impose discipline on the peasantry and to allow individuals to gain recourse for damages done to them.

The peasant population of a typical manor included individuals whose legal status ranged from slave to free individual. But most were *serfs,* who were legally bound to the soil but who also held a tenancy from which they could not be dispossessed. Thus, a serf was legally unfree but possessed both a precious right in a piece of land that ensured his livelihood and a place in a community that provided protection and a court of law through which rights could be protected. Serf status was passed on by inheritance, as was the tenancy to which a serf was attached. Powerful forces were at work in the ninth and tenth centuries among both seigneurs and peasants to merge slaves and free individuals into serfdom.

More important to peasants than their precise legal status were the obligations they owed their seigneur. These obligations, defined by manorial custom, varied greatly over Europe, but everywhere certain dues were imposed on peasants. Their chief obligation was labor service. On most manors serfs were required to spend three days a week tilling the demesne of the seigneur. In addition, they might be required to do extra days of work during the planting and harvesting seasons and to maintain roads and buildings. Often these labor obligations extended to the serfs' wives, who were required to perform such duties as spinning, cleaning, and preparing food in the seigneur's household. In addition to labor services, most peasants owed their seigneur some portion of the produce of their tenancies, which provided the seigneur with an important supplement to the produce of his own demesne. Peasants had to pay a tithe to support the local church; often tithes found their way into the seigneur's hands. Fees were assessed for the use of the manorial mill, bakery, and brewery—facilities the seigneur alone could afford to build and over which he maintained a monopoly. The seigneur collected a death tax from each peasant household when the tenancy passed from father to son and a tax from any peasant whose daughter married outside the manor. There were also, of course, fees and fines to be paid by peasants involved in litigation in the manorial court.

This system obviously provided the seigneur with many opportunities to enrich himself at the expense of the peasantry, and many exploited these opportunities to the fullest. There were however, limits. The seigneur was wholly dependent on the peasants for the one prime ingredient of the manorial economy—labor. Without peasant labor the seigneur's land would go uncultivated and his wealth and status in the noble world would diminish. There was no other source of labor. The seigneur thus had to act with some restraint toward his laborers if he hoped to get efficient and constant work from them. Peasants were in a position to damage the interests of an oppressive seigneur by willful neglect of crops, buildings, and animals or by calculated mischief. Killing, maiming, or even irritating peasants in the interest of exacting more from them might be more costly than just treatment according to custom. The weight of custom, which tended to fix obligations over long periods, acted as a powerful brake on rapacious seigneurs.

Peasant life in the ninth and tenth centuries was brutally harsh. At best, the manorial system provided a livelihood at subsistence level. Crop failure, sickness, or warfare could erase the thin margin separating subsistence from famine and death. Too many children could overtax the meager supply of food that could be extracted from a tenancy of fixed size (see Figure 17.3). The seigneur or his agents were always at hand, seeking any spare wealth. The simple, one-room, scantily furnished huts offered little comfort. Nor did the monotonous diet of bread, soup, beer, cheese, and eggs, with an occasional bit of meat, fish, or fruit. Yet there were compensations. The religious establishment, represented by the local priest, was ever present, offering solace in the face of life's hardships, including charity at especially desperate moments, and the hope of a better life beyond this world. Its ministrations at life's crucial moments—birth, marriage, death—helped to give dignity and significance to human existence, even in the midst of squalor and poverty. Membership in the village community provided the psychological security that stems from living among people long and intimately known. That same community provided an array of simple pleasures, often occasioned by the numerous religious holy days—beer drinking, gaming, singing, dancing—all capable of easing the burden of a life of bare subsistence.

FIGURE 17.3 A Peasant Family This miniature shows a peasant, his wife, and their two infant children. The scene suggests both close and affectionate family ties and the burden of children in a world of poverty. (Photothèque Armand-Colin, from Bibliotheque Nationale, Paris)

4. THE CHRISTIAN COMMUNITY IN THE WORLD OF LORDSHIP AND DEPENDENCY

During the late ninth and tenth centuries the complex processes at work to put into place a system of lordship and dependency posed new kinds of problems for the religious establishment. These difficulties resulted largely from the entanglement of religious officials in the world of lordship and noble dependency. By the ninth and tenth centuries, the ecclesiastical system held an immense amount of landed property. Its holdings were attached to bishoprics, monasteries, and individual churches and administered by bishops, abbots, and priests. Part of its possessions had come from gifts from the faithful, but much had been acquired in the form of fiefs

granted by kings and other powerful laymen, who expected church officials so favored to render services as any other vassals did. In order to protect their holdings in a world where self-help was the key to survival, ecclesiastical officials acted like other lords. They granted church lands as fiefs in return for military and political services and thus became lords in their own rights. Like their lay counterparts, ecclesiastical property holders forced the peasants on their lands into a servile condition and gave full attention to asserting their seigneurial authority. They too had to concern themselves with protecting their vassals, holding courts, and collecting dues. Such necessary concerns directed their efforts away from their pastoral duties. Lay leaders refused to invest any bishop or abbot with a fief unless he had the qualities of a good vassal, including military prowess and loyalty to the lord rather than to the Church as an institution. In effect, this system meant that secular leaders gained control over elections to ecclesiastical offices, often filling them with loyal kinsmen or proven vassals with little interest in spiritual matters. Secular lords treated church land received as fiefs as if it were private property, diverting the income to uses that had little to do with spiritual needs. This thoroughly secularized officialdom in control of ecclesiastical offices and property neglected discipline, education, charity, and moral guidance. Members of the lower clergy, usually appointed and controlled by the lords of the manors where parish churches were located, were unlettered, undisciplined, and undersupported. They tended to live much like the peasant population with whom they associated, marrying, raising children, and sharing the pleasures of the manorial community. They were constantly tempted to traffic in religious services in return for money. The level of religious life in lay society deteriorated badly; superstition, moral laxity, and corruption of ritual practices abounded. To some contemporary pious souls, especially those who harbored some sense of the original Christian community or even those who remembered the Carolingian reform effort, religious life had become a scandal worse than had ever been seen. Mammon had seemingly triumphed over God!

While recognizing the abysmal condition into which the Christian community had sunk, it remains necessary to note another dimension of the position of the religious establishment in the world of lordship and dependence. Its involvement in that world drew it more directly than ever into contact with the basic institutions and dynamic elements of society. Its leadership shared the mentality and felt the needs of western Europe's warrior aristocracy and peasantry. Such involvement prepared that leadership to shape a religious order that was responsive to reality. Even in the midst of a genuine religious crisis, evidence of that response began to surface. Clerical writers began to explore the theoretical implications of a social structure based on three orders, each with a special social responsibility: those who prayed, those who fought, and those who labored. The religious establishment gave the feudal contract a religious dimension by making the oath of fealty a key element in establishing the relationship binding two men together. Christian moral concepts began to shape a code of behavior known as *chivalry* that befitted the warrior life (see Chapter 18). Ecclesiastical leaders instituted two practices aimed at curbing violence in feudal society. One, called the Peace of God, sought to restrain acts of war against certain categories of people (the clergy, women, children); the other, called the Truce of God, tried to prohibit warfare during certain periods holy to all Christians (Sundays, major holy days, Lent). A monastic reform beginning in the tenth century, known as Cluniac monasticism (see Chapter 21), encouraged certain practices of piety that appealed strongly to the warrior nobility. The grouping of the peasantry into organized villages provided a setting for the development of a parish structure through which the Christian population could be reached. Thus, despite the institutional and spiritual disarray caused by the worldliness of the Christian establishment, its immersion in the world of lordship and dependency provided new arenas where it could assert its influence over the development of European society.

The tenth-century world of lordship and dependency, of dominant warrior landlords and subservient peasant laborers, does not usually receive a sympathetic evaluation. The record affirms the potential of such a system for violence and oppression. Not nearly so clear except to those who investigate in detail what happened in tiny areas to tiny groups of people is the potential of that same system to create effective order. Taking all the evidence into account, it seems safe to conclude that the system of lordship and dependency played a fundamental role in preparing a backward society for a new outburst of creativity. That system shaped small communities of people capable of concerted, disciplined action. These new groupings created a situation requiring collaborative action among peoples of different social status and talents. These collectivities nurtured capabilities that were especially suited to attending to western Europe's porous frontiers and exploiting its chief resource, its underutilized lands, forests, and rivers. It is not coincidence that western European society began a spectacular period of growth *after* the system of lordship and dependency was established.

SUGGESTED READING

Lordship and Dependence

F. L. Ganshof, *Feudalism*, trans. Philip Grierson, 3rd ed. (1964). Stresses the legal aspects of feudalism.

Marc Bloch, *Feudal Society*, trans. L. A. Manyon (1961). A classic, approaching feudalism from a sociological perspective.

Perry Anderson, *Passages from Antiquity to Feudalism* (1978). A Marxist perspective on feudalism and its origins.

Guy Fourquin, *Lordship and Feudalism in the Middle Ages*, trans. Iris and A. L. Lytton Sells (1976). Provides insights into how power was exercised in the feudal world.

Jean-Pierre Poly and Eric Bournazel, *The Feudal Transformation, 900–1200* (1990). Good on the formation of lordships.

Timothy Reuter, ed. and trans., *The Medieval Nobility. Studies on the Ruling Classes of France and Germany from the Sixth to the Twelfth Century* (1978). These essays provide conflicting views on the origins and role of the medieval nobility.

Georges Duby, *Rural Economy and Country Life in the Medieval West*, trans. Cynthia Postan (1968). The best work on manorial economy; provides translations of medieval sources.

Robert Fossier, *Peasant Life in the Medieval West*, trans. J. Vale (1988). A balanced treatment.

Pierre Bonnassie, *From Slavery to Feudalism* (1991). Examines the end of slavery between 500 and 1200.

Philippe Contamine, *War in the Middle Ages*, trans. Michael James (1984). Treats an important aspect of feudal society.

RETROSPECT

In a letter written in 593 or 594, Pope Gregory I called his contemporaries' attention to the strife, suffering, destruction, and injustice seen everywhere. "See what has befallen Rome, once mistress of the world," he mourned. "What is there now, I ask, of delight in this world?" In a way, Gregory's lament reflected an element of truth about the history of the early Middle Ages if one limits his or her attention to western Europe. Much of what had characterized Greco-Roman civilization had been lost there, and society was poorer. One can easily write, as many have, the history of the early Middle Ages in terms of the destruction of classical civilization and the onset of a dark age.

However, from a larger perspective much happened between A.D. 500 and 1000 to replace what had been lost. Three new civilizations—Byzantine, Islamic, and western European—had been shaped within the confines of the classical world. Each retained precious elements of the old order. Each developed new institutions and ideas to suit its needs and situation. An inventory of what people had fashioned in these difficult centuries gives ample evidence that these "dark" years deserve a decisive place in the continuum of history. By 1000 there were still "things of delight" in the world.

The emergence of three new civilizations was not the only transformation that occurred during the early Middle Ages. In addition to the creative forces at work within each, a new dynamism had developed in the form of interactions among these civilizations. The Greco-Roman world had tended to absorb existing cultures into a unified pattern that stood counterposed to the barbarian world. By 1000 lines of interaction and points of tension existed among civilized societies rather than between the civilized and uncivilized orbits. This situation was of decisive importance in shaping the future of each new society.

The period just reviewed belonged to the East; Byzantium and Islam far surpassed western Europe in every respect. This little-appreciated fact demands attention, for the accomplishments of the Byzantine and Islamic worlds in these centuries gave their peoples a proud sense of contribution to the creation of civilized life that other societies later forgot. None benefited more from the achievements of these leaders than the struggling western Europeans, whose future glory would have been different had it not been for what they absorbed from the East.

PART FOUR

THE CENTRAL AND LATE MIDDLE AGES, 1000–1500: THE RESURGENCE OF EUROPE

As the end of the first millennium of Christian history approached, some predicted that in fulfillment of ancient prophecy the world would end. In fact, the passing of that date did mark the end of the old world, but not in the way apocalyptic visionaries anticipated. As a result of a revival in western Europe during the period 1000–1300, sometimes called the central Middle Ages, the underdeveloped society of the early medieval world was transformed to create a vibrant order that elevated western European civilization to a new position in a world setting.

The sudden upsurge of a formerly backward society is not easy to explain. But as our account of the effervescent, creative centuries from 1000 to 1300 unfolds, there can be no doubt that growth was rooted in the foundations established in the old world that was supposed to end. The institutions connected with lordship and dependence, the religious establishment, and the treasure of learning stored up by Carolingian scholars provided basic patterns of organization, social control, thought, and belief that permitted men and women to apply their energies toward new ends: producing greater wealth; constructing larger political entities; shaping more complex class structures; creating new forms of thought and expression; exploring new spiritual realms; thrusting outward from their beleaguered world into new geographical areas.

Although this sustained burst of creativity enriched western society in every respect, it eventually reached its limits. During the fourteenth and fifteenth centuries a succession of challenges for which existing institutions could not provide instant solutions temporarily disrupted the development of western European civilization. The eventual response to that crisis of the late Middle Ages provided the impetus to western Europe's continued advance in the early modern era.

CHAPTER 18
Economic and Social Revival, 1000–1300

FIGURE 18.1 Medieval Farming This miniature used to illustrate an English psalter shows peasants plowing their fields. It indicates that medieval agriculture was a cooperative effort: Peasants combined their labor, draft animals, and equipment to till the manor fields. The heavy moldboard plow was a major technological advance of the Middle Ages: It was especially efficient in cutting through and turning over heavy soils. Producing yields sufficient to feed both people and livestock was a major problem. (The British Museum)

Throughout the early Middle Ages a major deterrent to growth was the severely limited and constantly uncertain level of material resources available to western European society. Between 1000 and 1300 that situation was dramatically changed by a major economic expansion accompanied by significant adjustments in the social order. These changes had their source at the base of society. Their agents were modest seigneurs, toiling peasants, peddler merchants, and simple artisans, whose collective efforts provided the material means that made possible the more spectacular accomplishments of the central Middle Ages in politics, religion, and culture.

1. POPULATION GROWTH

The forces that generated economic growth after 1000 were complex. However, one contributing factor is evident: The population of western Europe increased substantially between about 900 and 1350. This demographic change, reversing a decline that had extended from late antiquity until the Carolingian age, resulted in a doubling of the population of western Europe; one generally accepted estimate suggests that the population grew from about 35 million in 900 to about 70 million in 1350. Modern demographers do not yet fully understand the causes of this growth. There is some evidence that during this period Eurasia was relatively free from killer diseases, especially bubonic plague. Perhaps the curbing of the more destructive aspects of warfare and the availability of more and better food contributed. Some have even suggested that the prospects of a better society encouraged people to have more children. Whatever the causes, the simple fact was that for three centuries a constantly expanding population put pressure on the agricultural system for greater productivity and provided a larger work force that could be turned to new enterprises.

There remains a whole series of fascinating and important problems associated with the effects of population growth on the structure of medieval society. For example, it is clear that the population growth was not uniform across western Europe, but the geographic pattern and the regional impact of growth have not yet been clearly established. Neither is it clear how growth affected different age groups and social classes. The impact of increasing population on life expectancy, marriage patterns, size of households, and child rearing is still poorly understood. Virtually all one can say is that population increase affected all these matters so vital to people's lives. A better understanding of these issues will undoubtedly make it more obvious that population growth was a major dynamic force changing western European society during the central Middle Ages.

2. AGRICULTURAL EXPANSION

The most important aspect of economic growth between 1000 and 1300 was expansion of agricultural production. The manorial system, with its reservoir of managerial ability, disciplined labor force, and technical skills, provided the base for growth. At least five factors were involved in expanding on that base.

First, western Europe's climate improved during this period, especially in northern Europe. Milder winters, longer growing seasons, better distribution of rainfall, and fewer violent storms and excessive variations in temperature all combined to create an improved setting for agricultural pursuits.

Second, a large amount of land was put under cultivation for the first time as a result of an immense effort devoted to land clearance and peasant resettlement. Much of this land clearance involved pushing out the boundaries of existing cultivated areas, which in the early Middle Ages stood as isolated, often overpopulated islands of cultivation in vast stretches of forest. Now the forests were cleared, swamps were drained, and land was even recovered from the sea. In addition to this internal expansion European cultivators, organized by enterprising landlords, moved great distances to settle on virgin or underutilized land on the frontiers of western Europe. The chief areas of colonization were the German frontier east of the Elbe River, the Spanish lands being wrested from Moslem control, and southern Italy. It appears that the cultivated acreage in western Europe nearly doubled between 1000 and 1300.

Third, technological advances greatly increased the efficiency of the labor force, especially by supplying new sources of power. The adoption of the horseshoe and the development of new harnesses, especially the shoulder collar, permitted the more efficient horse to replace the ox as a draft animal. Although known since Roman times, water mills and windmills finally came into common use and were improved by the development of complicated power trains which allowed the motion from these mills to be applied to such tasks as grinding grain, sawing timber, and processing wool for cloth production. Traditional agricultural tools—plows, spades, hoes, scythes—were improved by more effective practices of metallurgy. Especially important was the increasing use of the wheeled, moldboard plow, which could cut through and turn over the heavy soils of northern Europe (see Figure 18.1). One suspects that these advances owed much to the ingenuity and experience of simple peasants searching for ways to make their labor easier and more productive. Whatever the cause, the result was greater productivity and the freeing of human labor for other productive uses.

Fourth, agricultural production was increased in quantity and variety by improved methods of tillage and animal husbandry. Irrigation systems were developed in some parts of western Europe. Increasing opportunities for exchange encouraged agricultural specialization, as in the vineyards of Burgundy and the great sheep-raising granges in England; such specialization not only brought variety to the productive system but also allowed for a much more efficient use of diverse types of land than cereal production did. Greater attention was given to the use of animal waste for fertilization. Of special significance was the spread after 900 of the three-field system of crop rotation to replace the traditional two-field system. Under this new system the tillable land on a typical large estate was divided into three open fields. Every year and in rotation, one field was left fallow, a second was planted in the fall with wheat or rye, and a third was planted in the spring with barley, oats, or legumes (such as beans or peas). Not only did the three-field system put more land under cultivation each year, it also improved the human diet by making available high-protein foods, such as beans, to supplement the mostly carbohydrate diet of earlier times and provided oats

to feed the increasing number of horses used as prime beasts of burden. Better seeds were developed to take advantage of local soil and weather conditions. And improvements in animal breeds produced better animals and more animal products, such as meat and wool.

Finally, entrepreneurship played a part in expanding agricultural production. Planning was required to free labor to clear new lands, to organize peasant resettlement in distant places, to apply new tools and techniques, and to launch specialized production. Ingenuity was involved in finding ways to dispose profitably of excess production. Innovative thinking was required to develop new seeds and improved livestock strains. The surviving medieval record tells us little about such matters, but entrepreneurship, exercised in small and undramatic ways, must certainly have been a key to one of the great advances in the history of agriculture.

Inadequate evidence makes it difficult to quantify with any accuracy the overall magnitude of the growth of agricultural production between 1000 and 1300. However, in crude terms the consequences are beyond doubt. The increased amount of land under cultivation and higher yields permitted everyone to live better and produced a surplus of food, which left more people free to devote their energies to activities other than subsistence agriculture. That critical difference made possible significant changes in all aspects of the society of the central Middle Ages.

3. THE REVIVAL OF TRADE AND MANUFACTURING

The expansion of agricultural production after 1000 stimulated the revival of trade and manufacturing. Trade had never entirely vanished from the western European scene, but it had declined steadily from late Roman times, so that by 1000 it was a minor factor in the total economic life of western Europe. Neither had manufacturing totally disappeared, but during the early Middle Ages manufacturing was restricted to the manorial setting, where only a limited range of products needed for local self-sufficiency was produced. During the late tenth and early eleventh centuries, a revival began in both commerce and manufacturing; it continued until the mid–fourteenth century. During this era commerce became the catalytic force in European economy, and new forms of manufacturing emerged to provide an expanded range of products for exchange. Among the factors contributing to the commercial and industrial revival were population growth, agricultural expansion, greater political order, outside stimuli, and western European political, military, and religious expansion. But to these must be added the labors and enterprise of men and women whose activities are for the most part only vaguely known to us.

In considerable part, commercial expansion was a story of the ability of western Europeans to gain a share of the flourishing commercial activity in the Byzantine and Moslem worlds (see Map 18.1). Beginning in the tenth century, Italian cities took the lead in expanding trading endeavors in the Mediterranean area. The Venetians steadily enlarged their contacts by sea with Constantinople and brought an ever-increasing volume of goods to the West. In the eleventh century Pisa and Genoa used their navies to loosen Moslem control over the western Mediterranean, and their merchants established trade relations with the Moslems in Spain and North Africa. As a result of the success of the early crusading movement (see Chapter 20), Italian cities established important commercial footholds in the Moslem world in the eastern Mediterranean. The conquest of Constantinople in 1204 during the Fourth Crusade gave the Venetians virtual control over Byzantine trade, especially in the Black Sea area. By the thirteenth century the efforts of Italian merchants were being reinforced by other traders from coastal cities in France and Spain; collectively they had become the dominant commercial force in Mediterranean trade. Nor were they content with their new commercial sphere of influence; already by 1300 European merchants were exploring trading opportunities in central Asia and China. The lifeblood of this international trade was luxury items, especially spices and fine cloth.

Meanwhile, another window to the East was opened on the northern and eastern fringes of Europe by Viking pirates. Their raiding ventures opened a path through the Baltic Sea and along the rivers of Russia to the Black Sea and Constantinople. Traders from many areas of northern Europe eventually followed the Vikings along this route, opening a vigorous exchange between the Baltic–North Sea area and Constantinople and the eastern Mediterranean. Eventually this northern trading zone began to develop a commercial life of its own, marking a major expansion of European commercial enterprise. The focal point of this northern trading complex came to be the cities of Flanders.

No less important than international trade was the growth of trade within Europe. In part, that growth was a result of the efforts of aggressive Italian and Flemish merchants to provide increasingly prosperous aristocrats with luxury goods. Their activities created an ever-widening network of routes, especially following the river systems of Europe, that eventually covered most of Europe. During the twelfth century, the chief meeting places of international traders were the fairs of Champagne in France. Here merchants from all over Europe came to display their wares to other merchants, who in turn carried their purchases to local markets and prize customers (see Figure 18.2). By the thirteenth century the fairs were increasingly giving way to permanent markets established in cities.

Complementing the traffic in luxury items was an ever-growing exchange of goods between formerly self-sufficient manors and villages and the growing towns. Local trade in such items as salt, wine, and metals had always existed. From the eleventh century onward, it broadened to provide the growing towns with foodstuffs and raw materials and to carry manufactured products of the towns back to the rural settlements. In volume and number of people involved, the local town-country exchange undoubtedly exceeded international trade.

The expansion of commercial activity in western Europe promoted the growth of manufacturing. By the twelfth century the towns began to offer opportunities for skilled artisans to make a single product for sale to their fellow townspeople and rural buyers or to merchants who distributed them wherever there was a demand. Artisan manufacturing, centered on the workshops of individual craftsmen, long remained a vital element of the town economy and put a vast

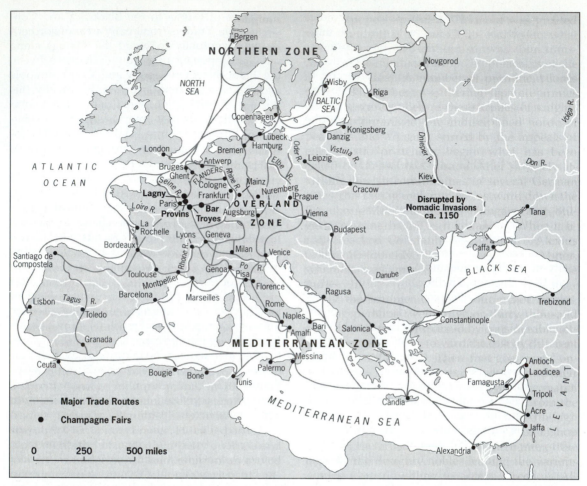

Map 18.1 **TRADE ROUTES, TWELFTH AND THIRTEENTH CENTURIES** This map shows the major trade routes developed during the twelfth and thirteenth centuries to link western Europeans with the East and to join major trading centers within western Europe. The crucial centers for the international trade linking East and West were located in northern Italy, especially Venice, Genoa, and Pisa, and in Flanders, especially Bruges and Antwerp. The internal routes, focusing especially in the towns of Champagne, where great international trading fairs were held annually, spread the products of the East from the Italian and Flemish centers over much of western Europe.

quantity of commonplace goods into the exchange system. By the thirteenth century some areas of Europe, particularly Flanders and northern Italy, had developed more complex manufacturing organizations based on the "putting out" system and "cottage" industry, applied to cloth manufacturing. Entrepreneurs purchased bulk quantities of raw wool raised in England by farmers specializing in sheep raising and transported it to Flanders, where it was processed through a series of steps including washing, carding, spinning, weaving, fulling, and dyeing. Each separate operation was performed by specialized laborers, many of them women, who worked for hire in their own homes. The high-quality finished product was distributed on an

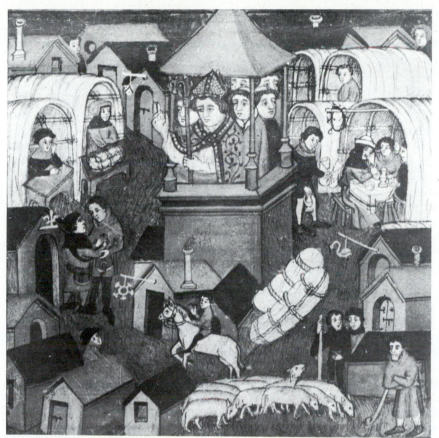

FIGURE 18.2 A Medieval Fair In this scene the bishop of Paris is giving his blessing to various merchants who are waiting for the opening of the fair held annually just outside Paris near the monastery of St. Denis. Such fairs provided a major setting for the exchange of goods from far and near. The presence of a figure so important as the bishop of Paris suggests that these fairs were viewed as a vital part of life. (Bibliothèque Nationale, Paris)

international scale by merchants contracted for by the entrepreneur. A comparable system for woolen production developed in such northern Italian cities as Florence.

There is no way to measure accurately what the revival of trade and manufacturing meant to the western European economy in quantitative terms. It seems safe to venture that by the thirteenth century the volume of trade and industry in western Europe surpassed that of the Greco-Roman world, and probably that of the contemporary Byzantine and Moslem economies as well. Agriculture was still the most important economic element, but the wealth from exchange and craftsmanship made a critical difference in the total economy of the West. Moreover, trade and industry increasingly supplied the dynamism that encouraged continued economic growth and diversification.

4. ECONOMIC CONSEQUENCES OF INCREASED PRODUCTION

The wealth generated by the increased agricultural, commercial, and industrial productivity of western Europe manifested itself in a hundred ways: better houses, bigger churches, more elaborate dress, greater quantities and varieties of food, more art and literature, more leisure. But aside from greater wealth, expanded productivity had more specific results that affected the fundamental structures of economic life.

First, economic growth spurred the growth of cities. Towns had never disappeared from western Europe. But between late antiquity and about 1000, they became primarily ecclesiastical, administrative, or defensive centers, sparsely populated and economically dependent on agriculture. Between 1000 and 1300 many of the old urban centers grew dramatically, and many new towns appeared. By 1300 there were European cities of considerable population: Some Italian towns, such as Venice, Milan, Florence, and Genoa, had populations of around 100,000; Paris may have had 80,000 people; and London had 50,000. The vast majority of medieval cities probably had populations of 10,000 or fewer, but these modest figures should not detract from their vitality. Spread widely across the European landscape and closely integrated with the countryside, these modest centers spurred the local agricultural economy and provided an outlet for excess rural population. More significant than their numbers was the fact that most urban residents earned their livelihood from trade and manufacturing, thus making the "new" urban centers quite different from the economically nonproductive towns of the early Middle Ages.

In terms of physical growth, many important towns of the era were simply enlargements of older episcopal, monastic, administrative, or military centers. Merchants and then artisans were attracted to these centers for many reasons: security, favor shown them by ruling authorities, access to rivers and roads, availability of buyers. Often they settled haphazardly outside the walls of the old center, their shops, stalls, and households creating a *suburb* (Latin for "under the city"). As commercial activity increased, the walls were extended to enclose the suburbs. Often the suburban marketplace became the center of urban life. During the central Middle Ages new towns were often established at locations favorable to commerce, and their physical development resembled that of the old centers.

A second consequence of economic expansion was the emergence of a money economy. Money had always circulated in western Europe, but only minimally until the eleventh century. Thereafter, its use rapidly expanded to meet the needs of commercial exchange and then began to affect agricultural production. The impact of the money economy was revolutionary. A whole new form of wealth emerged to challenge the monopoly held by land. Old economic relationships based on services and payment of obligations in kind were replaced by payments in money. By creating a common standard against which all values could be calculated, money

greatly speeded up the exchange process. Money could be accumulated in a way that labor services and produce could not, and such "savings" could be manipulated endlessly to exploit changing economic opportunities. The possession of money allowed people to specialize their economic activities and still have the means to obtain the full range of material goods they needed. In the face of the impact of an expanding money economy, perhaps it is not surprising that conservative moralists of the era warned with increasing frequency that money was the root of all evil.

A third major effect of economic growth was the transformation of agricultural production. The market for surplus food provided by the towns gave manorial lords and peasants alike money incomes with which they could embellish their lives with products from the town markets. This new potential for profit changed the emphasis on the manors from self-sufficiency to surplus production. Under this pressure the traditional system of servile dependency began to dissolve. The dissolution proceeded in two broad directions. In many areas of western Europe, especially in the twelfth century, seigneurs began to break their demesnes into tenancies which were rented to peasants for cash payments. At the same time, they commuted the labor obligations of their serfs and the dues owed them in kind to money payments. Serfs could afford to buy off their obligations because the town market offered them a chance to sell produce and save a little money. But many seigneurs moved in the opposite direction, expanding their demesne and managing its cultivation themselves, often concentrating on a specialized cash crop. Seigneurs who took this course often displaced peasants from their ancient tenancies, forcing them to work for wages or to seek new livelihoods in the towns. In either case, the old manorial system and servile dependence gradually dissolved over much of western Europe. In its place a variety of forms of agricultural exploitation emerged; all were dominated by the concern for profit, an end that could be achieved only by linking the countryside to the towns, their markets, and their money.

A fourth change nurtured by economic growth involved a new attitude as to the purpose of economic endeavor. No longer were producers content with self-sufficiency; they worked and planned to gain more worldly goods. They began to devise strategies and techniques that would increase wealth: lending money for profit, speculating in trading ventures, manipulating land for gain, saving money. A protocapitalist economic mentality was taking shape that prized economic growth rather than stability.

Finally, western Europeans had achieved such economic growth by 1300 that they had seized economic leadership in the vast area surrounding the Mediterranean—a leadership that would eventually be extended to the whole world. No longer did Byzantium and Islam stand as advanced economic centers to a backward western Europe. As we shall see later, political factors helped the advance of the Europeans, but it is beyond question that their enterprise played a vital role in establishing their economic leadership.

5. SOCIAL CHANGE: THE BOURGEOISIE

The economic growth of western Europe during the central Middle Ages brought major changes to the simple social order characteristic of the world of lordship and dependency. Perhaps the most significant change was the emergence of a new social group, the *bourgeoisie*. The shaping of this group resulted from the efforts of traders and artisans living in towns to define a place for themselves in a world lacking legal or social institutions that fitted their situation. In order to pursue their economic interests effectively, they had to seek various "liberties," or, more accurately, special privileges. Their effort slowly created for them a collective status that distinguished them socially from the clergy, noble warriors, and agricultural laborers.

As soon as men and women began to devote full time to commerce and manufacturing, they felt a basic need for personal freedom. Their livelihood depended on their ability to move about in a world that fixed people to fiefs and manors, to dispose of their property at will in a world where property was bound up in an intricate network of obligations, to apply their talents and labor to whatever opportunity arose in a world where long-sanctioned customs dictated how

people spent their time and efforts. And so the merchants and artisans of the towns struggled for personal freedom, using money payments, force, and persuasion to wring concessions of freedom from kings, lords, and bishops. So successful were they that by 1300 merely to breathe the air of a city for a year and a day meant personal freedom.

Although personal freedom was vital, it was not sufficient. Townspeople needed liberties that would allow them to determine their collective destiny, in terms of both defining relationships among themselves and regulating interactions with those outside their urban setting. To gain these added liberties, they sometimes banded together into associations to seek special privileges from those who had political authority over them and over the space their city occupied. Their efforts often resulted in a written document, called a *charter*, which defined their status and rights as a corporate body. Initially, such charters had to be fought for or purchased at a high cost, but acquiring a charter soon grew easier as kings, lords, and bishops realized the profits to be gained by having a thriving town on their domains. Charters varied greatly in content. The typical charter recognized the citizen body of the town as a corporation that could act legally. Usually charters granted personal freedom to the townspeople and defined what they owed to the granting authority. Finally, charters granted some degree of self-governance. In a few cases, especially in Italy, towns gained complete freedom; such towns were called *communes*. More commonly, the townspeople had only limited privileges of self-government.

In shaping political institutions, the townspeople experimented considerably. In most towns there was some degree of popular participation in political life, authority being vested in an elected council. In a typical commune the council usually possessed complete power to legislate, conduct courts, levy taxes, expend money for civic purposes, and negotiate with outside powers. Its only responsibility was to the citizens of the town. Many towns chose a chief administrative official—*mayor, burgomaster, podesta*—who functioned under the supervision of the council. Judicial affairs were entrusted to specially trained judges. Towns with only limited political freedom often had to respect the authority of a royal official, a bishop, or a representative of a feudal lord who exercised many powers in judicial and financial matters. Whatever the form of government, the towns quickly created an elaborate new body of law regulating civic affairs.

A grave problem in every urban center was the regulation of economic activity among merchants and artisans, a problem for which the rest of society had no solution. The usual answer was the establishment of *guilds* within each town. The merchants of a town often organized themselves into a single merchant guild; the artisans formed several craft guilds, one for each trade. The merchant guild existed primarily to protect the interests of merchants from outsiders and to restrain the members from taking unfair advantage of one another and their customers. Each guild enacted rules governing prices to be charged, trading practices to be observed, and the conditions under which trade could be conducted. The craft guilds similarly imposed regulations on their members concerning prices, quality of goods, conditions of labor, and quantity of production. They also controlled the conditions for entering a trade. Boys began as *apprentices* to a master, working from two to seven years under his guidance and living in his household. The apprentice then became a *journeyman* who worked for hire until he could satisfy the guild that he had developed adequate skill to become a *master.* Along with their regulative functions, merchant and craft guilds had social functions. Each usually had its own guildhall, where banquets, pageants, and religious affairs were conducted for the entertainment and edification of the members. Each guild also aided its members when sickness or death struck a family.

Like their rural contemporaries, city dwellers made technical innovations that aided their economic activities. Market facilities were created to allow the display of goods and money-changing operations. Sound coinage systems were established, especially by the Italian towns, whose coins were used in markets all over Europe. Insurance was developed to protect merchants against losses. Bookkeeping systems were devised to keep track of exchange operations and inventories. Merchants created ways to pool their resources for mutual benefit. Partnerships, called *commenda*, were formed in which one or more merchants provided capital to another merchant to conduct a specific trading enterprise in return for a specified share of the profit. Eventually permanent companies were formed in which investors made deposits and received regular dividends paid by those who actually conducted the business enterprise.

Particularly significant as a means of providing capital to promote commercial and industrial growth was the development of a credit system and of an institution specializing in credit services: the bank. Bills of exchange became available, allowing merchants to deposit money in one place in exchange for a receipt that could be used to pay for goods in another place. Money-lending for interest became common. At least in the early stages of commercial growth, the religious establishment strenuously opposed the lending of money for interest (usury) because it allowed people to profit from the misfortunes of others. Gradually, theologians and canon lawyers conceded that lenders who provided funds for investment in speculative activities were entitled to compensation for the risk. By the thirteenth century large-scale lending operations conducted by banks were a vital part of the economy and a source of great profit; among their best customers were high ecclesiastical officials.

The urban environment allowed greater social mobility than did the worlds of nobles and peasants. Trade and industry provided diverse opportunities for merchants and artisans to use their freedom and their talents to increase their wealth and better their social status. Urban political and guild structures created possibilities for individuals to play a part in shaping political decisions and even to achieve major leadership roles. Women also found a wider range of economic opportunities in the towns than were available to noble and peasant women. Aside from assisting their husbands in trading and manufacturing, women could engage in economic ventures independently. Widows of important merchants often continued their former husbands' trading enterprise. Many women were members of craft guilds and apparently practiced their craft alongside men, although often at lower wages. Although urban life permitted social mobility, in the period 1000–1300 bourgeois society tended to become stratified on the basis of wealth. An oligarchy of rich entrepreneurs, usually merchants, increasingly claimed special status and gained control of city governments and guilds. At the other end of the social spectrum from these patricians was a growing number of poor, exploited laborers who sometimes vented their discontent by rioting.

Perhaps the most tragic victims of medieval urban society were western Europe's Jews. Although during the early Middle Ages Jews were viewed as a unique social group and were subject to special legal restrictions, they were allowed and even encouraged to engage in commercial activity. On the basis of this experience Jews were active participants in the early expansion of trade, earning for themselves not only wealth but also a special place in many cities as a self-governing group centered around their synagogues. But by the twelfth century their situation began to deteriorate. As more Christians began to engage in trade and manufacturing, measures were taken to exclude Jews from these activities, driving them to rely on moneylending as a means of livelihood and causing them to be scorned as usurers as well as adherents of a religion increasingly attacked by a variety of Christian intellectual leaders. By the thirteenth century Christian bankers were taking over moneylending operations, devising whatever means they could to exclude their Jewish competitors from this lucrative business. Increasingly forced out of the mainstream of urban economic life, Jews were impoverished, forced into menial occupations, compelled to live in ghettos and wear distinctive clothing, and often savagely persecuted by kings, urban officials, and ecclesiastical authorities.

The urban environment generated its own cultural needs. Commercial and industrial pursuits required literacy, computing skills, and rational planning. The activities of the markets and shops raised a new range of moral problems and special kinds of spiritual longing. The physical circumstances unique to city life encouraged experimentation in architecture, sculpture, and painting. The interaction of people from many parts of Europe and the world beyond made city dwellers aware of cultural differences and raised questions about the validity of local customs. As a result of all these forces, cities became centers of educational, intellectual, and artistic change.

By 1300 the bourgeoisie was still not a very exalted social group; the nobility looked down on merchants and artisans, ecclesiastical leaders disapproved of many of their activities as immoral, and peasants were suspicious of the sharp practices of the "city slicker." Still, the bourgeoisie constituted a dynamic factor in the social order whose members would play an increasingly important role in shaping the future course of Western civilization.

6. SOCIAL CHANGE: THE NOBILITY

Between 1000 and 1300 the nobility remained the dominant social group, its power and influence still defined primarily in terms of lordship and noble dependency. However, changing economic conditions created new circumstances that affected the status and lifestyle of the nobility.

Land remained the basis of aristocratic wealth and high social status. However, in an expanding market economy the value of land depended less on granting it out in return for noble services than on exploiting it as a source of spendable income. In the face of this new reality nobles made significant changes in their use of land. The pressure to keep holdings intact as a source of wealth led to fundamental changes in inheritance patterns and family structures. The earlier practice of shared inheritance among all members of the family, including women, gave way to inheritance restricted to the eldest son. As inheritance patterns changed, the older extended family system in which descent was marked through both parents gave way to a patrilineal family structure in which noble descent was determined through the male line. Such changes solidified male domination over the noble family and constricted the status of younger sons, wives, and daughters. Even though the new inheritance system kept the family patrimony intact, changing economic conditions required new approaches to land exploitation. As noted earlier, some nobles consolidated their holdings into productive units they managed themselves. Many more abandoned the traditional manorial system to become landlords living on money rents paid by peasant tenants. This last course had its risks. In an age of steady inflation many aristocrats made the mistake of agreeing to long-term leases that provided them with fixed returns whose real value declined over time. As a consequence, their families saw their wealth and social status reduced; some even lost their noble status. Some nobles turned to commercial activities to bolster their wealth, either by extracting money payments from town governments in return for privileges or by investing in commercial ventures. Others associated themselves with the increasingly powerful royal governments as a way of enhancing their prestige and protecting lucrative private political jurisdictions. All these factors combined to bring about a more complex stratification of noble society, to limit mobility within that group, and to put greater constraints on the admission of outsiders.

The expanding economy allowed noble society to enjoy a more comfortable material life; in fact, the quest for material goods became an important objective of noble life and the display of material affluence a measure of status. Stone castles featuring more private chambers, fireplaces vented through chimneys, and improved sanitary facilities appeared all over Europe. The adornment of these residences stimulated aesthetic interests, and the urge to use them as places to display status prompted literary patronage; some nobles even became literate. For a price a typical noble could enjoy a much more varied diet than before, including sugar and exotic spices from the East and fine wine from southern France. A greater variety of clothing was available, especially fine woolens and imported silks.

The improved material standard of living was but one aspect of a subtle refinement of noble life. The essence of the new ethos was reflected in the code of *chivalry* that by the twelfth century had emerged to define ideal noble behavior. Chivalry was rooted in the values of the feudal warrior; it stressed loyalty, bravery, generosity, honor, and military prowess. From the eleventh century on, these values acquired new shades of meaning drawn from the changing realities surrounding noble life in a more affluent age and from Christian concepts that—at least in theory—converted the crude, brutal warrior of earlier times into the knight skilled in the practice of courtly manners. Under the code of chivalry the ideal noble was still defined as a warrior who required an elaborate training in the arts of war-

fare before receiving public recognition as a knight. However, chivalry restrained his behavior. He was now expected to treat knights against whom he fought according to rules of honor. In his conduct as a warrior he was obligated to avoid harming noncombatants (clergy, women, children), damaging church property, and disrupting religious activities. The ideal knight fought only for a "good" cause, such as crusading to spread the true faith or punishing evildoers who preyed on the weak. Under the chivalric code the warrior instinct tended to be channeled into carefully arranged engagements, called *tournaments*, where the martial arts were practiced under strict rules and amid a pageantry that featured mannered behavior more than bloodshed and booty taking.

A particularly distinctive feature of the code of chivalry was the role it gave to women. Whereas the old warrior society valued women little except as bearers of children, sources of dowries, and objects of sexual gratification, the code of chivalry made women objects of devotion, loyalty, and sentimental attachment. A true knight was expected to develop a set of manners that would make his presence pleasing to noblewomen. In aristocratic circles an elaborate code of courtly love encouraged unmarried knights to demonstrate their prowess by winning the love of a noble lady. The pursuit of the love of a lady called for patterns of behavior extending far beyond the ability to wield the tools of war, and it placed a higher value on virtues associated with women: graciousness, the capacity to give love, gentleness. In order to respond to the new attention extended to them, noblewomen were expected to develop modes of behavior suited to a more refined world in which males and females mixed in a courtly setting.

The code of chivalry certainly did not totally transform noble behavior. The twelfth- and thirteenth-century record is full of violence and oppression perpetrated by unruly nobles whose excesses could be effectively curbed only by constraints forcefully imposed by superior lords, especially kings. Whether chivalry improved the status of women remains a disputed question. In legal and economic practice their role remained restricted. The emergence of the patrilineal family structure placed them more surely than ever under male domination. The prime objects of

WHERE HISTORIANS DISAGREE

Origins of the Medieval Nobility

During much of this century historians of the Middle Ages have disagreed in explaining the origins of the medieval nobility, the class which dominated political, social, economic, and cultural life.

Early in this century there was general consensus on an interpretation that was given classic expression by the French historian Marc Bloch in his seminal work entitled *Feudal Society*. Reflecting a view of aristocracy rooted in the Ancien Régime in France, Bloch defined "nobility" as a social class enjoying specific hereditary privileges defined by law. He argued that such a class did not emerge until the twelfth century. Before then there had existed a loosely defined aristocracy, the members of which enjoyed social prominence based on their personal association with royalty and on favors—chiefly land grants and offices—flowing from that connection. This social group was destroyed in the tumult following the collapse of the Carolingian empire. Amid that chaos, "new," "self-made" men enjoying a monopoly on military power used that power to carve out a legally sanctioned position of privilege transmitted by blood. In brief, the European nobility was derived from the aggressive, ruthless feudal warriors.

Recent investigations have raised questions about this explanation. Many historians, especially those influenced by concepts of social structures formulated by social scientists, argue that noble status embraces more than inherited legal privileges. They claim that noble status involves factors such as wealth, power over others, lifestyle, and mental perceptions. Any effort to explain the origins of the medieval nobility that focuses on narrow legal concerns without considering these factors is faulted.

Bloch's thesis has been challenged on another ground. He argued that during the tenth and eleventh centuries there was a break in an established order which created an opportunity for "new" men to forge a unique social status for themselves. But recent historians have shown that in many cases there was biological continuity linking Carolingian noble families to noble families of the eleventh and twelfth centuries. It can be demonstrated that some warrior upstarts entered the ranks of nobility during the tenth and eleventh centuries, chiefly by marrying into old noble families. But their social ascent by attaching themselves to existing noble circles does not support the case for a "new" and different nobility in the twelfth century. The issue of the origins of the nobility must involve the study of noble status in the early Middle Ages.

Further complicating our understanding of the origins of the medieval nobility is a changing view of the relationship between noble status and the warrior element in society. It was once nearly axiomatic that by the twelfth century every warrior—every knight—was *ipso facto* a noble. Historians are no longer quite so positive. There is much evidence to suggest that many knights held an inferior social status. What seems to have been more important than simply being a warrior was membership in a new kind of family structure in which the material resources of each family were transmitted from father to eldest son rather than being divided among all members of the family, as had been the ancient Germanic custom. In other words, noble status in the central Middle Ages originated only with the advent of the patrimonial family structure, which permitted the concentration and transmission of wealth in a narrow circle of families.

Their disagreement on the origins of the medieval nobility leaves historians at a loss in explaining a key source of dynamism in the medieval world: the processes which allowed some people to establish a pattern of dominance over society.

marriage remained the improvement of the economic and political status of the family and the rearing of children who would sustain the family status. Some evidence suggests that the new place defined for noblewomen in the chivalric code required them to be sheltered and protected as sex objects unsuited to participate in the world of work and power. What was important about chivalry was its enlargement of the range of activity proper to noble status. That expanded vision served both to distance nobles from the rest of society and to add complexity to the social function served by the nobility.

Taken together, the forces working to transform the conditions of noble life during the central Middle Ages resulted in the definition of the nobility as a leisured class of gentlemen and ladies clearly distinct from the rest of society by birth, wealth, and modes of behavior. The basic elements developed during the central Middle Ages to distinguish this dominant class survived long after the end of the Middle Ages to determine the norms of genteel behavior and to define the privileges enjoyed by those claiming aristocracy.

7. SOCIAL CHANGE: THE PEASANTRY

The peasantry was also affected socially by the currents of economic change. During the twelfth and thirteenth centuries, there was large-scale freeing of serfs, especially in France, England, Flanders, Italy, and western Germany. Some peasants purchased their freedom; some gained it in return for colonizing new lands and others by leaving the manors for the city. A more important cause was the willingness of manorial seigneurs to surrender their rights to a serf's produce and services for money payments. In much of the West the serf was thus becoming a legally free tenant farmer, enjoying whatever benefits freedom brought but also losing the paternalistic protection the manorial lord had extended.

In a general way, the material life of the peasants improved during these centuries. Their incomes increased as results of their greater productivity and the inflationary trends that caused the prices they received for their produce to rise faster than the value of the obligations they owed. As they gained access to local markets, their diet became better, their health and life expectancy improved, and they were able to enjoy a wider range of products. As might be expected, significant gradations in peasant status emerged as turns of fortune allowed some peasants to acquire the use of more land than others and as some proved to be more skillful and intelligent than others.

Some evidence suggests that as serfdom declined the peasants gained a greater degree of self-determination than they had had when most of them were locked into the manorial structure, legally bound to the soil as a dependent population. Most peasants continued to live in small villages and had few contacts with the wider world. In some cases they banded together to gain special privileges from their political superiors, which allowed them to control some aspects of village life, much as town dwellers—the bourgeoisie—were doing. They also sometimes directly influenced the management of the resources of the local church. Free peasants had more opportunity to decide how they would exploit their rented lands and how they would dispose of their crops. They could leave their villages to take up farming where conditions were more favorable, or they could seek their fortunes as traders or artisans in the expanding urban centers.

However, we must not push too far in assessing the improved lot of the peasants, who still remained at the bottom of the social scale. Perhaps they were even further removed from the top because of the increasing complexity, refinement, and class consciousness of the nobility. Peasants became even more the object of scorn by the nobility, whose members assumed that their elevated status and expanding economic needs gave them the right to exploit the peasantry economically. For the most part, peasant life remained hard, poor, limited, and controlled by the dominant aristocracy. As was the case with the nobility and the bourgeoisie, the basic legal and social patterns shaping peasant life became so solidly fixed during the central Middle Ages that they would persist far into the future.

Taken together, the changes just described changed the face of western Europe between 1000 and 1300. It became more populous, richer, more diversified in productive capacity, more complex in social structure, and collectively stronger. These changes put into place fundamental economic and social structures that would endure for centuries to determine how people lived, worked, and interacted with one another.

SUGGESTED READING

Overview of the Central Middle Ages, 1000–1300

Christopher Brooke, *Europe in the Central Middle Ages, 962–1154*, 2nd ed. (1987).

John H. Mundy, *Europe in the High Middle Ages, 1150–1309*, 2nd ed. (1991).

Malcolm Barber, *The Two Cities. Medieval Europe, 1050–1320* (1992).

Taken together, these well-written works will provide excellent coverage of the period covered in Part Four.

R. W. Southern, *The Making of the Middle Ages* (1953). A brilliant essay, concentrating on the "silent" forces affecting society.

Susan Reynolds, *Kingdoms and Communities in Western Europe 900–1300* (1984). A challenging effort to identify collectivities that shaped society in the High Middle Ages.

Economic History

R. H. Bautier, *The Economic Development of Medieval Europe*, trans. Heather Karolyi (1971).

N. J. G. Pounds, *An Economic History of Medieval Europe* (1974).

Two excellent general surveys of economic history.

Georges Duby, *Rural Economy and Country Life in the Medieval West*, trans. Cynthia Postan (1968).

Léopold Genicot, *Rural Communities in the Medieval West* (1990).

Together these two works will provide a good picture of rural life.

Robert S. Lopez, *The Commercial Revolution of the Middle Ages, 950–1350* (1971). A persuasive defense of an interesting thesis.

Jean Gimpel, *The Medieval Machine: The Industrial Revolution of the Middle Ages* (1976).

Social History

Christopher Brooke, *The Structure of Medieval Society* (1971). Describes the general features of the medieval social order.

The following works treat more specialized aspects of medieval society, as indicated by their titles.

Frances Gies and Joseph Gies, *Marriage and the Family in the Middle Ages* (1987).

Christopher Brooke, *The Medieval Idea of Marriage* (1988).

David Herlihy, *Medieval Households* (1985).

Maurice Keen, *Chivalry* (1984).

C. Stephen Jaeger, *The Origins of Courtliness: Civilizing Trends and the Formation of Courtly Ideals, 939–1210* (1985).

Frances Gies and Joseph Gies, *Life in a Medieval Village* (1990).

Shalamith Shahar, *The Fourth Estate. A History of Women in the Middle Ages*, trans. Chaya Galai (1983).

Margaret Wade Labarge, *A Small Sound of the Trumpet: Women in Medieval Life* (1986).

Mary Erler and Maryanne Kowaleski, eds., *Women and Power in the Middle Ages* (1988).

Constance H. Berman et al., *The Worlds of Medieval Women: Creativity, Influence, Imagination* (1985).

Shalamith Shahar, *Childhood in the Middle Ages* (1990).

Michel Mollat, *The Poor in the Middle Ages. An Essay in Social History*, trans. Arthur Goldhammer (1986).

John M. Carter, *Sports and Pastimes of the Middle Ages* (1988).

Joseph Gies and Frances Gies, *Life in a Medieval City* (1969).

CHAPTER 19

The Restoration of Political Order: The Revival of Monarchy, 1000–1300

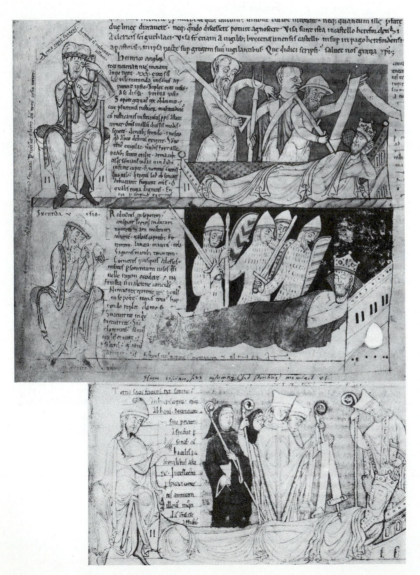

FIGURE 19.1 A Medieval King's Nightmares These drawings from a manuscript portray a dream of Henry I of England. He dreams that his royal power will not be sufficient to control the major elements of his subjects: the peasants, the nobles, and the clergy. Perhaps because he dreamed what he had to face, Henry I was more successful than most of his contemporaries in winning the support of his diverse subjects. (The President and Fellows of Corpus Christi College, Oxford)

While western Europe's lesser men and women were producing new wealth and rearranging their social relationships, its crowned heads and their agents were successfully engaged in rebuilding political structures capable of controlling much larger political communities than the principalities that had dominated tenth-century western Europe. By 1300 their efforts had produced a level of political order in the West that had not existed since the collapse of the Roman imperial regime. No less important, the major political entities created between 1000 and 1300 marked the origins of states that have persisted until the present. Although state building advanced over all of western Europe, we shall focus attention chiefly on political developments in Germany, Italy, England, and France.

The larger and more effective political entities that developed betweeen 1000 and 1300 emerged from shadowy tenth-century kingdoms ruled by weak monarchs whose power had been assumed by lords exercising private authority on a local level. In expanding their power and creating institutional forms to sustain it, successful rulers of the central Middle Ages drew on a rich tradition that defined the role of the state and its rulers: the distant memory of the Roman Empire; Germanic concepts of warrior kings; the Carolingian ideal of ministerial kingship; political theories derived from biblical history, Greco-Roman philosophy, and Roman law; concepts of lordship and dependence imbedded in feudal practices. But in the final analysis the growth of royal power resulted from the sustained creative efforts of individual rulers to take advantage of contemporary political realities.

1. THE HOLY ROMAN EMPIRE

The earliest effort at political reconstruction during the central Middle Ages involved an entity that later came to be known as the Holy Roman Empire. This state emerged from the combination of parts of the Carolingian kingdoms created by the Treaty of Verdun in 843: the kingdom of the East Franks and the kingdom of Lotharingia and its later subdivisions (see Maps 16.2 and 19.1). During the late ninth and early tenth centuries, royal power declined steadily in these kingdoms as local potentates carved out principalities, imposed their lordship over the local population, and joined hands to replace the Carolingian dynasty with rulers selected from local families. In the Kingdom of the East Franks—Germany—that process resulted in the formation of the virtually independent duchies of Saxony, Bavaria, Franconia, and Swabia, each reflecting pre-Carolingian Germanic tribal groupings whose ethnic ties gave each one internal solidarity and each led by a duke who claimed to exercise the public powers originally bestowed on the ducal office by the Carolingian kings. In Italy an even more chaotic mosaic of local lordships emerged at the expense of royal authority.

In Germany the drift toward localism was reversed by Otto I, the Great (936–973), whose father had been duke of Saxony prior to his election to the royal office. In effect, Otto I sought to restore rulership on the Carolingian model. He successfully compelled the dukes to accept royal overlordship, a struggle that led to the replacement of several ducal families with members of his own family. He earned fame as an effective warrior by inflicting a decisive defeat on Magyar invaders of Germany at the battle of Lechfeld in 955 and by encouraging miltary expansion, colonization, and missionary activity eastward into the Slavic world. His success in these ventures stemmed from his ability to strengthen the institutional base of royal power through an alliance with religious leaders. He made large grants of royal land to bishops and abbots, who became royal vassals, obligated to render to the king the military and political services needed to sustain royal authority. This policy, called *lay investiture*, gave the German ruler virtual control over appointments to ecclesiastical offices and the use of ecclesiastical property.

Once successful in uniting and defending his German kingdom, Otto was drawn into Italian affairs. Although the Carolingian example played a part in shaping this fateful decision, Otto turned south for more immediate reasons. Many Italians, including the popes, were looking for an outsider to curb local disorder and to protect them from Saracen and Magyar attacks. Some of Otto's powerful subjects, especially the dukes of Bavaria, were tempted to fish in those troubled waters in search of a power base from which to defy royal authority. After an initial

Map 19.1 **THE MEDIEVAL HOLY ROMAN EMPIRE** This map clearly illustrates the vast extent of the Holy Roman Empire at the death of Frederick I Barbarossa in 1190; it was soon enlarged even more when his successor, Henry VI, took control of the Kingdom of the Two Sicilies as a consequence of his marriage to the heiress to that realm. Not only did the size of the empire but also the ethnic and cultural diversity of its population made its governance difficult. After 1200 the major principalities and cities indicated on the map, especially those in Italy, became increasingly independent.

venture into Italy in 951 that resulted in his assumption of the title "king of Italy," Otto returned a decade later to solidify his position. In 962 Pope John XII crowned him "emperor," thus renewing the office Charlemagne had revived in 800. Otto forced his authority on the Italian nobility and entrusted the exercise of royal power to church officials, who became his vassals. In settling affairs in Italy, Otto I was forced to depose John XII, dictate the election of a more pliant successor, and impose the rule that no pope would be selected in the future without the approval of the emperor. This decision, which opened an era of German domination of the papacy, punctuated the fact that the emperor was the head of the Christian community, just as Constantine and Charlemagne had been.

From Otto I's death in 973 until 1056 his policies were continued with considerable success. In both Germany and Italy nobles were made subservient to imperial authority and their efforts to act independently in their local lordships were checked. The religious establishment continued its invaluable service to the emperor. To complement the administrative functions performed by clerical vassals, the emperors developed a corps of secular officials, called *ministeriales*, recruited from the nonfree population under terms that made them totally devoted to royal service. The empire was expanded by the absorption of the old Carolingian subkingdom of Burgundy-Arles. Poland, Bohemia, and Hungary all recognized imperial overlordship. The emperors and their ecclesiastical supporters skillfully wove around the imperial office a theocratic ideology that stressed the sacred role of the emperor as protector of Christendom, a "renewed" (albeit somewhat smaller) Carolingian Empire in the West that was coequal in dignity to the Byzantine Empire in the East (see Figure 19.2).

But the very success of the German emperors provoked opposition from a variety of sources. The nobility remained eager to escape imperial control whenever possible. Aside from the general dislike of foreign domination felt in Italy, the emerging Italian commercial cities were eager to establish their liberty at the expense of imperial control. Rulers in France and the Slavic world were suspicious of imperial designs on their territories. Following ancient Germanic custom, the royal office remained elective, making it constantly vulnerable to political maneuvering by ambitious secular and religious leaders. Moreover, long-established custom dictated that only the pope could bestow the imperial crown, leaving the German rulers vulnerable to challenges to their exalted place in Christendom. That matter became crucial when the Holy Roman Empire became the focus of attack by leaders of a powerful religious reform movement sweeping over western Europe (see Chapter 21).

By the middle of the eleventh century that reform movement found its leadership in the papacy, which for the previous century had been controlled by the emperors. The turning point came when Emperor Henry III (1039–1056), himself an advocate of religious reform, installed a German bishop, Leo IX (1049–1054), as pope. Under Leo's leadership, a circle of reformers, spearheaded by a monk named Hildebrand (later Pope Gregory VII), articulated the ideological and practical goals of reform. In ideological terms this group rediscovered the ancient tradi-

FIGURE 19.2 The Holy Roman Emperor as "Agent of Christ" This tenth-century ivory plaque shows Emperor Otto I offering a model of the cathedral church of Magdeburg to Christ, who is seated in majesty. It reflects the convictions not only that the emperor controlled the Church but also that he was the intercessor between Christ and the faithful Christians on earth. (The Metropolitan Museum of Art, Gift of George Blumenthal, 1941)

tion that insisted that the Christian community—the Church—is an earthly corporate body that must have its own head, its own law, its own resources, and its own liberty in order to fulfill its divine mission of leading humanity to salvation. By implication secular rulers were denied a role as divinely ordained directors of Christian life; at best, princes were agents of the Church, commissioned by ecclesiastical authorities to assist in directing Christian society and subject to priestly judgment in serving their role. In practical terms, the papal reformers proclaimed the need to purify the religious establishment of whatever impeded its freedom of action, including lay control over ecclesiastical offices and property, and to purge from the ranks of the clergy those who had attained office by lay appointment and who exploited religious offices, property, and services for unholy purposes. Although this radical reform program threatened many secular and ecclesiastical leaders, especially vulnerable was the Holy Roman emperor, who not only manipulated ecclesiastical property and offices to create subservient clergymen who sustained his power but also claimed, by virtue of his exalted office, the God-given right to direct the destiny of Christian society.

During Leo IX's pontificate, the papacy turned reforming ideology into a practical reform program that impinged directly on the existing political and ecclesiastical establishment. The role of the bishop of Rome, the successor of St. Peter as Christ's vicar on earth, as head of the Christian community was vigorously propagated throughout the West, often backed up by papal agents sent to intervene in local ecclesiastical affairs. In 1059 a papal decree provided that henceforth popes would be chosen by the College of Cardinals, a body of ecclesiastical officials centered in Rome who assisted the pope in carrying out papal administration; the emperor was deprived of any voice in papal elections except to approve what the cardinals decided. In that same year the papacy formed an alliance with the Normans, a new political force emerging in southern Italy and Sicily (see Chapter 20), thereby gaining a protector that could serve as a foil to the emperor. The papacy issued a steady flow of legislation seeking to eliminate immorality and corruption afflicting the clergy, a cause that was taken up by papally sponsored local church councils all over the West. That legislative program culminated in 1075, when Pope Gregory VII (1073–1085) decreed that lay investiture—that is, control by lay authorities over the election and installation of ecclesiastical officials and over the property associated with these offices—was illegal; henceforth these matters crucial to the liberty of the religious establishment would be decided from within that establishment. This act put the papacy onto a collision course with most of the kings and lords of western Europe, and especially the Holy Roman emperor, in a contest known as the *investiture struggle*.

Confronted with Gregory's prohibition of lay investiture, the reigning German king, Henry IV (1056–1106), chose to act as his predecessors had in dealing with the religious establishment. In 1075 he filled the vacant episcopal office of the key Italian city of Milan with a candidate of his choice and then defied papal efforts to undo his action. Whereupon in 1076 Gregory VII excommunicated the king, suspended him from office, and invited the Germans to elect a new king. A coalition of German nobles and bishops immediately informed Henry that unless he cleared himself of excommunication before the meeting of an assembly to be held in early 1077, he would be deposed; Gregory was invited to preside over the assembly. Henry's response was tactically brilliant. He went to Italy, where at Canossa he intercepted Gregory, already en route to Germany, and in the garb of a penitent begged the pope's forgiveness. After keeping the king waiting in the snow for three days, Gregory met his priestly responsibility by absolving the repentant sinner. Although the pope had won a moral victory, his action freed Henry to counterattack. During the next few years Henry neutralized his enemies in Germany, captured Rome, forced Gregory into exile, and in 1084 had himself crowned emperor by a pope he installed to replace Gregory.

But Henry's victory was a hollow one. Before his death in 1106 he lost control of Rome to the Normans, saw the reforming party resume control of the papal office, and suffered serious setbacks at the hands of the German nobility. Under his three successors, who ruled until 1152, imperial control in Italy virtually disappeared, usurped by independent towns, nobles, and the papacy. In Germany the royal office became a pawn of warring noble factions that demanded political concessions in return for their support of any candidate for the crown. In 1122 Emperor Henry V did settle the issue of lay investiture by joining the pope in accepting the Concordat of Worms, which provided that the ecclesiastical establishment would control election to church offices and the bestowal of the spiritual powers of those offices while the lands and secular powers associated with such offices would be invested by the king. While this compromise left German rulers with an important role in filling ecclesiastical offices, it deprived them of absolute control over what had long been a mainstay of their power, a subservient clergy willing to serve the ruler's political needs.

More significantly, the long struggle between popes and emperors led to a fundamental change in the power structure of the Holy Roman Empire. The incessant civil strife resulting from challenges to the emperor's authority by the papacy and its supporters created an opportunity for powerful noble families and ecclesiastical leaders to create local lordships over which the royal government had only vague claims of authority and little means of exercising effective control. This development undermined the Ottonian system of royal government, in which royal authority was based on the ruler's claim of being the God-ordained head of the Christian community. Having claimed its liberty, the religious establishment, led by the bishops of Rome, now claimed headship of Christian society, leaving the ministerial king with little upon which to base his right to direct the lordships being shaped in the Holy Roman Empire.

Despite the adverse impact of the investiture struggle, the Holy Roman Empire survived. At mid–twelfth century a new dynasty, the Hohenstaufens, undertook to rebuild imperial government. The first notable Hohenstaufen, Frederick I, Barbarossa ("Red Beard," 1152–1190), charted the new course. To establish an independent material base for royal power, he increased the royal domain, that is, the territory under direct control of the king, and entrusted its administration to nonnoble civil servants who owed their position and loyalty to the king. He also curried the support of Germany's growing cities by conceding liberties in return for financial support. He sought to use these resources as a means of enforcing specific rights over his subjects that he claimed belonged to him by virtue of his office as king and emperor. In general, Frederick's concept of regalian rights was based less on theocratic principles than on secular principles grounded in Roman law and in customs defining lordship and dependency.

Frederick's effort to assert his regalian rights led to a prolonged conflict with a variety of foes. In Germany he sought to collaborate with a few great noble families willing to become royal vassals in exchange for concessions that allowed them considerable power to dominate the lesser nobles in their extensive principalities. But a faction of these nobles, called the Welfs, constantly opposed the king, forcing him finally to break up the large principalities and grant territory to many lesser nobles willing to serve as royal vassals. In Italy an even more potent array of foes, called the Guelfs, faced Frederick. He initially enjoyed the support of the papacy, which granted him the imperial title in 1155, but that relationship soon turned hostile, chiefly because Frederick steadfastly insisted on asserting control over ecclesiastical appointments and property on the basis of rights he claimed adhered to his office. The result was a long battle between emperor and pope, marked by the emperor's attempt to select a pope favorable to imperial interests to replace Pope Alexander III (1159–1181), a true heir of Gregory VII in terms of protecting the liberties of the religious establishment; in 1177 Frederick finally recognized the legitimacy of Alexander, in effect conceding that his imperial office did not entitle him to control the papacy. Throughout this struggle the papacy was supported by the Norman kingdom of Sicily, which remained a constant threat to Frederick's position in Italy until 1186, when he arranged a marriage between his son and the heiress to that kingdom. Especially dangerous to Frederick's position were the rich commercial cities of northern Italy, whose wealth and independence were threatened by Frederick's aggressive efforts to reclaim rights in their governance which he claimed they had usurped. The cities responded by forming the Lombard League, which in 1176 inflicted a serious defeat on the imperial army. Finally, in 1183, Frederick and the Lombard League agreed on the Peace of Constance, which provided that the Italian cities would recognize Frederick's overlordship in return for his concession of specific rights that ensured their control over their internal affairs.

Despite his setbacks and compromises, when Frederick Barbarossa drowned in 1190 while leading the Third Crusade, he left behind the framework for a political system that had the potential to establish effective royal government over his sprawling empire. However, his successors were unable to sustain his program. His son, Henry VI (1190–1197), began his reign auspiciously by successfully claiming the throne of the kingdom of Sicily, acting decisively to check papal attempts to undermine Hohenstaufen power in Italy, and pursuing an aggressive policy that expanded Hohenstaufen influence in the eastern

Mediterranean. However, Henry's early death cut short his ambitious program and plunged the empire into an extended crisis centering around the issue of succession. His only heir was an infant son, Frederick, too young to succeed to his father. Rival candidates representing Hohenstaufen and Welf factions emerged in Germany to claim Henry's inheritance; their rivalry divided Germany into warring camps. The struggle there was complicated by the intervention of Pope Innocent III, King John of England, and King Philip II of France. The northern Italian cities sought to use this tumult to expand their independence from imperial control. As legal guardian of the young Frederick, Pope Innocent III assumed virtual control over the kingdom of Sicily. This complex and prolonged struggle was finally resolved in 1212, when Innocent's ward, Frederick, aided by Philip II of France and by Innocent, won the upper hand in Germany. His victory led to his election as king of Germany and soon after as Holy Roman emperor. Because of the disturbances affecting the empire during the years since his father's death, Frederick II faced a formidable task.

A gifted, educated, cosmopolitan figure whose talents caused some of his contemporaries to hail him as a wonder of the world (*stupor mundi*) while others branded him as irreligious, immoral, the Antichrist, Frederick II took a new approach to his imperial office. Almost immediately after his election in 1212, he made sweeping concessions that gave the papacy control over the German ecclesiastical establishment and assured German princes of extensive rights of government over their lordships. As he progressively disengaged himself from direct rulership over Germany, Frederick turned his energies toward creating in his homeland, the Kingdom of Sicily, a centralized, bureacratic state where the ruler would be absolute. His program for this regime was spelled out in a code of law, called the Constitutions of Melfi, issued in 1231. This document, strongly influenced by concepts drawn from Roman law and by the model of the Byzantine Empire, gave the king supreme authority as lawgiver and judge, set up a bureaucracy to control local affairs, and abolished privileges enjoyed by nobles, towns, and ecclesiastical officials. Frederick then attempted to impose a

comparable regime on Italy, a move that again activated the ancient enemies of the Hohenstaufens: the papacy and the Italian cities. Frederick battled this coalition with skill and flair for twenty years but was unable to establish control over Italy. During that interval imperial power in Germany practically vanished to the great advantage of local princes, high ecclesiastical officials, and towns. When Frederick II died in 1250, the prospects were indeed dim for the realization of one of the cherished ideals of medieval society—a Christian empire in which people who held one faith would enjoy one ruler and one law to guide them in the struggle for salvation. But what lay in the future must not obscure the fact that for three centuries prior to 1250 the Holy Roman Empire was the most prominent state in western Europe and that its rulers exercised an authority that provided stability to a large population occupying a considerable part of western Europe.

2. ENGLAND

While the German rulers struggled to govern their extensive empire, political consolidation progressed more effectively in England. During the first half of the eleventh century the effective monarchy established by Alfred and his successors (see Chapter 16) began to falter in the face of efforts by powerful nobles to create private lordships and new threats by Scandinavian invaders. When the last Anglo-Saxon king, Edward the Confessor (1042–1066), died without an heir, a struggle to decide the succession ensued that changed the course of England's history. The victor, a claimant from the Continent, William, duke of Normandy, led an invading army that defeated a rival Anglo-Saxon candidate, Harold, at the battle of Hastings in 1066 (see Color Plate 9). William's victory allowed the Conqueror to claim not only the royal title but also control over England.

From the beginning of his reign William I (1066–1089) based his authority on the powers claimed by his Anglo-Saxon predecessors. To ensure the resources needed to assert those powers and to establish his Norman followers as a new ruling elite in England, he adapted usages borrowed from the system of lordship prevailing in his continental duchy of Normandy to suit his situation in England. Claiming a large portion of England by right of conquest, he set aside extensive lands as a royal domain and then granted the rest to his Norman followers as fiefs. In return they became his direct vassals (called *tenants-in-chief* or *barons*), owing him services, chiefly military, in proportion to the size of their fiefs. Although his tenants-in-chief were allowed to subinfeudate their holdings and acquire their own vassals, William insisted that all subvassals owed first allegiance to the king. Through this arrangement the new king secured a substantial domain from which he derived significant income, the military service of about five thousand knights, and rights of lordship over the newly installed Norman nobility.

Working from this solid power base, William I laid the foundations for a government capable of asserting royal authority throughout his realm. The Anglo-Saxon Witan was replaced by the *Curia Regis* (the court of the king), to which tenants-in-chief and ecclesiastical leaders were summoned to fulfill their obligation as vassals to give counsel to their royal lord and to judge cases involving the king-lord and his vassals. The Anglo-Saxon units of local administration, the shires and hundreds, continued to operate as agencies through which the king kept in direct touch with the English populace in matters of justice, peacekeeping, and taxation. To complement the income from the royal domain, William continued to impose direct taxes on his subjects and to collect dues associated with vassalage. The king's zeal in this matter was demonstrated by the Domesday Book, a compilation drawn up in 1086 to record the results of a survey conducted by royal agents to ascertain fief by fief what the king's subjects possessed and how much they owed the king. The ecclesiastical establishment was drawn into support of the monarchy. William played a key role in filling high religious offices and extracting dues from church property. Such practices risked bringing down the wrath of the reformers who caused so much trouble for his contemporary, Emperor Henry IV. William avoided this danger by making generous gifts to the religious establishment, by respecting the liberty of church officials in conducting religious courts, and especially by championing religious reform in England, a cause pushed with special vigor by Lanfranc, a Norman reformer installed by William as archbishop of Canterbury.

The Norman conquest thus marked a watershed in English history. Aside from giving new vitality to the English monarchy, the coming of the Normans drew England into the vigorous economic, religious, and cultural movements that were revitalizing society on the Continent. To be sure, many of the unique aspects of traditional Anglo-Saxon society were slowly effaced during the next century, a development lamented by many in England then and later. But on the whole England benefited greatly from closer contacts with continental Europe.

During the century following William I's death, his successors (known as the Norman-Angevin dynasty) were energetic, capable kings who worked hard to expand royal power: the rough, brutal William II (1087–1100); the quiet, prudent, avaricious Henry I (1100–1135); the ambitious, tempestuous Henry II (1154–1189); and the colorful, romantic knight Richard I, the Lion-Hearted (1189–1199). Although these kings devoted considerable energy to protecting and managing their extensive continental holdings (see pp. 262–263 and Map 19.2), we shall concentrate here on their efforts to create a strong monarchy capable of ruling a unified state (see Figure 19.1).

Never far from the minds of any of these kings were the protection and expansion of the material and military resources upon which royal power depended. They were avid—too avid, many thought—in exploiting the royal domain, still a major source of royal income, collecting every possible due owed by royal vassals, and discovering new sources of income, especially customs duties on the expanding trade and direct taxes on property. Their military support depended primarily on the services rendered the king by his tenants-in-chief. However, the kings still maintained the ancient royal right to summon the *fyrd*, the army of all freemen in the realm. Toward the end of the twelfth century the kings began to allow those who owed them military service to make money payments, called *scutage* or shield money, in lieu of personal ser-

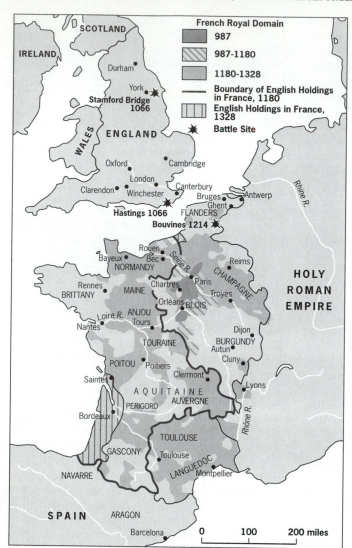

French Royal Domain

▨	**987**
▨	**987-1180**
▨	**1180-1328**
—	**Boundary of English Holdings in France, 1180**
▥	**English Holdings in France, 1328**
✴	**Battle Site**

SCOTLAND
IRELAND
Durham
York ✴
Stamford Bridge 1066
WALES
ENGLAND
Oxford ● Cambridge ●
London ●
Clarendon ● Winchester ● Canterbury ●
Bruges ● Antwerp ●
Ghent ●
Hastings 1066 FLANDERS
Bouvines 1214 ✴
Rhine R.
Rouen ● Reims ●
Bayeux ● Bec ●
NORMANDY
Chartres ● Paris ● CHAMPAGNE
Rennes ● Troyes ●
BRITTANY MAINE
Orléans ● BLOIS
Nantes ● Loire R. ANJOU
Tours ●
TOURAINE Dijon ●
BURGUNDY
Autun ●
POITOU Poitiers ● Cluny ●
Saintes ● Clermont ●
Lyons ●
A Q U I T A I N E
PERIGORD AUVERGNE
Bordeaux ● Rhône R.
TOULOUSE
GASCONY Toulouse ●
LANGUEDOC
NAVARRE Montpellier ●
SPAIN ARAGON
Barcelona ●

Seine R.

HOLY
ROMAN
EMPIRE

0   100   200 miles

Map 19.2 MEDIEVAL FRANCE AND ENGLAND
During the central Middle Ages it was in France and England that the greatest advances were made in consolidating power in royal hands. As the map suggests, England was not plagued with many deeply rooted local political entities, as was France. The map points up two trends that had a vital effect on the political destinies of France and England. First, it illustrates the steady shrinking of English holdings on the Continent. Second, it shows the success of the French kings in bringing much of that territory under direct royal control, thereby creating the territorial basis for a unified French kingdom.

vice; this income was used to hire mercenary troops. By the end of the twelfth century these efforts ensured that the English kings enjoyed a stronger financial and military base for their power than did any other rulers in Europe.

More innovative were steps taken by the twelfth-century English kings, especially Henry I and Henry II, to develop a royal administrative system capable of asserting the royal will, an effort given special impetus by the quest for financial resources. Drawing on the services of the personnel associated with the royal household and the Curia Regis, in which the king's tenants-in-chief were obliged to serve as part of their obligation to their royal overlord, the kings began to gather at their court a corps of individuals who devoted increasing amounts of time to administrative functions. The activities of these semipermanent royal servants soon began to focus on specialized administrative functions. As a result of this process four specialized departments of administration began to take shape during the twelfth century: the *Exchequer*, for collecting moneys due the king; the *Treasury*, for guarding and dispensing royal funds; the *Chancery*, for issuing royal orders and composing royal correspondence; and *royal courts of justice.* The routine business associated with these activities was increasingly performed by literate, non-noble civil servants whose livelihood and status depended on service to the king. A major responsibility of the central administrative apparatus was the supervision of the sheriffs, the royal officials charged with exercising the king's authority in the counties or shires that served as the local units of administration. This professionalized administrative system not only ensured that the bulk of the population became aware of royal authority but also placed increasingly insurmountable obstacles in the way of anyone with ambitions to carve out a private sphere of power.

Of particular significance in expanding royal power during the twelfth century was the development of a royal system of justice which provided one of the positive benefits of effective royal government. The expansion of royal justice was in large part a response to the confusion surrounding the existing system of justice under which various courts—shire, baronial, manorial, ecclesiastical, town—were conducted by judges of diverse competencies who applied different systems of law, procedures, and penalties. The kings' advisers sought to diminish this diversity by expanding the basic royal right to give justice in ways that would provide a system of justice common to all royal subjects, a step that had the added attraction of increasing the royal income derived from fees for court costs and fines.

The expansion of the royal system of justice advanced on many levels. The judicial functions previously performed by the barons acting in the Curia Regis began to be taken over by central judicial bodies directed by professional judges who held sessions at the royal court. The number of royal judges was increased by the introduction of a *circuit court system* under which itinerant judges were sent into the shires at set intervals to try cases in the name of the king. By comparing notes on their individual decisions and by following the guidance provided by judges serving the central courts, these itinerant judges began to shape a *common law* based on precedent that could guide them in deciding new cases. Royal judges sought to expand their jurisdictions

by intruding into judicial realms heretofore controlled by baronial, manorial, ecclesiastical, and town courts. Royal jurisdiction over criminal matters was expanded by legislation defining new crimes against the royal peace. Insisting that no person should lose property unjustly, the kings provided dissatisfied litigants involved in civil cases in the traditional courts an opportunity to purchase *writs* ordering a royal court to inquire into their cases. In effect, purchasing a writ amounted to transferring a civil dispute from the baronial, manorial, and town courts to the royal courts.

To encourage the use of royal courts, important innovations were made to ensure speedier and more efficient judicial processes: regularly scheduled court sessions, clearly fixed court fees, utilization of trained judges, uniform punishments. Significant in this respect was the introduction of the jury system. Building on an earlier practice of requiring subjects to tell under oath what they knew about some matter of public interest, Henry II ordered sheriffs to summon within their shires a *presentment* or *grand jury* made up of knowledgeable local residents who were required under oath to bring charges against those who had committed crimes in that area. On the basis of such testimony, the sheriffs could proceed to bring suspected criminals to trial. After trial by ordeal (see Chapter 13) was outlawed at the Fourth Lateran Council in 1215, comparable groups known as *petit* (little) juries began to be used to decide on the basis of evidence presented to them the guilt or innocence of those accused of violating the law.

The growth of royal power during the twelfth century occasionally brought the monarchs into conflict with the religious establishment. During the reign of William II, the clergy, led by Anselm, archbishop of Canterbury, challenged the monarch's right to appoint ecclesiastical officials; this quarrel was resolved by the Compromise of Bec in 1107, which allowed the church to elect its own officials but gave the king the privilege of investing these officials with the lands attached to their offices. A more serious clash arose in 1164, when Henry II issued his Constitutions of Clarendon, which sought to impose serious restrictions on the jurisdiction of ecclesiastical courts. The archbishop of Canterbury, Thomas à Becket, resisted what he considered to be an infringement on the liberty of the religious establishment and was murdered under circumstances that made it seem that Henry was responsible (see Figure 19.3). During the ensuing uproar Henry was forced to concede certain liberties to ecclesiastical courts. However, despite these challenges the English kings exercised considerable control over religious affairs, and the religious establishment gave its support to the monarchy. Unlike the Holy Roman Empire, England was spared the disruptive impact of a struggle with the clerical establishment.

During the twelfth century the English kings enjoyed remarkable success in expanding royal authority without encountering sustained resistance. However, implicit in the structure of the political system they created was a principle that eventually had to be confronted. Among other things, the English kings were lords whose dependent vassals—especially the great barons—had rights implicit in their status as vassals that must be respected. During the thirteenth century the kings were increasingly called upon to honor those rights, with the result that limits were imposed on the growth of royal power.

King John (1199–1216) was the first to be challenged. Inclined toward rashness and arbitrary action, he managed to suffer defeats at the hands of powerful enemies under circumstances that emboldened some of his subjects to challenge his authority. He became involved in a long struggle with King Philip II of France (see pp. 262–263) that forced him to impose a heavy burden on his subjects but that ended in a disastrous defeat that cost him most of his possessions in France. His situation was complicated when his effort to appoint an archbishop of Canterbury caused Pope Innocent III to suspend all religious services in England until the king bowed before papal authority. These setbacks finally goaded powerful nobles and clergy to meet in 1214 with the express purpose of organizing a rebellion aimed at curbing the king's tyrannical actions. John extricated himself from this crisis by signing the Magna Carta in 1215. Later celebrated as a charter of liberty, the Great Charter basically affirmed the traditional liberties of nobles, clergy, and townspeople. Its framers had no thought of destroying effective royal government; rather, they insisted on the principle that certain of the king's subjects had rights, defined by law, custom, and

FIGURE 19.3 Murder in the Cathedral: The Making of a Martyr This manuscript illustration shows agents of King Henry II murdering Archbishop Thomas à Becket in the cathedral at Canterbury. (The Walters Art Gallery, Baltimore)

contract, which the king must respect. But in doing so they began to define broad principles that curbed royal power in certain crucial areas, especially in taxation without the consent of those taxed and in arbitrary administration of justice without respect for the law.

The clash between the king and the privileged over the extent and limits of royal power continued throughout the reign of John's son,

Henry III (1216–1272). His costly foreign ventures and inept conduct of royal business caused exasperated nobles to resist him in several ways: They forced him to reissue the Magna Carta, compelled him to dismiss the foreigners who served him as advisers, formed a council of nobles to supervise the operation of the royal government, and finally incited a major rebellion. These efforts were ultimately thwarted by the inability of the king's opponents to agree on a course of action and by military measures taken against the rebels. In fact, these clashes hid a more fundamental development upon which Henry's successor, Edward I (1272–1307), capitalized to bring medieval English monarchy to its fullest development. Even during the troubled times of John and Henry III, royal government continued to grow in complexity and effectiveness to the point where many nobles, clergy, and townspeople began to share a sense of its vital importance to their interests. What modern historians have called a *community of the realm* was emerging, comprising powerful elements who shared a consciousness of belonging to a larger entity, a nation, and a concern that the king and his officials govern that realm in a way that would take their collective interests into account.

Edward I's reign represented an effort to solidify the position of the central government in such a way. He introduced administrative reforms intended to correct abuses of power by royal officials that led to complaints from the powerful interests those officials served. He took the initiative in enacting a series of fundamental laws which defined in more precise terms the rights and powers of the king and the manner in which these should be exercised. In pursuing this course of action, which on the whole strengthened royal government at the expense of the nobility, the religious establishment, and the towns, Edward made regular use of *Parliament* as an instrumentality through which the community of the realm could express its political concerns. The roots of this institution lay in advisory bodies, such as the Witan and its successor, the Curia Regis, to which kings had traditionally summoned their tenants-in-chief and high church officials to provide counsel in matters of state. By the thirteenth century it became the practice to add to such advisory bodies representatives who could speak for a broader spectrum of England's free population, a precedent that Edward I sanctioned in his Model Parliament of 1295, to which he summoned two knights from each shire and two burghers from each town to join the feudal barons and clergy in taking counsel with the king. Edward called meetings of Parliament primarily to serve his own purposes, especially to gain approval for additional taxes and for new legislation expanding royal power. However, Parliament did provide an institutional setting in which complaints against royal government could be voiced and suggestions for change proposed; from such pleas emerged the right of Parliament to initiate legislation binding on the king and the entire realm. Although its organization and powers still remained vague during Edward I's reign, its very existence reflected an essential feature of medieval England's political system: The king had to rule in a fashion that took into account the concerns and rights of at least some of his subjects. The sophisticated administrative, judicial, fiscal, and military apparatus that had evolved over three centuries allowed the king a wide latitude to act in ways that brought peace and order to the English populace, but there were "constitutional" limits beyond which royal power could not extend.

3. FRANCE

The emergence of effective monarchy proceeded more slowly in France than in England and under different circumstances. The medieval French state had its origins in one of the subdivisions of the Carolingian Empire created by the Treaty of Verdun in 843 (see Map 16.2), the Kingdom of the West Franks, over which, except for brief intervals, members of the Carolingian family ruled until 987. Under the last Carolingians royal power declined steadily, and the kingdom was fragmented into numerous small principalities controlled by powerful local lords. In 987 these lords, joined by the clergy, finally ended the Carolingian dynasty by electing as their king one of their own, Hugh Capet, count of Paris, whose descendants, called the Capetians, ruled France until 1328. The first four Capetians, who reigned from 987 to 1108, exercised almost no power outside their own domain, a modest territory around Paris (see Map 19.2). Throughout the rest of the kingdom powerful lords did as they pleased in their own principalities. The first Capetians did manage to establish a hereditary claim to the throne and to maintain the fiction inherited from the Carolingian world that the royal office was surrounded by a sacral quality which elevated its holder above all who were his subjects. The kings also claimed lordship over many local potentates, who were considered to be vassals owing services to their royal lord in return for the fiefs that made up their principalities.

For a long time these royal claims meant little in reality. Between 843 and 1108 the history of the Kingdom of France, which can be told only in terms of the history of each of the lordships into which it was divided (see Map 19.2), is primarily a study in political fragmentation. However, by the eleventh century a subtle change began to emerge. Local lords—dukes, counts, viscounts, castellans—began to establish more effective control over their principalities by a rigorous assertion of their rights of lordship. They exploited those rights to shape institutions that permitted them to amass sufficient military and fiscal resources to compel the obedience of their noble and servile dependents, to assume control over the administration of justice, and to command the support of the local religious establishment. This consolidation of local lordships was most notable in the great royal fiefs of northern France, especially Normandy, Flanders, Anjou, Maine, Champagne, Burgundy, and Blois. The effectiveness of such lords was exemplified by William, duke of Normandy, who was able to muster sufficient resources to conquer England. In southern France the royal fiefs such as Aquitaine, Gascony, and Toulouse remained more fragmented.

Until the early twelfth century the Capetian kings of France played no significant role in the process of local consolidation, but then the situation began to change. Louis VI (1108–1137) was able to establish effective control over his vassals in the royal domain and to create an administrative machinery that provided him sufficient resources to exercise the rights of lordship he claimed over vassals holding fiefs once granted by the king. With increasing frequency he acted as judge in cases involving his vassals, protected

weaker ones against stronger, controlled the succession of fiefs, and annexed disputed territories to the royal domain. Illustrative of his expanding strength was the decision of the dying duke of Aquitaine to entrust his daughter and heiress, Eleanor, to the protection of his overlord, the king of France. Louis VI promptly arranged for the marriage of his ward to his own son, setting the stage for the annexation of Aquitaine to the royal domain.

The modest progress made by Louis VI in expanding royal influence was threatened by a major crisis that emerged under his successor, Louis VII (1137–1180). In part the crisis resulted from Louis VII's political ineptitude, exemplified by the fate of his marriage to Eleanor. Not only did this patroness of troubadour poets and devotee of the ideals of courtly love fail to produce a male heir, it was also rumored that she had been unfaithful to the king when she accompanied him on the Second Crusade. Perhaps her behavior resulted from her own frustration, for she is alleged to have said that she had discovered she had married a monk instead of a king. As a result, the pious Louis divorced her and was forced to surrender her dowry, the duchy of Aquitaine. But the hapless king's major difficulty did not stem from his political and marital ineptitude. During his reign a sequence of events unfolded to create what historians call the Angevin "empire," comprising several major royal fiefs in France joined together in the hands of a single royal vassal. The architects of this conglomeration were the counts of Anjou, who through inheritance, conquest, and marriage alliances managed to establish hereditary claim to a substantial territory, including Normandy, Anjou, Brittany, Maine, and the Touraine (see Map 19.2). In 1151, by the accidents of inheritance, all these possession fell into the hands of a single family member, Henry. In 1152 that same Henry married the recently divorced Eleanor and acquired Aquitaine as her dowry. For all these territories Henry was vassal of Louis VII. Then in 1154, the already well endowed Angevin heir became Henry II, king of England. Obviously, his "empire" provided him with resources far exceeding those of his lord, the king of France, whose power was in serious jeopardy.

It remained for Philip II Augustus (1180–

1223) to respond to the challenge posed by the Angevin "empire"; he did so in a fashion that marked a turning point in the history of the medieval French monarchy. During the first two decades of his reign he maneuvered successfully to prevent his vassals, the English kings Henry II and Richard I, from solidifying their hold on their continental possessions. With the accession of John came an opportunity for more decisive action. When John allegedly violated the rights of one of his vassals on the Continent, Philip II exercised his right as John's overlord to summon his vassal to stand judgment for his conduct as a vassal, found the English king guilty of being an unfaithful vassal, and confiscated his fiefs. To carry out his sentence, Philip proceeded by force of arms to annex Normandy, Anjou, Maine, the Touraine, and parts of northern Aquitaine to the royal domain, a task made easier by John's troubles with his English subjects and with Philip's ally, Pope Innocent III. Philip's control of these territories was ensured by a victory in 1214 at the battle of Bouvines, where he crushed the forces of John and his anti-Hohenstaufen allies from the Holy Roman Empire. Philip II's victory provided the power base that allowed his successors to continue to bring territory under direct royal control as part of the royal domain. They employed various means of claiming territory: marriage alliances that permitted the Capetian family to inherit fiefs; confiscation of fiefs held by vassals judged unfaithful; recovery of fiefs held by vassals who died without heirs; purchase; conquest. King Henry III of England sought to thwart the expansion of the French royal domain by recapturing the fiefs lost to Philip II, but eventually, in 1259, was forced to agree to a treaty giving up his claims in France except for a small territory in Gascony. When the Capetian dynasty finally ended in 1328, the king or a close member of the royal family exercised direct control over most of the principalities that had once enjoyed virtual independence. What had been a political mosaic had become a consolidated kingdom.

More than territorial consolidation was involved in creating medieval France. The later Capetians, especially Philip II, Louis IX (1226–1270), and Philip IV, the Fair (1285–1314), worked vigorously to develop institutions that would allow them to govern their expanding realm effectively. To create an effective central administration at their capital in Paris, they adapted and expanded primitive institutions inherited from the early Capetians: the Curia Regis, a court of the king's vassals; the royal household (*hôtel*), made up of officials who looked after the personal needs of the royal family; and the *provosts*, agents who managed the royal estates. Out of these institutions gradually emerged an extensive central court staffed by full-time royal agents, often trained as lawyers, serving in specialized departments devoted to financial matters, administration of justice, and record keeping. The jurisdiction claimed by this central administration was constantly expanded by royal ordinances which drew on feudal practice, Roman law, classical political theory, and Christian ideology for precedents justifying the expansion of royal authority. By the reign of Philip IV the central administration had become a fully professionalized body of officials devoted to enhancing royal power and capable of asserting a collective force that guaranteed obedience to the royal will. Perhaps its power even exceeded that of the central government that served the English kings.

As the royal domain grew, the kings were faced with the monumental task of devising a system of local government. Unlike the situation in England, where kings were served by the ancient system of shires and sheriffs that allowed them to intervene directly in local affairs, the early Capetians had no means of exercising authority across most of their kingdom; local government was the monopoly of local lords. Philip II attacked this problem by creating special officials known as *baillis* (bailiffs), whose numbers and powers were increased by his successors. Usually selected from nonnoble personnel drawn from the royal court, these officials were assigned to specific territories within the royal domain to hold courts, collect taxes, and keep order in the name of the king; their enthusiasm for such pursuits was increased by the fact that their reward depended on what they exacted from the king's subjects. Louis IX established special officers called *enquêteurs* (investigators) to check on the conduct of the bailiffs and to report misdeeds to the central government. Although the local nobility continued to perform many political functions and to resist royal intrusion, the bailiffs, acting in the name of the kings, steadily assumed political functions once monopolized by local lords. Their efforts slowly imposed a common administration on France.

The broadening range of royal activities, especially waging war to expand and protect the royal domain and supporting the expanding royal administration, placed a heavy financial burden on the kings. A significant part of the royal income continued to be derived from royal lands, but other sources of revenue had to be found. Aside from feudal dues, fines, and fees for royal services, the royal government had few sources of regular income. As a result, the kings often had to resort to arbitrary exactions from any source possible: towns, the religious establishment, Jews, foreign bankers and merchants, nobles who fell out of royal favor. Especially during the reign of Philip IV, the measures used to satisfy the ravenous royal appetite for money produced complaints of royal tyranny and aroused widespread resistance.

Partly in reponse to their need for revenues, the Capetians instituted another practice that strengthened their authority. Expanding on the ancient practice of seeking counsel by callinng their vassals to the Curia Regis, they began in the fourteenth century to summon representatives of the three major social groupings (*estates*)—the nobles, the clergy, and the townspeople—to advise them and approve their policies. Philip IV convoked three of these *Estates General* to approve policies that extended his authority, thereby giving the impression that the entire nation supported his policy. The Estates General was much more a tool of the French monarchs than the English Parliament was, chiefly because the major power groups in France, especially the nobility, failed to develop a sense of shared interest in and concern for the affairs of the entire realm.

Throughout most of the long period during which the Capetians were consolidating their hold on France, they drew invaluable aid from both the papacy and the higher clergy in France. The kings bestowed wealth on the religious establishment, supported reform, took the side of the papacy in the investiture struggle, and respected religious liberties. In return, high church officials supported the royal claims to greater power and lent their wealth and talent to royal service. This fruitful relationship did not until the reign of Philip IV, who became embroiled in a bitter struggle with Pope Boniface VIII (1294–1303) over the extent of the king's power to tax ecclesiastical property and judge the clergy. As we shall see (Chapter 24), Philip IV won a stunning victory over the mighty head of Christendom, so long successful in thwarting the Holy Roman emperors. The explanation is clear: By the early fourteenth century the king of France possessed a power base that even the pope could not dissolve by simple command.

Amid both their travails and their successes the Capetians managed one more achievement: They endowed their royal office with an aura that made it seem to many a reflection of kingship at its best. The prestige of the Capetians is best exemplified by Louis IX, eventually recognized as a saint. In no small part because of his actual accomplishments, Louis was hailed in his own time as a lover of justice, model Christian, gallant knight, crusader, peacemaker, promoter of morality, ideal son, husband, and father—in short, the ideal Christian prince (see Figures 19.4 and 20.1). Although not all were endowed with Louis' talents, most of the Capetians shared at least some of that aura of excellence, proving them to be as skillful in fashioning an image as in shaping effective political institutions. That image did much to enhance their real power in France and throughout Europe.

Between 1000 and 1300 the political face of western Europe was certainly changed in ways that prefigured the future by political leaders seeking a solution to a problem that had persisted since the dissolution of the Roman Empire—how to create a stable political order capable of binding men and women into a large-scale community that promoted the common goals of its members. A succession of German rulers sought with some success to unite Germany and Italy into a single state guided by principles defined by Christian universalism; that effort ultimately failed, leaving in its wake a fragmented political order in Germany and Italy that would prevail far into the future and a dream of somehow finding a way to create a single European political community. In England and France equally resourceful leaders fashioned

FIGURE 19.4 A Queen at Work This manuscript illustration shows Queen Blanche of Castile, wife of King Louis VIII (1223–1226), keeping close watch over the education of her son, King Louis IX (1226–1270). Even while she was asserting her role as a mother, she was acting as regent for a kingdom that Louis IX inherited when he was an infant. Her son became a great king and a saint. (Bibliothèque Nationale, Paris, ms. fr. 5716)

institutions that allowed them to exercise sufficient authority over their subjects to ensure peace and order within a limited geographical area, but with constraints that left privileged groups sufficient liberty to ensure their role as partners in the task of governance; these rulers had laid the basis for nation-states as a prime factor in western Europe's political future.

SUGGESTED READING

The Holy Roman Empire

K. J. Leyser, *Medieval Germany and Its Neighbors, 900–1250* (1982). The best general history.

Josef Fleckenstein, *Early Medieval Germany*, trans. Bernard S. Smith (1978).

Timothy Reuter, *Germany in the Early Middle Ages, c. 800–1056* (1991).

Two excellent works on the origin of the Holy Roman Empire.

Horst Fuhrmann, *Germany in the High Middle Ages, c. 1050–1200*, trans. Timothy Reuter (1986).

Albert Haverkamp, *Medieval Germany, 1056–1273*, trans. Helga Brown and Richard Mortimer (1988).

Either of these works provides a sound treatment of the

crucial period in the history of the Holy Roman Empire.

J. K. Hyde, *Society and Politics in Medieval Italy: The Evolution of the Civil Life, 1000–1350* (1973). Effective survey of the complex history of medieval Italy.

Benjamin Arnold, *Princes and Territories in Medieval Germany* (1991). Helpful on medieval Germany's complex internal history.

R. Folz, *The Concept of Empire in Western Europe from the Fifth to the Fourteenth Century*, trans. Sheila Ann Ogilvie (1969). Treats the concepts undergirding the medieval ideal of universal empire.

Uta-Renate Blumenthal, *The Investiture Controversy: Church and Monarchy from the Ninth to the Twelfth Century* (1988). Reflects modern scholarship on a much-disputed problem.

England

Christopher Brooke, *From Alfred to Henry III, 871–1272* (1961). A brief, well-written survey.

Robin Frame, *The Political Development of the British Isles, 1100–1400* (1990).

M. T. Clanchy, *England and Its Rulers, 1066–1272: Foreign Lordship and National Identity* (1983).

Two fuller accounts stressing the evolution of political institutions.

Doris M. Stenton, *English Society in the Early Middle Ages (1066–1307)*, 4th ed. (1965). Particularly strong in relating economic, social, and cultural factors to political history.

R. Allen Brown, *The Normans and the Norman Conquest*, 2nd ed. (1985). Excellent treatment of Norman expansionism.

W. L. Warren, *The Governance of Norman and Angevin England, 1086–1272* (1987). A fine synthesis.

J. C. Holt, *Magna Carta*, 2nd ed. (1992). A fine analysis.

France

Elizabeth M. Hallam, *Capetian France, 987–1328* (1980).

Georges Duby, *France in the Middle Ages 987–1460: From Hugh Capet to Joan of Arc*, trans. Juliet Vale (1991).

Two excellent general surveys of the growth of the kingdom.

Jean Dunbabin, *France in the Making 843–1180* (1985). Especially good in its treatment of France's principalities.

Biographies

Peter Munz, *Frederick Barbarossa: A Study in Medieval Politics* (1969).

David Abulafia, *Frederick II. A Medieval Emperor* (1992).

A. J. MacDonald, *Hildebrand: A Life of Gregory VII* (1932).

David C. Douglas, *William the Conqueror: The Norman Impact upon England* (1964).

W. L. Warren, *Henry II* (1973).

Amy Kelly, *Eleanor of Aquitaine and the Four Kings* (1950).

Frank Barlow, *Thomas Becket* (1986).

John Gillingham, *Richard the Lionheart* (1978).

W. L. Warren, *King John*, rev. ed. (1978).

Michael Prestwich, *Edward I* (1988).

Jean Richard, *Saint Louis: Crusader King of France*, trans. Jean Birrell (1992).

CHAPTER 20
The Medieval Expansion of Europe, 1000–1300

FIGURE 20.1 **Departure on a Crusade** This scene depicts King Louis IX of France leaving Paris on the Seventh Crusade. It captures some of the solemnity surrounding the crusading movement. With their eyes seemingly on their distant goal in the Holy Land, Louis and his knights depart without a look backward at the group of monks blessing them. (The British Museum)

Linked with western Europe's economic and political revival was a decisive change in the relationship between the West and the world beyond. Between 500 and 1000 western Europeans had been almost constantly on the defensive. After 1000 that situation was reversed. During the next three centuries Europeans employed a variety of means to expand their sphere of influence over a wide area. These efforts marked the beginning of an outward thrust by western Europeans that would continue for centuries.

1. MISSIONARY EXPANSION

The expansionist urge that marked Christianity from its beginnings continued vigorously and successfully during the central Middle Ages. A major area of missionary expansion was in Scandinavia. While the first efforts to convert the Scandinavians began in the ninth century, the crucial era in the conversion of Denmark, Norway, Sweden, and Iceland came in the late tenth and eleventh centuries. In most cases the conversion process was initiated by the native rulers, but they received assistance in instructing their people and organizing a religious establishment from missionaries from England and Germany.

Meanwhile, Christianity was carried eastward into the Slavic world. In this area the major impetus for expansion was provided by the rulers of the Holy Roman Empire and their ambitious lay and ecclesiastical vassals. Beginning in the late tenth century, the Bohemians, Poles, and Hungarians were gathered into the Roman Catholic fold. Somewhat later missionaries accompanied the conquering Teutonic Knights, a military order that had originally served the crusading forces in the Holy Land, to convert the Wends, Prussians, Finns, Livonians, and Lithuanians living along the Baltic coast. During this same period missionary forces from the Byzantine Empire were spreading Christianity among the eastern Slavs, especially the Russians.

During the thirteenth century missionaries from the West made efforts to win converts among the Moslems of North Africa and the Near East, and some even ventured as far afield as the Mongol Empire and China. Although these ventures produced no significant results, they opened vast new prospects for the future.

Wherever the missionary effort succeeded—Scandinavia, central Europe, Iceland, the Baltic area—those who brought Christianity introduced their converts to many aspects of western European culture. As a consequence, the lives of people in newly converted areas were decisively changed; they were "Europeanized" in terms of their institutions and their way of thinking.

2. COLONIZATION AND COMMERCIAL EXPANSION

The western Europeans who thrust outward with the cross were often accompanied—and sometimes led—by others driven toward and beyond Europe's old frontiers primarily by economic interests. As we have already seen, one of the great accomplishments of western Europeans during the era from 1000 to 1300 was the opening and colonization of an extensive agricultural frontier on the eastern fringes of Europe—in today's terms, a territory comprising northern Poland, the eastern part of unified Germany, the Czech Republic, Slovakia, and Austria. This Germanic "drive to the east" had the support of the Holy Roman emperors and religious leaders, but mainly it was carried out by landowners and peasants seeking new lands to exploit. Their occupation of this frontier zone was accompanied by the implantation of western European institutions.

Likewise, between 1000 and 1300 merchants reached beyond Europe to establish a western European presence in a much larger world (see Map 18.1). Italian merchants wrested control of the Mediterranean seaways from the Byzantines and Moslems and established trading posts in Constantinople and several Moslem seaports in Syria, Egypt, and North Africa. Northern Europeans, spearheaded by the Vikings, established settlements at Novgorod, Smolensk, and Kiev; from these emerged the Kievan principality, which constituted the first effective state in Russia. After the armies of the Fourth Crusade conquered Constantinople in 1204, western European merchants established bridgeheads around the Black Sea, which opened access to the cities of Central Asia and China. Italian traders roamed across the Asian world, reaping rich profits and reporting the potential of that vast area in travel accounts such as that composed in the late 1200s by the Venetian Marco Polo. A few bold Europeans were finding their way toward the waterways leading eastward to India and the Indies. Simultaneously, Western seafarers were pushing southward along Africa's west coast, drawn chiefly by the fame of the gold mines of Senegal.

3. MILITARY EXPANSION IN SPAIN AND SOUTHERN ITALY

The outward movement of missionaries, colonists, and traders was often supported by military forces impelled by a variety of motives: land hunger, a quest for booty, a lust for adventure, religious zeal. Military expansionism manifested itself around the whole rim of the European heartland, but the thrust was aimed primarily toward the Mediterranean basin and into areas dominated during the early Middle Ages by Byzantines and Moslems.

One of the most important areas of expansion was the Iberian peninsula. When the Moors (as Moslems are called in Spanish history) conquered the Iberian peninsula in the eighth century, they failed to subdue small pockets of Christians in the extreme northwestern part of the peninsula. In the late eighth and early ninth centuries the Carolingians pushed across the Pyrenees to create the Spanish March in northeastern Spain from territory won from the Moors. Prior to 1000 several petty states developed in these Christian enclaves—León, Castile, Navarre, Aragon, and Barcelona. By the early eleventh century these states began to expand southward, generating a movement that soon turned into a war of liberation called the *Reconquista*. The disintegration in the early eleventh century of the once-powerful caliphate of Córdoba and the emergence of numerous warring Moslem principalities made Christian expansion easier. Given this opportunity, the militant Christians turned their energies to a common assault on the Moors. Large numbers of Christian knights from outside Spain, especially from France, joined the fray. Aside from a thirst for land, the warriors involved in the Reconquista were animated by a powerful religious spirit, as is illustrated by two great vernacular literary works written to celebrate the feats of Christian warriors against the

Moorish infidels, the *Song of Roland* and *The Cid*. The first phase of the Reconquista culminated in 1085 with the capture of the key city of Toledo. With the aid of Berber reinforcements from northwest Africa, the Moors were able to halt the Christian advance temporarily and by the mid–twelfth century even threatened to reclaim territory lost to the Christians. Shortly thereafter the Christian offensive was renewed, culminating in 1212 at the battle of Las Navas de Tolosa, where the Christian forces won a decisive victory over the combined forces of the Spanish Moors and their Berber allies. By 1300 the Christians had occupied all of the peninsula except a small region in the south called Granada (see Map 20.1).

Three major Iberian kingdoms—Castile (to which León was joined), Aragon, and Portugal—grew out of the territory rewon from the Moslems during the Reconquista. Each developed its own system of government, although all had certain basic similarities. Monarchy was the basic institution, and the kings steadily gained prestige as a result of their leadership of the Reconquista and the support of their cause by religious leaders, especially the papacy. The newly conquered lands gave them a chance to settle people as farmers or town dwellers under conditions that allowed the king to retain his authority. In each kingdom there emerged a powerful nobility, made up of warriors richly rewarded with grants of land in return for their services in the wars against the Moors. Although these nobles were often bound to the king by ties of vassalage, they posed a constant challenge to royal authority. Seeking to take advantage of the superior skills of some of their conquered subjects as traders and artisans, the kings also granted extensive privileges to the Moslem and Jewish communities in conquered Spanish cities. Like their contemporaries in England and France, the Spanish monarchs sought to develop centralized administrations, well-organized financial systems, and effective courts. Several thirteenth-century kings of Aragon and Castile legislated extensively to define royal powers, and they appointed local officials, comparable to the French bailiffs, to represent them. Both the nobles and the townspeople resisted the expansion of royal power and in the long run compelled the kings to accept limitations on their authority. In each kingdom there developed a *Cortes,* a representative body com-

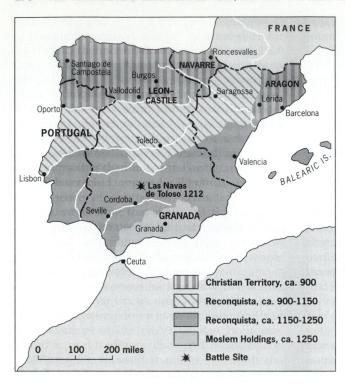

Map 20.1 CHRISTIAN EXPANSION IN IBERIA
This map shows the progress made by Spanish Christian warriors in reconquering the Iberian peninsula from the Moors during the Middle Ages. Three major kingdoms emerged from the Christian victories—Aragon, Castile (to which León was joined), and Portugal.

posed of nobles, ecclesiastical leaders, and townspeople with considerable power to limit royal decisions on a variety of matters, including taxation.

As the Iberian kingdoms developed, the society of each took on many features common to the rest of Christian western Europe. As a consequence, the Iberian world became an integral part of western European civilization. However, Spanish society retained its unique features, byproducts of the merging of Christian and Moslem institutions and ideas during the long period of the Reconquista. As a result, Spain played a special role in the medieval West as the channel through which many Moslem influences flowed into the mainstream of western European society.

Another area drawn into the western European sphere of influence by military force was southern Italy and Sicily, long controlled by the Byzantines and the Moslems. Norman warriors from northwest France were the aggressors here, coming first to southern Italy as adventurers who, in return for land, were willing to sell their military services to local rulers competing for power. Especially anxious for their services were Byzantine officials, who sought desperately to retain control over the area in the name of the emperor in Constantinople. Soon, however, these resourceful warriors, constantly reinforced by new adventurers from Normandy, succeeded in establishing dominance over their supposed masters. By the mid–eleventh century the papacy legally recognized a Norman principality in southern Italy; in return, the Normans agreed to support the papacy in its struggle with the Holy Roman emperors. These same aggressive warriors then wrenched Sicily from the Moslems, a victory recognized in 1130 when the papacy sanctioned the creation of the Kingdom of Sicily, embracing southern Italy and Sicily, with a prince of Norman descent, Roger II, as king. A strong monarchy was soon shaped, featuring a mixture of northern European feudal, Byzantine, and Moslem practices. The Kingdom of Sicily passed into Hohenstaufen hands at the end of the twelfth century and reached its apogee under Frederick II (see Chapter 19). Thereafter, the kingdom began to decline, chiefly because it became a pawn in the rivalry among various European states. But it remained in western European hands, a prize of expansion from which flowed political, economic, intellectual, and artistic influences that had an important effect on western Europe.

4. MILITARY EXPANSION: THE CRUSADES

The most dramatic manifestation of medieval western European expansion involved a succession of military campaigns, called the Crusades, that were directed toward the eastern Mediterranean world. Initially undertaken as religious wars against Islam for control of the holy places where Christianity had originated, these campaigns eventually involved a struggle to maintain a western European outpost in the Near East.

In part, the crusading movement began because political developments in the Near East offered western Europeans opportunities and inducements. As early as the ninth century, the vast Abbasid caliphate began to break up into independent caliphates bitterly contending with one another for territory and for the right to represent the true version of Islam. The rivalry was especially keen in Syria and Palestine, where Abbasid dominance was challenged by the aggressive Egypt-based Shiite Fatimid caliphate and the Byzantine Empire, which sought to reclaim territory it had once possessed as heir to the Roman Empire. In an effort to bolster its declining strength, the Abbasid dynasty brought a vigorous new force into the picture: the Seljuk Turks. They were a people of Asiatic origin who had entered the Moslem world in the tenth century, become converts to Islam, and used their military prowess to expand their influence. By the mid–eleventh century, the Seljuks established their dominance over Baghdad and made the Abbasid caliphs their puppets. They then turned their energies westward in an effort to enlarge their sphere of influence. This expansion brought them into conflict with the Fatimids and the Byzantine Empire and made the eastern Mediterranean world a confusing battleground. The Turkish menace became especially critical about 1070, when the Turks seized Jerusalem from the Fatimids and inflicted a crushing defeat on the Byzantines at the battle of Manzikert (see below). In the midst of this confusion, local Moslem leaders established several small principalities in Syria and Palestine; they were willing to make any arrangements that would thwart the efforts of their major rivals to establish dominance over this crucial territory.

The Byzantine Empire was also undergoing a crisis in the late eleventh century. After reaching its pinnacle under the greatest emperor of the Macedonian dynasty, Basil II (976–1025), the empire began to decline, in part because a succession of ineffectual rulers allowed the aristocracy to exploit the free peasantry that constituted the backbone of the imperial defense system. The Normans, who had already wrested southern Italy from imperial control, posed a growing threat to imperial control in the Balkans. The Italian city-states, especially Venice, challenged the Byzantine sea power. More seriously, in 1071, at the battle of Manzikert, Byzantine forces suffered a crushing blow from the Seljuk Turks, who in succeeding years conquered most of Asia Minor. This deepening crisis finally produced an effective ruler, Alexius Comnenus (1081–1118), who in his effort to recover Asia Minor began to appeal to the pope and the princes of western Europe for military help against the aggressive Turkish infidels, whom the Byzantines portrayed as a threat to all Christendom.

Despite the volatile situation in the east, there would have been no crusading movement without the confluence of various forces affecting western European society. Increasing material wealth provided the means for ambitious military undertakings, and the greater political order curbed local warfare and freed the war-loving aristocracy for foreign ventures. Changing patterns of landholding, which confined inheritance to eldest sons, created a large pool of young warriors seeking ways to make a fortune. The military potency of European society was being demonstrated by victories on the German, Spanish, and Italian frontiers. The Italian cities were eager to advance their commercial interests in the eastern Mediterranean. The long-standing religious animosity toward Islam was sharpened by the wars in Spain and Italy. The wave of religious reform sweeping over western Europe emphasized the idea that Christians must serve God by working through outward, active demonstrations of their piety. One way in which that activist impulse expressed itself was through an increasing interest in pilgrimages. Thousands of people joined organized voyages to holy places all over Europe and increasingly to the Holy Land, where their occasional victimization by warring Moslem factions heightened anti-Moslem feelings. The religious revival had an especially important impact on the chivalric ideal. Increasingly, it emphasized the responsibility of the true warrior to devote his prowess to holy war that would promote the cause of Christianity and scourge its enemies, especially the hated Moslem infidels.

It was Pope Urban II (1088–1099), a dedicated reformer eager to assert papal leadership over Christendom, who translated the opportunities emerging in the east and the forces of militancy surging through western European society into a specific form of military action. In 1095, after discussions with important ecclesiastical and lay leaders, Urban made public his plan in a stirring speech at Clermont in France. He called on Christian knights to put aside their petty quarrels and join forces under papal leadership in an armed pilgrimage to the east to achieve a variety of ends for the good of the true faith. This army would respond to an appeal that Alexius Comnenus made to the pope in the same year for aid in defending the Byzantine Empire against the Moslem Seljuk Turks. In return for this help Urban hoped to gain Byzantine recognition of papal supremacy over the whole Christian world, thus ending the schism that had occurred in 1054, when the pope and the patriarch of Constantinople had excommunicated each other. Finally, this force, aided by the Byzantines, would capture the holy places in Palestine as a supreme act of piety in the service of God. As an inducement to join his crusade, Urban proclaimed measures to protect the property and families of those willing to take up the cross and promised that each would be rewarded in heaven for fighting this holy war.

The pope's appeal at Clermont was greeted with shouts that it was God's will to do what Urban asked. That enthusiasm was soon transmitted over much of Europe by preachers of the crusading ideal. A number of prominent lords (but no kings) began gathering separate armies in various areas. Before these armies of knights could be organized, an undisciplined horde of peasants and artisans, stirred by the appeals of enthusiastic preachers, began what has been called the Peasants' Crusade. After savagely attacking Jewish communities in several German cities, this ragtag mob moved eastward down the Danube Valley and across Hungary and Bulgaria, causing havoc as it advanced. When it finally reached Constantinople, Emperor Alexius Comnenus quickly dispatched it to Asia Minor, where it was immediately annihilated by the Turks.

By the summer of 1096 four major armies, totaling perhaps twenty-five or thirty thousand armed knights accompanied by considerable retinues, began to move toward the east by different routes (see Map 20.2). Their first goal was Constantinople, where they expected to unite their forces for the attack on the Turks and the march to Jerusalem. The leaders of the armies from the west had no common plan of action. Although Urban II had designated a distinguished bishop to direct the crusading effort in the name of the papacy, the doughty nobles leading the various armies were unwilling to accept direction. Alexius Comnenus had expected mercenary contingents that he could simply take into his pay and order to do what he wished; the armies now converging on his capital were anything but soldiers for hire. Thus, Alexius had to negotiate an agreement with each leader. Eventually, by means that increased the distrust of the proud crusaders for the "Greeks" and of the Byzantines for the western "barbarians," Alexius persuaded each of the crusading leaders to swear a personal oath of allegiance to him and to promise to restore to Byzantine control conquered territories that had previously belonged to the empire. In return, he promised to provide supplies and military support.

In the spring of 1097 the crusaders began their march across Asia Minor, brushing aside modest Turkish resistance but paying little heed to their

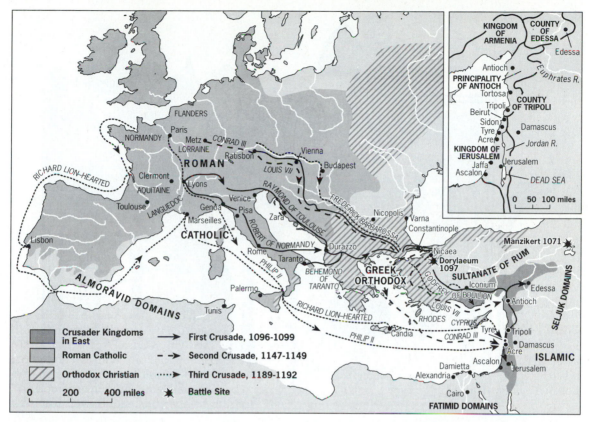

Map 20.2 **THE EARLY CRUSADES** This map shows the major land and sea routes taken by various crusading armies during the First, Second, and Third crusades. The leaders of the major armies are also indicated. The distances involved in these military ventures suggest the challenges faced by the crusaders. The First Crusade established the Latin Kingdom of Jerusalem, far removed from where the armies started their trek. Most of the successive crusades were prompted by the need to defend that kingdom from the Moslem forces that surrounded it.

promise to Alexius to liberate Asia Minor. This disregard for Byzantine interests, coupled with Alexius' failure to provide the hard-pressed crusading armies with promised supplies, virtually ended any hope of effective collaboration between the Byzantines and the crusaders. Once in Syria, the crusading force began to split up, chiefly because its leaders were anxious to ensure their private fortunes. One group left the main body to establish control over Edessa and its surrounding territory, while another, led by the Norman prince Bohemond, established an independent principality centered around Antioch. Not until July 1099 was Jerusalem captured by

the remaining crusaders, who vented their fury by slaughtering hundreds of its inhabitants (see Figure 20.2). Their victory, a remarkable feat considering how far the crusading armies had come and the severe tribulations they had faced for three years, made the First Crusade a success in the eyes of western Europeans.

In the wake of their triumph the crusading leaders disregarded both their pledge to Alexius to serve as his vassals and a papal plan to create a state subordinate to Rome. Instead, in 1100 they elected Baldwin of Flanders, count of Edessa, as king of the Latin Kingdom of Jerusalem. Baldwin retained a sizable territory around Jerusalem as

FIGURE 20.2 **The Capture of the Holy City, 1099** This manuscript illustration shows the crusaders making their final assault on Jerusalem in 1099 to mark the successful end of the First Crusade. Their victory ended with the slaughter of those shown defending the city. (Snark International/Art Resource)

the royal domain and granted out the principalities of Edessa, Antioch, and Tripoli as fiefs to major crusading leaders, each of whom became a royal vassal and in turn granted fiefs to his own vassals. Although the king claimed lordship over the princes of the major principalities and often acted in concert with them in the common cause of the Christian establishment, the Latin Kingdom of Jerusalem was unstable internally, constantly riven by princely rivalries and by the ambitions of newcomers from the west. A Latin patriarch of Jerusalem was installed, thus subordinating the Christian establishment to Roman authority. The native population was disturbed very little by the newcomers.

Once the Latin Kingdom of Jerusalem had been established, the defense of "Overseas"

(*Outremer*, as western Europeans called their distant outpost) became a major problem. Almost immediately after the capture of Jerusalem, most of the knights from the west returned home, having fulfilled the vow they had taken to liberate the holy places. Those who stayed took various steps to protect themselves. With the aid of Italian navies they seized the chief Mediterranean seaports in Syria and Palestine; this success allowed the Latins to control the sea routes facing the Latin Kingdom, which were of decisive importance in holding their position. They built a series of impregnable castles at strategic locations in the Holy Land. Before 1130 they established two military orders, the Knights Templar and the Knights Hospitaler; a third, the Teutonic Knights, developed somewhat later. These orders, modeled on monastic organizations, recruited members in the west who vowed to serve God by defending Christians living in and coming to the Holy Land and by raising troops and money to support the Christian establishment in the Holy Land. Despite these measures the Christian position remained tenuous, creating an ongoing concern that during the next two centuries repeatedly persuaded western Europeans to go crusading as a way of serving God. Almost every year some western European knights at least temporarily lent their efforts to defending the Latin Kingdom. On occasion, especially at moments of crisis in the Latin Kingdom of Jerusalem, efforts were made in the west to organize more substantial forces to defend the holy places, thus permitting historians to speak of successive "crusades."

The Second Crusade (1147–1149) was prompted by the loss of Edessa to the Moslems in 1144. Papal appeals for action attracted two kings as its leaders: Conrad III, Holy Roman emperor, and Louis VII, king of France. Despite such prestigious leadership, the crusading armies were virtually destroyed by the Turks in Asia Minor. When the two rulers did arrive in the Holy Land with remnants of their forces, their misdirected military efforts aided little in the defense of the Latin Kingdom.

During the years following the Second Crusade, more effective leadership began to emerge in the Moslem world surrounding the Christian holdings. The most brilliant of these new leaders was Saladin, whose success in uniting the Moslem forces of Egypt and Syria posed a powerful threat to the Latin Kingdom of Jerusalem. By 1187 he captured almost all the Christian holdings except Tyre, a few isolated castles, and the northern counties. When the news of this disaster reached the West, the pope called for a new crusade and received the promises of Henry II of England, Philip II of France, and Frederick Barbarossa of Germany to lead armies against Saladin. Frederick left first but was drowned en route. Henry II also died before he could begin his march; however, his successor, Richard the Lion-Hearted, stepped into his place. He and Philip, almost always at odds, made their way to the east by 1191. More concerned with undermining Richard's Angevin "empire" back in

France than crusading, Philip stayed on the scene only a minimum time. The colorful English king remained for over a year. After several inconclusive engagements with Saladin, Richard finally agreed to a truce that left Jerusalem in Moslem hands and allowed Christians to visit it. Aside from the return of a few coastal cities to Latin control, the Third Crusade did little to improve the Christian position.

The Fourth Crusade was initially prompted by Pope Innocent III. However, the pope soon lost control over the forces that were raised. To ensure transportation to the east, the crusading leaders turned to the Venetians, who invested far more in ships to transport the crusaders than the disappointingly small crusading force was able to collect. To resolve this problem, the Venetians and the crusading leaders agreed to support a claimant to the Byzantine throne in return for trade concessions for Venice and money and troops to help the crusaders attack Egypt. But having ensconced their Byzantine ally in the imperial office, they found him either unwilling or unable to deliver on his promises. The crusaders and the Venetians therefore decided to take Constantinople for themselves. Their attack was successful; the city fell into Western hands in 1204 and was savagely pillaged. The crusaders immediately established a Latin Empire of Constantinople and elected a Flemish noble as emperor and a Venetian cleric as patriarch of the Greek Orthodox church, thus reuniting the eastern and western Christian communities for the moment. Somewhat reluctantly Innocent III gave his sanction to the whole arrangement. The crusading nobles immediately began to carve out rich fiefs for themselves on Byzantine soil. The Venetians assumed control over the chief port cities of the empire, making them the real beneficiaries of the whole undertaking. The Latin Empire of Constantinople survived until 1261, when forces representing the legitimate Byzantine emperor recaptured Constantinople and ousted the usurpers.

By the beginning of the thirteenth century, the crusading movement was beginning to lose its appeal for western Europeans. In the minds of some the attack of Christians on other Christians during the Fourth Crusade made a travesty of the crusading ideal. The exploitation by the papacy of the crusading ideal as a means of rallying forces to attack such papal enemies as the Albigensian heretics (see Chapter 21) or Emperor Frederick II fueled antipathy in many quarters. Growing numbers in the West began to argue that peaceful missionary activity was a better way to convert the infidel Moslems than military force. The attraction of the Near East as a place to make a fortune waned in the face of the tenuous situation of the Christian establishment in the Latin Kingdom of Jerusalem.

Nonetheless, the continued existence of the beleaguered Christian outpost in the east as well as the ambitions of western Europeans seeking to use the crusading movement to promote political ends prompted new crusades during the thirteenth century. Pope Innocent III organized a fifth crusade, but he died before it could get under way in 1217. Seeking to strike the Moslem threat to the Christian position at its source, this crusade was directed toward Egypt, but an attempted expedition up the Nile ended in a resounding defeat. Emperor Frederick II led the next crusade, chiefly because he wanted to secure possession of the Holy Land, to which he had a legal right by virtue of his marriage to the heiress of the Latin Kingdom of Jerusalem. Through diplomacy he arranged a treaty in 1229 with the Moslems which restored Jerusalem to Christian control. But his victory was tainted in the eyes of many because at the time he occupied Jerusalem he was under sentence of excommunication imposed by the pope as punishment for Frederick's refusal to accept papal direction. In 1244 the Moslems again captured the Holy City. This loss prompted Louis IX of France to organize what amounted to the last major crusade (see Figure 20.1). His four-year stay in the Holy Land did little to strengthen the Christian position. In fact, his attempt at an Egyptian campaign increased the danger by providing the occasion for a strong, aggressive Moslem dynasty, the Mamelukes, to establish itself in Egypt.

The increasingly precarious position of the Latin Kingdom of Jerusalem was relieved temporarily in the mid–thirteenth century, when Christians and Moslems allied to save themselves from the Mongol threat. Early in the century a great leader, Genghis Khan, had transformed the Mongol nomads of Central Asia into a potent military force that swept over Eurasia and fashioned a huge empire stretching from China to central Europe. After 1260 the Mongol threat began to lessen, and the old hostilities between Moslems and Christians in the Near East were renewed. In 1291 the Mamelukes took the last Christian strongholds in the Holy Land. After nearly two centuries, the Latins had finally been ousted from Syria and Palestine.

So ended the most overt and dramatic manifestation of medieval western European expansionism. Historians are not unanimous in their assessments of the consequences of the crusading movement, but they agree that at least in some respects the effects were enduring. The Crusades generated an interaction between East and West which "educated" Europeans to new ideas, products, and styles of life. They extended and solidified western European commercial power. They decisively affected the histories of both the Byzantine Empire and the Moslem world, weakening the former and provoking the latter to a new aggressiveness that was to have a significant impact on Europe during the late Middle Ages and well into early modern times. Perhaps the most significant legacy of the crusading movement was the negative image of western Europeans it generated among people in the east: the greedy, faithless, crude warrior; the crafty, grasping merchant; the ambitious, worldly church official—all of whom would do anything to acquire land, wealth, and power. Such images poisoned East-West relationships for centuries.

However one judges the impact of the Crusades, the loss of Outremer should not detract from the importance of medieval expansionism in all its various forms in changing the position of western Europe with respect to the rest of the world. Extensive territories and their inhabitants in northern and central Europe, Spain, and southern Italy had been drawn permanently into the orb of western European civilization. The sphere of influence of Latin Christendom had been greatly enlarged. The commercial boundaries of western Europe had been vastly expanded. Their contacts with a larger world stretched the mental horizons of western Europeans far beyond what they had been in 1000. This outward thrust marked a preliminary step that eventually would lead to a revolutionary transformation of western Europe's position in a global setting.

SUGGESTED READING

Overviews of Medieval Expansion

J. R. S. Phillips, *The Medieval Expansion of Europe* (1988). A good introduction.

Archibald R. Lewis, *Nomads and Crusaders*, A.D. *1000–1368* (1988). Treats medieval European expansion in an intercontinental context.

Expansion in Spain, Southern Italy, and the Baltic

Anwar G. Chejne, *Muslim Spain. Its History and Culture* (1974). A fine introduction to Moslem Spain.

Thomas F. Glick, *Islamic and Christian Spain in the Early Middle Ages* (1979). Treats the interaction of Islamic and Christian societies.

Angus MacKay, *Spain in the Middle Ages: From Frontier to Empire, 1000–1500* (1977). Traces the rise of the Christian kingdoms.

Donald Matthew, *The Norman Kingdom of Sicily* (1992). A fine study of the birth of a new state in the Middle Ages.

The Crusades

P. M. Holt, *The Age of the Crusades. The Near East from the Eleventh Century to 1517* (1986). A helpful overview.

Jonathan Riley-Smith, *What Were the Crusades?* (1977). A stimulating analysis of the nature of the crusading movement.

Carl Erdmann, *The Origin of the Idea of Crusade,* trans. Marshall W. Baldwin and Walter Goffart (1977). A fundamental work stressing ideological factors.

Jonathan Riley-Smith, *The Crusades. A Short History* (1987).

Hans E. Mayer, *The Crusades,* trans. John Gillingham (1972).

Two fine short histories; perhaps the Riley-Smith work is better.

Erick Christiansen, *The Northern Crusades: The Baltic and the Catholic Frontier, 1100–1525* (1980). A full treatment of an overlooked aspect of medieval crusading.

Joshua Prawer, *The Crusaders' Kingdom: European Colonization in the Middle Ages* (1972). Portrays what happened to the Europeans in the Near Eastern environment.

Norman Daniel, *The Arabs and Medieval Europe,* 2nd ed. (1979). Treats European attitudes toward Islam.

Benjamin Z. Kedar, *Crusade and Mission: European Approaches Toward the Muslims* (1984). Examines the interactions between crusading and missionary concepts.

Michael Angold, *The Byzantine Empire, 1025–1204: A Political History* (1984). Will help the reader understand the Byzantine role in the Crusades.

Malcolm Cameron Lyons and D. E. P. Jackson, *Saladin: The Politics of Holy War* (1982). A perceptive study of a great Moslem leader.

CHAPTER 21
Religious Renewal, 1000–1300

FIGURE 21.1 **The Last Judgment** This magnificent scene carved above the main portal of the west façade of the Gothic cathedral at Chartres illustrates a fundamental idea of medieval Christian teaching: the Last Judgment, when Christ will make a final determination of the eternal lot of all people. Christ is surrounded by symbols of his glory and by life-size representations of individuals who played a role in the unfolding of the Christian drama. The scene conveys a powerful message to the faithful who might stray into sin: The time is at hand to enter the church and partake of grace-giving sacraments so that one will be ready to receive Christ's approval at the final hour. (Scala/Art Resource)

Between 1000 and 1300 powerful religious forces surged through western European society to bring about changes that some refer to as a medieval "reformation." The religious revival of the central Middle Ages was complex, involving diverse approaches to the structuring of Christian society and to the attainment of Christian perfection. It challenged many traditional assumptions about religion and society. It called forth a major intellectual effort that sought to discover in the rich Christian tradition guides that would help shape a fuller religious life. Its impact was felt at all levels of society. In its totality the reform movement provided the prime force binding all Europeans into a unified civilization. Thus, in a real sense, the medieval reformation constituted the central "event" in the history of the central Middle Ages.

1. THE ORIGINS OF THE REFORM MOVEMENT

As we have seen (see Chapter 17), in the tenth century religious life in western Europe was beset by serious problems. At the root of those problems was the immersion of the religious establishment in the system of lordship and dependency that dominated the contemporary society. Ecclesiastical property and offices were controlled by lay lords concerned chiefly with acquiring power and wealth, a system that produced religious leaders who shared the same concerns and an ignorant, impoverished, undisciplined lower clergy badly equipped to provide pastoral care for the lay population. Abuses of all kinds enveloped the administration of the religious services upon which the salvation of souls was believed to depend. The level of Christian spiritual life had reached a low point in spite of the power and wealth wielded by the worldly religious establishment.

In the midst of that difficult era signs of religious renewal began to appear. In large part this renewal was generated as a protest against a corrupt religious establishment, but it was also given impetus by men and women who recaptured from Christian tradition visions of perfection that prompted efforts to purify religious life. The first manifestations of renewal came in the monastic world, which for centuries had served as a focal point for those seeking spiritual perfection. During the tenth century monastic reforms were initiated in various parts of western Europe—Burgundy, Lotharingia, Italy, England—each stressing various patterns of renewal: escape from the heavy hand of secular control; denial of the corrupt material world in favor of poverty; a search for moral perfection; intensification of devotional practices; a quest for a better understanding of the Christian heritage. Here and there bishops sought ways to improve the moral lives of the lower clergy under their jurisdiction and to intensify the teaching of their flocks. Pious rulers, and especially their queens, began to patronize reform activities. Feudal potentates gave generous support to reformed monastic houses, became involved in new devotional practices sponsored by reformed monks, and even curbed their conduct as warriors out of respect for efforts to promote Christian peace. Even simple peasants and townspeople felt the pull of reform, as evidenced by their outcries against the wealth and corruption of those who claimed to direct their spiritual lives.

At its beginnings in the late tenth and early eleventh centuries, the quest for spiritual renewal was spontaneous, diffuse, disorganized, and lacking in specific direction. Although elements of spontaneity continued to surround the reforming effort until well into the thirteenth century, from the early eleventh century onward certain major trends dominated the medieval "reformation." One, spearheaded by the Roman popes with the support of some secular rulers and the intellectual establishment, sought to establish the "liberty" of the religious establishment, to perfect its organization, and to impose on the faithful a uniform discipline and doctrine. A second, focused chiefly in the monastic world but also drawing strength from intellectuals, probed for deeper spirituality, moral improvement, and more meaningful ways of worshiping God. A third involved a vibrant upsurge of popular piety that sought ways by which the poor and meek might share the promises of Jesus. In examining each of these major currents of religious reform separately, it must be remembered that they developed concurrently and constantly intersected, sometimes reinforcing each other and sometimes clashing.

2. PAPAL REFORM: THE QUEST FOR ORDER AND UNIFORMITY

The papacy became involved in the medieval religious revival relatively late. During the tenth and early eleventh centuries it had become bogged down in corruption and been dominated first by Roman nobles and then by the Holy Roman emperors. As a consequence, it asserted little influence over the Christian community of western Europe. The situation began to change in the middle of the eleventh century, when a circle of reformers established control over the papacy and spearheaded a movement called the Gregorian reform by later historians after one of its leaders, the monk Hildebrand, later Pope Gregory VII (1073–1085). These reformers were men of deep moral convictions and well schooled in Christian tradition. As we have seen (see Chapter 19), the Gregorian reformers argued that the Christian community should constitute a visible earthly community, a "Church" (ecclesia) as they would have put it, within which the attainment of salvation for all members must be the central concern. They believed with a passion that the community needed its own head, its own laws, its own resources, and its own liberty. On the basis of the ancient Petrine theory (see p. 158), they claimed for the bishop of Rome the divinely sanctioned authority to head the Christian community as Christ's earthly vicar. They argued that God entrusted to his vicar two kinds of divinely ordained power, spiritual and temporal. The pope held spiritual authority, which bestowed on him both the right and the duty to direct the activities of all ecclesiastical officials and to supervise all activities related to saving souls. By virtue of their office, lay princes were vested with temporal power to be used to repress the evil forces that impeded the faithful from gaining God's favors on earth and from earning eternal salvation, but always with the understanding that temporal power could be withdrawn if any prince did not use it in ways that served spiritual ends or if a prince went counter to the spiritual authority, which was always superior. Although this ideology was shaped from long-standing traditions, its articulation in the eleventh-century setting had revolutionary implications in terms of the governance of the Christian community. Most revolutionary of all was its challenge to another long-established tradition which had entrusted to Christian princes, such as Constantine, Charlemagne, and Otto I, a God-given responsibility to guide their subjects along the path leading to salvation.

As pope, Gregory VII acted to convert this ideology into a reform program that focused on concentrating authority in papal hands and on using that power to correct the evils that impeded the purification of Christian society. He launched an effort to free the religious establishment from lay control by prohibiting lay investiture of clergymen with their offices and lands, thereby opening a prolonged political struggle with the princes of western Europe, especially the Holy Roman emperors. He initiated a legislative program aimed at using papal authority to eliminate moral abuses among the clergy, especially the selling of church offices and services (simony) and clerical marriage. To ensure that these efforts at reform were observed, he charted a program aimed at centralizing ecclesiastical authority in papal hands. Even before his pontificate, the papal reformers had placed the responsibility of selecting popes in the hands of clergymen, the College of Cardinals, thereby putting the papal office beyond lay control. Gregory took important steps to make that body the nucleus of a papal administrative machine. Papal *decretals* (legislative enactments) were issued with increasing frequency, laying down regulations for church governance and clerical conduct. Papal legates were sent across Europe to enforce this legislation. The papacy encouraged regional church councils to enact measures aimed at correcting abuses wherever they existed in the Christian world. Provisions were made to expedite the appeal of difficult cases to Rome for settlement. Special attention was given to regularizing and increasing papal income so as to ensure independence of action.

Gregory VII did not live to see his program realized, but its basic tenets remained a powerful force in shaping Christian life for the next two centuries. The consolidation of papal power met resistance from many quarters, particularly from bishops and princes who believed that their ancient rights were threatened and from other reformers who saw the advance of papal authority as still another way of the pope's gaining power and wealth. But Gregory's successors, exemplified by popes such as Urban II (1088–1099) and Alexander III (1159–1181), pursued his policy of centralization with skill and persistence. Their efforts were abetted by their willingness to retreat from Gregory's radical position on the supremacy of ecclesiastical over secular power. This compromise led to mutual support between the papacy and secular princes in establishing a more effective ecclesiastical organization; many kings found such an organization useful in supporting their own efforts to curb stubborn nobles and towns. By the thirteenth century such popes as Innocent III (1198–1216), Honorius III (1216–1227), Gregory IX (1227–1241), and Innocent IV (1243–1254) presided over an immense organization capable of directing religious life all over western Europe in minute detail.

These thirteenth-century ecclesiastical monarchs controlled an elaborate central bureaucracy located in Rome called the papal *curia.* This body was divided into specialized departments dealing with finances, correspondence and records, judicial cases, doctrinal issues, and the discipline of sinners. It was staffed by trained clerical specialists who made careers of papal administration. The College of Cardinals, made up of churchmen especially selected by the pope, sat with the pope in special meetings (called *consistories*) to formulate major policies; its members often served as heads of the specialized departments that handled routine administrative matters. From the curia flowed a steady stream of legislation touching on every conceivable aspect of religious life. The papal judicial system handled an ever-increasing volume of cases appealed to Rome from throughout Europe. The Roman curia extended its authority beyond Rome through a system of papal agents, called *legates,* sent from Rome to supervise the enactment of papal orders. The legatine system, coupled with the curia's extensive correspondence and judicial appeals to Rome, kept the popes well informed about local affairs throughout Europe. A constantly increasing income—derived from papal property, gifts, fees for judicial services, payments for dispensations from papal regulations, and assessments levied on the lower clergy and the laity—sustained this huge organization.

The authority of St. Peter's vicar was extended downward through the age-old hierarchy of archbishops, bishops, and priests. From Greg-

ory VII's time until 1300 considerable effort was devoted to differentiating the status of the clergy from that of the laity and to defining the exact functions of each level within the clerical hierarchy. In that process papal control over the election and supervision of archbishops and bishops was extended, greatly limiting—although not eliminating—secular domination of the clergy. Each archbishop was entrusted with the supervision of several bishops in his *province,* and each bishop was empowered to direct the activities of the priests and laity residing in his *diocese.* Each of these officials headed a small-scale model of the papal curia, called a *cathedral chapter,* staffed by *canons* who had a voice in episcopal elections, advised their superiors, and carried out provincial and diocesan administration. That administration involved conducting judicial proceedings, collecting and dispensing revenues, managing episcopal property, and supervising parish priests, who were charged with administering the sacraments and preaching to the Christian populace. One of the major accomplishments of the era was the establishment across western Europe of a firm structure of local parishes through which Christian teachings could be delivered to all people. For the most part these territorial units, often coinciding with manors and agricultural villages or with specific quarters in urban centers, were freed from lay control over the appointment of priests and parish income and placed under episcopal direction.

Although by 1300 some were beginning to think otherwise, the inspiration behind this effort at centralization was not merely a quest for power. Popes, bishops, monks, and large segments of the laity genuinely believed that effective ecclesiastical organization was only a means by which a higher end could be realized: guiding the Christian flock toward observance of the one right way of behaving and believing that God had ordained as essential to salvation. As a consequence, a major aspect of the papal reform movement centered on defining and standardizing church law and doctrine to provide those in charge of the care of souls with norms governing Christian life and belief.

By the eleventh century there existed an immense body of law relating to Christian life that had been derived from many sources: scriptural injunctions, the writings of the early Church

Fathers, the acts of a long succession of church councils, the pronouncements of popes and bishops (some of which were forged), and legislation by Christian rulers. Many of the provisions of this body of law were confused and contradictory, and some no longer applied to contemporary realities. Moreover, the issues posed by the reform movement demanded new legal solutions. These problems produced a new breed of specialist to serve the religious establishment: trained lawyers working to create a consistent, organized body of law, called canon law, that would sustain the effort to create an independent religious community governed by its own rules. A decisive figure in the effort to create a "code" of law for the religious establishment was Gratian. In 1140 he published his *Decretum*, which represented an effort to apply the rules of logic to the vast body of past precedents in a way that would remove contradictions and produce a consistent set of laws. Gratian's work immediately became the guide for ecclesiastical administration and discipline. Among many other things, his code defined the powers of each rank of the clergy, the jurisdiction of ecclesiastical courts, crimes against the religious establishment and their punishments, the proper use of ecclesiastical income and property, and the manner of conducting religious ceremonies. Throughout the work ran one predominant idea—the supremacy of the papacy in the governance of Christendom. Subsequent codifications that incorporated new legislation greatly expanded canon law, and extensive commentaries aimed at relating its provisions to the real world greatly facilitated its application. By 1300 a powerful instrument for directing Christian society had been forged.

A comparable movement occurred with respect to doctrine. By 1000 there existed a rich body of teachings derived from diverse sources that dealt with Christian belief. Like the law, this material was disorganized, filled with contradictions, and interpreted in a variety of ways. To cope with this problem, another kind of specialist, the trained theologian, emerged. Operating primarily in the setting of monastic and cathedral schools and then universities, these theologians gradually worked out an approach to doctrinal issues that came to be called scholasticism (see Chapter 22). Working within the parameters provided by revealed truth contained in Scripture, scholastic theologians sought to use human reason to resolve by rules of logic the contradictions imbedded in doctrinal tradition. Beyond that, they sought to compile summaries that would set forth in logical, consistent, and holistic terms what constituted the essence of Christian belief. To achieve this end, the scholastics sought to weave all human knowledge into a theological framework which would provide a single body of truth that would provide an authoritative answer to any issue facing a Christian believer.

At the heart of the system of belief developed during the twelfth and thirteenth centuries stood the doctrines of grace, the sacraments, and good works. According to the theologians, God had created human beings in order that they might enjoy eternal salvation, human life being but a test of worthiness. Since humans were corrupted by original sin, the stain imposed on all by the disobedience of Adam and Eve, men and women needed God's grace to save them. That grace was bestowed through the sacraments instituted by Jesus as an essential part of his mission of redemption (see Figure 21.2). Although the grace that flowed from the sacraments was a gift bestowed by God out of his love for humanity, worthiness for that gift depended on the performance of good works pleasing to God.

At the Fourth Lateran Council, held in 1215 under the direction of Innocent III, the number of sacraments was set at seven. Each drew its efficacy by virtue of the fact that it was administered by duly anointed members of the clergy, without whose services no Christian could expect to be saved. *Baptism,* usually administered at infancy, removed the stain of original sin and initiated its recipients into the Christian community. *Confirmation,* usually received at adolescence, infused into Christians the Holy Spirit, strengthening their faith and fortifying them against the Devil at a particularly critical moment in their lives. *Extreme unction,* administered to those in danger of death, strengthened them at the moment they must face the judgment of the Almighty and removed from their souls the stain of minor (or venial) sins. *Marriage* sanctified the wedded state and family life. *Holy orders,* or *ordination,* conferred on select Christian males the priestly powers that permitted them to act as valid successors of Christ and the apostles in teaching the faith and administering the grace-

FIGURE 21.2 The Sacraments These scenes from a fourteenth-century manuscript illustrate three of the seven sacraments—baptism, the Eucharist, and marriage. According to the Church's teaching, only through participation in the sacraments could a Christian gain salvation. (Bibliothèque Nationale, Paris, ms. n. s. fr. 4509)

giving sacraments, especially the Eucharist and penance. The *Eucharist* was the sacrament by which Christ himself became present to the faithful. Its exact nature was not defined until 1215, when the Fourth Lateran Council pronounced the doctrine of *transubstantiation:* When a priest consecrated bread and wine at Mass, their substance miraculously changed into the body and blood of Christ, although their external attributes (color, shape, taste, etc.) remained the same. Partaking of this sacrament—receiving Communion—infused the grace of Christ's substance into the soul. No punishment was more terrible than excommunication—being cut off from receiving the Eucharist. The last sacrament was *penance*, whereby Christians who confessed their sins to a priest and resolved not to repeat them received God's forgiveness, provided that they made some sacrifice or did some good work assigned by the priest. Since the stain of sin barred one from heaven, Christians constantly needed to resort to a priestly confessor to ensure that their

souls, freed from original sin by baptism, were repurified by the removal of all stains caused by the sins they committed in the course of their lives. The Fourth Lateran Council decreed that the faithful must confess at least once a year.

Embroidered on the sacramental system was a rich set of practices sanctioned by the religious establishment that were counted as good works whose performance served to facilitate winning divine favor beyond the saving grace bestowed by the sacraments. By the thirteenth century Christians could avail themselves of an array of prayers and ritual ceremonies that served in every conceivable situation to invoke the help of God, Jesus, the Virgin Mary, and an army of angels and saints and to frustrate the hordes of demons that schemed under Satan's command to corrupt men and women. Opportunities abounded to offer material donations to churches and monasteries, to perform acts of charity, and to do penitential acts, such as fasting, abstaining from pleasures of the flesh, and venerating the relics of saints—all counted as good works. When coupled with the impresssive rites associated with administering the sacraments, involvement in these adjuncts to the sacramental system added a compelling emotional dimension to religious life that played a major role in making religion a central force in the lives of people from all levels of society.

The major fruits of papal reform—expanded liberty for the religious establishment, the centralized administrative system, the wide-ranging body of canon law, and the theological system that made the clergy essential to the salvation of all—permitted religious leaders to extend their influence into a wide range of matters involved in daily life. For example, it is difficult to treat any aspect of thirteenth-century European political life without encountering the influence of the papacy. Pope Innocent III offers a case in point. We need only recall how he manipulated the election of the Holy Roman emperors, finally arranging for his ward, Frederick II, to assume that office. He took an active role in directing affairs in the Kingdom of Sicily and in shaping the complex political interactions among the numerous Italian city-states. After a long quarrel he compelled Philip II of France to take back a wife he had repudiated. He forced or persuaded John of England and several other rulers to accept the status of vassal of the pope. Innocent was active in promoting the Fourth and Fifth crusades and in organizing a crusade against the heretical Albigensians of southern France, thereby helping the French kings to expand their royal domain. While not all of Innocent's ventures into European politics turned out the way he intended, the papal presence was a crucial factor in determining the political scene. Innocent's story was replicated in the careers of most thirteenth-century popes and, on a smaller scale, in those of countless bishops and priests. In the settings in which the ordinary affairs of people's lives were played out, ecclesiastical influences were everywhere present—in matters pertaining to the administration of justice, land transactions, oath taking, marriages, wills, crime, education, warfare, charity. Papal monarchs and their episcopal and priestly agents used religious weapons to gain political ends and political and economic pressures to advance ecclesiastical interests. Seldom in all history has a religious establishment been able to assert its independent authority so decisively in shaping the conduct of secular society as did the thirteenth-century Church in western Europe.

3. MONASTIC REFORM: SPIRITUAL SEEKING

While the quest for greater order in the organization of the Christian religious establishment and for standardization of its law and theology was advanced by popes, bishops, canon lawyers, and theologians, others sought a deeper spiritual understanding. Although those promoting reform on the papal model were always concerned with spirituality, it was in the monastic world that the urge to deepen the spiritual life found its most fruitful institutional setting; in some cases the spiritual forces that shaped monastic reforms derived from impulses welling up in the world of the laity.

In the year 1000 those interested in expanding their spiritual horizons faced a religious mentality of limited dimensions. Most Christians believed in a God perceived as a stern judge whose wrath might fall on helpless, sin-tainted humans at any time and in any form (see Figure 21.1). Human life was surrounded by constant danger from the Devil and his demons, present everywhere and armed with almost irresistible powers to entice men and women ever deeper into sin, for which God's anger would only be greater. The best humans could hope for was to do something that would be pleasing to God or that would persuade the legions of angels and saints who served the judgmental deity to intercede in their behalf. As a consequence, religious life was highly externalized. Men and women sought to propitiate God by offering their material goods, performing acts of charity, praying, and venerating relics of the saints. They searched for acts of penitence to win forgiveness for their sins. Always uppermost in people's minds was the hope for miracles whereby God or his agents would overturn the natural order to cure sickness, turn sure defeat in war into victory, save the harvest, or confound the Devil in his efforts to trap someone into sin. Building on this religious mentality, monastic spiritual seekers sought to deepen their understanding of God and to discover new ways of linking the human spirit to the divine. At first their prime concern was the enrichment of the spiritual life of the select few living the cloistered life, but eventually they widened their vision to embrace the spiritual condition of all Christians.

During the tenth and eleventh centuries the monastic reform movement was dominated by the Cluniac order. The monastery of Cluny had been founded in 910 by a pious lay prince under terms that freed the new foundation from lay control and dedicated its members to strict observance of the Benedictine rule. Cluny's first abbots sought to extend its influence by founding new houses or reforming corrupted existing houses, all of which were placed under the governance of the abbot of the motherhouse as a means of ensuring continued purity of life. As a consequence of the abbots' reforming zeal, by the eleventh century Cluniac monasteries existed all over Europe as centers of spiritual guidance. Cluniac spirituality emphasized an elaborate daily round of prayer and celebration of sacred rites as the main duty of the monks. The Cluniac liturgy was a splendid model of the kind of externalized religion that the contemporary world found so attractive. Many feudal aristocrats established close ties with Cluniac communities, chiefly to gain assurance that the monastic congregations they supported would include them in their prayers for the dead. As a prime sponsor of the Peace and the Truce of God, the Cluniac order made a notable contribution to curbing feudal warfare and promoting the concept of holy warfare as an act pleasing to God. And as promoters of the cult of saints and pilgrimages, the Cluniac monks provided an important outlet for the widespread urge for penitential actions pleasing to God.

By the end of the eleventh century the Cluniac movement began to lose its appeal, in part because of the excessive wealth of the Cluniacs, but more importantly because spiritual seekers increasingly found the externalized forms of piety promoted by Cluny unduly limited and not attuned to changing concepts of the nature of God, of human capabilities, and of the needs of Christian society, especially as highlighted by the Gregorian reform. These views tempered God's harsh judgmental qualities with a new emphasis on his love for humanity (see Figure 21.3) and

FIGURE 21.3 A Loving, Caring God This sculpture from Chartres Cathedral shows God creating Adam. This Creator is not the awful judge of the last day (see Figure 21.1). Rather, this scene reflects the new understanding of God that had such a powerful effect on the spirituality of the twelfth and thirteenth centuries. (Archives Photographiques, Paris)

on the human capacity to absorb God's love internally and to progress toward perfection through human powers born of human love toward other humans. The new piety especially extolled the virtue of poverty as a condition for personal perfection, a position that left the existing religious establishment open to criticism. The ideal of poverty led to a revival of hermit life based on the model provided by the desert fathers of the fourth and fifth centuries. Although most hermits of the eleventh and twelfth centuries pursued their search for perfection individually, the hermit ideal did produce the Carthusian order, established in France in the late eleventh century. Imposing on its members a severe regimen of poverty, fasting, and prayer as a means of opening the human heart to divine love, the Carthusian order impressed upon an admiring world a model of denial of the self and the world as a means of preparing to meet God.

The monastic movement that during the twelfth century played the most important role in shaping and projecting a new spiritual vision into the world was the Cistercian order. Founded in 1098 by a Benedictine who felt that the ancient rule was not being properly observed by the then-dominant Cluniacs, the Cistercian movement stressed the needs for separation from the world and for a simple life of prayer and physical labor. Cistercian houses were usually established on remote, uncultivated sites where the Cistercian monks and their lay brothers—peasants who bound themselves to monastic life by oath but followed a less austere life than did full members of the order—employed their labor, managerial skills, and technical ingenuity to create thriving agricultural establishments. Cistercian houses, both male and female, soon sprang up all over Europe, linked together by a unique governance system in which decisions affecting all houses were made collectively by the heads of individual houses meeting on a regular basis.

Especially influential in shaping the Cistercian order and its spiritual message was Bernard of Clairvaux (1090–1153), who entered the order in 1112 and almost immediately became its driving force. Bernard viewed monastic life as a preparation for action in the cause of God. That preparation was aimed at the inner spiritual development of each individual monk rather than at the elaborate, communally organized round of external religious acts that characterized Cluniac practice and that dominated the religious mentality of most contemporary Christians. Monks were now to practice physical deprivation, work, and prayer as a part of their spiritual training. Equally important were contemplation and devotion. Bernard's prescription for individual spiritual development focused attention on a loving God reaching out to unleash the potential of the human soul to participate in holiness. The human spirit could best reach back toward that God by contemplating the human, suffering Jesus and by seeking to share the feelings of Mary, Mother of God, of Jesus' disciples, and of those he taught as all of them lived in the presence of God made human for the salvation of other humans. Bernard was fully confident that the love and understanding flowing from such an approach to God would prepare human beings to go forth to fight sin and spiritual poverty without fear of corruption. In his own life he exemplified this new kind of spiritual activism. During his forty-year career in the Cistercian order, he was involved in many important events in Europe. He was the chief instigator of the Second Crusade, proclaiming that involvement was a manifestation of love for God and of service in the divine cause. He served the papacy doggedly in rooting out corruption in the clergy (he even censured papal conduct on occasion). He was a relentless foe of what he perceived as unorthodox and heretical thinking. He constantly hounded Europe's kings to improve their lives and their governments. He had no peer as a popular preacher and as a promoter of the use in the entire Christian community of the devotional practices that were at the heart of Cistercian spirituality. He and other Cistercians served as industrious soldiers of Christ whose chief armament was their sense of godliness derived from their inner spiritual life. Their target was the souls of individual men and women who possessed but did not properly use the power to make themselves better Christians.

Other developments in the monastic world of the twelfth century contributed to the deepening of religious life and the expansion of monastic influence on society. The number of monastic houses for women—nunneries—increased dramatically. These centers enlarged the visibility of women as models of piety and offered many of them opportunities for education and service. An order called the Augustinian Canons was organized as a means of improving the moral quality of the clerics who served in cathedral chapters. Its rule bound the canons to poverty, prayer, and moral excellence while permitting them to continue their responsibilities as pastors and episcopal administrators. Perhaps the most unusual application of the monastic model was the establishment of the crusading orders—the Templars, the Hospitalers, and the Teutonic Knights. Following a model defined by Bernard of Clairvaux, those who entered these orders took a monastic vow stressing obedience, poverty, and service to God as warriors defending the Christians in the Holy Land. Their activities in the cause of holy war earned these orders not only high respect but also immense wealth, which eventually led to their involvement in landholding, commerce, and moneylending.

The expansion of monastic involvement in the world and the search for new spiritual horizons reached a culmination in the early thirteenth century with the establishment of the *mendicant* (begging) orders, the Dominicans and the Franciscans. These orders were a response to new problems that increasingly challenged the clergy's traditional pastoral activities: the growth of urban life, with its unique institutions and tensions; the emergence of more sophisticated law and theology; the growing criticisms of the wealth and power of the ecclesiastical establishment; and doctrinal heresy. The mendicant movement sought to prepare brothers and sisters to serve God not by retreating to the cloister but by going into the world to address these problems without being burdened by material concerns or the stigma of wealth—which were widely believed to be barriers to spiritual perfection. To achieve this end, the mendicant orders insisted on absolute poverty after the model of Jesus and his disciples; neither the individual monk nor the corporate order was to possess wealth. Material support was to be derived from charity extended by those being served; begging for such charity was a key element of the vocation of the mendicants. Although the mendicants were mindful of the necessity of developing inner spiritual resources, the problems they sought to address as pastors called for the development of intellectual skills. As a consequence, their preparation for active monastic life stressed an education devoted to mastering the intricacies of canon law and theology and to developing the skills needed for effective propagation of Christian beliefs and practices.

The Dominican order drew its name from its founder, a Spanish canon named Dominic (1170–1221). He was inspired to found a new order as a result of a tour through southern France, where the Albigensian heresy (see pp. 289–290) was rampant despite the efforts of the local bishops and Cistercian monks to curb it. Dominic became convinced that orthodoxy would prevail only if preachers learned in theology and free from all suspicion of wealth mingled intimately with heretics to teach them the true faith. In 1215 Pope Innocent III authorized him to organize a new order dedicated to the destruction of heresy by preaching. The rule provided that Dominic's followers would commit themselves to complete poverty and to preaching; their collective activities would be directed by a master general and his subordinate priors who commanded the provinces into which the order was organized. The rule placed heavy stress on the education of each monk in theology and law. The Black Friars, or Friars Preachers, as the order came to be called, quickly established themselves as a major force across Europe, active in preaching and in controlling the formulation and teaching of theology in the universities. Their involvement in university education allowed them to play a major role in shaping the mentality of religious leadership during the thirteenth century.

The inspiration for the Franciscan order was supplied by one of the most appealing figures in all religious history, Francis of Assisi (1182–1226) (see Figure 21.4). The son of a wealthy Italian merchant, Francis, while still a young man who had previously enjoyed a worldly life, underwent a fundamental spiritual conversion that convinced him that he must imitate Jesus in a most literal sense. As he put it, he married "Lady Poverty" and turned his energy to preaching and performing charitable works. He was especially charismatic as a preacher, exuding joy and a sympathy for all God's creatures, especially unfortunate, suffering human beings. To his followers, he was "God's own troubadour," filled with happiness and love. Almost immediately both men and women began to follow him. They sur-

FIGURE 21.4 Francis of Assisi: "God's Own Troubadour" St. Francis of Assisi, portrayed here in a painting done by Cimabue ca. 1280, was perhaps the most powerful spiritual force in the thirteenth century. His ideas on poverty and love deeply affected many of those searching for religious values in his age. (Alinari/Art Resource)

tured organization and a discipline more formal than the founder's simple command that his followers imitate Jesus. The rule of absolute poverty was modified to allow the order to acquire wealth and to place greater emphasis on formal education as preparation for a preaching career. To many devoted Franciscans these compromises represented a denial of the Franciscan ideal; as a result of these concerns, the order was plagued by bitter internal conflicts. The Friars Minor, or Grey Friars, also met strong opposition from local clergy, who resented their exaltation of poverty and their effective skills as preachers and confessors. Despite these obstacles, the Franciscans asserted a powerful influence on religious life at all levels of society. Together, the Franciscans and the Dominicans became pillars of strength for the thirteenth-century religious establishment in terms of propagating its teachings, containing voices of dissent, and expanding spiritual consciousness.

4. POPULAR REFORM: ENTHUSIASM, DISSENT, HERESY

The highly visible efforts of reformers to impose order on religious life and to expand spiritual vision were accompanied by considerable religious ferment among people of modest social status. Reform of this kind manifested itself in the activities of diverse peoples: simple priests, maverick monks, peasants, merchants, artisans, women, even children. What motivated their efforts at religious renewal is difficult to discern. Perhaps they were stimulated by a deeper understanding of the Christian message brought to them by the priests and monks produced by the papal and monastic reform movements. Perhaps they were introduced to new religious ideas by the slowly expanding number of literate laypersons, especially in towns, who were able to explore sacred literature, especially the Bible, and articulate their own interpretation of its meaning. The social and economic changes affecting society at all levels created new pressures that provoked a rethinking of traditional religious values. In reviewing the evidence, one suspects that many simple, uneducated, illiterate people were able to extract from their limited knowledge of God's ways and of Jesus' message fresh religious

rendered their wealth, worked or begged for a livelihood, and preached a simple message of love for God and humanity. In 1210 Francis asked Innocent III for permission to organize a formal religious order that would practice absolute poverty and dedicate its efforts to preaching and good works. Innocent hesitated, feeling that Francis' demands on his followers were too severe and perhaps concerned that the simple message of love and repentance would breed a troop of dissenters with little regard for the machinery that the organized Church supplied for saving souls. Finally, however, he consented. Between then and 1226, when Francis died, the order grew rapidly, spreading to nearly every part of western Europe. As the order expanded, its governing rule was modified to provide a more struc-

insights that made their lives more meaningful. Whatever the source, there can be no question that the period 1000 to 1300 witnessed significant religious stirrings throughout the population.

One manifestation of popular religious ferment was the enthusiastic response of simple people to externalized cult practices aimed at seeking God's favor and doing penance for sins. Such people eagerly participated in the cult of relics and the veneration of saints. Simple people participated in pilgrimages to holy places, whether the holy place be a shrine located a few miles away or the scene of Jesus' earthly life in distant Palestine. The infamous Peasants' Crusade reflects the fervor aroused in the popular mind by the crusading movement; even more bizarre was the Children's Crusade of 1212, during which several thousand children were organized for an expedition to the Holy Land and proceeded as far as Marseilles in southern France before less pious merchants sold them into slavery.

Another manifestation of popular religious enthusiasm was the response given to charismatic preachers. Building their message around Jesus' poverty, humility, and love, these preachers often established bands of followers who shared their wealth, engaged in works of charity, cared for the sick, and worshiped in unique ways that emphasized emotion and intimate companionship. Some of these leaders spiced their exhortations to live like Jesus and his apostles with passionate attacks on the moral flabbiness of the clergy and the wealth of the contemporary religious establishment, thus making anticlericalism a regular part of popular religious reform. On occasion, this anticlericalism led to overt action against the established clergy. For example, between about 1050 and 1070, at the very moment when the Gregorian reform movement was gathering momementum, groups of lower-class dissidents called *patarenes* (ragpickers) by their enemies fiercely resisted the authority of bishops appointed to their office by secular rulers in several Italian cities, protesting episcopal wealth, abuse of power, and immorality. Again, in 1145, an Italian monk, Arnold of Brescia, so aroused the populace of Rome against the wealth and secular power of the papacy that the pope was forced to flee and succeeded in recapturing control of the city only by calling upon Emperor Frederick Barbarossa to use force to capture and execute Arnold.

On occasion such popular reform efforts went beyond what the religious and secular authorities would tolerate as dissent and thus became heresy in the eyes of those authorities. Such was the fate of the Waldensian movement. This group was inspired by Peter Waldo, a rich merchant from Lyons in France. In 1173 he gave away his wealth and took up a life of poverty in imitation of Christ—much as contemporary Carthusian and Cistercian monks were doing and as Francis of Assisi would later do. Soon after he began his preaching, Peter sought papal permission to establish a monastic order based on poverty. The pope denied his request, but Peter and his following continued their activity, gradually becoming more radical. Practicing poverty and a strict moral life reflecting many Cistercian ideas about sobriety, temperance, and simplicity, Waldensian leaders went among the common people, especially in urban centers, preaching and praying in the vernacular language. They condemned the clergy, arguing that all Christians could serve a priestly function, and denied the need for sacraments in gaining salvation. They developed their own ministers, both men and women, and their own ritual practices. Eventually they were accused of heresy, and the religious establishment undertook to suppress the movement. Some Waldensian groups, especially in France, returned to orthodoxy, but in northern Italy the movement withstood persecution and survived as a potent force of dissidence in many cities.

Far more radical were the Cathari (from a Greek word meaning "pure"), also called Albigensians (from Albi, the southern French city where the movement was especially strong). Their fundamental beliefs were rooted in a radical dualism, a concept that had originated in the Near East as early as the fourth century, probably as a result of the mixing of Christian and Zoroastrian ideas. The movement spread slowly westward from the Near East, finally reaching northern Italy and southern France in the tenth century. By 1200 its influence was felt throughout Europe, with its major center of strength in southern France.

The Cathari believed that two powers, good and evil, coexisted and constantly competed in the universe. Only things spiritual, including the human soul, were good. Everything material was evil, including the flesh within which the soul was entrapped and the earth itself. This position caused the Cathari to repudiate the God of the Old Testament, who had created the material world, and to deny the humanity of Jesus and the validity of what had been instituted in his name as instruments of salvation, including the earthly religious establishment, the ordained priesthood, and the sacraments, all of which in some way partook of the evil material world. True Cathari—the "perfect," as they called themselves—sought to liberate their souls by escaping the material world. They refused to marry, holding that human procreation was the greatest of all evils. They ate no meat, milk, or eggs, all of which were the products of sexual union. They owned no property and refused to shed blood. Allowances were made by the Cathari communities for those incapable of the rigorous life imposed on the "perfect." Second-grade Cathari, called "believers," were permitted to indulge in things material more freely, although "believers" hoped someday to join the ranks of the "perfect," who alone would be saved. The Cathari developed their own clergy, their own religious services, and their own rules of conduct. Their fervor and discipline produced communities that were remarkably resourceful in asserting political and economic dominance over the areas in which they lived. But above all else, the Cathari impressed those around them with their austerity and moral earnestness.

Needless to say, the unique beliefs and the material success of the Cathari aroused the ire of those outside their exclusive communities and brought charges of heresy against them. As a consequence, the ecclesiastical authorities moved to suppress the movement. Local bishops attempted to convert them by persuasion; that failing, they then hailed them before ecclesiastical courts to try to punish them under the provisions of canon law that provided death sentences for heresy. As we have noted, first the Cistercians and then the Dominicans tried to persuade the Cathari to return to orthodoxy. However, these measures failed, in part because of the dedication of the Cathari and in part because the movement had the support of many local nobles. Pope Innocent III finally took a more drastic step: He

enlisted the support of the French monarchy to mount a "crusade" against the heretics. This ferocious Albigensian Crusade (1209–1229) destroyed the main centers of Cathari power and exterminated many members of the movement. To hunt down those that remained, the papacy utilized a special court, the Inquisition, and empowered it to employ special legal techniques, including secret witnesses and torture, to identify suspected heretics and to bring them to trials that resulted in either their return to orthodoxy or their death. These drastic measures provided a final solution for Catharism, perhaps, however, at the cost of defining the care of souls in terms that irreparably damaged the image of an institution which claimed to serve the religion founded by Jesus.

5. CONSEQUENCES OF THE MEDIEVAL RELIGIOUS REVIVAL

During the thirteenth century there were increasing signs that the reform movement was losing its vitality. Most of the forces that had generated reforming ideas and practices during the eleventh, twelfth, and early thirteenth centuries had been successfully encapsulated into the formal structures of the religious establishment as official parts of its organization, its doctrine, its law, its ritual, its moral code, and its spirituality. Those that could not be assimilated were often eradicated or disregarded. There remains but one question: What were the consequences of all the energy spent trying to elevate the level of religious life? Historians have differed widely in their answers to this question, but perhaps most would accept certain outcomes of the medieval reformation.

First, the medieval reformation certainly strengthened the organization of the religious establishment. In contrast to its position in 1000, that establishment had by 1300 developed structures and processes that allowed the clergy, a group clearly distinguished from the rest of society, to impose one body of belief, one code of conduct, and one set of religious practices on the lay members of the Christian community. Seldom in history has an institution been in a position to direct society so decisively. But that position was not gained by accident; it was a consequence of sustained institution building.

Second, the reformation redefined the relationship between church and state. Whereas in 1000 the religious establishment was subordinated to secular powers whose authority was surrounded by a sacral aura, by 1300 the "Church" as a corporate body had defined for itself an area of liberty into which no other authority could intrude. Acting within this sphere, its officials were able to play a vital role in influencing societal development according to norms defined in religious terms. The existence of separate realms for church and state would powerfully affect Europe's future.

Third, the challenges posed by the effort to renew the religious life unleashed intellectual and artistic talents in ways that stretched the mental capabilities and artistic sensibilities of western Europeans far beyond the boundaries of the mentality existing in the year 1000. In short, the religious renewal sparked a cultural renaissance that might not otherwise have happened except for the troublesome issues raised by the intense search for God and for more effective ways of serving his will.

Fourth, the medieval reformation broadened the range of spiritual possibilities far beyond what had been available to Christians in the early Middle Ages. The probing for the meaning of religious life that occurred between 1000 and 1300 in the monastic world and among simple people produced spiritual concepts that greatly enriched Christian life. Of particular importance for the future of western Christianity was one result of medieval spiritual searching: There was an increasing conviction that within each individual follower of Jesus, whatever his or her social status might be, there existed a spiritual realm of infinite dimensions which each could explore and enrich by exercising powers inherent in human nature.

Finally, it can be argued that the medieval reformation caused as many religious problems as it solved. As its most notable monument, the medieval reformation created a powerful, rich, hierarchically structured institution deeply involved in the affairs of the world. In its theology and its law, that institution had defined a highly formal system of religion that claimed to place the keys to salvation into the hands of a distinctive spiritual elite. It remained to be seen whether society would continue to accept that monolithic system in its entirety. Would kings and princes allow religious leaders to direct many aspects of worldly society according to their own rules? Would men and women find the answers to their spiritual needs in the strictly defined system of belief and worship prescribed by the clergy? Was there any flexibility within this highly centralized, legalistic, formal religious structure to allow adjustment to changing times and ideas? In short, did one productive religious reformation create conditions that would soon demand another?

SUGGESTED READING

General Surveys of Church History

Bernard Hamilton, *Religion in the Medieval West* (1986). A valuable guide to the basic tenets and practices of the medieval Church.

Jeffrey Burton Russell, *A History of Medieval Christianity: Prophecy and Order* (1968).

Joseph H. Lynch, *The Medieval Church: A Brief History* (London and New York, 1992).

Either of these brief surveys will provide an excellent introduction to the major developments in medieval religious history.

Hubert Jedin and John Dolan, eds., *Handbook of Church History*, Vol. 4: *From the High Middle Ages to the Eve of the Reformation*, trans. Anselm Biggs (1970). A detailed history of religious life.

R. W. Southern, *Westsern Society and the Church in the Middle Ages* (1970). Stresses relationships between the Church and the world.

Reform: Papal, Monastic, Popular

Colin Morris, *The Papal Monarchy: The Western Church, 1050–1250* (1989).

I. S. Robinson, *The Papacy, 1073–1198: Continuity and Innovation* (1990).
Two excellent treatments of the development of papal power.
Jaroslav Pelikan, *The Christian Tradition. A History of the Development of Doctrine*, Vol. 3: *The Growth of Medieval Theology (600–1300)* (1978). A challenging treatment of the search for a uniform body of doctrine.
Christopher Brooke, *The Monastic World, 1000–1300* (1974).
C. H. Lawrence, *Medieval Monasticism: Forms of Religious Life in Western Europe in the Middle Ages* (1984).
Two good descriptions of various forms of medieval monasticism.
Rosalind and Christopher Brooke, *Popular Religion in the Middle Ages: Western Europe, 1000–1300* (1984).
A. I. Gurevich, *Medieval Popular Culture. Problems of Belief and Perception* (1988).
Two stimulating studies of the beliefs of common people.
R. I. Moore, *The Origins of European Dissent* (1977).
Malcolm D. Lambert, *Medieval Heresy. Popular Movements from Bogomil to Hus* (1977).
Thorough treatments of dissent and heresy with emphasis on the social factors involved.
R. I. Moore, *The Formation of a Persecuting Society. Power and Deviance in Western Europe, 950–1250* (1987). A brilliant treatment of changing attitudes toward dissent.
Bernard Hamilton, *The Medieval Inquisition* (1981). An objective treatment.
Walter L. Wakefield, *Heresy, Crusade and Inquisition in Southern France, 1100–1250* (1979). Excellent on the Cathari.

Biographies

Helene Tillmann, *Pope Innocent III*, trans. Walter Sax (1980).
Watkin Williams, *Saint Bernard of Clairvaux* (1953).
Adolf Holl, *The Last Christian*, trans. Peter Heinegg (1980). Treats Francis of Assisi.
Pierre Mandonnet, *St. Dominic and His Work*, trans. Mary Benedicta Larkin (1945).

CHAPTER 22
Intellectual and Artistic Revival, 1000–1300

FIGURE 22.1 Gothic Sculpture
These Gothic figures from the south portal of the cathedral at Chartres, France, illustrate the warmth and realism of Gothic sculpture. (Jean Roubier)

As in all other aspects of life, the pace of cultural activity quickened during the years between 1000 and 1300, resulting in an outpouring of creative work in thought, literature, and art. The foundations for this cultural outburst had been painfully shaped during a long apprenticeship culminating in the Carolingian revival; the immediate stimulus was provided by the powerful political, economic, social, and religious changes occurring after 1000. These achievements played an important role in giving western European civilization its unique character and in establishing western European preeminence in a world setting.

The cultural achievement of the central Middle Ages can best be understood by a topical approach concentrating on certain areas of cultural activity that dominated thought and expression. However, it is important to note that the cultural development occurring during the period from 1000 to 1300 had a chronological dimension. In broad terms, cultural change occurred in two phases. The first, which extended from about 1000 to 1170, was marked by vigorous exploration and experimentation that immensely expanded the cultural horizons, skills, and resources of thinkers, writers, and artists. As one American scholar put it, that era witnessed a "renaissance." Toward the end of the twelfth century the cultural climate began to change. The buoyant, questing spirit gave way to a concern for organizing and summarizing the diverse accomplishments of the earlier period. This age of synthesis, which extended across the thirteenth century, produced the most mature expressions of medieval culture, but its accomplishments lacked the freshness and spontaneity characteristic of the "twelfth-century renaissance."

The cultural life of the central Middle Ages was divided into two distinctive spheres. In one, Latin was the vehicle of expression. It was in that language that the prime sources of the Christian faith were enshrined: Scripture, the writings of the Church Fathers, the liturgy, canon law. And that was the language employed to explain the meaning of the faith. Those able to use that language, chiefly members of the clergy, became the "learned" in society, a group accorded high respect because its members had access to the written sources that opened the way to salvation. In the other cultural sphere, the languages of the people, the vernacular tongues, prevailed, first as spoken vehicles of communication and then as written languages devoted chiefly to expressing the interests, tastes, and values of the nobility. Although these two cultural spheres intersected and interacted, each made its own unique contributions to the cultural life of the central Middle Ages. In a real sense, the visual arts played an important role in bridging these two cultural spheres.

1. THE WORLD OF LEARNING: EDUCATION

In the world of the "learned" education was of crucial importance. During the early Middle Ages Latin increasingly became a foreign language that had to be learned by those seeking access to religious truth. This crucial need required schools designed primarily to sustain Latin literacy. What was taught in those schools and how it was taught became a prime factor in shaping the mentality of the learned world. As we have already noted (see Chapters 15 and 16), prior to 1000 educational activity was largely confined to monastic schools, although by 1000 a few modest cathedral schools still survived from Carolingian times, and in Italy some municipal schools continued. A curriculum based on the study of the seven liberal arts had been fixed, and basic textbooks defining the content and methodology of these disciplines had been established, chiefly during the Carolingian period (see p. 216). The monastic schools touched a narrow segment of the population and cultivated a limited range of intellectual interests.

During the eleventh and twelfth centuries the educational system underwent a significant expansion and a fundamental change in character. Part of the stimulus came from intellectual ferment within the monastic world (see Chapter 21). More decisive, however, was a shift in the social value of education. There was a mounting need for literate people able to serve the religious establishment, royal governments, and urban commercial enterprises. Education became the avenue by which increasing numbers could prepare themselves for career opportunities created by that demand. Cathedral and municipal schools were better prepared to meet this challenge than monastic schools were and enjoyed a remarkable growth in both number and size. Especially in the cathedral schools there was a marked intensification and expansion of the study of the seven liberal arts, particularly the *trivium*—grammar, rhetoric, and dialectic (logic). In the municipal schools in Italy, the study of law took on new vigor. Many of the most prominent cathedral schools of the early twelfth century, such as those at Paris, Chartres, Laon, and Reims, owed their fame to individual masters who specialized in one of the liberal arts and were thus able to enrich its content and methodology. In fact, being a master became a career in itself, marking the appearance of the professional intellectual as a key force in the world of learning. Since the content of grammar, rhetoric, and dialectic was derived chiefly from classical Latin models, cathedral schools became centers of more intensive and critical study of the Latin classics. The other four liberal arts (the *quadrivium*)—arithmetic, geometry, astronomy, music—were less important in training literate, articulate people to serve new social roles. Still, their content was constantly expanded, chiefly as a result of the renaissance of classical studies.

Toward the end of the twelfth century the monastic, cathedral, and municipal schools no longer met the needs of the world of learning. Because they were often dependent on a single master teaching a specialized discipline, they lacked continuity and curricular breadth. Also, their masters had opened up intellectual vistas and generated specialized scholarly interests that abbots, bishops, and town councils had little practical interest in fostering. Moreover, during the last half of the twelfth century western Europe was flooded with a huge body of new knowledge coming from the Greek and Moslem worlds. Primarily philosophical and scientific in content, this new knowledge challenged existing religious beliefs and demanded a level of learning well beyond that needed to prepare people for careers. The response was a new institution, the university, that consisted of a community of teachers and learners engaged in a collective effort to expand, organize, and transmit knowledge and intellectual skills.

The earliest universities, those at Bologna and Paris, came into existence about 1200; not long after, others emerged in various urban centers across Europe. Following a pattern already used by urban dwellers and by merchants and craftsmen seeking to establish places for themselves in society, the founders of universities organized themselves into self-governing corporations, or guilds (the general Latin term for "guild" was *universitas*). At Bologna the students, for the most part law students, formed a *universitas* to protect themselves against exploitation by townspeople and to regulate the teaching performance of their masters. At Paris the teachers of the arts in the city's episcopal school broke away from the bishop's control and founded a self-governing body, the faculty of the arts, to control the educational process. A crucial step in establishing a university was gaining legal recognition from a public authority—king, bishop, town council—which allowed the corporation to exercise certain privileges. The privileges claimed were wide-ranging, but one was vital: the right to grant a degree certifying that a learner had completed a specified program of training defined by a faculty. Once a guild of teachers and students had established its legal status, it developed its own internal governance structure and operating rules. This process was often lengthy and beset by fierce struggles within the *universitas*.

The core curriculum of the typical university was based on training in the seven liberal arts conducted by a faculty of masters of arts, each a specialist in one of the arts. For most students university training involved becoming acquainted with all of the arts, a program usually requiring four years of study and resulting in a bachelor of arts degree, which qualified its literate recipients for a variety of careers. Those wishing to teach the arts either in a university or in some other kind of school pursued their studies in one of the arts for another year or two and earned a master's degree. Those who aspired to a teaching career beyond instructing students in the liberal arts or who hoped to serve in high places as authorities on technical disciplines could pursue a doctorate in theology, law, or medicine. This degree required additional years of study, research, and public lecturing. At Paris, for example, the theology doctorate took at least thirteen years of study. Although the ultimate objective of university study was earning a degree, many students spent time at universities without earning degrees; simply having been at a university earned them preferment in advancing their careers.

The basic teaching method at universities focused on acquainting students with authoritative texts in the various disciplines. Usually these texts were works by ancient authors, but occasionally the works of "modern" authorities were added. Since books had to be hand copied, they were expensive and scarce. In the face of this problem, the master read the text (thus the origin of the lecture method, derived from the Latin word for "reading," *lectio*), and the students took notes. As the master read the text, he commented on the issues it raised, often citing the opinions of other authorities on each issue and employing logical argumentation to reconcile differences. The purpose of this enterprise was to convey fundamental truths and to train students in the art of defending those truths through argumentation (*disputatio*)—an art that required acquiring a body of knowledge, developing a capacity for logical thinking, and perfecting skills in oral argumentation. Proof of worthiness for a degree was established by a student's performance in a public examination. Such a test required the student to expound on a text, develop and defend a thesis with respect to it, and respond to challenges to the thesis posed by the examining masters. This method produced minds that held a high respect for established authorities, were adept at textual analysis, were skilled in reconciling contradictory positions by logic, and were inclined to settle differences by argumentation.

The early universities were communities of people rather than physical entities. Most classes were held in rented halls. Students took lodgings in private homes. In time, however, universities did take on a physical presence. Patrons began to endow establishments, called *colleges*, for housing and feeding students. The first such institution was the Sorbonne at Paris, named after its patron, Robert de Sorbon, a rich courtier. Chapels, manuscript-copying services, and libraries were built to serve those engaged in teaching and learning. Thus, a university quarter began to emerge in some medieval cities, usually a welcome—although not always peaceful—adornment to urban life.

University students were almost exclusively male and came from a mixed social background; predominantly they were the offspring of people of modest means—petty nobles, merchants, artisans, even affluent peasants—who saw education as a means of economic and social advancement. They ranged in age from fourteen or fifteen to thirty or thirty-five. Since universities were few, students gathered at each from afar, thus constituting a population of strangers in most university towns. Many were supported by their parents or by patrons—usually inadequately, if we can believe the constant pleas for funds voiced in surviving student letters. These letters, however, seldom talk of student expenditures in taverns and on other frivolous pursuits that are recorded in other surviving documents. Students clashed constantly with townspeople, who viewed them not only as foreigners, idlers, and wastrels but also as targets for exploitation. Since students were legally considered members of the clergy and of a privileged corporation, it was difficult for town governments to exercise legal control over them. Town-gown rivalry, often surrounded by bitter recriminations and even violence, became a regular part of urban life in every university center.

2. THE WORLD OF LEARNING: THE MEDIEVAL "SCIENCES"

The evolution of the medieval educational system promoted the structuring of intellectual activity into what medieval scholars would have called "sciences," by which they meant bodies of interrelated knowledge capable of describing and explaining meaningful segments of the total universe of knowledge. In a sense, each of the seven liberal arts constituted a science in the medieval scheme of things, and medieval scholars and teachers greatly enriched each of them. However, the chief monuments of medieval intellectual activity came in more exalted "sciences": theology (which embraced what we would call philosophy), or the study of God; law, or the study of human society; and nature, or the study of the material order. Aside from the challenging intellectual issues innate in each of these areas, various pressing problems in a changing society forced learned individuals to seek to bring order to what was known about each of these sciences and to try to find out more.

If the liberal arts can be counted among the

sciences in the medieval learned world, then perhaps the monument that marks their place in that world was the rich and varied body of literature written in Latin to serve the increasing number of Latin readers and speakers produced by the schools. That literature was strongly influenced in style and language by the classical Latin texts that provided the models upon which the study of grammar and rhetoric was based. Latin authors of the central Middle Ages demonstrated considerable skill in using these models in innovative ways. The Latin vocabulary was constantly enriched by the infusion of new words and by the redefinition of old meanings, and classical literary forms were modified to permit Latin authors to treat matters that concerned them in creative ways. Between 1000 and 1300 there was a great outpouring of Latin prose literature devoted to history, biography, saints' lives, devotional manuals, letters, and political polemics. Perhaps the most original Latin literature took the form of lyric poetry on religious themes, often composed to serve the needs of the liturgy. But medieval writers were equally adept at nonreligious poetry, as exemplified by many student songs, collectively called Goliardic poetry, celebrating drinking, sensual love, gambling, and other worldly themes. Unless serious attention is given to the vast body of literature written in Latin for an "educated" audience, little can be known about what happened in the medieval world, what people thought about that world, and how they felt about the human scene.

Beyond the active commerce of ideas fostered by Latin belles lettres were the higher realms of truth. The queen of medieval "sciences" was theology, not so much because of the number who mastered it (they were few) but rather because of the weight of the subject with which it dealt. Although it had always engaged Christian thinkers, theology made a quantum leap forward as a field of systematic investigation during the central Middle Ages. That advance was due in part to the urgent need felt by religious leaders seeking to unify and systematize basic religious teachings as an aspect of the effort to reform Christian society. But also stimulating theological activity were new methods of intellectual inquiry and new knowledge.

During the early Middle Ages theological inquiry sought primarily to understand and explain the meaning of certain authoritative texts that contained the divine truth—above all else, Scripture. The approach was primarily literary, seeking by careful reading and meditation to discover the levels of meaning contained in the word of God. In the eleventh century, a subtle change in the approach to sacred texts began to occur, providing the key to the emergence of the medieval "science" of theology. Prompted by their growing awareness of the contradictions in scriptural texts themselves and in the way in which past authorities had interpreted the revealed truth, scholars began to explore the extent to which human reason could be useful in grasping religious truth. In this pursuit they turned to the methodology of dialectic or logic, using the rules of formal thinking to test and demonstrate the validity of religious propositions.

The development of the "new" theology, not unlike the advent of the new "science" of later centuries, was slow and tentative, marked by deep suspicion on the part of advocates of traditional ways of exploring religious truths. A key figure in turning the tide was Anselm (1033–1109), abbot of the monastery of Bec in Normandy and later archbishop of Canterbury. A man of learning and unquestioned orthodoxy, Anselm proclaimed as his central intellectual tenet that faith should seek understanding, by which he meant that one steeped in revealed truth should strive to understand that faith in human terms. To demonstrate his point, he undertook to develop a logical proof of the existence of God, one that could stand on its own without depending on revelation. His famous proof, which has intrigued many generations of thinkers, legitimized human reason as a valid tool in the search to understand what revelation meant.

By the early twelfth century the study of dialectic and its application to various problems became a passion in the schools. A key figure in creating a science of theology based on dialectic was Peter Abélard (1079–1142). Son of a minor Breton noble family, Abélard studied with several leading masters in various cathedral schools in France and then became a successful master himself. His promising ecclesiastical career was disrupted by a love affair with one of his pupils, Héloïse, which led to a pregnancy, a secret marriage, a child, the emasculation of Abélard by

Héloïse's outraged kinsfolk, and the separation of the lovers. These "calamities," as Abélard put it, sent Héloïse to a nunnery and condemned Abélard to a life of wandering from monastery to monastery and school to school—perhaps always haunted by his memory of true love but also driven by an urge to know and understand more fully. Abélard's career was filled with controversy, stemming partly from his prideful, combative personality and partly from the force of his ideas, which posed a revolutionary challenge to traditional theological inquiry.

Superbly skilled as a logician, Abélard made a major contribution to systematizing the use of dialectic as a tool of theological inquiry. In a bold book entitled *Sic et Non* (*Yes and No*), he set down a series of cases in which revered authorities disagreed on fundamental doctrinal questions. His approach implied that only the use of reason could resolve these contradictions. Abélard also developed new insights into how human beings came to know. He maintained that the truth consists of concepts formed in the mind from the study of created things, such concepts being the nearest approximation to the perfect knowledge that is God. A philosopher's task is to organize in a logical fashion all that is known so as to create a mental image of God's universe. Abélard's dialectical approach to theology aroused strong opposition, led by the formidable Bernard of Clairvaux, which eventually resulted in an official condemnation of some of his teachings by a church council. But the opposition was to no avail, and the new theology became predominant. It was given special impetus by one of Abélard's students, Peter Lombard (1100–1160), who used the dialectical methodology as the basis for his *Sentences*. In it Peter employed logic to resolve contradictory positions contained in Scripture and the writings of the Church Fathers on a large number of topics relating to basic Christian doctrine. The result was a unified body of theology, systematically organized. The *Sentences* quickly became the basic text for teaching theology, and its dialectical methodology became standard.

The value of the dialectical approach became even more evident during the late twelfth and thirteenth centuries, when scholars in the West came into possession of a vast body of new knowledge derived from Greek philosophy and scientific knowledge along with the Moslem commentaries on that material. During the early Middle Ages western Europeans had lost contact with almost all of Greek philosophy and science. However, from as early as the ninth century Moslem scholars became deeply interested in this material, translated most of it into Arabic, and commented on it extensively (see Chapter 14). Beginning about 1150, this huge body of knowledge again became available in the West, first as a result of the labors of scholars working chiefly in Spain and Sicily to translate Arabic texts into Latin and then later as a result of translations made directly from Greek texts. The new material included most of Aristotle's writings, and he—the Philosopher, as Western thinkers soon called him—quickly became the leading authority on logical methods as well as philosophical and scientific learning. The new learning posed a serious challenge: Not only did it provide scholars with heretofore unfamiliar knowledge about a wide range of matters, especially the natural world, it also confronted them with logically demonstrated systems of truth that directly contradicted many basic Christian teachings.

The major concerns of thirteenth-century theologians, collectively called the Scholastics, centered on mastering the new knowledge, organizing it into a rational system, and reconciling it with Christian doctrine in a way that met the tests of logic without denying the faith. Their assault on these problems was motivated not only by the intellectual challenges innate in these issues but also by their urge to serve the religious establishment in its quest for doctrinal clarity and uniformity. These concerns, explored most intensely in the universities, evoked a variety of responses, often accompanied by bitter intellectual warfare that belies the notion that the Middle Ages was a time of uniformity and conformity in the realm of ideas.

One especially controversial approach to these fundamental issues was formulated by a group of scholars called the Averroists, after Averroës, a famous Moslem thinker who had commented extensively on Aristotle's works (see Chapter 14). The adherents of this school wholeheartedly accepted Aristotelian rationalism, arguing that reason was capable of defining an order of truth that had its own validity irrespective of the tenets of the faith. At the opposite pole was a school of thought that found Aristotelianism to be of little value in leading to the truth about the faith. This school reasserted the Platonic-Augustinian tradition that had long prevailed as the prime approach to theological wisdom. The most notable figure in this group was Bonaventura (1221–1274), a Franciscan teacher in Paris who later became head of the Franciscan order. Bonaventura argued that reason could not discover the ultimate truth, which must come to the intellect intuitively through an illumination from divine sources beyond the power of human reason. Although Bonaventura did not deny the value of a rational consideration of natural phenomena, he held that no fundamental truth would result; in fact, he was convinced that rationalism would ultimately end in doctrinal error.

But the most representative response to the major issues posed by the new knowledge was formulated by a succession of scholars who tried to reconcile revelation and reason. By far the most influential advocate of this approach was Thomas Aquinas (1225–1274), an Italian Dominican whose active career was divided between teaching at the university in Paris and serving at the papal court. During his career as teacher and scholar he produced a huge body of theological writing. His chief works, the *Summa contra Gentiles* and the unfinished *Summa Theologica,* reflect scholasticism in its most representative form. In all of his works Thomas begins with the assumption that God created the universe in such a way that all its parts fit together and have a single purpose. Every human being has the duty to know God and his works, and each has the ability to achieve that end as a result of powers inherent in human nature. There are two paths to this single, unified order of truth: revelation and reason. The task of the mind is to seek the truth by applying itself to those things that are the proper subjects for reason while accepting on faith those things that can be learned only by revelation. Thomas accepted on faith such doctrines as the Creation, the Trinity, and the Incarnation but applied reason to such problems as the existence of God, immortality, the operation of the natural world, the nature of government, and ethics. He was certain that reason directed to the proper ends and guided by sound methodology would provide the intelligence with an order of truth that fitted into the order of truth contained in revelation. If there is a conflict between revelation and reason, he felt, it results from faulty reasoning.

Following the rules of logic formulated by Aristotle and relying heavily on him for knowledge of subjects proper to human reason, Thomas measured the whole realm of human knowledge item after item with a view toward reconciling that knowledge with the revealed truth. His method consisted of a rigorously applied series of steps: formulating a proposition stating some aspect of the truth, setting forth all possible contrary positions, demonstrating the logical fallacies in these contrary positions, and finally showing the logical validity of the true position. Each single truth in Thomas' system is part of an interlocking structure of thought that relates all things to a perfect truth. The final result of his work—his *summae,* or summations— is a synthesis of all knowledge into one vast structure glorifying God and demonstrating the perfection of his creation in terms comprehensible to the human mind. The Thomistic synthesis perhaps best represents the overall spirit of medieval thought: the quest to integrate existing knowledge, both human and divine, into a single structure. New knowledge was seldom a concern of medieval theologians or philosophers.

Another "science" that developed during the central Middle Ages involved the systematic study of law. Although several universities had faculties of law, the major center of legal studies was at the University of Bologna. By the eleventh century strong pressures were being felt in society, especially in the religious establishment and the royal courts, to develop unified, consistent bodies of law as an instrument to promote order in society. However, the legal systems existing at that time were surrounded with confusion and contradictions. Like the theologians, students of law began to employ dialectic as a tool to resolve this problem. We have already noted the work of Gratian (see p. 282), who in his *Decretum* (1140) created a model compendium of canon law, based on the collection and rational reconciliation of a wide range of discordant precedents. Gratian's work became the basic text used in teaching canon law. A long succession of twelfth- and thirteenth-century canon lawyers continued the work of compilation and commentary; by the thirteenth century their labors had produced a highly sophisticated, consistent body of law essential to the governance of religious life in all its aspects.

The development of canon law was greatly stimulated by a revived interest in the study of Roman law. Except for a few places where written law had remained in use during the early Middle Ages, such as southern France and northern Italy, Roman law had long been neglected in the West. Then, in the eleventh century, its study was taken up with great vigor, mainly because the chief embodiment of Roman law, the Code of Justinian (the *Corpus juris civilis*), provided invaluable guidance in defining political authority. Civil lawyers spent their energies writing commentaries (called *glosses*) on the code to try to elucidate its meaning and relate its principles to existing society. Aside from producing an immense body of legal literature, their work decisively influenced the kind of law administered in the rising monarchies and shaped the concepts defining royal power. The legal concepts set forth by the students of Roman law prompted efforts to codify the confused bodies of customary law existing over much of western Europe. An example was the important treatise on English common law compiled by Henry Bracton in the thirteenth century.

Although a precise "science" of society did not emerge during the central Middle Ages, theologians and lawyers had much to say about the nature of human society and the political order. Discussions on these matters were spurred by a variety of influences: explorations by religious reformers of the ancient Christian concepts of the nature of the state and society; the conflict between church and state; the need to justify the claims of the new monarchies; the revival of Roman law; the recovery of classical Greek and Roman works on political theory (especially Aristotle). Gradually the serious study of political theory led to a new view of the nature of society and the political order. Traditional political thought, derived chiefly from Augustine, viewed the state as an instrument for suppressing the sinful nature of human beings; by filling this negative role, rulers prepared the ground for the spiritual perfection of human beings through the efforts of ecclesiastical leaders. Increasingly during the twelfth and thirteenth centuries the state came to be defined as an integral part of the natural order that asserted a unique and necessary positive force for the full realization of human potential.

Thomas Aquinas played an important role in articulating this view of the state. Strongly influenced by Aristotle, he argued that the state was a part of the natural order and existed to permit human beings to live in an ordered community where each could realize his or her innate potential for good. The proper form of government was a result of rational reflection on human needs. In Thomas' view, the ideal state was one in which various classes performed specific functions under the guidance of a just ruler in the interest of providing for the needs of all. Such a system ensured justice, which was the ultimate objective of government. Upon the ruler of the good state fell the heavy responsibility of discovering and applying the principles of natural law required to regulate human society in accord with the divine order. In discovering a positive role for the state as an instrument shaped by rational human actions for promoting human welfare, the political theorists of the central Middle Ages established the foundations for future study of the state and its functioning in a context which took existing realities into account.

In the "science" of the natural world the achievements of medieval thinkers seem pale by the standards of later ages. However, the central Middle Ages did witness one development of major significance for the study of the natural world. During the early Middle Ages thinkers had adhered to a view of nature rooted in Neoplatonism. This view considered the natural world to be an inferior order of reality that represented an illusory reflection of nonmaterial perfect forms. As this Neoplatonic concept was translated into a Christian idiom, nature came to be viewed as part of the universe corrupted by the Fall, lacking in any inherent order, subject to unpredictable alterations by transcendent forces. Given powerful impetus by a monastic ideal that spurned material things, early medieval thought was biased against serious concern with the study of the natural world in its own right. That view began to change by the twelfth century. The scholastic effort to unite all knowledge into a single truth and the vastly increased knowledge of nature resulting from the rediscovery of Greek and Moslem scientific works generated an effort to study the natural world as a fundamental dimension of God's created cosmos. That study led to the conclusion that the material world was good by virtue of being part of God's creation, that there was order in nature because it was part of God's perfect order, and that the natural world was intelligible to human reason. In short, nature had to be understood if theological and philosophical knowledge was to be complete. This fundamental shift in attitude constituted a prime achievement of the medieval search for truth. The discovery—perhaps rediscovery is a better term—of nature provided the starting point for great advances in knowledge.

The changing perspective on the natural world provided powerful impetus to an activity that was central to medieval natural science and eventually important to later advances in science—the mastery of the vast body of knowledge about the natural world that had been collected over the centuries by Greek, Hellenistic, and Moslem scholars. The preoccupation with accumulated knowledge about the natural world is amply illustrated in the field of medicine, which constituted a separate field of study in some universities, especially at Salerno in Italy. There the curriculum focused primarily on mastering Greek and Moslem medical texts. That same avid interest in accumulated knowledge about the natural world is evident in the writings of such theologians as Albertus Magnus (ca. 1206–1280), Thomas Aquinas' teacher at the University of Paris, whose voluminous writings on theology are filled with information about nature drawn chiefly from Aristotle's scientific works.

Despite this fascination with authority, tentative steps were taken to learn more about the natural world than was contained in the ancient texts. In medicine, for example, new knowledge was slowly added to the old as a result of information gleaned from observation of sick people, dissection of bodies of animals and humans, and study of the medicinal properties of plants. Especially noteworthy in encouraging the quest for new knowledge about nature was a group of scholars, most of them Franciscans, centered at Oxford University in the thirteenth century. Robert Grosseteste (1168–1253) and his pupil Roger Bacon (ca. 1214–1294) were its most distinguished members. These men insisted that the truth about the natural world could be gained only through observation and experimentation. Aside from his own experimentation in optics, Bacon raised questions about the blind trust which contemporaries had put in the scientific theories of ancient authorities, especially Aristotle. Such doubts, soon shared by others, had important implications for the exploration of nature, especially in such fields as astronomy and physics. Working at a somewhat less exalted level to expand knowledge about and control over the natural world were astrologers seeking to predict the future and alchemists trying to convert base metals into gold. And not to be overlooked in assessing the natural sciences in the Middle Ages were the increasing body of knowledge about natural phenomena and the advancing levels of technical expertise being accumulated by artisans and farmers engaged in the routine affairs of life. The ground was being prepared for an explosion of scientific knowledge.

3. BEYOND THE LEARNED WORLD: VERNACULAR LITERATURE

The learned world represented by the medieval schools and the Latin writings of theologians, lawyers, scientists, historians, poets, and polemicists involved a relatively narrow circle whose intellectual activities impinged on the lives of most people only indirectly at best. Beyond that narrow world was a larger circle of men and women who sought instruction and entertainment. During the central Middle Ages that world found its voice in vernacular literature, written in the tongues that people spoke in their daily lives about matters of which heretofore most of them had only spoken, not read. By 1000 the language map of western Europe had become a tower of Babel. That map had emerged slowly during the early Middle Ages out of three basic root languages: classical Latin, which evolved into the Romance tongues, such as French, Provençal, Italian, Spanish, and Catalan; Old German, out of which came German, English, Dutch, and the Scandinavian tongues; and Celtic, which evolved into Irish and Welsh. Each of these basic vernacular languages was further divided into local dialects, and many of them were enriched by extensive borrowings from each other and from Latin. Although how it happened is far from clear, the fact that between 1000 and 1300 writers did develop the capability of using these spoken languages to create literary works expressing unique ideas and feelings marked a major landmark in western European cultural development. Somehow that development must have been rooted in the dynamics of a changing world which created a need for and an interest in literacy other than in Latin. For the most part, those who created vernacular literature wrote for an audience of aristocratic laymen and laywomen, suggesting that it was at that level of society where the need was first felt. However, there is some evidence that their works were known and enjoyed by nonnoble townspeople and perhaps even peasants.

One form of vernacular literature that found wide favor among aristocratic audiences was the epic, a song setting down in writing the deeds of great warriors of the past that had been preserved in oral tradition. The great Anglo-Saxon epic *Beowulf*, composed about 800, recounts the adventures of a warrior living in a pre-Christian Germanic society. The epic genre is also illustrated by the Icelandic sagas, such as the anonymous twelfth-century *Poetic Edda* and the *Prose Edda* compiled in the early thirteenth century by Snorri Sturluson; both of these collections reflect a much earlier Scandinavian world dominated by the violent struggles of mythic heroes and pagan values. The chief Germanic epic, the *Nibelungenlied*, composed about 1200, reflects a tradition dating back to the time of the Germanic invasions and to the awesome deeds and terrible fates of heroic warlords and their formidable women. The chief *chanson de geste* ("song of deeds") produced in French was the *Song of Roland*, written about 1100 to retell the story of Charlemagne's expedition of 778 against the Moors in Spain, which ended in the defeat of the Frankish forces at Roncesvalles. However, the unknown author adorned his account of this historical event and its hero, Roland, with the ideals and customs characteristic of eleventh-century noble society; particular emphasis is given to Roland's prowess as a warrior, his loyalty to his lord, and his willingness to give his life to defend his faith. The same themes dominate the Spanish epic *Song of the Cid*, which glorifies the deeds of a famous knight involved in the Reconquista of Spain from the Moors.

The epic genre was soon rivaled by a new vernacular literary form, the lyric poem, which during the twelfth century enjoyed a tremendous vogue in the courtly circles of the chivalric nobility. This poetry developed first in Provence in southern France and soon spread over most of Europe. Its creators, called *troubadours*, were chiefly young noblemen whose lack of great fiefs and firm family ties rooted in proper marriages placed them on the fringes of noble society. Through their poetry they sought to expound their sensual love for a noble lady in a fashion that would earn them honor in her eyes and thus status in the society to which she belonged. The troubadours (called *trouvères* in northern France and *minnesänger* in Germany) projected a new set of values for noble society. Their poetry argued that the emotions associated with love—longing, suffering, anticipation of a lover's favor—had the power to ennoble just as much as did prowess in battle or loyalty to a male feudal lord. The search for self-understanding and the emotional probing associated with the quest for love refined the inner spirit and evoked patterns of behavior that combined to create the gentleman as the epitome of noble existence. The lyric writers thus played a crucial role in transforming the values and behavioral patterns upon which the concept of male excellence was based. They were also instrumental in attributing to women a vital role in shaping nobility, a role based on their sexuality and their power to give pleasure. The impetus for this new morality derived primarily from qualities innate in human nature, qualities having little to do with religious values. For this reason, troubadour poetry was viewed with grave misgivings by many religious leaders; perhaps also for this same reason, it enthralled noble society (see Figure 22.2).

Toward the end of the twelfth century, a third type of vernacular literature, the *romance*, began to rival epic and lyric poetry. Romances were stories combining a love theme with adventure, written chiefly to entertain court society; the immensely popular romances enjoyed the special patronage of high-placed noblewomen, such as Eleanor of Aquitaine. The adventure element in

FIGURE 22.2 Medieval Love This miniature showing a knight and a lady captured by love conveys the sense in which troubadour poetry saw love as a force capable of transforming behavior. (Universität Bibliothek, Heidelberg)

these stories was drawn from sources with vague roots in history, especially materials relating to the legendary King Arthur and his court. The authors of the romances used this "historical" material with complete freedom. The treatment of love in these stories reflected a continued probing of themes contained in troubadour poetry. The most gifted romance writers fashioned works with enduring appeal. Among them was Chrétien de Troyes, a late-twelfth-century French author who skillfully exploited the Arthurian material to create an intriguing picture of the ideal knight struggling to achieve chivalric excellence through pursuit of love and adventure and of the noble lady serving as a prime agent in shaping the consummate knight. Another writer, the thirteenth-century German Gottfried von Strasbourg, in his *Tristan and Isolde,* masterfully reveals the meaning of love in the lives of two who were its prisoners. *Parzival*, written by his countryman Wolfram von Eschenbach, is an appealing picture of a man pursuing an unobtainable ideal, symbolized by the Holy Grail. The

concepts of chivalry found their most mature expression in the romances. The themes and actions treated in them had a powerful impact on the behavior of the nobility for centuries and have continued to intrigue writers and audiences down to the present, influencing poetry, operas, and even modern musicals.

While the epics, lyrics, and romances were being written, sung, and read by nobles, other forms of literature evolved to appeal to the tastes and interests of nonnobles. Especially notable were dramas, *fabliaux,* and saints' lives. Although there was some interest in classical drama during the Middle Ages, as witnessed by the attempts of a tenth-century German nun, Hrotsvitha, to write plays in Latin modeled on Terence, medieval drama owed little to past examples. It began as part of the church liturgy; dramatized parts of services eventually moved outside the church into the marketplace. By the thirteenth century the guilds had taken over the responsibility for producing these dramas during religious festivals. Each guild presented one scene from a connected series of scenes that constituted an entire play. Several types of dramatic production developed: mystery plays, enacting scenes from the Bible; miracle plays, treating the highlights of saints' lives; morality plays, personifying human virtues and vices. The presentation of these serious, sacred dramas was punctuated by earthy language and comical portrayals of the key characters. The *fabliaux* were short tales recited in public squares to entertain the crowds. Whatever the subject—it could be almost anything—the *fabliaux* were always close to city life, representing everyday events in the lives of ordinary people. They were filled with vulgar humor and satire aimed especially at corrupt priests, betrayed husbands, and scheming women effective in getting what they wanted from young men. The most famous collection of *fabliaux* was *The Romance of Reynard the Fox*, made up of stories in which animals symbolize people and human characteristics. The spirit of *fabliaux* is also reflected in some of the tales told by Geoffrey Chaucer (ca. 1340–1400) in his *Canterbury Tales,* a highly entertaining collection of stories supposedly told by a group of pilgrims to entertain one another during their journey. Immensely popular were vernacular versions of stories telling of the heroic and miraculous deeds of the legions of Christian saints.

If one had to select a single author whose writings encapsulate the spirit and the art of medieval vernacular literature, it is likely that the choice would be Dante Alighieri (1265–1321). He was to medieval literature what Thomas Aquinas was to medieval theology. Dante was a product of the vibrant urban life of Florence. In his youth he fell in love with a girl named Beatrice, who later married someone else and died young. Beatrice became for Dante the ideal woman as defined by the code of courtly love. Dante was a learned man who wrote in Latin on a variety of subjects. He was also active in Florentine political life, ultimately suffering expulsion from the city because of his identification with a faction that lost control of the city government. While suffering what he called ''an undeserving exile,'' he wrote his masterpiece, *The Divine Comedy*, in his native Tuscan dialect. Outwardly, it tells of Dante's journey through hell, purgatory, and heaven. Tired, discouraged, and confused at the outset, the pilgrim slowly begins to comprehend the harmony, order, and purpose in the universe; his spirit is progressively uplifted and his soul cured of its discontents. Guided through hell and purgatory by the Latin poet Vergil and through heaven by his beloved Beatrice, he is permitted to see all things from the depths of hell to God himself. Within this framework Dante weaves with dazzling poetic skills a rich tapestry reflecting medieval thought. He is a philosopher, presenting with consummate skill the medieval idea that all things in the universe are ordered by God in a cohesive, intelligible scheme. He is a mystic, yearning to the depths of his soul to catch a glimpse of God so that his human disquiet may be satisfied. He is a love poet; Beatrice, his guide in heaven, is a symbol of human love, a purifying and uplifting emotion. He is a scientist, incorporating into his poem many medieval ideas about the structure of the physical universe. He is an admirer of Greek and Roman writers and thinkers, although he has to condemn them to hell as non-Christians. He is a keen political observer, full of fierce partisanship. On his long journey from the gates of hell to its very pit, where Lucifer chews up three great traitors, Brutus, Cassius, and Judas, Dante discusses with Vergil nearly every kind of sin, showing a deep understanding of human nature and its weaknesses. The ascent from hell through purgatory to the seat of God in heaven offers him an equal chance to discourse on every aspect of virtue. Few artists have grasped human life and human aspirations more fully or written of them with greater artistry.

4. IN ALL WORLDS: THE VISUAL ARTS

During the Middle Ages the visual arts were the media common to all, rich and poor, literate and illiterate, learned and ignorant. The era from 1000 to 1300 marked a decisive epoch in art history during which two major styles, Romanesque and Gothic, were perfected and left a mark on artistic expression in western Europe that still asserts an influence. Both styles were preeminently religious in inspiration, created primarily to provide suitable places of worship, but features of both were adapted for secular purposes. The religious establishment was the prime agency promoting artistic endeavor, but almost all elements of society provided support for artistic undertakings.

The Romanesque and Gothic architectural styles were the fruits of a long evolution. The starting point of medieval church architecture was the Roman basilica, the rectangular meeting hall. The early Christians placed their altars in the semicircular *apse* at the rear and conducted the Mass there. The *nave* provided space for the faithful participating in the sacred rites. Side aisles often flanked the nave. The upper walls of the nave rose above the side aisles and were pierced with windows that allowed light into the nave. A lateral aisle, called the *transept*, sometimes crossed the nave just in front of the apse, so that the early church took the form of a cross. Over the centuries, this basic ground plan of church architecture and the art that decorated it were considerably modified by influences from the Byzantine, Germanic, and Celtic worlds and by new creative forces emerging from daily life. During the central Middle Ages artists finally succeeded in blending these many tributaries into distinctive new styles.

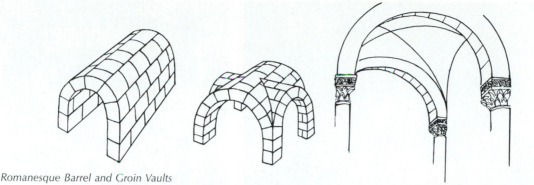

Romanesque Barrel and Groin Vaults

Romanesque architecture first appeared in the late Carolingian period and flourished until well into the twelfth century. Its main features are admirably illustrated by several churches still standing: Notre Dame la Grande in Poitiers, the cathedral of Saint Sernin in Toulouse, the cathedral church of Worms, the Abbey Church of Maria Laach in Germany, the church of Sant' Ambrogio in Milan, and the church of Sainte Madeleine at Vézelay in France (see Figure 22.3). The Romanesque style was characterized both by technical innovations and by a new spirit. The monastic world, especially the Cluniac reformers, played a dominant role in developing and spreading this style. The Cluniac emphasis on elaborate rituals and concern for providing the proper setting for the veneration of relics and for gatherings of pilgrims dictated that churches be large enough to house a number of chapels and accommodate great crowds. Architects also wanted to find a replacement for the traditional wooden roofs, which were so often destroyed by fire. The solution was a capacious church built entirely of stone.

So that liturgical needs could be met, the Romanesque style modified the basic ground plan of the traditional basilican structure. The nave was extended beyond the transept to create a *choir*, a space where the main altar was located and where the clergy and monks could gather for worship. The side aisles were also extended around the choir, creating a passageway or ambulatory that encircled the nave and the choir. A series of chapels was constructed off the side aisles and the choir ambulatory, providing spaces for many simultaneous religious services

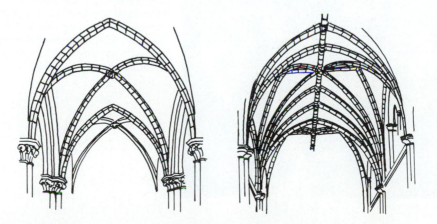

Gothic Ribbed Vault

FIGURE 22.3 Romanesque Art These photos of the church of Sainte Madeleine at Vézelay in France illustrate some of the main features of Romanesque art. The nave (top right) features round ribbed arches, heavy columns, and thick walls pierced by small windows. Above the main portal (upper left) is a sculptured complex showing Christ instructing his disciples; comparable scenes over entrances were usual in Romanesque churches. The many capitals atop the pillars (lower left) of the nave and the porch leading to the main entrance provided space for carved scenes illustrating biblical themes. Romanesque sculpture was less concerned with realism than with reminding viewers of a religious truth and with moving their emotions. (Nave, Marburg; portal, Scala/Art Resource; sculpture, Marburg/Art Resource)

and for special shrines to display relics. To replace the wooden roof, architects developed techniques that allowed them to throw a barrel vault made of stone over the full length of the nave and choir and the side aisles. These heavy roofs were supported by massive stone walls. Where openings were needed through these walls—such as passages between the nave and the side aisles—round arches set on heavy pillars were used to support the structure above the opening. Groin vaults, again supported by arches and pillars, were evolved to cover the square or rectangular area where the axis of the nave and the choir was crossed by the transept (see illustration, p. 305). However, the barrel vault system of creating a stone roof was satisfactory only for relatively small structures. As the Romanesque style evolved, architects developed a method of building stone roofs over larger naves and choirs. They begin to break up the long barrel vault with rib arches crossing the nave and choir and resting on pillars on opposite sides of the nave and the choir. This technique created a series of bays, or "squares," marked off by pillars at each of the four corners. Each bay could then be covered with cross vaults. The space between the rib and the cross vaults could be filled in with relatively light stone pieces, reducing the roof weight and concentrating its downward thrust on the pillars at the corners of each bay (see illustration, p. 305). Despite these innovations, the stone vaulting covering the structure remained massive and exerted tremendous downward and outward thrust. For this reason Romanesque churches required heavy walls and massive internal columns; the few windows had to be kept small. Thus the typical Romanesque structure had an atmosphere of muted darkness and mystery that was not dispelled by the decorative paintings on piers, arches, and walls and by the candles that supplied artificial light. Yet this atmosphere was also due to the religious mentality of an age that viewed the church as God's citadel standing against a world filled with evil forces, a sacred fortress where men and women could commune with the God who protected them from the howling demons and the frightening forces of nature that raged outside this holy refuge (see Figure 22.3).

By the mid–twelfth century the European world was changing rapidly, and the new environment produced a new architectural style, the Gothic. It appeared first in Ile de France, the domain of the Capetians; the earliest full-scale Gothic church was the Abbey Church of Saint Denis near Paris, built in 1137–1144 by Abbot Suger, the adviser to kings Louis VI and Louis VII. From here the Gothic style spread over much of Europe.

The Gothic style evolved out of a desire for height and light in churches, a desire derived largely from new intellectual and spiritual concepts that fostered a more rational view of God and saw his chief attributes in terms of reason, light, and proportion. The Gothic church was an attempt to leave behind the mystery-shrouded, awesome world of the Romanesque and to create a setting in which the attention of anyone entering the structure would be drawn upward toward the light and purity of paradise—the paradise Dante pictured in poetry. Among the Gothic structures that achieve this effect magnificently are the cathedrals at Paris (Notre Dame), Chartres, Reims, Amiens (see Figure 23.4), Strasbourg, and Bourges in France; at Lincoln, York, and Salisbury in England; and at Cologne in Germany.

Technically, this transformation was made possible by the pointed arch, which carried thrust downward, and the ribbed vault, used to concentrate the thrust at a few points. Architects were able to combine them to fashion tremendously tall skeletons of stone whose weight flowed to earth through a series of slender pillars (see illustration, p. 305). The outward thrust, greatly reduced by the pointed arches and concentrated by the rib vaults, could be offset by thickened columns at the outside of the building or by flying buttresses, pillars set away from the main structure and joined to it by bracing arches high above the ground. Thin walls, supporting nothing but their own weight, could be filled in between the pillars. More important, light could be let into the structure by great arched windows cut through the thin walls. These windows, often interlaced with delicate decorative stonework, pierced the lofty clerestory and the side aisles, and majestic round windows were placed high above ground level at the ends of the nave, the choir, and the transept. The windows were often filled with many-hued stained-glass figures or scenes that suffused the interior with a breathtaking display of colored light (see Figure 22.4 and Color Plate 10).

Nearly every other visual art was put to work to decorate medieval churches. The exterior of a Romanesque church was generally plain except for the west façade, where the great arches built to provide doorways leading to a nave and side aisles provided a setting for sculpture. As illustrated by the church at Vézelay, these spaces were filled with massive, highly symbolic sculpture done in high relief; they portrayed human figures, animals, and abstract decorative patterns. A favorite subject was the Last Judgment, in which a stern Christ was portrayed relegating men and women to heaven or hell (see Figures 21.1 and 22.3). Within a Romanesque church there was more sculpture, chiefly decorative carving adorning the massive piers. The wall spaces were decorated with frecoes portraying scriptural scenes, particularly those that stressed the suffering of Christ and his judgment on humanity. Romanesque sculpture and painting are somber, with human beings portrayed as small, powerless, and dependent, surrounded by symbols of the terrors that beset spiritual life; they grip the emotions rather than the mind.

Gothic architecture brought about changes in the other arts. The exteriors of Gothic churches provided innumerable places for decorative sculpture, giving stone carvers an opportunity to experiment with a fantastic array of decorative motifs. Statues, sometimes executed in the round as well as in relief, became more realistic and humanistic, concerned more with expressing the human qualities of Jesus, the Virgin, the apostles, and the saints (see Figures 21.3, 22.1, and 22.4). The interior of Gothic churches offered less space for painting and sculpture than Romanesque churches did; decoration was concentrated chiefly on columns and arches. Not images but light fills the Gothic church. The painted walls of the Romanesque church were replaced with stained-glass windows. Their creators drew their themes chiefly from scriptural sources, but in their renditions they reflected the daily activities of medieval people in amazing detail. The stained glass at Chartres and in the beautiful Sainte-Chapelle built by Louis IX in Paris enthrall the viewer.

A variety of minor arts was employed to adorn these structures and to serve in carrying out religious services. Skilled metalwork was used for door handles and hinges, candleholders, chalices and pitchers, reliquaries, and railings to divide the space within the church. Woodwork provided pulpits and highly adorned seats for the celebrants of sacred services. Intricate needlework was employed to create splendid vestments for the clergy and tapestries to cover wall spaces. Skilled copyists and miniature painters fashioned beautiful liturgical books: Bibles, missals, psalters, hymnals. Ivory carvings were used to fashion covers for these books. In all these forms, artists demonstrated highly developed skills and imagination to create works that fitted the grand style dictated by the architecture and that reinforced the atmosphere of sanctity proper to holy places. Attendance at religious services constantly exposed the entire population to a dazzling display of the visual arts.

Another art associated with religious activity, music, also developed significantly during the central Middle Ages. Church music consisted primarily of melodies with verses taken from Scripture (especially the psalms) or composed for liturgical events (such great hymns as *Dies Irae* and *Stabat Mater* came from the Middle Ages). Gregorian chant (its alleged inventor was Pope Gregory I), or *plainsong*, developed as early as the sixth century. At first the singing was in unison, but over the centuries variations worked on plainsong developed into contrapuntal music. By the thirteenth century, complex and moving contrapuntal compositions, rendered by many voices and various instruments, filled the churches with sounds almost as heavenly as the light that poured through the stained-glass windows.

The great Romanesque and Gothic cathedrals and abbey churches commanded the best artistic talent and the bulk of the wealth that medieval society had to devote to art. However, the splendid artistic achievement they represent should not let us forget that there were other lines of artistic pursuit. The landscape was dotted with hundreds of small, simple parish churches, each a monument to the small community through whose efforts it had been built. These structures and their decor usually reflect Romanesque or Gothic styles, but often wonderfully creative local touches make one wish more was known about their creators. Living quarters for bishops

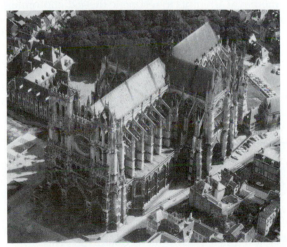

FIGURE 22.4 The Gothic Style The splendid church of Notre Dame at Amiens in France exemplifies the Gothic style. Its lofty nave (top left) is vaulted with pointed arches whose ribs carry weight down to the columns flanking the nave. Note the high arches that lead to aisles on either side of the nave. Above these arches is the clerestory, pierced by huge windows lighting the nave; the expanse can be seen in the apse at the far end of the building. The aerial view of the structure (bottom left) shows the flying buttresses used to offset the outward thrust of the roof on its supporting stone skeleton. Also evident is the transept crossing the nave. The façades of the main structure and the transept were decorated with numerous sculptures. Greeting those who entered the south transept was the "Golden Virgin" (top right), a wonderful example of the warmth and realism of Gothic sculpture. (Aerial view, Aerofilms, England; nave and sculpture, Archives Photographiques, Paris)

and the cathedral clergy and for monastic communities were constructed in both the Romanesque and Gothic styles. Many feudal castles, massive rather than elegant or comfortable, were built in the Romanesque style. In the towns, especially from the thirteenth century onward, beautiful town halls and guildhalls were constructed, putting Gothic principles to new uses. These buildings were decorated with paintings and carvings and furnished with skillfully wrought furniture and utensils for daily living. These structures were impressive signs that the religious system never completely absorbed the inspirations or energies of artists.

5. THE UNDERLYING SPIRIT OF MEDIEVAL CULTURE

Certainly it is not easy to find a common denominator for Thomas Aquinas, Dante, the architects and sculptors who built the churches at Poitiers, Amiens, and Chartres, the troubadours, the romance writers, and the authors of *fabliaux*. However, the more one experiences medieval thought and expression, the more one senses an underlying, unifying spirit.

Medieval thought, literature, and art are permeated by a quest for truth and light beyond the world of human existence. This reaching out of the mind and the imagination sprang from the almost universal belief that God controlled the universe and that it was the duty of mortals to know and worship him. The artist and the writer stood in awe of God and humbly used their talents to serve him. Medieval culture viewed as a whole, therefore, has an atmosphere of otherworldliness and of surrender to a power beyond human understanding.

Yet intertwined with this aspiration toward and submission to the Divine is a warm, sympathetic feeling for humankind. Medieval people believed that a human being was God's finest creation. Artists and writers were never disdainful of human powers and potentialities. They took joy in presenting humanity as it was and wrestled constantly with the problem of understanding human nature more fully.

The medieval genius shines forth most singularly in attempts to synthesize these two outlooks. Thinkers, writers, and artists seldom felt that otherworldliness and secularism, spirituality and humanism were contradictory terms. They respected their own powers enough to believe that they could reach out toward God—by building higher cathedrals or by putting together greater *summae* of knowledge or by flights of poetic fancy. Yet they were filled with a faith great enough to believe that their human quest would lead them to a power infinitely greater than themselves and that an ultimate illumination would allow them to realize their full potential as God's creatures. The best cultural artifacts of the Middle Ages are permeated with an intellectual and emotional tension stemming from an effort to accommodate the divine and the human, the spirit and the flesh, the sacred and the secular, faith and reason. Becoming involved with the medieval attempts to reconcile these dichotomies reminds one that medieval thinkers and artists staked out cultural frontiers that would give shape to cultural activity far into the future.

SUGGESTED READING

General Surveys

John W. Baldwin, *The Scholastic Culture of the Middle Ages, 1000–1300* (1971). A perceptive, brief survey.

Philippe Wolff, *The Cultural Awakening,* trans. Anne Carter (1968).

Robert L. Benson and Giles Constable, eds., *Renaissance and Renewal in the Twelfth Century* (1982).

These two works provide insight into the forces bringing about cultural revival.

Jacques Le Goff, *Medieval Civilization 400–1500,* trans. Julia Barrow (1988). Helpful on the social and mental context within which medieval culture took shape.

W. R. Cook and R. B. Herzman, *The Medieval World View: An Introduction* (1983). Suggestive on a big subject.

The Learned World

Jacques Le Goff, *Intellectuals in the Middle Ages,* trans. Teresa Lavender Fagan (1992).

Alan B. Cobban, *The Medieval Universities: Their Development and Organization* (1975).

Stephen C. Ferruolo, *The Origins of the Univeristy. The Schools of Paris and Their Critics* (1985).

These two works will clarify the origins and the working of medieval universities.

Michael Haren, *Medieval Thought: The Western Intellectual Tradition from Antiquity to the Thirteenth Century* (1985). Especially good in showing continuity between the ancient and medieval worlds.

John Marenbon, *Later Medieval Philosophy (1150–1350): An Introduction* (1987). A clear treatment; should be used with Marenbon's volume on an earlier period cited in Chapter 14.

Etienne Gilson, *History of Christian Philosophy in the Middle Ages* (1955). A classic detailed treatment.

Harold J. Berman, *Law and Revolution: The Formation of the Western Legal Tradition* (1983). A seminal study rich in insight.

A. C. Crombie, *Medieval and Early Modern Science,* 2nd ed., 2 vols. (1959). A good survey.

J. H. Burns, *The Cambridge History of Medieval Political Thought, c. 350–c. 1450* (1988). A detailed treatment.

Literature and Art

W. T. Jackson, *The Literature of the Middle Ages* (1960). A useful survey. More valuable is reading medieval literary works; the works mentioned in this chapter are easily available in excellent translations.

Peter Dronke, *Women Writers of the Middle Ages. A Critical Study of Texts from Perpetua (d. 203) to Marguerite (d. 1310)* (1984). Highlights some unsung individuals.

Joachim Bumke, *Courtly Culture: Literature and Society in the Middle Ages,* trans. Thomas Dunlap (1991). Fascinating details on courtly society.

Marilyn Stokstad, *Medieval Art* (1986). A comprehensive survey.

Henri Focillon, *The Art of the West in the Middle Ages,* 2nd ed., 2 vols., trans. Donald King (1969). A masterful, detailed treatment with excellent illustrations.

Georges Duby, *The Age of the Cathedrals: Art and Society, 980–1240,* trans. Eleanor Levieux and Barbara Thompson (1981). A challenging attempt to interrelate art and social developments.

Christopher Wilson, *The Gothic Cathedral* (1989). A stimulating treatment.

Jean Gimpel, *The Cathedral Builders,* trans. Teresa Waugh (1984). Describes the techniques of medieval builders.

Henry Adams, *Mont-St. Michel and Chartres* (1913). A classic work contrasting the spirits of Romanesque and Gothic art.

Erwin Panofsky, *Gothic Architecture and Scholasticism* (1951). Interrelates the intellectual and artistic worlds.

CHAPTER 23

Transition in Economic, Social, and Political Structures, 1300–1500

FIGURE 23.1 Medieval Siege Warfare This scene portrays the siege of an English castle in southern France by French forces during the Hundred Years' War. It illustrates very accurately the main weapons used in warfare. Engagements of this type drained large amounts of resources from both the English and the French royal governments. Providing the needs of the armies in these encounters often resulted in the pillaging of the countryside, which disrupted agricultural production and commercial exchange and caused untold misery to many. (The British Museum)

B y about 1300 the forces of growth, expansion, revival, and renewal that had propelled western European society forward during the preceding three centuries showed signs of faltering. As a result that society began to encounter stresses and tensions that laid bare the limitations inherent in the medieval pattern of civilization and that required adjustments in institutions and mentalities in order to cope with problems stemming from those limitations. The fourteenth and fifteenth centuries thus became an age of transition marked by developments in political, economic, social, religious, intellectual, and artistic life which transformed the medieval order in significant ways. What emerged was the early modern European world, whose roots were in the medieval world but whose institutional and ideological configuration was sufficiently different to mark a turning point in the history of western European civilization.

1. ECONOMIC AND SOCIAL TENSIONS AND READJUSTMENTS

Perhaps the most obvious sign of changing times came in economic and social life. By 1300 the long period of economic growth that western Europe had enjoyed since about 1000 (see Chapter 18) was ending. For the next century and a half contraction and depression became the order of the day in many aspects of economic life that had been of crucial importance to the prosperity of the eleventh, twelfth, and thirteenth centuries. Amid the economic dislocation new ways of organizing and conducting economic activity began to emerge that pointed toward early modern times. Economic changes were accompanied by social disequilibrium and adjustment. Although the nature and impact of economic and social dislocation and the responses to the changing scene varied from region to region, certain broad patterns affected western Europe generally.

A powerful engine of economic growth of the period from 1000 to 1300 had been sustained population growth. After 1300 western Europe suffered a dramatic population decline. Surviving evidence suggests that by 1300 the population level had begun to outstrip the food supply. That situation, coupled with unfavorable climatic conditions, produced a succession of famines in the early decades of the fourteenth century that began to reduce the population. Then came a demographic catastrophe in the form of a devastating pestilence: the Black Death, an epidemic of bubonic plague that first spread over Europe with deadly effect between 1347 and 1350 and then returned periodically during the next two centuries. The scourge was brought to Europe from the east by rats infested with fleas whose bites transmitted the bacilli to the human bloodstream. Once the disease was loosed in western Europe, it caused an immense loss of life among a population made vulnerable by malnutrition and primitive sanitation conditions. The best estimates suggest that a third of Europe's population was wiped out between 1347 and 1350. Periodic recurrence of the plague continued the downward spiral of the population, so that by the early fifteenth century western Europe had barely half as many people as it had had in 1300. Such a drastic demographic change had massive effects on levels of production, the demand for goods, the labor supply, prices, social relationships, and mass psychology (see Figure 23.2).

While population decline was a prime force in disturbing established economic patterns, it was only one factor. The economy also suffered from structural limitations rooted in the traditional system of production and from disruptive forces outside the economic system. Especially damaging to economic life during the fourteenth and fifteenth centuries was the reduction of commercial exchange. The population decline drastically reduced demand and limited the productive processes that supplied goods for exchange. Political disturbances in eastern and central Asia ended opportunities to penetrate new areas of commercial opportunity. The rise of the Ottoman Empire disturbed the favored position that Italian merchants had long enjoyed in the eastern Mediterranean. Under the pressure of a depressed economy the merchant guilds that had promoted commercial growth prior to 1300 increasingly imposed restrictions on the flow of goods, chiefly in an effort to create and protect the monopoly they held over local and regional trade. Self-governing cities found it difficult to cooperate for mutual benefit. The most successful effort of this kind was the Hanseatic League, which linked about eighty cities in northern Ger-

FIGURE 23.2 The Plague This painting captures the terror inflicted on the population of a city by the Black Death. Even while shrouding the dead for burial, people were suddenly struck down, as is the man shown falling to the ground. Neither the prayers of the clergy nor the pleas of the saints, represented in this scene by St. Sebastian, could help. (The Walters Art Gallery, Baltimore)

governments in an effort to force wages down and fix prices; they also joined landowners to pressure royal governments to pass legislation to freeze wages, such as the English Statute of Laborers (1351). Craft guilds, which had once promoted industrial production, increasingly enacted restrictive rules limiting the volume of production, setting prices, excluding the products of outsiders, barring technical changes, and limiting entrance into each craft. The general effect of such measures was to depress industrial production and to disrupt established patterns of manufacturing long dominated by independent craft workers. Better able to adapt to new conditions were some large-scale industries, such as the wool industry and mining, where new organizational patterns, technologies, and practices of capital accumulation were applied.

Agricultural production was likewise depressed and dislocated. Widespread and persistent warfare ravaged many lands. Colonizing opportunities had nearly disappeared. Famine and plague decimated the rural labor force and sharply reduced the urban demand for food products, especially cereal grains. Large areas of marginal land were taken out of production, dislocating many agricultural workers. Many landowners responded to the depressed economy by hastening along the dismantlement of the traditional manorial system, a process which had already begun before 1300. Some rented their domains to enterprising peasants eager to gain access to more land. Others enclosed their manors in order to concentrate on specialized crops and livestock raising; these operations increasingly depended on hired labor.

Economic dislocation and contraction led to widespread social tension and disturbances in the later Middle Ages. As we noted earlier, even before 1300 Europe's aristocracy was becoming stratified, chiefly on the basis of wealth. That stratification continued and became even more pronounced during the late Middle Ages. These were tenuous times for the highest nobility, not only because changing economic conditions strained their fortunes but also because the unsettled political situation demanded their involvement in violent factionalism and civil war if they were to retain their positions of prestige and power. Some did not survive the murderous conflicts. However, those aristocratic families

many, Scandinavia, and the Low Countries into a cooperative trading enterprise. But ultimately the League declined, chiefly because its members refused to sacrifice local interests.

Industrial production experienced a comparable constriction. Labor shortages increased labor costs to the point where many kinds of industrial production were unprofitable in a setting where demand for goods was depressed by population decline. To redress this situation, some manufacturers began to manipulate urban

that did survive maintained their fortunes and increased their privileges, so that their social position became more distinct than ever. Increasingly, these powerful nobles owed their status to their close connections to the monarchs. The high aristocracy pursued an ever more splendid and exclusive lifestyle; it was based on an exaggerated practice of behavior patterns dictated by the code of chivalry.

Although many lesser nobles were also sorely tested by the agricultural depression, they solidified their position as a country gentry asserting a powerful influence over local life. The key to their success was the careful management of production on their landholdings and the exploitation of the local labor supply. They often strengthened their local position by allying themselves with great nobles and by seeking favors from royal governments. While duly impressed by the lifestyle of the great nobles, the lesser nobles were not able and did not try to imitate it. They began to develop a simpler lifestyle attuned to the activities of the small country estate and the local town. By 1500 this gentry had become a powerful force interested primarily in order and stability and support for their economic interests; they became a source of support for the increasingly strong kings. Thus, by 1500 a powerfully entrenched aristocracy continued to dominate society. However, its inner structure as a class was being altered, and its power base was shifting from the relationships once defined in terms of lordship and noble dependence to those defined by birth, wealth, and royal favor.

The peasant world also underwent significant changes during the late Middle Ages. The last vestiges of servile dependence in western Europe had virtually disappeared. While this development improved the legal status of most peasants, it deprived many of the economic security that had characterized serf status in earlier times. Population decline and the dismantling of manors seriously disrupted community groupings that had been a vital part of peasant life. Economically, peasants were thrown more and more on their own as renters or hired laborers, sometimes with disastrous results in a period of limited economic opportunity. Hard-pressed landlords preyed on peasant misfortunes to force on them added financial obligations, higher rents, and lower wages. Royal taxes fell heavily on the peas-

ants, and the wars that their taxes supported often ravaged their farms. With reduced opportunities in the troubled cities and a vanishing frontier, many peasants were trapped in a position of poverty and oppression. They expressed their discontent by frequent and violent rebellions, typified by the *Jacquerie* in France in 1358 and the Peasants' Revolt in England in 1381 (see Figure 23.3). Most of these rebellions were brutally crushed by kings, nobles, and clergy. Despite the generally grim condition of peasant life in the later Middle Ages, there were peasants who succeeded in increasing their landholdings either by purchase or by renting and who found ways of expanding their productivity and wealth in a volatile economic setting. This element of the peasant class would eventually make important contributions to the agricultural recovery of western Europe (see Color Plate 11).

Equally disadvantaged and discontented were certain elements of the urban population. The depression in manufacturing and exchange reduced many small-scale artisans and shopkeepers to the status of laborers for hire or to the ranks of the unemployed. They were also increasingly deprived of a significant voice in urban government such as they had enjoyed during the twelfth and thirteenth centuries. Dominated by rich entrepreneurs, city governments and the guilds sought to regulate the economic activities and wages of urban laborers more stringently. As their status as full members of the urban bourgeois community disintegrated, this element of the urban population demonstrated their discontent by frequent rioting and rebellion, which usually yielded little more immediate benefit to the urban poor than the peasant revolts did for their propagators.

The social group making the greatest advance in the fourteenth and fifteenth centuries was an elite segment of the bourgeoisie engaged in capitalistic ventures. Their success was exemplified by the Medici and the Bardi in Italy, the Fuggers in southern Germany, Jacques Coeur of France, and some of the entrepreneurs associated with the Hanseatic League. Members of this group amassed huge fortunes in such fields as banking, moneylending, and the wool industry. Pursuing techniques characteristic of early modern capitalism (see Chapter 28), these entrepreneurs increasingly determined the course of economic

FIGURE 23.3 Peasant Violence Pressed by a variety of miseries, peasants often resorted to violence in the late Middle Ages, as illustrated in this drawing showing peasants attacking a knight with axes and daggers. (Bibliothèque Nationale, Paris, ms. fr. 87)

market. Innovative techniques for accumulating capital and organizing large-scale commercial and manufacturing enterprises were being devised. New technological advances were being made and were being applied more widely—water mills in the textile industry, better mining techniques, printing, improved shipbuilding, the compass, the astrolabe, gunpowder. New frontiers were opening by way of the seas that washed Europe's western shores. All these forces pointed toward new economic growth in western Europe. It was obvious, however, that this growth would be achieved in ways different from those that had prevailed in medieval Europe.

2. MONARCHY UNDER STRESS: FRANCE, ENGLAND, SPAIN

One of the major achievements of the central Middle Ages was the creation in France, England, and Spain of large political communities ruled by monarchs who devised techniques of governance that increasingly allowed them to compel their subjects to observe common rules in certain spheres of political behavior. Within each of these medieval states monarchs recognized the privileged political status of nobles, religious leaders, and urban corporations by allowing these groups to exercise certain rights of lordship over their dependents. As the fourteenth century progressed, various pressures, some stemming from economic decline and social unrest and others from limitations inherent in the medieval political system, began to upset the delicate balance between the central and local spheres of authority. These tensions combined to disrupt the orderly operation of royal governments temporarily and check the expansion of royal power. However, the political disorder proved to be transitory; eventually the consolidation of central authority as the prime force in political life resumed, leading to the establishment of early modern national states.

During the later Middle Ages the royal governments in both France and England had to face monumental internal problems emerging from the economic depression and social dislocations, the efforts of privileged groups to extend their powers to serve selfish interests, and disruptive

development. They seized political control of most city governments and found favor with kings. Culturally they were able to patronize the learning and art associated with the Renaissance, allowing them to play a decisive role in shaping the cultural environment of western Europe. In a sense, this group now represented the bourgeoisie; others who had formerly been counted in this class—simple artisans and small shopkeepers—were becoming a group apart, a laboring class. The new bourgeoisie was destined to play a major role in the future of the West.

By about 1450 the worst of the economic and social stresses of the late Middle Ages were over, and there were signs of recovery everywhere. The population had begun to grow again. The agricultural system became more productive, chiefly as a result of a more rational management of land and labor in relation to the realities of the

clashes over succession to the throne. These challenges were complicated by a prolonged military struggle, called the Hundred Years' War (1337–1453), that placed demands on each monarchy far exceeding its traditional military and financial resources. That struggle was an extension of a conflict that had begun in the twelfth century over possessions held on the continent by English kings as fiefs from the French kings (see Chapter 19). Although the French rulers had reclaimed most of these territories by the early thirteenth century, England still held important possessions in Aquitaine (see Map 23.1) which the French kings constantly sought to recapture. French and English interests also clashed in Flanders, where the English sought to check French expansion in order to protect the Flemish woolen industry, which depended on English raw wool, and in Scotland, where the French supported the efforts of the Scots to win independence from England.

These festering issues were brought to a head when in 1328 the last member of the direct Capetian line died. Although England's Edward III (1327–1377) had the best hereditary claim to the French throne, the Estates General selected as king Philip of Valois, who represented a collateral line of the Capetian family. Philip VI's aggressive policy in Flanders and his confiscation of Aquitaine in 1337 on the grounds that Edward had refused to honor his obligations as a vassal led Edward to assert his claim to the French throne and to undertake a war to make good his claim.

The first phase of the Hundred Years' War, which lasted until 1360, was nearly fatal to France. English armies won two great battles at Crécy (1346) and Poitiers (1356), where English longbowmen clearly bested the flower of the French nobility. At Poitiers, King John of France (1350–1364) was captured and taken to England. An internal crisis ensued in France, marked by an effort by some leaders acting in the name of the Estates General to take control of the government, by a peasant rebellion called the *Jacquerie*, and by the ravaging of a large part of France by bands of unpaid mercenary soldiers upon whose services kings on both sides were increasingly forced to rely. Eventually John bought his release by accepting the Treaty of Brétigny (1360), under which he agreed to pay a huge ransom and to give Edward III full title to Guienne as well as a

small territory in northern France, including the key port of Calais. Edward renounced his claim to the French throne.

The Treaty of Brétigny did not, however, end the ancient rivalry. The next phase of the war, which extended from 1364 to 1415, saw sporadic but indecisive fighting. Effective military action was impeded by serious internal problems in both of the rival kingdoms. France enjoyed a brief recovery under Charles V (1364–1380), who rebuilt French military strength and increased royal income to the point where he seriously threatened England's hold on Guienne. However, these gains were undone during the reign of his pitiful successor, Charles VI (1380–1422). A minor when he became king and later the victim of spells of insanity, Charles VI often required regents to act in his stead. His uncle Philip, duke of Burgundy, and his brother, Louis, duke of Orléans, became bitter rivals to fill that role, each joined by a faction of self-seeking nobles. The rivalry between the Burgundians and the Armagnacs (partisans of Louis) plunged France into internal chaos from which most of the population suffered badly.

England was hardly less troubled during these years. Edward III ruled until 1377 amid deepening trouble. To pay for the increasingly costly war against France, he was forced to turn to Parliament to win approval for new taxes. Its members, who represented the forces of privilege in England, responded by claiming a role in deciding how money was spent, controlling royal officials, and initiating legislation through petitions presented to the king. The advancing power of Parliament became particularly notable in the reign of Richard II (1377–1399). His reign was troubled by economic and social problems that led to the Peasants' Revolt in 1381 and by dissatisfaction among the nobles with the king's allegedly autocratic ways. Eventually, Parliament deposed Richard II and chose in his place Henry IV (1399–1413), whose sole right to rule was based on Parliament's approval. Obviously, that institution had assumed a crucial role in political life. However, Parliament proved neither capable of directing the kingdom nor willing to trust the king to do so. It became a forum for agitation by noble factions aimed at dominating the king in order to gain greater privileges.

Henry V (1413–1422) hastened both England and France on their troubled ways by reopening

Map 23.1 THE HUNDRED YEARS' WAR In the Hundred Years' War the English fought to regain their once-extensive possessions in France (see Map 19.2), and the French sought to add these territories to the royal domain. The map shows the ebb and flow of that prolonged struggle. When the war began in 1337, England held only a modest territory in southwest France. At the height of their fortunes in the first half of the fifteenth century, they controlled most of northern France. But not for long. When the war ended in 1453, the French had driven them off the Continent except for the city of Calais.

the Hundred Years' War. In 1415 he invaded France and crushed a French army at Agincourt. With the support of the Burgundian faction, he established control over most of France north of the Loire River. In 1420 he forced the humiliating Treaty of Troyes on Charles VI. By its terms, Henry married Charles' daughter and was made heir to the French throne, thereby disinheriting the legitimate heir to the throne, the dauphin Charles. Generous concesssions were made to the duke of Burgundy for his support of the English. The French kingdom seemed on the verge of dismemberment.

But the English were not to enjoy their triumph for long. After both Henry V and Charles VI died in 1422, leaving the infant Henry VI as king of both nations, the French began to recover from what seemed disaster. The rallying point was the dauphin Charles, whose fortunes took a decisive turn in 1429, when a simple peasant girl, Joan of Arc, came to him claiming that God had revealed to her that Charles must free France of the English and assume the crown that rightly belonged to him. Her message bestirred the dispirited Charles and pumped new confidence into the many royal officials, military captains, nobles, and simple soldiers who were loyal to the house of Valois. Joan herself was with the army that in 1429 defeated an English army besieging the key city of Orléans, a victory that was followed by Charles' coronation as king. These events marked the beginning of a series of French triumphs which Joan did not live to see. In 1430 she was captured by the Burgundians and turned over to the English, who put her on trial before an ecclesiastical court that convicted her of heresy and ordered her burned at the stake in 1431.

Joan's dream of a reborn France soon came to pass. Under Charles VII, royal power made a remarkable recovery. Well served by excellent ministers, Charles was able to build a well-trained army paid for by the king, thus ending his dependence on a feudal army and trouble-making mercenaries. That army won victory after victory against the English, who by 1543 held only Calais. In 1439 the Estates General granted the king power to impose a direct tax, called the *taille,* on his subjects. Although many powerful nobles in France continued to act in their own interest, political life focused more and more on the royal government with its increasing ability

to establish order, curb the irresponsible behavior of the princes, and tap the growing sense of pride and shared interest felt by many subjects who increasingly thought of themselves as French. When Charles VII died in 1461, his son, Louis XI (1461–1483), inherited a solid base from which to rule what had become a national state (see Chapter 27).

England was in a less happy state during much of the fifteenth century, chiefly because of a deepening factionalism among a few privileged families seeking control of the government as a means of enhancing their power. Surrounding themselves with private armies, these factions pushed England toward a civil war. That struggle, the War of the Roses, so called because the opposing forces adopted the red and the white rose as their symbols, pitted against each other supporters of two rival families with claims to the throne, the Lancastrians and the Yorkists. While this struggle for the crown raged, the regular processes of orderly government were disrupted. Tyranny, intrigue, murder, confiscation of property, and pursuit of private ends were the order of the day. Finally, in 1485, Henry Tudor, a Lancastrian, defeated his Yorkist rival, King Richard III, in a pitched battle at Bosworth Field and assumed the throne as Henry VII. Although Henry's claim to the crown was extremely tenuous, the nation, weary of civil disorder, was willing to follow anyone who promised to restore peace and security. The desire for order was strong among the lesser nobles, the gentry made up chiefly of rural landowners, the prosperous peasant yeomen, and the well-to-do bourgeoisie. Taken together, these elements constituted a substantial force willing to support effective royal government. The old noble factions were badly discredited as a result of their brutal, self-seeking conduct during the War of the Roses. As a result, the new king had considerable freedom to act as he pleased. Henry used the opportunity to fashion a strong central government that united the English people into a nation (see Chapter 27).

The three major Iberian kingdoms—Aragon, Castile, and Portugal—also had their difficulties during the late Middle Ages. By 1300 the holy war against the Moslems had ceased to be the significant factor in Spanish affairs, for the Moslems had been confined to the narrow territory of Granada (see Map 20.1). The Christian kingdoms then turned on one another, competing bitterly for territory. At the same time almost constant civil strife raged within each kingdom, replicating the struggles in England and France. Castile was plagued by a long series of disputed successions that undermined royal authority. Aragon's internal order was compromised by the aggressive overseas policy pursued by its kings, especially in Italy, a policy seldom favored by the nobility, and by conflict between the landed and commercial interests. These senseless quarrels finally began to abate in 1469 when the heiress of Castile, Isabella, married Ferdinand, the heir of Aragon. In 1479, when this couple had succeeded to both thrones, they quickly took steps to end the strife, unify their lands into a single state, and impose stronger royal control over their subjects (see Chapter 27). The Portuguese kings did not meet such violent resistance as did the other Iberian kings, and their heroic struggle to prevent Castile from absorbing Portugal won them broad internal support. They also promoted commercial ventures throughout the fifteenth century, backing Portuguese merchants who expanded southward along the African coast and found lucrative markets.

Thus, by the end of the fifteenth century the major monarchies formed in western Europe during the central Middle Ages had survived a succession of tests. During the age of transition each faced challenges that created new pressures and fresh opportunities for strengthening central government as the only effective agency capable of addressing the common problems and shared interests that increasingly linked together the lives of large numbers of subjects living in what was perceived as a national political community. Medieval kingdoms were becoming early modern nation-states.

3. THE HOLY ROMAN EMPIRE: THE END OF THE UNIVERSAL STATE

Between 950 and 1250 one of the chief political entities in western Europe had been the Holy Roman Empire. Embracing Germany, Italy, and the western fringes of the Slavic world, this state represented an effort to realize a political ideal—a Christian commonwealth uniting all Christian people under a single Christian prince through whose guidance God's plan could be realized (see Chapter 19). After the death of the last great medieval emperor, Frederick II, in 1250, the ideal of a Christian commonwealth lived on, but in reality the medieval Holy Roman Empire began to fragment into a variety of political entities.

In Germany, after a interval without a ruler (called the Interregnum, 1250–1273), the German nobility exercised its long-established right of election to bestow the imperial crown upon a succession of rulers from three different families—the houses of Hapsburg, Luxembourg, and Bavaria—only to repudiate each family in turn when its elected representative threatened to become too powerful. While demonstrating their unwillingness to accept a ruler with any effective power, the nobles, clergy, and townspeople successfully extended their independence from the central government to constitute a mosaic of territorial entities each determining its own political course. The emerging political structure of Germany was given legal definition by Emperor Charles IV (1347–1378), who in 1356 issued a decree called the Golden Bull. It provided that the German ruler would be chosen by seven princes designated as electors: the archbishops of Cologne, Trier, and Mainz and the princes of Saxony, Brandenburg, the Palatinate, and Bohemia. Each elector was granted almost complete independence within his own territory. Other princes and cities demanded and gained the same kind of independence enjoyed by the electors, making the empire little more than a confederation of hundreds of independent political entities. The emperor could call together the princes, church leaders, and representatives of the towns in meetings called *diets*, but he lacked any means of enforcing decisions; he had no national army, no tax system, and no court system. Within their small principalities, many princes created stable, well-organized political systems—Germany was not a lawless land by any means. But in contrast to what was happening in England, France, and Spain during the late Middle Ages, a unified national state failed to emerge in Germany, a condition that would affect German history far into the future.

In Italy, where imperial authority had always been resisted, the trend toward decentralization was even more pronounced after 1250. In theory the ruler elected by the Germans and crowned emperor by the pope still claimed dominion in Italy, and from time to time some Italians did seek to have him exert his authority. After the early fourteenth century, the emperors seldom even tried to exercise any influence over their Italian realms, and a welter of independent states emerged.

In southern Italy the old Norman-Hohenstaufen state was divided after 1282 into the Kingdom of Naples, ruled by a French prince, and the Kingdom of Sicily, ruled by a member of the royal family of Aragon. Their rivalry and misrule brought steady decline to this once-rich area. Finally, in 1435, the two kingdoms were united under Aragonese rule. In central Italy the Papal States dominated. Papal overlordship was bitterly resisted by the local nobles, and it was badly compromised by the absence of the papacy from Rome during much of the fourteenth century (see Chapter 24). However, during the fifteenth century a succession of able, ruthless popes restored their authority, making the Papal States a major force in Italian political life.

Northern Italy was divided among many city-states which had forced concessions from their political overlord, the Holy Roman emperor, that ensured each its political independence. After the death of Frederick II, they battled one another for land, trading advantages, power, and security. Some of the more powerful of the city-states, especially Milan, Venice, and Florence, were able to impose their rule on smaller neighboring cities to create territorial entities that tended to dominate the political life of northern Italy. These cities provided the setting for a powerful cultural movement, the Renaissance, that played a decisive role in the transition from the medieval to the early modern world (see Chapter 25).

Internally, the political system of most of the city-states tended to move from an order with considerable citizen participation toward a system dominated by a single individual (a *signore*, "lord") or by an oligarchy of the rich. In Milan, for example, first the Visconti family and then after 1447 the Sforzas established a regime of despots under whose direction Milan grew rich and expanded its territories. Florence resisted despotism longer; in fact, through most of the period Florence retained the façade of a republican form of government that allowed its citizens considerable power to decide public issues. Gradually there emerged a behind-the-scenes power that used patronage, bribery, and personal influence to shape political decisions. After about 1430 that role was played by members of a rich banking family, the Medicis. Although they held no exalted titles, the Medicis in effect ran Florence as if they were despots. Venice always remained subject to an oligarchy of rich merchants whose methods did not differ greatly from those of the despots. The turbulent, strife-filled times promoted a new style of politics, described brilliantly in Machiavelli's *The Prince* (see pp. 344–345), which placed heavy emphasis on the absolute sovereignty of the state, its right to create its own moral sanctions, and its superiority over its subjects. Many historians have seen these developments as prototypes for the powerful national monarchies that came to dominate in western Europe at the beginning of the early modern period. Despite the innovative political practices of the Italian Renaissance states, the fragmentation of the peninsula doomed Italy to weakness and prepared the way for a long era during which the many states of Italy became pawns in the power politics practiced by the national states of early modern Europe.

4. THE CHANGING SCENE IN EASTERN EUROPE AND THE MEDITERRANEAN WORLD

While the internal structures of the western European states were undergoing transformations during the age of transition, other highly significant political changes were unfolding along western Europe's eastern and southeastern frontiers that would alter the relationships that had been established between the West and these eastern areas between 1000 and 1300 (see Map 23.2).

Perhaps the most significant development was the demise of the Byzantine Empire. That long-established fixture on the medieval political map never fully recovered from the attacks of the Seljuk Turks in the late eleventh century and the capture of Constantinople by western Europeans in 1204 during the Fourth Crusade. After

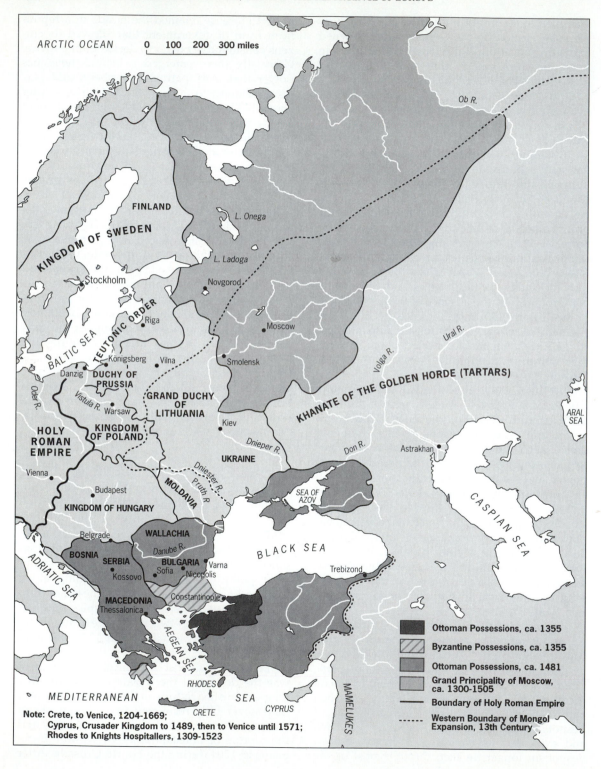

ARCTIC OCEAN

0 100 200 300 miles

Ob R.

FINLAND

KINGDOM OF SWEDEN

L. Onega

L. Ladoga

Stockholm

Novgorod

Moscow

TEUTONIC ORDER

Riga

Ural R.

BALTIC SEA

Königsberg

Vilna

Smolensk

KHANATE OF THE GOLDEN HORDE (TARTARS)

Volga R.

Danzig

DUCHY OF PRUSSIA

GRAND DUCHY OF LITHUANIA

Oder R.

Vistula R.

Warsaw

Kiev

ARAL SEA

HOLY ROMAN EMPIRE

KINGDOM OF POLAND

UKRAINE

Dnieper R.

Don R.

Astrakhan

CASPIAN SEA

Vienna

Dniester R.

Pruth R.

SEA OF AZOV

Budapest

MOLDAVIA

KINGDOM OF HUNGARY

BLACK SEA

Belgrade

WALLACHIA

Danube R.

BOSNIA

SERBIA

BULGARIA

Varna

Trebizond

Kossovo

Sofia

Nicopolis

ADRIATIC SEA

MACEDONIA

Constantinople

Thessalonica

AEGEAN SEA

RHODES

MEDITERRANEAN   SEA   CYPRUS

CRETE

MAMELUKES

Note: Crete, to Venice, 1204-1669;
Cyprus, Crusader Kingdom to 1489, then to Venice until 1571;
Rhodes to Knights Hospitallers, 1309-1523

■ Ottoman Possessions, ca. 1355
▨ Byzantine Possessions, ca. 1355
■ Ottoman Possessions, ca. 1481
■ Grand Principality of Moscow, ca. 1300-1505
— Boundary of Holy Roman Empire
--- Western Boundary of Mongol Expansion, 13th Century

the Europeans were finally ousted in 1261, a fatal illness afflicted the empire. Civil strife slowly sapped the strength of its government. The Italian city-states, led by Venice, deprived the empire of much of its trade, and bit by bit its territory was pared away, first by Slavic princes in the Balkans and then by the Ottoman Turks. The emperors of the fourteenth and fifteenth centuries appealed desperately to the West for help but received little. Finally, in 1453, the Ottomans captured Constantinople and made the city their capital under the name Istanbul. The fall of Constantinople ended forever the Christian power that had so long shielded western Europe from the threat of the Moslems and had contributed so much to spreading civilized life to central and eastern Europe.

The Ottoman victory marked a renewal of the threat of Moslem aggression against the West, a danger that western Europeans had not faced for centuries. The Ottoman Turks were originally Asiatic nomads who had been uprooted and pushed westward by Mongol expansion in the thirteenth century. They had settled in Asia Minor and accepted Islam. Under their first great ruler, Osman (or Othman, whence the term Ottoman) (1290–1326), the new state began to expand in Asia Minor and then into the Balkans, largely at the expense of the Byzantine Empire. Early in the fifteenth century, Ottoman power was nearly destroyed by Tamerlane, a Mongol warrior who sought to reconstruct the empire of Genghis Khan (see Chapter 20). The collapse of Tamerlane's empire soon after his death in 1405 allowed the Ottomans to resume their expansion. They completed the conquest of the Byzantine Empire by 1453. Early in the sixteenth century, they conquered Syria, Palestine, and Egypt. As the Middle Ages ended, their vast empire loomed as a major threat to the West.

As the Ottoman Turks extended their territorial sway, they fashioned political institutions that gave their empire strength and stability. The Ottomans constituted an elite claiming supremacy over their subjects, many of them Christians, by right of conquest. They retained a strong sense of community based on their ethnic identity and their religion. The Ottoman state was headed by the *sultan*, whose extensive power over all aspects of life was based on his claim to be the successor of Muhammad and empowered to interpret the Moslem law that all followers of Allah were required to obey. A well-organized bureaucracy developed, modeled on both Byzantine and Abbasid models. Local units of government were developed across the empire to carry out the sultan's policies, collect taxes, and administer justice. In practice, the Ottoman regime allowed local communities broad authority to regulate their own affairs as long as they did not disrupt internal peace or challenge the sultan's supreme power. Aside from taxes, the Ottomans extracted human resources from their subject population to sustain their regime. Young boys, often of Christian or Jewish origin, were taken as slaves, converted to Islam, and trained for specialized duties in the civil service or the army. The military corps created from these slaves, called the Janissaries, developed into a highly professional, dedicated force that played a key role in Ottoman expansion and in maintaining Ottoman domination over the large empire. Young girls were also enslaved to serve in Ottoman harems, including that of the sultan, from which successors to the throne were selected.

Central and eastern Europe began to assume a modern shape in the wake of the decline of the Holy Roman and Byzantine empires. The south coast of the Baltic Sea was dominated by Germans, an expansion spearheaded by the crusading order of the Teutonic Knights, who brought traders, missionaries, and agricultural colonists in their wake. Their presence filled the Slavs of central Europe with an abiding distrust and fear of the Germans. The Germanic threat resulted in a union of the ruling houses of Poland and Lithuania under the Lithuanian prince Jagiello, who married a Polish princess and governed both

Map 23.2 CENTRAL EUROPE AND WESTERN ASIA, CA. 1500 This map shows the major political entities in central Europe and western Asia about 1500. Especially threatening to Poland, Lithuania, and Hungary—and to western Europe in general—were two rapidly expanding powers: the Ottoman Empire and the Grand Principality of Moscow (the future Russia).

states as King Ladislas II (1386–1434). The house of Jagiello exerted strong military pressure on the Baltic Germans and the Russian states to the east during much of the fifteenth century, but it never succeeded in creating an effective government for its huge kingdom. To the south, Hungary continued to develop, but its energies were increasingly absorbed in defending itself against the Ottoman Turks and holding back ambitious German nobles bent on taking the Hungarian throne. Until the Ottomans seized control of the Balkans at the end of the fourteenth century, a flourishing Serbian kingdom, created at the expense of the declining Byzantine Empire, dominated that area; after its destruction by the Ottomans, the Hungarians stood as western Europe's outpost against the Turks. Farther east a vigorous Russian state was emerging. We shall return to the story of its development later (see Chapter 32). Suffice it to say here that by 1500 Russia, whose ruler took the title *tsar* (*"caesar"*) to befit his claim that his realm was the "third Rome," was beginning to play an important role in determining the fate of eastern Europe.

SUGGESTED READING

Overview of the Period 1300–1500

Robert Fossier, ed., *The Cambridge Illustrated History of the Middle Ages,* Vol. 3: *1250–1520,* trans. Sarah Hanbury Tenison (1986).

Denys Hay, *Europe in the Fourteenth and Fifteenth Centuries,* 2nd ed. (1989).

George Holmes, *Europe: Hierarchy and Revolt, 1320–1450* (1975).

Any of these three works will provide an excellent overview of the major developments during the period.

Western European Political Development

George Holmes, *The Later Middle Ages, 1272–1485* (1962).

Trevor Rowley, *The High Middle Ages* (1986).

Either of these works will provide a clear picture of political developments in late medieval England.

John A. F. Thompson, *The Transformation of Medieval England, 1370–1529* (1983). A good picture of social change.

John Gillingham, *The War of the Roses: Peace and Conflict in Fifteenth-Century England* (1981). Stresses the political and military aspect of England's internal strife.

P. S. Lewis, *Later Medieval France: The Polity* (1968). Good on political institutions; see also the study by Duby cited in Chapter 19.

Christopher Allmond, *The Hundred Years' War: England and France at War c. 1300–c. 1450* (1988). A well-done treatment stressing the effects of the war.

F. R. H. DuBoulay, *Germany in the Later Middle Ages* (1983).

Joachim Leuscher, *Germany in the Late Middle Ages,* trans. Sabine MacCormack (1980).

Either of these two works will provide a good overview.

Giovanni Tabacco, *The Struggle for Power in Medieval Italy: Structures of Political Rule,* trans. Rosalind Brown Jensen (1989). A difficult but rewarding study.

Bernard Guenée, *States and Rulers in Later Medieval Europe,* trans. Juliet Vale (1985). A comparative study of late medieval political institutions.

Richard W. Kaeuper, *War, Justice and Public Order in England and France in the Later Middle Ages* (1988). A challenging analysis of political change in the later Middle Ages.

Eastern European Political Developments

Donald M. Nicol, *The Last Centuries of Byzantium, 1261–1453* (1972). A clearly presented account.

Halil Inalick, *The Ottoman Empire: The Classical Age, 1300–1600,* trans. Norman Itzkowitz and Colin Imber (1973). The best treatment of a subject not always given an objective evaluation.

John V. A. Fine, Jr., *The Late Medieval Balkans. A Critical Survey from the Late Twelfth Century to the Ottoman Conquest* (1987). A fine treatment of a neglected subject.

Robert O. Crummey, *The Formation of Muscovy 1304–1613* (1987). A good synthesis of a difficult period in Russian history.

David Morgan, *The Mongols* (1986).

Economic and Social History

C. M. Cipolla, *Before the Industrial Revolution: European Society and Economy, 1000–1700* (1976). Effectively places late medieval economic and social history in a larger context.

Harry A. Miskimin, *The Economy of Early Renaissance Europe, 1300–1460* (1969). A detailed study; more general treatments can be found in the works of Bautier and Pounds, cited in Chapter 18.

Specialized aspects of late medieval economic and social history are treated in the following works.

Johannes Schildhauer, *The Hansa: History and Culture,* trans. Katherine Vanovitch (1985).

Robert S. Gottfried, *The Black Death: Natural and Human Disaster in Medieval Europe* (1983).

Graham Twigg, *The Black Death: A Biological Reappraisal* (1984).

Joel T. Rosenthal, *Nobles and Noble Life, 1295–1500* (1976).

Michel Mollat and Philippe Wolff, *The Popular Revolutions of the Late Middle Ages,* trans. A. L. Lytton-Sells (1973).

Biographies

Marina Warner, *Joan of Arc: The Image of Female Heroism* (1981).

Anne Barstow, *Joan of Arc: Heretic, Mystic, Shaman* (1986).

CHAPTER 24

Transition in Religion and Thought, 1300–1500

FIGURE 24.1 **Pope Boniface VIII** This fresco from the Church of St. John Lateran in Rome shows Pope Boniface VIII proclaiming the great jubilee held in Rome in 1300. The artist, perhaps Giotto, catches something of the autocratic spirit of the proud pontiff whose efforts to assert papal authority led to deep trouble for the Church. (Alinari/Art Resource)

The tensions that beset and transformed western European economic, social, and political structures during the fourteenth and fifteenth centuries were also felt in religious life. After 1300 the religious establishment, which had earlier decisively influenced all aspects of human activity, encountered increasing difficulties in asserting its traditional leadership role. Its leaders, its system of government, and its teachings were challenged on many fronts. From one perspective many of these challenges represented a continuation of the reforming spirit that had characterized religious life between 1000 and 1300. However, others stemmed from new forces unleashed by the troubled times marking the late medieval age of transition. Increasingly, the directive forces in the religious establishment failed to discover effective ways to respond to the mounting challenges.

1. THE CRISIS IN RELIGIOUS LEADERSHIP

One of the major results of the reform movement of the central Middle Ages had been the creation of a centralized system of church governance. By 1300 that system consisted of a hierarchy of ecclesiastical officials, headed by the bishop of Rome, that claimed for itself an independent sphere of authority that allowed it to define and control belief and discipline for the entire Christian community of western Europe. As that structure evolved, it met resistance in many quarters, centering especially on what the limits of ecclesiastical authority were and how religious officials should use their power. During the late Middle Ages that resistance stiffened to the point of creating a crisis in religious governance.

The most dramatic challenge to that system focused on its very center: the papacy. The authority of the papal office was brought to its apogee by the talented popes of the thirteenth century who claimed for themselves a God-given right to exercise "the fullness of power" over all Christians, by which they meant they had the right to make final decisions affecting any aspect of Christian society. When Pope Boniface VIII (1294–1303), a vain, ambitious figure described by Dante as "prince of the new Pharisees" (see Figure 24.1), sought to impose that claim, he en-

countered vigorous resistance from the kings of England and France. The resultant struggle opened a long sequence of events that eventually weakened not only papal authority but also the medieval system of religious governance.

Boniface clashed with these kings over issues that had long been bones of contention between the papacy and the civil authorities. His first setback came when he attempted to stop Edward I of England and Philip IV of France from imposing new taxes on the clergy and church property in their realms to help finance their wars against each other. In a pronouncement (called a *papal bull*) entitled *Clericis laicos,* which was intended to be binding on all Christians, Boniface forcefully maintained that taxes could be laid upon the religious establishment only with papal consent; his case was based on the "liberties" of the ecclesiastical establishment and the right of the head of that establishment to command the obedience of secular rulers. Edward and Philip responded by cutting off revenues from their kingdoms to Rome, forcing Boniface to retreat from his position. Before long Boniface and Philip again clashed, this time over the question of whether the king had jurisdiction in legal cases involving the clergy. Again the strong-minded pope stated his case unequivocally. In a bull entitled *Unam sanctam* (see Historians' Sources, p. 329) he not only claimed the exemption of the clergy from secular justice but also insisted that kings and all other Christians must subject themselves to the pope to be saved. Philip countered with a masterful propaganda campaign which discredited the pope in the eyes of the French public, including many French clergymen. He capped that campaign by sending his agents to Italy to capture Boniface. They were successful, and the pope escaped what might have been an even more painful defeat by dying. St. Peter's vicar had suffered a humiliating defeat at the hands of strong kings intent on asserting greater control over the ecclesiastical establishment in their realms.

Philip IV capitalized on his victory by using his influence over the College of Cardinals to ensure the election of a French bishop as Boniface's successor. In 1309, aware that he would be unwelcome in the turbulent Papal States, the new pope took up residence at Avignon, a city located on the east bank of the Rhone River, just outside

French territory. Until 1377 this city remained the residence of the papacy. During these years of what the Italian writer Petrarch called the "Babylonian Captivity"—referring to the episode in Jewish history when God's chosen people were held captive in Babylon by the sinful Chaldeans, now equated with the French monarchy—the prestige of the papacy suffered badly. The king of England and the Holy Roman emperor used the excuse that the popes were pawns of the French kings to expand their control over ecclesiastical affairs in their realms. Many Christians were troubled by the fact that the pope's claim to power was based on succession to St. Peter as bishop of Rome, not Avignon. These critics were not impressed by the plea of the papacy that Rome was not safe; neither had it been for Peter nor for many earlier popes. The Babylonian Captivity caused scholars and writers to raise major questions regarding church government and to arrive at answers that challenged papal supremacy.

The Avignon popes were extremely active in pursuing policies intended to strengthen papal control over the ecclesiastical organization. Several of the Avignon popes were highly skilled administrators whose efforts brought the long-standing trend toward centralization of religious organization to a culmination. Their most pressing concerns were financial. Affected by the economic despression gripping all of western Europe and cut off from the traditional revenues from their control of the Papal States in Italy, the Avignon popes worked hard to exploit old sources of revenue from all across Europe and to develop new forms of income. Among other things, they resorted to increasing assessments on local churches; "reserving" for themselves the right to fill major ecclesiastical offices in return for payment of a price; granting dispensations from the regulations of canon law in return for fees; selling indulgences which allowed sinners to do penance by making payments in money; and requiring adjudication of cases involving violation of canon law in papal courts for which fees and fines were collected. The concern with expanding financial resources and judicial activities required a huge expansion of the bureaucracy of the papal curia. In terms of revenues, subordinates, and business transactions, the Avignon popes were actually more powerful than even their thirteenth-century predecessors.

This emphasis on organizational affairs posed serious threats to papal prestige. The papal bureaucracy was increasingly open to charges of corruption involving the sale of offices and acceptance of bribes to ensure the desired outcome of requests for papal favors or judicial cases tried in papal courts. With increasing frequency, major ecclesiastical offices were sold to people who never occupied them or who purchased more than one; absenteeism and pluralism led to widespread neglect of the responsibilities attached to key religious offices. Bishops and abbots in all parts of Europe resented the growing papal interference in local religious affairs and tried to escape papal control, often by turning to their kings, who gladly protected them—for a price. Papal taxation aroused bitterness and resistance everywhere. Edward III of England reflected the dislike of the money-grubbing popes when he said "The successor of the Apostles was ordered to lead the Lord's sheep to the pasture, not to fleece them." The officials of the papal curia spent much of this wealth on luxurious living; a symbol of their luxury was the splendid papal palace built in Avignon. The ecclesiastical lifestyle of the city, which Petrarch called "the sewer of the world," aroused the bitter anger of many in Europe whose lot was poverty and suffering in the wake of the Black Death and widespread economic depression. The Avignon popes seemed powerless to curb these excesses and thus suffered the blame.

The Babylonian Captivity finally ended in 1377 with the return of the reigning pope to Rome. However, when he died in 1378, the complex maneuvers of the College of Cardinals to replace him ended with two popes, one in Rome and another in Avignon. Thus began the Great Schism, forty years during which the Christian community was headed by two popes directing two administrations, two tax systems, two sets of Church courts. All western Christendom wondered who was in charge of the keys to the heavenly kingdom. Those who were not confused sought to take advantage of the situation; their efforts were abetted by the politicking of rival popes seeking to gain sufficient allies to oust what each called the anti-pope. Many princes thought in terms of supporting the pope who offered the most advantageous concessions in terms of controlling the ecclesiastical establishments within their realms. Few took seriously the

HISTORIANS' SOURCES

Boniface the VIII: "Unam Sanctam"

In 1302 Pope Boniface VIII issued the following official pronouncement (called a bull) entitled "Unam Sanctam" as a response to claims made by the French king, Philip IV, to try in a royal court a French bishop charged with treason. From it the historian can gain a sense of what medieval popes meant by "fullness of power" and why secular rulers felt that their authority was threatened.

The true faith compels us to believe that there is one holy catholic apostolic church, and this we firmly believe and plainly confess. And outside of her there is no salvation or remission of sins. . . . In this church there is "one Lord, one faith, one baptism" (Eph. 4:5). For in the time of the flood there was only one ark, that of Noah, prefiguring the one church, and it. . . . had but one helmsman and master, namely, Noah. . . . Therefore there is one body of the one and only church, and one head, not two heads, as if the church were a monster. And this head is Christ and his vicar, Peter and his successor; for the Lord himself said to Peter: "Feed my sheep" (John 21:16). And he said "my sheep," in general, not these or those sheep in particular; from which it is clear that all were committed to him. If therefore Greeks or anyone else say that they are not subject to Peter and his successors, they thereby necessarily confess that they are not of the sheep of Christ. For the Lord says in the Gospel of John, that there is one fold and only one shepherd (John 10:16). By the words of the gospel we are taught that the two swords, namely, the spiritual authority and the temporal are in the power of the church. . . . Whoever denies that the temporal sword is in the power of Peter does not properly understand the word of the Lord when he said: "Put up thy sword into the sheath" (John 18:11). Both swords, there-

fore, the spiritual and the temporal, are in the power of the church. The former is to be used by the church, the latter for the church; the one by the hand of the priest, the other by the hand of kings and knights, but at the command and permission of the priest. Moreover, it is necessary for one sword to be under the other, and the temporal authority to be subjected to the spiritual. . . . According to the law of the universe all things are not equally and directly reduced to order, but the lowest are fitted into their order through the intermediate, and the lower through the higher. And we must necessarily admit that the spiritual power surpasses any earthly power in dignity and honor, because spiritual things surpass temporal things. We clearly see that this is true from the paying of tithes, from the benediction, from the sanctification, from the receiving of the power, and from the governing of these things. For the truth itself declares that the spiritual power must establish the temporal power and pass judgment on it if it is not good. . . . Therefore if the temporal power errs, it will be judged by the spiritual power, and if the lower spiritual power errs, it will be judged by its superior. But if the highest spiritual power errs, it can not be judged by men, but by God alone. For the apostle says: "But he that is spiritual judgeth all things, yet he himself is judged of no man" (1 Cor. 2:15). Now this authority, although it is given to man and exercised through man, is not human, but divine. For it was given by the word of the Lord to Peter, and the rock was made firm to him and his successors, in Christ himself, whom he had confessed. For the Lord said to Peter: "Whatsoever thou shalt bind on earth shall be bound in heaven: and whatsoever thou shalt loose on earth shall be loosed in heaven" (Matt. 16:19). Therefore whosoever resisteth this power thus ordained of God, resisteth the ordinance of God (Rom. 13:2). . . . We therefore declare, say, and affirm that submission on the part of every man to the bishop of Rome is altogether necessary for his salvation.

SOURCE: Oliver J. Thatcher and Edgar Holmes McNeal, *A Source Book of Medieval History. Selected Documents Illustrating the History of Europe in the Middle Ages* (New York: Charles Scribner's Sons, 1905), pp. 314–317.

claim of either pope to be spiritual leader of Europe; popes who competed with each other and encouraged the division of Christendom seemed little better than greedy politicians.

As a result of the schism and the increasing corruption, many leaders—bishops, canon lawyers, theologians, and even princes—began to search for ways of ending what seemed a scandalous situation. Their search eventually focused on an institution that had played a major role in the early history of the Christian establishment: a general council. The advocates of the conciliar theory argued that an ecumenical assembly of bishops possessed an authority superior even to that of the pope and thus provided a legitimate means of healing the schism and reforming the clergy. As a result of conciliar agitation four general councils were held between 1409 and 1449, each a stormy affair marked by limited results. The Council of Pisa (1409) addressed the issue of the schism but ended with the installation of a third pope to further complicate that problem. The Council of Constance (1414–1418) finally succeeded in restoring a single pope and articulating the principle of the supreme authority of councils in ecclesiastical governance. In the subsequent two councils the popes devoted singular attention to disarming this dangerous threat to papal authority, a task made easier by disagreements among ecclesiastical leaders representing different nations. A major tactic used by the popes to curb the claims of the conciliarists to supremacy in religious affairs was to seek support for papal authority from secular rulers by making concessions extending their control over the clergy and ecclesiastical income. These concessions limited papal power and hastened a trend toward the creation of "national" churches.

Probably the greatest failure of the conciliar movement was its inability to institute meaningful reform. Despite numerous attempts to enact legislation aimed at curing many of the ills afflicting the ecclesiastical establishment and religious life, the members of the councils were never able to agree on a practical reform program. A major obstacle to reform stemmed from the fact that the councils were dominated by clergymen whose conduct would have made many of them the chief target of reform. When the last council disbanded in 1449, most people had lost confidence in this means of revitalizing the religious system. The greatest influence of the conciliar movement was indirect: It raised fundamental questions about the traditional religious organization and caused many to conclude that the pope's claim to the "fullness of power" was not divinely ordained.

The popes of the last half of the fifteenth century concentrated on strengthening their control over the Papal States in Italy and on making their state a decisive force in the many power struggles raging in Italy in this period. On the whole, they were successful in establishing the Papal States as a preeminent power in Italian affairs. But the methods they employed led many to view the pope as nothing more than a secular prince, scheming, bribing, and brawling to get what he desired for himself, his family, and his friends. That impression was given greater credence by the role the papacy played as patron of Renaissance cultural activity, a role that immersed the papal court in a wide range of worldly activities that seemed to have little to do with the vicarship of Christ. With increasing frequency the popes conceded control of the religious establishment outside Rome and Italy to secular princes in return for nominal recognition of papal supremacy. These developments combined to deprive the papacy of the moral authority that had been its chief source of influence in the thirteenth century, and without that authority the papacy was in no position to command the respect and veneration of large numbers of Christians, as the beginning of the Protestant Reformation soon made evident.

The disarray in church governance resulting from the problems besetting the papacy and the decay of papal prestige was compounded by a steady deterioration of the effectiveness of the entire body of the clergy in the performance of pastoral and administrative responsibilities. A variety of factors combined to distract the secular clergy, charged with everyday ministry to the Christian populace, from its central function and to provide a basis for charges of corruptness and moral laxness against its members. The tone guiding the behavior of the upper clergy was set by popes and the powerful officials of the papal curia, especially the cardinals, whose vast entourages, immense wealth, and talent for political machinations indeed made them "princes of the Church" and targets of criticism. Following the

FIGURE 24.2 Misconduct of Monks Some of the most savage criticism of the late medieval church was aimed at the monastic establishments. These scenes reflect some of the causes of that criticism. Left, a monk and his mistress are held in stocks for passersby to jeer at. Right, a monk drinks excessively. (The British Library)

model of the cardinals, many bishops found the lure of political and social life surrounding the courts of kings and great nobles irresistible. In the face of the fiscal pressures resulting from a declining income in an era of depression, the price demanded by popes and kings to secure appointment to their office, and heavy papal and royal taxes, most bishops were left with little choice except to wring money from their flocks. Some bishops were tempted to meet these demands by requiring payment from the faithful for religious services and by offering lower ecclesiastical offices for sale. Ordinary priests who paid for their offices tried to recoup their costs by similar tactics. Both bishops and priests sought to hold several ecclesiastical offices at once; pluralism led to absenteeism. Absentee clergy often turned religious duties over to poorly trained, poorly paid clerks little suited to guide spiritual life. Divine services, instruction, confessions, preaching, and counseling were slighted, leaving Christians who had religious problems lost, unhappy, and even angry.

Monasticism, long a source of spiritual searching and religious renewal, also suffered stagnation. Between 1300 and 1500 not a single new monastic order of any importance was established, and many of the established orders failed to provide effective spiritual leadership. The Franciscans and the Dominicans were the most powerful and active orders during the later Middle Ages, continuing their work as preach-

ers, confessors, and educational leaders. However, both orders attained increasing wealth and became engaged in a quest for power both within the religious establishment and in secular society. In the older Benedictine and Cistercian orders monks and nuns were lax in observing the rules governing discipline and morality. Little attention was paid to the quality of recruits entering monasteries and nunneries; many were aristocratic ladies who could not find husbands, landless younger sons of noble families, and commoners who sought to escape the hardships of life. Absentee abbots thought more about garnering income from monastic properties than about directing the spiritual lives of their charges. As the late medieval age of transition progressed, monastic life increasingly came to be held in low repute. Its bad reputation was mirrored with special force in late medieval literature, such as Boccaccio's *Decameron* and Chaucer's *Canterbury Tales*, both of which equate monastic life with greed, immorality, and hypocrisy (see Figure 24.2).

The combination of challenges to its authority and its own mismangement of the internal governance of the religious establishment led to increasing criticism of the religious leadership by many Christians. In their minds the institutional establishment that claimed the right to direct Christian life was too rich, too powerful, too bloated with self-serving officials. The ecclesiastical establishment had become concerned chiefly with sustaining its power and wealth at the expense of a vast community of faithful already deeply troubled by a variety of economic, social, and political dislocations and disturbed by deep spiritual concerns. One of the most impressive creations of the central Middle Ages was in need of an overhaul.

2. SPIRITUAL DISQUIET

While its system of governance was encountering difficulties that increasingly limited its ability to control the Christian community, the religious establishment was confronted with numerous signs of religious discontent welling up in the tension-filled society of the age of transition. Chiefly as a result of the intense effort by the ecclesiastical hierarchy and the intellectual establishment to impose uniformity of belief and practice on religious life during the central Middle Ages, Roman Catholicism had by 1300 become a highly formalistic religion in which piety was equated with participating in prescribed rituals, receiving the sacraments, and conforming to regulations governing behavior prescribed by canon law. There had, of course, been Christians before 1300 whose spiritual needs were not fully satisfied with that kind of religious experience; their efforts at "reform" had played an important part in the religious revival of the central Middle Ages. Such searching continued in the later Middle Ages, intensified and reshaped by the changing social setting.

Spiritual searching and dissatisfaction took many forms. One of the most important was an increase in the number of mystics, that is, persons who believed they could experience and know God directly without mediation by other persons or institutions. Mysticism was present throughout the Middle Ages; St. Bernard and St. Francis of Assisi were mystics. But the fourteenth and fifteenth centuries produced an especially large number of people who sought ways to experience a personal vision of God. Many of the most influential were simple men and women who never wore clerical garb, like Joan of Arc. None was more prominent than Catherine of Siena (1347–1380). On the basis of visions of Christ she claimed to have experienced, she proclaimed an intensely personal kind of spirituality which she not only shared with others by word

of mouth during her extended travels and numerous letters that circulated all over Europe but which she also put into practice through her efforts to help the poor, the sick, criminals, and the downtroddden. So great was her fame that she earned a reputation as a saint in her own lifetime. Although she, as well as many like her, was never seriously at odds with the religious establishment, Catherine practiced a kind of Christianity unfamiliar to contemporary religious officials.

The activities of mystics sometimes resulted in the formation of communal movements that operated almost independently of the established religious system. A prime example was the Brethren of the Common Life (and its female counterpart, the Sisters of the Common Life), founded by a lay preacher named Gerard Groote (1340–1384), who was one of the many spiritual heirs of the great German mystic Meister Eckhart (1260–1327). This loosely knit movement was a product of a new kind of piety called the *devotio moderna*, which stressed prayer, love, and direct communion with God. Devotees of the new piety joined together as brothers and sisters in communities in which they shared their worldly goods, joined in common worship, confessed their sins to one another, devoted themselves to works of charity, sought to educate members of the community, and even produced their own devotional literature. One of the best examples of that literature, still read today as a spiritual guide, is Thomas à Kempis' *Imitation of Christ*. The many communities of the Brethren seldom strayed into heresy, but their piety, their puritanical life, and their mysticism set them apart. Not surprisingly, the Brethren were often attacked for spreading dangerous ideas; perhaps there was some substance to this charge in view of the fact that such important later reformers as Erasmus and Martin Luther were educated in their schools. Akin to the Brethren were the Beguines, associations of laywomen who led a common life, committed themselves to chastity and good works, and supported themselves by working or begging. Similar communities of men, called Beghards, were also established. More radical were the Brethren of the Free Spirit, who among other things denied the existence of sin on the basis of their belief that God existed in all things, an idea that resulted in their condemnation.

The fourteenth and fifteenth centuries produced a hardier crowd of critics—usually condemned as heretics—who voiced ideas that called for radical changes in the religious establishment. Some were intellectual figures, such as Marsiglio of Padua, whose book, *The Defender of the Peace* (1324), mounted a devastating attack on the claim of the religious establishment to exercise superior authority over society. Marsiglio argued that ultimate authority in any community derives not from God but from the will of the members making up that community. The will of the community expresses itself through the state, whose authority is sovereign. Any claim of the religious authorities to independent authority is thus a fiction. Marsiglio advocated that the religious establishment be deprived of its wealth and privileges and be made a branch of government, subservient to the ruler in whom authority was vested by the will of the political community. He argued that the "Church" as a community of all Christians should be ruled by a council representing all elements in Christian society, not by a clerical hierarchy headed by the pope. He denied that the papal office had divine sanction; the pope was simply an ecclesiastical administrator whose powers were defined by the Christian community and who could be limited in any way that community wished. Not surprisingly, Marsiglio was excommunicated by the papacy and his book was condemned.

Somewhat later, John Wycliffe (1320–1384), a teacher and scholar at Oxford, raised equally serious issues about the prevailing practice of Christianity. Wycliffe's critique of the religious establishment stemmed not only from his reflections on matters of faith but also from his sympathy with the growing tide of anticlericalism and antipapalism emerging in an England troubled by the Avignon papacy, the burdens of the Hundred Years' War, and internal political and economic stresses. He first voiced his concerns about the ecclesiastical system by arguing that it had abused its right to hold property and that all Church property should be confiscated by the state. Later he advocated the destruction of the whole clerical hierarchy on the ground that salvation depended not on the clergy but on grace flowing from God; every person was his or her own priest in terms of establishing a relationship with the divine. Here, of course, he was striking a blow at a key idea on which the medieval religious establishment based its institutional po-

sition: the idea that salvation depended on the ministry of a clergy set apart from and above the laity by the sacrament of ordination. Wycliffe also attacked many of the religious practices currently in use—elaborate rituals, prayers to saints, veneration of relics, pilgrimages, and the like. He even questioned the validity of the sacraments as necessary to salvation. He argued that Scripture alone must be the authority for Christian doctrine and began to translate the Bible into English so that all could read it. Although Wycliffe was soon condemned as a heretic and forced to leave Oxford, his teachings attracted many followers, known as the Lollards, and for many years Lollard preachers and writers spread their master's ideas in England. In time, however, they came to challenge all authority; with the support of Parliament the English kings joined the clergy in destroying the movement.

Wycliffe's ideas had their most significant effect not in England but in Bohemia. The leading disciple there was John Huss (ca. 1373–1415), a priest who taught at the University of Prague. When his preaching of Wycliffe's precepts raised a protest from the clergy and ruling faction, most of whom were German and were passionately hated by the native Czechs, Huss became a national hero in Bohemia. Like Wycliffe, he too was excommunicated. Eventually, Huss sought and received permission to appear before the Council of Constance to defend his teaching. Once in Constance, however, Huss was imprisoned, tried, and executed as a heretic in 1415. A rebellion immediately broke out in Bohemia and raged until 1436. Crusade after crusade was preached by the papacy against the Hussites; several German armies, led by an emperor who was anxious to reclaim Bohemia, were soundly thrashed by the aroused Bohemians. Eventually peace was restored when certain religious concessions were granted to the Hussites. However, a faction of the followers of Huss and Wycliffe, called Taborites, was not satisfied by these concessions and became practically a church apart in Bohemia during the last years of the Middle Ages.

Manifestations of religious ferment and frustration took many other forms during the fourteenth and fifteenth centuries. Any number of fiery preachers proclaimed the end of the world and the coming of God's wrathful final judgment. Wildly emotional cults, such as the Flagellants, who whipped one another to atone for the world's sins, preyed on people's religious sensibilities, especially in times of great crises such as the Black Death. Brutal massacres of the Jews in the name of Christian righteousness marred the histories of many cities. A fear of witches flourished on an unprecedented scale, accompanied by numerous trials of those suspected of witchcraft. Increasingly, people sought assurances of salvation by purchasing indulgences, which they believed would ensure that the punishment due for sins would be removed. Never were relics more appealing or more brazenly manipulated, as illustrated by Chaucer's pardoner, always equipped with his bag full of "pigs' bones" for sale to gullible sinners. Literature, art, and sermons were preoccupied with death in particularly horrible forms. All of these unusual forms of religious expression reflected a psychology of fear and uncertainty that sometimes reached the proportions of mass hysteria.

Of course, amid this ferment religious life went on in conventional ways. The established structures of ecclesiastical governance continued to operate, people attended Mass, received the sacraments, prayed, tried to observe church law, sinned, and were forgiven. However, the intensity and variety of discontent pointed toward an emerging religious crisis. Neither the gentle mystics nor the fiery-tongued rebels, neither the adherents of the occult nor the victims of hysteria, were completely at home in the Roman Catholic church. People were striking out in all directions, questioning ritual, organization, and dogma. But the institution that claimed to care for the souls of the disturbed and the dissatisfied either ignored the quest for religious satisfaction or ruthlessly crushed the discontent. It was failing its central mission: to meet the basic religious needs of its vast flock. More important, it seemed unable to discover ways of restoring its power to cure souls.

3. INTELLECTUAL FERMENT AND RELIGIOUS VALUES

The influence exercised by the religious establishment over medieval society was further weakened by fundamental shifts in intellectual life in the late medieval age of transition. Be-

tween 1000 and 1300 ecclesiastical leaders seeking to shape society according to Christian concepts received powerful support from an intellectual establishment working to define law and doctrine in terms that would apply universally to a united Christian community and to merge all knowledge into one order of truth which would sustain the Christian worldview. After 1300 intellectuals began to pursue lines of thought that challenged the worldview upon which the authority of the religious establishment was founded and to formulate new interpretations of what constituted truth and right values. Although this transformation was not dramatic, it marked a significant step in the transition to the modern world.

Outwardly, the life of learning continued down familiar paths. The universities remained the focal points of scholarship and teaching in the liberal arts, theology, law, medicine, and science, and most intellectuals continued to pursue knowledge and truth within the institutional framework of the university system. The scholastic method, which since the twelfth century had been employed to establish knowledge and understanding through the application of logical tests to propositions concerning the divine, humanity, and nature, continued to dominate theological and philosophical inquiry. But the emphasis and objective of intellectual endeavor underwent subtle changes. The quest, exemplified by the works of Thomas Aquinas, to synthesize divine and human knowledge, to reconcile revelation and reason in a fashion that would produce a single, all-embracing, consistent order of truth failed to establish dominance over theological and philosophical discourse. For some intellectuals Aquinas' approach raised so many problems that they despaired of reconciling revelation and reason into one complete order of truth. Still others began to attack the basic proposition that faith and reason were compatible. Thus, by 1300 analysis began to take precedence over synthesis and became the keynote to intellectual inquiry during the late Middle Ages.

Not long after Aquinas' death in 1274, such issues led to the formulation of approaches that redirected theological and philosophical inquiry. The Franciscan scholar John Duns Scotus (ca. 1266–1308) argued with great force that God's freedom and power were so exalted that all attempts to describe his attributes rationally imposed untenable limits on divine power. In effect, Duns Scotus was saying that theology was not a proper matter for rational speculation. This trend of thought was expanded by William of Ockham (ca. 1300–1349), an English Franciscan who taught at Oxford. A skilled logician, Ockham assailed the basic rational supports of Thomistic theology. In his mind knowledge of such things as the existence of God and the immortality of the soul came only by intuition and mystical experience. Theology and philosophy thus became separate "sciences," incapable of reconciliation. In defining the realm of reason, Ockham argued that only by sense perception of individual objects could humans know; in this respect he was a philosophical *nominalist,* repudiating the long tradition that ideas constituted the ultimate reality (philosophical *realism*). Duns Scotus and William of Ockham gained powerful disciples who followed up the assault on Thomism. Their attacks shattered the thirteenth-century confidence in establishing one all-embracing truth and with it a powerful prop of the religious establishment.

These challenges to Thomism led thinkers to explore a variety of new issues in new ways. Since reason was distinct from faith, political theorists like Marsiglio of Padua constructed new concepts of the governance of church and state that were especially destructive to theologically based justifications of ecclesiastical power over the social order. The attack on rational theology nourished mysticism and opened the way for the radical theological concepts of Wycliffe and Huss. Many intellectuals, disillusioned by the barren exercises of late medieval scholasticism, found intellectual sustenance in classical literature and philosophy, drawing from these sources a secular, humanistic worldview and value system. Especially pregnant for the future was the growing interest in the material world. Following Ockham's argument that rational inquiry must confine itself to tangible objects, scholars, especially at the universities of Paris and Oxford, produced a considerable body of scientific knowledge and provided significant corrections to Greco-Arabic scientific generalizations. Their efforts laid the groundwork for the revolutionary scientific discoveries of Copernicus, Galileo, and others in the sixteenth and seventeenth centuries.

As intellectual life became more pluralistic and more oriented to worldly, secular concerns, the potential for criticism of the ecclesiastical establishment increased, and that establishment's ability to control intellectual activity for its own benefit decreased.

4. NEW FORCES AND THE RELIGIOUS ESTABLISHMENT

While the religious establishment encountered deepening difficulties in managing its internal affairs and containing religious and intellectual currents that challenged its position, it had to contend with powerful forces outside the sphere of religion that threatened its leadership and depleted its following. Many of these forces portended a new era in western European history; they will receive fuller treatment later. Here, it is important that they be noted as threats to the ecclesiastical dominance.

The aggressive national states beginning to take shape in the fifteenth century represented one such force. Although still observant, even enthusiastic, Christians, ambitious rulers sought to limit and dominate the religious establishment in their realms. Their ambitions were given impetus by a widespread perception of corruption in the religious establishment and by intellectual currents that argued for secular direction of earthly society. In England kings and Parliament joined in enacting laws to prevent the papacy from taxing church property and controlling ecclesiastical appointments. In France the royal government worked steadily, often with the help of the French clergy, to establish a "Gallic" church independent of the papacy and subservient to the crown. In Spain, late in the fifteenth century, the monarchs even undertook to reform the religious life independently of the papacy. These cases were all clear indications that as 1500 approached, "national churches" were becoming a reality at the expense of the "universal Church" of the Middle Ages.

Equally threatening to the domination of society by the religious establishment and a religious mentality was the capitalistic ethos that was emerging in economic life, especially among urban patricians but also among members of the rural gentry and affluent peasants. Challenging the ancient Christian distrust of wealth and materialism, this new ethos viewed wealth and its acquisition as a positive force in society. Its adherents would have liked to see the wealth held by the ecclesiastical establishment put to new uses. Most of them paid little heed to religious arguments condemning the charging of interest, price manipulation, and profit seeking. Implicit in the capitalist ethos was a mentality oriented toward competition, worldliness, individualism, pragmatism, and a work ethic—all values that did not fit easily into the traditional concept of how the drama of salvation should be played out.

Finally, a new breed of thinkers, writers, and artists, sometimes collectively called *humanists,* was emerging to criticize many teachings and practices supported by the medieval religious establishment. The new humanism, developing first and most vigorously in Italy and then spreading to other parts of western Europe, found its intellectual sustenance and its aesthetic values in classical rather than medieval models. While not anti-Christian, humanism nurtured a worldview that gave greater prominence to human life in a worldly setting than did the view long promoted by the religious leaders in the name of Christian truth.

The stressful internal difficulties and the challenging outside forces that combined to undermine the authority of the religious establishment in the later Middle Ages provided the surest indication that an epoch was ending. Admittedly the stresses and strains affecting political, economic, and social institutions all pointed toward the transformation of the basic structures characteristic of medieval western European civilization. However, for centuries the religious establishment—the Church—had been the main force giving that civilization its cohesion, its direction, and its distinctive features. The faltering of that establishment truly heralded the end of an epoch in western European history.

SUGGESTED READING

Problems of Religious Organization

Francis Oakley, *The Western Church in the Later Middle Ages* (1979).

Steven Ozment, *The Age of Reform (1250–1530). An Intellectual and Religious History of Late Medieval and Reformation Europe* (1980).

Two excellent treatments of all aspects of religious history.

John Bossy, *Christianity in the West, 1400–1700* (1985). A stimulating interpretation of religious change.

Yves Renouard, *The Avignon Papacy, 1305–1403,* trans. Denis Bethell (1970). A concise survey.

Walter Ullmann, *The Origins of the Great Schism: A Study in Fourteenth-Century Ecclesiastical History* (1948). A careful analysis of the factors that produced the Great Schism.

Brian Tierney, *Foundations of the Conciliar Theory: The Contributions of the Medieval Canonists from Gratian to the Great Schism* (1955). Stresses the legal basis for conciliar ideas.

Antony Black, *Council and Commune: The Conciliar Movement and the Fifteenth-Century Heritage* (1979). Discusses the ideas of the conciliarists in the context of history and theology.

New Religious Movements

Rufus M. Jones, *The Flowering of Mysticism: The Friends of God in the Fourteenth Century* (1939).

James M. Clark, *The Great German Mystics: Eckhart, Tauler, and Suso* (1949).

Anne Bancroft, *The Luminous Vision: Six Medieval Mystics and Their Teachings* (1982).

Any of these three titles will help the reader to understand the nature and influence of late medieval mysticism.

Albert Hyma, *The Christian Renaissance: A History of "Devotio Moderna,"* 2nd ed. (1965). A full treatment of a movement that deeply affected late medieval religious life.

Richard Kieckhefer, *Unquiet Souls: Fourteenth-Century Saints and Their Religious Milieu* (1984). Rich in insights into the nature and causes of religious "unquiet" in the fourteenth century.

Norman Cohn, *The Pursuit of the Millennium: Revolutionary Millenarians and Mystical Anarchists of the Middle Ages,* rev. ed. (1970). A brilliant description of aberrant religious movements in the later Middle Ages.

Malcolm Lambert, *Medieval Heresy: Popular Movements from Bogomil to Huss* (1977). An excellent synthesis.

Intellectual Movements

Georges Duby, *Foundations of a New Humanism, 1280–1440,* trans. Peter Price (1966). A remarkable synthesis linking many aspects of late medieval cultural history.

Gordon Leff, *The Dissolution of the Medieval Outlook: An Essay on Intellectual and Spiritual Change in the Four-teenth Century* (1976). A perceptive but challenging interpretation of late medieval intellectual development.

Alistar McGrath, *The Intellectual Origins of the European Reformation* (1987). A good analysis of theological trends in the later Middle Ages.

RETROSPECT

The era from 1000 to 1500 was of decisive importance in shaping the essential features of western European civilization. The first three centuries of that period were marked by remarkable developments that changed every aspect of the "backward" society that had been so painfully pieced together during the five hundred years immediately following the collapse of the Roman order. The fruits of that sustained, creative activity were abundant: increased material wealth; larger, more stable political communities; a more complex social structure; expanded mental and spiritual horizons; a deepened understanding of the human condition; and enlarged capabilities for expression. Many of the creations of medieval society would remain essential features of western European society almost to the present: national states; urban complexes; agricultural and commercial organization; representative government; legal systems; a centralized religious establishment; vernacular languages; Romanesque and Gothic art; universities; commercial and agricultural technologies. And the era had another equally important dimension: While gathering strength internally, western European society began to thrust outward into the world beyond its boundaries, taking the first decisive steps toward the establishment of western European preeminence on the world scene. Any attempt to understand either subsequent western European or world history must take into account the achievements of the Middle Ages; such an effort will dispel the long-held view that that was a "dark age."

By 1300 the dynamism that had produced the great leap forward of western European society began to diminish, leading to an era of stressful transition. In part the troubles of the late medieval era stemmed from a series of unpredictable events: a demographic catastrophe that caused massive economic, social, and psychological dislocations; dynastic crises that disrupted the orderly succession of rulers and produced singularly incompetent rulers; misguided political ambitions that led to prolonged, destructive wars; overblown claims to authority in the name of religion; shifts in the power structure in lands lying to the east of Europe's frontiers. Effective responses to the disruptions caused by these events were made difficult by conflicting positions inherent in the institutional structures, thought patterns, and value systems shaped prior to 1300. In fact, those dichotomies were themselves sources of deepening tensions during the later Middle Ages. The medieval ideal of a Christian commonwealth produced sharp disagreement about the leadership of that commonwealth and threats to deep-seated localism. Progress toward the formation of nation-states led to conflicts between royal authority and private privilege. The monolithic religious establishment encountered difficulty in containing the ferment that sought new ways of understanding and living the Christian life. The international, profit-seeking, individualistic enterprises at the cutting edge of economic development were impeded by localistic, monopolistic, self-sufficient economic structures. Faith and reason, Latin and vernacular cultures, religious and secular values vied for people's minds.

However, despite the severity of the crises afflicting western Europe between 1300 and 1500 and the grim prophecies of impending doom uttered by some late medieval millenarians, the end of a civilizational order was not at hand. The institutional patterns and value system fashioned during the central Middle Ages showed remarkable resiliency under pressure. By 1500 it was becoming clear that that system had potential for further development. What we call "modern" Europe was the product of a new burst of creativity which shaped a society with its own distinctive features but with its roots in the Middle Ages. The history of modern Europe is inexplicable and unintelligible without a knowledge of those roots.

PART FIVE

EARLY MODERN TIMES: THE RENAISSANCE TO THE EIGHTEENTH CENTURY

During the second half of the fifteenth century, new developments began to sweep over Europe. What historians call the Middle Ages was ending and early modern times were beginning.

The precursor of change was the Renaissance, which was born in the urban societies of northern Italy during the fourteenth and fifteenth centuries. With roots in classical and medieval civilizations, Renaissance culture developed thought, art, and values that would characterize early modern times.

Several striking changes followed that would alter the course of European history. First, new monarchs succeeded in taking major steps toward creating national states with strong central governments. Second, Europe expanded dramatically as these national states supported the establishment of empires around the globe. Third, the Reformation of the sixteenth century permanently destroyed the unity of the western Christian Church and entwined religion, politics, and violence in new ways.

Other changes proceeded more slowly but no less importantly. Most people remained tied to agriculture and their small villages. However Europe's medieval economy increasingly gave way to commercial capitalism, and during the eighteenth century the agricultural revolution and the spread of cottage industry foreshadowed the greater changes that were to come. The landed aristocracy generally retained its power but was forced to absorb new members into its ranks and face growing challenges from middle-class merchants and entrepreneurs. The dominant cultural trends continued to reflect the tastes of the elite classes.

Finally, the scientific revolution and the Enlightenment of the seventeenth and eighteenth centuries would eventually help undermine the traditional order of early modern Europe and provide an intellectual foundation for the modern society of the nineteenth and twentieth centuries.

CHAPTER 25
The Renaissance: Italy

FIGURE 25.1 Leonardo da Vinci, ***The Virgin of the Rocks,*** **ca. 1485** With Leonardo da Vinci (1452–1519), Renaissance painting, with its emphasis on humanism, reached its peak. In this painting, the Virgin is a beautiful woman and the Christ child is a playful, cuddly little boy. The rock formation is authentic, and the plants are identifiable specimens. (Archives Photographiques, Paris)

While most of European society during the fourteenth century was still medieval, Italian society was already changing, developing some of the characteristics that would become common during the early modern period. Most important, Italian society produced a new culture with roots in both the medieval Christian civilization and the classical Greek and Roman civilizations. This culture, called the Renaissance, would continue to grow in Italy during the fifteenth century and then spread throughout Europe. The Renaissance became a basis upon which thought, literature, and art during the early modern period rested.

1. ITALIAN ORIGINS

Although historians have debated the causes for the rise of the Renaissance in Italy, they usually point to a few factors that distinguish Italy, and particularly northern Italy where the Renaissance was centered, from the rest of Europe.

Above all, northern Italy was unusually urbanized—there were more and larger cities than in most other areas of Europe. The first and most important Renaissance city was Florence, but other cities such as Venice, Pisa, and Milan also became centers of the Italian Renaissance. By the fourteenth century these cities had gained economic prosperity from long-distance trade, commerce, industry, banking, and particularly the production of luxury goods.

These cities marshaled their economic strength to expand and gain power over surrounding lands once controlled by the landed aristocracy. They also took advantage of the exhausting struggles between the Holy Roman emperor and the papacy, two powers that might have been strong enough to hinder the growing political independence of the cities. Political life within the cities became dynamic, often chaotic, but most of the time it was controlled by the new commercial elite.

The society of these large, commercial cities became more fluid as position began to be determined more by wealth than by blood. Medieval aristocratic strictures were weakened. The urban elite, continually infused with new members of the wealthy bourgeoisie and outside talent attracted to the vibrant cities, participated in commercial and industrial exploits—activities usually rejected as inappropriate to the aristocracy elsewhere in Europe. Wealthy leaders of the guilds that dominated commercial and industrial life gained new standing and power. Within the elite there were a large number of relatively young people, more aggressive and individualistic than traditional groups elsewhere.

This urban elite needed to be literate and well educated in practical matters. Schools arose to serve them and taught a curriculum appropriate to their practical interests. The elite also had great wealth to spend, and they turned to culture in general and art in particular. They may have wanted art as an investment, as a means of promoting their own political and social ambitions, or as a matter of civic pride. In any case they became patrons of the arts. Now art was being produced not only for clerical and traditional aristocratic patrons but also for rich, middle-class, and urbanized aristocratic patrons who had different outlooks.

As the demand for art grew, so did the prestige of the artist. In medieval society artists had been little more than low-paid artisans. In Renaissance society they became well-paid professionals and part of a respected intellectual elite that included writers and philosophers.

Finally, the physical and human environment of the Italian cities included advantages not present elsewhere in Europe. The remains and traditions of Greco-Roman civilization were still evident in Italy and its cities. Moreover, these cities, thanks to their proximity to the Near East and their commercial and political ties to the Byzantine lands, often came into contact with the sophisticated Byzantine culture.

Thus the thriving Italian urban society—with its commercial wealth, its political independence, its social fluidity, its schools, its artists, its intellectual elite, and its cultural environment—was the fertile ground in which the Renaissance first grew.

2. GENERAL NATURE

The term *renaissance* means "rebirth." One of the central characteristics of the Renaissance was the self-conscious revival of classical civilization and the sense of creating something different from medieval civilization. Renaissance scholars rejoiced in discovering, mastering, and making available the cultural products of Greece and Rome. At the same time they criticized medieval Scholasticism and medieval culture in general. They envisioned themselves as being part of a new civilization based on a revival of classical civilization intertwined with the purest elements of Christian civilization.

The emphasis on reviving classical civilization reflected a greater concern with secular life. The medieval focus on theology—concern with the spiritual world and formal religious doctrines—changed toward a focus on human beings, their nature and their actions. Medieval Christian theologians had distrusted the flesh as an enemy of the spirit and human wisdom as unable to perceive divine truth by rational processes unless guided by Christian inspiration. Renaissance scholars and artists glorified the human form as beautiful and the human intellect as capable of discovering all truth worth knowing. They viewed human beings as three-dimensional, part of an immediate, concrete, recognizable physical environment.

However, care must be taken in characterizing Renaissance culture as secular. The Renaissance was not antireligious; there was no fundamental questioning of Christian beliefs in this still-religious age. Much of the secularism of the Renaissance was in a Christian and even a pious context. Part of the concern with reviving secular classical civilization stemmed from a desire to better understand early Christianity and Christian principles. Moreover, the secularism of the Italian Renaissance was not a sharp, sudden break with the immediate past. Secular interests had never completely died out, even at the peak of the Church's prestige in the Middle Ages. The twelfth century had already witnessed a revival of interest in classical civilization. It would be better to say that during the Italian Renaissance there was a significant intensification of the secular spirit in thought, literature, and art, all still within a fundamentally Christian environment.

Individualism was another important facet of the Renaissance spirit. In this respect, the difference between the medieval and Renaissance spirits was primarily one of degree. Christianity did much to elevate the dignity of the individual soul and the individual personality. But the medieval clergy had feared pride as a sin. They had taught that the individual ego must be carefully held in check. Medieval monasticism had attempted to suppress the individual ego and submerge it in the group. In practice, then, medieval Christianity had tended to be collectivist. Church artists and writers usually had not signed their names to their work, which was supposed to contribute only to the greater glory of God. Renaissance individualism was prideful, even lusty. People of accomplishment were self-consciously confident, even boastful. They wanted the glory that their work would bring them. People such as Boccaccio (1313–1375), Alberti (1404–1472), Machiavelli (1469–1527), and Cellini (1500–1571) were proud of their identity and uniqueness.

Many of these great scholars and artists displayed another element of the Renaissance ideal—versatility. The educated person of the Middle Ages had usually been a specialist—a theologian or church artist or administrator. But the most renowned Renaissance schoolteachers taught many subjects in addition to the traditional formal ones—dancing, fencing, poetry, and vernacular languages, to mention a few. Many of the Renaissance schools broadened the old theology-oriented seven liberal arts and made much greater use of pagan classical literature and philosophy in the curriculum. One of the most popular books in Europe in the sixteenth century was Castiglione's *Book of the Courtier*. The ideal courtier, said Castiglione, is not only a gentleman and a scholar but also a man of action—a soldier and an athlete. Probably the best illustration of versatility in any age is Leonardo da Vinci (1452–1519). This revered Renaissance figure, one of the most celebrated painters of all time, was also an able sculptor, architect, mathematician, philosopher, inventor, botanist, anatomist, geologist, and engineer.

Finally, the Renaissance was urban and socially limited. While many products of the Renaissance were public and even unavoidable in Italian cities, only an elite participated in or directly supported the Renaissance. The majority of the urban population was made up of wage earners, day laborers, domestic servants, and unemployed people. They lived near or below subsistance level and often depended on charity to survive. Most who were somewhat better off—skilled workers and small merchants—lacked formal education and were far from wealthy. In the countryside access to the culture of the Renaissance was even more limited. Despite Italy's relatively urban environment, most people remained tied to the land. There only a few had enough for more than a minimum of needs and even fewer had the time or money for a formal education. In short, the Renaissance scarcely touched most people in the cities and was unheard of in the countryside.

The Renaissance was also of different significance for women than men, even among the elite. On the one hand, women often participated with men in the new urban schools and played a growing role within the household. Indeed, marriage patterns often resulted in widowed women retaining the family's wealth while not remarrying, giving them considerable economic freedom. Some women did manage to become Renaissance humanists and artists, a few of whom, such as the writer Vittoria Colonna (1492–1547) of Marino and the sculptor Properzia Rossi (ca. 1490–1530) of Bologna, became well known and celebrated in circles of humanists and artists. Perhaps the most famous Renaissance woman was Christine de Pisan (ca. 1364–ca. 1431), who was born in Venice but lived in France. She wrote several poems and books, the most widely read of which was *The City of Ladies*. On the other hand, women during the Renaissance were losing some of the status and public position they had held during the Middle Ages. More than before, they were relegated to domestic life, where they played a supportive, decorous, and sexually inferior role to their husbands. This changing status was particularly evident within the rising middle class, but even noblewomen lost power and the independence they had enjoyed when medieval courtly manners and love had held sway. Women were generally excluded from active, public participation in the culture and society of the Renaissance.

3. HUMANISM

During the fourteenth century, Italy witnessed the rise of humanism. Historians have debated the exact meaning of Italian humanism. Narrowly defined, it means classical scholarship—the study of original Latin or Greek manuscripts.

Broadly defined, it means the recovery of classical manuscripts, educational reform to include greater emphasis on classical scholarship, a rejection of medieval Scholasticism and professionalism, and an optimistic emphasis on human beings—on their capabilities as powerful, rational Christian and secular beings on this earth. Understood in this broad sense, humanism encompasses in its literature, its educational reforms, and its philosophy the main characteristics of the Italian Renaissance.

Literature

The characteristics of Renaissance humanism are richly illustrated by the Italian literature of the fourteenth century. The best of that literature was produced by the Tuscan Triumvirate—so called because it consisted of three men who lived in Florence in the old Etruscan province of Tuscany. The first was Dante Alighieri (1265–1321). In an earlier section (see Chapter 22) we discussed Dante as the greatest of the late medieval writers. His masterpiece, *The Divine Comedy*, is so full of medieval Christian lore and theology that it has been called a *Summa Theologiae* in poetry. Nevertheless, there is so much of the humanistic spirit in *The Divine Comedy* and in Dante's other writings that he also belongs to the Renaissance. In the "Inferno" of *The Divine Comedy*, Dante paints vivid, sensuous word pictures that seem to characterize this world rather than the next. The blazing fires and sulfurous fumes of hell, the cries of lament and curses of the damned come alive in our imagination. Furthermore, the author venerates such pagan classical writers as Vergil and Cicero to a much greater degree than had the medievalists (although a number of medieval writers had tried to make Vergil a Christian).

Dante's other major writings are even more humanistic. His love lyrics, written in his native Tuscan vernacular and addressed to Beatrice, are among the most beautiful in any language. In fact, Dante's writings greatly enriched the Florentine dialect and eventually raised it to the status of the national language of Italy.

Dante was also versatile; he was a man of public affairs as well as of letters. An active participant in the turbulent politics of Renaissance Italy, he was exiled from his native Florence when his faction lost. Dante even went so far as to fill hell in *The Divine Comedy* with his political enemies.

Petrarch (1304–1374), the second of the Tuscan Triumvirate, is often considered the father of Italian humanism. In both his writing and his life he rejected medieval Scholasticism and culture as inferior to classical culture. He argued for the recovery of classical manuscripts, the mastering of Latin, and educational reform. He is best known for his superbly crafted letters to great figures of the past, such as Cicero, Vergil, Livy, and St. Augustine, and for his love sonnets in the Tuscan vernacular to Laura, a married woman whom he saw at Mass and loved from afar.

Boccaccio (1313–1375) did for Italian prose what Dante and Petrarch did for Italian poetry. In his *Decameron*, a collection of one hundred tales or novelettes, Boccaccio exhibits little Christian restraint. He relates bawdy romances with skill and grace, condoning and even glorifying the seamy side of human nature.

Classical Manuscripts

The passionate quest for Latin and Greek literary manuscripts sometimes conflicted with the creation of original Italian literature by siphoning off the interest and energy of the writers. This conflict is illustrated by Petrarch, who rather early in life ceased writing what he called his "worthless" lyrics in order to discover lost classical manuscripts and to copy their style. He did succeed in bringing to light many priceless classical literary gems, but his epic *Africa* (relating the exploits of Scipio Africanus), written in Latin after the style of Vergil's *Aeneid*, lacks spontaneity and is all but forgotten.

Petrarch interested Boccaccio in the recovery of Greek and Latin manuscripts, and the search soon spread. Popes, princes, rich merchants, and bankers subsidized the humanists. In the fifteenth century, Italy was busy with professional humanists hunting for, copying, translating, and editing ancient manuscripts.

Educational Reform

Working with classical manuscripts was related to a broader educational reform encompassed in the humanist movement. Humanists such as Petrarch argued that medieval schooling had been too narrow, that the goal of education should be to produce more rounded, eloquent, virtuous individuals who were able to pursue the good life. Classical literature became a larger part of an educational curriculum that increasingly stressed practical learning. Educational reformers such as Pietro Paolo Vergerio (1349–1420) and Vittorino da Feltre (1378–1446) modified the Scholastic tradition and infused the curriculum with physical exercises, music, philosophy, Latin, and Greek as well as classical literature.

Philosophy

The study of classical masterpieces led to a variety of philosophical inquiries. This phase of humanism had many facets, including a new stress on the rational capabilities of humans, the development of a critical attitude, and a change in the concept of politics.

In 1396 Manuel Chrysoloras, a Byzantine scholar from Constantinople, was invited to Florence. He and other Greek scholars stimulated the study of Greek manuscripts during the fifteenth century. This study led to a revival of interest in Platonism and the establishment of the Platonic Academy in Florence under Marsilio Ficino (1433–1499) and Pico della Mirandola (1463–1494). They believed that, properly understood, Platonic philosophy and Christianity were compatible. They argued that human beings had great freedom and abilities, above all an ability to use will and reason to strive for the good life.

Another element of the humanistic view of life was the development of an analytic attitude. When Lorenzo Valla (1407–1457) proved by linguistics that the Donation of Constantine was a forgery, the scholarly and secular-minded pope raised no objections, although this was one of the documents upon which the papacy had based its claims to temporal power in the West. In fact, Pope Nicholas V made Valla his secretary. By making this discovery, Valla established himself as the father of modern critical historical scholarship.

The Florentine Niccolò Machiavelli (1469–1527), in his celebrated *The Prince*, suggested that Christian morals have little to do with the actual practice of politics (see p. 321). To acquire and maintain political power, the prince (or ruler or governing officials) must be willing to use both amoral and ruthless means. Since politicians, like all human beings, are self-seeking animals, the prince should assume that all rival princes and even his own lieutenants are conspiring for his power. Therefore, the prince should be willing to set his own chief subjects against each other and maneuver them into impotence. A wise prince deceives and treacherously attacks his foreign rivals at the most favorable moment before they can do the same. While Machiavelli was trying to remedy the deplorable reality of a divided Italy overrun and pillaged by more powerful foreign enemies, he also reflected the reality of secular attitudes and politics in fifteenth- and sixteenth-century Italy. His was a political theory that separated politics from ethics, stressing how people behaved rather than how they ought to behave. Few books have had more influence on, or been more descriptive of, modern political thought and practice.

4. FINE ARTS

Several characteristics of the Italian Renaissance are vividly illustrated in the Italian fine arts of the fourteenth, fifteenth, and sixteenth centuries.

Painting

Medieval painting in Europe had been closely allied with the Church. Painters deliberately penalized human flesh in order that the spirit might shine forth unimpeded. The figures, nearly always saints, were stiff, haggard, flat, and elongated. The physical world too was blanked out with solid gold backgrounds. The styles were stereotyped.

In the early fourteenth century Giotto, a contemporary of Dante, began to break this medieval mold of artistic custom by humanizing his figures and painting functional landscape backgrounds. Giotto's subject matter was almost entirely religious, but his treatment of it was such that the humanistic spirit made definite advances at the expense of the medieval. In the early fifteenth century Masaccio greatly developed the

trend begun by Giotto a century earlier. He increased the illusion of depth by introducing atmospheric perspective and by further developing linear perspective. He also introduced the principle of the known light source, which thereafter replaced diffused light in painting. His nude human forms were further rounded and humanized (see Figure 25.2). His landscape backgrounds were realistic and detailed. With Masaccio and later painters such as Giovanni Bellini (see Color Plate 12) and Botticelli (see Figure 25.3), the transition from medieval to Renaissance painting was completed and the stage set for such towering geniuses of the Italian High Renaissance as Leonardo da Vinci, Michelangelo, Raphael, and Titian.

It would be difficult to find a more representative figure of the Italian Renaissance than Leonardo da Vinci (1452–1519). All the colorful facets of the Renaissance spirit are richly illustrated by the career and work of this versatile genius. Leonardo was an illegitimate child, as were a number of the famous figures of the Renaissance. He was born near Florence and began his career there, but some of his most productive years were spent in the employ of the duke of Milan. He finally followed King Francis I to France, where he died. Like most Renaissance artists, Leonardo dealt primarily with religious subject matter; but, also like the others, his treatment of it was more secular and human. In his *Virgin of the Rocks* (see Figure 25.1), for instance, Leonardo creates with exquisite grace and beauty the Virgin Mary and the Christ child. The Virgin, however, is the loveliest of women, and the Christ child is a plump and playful baby boy. The characters are human, not divine. The background is a strange rock formation, naturalistic enough to reveal a keen interest in this material earth and yet arrestingly abnormal. The plant forms in the background are actually identifiable. Leonardo's *Last Supper* depicts the reactions of the twelve disciples to Christ's words, "One of you shall betray me." This celebrated fresco, exhibiting the artist's complete mastery of technique and draftsmanship, is essentially a study in human psychology—a subject in which Leonardo showed a special interest. The famous *Mona Lisa* is not religious in subject matter; it is the portrait of a real woman. The mysterious half smile—the

mouth smiles but the eyes do not—so captivates the viewer that one is likely to overlook other features of the picture, including the hands, which are said to be the most sensitive ever painted.

Michelangelo (1475–1564) is second only to Leonardo da Vinci as a versatile Italian High Renaissance genius. Since Michelangelo was primarily a sculptor, his painting is sometimes called "painted sculpture." Although a Florentine, much of his life was spent in Rome, where he labored in the service of the popes. His greatest painting was the ceiling fresco in the Vatican Sistine Chapel. The hundreds of individual figures, representing nine scenes from the book of Genesis, marvelously blend together into one harmonious whole. Later Michelangelo painted *The Last Judgment* as an altarpiece for the same chapel. The Christ in this picture is more like a pagan giant than the Jesus of medieval Christianity.

Some critics believe Raphael (1483–1520) to be the greatest painter of all time; others say that he merely synthesized the original work of others. The output during his brief life was enormous. His favorite subjects were religious, but his Madonnas were feminine, gracious women and his Christ child pudgy and mischievous. His best-known paintings, the *Sistine Madonna* and the *Madonna of the Chair*, both in oil, well illustrate this secular treatment of a sacred theme. Many of his vivid portraits are of lay princes and tycoons (see Color Plate 13). His monumental fresco *The School of Athens* reveals the veneration felt for the glory of Greece during the Renaissance.

The fourth of the great painters of the Italian High Renaissance was Titian (1477–1576). A citizen of Venice, the most powerful commercial city of the fifteenth and early sixteenth centuries, Titian reflected the humanistic spirit of the Renaissance to an even greater degree than his three renowned contemporaries. Although a

FIGURE 25.2 **Masaccio,** *Expulsion of Adam and Eve* Masaccio, early in the fifteenth century, developed still further the trend toward humanism and naturalism begun a century earlier by Giotto. His *Expulsion of Adam and Eve from the Garden of Eden* depicts a religious subject in a human, realistic, and detailed manner. The nude figures are rounded and individualized. (Alinari/Scala Art Resource)

FIGURE 25.3 Botticelli, *Adoration of the Magi,* ca. 1477 The theme of this painting is religious, with the Christ child in the center. However, the human figures are depicted with individualism, and the models (Lorenzo de Medici kneeling next to the Christ child; the artist, Botticelli, standing proudly to the far left) are secular and contemporary. (Uffizi/Art Resource)

considerable portion of his painting was of religious subjects, his focus was nearly always the pomp and pageantry of the Church rather than its teachings. But a large part of his subject matter was more secular. The wealth and brilliance of Venice, overflowing with cargoes of luxurious fabrics, tapestries, and gems from the east, provided a challenging array of sensuous and colorful material for the artist to depict. And in the use of color, particularly vivid yellows, reds, and

blues, Titian had no peer. He painted the hair of his women a reddish gold hue that has come to be called titian. His portraits of some of the great lay personages of the sixteenth century, such as Francis I of France, Emperor Charles V, and Philip II of Spain, are masterful character studies. With Titian, the break with medieval painting begun by Giotto and Masaccio and widened by Leonardo, Michelangelo, Raphael, and many other great Italian painters was completed.

Niccolò Machiavelli: *The Prince*

The Italian Renaissance developed in an environment in which politics took on an increasingly competitive, secular tone. Within each Italian state, parties fought for power while at the same time the states fought one another for advantage. After 1492 Italy was invaded numerous times by Spain, France, and the Holy Roman Empire. These developments are reflected in the life and work of the great Renaissance political theorist Niccolò Machiavelli (1469–1527).

Machiavelli initiated his career in the Florentine civil service in 1498. He rose to important diplomatic posts within the government but was forced into retirement when the Medici family came back to power in 1512. He never gave up hope of returning to favor, and he wrote his most famous work, The Prince *(1513), in part as an application to the Medici rulers for a job in the Florentine government. The book has since become a classic treatise in political theory, above all for the way that it divorces politics from theology and metaphysics. The following selections from* The Prince *illustrate its style and main themes.*

It now remains to be seen what are the methods and rules for a prince as regards his subjects and friends. And as I know that many have written of this, I fear that my writing about it may be deemed presumptuous, differing as I do, especially in this matter, from the opinions of others. But my intention being to write something of use to those who understand, it appears to me more proper to go to the real truth of the matter than to its imagination; and many have imagined republics and principalities which have never been seen or known to exist in reality; for how we live is so far removed from how we ought to live, that he who abandons what is done for what ought to be done, will rather learn to bring about his own ruin than his preservation. A man who wishes to make a profession of goodness in everything must necessarily come to grief among so many who are not good. Therefore it is necessary for a prince, who wishes to maintain

Source: From *The Prince and the Discourses* by Niccolò Machiavelli, translated by Luigi Ricci and revised by E. R. P. Vincent (1935), pp. 56, 65–66, by permission of Oxford University Press.

himself, to learn how not to be good, and to use this knowledge and not use it, according to the necessity of the case. . . .

It is not, therefore, necessary for a prince to have all the above-named qualities, but it is very necessary to seem to have them. I would even be bold to say that to possess them and always to observe them is dangerous, but to appear to possess them is useful. Thus it is well to seem merciful, faithful, humane, sincere, religious, and also to be so; but you must have the mind so disposed that when it is needful to be otherwise you may be able to change to the opposite qualities. And it must be understood that a prince, and especially a new prince, cannot observe all those things which are considered good in men, being often obliged, in order to maintain the state, to act against faith, against charity, against humanity, and against religion. And, therefore, he must have a mind disposed to adapt itself according to the wind, and as the variations of fortune dictate, and, as I said before, not deviate from what is good, if possible, but be able to do evil if constrained.

A prince must take great care that nothing goes out of his mouth which is not full of the above-named five qualities, and, to see and hear him, he should seem to be all mercy, faith, integrity, humanity, and religion. And nothing is more necessary than to seem to have this last quality, for men in general judge more by the eyes than by the hands, for every one can see, but very few have to feel. Everybody sees what you appear to be, few feel what you are, and those few will not dare to oppose themselves to the many, who have the majesty of the state to defend them; and in the actions of men, and especially of princes, from which there is no appeal, the end justifies the means. Let a prince therefore aim at conquering and maintaining the state, and the means will always be judged honourable and praised by every one, for the vulgar is always taken by appearances and the issue of the event; and the world consists only of the vulgar, and the few who are not vulgar are isolated when the many have a rallying point in the prince.

Sculpture

In sculpture, the artist without peer in any age is Michelangelo. It is true that he had Roman copies of the sculpture of Hellenic Greek masters such as Praxiteles and Scopas to guide and inspire him. But the gifted Florentine was no mere copier. The Greek masterpieces, for all their beauty and grace, were idealized types—half human, half divine. Michelangelo and his lesser-known immediate predecessors and contemporaries added a typically Renaissance characteristic to sculpture: individuality. The statues of the Italian Renaissance are not only human beings but also human individuals. Even Michelangelo's *Pietà*, which represents the mother of Jesus holding the dead body of her son as she looks down piteously, is a study in human emotions. The helplessness and hopelessness of the huge, all-engulfing mother display human resignation at the finality of death—not the Christian hope of resurrection and eternal life. His *Moses* portrays the fierce and rugged strength of man, not God. Moses' beard, as crude as icicles beneath a water tank in the month of January, displays the sculptor's ability to distort deliberately for effect. The three-dimensional medium of marble enabled Michelangelo to exploit to the full his favorite subject, the masculine nude. Numerous statues of David are used to convey not only the virile muscular power but also the agile grace of the male animal. His *Dying Slave* (see Figure 25.4) is a sublime portrayal of both the human form and the human spirit struggling to free themselves from bondage. Some critics think that the great sculptor's finest genius is displayed in the companion statues of two members of the Medici family—Lorenzo, the contemplative type, and Giuliano, the man of action. In these two pieces the master craftsman and artist exhibits every technique of sculpture. The work of Michelangelo is probably our best example of the Renaissance glorification of the human being.

The subject of Renaissance sculpture cannot be dismissed without brief mention of the work of Benvenuto Cellini. His work in gold and silver was of an exquisite delicacy that has never been equaled. His most famous larger work is the bronze statue of Perseus holding up the Gorgon's head. In this amazing conglomeration of unrealities, Cellini showed complete disregard of all accepted traditions and standards, yet with

FIGURE 25.4 Michelangelo, *The Dying Slave* The genius of Michelangelo, master sculptor of the Renaissance, is exemplified in this work, *The Dying Slave*, now in the Louvre, which glorifies both the human form and the human spirit. (Courtesy Michigan State University)

happy results. Such bold and original pioneering was typical of the self-confident, secular nature of the Renaissance mind.

Architecture

Renaissance architecture, like Renaissance sculpture, drew heavily from Greek and Roman sources (see Figure 25.5). From Greece by way of Rome came columns (now merely decorative) and horizontal lines; from Rome came the dome, the arches, and the massiveness that character-

FIGURE 25.5 Circle of Piero Della Francesca: An Ideal Town This mid–fifteenth-century townscape painting expresses ideals of Italian Renaissance architecture: geometry, logic, individuality with order, lightness, and spaciousness. (Anderson/Art Reference Bureau)

ized Renaissance buildings. All of these features (except massiveness) represented a revolt against the Gothic architecture of the later Middle Ages, although the Gothic style had never gained much of a foothold in Italy.

The two greatest monuments of Italian Renaissance architecture are the dome of the cathedral in Florence and St. Peter's Basilica in Rome. The Florentine cathedral is essentially Tuscan Gothic. Its ornate rectangular façade and bell tower reflect both Byzantine and Islamic influences. But its most distinguishing feature is its gigantic octagonal dome, designed and constructed by Brunelleschi in the early fifteenth century. This symbol of the grandeur of ancient Rome served as a model for such later great domes as St. Peter's in Rome, St. Paul's in London, and the Capitol building in Washington, D.C.

But the most grandiose achievement of Renaissance architecture is St. Peter's. This magnificent structure was to the Renaissance era what the Pyramids, the Parthenon, the Colosseum, and the Gothic cathedrals were to their respective epochs. It was built by the popes during the sixteenth and early seventeenth centuries at a cost that shook all western Europe religiously and politically. Its numerous architects drew primarily on classical Greek and Roman sources for their inspiration. Even seventeenth-century baroque features eventually entered into its design. Raphael served for a time as chief architect, and Michelangelo designed the dome. One has to

step inside St. Peter's to appreciate the breathtaking grandeur of this awesome structure. Its lofty proportions and gigantic pillars, its brilliant paintings and sculptures, its gold, marble, and mosaic decorations all glorify the material things of this world as well as the spiritual aspects of this world and the next.

Music

Music was another field of art in which many original contributions were made during the Renaissance period, particularly the sixteenth century. Although most of these developments occurred in northern Europe, especially the Netherlands, Italy was a scene of some importance. Instrumental music became popular, and great improvements were made in the instruments. The harpsichord and the violin family of instruments came into existence. Musical techniques such as major and minor modes, counterpoint (the blending of two contrasting melodies), and polyphony (the interweaving of several melodic lines) rapidly developed. The most illustrious musician of the sixteenth century was Palestrina, chief musician to the pope and probably the greatest master of polyphonic music of all time. Although most of the music of the Renaissance still centered about the Church, it was now more sensuous and versatile. Moreover, new secular forms appeared. The madrigal, popular throughout Europe in the late sixteenth century, was a musical rendition of stanzas of secular lyrical poetry. Renaissance musicians laid the foundations for modern classical music in all its major forms—concerto, symphony, sonata, oratorio, and opera.

5. DECLINE

During the sixteenth century, the Italian Renaissance lost some of its vigor and originality. Certainly this loss did not occur overnight. For decades, and even into the seventeenth century, Italy was recognized as a center of the fine arts and cultural sophistication. Italian art, heavily patronized by the Church, retained much of its momentum. However, the center of Renaissance activity was shifting from Italy to northern Europe, paralleling the shift of commerce from the Mediterranean to the Atlantic. When Venice, Florence, and Milan were the most prosperous commercial and banking centers in Europe, they were the most vigorous seats of Renaissance culture. With the shifting of the trade routes to the west, their cultural vigor declined.

Other sixteenth-century developments probably played a role in the decline of the Italian Renaissance. The invasions of Italy by the French, Spanish, and German armies and the general military and political instability of the sixteenth century seem to have contributed to the decline. The flowering of culture and relative political stability in other parts of Europe may have made Italy a less important or attractive cultural center. In any case, cultural momentum shifted northward as the Renaissance spread outside of Italy.

SUGGESTED READING

General

G. A. Brucker, *Renaissance Florence,* rev. ed. (1983). A useful book on Renaissance Florence.

J. Burckhardt, *The Civilization of the Renaissance in Italy* (1867, 1983). A classic that has influenced all subsequent studies of the subject.

P. Burke, *The Italian Renaissance* (1986). A recent interpretation.

J. R. Hale, *Renaissance Europe: The Individual and Society, 1480–1520* (1978). Strong on individualism.

C. Klapiche-Zuber, *Women, Family, and Ritual in Renaissance Italy* (1985). Useful essays on social life and women.

I. Maclean, *The Renaissance Notion of Women* (1980). Assumptions about women by Renaissance intellectuals.

L. Martines, *Power and Imagination: City-States in Renaissance Italy* (1980). A highly respected recent study.

Humanism

Paul O. Kristeller, *Renaissance Thought: The Classic, Scholastic, and Humanistic Strains* (1961). A highly respected study of Renaissance thought.

A. Rabil, ed., *Renaissance Humanism* (1988). A multivolume collection of essays on all aspects of humanism.

Q. Skinner, *Machiavelli* (1981). A solid, well-written account.

C. Trinkaus, *The Scope of Renaissance Humanism* (1983). A detailed survey.

The Fine Arts

James Beck, *Italian Painting of the Renaissance* (1981). A good recent study.

Bernard Berenson, *The Italian Painters of the Renaissance* (1968). A classic.

Sources

B. Castiglione, *The Book of the Courtier* (1976). Contemporary textbook for gentlemanly behavior.

B. Cellini, *Autobiography* (1956). The artist's own account of an adventuresome life.

N. Machiavelli, *The Prince* (1961). A classic of political theory.

P. Taylor, *The Notebooks of Leonardo da Vinci: A New Selection.* Well illustrated.

CHAPTER 26
The Renaissance: The North

FIGURE 26.1 Albrecht Dürer, *The Four Horsemen of the Apocalypse,* ca. 1497–1498 In this woodcut the great German artist Albrecht Dürer exhibits a skill in his engraving and woodcutting that matched the painting genius of his Italian contemporaries Leonardo and Michelangelo. His painting of this apocalyptic scene reveals the piety, mysticism, and concern with death that were important elements of the northern Renaissance. (The Art Museum, Princeton University)

The northern Renaissance occurred later than the Italian Renaissance and was in large measure imported from Italy. Although northern scholars such as Chaucer visited Italy as early as the fourteenth century, it wasn't until the late fifteenth century, when journeys by scholars, students, and merchants to Italy were commonplace, that the Renaissance flowered in the north. The northern Renaissance also had its own roots and characteristics. It was located more in the courts and universities than in large commercial cities. Northern humanism was more intertwined with Christian pietism than in Italy. In a broad sense, the northern Renaissance sought to humanize Christianity, to reconcile the sacred and the secular.

1. NORTHERN HUMANISM

The trend toward humanism as a basic attitude toward life began in earnest in northern Europe in the late fifteenth century. One of the central figures of northern humanism was Johann Reuchlin (1455–1522), a German scholar. After a sojourn in Italy during which he became imbued with the ideas of the Italian humanists, Reuchlin undertook to introduce the new classical learning into Germany. Specifically, he sought to broaden and enrich the university curriculum by establishing the study of the ''un-Christian'' Hebrew and Greek languages and literature. The Church and university interests vested in the medieval order of things attempted to thwart him, invoking the Inquisition to try him on grounds of heresy. Reuchlin fought back courageously and enlisted a large and enthusiastic following. Eventually the pope condemned him to silence. However, the victory really lay with Reuchlin and his humanist supporters. During the first few decades of the sixteenth century the new humanistic curriculum became established in all the major universities of Germany.

Meanwhile, in England a group of Oxford professors was accomplishing with less opposition what Reuchlin had fought for in Germany. John Colet (1467–1519) was the most prominent member of this group. He, too, visited Renaissance Italy. In true northern humanistic fashion he gave a critical and rational slant to his preaching and teaching of the Scriptures at Oxford. Probably the greatest of Colet's contributions to the new learning was the founding of St. Paul's grammar school in London, with a largely classical curriculum. To guarantee its humanistic orientation, he chose as trustees a guild of London merchants. St. Paul's soon became a model for many other such schools throughout England.

The most famous of the early-sixteenth-century English humanists was Sir Thomas More (1478–1535), Lord Chancellor of the Realm. More's *Utopia*, like Plato's *Republic*, blueprinted an earthly, not a heavenly, paradise. In picturing his ideal commonwealth, More indicted the social, religious, and political events of his own time. Utopia was a society in which private property and profits were unknown. Much attention was given to public health and education. The economy was planned and cooperative. War was outlawed except in self-defense. Religious freedom was granted to all but atheists. Although More eventually was to accept death by beheading rather than recognize Henry VIII as head of the English church in place of the pope, his ideal society was ethical and secular. Humans through their own wisdom, he believed, could create their own perfect world here on earth.

Towering above all the other northern humanists was Desiderius Erasmus (1466–1536). Erasmus was born in Rotterdam in the Netherlands, the illegitimate son of a priest. Reared as an orphan, he was educated in a school run by the Brethren of the Common Life, a pietistic order of laymen that taught the Greek and Latin classics and emphasized simple inner piety rather than ritual and formal creed (see Chapter 24). (Martin Luther, the great contemporary and adversary of Erasmus, also attended a school of the Brethren of the Common Life.) At the age of twenty-one Erasmus entered an Augustinian monastery (again like Luther) and was eventually ordained. Instead of serving as a priest, however, he studied his beloved classics—a pursuit he was to continue at the Sorbonne and for the rest of his life.

Erasmus' vast erudition combined with his great personal charm made him a much-sought-after man. His first book was *Adages*, a collection of wise sayings of the Greeks and Romans with his own comments. It was an immediate success, and other books soon followed. His greatest work was *The Praise of Folly*, in which he ridiculed with subtle humor and delightful satire the ignorance, superstition, credulity, and current practices of his day, particularly those connected with the Church. The folly that he praised was a very human lightheartedness, a sense of humor. Wherever Erasmus went—France, England, Italy, Switzerland, Germany, the Netherlands—he was received with admiration and awe. No other individual so advanced the cause of northern humanism by popularizing the study of the Greek and Latin classics.

In addition to popularizing the new humanistic learning north of the Alps, Erasmus is significant in history for at least two other reasons—his influence on religious and social reform and his efforts to humanize and intellectualize Christianity. He was at his best when laughing to scorn the abuses and superstitious practices of the Roman Catholic church. The taking of money from the poor and ignorant masses by wealthy and corrupt clergy, the veneration of relics, and unquestioning belief in the miraculous were in the eyes of Erasmus beneath the contempt of enlightened men and women. But he was clever enough to sheathe his barbs with humor, thus making them more subtle and effective. Erasmus, however, was no Protestant. When Martin Luther first began his attacks on the Roman Catholic church, Erasmus thought that he was merely seeking to correct glaring abuses and hailed him as a fellow spirit. But when Erasmus discovered that the German reformer was primarily interested in doctrinal reform and that the Protestants were as dogmatic as the Roman Catholics, Erasmus would have nothing more to do with him. Nevertheless, Erasmus' incessant attacks on the abuses of organized Christianity undoubtedly encouraged both Protestant and Roman Catholic reformers.

Erasmus made great efforts to humanize Christianity. Although he never did specifically say so, the implication running through his writings is that Jesus was also a human being—a person to emulate. Erasmus would bypass formal creed, dogma, ritual, organization, and seek the "historical" Christ. Erasmus attempted to steer Christianity into a practice of following the example of a humanized Christ, stressing love, piety, civic virtue, and the best of classical values.

2. LITERATURE

During the late fifteenth and early sixteenth centuries Renaissance literature in the North was closely connected to the spirit of northern humanism with its stress on combining classical scholarship and Christian concerns. Scholars and educators such as Ulrich von Hutten (1488–1523) in Germany, Jacques Lefèvre d'Étaples (1454–1536) in France, Francisco Jiménez de Cisneros (1436–1517) in Spain, and William Grocyn (ca.1446–1519) in England helped establish traditions of literary humanism in their countries. During the middle of the sixteenth century Renaissance literature in the north became more distinctly secular. The most important literary developments in the decades from the mid-sixteenth to the early seventeenth centuries were in England, France, and Spain.

The reign of Elizabeth I (1558–1603) was a period of great energy and optimism in England. Elizabeth herself, like a few other elite women of the period, was educated according to the precepts of the Renaissance. All this was reflected in the literary outpourings of the period. England became "a nest of singing birds" such as the world had never seen or heard. Edmund Spenser's *Faerie Queen* (1590) glorified the versatile individual of the Italian humanists, particularly the ideal set forth by Castiglione in his *Book of the Courtier*. Christopher Marlowe (1564–1593) in his brief life wrote human-centered plays of such caliber that some critics think he would have achieved the stature of Shakespeare had he lived. His *Tamburlaine the Great* and *Edward II* treat the worldly drama of royal ambition. The central figure in *The Jew of Malta*, a forerunner of Shylock, is a product of the revived commercial capitalism. *Doctor Faustus* dramatizes the theme, later immortalized by Goethe, of the intellectual who in true Renaissance fashion sold his soul to the devil in return for earthly knowledge and pleasure.

Mightiest of all the writers of the English Renaissance was William Shakespeare (1564–1616). Although his lyrical poetry was beautiful, his most important work was in drama. Here he was heavily indebted to his contemporary, Christopher Marlowe, as well as to the ancient Greek and Roman dramatists. Marlowe developed the blank verse form, which Shakespeare perfected. In plays such as *Hamlet, Macbeth, Othello, King Lear, The Merchant of Venice, As You Like It, Henry IV, Romeo and Juliet*, and *Julius Caesar*, Shakespeare displayed a mastery of every known technique of the dramatic art.

More important for the student of history, he exemplified and dramatized the secular spirit of the Renaissance. The individual is Shakespeare's subject matter. Rugged, distinctive human personalities are the heroes and villains of his plays. No human emotion, aspiration, or psychological conflict escapes his eye. On the whole, Shakespeare, unlike the Greek dramatists, makes each person the master of his or her own fate. Admiration for Greece and Rome, a keen interest in newfound lands, the first stirrings of modern natural science, the commercial revolution and social problems arising from the emergence of the capitalistic middle class, the rise of national monarchy and a national patriotic spirit—all enter into the fabric of the plays.

The two chief figures in French Renaissance literature were François Rabelais (1494–1553) and Michel de Montaigne (1533–1592). Rabelais was a renegade priest, bored physician, and loving student of the classics. Although he stumbled quite by accident and late in life upon his gift for writing, he turned out to be one of the great creative geniuses in the history of literature. His masterpieces are *Pantagruel* and *Gargantua*. They are fantasies about two completely unrestrained giants who wallow and revel unashamedly in sensual pleasures. These works are an open assault on Christian moral standards and restraints. The wit is coarse and lewd and sympathetic toward the frailties of human nature. Rabelais' rich imagery, his marvelous gift of expression, and his graceful artistry combine to make him one of the founders of modern French prose.

Montaigne was a prodigy born of a wealthy family. Like Rabelais, he was an ardent lover of the classics. The result of his life of study and reflection was his *Essays*. Montaigne was a skeptic. To arrive at reliable truth, he believed, one must rid oneself of all religious prejudice. He was a moral and spiritual relativist, rejecting all absolutes. Unlike his successors of the eighteenth-century Enlightenment, he distrusted the authority of human reason. Unable to replace the authority of Christian dogma with any other firm conviction, Montaigne was nearly always negative in his conclusions. But he immensely enjoyed this game of intellectual hide-and-seek. In fact, Montaigne believed that the chief purpose of life is pleasure—not the "eat, drink, and be merry" pleasure of Rabelais, but urbane, sophisticated, restrained, intellectual pleasure. The influence of Montaigne has been enormous—obviously on essayists from Bacon to Emerson and later, but also on the development of modern rationalism in general.

Standing out above all others in Spanish Renaissance literature are Miguel de Cervantes (1547–1616) and Lope de Vega (1562–1635). Cervantes was a contemporary of Shakespeare, the two dying within a few days of each other in 1616. Cervantes' early life, like Shakespeare's, is obscure. In time he became a soldier of fortune, fought heroically and was wounded in the great naval battle of Lepanto with the Turks, suffered a five-year imprisonment in Algeria, and finally served as a quartermaster for Spain's Invincible Armada. In poverty-stricken later life he settled down to write his famous novel *Don Quixote*. This masterpiece of Spanish literature relates with urbane grace and humor the adventures of a confused knight who filled his noble head too full of the lore of chivalry and his groom, Sancho Panza. Sancho, a squat plebeian on a donkey, and Don Quixote, an emaciated knight on a tall, lean horse, go about Spain from one delightfully charming adventure to another. Cervantes' most immediate purpose was to satirize what was left of medieval chivalry. At a deeper level he probes the balance between the idealism of Don Quixote and the realism of Sancho Panza, revealing that there is some of each in all of us. Finally, since all types and classes of people throughout Spain are lucidly portrayed, *Don Quixote* is a valuable historical source for descriptions of life in sixteenth-century Spain.

Lope de Vega wrote a fabulous number of works in practically every known genre. His plays alone exceed in number those of any other writer, whether we accept the writer's own claim to at least eighteen hundred or recognize only the five-hundred-odd plays that can be accounted for today. The secular person, pictured in every conceivable dramatic situation, is the hero of the great Spanish playwright.

FIGURE 26.2 The Gutenberg Bible An illuminated page from the Gutenberg Bible, after a facsimile. This forty-two-line Bible, printed by Johannes Gutenberg in about 1456, is the earliest known book printed by movable type in the Western world. The craftsmanship exhibited by this illustration is remarkable. Gutenberg's invention launched a revolution in communications. (Rare Book Division, New York Public Library, Astor, Lennox and Tilden Foundations)

Thus the writers of the northern Renaissance had much in common. Their chief interests were contemporary human beings and the exciting, rapidly expanding material world around them. They were inspired by the classical literature of Greece and Rome. They were on the whole nationalistic and wrote in the new national vernaculars.

3. PRINTING WITH MOVABLE TYPE

The spread of humanism and literature in general was stimulated by the invention of printing on paper with movable type. In ancient and medieval times manuscripts had been written and copied in longhand on parchment or papyrus, a slow and costly process that greatly retarded the dissemination of knowledge. In the fourteenth century printing from carved wooden blocks came to western Europe from China by way of the Moslem world and Spain. This process too was tedious, costly, and limited. Also from China came paper made of various fibers—silk, cotton, or flax. Paper was a great improvement over parchment or papyrus for purposes of mass production. (Even the art of printing by movable type itself was a Chinese [Korean] invention, although this is not believed to have influenced its invention in the Western world.)

Johannes Gutenberg set up the first practical printing press using movable type in Europe at

FIGURE 26.3 Matthias Grünewald, *The Crucifixion*, ca. 1510–1515 This northern Renaissance painting from the Isenheim Altarpiece by the German artist Grünewald combines a deeply pious subject matter reminiscent of late Gothic traditions with Renaissance perspective and individualism. (Musée Unterlinden, Colmar)

Mainz in western Germany. The Gutenberg forty-two-line Bible printed in about 1456 is the earliest known book to be printed by the new process (see Figure 26.2). The invention was an immediate success and spread quickly to all the other countries of western Europe. It is estimated that by the end of the fifteenth century more than twenty-five thousand separate editions and nearly 10 million individual books had been printed. Printing was now much cheaper, quicker, and more accurate.

Its effects spread beyond a greater access to religious and secular literature. The printing press encouraged the growth of literacy and made the spread of political and commercial documents easier. Cheaply produced pamphlets and books became a medium for social, religious, and political debate. The new availability of written materials made a variety of studies available to women otherwise hindered from formal training. News sheets would make events much more current to readers in the seventeenth and eigh-

teenth centuries. The printing press would prove crucial to the spread of ideas during the scientific revolution and Enlightenment (see Chapters 35 and 36).

4. ART, ARCHITECTURE, AND MUSIC

Northern Renaissance art was influenced by Italian art and shared many of its characteristics, but it had stronger roots in the Christian, pietistic culture of the late Middle Ages. In general the subject matter of paintings was less secular than that of Italian Renaissance paintings. Northern artists tried to bring the concrete details of Christian life into immediate focus and with great emotional impact (see Figure 26.3).

The most noteworthy fifteenth- and sixteenth-century painters in the north were the Flemings (Belgians) and the Germans. The Van Eyck brothers, Hubert and Jan, lived in Ghent in

FIGURE 26.4 Jan van Eyck, *The Virgin and Chancellor Rolin* The van Eyck brothers, Hubert and Jan, of Ghent in the Netherlands, were fifteenth-century contemporaries of Masaccio. This painting illustrates the clear, naturalistic perspective, the precision of line and detail, and the religious theme that were characteristic of northern Renaissance painting. (Scala/Art Resource)

the Flemish Netherlands in the fifteenth century. Like Masaccio, their Italian contemporary, they brought to near completion the transition from medieval to Renaissance painting (see Figure 26.4). Their greatest joint work is *Adoration of the Mystic Lamb*. Not the least of their contributions to painting was the development of oil as a medium. It was from them that Leonardo da Vinci learned to work in this medium, which he perfected in such masterworks as *Mona Lisa* and *Virgin of the Rocks*.

In sixteenth-century Germany, Albrecht Dürer of Nuremberg and Hans Holbein the Younger of Augsburg were the leading painters. Dürer was a master craftsman of delicate and graceful line. Probably for this reason, his woodcuts and engravings are better than his paintings, and in these media he is without peer in any age (see Figure 26.1). Holbein was a skillful sketcher and woodcutter, but he made his greatest contributions in the field of portrait painting. He painted several portraits of Erasmus and illus-

trated Erasmus' *Praise of Folly* with pen-and-ink drawings. Many of his most productive years were spent in England in the employ of Henry VIII. Among his greatest portraits are those of Henry VIII (see Figure 27.1), Edward VI, Mary Tudor, and Sir Thomas More.

Renaissance architecture was less prominent in the north. The largest Renaissance structure outside Italy is the vast Escorial near Madrid, which Philip II of Spain built as a royal palace and mausoleum. Its rugged massiveness, rectangular shape, and horizontal lines typify the Renaissance style. Some of the best examples of northern Renaissance architecture are the Renaissance wing of the Louvre in Paris and some of the largest châteaux along France's Loire River. This architecture was essentially derivative; the French Renaissance châteaux were really fortresses being played with.

The music capital of the Western world during the Renaissance period was the Netherlands. It was from the Flemings that the Italian Renaissance musicians, including Palestrina, derived much of their knowledge and inspiration (see p. 350).

5. SIGNIFICANCE OF THE RENAISSANCE IN HISTORY

In retrospect, then, it is apparent that the Renaissance was part of a transition from the Middle Ages to the early modern period. In some measure it was a rebirth of the classical civilizations of Greece and Rome, but it was not merely that. There was much in the Renaissance that was fresh and original, and there was a self-consciousness among Renaissance scholars, writers, and artists that they were part of something new.

In some ways the Renaissance represented a new emphasis on secularism and a rejection of the scholastic Christian culture of the Middle Ages, particularly in Italy. Yet in other ways it remained fundamentally a Christian civilization and an era that, in our terms, was quite religious. Indeed, the depth of religious sentiment during the Renaissance, particularly in the north, is revealed by the Reformation.

The intellectual and cultural themes established during the Renaissance would continue to grow throughout the early modern period. As we shall see, their effects would be felt in the politics, the commerce, and the society of Europeans during the sixteenth, seventeenth, and eighteenth centuries.

SUGGESTED READING

General

J. Huizinga, *The Waning of the Middle Ages* (1954). A superb interpretation important for an understanding of the early northern Renaissance. (See also items at the end of Chapter 25.)

Northern Humanism

E. H. Harbison, *The Christian Scholar in the Age of the Reformation* (1956). By a leading scholar in the field.

J. Huizinga, *Erasmus and the Age of the Reformation* (1957). Probably the best single volume on Erasmus.

R. Marius, *Thomas More: A Biography* (1984). A recent study.

M. M. Philips, *Erasmus and the Northern Renaissance*, 2nd ed. (1981). A good general study.

England, France, and Germany

M. Dowling, *Humanism in the Age of Henry VIII* (1986). An informative history of English humanism.

L. Febvre, *Life in Renaissance France* (1977). A highly respected account.

Werner L. Gundersheimer, ed., *French Humanism 1470–1600* (1969). A solid collection of essays.

J. H. Overfield, *Humanism and Scholasticism in Late Medieval Germany* (1984). Focuses on universities.

Lewis Spitz, *The Religious Renaissance of the German Humanists* (1963). Broad and well written.

Art and Printing

Elizabeth Eisenstein, *The Printing Press as an Agent of Change* (1978). A superb, exhaustive interpretive study.

W. Stechow, *Northern Renaissance Art: 1400–1600* (1966). A useful survey.

CHAPTER 27
The Rise of National States

FIGURE 27.1 Hans Holbein the Younger, *Portrait of Henry VIII*, 1540 Henry VIII and his father, Henry VII, were two of the most forceful of the new monarchs who arose in Europe between 1450 and 1550. These monarchs increased the power of the central government as well as their own personal power. (Alinari/Art Resource)

In the fifteenth and sixteenth centuries, monarchs in western Europe succeeded in creating powerful national states. These monarchs, often referred to by historians as the "new monarchs," aggressively built their dynastic power in three main ways. First, they undermined their competitors, above all the feudal barons. Monarchs turned to members of the lesser nobility and the middle class for backing. Second, they developed new methods of financial and administrative support. National taxes gave monarchs new, independent sources of income, and expanding governmental bureaucracies staffed by officials who owed allegiance to the monarchs extended royal authority throughout the land. Third, they brought the Church more under their command. In some cases they gained the right to appoint church officers within their lands; in other cases they actually established new official churches.

The new monarchs used other methods as well and took advantage of developments occurring at that time. Applying principles of dynastic succession, they married to expand and unify their lands. They increased their income by promoting and tapping into reviving commerce, which brought with it a moneyed economy and a prosperous middle class. With their greater financial resources, new monarchs established standing professional armies that could use the new military tactics and technology that were lessening the importance of the independent mounted armored knight. They suppressed internal violence and made law enforcement more the responsibility of their own agents. To legalize their growing power, the monarchs utilized the principles of Roman law, which considered kings to be sovereigns in whose hands the welfare of all the people was placed.

The most important of these new monarchs arose in Spain, France, and England. Although other factors retarded unification in Italy and Germany until the nineteenth century, Spain, France, and England were already well on their way to becoming powerful national states in the late fifteenth century.

1. SPAIN

Spain became the most powerful and influential of the new states at the opening of the early modern era. The energy and enthusiasm that Spain displayed at this time may be attributed in part, at least, to her long and finally successful struggle against the Moors. By the middle of the thirteenth century the Moors had been driven out of the entire Iberian peninsula except for the southernmost province of Granada. Furthermore, the numerous medieval feudal holdings in what is now Spain had been consolidated into four large kingdoms—Castile, Aragon, Granada, and Navarre (south of the Pyrenees). The marriage of Ferdinand of Aragon and Isabella of Castile in 1469 united to some extent the two largest kingdoms. During their reign (1474–1516)[1] Granada and Navarre were conquered and ties between their lands were strengthened. Thus, within a forty-seven-year span from 1469 to 1516 the Spanish national state was created.

Ferdinand and Isabella strove for political and religious unity. In order to suppress the jealous nobility further, they allied themselves with *hidalgos*—members of the lesser nobility—and the middle class, leaning heavily on them for financial and administrative assistance. In return, the joint sovereigns did everything in their power to advance their fortunes. Vigorous enforcement of law and order, stabilization of the currency, building of roads and bridges, tariff protection of home industries—all served to advance the economic prosperity of Spain in general and the middle class in particular. This commercial expansion was greatly enhanced in 1492 with the "discovery" of the New World in the name of Spain. The ensuing profits and loot further strengthened the hands of the Spanish sovereigns by freeing them from dependence on the Cortes (the representative bodies dominated by the nobility) for funds.

In religious affairs, also, Ferdinand and Isabella gained power over the Church and unified their country. They acquired the right to appoint bishops, reformed the Church, and gained access to some of its wealth. By the end of their reign, the Church in Spain was in effect at the command of the Spanish state. Against the two non-Christian groups in their realm, the Jews and the Moslems, the "Catholic sovereigns" waged a cam-

---

[1]Isabella ruled Castile from 1474 to 1504, and Ferdinand ruled Aragon from 1479 to 1516.

paign of conversion or expulsion. The Jews had long been objects of hatred and persecution in Christian Europe. In part this hatred derived from religious differences, but there was also an economic factor. Church laws against usury had given the Jews a monopoly on moneylending, a precarious but often profitable activity. The envy and hatred of the Christians led to periodic outbreaks of violence. In the late fourteenth century, an outbreak of unusual severity forced many Spanish Jews to seek safety in outward conversion. But these Marranos, as the pseudoconverts were called, were the object of increasing suspicion. Finally, Ferdinand and Isabella, despite some reluctance, introduced the Inquisition into Spain. At the mercy of this court, the Marranos were terrorized by imprisonment, torture, and loss of life and property. In 1492 the remaining Jews were ordered to leave the country. The exiles thus banished (estimated to be in the neighborhood of one hundred fifty thousand) took much of their wealth and all their economic energy and skills with them.[2]

Shortly afterward the Moslems suffered a similar fate. Upon surrendering their last stronghold in Granada, in 1492, they had been promised religious freedom in return for submission to the political authority of the Spanish crown. However, again the "Catholic sovereigns" yielded to the increasing pressure of religious intolerance, and in 1502 the Moslems were ordered to accept Christianity or leave Spain. Although thousands did leave, even more thousands remained and went through the farce of outward conversion. But these "converts," called Moriscos, only delayed their fate. In the two succeeding reigns they too were persecuted and expelled.

Spain, then, was unified religiously under the crown, but at an economic and intellectual cost. Nevertheless, territorially consolidated and politically unified by Ferdinand and Isabella and their successor, Charles V (see p. 368), enriched by the wealth of the New World, and inspired by the crusading zeal of a purified and triumphant religion, Spain was to be the most powerful and influential of the new national states

during the first century of the early modern era (see Figure 27.2 and Map 27.2).

2. FRANCE

The reign of Louis XI (1461–1483), known as the "Spider King," may be said to mark the beginning of France as a modern national state. Louis came to the throne of France eight years after the end of the Hundred Years' War with England. His predecessor, Charles VII, had used the war emergency to obtain powers over taxation (*taille*) and a standing army for the crown. During the last phase of the war a great upsurge of French national spirit, aided by the exploits of Joan of Arc, made possible, at long last, the expulsion of the English invaders. Louis XI put these inherited advantages to clever use. First of all, he set out to crush the power of the feudal nobility who had taken advantage of the royal distress during the Hundred Years' War to assert their virtual independence of the crown. By craft and direct military force he broke up the league the insubordinate nobility had formed against him and reduced the individual nobles to submission. In order to achieve this goal, Louis utilized the rising middle class. In return for its support he placed many members of this class in his councils and in key administrative posts, enabling some to enter the nobility. He also did what he could to foster commerce and industry. Roads, harbors, and waterways were improved. Shipbuilding, commerce, and industry were encouraged by royal subsidies and protective regulation.

Louis XI virtually completed the territorial consolidation of what would become the French national state (see Map 27.1). He brought province after province under direct royal control, until by the end of his reign France had acquired most of its modern territory. This expansive movement brought Louis XI into conflict with Charles the Bold of Burgundy. Charles the Bold (perhaps "the Rash" would have been a more accurate title) had inherited rich and strategically located territories that included the Netherlands, the duchy of Burgundy, and the free county of Burgundy. These he hoped to consolidate into a great national state—the old Middle Kingdom of Charlemagne's grandson Lothair—between France and Germany. Had he succeeded in doing

---

[2]The Jews had earlier been expelled from England, France, and the German states.

FIGURE 27.2 Ferdinand and Isabella A coin of Ferdinand and Isabella, sovereigns of Spain. Spain was the most powerful of the new national monarchies and her coins enjoyed wide circulation in Europe and predominance in the Spanish and English empires in North and South America during the sixteenth, seventeenth, and eighteenth centuries. The Spanish piece-of-eight was commonly called the "dollar," and in 1787 the dollar was adopted by the United States as its standard unit of value. (American Numismatic Society)

so, the course of history might have been changed significantly. However, Charles the Bold was killed battling the Swiss, and his successor, Mary, was unable to prevent Louis XI from seizing the duchy of Burgundy, Picardy, and part of Flanders. (The abortive Burgundian "Middle Kingdom" has been a battleground between France and Germany throughout much of the modern period.) Thus consolidated and enlarged, France was to play a dominant role in European affairs in the centuries that followed.

Louis XI's schemes, however, did not include the betterment of the condition of the lower classes. Having paid for his ambitious programs with heavy taxes but having received little in return, the lower classes remained disaffected and discontented.

3. ENGLAND

Early modern times, so far as English history is concerned, may be said to have begun with the reign of Henry VII (1485–1509), the first of the Tudor dynasty. The political unity of the English national state had been brought about as early as 1066 by William the Conqueror (aided to a considerable degree by geography). However, the feudal system, with its decentralization of administration and society, the Hundred Years' War with France (1337–1453), and the Wars of the Roses (1455–1484) between the rival houses of Lancaster and York, had by the last quarter of the fifteenth century brought England to a state of turmoil bordering on anarchy. Henry Tudor acquired the English throne by victory on the battlefield over the Yorkist King Richard III, who was slain. Himself a member of the Lancastrian family, Henry ended the bloody dynastic feud by marrying Elizabeth of York.

The most pressing task confronting the strongwilled new monarch was the suppression of the turbulent nobility. The great feudal barons had taken advantage of the decades of civil war and the long rule of a weak king prior to the war to defy royal authority. They retained their own private armies and overawed the local courts. At once and with great vigor Henry VII proceeded

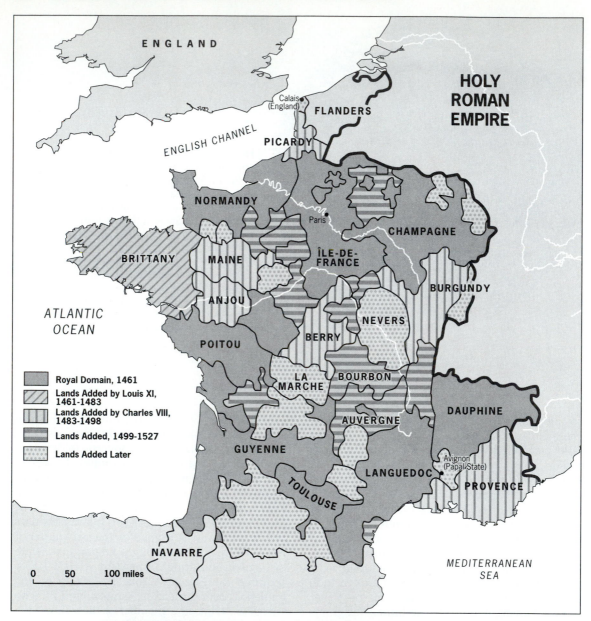

Map 27.1 THE UNIFICATION OF FRANCE, 1461–1527 During the first half of the fifteenth century, France was divided and the monarchy was weak. As indicated by this map, between 1461 and 1527 French monarchs succeeded in bringing most of modern France under their control.

Hapsburg Dominions

Ottoman Empire

Boundary of the Holy Roman Empire

Map 27.2 EUROPE, 1526 This map indicates how widespread the Hapsburg dominions were under Charles V. In addition, Charles V exercised some indirect control over most of the territory within the Holy Roman Empire as its selected emperor. As the Spanish monarch, his lands included Spanish holdings in the New World. The map also shows France nearly surrounded by its Hapsburg rivals and the Islamic Ottoman Empire was a threat to Christian Europe.

to enforce the laws against livery and maintenance,[3] thereby destroying the illegal feudal armies. Since the regular local courts were too weak to proceed against the nobility, Henry set up his own Court of Star Chamber, which, backed by the royal army, was able to overawe the most powerful barons and bring them to justice and to submission to the crown.

In these undertakings Henry VII had the support of the lesser gentry and the middle and lower classes, all of whom yearned for peace and order. The middle class, particularly, desired stability for the sake of its growing business activi-

---

[3]So called from the practice of the peasantry's wearing the lord's badge or livery, signifying membership in his private army, in return for the lord's promise to maintain (support) them in courts of justice.

ties, and it was with this class that the Tudors allied themselves. Henry selected many of his counselors and administrators from the ranks of the bourgeoisie. He made favorable commercial treaties with the Netherlands, Denmark, and even Venice, the jealous queen of the rich eastern Mediterranean trade. Navigation acts were passed to protect English shippers. Henry's frugality and careful collection and handling of revenues not only were good business but also freed the king of dependence upon Parliament for funds.

Henry VII died in 1509, but he passed along to his glamorous son, Henry VIII (see Figure 27.1), a united and orderly national state and a well-filled treasury. And under his granddaughter, Elizabeth, England rose to a position of first-rate importance in European affairs.

4. ITALY, GERMANY, AND THE HOLY ROMAN EMPIRE

Italian- and German-speaking people have played a vital role in European history, particularly in making important contributions to the arts and sciences. However, they did not achieve political unity at the opening of the early modern period, and that disunity created political problems that persisted into the nineteenth and twentieth centuries.

At the opening of the early modern period the Italian peninsula was divided into five major independent states: the Kingdom of Naples, the Papal States, Florence (Tuscany), Venice, and Milan. The Kingdom of Naples, the poorest of the Italian states, occupied the southern third of the peninsula and at times the large island of Sicily (see Map 27.3). During the fifteenth and sixteenth centuries it was a bone of contention over which France and Spain repeatedly fought. The Papal States occupied the central portion of the peninsula. These states were ruled by the pope not only as a supreme pontiff but also as political head. Florence and Venice, republics in name, were dominated by rich banking and commercial families. Milan, another thriving center of commerce, was ruled by an autocratic duke.

The main reason for Italian disunity in the early modern era was the long tradition of independence among the city-states. There the spirit of local rather than national pride and loyalty prevailed. Instead of forging common bonds, the major Italian city-states such as Florence, Venice, and Milan competed with one another for control over the smaller ones, such as Ferrara, Modena, and Mantua. Possibilities of unification under the papacy or the Holy Roman emperor were undermined by a long history of struggles between these two powers. For a while, the Treaty of Lodi (1454–1455), which allied Florence, Milan, and Naples, and alliances between Venice and the Papal States created a balance of power and some stability on the Italian peninsula. But this stability broke down in 1494. In the following decades Italy was repeatedly invaded by France and the Holy Roman Empire. The political division of the Italians in an age of powerful national states continued to be a standing invitation to aggression against them.

During the fifteenth century German-speaking peoples remained split up into more than three hundred virtually independent units. The only political bond among them was the impotent government of the Holy Roman Empire. This ramshackle institution—a survival of the organization set up by Charlemagne in 800 and revived by Otto the Great in 962—purported to be a restoration of the old Roman Empire, but it never was. In the Middle Ages, when the Spanish, French, and English sovereigns had been consolidating their territories and their authority, the German emperors had been frittering away their time and energy trying to bring Italy under their control. While they were away from Germany on these quixotic ventures, the local feudal barons had conspired against them, consolidated their own power, and built up hereditary states of their own within the empire. Meanwhile, territory after territory had slipped from under the emperor's control, until by the opening of the early modern period the Holy Roman Empire included for all practical purposes only the German-speaking states plus Czech-speaking Bohemia.

Eventually seven of the emperor's most prominent subjects gained the right to elect him. This elective feature not only diminished the prestige of the emperor but also forced candidates to bribe the electors and bargain and promise away any chance of strengthening the imperial office. Since the emperor had no sure income,

Map 27.3 ITALY, 1454 Italy was unable to overcome her political divisions, with the large but weak Kingdom of Naples controlled by outside powers, the center controlled by popes oppposed to national unification, and the rich, urbanized north divided among competing states.

he had no military force with which to enforce his will. Even to defend the empire, he was forced to call upon his subject princes to furnish troops. The lawmaking and taxing powers lay in the hands of the Diet, which was composed of three houses: the house of electors, the house of lesser princes, and the house of representatives of the free imperial cities. The Diet had no regular time or place of meeting and was seldom able to reach agreement on any important question. In the late fifteenth century an imperial court was set up to settle disputes between member states. However, lacking any means of enforcing its decisions, this instrument too proved ineffective.

The one factor that gave any semblance of vitality to the Holy Roman Empire was the Hapsburg family. A Hapsburg was first elected em-

peror in 1273. After 1438, with only one brief exception, no one but a Hapsburg was elected until the empire finally died at the hands of Napoleon in 1806. By marriage and diplomacy, the Hapsburgs expanded their original Austrian lands until at the opening of the early modern period they possessed one of the largest and richest dynastic estates in Europe. Although, therefore, the Holy Roman emperor as emperor was virtually powerless, as head of the house of Hapsburg he was one of the most influential of monarchs. Nevertheless, all efforts of the Hapsburgs to strengthen the central government of the empire foundered on the rocks of German particularism—the local interests of the jealous princes.

During most of the first half of the sixteenth century the house of Hapsburg was headed by

FIGURE 27.3 Emperor Charles V This sixteenth-century engraving by Sichem shows Emperor Charles V with symbols of the Holy Roman Empire: sword and crossed globe. (The Bettmann Archive)

Emperor Charles V (see Figure 27.3). Charles V inherited from his parents and four grandparents a vast array of territories and claims. From his grandfather Maximilian he inherited the Hapsburg provinces generally spoken of as Austria, to which were added in Charles' lifetime Hungary, Bohemia, Moravia, and Silesia. As a Hapsburg, he also inherited a good claim to the imperial crown of the Holy Roman Empire. From his grandmother Mary he inherited the Burgundian lands: the free county of Burgundy (Franche-Comté), the Netherlands, Luxembourg, Flanders, Artois, and claims to the duchy of Burgundy and Picardy, which had been seized by Louis XI. From his grandfather Ferdinand he received Aragon, the Kingdom of Naples, and numerous islands in the Mediterranean. From his grandmother Isabella he received Castile and a claim to the entire Western Hemisphere based

on the papal Line of Demarcation (1493) and the Treaty of Tordesillas (1494). And from Ferdinand and Isabella jointly, he inherited Granada and Spanish Navarre.

The very size of Charles V's far-flung holdings spelled perpetual trouble (see Map 27.2). The language problem alone was appalling. To this were added differences in local customs, tastes, and eventually religion. Moreover, Charles V was sure to become involved in all the major international conflicts of Europe. Born and reared in the Netherlands, Charles was accepted in Spain only after a serious opposition and open revolt. His efforts to strengthen the government of the Holy Roman Empire and to raise money and troops there were frustrated by the local German princes. Finally, the Lutheran revolt further split the empire and completely shattered the personal power of Charles in Germany.

5. INTERNATIONAL RIVALRIES, 1516–1559

The rise of national states failed to bring peace to Europe. The national monarchs, supported by the bourgeoisie, had justified their own aggrandizement on the grounds that it was necessary to end the interminable feudal wars, and they had in fact established a large measure of internal law and order. However, the little feudal wars were followed by big national and dynastic wars. Although these monarchs established modern diplomatic institutions (earlier developed by the Italians in the fifteenth century), such as permanent ambassadors, they also utilized larger armies and new military technology in their wars.

Throughout the sixteenth century international strife revolved around the house of Hapsburg. Charles V found himself almost continually at war with Francis I of France. Each feared the other's power. Francis I had continued the process initiated by his predecessors of increasing the power of the French monarchy, above all by securing new revenues through the sale of governmental offices, by swelling the state bureaucracy, and by gaining the right to appoint France's bishops and abbots. Francis vigorously contested Charles' election as Holy Roman Emperor. They fought over conflicting territorial claims in Italy and the Burgundian lands and along the French-Spanish border. Charles won

nearly all the battles, but he was never able to make his victories permanent.

The relations between Charles of Hapsburg and England were limited to a personal family quarrel. When Henry VIII sought an annulment of his marriage to Catherine of Aragon, the aunt of Charles V, Charles used his influence with the pope to block the proceedings, thus touching off a chain of events that ended with Henry taking over the Church in England and separating it from the Roman Catholic church. It was under Charles' son, Philip II, that conflict between Spain and England was brought to a climax.

Among Charles V's more concrete achievements were his marriage to Isabella of Portugal, which brought about a brief union of Spain and Portugal under Philip II, and his repulse of the Ottoman Turks. The Ottoman Turks had migrated to Asia Minor from Central Asia in the thirteenth century, converted to Islam, and by the beginning of the sixteenth century had built an empire that extended from Egypt to the Danube. Under Suleiman the Magnificent (1520–1566), their ablest ruler, they crushed the Hungarians at Mohacs (1526), swept across Hungary, and in 1529 laid seige to Vienna, the capital city of Hapsburg Austria. At the same time they con-

quered all of North Africa as far west as Morocco, and their fleets dominated the Mediterranean. It was feared that all western Christendom might fall to the Moslems. At this point, Charles V rallied the forces of the empire and the Hapsburg provinces and drove the Turks back into Hungary. His captains also administered some defeats to the Moslem Barbary pirates in the western Mediterranean.

In 1555 Charles V began to divide his holdings between his son, Philip II, and his brother, Ferdinand. To Philip he gave the Burgundian provinces and Spain, with its appanages in Italy, the Mediterranean, and the New World. To Ferdinand he gave the Austrian provinces and successfully promoted Ferdinand's candidacy to the crown of the Holy Roman Empire. Henceforth there were two branches of the Hapsburg dynasty—Austrian and Spanish—both of which would long continue to play important roles in European and world history.

In 1559 the Treaty of Cateau-Cambrésis ended the dynastic wars between the Hapsburgs and the French Valois kings. Spain gained dominance in Italy, the center of power in Europe shifted to Spain, and a new era of revolts and wars entwining religion and politics unfolded.

SUGGESTED READING

General—The Fifteenth and Sixteenth Centuries

B. Guenée, *States and Rulers in Later Medieval Europe* (1985). Analyzes the forces underlying Europe's state system.

De Lamar Jensen, *Renaissance Europe: Age of Recovery and Reconciliation* (1981). A good recent treatment.

Eugene F. Rice, Jr., *The Foundations of Early Modern Europe, 1460–1559* (1970). The best general survey of the period, with an excellent bibliography.

The New National Monarchies

M. V. C. Alexander, *The First of the Tudors: A Study of Henry VII and His Reign* (1980). A good biography.

J. H. Elliott, *Imperial Spain, 1469–1716* (1964). An excellent account of Spanish history during this period.

A. Goodman, *The New Monarchy: England, 1471–1534* (1988). Brief and insightful on the Tudor monarchy.

H. Kamen, *Spain 1469–1714* (1983). A useful survey.

R. J. Knect, *Francis I* (1982). An authoritative study.

J. H. Shennan, *The Origins of the Modern European State* (1974). An excellent brief analysis.

Italy, Germany, and the Holy Roman Empire

M. F. Alvarez, *Charles V* (1975). A well-written biography of this outstanding figure.

G. Benecke, *Society and Politics in Germany, 1500–1750* (1974). Early chapters cover the period well.

D. Hay and J. Law, *Italy in the Age of the Renaissance* (1989). A good recent survey.

H. B. Koenigsberger, *The Hapsburgs and Europe: 1516–1660* (1971). A solid account of Hapsburg rule.

International Rivalries

J. R. Hale, *War and Society in Renaissance Europe* (1986). Relates war to political and social developments of the period.

CHAPTER 28

European Expansion, Commercial Capitalism, and Social Change

FIGURE 28.1 Columbus Discovers the New World This illustration is from a letter of Columbus to the treasurer of the king of Spain, published in Basel a year after his first voyage. Here the Spaniards are offering the Indians gifts as they approach the West Indian island. The Indians are portrayed as naked and perhaps even childlike, emphasizing the European perception of them as lesser, uncivilized beings. Pictures such as this excited the wonder and greed of many Europeans. (NYPL Picture Collection)

The rise of national states was closely associated with the expansion of Europe and new economic development. The monarchs who created national states supported voyages of discovery and the overseas conquests that resulted. They took advantage of the wealth that poured in to finance their growing governments and their wars. They also allied themselves with the rising middle class against the feudal aristocracy. The strength of this middle class lay in its commercial wealth and its use of capitalistic methods to gain that wealth. Together, this European expansion and economic development represented a new level of power and wealth that would make Europe dominant over large parts of the globe.

1. THE AGE OF DISCOVERY

In the late fifteenth and early sixteenth centuries European mariners made a series of daring voyages in which they "discovered" not only the New World but also new and much better routes to the East (see Map 28.1). These voyages were made possible by a number of recent developments. Important improvements in the technology of shipping and navigation were being made. New armaments and military tactics gave Europeans advantages over those resisting them. Commercial and organizational skills increased the chances of success for these risky voyages. The governments of the national states along the Atlantic coast promoted these voyages and provided needed financial support. Their principal motive was a desire to bypass the Venetians, the Moslems, and the land barriers that separated them from the riches of the East. But there was also a powerful outward impetus in the spirit of inquiry and adventure kindled by the Renaissance interest in the secular world and in the Christian missionary zeal that had always been a spur to expansion.

The first to begin these voyages in the fifteenth century were the Portuguese. During the first half of the fifteenth century, Prince Henry the Navigator (1394–1460) established a school of navigation and base of operations on the southwestern tip of Portugal from which he sent expeditions down the west coast of Africa. In addition to curiosity, his motives were mercenary and religious: He wanted to capture the gold trade in western Africa and hoped to find the legendary Christian kingdom of Prester John. A broader goal of this Portuguese effort was to find a new route around Africa to India. Pushing steadily down the coast of West Africa, the Portuguese developed a lucrative trade in gold, ivory, sugar, and slaves. In 1488 Portuguese explorers rounded the Cape of Good Hope. In 1498 Vasco da Gama, in what was probably the greatest voyage in the history of navigation, reached India, the object of the quest. Vasco da Gama was out of sight of land ninety-three days—three times as long as Columbus on his voyage to the New World. That the Portuguese knew what they were up to is proved by the fact that Vasco da Gama's return cargo sold for sixty times the cost of the expedition. These glad tidings sent a host of Portuguese adventurers hurrying to the East Indies, where they carved out a huge commercial and political empire. One of these adventurers, Pedro Cabral, swinging too far westward, touched the eastern bulge of South America, thus laying the basis for Portugal's claim to Brazil. With their discovery of this all-water route to the East, the Portuguese broke the Arab and Venetian monopoly over the spice trade. From that point on, the center of commercial activity shifted westward toward the Atlantic seaboard.

Meanwhile, Spain was sending its mariners westward, for by the late fifteenth century most educated people in western Europe assumed that the earth was round, although they greatly underestimated its size. Many navigators therefore believed that the East Indies could be reached by sailing west. The first European to attempt it was Christopher Columbus. (Nothing had come of the tenth-century voyages to Greenland and northern America of the roving Norsemen Eric the Red and Leif Ericson.) Columbus was born in Genoa but moved to Portugal. When, however, Portugal failed to support his proposed westward voyage, he turned to Queen Isabella of Castile, who gave him the necessary backing. His three ships touched a West Indian island on October 12, 1492 (see Figure 28.1). Thinking that the West Indies were islands off the east coast of Asia, Columbus made three further voyages in the hope of bypassing these barriers and sailing on to his real goal, the East Indies. Instead, he

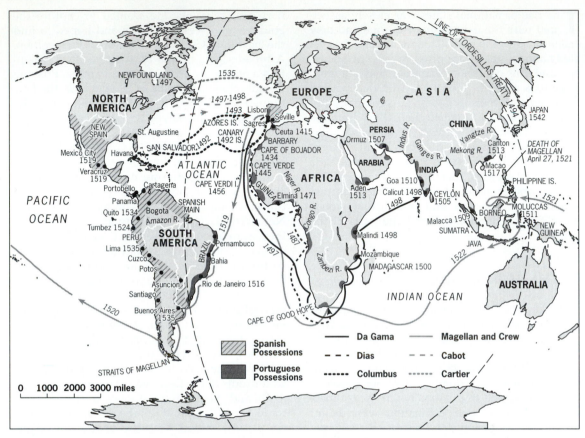

Map 28.1 EXPLORATION AND CONQUEST, FIFTEENTH AND SIXTEENTH CENTURIES This map shows the routes taken by some of the early explorers. It indicates some of the distinctions between the Portuguese and Spanish empires—the Portuguese concentrated in Africa and the East and focused primarily on sea power and trading posts; the Spanish concentrated in the New World and focused primarily on conquest and colonization. Early English and French efforts were more limited and farther north.

was turned back by the South and Central American mainlands and died disappointed, not having realized the magnitude of his discovery.

But others soon realized it, and in the first half of the sixteenth century Spanish expeditions to the New World multiplied. In 1493 the pope drew a line of demarcation dividing the non-Christian world between Spain and Portugal. This line was somewhat altered in favor of Portugal the following year by the Treaty of Tordesillas. Since all of North and South America except the eastern part of Brazil and most of Greenland fell to Spain, the Spanish sailors continued to move westward. Juan Ponce de León,

Hernando de Soto, and Juan Vásquez Coronado explored the southern part of what is now the United States. Balboa crossed the Isthmus of Panama and looked out upon the Pacific Ocean. In 1519 Ferdinand Magellan set out around the world by way of the Strait of Magellan. Although he himself was killed in the Philippines, in 1522 one of his ships completed the circuit. Also in 1519 Hernando Cortez began the conquest of the Aztec Empire in Mexico. In 1531–1532 Francisco Pizarro conquered the Inca Indians in Peru.

The other two national states, England and France, were relatively inactive in discovery and exploration during the fifteenth and early sixteenth centuries. The English crown did, however, sponsor voyages to northern North America by the Italian mariner John Cabot in 1497–1498. These voyages became the basis for England's claims to North America, where England later built a great empire. The French government sponsored Jacques Cartier, who in 1535 sailed up the St. Lawrence to what is now Montreal and claimed Canada for France. Nonetheless, it was not until the seventeenth century that Spain and Portugal were replaced as the world's leading imperial powers.

2. THE FOUNDING OF THE SPANISH NEW WORLD EMPIRE

Although much of the Western Hemisphere at the beginning of the sixteenth century was sparsely inhabited by native or "Indian" tribes, the Spaniards encountered two highly organized societies: those of the Aztecs in Mexico and the Incas in Peru.

The first inhabitants of the Western Hemisphere are generally believed to have immigrated from Asia across the Bering Strait some 10,000–20,000 years ago and perhaps much earlier. They organized into numerous tribes throughout North, Central, and South America.

The first of these tribes to build a highly organized society were probably the Olmecs, who flourished between 1200 B.C. and 400 B.C. in southeastern Mexico, but little is known of this civilization. Other societies developed, but perhaps the best known of these early civilizations was the Maya in southeastern Mexico and Central America. Between A.D. 300 and 900, the Maya developed large urban religious centers. Their writing was a combination of pictures and ideographs. Their best art was brightly colored pottery, gems, gold and silverware, and sculpture. Probably their most remarkable creations were a system of mathematics based on the decimal (actually vigesimal) system and a calendar based on astronomy, both of which were in advance of those used in contemporary Europe. Their massively walled stone cities were connected by elaborately paved roads. Between about A.D. 700 and 900 the Mayan civilization collapsed, perhaps because of a combination of increasing warfare and agricultural exhaustion—the reasons

are unclear. Between 950 and 1200 the Toltecs gained control over what had been some Mayan territory and lands further north.

In the fourteenth century the warlike Aztecs came down from the north and founded a city on an island in Lake Tezcoco—the present Mexico City. From this base they formed alliances that enabled them to conquer and organize a military empire or confederacy comprising most of what is now southern and central Mexico. Theirs was the gift of military and political organization. They developed an elaborate, though stern, system of justice. The Aztecs borrowed many aspects of their culture and religion from previous civilizations. Their religion was important and highly organized. Several thousand priests, both regular and secular, tended the impressive temple and supervised education and morals. The numerous gods were headed by the terrible war god, who demanded human sacrifice, usually prisoners of war. And yet the rank-and-file Aztecs were gentle lovers of poetry and art. Flourishing commerce, agriculture, and mining added to the wealth obtained by conquest.

An even more colorful civilization was that of the Incas on the Andean Plateau of South America. In the fourteenth century the Inca Indians began to extend their sway over their neighbors until their empire covered an area fifteen hundred miles long and three hundred miles wide—including present-day Ecuador, Peru, and parts of Bolivia and Chile. An elaborate system of roads and communications tied this vast and lofty empire together. The all-powerful Inca ruler was treated as a god. However, he had a body of advisers and administrators chosen from the upper classes. The state claimed control over all land and production. The regimented lower classes did all the work under close supervision and shared from the common stores. A high degree of specialization was practiced. Agriculture was well advanced, and huge terracing and irrigation projects had been developed to overcome the difficulties of the Andean terrain. Religious worship, particularly of the sun god, was an important feature of national life. Outstanding were Incan pottery, architecture, textiles, and gold and silver ornamental objects.

The native American civilizations were no match for the marauding Europeans. Spanish military men, particularly those of the lesser no-

FIGURE 28.2 The Aztec Perception of the Spanish Although there are many Spanish records of the Spaniards' arrival and explorations in the New World, this Aztec manuscript (ca. 1519–1522) is one of the few surviving Indian versions of the coming of the Europeans. This illustration shows Cortez arriving in Mexico. Note the depiction of some of the crucial elements of Cortez' conquest: the sword, the horse, the flag, and the cross. (Biblioteca Apostolica Vaticana, Rome)

bility (*hidalgos*), were part of a centuries-old tradition of crusading for Church, crown, and profit. Cortez, with a band of some six hundred soldiers and eighteen horses, overcame the Aztecs by a combination of alliances, treachery, tactics, weapons, and determination. He took advantage of divisions and hostilities between the Aztecs and the subject tribes as well as the Aztec belief that the Spaniards were ancient gods whose return had long been expected. Once inside the capital city, the Spaniards were too strong to be expelled. They slaughtered and looted the poorly armed Aztecs without mercy (see Figure 28.2).

Even more spectacular was the conquest of the Incas. Like Cortez, Pizarro used disunity within the Incan Empire as well as trickery and brutality to defeat the Incas. At one point, Pizarro enticed the Incan emperor into a conference. At a given signal Pizarro's small but well-armed band of Spanish soldiers fell upon the splendidly dressed but primitively armed Incan troops and slew them by the thousands. Pizarro promised to free the Incan chieftain in return for a ransom of gold objects sufficient to fill a room seventeen by twenty-two feet to a height of nine feet, plus a larger amount of silver. This ransom was collected and paid, but Pizarro, who had never really intended to free the emperor, had him put to death anyway.

Spanish administrators soon replaced these conquerors, and throughout the sixteenth century Spaniards flocked to the New World. By 1607, when the first permanent English colony was founded in North America, a quarter of a million Spaniards had settled in the vast Spanish Empire stretching from what is now Arizona to Cape Horn. A number of distinguished missions and cathedrals had been erected, and several thriving universities had been founded. The native civilizations had been almost wholly destroyed and replaced by the Christian civilization of Spain.

3. CAPITALISM AND THE COMMERCIAL REVOLUTION

The discovery of the New World and of all-water routes to the Far East fueled an expansion of European commerce that was already under way. A crucial aspect of this expansion was the development of capitalistic methods. The use of capitalistic methods and the scale of commercial growth was so great that the term *commercial revolution* is used to describe it.

The term *capitalism*, stripped to its barest essentials, means a system whereby private individuals put money to work to make more money. Individuals, competing in a market to maximize their profits, determine what to produce, how to produce it, and what price to charge. It involves, among other things, private property, the profit motive, a substantial amount of free enterprise, the hiring of labor for wages, and the lending of money for interest.

Elements of capitalism had been in existence for centuries, but to a lesser degree and in much more limited form than during the sixteenth century. During most of the Middle Ages agriculture operated at only a subsistence level and was carried out under feudal restrictions. Commerce was a trickle of luxuries for the rich and necessities such as iron, implements, and salt. Guilds hampered commercial and industrial enterprises. The Church supported the concept of the "fair price" rather than competitive pricing and frowned on the lending of money for interest (usury).

During the eleventh century, commercial activities began to revive, and by the thirteenth century a pronounced recovery was under way. The Crusades contributed to this revival. The huge movement of men and supplies from western Europe to the Holy Land enriched the merchants and shippers of Venice and other Italian cities. Some of them set up permanent trading posts in the Near East and introduced the luxuries of the materially more advanced Moslem and Byzantine worlds to western Europe. The Fourth Crusade, which the Venetians diverted to the looting of Constantinople, was particularly fruitful. The Venetians seized not only a great hoard of gold and silver in the stricken eastern imperial capital but also a large part of the territory of the Byzantine Empire itself. This wealth flowed into the stream of western European commerce.

Foremost among the centers of this newly revived commerce and capitalism were the city-states of northern Italy, such as Venice, Genoa, Florence, and Milan. Venice was the queen of the Mediterranean in the thirteenth, fourteenth, and fifteenth centuries. After crushing the sea power of her chief rival, Genoa, in the fourteenth century, Venice enjoyed a virtual monopoly over the lucrative trade with the East. At the peak of its prosperity, Venice's merchant marine numbered some thirty thousand sailors. Milan was the starting point of the overland traffic across the Alps to northern Europe. In the late fourteenth century Milan gained control of the port city of Genoa. Florence manufactured large quantities of fine woolen textiles on a capitalistic basis, and in the fourteenth and fifteenth centuries it was the banking capital of the Western world. The Medici family alone at one time possessed dozens of branch banks scattered throughout western and central Europe.

In northern Europe, the Hanseatic League, composed of some eighty German Baltic and North Sea cities, enjoyed a brisk trade in such commodities as fish, furs, grain, and timber. In southern Germany and the Rhine Valley, numerous trading centers such as Augsburg, Nuremberg, and Cologne sprang up along the overland route between Italy and northern Europe. Finally, the Netherlands, Paris, and London shared in this early period of revived commercialism.

As the main trade routes shifted from the

Mediterranean to the Atlantic during the fifteenth and sixteenth centuries, new commercial centers to the west began to flourish. Contrary to what one might have expected, Spain, surfeited with gold and silver from Mexico and Peru, never developed a thriving commercial capitalism. And although Lisbon became the first great terminus of goods pouring in from the East, the Portuguese, like the Spanish, were so preoccupied with their vast overseas empire that they neglected the marketing opportunities in Europe itself.

These lucrative opportunities were first seized by the Dutch. Enterprising Dutch merchants purchased the goods in Lisbon, shipped them to the Netherlands, and sold them at a nice profit throughout northern and western Europe (see Figure 28.3). In the sixteenth century Antwerp, with its excellent harbor and location, was the leading commercial center in Europe. In the seventeenth century, following the sack of Antwerp in 1585 by Spanish troops, Amsterdam and London led the commercial world. The Dutch even took advantage of their newly won independence from Spain and of Portugal's temporary conquest by Spain in 1580 to seize the best part of Portugal's eastern empire, the area of present-day Indonesia.

Another phase of the commercial revolution was the advent of more bounteous supplies of commodities. Spices, coffee, tea, sugar, dyes, tropical fruits, fine textiles, tapestries, and precious stones, long known but in scarce supply and too expensive for all but the very rich, now came into Europe in ever-increasing volume. From the New World came potatoes, corn, tobacco, and chocolate (all of which had previously been unknown to Europe), new dyes and medicines, gold and silver.

The trade in slaves also swelled the rising stream of commerce. This early modern traffic in human beings was carried out in the later fifteenth century by the men of Portugal's Prince Henry the Navigator. It was later taken over by the Spaniards to supply labor for their empire in the New World. The native Indian populations were decimated by disease and the harsh conditions imposed by the Spaniards. Those who survived proved to be poor slave laborers. The Spaniards thus turned to tropical Africa to supply slaves for their mines and plantations. Thou-

FIGURE 28.3 Jan Gossaert, *Portrait of a Merchant*, ca. 1530 This portrayal of a banker by the Flemish painter Gossaert reflects the spirit of commercial capitalism. This serious, self-assured banker works with pen in hand and business letters in the background. His clothes and rings reveal controlled wealth. (National Gallery of Art, Washington, D.C.; Alisa Mellon Bruce Fund)

sands of Africans were bought from local chieftains and crowded into the holds of ships. Many of them died during the crossings, but the survivors were sold like cattle for a high price in the New World markets. So heavy was this immensely profitable traffic that the racial and social complex of New World society was drastically altered.

New types of business organizations were developed to accommodate the expanding volume of commerce. *Chartered companies* were organized to bypass the medieval guilds, which were unable or unwilling to meet the new demands. The most efficient type of chartered company proved to be the joint stock company. The members of a joint stock company pooled their resources, hired or elected their management, and shared in the profits in proportion to the amount of stock owned. In this way permanence was achieved, since the stock of any individual member could be bought or sold while the company remained intact.

Two of the earliest joint stock companies were the British East India Company, founded in 1600, and the Dutch East India Company, founded two years later. The British company was given not only a trading monopoly over British India but political control of the area as well. The Dutch company was given a monopoly over all Dutch trade east of the Cape of Good Hope. Annual profits of 300 percent were not uncommon for these giant companies. The annual profits of the Dutch East India Company never fell below 12 percent over a period of two hundred years.

Banking expanded in proportion to commerce. In the sixteenth century the Fugger family of Augsburg occupied the place in the financial world that the Medicis of Florence had held in the fifteenth. Jacob (the Rich) Fugger loaned Charles V the money with which he bribed his way to the emperorship of the Holy Roman Empire. In the seventeenth century the Bank of Amsterdam and the Bank of England were founded on a seminational basis. Both of these banks were really private joint stock companies, but in return for certain monopolies, such as the handling of government funds and the issuance of currency, they were obliged to accept a degree of government regulation. Banks of this size were able to mobilize sums of money and credit sufficient not only to launch and control large-scale commercial ventures but to influence government as well.

The commercialization of agriculture was of especially great significance. In some areas, particularly England, it sped up the process of combining smaller plots of land oriented toward subsistence farming into larger plots of land specializing in certain crops or herding for export. The commons—land available for the use of poor tenants—was taken away by large commercial landlords. Increasingly, small farmers were turned into wage laborers, either on the lands of commercial farmers or in the cities. The ranks of the landless poor swelled, while the productive commercial farmers gained wealth.

Industrial activity expanded in this period, particularly mining, shipbuilding, printing, armaments, and textiles, but guilds and governmental restrictions hindered the spread of capitalistic methods in these industries. The greatest expansion of capitalistic practices came with the growth of the domestic, or "putting-out" system. Merchants or entrepreneurs would purchase raw materials and distribute them to artisans, who would do the piecework in their cottages. Then the entrepreneur would collect the finished products, pay the cottagers for their work, and market the goods at a profit. While this system had certain advantages, it limited the volume of production. Until the coming of the machine and the factory system in the late eighteenth and early nineteenth centuries, therefore, large-scale capitalism was to remain commercial rather than industrial.

Part of this commercial revolution was fueled by the extraordinary rise in prices during the sixteenth century. This price inflation was probably related to the dramatic influx of gold and silver from the New World into Europe. However, historians now point to other causes for the price inflation that were perhaps more important. Population grew rapidly during the sixteenth century, particularly in western Europe and in urban areas. Many areas experienced a more than 50 percent increase. England's population almost doubled, while London's population grew by over 400 percent. All these people were competing for goods with each other and with governments. Tempted by the new gold and silver in their hands and pressured by greater expenses, governments spent more and went massively into debt; some governments responded by devaluing their currencies, making matters even worse. All these forces combined to push the demand for goods beyond the available supplies. Traders, merchants, and commercial farmers were in a particularly good position to benefit from the rising prices for commodities, which encouraged them to invest in commercial activities.

4. MERCANTILISM

Governments attempted to exercise some control over economic developments. From the beginning of the Age of Discovery in the late fifteenth century until the end of the eighteenth century, all the governments of western Europe except the Dutch Netherlands pursued a policy that has come to be called *mercantilism*. Mercantilism was, in essence, economic nationalism. While the monarchs of the new national states were consolidating their political power, they were also attempting to unify and centralize their national economies. Efforts were made to standardize national currencies and weights and measures. Internal commerce was encouraged by improving communications and reducing or removing internal tariff barriers. These efforts, however, were only partially successful. More attention was paid to the aggrandizement of each nation's economy at the expense of its neighbors. The basic assumption of mercantilist theory was that gold and silver are the true measure of national prosperity and power. Gold and silver, the mercantilists believed, in addition to being convenient media of exchange, could purchase anything—consumer goods, armies, navies, and administrative personnel. Spain's good luck in Mexico and Peru and its sixteenth-century brilliance and influence undoubtedly strengthened this view.

Spain alone was fortunate enough to come upon the gold and silver directly. All the other states had to devise more roundabout means of acquiring the precious metals. The favorite device was to seek a favorable balance of trade. The importation of expensive manufactured goods was discouraged by high tariffs, whereas the exportation of manufactures was encouraged, if need be, by subsidies. The reverse was true of inexpensive raw materials. The national aim was to buy low and sell high. Colonies were sought as sources of raw materials and markets for manufactured goods. But the colonies were not to be permitted to compete with the manufacturers and shippers of the mother country. Navies were advocated for the protection of the colonies. Sometimes the mercantilists closely regulated a nation's manufactures with a view to maintaining a reputation for high quality abroad. This phase of mercantilism reached its highest development in France in the seventeenth century under Louis XIV's economic minister, Jean-Baptiste Colbert. It was not until the latter part of the eighteenth century that the British economist Adam Smith and the French Physiocrats began to undermine faith in the validity of mercantilist principles and to prepare the way for an era of *laissez-faire*, or free, trade.

5. POLITICAL AND SOCIAL CONSEQUENCES

One immediate political consequence of the rise of commercial capitalism in western Europe was the strengthening of royal absolutism. The monarchs made use of the merchants and bankers in order to increase their own power at the expense of the rival nobility. More money was now available for the royal treasury and the royal army, even if it had to be borrowed. The middle classes, of course, shared the benefits of their alliance with the royal monarchs. Many members of the bourgeoisie were appointed to key positions in the royal administrations. With their increased wealth came increased social and political influence. The strongholds of their influence were the towns and cities whose growth paralleled the expansion of commerce. Western European society was becoming more urban—yet another change from the medieval pattern.

As the power of the national monarchs and the middle class grew, the position of the old nobility weakened. Their wealth and power were based on land, and now money was of growing importance. The inflation of prices further hurt the old nobility in relation to the moneyed bourgeoisie. Not overnight, but slowly and unevenly over decades and centuries, the old nobility of western Europe was losing social and political influence. Money was more easily acquired than blue blood or title. Feudal class lines were weakening, making possible a more fluid social structure and future political change.

Yet in some ways the nobility was not being replaced but was rather being infused with new, though suspect, blood. The successful, wealthy middle class generally dreamed of joining the privileged nobility rather than replacing it as a social class. They did just that by purchasing aristocratic titles, acquiring large estates, and marrying into the nobility. Moreover, various opportunities were grasped by bolder but less established members of the nobility. Many nobles of minor importance in Spain were able to become wealthy and powerful in Spanish lands overseas. In England and the Netherlands many members of the aristocracy openly engaged in business operations, thereby adjusting successfully to changing economic conditions.

The ascendance of the middle class and the changes within the nobility did not bring an immediate improvement in the condition of the lower classes. Indeed, the *nouveaux riches* often proved to be harsher taskmasters than the older aristocracy, who had stronger ties to medieval traditions of social responsibility. The urban wage earners were especially hard hit by the inflation. More were attracted to the cities of western Europe than could be employed, swelling the ranks of the unemployed and forcing many to return to the land as agrarian laborers—the landless poor. Sixteenth-century cities, while increasing in size and number, witnessed an even greater growth of poverty, begging, vagrancy, and crime (see Figure 28.4). As the demand for food overwhelmed the supply toward the end of the century, hunger and starvation spread.

In the countryside, landlords and those wealthier peasants who adapted well to the commercialization of agriculture profited. They were able to sell their surplus crops in cities at inflated prices. More broadly, those peasants in western Europe who had converted their feudal dues to money payments came out ahead, for those payments were fixed despite the rise in prices. But those who profited from the commercialization of agriculture and the rise in prices usually left in their wake large numbers of peasants worse off than before. Landlords who became distressed were likely to pass their hardships along to the peasantry. Peasants who prospered tended to purchase the land of the unfortunate, further dividing the peasantry into the relatively rich and the poor. The number of landless poor grew. Peasant revolts became common throughout Europe in the sixteenth century.

Finally, commercial capitalism probably diminished women's economic status. Most women still worked in traditional occupations—remaining in the countryside, assisting in their husbands' trades, or engaging in typical women's jobs such as domestic service, midwifery, and nursing. In the newer commercial, industrial, or professional occupations stimulated by commercial capitalism, women were usually either excluded or relegated to the lower-status and lower-paid jobs such as carding and spin-

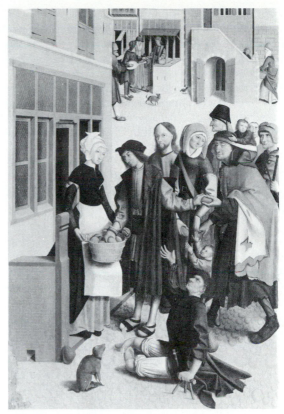

FIGURE 28.4 Cornelius Buys, *Feeding the Hungry* This early-sixteenth-century painting shows a domestic from a wealthy household distributing bread to the urban poor. Many in the growing cities had to rely on private charity such as this to survive. (Rijksmuseum-Stichting, Amsterdam)

ning wool. As work became increasingly defined as labor for paid wages, the domestic tasks performed by women lost their status as work. Ultimately some women would gain options for greater independence from the spreading commercial capitalism, but they had much to overcome.

6. EUROPEAN DOMINATION OF THE GLOBE

Thus we see that Europe's agricultural, collectivist, "fair price" economy was being transformed into a much more dynamic, urban, competitive, profit-motivated economy. The rise of commerce and capitalism not only changed the nature of European society but also provided much of the explosive force that enabled tiny Europe to dominate most of the rest of the world.

During Europe's Age of Discovery much of the Western Hemisphere, southern Asia, and the coastal areas of Africa were quickly brought under European domination. This amazing expansion continued until by the end of the nineteenth century practically the entire world was dominated by Europe and European civilization. Spanish, Portuguese, English, French, and Dutch colonists, followed later by the nationals of all the other European countries, flocked to the New World, taking their western Christian culture with them. The brilliant Aztec and Incan civilizations of Mexico and Peru were destroyed. The tribes of American Indians were exterminated, absorbed, or confined to reservations. The Moslem, Hindu, Buddhist, and Confucian civilizations of Asia and Africa were not so quickly or extensively destroyed, but they were clearly affected. The details of European expansion (and eventual contraction) constitute a considerable portion of the history of Western civilization since the sixteenth century.

SUGGESTED READING

The Age of Discovery

C. M. Cipolla, *Guns, Sails, and Empires: Technological Innovation and the Early Phases of European Expansion, 1400–1700* (1965). Stresses the connections between technology and successful expansion.

J. H. Parry, *The Age of Reconnaissance* (1963). A good survey of the causes and consequences of the early voyages.

G. Scammell, *The First Imperial Age: European Overseas Expansion, 1400–1715* (1989). A good recent introduction to the whole period.

V. B. Thompson, *The Making of the African Diaspora in the Americas, 1441–1900* (1988). Informative history covering the Atlantic slave trade and more.

E. R. Wolf, *Europe and the People Without History* (1982). Excellent, providing an alternative perspective on expansion.

Overseas Empires

Charles R. Boxer, *The Portuguese Seaborne Empire* (1970). An excellent study of the Portuguese Empire.

B. Keen and M. Wasserman, *A Short History of Latin America* (1984). A useful recent text.

L. McAlister, *Spain and Portugal in the New World 1492–1700* (1984). A broad survey of the Southern American empires.

K. Sale, *The Conquest of Paradise: Christopher Columbus and the Columbian Legacy* (1991). A radical reinterpretation with an ecological perspective.

Commercial Capitalism and Social Change

F. Braudel, *Civilization and Capitalism, 15th–18th Century,* trans. S. Reynolds, Vol. 2: *The Wheels of Commerce* (1982). Highly acclaimed and sophisticated.

R. Bridenthal, C. Koonz, and S. Stuard, eds., *Becoming Visible: Women in European History,* Second Edition (1987). Contains good material on this period.

C. M. Cipolla, *Before the Industrial Revolution: European Society and Economy* (1980). Particularly good on demographic and economic change.

Ralph Davis, *The Rise of the Atlantic Economies* (1973). Contains a good survey of sixteenth-century economic history.

H. Kamen, *European Society, 1500–1700* (1984). A general history of social structure and life.

P. Kriedte, *Peasants, Landlords and Merchant Capitalists* (1983). A Marxist interpretation of economic and social change.

A. K. Smith, *Creating a World Economy: Merchant Capital, Colonialism, and World Trade, 1400–1825* (1991). A recent analysis connecting expansion and commercial capitalism.

CHAPTER 29
The Reformation

FIGURE 29.1 Lucas Cranach the Younger, *Protestant Reformers,* 1543
This painting shows some of the crucial figures of the Protestant Reformation. In the center stands Elector John Frederick of Saxony, whose family protected Luther and other Protestant reformers. Luther is to the far left, his associate Philip Melanchthon is to the far right, and between Melanchthon and Frederick is Huldreich Zwingli, a leading reformer in Zurich. (Toledo Museum of Art, Toledo, Ohio; gift of Edward Drummond Libbey)

Sixteenth-century Europeans were intensely interested in religion. Although Renaissance culture, political developments, and commercial expansion were of great concern, the Church was still at the very center of their lives. The Reformation probably touched more people than any other development of the sixteenth century.

The Protestant Reformation, initiated in the second decade of the sixteenth century by Martin Luther, swept through much of northern Europe. Reform within the Roman Catholic church, often called the Catholic Reformation, followed and included both internal reforms initiated independently of the Protestant Reformation and reforms undertaken to counter Protestantism. In the end, the Reformation split western Europe into hostile religious camps, destroying the medieval unity of the western Christian Church.

1. BACKGROUND

In the late Middle Ages, discontent with the Church grew. Large numbers of people felt spiritually dissatisfied with what the Church offered. Greatly concerned with their own salvation and with leading a more pious life, people looked outside the formal institutions of the Church for guidance and examples. The growth of lay religious organizations such as the Brethren of the Common Life, the popularity of traveling preachers, the continuing search for mystical experiences, and the graphic pious art all testified to widespread and deep spiritual needs that were not being met through the traditional Church. The church hierarchy seemed to have departed too far from the spirit and practices of the apostles and early fathers.

People voiced other complaints about the Church, particularly about many abuses that arose during the fourteenth and fifteenth centuries, when the Church was torn by the Babylonian Captivity, the Great Schism, and the struggles between popes and councils (see pp. 327–332). The lack of education and the worldliness of the clergy, the sale of church offices and services (simony), the favoring of relatives for lucrative church offices (nepotism), and the holding by one man of more offices than he could ade-

quately serve (pluralism)—all were subjects of loud and growing complaint. Many of the higher clergy, even the popes, became preoccupied with their own secular concerns and Renaissance culture. Those who recognized a need to remedy these problems were unable to do enough until it was too late. Eventually the church hierarchy took steps to remedy abuses, but not until much of western Christendom had already left the Roman Catholic fold.

In addition to these spiritual dissatisfactions and complaints about abuses within the Church, other developments made certain areas of Europe fertile for the growth of reform movements. In Germany the Holy Roman Empire lacked the political unity that had helped national monarchs in Spain, England, and France gain control over their national clergy and access to the accumulated wealth of the Church. Local governments grew jealous of the immunity from civil laws and taxation enjoyed by the clergy. People resented the drain of wealth to the clergy and the institutions of the Church outside their territories, especially in Italy. These localities supported lay preachers, who gave numerous popular sermons throughout the year. In some of these same areas, particularly in university towns, Christian humanism took hold. Thanks to the printing press, criticisms of the Church by Erasmus, Ulrich von Hutten, and other humanists became widespread.

For the most part, this growing dissatisfaction with the Church was not revolutionary and did not yet challenge the fundamental doctrines of the Church. There was no widespread sense that the Church was about to be torn apart or that the only alternative was to make a complete break from it. On the other hand, the depth of the problems facing the Church is indicated by the radical reform movements occurring prior to the sixteenth century. As early as the fourteenth century reformers such as John Wycliffe in England and Jan Huss in Bohemia had voiced their protests against the Church. These protests turned into threatening movements of heretical dissent and social revolt, and authorities put them down only with great difficulty. When movements of dissent and revolt against the Church arose in the sixteenth century, they proved to be too powerful and well supported to be suppressed.

2. LUTHERANISM

The Protestant Reformation was composed of four major distinct but related movements—Lutheranism, Calvinism, Anglicanism, and Anabaptism. From these four main stems have sprung the hundreds of Protestant denominations that exist today. The Lutheran revolt was first in point of time.

Martin Luther (1483–1546) was the son of an ambitious miner living in central Germany (see Figure 29.2). At a boarding school run by the pietistic Brethren of the Common Life he, like his contemporary Erasmus, was introduced to a type of Christianity that emphasized simple piety rather than dogma and ritual. Later, at Erfurt University, he received a traditional liberal arts education. He was an excellent student. However, upon the completion of his undergraduate course and just as he was ready to begin study of the law, he suddenly renounced the world and entered an Augustinian monastery. This decision was no passing whim. As a child, Luther had been much concerned about the fate of his soul, and throughout his university days, his religious yearning had increased.

But the young friar found no satisfaction in the monastic life of the sixteenth-century Church. He scourged himself, donned beggar's garb, and went out among his former fellow students with sunken cheeks and gleaming, feverish eyes. It was not until, on the advice of a perceptive supervisor of his monastic order, he began to read the writings of St. Augustine and St. Paul that Brother Martin found the answer to his lifelong quest. On reading in Paul's Letter to the Romans (1:17) "the just shall live by faith," he concluded that here was the true means of salvation—not good works, sacraments, and rituals, but simple faith in Christ. Over a period of years he developed a theology based on the fundamental concept that righteousness is a gift of grace from God attained by faith in Christ's righteousness—justification by faith alone.

In the meantime Luther had become a member of the faculty of the newly founded University of Wittenberg in Saxony. For several years he taught philosophy and theology, quite unaware that his belief in salvation by faith alone was in fundamental conflict with the dogma of

FIGURE 29.2 Lucas Cranach the Elder, *Martin Luther*, 1521 Martin Luther often referred to himself as "a peasant, the son of a peasant." His father, though of peasant stock, was an ambitious miner who moved into the ranks of the bourgeoisie. A complex character, Luther had the brilliant mind and personal force of one of the great leaders and movers of history. (Culver Pictures)

his church. Students flocked from afar to listen to him.

In 1517 a friar named Johann Tetzel came into the vicinity of Wittenberg, selling indulgences on behalf of the pope and Prince Albert of Brandenberg. According to the doctrine of indulgences, which had arisen in the late Middle Ages, Christ and the saints, by their good works while on earth, had accumulated in heaven a treasury of excess merit that the pope could apply to the credit of penitent sinners. People came to believe that the purchase of indulgences would shorten or eliminate a stay in purgatory for them or their loved ones. By the opening of the sixteenth century the dispensing of this vague, extrasacramental means of grace had become hardly more than a money-making venture. Huge sums from all over Europe were taken to Rome for the construction of St. Peter's or for other costly papal projects.

On October 31, 1517, Martin Luther posted on the church door in Wittenberg his Ninety-Five Theses, or propositions, concerning the doctrine of indulgences, which he proposed to be debated publicly. It did not occur to him that this event would mark the beginning of an upheaval to subside only after nearly half of western Christendom had broken away from the Roman Catholic church. He was astonished and at first dismayed to find himself suddenly the national hero of all the various disgruntled elements throughout Germany. When, however, two years later in a public debate at Leipzig Luther finally realized that his position was hopelessly at odds with that of the Church, he lost no time in making the break clean. He published a series of pamphlets in which he violently denounced the pope and his organization and called on the German princes to seize the property of the Church and make themselves the heads of the Christian church in Germany.

A papal bull of excommunication (which Luther publicly burned) soon followed. A few months later Emperor Charles V called the troublesome monk to appear before the Diet of the Holy Roman Empire at Worms (1521). There Luther boldly refused to recant and was outlawed by the highest civil authority in Germany. Although Luther remained under this death sentence with a price on his head for the rest of his life, he was protected by his prince, the elector of Saxony, and German public opinion (see Figure 29.1).

By this time all Germany was in religious and social turmoil. Nearly everyone with a grievance of any kind was looking to Luther for leadership. Religious zealots, such as the Anabaptists, began preaching individualistic and more radical doctrines in his name, and he found it necessary to repudiate them. Taking a somewhat more conservative stand, he decided that only those features of the Roman Catholic church that were opposed to the Scriptures ought to be rejected. In the early stages of the conflict Erasmus and many other humanists thought they saw in Luther a kindred spirit, but this alliance was short-lived. Erasmus soon found Luther to be as dogmatic and uncompromising in matters of doctrine as the Roman Catholic theologians, if not more so. Moreover, Luther's rebellion against the Catholic church did not make him more tolerant of those outside the Christian fold. He favored deporting Jews and burning their synagogues.

Luther also found it necessary to break with a group of rebellious peasants in south Germany. The condition of the peasants was bad and growing worse. The landed aristocracy, themselves losing ground to the rising middle classes, were depriving their peasants of long-established manorial rights such as free use of meadows and woodlands. In 1524 widespread disturbances broke out in southwestern Germany. The next year the peasants published a list of demands, including an end to serfdom, elimination of certain taxes, confiscation of church property, and reform of the clergy. When these were refused, the peasants rebelled in the name of Luther, whom they believed to be against all oppressive authority. Luther was sympathetic with some of their demands, particularly the confiscation of church property and reform of the clergy, but otherwise he proved to be socially and politically too conservative. He rejected their attack on authority as too broad and pleaded with them to refrain from violence. When the rebellious peasants did not follow Luther's advice and continued their violent uprisings in Luther's name, he repudiated them and called on the civil authorities to suppress the revolt by force. The armed authorities did so with a vengeance.

Luther's message, and Protestant reform in general, appealed to many others for a variety of reasons. Governments were interested in breaking the papacy's control over churches—and the revenues controlled by those churches—in their territories. Princes and independent cities could thereby benefit politically and economically from reform. Merchants and artisans resented the freedom from taxation enjoyed by Catholic religious orders and the privileged position of priests. Lutheranism spread most rapidly in the cities and towns of Germany. Certain noblewomen in Catholic areas became powerful supporters of the reform movement. Leaders such as Marguerite of Navarre (1492–1549), sister of Francis I of

France, and Mary of Hungary (1505–1558), queen of Hungary and regent of the Netherlands, used their positions to protect both reformers and humanists.

Luther's new religion, as he eventually formulated it, made the Scriptures the sole authoritative source of Christian dogma. That all might have access to the Bible, he translated it into German.[1] He conceived of the Church as the whole body of believers in Christ, not the Roman Catholic church or any other specific organization. He abolished the hierarchy of pope, cardinals, and bishops, and he reduced the importance of the clergy in general, proclaiming the priesthood of all believers. The ritual of worship was made much simpler. Of the seven sacraments of the Roman Catholic church, Luther kept only the two he found mentioned as sacraments in the Bible: baptism and the Eucharist. He rejected the Roman Catholic doctrine known as transubstantiation (see p. 283). Luther interpreted the scriptural passages that refer to the Holy Eucharist, or Lord's Supper, to mean that during the administration of the sacrament Christ's body somehow enters into the bread and the wine, but the bread and wine remain—consubstantiation. He denied the Roman Catholic belief that a sacrifice is involved. He abolished monasteries and the celibacy of the clergy. Luther himself married a former nun. Although Luther refused to allow women formal roles as preachers or teachers, some women such as Elizabeth of Braunschweig and Argula von Grumbach played important roles in spreading Lutheranism. In general, he sharply distinguished religious matters from political and social matters, leaving the believer spiritually free and the secular rulers in charge of political and social matters.

The Emperor Charles V was greatly distressed by this religious revolution, which further divided his scattered and chaotic empire. Many German princes saw in Lutheranism a chance to increase their own political and financial independence from Charles V and the Italian papacy. Although determined to suppress the Protestants, Charles V was too busy with his wars against the French and the Turks to make much headway. Years of indecisive fighting between the Roman Catholics under Charles V and the Protestants ended in 1555 with the compromise Peace of Augsburg. Each of the more than three hundred German princes was left free to choose between Lutheranism and Roman Catholicism; his subjects were to abide by his choice. Luther himself died in 1546, just before the fighting began. By this time, Lutheranism had triumphed in the northern half of Germany and soon had spread, under the leadership of the Scandinavian monarchs, to Denmark, Norway, Sweden, and most of the Baltic provinces (now Latvia, Estonia, and Finland), which were then under Swedish control. In addition, Lutheranism heavily influenced all later Protestant movements, the most important of which was Calvinism.

3. CALVINISM

John Calvin shares with Luther the position of first importance in the founding of Protestant Christianity. Born in France in 1509, John Calvin was twenty-six years younger than Luther. He was the son of a lawyer who was secretary to the bishop of Noyon in Picardy. Young Calvin had a radiant personality that made for warm friendships. Long association with aristocratic friends probably accounted for his elegant manners. His father sent him first to the University of Paris for a thorough grounding in the humanities and theology and then to the best law schools in France. Upon finishing his legal training, he entered a humanistic literary career. Suddenly, at the age of twenty-four, after reading Luther's writings and having an intensely personal religious experience, Calvin converted to Protestant Christianity.

The zealous young reformer soon aroused the ire of both Roman Catholic authorities in France and the French government and was forced to flee for his life. Calvin then spent the next two years in hiding writing the first edition of *The Institutes of the Christian Religion*. Published in Basel, Switzerland, when Calvin was only twenty-six, this theological treatise was to become the most influential writing in the history of Protestantism. Its precise, forceful logic reveals

---

[1]Luther's translation was in such excellent German that it had great influence on the standardization of the modern literary German language.

the fine legal training and powerful intellect of the author. Its lucid, facile style influenced the formulation of modern literary French. It immediately made Calvin an important name in literary and theological circles.

Probably Calvin's most significant contribution to Christian theology is his sublime concept of the majesty of God. To the author of the *Institutes*, the Divine Creator is so majestic and awe inspiring, and human beings so insignificant by comparison, that salvation by election, or *predestination*, as it is more often called, seems to follow logically. According to Calvin, God in the beginning planned the whole universe to the end of time. For unfathomable reasons of his own, God selected those human beings who would be saved and those who would be damned. He planted in the minds of the elect a saving faith in Christ and an insatiable desire to live the Christian life and to bring about the Kingdom of God on earth. In no other way could one acquire this faith and this desire. Calvin based this doctrine on the Scriptures (particularly the writings of St. Paul), which he considered to be the sole authoritative source for Christian theology. St. Augustine, the most influential of the early Church Fathers, and Luther also believed in salvation by election, but neither they nor anyone else had ever spelled out the doctrine so precisely.

Shortly after the publication of the *Institutes*, Calvin went to Geneva. That city, like most of the rest of Switzerland, was in the throes of a religious and political revolt brought on partly by the influence of Luther and the native Swiss reformer Huldreich Zwingli (1484–1531). At first accepted by Protestant leaders, then rejected, Calvin finally returned in 1540 to try to make Geneva a model city of God on earth. Calvin, by sheer force of personality and intellect, soon rose to a position of great power in the city. He brought the town council, which was remarkably democratic and representative for the sixteenth century, under the dominance of a consistory composed of Protestant pastors and laity. Under Calvin's leadership the town council and the consistory set up a strict system of blue laws. Churchgoing was compulsory. Dancing, card-playing, theatergoing, drinking, gambling, and swearing—all were forbidden. Enforcement was vigorous and penalties severe, even for the six-

teenth century. The most famous penalty was the burning of Michael Servetus, an eccentric amateur scientist and theologian whom the Roman Catholic church had already condemned to death for heresy.[2] Servetus escaped his Catholic persecutors in Lyon and went to Geneva. When he arrived, he was seized, tried, convicted, and burned at the stake.

Calvinist ritual was even simpler than that of the Lutherans. The worship service consisted of preaching, praying, and psalm singing. Like Luther, Calvin retained only two of the seven sacraments—baptism and the Holy Eucharist, or Lord's Supper. But to Calvin, Christ was present only in spirit in the bread and wine and only for the elect. Calvin patterned his system of church government after that of the very earliest church as described in the Bible (Acts of the Apostles). The local churches were governed by laymen called *elders* who were elected by the congregations. A measure of unity in faith and practices was maintained by means of a hierarchy of representative assemblies.

During the second half of the sixteenth century it was Calvinism rather than Lutheranism that became the most dynamic force in Protestantism. Protestant Christians came from many countries to sit at the feet of Calvin and to study at the University of Geneva, which he founded. John Knox, who came from Scotland to study under Calvin, called the Genevan theocracy "the most perfect school of life that was ever on earth since the days of the apostles." Calvinists combined vigorous evangelical appeals with a systematic theology and a well-organized church. The Calvinist ethic of "the calling" to one's station on earth, no matter what it was, dignified striving and hard work.

Calvinism became dominant in most of Switzerland (Swiss Reformed), the Dutch Netherlands (Dutch Reformed), Scotland (Presbyterian), and the German Palatinate. It also had a strong minority following in England (the Puritans) and a smaller but vigorous following in France (the Huguenots), Bohemia, Hungary, and Poland. The Calvinists played an important part

---

[2]The most serious of Servetus' heretical views were his denial of the Trinity, which cast doubt on the divinity of Christ, and his rejection of childhood baptism.

in the founding of the United States, particularly the Puritans in New England, the Dutch Reformed in New York, and the Scotch-Irish Presbyterians along the frontiers of all the original states. Such well-known denominations in present-day America as the Congregationalists, the Presbyterians, and the Baptists are Calvinist in origin.

4. ANGLICANISM

The foundations of the Reformation in England had been developing for many years before it was actually initiated by the actions of King Henry VIII (1509–1547). Lollardy, a movement of religious and social dissent stretching back over a hundred years, persisted as an underground movement into the sixteenth century. Humanism and anticlerical sentiments were gaining in strength. In 1525 William Tyndale (1494–1536), influenced by Luther, started printing an English translation of the Bible. However, the occasion of the beginning of the Reformation in England was the desire of Henry VIII for a new wife and a male heir. Catherine of Aragon, to whom he had been married for eighteen years, had given him only a daughter, Mary. When it became apparent that Catherine would have no more children, Henry decided to ask the pope to annul the marriage. The pope, however, was in no position to grant the annulment. Catherine was the aunt of Emperor Charles V, whose troops were at that very moment in control of the city of Rome. When Henry finally realized the pope was not going to accommodate him, he took matters into his own hands. At his bidding a subservient Parliament passed the Act of Supremacy (1534), making the king of England, not the pope, head of the Church in England. Later the monasteries, strongholds of papal influence, were dissolved and their holdings confiscated by the Crown. Meanwhile, Thomas Cranmer, whom Henry made archbishop of Canterbury, had arranged the annulment, and Henry had married Anne Boleyn. (He was to marry six times in all.) Henry was, of course, excommunicated by the pope.

But Henry VIII was no Protestant. In the days before the annulment controversy the pope had given him the title "Defender of the Faith" for his anti-Lutheran writings. Now he had Parliament pass the Six Articles reaffirming the Catholic position on all controversial doctrinal points except that of papal supremacy. Protestants, on the one hand, and Roman Catholics who refused to acknowledge the headship of Henry VIII in place of the pope were persecuted with equal severity.

It was during the reign of Henry VIII's young son, Edward VI (1547–1553), that the Anglican church first became Protestant. Archbishop Cranmer drew up a Book of Common Prayer and Forty-two Articles of Faith that were definitely Calvinist in flavor. Edward VI was succeeded by his elder sister, Mary (1553–1558), who was the daughter of Catherine of Aragon and a devout Roman Catholic. Mary's ambition was to restore her kingdom to the Roman Catholic fold. Her first step was to marry her cousin, Philip II of Spain, the most powerful champion of resurgent Roman Catholicism in all Europe. Next she asked and received papal forgiveness for her wayward people. Finally, "Bloody Mary" burned at the stake some three hundred Protestants, including Archbishop Cranmer. But Mary's marriage to a man soon to be king of Spain, England's most dangerous rival, and her persecutions were extremely unpopular in England; in the long run her policies hurt rather than helped the Roman Catholic cause there.

Elizabeth I (1558–1603), the Protestant daughter of Anne Boleyn, followed Mary on the English throne. This high-spirited, cynical, and politically minded queen found theology tiresome. Her chief interest was to find a satisfactory compromise that would unify her people. During the course of her long reign the Anglican church became definitely, but conservatively, Protestant. Cranmer's Book of Common Prayer was readopted with slight alterations. The Forty-two Articles were changed to the Thirty-nine. Some of the more controversial doctrinal points that seemed to prevent the various Protestant sects from uniting were reworded. Although celibacy of the clergy was abandoned, the episcopal system (government of the church by bishops) was retained. A rather elaborate ritual was adopted. Two of the sacraments, baptism and the Eucharist, were retained.

Although the great majority of the English people appeared to have accepted Elizabeth's compromise settlement, two groups remained dissatisfied. One was an extreme Calvinist element that sought to "purify" the Anglican church of all remaining traces of Roman Catholicism. These Puritans were to increase in strength until, under Oliver Cromwell's leadership in the next century, they gained temporary control of the country. The Roman Catholic minority, on the other hand, lost steadily in numbers. The support that some Roman Catholics gave to Philip II's attempt to conquer England and to the effort of Mary, Queen of Scots (a Roman Catholic), to overthrow Elizabeth (see Chapter 30) tainted all of them with the suspicion of treason and played into Elizabeth's hands. By the end of her reign, England was one of the Protestant countries of Europe.

5. THE ANABAPTISTS

Some reformers believed that Luther, Calvin, and the Anglican leaders had not gone far enough. They would break more sharply with all the existing institutions of the early sixteenth century—political, economic, and social as well as religious. Hence the term *radical* is often applied to them. Since these "radicals" were highly individualistic in their approach to religion, it is difficult to generalize about the many sects with their widely differing views and points of emphasis.

Generally, these sects tended to emphasize the evilness of the world, the mystical communion with God, the Second Coming of Christ, and the righteousness of the poor in their struggle against the rich. In some cases, religious reform became a means of social reform—a revolt of the poor against the rich.

These sects commonly rejected the doctrine of infant baptism. The true Christian, they believed, was one who was "born again" and baptized as an adult according to Scripture. Those who had been baptized as infants must be rebaptized. Anabaptism means *re*baptism. The Anabaptists believed that the true church of Christ on earth is a gathered church composed only of born-again Christians. The Anabaptists attempted to live lives of uncompromising holiness as dictated by the Bible or by the Holy Spirit speaking directly to each individual. These sects refused to recognize or participate in civil government, take oaths of allegiance, recognize titles, or serve in armed forces. Some practiced a shared economy. Most of them were poor. They were feared and persecuted by Roman Catholics, Lutherans, Calvinists, Anglicans, and secular leaders alike.

A few of the early Anabaptist leaders were violent activists, such as Thomas Müntzer, who inflamed the peasant rebels of southwest Germany, and John of Leyden, who set up a violent dictatorship in Münster in northwest Germany. This bizarre "heavenly Jerusalem" held out for more than a year against besieging Lutheran and Roman Catholic armies. The leaders were then tortured to death and their bodies hung in iron baskets from a church tower as a warning to radical dissenters. But the great majority of the Anabaptist leaders were pious and gentle—in fact, pacifists. Conrad Grebel, the first prominent Anabaptist leader, was a humanist from an upper-class family of Zurich, Switzerland. Probably the most successful and influential of all the Anabaptist leaders was the convert Menno Simons, a gentle former Roman Catholic priest from the Dutch Netherlands. His followers, the Mennonites, spread throughout much of western Europe and later the United States. Also in the Anabaptist tradition was the Society of Friends, commonly known as Quakers. Founded by George Fox in England in the mid–seventeenth century, this pietistic and pacifistic sect has spread to many parts of the world.

6. CATHOLIC REFORM

The rise of Protestantism touched off an aggressive Catholic reform movement during the 1530s and 1540s, but even before this movement some efforts to revitalize Roman Catholicism had already taken place. In Spain, around the turn of the sixteenth century, Cardinal Ximenes had forestalled a possible protest movement by enforcing strict discipline on the clergy and waging bitter warfare against heresy. During the first few decades of the sixteenth century several religious orders such as the Theatines, the Capuchins, the Barnabites, and the Ursulines were founded and dedicated themselves to clerical reform and education within the Catholic church. Even before the revolt of Luther and Calvin, Catholic leaders from several countries pushed for the calling of a general council to authoritatively enact badly needed reforms. However, the secular interests of the Renaissance popes and the popes' fears that an assertive reform council might again challenge the absolute authority of the papacy prevented a coordinated European-wide reform. The last council to meet before the Reformation, the Fifth Lateran Council (1513–1517), bowed to the pope's control and enacted no major reforms.

After the 1520s and 1530s, with area after area becoming Protestant, countermeasures of a rather drastic nature became imperative. There were two schools of thought concerning the proper course of action. One, led by the liberal Cardinal Contarini of Venice, advocated compromise and conciliation. Contarini eventually went so far as to meet with Melanchthon, a close friend of Luther and an important figure in the Lutheran revolt, in earnest quest of an acceptable compromise. They were unsuccessful; the two religions appeared to be incompatible. The other school of thought was led by the conservative Cardinal Caraffa of Naples. Caraffa believed that many corrupt practices in the Church needed to be reformed but that no compromise whatever should be made in the dogma. He believed that the Protestants were heretics and could reunite with the Roman Catholic church only by recanting and submitting to the pope. This is the school of thought that triumphed, and Caraffa became Pope Paul IV. The upshot of this line of thinking was the calling of a Church council at Trent, an imperial city in northern Italy.

The Council of Trent

The Council of Trent, which was in session off and on for eighteen years from 1545 to 1563, was probably the most important council in the history of the Roman Catholic church. The popes skillfully controlled its membership and voting procedure. The ultimate decisions of the council were in two categories: dogmatic and reformatory. In matters of faith or dogma, all the traditional doctrines of the Church were reaffirmed and redefined, especially controversial ones such as the sacraments, transubstantiation, auricular confession, celibacy of the clergy, monasticism, purgatory, invocation of the saints, veneration of relics, and indulgences. The dogmatic canons

and decrees of the council concluded: "Anathema to [accursed be] all heretics! Anathema! Anathema! Anathema!" The council also took stern measures to stop corrupt practices. Simony, nepotism, pluralism, and immorality and ignorance among the clergy were condemned. Schools for the education of the clergy were advocated. Bishops were admonished to exercise closer supervision and discipline over the lower clergy. To implement its canons and decrees, the council endorsed the Inquisition, which had recently been set up in Rome to combat heresy, and inaugurated the Index of Forbidden Books to prevent the reading of heretical literature except by authorized persons. Both instruments were placed under papal control and supervision.

Thus the Roman Catholic church at last spoke out, selected its weapons, and girded itself for more effective battle against the Protestants. At its service was the militant new Society of Jesus.

The Society of Jesus

The founder of the Society of Jesus, Ignatius Loyola (1491–1556), was a member of the Spanish lesser nobility, and until early middle life he was an obscure soldier (see Figure 29.3). In a battle with the French his leg was crushed by a cannonball. During the months of agony and convalescence Loyola read lives of the Christian saints and underwent a deep spiritual conversion. He determined to devote his tremendous energies and latent talents to the service of the Roman Catholic church—to become a soldier of Christ, the Virgin Mary, and the pope. He set off for the University of Paris to begin his education. Loyola was, however, neither a scholar nor a theologian but a man of action. He soon began to attract a band of followers, with whom he organized the Society of Jesus.

The Jesuit order, as the Society of Jesus was commonly known, was founded along military lines. Absolute and unquestioning obedience was the first requirement. Loyola admonished his followers, ". . . if she [the Church] shall have defined anything to be black which to our eyes appears to be white, we ought in like manner to pronounce it to be black." Applicants for membership were carefully selected and trained. For the spiritual guidance and inspiration of the

WHERE HISTORIANS DISAGREE

The Meaning of the Reformation

Most historians agree that the Reformation was of major significance, but when they address the more difficult questions of its exact causes and nature, agreement ends.

Before the twentieth century, historians often confused their own religious preferences with historical analysis, becoming more interested in assigning blame or praise. Protestant scholars focused on the corruption of the Roman Catholic church, the heroic piety of Protestant figures, and the positive force of the Protestant Reformation in the modern world. Catholic scholars contended just the opposite, arguing that there had been no crying need for doctrinal reform, that the Protestant leaders were self-centered and ignorant theologians, and that the Protestant Reformation was to blame for the flood of secularization in the West.

Most twentieth-century historians look at the Reformation in more complex terms. Many favor sophisticated religious and cultural interpretations of the Reformation. These historians argue that the Reformation grew out of deep and widespread spiritual longing and dissatisfaction with the practices of the Catholic church. They emphasize that whatever other qualities Protestant leaders may have had, they were deeply religious people whose reforming doctrines and practices appealed to the spiritual and cultural needs of many. These historians also stress the spiritual concerns revealed in Catholic reform. To these historians, the sixteenth century was an age of religious reform.

Other historians think of the Protestant Reformation in primarily political terms. They stress that the time was ripe for the Reformation not only because of religious tensions but also because secular authorities favored it. They emphasize that vast numbers of people became Protestant or remained Catholic (or reconverted) because their political leaders demanded it. They view the various religious movements of the sixteenth century as associated with nationalism. They believe it to be significant that the Protestant Reformation began in Germany, where there was no strong central government and where Luther strongly and openly appealed to German nationalism against Rome. By contrast, the strong rulers of France and Spain were able to extract such concessions from the pope as to create what amounted to a Gallican church and Spanish Catholic church, while successfully withstanding the Protestant challenge. The various Calvinistic churches were generally set up along national lines, such as the Swiss, Dutch, German, and Scottish Reformed churches. And of course the Anglican church was a national church.

Still other historians interpret the Reformation from an economic perspective. They point out the hunger for the rich lands held by the Roman Catholic church, the resentment over the tax exemption of these lands and the draining away of money to Rome, and the opposition of the commercial class to the Church's ban on usury. Related to these points is the "Weber thesis." Max Weber and other scholars have argued that the hard work and asceticism which Calvinism stressed fit well with the emerging spirit of capitalism, which emphasized hard work, saving, and reinvestment. Thus Calvinism appealed particularly to people in commercial centers in Holland, England, Switzerland, and New England. From this perspective, then, Protestantism helped solve various economic problems of the era.

The long history and depth of these controversies over the meaning of the Reformation reveal how difficult the evaluation of major religious change can be.

FIGURE 29.3 Ignatius Loyola (1491–1556) Ignatius Loyola, by founding the Society of Jesus (the Jesuits), played a key role in the Catholic Reformation. Although not as scholarly as Luther or Calvin, he was a superb organizer and leader. (Culver Pictures)

priests, the Jesuits were nearly always the best trained, the most popular, and the most influential. As teachers, they were usually more highly educated, devoted, and attractive than their competitors. They have always been keenly aware of the power of education, especially for the very young. "Give me the child, and I care not who has the man." The Jesuits soon gained control of education in most Roman Catholic countries.

These dedicated soldiers of Christ also made the best missionaries. In North and South America the dauntless Jesuits went among the Indians and converted most of them to Roman Catholic Christianity. In the Far East, Francis Xavier, second only to Loyola himself in Jesuit history, converted tens of thousands.

Not the least important of Jesuit activities was that of gaining the confidence of kings, princes, and other political personages, and thereby influencing state policy. This militantly zealous order was a powerful stimulant to the wavering cause of Roman Catholicism. In Italy, Spain, Portugal, and Ireland, where Protestantism had only a weak foothold, the Jesuits helped stamp it out altogether. In France and Belgium they helped to turn the tide against the Protestants. In southern Germany, Poland, and the Austrian Hapsburg lands, all of which seemed to be on the verge of going Protestant, the Jesuits reversed the trend and helped make those lands strongholds of Roman Catholicism.

members of the Society, Loyola wrote the *Spiritual Exercises*. The *Exercises* guide the member through a solid month of concentrated meditation, a week each on the horrors of sin, the life of Christ to Palm Sunday, his suffering and crucifixion, and his resurrection and ascension. This remarkable work has proved to be a powerful tool for training and rededication. Jesuits served as priests, teachers, medics, diplomats, or in almost any other capacity suitable to their talents and training—but always with the interests of the Catholic church in mind. After years of service a few of the most outstanding were admitted to the highest circle of officers, who, under a general elected for life and residing in Rome, governed the order.

Loyola's high standards, far from deterring applicants, served as both a challenge and an attraction. The Society of Jesus grew rapidly. As

7. WOMEN AND THE REFORMATION

As with the Renaissance, scholars question whether the Reformation benefited women socially or in any aspect of public life. Although Luther may have encouraged greater sharing within the household—the ideal of the companionate marriage—and acceptance of sexuality within the marriage, it is difficult to argue that his reforming ideas greatly improved the condition of women. In his eyes, women were expected to be satisfied to be pious wives, mothers, and household managers, remaining clearly under the authority of their husbands. Despite some advocacy of mutual cooperation within the

FIGURE 29.4 Angela Merici (1474–1540) Catholic reform was supported by the growth of women's organizations such as the Ursulines. Here the founder of the Ursulines, Angela Merici (1474–1540), is shown on her deathbed. (Ursuline Provincialate)

marriage, Calvin also rejected female independence and placed the husband at the head of the household.

The Protestant abolition of monasteries included women's religious orders, thereby eliminating one of the few occupational outlets available to sixteenth-century women. Protestantism offered no comparable alternative for the thousands of women who left the often socially prestigious Catholic convents. Only well into the seventeenth century and in certain Protestant sects such as the Quakers did women start to play a public role as preachers.

Catholic reform also resulted in few if any significant changes for women. Only the growth of pious Catholic women's organizations, such as the Ursulines (see Figure 29.4), who were de-voted to teaching girls, and the Carmelites, under the leadership of the influential Saint Teresa of Avila (1515–1582), gave women some opportunity to play a more active role within the Church.

If the direct effect of the Reformation on women is uncertain, it is clear that women during that era suffered from an explosion of witch-hunts and prosecutions for infanticide. The belief in witchcraft dated back for centuries, but it was not until the sixteenth century that large numbers of women were actually prosecuted and put to death on charges of witchcraft. Protestants and Catholics alike charged women, usually older, lower-class women living in rural villages, with the heretical crime of making a pact with the devil and causing harm to their enemies. Tens of thousands of women were tried for witchcraft, and perhaps a third of them were put to death.

Concurrent with these witchcraft hunts of the Reformation era came a flood of prosecutions for infanticide. While authorities prosecuted far fewer women for infanticide than for witchcraft, those prosecuted were more likely to be found guilty and executed. Usually the objects of these prosecutions were poor, unmarried younger women living in cities.

How much the Reformation itself had to do with this wave of lethal prosecutions of women is unknown. Perhaps more important were the growing efforts by the state to regulate behavior, the environment of fear during this period, and the general suspicion of women outside the norm in this male-dominated society. In any case, during the sixteenth and seventeenth centuries both Catholic and Protestant authorities, whether religious or secular, found sufficient theological and civil justifications to carry out these prosecutions that cost so many women their lives.

8. SUMMARY

Protestantism grew out of a widespread desire for greater spiritual satisfaction and correction of abuses within the western Christian Church. Political and economic factors soon came into play to broaden the appeal and strength of the Protestant Reformation. Towns, princes, and kings saw the advantages of acquiring control over religious institutions and the tremendous wealth

FIGURE 29.5 Adriaen van de Velde, *Fishing for Souls,* 1614 This allegory of the religious struggle during the Reformation shows Protestants on the left and Catholics on the right competing for souls in the waters that divide western Christendom. Above the fray, God's rainbow unites them all. (Rijksmuseum-Stichting, Amsterdam)

controlled by these institutions. This wealth and control served to strengthen their own political power. Since religious affiliation was viewed as integral to political and social order, conversion of political leaders eventually meant conversion of most of their people.

Initially Lutheranism was the dominant Protestant denomination, but in the second half of the century Calvinism became the most dynamic. By the end of the third quarter of the sixteenth century, Protestantism had triumphed in the northern half of the Germanies, in Scandinavia, in most of the Baltic provinces, in most of Switzerland, in the Dutch Netherlands, in Scotland, and in England. In addition, it had gained a strong minority following in France, Poland, Bohemia, and Hungary.

No matter how much the various Protestant denominations disagreed among themselves, most shared beliefs that put them at odds with the Roman Catholic church. They believed in justification by faith alone. They believed that the Roman Catholic church had departed so far from

the spirit and practices of the apostles and early Fathers that it could no longer be considered God's appointed custodian of the Christian religion. Scripture alone, not the decisions and traditions of the Roman Catholic church, was their sole authoritative source for Christian dogma. They emphasized the direct relationship between human beings and God. They thought of the Church as a priesthood of all believers. They rejected papal supremacy, the divine sanction of the Roman Catholic church, the celibacy and indelible character of the priesthood, monasticism, and such other characteristic Roman Catholic doctrines as purgatory, transubstantiation, invocation of saints, and veneration of relics.

The Roman Catholic church was not impotent in the face of these challenges. It had already initiated some internal reform efforts of its own prior to the outbreak of Protestantism, and those reform efforts grew throughout the sixteenth century. It also initiated a broad-based counter-Reformation to strengthen its hold in areas that remained Roman Catholic and to try to regain areas lost to Protestants. Despite some successes, however, it was never able to reconquer or reconvert the territories in which Protestants had gained a clear majority (see Figure 29.5, p. 393).

The Reformation definitively split western Christendom into hostile religious camps, and this religious hostility would spill over into decades of bloody wars and revolts.

SUGGESTED READING

General

De Lamar Jensen, *Reformation Europe, Age of Reform and Revolution* (1981). A very good work.

H. Koenigsberger and G. Mosse, *Europe in the Sixteenth Century* (1987). A broad survey with bibliography.

R. L. de Molen, *Leaders of the Reformation* (1984). Portraits of key figures.

S. Ozment, *The Age of Reform, 1250–1550* (1980). A broad, respected interpretation.

L. W. Spitz, *The Protestant Reformation* (1985). A solid, recent survey.

Lutheranism

E. Erikson, *Young Man Luther: A Study in Psychoanalysis and History* (1962). A highly important and influential interpretation.

H. G. Haile, *Luther: An Experiment in Biography* (1980). A modern treatment.

R. W. Scribner, *The German Reformation* (1986). A balanced treatment of Luther and the German Reformation.

Calvinism

W. Bousma, *John Calvin: A Biography* (1987). Calvin in his historical context.

W. E. Monter, *Calvin's Geneva* (1967). A fine study of the Reformation in Geneva.

Anglicanism

A. G. Dickens, *The English Reformation* (1974). The best survey.

J. J. Scarisbrick, *The Reformation and the English People* (1985). A short survey.

The Anabaptists

C. Clasen, *Anabaptism, A Social History, 1525–1618* (1972). Connects religious and social history.

M. Mullett, *Radical Religious Movements in Early Modern Europe* (1980). An excellent survey.

Catholic Reform

N. Davidson, *The Counter-Reformation* (1987). A solid, brief survey.

J. Delumeau, *Catholicism Between Luther and Voltaire* (1977). A respected interpretation of Catholic reform.

J. C. Olin, *The Autobiography of St. Ignatius Loyola* (1974). The life and ideas of the founder of the Jesuits.

Women and the Reformation

M. J. Boxer and J. H. Quataert, eds., *Connecting Spheres: Women in the Western World, 1500 to the Present* (1987). Includes useful material on the period.

R. Bridenthal, C. Koonz, and S. Stuard, eds., *Becoming Visible: Women in European History, Second Edition* (1987). Includes a good chapter on this period.

B. Levack, *The Witch-Hunt in Early Modern Europe* (1987). An excellent analysis with focus on causes.

CHAPTER 30
Politics and the Wars of Religion

FIGURE 30.1 François Dubois, *St. Bartholomew's Day Massacre* This painting of the St. Bartholomew's Day Massacre in 1572 by François Dubois, a contemporary Protestant painter, shows soldiers indiscriminately killing Huguenots in Paris. (Musée Cantonal des Beaux-Arts, Lausanne)

The Peace of Augsburg in 1555 brought an end to war between Catholics and Lutherans in Germany, and the Treaty of Cateau-Cambrésis in 1559 ended the Hapsburg-Valois wars. But these halts to long conflicts did not bring an end to the bloodshed. On the contrary, the period between 1560 and 1648 witnessed an outbreak of revolts, massacres, civil wars, and international wars that was unprecedented. While people in several areas suffered, the most intense and extended fighting occurred within the boundaries of the Holy Roman Empire. By the end of the Thirty Years' War in 1648, probably a third of the German population had died from the war.

Certainly religious differences were involved in these conflicts and accounted for the ferocity of the struggles (see Map 30.1). But politics and greed were also intertwined, with leaders vying for political gain and mercenaries thirsty for loot. Both crossed religious lines to make war for their own purposes.

1. THE CRUSADE OF CATHOLIC SPAIN

Emperor Charles V had bequeathed the greater part of his vast empire to his son Philip II (1556–1598) (see Figure 30.2). In addition to Spain, Philip's inheritance included the Netherlands, Franche-Comté, Milan, the Kingdom of Naples, Sardinia, and the Spanish Empire overseas. In 1580 Philip conquered Portugal in the name of his Portuguese mother and became master (at least in name) of Portugal's huge eastern empire.

Philip II, unlike his father, was a native Spaniard. He utilized the gold and silver flowing in a steady stream from the New World and the lucrative commerce of the East Indies and the busy Netherlands in the interests of Spain. Ignoring the Cortes and the local rights of Aragon and tending personally to the myriad details of government, the meticulous and stubborn Philip brought Spain under his sway to an extent that Ferdinand and Isabella and Charles V had never been able to do. With the best army in Europe and the will to use it, there is little wonder that the king of Spain was the most feared man in western Christendom.

The Roman Catholic church was of great importance to Philip II. He conceived it to be his chief mission in life to use the great wealth and power of Spain to restore the dominion of the Roman Catholic church over all of western Christendom. In the Netherlands, in England, and in France, Philip II threw the might of Spain on the side of the Roman Catholics in their counteroffensive against the Protestants.

Revolt in the Netherlands

Unlike his father, Philip II was considered by the Netherlanders to be an unsympathetic foreigner who taxed their prosperous commerce and industry for the benefit of Spain. The absolutist monarch and his Spanish administrators also overrode the traditional political privileges of the nobles and the cities in the Netherlands. Nonetheless, religion was the foremost cause of dissension. By the mid–sixteenth century, nearly half the people in the Netherlands had become Protestant. Most were Calvinists, but a considerable number were Anabaptists. Philip II, who would tolerate no heresy in his empire, took stern measures to stamp out Protestantism. The Inquisition was used to enforce the laws against heresy. In 1566, bands of outraged Protestants began to deface Roman Catholic churches. Philip thereupon dispatched Spanish troops under the duke of Alva to reduce the Netherlands to submission. A six-year reign of terror followed, during which thousands were put to death.

Far from being cowed, however, the Netherlanders resisted fiercely. They found a brilliant leader in William of Orange, or William the Silent, as he came to be known. They took to the sea, playing havoc with Spanish commerce and communications. When, in 1580, Philip conquered and annexed Portugal, the hardy Dutch "Sea Beggars" seized the richest parts of the Portuguese Empire in the East Indies. The Spanish infantry quickly overran the ten southern (Belgian) provinces, but against the seven northern (Dutch) provinces, made up largely of islands and peninsulas and skillfully defended by the Dutch fleet, Spain's armies could make little headway. Most of the Protestants soon fled north from the Spanish-occupied southern provinces. Likewise, most of the Roman Catholics fled south from the Protestant-dominated north. In 1579 the ten Roman Catholic southern provinces (now Belgium), fearful of the growing power of the

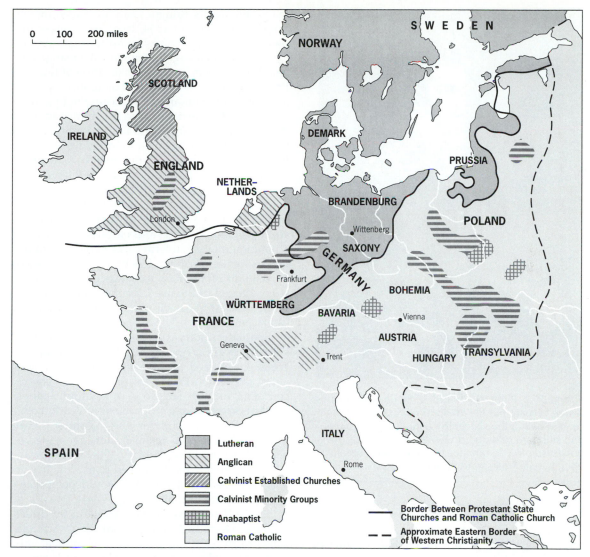

Map 30.1 RELIGIOUS MAP OF EUROPE, CA. 1560 This map indicates the religious divisions in Europe during the Reformation. In the turmoil between 1560 and 1648, most of those areas that had already turned Lutheran or had established Calvinist churches would remain Protestant. Those areas in which Protestant groups were in the minority would be subject to pressures and change.

Protestant northern provinces (which also spoke a different language), submitted to the Spanish yoke. The seven northern provinces, however, banded together in the Union of Utrecht and continued the struggle for independence. When in 1584 William the Silent was assassinated by a hireling of Philip II, other able leaders arose to take his place. Finally in 1609, eleven years after Philip's own death, Spain agreed to a twelve-year truce, and in 1648 Spain recognized the complete independence of the Dutch Netherlands, as the seven northern provinces are commonly called. In the seventeenth century the little Dutch republic led the world in commerce, bank-

FIGURE 30.2 Philip II Philip II of Spain was the most feared monarch in the Western world during the second half of the sixteenth century. A meticulous and stubborn ruler, he struggled to extend his own power and the dominance of the Roman Catholic church over Protestantism. (Alinari/Scala/Art Resource)

ing, and painting and was second to none in science and philosophy.

Thus Philip II's crusade in the Netherlands was only partly successful. He saved the southern provinces for Spain for another century, and for the Roman Catholic church, but the Dutch provinces, the richest in his empire, were lost both to Spain and to the Church.

Struggles with England

Most grandiose of all Philip II's crusading efforts was his attempt to restore wayward England to the Roman Catholic fold. His first move was to marry England's Roman Catholic queen, Mary Tudor. They wed in 1554, two years before his own rule over the Spanish Empire began. However, Mary's marriage to the king of a feared and hated rival power and her persecution of English Protestants only increased her own unpopularity and that of the Roman Catholic cause in England. Moreover, the marriage failed to produce an heir. When Mary died in 1558, Philip sought to continue his influence in England by trying to marry her successor, Elizabeth. But Elizabeth, a Protestant and high-spirited English patriot, refused.

Elizabeth proved to be one of England's ablest monarchs (see Figure 30.3). In style and policy, she was a *politique*—a ruler who avoided strong religious stands and emphasized moderation, pragmatism, tolerance, or avoidance in religious matters. For her, like other *politiques* such as William of Orange, religious concerns were subordinated to the need for political unity. She guided the Anglican church to a moderate Protestant position.

Spain's military successes led Elizabeth to support Spain's opponents. In the 1570s and 1580s she signed an alliance with France and aided the Dutch Protestant rebels. She also encouraged English sea dogs to plunder Spain's treasure ships sailing from its New World colonies—indeed, to plunder the colonies themselves. When in 1587 Spanish plots against Elizabeth clearly implicated Mary, Queen of Scots (a Catholic), Elizabeth was forced to execute her. It was then clear that England would not peacefully rejoin the Catholic fold.

Philip II tried to conquer England by direct military action. In 1588 his "Invincible" Armada sailed forth—130 ships, many of them great galleons. Aboard was a formidable Spanish army. The Armada was to go first to the Netherlands and pick up additional soldiers. In the English Channel it met the somewhat larger English fleet, composed mostly of smaller but swifter and more heavily armed ships. The Spaniards fought well until finally their formation was broken by English fire ships sent into their midst. Once scattered, the Spanish ships were no match for the English fleet. Storms played a major role in the loss of Spanish ships, and only about half the ships ever reached Spain. It was at this point that England began to wrest control of the seas from

FIGURE 30.3 **Marcus Gheeraert,** *Queen Elizabeth I* Marcus Gheeraert's portrait of Queen Elizabeth I shows this monarch at the height of her power (a picture of her victory over the Spanish Armada in the background, the crown to her right, her right hand on the globe) and wealth (her jewel-laden attire). (Cooper-Bridgeman Library)

Spain. Not only had Philip II failed to exterminate Protestantism in England, but the Roman Catholic cause there was now tainted with treason, and Protestantism was stronger than ever.

Confronting the Ottoman Turks

In the sixteenth century, the Ottoman Empire under Suleiman had grown in power to its greatest extent. Victories over Christian troops in Hungary had threatened central Europe. Ottoman fleets dominated large parts of the Mediterra-

nean. The Hapsburgs had traditionally led in the struggle against the Ottomans and Islam in general, and Philip II took up the challenge with vigor. Under the urging of the pope, Venice, Genoa, and Spain amassed a fleet of more than two hundred vessels under the command of Philip's illegitimate half brother, Don Juan. In 1571 this fleet caught and annihilated the somewhat larger Turkish fleet off Lepanto on the coast of Greece. This was one of the few clear-cut successes of Philip's career. Lepanto greatly diminished the Turkish menace to Christendom by sea.

2. THE RELIGIOUS WARS IN FRANCE

In France and Germany during the late sixteenth and first half of the seventeenth centuries, struggles between Protestants and Catholics combined with conflicts between different political factions to break out into bitter wars, usually called the Wars of Religion.

In France Calvinism had made slow but steady progress during the reigns of Francis I (1515–1547) and Henry II (1547–1559) in spite of vigorous persecution by those Roman Catholic monarchs. By 1559 the Huguenots, as the French Calvinists were called, numbered possibly a twelfth of the total population. However, since their ranks included many of the prosperous bourgeoisie and some of the greatest noble families of France, their influence was far greater than their numbers would indicate. Enmity between the Huguenots and the Roman Catholics, which had smoldered under the strong rule of Francis I and Henry II, broke into open and consuming flame under Henry II's three ineffective sons, who ruled in succession from 1559 to 1589. All three were dominated by their powerful and ambitious mother, Catherine de Médicis. This situation invited political as well as religious faction and intrigue, and in the civil wars that followed politics and religion were intertwined.

The leadership of the Roman Catholic faction was assumed by the powerful Guise family; that of the Protestants by the influential Bourbon family, who were related to the royal line. The first eight years of fighting were ended in 1570 by an uneasy truce. However, Catherine de Médicis became fearful of the growing influence of the Huguenots. She turned for support to the Catholic Guises, and under their influence she agreed to a plan to massacre the Huguenots. At a given signal at midnight, August 24, 1572 (St. Bartholomew's Day), the Roman Catholics in Paris fell to slaughtering the Protestants (see Figure 30.1). The massacre soon spread to the provinces and went on for a number of weeks. Thousands of Huguenots were slain.

The ablest of the Huguenot leaders, young Henry (Bourbon) of Navarre, escaped and rallied the remaining Protestant forces for the war that was now renewed in earnest. The wealth and energy of the numerous bourgeois and noble members of the Huguenot faction, plus the brilliance of their dashing young leader, offset the superior numbers of the Roman Catholics. Eventually Henry III, the third son of Catherine de Médicis to rule France, organized a moderate Roman Catholic faction to stand between the uncompromising Guise faction and the Protestants. The struggle now became a three-cornered "War of the Three Henrys" (Henry, duke of Guise, Henry of Navarre, and Henry III, king of France). Philip II of Spain threw his support to Henry, duke of Guise. Henry III, now regarding Henry, duke of Guise, as the greater menace to his own royal authority, had him assassinated in 1588. The next year an agent of the Guises assassinated Henry III. This left Protestant Henry of Navarre, by right of succession, King Henry IV of France. However, it was only when he abjured Protestantism four years later and went through the formality of becoming a Roman Catholic that the great majority of his subjects, who were Roman Catholics, allowed him to enter Paris and be legally crowned. "Paris is worth a Mass," he is alleged to have remarked. Five years later (1598) he issued his famous Edict of Nantes, which, by granting tolerance to the Protestant minority, ended religious strife in France for nearly a century.[1] By these acts, Henry revealed himself as a *politique*, favoring national unity over religious concerns. He enjoyed some of the same success and popularity as other *politiques*, such as Elizabeth I in England and William of Orange in the Netherlands.

3. THE THIRTY YEARS' WAR IN GERMANY

The Peace of Augsburg (1555), which had brought to a close the first armed conflict in Germany between the Roman Catholics and the Lutherans, proved to be only an uneasy truce. Since the signing of the treaty, which recognized only Roman Catholics and Lutherans, the Calvinists had made strong headway in several states of the Holy Roman Empire and demanded equal

---

[1]The Huguenots rose up in a brief rebellion (1627–1629) against Cardinal Richelieu when he removed their military and political privileges.

FIGURE 30.4 The Thirty Years' War This print shows Magdeburg, where in 1631 one of the battles of the Thirty Years' War was fought. The last and the bloodiest of the religious wars that accompanied the Reformation, the Thirty Years' War devastated much of Germany and exhausted its participants. (NYPL Picture Collection)

recognition. Furthermore, lands of the Roman Catholic church were constantly being secularized in Protestant areas in violation of the treaty. On the other hand, the Roman Catholics, being more aggressive as a result of the clarification of their position by the Council of Trent and the activities of the militant Jesuits, talked of exterminating Protestantism in the Holy Roman Empire and recovering all their lost lands and souls. In alarm, the Protestants formed a defensive league. The Roman Catholics countered by forming a league of their own.

The increasing tension finally erupted into the Thirty Years' War (1618–1648) (see Figure 30.4). In this war the religious issue was complicated and often confused by political and dynastic issues. The individual princes of the empire were struggling to maintain or even increase their independence from the emperor. The Hapsburg dynasty, both Austrian and Spanish, threatened to become so powerful that the apprehensive Bourbons of France entered the war against them. The upshot was that eventually the Roman Catholics, the Holy Roman emperor, and the

Hapsburg dynasty (the emperor was an Austrian Hapsburg) formed one faction against which were arrayed the Protestants, most of the individual princes of the empire, and the Bourbons.

The long-brewing Thirty Years' War began in 1618 when a group of Bohemian nobles, mostly Calvinists and fearful of losing both their religious and their political rights, declared their Hapsburg ruler deposed and chose the Calvinist elector of the Palatinate as their king. The Hapsburg Holy Roman emperor, aided by the Roman Catholic League and by Hapsburg and Roman Catholic Spain, took the field and easily crushed both Bohemia and the Palatinate. Hundreds of Calvinist Bohemian nobles were executed and their property confiscated. Protestantism was outlawed in Bohemia. The Calvinist Palatinate was annexed to Roman Catholic Bavaria. This quick, crushing victory by Roman Catholic and imperial forces frightened not only the Protestant princes of northern Germany, but also the Protestant neighboring states.

In 1625 Lutheran King Christian IV of Denmark, who held numerous bishoprics in Germany that had been illegally secularized, entered the war against the Roman Catholic and imperial forces. Christian IV was aided by English subsidies and numerous German Protestant princes. At this critical juncture a brilliant soldier of fortune, Albrecht von Wallenstein, offered his services to the emperor. This military genius raised a volunteer army of fifty thousand adventurers of various nationalities. Wallenstein's army, together with the regular imperial and Roman Catholic forces, defeated Christian IV and drove him out of Germany. The Danish king was deprived of nearly all his German holdings. Upon the conclusion of this phase of the war in 1629, the victorious emperor issued the Edict of Restitution, restoring to the Roman Catholic church all the lands illegally secularized since the Peace of Augsburg—more than a hundred tracts, large and small.

The whole Protestant world was now genuinely alarmed at the resurgent power of the Roman Catholics. The German princes were faced with the loss of their powers to the Holy Roman emperor. The French Bourbons were concerned about the rapidly growing strength of the Hapsburgs. At this juncture another Protestant champion stepped forward—Gustavus Adolphus of Sweden. This Lutheran "Lion of the North" was a military leader of great ability. Furthermore, he was well backed by French gold. Gustavus Adolphus led his army victoriously through the Germanies, gaining allies among the Protestant princes as he went. The Hapsburg emperor hastily recalled the ambitious Wallenstein, whom he had dismissed upon the conclusion of the Danish phase of the war. Two of the ablest military commanders of early modern times now faced each other. In the battle of Lützen (1632) Wallenstein was defeated, but Gustavus Adolphus had been killed and the victory was far from decisive. Fortunately for the Protestants, Wallenstein was dismissed and two years later was assassinated. Since Sweden had failed to turn the tide of the war, the Bourbon king of France in 1635 threw the full weight of his military might directly into the fray. For thirteen more years the war dragged on until all participants were exhausted. The Treaty of Westphalia in 1648 finally brought the struggle to a close (see Map 30.2).

In general, thanks largely to the intervention of France, the Roman Catholics, the Holy Roman emperor, and the Hapsburgs suffered a setback. Not only were the Roman Catholics thwarted in their efforts to exterminate Protestantism in Germany, but the Calvinists now gained equal status with the Lutherans and Roman Catholics in the Holy Roman Empire. The Holy Roman Empire practically fell apart. According to the terms of the Treaty of Westphalia, each of the more than three hundred individual princes could now make his own treaties. Three of the most important princes, the rulers of Brandenburg, Bavaria, and Saxony, made sizable additions to their territories. Sweden gained strategic territories along the German Baltic and North Sea coasts. France gained the important bishoprics and fortress cities of Metz, Toul, and Verdun and the province of Alsace except for the free city of Strasbourg. The complete independence of Switzerland and the Dutch Netherlands was officially recognized. The Austrian Hapsburgs retained their hereditary possessions but lost prestige as emperors of a disintegrating Holy Roman Empire. Also, their relative position declined as that of France rose. The Spanish Hapsburgs fared worse. After eleven more years of fighting with France they yielded a strip of the Spanish Netherlands and another strip along the Spanish border to France. Spain's days of greatness were finished.

The immediate effect of the Thirty Years' War on Germany was disastrous. For three decades hostile German and foreign armies had tramped back and forth across Germany, killing, raping, and looting the defenseless inhabitants. In the wake of Wallenstein's army of fifty thousand, for instance, swarmed one hundred fifty thousand camp followers bent on plunder. To the usual horrors of war was added religious fanaticism. Some 30 to 40 percent of Germany's inhabitants lost their lives from this war. Many years would be required for Germany to recover from these wounds.

The Thirty Years' War was the last and the bloodiest of the religious wars that accompanied the Reformation. Although there would still be much religious strife and controversy, the religious map of Europe would henceforth change very little. After 1648 political rather than religious affairs would occupy center stage in the Western world.

Map 30.2 EUROPE, 1648 This map of Europe after the Treaty of Westphalia in 1648 shows that what would eventually become unified into Germany during the nineteenth century was still greatly divided within a Holy Roman Empire that was weaker than ever. With the rapid decline of Spain, most political conflict in the century after 1648 would be among France, England, Austria-Hungary, and Brandenburg-Prussia.

SUGGESTED READING

General

R. Dunn, *The Age of Religious Wars, 1559–1689* (1979). A good, brief survey.

G. Parker, *Europe in Crisis, 1598–1648* (1979). A survey and interpretation of this period as one of general crisis.

T. Rabb, *The Struggle for Stability in Early Modern Europe* (1975). Analyzes the "crisis" interpretation.

The Crusade of Catholic Spain

W. T. MacCaffrey, *Queen Elizabeth and the Making of Policy, 1572–1588* (1982). A good recent analysis.

C. Martin and N. Parker, *The Spanish Armada* (1988). Provides some new insights.

G. Mattingly, *The Armada* (1959). Brilliantly shows the impact of the Armada's failure on all of Europe.

Geoffrey Parker, *Spain and the Netherlands, 1559–1659* (1979). A clear introduction.

P. Pierson, *Philip II of Spain* (1975). A well-written biography.

J. Ridley, *Elizabeth I* (1988). A good recent biography.

Religious Wars in France

M. Greengrass, *France in the Age of Henri IV* (1984). A fine recent history of this crucial period.

J. H. M. Salmon, *Society in Crisis: France in the Sixteenth Century* (1975). Focuses on French institutions.

The Thirty Years' War

P. Limm, *The Thirty Years' War* (1984). A brief survey with accompanying documents.

T. K. Rabb, ed., *The Thirty Years' War* (1981). A collection of differing interpretations of the war and its significance.

CHAPTER 31

Society, Faith, and Culture in the Seventeenth and Eighteenth Centuries

FIGURE 31.1 **Thomas Gainsborough,** *Miss Catherine Tatton* Although the middle class was growing during the early modern era, the culture of the period was still dominated by the aristocracy. This portrait of an aristocratic lady by Thomas Gainsborough (1727–1788) reflects the luxury and tastes of the eighteenth-century aristocracy, which commissioned many such paintings. (Scala/Art Resource)

For most people the structure of society, the way of life, and the relevant social institutions changed only slowly throughout most of the seventeenth and early eighteenth centuries. More rapid change occurred thereafter, but it was usually concentrated in certain areas and classes. Despite the continued rise of the bourgeoisie and considerable political change, the aristocracy remained socially dominant and governments headed by kings generally continued to centralize their power. Religious faith remained of great importance to most people, but after the middle of the seventeenth century new religious movements such as pietism were no longer the revolutionary force they had been during the previous century. The literature and arts of the period reflected the spirit of royal absolutism and the values of the aristocracy, with their exaltation of kings, princes, and nobility and also their concern for order and form.

1. SOCIETY

Population Growth

One of the greatest sources of change in Western society has been population growth. As we have seen (see pp. 377–380), European population grew substantially during the sixteenth century, putting pressure on economic life, adding to social turmoil, and creating changes in the quality of life for different classes of people. This population growth leveled out during the first two decades of the seventeenth century. On the whole, during the seventeenth century Europe's population was able only to maintain itself or grow slightly. In some areas population declined markedly. The typical enemies of population growth were poverty, disease, famine, and war. Most people lived close to the subsistence level. Any disturbance—a poor harvest, a natural catastrophe, a war—quickly used up their meager reserves of food and opened the door to hunger, declining health, disease, and famine. The Thirty Years' War was particularly devastating, leading to a decline in the German population of some 40 percent during the first half of the seventeenth century. The relatively late age of marriage—late twenties for men, mid-twenties for women—also helped keep down the number of births in a so-

ciety in which life expectancy was short and only about half of the babies born would reach maturity.

During the eighteenth century, particularly after the 1730s, the European population grew sharply—from approximately 110 million in 1700 to 190 million in 1800. Although the causes are unclear, it seems that an increasing birthrate and declining death rate were achieved by earlier marriages, better and more regular nutrition, fewer plagues, and less devastating wars. Agricultural and commercial prosperity, along with continuing improvements in transportation facilities, diminished the periodic famines in many areas. In particular, historians credit the introduction of the potato from the New World and its widespread cultivation in eighteenth-century Europe with crucially increasing supplies of nutritious food. More effective urban sanitation and increased use of quarantines probably improved health. Medical practices were not one of the causes of population growth. Certainly some progress was made in medical knowledge and there were a few better hospitals in eighteenth-century Europe than before. But with the exception of developing smallpox inoculation, which was little used outside England until the nineteenth century, eighteenth-century doctors, hospitals, and medicines probably caused more deaths than they prevented.

There was an ironic price to pay for this eighteenth-century increase in population. Greater competition for food drove prices up while that same competition for jobs usually drove wages down. At the same time that more people were able to survive, more experienced hunger and poverty. The poor were forced to wander and migrate more than ever.

Social Structure

Seventeenth- and eighteenth-century people viewed their society as divided—into different occupational groups and classes—and hierarchically ordered—the different groups and classes ranked from high to low status by birth, office, wealth, or education. Mobility between these ranked orders of society was viewed as the exception. People considered the social order to be relatively rigid and correct. In fact, however, mobility and change occurred. Wealth, education,

FIGURE 31.2 Louis le Nain, *The Cart*, 1641 In contrast to most seventeenth-century artists, le Nain shows the life of the French peasantry. This farmyard scene (notice the mixture of ages), so typical of the countryside, contrasts sharply with the life of the aristocracy. (The Louvre, Paris)

and new opportunities for governmental service opened avenues for middle-class merchants, bankers, and professionals as well as the gentry to move into the ranks of the aristocracy. Nevertheless, social mobility was never the option for many, as it would become during the nineteenth and twentieth centuries.

As in previous centuries, the aristocracy enjoyed the highest status and the greatest number of privileges. Their position was defined not by wealth but by title and blood. Some were fabulously rich, but others were relatively impoverished. However, an aristocrat was expected to have enough wealth to fulfill costly political, social, and military functions. Usually that wealth derived from the lands they owned, and most of it was protected by numerous exemptions from taxes.

Below the aristocrats were the clergy and commoners. In these groups there were ordered ranks as well. In the cities the wealthiest merchants, particularly those from "old families," were on top. They enjoyed some of the distinctions of rank and power that aristocrats had, and some were granted aristocratic status. Below them were guild members, followed by artisans and unskilled workers. In the countryside the ownership of land usually determined status. The

wealthiest landowners, often called the gentry, performed many of the functions of the landed aristocracy. Below them, landowning peasants enjoyed some position, leaving the landless peasants toward the bottom—though even they were in a higher position than those who were still serfs and bound to their masters.

Within this social structure, it was the group rather than the individual that was supposed to be of primary importance. First came the family and the household, then the local community, finally the larger social order with its various orders and hierarchies. In our sense of the term, national identity was still of secondary importance for most people.

Rural Life

Seventeenth- and eighteenth-century Europeans lived predominantly in rural settings. In western Europe approximately 80 percent still lived in the countryside; in the less urbanized eastern Europe the percentage was even higher. In rural areas life was centered on the traditional village (see Figure 31.2). Most villages were small, ranging in size from a few families to little over a hundred families. There life was communally oriented: villagers knew each other, strangers stood out, and almost all effective authority was local. Community pressures limited what we today would consider the rights of dissent and privacy. The local church or manor served as a center of communal activities. Still relatively isolated, villages had to be self-sufficient. When bad harvests occurred, as they did on a regular basis, help from outside was rarely available.

Most people were relatively poor, living in small, crowded structures. Inside there few furnishings or possessions. At one end was a stone hearth for light, cooking, and heat, but shortages of fuel (wood and peat) meant people suffered from the cold. Bread and grain products made up most of their meals, though in various areas meat, vegetables, fruits, and dairy products supplemented their diets. If they owned or had rights to land, they could raise their own food. Even this was of little help when the crops failed.

During this period the traditional pattern of rural life was slowly being altered. The traditional village was experiencing intrusion from the outside, change in its age-old pattern of life, and loss of people to the growing cities. The political isolation of the village was being broken by the increased presence of officials from the growing central governments, by the growing absence of the local nobility (who were attracted to the courts and capital cities), and by the decline of communal political institutions. Above all, economic life was being changed by the agricultural revolution and the spread of cottage industry—both of these facilitated by improving means of transportation.

The Agricultural Revolution At the beginning of the seventeenth century, crops and animals were raised in western Europe much as they had been since the Middle Ages. Most fields were open and divided into various strips of land. Crops were rotated and land allowed to lie fallow (unplanted) one out of every two or three years to keep the soil fertile. Large strips of land were set aside as "commons"—open areas where villagers grazed their animals and gathered food and hay. Decisions about crops, animals, and land use were usually determined by tradition and the practices of the community.

During the seventeenth and eighteenth centuries, changes in agricultural production initiated in Holland spread to England and then to other areas of western Europe. These changes were so important that they have been called an agricultural revolution. New crops such as potatoes, turnips, and clover were introduced. New methods of rotating crops, such as from grains to tubers (potatoes and turnips) to hay (grasses for animal fodder), were developed. Fertilization of the soil was increased by using manure from larger animal herds. These changes enabled farmers to eliminate fallow land. In addition, Dutch innovators developed methods of draining wetlands so that new crops and methods could easily be introduced. They also experimented with breeding to create new strains of more productive cattle.

In the early eighteenth century, the new crops and methods spread to England. Charles "Turnip" Townsend experimented with crop rotation and the use of turnips and clover. His contemporary and compatriot, Jethro Tull, advocated the use of a seed drill, which made planting more efficient and productive. Another Englishman, Robert Bakewell, improved the existing types of sheep and cattle by selective breeding.

These changes were sometimes connected to the enclosure of open fields and commons, particularly in England. The consolidation and enclosure of scattered strips and farms allowed larger landowners the freedom to apply new agricultural methods. Enclosures had been used in Great Britain since the sixteenth century, but the profits that could be made in commercial agriculture employing new crops and methods stimulated numerous landlords to seek enclosures during the eighteenth century. After 1750 Parliament authorized a wave of enclosures that transformed the British countryside. While these enclosures hastened the agricultural revolution, they left large numbers of rural poor unable to survive as small farmers. Many of them were forced into the ranks of rural or urban workers.

Cottage Industry During the seventeenth and eighteenth centuries, "cottage industry," or the "putting-out system," expanded greatly in rural areas. According to this system, a merchant-capitalist provided raw materials (usually for production of textiles such as wool or linen) and sometimes equipment (such as a handloom or spinning wheel) to peasants. Peasants, working in their cottages, turned these raw materials into

FIGURE 31.3 Cottage Industry Most cottage industry was in textiles. Here the various members of a rural household in Ireland work together, beating and combing flax into linen, which will be spun and woven. (The Mansell Collection)

finished products—spinning and weaving wool into cloth (see Figure 31.3). The merchant periodically returned, paid for the peasants' labor by the piece, and distributed the finished products to distant markets. The pay was low, lower than that offered in cities, but it was enough to help large numbers of peasants and rural workers to survive. The growth of cottage industry during the eighteenth century, particularly in Great Britain and parts of France and Germany, helps explain how so many people could remain in rural areas.

Urban Life

Cities grew during the seventeenth and eighteenth centuries, but unevenly. Until the middle of the eighteenth century, most of the growth was in the capital and port cities, particularly in northern and western Europe. These cities swelled with the growth of central governments and commerce. After the 1750s new cities arose and small cities grew, reflecting the general population growth and new concentrations of agricultural and industrial activity, particularly in Great Britain.

This urban growth meant greater prosperity for some, but a large percentage of the urban masses were not beneficiaries. They continued to live precariously at little more than a subsistence level. The poorest were the hardest hit by the surplus of labor, inflation, and disasters such as war, disease, and failed harvests. In bad times, food riots were common. As traditional ways of aiding the poor—through the Church or private charity—were overwhelmed, cities tried to control begging and enact various sorts of poor relief. Legislation, such as the English Poor Laws, required the impoverished to work on public projects or in workhouses and provided some training, but laws such as these were often not carried out or were used more to control and discipline the poor than to help them.

However, there were more kinds of food, more goods, and more opportunities in cities. Artisans and skilled workers lived relatively comfortable lives. Those who found regular unskilled jobs as haulers or domestic servants were probably better off than the rural poor. Many worked or supplemented their income on small plots of land within or just outside the city; some cities owned large tracts of land and hired people to farm them.

Those who benefited most from improvements in the standard of living were the middle and aristocratic classes, particularly those taking advantage of the opportunities in commerce and industry and in the expanding governmental bureaucracies. A growing class of urban professionals attended institutions of higher education. In an expanding number of colleges they joined young aristocrats sent by families who felt that more education and culture were appropriate to members of the aristocracy. The middle classes continued to use their wealth to enter the aristocracy through the purchase of titles and offices, the acquisition of large estates, and judicious marriages.

The Family

The family, so central to social life and the socialization of future generations, is usually one of our most conservative institutions, evolving only gradually over time. This pattern of subtle, slow change held true for most of the seventeenth and eighteenth centuries.

The family functioned as both a social and an economic unit. In this household economy (or family economy), everyone who could worked for the good of the household. Husband, wife, children, servants, and apprentices were part of this unit of production and consumption. Even those who earned wages elsewhere usually sent part of their earnings back to the family. Children

were often sent away to other households when they could earn more outside their own family.

Child rearing and attitudes toward children were strikingly different from those of today. Children were generally not at the center of family life nor of primary concern. Girls were less valued than boys, reflecting women's subordination to men. Infanticide, though illegal, was not unknown, abandonment was a common practice, and what we would consider neglect was more often the rule than the exception. Much of this behavior may be explained by the high rate of infant mortality (some 30 to 50 percent of children died within the first five years of life), the generally precarious state of the household economy, and simple poverty. Certainly the lack of birth control may have played a role: Modern methods were unknown, the unreliable method of withdrawal was discouraged or condemned, and abortion was dangerous. Parents usually had to view those children who survived not only as family members but as assets or liabilities in the survival of the family. With life so precarious for their children, any great emotional involvement with them was risky.

It was once thought that most people lived in extended families—more than one married couple and their children in the same household; however, most historians now agree that as a rule people lived in a nuclear family household consisting of one couple and their children. Nevertheless, the typical family household during the sixteenth, seventeenth, and most of the eighteenth centuries was a much more populated, public place than the household of a modern nineteenth- or twentieth-century nuclear family. At various times a variety of relatives lived in or moved through the household, as did domestics and laborers. The household was far more open to members of the community and pressures from the community at large. The father, older children, other relatives, and community adults in general participated with the mother in raising and socializing young children.

Marriages continued to be entered into for primarily economic and social reasons. The land, wealth, skills, and position one held were the most important considerations in contemplating marriage; sentiment, particularly being in love, played a secondary role. Children were the expected product of a successful marriage. Typically, a married woman gave birth to more than five children, though the odds were that many of those would fail to reach adulthood or even get beyond the first few years of childhood. Marriages whether happy or not, were expected to last. Divorce, though permitted in Protestant communities, was in most cases difficult if not impossible. Separation was more accepted, but death, which often struck people at a relatively young age, was usually the only way out of an unsuccessful marriage.

Within the middle and upper classes, a significant change came during the second half of the eighteenth century. Sentiment became more important as a motivation for marriage; economic and social considerations, while still important, were not quite as dominant as before. Premarital sex and sex outside of marriage were on the increase, as evidenced by the growing number of births registered within a few months of marriage and by the rising rates of illegitimacy. People were marrying at an earlier age and moving around more. Child rearing and homemaking were being turned into a woman's profession in middle-class households. Along with the rising likelihood that most babies born would survive came a changing perception of children as more special, precious, and loved—not miniature adults to be used, as they had more often been perceived in the sixteenth and seventeenth centuries. Indeed, what was happening during the second half of the eighteenth century was a slow transformation to the modern family, which would come into bloom with the spread of industry and the dominance of the middle class during the nineteenth century.

Women

Women, while continuing to play a subordinate role to men, were central to the economic well-being of the family among the lower classes. Their work started when they were children, helping with the lighter tasks of farming or cottage industry. In her early teens, a girl often left home to work as a servant, trying to gain skills and money for her future marriage and the establishment of a new household. As a married woman, she could expect to spend much of her time pregnant (five or more pregnancies were not unusual) and involved with child care. But her tasks as childbearer and child rearer were no more important than her other economic and social functions. In addition to the standard household chores, women were expected to work as much as possible. Women participated in the collecting and threshing of grain, took primary responsibility for gardening, raised poultry, supervised and processed dairy production, and shared in the manufacture of household items and products for commerce (particularly spinning) as the putting-out system spread. When women worked in wage-earning occupations, it was generally at less pay and in lower-status positions than men. The line between acceptable "women's work" and "men's work" widened as the emphasis on women's domestic responsibilities grew. Within the household women were legally subordinate to their husbands and generally expected to be subject to his authority. Outside a household, women were particularly vulnerable. They lacked many legal rights and were denied most alternatives for independent employment. There were some occupations open to women, such as glove making, spinning yarn, midwifery, and nursing, but the status and pay of these occupations were often diminished because of their association with women.

Middle- and upper-class women had fewer opportunities for participation in economic life. Respectable careers open to unmarried middle-class women were limited to those of governess or lady-in-waiting. Once married, the middle-class woman was at the center of the family, but for any real economic independence she had to wait for the death of her husband. More than lower-class women, middle-class women were increasingly seen as responsible for upholding standards and supervising the help within the home. Most aristocratic women were similarly limited in the economic roles they played, but they could turn to influential social and cultural roles (see Chapter 36). Some, such as Queen Christina in seventeenth-century Sweden, Maria Theresa in eighteenth-century Austria, and Catherine the Great in eighteenth-century Russia, became rulers. Others, such as Maria de Médicis in seventeenth-century France, became surrogate rulers or royal regents. More often, they held privileged positions in royal courts and served as unofficial advisers. As courtiers women could gain position, wealth, and prestigage for themselves and their families.

2. FAITH: THE GROWTH OF PIETISM

After the end of the Wars of Religion in the mid–seventeenth century, a relative status quo existed between Catholicism and Protestantism. While hostility still existed among the believers of different Christian faiths, it no longer broke out into the violence and revolution characteristic of the Reformation era. Religious life remained centered in the local parish. In his church, the priest or pastor conducted services and supervised various charitable and educational activities. Although most people retained an allegiance to the established Catholic or Protestant churches, some new religious movements did arise during the seventeenth and eighteenth centuries. The most important were a number of pietistic sects which stressed the importance of active faith in leading a religious life.

In Germany Philipp Spener (1635–1705) and Count Zinzendorf (1700–1760) became leaders of pietist movements of considerable dimensions. Spener, a Lutheran pastor, recoiled from the formal officiousness that his church had fallen into after the heated religious strife of the sixteenth and early seventeenth centuries. He minimized dogma and external forms in favor of inner piety and holy living. His largely Lutheran following included some of the leading intellects of Germany. Count Zinzendorf, a well-to-do Saxon nobleman, undertook to restore the Bohemian Brethren, the persecuted and scattered followers of the early-fifteenth-century reformer Jan Huss. He called his group the Moravian Brethren. The Moravians, too, shunned intricate dogma and formal ritual. They set up model communities based on brotherly love, frugal living, hard work, and inner piety.

In Lutheran Sweden, Emanuel Swedenborg (1688–1772), a distinguished scientist, inventor, and public servant, founded a movement somewhat like the Moravian Brethren, based on his visions, which he took to be direct revelations of God. Swedenborg wrote several learned theological works stressing inner and outward piety and individual communion with God.

England, however, was the seat of the most widespread and influential pietistic movements of the seventeenth and eighteenth centuries. The first was the Society of Friends, or Quakers, as they were generally called, founded by George Fox (1624–1691). Fox, a man of great energy and stubborn independence, detested formalism in religion as well as in society and government. He believed that true Christianity is an individual matter—a matter of plain, pious living and of private communion with God under the guidance of a divine "inner light." Opposed to war, rank, and intolerance, the Quakers refused military service, the use of titles, and the taking of oaths. In these respects the Quakers were different from most of the other pietists. They were considered dangerous to the established order and were severely persecuted.

A more moderate and popular pietist movement was Methodism. The prime mover in Methodism was John Wesley (1703–1791). John Wesley and his brother, Charles, became converted to a more fervent, evangelical type of Christianity. When the Anglican churches closed their doors to John Wesley, he preached emotional sermons to huge throngs in the streets and fields. George Whitefield, the most eloquent of all the early Methodists, electrified tens of thousands in England and America and converted many to pietistic Christianity. The real founder of Methodism in the American colonies was Francis Asbury (1745–1816), who in many respects duplicated the work of John Wesley in England. In both England and America the Methodists grew rapidly in numbers, mostly among the middle and lower classes.

The various pietist groups were definitely not political revolutionaries. They were intensely interested in social reform—in education, health and sanitation, temperance, penal reform, and abolition of the slave trade. But they hoped to achieve these reforms by private charity rather than political action. They tended to accommodate themselves to the political status quo in the belief that spiritual and social conditions could be improved within that framework of government.

3. CULTURE

The cultural styles of the seventeenth and eighteenth centuries reflected the dominance of royal and aristocratic tastes—particularly in the baroque, classical, and rococo styles. The main exceptions were in the Dutch Netherlands and eighteenth-century England, where paintings and literature often reflected the tastes of the ascending middle class. Bridging the middle and upper classes were the scientific revolution and the Enlightenment, two intellectual and cultural developments of great importance that will be examined on their own in Chapters 35 and 36.

Literature

The reign of Louis XIV (1643–1715) was the golden age of French literature. The elegance, the sense of order, and the formalism of the court of the Grand Monarch were all reflected in the literature of the period, sometimes called the Augustan or classical period of French literature. It was in the field of drama that the French writers attained their greatest success. Corneille wrote elegant tragedies in the style of and often on the same subjects as the ancient Greek tragedies. The struggles of human beings against themselves and against the universe furnish the dramatic conflicts. Corneille's craftsmanship and style are handsomely polished, though often exalted and exaggerated.

Even more exquisitely polished were the perfectly rhymed and metered couplets of Racine's tragedies: *Andromaque* relates the tragic story of Hector's wife after the death of her husband at the hands of Achilles and the ensuing fall of Troy. *Phèdre* is about the wife of the legendary Greek king Theseus who falls in love with her stepson. This story had also been the subject of plays by Euripides, Sophocles, and Seneca.

One of the greatest of all the French dramatists was Molière. In his charming and profound comedies—such as *Tartuffe*, *Le Misanthrope*, and *Les Femmes Savantes (The Learned Ladies)*—Molière devastatingly portrays and satirizes the false, the stupid, and the pompous: egotists, pedants, social climbers, false priests, quack physicians. The tragic conflicts and personality types of Cor-

neille, Racine, and Molière are universal and eternal.

Perhaps the most popular novel of the period was *Grand Cyrus*, a historical romance by Madeleine de Scudéry. The fact that this book was published under the name of her brother Georges indicates some of the difficulties women faced in cultural pursuits.

Other major French writers of the age of Louis XIV were Blaise Pascal, the scientist and mathematician who also wrote the marvelously styled *Provincial Letters* against the Jesuits and the deeply reflective *Pensées (Thoughts);* Madame de Sévigné, who wrote almost two thousand letters to her daughter, each a work of art; and the duke of Saint-Simon, who spent the latter part of his life writing forty volumes of *Mémoires*. Madame de Sévigné and the duke of Saint-Simon, both of whom were eyewitnesses at the court of Louis XIV, constitute two of the most important sources we have for the history and life of that period.

The common denominator among all these writers is their emphasis on and mastery of elegant and graceful form. In this emphasis they reflect the spirit of royal absolutism at its height. However, form is valued not merely for its own sake but as an artistic clothing for subtle and critical thought. French literature in the late seventeenth century overshadowed that of all other countries of Europe, much as did French military and political influence. The lucid, graceful French language became the fashionable language of most of the royal courts and courtiers on the European continent.

French literature in the eighteenth century continued for the most part in the classical vein. Voltaire wrote dramas and poems carefully tailored to the dictates of classical formalism. His prose works exalted logic and the ideals of Greece and Rome. Only Rousseau among the major eighteenth-century French writers departed from the classical spirit to anticipate the romanticism of a later era.

Next to France, England produced the most important literature in the seventeenth and early eighteenth centuries, and like the French, the English authors generally wrote in the classical vein. The giant of English letters in the mid–seventeenth century was John Milton (1608–1674). This learned Puritan was steeped in the literature of ancient Greece and Rome. His exquisite lyrics *L'Allegro* and *Il Penseroso* and incomparable elegy *Lycidas* are thickly strewn with references to classical mythology. The conscientious Milton contributed much of his great talent and energy to public affairs. During the Puritan Revolution he went blind while working as a pamphleteer for the Puritan cause and secretary for Oliver Cromwell. The chief literary product of this period of his life is *Areopagitica*, probably the noblest defense of freedom of the press ever penned. Milton's masterpiece is *Paradise Lost*, written in his blindness and after the restoration of the Stuart kings had ruined his public career. *Paradise Lost* is a poem of epic proportions based on the Genesis account of the rebellion of Satan against God and the temptation and fall of human beings. This majestic theme is treated in stately blank verse of formal elegance. Even in this deeply religious work, Holy Writ is interwoven with classical pagan myth.

The two greatest poets to succeed Milton were John Dryden in the late seventeenth century and Alexander Pope in the early eighteenth century. Both were satirists, both displayed a massive knowledge of Greek and Roman lore, and both wrote chiefly in the formal rhymed couplets typical of the classical period. In the precision of their form, as in the sharpness of their satire, their appeal was to reason rather than to emotion.

The eighteenth century in English literature was an age of great prose. Following the upheavals of the seventeenth century, the Puritan and Glorious revolutions, it was a time of political and religious bitterness and bickering. In pungent and incisive prose Jonathan Swift, in his *Gulliver's Travels* and political essays, and Richard Sheridan, in his numerous dramas, pilloried the fops, pedants, bigots, and frauds of the day, much as Molière had done a century earlier across the Channel. It was in the eighteenth century that the English novel was born. More than other literary forms, it was aimed at and reflected the tastes of England's rising middle class. Samuel Richardson, in *Clarissa Harlowe*, and Henry Fielding, in *Tom Jones*, used this medium to analyze human personality, emotions, and psychology, just as Corneille and Racine had used the poetic drama in France for the same purpose.

In the eighteenth century several writers—

Robert Burns in Great Britain, Rousseau in France, Schiller and Goethe in Germany—anticipated romanticism (see Chapter 41). But the prevailing spirit in eighteenth- as in seventeenth-century literature was classical. Precision, formalism, and ofttimes elegance marked the style. Ancient Greece and Rome furnished the models. The appeal was generally to reason. The royal monarchs and their courts had little to fear from this literature. They could derive comfort from its formal order and laugh with the rest of the world at its satire, which was aimed at humankind in general rather than at the ruling regimes.

Painting and Architecture

If the literature of the seventeenth and eighteenth centuries did not offend the absolutist kings and their aristocratic courtiers, the visual arts of the period usually glorified them (see Color Plate 17). The dominant style of painting and architecture during the seventeenth century was baroque, which used elaborate swirling forms and colors to achieve dramatic, emotional effects. The baroque style was originally associated with the Roman Catholic Reformation and reflected the resurgence of a revitalized Roman Catholic church led by the militant Jesuits. Later its massive and ornamental elegance reflected the wealth and power of the absolutist monarchs and their courts, then at the peak of their affluence.

The most popular of the baroque painters of the early seventeenth century was the Fleming Peter Paul Rubens (1577–1640). After studying the work of the Italian High Renaissance masters, Rubens returned to Antwerp and painted more than two thousand pictures, many of them huge canvases. He operated what amounted to a painting factory, employing dozens of artists who painted in the details designed and sketched by the master. Rubens, a devout Roman Catholic, first painted religious subjects (see Color Plate 14). His later subjects were pagan mythology, court life, and especially voluptuous nude women—all painted in the most brilliant and sensuous colors (see Figure 31.4).

Spain boasted two of the greatest seventeenth-century painters: El Greco and Velásquez. El Greco, whose real name was Domenikos Theotokopoulos, was a native of the Greek island of Crete (hence "The Greek"). After studying the

FIGURE 31.4 Peter Paul Rubens, *Henry IV Receiving the Portrait of Marie de Médicis,* 1621–1625 Rubens was commissioned by Marie de Médicis, widow of King Henry IV of France, to paint this allegorical scene showing Henri IV considering a proposed marriage to Marie de Médicis. The swirling lines, dramatic perspective, rich color, and opulence are typically baroque. (The Louvre, Paris)

Italian Renaissance masters, he settled down in Toledo and developed a style of his own. By deliberate distortion and exaggeration he achieved sensational effects. *View of Toledo, St. Jerome in His Study,* and *Christ at Gethsemane* illustrate his genius. El Greco's favorite subject was the reinvigorated Church of the Roman Catholic Reformation. Considered by his contemporaries to be a madman, he is now regarded as the forerunner of several schools of nineteenth- and twentieth-century painting. Velásquez was a painter of great versatility. Although much of his earlier work was of a religious nature, he also painted genre subjects (depicting the life of the common people) and later portraits. He is considered one of the greatest of portrait painters. As official court painter, he exalted and glorified the Spanish royalty and ruling classes at a time when they had really passed their peak in world affairs.

During the second half of the seventeenth and then the eighteenth century, classicism, with its greater emphasis on control and restraint, gained favor. Good examples of classicism are in the works of the French artists Nicolas Poussin and Claude Lorraine (see Color Plate 15). Poussin spent most of his life in Italy studying the Renaissance masters. Although his biblical and mythological scenes are more vibrant and pulsating than the Italian Renaissance paintings that inspired them, they are much more serene, subtle, and controlled than the works of Rubens and El Greco.

In eighteenth-century Great Britain, Joshua Reynolds, Thomas Gainsborough, George Romney, and Sir Thomas Lawrence vied with one another for commissions to paint the portraits of royalty and aristocracy. The results were plumes, jewels, buckles, silks, brocades, and laces in dripping profusion (see Figure 31.1).

FIGURE 31.5 The Baroque Style This photo is of the interior of the basilica St. Andrea della Valle, which was built in the latter part of the seventeenth century. It well illustrates the elaborate, gaudy splendor of the baroque style, the hallmark of the age of royal absolutism and affluence. In this case the royal monarch was the pope, ruler of a Church reinvigorated by the Roman Catholic Reformation. (Alinari/Scala/Art Resource)

In the Dutch Netherlands painting did not reflect royal and aristocratic tastes. Here in the busy ports and marketplaces commerce was king, and the great Dutch painters of the seventeenth century, notably Frans Hals, Jan Vermeer, and Rembrandt van Rijn, portrayed the bourgeoisie and common people (see Color Plate 16). Rembrandt is universally recognized as one of the greatest artistic geniuses of all time. As a portrayer of character he has never been surpassed. His mastery of light and shade (*chiaroscuro*) made it seem as if the very souls of his subjects were illumined. *Syndics of the Cloth Guild*, *The Night Watch*, and *The Anatomy Lesson of Dr. Tulp* (see p. 443) are among his most powerful portrait studies. These three paintings also vividly depict the commercial prosperity, the festive urban life, and the growing interest in natural science in the seventeenth-century Dutch Netherlands.

Baroque architecture, like baroque painting, was an elaboration and ornamentation of the Renaissance and a product of the Roman Catholic Reformation (see Figure 31.5). In the late sixteenth, the seventeenth, and the eighteenth centuries Jesuit churches sprang up all over the Roman Catholic world. The most important and one of the best examples of the baroque style is the Jesuit parent church, Il Gesù, in Rome. Also, like the painting, baroque architecture was later used to represent the gaudy splendor of the seventeenth- and eighteenth-century absolute monarchs and their courts.

Towering over all other monuments of baroque architecture, much as St. Peter's towered over all other Renaissance structures, was the Versailles Palace of Louis XIV (see Figure 32.1). The exterior of Versailles is designed in long, horizontal, classic lines. The interior is lavishly decorated with richly colored marbles, mosaics, inlaid woods, gilt, silver, silk, velvet, and brocade. The salons and halls are lighted with ceiling-to-floor windows and mirrors and crystal chandeliers holding thousands of candles. The palace faces hundreds of acres of groves, walks, pools, terraces, fountains, statues, flower beds, and clipped shrubs—all laid out in formal geometric patterns. So dazzling was this symbol of royal absolutism that many European monarchs attempted to copy it. The most successful attempt was Maria Theresa's Schönbrunn Palace in Vienna.

In England Sir Christopher Wren was the greatest architect of the baroque period. The great fire that destroyed most of the heart of London in 1666 provided Wren with an opportunity to build numerous baroque structures. His masterpiece is St. Paul's Cathedral, with its lofty dome and columns.

In the eighteenth century, architecture tended to become less massive, relying heavily on multiple curves and lacy shell-like ornamentation. This style is usually referred to as rococo. One of the best examples of the rococo style is Frederick the Great's Sans Souci Palace at Potsdam. The rococo style, like the baroque, represented an age of royal and aristocratic affluence.

Music

The classical spirit pervaded the music of the seventeenth and eighteenth centuries as it did the literature and the visual arts; and like the literature and the visual arts, the music was an outgrowth of Renaissance developments.[1] The piano and the violin family of instruments, whose fore-

bears appeared in the sixteenth century, developed rapidly in the seventeenth. In the late seventeenth and early eighteenth centuries, three Italian families, the Amati, the Guarneri, and the Stradivari, fashioned the finest violins ever made. The seventeenth century was also marked by the rise of the opera. Alessandro Scarlatti in Italy, Jean-Baptiste Lully in France, and Henry Purcell in England popularized this grandiose combination of music and drama. The eighteenth was the great century of classical music—the age of Bach, Handel, Haydn, and Mozart.

Johann Sebastian Bach (1685–1750) was a member of a German family long distinguished in music. Noted in his own lifetime chiefly as an organist, he composed a vast array of great music for organ, harpsichord, and clavichord (forerunner of the piano), orchestra, and chorus, much of which has been lost. Most of Bach's compositions were religiously inspired, and he holds the same position in Protestant music that the sixteenth-century Palestrina does in the music of the Roman Catholic church. Bach was not widely appreciated in his own day. It was not until Felix Mendelssohn "discovered" him in the nineteenth century that he became widely known.

George Frederick Handel (1685–1759) was born in central Germany in the same year as Bach and not many miles distant. He studied Italian opera in Germany and Italy and wrote forty-six operas himself. He became court musician of the elector of Hanover. Later he made his home in England, as did the elector, who became King George I of England. Handel wrote an enormous quantity of music, both instrumental and vocal. All of it is marked by dignity, formal elegance, and melodious harmony—fitting for and appreciated in an age of royal splendor. His best-known work is the majestic oratorio *The Messiah*, heard every Christmas season.

Franz Joseph Haydn (1732–1809), unlike Handel, was primarily interested in instrumental music; he was the chief originator of the symphony. During his long career in Vienna, which he helped to make the music capital of the world, he wrote more than a hundred symphonies in addition to scores of compositions of other forms of music, particularly chamber music. It was in his hands that orchestral music really came into its own. All his work is in the formal, classical style. He became a friend and an important source of inspiration for the younger Mozart.

---

[1]Some music historians designate the music of the seventeenth and early eighteenth centuries, including that of Bach and Handel, as baroque, which was a forerunner of classical.

FIGURE 31.6 **Pieter Brueghel the Younger,** *Flemish Country Festival* This early-seventeenth-century painting shows one of the many typical festivals that took place during the year. Often such festivals were occasioned by religious holidays and celebrations. Here the lines between religion, social life, and popular culture blur as villagers gather and celebrate. (Galleria Sabauda, Turin/ Art Resource)

Wolfgang Amadeus Mozart (1756–1791) is regarded by many students as the greatest musical genius of all time. Born in Salzburg, he spent most of his adult life in Vienna. Mozart began composing at the age of five (possibly four), and gave public concerts on the harpsichord at the age of six. At twelve he wrote an opera. Before his untimely death at the age of thirty-five, he wrote more than six hundred compositions in all the known musical forms. Symphonies, chamber music, and piano sonatas and concertos were his favorite forms. His best-known operas are *The Marriage of Figaro, Don Giovanni,* and *The Magic Flute.* In the masterful hands of Mozart the classical style reached the peak of its perfection. Never had music been so clear, melodic, elegant, and graceful.

Popular Culture

The formal literature and the baroque art of the seventeenth and eighteenth centuries reflected the concerns and tastes of the elite classes. However, the lower classes were not without cultural outlets that fit their lives and were available to them.

Numerous festivals and public ceremonies occurred throughout the year (see Figure 31.6). Some reflected the seasons, which were of particular importance to societies so dependent on agriculture, while others reflected events on the Christian calendar, such as Christmas and Easter. Traditional weddings involved a community procession and festivities as well as a religious ceremony. Music, dancing, feasts, game, and play were part of these festivals and community events.

Sports also brought communities together and were often violent. The most popular involved animals, such as cockfighting and dogfighting. Others, such as soccer and cricket, became more organized, sometimes drawing large crowds.

Literacy was growing, thanks to the printing press, the demands of business, and more primary schools. Some 40 to 60 percent of the population in England and France could read by the end of the eighteenth century, and this was reflected in the growth of popular literature. Stirring religious tracts as well as romances of chivalric valor were widely circulated.

Finally, the line between elite and popular culture was not very sharp. Members of all classes could be found at village festivals and sporting events. The middle and upper classes read some of the same popular literature enjoyed by the lower classes, while the lower classes had some access to the plays, art, and architecture that reflected elite tastes.

SUGGESTED READING

General

F. Braudel, *The Structures of Everyday Life: The Limits of the Possible* (1982). A massive, highly respected social history.

H. Kamen, *European Society, 1500–1700* (1985). A solid survey.

I. Woloch, *Eighteenth Century Europe, Tradition and Progress, 1715–1789* (1982). Emphasizes social history and popular culture.

Society

P. Ariés, *Centuries of Childhood: A Social History of Family Life* (1962). A path-breaking work.

J. V. Beckett, *The Aristocracy in England* (1986). A good recent study.

J. Blum, *The End of the Old Order in Rural Europe* (1978). Excellent comparative study.

M. W. Flinn, *The European Demographic System, 1500–1820* (1981). A recent survey.

A. Fraser, *The Weaker Vessel: Woman's Lot in Seventeenth-Century England* (1985). Portraits of seventeenth-century women.

P. Laslett, *The World We Have Lost* (1965). A classic study of English society during the period.

E. Shorter, *The Making of the Modern Family* (1975). Interpretive, controversial, and well written.

L. Stone, *The Family, Sex and Marriage in England, 1500–1800* (1977). A sophisticated interpretation.

L. Tilly and J. Scott, *Women, Work and Family* (1978). A highly respected work.

J. de Vries, *European Urbanization, 1500–1800* (1984). Broad recent survey.

Faith

A. Armstrong, *The Church of England, the Methodists, and Society 1700–1850* (1973). A broad survey.

G. R. Cragg, *The Church and the Age of Reason* (1961). A solid survey.

Culture

A. Adam, *Grandeur and Illusion: French Literature and Society 1600–1715* (1972). A thorough survey of French literature and its relation to seventeenth-century society.

P. Burke, *Popular Culture in Early Modern Europe* (1978). Focuses on ordinary people.

J. Held, *Seventeenth and Eighteenth Century Art: Baroque Painting, Sculpture, Architecture* (1971). A useful general survey.

C. Palisca, *Baroque Music* (1968). Excellent survey.

C. Rosen, *The Classical Style: Haydn, Mozart, Beethoven* (1972). Excellent study.

I. Watt, *The Rise of the Novel: Studies of Defoe, Richardson, and Fielding* (1957). A good introduction.

CHAPTER 32

Royal Absolutism in Western and Eastern Europe

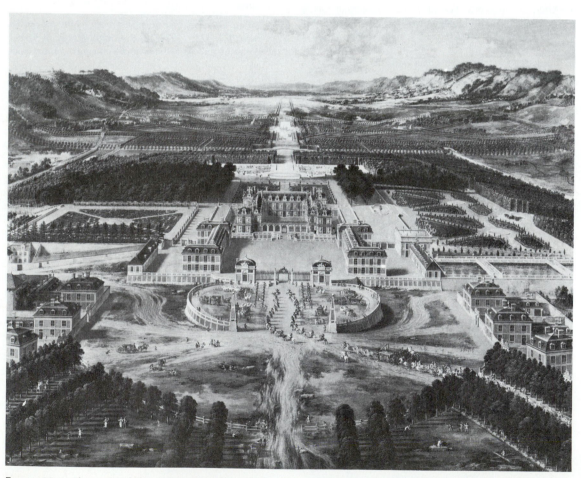

FIGURE 32.1 **Pierre Patel the Elder,** *Versailles,* **1668** This painting shows Louis XIV's palace and grounds at Versailles in 1668. The scale and order of Versailles reflected the grandeur of the French monarchy at its height. Other European monarchs modeled their palaces after Versailles in an attempt to increase their own prestige. (Lauros-Giraudon/Art Resource)

During the seventeenth and eighteenth centuries, several monarchs in western and eastern Europe increased the power of their central governments and elevated themselves as holders of that power. These monarchs often justified their absolute powers as a divine right and surrounded themselves with advisers and admirers who supported royal absolutism. While in some countries the trend was away from monarchical power, royal absolutism became the dominant political development of this period.

1. ABSOLUTISM IN WESTERN EUROPE: FRANCE

France was the most powerful nation in western Europe throughout most of the seventeenth and eighteenth centuries. Under Louis XIV royal absolutism not only reached its peak in France but also served as a model that other monarchs sought to emulate.

While French monarchs had been gaining power for their central government and themselves since the fifteenth century (see pp. 362–363), the immediate roots of royal absolutism in France go back to the reign of Henry IV (1589–1610).

The Roots of French Absolutism

When Henry IV became king of France in 1589, his country was torn by several decades of bitter religious war. Respect for law and order had broken down. The feudal nobility had in many cases reasserted its own authority. The finances of the central government were in chaos. Roads and bridges were in disrepair. French prestige abroad was at a low ebb; even the city of Paris was garrisoned by the Spanish troops of Philip II.

Henry of Navarre, the first of the Bourbon dynasty to rule France, set out to change all this. The new king, in his prime at the age of thirty-six, was debonair and witty, courageous, generous, and optimistic. His slogan "A chicken in the pot of every peasant for Sunday dinner" was more than an idle phrase; it is little wonder that *Henri Quatre* became the most popular monarch in French history. The romantic Henry had in the duke of Sully an able, methodical administrator to serve and steady him. The most urgent task

was to restore the authority of the central government. This Henry set out to do by vigorously suppressing brigandage and enforcing the law. The lesser nobility was brought to heel directly and quickly. The powerful nobility was dealt with more gingerly, but by the end of Henry's reign real headway had been made toward reducing the nobles to obedience to the central government.

Henry and Sully launched a comprehensive program of economic reconstruction. Agriculture and commerce benefited from the increased security of life and property, from the repair of roads, bridges, and harbors, and from the freeing of internal and external commerce from many obstructions and tariff barriers. Marshes were drained for farming. Better breeding methods were introduced. Peasants' livestock and implements were protected against seizure for debt or taxes. New industries producing glass, porcelain, lace, tapestries, and fine leather and textiles were subsidized and protected by the state. Silk culture, which brought vast wealth to France, was introduced. Sully's efficient administration of expenditures resulted in a budget surplus for the first time in many years.

Henry defused the religious turmoil that had weakened France by granting religious toleration to the Huguenot minority. A *politique*, Henry abjured Protestantism in order to gain acceptance as king of an overwhelmingly Roman Catholic nation. The Edict of Nantes, which Henry IV issued in 1598, granted the Huguenots not only complete freedom of conscience and limited public worship but also civil and political equality. Moreover, they were given military control of some two hundred fortified cities and towns as a guarantee against future oppression.

Having laid the foundations for royal supremacy, economic health, and religious toleration, Henry IV in the last years of his reign devoted an increasing amount of attention to foreign affairs. His goal was to make France first secure and then supreme in Europe by weakening the power of the Spanish and Austrian Hapsburgs. In 1610 he readied his armies for a campaign, but just as he was preparing to join them he was assassinated by a fanatic.

After fourteen years of retrogression under Henry IV's Italian wife, Marie de Médicis, and their young and inept son Louis XIII (1610–1643),

Cardinal Richelieu gained active control over the government of France. Although technically a mere servant of the fickle Louis XIII, the masterful cardinal made himself so indispensable that for eighteen years (1624–1642) he held firm control over French affairs. Handsome, arrogant, and calculating, Richelieu was a true Machiavellian. His twofold policy, from which he never veered, was similar to that of Henry IV—to make the royal power supreme in France and France supreme in Europe.

Believing the high nobility and the Huguenots to be the chief threats to royal absolutism, Richelieu crushed them both. With the royal army at his disposal, he boldly destroyed the castles of nobles who remained defiant, disbanded their private armies, and hanged a number of the most recalcitrant. The special military and political privileges that the Huguenots enjoyed under the Edict of Nantes were considered by Richelieu to be intolerable, giving them the status of a state within a state. After a bloody two-year struggle, he stripped the Huguenots of these privileges, although he left their religious and civil liberties intact.

In order to dilute local political influence, which in some provinces was still strong, the dynamic minister divided France into some thirty administrative districts called *généralités*, each of which was placed under the control of an *intendant*,[1] who was an agent of the crown. These *intendants* were chosen from the ranks of the bourgeoisie and were shifted around frequently lest they become too sympathetic with the people over whom they ruled. The royal will was thus further extended throughout France.

Although Richelieu was a cardinal in the Roman Catholic church, he did not hesitate to plunge France into the Thirty Years' War in Germany on the side of the Protestants. His purpose, of course, was to weaken the Hapsburgs, chief rivals of the French Bourbons for European supremacy. When Richelieu died in 1642, he had gone far toward bringing to fruition Henry IV's policies of royal supremacy in France and French supremacy in Europe. Richelieu, however, did not share Henry IV's concern for the common people. Their lot became harder under the imperious and ruthless cardinal, at whose death they rejoiced.

Richelieu was succeeded by his protégé, Cardinal Mazarin. Louis XIII's death in 1643, one year after that of his great minister, left the throne to Louis XIV (1643–1715), a child of five. Mazarin played the same role in the early reign of Louis XIV that Richelieu had played during most of the reign of Louis XIII. From the death of Richelieu in 1642 until his own death in 1661, Mazarin vigorously pursued the policies of his predecessor. The Thirty Years' War was brought to a successful conclusion. Between 1648 and 1652, he put down the *Fronde*—a series of uprisings by disgruntled nobility and townspeople. All who challenged the crown's authority were crushed. When Marazin died in 1661, he passed along to young Louis XIV a royal power that was unprecedented and a national state that was easily the first power of Europe.

Louis XIV and His Government

Louis XIV was twenty-three years old when, in 1661, he stepped forth as the principal actor on the world's gaudiest stage. Young Louis was well fitted for the part. He had a sound body and a regal bearing. His lack of intellectual brilliance and deep learning were more than offset by a large store of common sense, a sharp memory, a sense of responsibility, and a capacity for hard, tedious work. From his Spanish mother, from Mazarin, and from his tutors he had gained the conviction that he was God's appointed deputy for France. In Bishop Bossuet he had the most famous of all theorists and exponents of royal absolutism. Bossuet in numerous writings argued that absolute monarchy is the normal, the most efficient, and the divinely ordained form of government. He contended that, furthermore, the royal monarch, the image of God and directly inspired by God, is above human reproach and accountable to God alone. These ideas as acted out by Louis gained and held the ascendancy throughout the continent of Europe during the late seventeenth and most of the eighteenth centuries.

Absolute though he might consider himself (the words "L état, c'est moi" ["I am the state"]

---

[1] The *intendants* had existed before Richelieu's time, but he greatly increased their power and functions.

are often attributed to him), Louis could not possibly perform all the functions of government personally. Actually, the great bulk of the decisions and details of government were handled by a series of councils and bureaus and were administered locally by the *intendants*. Distrusting nobles, Louis appointed members of the middle class to the important offices of his government. As supervised by the industrious Louis XIV, however, the administrative machinery worked smoothly and efficiently. In fact, it was the envy of his fellow monarchs and probably constituted his most constructive achievement. There was no semblance of popular participation in government. The role of the people was to serve and obey; in return, they enjoyed reflected glory and received such benefits as the monarch might be willing and able to bestow on them.

In line with Louis XIV's concept of divine right absolutism, he believed that he should have a palace worthy of God's chief deputy on earth. Hating tumultuous Paris, congested and crowded with vulgar tradespeople, he selected Versailles, eleven miles southwest of the city, to be the new seat of government. There as many as thirty-five thousand workmen toiled for thirty years, turning the marshes and sandy wastes into the world's most splendid court (see Figure 32.1). Around his court Louis XIV gathered the great nobles of France and turned them into court butterflies (see Figure 32.2). He subsidized and brought to Versailles the leading French artists and literacy figures. But this great monument to royal absolutism was not beloved by all. The balls, parades, hunts, and social ritual were not sufficient to absorb the energy of the vivacious and ambitious nobility of France. The court seethed with gossip, scandal, and intrigue. Nor did the hard-toiling, heavily taxed French masses, who were supposed to enjoy the reflected glory of the monarch, always appreciate such extravagant glamour. Indeed, there were increasing expressions of discontent.

Colbert and the French Economy

Louis XIV was fortunate to have at his command during the first half of his reign a prodigious financial manager. Jean-Baptiste Colbert (1619–1683) was an inordinately ambitious social climber who realized that, because of his bourgeois origin, his only means of advancement was through indispensable service to the king. An engine of efficiency, he toiled endlessly, supervising the countless details of the French economy.

Under Colbert, mercantilism reached its peak. French industries were protected by prohibitive tariffs, while exports and new industries were subsidized. Raw materials, however, were strictly husbanded. Imperial and commercial activities in India and North America were vigorously promoted. To protect this growing empire and the commerce it generated, a large navy was built. But Colbert did not stop with these traditional mercantilist practices. In order to gain a worldwide reputation for the uniformly high quality of French products, all manufacturing was subjected to the most minute regulation and supervision. So many threads of such and such quality and color must go into every inch of this textile and that lace. A veritable army of inspectors enforced the regulations. This extreme policy of mercantilism, the economic adjunct to royal absolutism, has come to be called Colbertism. It achieved its immediate end so far as quality and reputation were concerned, but it stifled initiative and retarded future industrial development. That Colbert was able to balance the budget and achieve general economic prosperity in the face of Louis XIV's lavish expenditures, including the building of Versailles, was a remarkable feat. It is well, however, that Colbert died in 1683, for Louis' wars of aggression eventually wrecked most of the great minister's work. Much of Europe copied Colbert's policies and techniques during the latter part of the seventeenth and most of the eighteenth centuries.

Absolutism and Religion

It was virtually inevitable that Louis XIV's concepts of divine right monarchy would have religious repercussions. First, they ran counter to the papal claims of authority over the French clergy. Numerous conflicts between the king and pope resulted in a statement of Gallican Liberties, which greatly freed the French church from Roman domination. Second, Louis' absolutism ran afoul of the Jansenists, an influential group within France's Catholic church that emphasized predestination, inner piety, and the ascetic life.

FIGURE 32.2 Charles Lebrun, *Chancellor Seguier* Chancellor Seguier, a patron of the seventeenth-century French artist Lebrun, is shown here as an ambitious courtier to Louis XIV. In formal robes, this member of France's new nobility (*noblesse de robe*) is attended by pages as if he were a monarch. (The Louvre, Paris)

Eventually the Jesuits persuaded the pope to declare Jansenism heretical and aroused Louis XIV against the Jansenists. He outlawed the sect and destroyed its buildings. Finally, Louis XIV moved against the Huguenots—France's Protestants. In 1685 he revoked the Edict of Nantes and the Protestant religion was outlawed. Although Huguenots were forbidden to emigrate, many—probably a quarter million—succeeded in doing so, taking much of their wealth and all their economic knowledge and skills with them to Protestant areas of Europe and America.

Louis XIV's Wars of Aggression

The Sun King was not content to rule the world's most powerful nation. He wanted to expand France's borders. Louis' war minister, the marquis of Louvois, organized France's huge military establishment on a scientific and businesslike basis, replete with supply depots and hospitals. He introduced strict discipline, uniforms, and marching drills. Sébastien de Vauban was one of the great designers of fortifications and of siege operations. It was a common saying that a city defended by Vauban was safe and that a city besieged by Vauban was doomed. Henri-Jules Condé was an able and dashing military leader and the viscount of Turenne a masterly planner of campaigns and battles.

During the last four decades of his seventy-two-year reign Louis XIV fought four wars of aggression, at times unifying most of the other military powers of western Europe against him. By the end of the Dutch War in 1678, Louis XIV had gained some valuable territories. But the tide turned. His final struggle, the War of the Spanish Succession, lasted eleven years (1702–1713) and resulted in a series of defeats. Beaten and exhausted, Louis XIV was forced to accept the Treaty of Utrecht (1713). He was left with little more than he had started with some fifty years earlier.

Louis XIV lived only two years after the signing of the Treaty of Utrecht. He had long outlived his popularity. As the body of the grandest of all the absolute monarchs was drawn through the streets of Paris, some of his abused people cursed in the taverns as the coffin passed.

The Decline of French Absolutism

The French monarchy never again achieved the power it had wielded under Louis XIV. Certainly France remained a first-rank power with a large army, a centralized bureaucracy, and a growing economy. But between 1715 and 1789 the monarchy slowly declined.

Expensive wars and unreformed taxation policies left the treasury depleted after Louis XIV's death. The clergy and nobility retained most of their immunity from taxation despite the efforts of several ministers to break those privileges. The debt grew, and the monarchy was weakened by its inability to reform its finances to lessen the burden of that debt.

Underlying these political and financial problems was a resurgence of the aristocracy. In the decades between 1715 and 1789 the monarchy was faced by an increasingly assertive aristocracy anxious to recapture some of its old political power. Ambitious aristocrats thwarted the kings' efforts to reform taxes. They set themselves up as centers of aristocratic opposition to the monarchy, above all through their control of the *parlements* (law courts).

Thus, by the middle decades of the eighteenth century, the French monarchy had clearly declined from its heights under Louis XIV. When problems came to a head in the 1780s, the king was unable to handle them and the monarchy was toppled by a great revolution.

2. ABSOLUTISM IN EASTERN EUROPE

At the beginning of the seventeenth century eastern Europe exhibited certain characteristics that set it in sharp contrast to western Europe. Economically, the states east of the Elbe River were less commercially developed than those in western Europe. Estate agriculture (large landed estates owned by lords and worked by their serfs) remained the rule. Socially, the landed aristocracy dominated these areas to a greater extent than in western Europe. Indeed, this aristocracy had generally succeeded in reversing the medieval trends toward greater freedom for the peasantry and the growth of towns. During the fifteenth, sixteenth, and seventeenth centuries serfdom was reimposed with greater severity than ever, and the landed aristocracy won in its struggle with competing urban centers. Politically, many areas lacked the strong central government found in the western European states.

The most significant political developments in central and eastern Europe during the seventeenth and eighteenth centuries were the rise of Prussia, the centralization of Austria, and the expansion of Russia, three states that developed strong national governments and powerful monarchies. At the opening of the seventeenth century, the two chief powers in central and eastern Europe were the Ottoman and Hapsburg empires. Although the Islamic Ottoman Turks had been restrained by Hapsburg military power in the sixteenth century on both land and sea, they were about to renew their effort to conquer Christian Europe. The Austrian Hapsburgs, in addition to disputing the control of southeastern Europe with the Turks, dominated the Holy Roman Empire, which included all the German states. In northeastern Europe, Sweden, Prussia, Poland, and Russia competed for hegemony. Among all these powers, Prussia and Russia had hitherto been the least conspicuous in world affairs. During the seventeenth and eighteenth centuries, Prussia and Russia would become major powers and assume an active role in international politics.

The Hohenzollerns and the Hapsburgs

The political history of Prussia is in large measure the history of Hohenzollern family rulers. In 1415 the Hohenzollerns became rulers of Brandenburg (1415), a bleak and thinly populated little province within the Holy Roman Empire. In the centuries that followed until they were finally overthrown at the end of the World War I in 1918, they followed a threefold policy: militarism and territorial aggrandizement, paternal despotism, and centralized bureaucracy. The first to take major steps toward making Brandenburg an important power was Frederick William (1640–1688), the Great Elector. One of the ablest of all the Hohenzollerns, he acquired several new territories at the end of the Thirty Years' War. He centralized and administered the governments of his scattered territories with energy and skill. He won in his struggles with the Estates, the representative assemblies of the realm, gaining the crucial power to collect taxes and eliminating the Estates as a functioning institution. He established and strengthened his standing army. He managed an important compromise with the landed aristocracy, allowing them complete control over their serfs but committing them to his government as members of his bureaucracy and his military officer corps. He protected the native industries, improved communications, and aided agriculture. In a most intolerant age he followed a policy of religious toleration. When Louis XIV revoked the Edict of Nantes in 1685, Frederick William welcomed thousands of industrious Huguenots to Brandenburg. At the death of the Great Elector in 1688, Brandenburg was on the road to becoming a great power.

The next Hohenzollern, Frederick I (1688–1713), acquired the title of king for the dynasty. The Hapsburg Holy Roman emperor in 1701 granted Frederick the title in return for aid against Louis XIV in the War of the Spanish Succession. Frederick I chose Prussia rather than Brandenburg for the name of his kingdom, since Prussia was outside the Holy Roman Empire and a free sovereign state. Hence Brandenburg became Prussia.

From 1713 to 1740 Prussia was ruled by a vigorous militaristic autocrat, Frederick William I (since he was the first Frederick William to be king). Unquestioned absolutism, machinelike centralized bureaucratic administration, and, above all, militarism were his obsessions. He built the Prussian army into the most efficient and one of the largest fighting forces in Europe. And yet Frederick William was so efficient and miserly that he was also able to pass along to his talented son, Frederick II, a well-filled treasury.

In the same year (1740) that Frederick II became King of Prussia, Maria Theresa became archduchess of the Austrian Hapsburg dominions. During the second half of the seventeenth century the Austrian Hapsburgs had successfully carried out a policy of centralizing their power in those lands they directly controlled (rather than the Holy Roman Empire) and expanding to the east. The monarchy improved its administration, established a powerful standing army, gained at least a fragile allegiance of the nobility, and acquired territories at the expense of the Ottoman empire and Poland.

In 1740 Frederick II challenged Maria Theresa's authority by marching his troops into Silesia, one of the richest of the Hapsburg provinces. This Machiavellian act by the young Prussian king plunged most of the major European states into a series of wars for the mastery of central Europe. The War of the Austrian Succession lasted for eight years (1740–1748). Maria Theresa successfully repelled the Bavarians, Saxons, French, and Spaniards, but she was unable to dislodge Frederick II from Silesia. Frederick, on his part, cynically deserted his allies as soon as he had achieved his own purposes.

The Hapsburgs, however, had no intention of being thus despoiled of one of their fairest provinces by the upstart Hohenzollerns. Proud rulers over territories many times the size and population of Prussia and for centuries emperors of the Holy Roman Empire, they viewed the Hohenzollerns with condescension. Maria Theresa's able diplomat, Count Kaunitz, was soon at work lining up allies.

Frederick was not one to wait for his enemies

FIGURE 32.3 Frederick II Before His Troops During the seventeenth and eighteenth centuries, the rulers of Brandenburg-Prussia used their armies to build up the state, making it one of the major powers of eastern and central Europe. Here, Frederick II of Prussia is shown in a characteristic military pose, exemplifying the strong alliance of the monarchy and army. (The Mansell Collection, London)

Having so narrowly escaped destruction, Frederick the Great spent the remaining twenty-three years of his life reconstructing his war-ravaged territories. He encouraged agriculture, subsidized and protected industry, and invited immigrants into his well-governed territories. At no time, though, did he neglect his war machine. In 1772 he joined Austria and Russia in the first partition of Poland. Frederick took West Prussia, thus joining East Prussia with the main body of the Prussian state. When Frederick II died in 1786, Prussia had been raised to the status of a great power, sharing the leadership of central Europe equally with Austria. During his reign Prussia's size and population had more than doubled, and its military exploits pointed to a spectacular future (see Map 32.1).

Russia and the Romanovs

While Prussia was becoming a great power in central Europe, Russia was rising to prominence to the east. The first of the grand dukes of Muscovy under whom Russia took on the shape of a modern national state was Ivan III (1462–1505). In 1480 Ivan III defeated the rapidly declining Mongols and limited their power in Russia to the southeastern area. Ivan greatly extended his sway to both the north and the west by military conquest. After his marriage to Sophia Palaeologus, heiress to the now-defunct Byzantine (Eastern Roman) Empire, Ivan declared himself successor to the Eastern Roman Caesars—hence the title "tsar." When he died, the foundations of a Russian national state had been laid (see Map 32.2).

Ivan IV (1533–1584), "the Terrible," added both to the authority of the Russian tsars and to the territories over which they ruled. He destroyed the remaining power of the Mongols in southeastern Russia and annexed most of their territory. It was during Ivan IV's reign that Russia's conquest of Siberia was begun. Half a century later the Russian flag was planted on the shores of the Pacific.

The twenty-nine years following the death of Ivan IV are known as the Time of Troubles (1584–1613). Weak rulers and disputed successions resulted in such anarchy that the Poles were able

to strike first. As soon as he became aware of their designs, he opened hostilities by overrunning Saxony (see Figure 32.3). Thus began the Seven Years' War (1756–1763). Frederick, with his slender resources, soon found himself at bay; the four greatest military powers on the continent of Europe were closing in on him from all directions. After tenaciously holding his enemies off for six years, defeat appeared to be near. Then in 1762 the Russian Tsarina Elizabeth, one of his bitterest enemies, died and was succeeded by the ineffective Peter III, who was an ardent admirer of Frederick II and who put Russia's forces at the disposal of Prussia. Although Peter III was soon murdered by a group of his own officers and court nobility and Russia withdrew from the war, the remaining allies had no further stomach for the fight. The Peace of Hubertusburg in 1763 left things as they had been at the beginning of the war, with Prussia retaining the controversial Silesia. In the same year the Treaty of Paris brought to a close the colonial struggle between Great Britain and France in India and North America, leaving Great Britain master of both.

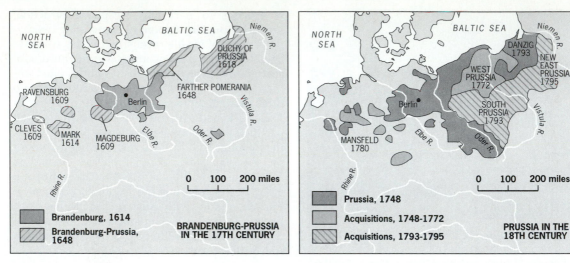

Map 32.1 THE GROWTH OF PRUSSIA, 1614–1807 These maps show the growth of Brandenburg-Prussia during the seventeenth and eighteenth centuries. The maps reveal the lack of connections among many of Brandenburg-Prussia's lands; one of Prussia's long-term goals in the eighteenth and nineteenth centuries was to connect those territories it already controlled as well as to expand its holdings.

to capture Moscow and hold it briefly. To end the political chaos, a group of leading nobles in 1613 chose Michael Romanov as tsar.

The early decades of the Romanov dynasty, which was to rule Russia until the Revolution of 1917, were not easy. There were great popular discontent and numerous uprisings between the late 1640s and the early 1670s as the lower classes rebelled against the nobles and the central government, who were making serfdom even more onerous and life for townspeople more difficult. The discontent reached a climax with the revolts led by Stenka Razin in the late 1660s and early 1670s. Razin was finally caught and executed, thus ending that series of threats. During this same period problems within the Russian Orthodox church broke out as many, known as the Old Believers, rejected liturgical changes initiated by the patriarch of Moscow. The effect of this controversy was to drive the Church into greater dependence on the secular government. Nevertheless, by the final decades of the seventeenth century the Romanov tsars had managed to overcome these problems, improve the central administration, and extend their authority. They

gradually established commercial and cultural contacts with the West. Increasing numbers of traders, artisans, and adventurers from central and western Europe, particularly Germany, came to Russia to seek their fortunes. Thus the stage was set for Russia to become more fully involved in European affairs. This involvement became especially important during the reign of Peter the Great.

Peter I (1689–1725) was an unusually large, vigorous, and ambitious individual. At the age of seventeen he seized the reins of government from his elder sister. For the next thirty-six years he devoted his boundless energy to the twofold policy of strengthening his own authority and his military forces and of gaining access to the west on the Baltic and Black seas.

Peter concluded that one of the best ways to increase his own political and military power was to copy Western practices. He traveled in western Europe and learned much about Western customs and techniques, which he proceeded to introduce into Russia. After crushing a revolt of his bodyguard with a ruthlessness that cowed all potential troublemakers, he adopted the bu-

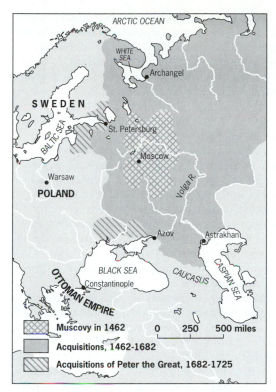
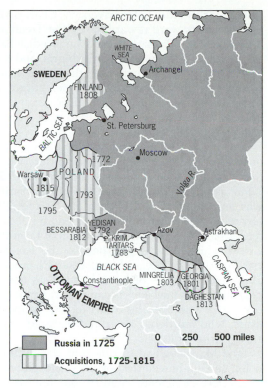

Map 32.2 THE GROWTH OF RUSSIA IN THE WEST These maps show the steady expansion of Russia to the west and south, acquiring access on the Baltic and Black seas under Peter the Great and extending its territories further in the course of the eighteenth century.

reaucratic system of western European monarchs in both central and local government to make his authority more absolute. Western technicians were brought to Russia in large numbers, and new industries were subsidized and protected by mercantilist policies. Western, particularly French, social customs were introduced to the upper and middle classes of Russian society. Women were brought out of seclusion, and the long beards and flowing Oriental robes of the men were banned. These reforms hardly touched the peasant masses, who were increasingly tied down in a system of serfdom bordering on slavery—a process that had been going on in Russia throughout the sixteenth and seventeenth centuries. When the patriarch of the Russian Ortho-

dox church opposed the tsar's authority and some of his Westernizing policies, Peter abolished the patriarchate. Henceforth, the Orthodox church was a powerful instrument of the Russian government. But Peter the Great's chief concern was always his military establishment. He built a navy and patterned his conscript army after that of Prussia. By the end of his reign, Russia had one of the major fighting forces of Europe.

When Peter became tsar, Russia had no warm-water access to the west. Sweden held the coveted shores of the Baltic Sea, and the Ottoman Turks occupied the territory north of the Black Sea. Peter's efforts to dislodge the Ottoman Turks were not very successful, but after an extended, costly war with Sweden, in which Peter lost the early battles to his adversary, Charles XII, Peter's efforts were rewarded. By the Treaty of Nystad in 1721, Russia received the Swedish Baltic provinces of Livonia, Estonia, Ingria, and Karelia. On the Neva River near the Baltic, Peter built a new, modern capital, St. Petersburg, facing the west. At his death in 1725, Russia was a great and growing power ready to play a major role in European affairs.

Peter the Great was followed by a succession of weak or mediocre rulers. After an interval of thirty-seven years, Catherine the Great (1762–1796) ascended the Russian throne. Catherine was an obscure princess from one of the little German states. She had been married for political reasons to young Peter III, grandson of Peter the Great, while he was still heir to the Russian crown. After he became tsar, Peter III quickly alienated all classes of his subjects. Less than a year after her husband became tsar, Catherine conspired with a group of aristocratic army officers, who murdered Peter and declared Catherine tsarina of Russia.

The Machiavellian tsarina prided herself on being an enlightened despot, as was fashionable in the late eighteenth century, but few of her enlightened ideas were translated into political or social deeds. Some apparent reforming efforts ended when Russian serfs rose in one of the greatest insurrections in history. In 1773, under the able leadership of a Don Cossack, Pugachev, hundreds of thousands of serfs marched against their masters. The rebellion was put down with difficulty. The cruel repression left Russian serfs almost as slaves to the privileged nobility.

Catherine the Great followed an aggressive foreign policy. Peter the Great had reached the Baltic by despoiling the Swedes. Catherine reached the Black Sea, the Balkan peninsula, and the heart of Europe by defeating the Turks and destroying Poland. When she finally died in 1796, Russia was a nation ominous in size and power and a major factor in European and world affairs.

Poland, Sweden, and the Ottoman Empire

By the end of the eighteenth century, Prussia and Russia were rising, major powers in Europe. Poland, Sweden, and the Ottoman Empire did not fare so well.

Poland, at the opening of the eighteenth century, was the third largest country in Europe, exceeded in size only by Russia and Sweden. In the sixteenth and seventeenth centuries it had appeared that Poland would become a major power. Taking advantage of Russia's Time of Troubles (1584–1613), the Poles had captured Moscow. In the latter part of the century they had saved Vienna from the Turks.

Actually, however, the Polish nation was far from strong. Sprawling over a large area between Russia and the German states, it enjoyed no natural boundaries either to the east or to the west. The eastern half of its territory was inhabited by Russian-speaking people. The northern provinces were peopled largely by Latvians, Lithuanians, and Germans. There were also many Germans in the west. Religious cleavages followed the language lines.

Moreover, there was no strong middle class to vitalize Poland's economy. In the late Middle Ages a sizable overland commerce between the Black and Baltic seas had flowed across Poland. But with the shifting of commercial routes and centers to the west in the early sixteenth century, Poland's commerce had withered. Furthermore, the Polish nobility, jealous of its own power and fearful of an alliance between the bourgeoisie and the king, deliberately penalized commerce with severe restrictions. The great mass of the people were serfs, tilling the soil of the powerful nobility.

In the face of so many divisive forces, only a strong central government could have made Poland into a stable national state. But here lay Poland's greatest weakness. The kingship was elective, and the great nobles who held the elective power saw to it that no strong king ever came to the throne. During the eighteenth century the kings were all foreigners or puppets of foreign powers. The legislative Diet was completely monopolized by the nobility. So that each noble's rights were safeguarded, unanimity was required for the passage of every measure. This system guaranteed virtual political anarchy. National spirit was weak. The all-powerful nobles were far more concerned for their own private interests than for the well-being of the nation.

It would have been surprising had such a power vacuum as eighteenth-century Poland not invited the aggression of its ambitious neighbors.

In 1772 Catherine the Great and Frederick the Great bargained to take slices of Polish territory. The somewhat less greedy Maria Theresa of Austria, fearful of being outdistanced by Russia and Prussia, joined them. This aggression at long last stirred the Poles to action. Sweeping reforms were passed, improving the condition of the peasants and the bourgeoisie and giving the king and the Diet power to act effectively. But it was too late. They were no match for the professional armies of Russia, Prussia, and Austria, who in 1795 divided the remainder of Poland among themselves.

Poland was not the only victim in eastern Europe of the powerful Russian, Prussian, and Austrian armies. Sweden and the Ottoman Empire also declined, both relatively and actually. Sweden had become the dominant military power in northern and eastern Europe under Gustavus Adolphus in the early seventeenth century. At the opening of the eighteenth century Sweden was second only to Russia in size among the nations of Europe, holding large areas east and south of the Baltic in addition to the homeland. However, its population and resources were too small to hold such far-flung territories, which were coveted by the ambitious and growing Prussia and Russia, for very long. Charles XII made a spectacular effort to hold them, but in the end he lost all his trans-Baltic territories except Finland, and he dissipated Sweden's strength in doing so. Sweden has never been a major power since.

The Ottoman Turks, after reaching the gates of Vienna early in the sixteenth century and again late in the seventeenth century, weakened rapidly. The Treaty of Karlowitz in 1699 limited their power in Europe to the Balkan peninsula and a strip of territory north of the Black Sea. Their two serious defeats at the hands of Catherine the Great marked the beginning of the breakup of the Ottoman Empire.

By the end of the eighteenth century, the three dominant powers in central and eastern Europe were the relatively static Austrian Hapsburg Empire and the two rapidly rising states—Prussia and Russia (see Map 32.3). Each of these states, like France in western Europe, had developed strong central governments with standing armies, large bureaucracies, and organized systems of taxation under the monarch's control.

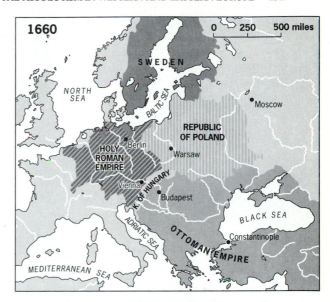

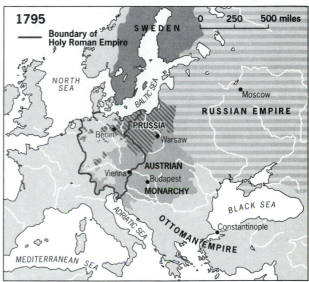

Map 32.3 EASTERN EUROPE, SIXTEENTH–EIGHTEENTH CENTURIES Between the sixteenth and eighteenth centuries, political power in central and eastern Europe shifted fundamentally. The first map shows Sweden, the Holy Roman Empire, Poland, and the Ottoman Empire in the sixteenth and early seventeenth centuries. The second map shows that by the end of the eighteenth century, these powers except for Sweden had all but been replaced by Prussia, the Russian Empire, and the Austrian Empire, and Sweden's holdings had been diminished by Russian Expansion.

SUGGESTED READING

General

P. Anderson, *Lineages of the Absolutist State* (1974). A good Marxist analysis.

R. N. Hatton, *Europe in the Age of Louis XIV* (1979). A well-illustrated survey.

D. McKay and H. Scott, *The Rise of the Great Powers, 1648–1815* (1983). A good survey.

D. Pennington, *Europe in the Seventeenth Century* (1989). A recent introduction.

Absolutism in Western Europe

W. Beik, *Absolutism and Society in Seventeenth-Century France* (1985). A well-written interpretation of French absolutism.

W. F. Church, ed., *Louis XIV in Historical Thought* (1978). Conflicting interpretations of Louis XIV.

P. Goubert, *Louis XIV and Twenty Million Frenchmen* (1970). A respected study of French society and politics.

H. Rowen, *The King's State: Proprietary Dynasticism in Early Modern France* (1980). Analyzes the theory of Louis XIV's rule.

V. L. Tapié, *France in the Age of Louis XIII and Richelieu* (1974). A good survey.

A. Trout, *Jean-Baptiste Colbert* (1978). Analyzes his economic policies.

Absolutism in Eastern Europe

P. Coles, *The Ottoman Impact on Europe, 1350–1699* (1968). A well-written study.

N. Davies, *God's Playground: A History of England*, Vol. 1; *The Origins to 1795.* (1981). A full introduction.

P. Dukes, *The Making of Russian Absolutism: 1613–1801* (1982). A solid survey.

R. J. Evans, *The Making of the Hapsburg Empire, 1550–1770* (1979). A solid, recent account.

H. Holborn, *A History of Modern Germany 1648–1840* (1966). The best on the subject.

H. C. Johnson, *Frederick the Great and His Officials* (1975). Focuses on Prussian administration.

H. W. Koch, *A History of Prussia* (1978). A good analysis of the rise of Prussia.

I. de Madariaga, *Russia in the Age of Catherine the Great* (1981). Highly regarded recent study.

M. Roberts, *Sweden's Age of Greatness* (1973). A good summary of Sweden during this period.

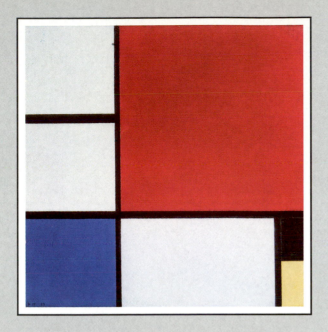

PLATE 31. Piet Mondrian, *Composition*, 1929
The twentieth-century trend away from art that represents external reality toward abstract art was carried to an extreme by the Dutch painter Piet Mondrian (1872–1944). Here he uses only black, white, and the three primary colors to express his logical, harmonious vision. (National Museum, Belgrade: Scala/Art Resource)

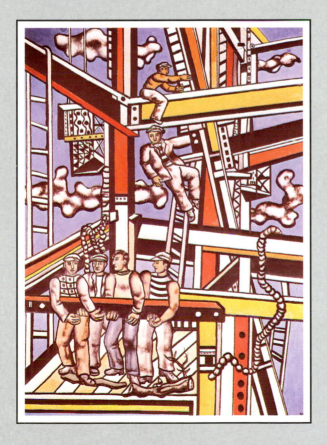

PLATE 32. Fernand Léger, *The Great Constructors*, 1950 This painting by the French artist Léger (1881–1955), reflects several trends in twentieth century art. Clearly this is an urban scene, showing construction workers and the steel frame of a skyscraper; yet the lines, proportions, and colors scarcely conform to reality. Elements of expressionism—the attempt to convey a feeling about people in this mechanical age—and abstract art—the concern with nonrepresentational lines and colors—abound in this work. (Musée de Biot, France: Josse/Art Resource)

PLATE 29. Max Ernst, *Europe after the Rain,* 1940–1942 Max Ernst (1891–1976) became a leader of the surrealists during the 1920s. He painted *Europe after the Rain* while hiding in Paris during World War II. The painting seems to represent the illogical horror and destruction of that era, and it stands as a perhaps prophetic warning to us all. (Wadsworth Atheneum, Hartford, Ella Gallup Sumner and Mary Catlin Sumner Collection)

PLATE 30. Salvador Dalí, *The Temptation of St. Anthony,* 1947 Surrealism, a relatively popular style of twentieth-century painting, emphasizes the power of dreams and the unconscious. The aim is to depict an unfiltered psychic reality that visually may seem shocking and impossible. One of the most well known surealists was Salvador Dalí (1904–1989). Here the subject is apparently traditional (St. Anthony trying to fend off temptations), but the painting has the feeling and appearance of an improbable nightmare. (Musées Royaux des Beaux-Arts de Belgique, Brussels)

PLATE 27. James Ensor, *Intrigue,* **1890**
During the late nineteenth century a
sense of dissatisfaction and a criticism of
middle-class life grew. This is reflected in
expressive paintings such as those by the
Belgian painter James Ensor (1860–
1949). Here people are shown as indis-
tinct from the obnoxious masks they
seem to wear. (Royal Museum of Fine Arts,
Antwerp)

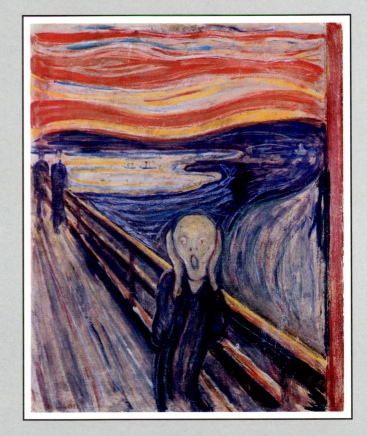

PLATE 28. Edvard Munch, *The Scream,*
1893 Like Ensor, Edvard Munch (1863–
1944) expressed an undermining of middle-class life, but on a deeper, more individual level. In *The Scream,* a nightmare-
like fear is revealed, reflecting an anxiety
and a turning inward toward the unconscious that was growing in late-nineteeth-
century intellectual and cultural circles.
Similarities to van Gogh's paintings can
be seen in how paint is used boldly to
express emotion. (National Museum, Oslo)

PLATE 25. Paul Cézanne, *Mont Sainte-Victoire*, 1902–1904 Cézanne (1839–1906) had roots in impressionism but ultimately rejected it. He tried to display the essence rather than the surface of reality by emphasizing the geometric principles of form and an analytic understanding of color. This landscape is one of a series of paintings of Mont Sainte-Victoire in southern France. Both Cézanne and van Gogh created foundations for twentieth-century painting. (Philadelphia Museum of Art, George W. Elkins Collection)

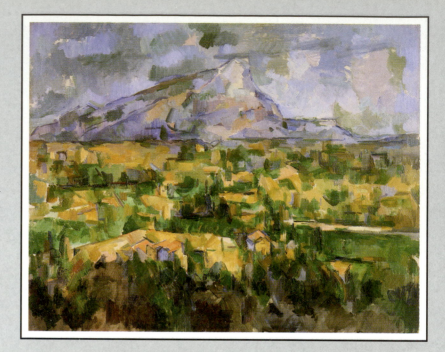

PLATE 26. Vincent van Gogh, *The Starry Night*, 1889 Like Cézanne, van Gogh (1853–1890) had roots in impressionism but went beyond it. He was able to express his own intense emotions in bold, dynamic paintings. Here he seems to have poured himself into this scene he painted toward the end of his life while at a sanatorium in St.-Rémy. The scene swirls with color applied in distinct, broad strokes. It is not a scene of reality one might see, but rather an expression of feelings that mingles with external reality. (Oil on canvas, 29 x 36¼". Collection, The Museum of Modern Art, New York; acquired through the Lillie P. Bliss Bequest)

PLATE 23. Auguste Renoir, *Le Moulin de la Galette à Montmartre*, 1876 Impressionist painters emphasized the appearance of things as one might see them at a glance. Using new techniques that emphasized applying dabs of colors to the canvas so the eye could mix them, these paintings had great immediacy. Here Renoir (1841–1919), a leading French impressionist most known for his fleshy, optimistic paintings, portrays a festive scene at a Parisian outdoor dance hall. Youthful middle- and working-class figures brim with health and pleasure in this artificial urban environment. (Musée d'Orsay, Paris; Scala/Art Resource)

PLATE 24. Georges Seurat, *A Sunday on La Grande Jatte*, 1884–1886 Some neo-impressionists such as the French artist, Georges Seurat (1859–1891), reflected the growing influence of science during the second half of the nineteenth century. Using a compulsive style of painting based on the latest scientific understanding of light and color, Seurat carefully composed this canvas portraying the urban bourgeoise at leisure. The scene emphasizes the inhibited stiffness of this class, its emotional separation from other classes, and the isolation of individuals and small groups within the bourgeoisie. (Oil on canvas, 207.6 × 308 cm, Helen Birch Bartlett Memorial Collection, 1926.224. © 1993 The Art Institute of Chicago.)

PLATE 21. Eugène Delacroix, *Entrance of the Crusaders into Constantinople*, 1840 Romantic painters such as Delacroix (1793–1863) often glorified the medieval past and the exotic. In this dramatic scene, Byzantine patricians humble themselves before the intruding Crusaders. The scene swirls with passion and color—a romantic vision of the past in sharp contrast to the reality of mid-nineteenth century France. (The Louvre, Paris)

PLATE 22. Gustave Courbet, *The Stone Breakers*, 1849 Realism rejected almost all elements of the Romantic movement. Realistic artists such as Courbet (1819–1877) depicted the mundane, everyday life of workers. Here he portrays stone breakers as a passerby might see them. While there is dignity in their work, Courbet does not glorify them or nature. (Staatlichen Kunstsammlungen, Dresden)

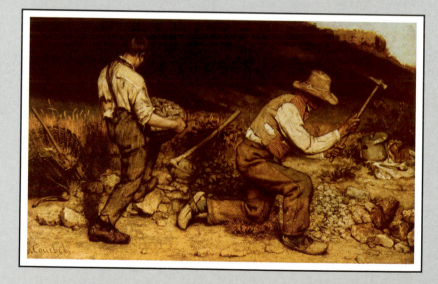

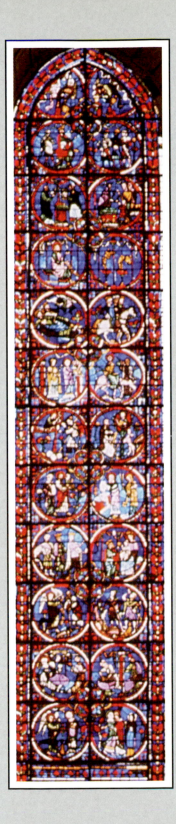

PLATE 10. Stained Glass One of the most stunning features of a Gothic church was its stained-glass windows. Although the effect such windows created is impossible to capture in a photograph, the one shown here from the cathedral at Laon in France shows how an artist could use different-colored pieces of glass to tell a story, usually from sacred history. This window treats the childhood of Jesus. (Archives Photographiques, Paris: Jean Feuillie © C.N.M.H.S./S.P.A.D.E.M.)

PLATE 11. A Winter Scene Very popular in the late Middle Ages were illustrated books of hours used for private devotions. A splendid example was one created for the duke of Berry. It contained a painting for each month of the year. The one below is for February. (Musée Condé/ Chantilly: Giraudon/Art Resource)

PLATE 12. Giovanni Bellini, *Transfiguration of Christ,* **Late 1480s** Giovanni Bellini (1430–1516) was one of the leading painters of the Italian Renaissance. In the *Transfiguration of Christ,* the sacred figures, Peter, James, and John, crouch below Christ, who stands calmly between Moses and Elijah. In the background is a fifteenth-century town and the hills of northern Italy. The individualism of the figures, the depth and realism of the landscape, the immediacy of the scene, and the religiosity of the subject matter were characteristic of Renaissance art. (Museo di Capodimonte, Naples: Scala/Art Resource)

PLATE 13. Raphael, *Portrait of a Man,* **ca. 1503** While Renaissance artists typically painted religious scenes, they also painted secular scenes—often reflecting the tastes and characters of their patrons. Raphael is considered the central painter of the High Renaissance. In portraits such as this, he conveyed the strength and individuality of important secular men without resorting to flattery or conventions. (Borghese Gallery, Rome: Scala/Art Resource)

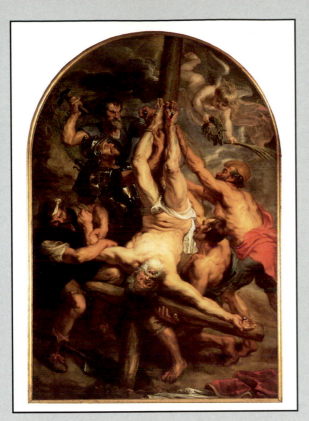

PLATE 14. Peter Paul Rubens, *The Crucifixion of St. Peter*, 1642 Baroque paintings are often extraordinarily dynamic and rich. This is particularly so in the large paintings of Rubens. In this altarpiece, the subject matter is religious, but the feeling of the painting is not one of calmness or piety. The heroic, heavily muscled figures are caught in a moment of dramatic struggle; color and lines create a sense of movement; details are carefully rendered creating a sense of realism. (Church of St. Peter, Cologne. Fotografie Wim Cox)

PLATE 15. Claude Lorraine, *The Marriage of Isaac and Rebekah (The Mill)*, 1640 This painting, with foreground figures framed by trees under a radiant sky, reveals certain characteristics of the classical style: the geometrically balanced Italian landscape, the figures in classic dress, and the general calm and discipline of the scene. Compared to the dynamic, dramatic nature of Rubens' Baroque style, the classical style is logical and restrained. Claude Lorraine (1600–1682) and Nicolas Poussin (1594–1665) helped make classicism popular in France during the seventeenth century. (Reproduced by courtesy of the Trustees, The National Gallery, London)

PLATE 16. Jan Vermeer, *The Painter's Studio*, ca. 1665 Dutch artists often painted interior scenes depicting popular and middle-class life. In this painting a woman poses as an allegorical figure of fame. Light spreads smoothly through a window in front of her, affecting everything in the studio. A map, something particularly crucial for the commercial Dutch, hangs below a geometrically precise candelabra. (Kunsthistorisches Museum, Vienna)

PLATE 17. Antoine Watteau, *A Pilgrimage to Cythera*, 1717 During the early modern period, painting often reflected the tastes of the dominant aristocracy. This was particularly so in eighteenth-century France. This theme is one of classical mythology, but the figures are like eighteenth-century aristocrats gracefully at play in an idyllic garden of nature. The line between life and the roles they are playing blurs in this lush scene. (The Louvre, Paris)

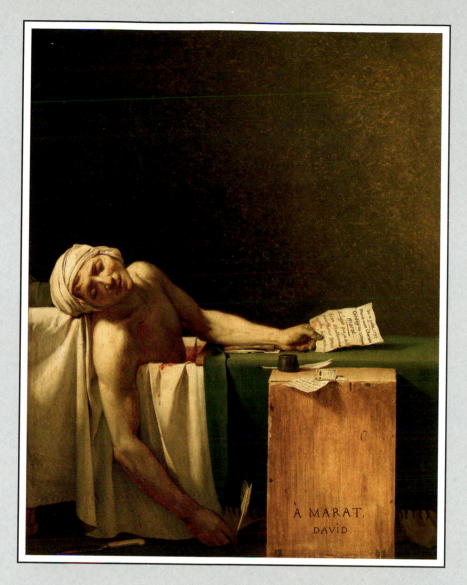

PLATE 18. Jacques-Louis David, *The Death of Marat*, 1793 The French artist David was an active figure in the French Revolution. Here he shows the death of Marat, one of the chief leaders of the radical second phase of the Revolution. Marat was working in his bathtub when Charlotte Corday assassinated him. The subject matter and the political message are in sharp contrast to earlier eighteenth-century art, which reflected aristocratic tastes. (Musées Royaux des Beaux-Arts de Belgique, Brussels)

PLATE 19. John Constable, *The White Horse,* **1819**
Like many romantic painters, John Constable (1776–1837) was fascinated by nature. Here he depicts a rural scene that is naturalistic (a real scene the viewer might come across) and idyllic. The painting, with its vast living sky and detailed foliage, pulls the viewer into nature. The reality of this image of rural life in nature was already starting to disappear as commercial agriculture, industrialization, and urbanization spread throughout England. (Copyright The Frick Collection)

PLATE 20. Joseph Mallard William Turner, *The Fighting Temeraire,* **1839**
Turner is considered the greatest of the English romantic painters. In paintings dominated by light and color, he depicted heroic, tragic struggles mirrored by the overwhelming forces of nature. Here an antiquated battleship sails off into the eternity of the setting sun. The grand ship of the past is replaced by a modern steamship, the smoke from its stack merging into the clouds that frame the sun. (National Gallery, London: Art Resource)

PLATE 7. Christ, Ruler of the Universe This mosaic from the cathedral of Cefalu in Sicily portrays a theme often treated by Byzantine artists. It reflects the skill of Byzantine artists in conveying a spiritual message visually. (Scala/Art Resource)

PLATE 8 *(right).* **Christ Enthroned** This manuscript illumination from the Irish Book of Kells represents one of the major art forms of the early Middle Ages. Churches and monasteries and their patrons prized sacred books decorated with such illuminations highly. (Trinity College Library, Dublin)

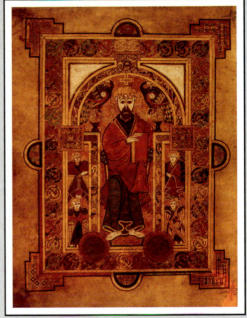

PLATE 9. A Medieval Battle As the Latin lettering says, this scene from the Bayeux Tapestry shows the English and French in battle. This remarkable weaving, nearly 240 feet long, portrays a series of episodes involved in William of Normandy's successful effort to conquer England in 1066. (Scala/Art Resource)

PLATE 4. A Room in a Roman Villa
This photo shows a reconstructed room from an aristocrat's villa near Pompey. The decoration of such rooms occupied much of the attention of Roman artists. Paintings dealing with history and nature adorned wall spaces, while elaborate mosaics covered the floors. Examples of such paintings are shown below. (The Metropolitan Museum of Art, Rogers Fund, 1903)

PLATE 5. Aeneas at the Doctor Inspired by Vergil's *Aeneid,* this scene from a villa at Pompeii shows a doctor treating Aeneas; his weeping son stands by while Venus appears with healing herbs. (National Museum, Naples: Scala/Art Resource)

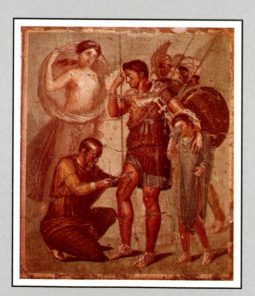

PLATE 6. The Countryside This scene formed part of the decoration of a magnificent villa built by Emperor Hadrian near Tivoli. The bucolic countryside was a favorite subject of Roman artists and writers. (Monumenti Musei e Gallerie Pontificie, Vatican)

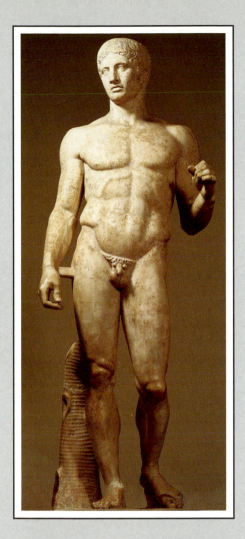
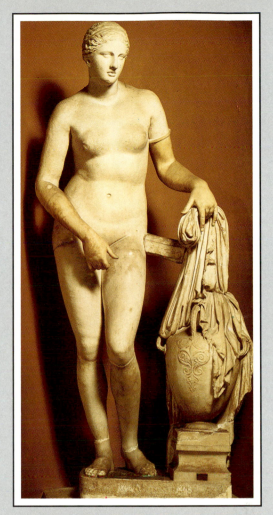

PLATE 3 *(left and right)*. **Ideal Greek Humans** These two statues, both Roman copies of Greek originals, reflect the search by Greek artists to represent ideal human beings. The male figure by Polyclitus (fl. ca. 450–420 B.C.) portrays a spearbearer. The female figure by Praxiteles (fl. ca. 350 B.C.) portrays Aphrodite, the goddess of love. These statues reflect the Greek genius for creating a calculated symmetry of the parts of the body without sacrificing the sense that one is observing a living human about to move. (Left, National Museum, Naples: Scala/Art Resource; right, Vatican: Scala/Art Resource)

PLATE 1. Gudea of Lagash (Ruled ca. 2150 B.C.) This is one of several surviving statues of Gudea, a very active ruler of the Sumerian city of Lagash. Represented in prayer, the ruler's expression reflects the spirit of resignation which characterized the Sumerian worldview. The stylized features and the immobility surrounding the human figure were characteristic of Mesopotamian sculpture. (The Metropolitan Museum of Art, Harris Brisbane Dick Fund, 1959)

PLATE 2. Egyptian Temple This photo shows the remains of a massive temple built in honor of Amon-Ra at Karnak in the time of Rameses II (1299–1232 B.C.), when the Egyptian empire was at its height. The structure marked the culmination of a long tradition of temple building. The huge columns defined an inner hall which rose above side aisles also defined by columns. The columns contained numerous reliefs and hieroglyphic texts exalting Amon-Ra and the feats of the pharoah. (M. Timothy O'Keefe/Bruce Coleman)

CHAPTER 33

The Challenge to Absolutism: England and the United Netherlands

FIGURE 33.1 The English Cabinet This scene shows Robert Walpole, who served as prime minister of England from 1721 to 1742, presiding over a session of the cabinet. Walpole and the other cabinet members shown here were all members of Parliament and belonged to the majority party in that body. In sessions such as this they decided upon the major policies to be followed by the government; their control of Parliament allowed them to enact their decisions. Thus, the cabinet became the effective executive power in Great Britain, a position that it still holds today. The emergence of the cabinet system was one of the major outcomes of the bitter political struggle in seventeenth-century England. (The Bettmann Archive)

While royal absolutism dominated the political scene in France and elsewhere on the Continent, England and the United Netherlands moved toward a form of government that placed limitations on the authority of the executive and the power of the state. In these two nations a constitutional system was emerging that gave a representative body the authority to define the law and sought to create a balance between the power of the state and the rights and liberties of citizens of the state. The constitutional changes made in England and the United Netherlands during the seventeenth century strongly influenced later struggles against absolutism in many parts of the world.

1. EARLY STUART ATTEMPTS AT ABSOLUTISM

The absolutism shaped by the Tudors (see Chapters 27, 29 and 30) was subjected to serious challenges during the seventeenth century. "Good Queen Bess" died in 1603 without a direct heir. She was succeeded by a distant cousin, James Stuart (1603–1625), king of Scotland. He was an avowed absolutist, but he was woefully ignorant of the delicate workings of the Tudor political system and not suited by temperament for the hard work or gifted with the political adroitness needed to keep that system going. His political ineptitude contributed to a progressive breakdown of the Tudor system and to a polarization of political forces.

But not all the troubles of James I's reign were the makings of a king known in his own days as "the wisest fool in Christendom." New problems were facing England that threatened the general satisfaction most people had felt toward Tudor governance. Major economic changes were in process, creating new opportunities for highly profitable investments in agriculture, manufacturing, and trade. Those who benefited most from these changes, the lesser nobility (the gentry) and merchants, were increasingly insistent on having a voice in shaping royal policies affecting their economic interests and on limiting arbitrary royal interference that curbed their freedom of action. These same changes were adversely affecting other groups, especially rural tenants and laborers, thereby fostering popular discontent. A major realignment of power was taking shape in Europe, marked by the ascendancy of France. This development encouraged the English rulers to seek closer ties with their traditional enemy, Spain, a course that many still basking in the glories of the victory over the Armada viewed as unpatriotic.

The very structure of the Tudor political system lacked key elements required for effective absolutism. Too much depended on the personal qualities of the monarch and a narrow circle of royal advisers. England lacked a well-developed bureaucracy and a well-organized military force to support the ruler's absolute authority. The central government had limited control over local government, which was dominated by the local gentry, the members of which were jealous of their offices and protective of their local interests. The traditional system of common law served to limit arbitrary acts by the royal government. Most serious of all were the limited financial resources of the Crown. It could not manage on the traditional sources of revenue from royal lands, customs duties, and feudal dues. Additional income could be derived only from taxes, which Parliament had long since established its right to approve. If absolutism were to continue, significant political reforms aimed at increasing the power of the monarch would be required. Such changes posed a threat to powerfully entrenched interests in England.

Another increasingly acute source of tension involved religious issues. Many people, including an important segment of the gentry and the merchants, were not satisfied with the Anglican settlement carried out during Elizabeth's reign (see Chapter 30). The major dissenters were the Puritans, who wanted reforms that would make the established religion more "Protestant": simpler ritual, more emphasis on Scripture, less episcopal control over local churches. There also remained many Roman Catholics who hoped to undo the Reformation; their presence was a cause of constant concern for all Protestants.

During James I's reign these issues found their focus in Parliament, especially in the House of Commons, a body that theoretically represented the entire English populace but was actually dominated by the country gentry, merchants, and lawyers. The king was forced to summon Parliament because of the increasing need for funds. Although Parliament usually provided some financial aid, its members constantly raised issues that challenged royal policy. They criticized James I's royal advisers for corruption, favoritism, and incompetence. They questioned his unwavering support of Anglicanism and his lenient policy toward the Catholics. They condemned the alliance he made with Spain early in his reign and his failure to support the Protestant cause when the Thirty Years' War began in 1618. James responded by repeatedly dismissing Parliament. He then tried to utilize other means of raising money, but these efforts were challenged in the courts as contrary to custom and therefore illegal. The king answered by dismissing judges, which led to more parliamentary criticism. Throughout this long series of clashes, Parliament proved itself to be an undisciplined, intemperate body. But its confrontations with the king heightened the fear that the royal government was bent on extending its prerogatives to the point where customary political processes, traditional rights, and the law would be subverted, opening the way to tyranny.

Under James' successor, Charles I (1625–1649), the conflict deepened into civil war. Charles was no less stubborn than James in his insistence on royal supremacy and in his refusal to bend before the claims of Parliament and the courts. The king's major problem continued to be a need for funds, a need made more desperate by a blundering foreign policy that resulted in costly but unsuccessful military ventures in France and Spain. To Charles' requests for additional taxes Parliament responded by continuing to challenge royal policy on a variety of issues. Increasingly, the leaders of Parliament began to make specific their definition of what they meant by royal violation of the traditional system and the law. Their views found particularly forceful expression in the Petition of Rights submitted to the king in 1628. This bold document demanded that the king desist from various illegal acts: imposing martial law in peacetime, levying taxes without Parliament's approval, imprisoning citizens without trial, and quartering soldiers with private citizens. Desperate for money, Charles accepted the Petition of Rights, thereby admitting that he had acted illegally. But when Parliament in its next session, in 1629, insisted that the king respect the petition's provisions on taxation, Charles dismissed it over the bitter protests of its leaders.

For the next eleven years Charles ruled without Parliament. To do so, he was forced to rely on a variety of means of raising funds that pushed royal authority to the limits of legality. Ultimately, it was Charles' religious policy that forced him once again to confront his enemies on their own ground—in Parliament. With Charles' support, his chief religious adviser, William Laud, archbishop of Canterbury, initiated a vigorous "reform" aimed at giving greater emphasis in the Church of England to elaborate rituals, episcopal authority over local churches, and the doctrine of free will. To the Puritans Laud's reforms were detestable, the very opposite of the most fundamental precepts of Calvinistic Protestantism. Many fled to the New World in search of a setting where they would have the freedom to institute real Protestantism. Laud's policies even alarmed some Anglicans, who sensed that England was on a course that would lead it back to Roman Catholicism. But it was the absolute refusal of the Scotch Presbyterians to accept the "beauty of holiness," as Charles called Laud's reforms, that precipitated a crisis. In 1639 they revolted and invaded northern England, creating a military crisis that forced Charles to summon Parliament into session in 1640 in order to raise money to resist the Scottish threat to the kingdom.

The first Parliament of 1640, called the Short Parliament, was dismissed after three weeks because it again challenged royal authority. But the Scots continued to press, and Charles was forced to capitulate. He summoned the Long Parliament, so called because it was to sit for twenty years. With an amazing show of unity Parliament proceeded to legislate the end of Stuart absolutism. It forced Charles to sacrifice his chief ministers, including Laud. It abolished the hated extraordinary courts, including the Star Chamber and the Court of High Commission, which had long been tools used by the Crown to avoid the common law. An act was passed requiring a meeting of Parliament every three years and curbing the power of the king to dismiss Parliament. Severe limitations were placed on the king's power to tax without parliamentary approval. To all of this Charles acceded, chiefly because he needed money to fight the Scots.

Up to this point Parliament had succeeded brilliantly in legislating what amounted to a bloodless revolution that established limited monarchy. But the parliamentary forces then began to divide over the question of how to use Parliament's power. In general, its leadership was forced into directions that caused alarm in many quarters and drove many back toward support of the king, who gave every sign that he would resist being a limited monarch. Suspicion of his intentions caused parliamentary leaders to remove control of the administration and the army from his hands and to impose taxes that seemed as burdensome as those imposed by Charles earlier. Religious opinion in Parliament moved in the direction of ending Anglicanism "root and branch" in favor of some form of Presbyterianism. This mounting extremism caused many influential leaders to believe that Parliament was setting a course that would upset the established order. The division in the parliamentary ranks emboldened Charles to try to restore his control; he went so far in early 1642 as to attempt to arrest the leaders of Parliament. This action was a call to arms, pitting against one another elements of a ruling class that had lost its community of interest, an interest that had long focused on the monarch.

2. CIVIL WAR, COMMONWEALTH, AND PROTECTORATE, 1642–1660

The opening of armed strife divided England along lines that defy easy definition. The opposing forces did not represent clear-cut economic interests or social classes. A considerable following, soon known as the Cavaliers, rallied around Charles, who represented himself as the champion of the established order against the political and religious radicals in Parliament. The backbone of the Cavalier forces came from the great noble families and their clientele among the country gentry living in the more economically backward areas of northern and western England. Although the opposition, called the Roundheads, also had noble supporters, it drew its main strength from lawyers, the gentry of the south and east, and the commercial interests; many from these elements were Puritans. This core was soon reinforced by advocates of radical political and economic changes favoring the poor and oppressed. In the intricate matter of choosing sides there figured complex personal factors—family ties, friendships, personal loyalties—much after the fashion of the American Civil War.

The first phase of the civil war lasted through 1646. While neither side was prepared militarily, for a time the Cavaliers seemed to have the upper hand. But the Roundheads had forces working in their favor: support by the navy, domination of the richest part of England, control over the regular administrative system and Parliament, the power to vote taxation. In 1643 the Roundhead cause was bolstered by an alliance with the Scots. But ultimately the outcome of the struggle was determined by the success of the Roundheads in creating an effective army. The chief architect of the victorious army was a simple farmer with strong Puritan convictions, Oliver Cromwell. He organized a cavalry regiment of disciplined, deeply religious recruits who proved more than a match for the Cavalier forces they faced. His system was soon applied to the entire Roundhead force to create the New Model Army, made up of highly motivated troops paid and equipped in a businesslike fashion. It quickly proved itself superior to the Cavalier army, so that by 1646 the Cavalier army was crushed and Charles was forced to surrender.

However, with victory within their grasp, the Roundheads were unable to work out an acceptable settlement. Moderate leaders in the Roundhead camp wished to establish a limited monarchy and a Presbyterian religious order. Charles remained unwilling to accept such a settlement and raised fears of a renewal of the civil war by fleeing his captors and allying himself with the Scots. More ominous was the increasing prominence of Roundhead leaders who demanded a more radical religious reform favoring the independence of local churches and freedom of conscience. These religious Independents were supported by various political radicals, most notably the Levellers, who advocated the end of monarchy, democratic elections, and the redistribution of wealth. These religious and political radicals dominated the New Model Army, where discontent was fed by the fact that pay was considerably in arrears. Fearful that the radicals would seize complete control, the moderate

Roundheads ordered the army demobilized. They turned back to the king, who suddenly expressed considerable enthusiasm for parliamentary control over the monarchy as well as for Presbyterianism. The Independents, led by Cromwell, would not be denied. They destroyed the hope of Charles and his Scottish army in a single battle in 1648 and, along with it, the cause of the Cavaliers and the moderate Roundheads. Backed by the New Model Army, Cromwell acted decisively to ensure the position of the Independents. He purged the Long Parliament of all members not dedicated to his cause and gave the so-called Rump Parliament chief authority in the land. It immediately legislated out of existence the Anglican church, the House of Lords, and the monarchy. And at Cromwell's urging it decreed the execution of the king in 1649 on the grounds that he was "a tyrant, traitor, and murderer."

For eleven years after Charles I's death Cromwell and his Independents sought to rule England without a king. Always in a minority and dependent on the army, the Cromwellians experimented with various forms of government but ultimately failed to establish an acceptable order. They first sought to create a republican form of government called the Commonwealth. A one-house Parliament was made the supreme authority, with a state council of forty-one members charged with conducting the daily affairs of government. Under Cromwell's guidance this government pursued several positive policies. Considerable toleration was extended to all Protestants, a policy that required curbing political and religious extremists in the army. Effective, albeit severe measures were taken to subdue the rebellious Irish and Scots. An aggressive foreign policy, aimed at promoting English commercial and colonial interests, was undertaken. Navigation acts were passed to ensure that trade within England's emerging empire would be monopolized by England. None of these policies, however, helped to popularize the Commonwealth. The Cromwellians could not shed their image as regicides, Puritan extremists, and political radicals (see Figure 33.2). Resistance to the Commonwealth grew steadily. Cromwell ultimately blamed the failure of the Commonwealth on what he considered the self-serving leaders of Parliament, causing him to take steps to curb its

Oliver seeking God while the K. is murthered by his order.

FIGURE 33.2 A Satire on Cromwell The deep religious fervor of the Puritans and the taint of regicide that lingered throughout the Commonwealth and the Protectorate are satirized here as Oliver Cromwell is shown at prayer while Charles I is being executed. (NYPL Picture Collection)

power and to act without it—a course that convinced many that Cromwell was no less a tyrant than his royal predecessors.

In pursuit of what he called a "healing and settling" course for England, Cromwell tried one more experiment, called the Protectorate. A written constitution was drawn up that entrusted power to a lord protector (Cromwell), who was advised by a Council of State and guided by a one-house Parliament elected by property holders. From the beginning the lord protector and Parliament clashed on most issues, largely because the elected Parliament represented political and religious positions that ran contrary to the convictions of those who alone could assure Cromwell's continued dominance, the "godly" men of the New Model Army. To sustain his power Cromwell was forced to impose a virtual military dictatorship that aroused resistance across a wide spectrum of opinion and bred conspiracies that constantly threatened public order. More and more people began to see the restoration of monarchy as an alternative to Cromwell's regime. In fact, in 1657 Parliament asked Cromwell to become king, an honor he declined; but he did agree to remain lord protector for life. Thus, when he died in 1658, the wheel had come nearly full circle: A man who had led his soldiers to the abolition of monarchy had himself become king without title.

Cromwell was succeeded as lord protector by his son Richard, but this weak figure was soon swept aside by forces favoring the restoration of monarchy. By 1660 elements in the New Model Army joined with people of property and commerce to end the Protectorate. The Long Parliament voted to dissolve itself. A new Parliament was elected and in 1660 invited Charles Stuart, the son of Charles I, to return from exile and assume the crown.

3. THE RESTORATION, 1660–1688

The Restoration that brought the Stuarts back to the throne also saw the reestablishment of both houses of Parliament, the Anglican church, the traditional courts of law, and the old system of local government. However, what seemed outwardly to be a return to the system that had prevailed before the execution of Charles I by no means resolved the basic problems that had divided England since 1603, particularly those involving the relationship between king and Parliament and the religious establishment. Nor did it negate the advancing claims of England's gentry and merchants to a decisive voice in political decision making. Between 1660 and 1688 political tensions continued, although at a less violent level than had been the case in the preceding two decades.

The reign of Charles II (1660–1685) began in a climate of forgiving compromise. The king and Parliament joined in repealing all the acts of the Commonwealth and the Protectorate. Only a few Cromwellians were punished for their part in killing Charles I. Confiscated properties were returned to their original owners. The king was assured of a sizable income on a regular basis, but he was deprived of many ancient rights that had allowed his predecessors to exact taxes without approval of Parliament. Not only was control of taxation reserved to Parliament, but the Triennial Act was passed to ensure that it would meet every three years whether or not the king so wished. However, this settlement did not get to the basic political issue: Where did ultimate authority rest? Even more disconcerting was the religious settlement embodied in a series of parliamentary acts passed in 1661 and 1662 and known as the Clarendon Code after Charles II's chief adviser, the earl of Clarendon. These acts not only reestablished the Anglican church but also made it illegal for nonconformist Protestants, including Independents and Presbyterians, to meet for religious purposes, to conduct services in their own way under the leadership of their own preachers, and to hold local political offices. In brief, the Clarendon Code promised to nonconformists (that is, non-Anglicans) little better than criminal status.

Dissatisfaction stemming from these issues once again surfaced in Parliament. The discontent was intensified by a series of disasters that befell England during the early years of Charles' reign. He involved England in a war with the Dutch that led to a humiliating defeat. In 1665 a plague struck England, followed the next year by a fire that destroyed most of London. Many God-fearing English felt that these misfortunes were divine retribution for the immorality of the royal court, where the model of profligacy was set by the king himself. Parliament reacted to public wrath over religious issues by forcing Clarendon out of office in 1667 and to a failed foreign policy by becoming stingier in approving taxes. Charles paid little heed to the growing opposition, choosing instead to pursue two policies he personally favored: an alliance with France and religious tolerance in England that would permit Roman Catholics to worship freely. In 1670 he signed a secret treaty with Louis XIV by which he agreed, in return for a subsidy, to join France in a war on the Dutch and to promote the Catholic cause in England; when the terms of this treaty became known, anti-Catholic and anti-French sentiment reached fever pitch. In 1672 Charles issued a Declaration of Indulgence, which set aside the laws restricting the practice of Roman Catholicism. An outraged Parliament forced the king to withdraw the Declaration of Indulgence and passed the Test Act (1673), which excluded Catholics from all public offices. And when Charles joined France in another unsuccessful war against the Dutch in 1672–1674, Parliament forced him to seek peace by refusing financial support.

As his reign progressed, Charles showed considerable ingenuity in neutralizing his opponents in Parliament. Increased tax returns resulting from an improving economy coupled with Louis XIV's subsidies minimized Parliament's ability to pressure the Crown by denying taxation. More significantly, Charles skillfully built a political following—an embryonic "party"—devoted to a strong monarchy and Anglicanism. Its members, scornfully dubbed "Tories" (a term used to designate Irish bandits) by the opposition, could often control Parliament in support of the king. An opposing "party," committed to parliamentary supremacy and religious tolerance for all Protestants, was also formed; its members were called "Whigs" (after a term used to designate Scottish horse thieves and murderers). Charles' successes led many to feel that absolutism was returning to England. But one obstacle kept Charles from totally controlling English political life: a rising fear that the king was determined to restore Catholicism.

James II (1685–1688) inherited a strong position from his brother, based in large part on the Tory majority in Parliament, a sound financial position, and the legitimacy of his claim to the throne. But he soon dissipated this strength by his open avowal of Catholicism and attempts to improve the position of Catholics in England, which neither the Tories nor the Whigs would tolerate. When in 1688 a son was born to James and his Catholic wife and baptized in the Catholic faith, ensuring that the Stuart dynasty would be perpetuated by a Catholic successor, Tory and Whig leaders invited James' Protestant daughter, Mary, and her husband, William of Orange, the stadholder of several provinces in the Dutch Netherlands, to assume England's throne. When William invaded England in late 1688, the great

majority of the people rallied to his side; James II fled to France. For a second time, the unhappy Stuarts had been forced off England's throne, but this time the revolution was bloodless.

4. THE GLORIOUS REVOLUTION AND ITS CONSEQUENCES

Unlike the execution of Charles I, the flight of James II did not lead to radical political experimentation. Instead, what the English call a Glorious Revolution was carried through in the form of several fundamental legal enactments that established the basis for England's future constitutional system.

Immediately after the triumph of William and Mary, Parliament declared the throne vacant by reason of James' abdication. It then voted to grant the crown to William III and Mary as co-rulers, thereby establishing Parliament's control of the throne. A Bill of Rights was passed in 1689 that set forth clear limits on royal power. This fundamental charter assured the members of Parliament of the right of free speech and immunity from prosecution for statements made in debate. It forbade a variety of acts that had long been the basis of royal absolutism: taxing without the consent of Parliament, suspending laws passed by Parliament, maintaining a standing army in peacetime, requiring excessive bail, depriving citizens of the right to trial in the regular courts, interfering with jurors, and denying people the right to petition the king. The Bill of Rights implied that government was based on a contract between ruler and ruled, a concept of government increasingly attractive among "enlightened" leaders in western Europe. This theory of government was set forth with special force by John Locke in his *Two Treatises on Civil Government*, published in 1690 (see pp. 464, 468, 473). Locke argued that a government was the product of a contract entered into by rational people in order to establish an authority capable of protecting rights that belonged to all humans by the laws of nature: the rights of life, liberty, and property. Any government that violated these natural rights broke the contract that had brought it into existence; in this event its subjects had a right to correct or even overthrow it. To settle the long-standing religious issue, a Toleration Act was passed that allowed religious freedom to Puritans and Independents but not to non-Protestants. Finally, the Act of Settlement was enacted in 1701 to ensure that none but Protestants could inherit the throne.

The initial settlement marking the Glorious Revolution certainly resolved some fundamental issues that had troubled England for nearly a century. However, there still remained problems to be addressed. Under William's leadership England's foreign policy underwent a basic reorientation which called on the nation to commit its resources to a long, burdensome but eventually successful series of wars in many parts of the globe to prevent France from establishing world dominance (see Chapters 32 and 34). Closer to home the Irish problem was resolved to England's advantage. Early in his reign William led an army into this unhappy land, where discontent had long festered and which now became a center of Stuart intrigue—funded by the French—aimed at recovering the English throne. Having established control by force, William instituted a policy aimed at the suppression of Roman Catholicism and at reducing Ireland to colonial status, a policy that provided expanded opportunity for English landlords to uproot Irish Catholic landowners and take possession of their property. Scotland enjoyed an easier fate in the face of increasing English power. Early in his reign William began negotiations with the Scots that finally bore fruit after his death. In 1707 Parliament passed the Act of Union, which joined the two kingdoms into a single nation henceforth known as the United Kingdom of Great Britain. The settlement gave the Scots a liberal number of seats in Parliament and guaranteed their Presbyterian religious establishment.

A major consequence of the Glorious Revolution was Parliament's increasing involvement in the conduct of affairs of state. Partly this expanded role was a consequence of the fundamental principle established by the settlement of 1688–1689: the need for parliamentary approval of important political decisions. No less important was the royal need for additional funds. Chiefly as a result of the burdens of global war, annual government expenditures had increased threefold between the reign of Charles II and that of William and Mary. To meet these expenditures, the monarchs had to call Parliament nearly every year. These frequent sessions of Parliament required that the royal government pay special attention to the election process in order to gain sufficient votes from qualified voters—chiefly property owners—to secure a majority in Parliament that was willing to support royal policy. Because Parliament was increasingly important, party strife between Whigs and Tories became a decisive feature of political life. Party leaders played an ever-larger role in counseling the rulers and overseeing public affairs. This ever-increasing identification of Parliament with the management of the nation's affairs probably did more than the noble principles of the Bill of Rights to secure parliamentary control of public life.

These developments raised a major constitutional issue: How should the Crown and Parliament interact so that the monarchy could discharge its executive functions in a way acceptable to Parliament? Certainly, the Glorious Revolution in no sense sought to deprive the Crown of the responsibility for administering affairs of state; but just as certainly, that settlement made the traditional executive system inadequate. For centuries English monarchs had relied on powerful ministers of their own choice and responsible to them alone to assist them in conducting government affairs and shaping policy. In the face of the new reality posed by the supremacy of Parliament, that system was no longer workable. The need for a new mechanism of interconnecting Crown and Parliament became especially obvious during the reigns of the first members of the Hanoverian dynasty, George I (1714–1727) and George II (1727–1760), both of whom spoke English poorly and were more interested in affairs in Germany than in England.

The answer was the *cabinet system,* under which royal ministers were increasingly chosen from members of the House of Commons on the basis of their ability to secure parliamentary approval to carry on the affairs of state in the name of the monarch. Since the Commons tended to divide into parties, it was only prudent for the rulers to seek the leaders of the majority party in the House of Commons for appointment as ministers responsible for exercising executive functions. Those chosen to constitute the cabinet of ministers slowly learned to accept mutual responsibility for the formulation and execution of policy and to assert their collective influence in ensuring that their party followers in Parliament supported their program. If the cabinet failed to command a majority in the House of Commons, its members had to surrender their positions as ministers in favor of a new cabinet that did have a parliamentary majority. One member of the cabinet, eventually called the *prime minister*, came to be recognized as the leader and spokesperson of the whole group; a major qualification for this designation was leadership of the majority party in the Commons.

Although Queen Anne (1702–1714) relied heavily on John Churchill, duke of Marlborough, to conduct her government, the key figure in shaping the cabinet system was Robert Walpole (see Figure 33.1). A longtime member of the Commons, he became George I's chief minister in 1721, primarily because of his leadership of the dominant Whig party in the Commons. From then until 1742 he virtually ran England by surrounding himself with fellow ministers who could control votes in Parliament and who would follow his leadership. Walpole proved to be a master at dispensing patronage and manipulating elections as a means of sustaining a Whig majority in Parliament and maintaining discipline among his Whig followers. Not until he lost control of the Commons over a foreign policy issue was he forced to relinquish his position as prime minister. However, the king had little choice but to appoint another prime minister and cabinet that could command a majority in Parliament. Henceforth to the present, the executive functions of government in Great Britain would be carried out in the name of the monarch by a circle of party leaders who could command a majority in the House of Commons but who were likewise required to render account to that body for their conduct of public affairs.

The Glorious Revolution marked a turning point in Great Britain's history. Two great decisions had been reached. First, royal absolutism had been repudiated in favor of a limited monarchy in which ultimate authority was entrusted to an elected Parliament. Second, religious uniformity had given way to religious toleration for all Protestants. The resolution of these issues restored Great Britain's internal stability and provided a basis for its rapid advance to the status of world power. However, the "revolution" had its limitations. The right to vote in parliamentary elections and eligibility for election to a seat in the House of Commons were limited to a narrow circle of men of wealth, chiefly landowners and merchants. The apportionment of seats in the House of Commons had less to do with ensuring that each seat represented the same number of people than with guaranteeing "safe" seats to prominent families. The Glorious Revolution was a victory for a narrow oligarchy of entrepreneurial landowners and merchants who had successfully taken advantage of changing economic conditions to establish themselves as the wealthiest segment of the English population. Until the nineteenth century these "gentlemen" dominated Great Britain in a fashion that served their collective interests.

5. THE UNITED NETHERLANDS

Absolutism was also successfully challenged during the seventeenth century by the Dutch. Their success led to the creation of a new nation in which prevailed a political and social environment that allowed the Dutch to forge themselves a leadership role in European commerce, banking, and intellectual and artistic life. That new nation emerged from the Dutch refusal to accept the absolutist system that Philip II of Spain attempted to force on them (see Chapter 31). Although Philip II was able to impose Spanish rule over the ten southern provinces of the Netherlands (now Belgium; see Map 33.1), the seven northern provinces resisted and by 1609 had established effective independence as the United Provinces of the Netherlands; their independence was officially recognized by the Treaty of Westphalia in 1648.

The new state adopted a republican form of government. Each province, ruled by an elected executive (called the *stadholder*) and a provincial representative assembly, retained extensive control over local affairs. Although most of the stadholders came from the landed aristocracy, especially from the House of Orange, a powerful family that had played a crucial role in the struggle for independence, the provincial governments over which they presided were dominated by commercial and financial leaders who resisted the establishment of a strong central government. The only truly national political institution was the Estates General, made up of delegates from each province who acted only on instructions from the provincial governments. It en-

Map 33.1 THE UNITED PROVINCES, 1609 This map illustrates how small a territory the Dutch Republic occupied in its golden age—no larger than a corner of England. Yet through the cities of this small area flowed much of the commerce of the seventeenth and eighteenth centuries. With that commerce came a flow of money that made such cities as Amsterdam the financial centers of the world.

joyed limited powers and asserted very little direction over national affairs. The citizens of the Dutch Netherlands enjoyed considerable freedom to pursue their personal and collective interests. Particularly noteworthy was religious freedom. The Reformed church, strongly Calvinist in doctrine and practice, was established by law, but other religious groups, including Roman Catholics and Jews, were tolerated, a fact that attracted religious refugees from other European nations.

The Dutch Netherlands, a nation of only about a million, made its chief mark on the seventeenth-century world in commerce and finance. That success was based on the seafaring skills of its people and the entrepreneurship of its vigorous bourgeoisie. Those talents, developed over many centuries, allowed the Dutch to become world leaders in commerce. Experienced Dutch sailors plundered Spanish commerce and

overseas colonies to reap a rich reward. When Spain temporarily annexed Portugal in 1580, the Dutch seized most of Portugal's lucrative holdings in the East Indies. The Dutch East India Company, set up in 1602 to develop trade with the East Indies, returned huge profits to its stockholders during the entire seventeenth century. The Dutch also established a flourishing colony in North America. In addition, Dutch traders took advantage of their favorable geographical position to gain a near-monopoly on the carrying trade of Europe. A large proportion of Europe's ships were built in Dutch shipyards.

The extensive trading activities of the Dutch produced a huge flow of wealth into the hands of Dutch merchants. This capital allowed them to become Europe's leading moneylenders, serving princes, merchants, and landowners willing to pay for the use of Dutch capital. The financial activities of the Dutch were institutionalized in the Bank of Amsterdam, set up in 1609. It became a model for national banks later established elsewhere in western Europe. Its location in Amsterdam reflected the fact that that city had become the world's chief commercial and financial center.

The wealth and freedom of Dutch society generated a vigorous cultural outburst. Some of the chief intellectuals in Europe found refuge in the United Provinces, including the philosophers René Descartes from France, John Locke from England, and Baruch Spinoza, a Jewish refugee from Portugal. Among the notable Dutch intellectuals was Hugo Grotius, whose *On the Law of War and Peace* was the first great treatise on international law and has remained a classic on the subject ever since. Freedom of the press enabled the United Provinces to become the leading European center of book publishing. This was also the golden age of Dutch painters. While baroque painters in other countries were glorifying royalty and nobility, Jan Vermeer, Franz Hals, and, above all, Rembrandt van Rijn were celebrating the spirit of Dutch society by dignifying—sometimes glamorizing—the middle and lower classes (see Figure 33.3). Dutch scientists played an important role in advancing the scientific revolution, including the invention of the telescope and the microscope. All of these activities gave the Dutch an important role in western European intellectual and artistic life.

As the seventeenth century drew to a close,

FIGURE 33.3 Rembrandt van Rijn, *Syndics of the Cloth Guild* In the Dutch Netherlands of the seventeenth century, commerce was king. Under the leadership of such men as are shown here, the tiny Dutch Netherlands attained a first-rank position in the world of science, philosophy, and trade. Rembrandt, one of the greatest portrait painters of all time, was probably also the greatest of the baroque painters. (Fotocommissie Rijksmuseum, Amsterdam)

the Dutch preeminence in commerce and banking began to decline, especially in the face of England's sea power and France's land might. But that decline could not efface the notable contributions of the Dutch to seventeenth-century western European civilization, a contribution due at least in part to the freedom enjoyed by Dutch citizens to assert their talents as they chose.

SUGGESTED READING

General Treatments

Barry Coward, *The Stuart Age. A History of England 1603–1714* (1980). A fine overview of Stuart England.

Derek Hirst, *Authority and Conflict: England, 1603–1658* (1986).

J. R. Jones, *Country and Court, England, 1658–1714* (1978). Taken together, these two volumes give a balanced treatment of the period.

Christopher Hill, *A Century of Revolution, 1603–1714*, 2nd ed. (1991). A provocative study from a Marxist perspective.

C. G. A. Clay, *Economic Expansion and Social Change: England, 1500–1700,* 2 vols. (1984). An excellent synthesis, rich in details.

From Civil War to Glorious Revolution

Robert Ashton, *The English Civil War: Conservatism and Revolution, 1603–1649,* 2nd ed. (1989). Good on issues.

Ann Hughes, *The Causes of the English Civil War* (1991). A challenging overview of the causes of the Civil War.

G. E. Aylmer, *Rebellion or Revolution? England, 1640–1660* (1986). A balanced treatment of the civil war and the era of Cromwell.

Ronald Hutton, *The British Republic, 1649–1660* (1990). Excellent on the political affairs of Cromwell's age.

Christopher Hill, *The World Turned Upside Down: Radical Ideas During the English Revolution* (1972). An important work on radicalism.

Patrick Morrah, *Restoration England* (1979). A good social history.

John Miller, *The Glorious Revolution* (1983). A brief, thoughtful description and assessment of the Glorious Revolution.

Lois G. Schwoerer, ed., *The Revolution of 1688–1689: Changing Perspectives* (1992). Presents various views on the nature and significance of the Glorious Revolution.

P. Laslett, *The World We Have Lost,* 2nd ed. (1971). A brilliant evocation of the English society of about 1700.

The Dutch Netherlands

Charles Wilson, *The Dutch Republic and the Civilisation of the Seventeenth Century* (1968).

K. H. D. Haley, *The Dutch in the Seventeenth Century* (1972).

Either of these two titles will provide a good overview of Dutch society in its most glorious age.

Jonathan I. Israel, *Dutch Primacy in World Trade, 1585–1740* (1989). An excellent description of Dutch economic activity in a world setting.

Simon Schama, *The Embarrassment of Riches. An Interpretation of Dutch Culture in the Golden Age* (1988). A brilliant portrayal of social life.

Biographies

Pauline Gregg, *King Charles I* (1981).

Antonia Fraser, *Cromwell. The Lord Protector* (1973).

Barry Coward, *Cromwell* (1991).

Antonia Fraser, *Royal Charles: Charles II and the Restoration* (1979).

S. B. Baxter, *William III and the Defense of European Liberty* (1966).

CHAPTER 34

Overseas Colonization and the Competition for Empire

FIGURE 34.1 The Taking of Quebec, 1759 This eighteenth-century engraving shows British forces capturing Quebec from the French in 1759. This victory was a major turning point in the eighteenth-century competition for world empire. (Library of Congress)

During the seventeenth and eighteenth centuries the European nations intensified their competition for overseas possessions and commerce. They were spurred on in large part not only by the riches that flowed to Europe from these possessions but also by a conviction that overseas possessions enhanced the power of nations. Whereas Spain and Portugal had led the way beyond the Atlantic frontier during the sixteenth century, England, France, and the United Netherlands threw themselves vigorously into colonization and commercial expansion during the seventeenth and eighteenth centuries and soon outstripped their older rivals. As large as the world beyond western Europe was, the competition for it led to struggles among the leading European powers which decisively affected the power relationships among the competing nations. And while Europeans colonized, traded, and competed around the globe, European civilization spread with them, impacting with varying results on the native populations encountered by the Europeans. The seventeenth and eighteenth centuries marked a turning point in the establishment of western European domination over much of the world. No less significantly, European expansion laid the basis for a global economy.

1. THE NEW WORLD: THE ENGLISH, THE FRENCH, AND THE DUTCH

One of the areas attracting the English, French, and Dutch was the New World, where all three established colonies during the seventeenth century and soon became embroiled in bitter rivalry for dominance. Spain and Portugal still retained their vast empires in Central and South America and during the seventeenth and eighteenth centuries continued to earn rich returns from their enterprises. Having exhausted the easy hauls of gold and silver, the Spanish and Portuguese turned their energies toward creating large plantations worked by oppressed natives and imported African slaves to produce agricultural products marketable in western Europe. Their presence in South and Central America forced the attention of the English, French, and Dutch toward North America and the Caribbean area.

The English were the most successful colonizers in North America. Although some settlers left England to escape political and religious oppression, most were lured by the prospect of cheap land. Colonizing ventures were organized by joint stock companies chartered by the government or by individuals granted huge tracts of land for the purpose of colonization. Between 1607, when the first English colony was planted at Jamestown, Virginia (see Figure 34.2), and 1733, when the last colony was founded in Georgia, England established control of the Atlantic seaboard from Maine to the Spanish colony in Florida. In the thirteen colonies a stable order soon emerged that had a growing potential to supply England with not only raw materials and agricultural products but also markets for manufactured goods. Before long settlers were pushing westward from England's coastal colonies in search of new lands to occupy. English explorers and traders penetrated into the Hudson Bay area in Canada and claimed for England a huge territory, where a profitable fur trade soon developed. Flourishing English colonies were established in the West Indies, especially in Barbados, Jamaica, and Bermuda. In this area the English concentrated on developing profitable sugar plantations, utilizing African slaves as a labor supply.

France also undertook to colonize in the New World, although not as successfully as England. The first French colony in the New World was established by Samuel de Champlain at Quebec on the St. Lawrence River in 1608. Champlain later explored and claimed for France the entire St. Lawrence Valley from the Atlantic to the Great Lakes. Toward the end of the seventeenth century, during the reign of Louis XIV, the French extended their holdings in North America by exploring and claiming a huge territory called Louisiana, stretching down the Mississippi Basin from the Great Lakes to the Gulf of Mexico. The French also established prosperous colonies in the West Indies, especially on Martinique and Guadeloupe, where sugar production was the major economic activity. Except for the West Indies, settlers were slow to come to France's vast, rich lands in the New World, in part because of governmental policy. France closed its empire to non-Catholics, thus excluding an element so important in populating England's colonies—the religiously dissatisfied. By

FIGURE 34.2 The New World Frontier This representation of the first settlement at Jamestown, Virginia, suggests something of the drastic changes that affected those who left European society—symbolized by the great ship standing at anchor—to face the wilds of the New World. (Culver Pictures)

adopting a policy of land allocation that favored the aristocracy, the French government made it difficult for commoners to obtain land overseas. The opportunities for profit offered by the fur trade also discouraged agricultural settlement. When England seized France's American empire in 1763, perhaps no more than eighty thousand settlers lived in New France, compared with the 2 million inhabitants of the English colonies. But that sparse population left its imprint, especially in the form of Roman Catholicism, the French language, and social practices established by settlers in the St. Lawrence Valley and southern Louisiana—marks that persist to the present.

The Dutch also became involved in the colonization of North America. In 1621 the Dutch West India Company was chartered to undertake colonizing and commerce in the New World. In 1624 a Dutch colony was planted on Manhattan Island, a location especially attractive because of its potential as a center from which trade could be controlled. Soon other Dutch communities were established in the valleys of the Hudson, Connecticut, and Delaware rivers. However, the Dutch did not push their colonizing effort very

seriously. Their interest was chiefly in trading, which led them to concentrate their energies on the more profitable East Indies. In 1664 the English seized New Netherland, ending Dutch colonization in North America.

2. EUROPEAN PENETRATION OF THE FAR EAST AND AFRICA

During the sixteenth century, Portugal was the dominant European power in the Far East. In the seventeenth century, however, the Dutch, English, and French aggressively entered into the area (see Map 34.1). The Dutch were the first. In 1602 all the competing Dutch companies interested in Far Eastern trade were joined into a single Dutch East India Company, to which the Dutch government gave almost complete freedom of action. The company soon drove the Portuguese out of the East Indies and established a trading empire that embraced Sumatra, Java, Borneo, the Moluccas, the Celebes, the Malay peninsula, and Ceylon. The English tried to seize a share of this rich area, but they were rebuffed

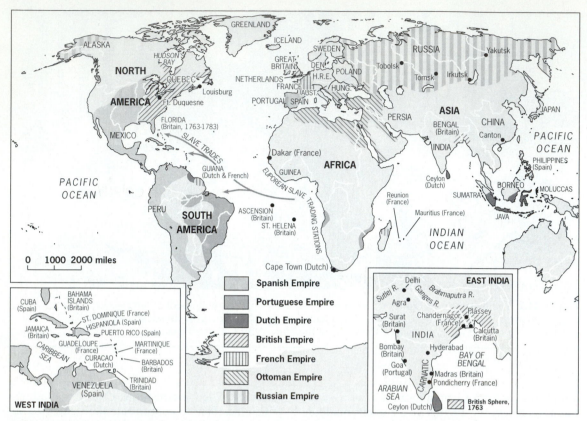

Map 34.1 OVERSEAS POSSESSIONS, 1763. This map shows the extent to which the major European powers had established control over the world by the middle of the eighteenth century. It especially points up the success of England in the quest for overseas possessions. The rich trade flowing between Europe and the overseas possessions had become a vital factor in the economies of these nations. Increasing its overseas possessions and trade was of vital importance to every European state.

by the Dutch as early as 1623. To safeguard the sea route to the Indies, the Dutch established a colony at the Cape of Good Hope in South Africa. Its growth was slow, but the Dutch influence was eventually strong enough to influence the history of South Africa to the present. The Dutch East India Company's interests in the East Indies were represented by a governor-general with headquarters in Java, who in turn set up several other fortified governmental centers throughout the island empire. For years after, the Dutch continued to profit from their holdings in the Indies. They demonstrated remarkable skill in utilizing the native agricultural economy to produce commodities such as spices that were in great demand in western Europe. Consequently, their presence disturbed the existing patterns of life in the area very little. The Dutch also made attempts to penetrate China and Japan but enjoyed only limited success, chiefly because neither the Chinese nor the Japanese welcomed Europeans or their products.

Although shut out of the East Indies by the Dutch, the English soon carved out their own niche in the Far East. An English East India Company was chartered in 1600 and given a monopoly on English trade in the East. This company concentrated chiefly on India, slowly forcing the

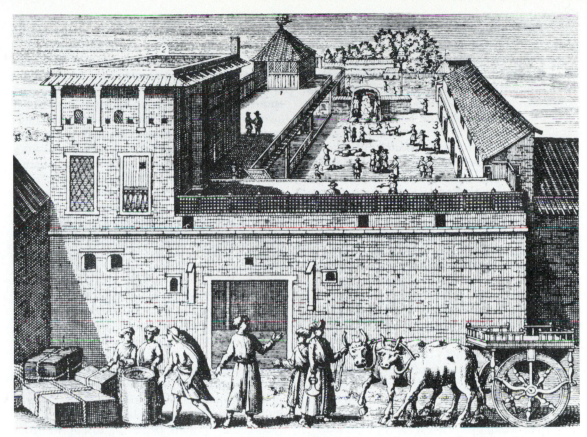

FIGURE 34.3 A Refuge in a Foreign World. This drawing shows a European factory, or trading settlement, built in seventeenth-century India. Within the confines of such structures were warehouses, places of residence, market facilities, and even a church. The structure illustrates how the Europeans isolated themselves from the native population in the Far East. (The Bettmann Archive)

Portuguese to let English traders into that rich land. The company founded its own "factories" (trading posts) at key locations—Surat, Madras, Bombay, and Calcutta (see Figure 34.3). For a long time the East India Company was content to exploit the trading opportunities available in these cities; the merchants interfered little with Indian affairs and had little influence on Indian society. Eventually, however, they had to contend with another European rival in India. In 1664, the French organized their own East India Company, which soon established an outpost at Pondicherry. From this center the French company built up an expanding sphere of influence in India and a prosperous trade that returned large profits.

During the seventeenth and eighteenth centuries, western Europeans made significant inroads into sub-Saharan Africa. Again the Portuguese had been the early leaders, but they were eventually joined by others. It was the establishment of the plantation system in the New World that sparked Europeans' new interest in Africa. The plantations needed labor; African slaves could provide that commodity. Portuguese, Dutch, English, French, and North American traders and adventurers, acting with the support of their governments, established a series of trading posts along the West African coast stretching from modern Senegal to Angola chiefly for the purpose of purchasing slaves to be transported to the New World. The lure of these markets for human beings soon asserted a sinister effect on the native African population far inland from the slave coast.

3. THE IMPACT OF EUROPEAN EXPANSION: NATIVE AMERICANS

The increasing presence of European colonists and traders around the globe during the seventeenth and eighteenth centuries had a significant effect on the native populations of the areas to which Europeans went. In many ways these encounters between Europeans and natives set a pattern that was to impose a bitter heritage on the modern world.

Of all the non-Europeans who felt the impact of the Europeans, the native Americans—American Indians—were perhaps most immediately and drastically affected. Their long-established patterns of life, ranging from the sophisticated civilizations of the Incas in Peru and the Aztecs and Maya in Mexico and Central America to the pastoral and hunting cultures of the North American Indians, were irreparably disrupted by the onslaught of the intruders.

We have already described the destructive impact of the Spanish and Portuguese *conquistadores* on the Aztec, Maya, and Inca civilizations. During the seventeenth and eighteenth centuries, the dislocation continued. The Spanish and the Portuguese had put into place an administrative system that allowed them to dominate political, economic, and social conditions with little regard for the established patterns of native life. Since their fundamental concern was their own enrichment, they viewed the Indians chiefly as laborers on the expanding plantation system and in the mining enterprises from which huge profits could be gleaned. To add to the disruption of native social and economic life, the European masters imported large numbers of black slaves from Africa. Despite their dominance and their disdain for the native Americans, the Europeans in Latin America were never numerous enough to destroy the native American cultures com-

pletely. With passing time their blood and their culture intermingled with those of the native Americans. As a result, significant elements of native American culture were assimilated into the dominant European pattern of life, especially in family structure, agricultural techniques, art motifs, and even religion. Although the ancient Indian civilizations of Central and South America were disrupted forever, enough Indian culture survived to give Latin American society a special hybrid character that has survived to this day.

The Indians of North America suffered a different, and perhaps crueler, fate. In general, the interactions between French settlers and the Indians were not particularly disruptive to Indian society, chiefly because the French were few in number and usually more concerned with trade than land occupation. The English settlers pursued a more ruthless course. From the beginning they were chiefly interested in occupying and exploiting the land, an intention that in the final analysis demanded the displacement of the natives. Although English-Indian relationships were occasionally marked by friendliness and mutual assistance, the English colonial establishment almost from the beginning asserted inexorable pressures on the Indians. As a consequence, the Indians began to disappear from "new" America; their demise was often accompanied by conniving and brutality on the part of the settlers, who began to perceive themselves as the real "Americans." In an effort to protect their land, the Indians fought back savagely. In their struggle for survival they inevitably became embroiled in the mounting rivalry between the English and French for control of North America, a course that made them even more vulnerable. Their resistance nourished a feeling among the colonists that the native Americans were inferior savages whose extermination would best serve everyone's interests. The British government struggled from afar to establish an Indian policy aimed at respecting Indians' rights to their lands and dealing with them honorably in resolving conflicts. But the land-hungry settlers paid little heed and proceeded with the grim business of displacing or exterminating the Indians in the vast Indian stronghold lying between the Appalachians and the Mississippi. The resultant dislocations completely undermined the foundations of native American culture and condemned the Indians to a long-standing inferior status.

4. THE IMPACT OF EUROPEAN EXPANSION: THE FAR EAST

In contrast with the dislocation of native life that marked the coming of the Europeans to the New World, Europeans' impact on the peoples of the Far East was far less disruptive. Few Europeans went to that part of the world; those who did were seeking trading opportunities rather than land upon which to settle. The newcomers isolated themselves in trading depots located in seaboard cities in India and the East Indies, where their contacts with and influence on the natives were slight.

When the Europeans first became involved in India, they encountered a strong state led by other foreigners, the Islamic Moguls, a branch of the Mongol horde of Tamerlane, who early in the sixteenth century had conquered and imposed unity on India. Mogul rule brought prosperity to India's upper classes and created a brilliant chapter in India's already rich cultural history. As the seventeenth century progressed, however, Mogul power began to decline. Political power increasingly fell into the hands of native Indian princes, a development that proceeded rapidly during the eighteenth century. Because this situation aided both the English and the French in establishing their commercial interests in India, the intruders encouraged political localism. Thus, their presence had an impact on the political structure of India but in no sense a determining influence until much later.

Indian society retained both its cohesion and its unique identity despite the presence of the foreigners, be they Islamic Asiatics or Christian Europeans. India's long-established primary social institutions—the family, the village, and the caste system—exercised a decisive role in shaping the lives of most Indians, who were little affected by those who wielded political power. Undergirding these ancient social institutions was a conservative mentality rooted in the religious beliefs and practices embodied in Hinduism and sustained by Hindu priests, called Brahmins, who played a powerful role in directing Indian life. Indians were inclined to accept their situation in the present world because they believed that each individual's lot represented a necessary step in the progression toward ultimate fulfillment in another world. Progress, competition for wealth, and the search for new things did not hold the same attraction for Indians as for Europeans. Indians were not impressed by European civilization. They were convinced that they had reflected as deeply on human problems as the foreigners had and had arrived at superior answers. Indians could point to a remarkable art and literature as proof of the vitality of their way of life. Little the Europeans could offer to India seemed able to improve on Indian institutions and values. The outsiders found that a few hundred soldiers and a few cannon could not shake the Indians' confidence in their village and family life, their caste system, their religion, and their culture. Moreover, the continued existence of the basic pattern of Indian civilization in no way impeded the Europeans from reaping huge profits from their commercial enterprise in India. Only slowly and almost imperceptibly did the European way of life make any significant impression on India. And as time passed, Europeans developed a deep respect for some aspects of Indian civilization.

The Dutch presence in the East Indian world likewise had little influence on native society. In fact, the Dutch found it in their interests to sustain the existing order because it lent itself easily to commercial arrangements favorable to the outsiders.

The other major cultural centers in the Far East—China and Japan—were also little affected by the intrusion of Europeans during the period from 1500 to 1800. Again, this was a consequence of the vitality of the native civilizations. In China the Manchu dynasty established a strong political regime during the seventeenth century that brought internal peace, prosperity, and a revitalization of Chinese social, religious, and cultural life along traditional patterns. Chinese civilization came to be greatly admired in Europe in the eighteenth century. However, the Manchus carefully controlled the activities of Western traders—called "Ocean Devils" by the Chinese—with the consequence that European influences were barely felt in China. Japan also enjoyed internal stability under the rule of the Tokugawa shoguns, who in the early seventeenth century established firm control over Japan's ancient feudal system and encouraged a close adherence to ancient social, cultural, and religious customs and values. The new rulers soon adopted a policy of excluding all Europeans from access to Japan, a policy of isolationism that continued until the nineteenth century and that ensured that European influences would be minimal.

5. THE IMPACT OF EUROPEAN EXPANSION: SUB-SAHARAN AFRICA

European expansion into sub-Saharan Africa during the seventeenth and eighteenth centuries had a decisive effect on the societies existing in that vast territory. The centuries prior to 1500 had witnessed the formation of several prosperous states across a wide belt of territory south of the Sahara from the Atlantic to the Indian oceans and then far southward along the east coast of Africa. These states—Ghana, Mali, Songhay, the kingdoms of Hausaland, and the Swahili city-states on the east coast of Africa—were strongly influenced by the Islamic religion, culture, and technology from North Africa. However, in all of them the imprint of much older native African cultures was also strongly felt, producing an amazingly cosmopolitan culture, especially in the cities that dominated these states. The remarkable affluence of these states depended on a vigorous trans-Saharan and Indian Ocean trade that carried gold, ivory, slaves, and many other products northward to the Islamic and European worlds and eastward to India. In fact, many of these states had been brought into existence by enterprising native chieftains who organized extensive realms so as to control more effectively the trading ventures that brought such great riches. Because their existence depended so heavily on trade and because the techniques their rulers borrowed to assert their power had little impact on the great bulk of the native population, these states tended to be unstable. Nonetheless, their creation and their active intercourse with outside cultures marked an important stage in the development of sub-Saharan Africa and its involvement with the larger world. Farther to the south, beyond the sphere of Islamic influence, the native population continued its agricultural existence according to ancient customs, as yet little touched by developments to the north.

These developments in pre-1500 sub-Saharan Africa created a situation that made Africa particularly susceptible to the onslaught of the western Europeans, chiefly because the destinies of so many African states were tied directly to trade with the outside world. Coming by sea to the Atlantic coastal areas of sub-Saharan Africa, the Europeans very quickly caused a redirection of trade routes. Whereas the traditional trade routes plied by African traders had been oriented northward toward the Mediterranean world and eastward toward the Indian Ocean, attention now shifted toward the Atlantic coasts of Africa that gave access to western Europe and the expanding European empires in the New World and the Far East. The European newcomers made little effort to settle in sub-Saharan Africa, chiefly because they could get what they wanted by doing little more than establishing a few trading posts on the Atlantic shores of Africa. What they wanted were the valuable raw materials of Africa, especially gold, and then before long the Africans themselves—as slaves to perform the arduous labor of creating a rich agricultural establishment in the New World. Throughout the seventeenth and eighteenth centuries massive numbers of black Africans—perhaps as many as 11 or 12 million—were uprooted from their native soil, sold into the hands of English, French, Dutch, Portuguese, Spanish, and American slave traders, packed into ships that transported them under inhuman conditions to the New World, and auctioned off to white masters to toil as chattels on the plantations and in the mines of the New World. This traffic in human beings and the cheap labor it supplied resulted in huge profits that became a major source of capital formation in the western European world. In a real sense, the slave trade and slave labor underpinned the rising level of prosperity enjoyed by many people in both Europe and the New World who were not directly involved in either trading or exploiting slaves.

As the Europeans opened slave stations along the coasts of sub-Saharan Africa, significant new political alignments arose in Africa. African kingdoms along or with access to the West African coast flourished as a result of their domination of the trade flowing from inland Africa into the hands of European traders. Among the most prominent of these kingdoms were Oyo, Benin, Asante, Kongo, and Ngola. Often the ruling elements of these kingdoms became prime agents in supplying slaves to the Europeans, leading them to intervene among inland tribes to find slaves to sell. Native chiefs living inland likewise became caught up in the slave trade. Armed with guns supplied by Europeans, the native tribes began to wage war on one another as a means of procuring slaves. The Europeans asserted subtle influences on the coastal states in order to enhance their own trading interests, thus promoting a slow deterioration of the capability of the Africans to control their own destiny. As the demand for slaves increased and the prices commanded by the African slave suppliers rose, European traders moved farther and farther south along the west coast of Africa to turn the attention of more and more native Africans toward serving European trading interests, especially slavery, with the same disruptive consequences. On the east coast of Africa the European presence was equally disruptive. Here the Portuguese effort to seize control of the trade in gold and copper that flowed from central Africa through the Swahili city-states toward Persia and India brought about a decline of those cities and the brilliant civilization they supported. Only deep in the central part of Africa did the native population remain relatively free of the impact of European intrusion.

On the whole, the development of sub-Saharan Africa was seriously impeded by the encounter of its peoples with the western Europeans during the seventeenth and eighteenth centuries. Africa's human resources were depleted, its natural resources plundered, and its political and social structures disrupted. The Europeans gave little in return, especially when compared with what the Moslems of North Africa had contributed to the enrichment of sub-Saharan Africa prior to 1500. Despite the traumatic consequences of European expansion in this era, the Africans retained many elements of their native tradition, which would reemerge later as a significant aspect of their liberation from European domination. And those who were uprooted from Africa took elements of their native culture with them that helped sustain their miserable lives as slaves and that eventually asserted an influence on the civilization of the New World.

6. THE STRUGGLE FOR OVERSEAS EMPIRE

In spite of the vast lands available in the New World and rich trading opportunities to exploit in the highly civilized East and sub-Saharan Africa, the aggressive European nations could not keep out of one another's way in their overseas expansion. As a consequence, their rivalry became global, and the outcome of their struggles began to determine the destinies of peoples only remotely involved in the affairs of Europe.

During the seventeenth and eighteenth centuries the competition for empire was rooted in two interrelated factors: the essential importance of overseas trade to the expanding economies of the major European nations and the policy of mercantilism practiced by most European powers.

The growing importance of overseas commerce not only to national economies but also to people's daily lives was abundantly clear. New products from abroad—among others, spices, sugar, tobacco, cotton, silk, and tea—were in high demand; some of them even became necessities. So also were some manufactured goods from the Far East, especially cotton textiles and chinaware. Colonists needed the products of European manufacturers. The desire of traders to transport these goods stimulated shipbuilding. The distribution of products from colonial and commercial outposts created new opportunities for merchants. The funding of overseas trading and colonizing ventures stimulated the development of banking and credit. The profits garnered from overseas trading activities not only improved the standard of living of those who earned the profits but also became a prime source of capital for investment in western European agriculture, manufacturing, and commerce. Even governments relied on the gains from overseas trade to provide taxes and loans. In short, Europe's economy had been given a new and vital dimension by its global involvement. Control of that economy was vital to the well-being of each European nation, even to the point of fighting others for a share of the lucrative overseas trade.

The realities of seventeenth- and eighteenth-century economic life found expression in the widely accepted economic policy of mercantilism, which accentuated the importance of overseas trade and colonies to every nation. Mercantilist policy was based on the conviction that the economic well-being of a nation depended on governmental management of exchange operations in a way that would produce a favorable balance of gold and silver coming into the economy. Colonies were viewed as a source of cheap food and raw materials and an outlet for manufactured goods that would return a profit to the mother country. Such a view made the accession and careful management of colonies crucial to each nation that aspired to be rich, and thus powerful. Especially important was the need for each nation to monopolize trade with its own colonies, which placed a premium on developing naval power and regulating economic life in the colonies. Likewise, mercantilism dictated that each nation make every effort to restrict the colonizing ventures of rival nations and to deprive them of their colonial possessions whenever possible. Adherence to mercantilist policy meant that every conflict among the major European nations in the seventeenth and eighteenth centuries was extended to their colonies and that every major peace settlement included a redistribution of overseas possessions.

The competition for the fruits of overseas empires began in the sixteenth century with the English and Dutch assaults on Spanish and Portuguese trading activities and overseas holdings. Initially the Dutch won the advantage, but by the middle of the seventeenth century England began to play a more aggressive role in the competition for empire and trade, a development that was one of the major outcomes of the seventeenth-century political upheaval that put control of the English state into the hands of the country gentry and the merchants. As early as 1651 England passed its first Navigation Act, which provided that all goods coming to and from England and its overseas possessions must be carried in English ships. This policy posed a challenge to the commercial interest of the Dutch, who were especially successful in providing shipping services to other nations. It also encouraged the growth of the English merchant fleet and the navy, which had been badly neglected during the early Stuart period. On three different occasions between 1651 and 1688, England engaged the Dutch in warfare. As a result, Dutch commercial ascendancy began to be undermined while England's commercial power grew. Indicative of the shifting balance was the seizure of the Dutch North American colonies by the English.

Toward the end of the seventeenth century both the English and the Dutch began to see that France was their chief threat, for France too became increasingly committed to expanding its colonial and commercial power. The result was an Anglo-Dutch alliance made by William of Orange when he became king of England in 1689. No longer the major sea power in Europe, the Dutch were increasingly content to keep their already established holdings in the East Indies, to continue their declining but still profitable carrying trade, and to reap great profits as the chief bankers and moneylenders of Europe.

From 1689 to 1763 England and France fought each other regularly in Europe (see Chapter 32 for the European aspect of these wars), and each engagement had its repercussions abroad (see Map 34.1). Several times during the War of the League of Augsburg (1688–1697), English and French forces engaged in North America, where the war was called King William's War. Neither in Europe nor in America was the action decisive, and no changes were made in the holdings of either combatant. England had more success during the War of the Spanish Succession (1702–1713). In North America, where the struggle was called Queen Anne's War, England captured Acadia (Nova Scotia) and received recognition of its claims to Newfoundland and Hudson Bay. From France's ally, Spain, England received Gibraltar and Minorca, ensuring access to the Mediterranean. Spain also granted to England the right to supply Spain's colonies with slaves (the *asiento*) as well as the privilege of sending one ship a year to the Spanish colonies in America. These concessions ended Spain's long effort to close its empire to outsiders and gave England the advantage over other nations in exploiting the trading opportunities provided by the Spanish overseas holdings.

From 1713 to 1740 England and France remained at peace. During this calm neither nation was idle in overseas matters. France, realizing the weakness of its position, was especially active in North America. It tried to protect its holdings from English sea power by building a strong fort at Louisburg at the mouth of the St. Lawrence. The French also began to construct and garrison a series of forts to make its hold on the vast territories it claimed along the St. Lawrence valley through the Great Lakes region and down the Mississippi Valley more secure. England concentrated its efforts on widening the commercial breach it had made in Spain's empire in 1713. However, English colonists in North America were steadily advancing westward beyond the Appalachians toward a confrontation with the French for control of the Ohio Valley, where a powerful coalition of native American nations, the Iroquois Confederacy, still held the balance of power. A new European war in 1740, the War of the Austrian Succession, led to a sharp conflict between England and France in both America (King George's War) and India. At the end of the war in 1748 each power restored its spoils to the other, England giving up Louisburg and France restoring Madras.

An eight-year truce ensued in Europe, each side preparing desperately for the struggle that everyone knew would soon reopen. In North America, the French renewed their effort to build a barrier against the westward expansion of the English colonies, focusing their attention now on the Ohio Valley. The inevitable clash came in 1755, when a British attempt to oust the French from Fort Duquesne, at the present site of Pittsburgh, was defeated. The battle in America was clearly joined; one power must destroy the other. In India a no less dramatic struggle was shaping. Although the French had entered the scene in India later than the English, by 1740 they had created a position of some strength. Between 1740 and 1756 the French and British each sought to take advantage of the deepening political crisis in India that resulted from the decline of Mogul power to wring from native Indian princes and political factions concessions that strengthened its own position. Competition became so vicious that soon an undeclared war was on.

Thus, at the opening of the Seven Years' War (called the French and Indian War in America) in 1756, France and England were pitted against each other on three continents. In that war England, led by William Pitt, threw its chief efforts into the colonial war and won a smashing victory. In North America the French, with considerable support from their native American allies, held their own until 1757. After that the superior British forces, supported by the navy, overpowered the French outposts one by one. The decisive blow came in 1759, when the British captured Quebec, opening all Canada to the British (see Figure 34.1). British naval units captured the chief French holdings in the West Indies. In India, Robert Clive, a resourceful agent of the East India Company, won a decisive victory for the British at the battle of Plassey in 1757 and enlarged England's sphere of influence by conquering several native Indian states.

The Seven Years' War ended in 1763 with the Treaty of Paris. France surrendered Canada and all Louisiana east of the Mississippi (except New Orleans) to England. Spain, which had been an ally of France, ceded Florida to England. By a special treaty France compensated Spain for this loss by giving Spain the rest of Louisiana (west of the Mississippi). All French possessions in the West Indies except Guadeloupe and Martinique also fell to England. France's empire in India likewise went to Britain. The French were permitted to enjoy trading privileges in India and to keep Pondicherry, but Britain controlled the chief centers of trade, ending any hope of a French recovery of power there. The Treaty of Paris closed an era in European expansion. Although the Dutch and Spanish still had extensive holdings abroad, Great Britain had fought its way to supremacy in colonial and commercial affairs. The English could now turn to the exploitation of that empire.

Since Columbus' voyage the Europeans had wrought an important change around the world. Energetic colonizers had planted European civilization on the soil of the New World. Enterprising merchants had begun to tap the wealth of a considerable part of the Far East and sub-Saharan Africa, creating for the first time a global economy in which the level of prosperity in European nations was directly related to their access to the labor and products of peoples all over the earth. European patterns of civilization had begun to alter the lives of peoples who had developed their own cultures long before the Europeans came. For good or bad, the Europeanization of the world had begun. And from then on, European history never ceased to have a global scope.

SUGGESTED READING

European Expansion

J. H. Parry, *Trade and Dominion: The European Overseas Empires in the Eighteenth Century* (1971).

Holden Furber, *Rival Empires of Trade in the Orient, 1600–1800* (1976).

Either of these studies will provide an excellent account of the building of commercial empires.

Alan K. Smith, *Creating a World Economy: Merchant Capital, Colonialism, and World Trade, 1400–1825* (1991). Treats the major factors involved in the emergence of a global economy.

The Impact of European Expansion

Bernard Bailyn, *The Peopling of British North America: An Introduction* (1986).

W. J. Eccles, *France in America*, rev. ed. (1990).

These two works will help the reader understand the occupation of North America by Europeans.

Gary B. Nash, *Red, White, and Black. Peoples of Early America*, 2nd ed. (1982). An interesting study of interactions among different peoples in colonial America.

Wilcomb E. Washburn, *The Indian in America* (1975). A good survey.

Karen Ordahl Kupperman, *Settling with the Indians: The Meeting of English and Indian Cultures in America, 1580–1640* (1980).

James Axtell, *The Invasion Within: The Contest of Cultures in Colonial North America* (1985).

Two excellent studies of the impact of European civilization on native American life.

Richard White, *The Middle Ground: Indians, Empires, and the Republics in the Great Lakes Region, 1615–1815* (1991). A brilliant analysis of what happened to Indians caught between European rivals for power in North America.

James Lockhart and Stuart B. Schwartz, *Early Latin America: A History of Colonial Spanish America and Brazil* (1983).

Mark A. Burkholder, *Colonial Latin America* (1990).

Either of these two excellent surveys will provide information on the fate of Indian civilizations in Latin America.

Stanley Wolpert, *A New History of India*, 4th ed. (1992). The appropriate parts of this work will provide a good introduction to Indian society at the time of the European intrusion.

Roland Oliver and Anthony Atmore, *The African Middle Ages, 1400–1800* (1981). A clear treatment of a complex subject.

James A. Rawley, *The Transatlantic Slave Trade: A History* (1981). A balanced account.

Patrick Manning, *Slavery and African Life: Occidental, Oriental and African Slave Trades* (1990). Excellent on the impact of slave trade on African culture.

Imperial Rivalry

W. L. Dorn, *Competition for Empire, 1740–1763*, rev. ed. (1963). A classic work.

CHAPTER 35
The Scientific Revolution

FIGURE 35.1 Isaac Newton Isaac Newton (1642–1727) became the leading figure of the Scientific Revolution, employing the new methods of science and drawing together discoveries in astronomy and physics to create a systematic explanation of the physical laws of the universe. This portrait suggests his youthful vigor and keenness. He was still in his twenties when he developed some of his greatest theories. (The Bettmann Archive)

Until the seventeenth century even the most learned scholars of Europe agreed with the standard medieval understanding of the physical nature of the earth and the universe. This medieval understanding was based on the views of the fourth-century B.C. Greek Aristotle, as modified by Ptolemy and medieval Christian scholars. According to this Christian medieval understanding the earth was stationary and in the center of the universe. Around it moved the planets, the sun, the stars, and the heavens in an ascending series of spheres. This universe was finite and focused on the earthly center of God's concern. "Scientific" investigation generally took the form of making deductions from accepted, authoritative medieval assumptions about the physical universe. The questions asked were usually the more philosophical or theological ones of ultimate causes for an event—guesses as to why something had occurred.

During the seventeenth century a relatively small number of scholars undermined this medieval understanding of nature and replaced it with a modern scientific view. According to this new scientific view, the earth was a moving body and no longer at the center of the universe. Rather, it, along with the planets, moved around the sun in an infinite universe of other similar bodies. Scientific investigations generally took the form of observing, measuring, experimenting, and coming to reasoned conclusions through the use of sophisticated mathematics. Medieval assumptions about the physical universe were viewed with a skeptical eye. The questions asked were usually the more concrete, pragmatic ones of *how* an event had occurred rather than the ultimate reasons for *why* such an event had occurred. The new scientific synthesis was one of a mechanistic universe of forces acting according to mathematically expressible laws and open to human reason and investigation.

Until the eighteenth century the impact of this modern scientific view, known as the Scientific Revolution, was limited. Nevertheless, it was an intellectual revolution of great significance, for with it Western civilization was making a turn from its medieval assumptions and embarking in a direction unique among the cultures of the world. Science would grow to become one of the main factors distinguishing the West and accounting for its power and dynamism.

1. CAUSES AND SPREAD

There were several causes for the development and spread of the Scientific Revolution, some of which extend back to the late Middle Ages and Renaissance. Medieval universities had been growing for some time and included the study of philosophy and other subjects that would be central to the Scientific Revolution, including astronomy, physics, and mathematics. Certainly the emphasis and the greatest prestige were accorded to theology and nonscientific study in these medieval universities, but nevertheless there were places on the faculty for many of the central figures of the Scientific Revolution, such as Galileo and Newton.

The Renaissance involved a search for classical writings. The discovery of Greek authorities who contradicted Aristotle and the growth of Neoplatonism as an alternative to Aristotelian thought in Renaissance Italy encouraged scholars to question medieval scientific assumptions. The Renaissance stimulated interest in analyzing and describing physical reality, a key concern of the Scientific Revolution. The Renaissance was also an age of commercial and geographic expansion in the West, which created a demand for new instruments and precise measurements, particularly for navigation on open seas. This demand encouraged scientific research, especially in astronomy and mathematics. In turn, the better instruments developed during the Renaissance helped scholars make accurate measurements, something crucial for the new science. During this same period, the printing press was invented, which facilitated the dissemination of the new science, even if initially to only a select few.

The Reformation played a mixed role in the Scientific Revolution. Generally, both Catholics and Protestants criticized the scientific discoveries that so threatened the medieval Christian view of the universe. During the sixteenth century there was perhaps more room within the Catholic church for scientific research than among Protestants, but by the middle of the seventeenth century this was clearly not the case. By then the Counter-Reformation Catholic church had turned into an enemy of much of the new science, while Protestants began to accept it. This was particularly so in England, where the Puritans encouraged the new science and where it took hold most firmly.

During the seventeenth century, governments supported science, in part hoping that scientific inquiry would yield discoveries that would increase the power and prosperity of the state. With governmental support scientific academies were established and played a significant role in the advancement of science. The earliest and most important of these were the Royal Society in England, chartered in 1662 by Charles II, and the Académie des Sciences in France, founded by Colbert four years later. These organizations and others patterned after them furnished laboratories, granted subsidies, brought scientists together to exchange ideas, published their findings, and encouraged scientific achievement generally. They also helped make scientists a more socially acceptable group and contributed to the creation of a new set of values supportive of the new science.

Finally, religious and psychological factors played an important, if difficult to evaluate, role in the development and spread of the Scientific Revolution. Many of the new scientists had strong, though not always traditional, religious motives for their work, particularly a desire to gain insight into the perfection of God's universe.

2. ASTRONOMY AND PHYSICS: FROM COPERNICUS TO NEWTON

The first branches of modern natural science to attract systematic attention were astronomy and physics. Discoveries in these fields would dramatically alter the perception of nature and the earth's place in the universe.

Nicolaus Copernicus

The first steps were taken in the sixteenth century by Nicolaus Copernicus (1473–1543), a Polish clergyman interested in astronomy, astrology, mathematics, and church law. Like so many other northern European scholars in the fifteenth century, he crossed the Alps to study in an Italian university. There he was influenced by the rediscovery of Greek scholarship, particularly Platonic and Pythagorean thought, that differed

from the accepted, mathematically complex Aristotelian-Ptolemaic tradition. This rediscovered Greek thought emphasized the importance of a hidden, simpler, mathematically harmonious reality underlying appearances. With a religious, mystical passion, Copernicus sought a simpler mathematical formulation for how the universe operated. This search convinced him that the earth was not the center of the universe but rather that the sun was the center. Moreover, the earth was not stationary but moved in perfect divine circles around the sun, as did other bodies in the universe. This change from an earth-centered (geocentric) to a sun-centered (heliocentric) universe has come to be known as the Copernican revolution (see Figures 35.2 and 35.3).

Copernicus worked on his heliocentric model of the universe for almost twenty-five years, but, fearing the ridicule of the laity and the ire of the clergy, he did not have it published until 1543, the year of his death. Few knew of his views and even fewer accepted them. Nevertheless, their significance and their threat to the Christian conception of the universe would be recognized and condemned by both Catholic and Protestant authorities, who would denounce the Copernican system as illogical, unbiblical, and unsettling to the Christian faith. Nevertheless, his views would stimulate other scholars investigating the physical nature of the universe.

Tycho Brahe

After Copernicus, the most important astronomer of the sixteenth century was a Danish aristocrat, Tycho Brahe (1546–1601). He persuaded the king of Denmark to support him, and he built the most advanced astronomy laboratory in Europe. There he gathered unusually accurate, detailed information about the planets and stars, even though the telescope had not yet been invented. Particularly important were his discoveries of a new star in 1572 and a comet in 1577, both of which undermined the Aristotelian assumptions about a sky of fixed, unalterable stars moving in crystalline spheres. He did not share Copernicus' belief in a heliocentric universe, nor did he grasp the sophisticated mathematics of the day. He believed that the earth remained the stationary center of the universe, as argued by Aristotle and Ptolemy, but he concluded that the

FIGURE 35.2 The Medieval View of the Universe
This woodcut (1559) shows the traditional Ptolemaic conception of the universe. At the center is the earth, surrounded by ascending spheres of air, fire, the sun, the planets, the stars (''firmament''), the crystalline ring, and the ''primum mobile.'' (The British Museum)

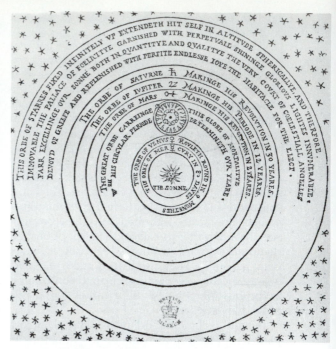

FIGURE 35.3 The Copernican Conception of the Universe (Woodcut, 1576) At the center is the sun, surrounded by the circling planets (one of which is the earth), all bounded by an infinity of stars and the heavens. One of the central developments of the Scientific Revolution was the replacement of the Ptolemaic geocentric by the Copernican heliocentric conception of the universe. (The British Museum)

other planets revolved around the sun, which itself moved around the earth and moon. However, the astronomical observations he gathered would be used by other scholars who became convinced that the earth moved around the sun.

Johann Kepler

Tycho Brahe's assistant, Johann Kepler (1571–1630), built upon Brahe's observations while returning to the Copernican heliocentric theory. A German Lutheran from an aristocratic family, Kepler believed there was an underlying mathematical harmony of mystical significance to the physical universe. He sought such a mathematical harmony that would fit with Brahe's observations. His most important findings were the

three laws of planetary motion, proposed between 1609 and 1619: first, that the planets moved in ellipses around the sun; second, that their velocity varied according to their distance from the sun; and third, that there was a physical relationship between the moving planets that could be expressed mathematically. He thus further undermined the Aristotelian universe accepted by medieval thought and provided support for the Copernican revolution. Moreover, he extended the Copernican revolution in ways that would be fully realized by Galileo and Newton.

Galileo Galilei

The Italian astronomer, physicist, and mathematician Galileo Galilei (1564–1642) believed, like Copernicus and Kepler, that there was a hidden harmony to nature. He felt that this harmony could be discovered through experimentation and mathematics. He investigated motion through controlled experiments and demonstrated that motion could be described mathematically. He showed that bodies once set into motion will tend to stay in motion and described the speed of falling bodies mathematically. He thus undermined Aristotelian physics and established rules for experimental physics.

Galileo then moved on to astronomy, using a telescope he built in 1609. The telescope revealed to Galileo that the moon had a rough surface not unlike the earth's, that Jupiter had moons, and that the sun had spots. He confirmed the Copernican hypothesis and provided support for the view that other heavenly bodies were like the earth and imperfect. By implication, this finding meant that the natural universe was ordered and uniform, without the hierarchical distinctions of the accepted medieval view.

Galileo aggressively published and defended his views against detractors, most notably in *Dialogue on the Two Chief Systems of the World*, published in Italian in 1632. This text brought him into conflict with conservative forces in the Catholic church, which condemned his theories at an inquisition in 1633, forcing him to recant.

Isaac Newton

The uphill trail blazed by Copernicus, Brahe, Kepler, and Galileo was continued on to a lofty peak by Isaac Newton (1642–1727) (see Figure 35.1). As a student at Cambridge University, he distinguished himself enough in mathematics to be chosen to stay on as professor after his graduation. Starting in his early twenties, Newton came forth with some of the most important discoveries in the history of science—or indeed of the human intellect. He developed calculus and investigated the nature of light. He formulated and described mathematically three laws of motion: inertia, acceleration, and action/reaction. He is probably best known for the laws of universal attraction, or gravitation. The concept matured and was refined in Newton's mind over a period of years. As it finally appeared in 1687 in his *Principia (The Mathematical Principles of Natural Knowledge)*, the law is stated with marvelous simplicity and precision: "Every particle of matter in the universe attracts every other particle

with a force varying inversely as the square of the distance between them and directly proportional to the product of their masses." This law, so simply expressed, applied equally to the movement of a planet and a berry falling from a bush. The secret of the physical universe appeared to have been solved—a universe of perfect stability and precision.

What Newton had done was to synthesize the new findings in astronomy and physics into a systematic explanation of physical laws that were true for earth as well as for the heavens. This Newtonian universe was uniform, mathematically describable, held together by explainable forces, atomic in nature. The universe was essentially matter in motion.

Like most other figures of the Scientific Revolution, Newton was profoundly religious; he believed in God and a God-centered universe, as well as alchemy. By the later years of the seventeenth century and the beginning of the eighteenth century, the new science was becoming more acceptable than it had been for Newton's predecessors, as is illustrated by his career. He became a member of Parliament and served for many years as director of the Royal Mint. He was knighted by Queen Anne. His acceptance, as contrasted with the ridicule and persecution suffered by Copernicus and Galileo, indicates the progress that had been made by the scientific community between the sixteenth and the eighteenth centuries.

3. SCIENTIFIC METHODOLOGY

The scientists who made discoveries in astronomy and physics succeeded in undermining the medieval view of the universe as stable, fixed, and finite, with the earth at its center. They replaced it with a view of the universe as moving and infinite, with the earth merely one of millions of bodies, all subject to the laws of nature. In the process they were also developing and using new methods of discovery, of ascertaining how things worked, and of determining the truth. Indeed, at the heart of the Scientific Revolution was the new methodology of science. According to this new methodology, earlier methods of ascertaining the truth, which primarily involved referring to traditional authorities such as Aristotle, Ptolemy, and the Church and making deductions from their propositions, were unacceptable. The new methodology emphasized systematic skepticism, experimentation, and reasoning based on observed facts and mathematical laws. The two most important philosophers of this new scientific methodology were Francis Bacon and René Descartes.

Francis Bacon

Francis Bacon (1561–1626) was a politician and was once lord chancellor of England under James I. He had a passionate interest in the new science. He rejected reliance on ancient authorities and advocated that scientists should engage in the collection of data without holding preconceived notions. From that information, scientific conclusions could be reached through inductive reasoning—drawing general conclusions on the basis of many particular concrete observations. He thus became a proponent of the empirical method, which was already being used by some of the new scientists. In addition, he argued that true scientific knowledge would be useful knowledge, as opposed to medieval Scholasticism, which he attacked as too abstract. He had faith that scientific discoveries would be applied to commerce and industry and generally improve the human condition by giving human being great power over their environment. He thus became an outstanding propagandist for the new science as well as a proponent of the empirical method (see Figure 35.4). He did not, however, have a good understanding of mathematics and the role it could play in the new science. Descartes did.

René Descartes

René Descartes (1596–1650) was born in France and received training in Scholastic philosophy and mathematics. He spent his most productive years as a mathematician, physicist, and metaphysical philosopher in Holland. In 1619 Descartes perceived connections between geometry and algebra that led him to discover analytic geometry, an important tool for scientists. He expressed his philosophy and scientific methodology in his *Discourse on Method* (1637), a landmark in the rise of the scientific spirit. It was an eloquent defense of the value of abstract reasoning.

FIGURE 35.4 Title Page of Bacon's *Novum Organum* This title page from Francis Bacon's *Novum Organum* (*New Instrument*), published in 1620, shows a ship of discovery sailing out into the unknown. Below is the quotation "Many shall venture forth and science shall be increased." (The Bettmann Archive)

He would question all authority no matter how venerable—be it Aristotle or the Bible. He tried to remove systematically all assumptions about knowledge to the point where he was left with one experiential fact—that he was thinking. "I think, therefore I am" he believed to be a safe starting point. From this starting point he followed a rigorous process of deductive reasoning to come to a variety of conclusions, including the existence of God and the reality of the physical world. He argued that the universe could be divided into two kinds of reality: mind, or subjective thinking and experiencing, and body, or objective physical substance. According to this philosophy, known as "Cartesian dualism," the objective physical universe could be understood in terms of extension and motion. "Give me extension and motion," said Descartes, "and I will create the universe." Only the mind was exempt from mechanical laws.

Descartes, like Bacon, rejected Scholastic philosophy as not useful (although his deductive method had similarities to the reasoning used in Scholastic thought). He emphasized the power of the rigorous, reasoning individual mind to discover truths about nature and turn them to human needs. Unlike Bacon, he emphasized mathematical reasoning, not empirical investigation. By challenging all established authority, by accepting as truth only what could be known by reason, and by assuming a purely mechanical, physical universe, Descartes was in dispute with medieval thought and established an influential philosophy and methodology for the new science.

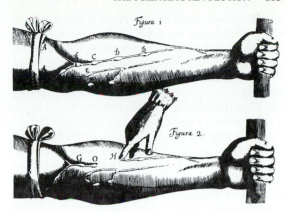

FIGURE 35.5 Modern Anatomy This illustration from an anatomy book published in 1639 by William Harvey shows the circulation of blood. Harvey's empirical, descriptive approach was typical of the new science. (Art Resource)

4. OTHER DISCIPLINES

The individuals who made the great discoveries of the Scientific Revolution all used, to varying degrees, the new scientific methodologies promoted by Bacon and Descartes during the first half of the seventeenth century. Clearly astronomy and physics led the way, but important discoveries were made in other sciences as well.

In the sixteenth century Vesalius, a Fleming living in Italy, wrote the first comprehensive textbook on the structure of the human body to be based on careful observation. Because he dissected many human bodies in order to make his observations, he ran into serious opposition from clerical authorities. In disgust he gave up his scientific studies and became the personal physician of Emperor Charles V. In the seventeenth century William Harvey, an Englishman who also studied in Italy, discovered the major principles of the circulatory system, thus making it possible for surgeons to operate on the human body with somewhat less fatal consequences than had previously been the case (see Figure 35.5). Vesalius and Harvey are regarded as the founders of the science of anatomy.

In the seventeenth century, an Irish nobleman, Robert Boyle, laid the foundations for modern chemistry by attacking many assumptions inherited from the ancients and by beginning the systematic search for the basic physical elements. He relied on the experimental method and argued that all matter was composed of atoms. He discovered a law of gases that still bears his name.

The language in which science is expressed is mathematics. In the early seventeenth century a Scotsman, Sir John Napier, invented logarithms, by which the process of multiplying and dividing huge numbers is greatly simplified. Shortly afterward the system was applied to the slide rule. About the same time, René Descartes adopted the symbols now used in algebra and devised analytic geometry, a method of combining and interchanging algebra and geometry. In the latter part of the seventeenth century Newton and the German Wilhelm Leibnitz, working independently, invented calculus, upon which many of the most intricate processes of advanced science and engineering are dependent.

During the seventeenth century some of the basic scientific instruments were invented. Both the telescope and the microscope were products of the Dutch Netherlands. However, it was Galileo who first used the telescope in systematic astronomical observations. Antoni van Leeuwenhoek, a Dutchman, was the chief pioneer in the use of the microscope. He discovered bacteria two hundred years before Pasteur learned how to combat them; he also observed the cellular structure of plant and animal tissue, the structure of the blood, and its circulation through the capillary system. Another Dutchman, Christiaan Huygens, invented the pendulum clock, making possible the precise measurement of small intervals of time for the first time in history.

The methods and discoveries of the Scientific Revolution spread to disciplines outside of what are usually considered the sciences. A good example is political theory, with the seminal thought of Thomas Hobbes (1588–1679) and John Locke (1632–1704).

Hobbes gained contact with the new sciences from several quarters. As a young man he served as a secretary to Francis Bacon. While traveling on the continent, he came into contact with Descartes and Galileo. He studied the writings of William Harvey. Hobbes acquired an expertise in both geometry and optics. Toward the middle of his life Hobbes became involved in the political events of his times and turned his attention to political theory. Dismayed by the civil strife raging during the civil war in England, Hobbes developed a political theory justifying absolutism in the name of law and order. In his *Leviathan* (1651), Hobbes started from a very few principles about human nature and rigorously deduced explanations for the founding and proper functioning of the state. He argued that human beings are most concerned with the preservation of their own lives, the avoidance of pain and pursuit of pleasure, and striving for power to protect themselves and get what they want. In the hypothetical state of nature, people are in a continual competitive struggle with one another. Self-interest and reason eventually lead people to exit the state of nature by way of a social contract among themselves. This social contract creates and grants massive powers to a sovereign, who uses those powers as necessary to keep the peace. Hobbes, like other seventeenth-century scientists, assumed a mechanistic, materialistic universe. His reasoning was much like Descartes'—rigorous, mathematical, and deductive. In the end, Hobbes concluded that absolutism was in accordance with natural law, though his method of reasoning pleased neither kings nor aristocrats.

Locke was also heavily influenced by the new seventeenth-century science. He acquired a medical education at college, read the works of leading scientific thinkers such as Francis Bacon and Isaac Newton, and was a friend of Robert Boyle. Like Hobbes, Locke was involved in some of the political events of his times. Locke also started with human beings in a state of nature, made some basic assumptions about the human condition, and traced the exit from the state of nature by way of a social contract. Yet Locke came to some significantly different conclusions. Assuming that human beings were not quite so self-centered and that things in the state of nature were not so bad, Locke argued that the sovereign had far fewer powers than Hobbes had claimed and that individuals retained the right to revolt under certain circumstances. Applying reasoning similar to that of seventeenth-century scientists, Locke concluded that British constitutionalism was in accordance with natural law.

Thus both Hobbes and Locke extended the Scientific Revolution to new fields. While their conclusions differed, they set a new standard for political theory, becoming two of the most influential political theorists of modern times.

5. IMPACT

By the end of the seventeenth century, the Aristotelian medieval world view had been broken and replaced by the Copernican-Newtonian worldview. The methodology of modern science was established. Scientists had created the foundations for the modern sciences of astronomy, physics, mathematics, chemistry, and anatomy, and study in other disciplines was under way.

Although the new scientists' work had gained some acceptance, their ideas were still known to only a few. Only a small group of people actually participated in this revolution in science. Most were men. Certainly some women overcame barriers and did participate. Margaret Cavendish (1623–1673) wrote works on natural philosophy and the scientific method. Maria Sibylla Merian (1647–1717) became a leading entomologist. Other women participated in scientific research. But men were reluctant to recognize them, and women were generally excluded from scientific societies. Moreover, the findings of the new sciences were not used to liberate women from traditional assumptions or roles, but rather to reaffirm notions of women's inferiority.

The impact of science on the masses remained minimal during the seventeenth century. Some members of the wealthy elite supported and were influenced by the new sciences, seeing potential benefits from them. But even they were few in number. It was not until the Enlightenment of the eighteenth century that the ideas of the Scientific Revolution spread widely and were applied in new ways.

SUGGESTED READING

General

J. Ben-David, *The Scientist's Role in Society* (1971). A sophisticated social interpretation.

A. R. Hall, *The Revolution in Science, 1500–1750* (1983). Full of detail.

M. Jacob, *The Cultural Meaning of the Scientific Revolution* (1988). A strong interpretation.

L. Schiebinger, *The Mind Has No Sex? Women in the Origins of Modern Science* (1989). An informative recent study.

A. G. R. Smith, *Science and Society in the Sixteenth and Seventeenth Centuries* (1972).

Astronomy and Physics

S. Drake, *Galileo* (1980). A brief study.

F. Manuel, *A Portrait of Isaac Newton* (1968). Uses a psychoanalytic perspective.

E. Rosen, *Copernicus and the Scientific Revolution* (1984). A good recent study.

R. S. Westfall, *Never at Rest: A Biography of Isaac Newton* (1981). An excellent biography.

Scientific Methodology

T. S. Kuhn, *The Structure of Scientific Revolutions* (1962). An important, influential interpretation of the Scientific Revolution.

Other Disciplines

P. Laslett, *Locke's Two Treatises of Government* (1970). Includes an introductory analysis with the texts.

C. B. MacPherson, *The Political Theory of Possessive Individualism: Hobbes to Locke* (1962). A controversial Marxist interpretation.

Sources

M. B. Hall, ed., *Nature and Nature's Laws: Documents of the Scientific Revolution* (1970). A good collection.

CHAPTER 36
The Enlightenment

FIGURE 36.1 *Madame Geoffrin's Salon,* **1755** Meetings in aristocratic Parisian salons such as this were typical of the Enlightenment. Here thinkers, artists, musicians, writers, and aristocrats exchanged views and helped spread the philosophy of the Enlightenment. (Giraudon/Art Resource)

As a period of intellectual history, the eighteenth century is usually referred to as the Enlightenment, or the Age of Reason. The Enlightenment was initiated toward the end of the seventeenth century by a number of intellectuals who attempted to popularize the ideas of the Scientific Revolution. During the eighteenth century this popularization continued, and new attempts were made to apply the methods of natural sciences to human behavior and social institutions. Western thinkers were speculating on the broader meaning of science—its ethical, political, social, and economic implications. They subjected almost everything to the critical standard of reason. In doing so, Enlightenment thinkers rejected the assumptions of their medieval and Renaissance predecessors, who had looked to the Christian or classical past for guidance. Enlightenment thinkers argued for reform and change. They felt that people were ready to shrug off the shackles of tradition and custom and participate in the progress of civilization; to these optimistic intellectuals, people were ready to become enlightened.

The Enlightenment was limited in some respects. During the eighteenth century the Enlightenment was centered in western Europe. Moreover, Enlightenment thought spread primarily to only the elite of the urban aristocracy and middle classes. Nevertheless, the ideas and attitudes developed during the Enlightenment would come to dominate most parts of Western civilization over the next two centuries.

1. ENLIGHTENMENT CONCEPTS

Although Enlightenment thinkers differed widely among themselves, they shared a belief in certain broad concepts that together make up the philosophy of the Enlightenment. The three most important concepts were reason, nature, and change and progress.

Enlightenment thinkers argued that all assumptions should be subjected to critical and empirical reasoning. Traditional institutions or customs should not be accepted because they have been long-lasting but rather should be examined critically and held up to the standard of reason. True knowledge is gained empirically.

All we know and all we can ever know is what we perceive through our senses and interpret with our reason. There are no such things as innate ideas or revealed truth.

Enlightenment thinkers believed that nature is ordered, functions reasonably, and constitutes a standard for judgment. Nature is governed by a few simple and unchangeable laws. Those who think they can change one of these laws—who think they can, by praying, for instance, bring down rain on parched crops and perchance a neighbor's unroofed house—are dupes of their own egotism. Nature does not act capriciously. Proper empirical analysis will show that nature functions in line with the laws of reason. Nature is good and beautiful in its simplicity. Human beings have corrupted it with their complex political, social, and religious restrictions. A move to nature is a move toward wholesome vigor and freedom.

Most Enlightenment thinkers felt that change and progress work hand in hand as human beings work to perfect themselves and their society. Change should not be viewed with distrust as a deterioration from a previously superior, more perfect state of things. Change, when dictated by reason and in line with nature, liberates individuals and should be pursued. Such change contributes to individual and social progress on earth. Human beings are naturally rational and good, but the proponents of mystic religions have distorted human thinking and prevented proper progress by preaching false doctrines of original sin and divine moral laws. Rid people's minds of these religious hindrances, and they can and will build a more perfect society for themselves.

The concepts of reason, nature, and change and progress worked together in the minds of Enlightenment thinkers and generally formed a structure for their more specific ideas. Enlightenment thinkers used reason and nature to criticize institutions and customs of the past that still dominated their eighteenth-century society. Reason and nature further guided these thinkers as they determined what changes should take place. They felt that as individuals and societies made appropriate changes, human life would become more informed by reason and more compatible with nature. They believed that human beings were on the verge of enlightenment—of great progress—if people would simply open their eyes and become mature, reasoning adults. This progress would take the form of people leading increasingly happier, freer, more moral lives.

2. THE *PHILOSOPHES*

Enlightenment ideas were put forth by a variety of intellectuals who in France came to be known as the *philosophes* (see p. 470). *Philosophes* is French for "philosophers," and in a sense these thinkers were rightly considered philosophers, for the questions they dealt with were philosophical: How do we discover truth? How should life be lived? What is the nature of God? But on the whole the term has a meaning different from the usual meaning of "philosopher." The *philosophes* were intellectuals, often not formally trained or associated with a university. They were usually more literary than scientific. They generally extended, applied, popularized, or propagandized ideas of others rather than originating those ideas themselves. The *philosophes* were more likely to write plays, satires, histories, novels, encyclopedia entries, and short pamphlets or simply participate in verbal exchanges at select gatherings than to write formal philosophical books.

It was the *philosophes* who developed the philosophy of the Enlightenment and spread it to much of the educated elite in western Europe and the American colonies. Although the sources for their philosophy can be traced to the Scientific Revolution in general, the *philosophes* were most influenced by their understanding of Newton, Locke, and English institutions.

The *philosophes* saw Isaac Newton as the great synthesizer of the Scientific Revolution who rightly described the universe as ordered, mechanical, material, and only originally set into motion by God, who since then has remained relatively inactive. Newton's synthesis showed to the *philosophes* that reason and nature were compatible: Nature functioned logically and discernably, and what was natural was also reasonable. Newton exemplified the value of reasoning based on concrete experience. The *philosophes* felt

that his empirical methodology was the correct path to discovering truth.

John Locke (1632–1704) agreed with Newton but went further. This English thinker would not exempt even the mind from the mechanical laws of the material universe. In his *Essay Concerning Human Understanding* (1690), Locke pictured the human brain at birth as a blank sheet of paper on which nothing would ever be written except by sense perception and reason. What human beings become depends on their experiences— on the information received through the senses. Schools and social institutions can therefore play a great role in molding the individual from childhood to adulthood. Human beings were thus by nature far more malleable than had been assumed. This empirical psychology of Locke rejected the notion that human beings were born with innate ideas or that revelation was a reliable source of truth. Locke also enunciated liberal and reformist political ideas in his *Second Treatise on Civil Government* (1690), which influenced the *philosophes*. On the whole Locke's empiricism, psychology, and politics were appealing to the *philosophes*.

England, not coincidentally the country of Newton and Locke, became an admired model for many of the *philosophes*. They tended to idealize it, but England did seem to allow greater individual freedom, tolerate more religious differences, and evidence greater political reform than other countries, especially France. England seemed to have gone furthest in freeing itself from traditional institutions and accepting the new science of the seventeenth century. Moreover, England's approach seemed to work, for England was experiencing relative political stability and prosperity. The *philosophes* wanted to see in their own countries much of what England already seemed to have.

Many *philosophes* reflected the influence of Newton, Locke, and English institutions, but perhaps the most representative in his views was Voltaire (1694–1778) (see Figure 36.2). Of all the leading figures of the Enlightenment, he was the most influential. Voltaire, the son of a Paris lawyer, became the idol of the French intelligentsia while still in his early twenties. His versatile mind was sparkling; his wit was mordant. An outspoken critic, he soon ran afoul of both church

FIGURE 36.2 Frederick the Great with Voltaire Voltaire, seated, talks with Frederick the Great. This picture reveals the image of the great Enlightenment thinker at work with books, papers, and pen and with the international stature sufficient to gain the ear of enlightened despots such as Frederick. Yet Frederick's enlightenment may have been more form than substance. (Bibliothéque Nationale, Paris)

FIGURE 36.3 The Encyclopedia This engraving from one of the many technical articles in the *Encyclopedia* shows workers preparing type for printing, with details of materials used in the process. It reveals the optimistic faith in the ease and practicality of learning that was typical of Enlightenment thought. (French Embassy Press and Information Division)

and state authorities. First he was imprisoned in the Bastille; later he was exiled to England. There he encountered the ideas of Newton and Locke and came to admire English parliamentary government and tolerance. In *Letters on the English* (1733), *Elements of the Philosophy of Newton* (1738), and other writings, he popularized the ideas of Newton and Locke, extolled the virtues of English society, and indirectly criticized French society. Slipping back into France, he was hidden for a time and protected by a wealthy woman who became his mistress. Voltaire's facile mind and pen were never idle. He wrote poetry, drama, history, essays, letters, and scientific treatises—ninety volumes in all. The special targets of his cynical wit were the Catholic church and Christian institutions. Few people in history have dominated their age intellectually as did Voltaire.

The work that best summarizes the philosophy of the Enlightenment is the *Encyclopedia*. The *Encyclopedia* was a collaborative effort by many of the *philosophes* under the editorship of Denis Diderot (1713–1774) and Jean le Rond d'Alembert (1717–1783). This gigantic work undertook to explore the whole world of knowledge from the perspective of the *philosophes*. Its articles on subjects ranging from music to machinery expressed the critical, rationalistic, and empiricist views of the *philosophes* (see Figure 36.3). The practicality of science and knowledge in general was emphasized. One of the work's main messages was that almost anything could be discovered, understood, or clarified through reason. An

The *Philosophes*

Enlightenment thinkers often referred to themselves as "philosophes," which is technically the French word for philosophers. The term had a special meaning bound up with the spirit of the Enlightenment. This is dealt with directly in the following selection, "The Philosopher," from the Encyclopedia. *It has traditionally been assumed that Diderot is the author of "The Philosopher," but it may have been written by another person, perhaps Du Marsais. In any case, it is an authoritative treatment of the topic according to Enlightenment precepts.*

Other men make up their minds to act without thinking, nor are they conscious of the causes which move them, not even knowing that such exist. The philosopher, on the contrary, distinguishes the causes to what extent he may, often anticipates them, and knowingly surrenders himself to them. In this manner he avoids objects that may cause him sensations that are not conducive to his well being or his rational existence, and seeks those which may excite in him affections agreeable with the state in which he finds himself. Reason is in the estimation of the philosopher what grace is to the Christian. Grace determines the Christian's action; reason the philosopher's.

Other men are carried away by their passions, so that the acts which they produce do not proceed from reflection. These are the men who move in darkness; while the philosopher, even in his passions, moves only after reflection. He marches at night, but a torch goes on ahead.

The philosopher forms his principles upon an infinity of individual observations. The people adopt the principle without a thought of the observations which have produced it, believing that the maxim . . . so to speak, of itself; but the philosopher takes the maxim at its source, he examines its origin, he knows its real value, and

SOURCE: Merrick Whitcomb, ed., "French Philosophers of the Eighteenth Century," in *Translations and Reprints from the Original Sources of European History*, Vol. VI, No. 1 (Philadelphia: University of Pennsylvania Press, 1898), pp. 21–23.

only makes use of it, if it seems to him satisfactory.

Truth is not for the philosopher a mistress who vitiates his imagination, and whom he believes to find everywhere. He contents himself with being able to discover it wherever he may chance to find it. He does not confound it with its semblance; but takes for true that which is true, for false that which is false, for doubtful that which is doubtful, and for probable that which is only probable. He does more—and this is the great perfection of philosophy; that when he has no real grounds for passing judgment, he knows how to remain undetermined.

The world is full of persons of understanding, even of much understanding, who always pass judgment. They are guessing always, because it is guessing to pass judgment without knowing when one has proper grounds for judgment. They misjudge the capacity of the human mind; they believe it is possible to know everything, and so they are ashamed not to be prepared to pass judgment, and they imagine that understanding consists in passing judgment. The philosopher believes that it consists in judging well: he is better pleased with himself when he has suspended the faculty of determining, than if he had determined before having acquired proper grounds for his decision. . . .

The philosophic spirit is then a spirit of observation and of exactness, which refers everything to its true principles; but it is not the understanding alone which the philosopher cultivates; he carries further his attention and his labors.

Our philosopher does not believe himself an exile in the world; he does not believe himself in the enemy's country; he wishes to enjoy, like a wise economist, the goods that nature offers him; he wishes to find his pleasure with others; and in order to find it, it is necessary to assist in producing it; so he seeks to harmonize with those with whom chance or his choice has determined he shall live; and he finds at the same time that which suits him: he is an honest man who wishes to please and render himself useful.

underlying current was criticism of the irrational and of whatever stood in the way of the Enlightenment, whether it was religious intolerance or traditional social institutions. The first volume appeared in 1751. Its threat to the status quo was recognized by governmental and church authorities, who censored it, halted its publication, and harassed its editors. Thanks in great part to the persistence of Diderot, who fought the authorities and dealt with a difficult group of contributing authors, the project was completed with the publication of the final volume in 1772. The *Encyclopedia* sold well and played an important role in the penetration of Enlightenment ideas outside the major cities and courts.

By this time the Enlightenment was evolving to a different stage. The *philosophes* were becoming more quarrelsome among themselves. This disagreement reflected a greater acceptance of the fundamental philosophy of the Enlightenment, for the debates tended to center on how far Enlightenment concepts could be extended. Some *philosophes,* such as Baron d'Holbach (1723–1789), verged on atheism in attacks on organized religion. Others, such as Marie-Jean de Condorcet (1743–1794), were so optimistic that they almost made a religion out of progress itself. Enlightenment thinkers were also tending to specialize. Some laid the foundations for the development of the social sciences during the nineteenth century. For example, Cesare Beccaria (1738–1794) contributed works on modern criminology and penology, and Adam Smith (1723–1790) wrote what would be the fundamental text of classical economics. Finally, some Enlightenment thinkers took more challenging positions, often contradicting some of the ideas of the Enlightenment itself and providing a transition to the succeeding intellectual traditions. The most important example of these thinkers is Jean-Jacques Rousseau (1712–1778).

One of the most original thinkers and writers of all time, Rousseau crusaded for a return to nature—beautiful, pure, simple nature. The message struck home in a society weary of arbitrary and often corrupt governmental bureaucracy and an oppressively artificial and elaborate code of social etiquette. Rousseau was lionized. Great ladies, including the queen of France, began playing milkmaid. In his novel *La Nouvelle Hé-*

loïse, Rousseau extolled the beauties of free love and uninhibited emotion. In *Émile* he expounded the "natural" way of rearing and educating children. He would let children do what they like and teach them "practical" knowledge. Rousseau shared much with other *philosophes,* even contributing to the *Encyclopedia,* but after the 1750s he broke from them for personal as well as intellectual reasons. In *The Origin of Inequality among Men* (1753), Rousseau argued that civilization was not necessarily a progressive boon to humanity, that human beings had lost much since their exit from the state of nature. In *The Social Contract,* Rousseau became one of the few *philosophes* to make a fundamental contribution to political theory. Rousseau generally placed greater faith in emotion, feeling, and intuition than in reason. In this he was a forerunner of the romantic spirit and expounded its principles long before that movement reached its peak.

The *philosophes* had a self-conscious sense of a spirit of enlightenment. They felt that they were leading a mission of liberation, that by striking the match of reason the darkness of the past would be dispelled and humanity would quickly and easily liberate itself. By becoming thus enlightened, humanity could move from childhood to adulthood. They attacked war and the military values of the traditional aristocracy. They rejected artificial social distinctions. They lauded most forms of freedom, including freedom of the press, speech, and religious belief. They supported the application of science to economic activity, a view appealing to the middle class and liberal aristocracy. They believed that their eighteenth-century civilization was ready for enlightenment and the great progress that would result. Yet the optimism of most of the *philosophes* was not wild-eyed; indeed, there was an underlying current of pessimism in the works of thinkers such as Diderot, the marquis de Sade, Rousseau, and even Voltaire.

In characterizing the *philosophes,* historians have disagreed. Some view the *philosophes* as shallow, self-concerned dilettantes who had few deep or original ideas and who were afraid of real reform. Most historians, however, argue that the *philosophes* were thoughtful, sincere thinkers who performed an important service by laying the intellectual foundations of modern society.

3. WOMEN AND THE SOCIAL CONTEXT

There were several centers of Enlightenment thought in the cities and courts of Europe, particularly western Europe, but the heart of the Enlightenment was in Paris. Gatherings were regularly held in the salons of several wealthy Parisian patrons, usually women of the aristocracy or upper middle class such as Madame du Deffaud or Madame Geoffrin (see Figure 36.1). There the *philosophes* met with one another and members of the international upper middle class and aristocratic elite. They debated the ideas of the Enlightenment in an environment lush with art, music, and wealth. These gatherings facilitated the spread of Enlightenment ideas among social and intellectual elites and added much to the social respectability of intellectuals.

As patrons and as intellectual contributors to these gatherings, women played an important role in the Enlightenment. Women such as Madame Geoffrin provided essential financial support to several *philosophes,* particularly for the *Encyclopedia.* Other women corresponded by letter with leading intellectual, political, and social figures throughout Europe, using letter writing as an art just as conversation was an art in the salons. The salons were open to women with the right intellectual or social qualifications. The *philosophes* tended to support improving the education and position of women. The Enlightenment emphasis on individualism theoretically and in the long run led toward accepting the idea of political and social equality between men and women. Nevertheless, it cannot be said that the *philosophes* advocated equal rights for women in a modern sense nor that they challenged fundamental assumptions about the subordinate public roles appropriate for women. One of the few people to argue for real change in the condition of women in the eighteenth century was Mary Wollstonecraft (1759–1797). In 1792 she published *Vindication of the Rights of Women,* but generally her plea for equal rights for all human beings fell on deaf ears.

Meetings in Paris salons were paralleled by smaller meetings in other French and foreign cities as well as by less organized meetings in coffeehouses and the homes of the liberal aristocracy. Enlightenment ideas were read and discussed in local academies, Freemason lodges, societies, libraries, and clubs.

4. ENLIGHTENMENT AND RELIGION

The Enlightenment was profoundly secular in character, but religion played an important role. Very few Enlightenment thinkers were either atheists or traditional Christians. Most were skeptics influenced by the arguments of Pierre Bayle (1647–1706). Many believed in some form of deism. They believed that this wonderful mechanism called the universe could not have come into being by accident. Some infinite Divine Being must have created it and set it in motion. However, the finite mind of human beings cannot comprehend the infinite. Therefore, God is unknowable. Furthermore, God, having set his perfect mechanical laws into motion, will never tamper with them or interfere in human affairs. God is impersonal.

It is readily apparent that the beliefs of the *philosophes* were in conflict with the doctrines of the Christian churches—Roman Catholic, Protestant, and Orthodox alike. Christian theologians argued that God remained active in the universe, that God's ways are revealed through religious literature and institutions, and that faith constitutes a valid alternative to reason. Enlightenment thinkers and Christian leaders were soon engaged in debate, spending much time and effort attacking each other. In countries such as France and Italy, where clerics were strongly entrenched in government, they censored the writings of the *philosophes* and sought to interrupt their work. In the long run, however, the ideas of the Enlightenment spread, and the Church probably lost more than it gained by so ardently attacking the *philosophes* and their ideas.

In general the Enlightenment promoted toleration toward religious minorities, whether Christian or otherwise. For example, Enlightenment thinkers such as Locke in England and Baron de Montesquieu in France were among several who attacked discrimination against Jews. While the century did not witness an end to anti-Semitism, monarchs and political leaders influenced by the Enlightenment lessened some dictates against Jews in Austria, France, Prussia, and Portugal.

5. POLITICAL AND ECONOMIC ASPECTS OF THE ENLIGHTENMENT

Enlightenment thinkers devoted much thought to matters of government. If human beings are by nature rational and good, then surely, if given the opportunity, they can devise for themselves efficient and benevolent political institutions. Corrupt tyrannies were no longer tolerable. Of the numerous "enlightened" thinkers in the field of political science, three stand out above the others in influence: Locke, Montesquieu, and Rousseau.

Locke's most eloquent plea was for the natural rights of human beings, which are life, liberty, and property. He theorizes, in his *Two Treatises on Civil Government,* that to safeguard these rights individuals voluntarily contract to surrender a certain amount of their sovereignty to government. The powers of the government, however, whether it be monarchical or popular, are strictly limited. No government may violate the individual's right to life, liberty, and property. If it does, the people who set it up can and should overthrow it. These ideas were fundamental in the thinking of the makers of both the French and the American revolutions. Jefferson wrote many of Locke's ideas into the Declaration of Independence, frequently using his exact words. They likewise appear in the U.S. Constitution and in numerous French declarations of liberty.

Baron de Montesquieu (1689–1755) was less a theorizer than a discerning student of history and shrewd analyst of political systems. His masterpiece is *The Spirit of the Laws.* Although a great admirer of the English government after the Glorious Revolution, Montesquieu came to the conclusion that different types of government are best suited to various conditions. For instance, absolute monarchy is best for countries of vast area, limited monarchy for countries of moderate size like France, and republics for small states like Venice or ancient Athens. Not only did he approve of Locke's doctrine of limited sovereignty, but he specified how it can best be secured—by a separation of powers and a system of checks and balances. The powers and functions of government should be equally divided among king, lords, and commons, each one being checked by the other two. This theory was probably Montesquieu's greatest practical contribution to the science of government. The principle was incorporated into the U.S. Constitution—kings, lords, and commons becoming the executive, judicial, and legislative branches of government.

Rousseau offered a more radical political theory. This morbid, erratic genius based the conclusions in his *Social Contract* and his *Second Discourse* upon pure imagination. People in the state of noble savagery were free, equal, and happy. It was only when some began marking off plots of ground, saying "this is mine," that inequality began. In order to restore their lost freedom and happiness, people entered into a compact, each with all the others, surrendering their individual liberty to the whole. Since sovereignty is indivisible, the general will is all-powerful. Although Rousseau never made it clear just how the general will would actually operate in practice, he apparently assumed that the individual would be free by virtue of being part of the general will. Rousseau had great influence on the leaders of the second and more radical phase of the French Revolution.

Some of the eighteenth-century planners of the better life through reason turned their thoughts to economics. Since the late fifteenth century, mercantilism had been the dominant economic theory and practice in western Europe. This system of regulated nationalistic economy reached its peak in the seventeenth century. Only the Dutch Netherlands held out for free trade. But if, according to the fundamental assumptions of the Enlightenment, the universe is run by a few simple mechanical laws, why should there not be a similar natural order in the field of economics? A group of French Physiocrats, led by François Quesnay, personal physician to Louis XV, began to teach that economics has its own set of natural laws, that the most basic of these laws is that of supply and demand, and that these laws operate best when commerce is freed from government regulation. This doctrine came to be known as *laissez-faire* (or free trade and enterprise).

The chief developer of the theory of laissez-faire was Adam Smith, a Scottish professor of philosophy who associated with the Physiocrats while sojourning in France. His *Wealth of Nations,* published in 1776, has remained the bible of laissez-faire economics ever since. The ideas of the French Physiocrats and Adam Smith strongly influenced the leaders of the American and French revolutions.

6. ENLIGHTENED DESPOTISM

While critical and combative, the *philosophes* were not political or social revolutionaries. They hoped for fairly painless change from above rather than a revolutionary transfer of power to the still-unenlightened masses. Many followed Voltaire in believing that enlightened despotism was the form of government that offered the greatest chances for enactment of enlightened reforms. By the middle of the eighteenth century several monarchs found these views attractive, styled themselves as enlightened monarchs, and attempted to enact reforms that at least appeared to fit with Enlightenment thought. These monarchs have been distinguished from their predecessors and termed "enlightened despots." To what extent this is a valid characterization of their rule remains to be seen.

The most sensational of the enlightened despots was Frederick the Great of Prussia (1740–1786). Frederick had from boyhood loved music, poetry, and philosophy. At the end of the Seven Years' War (1756–1763), the second of his two wars of aggression, he settled down as a model enlightened despot and attempted to apply the laws of reason to statecraft. Frederick was an avid reader of the French philosophers. He even invited Voltaire to visit him at Potsdam, but Prussia was not big enough to hold two such egos at once. The two quarreled and, after several years, parted.

Frederick made much of religious toleration. However, he continued to penalize the Jews and never ceased to ridicule Christians of all denominations. He was a strong advocate of public education, although he spent very little on it in comparison with what he spent on his army. The centralized Prussian bureaucracy became the most efficient government in Europe. True to the prevailing thought of the Enlightenment, however, he had no faith in popular self-government. Nor did he make a move to free the serfs or end the feudal system in Prussia. Probably the most lasting of Frederick's contributions to Prussia were his codification of the law and improvements in the administration of justice. In the field of economics, Frederick was a mercantilist, although he did share the Physiocrats' appreciation of the importance of agriculture.

The most sincere of all the enlightened despots was Joseph II of Austria (1780–1790). Unfortunately, he lacked the practical sagacity of Frederick the Great. His well-meaning but ill-conceived efforts to centralize the administration of the far-flung Hapsburg territories, to replace the numerous languages of his subjects with German, to secularize the strongly entrenched Roman Catholic church, and to free the serfs in a society still based on feudalism all backfired.

Other monarchs, such as those of Sweden, Sardinia, Spain, and Portugal, attempted or enacted reforms that could be seen as enlightened. Even in Russia, Catherine the Great made apparent efforts at enlightened reforms, but ultimately she did not put most of those reforms into practice.

Significantly, France alone of the great powers on the Continent failed to produce an even faintly enlightened despot. Upon attaining the French throne in 1774, the well-meaning Louis XVI appointed the Physiocrat Turgot as minister of finance. Turgot, a friend of Voltaire, initiated a program of sweeping reforms that might have forestalled the French Revolution. However, within two years' time the powerfully entrenched vested interests persuaded the weak-willed king to dismiss him.

Whether there was a phenomenon of enlightened despotism occurring during the eighteenth century, remains a debated question among historians. If there was, it was usually a matter more of form than of content. Several eighteenth-century monarchs acted in certain enlightened ways, believed themselves to be enlightened, admired some of the *philosophes,* and were admired in return. Several supported culture, favored a less religious and more rational justification for their rule, and consulted with *philosophes*. Yet most of their "enlightenment" was superficial. Many of the reforms they made were simply an update in the long process of making the central government more effective and powerful. Few tried to enact fundamental social, political, or economic reforms dictated by Enlightenment thought, and even those who tried, such as Joseph II, generally failed to effect those reforms.

7. CONCLUSION

Enlightenment thinkers applied and popularized a secular, rational, reformist way of thinking that undermined the intellectual foundations of traditional society. Their ideas threatened the Church more than any other institution, and one of the legacies of the Enlightenment was a widening gap between religiously influenced ideas and accepted scholarly thought. These thinkers, probably unknowingly, laid the intellectual foundations for the revolutions that swept Europe and America from the last quarter of the eighteenth century to the mid–nineteenth century. Moreover, their way of thinking and the ideas that arose from it would form the intellectual core of the liberal middle-class ideology that was ascendant during the nineteenth century and is still strong in the twentieth century.

SUGGESTED READING

General

C. Becker, *The Heavenly City of the Eighteenth-Century Philosophers* (1932). An influential, thought-provoking classic.

P. Gay, *The Enlightenment: An Interpretation*. Vol. I: *The Rise of Modern Paganism*. Vol. II: *The Science of Freedom* (1969). Detailed treatment by a leading authority.

N. Hampson, *The Enlightenment* (1982). A highly respected survey.

The Philosophes

T. Bestermann, *Voltaire* (1969). A solid biography.

A. M. Wilson, *Diderot* (1972). An excellent biography.

The Social, Political, and Economic Context

L. Krieger, *Kings and Philosophers, 1689–1789* (1970). A broad survey making connections between thought and politics.

H. Payne, *The Philosophes and the People* (1976). Focuses on the gap between the *philosophes* and the people.

P. Quennell, ed., *Affairs of the Mind: The Salon in Europe and America from the 18th to the 20th Century* (1980). Emphasizes the role of women.

S. I. Spencer, ed., *French Women and the Age of Enlightenment* (1984). Covers important aspects of the topic.

Enlightened Despotism

H. Scott, *Enlightened Despotism* (1990). A good recent analysis.

E. Wangermann, *The Austrian Achievement, 1700–1800* (1973). A good study of enlightened monarchs.

Sources

L. G. Crocker, ed., *The Age of Enlightenment* (1969). A good anthology.

P. Gay, ed., *The Enlightenment: A Comprehensive Anthology* (1973). A good selection of documents.

RETROSPECT

During the fourteenth and fifteenth centuries, various tensions and a weakening of social institutions marked the transformation of the medieval world. During the fifteenth and sixteenth centuries, the institutions and developments that would characterize early modern times grew out of the changing medieval system.

The first challenge to the medieval system came in the cities of northern Italy during the fourteenth and fifteenth centuries. There the ideas, values, and culture of the Renaissance arose. Although rooted in the medieval world, scholars, writers, and artists began looking back to classical Greece and Rome for models instead of accepting medieval scholastic authority. Cultural leaders focused more on individual human beings living in a concrete, material, Christian world rather than on medieval theology. The social and cultural elite were becoming more self-centered, proud, versatile, and materialistic. These Renaissance qualities produced new, vibrant literature and art, making northern Italy the cultural center of the West.

During the fifteenth and sixteenth centuries the Renaissance spread from Italy to northern Europe, particularly to the courts of princes and kings and to university towns. There the Renaissance took on a more piously religious character as northern humanists tried to reconcile Christian and classical cultures.

In place of the declining feudal monarchies and empires arose the national or territorial state, which became the dominant political institution of the early modern era. The rise of the national states ended the independence of numerous feudal lords by bringing them under the authority of national monarchs. Talented monarchs such as Ferdinand and Isabella in Spain, Louis XI in France, and Henry VII in England increased their own power and established foundations for the continued growth of national monarchical power. Those areas that did not unify into national states, such as in Germany and Italy, suffered from political weakness.

National monarchs encouraged Europeans to expand into the non-Western world. Voyages of "discovery" soon led to commercial trade, spreading Christianity, and political control. During the fifteenth and early sixteenth centuries, Portugal and Spain led in this expansion of Europe. England, France, and the Netherlands soon followed. By the end of the sixteenth century, large parts of the rest of the world, particularly in the Western Hemisphere, southern Asia, and coastal Africa, had come under European economic and political domination.

The expansion of Europe was also stimulated by new economic developments. Europe's medieval economy, characterized by subsistence agriculture, monopolistic guilds, and localism, slowly gave way to capitalistic practices and institutions. Increasing population and rising prices spurred commerce and created social turmoil, with the poorer peasants suffering the most. The old landed aristocracy was now threatened by newcomers into the class and by a new middle class of aggressive entrepreneurs, merchants, bankers, and lawyers. It is true that the bourgeoisie sought most of all to enter the ranks of the nobility and did so whenever possible, and that the nobility held the upper hand politically and socially for two or three more centuries. But by 1600 class lines had become more fluid.

The fifteenth and sixteenth centuries were marked by a deepening concern for religious matters. During the 1500s the western Christian church, which had monopolized religious life and strongly influenced the intellectual, political, and economic life of Europe during the Middle Ages, was split asunder by the Reformation. Great religious leaders such as Martin Luther and John Calvin broke from the Roman Catholic church and laid the foundations for the various Protestant churches. Much of northern Europe became Protestant. This advance of Protestantism stimulated reform efforts already underway within the Roman Catholic church. Catholic doctrine was forcefully affirmed at the Council of Trent, and new religious orders such as the Jesuits reinvigorated the Church.

The religious struggles of the Reformation combined with political forces to give rise to the

Wars of Religion. From the middle of the sixteenth to the middle of the seventeenth centuries, much of Europe was struck by war and political turmoil that was connected to religious issues. The most devastating of these wars was the Thirty Years' War, which broke out in Germany in 1618 and was not concluded until 1648 with the Peace of Westphalia.

The economy and society—rural, based on agriculture, and with a vast mass of peasantry dominated by the privileged aristocracy—changed only slowly during most of the seventeenth and eighteenth centuries. Gradually the central governments, the growing cities, and the middle classes altered life within the traditional village. The pace of social change quickened in the mid–eighteenth century as population grew, agriculture was revolutionized, and cottage industry spread. Religious affiliations changed little; established Catholic and Protestant churches remained committed to the hierarchical social order and the dominant political systems of their states. Even the numerous pietist and quietist religious sects that arose during this period passively accepted, for the most part, the political authority of the established and usually absolutist governments.

The baroque and classical styles, which prevailed in literature and the arts in western Europe throughout most of the seventeenth and eighteenth centuries, generally harmonized with and often exalted the absolutist monarchs and their courts. These styles stressed a combination of grandeur, richness, and order that appealed to monarchs and the privileged orders, who so often were the patrons of the arts.

The seventeenth and eighteenth centuries were the apogee of royal absolutism as a form of government in the Western world. The clearest example of royal absolutism in western Europe arose in France, where under Henry IV, Richelieu, Mazarin, and Louis XIV, the Bourbon monarchy achieved a degree of control that was unprecedented and a position of dominance in Europe. European history during the years 1661–1715 has been called the age of Louis XIV. Louis and his court were the envy of all other monarchs, who sought to emulate them. France possessed a military strength so great that the major states of western and central Europe working in combination held France in check only with difficulty.

Royal absolutism also dominated the political forms of central and eastern Europe during the seventeenth and eighteenth centuries. There the most important political developments were the rise of two military despotisms—Prussia and Russia. The Hohenzollerns of Prussia, consistently pursuing the policies of royal absolutism, militarism, and territorial aggrandizement, more than doubled their territory and population and challenged Austria for the leadership of the German-speaking world. Russia, under two strong absolutist monarchs, Peter the Great and Catherine the Great, defeated Sweden and the Ottoman Turks and gained valuable territory facing the West. Poland, which failed to develop a strong central government, disappeared from the map, carved up by Russia, Prussia, and Austria.

PART SIX

REVOLUTION, INDUSTRIALIZATION, AND NATIONALISM, 1776–1914

During the last quarter of the eighteenth century political and economic revolutions were initiated that would transform Western civilization. So massive were the changes stemming from these revolutions that historians usually mark this period as the beginning of modern times.

The first political revolution occurred in America, where in 1776 the British colonies revolted and declared their independence as the United States. The American Revolution was followed by the French Revolution of 1789, which was of considerably greater significance, for it represented an almost complete overthrow of traditional institutions in a powerful country in the heart of Europe. During the succeeding two decades, the ideas and reforms of the French Revolution spread throughout Europe. New uprisings and revolutions, generally inspired by some of the same goals as the French Revolution, occurred in several areas during the 1820s, 1830s, and 1840s.

The more subtle but even more historically significant revolution of this period was economic: the Industrial Revolution. Starting in Great Britain, the Industrial Revolution spread to continental Europe and other areas of the world over the course of the nineteenth century. As economic activity shifted from the farm to the factory, cities grew, classes changed, and society itself was transformed.

These political and economic revolutions were in great part responsible for the growth of a number of ideologies—sets of ideas and beliefs that moved people, groups, and governments to demand action in important, compelling ways throughout the nineteenth and early twentieth centuries. Liberalism, conservatism, and socialism became very influential, but perhaps the most powerful was nationalism, which became a potent force for national unification, international competition, and imperialism.

CHAPTER 37
The American Revolution

FIGURE 37.1 "In Order to Form a More Perfect Union" This painting by Junius Brutus Stearns depicts the Constitutional Convention in session in Philadelphia in 1787 with George Washington presiding. At times the proceedings of the Convention were less sedate and reflective than this scene portrays; nonetheless, it catches the sense of high purpose the delegates believed they were serving in seeking to strengthen the new nation. (The Granger Collection)

The age of revolutions opened in a somewhat unexpected setting—in the British colonies in North America. There, by force of arms, the American colonists rejected British rule and established the new nation of the United States of America. Historians are not agreed on whether the course followed by the Americans represented merely a war of independence or a revolution in the fundamental sense of changing traditional society. However, to many contemporaries both in America and in Europe something fundamental happened in America between 1776 and 1800 that heralded the beginning of a new era in western European history. Placed in a global setting, the American Revolution was a major event in shaping the modern world.

1. AMERICAN COLONIAL SOCIETY

The American Revolution was a complex movement, but behind it lay one fundamental fact: During the century and a half prior to 1776, American society had become different from that prevailing in Europe. Its uniqueness was due chiefly to the fact that European immigrants and their offspring had to adapt traditional European patterns of life in order to survive in a new environment. As a consequence, many colonists came to think of themselves as a separate people. That perception, coupled with Great Britain's effort to bend colonial society to British purposes without taking into account the changes that had occurred across the Atlantic, led the colonials to act in the name of independence and nationhood.

By 1776 an obvious sign of the vitality of British colonial society was its large population, which had reached about 2.5 million. During the eighteenth century population had grown faster in America than in Europe. The growth was in large part due to emigration from Europe and Africa; by 1776 African Americans constituted 20 percent of the population. Americans of European descent were also reproducing more rapidly than was the case in Europe, largely because of a longer life expectancy resulting from a healthier environment and the fact that earlier marriages were made possible in a setting where it was easier to establish a new household than it was in Europe.

The rapidly growing population had created a bustling economy in the American wilderness. Its backbone was a diverse agricultural establishment, ranging from small, independently owned family farms in New England and the Middle Atlantic colonies to great plantations worked by slaves in the southern colonies. The American soil and climate permitted a variety of crops: grain, tobacco, cotton, rice, indigo, vegetables, fruits, livestock. After the first hard years of the seventeenth century the colonists were more than able to feed themselves; some of their crops, especially tobacco, also found markets in Europe. And off to the west lay areas of rich, unexploited land to attract the growing population.

The colonies had not neglected commerce and industry. In the face of formidable obstacles, colonial merchants, especially in New England and the Middle Atlantic colonies, slowly developed commercial exchanges within America and then extended their activities to Great Britain, the West Indies, and continental Europe. The bulk of the international trade involved colonial raw materials, which were exchanged for European manufactured goods, sugar and rum from the West Indies, and above all slaves from Africa. By 1776 the colonists were producing considerable amounts of manufactured goods, sometimes in defiance of British mercantilist regulations. An important by-product of commercial and manufacturing activity was the emergence of small but vigorous cities. The American colonists were by no means economically self-sufficient, but neither were they totally dependent on Great Britain and Europe. American entrepreneurs were increasingly intent on expanding their economic interests and minimizing external constraints.

By 1776 American society was becoming stratified into a class structure that bore an outward resemblance to the society of Great Britain. Although there were significant contrasts marking the social order from region to region in America, everywhere an aristocracy of wealth made up of merchants, plantation owners, and successful professionals dominated many aspects of life and grew increasingly conscious of its status. A large, enterprising group of free farmers, shopkeepers, and artisans ranked below the aristocracy. Still lower on the social scale were the numerous tenant farmers and laborers—a group that was increasing in size and economic deprivation. Finally, there were African slaves, who were legally considered to be property without any rights and subject to whatever treatment their masters chose to impose on them; the lot of African Americans was made even worse by the assumption among European Americans that they were inferior creatures. However, social stratification in America was neither as rigidly defined nor as inflexible as the class structure in Europe. The chief forces that sanctioned aristocratic status in Europe—birth, royal favor, tradition, unique lifestyle—simply did not exist in America. Few European aristocrats emigrated to America; the family trees of most American aristocrats had shallow roots. America had no peasant class condemned to semidependent status by ancient custom defining their relationships with landlords; although many emigrants originally went to America as indentured servants bound by contract to serve a master, most of them gained their freedom by fulfilling their contracts and became independent farmers. Since aristocratic status depended chiefly on wealth gained in America through farming or commercial activity, it was possible for a capable, enterprising, and lucky individual of low status to advance to aristocratic status by amassing a fortune. The frontier also offered an escape for those threatened with being made dependent. Colonial conditions thus loosened the bonds of aristocratic society and provided a measure of freedom for people of lesser status and modest means—except for African slaves.

Early American society was patriarchal in structure, dominated by males whose authority as heads of the basic social unit, the family, allowed them to dominate women and children. That system was sustained by English law, which prevailed everywhere in the colonies, and by a social code that stressed the virtue of submission of women and children to male authority. The system made women legally subject to their husbands and barred them from participation in almost all aspects of public life. In the typical household, whether on a farm or in a city, women were expected to carry out an array of tasks generally viewed as "women's work": preparing food, making clothing, tending animals, caring for a garden, raising children. Particularly harsh was the treatment of slave women. Although slaves were permitted to maintain nuclear family units, the traffic in slaves often dis-

rupted these households, leaving slave women with the burden of caring for their children alone. In response to such uncertainties extended family networks developed in the slave population. Slave women were frequently sexually abused by their masters. In the upper classes, women of wealthy families enjoyed considerable comfort and leisure but little independence. The cities offered some opportunity for single women and widows to lead a more independent life as nurses, teachers, or shopkeepers. But on the whole colonial women had almost no opportunity to assert their talents beyond the confines of the household.

Religious life in colonial America assumed forms that slowly eroded the role that religion had long played in Europe as a buttress of the established order. Generally, the founders of each colony attempted to define a single religious establishment for that colony, usually based on a European model. One such establishment was the Puritan order that emerged in New England. Based on Calvinist theology and on the principles of local control of each congregation by those who believed themselves to be saved, simple ceremonies involving Scripture reading and preaching, and austere moral codes, the Puritan congregations exercised a powerful influence on the manners and morals of New England society. However, the Puritans were never able to exclude from their society those who would not conform to their religious system and eventually were forced to tolerate dissenters. Elsewhere an effort was made to implant Anglicanism as practiced in Great Britain. A variety of factors combined to make the Anglican church in America different from that in Great Britain. No Anglican bishoprics developed in America, and there was a shortage of educated clergymen trained to sustain the elaborate Anglican services. As a consequence, a hierarchically directed Anglican system capable of imposing uniform doctrines and rituals failed to develop. The Anglican establishment moved in the direction of a congregational system that allowed considerable latitude to local leaders and considerable toleration of differences. To some extent the other structured religions established in colonial America, especially Lutheranism and Roman Catholicism, found it difficult to maintain uniformity and conformity to traditional practices. Successive waves of immigrants from various parts of Europe constantly brought new religious sects to America. The influence of the traditional religious establishments was further challenged from the 1730s onward by a powerful revival movement called the Great Awakening, whose proponents emphasized a personal relationship with the Divine rather than authoritarian direction as the key to salvation. Appealing powerfully to those of precarious economic means and to women, this new piety created a variety of new religious congregations at the expense of older establishments. Still another stream of religious diversity began to emerge in slave society, where religious practices that mixed Christianity with African usages began to take shape as a fundamental element of African-American life. Religious diversity, toleration, and freedom came to be accepted in America to a degree unknown in Europe.

Prior to 1776 the colonists distinguished themselves only modestly in cultural activities. They did establish lower schools and colleges in an attempt to prepare people for careers. Newspapers and book publishers appeared in many areas. The rudiments of a distinct architectural style emerged. But in the main American cultural life depended on western Europe. Perhaps the most notable cultural development of the colonial era was the ability of some colonists to keep abreast of Europe's chief intellectual and cultural movements, especially those associated with the Enlightenment and science, from which were derived ideas that asserted a powerful influence over the colonial mentality at the time of the founding of the new nation.

Especially significant in setting the stage for the rebellion in America were developments involving the way the American colonies were governed. In theory the colonies were part of Great Britain, over which the British monarch and Parliament ruled through the same mechanisms that prevailed in Britain. In practice each colony slowly developed its own local government, which operated with only limited direction by the royal government in Britain. Each colony had a governor, usually appointed by the monarch, who represented the authority of the Crown and who provided a channel through which the concerns of the colonists were conveyed to the British government. Each colony (except Pennsylvania) had a two-house legislature, the lower house elected by male property owners and the upper house appointed by the king or the colonial governor. The property qualifications were such that a much larger proportion of male colonials was eligible to vote than was the case in Britain; as a consequence, colonial legislatures reflected a broader spectrum of society than did the British Parliament. The powers of colonial legislatures were never clearly defined, but in general they had extensive authority to control local affairs and to levy taxes. The governors had nearly absolute power of veto over the legislatures, but they were not usually in a position to exercise that power because they depended on legislatures for their salaries and operating funds. The colonists developed a system of courts patterned after the British court system, and they enjoyed the legal rights of British subjects as incorporated in English common law. Although the Americans recognized that the British government had authority over them, their system of local government encouraged them to feel that they had a right to decide their own political destiny. One hundred fifty years of experience in self-government created a breach wider than the Atlantic between Great Britain and its American colonies.

Although by 1776 there were large differences between the American and British societies, these differences did not preordain an American effort to establish independence. Most colonists still felt that they were British and were still attached to a European tradition. What eventually aroused American resistance to British rule was a conviction that the British were denying their American subjects the right to sustain the tradition they shared. That perception drew much of its substance from the fact that American society had become different, causing the Americans to view tradition in a different way than did their masters across the Atlantic.

2. THE AMERICAN REVOLUTION: FROM SALUTARY NEGLECT TO WAR

For a long time the unique society emerging in America was little understood in Great Britain. In conformity with mercantilist thought, the British authorities viewed America as a source of scarce raw products and a market for manufactured goods. This view was legislated by the Navigation Acts of the mid–seventeenth century, which implied that Britain would act politically and economically to shape the colonial economy to serve its own interests. It was assumed that the colonists would benefit by conforming to British direction. However, until the mid–eighteenth century the British government was lax in enforcing its mercantilist policies. Entrenched commercial interests in England resisted government interference in private enterprises that profited greatly from colonial trade. The British Crown failed to develop an administrative system in England to supervise the colonies. England was badly served by its officials in America, most of whom owed their offices to political favors or bribery rather than competence. In the meantime, the colonists grew accustomed to doing what they wished economically and politically.

With the end of the Seven Years' War in 1763, Britain began to change its policy in the direction of tightening control over its colonial empire. The vast lands won from the French needed some kind of administration that would ensure their utilization in ways that served British interests as well as deal with the Indian population, whose frustrations were expressed with frightening emphasis by a general Indian uprising in 1763, led by the Ottawa chief, Pontiac. Great Britain was faced with a huge debt, which from a British perspective had been incurred in part to save the Americans from the French and the Indians; it was time for the colonials to share that burden. Britain's rapidly growing population and the increasing importance of manufacturing to its economy had produced a mounting need for imported foodstuffs and for larger markets for manufactured goods. All of these considerations prompted legislation, such as the Grenville (1764–1765) and Townshend (1767) acts, which were designed to increase revenues, control the distribution of lands annexed from the French, and tighten administration in America.

The colonists were hardly in a mood to bend before British interests after so long enjoying the "salutary neglect" of earlier years. They felt they had made sufficient contributions to the British victories in the wars of the first half of the eighteenth century to relieve them of further responsibility. They resented what they felt was treatment as inferiors by the British forces sent to drive the French and Indians out of land that they increasingly believed belonged to them as the real "Americans." The American population was growing even faster than that of Great Britain, creating powerful pressures to expand the American economy and to move westward into the territories won from the French. The growing demand for manufactured goods created an unfavorable balance of trade, which increasingly made many Americans debtors to England. To correct this situation, the Americans needed to increase their native manufacturing and expand their markets in Europe, both of which ran counter to British mercantilist policy. A depression following the Seven Years' War sharpened the growing tension.

The Americans reacted to Britain's changing policy with fiery speeches, boycotts of British goods, protest meetings (such as the Stamp Act Congress of 1765), and occasional riots. They complained that they were being taxed without representation in Parliament and that their own legislatures, long the chief source of governing regulations, were being disregarded. Although the British reaction to the American resistance was inconsistent, the British government pressed on in its effort to tighten its hold on America. It increased its military presence in America and ordered royal officials to seize American property in ways that paid little heed to British law. Between 1768 and 1774 sterner measures, such as the Tea Act, the "Intolerable Acts," and the Quebec Act, were imposed to bring the colonials under tighter control. Resistance in America spread, reflected by the meeting of the First Continental Congress in 1774. And it was fed by growing ideological radicalism, which focused on the British violation of fundamental rights as justification for demanding independence and self-government.

In Great Britain some leaders realized the danger and even sympathized with the principles upon which the protests of the colonists were based. But those sharing these concerns could neither muster support for conciliatory actions that would reassure the considerable segment of the colonial population still not ready to break with Britain nor bring about a fundamental change of policy that would take into account the realities surrounding the relationships with the colonists, whose interests no longer coincided with those of the mother country. The British leaders agreed on only one thing: that it was an act of rebellion and a perversion of the British constitution to claim that British subjects had a right to disobey laws passed by Parliament, as indeed Americans were doing with increasing frequency. This attitude prompted an increase in the British armed forces in America, an action that appeard to reinforce King George III's words: "Blows must decide whether they are to be subject to the Country or Independent."

Indeed, it came to blows. Armed hostilities opened in April 1775, when American militiamen challenged British forces in skirmishes at Lexington and Concord. In May 1775 the Second Continental Congress assembled. Although some of its members still held out for attempts at reconciliation with England, those ready to break with Great Britain prevailed, giving emphasis to their position by appointing George Washington as commander of America's armies. The hour had come to settle the long-debated issues on the field of battle.

When the war began, Britain's larger population and superior resources seemed to doom the cause of the poor, disorganized rebels. In fact, the British government took the rebellion lightly; one royal official characterized the rebels as a "rude rabble without a plan." But such a view proved erroneous. It did not take into account Britain's ineffective military leadership, its distance from the war zone, and the determination of the rebels. For almost a year after the encounters at Lexington and Concord, the main British forces were pinned down in Boston by an American militia drawn chiefly from New England. The Second Continental Congress proceeded with its plans for raising money, recruiting and supplying a military force, and seeking allies. A variety of actions was taken to transfer power from British officials into the hands of American authorities. Most significant of all, once the shooting started, opinion in America moved rapidly toward acceptance of the idea of independence.

Popular sentiment in favor of independence crystallized in 1776, when several colonies instructed their delegations to the Second Continental Congress to break with Britain. On July 4, 1776, Congress issued the Declaration of Independence, crafted chiefly by Thomas Jefferson. Its magnificent preamble, which leaned heavily on the political philosophy of John Locke and European disciples of the Enlightenment, justified rebellion on the grounds of "self-evident" truths that bestowed on all people certain natural rights that must be protected by governments which derive their power from the consent of the governed. The Declaration set forth a long list of ways in which the British government had violated these "inalienable" rights. It therefore had no claim to the allegiance of its subjects, who were entitled to form a new contract to ensure those rights. For many, the Declaration of Independence elevated the struggle above mere revolt; it became a struggle for an "enlightened" polity. The principles enunciated in the Declaration would inspire later generations to act in the name of rights so fundamental that they were beyond the authority of any government.

However, Americans were far from united behind the cause of independence. Many—perhaps 20 percent—opposed independence and the war. Some of these loyalists—contemptuously dubbed "Torries" by Americans who called themselves "Patriots"—fled to Canada and Great Britain; those who remained were a source of concern to American leaders and a target of British efforts to promote dissension. Many Americans were essentially neutral; only under duress did these neutrals contribute to the war effort. Some African-American slaves saw the war as an opportunity to shed their shackles and enjoy the liberty of which the Patriots spoke so much. Loyalists and British alike tried to exploit this hope; the fear of slave revolts dampened enthusiasm for the war in the southern colonies. Even among the patriots there was perpetual disagreement on how to conduct the struggle for independence. The fact that the Americans did sustain their cause in the face of these divisions was remarkable. In part, success was due to the leadership provided by men like George Washington, John Adams, Thomas Jefferson, and Benjamin Franklin, all of whom demonstrated considerable talents for leading armies, organizing resources, rallying popular support, and negotiating with foreign powers.

The war itself unfolded indecisively during 1776 and 1777 (see Map 37.1). While there were

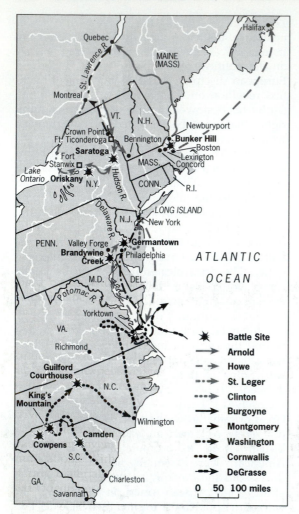

Map 37.1 REVOLUTIONARY WAR CAMPAIGNS This map portrays at least in broad outline the central strategy involved in the revolutionary war. With their main strength concentrated in New York City, where they could be reinforced by sea, the British tried to cripple the Americans first by attempting to seize control of the Hudson Valley and then by an extended campaign to win the South. The Americans countered both of these moves successfully while containing the main British forces in New York, New Jersey, and eastern Pennsylvania.

victories and defeats on both sides, the British seemed to be gaining the upper hand, especially when they undertook a major campaign in the Hudson Valley aimed at isolating New England from the other colonies. However, that bungled campaign ended in October 1777 with the surrender of a major British force at Saratoga. This victory not only raised the flagging American spirits but also was decisive in persuading a hesitant France to commit itself to the American cause. In 1778 a formal alliance was concluded, and France began to supply needed money, ships, and troops. Subsequently, other European powers showed increasing friendliness toward America; Spain and the Dutch eventually declared war on Britain, and several other nations threatened to do likewise. Britain now had a world conflict on its hands; the pressure on America was considerably relieved.

After 1777 the military activity spread over a large area. The British concentrated their main force in New York City, where it could be reinforced by sea. In a series of hotly contested engagements in New York, New Jersey, and eastern Pennsylvania the Americans managed to contain the British forces and avoid a decisive defeat in the crucial Middle Atlantic area. The British undertook a major offensive in the South in 1780 and 1781. Their campaign ended in a stunning defeat at Yorktown, Virginia, in October 1781. This was the last major battle of the war. By 1781 Britain was anxious to end a costly war that was threatening its position around the world. Prolonged negotiations involving not only Britain and America but also France and Spain finally ended with the Treaty of Paris in 1783. By its terms Britain recognized American independence and ceded to the Americans all territories east of the Mississippi from Canada to Spanish Florida. The new nation had won a magnificent victory.

3. THE AMERICAN REVOLUTION AND SOCIAL CHANGE

While the Americans were winning their war of independence against a somewhat inept mother country, a variety of developments occurred within American society that resulted in a political and social order sufficiently different from traditional society to make it unique in the contemporary world. Although many changes were pragmatic responses to the realities stemming from independence and war, the thrust toward restructuring society and government found inspiration in the concept of republicanism. Rooted in a tradition that reached back to ancient Greece and Rome, republicanism visualized the ideal society as one composed of independent property owners living as equals in small communities under a government exercising only limited power and controlled by its constituents. In such a society the natural virtue of people would constrain anyone from infringing on the rights of others and would allow all to pursue their individual interests according to their individual talents. It was the success the Americans achieved in moving toward the republican ideal that caught the attention of a world standing on the brink of other, more drastic revolutions.

The first important efforts at reordering society on republican principles were made within the several states (as the colonies were called after July 4, 1776). New governments, reflecting a mixture of elements draw from British political practices, colonial political experience, and theoretical concepts derived from Enlightenment thought, were formed in all the states. The framers of these governments were concerned above all else with protecting the people's liberties from tyrannical governments. Nearly every state drew up a written constitution that carefully defined the structure and functions of government. Elaborate bills of rights, stressing individual rights, were included in the constitutions. Since sovereignty rested with the people, all official positions were filled by elections and the right to vote was extended. Two-house legislatures were established in most states, the lower houses being controlled by property-holding male voters and the upper houses being selected by members of the lower chambers. Systems of representation were devised to ensure that each elected representative spoke for roughly the same number of voters. Legislatures were given wide-ranging powers that ensured their control over public affairs and especially over executive officials, who were universally suspected of being the chief instigators of tyranny. Independent judiciaries were almost universally adopted. The concept of separation of powers was thereby incorporated into the new state governments, signifying a strong conviction that the powers of government must be limited by constitutional safeguards. Taken as a whole, the state constitutions framed between 1776 and 1780 inaugurated a degree of popular control over government unknown in the contemporary world, although none of them was completely democratic.

The Revolution brought about changes in other areas of life as significant as those altering the political structures. Several states took steps to disestablish state-supported churches, to institute religious toleration, and in general to separate political and religious life. Many states passed new land laws that tended to make it easier to gain ownership of property. Especially significant was the abolition of primogeniture, a system of inheritance which provided that the eldest son receive all his father's land. Slavery was abolished in some northern states, in part at least because this institution seemed out of place in a society dedicated to the principles set forth in the Declaration of Independence. However, slavery survived the American Revolution in the southern and border states, perhaps reinforced by arguments devised by its defenders to counter those who claimed that bondage was inappropriate in a society founded on the principle that all were created equal. Efforts were made to expand educational opportunities and to take more adequate care of society's unfortunates. In the name of republicanism people spurned the old social customs that called for deference to aristocrats and replaced them with behavior patterns that reflected greater egalitarianism. Even the lot of women improved somewhat, although on the whole few changes were made in the legal constraints that kept women subject to men. In writing to her husband, John, in 1776 Abigail Adams chided him to "remember the ladies" in his schemes to increase liberty in America. Women came to be credited with playing a major role in building the virtues on which a republican society must rest. And expanding opportunities for occupations outside the household began to emerge for women. All these liberalizing movements pointed toward even greater freedom in the future.

Quite accidentally, the Revolution had an important leveling effect in terms of the distribution of wealth. Inflation, caused by the efforts of the Americans to pay for the war with paper money, wiped out fortunes, aided debtors, and allowed new fortunes to be built. Many established merchants suffered heavy losses from the disturbance of exchange patterns that had existed before independence, but new opportunities in trade and industry emerged once America was free from the British commercial system. Small farmers flourished during the war, bolstered by easy money and high prices. Under these varied pressures, the prerevolutionary social order did not survive intact. Again, a greater degree of social mobility, equality, and personal freedom emerged to characterize life in the new nation.

4. LAUNCHING THE NEW NATION

Once independence had been declared, the American leaders were faced with creating a central government. Formidable barriers challenged them in that task. Any movement toward a national political system had to take into account the forces working to liberalize society and the widespread republican distrust of large-scale government. The existence of thirteen separate states insistent on independence of action created a welter of contradictory interests. But there were forces working in favor of national union: the need for cooperation in a war for survival; the dangers inherent in a world of large, ambitious nations; and the sense of a shared experience in creating a new society in the American wilderness. In the end these forces drove sensible leaders toward forming a national government despite the formidable obstacles.

The first attempt at forming a national government was carried out by the Second Continent Congress. Dominated by men who had a deep distrust for strong government over which the populace had no control, the Congress shaped the Articles of Confederation, finally approved by all of the states in 1781. The Articles established a loose union of thirteen nearly independent states headed by a central government that could not compel the states to do anything but could only encourage them to cooperate. Despite the fact that this government had guided the new nation to victory over the British and made provisions for handling territories won from Great Britain, the inadequacies of the confederation, the self-serving actions of state governments, and a rising tide of social discontent eventually generated sentiment in favor of a stronger national government. As a result, in May 1787 a constitutional convention was summoned to consider revising the Articles of Confederation.

The convention immediately decided to scrap the Articles and write a new constitution (see Figure 37.1). Once this task was undertaken, the delegates found themselves in broad agreement on many crucial issues. They agreed that a republican form of government based on a written constitution enumerating the powers of the central government was necessary, that there must be popular control over the central government, that there must be a separation of powers with built-in checks among the various branches of government, that the states must enjoy jurisdiction in matters specifically reserved for them, and that the central government must have authority to deal independently with matters affecting the national interest. Working from these premises, the delegates forged a constitution outlining the basic framework for a new government. A two-house legislature, an elected president, and a national judiciary were established. Each branch was assigned specific functions, and an elaborate system of internal checks was devised to constrain each branch from exercising too much power. The powers of the national government were specifically enumerated, while other powers were reserved to the states. However, specific provisions were made allowing the central government to coerce the states in those matters over which it had jurisdiction. This principle of federalism was a unique feature of the new government. A major roadblock centering on the fears of smaller states was overcome by a compromise providing equal representation of each state in one branch of the legislature, the Senate, and representation in proportion to population in the other, the House of Representatives. To ensure a degree of flexibility, provisions were made for amending the Constitution.

By 1789 a sufficient number of states had approved the new constitution to allow the new government to begin operations with George Washington as president and with a Congress controlled by Federalists, that is, those who supported the Constitution and a strong national government. During the next decade the new government proved its worth. Congress enacted legislation that filled in vital details not provided in the Constitution: a Bill of Rights forbidding infringement on the basic rights of individuals; a federal court system; and administrative departments to assist the president in discharging his responsibilities. Taxes were levied and collected, public credit was established, and new states were added to the nation as a part of the process of utilizing the vast territory ceded by Britain in 1783. As president, Washington conducted himself in a way that gave the office dignity and allayed deep-seated fears of executive tyranny. Under the guidance of his cabinet, especially Alexander Hamilton as secretary of the treasury

and Thomas Jefferson as secretary of state, policies were formulated that helped to restore prosperity and to steer the fledgling nation along a path of neutrality in the stormy international scene agitated by the French Revolution.

Despite the successes of the new government under Washington and his successor, John Adams, there was mounting discontent with the Federalists who dominated it (see Figure 37.2). This party made it increasingly clear, especially through the policies promoted by Alexander Hamilton, that it intended to make the central government as strong as possible and to bind the wealthy to the cause of strong central government by favoring their economic interests. This direction aroused opposition not only from those who felt their economic interests threatened but

FIGURE 37.2 Congressional Debate This cartoon shows a ''discussion'' in the House of Representatives in 1798 between a Vermont Republican (with the tongs) and a Connecticut Federalist (with the cane). It reflects the intensity of party strife just prior to the key election of 1800. (New York Public Library Picture Collection)

also from those who were philosophically suspicious of strong government, those who were committed to human equality, and those who were confident of the political wisdom of the common people—ideas powerfully reinforced by the French Revolution. This opposition began to rally around Thomas Jefferson to form a new party, called the Republicans (not to be confused with the present Republican party, founded in 1854). The emergence of political parties added an element to the new political system that the makers of the Constitution had not foreseen. In a close and bitter election in 1800, Jefferson and the Republicans won the presidency in what has been called "the Revolution of 1800." Perhaps it would be more accurate to say that this election completed the revolution begun twenty-five years earlier. It provided final proof of the workability of the new government by demonstrating that the voters controlled the state and that they did not have to rebel to force a government to be responsive to the wishes of a majority.

Between 1775 and 1800 the Americans had put on an impressive display for a changing world. By force of arms they had rid themselves of a political regime they perceived to be tyrannical. To replace it, they had fashioned, by a rational process, thirteen state governments and a national government capable of effective governance but restricted from abusing the rights of citizens. These governments proved sensitive to popular control and made the exercise of popular sovereignty a fact. Liberal, enlightened people everywhere saw their ideals become a reality in America. Here was inspiration and guidance for those elsewhere who aspired to change society. Many believed, as the German poet Goethe put it, "America, thou hast it better/Than has our Continent, the old one." The age of revolutions had been launched in practice as well as in theory.

SUGGESTED READING

Colonial Society

Daniel J. Boorstin, *The Americans: The Colonial Experience* (1958). A challenging portrait.

James A. Henretta and Gregory H. Nobles, *Evolution and Revolution. American Society, 1600–1820* (1987). A stimulating treatment of many aspects of colonial society.

Jack P. Greene, *Pursuits of Happiness: The Social Development of Early Modern British Colonies and the Formation of American Culture* (1988). A challenging analysis of the social and cultural development of England and its colonies.

Edwin J. Perkins, *The Economy of Colonial America*, 2nd ed. (1988). A brief but effective description of the colonial economy.

Donald R. Wright, *African Americans in the Colonial Era: From African Origins Through the American Revolution* (1990). A brief but insightful overview.

Patricia U. Bonomi, *Under the Cope of Heaven: Religion, Society, and Politics in Colonial America* (1986). A broad survey stressing the vitality of colonial religious life.

Mary Beth Norton, *Liberty's Daughters: The Revolutionary Experience of American Women* (1980). A fine study.

The Revolutionary Era

Edmund S. Morgan, *The Birth of the Republic, 1763–1789*, rev. ed. (1977). A brief account of major events.

Bernard Bailyn, *The Ideological Origins of the American Revolution*, enl. ed. (1992). A brilliant study.

Marc Egnal, *A Mighty Empire. The Origins of the American Revolution* (1988). A challenging treatment stressing the role played by upper-class factions in the struggle against Great Britain.

Pauline Maier, *From Resistance to Revolution: Colonial Radicals and the Development of American Opposition to Britain, 1765–1776* (1991). An excellent analysis of changes in opinion leading to the Revolution.

Robert Middlekauff, *The Glorious Cause: The American Revolution, 1763–1789* (1982). A full narrative account.

Jeremy Black, *War for America. The Fight for Independence, 1775–1783* (1991). A good military history.

Merrill Jensen, *The American Revolution Within America* (1974). Stresses the impact of the Revolution on American society.

The New Nation

John C. Miller, *Toward a More Perfect Union: The American Republic, 1783–1815* (1970). A good narrative account of the first years of the new nation.

Richard B. Morris, *The Forging of the Union, 1781–1789* (1987). A superb analysis of the path toward the Constitution.

Gordon S. Wood, *The Creation of the American Republic, 1776–1787* (1969). Especially good on the growth of republican thought.

Richard B. Bernstein with Kym S. Rice, *Are We to Be a Nation? The Making of the Constitution* (1987). An exciting account of the Constitutional Convention.

CHAPTER 38
The French Revolution, 1789–1799

FIGURE 38.1 Jacques-Louis David, *The Tennis Court Oath,* **June 20, 1789** This painting by the sympathetic artist Jacques-Louis David glorifies a crucial step in the French Revolution when the leaders of the newly formed National Assembly swore to draw up a constitution for France. In the center representatives of the three estates—clergy, nobility, and commoners—join in a cooperative gesture. (French Embassy Press and Information Division)

In 1789 the French monarchy was brought to its knees by one of the greatest and most far-reaching upheavals in the history of Western civilization—the French Revolution. During the following ten years revolutionaries eliminated the centuries-old French monarchy, overturned the social system of France's old regime, and transformed France's religious institutions. Underlying these changes was the spirit of the Revolution, best summarized by its slogan: *Liberté, Égalité, Fraternité* ("Liberty, Equality, Fraternity").

The Revolution was so fundamental, so dynamic, and so threatening that it could not be contained within France. The news alone of what was happening in France spread fear among those hoping to maintain the status quo and stirred the hopes of those longing for change. Then by force of arms the French carried the ideas and institutions of the Revolution beyond France's borders. For France, and for much of Western civilization, the Revolution was a watershed that would mark the beginning of the modern world.

1. THE LAST DAYS OF THE OLD REGIME IN FRANCE

France at the succession of Louis XVI, though somewhat weakened by the defeats and failures of Louis XV, was still the richest and most influential nation in continental Europe. During the course of the eighteenth century, France's commerce and prosperity had steadily increased. Half of all the specie in Europe was to be found in France. The French enjoyed a relatively high standard of living. It is not, therefore, to desperation born of poverty that one must look as an explanation for the French Revolution but rather to frustration caused by existing institutions—social, religious, political, economic—that had failed to adjust to changing conditions.

French society on the eve of the French Revolution was divided into three distinct orders, or *estates*. The first estate was the clergy, numbering approximately one hundred thousand out of a total population of some 24 million. The Catholic church in France owned over 10 percent of the land—the best land—and from its lands and

tithes and fees enjoyed an income probably half as large as that of the government itself. It controlled all educational institutions and censored the press. It monopolized public worship and continued to harass all other religious groups at a time when the spirit of religious tolerance was rising throughout most of the Western world. The clergy itself was sharply divided. The upper clergy—the bishops and the abbots—were rich and powerful. They were drawn exclusively from the ranks of the aristocracy and were generally looked upon by most of the lower clergy and the common people as parasites. The lower clergy—the priests and the monks—came from the lower classes. The income of the priests was modest. They shared the lives of the people they served and were generally popular, but they had almost no influence on church policy.

The second estate was the nobility, numbering approximately four hundred thousand. The nobility owned over 20 percent of the land of France but was exempt from all direct taxation. The richest of them lived at Versailles as absentee landlords, where they hunted, intrigued, made love, and read the books of the *philosophes* of the Enlightenment. They were reputed to possess the best manners and the worst morals of any class in Europe. The most haughty of the nobility—the most jealous of their rights—were the newcomers, the *noblesse de la robe* (nobility of the gown). They were former rich bourgeois who had purchased judgeships in one of the high law courts. They led the newly reassertive eighteenth-century French aristocracy that had, since the death of Louis XIV in 1715, recouped some of their power and influence at the expense of the king and the bourgeoisie. By the second half of the eighteenth century, almost all high governmental posts were held by the nobility. This nobility was emboldened to challenge the authority of the monarchy when it sought reform and to assert ancient rights and privileges that had fallen out of use against those below them.

The third estate was composed of commoners—the bourgeoisie, the proletariat, and the peasantry—and comprised about 96 percent of the total population. Of all the social and economic groups in France in 1789, the bourgeoisie were probably the most frustrated. They were business and professional people—bankers, merchants, shopkeepers, and lawyers—who had grown into a middle class between the nobility and the peasantry. By the late eighteenth century France's upper bourgeoisie had gone as far as their wits and energy could take them. Some had become richer by far than most of the nobility—only to find the highest levels of government and society closed to them. Others, less wealthy but well educated and ambitious, resented the second-class status assigned to them by the nobility. Perhaps most frustrated were young lawyers and administrators who lacked social, economic, and political positions to match their talents and expectations.

The urban populace was a mixture of groups—wage earners, servants of the rich, artisans, and the unemployed. There was enough distress among them to create tensions—tensions that would increase with the maladjustments caused by the Revolution. During the course of the eighteenth century, the price of bread had risen three times as fast as wages. Paris was the only city in France with an urban populace large enough to make its influence strongly felt. There it included about three hundred thousand citizens (about half the total population of the city)—enough to play a significant role in a revolution.

In 1789 at least 90 percent of the French people were peasants, tillers of the soil. Although they were probably better off than most peasants elsewhere in Europe (they owned at least 30 percent of the land, and serfdom had virtually disappeared), they were on the whole discontented. Most peasant-owned land was subject to feudal dues. Probably a majority of the peasants owned no land at all but were sharecroppers who gave up 50 percent of their produce to the lord in addition to the feudal dues (the fees paid by the peasant for use of the lord's mill, oven, wine press, and breeding stock, death taxes, inheritance taxes, and sale-of-property taxes). Not only were peasants forbidden to hunt; they could not even protect their crops from the lord's hunting parties—nor, for that matter, from the game itself. Although French peasants no longer had to donate their labor to the lord, they were still required to furnish so many days' labor for roads and public works. On them fell nearly all the direct taxes levied by the national government.

Altogether, peasants gave up much of their income in taxes to their landlords, the Church, and the state.

The life of the peasantry too had evolved only slowly since the Middle Ages. Peasants generally lived in little rural villages, their houses close together. Each house usually consisted of one room with a dirt floor, thatched roof, and neither chimney nor glass windows. Livestock frequently lived under the same roof. The peasants' daily diet was made up almost entirely of dark bread and wine; meat was reserved for special occasions. Entertainment centered around the Church. On Sundays and holy days, of which there were many, the peasants' attire and attitudes were festive and gay. Ambitious young French peasants, unlike the peasants in most other parts of Europe, did have opportunities for advancement. Many engaged in cottage industry. A peasant could buy some land, become a priest or the lord's steward, a blacksmith or an innkeeper, or seek a new life in the city. Only relatively few, of course, would succeed.

The government of France was arbitrary. Usually the king's decree was, in effect, law. The Estates General, the French counterpart of the British Parliament, had not met for nearly two centuries. Justice was capricious and corrupt. There were 237 different codes of law to confuse litigants. There were no juries as in Great Britain. The king could arrest and imprison at will (although Louis XV and Louis XVI seldom did). The judges of the thirteen superior courts, called *parlements*, purchased or inherited their titles and were all members of the nobility. It was therefore impossible for a commoner to obtain justice in a case against the nobility. The arbitrariness and inherent injustice of this system, which had long been taken for granted, clashed with the widely circulated ideas of the Enlightenment.

2. THE BREAKDOWN OF THE OLD REGIME

In the decades preceding the Revolution the monarchy was beginning to weaken. Aristocrats in institutions such as the *parlements* (law courts) were challenging the king. The central government was losing control over political debate.

Louis XV (1715–1774) was not a popular or skilled king, and the costly French defeat in the Seven Years' War (1756–1763) only made matters worse. By the 1780s, the monarch's political authority was being seriously undermined.

It was a conflict over finance that set into motion a series of events that culminated in the breakdown of the monarchy and the Old Regime in France. Louis XVI had inherited a large and constantly growing national debt. It was not excessive for a nation as rich as France; Great Britain and the Netherlands had higher per capita debts. But when combined with the exemption of the nobility and the clergy and much of the bourgeoisie from direct taxation and the extravagant cost of maintaining the military establishment and servicing the national debt (most of which had been incurred by past wars), it spelled eventual bankruptcy. Furthermore, France lacked an adequate banking system and was still burdened with the corrupt system of tax collection (called tax farming) that allowed much revenue to be diverted from the treasury into the pockets of private collectors.

Upon assuming the throne, Louis XVI appointed the Physiocrat Turgot, a friend of Voltaire, as minister of finance. Turgot initiated a series of sweeping reforms designed to clean up the mess. However, those with vested interests in the old system brought about his dismissal at the end of two years, and his reform measures were rescinded. A succession of ministers then tried all kinds of palliatives, such as borrowing, pump-priming expenditures, and better bookkeeping, but to no avail. By 1786 the debt was 3 billion livres,[1] and the annual deficit had reached 125 million. Bankers refused to lend the government more money. In a desperate effort to save his regime, Louis called an Assembly of Notables in 1787 and attempted to persuade the nobles and the clergy to consent to be taxed. But the privileged orders refused and demanded, instead, a meeting of the Estates General, thinking that they could control it and thereby assert their

own interests. Pressured by a virtual revolt of his own nobility, the king gave in.

3. THE TRIUMPH OF THE THIRD ESTATE

During the early months of 1789 elections were held for members of the Estates General. All France was agog with excitement. Hundreds of pamphlets appeared, and there was widespread public debate. By tradition, each of the three estates, the clergy, the nobility, and the commoners, elected their own representatives. All males who had reached the age of twenty-five and paid taxes were permitted to vote. Since the third estate, which included the bourgeoisie, the peasantry, and the urban populace, comprised more than nine-tenths of the total population, it was given as many seats as the other two combined. However, by tradition the three estates sat separately and each group had one vote.

By April 1789 the delegates began to arrive at Versailles. Goodwill prevailed. Violent revolution was far from anyone's mind. The delegates came armed only with *cahiers,* the lists of grievances that had been called for by the king. Of the six hundred representatives of the third estate, not one was a peasant. Except for a handful of liberal clergy and nobles who were elected to the third estate, they were all bourgeois. Nearly all the members of the third estate, as well as many members of the two privileged estates, were acquainted with the philosophy of the Enlightenment. They held inflated hopes of quickly solving long lists of problems that had been growing for years.

The first formal session was held on May 5. Immediately a sharp debate began over the method of voting. The two privileged estates demanded that, according to custom, the three estates meet separately and vote by order—that is, each estate cast one vote. This procedure would mean that all attacks on privilege and inequality would be defeated by a vote of two to one. The third estate demanded that the three estates meet jointly and that voting be by head. Thus all measures for fundamental reform would pass, for not only did the third estate have as many members as the other two combined, but a number of lib-

---

[1] The livre was technically worth about twenty cents, but its purchasing power in the eighteenth century was much greater than that of the late-twentieth-century American dollar.

HISTORIANS' SOURCES

Signs of Revolution in France

To some sensitive observers of the time, the signs of revolution were at hand during the late 1780s. One of these observers was Arthur Young (1741–1820), a British farmer and diarist best known for his writings on agricultural subjects. Between 1787 and 1789 he traveled extensively throughout France, keeping a diary of his experiences. In the following selection from that diary, Young notes deep dissatisfaction among the French.

PARIS, OCTOBER 17, 1787

One opinion pervaded the whole company, that they are on the eve of some great revolution in the government: that every thing points to it: the confusion in the finances great; with a *deficit* impossible to provide for without the states-general of the kingdom, yet no ideas formed of what would be the consequence of their meeting: no minister existing, or to be looked to in or out of power, with such decisive talents as to promise any other remedy than palliative ones: a prince on the throne, with excellent dispositions, but without the resources of a mind that could govern in such a moment without ministers: a court buried in pleasure and dissipation. . . .

Pressured by discontent and financial problems, Louis XVI called for a meeting of the Estates General in 1789. In anticipation of the meeting of the Estates General, the king requested and received cahiers, lists of grievances drawn up by local groups of each of the three Estates. These cahiers have provided historians with an unusually rich source of materials revealing what was bothering people just before the outbreak of the Revolution in 1789. The following

SOURCES: Arthur Young, *Arthur Young's Travels in France During the Years 1787, 1788, 1789*, 4th ed., ed. Miss Betham-Edwards (London: Bell, 1892), pp. 97–98; "Cahier of the Grievances, Complaints, and Protests of the Electoral District of Carcassonne . . ." from James Harvey Robinson, ed., *Readings in European History*, Vol. II (Boston: Ginn, 1904), pp. 399–400.

is an excerpt from a cahier *from the Third Estate in Carcassonne.*

8. Among these rights the following should be especially noted: the nation should hereafter be subject only to such laws and taxes as it shall itself freely ratify.

9. The meetings of the Estates General of the kingdom should be fixed for definite periods, and the subsidies judged necessary for the support of the state and the public service should be noted for no longer a period than to the close of the year in which the next meeting of the Estates General is to occur.

10. In order to assure to the third estate the influence to which it is entitled in view of the number of its members, the amount of its contributions to the public treasury, and the manifold interests which it has to defend or promote in the national assemblies, its votes in the assembly should be taken and counted by head.

11. No order, corporation, or individual citizen may lay claim to any pecuniary exemptions. . . . All taxes should be assessed on the same system throughout the nation.

12. The due exacted from commoners holding fiefs should be abolished, and also the general or particular regulations which exclude members of the third estate from certain positions, offices, and ranks which have hitherto been bestowed on nobles either for life or hereditarily. A law should be passed declaring members of the third estate qualified to fill all such offices for which they are judged to be personally fitted.

13. Since individual liberty is intimately associated with national liberty, his Majesty is hereby petitioned not to permit that it be hereafter interfered with by arbitrary order for imprisonment. . . .

14. Freedom should be granted also to the press, which should however be subjected, by means of strict regulations, to the principles of religion, morality, and public decency. . . .

eral clergy and noblemen sympathized with the cause of reform. Both sides realized that the outcome of this issue would be decisive.

On June 17, after six weeks of fruitless haggling, the third estate, bolstered by the support of a few priests from the first estate, declared itself to be the National Assembly of France and invited the other two estates to join it in the enactment of legislation. Three days later, on June 20, when the members of the third estate arrived at their meeting hall, they found it locked. Adjourning to a nearby building used as an indoor tennis court, they took the "Tennis Court Oath," vowing never to disband until France had a constitution (see Figure 38.1). It was the third estate's first act of defiance. On June 23 the king met with the three estates in a royal session at which he offered many liberal reforms but commanded the estates once and for all to meet separately and vote by order. The king, his ministers, and members of the first two estates filed out, but the representatives of the third estate defiantly remained seated. When the royal master of ceremonies returned to remind them of the king's orders, Count Mirabeau, a liberal nobleman elected by the third estate, jumped to his feet and shouted, "Go and tell those who sent you that we are here by the will of the people and will not leave this place except at the point of the bayonet!" When the startled courtier repeated these words to his master, Louis XVI, with characteristic weakness, replied, "They mean to stay. Well, damn it, let them stay." A few days later he reversed himself and ordered the three estates to meet jointly and vote by head. The third estate had thus won the first round.

The monarchy might have still been able to reassert control had not the new National Assembly received unexpected support from two sources, the Parisian populace and the French peasantry. Both had been suffering from unusually poor economic conditions initiated by poor harvests. Revolutionary events raised expectations in these hard times, making both groups unusually volatile. The first important disturbances came in Paris. In early July alarming news began to arrive that the king was calling the professional troops of the frontier garrison to Versailles. It appeared that he was at last preparing to use force. At this critical juncture, the Parisians countered the threat of force with force. On July 14 a riotous crowd searching for arms marched on and destroyed the Bastille, a gloomy old fortress prison in a working-class quarter that symbolized the arbitrary tyranny of the old regime (see Figure 38.2). (July 14 has long been celebrated as the French national holiday.) This show of force stayed the king's hand.

At the same time the forces of order were faced with uprisings in the countryside. During July and August peasants revolted against their lords throughout France, burning tax rolls, attacking manors, reoccupying enclosed lands, and generally rejecting the burdens of feudalism. These revolts were further inflamed by what has come to be known as the Great Fear—unfounded rumors that brigand bands, perhaps raised by nobles, were creating havoc everywhere. A panic swept the countryside. Many nobles fled from France (the *émigrés*). For all practical purposes, feudalism came to an end. The legal end of feudalism came on August 4 during a night session of the National Assembly, when, in an effort to make the best of a bad situation, one nobleman after another stood up and renounced his feudal rights and privileges.

These defeats suffered by the forces of order enabled the third estate in the National Assembly to take further actions. The most important of these actions occurred on August 26, when the National Assembly proclaimed the Declaration of Rights of Man and the Citizen. This document, which followed the English Bill of Rights by an even hundred years and preceded the American Bill of Rights by two years, was replete with the phrases of the philosophers of the Enlightenment. "Men are born and remain free and equal in rights." The natural rights were declared to be "liberty, property, security, and resistance to oppression." Liberty of opinion "even in religion," freedom of the press, and freedom from arbitrary arrest were all proclaimed. But despite the important role women had played in the Revolution, it was only men who were named as gaining these new rights (see Figure 38.3).

The forces of privilege and reaction, however, still had to be brought to terms. The king not only refused to sign the August decrees but began once more to assemble troops around Versailles and Paris. In answer to this new threat of

FIGURE 38.2 The Storming of the Bastille The storming of the Bastille represented the first act of crowd violence of the French Revolution. Actually, the crowd of Parisians was merely looking for arms to defend itself against rumored attack by the forces of the king. However, the Bastille was believed to have held hundreds of political prisoners and was a symbol of all that was oppressive under the Old Regime. Its fall symbolized a direct blow for freedom and stayed the hand of the king, who was contemplating suppressing the defiant third estate. (Culver Pictures)

force, on October 5 and 6 a huge mob of Parisian women marched eleven miles to Versailles, surrounded the palace, and with the help of the bourgeois National Guard forced the king to accompany them to the city, where he became a virtual prisoner of the populace. As the carriage bearing the royal family rolled toward Paris, the surrounding crowd shouted jubilantly, "We have the baker, the baker's wife, and the little cook boy! Now we shall have bread!" A few days later the National Assembly moved its sessions to Paris, where it increasingly came under the influence of the radical populace of the great city. The third estate had triumphed.

4. MAKING FRANCE A CONSTITUTIONAL MONARCHY

The National Assembly could now at last settle down to the task of transforming French institutions. During the next two years the Assembly passed a series of sweeping reforms that may be conveniently classified as follows.

Judicial

The *parlements* and the manorial and ecclesiastical courts with their arbitrary procedures and overlapping jurisdictions were swept away. An

FIGURE 38.3 Women in the Revolution This contemporary print shows the crowd of Parisian women who marched out to the king's palace in Versailles and forced him to return with them to Paris, where he would be more under the control of the populace. These women were recognized as revolutionary heroines. (Historical Pictures/Stock Montage)

orderly system of lower and higher courts was established. The administration of justice was decentralized and democratized. Judges were to be elected for six-year terms. Torture was abolished. In criminal cases juries were to be used for the first time in French history.

Economic

In accordance with the doctrine of laissez-faire, guilds, labor unions, and trading associations were abolished. All occupations were declared open to all classes. Feudal obligations, including labor on the public roads, had already come to an end on the night of August 4. Internal tolls and customs were abolished.

Financial

The complex, unequal taxes, both direct and indirect, were swept away. They were replaced by a tax on land and a tax on the profits of trade and industry. Both were uniform and no one was exempt. Tax farming was at long last abolished. Expenditures were henceforth to be authorized only by the national legislature. To meet the pressing financial needs of the government, the National Assembly issued paper money called *assignats* to the value of 400 million livres. To back up this paper money, the property of the Roman Catholic church, valued at approximately that amount, was confiscated.

Religious

The seizure of its property was the first step toward the nationalization of the Church. Monasticism was abolished. The clergy was to be elected by the people (including non–Roman Catholics) and their salaries paid by the state. The bishops were reduced in number, wealth, and power. They were no longer to be invested by the pope. These measures were incorporated in the Civil Constitution of the Clergy, to which all members of the clergy were required to take an oath of allegiance in order to perform their functions and draw their salaries. The pope, whose control over the organization and the clergy of the French church would have been broken, declared the Civil Constitution of the Clergy to be founded upon heretical principles and ordered the clergy to refuse to take the oath of allegiance. A majority of the clergy, including nearly all the bishops, followed the pope's command. The defection of the "nonjuring clergy" and of thousands of their devoted parishioners was the first serious split in the ranks of the revolutionists.

Political

Under the new constitution, which was completed in 1791, the judicial, legislative, and executive powers of the central government were separated. Lawmaking was given to the single-chamber Legislative Assembly of 745 members elected for two-year terms. Voting, however, was limited to males at least twenty-five years of age who paid taxes equivalent to three days' wages. It is estimated that some 4 million adult males ("active" citizens) could meet these qualifications and that some 2 million remained "passive" citizens. Actually to sit in the Legislative Assembly required the payment of taxes amounting to fifty-four livres. Only some seventy thousand Frenchmen could meet this qualification, and the weight of power fell to the bourgeoisie. The king was granted a suspensive veto over all but financial and constitutional measures, but three successive legislatures could pass a bill over the king's veto. The conduct of foreign relations was left in the hands of the king, but he could not declare war or make treaties without the consent of the Legislative Assembly. The king's expenditures were limited to a sum voted by the legislative body. France was greatly decentralized. For purposes of local government and administration, the country was divided into eighty-three departments, each of which was administered by a small elected assembly. The execution of the national laws was placed almost entirely in the hands of the local authorities.

In October 1791 the National Assembly, having completed its work, gave way to the Legislative Assembly, which had recently been elected under the new constitution. Within a brief span of two years and with very little bloodshed, France had been made over. The monarchy had been limited and made subject to a written constitution. The Roman Catholic church had been subordinated to the state. Feudalism had come to an end. Individual rights and liberties and legal equality for men, if not women, had been defined and established.

5. FOREIGN WAR AND THE FAILURE OF THE MODERATE REGIME

The new government so optimistically launched lasted less than a year. The chief gainers in the French Revolution thus far had been the bourgeoisie and the peasants. The bourgeoisie had gained political control over the country as well as greater social mobility. Most adult male peasants, who constituted the bulk of the French male population, could now vote, and all of the peasantry was at least free from feudal obligations. To the many peasant landowners who owned their land before the Revolution were now added others who had seized the lands of émigré nobles or had purchased confiscated church lands. Most of the bourgeoisie and the landowning peasants were satisfied and wished to see the Revolution stop where it was, lest they lose their sacred property and their political dominance.

However, other groups were quite dissatisfied. The royal family, the aristocracy, most of the clergy, and the army officers yearned for the restoration of their privileges. And many of Paris's urban populace, both men and women, wanted to see the Revolution continued in a more radical way. They had gained little except theoretical rights and legal equality. Owning no property, they could not vote. Yet they had supplied much of the physical force that had saved the third estate and made the moderate reforms possible.

Leadership for these disgruntled groups was found among radical members of the bourgeoisie, who came to favor overthrow of the monarchy and extension of the Revolution. These radicals, although a definite minority, were well organized and ably led. They came together in numerous clubs, which were formed to debate and plan political matters. The most important was the Jacobin Club. Although the Jacobins were and remained predominantly intellectual bourgeoisie and were moderate at first, they gradually became the most radical group in France. Three Jacobin leaders came to tower over all others. Jean-Paul Marat, Swiss by birth, was an inordinately ambitious and frustrated physician and scientist turned popular journalist (see Color Plate 18). His was the gift of rabble-rousing journalism. He incessantly demanded the beheading of all those leaders who opposed the further extension of the Revolution. Georges-Jacques Danton, a former lawyer in the king's council, was a thundering orator of great energy and ability. Maximilien de Robespierre was also a lawyer. This determined idealist was influenced by Rousseau and bent upon the creation of a virtuous republic.

Events soon played into the hands of the radicals. The kings of Austria and Prussia, fearful of the spread of revolutionary ideas to their own lands and urged on by the French émigrés, began to make threatening moves and to issue meddlesome warnings to the French revolutionaries. In France the reactionaries believed that a successful war would enhance the prestige and power of the throne and that a defeat would result in the restoration of the Old Regime. Most of the radicals believed that war would expose the inefficiency and disloyalty of the king and bring about his downfall. When, therefore, in April 1792 Louis XVI appeared before the Legislative Assembly to request a declaration of war against Austria and Prussia, only seven negative votes were cast. Thus lightly was begun a series of wars that was to last twenty-three years and embroil most of the Western world.

The French armies, almost leaderless since nearly all the high-ranking officers were members of the nobility and had either fled or been deposed, were badly defeated. As the Austrian and Prussian armies advanced toward Paris, there was panic in the city. The king, who had already forfeited his credibility when he attempted to flee the country in June 1791, was now rightly suspected of being in treasonable communication with the enemy. A huge Parisian crowd of men and women advanced on the king's palace. The royal family fled for its life to the Legislative Assembly. The interior of the palace was wrecked, and several hundred of the Swiss Guards were slain. The Legislative Assembly suspended and imprisoned Louis XVI and called elections for a national convention to draw up a new constitution to take the place of the one that had just failed.

6. THE TRIUMPH OF THE RADICALS AND THE REIGN OF TERROR

The elections to the constitutional convention took place in an atmosphere of panic and violence. During the interim between the overthrow of the limited monarchy and the meeting of the convention, Danton assumed emergency leadership of the nation. Feverishly he superintended the gathering of recruits and rushed them to the front. As the recruits were preparing to leave Paris, rumors spread that their wives and children would be murdered by the reactionary clergy and nobles. Violent elements began murdering members of the nonjuring clergy and reactionary nobles who were being held in the prisons of Paris. During the first three weeks of September 1792 more than a thousand such victims were massacred. In the elections of the National Convention, held amid this hysteria, the radicals won a sweeping victory. Most of the conservative elements fearfully stayed away from the polls.

In the National Convention a long-simmering struggle between different Jacobin factions came to a head. The Girondins, so called because many of their leaders came from the vicinity of Bordeaux in the department of the Gironde, had once been the dominant and most radical faction of the Legislative Assembly—the Left.[2] In the National Convention the Girondins found themselves on the Right. The new Left was made up of the Jacobin followers of Marat, Danton, and Robespierre, mostly from the city of Paris. They came to be called the Mountain, since they occupied the highest seats in the convention hall. This radical convention, elected for the purpose of drawing up a new constitution, was to rule France for the next three years (1792–1795).

The first act of the National Convention was to declare France a republic. The next move was to dispose of the king. After a close trial he was found guilty of treasonable communication with the enemy and sent to the guillotine—an instrument adopted by the revolutionists for the more mechanical and humane beheading of the condemned (see Figure 38.4). The execution of Louis XVI, accompanied by proclamations of world revolution by the evangelical Jacobins, sent a shudder of horror through the royal courts of Europe. Furthermore, the hastily recruited French revolutionary armies, which had checked the Austrians and Prussians at Valmy in September 1792, had taken the offensive and overrun the Austrian Netherlands.

Austria and Prussia were now joined by Great Britain, the Dutch Netherlands, Spain, Portugal, Sardinia, and Naples in a great coalition

---

[2] The present political connotation of the terms *right* and *left* derives from this period. In the revolutionary assemblies the conservatives sat quite by chance on the speaker's right, the liberals and radicals on his left.

FIGURE 38.4 Execution of Louis XVI In January 1793 Louis XVI was executed by guillotine in a public square before troops and a large crowd of citizens. Here the scene is portrayed as a triumph of the Revolution. (The Bettmann Archive)

bent upon the destruction of the French Revolution and the restoration of the Old Regime. The French armies were unable to stand up to such an array of armed might. But the defeats and invasions were not the worst disasters to confront the revolutionary government. The peasants of the Vendée region in western France, who had been stirred up by the nonjuring clergy, rebelled against the radical government. The rebellion spread until some sixty of the eighty-three departments were involved. Major provincial cities such as Bordeaux, Lyons, and Marseilles were in revolt. Toulon, the chief French naval base on the Mediterranean, invited the British fleet in. Inside the convention itself many of the moderate Girondins were sympathetic to the rebels.

Faced with what seemed to be inevitable disaster to their radical cause and indeed to the Revolution itself, the leaders of the Mountain decided on drastic action. For support they turned to the Paris Commune, as the city government

was called, which was controlled by radicals, and the *sans-culottes*—the common laborers, small shopkeepers, and artisans who wore trousers rather than the aristocratic knee breeches (or *culottes*). The men and women of this urban populace had already played an important role in the Revolution by opposing the old forces of order and supporting the leaders of the third estate at crucial times, such as in the storming of the Bastille. By 1793 they wanted to carry the Revolution further, and for the next two years their wishes and actions would have considerable weight in France. Economically, they favored price controls to keep the cost of bread down and other governmental intervention in the economy to narrow the gap between rich and poor; they envisioned a society of small shopkeepers, artisans, and small farmers as ideal. Politically, they were antimonarchical and strongly republican, indeed favoring as much direct democracy as possible. While leaders of the Mountain did not fully agree with the *sans-culottes*, they were willing to work with them. On June 2, 1793, the National Convention, now dominated by the Mountain and surrounded by a threatening Paris crowd urged on by *sans-culottes* leaders, voted the expulsion and arrest of twenty-nine Girondin leaders. Having thus silenced all opposition within the convention, the leaders of the Mountain and their followers inaugurated a "reign of terror" against their political enemies. Their goals were to unite France and to save and extend the Revolution.

The National Convention delegated unlimited powers to a Committee of Public Safety, composed of twelve men working in secret. The most influential member of this all-powerful committee was Robespierre. At its call was the Committee of General Security, a national police force. A Revolutionary Tribunal was set up to try, condemn, and execute suspects without the usual legal procedure and as quickly as possible. Members of the National Convention were sent out in pairs to carry the Terror to every nook and cranny of France. Although tens of thousands of persons, possibly half a million, were imprisoned during the Reign of Terror, only some twenty-five thousand are believed to have been executed. This drastic policy was remarkably successful. The disaffected elements were quickly silenced and the rebellions quelled. The defense of the republic was entrusted to Lazare Carnot. A *levée en masse* (general call-up) was ordered. All men, women, and children were called to the colors. The able-bodied young men were rapidly trained and rushed to the front. Everyone else contributed to the war effort on the home front. This common activity for defense of country produced a high state of morale—the first mass national patriotism in history. Able new officers were found. The armies of the coalition were defeated on every front and hurled back beyond the frontiers.

While Robespierre and his associates were saving the Revolution, they were also busy extending it to more radical ground. Robespierre was determined to make France a utopian republic where virtue and fraternity would reign supreme. During the emergency of 1793 a maximum price was placed upon the necessities of life for the protection of consumers, particularly the *sans-culottes*. Efforts were made to control inflation by forcing people to accept the badly inflated *assignats* at their face value. New measures made it easier for peasants to acquire land. The metric system was adopted; the Louvre Palace was turned into an art gallery; the national library and national archives were founded; a law (never implemented) provided for a comprehensive national system of public education. Women adopted the flowing robes and hairstyles of ancient Greece. Silk knee breeches, the symbol of aristocracy, gave way to trousers. Titles of all kinds were discarded and "Citizen" and "Citizeness" substituted. Even the calendar was revolutionized. The months were made equal and named after the seasons. Weeks were made ten days long, with one day of rest (thereby eliminating Sunday, a day of traditional Christian importance). The Year 1 was dated from September 22, 1792, the date of the declaration of the republic. However the Jacobins took no radical steps for women. Rather, they rejected women's participation in politics and outlawed women's associations.

Meanwhile, discontent with Robespierre and his policies was increasing. The defeat of the invading armies of the coalition and the suppression of the internal rebellion appeared to most people to remove the justification for the Terror, yet the Terror was intensified. Robespierre felt that the republic of virtue for which he yearned had eluded him. When Danton counseled moderation, Robespierre sent even him and his most prominent followers to the guillotine. No one, not even the members of the National Convention, felt safe any longer. Finally, in July 1794, the Convention found the courage and the leadership to overthrow Robespierre and send him to his own guillotine.

7. REACTION AND THE RISE OF NAPOLEON

Since Robespierre was overthrown on July 27, which was 9 Thermidor by the revolutionary calendar, the reaction that followed is known as the Thermidorian Reaction. The propertied bourgeoisie, who quickly gained control of things, had been frightened and angered by the restrictive measures of Robespierre's regime. All such measures still in force were repealed. The Terror was brought to an end and the chief terrorists executed. Armed bands of bourgeois hirelings went around for some time beating or killing Jacobins. Many individuals, weary of discipline and restraint, reveled in an outburst of licentious living. In 1795 the National Convention finally got around to the task for which it had been elected three years earlier: the drawing up of a new constitution. The resulting constitution reflected conservative reaction. Only property owners could vote for members of the legislative bodies. Executive functions were placed into the hands of five directors, who were chosen for five-year terms by the two legislative bodies. In October 1795 the National Convention turned over its powers to the Directory, the name that was given to the new government.

The Directory (1795–1799) was staffed by men of reasonable competence, but they were unable to restore tranquility. Though peace had already been made with Spain and Prussia, war with Great Britain, Austria, and Sardinia dragged on. Government finances were chaotic, and brigandage was rife. More and more people longed for a strongman who could bring peace abroad and order at home. Napoleon proved to be the man, and the story of his rise to power will be told in the next chapter. When in November 1799 Napoleon overthrew the Directory and made himself dictator, the French Revolution had run full cycle from absolute Bourbon monarchy to absolute Napoleonic dictatorship.

SUGGESTED READING

General

F. Furet, *Interpreting the French Revolution* (1981). An influential new interpretation.

L. Hunt, *Politics, Culture, and Class in the French Revolution* (1984). Analyzes the creation of a new political culture in the Revolution.

R. R. Palmer, *The Age of the Democratic Revolution*, 2 vols. (1959, 1964). Places the French Revolution in a broader transatlantic context.

S. Schama. *Citizens: A Chronicle of the French Revolution.* (1989). A vivid, revisionary account.

D. Sutherland, *France, 1789–1815: Revolution and Counter-Revolution* (1986). Stresses connections between social and political conflict.

The Old Regime and the First Phase of the Revolution

W. Doyle, *Origins of the French Revolution* (1988). Encompasses recent research.

G. Lefèbvre, *The Coming of the French Revolution* (1947). By one of France's leading authorities, it covers the first phase of the Revolution.

M. Vovelle, *The Fall of the French Monarchy* (1984). Emphasizes the social aspects of the Revolution, especially the role of the popular classes.

Second Phase

T. Blanning, *The Origins of the French Revolutionary Wars* (1986). A good study of the revolutionary wars.

N. Hampson, *The Terror in the French Revolution* (1981). Effectively covers the radical stage of the Revolution.

M. Lyons, *France under the Directory* (1975). A good brief treatment.

R. R. Palmer, *Twelve Who Ruled: The Committee of Public Safety During the Terror* (1970). Best book on the Reign of Terror.

A. Soboul, *The Parisian Sans-Culottes and the French Revolution 1793–1794* (1964). The most highly respected analysis of the *sans-culottes*.

Sources

J. H. Steward, *A Documentary Survey of the French Revolution* (1951). Excellent, broad collection of documents.

CHAPTER 39

The Era of Napoleon, 1799–1815

FIGURE 39.1 **Jacques-Louis David,** *Napoleon's Coronation* This painting by David was intended to glorify Napoleon at the height of his powers. Having just crowned himself emperor with a laurel wreath (alluding back to Roman emperors) in an 1804 ceremony presided over by Pope Pius VII (on his right), Napoleon prepares to crown Josephine as empress. (Alinari/Art Resource)

No individual in modern times has enjoyed a more meteoric career than Napoleon Bonaparte, the modern counterpart of Alexander the Great and Julius Caesar. He was essentially a product of the Enlightenment and the French Revolution. He rose to power in France quickly, both undoing and securing changes initiated during the French Revolution. As he extended his rule throughout Europe by military conquest, he spread revolutionary forces of change to other lands.

1. NAPOLEON'S RISE TO POWER

Napoleon was born on the French island of Corsica in 1769. At the age of nine he was sent to a military school in France. An unusually self-reliant individual, he studied history, geography, and mathematics. At sixteen he received his commission as second lieutenant of artillery. During several years of boring garrison duty he stuffed his photographic mind with history, the classics, and the philosophy of the Enlightenment.

The French Revolution provided unprecedented opportunities for soldiers of talent to rise in the officer corps. Most of the prerevolutionary army officers were nobles and had fled the country or been deposed. Moreover, the expanded size of the army created a new demand for skilled officers. Napoleon took advantage of his opportunities. In 1793 he gained attention in the recapture of Toulon. In 1795 Napoleon was again called upon, this time by the National Convention, which was threatened by a Parisian crowd. Using artillery—his famous "whiff of grapeshot"—Napoleon quickly dispersed the crowd and became the hero of the Convention. He used his new prominence to secure command of the French army still fighting in northern Italy. Napoleon's dynamism and skill quickly galvanized the lethargic French forces, who defeated the Austrians and Sardinians and forced them to sue for peace. He personally negotiated a favorable peace with Austria and sent back glowing reports of his exploits.

Napoleon then turned toward France's most formidable opponent, the British. The British navy was too powerful for France to dare an invasion of the British mainland. Napoleon concluded that an expedition to Egypt would be a telling blow to British commerce with its colonies and to the British Empire in general. Moreover, it might prove to be an unexpected thrust and thus an easy victory, something to contribute to Napoleon's image as a daring, heroic conqueror. Militarily, the expedition was a failure; Admiral Nelson (1758–1805) decisively defeated the French fleet at the Battle of the Nile on August 1, 1798. Yet Napoleon avoided personal disaster by slipping back to France with a few chosen followers and cleverly managing the reports that arrived from Egypt.

Meanwhile, matters were turning worse for France's government, the Directory. The expedition to Egypt prompted Great Britain, Austria, and Russia to join in a second coalition against France. By 1799 French armies had suffered defeats and France was threatened with invasion. Internally, support for the Directory was weakening as the economic situation worsened and as political factions vied for power. One of the conservative factions, led by Abbé Sieyès (who was already one of the directors), concluded that the Revolution had gone too far. The members of this faction wanted to return to a more authoritarian form of government which would respect the changes initiated during the first, moderate phase of the Revolution in 1789. This situation provided Napoleon with another opportunity. Sieyès and others conspired with Napoleon to overthrow the Directory in a coup d'état. This coup occurred on 18 Brumaire (November 9, 1799). Napoleon was only thirty.

2. THE CONSULATE—PEACE AND REFORM, 1799–1804

Having seized power by conspiracy and force, Napoleon had a constitution drawn up to conceal what amounted to a military dictatorship under the cloak of parliamentary forms. He gave himself the title of first consul with the power to appoint key civilian and military personnel, declare war and make treaties, and initiate all legislation through a hand-picked Council of State. Two other consuls without any significant powers served as camouflage. Two legislative bodies were selected from a list of candidates elected by all adult French males. But since they could not propose new laws, their power was very limited. Thus the voters were led to believe that they were participating in the government, whereas in reality their voice was but faintly heard. Local government was again brought under the strict control of the central government by placing each of France's eighty-three departments under the control of a powerful agent of the central government called a *prefect*.

Napoleon lost no time in making a treaty (1800) with the United States, bringing to an end a two-year undeclared naval war that had grown out of French seizures of American vessels and the pro-British, anti-French policies of John Adams' administration. Slipping over the Alps with a French army, Napoleon crushed the Austrian army in northern Italy in the battle of Marengo, knocking Austria out of the Second Coalition. Tsar Paul of Russia was cajoled with flattery and promises into making peace. Even Great Britain was persuaded to sign the Peace of Amiens in 1802. Shortly thereafter Napoleon cut his losses in North America and sold Louisiana to the United States.

Napoleon next proceeded to gain social support for his rule and create new permanent institutions. He approved the end of feudal privileges and the transfers of property, thereby winning favor with the peasantry. By affirming property rights as inviolable and formal equality before the law for adult males, he gained support from the middle class. He also welcomed back all but the most reactionary émigrés, most of whom had been part of France's old aristocracy. He deterred opposing groups by creating a secret police force under Joseph Fouché and suppressing political organizations. For those who displayed loyalty and achieved the most, he created the prestigious Legion of Honor.

Some of these measures were institutionalized in Napoleon's most important reform, the creation of the Civil Code of 1804 (the Napoleonic Code), which would later be copied by many other nations. The Civil Code, along with other codes of criminal and commercial law, reduced the dozens of different legal codes in existence. In general they affirmed the reforms sought in the beginning stages of the French Revolution while rejecting the more radical measures

enacted after 1792. But for women, the code was a clear defeat. Rather than granting them legal or political equality, it gave authority over the family to men and left married women legally and economically dependent on their husbands.

Napoleon was keenly aware of the political and social importance of religion. "Always treat the pope," he counseled his diplomats, "as if he had 200,000 men." He himself was a deist and a cynical moral relativist, believing that God was "always on the side with the most cannon." One of his first steps was to make peace with the pope and end the ten-year struggle between the French revolutionary governments and the Roman Catholic church. After arduous negotiations, the first consul and the pope signed the Concordat of 1801, which was to govern the relations between the French state and the Catholic church until the beginning of the twentieth century. The Catholic religion was declared to be the religion of the majority of the French people, but freedom for other religions was also to be protected. The state was to appoint bishops, but only the pope could invest them in their offices. The bishops were to appoint and discipline the lower clergy, thus restoring the traditional episcopal principle of the Church. The salaries of the clergy were to be paid by the state, and the clergy were to take an oath of allegiance to the state. The pope accepted the permanent loss of church property seized by the National Assembly. While the Catholic clergy was never pleased with the Concordat (indeed, Pope Pius VII eventually renounced it), it ended the religious cleavage that had harassed France since the early days of the Revolution.

Napoleon initiated several other institutional reforms. He established the Bank of France to handle government funds and issue paper money. He brought order and efficiency to government finances. He created a long-lasting system of secondary schools tied to the University of France. He established several professional and technical schools.

The first five years of Napoleon's rule were spectacularly successful. Law and order at home and peace abroad had been attained. Financial stability, equal and efficient justice, religious tranquillity, and the foundations of an effective educational system had all been achieved. Public morale was high. However, Napoleon was not satisfied with his accomplishments. He yearned for more glory. In 1804 he crowned himself emperor of the French and sought further fields to conquer (see Figure 39.1).

3. THE EMPIRE—WAR AND CONQUEST

Great Britain, France's inveterate foe, had become increasingly alarmed at Napoleon's growing strength. Napoleon had not only continued to build up his military forces but had also taken advantage of the Peace of Amiens to further his commercial and imperial schemes at Great Britain's expense. Before the end of 1803 the British government declared war and the next year joined with Austria and Russia to form a third coalition against France. This was what Napoleon expected and wanted. He soon appeared at the English Channel at the head of a force sufficient to conquer the British Isles, if only the twenty-four-mile water barrier could be crossed. In the Channel, however, lay the world's mightiest fleet, commanded by the greatest of all Britain's admirals, Lord Nelson. Meanwhile, Napoleon was watching the movements of the Austrians and Russians and readying his own army. When the time was ripe, he suddenly marched his army eastward, surrounded an exposed Austrian army at Ulm in southwest Germany, and forced it to surrender. But the day after Ulm, Nelson sighted the combined French and Spanish fleets off Cape Trafalgar on the southwest point of Spain and annihilated them (October 21, 1805). Although Nelson was killed early in the battle, his victory saved Great Britain from the menace of a Napoleonic invasion and limited the scope of the French emperor's conquests to the continent of Europe.

On land, however, Napoleon seemed invincible. Moving his army eastward from Ulm, he met and crushed the oncoming combined forces of Austria and Russia at Austerlitz. Austria immediately sued for peace, and the demoralized Russians retreated toward their home country. At this juncture Prussia declared war on Napoleon. The time was inopportune, and the Prus-

sian army was no match for Napoleon. At Jena and Auerstädt Napoleon overwhelmed and virtually destroyed the Prussian forces (1806). Two weeks later the French were in Berlin. Hearing that the Russian troops were re-forming in Poland, Napoleon moved eastward to meet them. After being held to a draw by the Russians in a blinding snowstorm at Eylau, he defeated them decisively a few months later in the great battle of Friedland (1807). Tsar Alexander I now sued for peace. Although the Treaties of Tilsit (July 1807) were technically between equals, they actually left Napoleon master of the European continent and Alexander I only a junior partner. Russia was given a free hand to deal with Turkey in eastern Europe but was not permitted to take Constantinople, the prize the Russians most desired. In return for a dominant hand in eastern Europe, Alexander promised to join Napoleon against Great Britain and to force Sweden to do so. Tilsit recognized the changes that Napoleon had already made in central and western Europe and left him free to make any others he wished.

Between 1806 and 1808 Napoleon remade the map of Europe. The puppet Duchy of Warsaw was created out of part of Prussia's (and later, part of Austria's) Polish territory. Prussia's territory west of the Elbe was made a part of the kingdom of Westphalia, over which Napoleon's youngest brother, Jerome, was made king. Prussia was thus virtually halved in size. The Holy Roman Empire was at long last abolished and its hundreds of little principalities greatly consolidated. A strip of German territory along the North Sea was annexed outright to France. The rest of German territory west of the Elbe was brought into the Confederation of the Rhine, with Napoleon as protector. Napoleon's younger brother Louis was made king of Holland; but when Louis began to favor the interests of his Dutch subjects over those of the French Empire, Napoleon deposed him and annexed his territory to France. The Italian peninsula was brought under French dominance. The coastal areas along the northeastern Adriatic Sea were detached from Austria and annexed to France. In 1808 Napoleon overthrew the weak Spanish royal house and made his elder brother, Joseph, king of Spain. Shortly before, the Portuguese royal family had fled to Brazil at the approach of a French army. Denmark (including Norway) became Napoleon's most faithful ally.

Thus, by 1808, most of Europe was under French control or French influence (see Map 39.1). No other conqueror has so dominated Europe. In all those territories under direct French control, Napoleon's "enlightened" institutions and administrative efficiency were introduced. The rest of Europe, impressed with the effectiveness of the French revolutionary ideas and institutions, adopted many of them voluntarily.

4. DECLINE AND FALL OF THE EMPIRE

A number of factors contributed to the decline and fall of the Napoleonic empire. One of the most obvious was British sea power. Because of it, Great Britain alone of the European powers was able to withstand the Napoleonic military onslaught. After Trafalgar had dashed Napoleon's hopes of invading the British Isles, he sought the destruction of "perfidious Albion" by economic pressure. In order to wreck the economy of the "nation of shopkeepers," he attempted to blockade the entire continent of Europe against British shipping. All British goods were confiscated. French privateers were set upon British merchant ships. These measures, known as "the Continental System," did cause Great Britain distress. However, with control of the sea, Great Britain was able to apply a more effective counterblockade against the Napoleon-dominated Continent. The Continental System created an ever-increasing resentment against Napoleon's rule in France's satellite states.

Another factor that undermined the Napoleonic empire was the rise of a national spirit among the subject peoples. The mass spirit of intense patriotism or nationalism, which had had its origin in France during the *levée en masse* of 1793, spread to the rest of Europe in the wake of Napoleon's conquering armies. The first people to rebel openly against the French yoke were the proud Spaniards. Hardly had Napoleon's brother Joseph been placed on the Spanish throne when his unwilling subjects rose up and chased him out of Madrid. The superior French armies, even when led by Napoleon himself, were ineffective against the hit-and-run guerrilla tactics invented by the Spaniards. The British government, observing Napoleon's predicament in Spain, sent an army under Arthur Wellesley, the future duke of Wellington, to exploit the situation. Spain became a running abscess that drained away much of Napoleon's military strength. Meanwhile, Prussia, after the humiliation of Jena, had begun a rejuvenation under the leadership of Baron von Stein. Partly in secret and partly in the open, the Prussians modernized their army and their civil institutions and prepared for the day of liberation. In 1809 Austria declared war on Napoleon in a premature effort to free itself from subservience to the French emperor. Although Austria was once more defeated, the heroic valor with which the Austrian armies fought served notice of the rising spirit of national pride and resistance. Napoleon could no longer enjoy the advantage of commanding soldiers fired with the heady wine of nationalism against lethargic professional armies.

The beginning of the end was a disastrous campaign against Russia in 1812. With their own interests pulling them apart, the alliance between Alexander I and Napoleon became strained. Napoleon, against the advice of his closest associates, decided to invade Russia. Amassing an army of six hundred thousand, the mightiest army ever assembled up to that time, he plunged into the vastness of Russia. Many of his troops, however, were unwilling conscripts from the puppet states. The Russian army retreated into the interior of the huge country, following a scorched-earth policy and drawing Napoleon ever farther from his base of supplies. Finally, after the bloody battle of Borodino about seventy-five miles from Moscow, Napoleon's hosts entered the city. But Alexander I refused to make peace. A fire destroyed much of Moscow, leaving the invaders without shelter in the face of approaching winter. Napoleon began his retreat too late. The Russian winter caught his forces burdened down with loot. Tens of thousands froze or starved. Russian cossacks, riding out of the blizzards, cut down or captured other thousands. Of the six hundred thousand men who marched into Russia, no more than one hundred thousand returned.

Map 39.1 EUROPE, 1810 This map shows the Napoleonic empire at its height. Generally, French revolutionary and Napoleonic institutions spread most in those areas closest to France and under its direct control. Napoleon's empire was weakened when he tried to extend his control to Europe's geographic extremes—Spain and Russia.

WHERE HISTORIANS DISAGREE

Who Was Napoleon?

Few individuals in history have inspired such passionate debate as Napoleon. In part, this controversy is a result of his meteoric rise to the heights of power and his string of military conquests. And in part, it is a consequence of the charismatic quality of his leadership. He combined personal dynamism and charm, which created faith in masses of followers and enabled him to dominate many of those with whom he came into contact. The debate is also related to difficulties separating the myth of Napoleon from the reality of Napoleon. Finally, all sides of the debate can find some support in the varied, contradictory legacy of Napoleon's intentions and deeds. Therefore it is not surprising that historians have bitterly disagreed over how to characterize Napoleon.

Many historians argue that Napoleon was fundamentally a dictator. They point to the methods he used to acquire power—the fame associated with military prowess, the coup d'état, and the plebiscite that seemed to affirm his power democratically without offering a real choice—as methods typical of modern dictators. They also point to his actions after acquiring power—crowning himself emperor, eliminating freedom of speech and press, removing the substance from representative institutions, initiating a systematic crackdown on political opponents, and creating a secret police—as characteristic of military dictatorships.

Other historians see him as a preserver of the Revolution. They stress his familiarity with Enlightenment ideas and his early support of the French Revolution. They point out that Napoleon did affirm the end of feudalism, the overthrow of the old aristocracy, the establishment of equality before the law for men, and the rights of property. They also argue that his most important service may have been in spreading the ideas and institutions of the Revolution beyond France's borders—in particular, the rejection of aristocratic privilege and the spread of the Napoleonic Code. In short, Napoleon affirmed the fundamental reforms of the early French Revolution, institutionalized them, and then helped spread them elsewhere in Europe.

Still other historians argue that Napoleon is best viewed as the last in a line of eighteenth-century enlightened despots. They point out that like other enlightened despots, such as Frederick the Great of Prussia and Joseph II of Austria, Napoleon was most interested in maximizing the political and military power of the state. Like them, he saw that to do so required centralizing and rationalizing the government, improving finances, codifying laws, and supporting the armed forces. He shared their tendency to make religious concerns secondary to political unity and to gain support through the creation of educational institutions. Thus, from an eighteenth-century perspective, Napoleon is recognizable as an enlightened despot.

Many historians argue that individual leaders, even those as extraordinary as Napoleon, do not decisively affect history's mainstream. More important are the forces, circumstances, and people that surround them. Other historians maintain that individuals, above all the rare charismatic leaders such as Napoleon, can have significant historical consequences.

Which of these interpretations best fits the historical record depends greatly on the perspective of the viewer and on what aspects of Napoleon's personality and rule are emphasized. At the same time, how much can be attributed to the actions of any historical figure must be kept in mind in deciding exactly who was Napoleon.

Napoleon dashed back to France to raise fresh conscripts, but the flower of French manhood was gone. One nation after another rose up to join the Russians in a war of liberation. At Leipzig in central Germany, in October 1813, Napoleon was at last decisively defeated. The next year the allies entered Paris and exiled Napoleon to the island of Elba, off the coast of Italy. When the allies began to squabble over the peace settlement, Napoleon escaped back to France and raised another army, but he was finally defeated in June 1815 by the duke of Wellington and the Prussians under Marshal Blücher at Waterloo in Belgium. This time he was imprisoned on the island of St. Helena in the South Atlantic, where six years later he died.

5. OVERSEAS EFFECTS: LATIN AMERICA

One vast area outside Europe upon which the impact of the revolution of Napoleon was strong and immediate was Latin America. During the eighteenth century, discontent with colonial rule had been steadily mounting in the Spanish and Portuguese colonial empires in North and South America. As in the thirteen English colonies in North America, the resentment was directed primarily against economic and political restrictions. As the native-born "Creoles" had come to outnumber the Spanish- and Portuguese-born settlers, the ties of loyalty to the mother countries had become more and more tenuous. The liberal writings of the French and British philosophers of the Enlightenment were smuggled into Latin America and made their converts, particularly among young intellectuals. These liberal Latin Americans could not help being impressed by the successful revolt of the English colonies to the north and the setting up of a liberal New World republic. The French Revolution had an even more profound influence on them. When, therefore, Napoleon overthrew Ferdinand VII of Spain and placed his own brother, Joseph Bonaparte, on the Spanish throne, the colonies' sentiments of loyalty for the mother country, which were already weak, became confused.

By 1810 the colonies were in open revolt. As with the English colonists three decades earlier, the cause of the Latin American revolutionists

FIGURE 39.2 Simon Bolívar Here, in heroic pose, Simon Bolívar is shown leading the struggle to liberate South America from Spanish rule. The painting is modeled on a well-known work by David showing Napoleon leading his troops across the alps. (The Granger Collection)

seemed hopeless. In addition to the regular Spanish troops, they had to struggle against most of the wealthy Spanish settlers and the local Roman Catholic hierarchy. Eventually two brilliant young leaders, Simón Bolívar and José San Martín, emerged to overcome the seemingly impossible obstacles and to lead the South American revolutionists to success (see Figure 39.2). By 1822 the independence of Spanish South America was won. In the same year the issue was decided in Spain's Central American colonies and in Mexico, which then included the southwest quarter of what is now the United States. In all the former Spanish colonies, republics were established, although a long period of troubled apprenticeship preceded the establishment of effective popular governments. Real stability has continued to be a problem for the Central and South American nations.

In the huge Portuguese colony of Brazil, the independence movement was delayed by the flight of the Portuguese royal family to Brazil in 1807. However, the return of the king to Portugal six years after Napoleon's fall and the efforts of the Portuguese government to reimpose colonial status on Brazil quickly fanned the embers of revolt into flame. In 1822 the Portuguese king's son, Pedro, whom he had left behind as regent, yielded to native pressure and declared himself king of independent Brazil. In all of free Latin America the Napoleonic Code was adopted as the basis of civil law, and the impact of the Enlightenment on political institutions was clearly visible.

6. THE SIGNIFICANCE OF THE FRENCH REVOLUTION AND NAPOLEON

The French Revolution and its Napoleonic sequel had a profound effect on the course of history. Like Pandora when she lifted the lid of that fateful box, they let loose forces and ideas that have influenced and shaken the world ever since, especially the revolutionary ideals of *Liberty, Equality, Fraternity*. Originally conceived in the eighteenth century by the philosophers of the Enlightenment, they were born materially in the American and French revolutions and spread by Napoleon.

In the era of the French Revolution, the ideal of *liberty* meant freedom from arbitrary authority—political, religious, economic, or social. It meant freedom of speech, press, conscience, assembly, person, and profession and the sacredness of property. During the moderate first phase of the French Revolution, a great deal of progress toward these goals was made; in the tumultuous, bloody second phase, a good deal was lost. Under Napoleon's rule there was no political liberty. However, he claimed that the efficiency, prosperity, and honor of his regime more than made up for the lack of popular government, for which, he believed, the world was not yet ready.

Equality meant essentially equality under the law and equality of opportunity for gain and advancement. In general, it did not apply to women, even though women had played important roles during the Revolution and had hoped

for gains that never came. It was only during the brief dominance of Robespierre that even partial social equality of all male citizens became a goal. Napoleon's law codes were a great boon to the more moderate kind of equality among men. The codes left women devoid of political rights and legally dependent on men.

Fraternity manifested itself in the mass movements (sometimes violent) for reform, in the comradeship in the conscripted armies, and above all in the new popular and dynamic spirit of nationalism. These forces, released by the American and French revolutions, spread first to the rest of Europe, then to Latin America, and eventually to the rest of the world. Much of the history of the world since the era of the French Revolution has revolved around these forces.

In another sense, the French Revolution and the Napoleonic era constituted a decisive political watershed marking the beginnings of modern times. The French Revolution opened the road to constitutional government and democratic institutions. Although there would be numerous reversals, constitutional governments and democratic institutions would generally flourish over the course of the succeeding two centuries and come to characterize politically modern times. The administrative bureaucracy and legal codes established during the Napoleonic era would be imitated and also come to characterize modern political systems.

Finally, the French Revolution and the Napoleonic era provided two images that would invite study and imitation throughout the nineteenth and twentieth centuries. The first image was that of the successful popular revolution. While the French Revolution was not the first revolution, it was the one that occurred in the heart of Western civilization and toppled not only the government but the major institutions of traditional society. This revolution would inspire revolutionaries and warn those representing the status quo for decades to come. The second image was that of Napoleon as a nationalistic, charismatic leader who could suddenly grasp power and exert his will with great effect. During the nineteenth and twentieth centuries, this powerful image would inspire individuals who envisioned themselves as potential Napoleons and people who yearned for easy, decisive solutions to deeply felt problems.

SUGGESTED READING

General

P. Geyl, *Napoleon, For and Against* (1949). A good study of changing interpretations of Napoleon.

J. C. Herold, *The Age of Napoleon* (1983). An entertaining, well-written survey.

R. Jones, *Napoleon. Man and Myth* (1977). A fine treatment.

G. Lefèbvre, *Napoleon*, 2 vols. (1969). A scholarly treatment by a leading authority.

F. Markham, *Napoleon* (1966). An excellent biography.

France

L. Bergeron, *France under Napoleon* (1981). A good analysis.

R. B. Holtman, *The Napoleonic Revolution* (1967). Good on domestic policy and propaganda.

The Empire

D. Chandler, *The Campaigns of Napoleon* (1966). Focuses on military history.

O. Connelly, *Napoleon's Satellite Kingdoms* (1965). A good study of Napoleonic rule in Europe.

F. Markham, *Napoleon and the Awakening of Europe* (1965). A good study of Napoleon's influence outside of France.

W. S. Robertson, *The Rise of the Spanish-American Republics* (1965). A good brief account.

J. Tulard, *Napoleon: The Myth of the Savior* (1984). A biography that also covers the empire well.

CHAPTER 40
The Industrial Revolution

FIGURE 40.1 François Bonhomme, *Workshop with Mechanical Sieves,* 1859 This realistic painting of a factory interior in France shows the mixture of raw material (zinc ore), machines, and division of labor that epitomized the Industrial Revolution. Men, women, and children work together in this dismal environment; but the men have the more skilled jobs (a foreman sits in the rear to the left), while the women and children are assigned to the less skilled jobs (sorting and splitting chunks of ore). (Conservatoire Nationale des Arts et Métiers)

The term *Industrial Revolution* refers to the vast economic and social changes initiated in Great Britain during the last few decades of the eighteenth century and spreading to the Continent and other parts of the world during the nineteenth and twentieth centuries. It involved a shift from production by individuals alone or in small groups using hand tools powered by muscles, wind, and water to production by organized groups of people in factories using machinery powered by steam. These changes in the methods of production resulted in sustained economic growth. In the process of industrializing, nations experienced rapid population growth and a general shift from a rural society based on agriculture to an urban society based on manufacturing. Along with the French Revolution, the Industrial Revolution set into motion changes that would transform almost all aspects of life in the West during the nineteenth and twentieth centuries.

1. THE COURSE OF THE INDUSTRIAL REVOLUTION

The Industrial Revolution began in Great Britain for several reasons. Demand for the production of goods in Great Britain was growing rapidly during the eighteenth century, thanks to relatively widespread domestic prosperity, a growing population, and abundant markets within Britain's large colonial empire. Great Britain was well positioned to meet this growing demand for goods. It had an abundance of conveniently located raw materials, such as coal and iron. Investment capital amassed from merchants and landowners was available to enterprising entrepreneurs through family connections, partnership arrangements, and banks. Thanks to their leading role in the eighteenth-century agricultural revolution, Britain's farmers could more efficiently produce food for urban populations (see pp. 408–409). A large, mobile force of both skilled and unskilled workers provided industrial entrepreneurs with a cheap supply of labor. The hindrances to commerce and industry so common in other countries were not present to the same degree in Great Britain. British transportation facilities were good, there were fewer governmental restrictions on commerce, and wealthy citizens did not disdain involvement in commerce and industry. Britain's government had been stable since 1689 and was strongly influenced by capitalistic landowners, merchants, and bankers.

British inventors and entrepreneurs responded to these conditions by developing new machines, sources of power, transportation facilities, and factories. These new developments increased production and trade tremendously and made Great Britain an early leader in the Industrial Revolution. By the middle of the nineteenth century, Great Britain was the first industrialized society. It was urbanized, covered with railway lines and canals, and dotted with factories. It produced far greater quantities of textiles, metals, and machines than any other country.

During the eighteenth century, nations on the Continent lacked this combination of circumstances so conducive to British industrialization. In addition, between 1789 and 1815 the Continent suffered from the economic, social, and political turmoil of the French revolutionary and Napoleonic periods. After 1815, and particularly after 1830, the Industrial Revolution spread, first to Belgium, shortly thereafter to France, parts of Germany, and the United States, and later to other areas of Europe (see Map 40.1). At first Continental entrepreneurs copied British inventions and imported skilled British laborers and technicians. Governments recognized the British lead and became more directly involved in promoting industrialization by supporting the construction of railways, subsidizing certain industries, and erecting protective tariffs for domestic industries. By the end of the nineteenth century, countries that had once lagged far behind Great Britain were competing successfully for industrial markets.

2. TECHNOLOGY AND TRANSPORTATION

Probably the most dramatic change the Industrial Revolution brought about was the continual creation of new technology and transportation facilities (see Figure 40.2). A virtual explosion of inventions increased productivity and mechanized productions, above all in textiles, mining, and metallurgy. The steam engine provided a vast new source of reliable power. New roads,

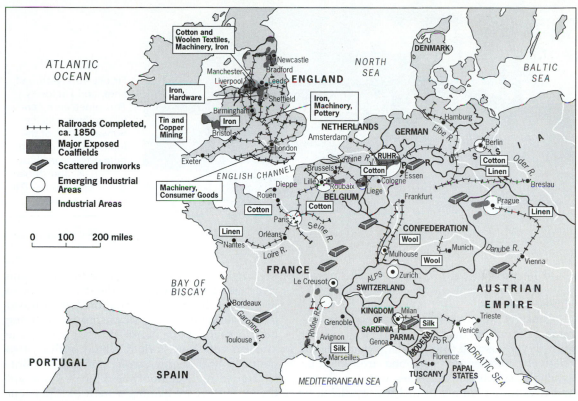

Map 40.1 **THE INDUSTRIAL REVOLUTION IN EUROPE, 1850** This map reveals the spread of industrialization in Europe in 1850 by indicating the location of railroads, coalfields, and ironworks and showing which areas of Europe were becoming industrial centers.

canals, and especially railroads provided regular, inexpensive means of transportation for people and materials.

The cotton textile industry was the first to become mechanized. In 1733 John Kay invented the flying shuttle, which doubled the speed at which cloth could be woven. In 1764 James Hargreaves hitched eight spindles to his wife's spinning wheel instead of one. The result was the far more efficient spinning jenny (named after his daughter Jenny). The number of spindles was soon multiplied. Five years later, Richard Arkwright patented the water frame, a system of rollers driven by water power, which spun a much finer and firmer thread than the jenny. In 1779 Samuel Crompton, combining the principles of the spinning jenny and the water frame, produced the hybrid spinning mule—a great im-

provement over both. In 1785 Edmund Cartwright invented the power loom.

The mechanization of both spinning and weaving greatly increased demand for cotton. In 1793 a young American, Eli Whitney, invented the cotton gin, which helped meet this demand. Removing the seeds from cotton fiber by hand was a tedious process; one person could separate only five or six pounds a day. Cotton was therefore grown only in small patches. Whitney's gin not only made possible an adequate supply of cotton for Britain's mills but also brought into existence the huge cotton plantations worked by black slaves in the American South.

Meanwhile, better sources of power were being developed. In 1769 James Watt significantly improved on earlier inefficient steam engines and invented the first steam engine that

FIGURE 40.2 Railroad, Ship, and Factories This nineteenth-century print shows the outward signs of the Industrial Revolution: railroads, steamships on canals, and smoke-belching factories. (The Bettmann Archive)

could be used to drive machinery. The power that could be generated by the steam engine was almost unlimited.

Constant improvements were made in the mining of coal and the production of iron, crucial for heavy industrialization. As large quantities of relatively inexpensive coal and iron became available, still better machines were produced and a sufficient supply of fuel was available to drive them.

An integral part of the Industrial Revolution was the improvement of transportation and communications. Without both, sufficient quantities of raw materials to feed the hungry machines and adequate markets to absorb the finished products would not have been available. Moreover, the massive population shifts accompanying industrialization would have been much more difficult.

The last decades of the eighteenth century and the first decades of the nineteenth were a time of road and canal building in Great Britain, France, and the United States. Around the turn of the century Thomas Telford and John Mc-Adam in Great Britain pioneered in the construction of well-drained and -surfaced roads. In Great Britain canals were particularly useful for transporting coal. In the United States the completion of the Erie Canal in 1825 opened up the Great Lakes region to lucrative world communications and ensured the primacy of New York City as the chief port and metropolis of the United States.

A more dramatic revolution in transportation came with the application of the steam engine to locomotion. In 1807 Robert Fulton demonstrated the practicability of the steamship by steaming his *Clermont* the one hundred fifty miles up the Hudson from New York to Albany in thirty-two hours. In 1825 George Stephenson in Great Britain convincingly demonstrated the usefulness of the locomotive by hauling a train of thirty-four cars twenty-five miles at twelve miles an hour. By the middle of the nineteenth century, railway lines covered Great Britain and were spreading rapidly on the Continent and in North America. The railroad transported people and material, opened up areas to commerce and urban growth, constituted a major source of demand for industrial products such as coal and iron, and symbolized the spread of the new industrialized society.

3. THE FACTORY SYSTEM

Many of the components of the Industrial Revolution were brought together by the development of the factory system (see Figure 40.1). Industrial capitalists invested considerable funds in machines, buildings, and raw materials. They trained workers to do specific jobs in conjunction with artificially powered machines, which increasingly determined the pace and nature of the work. Industrial capitalists organized the process of producing goods into a series of steps and specialized tasks. Their new factories pumped out unprecedented quantities of manufactured goods.

Before the factory system was instituted, goods were produced either by craft guilds or under the domestic, or "putting out," system (see Chapter 31). Under this system workers did as much or as little work as they wished without supervision. The operations were necessarily small in scale, much time was lost distributing the raw materials from cottage to cottage and collecting the finished products, and uniformity of quality was virtually impossible to attain.

The spread of the factory system spelled the end of the domestic system of manufacturing. The rise of the factory system resulted in a tremendous growth of productivity in manufacturing and a seemingly fantastic increase of manufactured goods. Artisans, although not immediately displaced, found it increasingly difficult to compete with factories that were producing similar products much more rapidly and inexpensively. As the factory system took hold, hastily and cheaply built living quarters for workers and their families were crowded around factories. This factory system was the origin of the modern mill town and industrial city. It also contributed to the dramatic urbanization of industrial societies in the nineteenth century and fundamental changes among social classes in these societies.

4. SOCIAL CHANGES

Population Growth and Urbanization

A large variety of far-reaching social changes are related to the Industrial Revolution. The broadest changes were demographic. Population increased dramatically. In Great Britain population grew from about 9 million in 1780 to almost 21 million in 1850. European population as a whole rose from about 188 million in 1800 to 266 million in 1850. The exact causes of this explosion of population are difficult to pinpoint, but it was probably a result of a declining death rate (thanks to a decline in epidemics and an increase of food supplies) and a rise in the birthrate (caused by earlier departure from home, earlier marriage, and earlier childbearing in an increasingly mobile population).

A more direct result of industrialization was the shift of population from rural to urban areas and the growth in size and number of cities. In England and Wales in 1800 about 17 percent of the population lived in cities of over twenty thousand inhabitants. By 1850 the figure grew to about 35 percent. London alone grew from less than 1 million inhabitants in 1800 to over 2.5 million by 1850. Smaller cities and towns were also growing, so that by midcentury half of Britain's population lived in urban areas. This pattern was being repeated in other areas of Europe as they industrialized. Most of the urban growth was fueled by internal migration. These new emigrants crowded together in cities, often in neighborhoods where there were people from their own rural regions. Many would maintain ties to their old rural communities, temporarily returning when work was scarce. Not all came to work in factories; a large number of men were employed in the building trades, and many women came to work as domestics.

The consequences of this rapid urbanization were all too apparent. Already overcrowded, devoid of mass transportation facilities, and equipped at best with vastly inadequate sanitation facilities, the cities became more densely packed and unhealthy each year. In bad times they became centers of unemployment as much as they were markets for jobs in good times. In this urban environment women had to manage with less pay than men; meager pay or loss of a job forced a growing number of women into prostitution. Urban crowding and poverty provided fertile ground for the growth of crime. The creation of modern urban police forces in London and Paris was more a symptom of the growing crime rate than a solution to it.

At the same time, the cities had a vibrancy and an image of opportunity that continued to attract people; often the alternatives available in the countryside were even less appealing hovels and rural slums.

Social Classes

Even before the Industrial Revolution, the French Revolution had altered many people's perceptions of the social order. Industrialization added economic and social foundations to this new understanding of society. People viewed themselves less as part of a rigid, ranked, ordered society and more as part of a flexible society of a few classes with mobility between classes being both possible and proper. Class membership was not a formal designation but a description of the amount of money, the type of work, the style of life, and the beliefs of people. Nevertheless, this does not mean that society had in reality become egalitarian. As in previous centuries, there remained sharp differences between different classes of people.

The two classes most firmly tied to the traditional rural society, the aristocracy and the peasantry, were doomed by the Industrial Revolution. Over the nineteenth century they would decline in number, wealth, position, and influence. Yet the extent and speed of this decline should not be overestimated. It was not until the second half of the nineteenth century that urban dwellers outnumbered rural populations in even the most industrialized nations; in some countries, such as France, the small farm was more the rule than the exception. Moreover, the aristocracy remained influential even in industrializing nations, commanding considerable wealth and prestige. Aristocrats still dominated many localities, staffed the upper levels of government, and controlled certain professions such as the diplomatic and military officer corps.

The middle classes as a whole and the industrial bourgeoisie in particular grew in number and profited from the Industrial Revolution. Those who benefited most were the large factory owners, bankers, and merchants, who amassed great fortunes and rose toward the top of society. The smaller factory owners, professionals, shopkeepers, and "white-collar" workers who made up the various ranks of the middle class also benefited. They gained their wealth by mental rather than physical labor and by the investment or manipulation of capital. This middle class tended to favor liberal reforms and believe in certain values such as hard work, thrift, careers open to talent, and prudence. Over time they outdistanced their two main competitors: the aristocracy, which remained dependent on the traditional society and rural economy, and the artisans, who were increasingly unable to compete with factory production. Though still a minority (even in the largest cities such as Paris they constituted no more than 25 percent of the population), the middle classes gained in prestige, political power, and cultural influence thanks to their growing wealth and numbers. During the second half of the nineteenth century they would gain dominance over much of Western society.

The urban working classes changed, grew, and suffered during the Industrial Revolution. Many of these workers were domestics, and this class grew still larger as the middle classes gained the wealth to hire them. Artisans remained a large class throughout the nineteenth century. On the whole they commanded better pay than the less skilled factory workers, and their products were demanded by wealthier purchasers. However, new factories increasingly displaced the artisans, and they often reacted radically, sometimes violently, to the changes brought about by industrialization. They tended to join radical political organizations, lead in union-organizing activities and strikes, and be the most active elements of violent and revolutionary protests. After midcentury this class would decline in size.

The industrial proletariat was the newest class. Demand by new factories swelled the ranks of the factory workers. Large numbers of surplus agricultural workers and displaced artisans were absorbed into factory work along with part of the overall increase in population. It was this industrial proletariat that most visibly grew with industrialization and stood in most striking contrast to the industrial bourgeoisie.

Factory workers were ruthlessly exploited by factory owners, particularly during the early stages of the Industrial Revolution. Wages for a workweek of six or seven days at twelve to sixteen hours per day were kept to a subsistence level. Unmarried women and orphaned children were more cheaply and easily exploited than men and were thus employed in the new factories. Contracts were made with orphanages for the employment of children. Young children were marched off before daybreak to work all day in the factories. If they fell behind the pace set by the machines, they were beaten (see Figure 40.3). Sometimes they were chained to their machines.

After the first few decades of the Industrial Revolution, a pattern of hiring whole families to work in the new factories emerged. Although this system meant that the amount of wages nec-

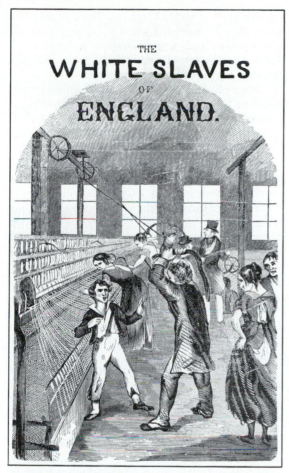

FIGURE 40.3 Child Labor This woodcut, dated 1853, portrays the supervisor of an English cotton factory whipping a young boy. Incidents similar to this were not uncommon during the first phase of the Industrial Revolution. Such conditions spurred speculation on ways to control industrial capitalism. (New York Public Library)

essary for subsistence was kept to a minimum, it at least allowed the working-class family to stay together. By the middle of the nineteenth century the practice of hiring families and children was declining, but life for the industrial working class remained oppressive. The factories and mines were dark, dirty, and dangerous. The dwellings of the workers were likely to be hovels clustered around smoky, noisy mills or mine entrances.

The workers were frequently compelled to spend their wages at company stores, paying monopoly prices arbitrarily set by the owners. Work lost its dignity. The factory workers were disciplined to the clock and the machine. The dull, monotonous, robotlike repetition of a single operation on a machine brought workers none of the satisfaction and pride of skilled craftsmanship.

Many historians and social scientists argue that statistics show that the early factory workers received higher wages and enjoyed a better standard of living than they had ever had as agricultural or urban workers. Clearly, industrial workers were reaping material benefits from the Industrial Revolution after 1850, but in the years before 1850 workers may have lost more than they gained. Certainly the life of the agricultural laborer or artisan should not be romanticized: The conditions of work and life among the agricultural and urban poor had always been hard. But industrial work involved vast changes that were extraordinarily painful. The longer hours, greater insecurity, limits on freedom, and more frequent unemployment of the uprooted slum-dwelling factory worker of the early nineteenth century do not appear in statistics of wages and prices (see Figure 40.4). The overall picture of the industrial proletariat during the first half of the nineteenth century is dismal and can justly be characterized as a new kind of slavery—slavery to the machine and the machine owner.

One of the industrial proletariat's first reactions was violence. Throughout the winter of 1811–1812, when the pressure of the Napoleonic war and the blockade against British commerce was added to the maladjustments of the Industrial Revolution, a wave of personal violence and machine smashing swept (the Luddite riots) through Great Britain. Parliament, composed entirely of members of the property-holding classes, quickly made industrial sabotage a capital offense and suppressed violence with a heavy hand. Several dozens of offenders were hanged. However, sporadic outbreaks of violence continued for several years. This story was repeated in other countries as the Industrial Revolution spread. In the United States in the middle decades of the nineteenth century, violence broke out among the Irish immigrants working in the anthracite coal mines of eastern Pennsylvania. The exploited miners formed secret terror

societies called Molly Maguires. For a number of years they intimidated, even murdered, unpopular bosses and uncooperative nonmembers. They were eventually ferreted out by civil authorities and ruthlessly suppressed.

More peaceful efforts of the industrial proletariat to bring group pressure to bear on their employers by organizing unions also met with defeat at first. In 1799 and 1800 the British Parliament passed the Combination Acts, which outlawed all labor combinations organized for the purpose of securing better wages, hours, or working conditions. In 1824 trade unions were legalized in Great Britain, but their activities were still severely restricted. In other countries strikes and union activities were outlawed. In some cases, as in the United States, the owners themselves organized for the purpose of breaking up labor unions. Private detectives and police were set upon labor leaders, who were beaten, fired, and blacklisted. It was not until the second half of the nineteenth century that labor unions were able to make consistent headway in major struggles with employers.

Nevertheless, factory workers and other elements of the working classes managed to assert themselves in various ways even during the first half of the nineteenth century. Many local working-class organizations were established and survived. A few larger organizations, such as the Grand National Union in Britain, had at least a temporary life. Strikes, whether legal or illegal, were numerous and widespread if not always well organized. There were even significant working-class political movements in this early period, the most important of which was Chartism in Great Britain. Chartism, organized by the London Working Men's Association, arose in the 1830s and 1840s. Chartists agitated for various political and economic reforms and at times

FIGURE 40.4 Gustave Doré, *A London Slum* This woodcut by Doré portrays the squalor of an overcrowded London slum in the early nineteenth century. (Prints Division, New York Public Library, Astor, Lenox, and Tilden Foundations)

seemed to be a powerful, organized, even revolutionary threat in England. Although the movement broke up by midcentury without having achieved its goals, it did reveal some of the potential political strength of an organized working class.

The Family and New Social Institutions

Industrialization had a strong impact on social institutions during the nineteenth century. Some of the most subtle but significant and long-lasting changes took place in the family, particularly the middle-class family.

During the nineteenth century, what many historians and sociologists call the "modern family" predominated in the West, particularly in western Europe and the United States, and above all within the middle classes. Compared with the family of early modern times, this modern family was more tied together by emotional bonds, more child-centered, and more private. Within the middle-class modern family, which increasingly served as an accepted standard for all families, there was a growing division of roles and labor between the sexes. Ideally the middle-class man was authoritative, competent, and controlled. His wife was supposed to be deferential, emotional, and even frail—almost on a pedestal as a showpiece of success and propriety (see p. 524). Men increasingly specialized in the competitive world of work outside the home, while women specialized in domestic management. Proper middle-class women were excluded from almost all paid occupations, with the exception of such jobs as governess or elementary-school teacher, which were directly connected to the domestic role. Home was idealized as a "haven in a heartless world" of ruthless industrial capitalism to which the husband returned after work. The wife was to provide the emotional support for the husband, who supplied the money to support the household. The wife was to make sure the house was clean, the meals were served. In addition to being in charge of any domestic servants (a requirement for any middle-class home), she was supposed to be the all-caring mother. She was likely to have fewer children—two or three rather than five or six of an earlier era. At the same time, those that were born were more likely to survive. Her children were at the center of the family, and their childhood was extended longer than ever before. The middle-class child was not viewed as an economic asset but as a fulfilling "product" of a good home.

Outside the middle class, patterns differed. In aristocratic families, the wider social and political connections remained important and still played a major role in the selection of marriage partners. In peasants' and artisans' families, the household economy was still a reality. In industrial working-class families, women were more likely wage laborers, though for less pay and in lower-status positions than men. Often women were able to find employment when men could find none, which weakened the traditional roles within the family. The stresses on the working-class family were so great that many broke apart, leaving a growing number of women to work and manage a household on their own.

Other social changes exacerbated by industrialization, such as poor housing, lack of public transportation, horrible sanitation, child labor, and periodic unemployment, did not go unnoticed. Many within the wealthier classes remained most comfortable supporting charitable institutions and self-help organizations, which proliferated during the nineteenth century. They tended to view the suffering of the poor as inevitable or as a matter of morals—something the poor brought upon themselves. Others saw the suffering as something caused by society, a social problem. Demands for social reforms by government intervention grew. Many of these demands came not simply from enlightened observers but from fear. Epidemics periodically swept cities. Popular unrest and crime seemed to explode during periods of economic decline. While it was the poor who were usually the victims, these social problems threatened all. In 1833 Britain outlawed the employment of children under nine years of age and restricted the hours of employment of older children. Public health organizations, sanitary codes, and housing regulations spread after the 1830s and 1840s. Governments took on greater responsibility for primary and secondary education. By midcentury, governments in industrializing areas had passed several laws to restrict child labor and control a few of the worst social conditions accompanying indus-

Elizabeth Poole Sandford: Woman in Her Social and Domestic Character

Industrialization had its effects on middle-class women. As the wealth and position of these women rose in a changing economic environment, previous models of behavior no longer applied. A variety of books and manuals appeared to counsel middle-class women on their proper role and behavior. The following is an excerpt from one of these, Woman in Her Social and Domestic Character *(1842), written by Elizabeth Poole Sandford.*

The changes wrought by Time are many. It influences the opinions of men as familiarity does their feelings; it has a tendency to do away with superstition, and to reduce every thing to its real worth.

It is thus that the sentiment for woman has undergone a change. The romantic passion which once almost deified her is on the decline; and it is by intrinsic qualities that she must now inspire respect. She is no longer the queen of song and the star of chivalry. But if there is less of enthusiasm entertained for her, the sentiment is more rational, and, perhaps, equally sincere; for it is in relation to happiness that she is chiefly appreciated.

And in this respect it is, we must confess, that she is most useful and most important. Domestic life is the chief source of her influence; and the greatest debt society can owe to her is domestic comfort: for happiness is almost an element of virtue; and nothing conduces more to improve the character of men than domestic peace. A woman may make a man's home delightful, and may thus increase his motives for virtuous exertion. She may refine and tranquillize his mind,—may turn away his anger or allay his grief. Her smile may be the happy influence to gladden his heart, and to disperse the cloud that gathers on his brow. And in proportion to her endeavors to make those around her happy, she will be esteemed and loved. She will secure by her excellence that interest and regard which she might formerly claim as the privilege of her sex, and will really merit the deference which was then conceded to her as a matter of course. . . .

Perhaps one of the first secrets of her influence is adaptation to the tastes, and sympathy in the feelings, of those around her. This holds true in lesser as well as in graver points. It is in the former, indeed, that the absence of interest in a companion is frequently most disappointing. Where want of congeniality impairs domestic comfort, the fault is generally chargeable on the female side. It is for woman, not for man, to make the sacrifice, especially in indifferent matters. She must, in a certain degree, be plastic herself if she would mould others. . . .

Nothing is so likely to conciliate the affections of the other sex as a feeling that woman looks to them for support and guidance. In proportion as men are themselves superior, they are accessible to this appeal. On the contrary, they never feel interested in one who seems disposed rather to offer than to ask assistance. There is, indeed, something unfeminine in independence. It is contrary to nature, and therefore it offends. We do not like to see a woman affecting tremors, but still less do we like to see her acting the amazon. A really sensible woman feels her dependence. She does what she can; but she is conscious of inferiority, and therefore grateful for support. She knows that she is the weaker vessel, and that as such she should receive honor. In this view, her weakness is an attraction, not a blemish.

In every thing, therefore, that women attempt, they should show their consciousness of dependence. If they are learners, let them evince a teachable spirit; if they give an opinion, let them do it in an unassuming manner. There is something so unpleasant in female self-sufficiency that it not unfrequently deters instead of persuading, and prevents the adoption of advice which the judgment even approves.

SOURCE: Mrs. John Sandford (Elizabeth Poole Sandford), *Woman in Her Social and Domestic Character* (Boston: Otis, Broaders and Co., 1842), pp. 5–7, 15–16.

trialization. But many of these laws were not effectively enforced until the second half of the century. Moreover, it was not until after 1850 that governmental programs such as urban planning, public sanitation (sewers and piped water), and urban transportation (horse-drawn and electric streetcars) had a real impact.

5. NEW ECONOMIC AND SOCIAL THOUGHT

Like the French Revolution, the Industrial Revolution and the social changes related to it were accompanied by new theories and doctrines. The increasingly dominant set of ideas, values, and beliefs—or ideology—was liberalism. Most middle-class liberals applauded both the Industrial and French revolutions while rejecting some of their "excesses" (see Chapter 43). Economic liberalism was more directly related to the economic and social changes accompanying industrialization. Socialism was another newer and more critical line of thought. Like economic liberalism, socialism directly related to industrialization, but not from the perspective of the middle class. Over the course of the nineteenth century, socialist ideology would grow and become the main alternative to economic liberalism.

Economic Liberalism

The growing middle classes, who were prospering from the Industrial Revolution, found intellectual support and justification for their interests in the doctrine of economic liberalism. This doctrine was best stated by the Scottish philosopher Adam Smith in his classic *Wealth of Nations* (1776). The essence of Smith's theory is that economics, like the physical world, has its own natural laws. The most basic of the economic laws is that of supply and demand. When left to operate alone, these laws will keep the economy in balance and, in the long run, work to the benefit of all. If the sanctity of property and contracts is respected, competition and free enterprise will provide incentive and keep prices down. Government regulations and collective bargaining only impede the workings of the natural laws of economics and destroy incentive. Government

should therefore follow a policy of laissez-faire, limiting its activities in the economic field to enforcement of order and contracts, public education and health, national defense, and in rare instances the encouragement of necessary industries that private enterprise does not find profitable. Here was a theory ready-made for the industrial capitalists, who already held all the trump cards.

A strong boost was given to laissez-faire thinking by a young Anglican clergyman, Thomas Malthus, who in 1789 published his *Essay on Population*. Malthus argued that since population increases by a geometric ratio whereas the food supply increases by only an arithmetic ratio, it is a basic natural law that population will outstrip the food supply. This alleged law has two important implications. One is that nothing can be done to improve the lot of the masses. If their condition is temporarily bettered, they will immediately produce children in such numbers that the food supply will be outstripped and starvation will threaten all. Only poverty and privation hold them in check. The second implication is that the rich are not to blame for the misery of the poor; the poor are themselves responsible because of their incontinence. These ideas were so soothing to so many of the book-buying upper classes that Malthus quickly attained fame and wealth.

David Ricardo supplied further support for policies of economic liberalism. Having made a fortune in stock market speculation while still a young man, Ricardo purchased a seat in Parliament and spent the rest of his life thinking and writing on economics. In *The Principles of Political Economy and Taxation* (1817), he propounded the law of rent and the iron law of wages. Rent is determined by the difference in productivity of land. Take off all restrictions and subsidies, and the poorest land will go out of cultivation, reducing the rent on the more productive lands proportionately. He argued for this idea so forcefully that it played an important part in the repeal of England's Corn Laws, which had maintained the price of grain at an artificially high level. Lower grain prices meant lower bread prices, which enabled industrial capitalists to pay lower subsistence wages to their workers. More important in economic thinking was Ricardo's iron law of wages, according to which the natural wage is the subsistence level and the market wage tends to conform to it. Raise the market wage, and workers will multiply so rapidly that soon the law of supply and demand will bring the market wage down below the subsistence level. Then the workers will die off from malnutrition and disease and slow down their reproduction rate. Eventually, they will become so scarce as to be able to bid the market wage up above the natural wage. Always, though, the pull is toward the subsistence level. This theory again was music to the ears of the industrial capitalists.

These economic liberals, being some of the earliest thinkers to analyze the economics of industrial capitalism, are often called the classical economists. Their ideas were popularized in Great Britain and spread to the Continent. There they were modified and expounded by men such as Jean-Baptiste Say and Frédéric Bastiat.

A related stream of economic liberalism was initiated by the British Utilitarian philosopher Jeremy Bentham as early as 1789, in his *Principles of Morals and Legislation*. Bentham was an eighteenth-century materialistic rationalist who lived on until 1832, bridging the eighteenth and nineteenth centuries with his life and thought. The Utilitarians believed that the useful is the good and that the chief purpose of government and society is to achieve "the greatest good to the greatest number." But since every individual is the best judge of his or her own best interests, the surest way to achieve general happiness is allow individuals to follow their own enlightened self-interest. Individualism, then, is the best safeguard of the general welfare. At the same time Bentham himself and several of his followers saw the necessity for the state to act for the common welfare. Utilitarians became active during the middle decades of the nineteenth century in promoting legislation and creating governmental bureaucracies to handle some of the economic abuses and social problems connected with the Industrial Revolution.

Over the nineteenth century, economic liberalism evolved as industrial capitalists proved unwilling to adhere to laissez-faire when it did not suit their interests, as the economic and social inequities of industrialism became too abhorrent to humanitarian sensibilities, and as perceptive criticisms of economic liberalism became persuasive. The most influential thinker to lead in this evolution of economic liberalism was John Stuart Mill (1806–1873). Mill, a child prodigy, was brought up to be a good Benthamite. However, he was too sensitive and humanitarian to remain in the hard materialist camp of the Utilitarians. Moreover, living a generation after Smith, Malthus, Ricardo, and Bentham, he was able to see some of the social effects of the Industrial Revolution. Although Mill in no way rejected private property and free enterprise, he believed that in the industrial age restrictions must be instituted by the state for the protection of the poor. Although production is bound by the laws of supply and demand, the distribution of goods is not. Public utilities such as railroads, gas, and waterworks are natural monopolies and should be owned by the state. The state should provide free compulsory education for all and regulate child labor. He favored income and inheritance taxes as economic equalizers. Mill's chief work on economics, *Principles of Political Economy*, was published in 1848. Mill was also the first influential philosopher in modern times to advocate equal rights for women. His *Subjection of Women*, which appeared in 1869, came to be considered the classic statement on the subject of women's rights. In his later years he considered himself a moderate socialist. More than other nineteenth-century liberals, many of his views fit those of twentieth-century liberalism.

Utopian Socialism

During the first phase of the Industrial Revolution the economies of the industrialized countries belonged to the bourgeoisie in thought as well as in deed. The theories of the economic liberals enjoyed ascendancy. The hard-pressed proletariat, though increasingly disconcerted, did not formulate new economic theories. However, as early as the opening of the nineteenth century, a number of intellectuals from the upper classes began to question the fundamentals of the existing system, such as private property and private enterprise for profit. They stressed the need for economic planning and wanted to base society on cooperation and community rather than competitive individualism. The ideas of these intellectuals were speculative and had limited impact, particularly when compared with those of Marx and other hard-headed socialists of the later nineteenth century. A number of these early, speculative intellectuals came to be called Utopian Socialists.

One of the first Utopian Socialists was the French nobleman Henri de Saint-Simon (1760–1825). He and his followers believed that society should be reorganized on a "Christian" basis, that all should work, and that the inheritance of private property should be abolished. His ideal society would be run according to the formula "from each according to his capacity, to each according to his deserts." Women would be elevated from their unequal social positions. Saint-Simon would reward superior artists, scientists, engineers, and businesspeople according to their merits. But he laid down no plan of action for achieving his ideal society.

Charles Fourier (1772–1837), a Frenchman of middle-class origin, advocated doing away with economic competition, the source of so much evil. In his utopian society, agriculture and industry would be carried on by voluntary cooperatives whose members would pool their resources and live in communal apartment houses. Housework and child care would be a communal responsibility. Women, like men, would have rights to work and to their own money. Distribution of goods and profits would be based on a mathematical formula: workers, five-twelfths; capitalists, four-twelfths; management, three-twelfths. Although Fourier's elaborate plans included many impractical ideas, some of his ideas found their way into practice.

A step forward in socialist thinking was taken by Louis Blanc (1811–1882), another middle-class Frenchman. Louis Blanc wanted to abolish the evils of selfish competitive capitalism by setting up a system of social workshops. The government would lend money to voluntary workers' cooperatives, which would establish and run the workshops. Distribution of the proceeds would be according to the formula "from each according to his ability, to each according to his need," the formula later adopted by Karl Marx.

A different kind of Utopian was Robert Owen (1771–1858). Born in Wales, Owen quickly made an industrial fortune in Manchester and bought large cotton mills in New Lanark, Scotland. Early in the nineteenth century he set out to make New Lanark a model socialist utopia. Wages were raised, hours shortened, working conditions improved, child labor abolished, educational and recreational facilities provided, sickness and old-age insurance established. Owen spent the rest of his life and fortune drawing plans for and setting up model socialist communities. Several were established in America, notably New Harmony, Indiana. All were short-lived; nor was Owen's benevolent example followed by other industrialists.

The Utopian Socialists were all strongly influenced by the materialistic rationalism of the eighteenth-century Enlightenment. They recognized some of the deeper significance of the Industrial Revolution and the alternatives it presented. They attacked the unbridled pursuit of profits in an unregulated economy. They attempted to show how a well-organized community or state could eliminate the misery of industrial capitalism and create a society of happy people. They opposed existing organized religion, although Saint-Simon believed that his ideal society should be dominated by a new social Christianity—a brand of Christianity that had never yet been tried. Most of the Utopian Socialists had little influence on their own times. They did, however, start a trend of economic and social thought that was to become influential. During the second half of the nineteenth century a more virile type of socialism would arise. For the most part, this later socialism would be organized and revolutionary and bear the stamp of Karl Marx.

Marxian Socialism

During the second half of the nineteenth century a stronger type of socialism was formed—a type whose foundations were established in the social and intellectual atmosphere of the 1840s. For the most part, this socialism would be organized and revolutionary and bear the stamp of its founder, Karl Marx (1818–1883).

Marx was born into a German middle-class family. His father was a Jewish lawyer who had converted to Christianity. A brilliant student, Karl Marx attained his doctorate in philosophy and history, but he was denied an academic position because of his radical views. After embarking on a career in journalism, he was exiled from Germany and later from France because of his radical ideas. He spent the last thirty-four years of his life in London working on his ideas and trying to build organizations to put them into action. Marx collaborated with his friend Friedrich Engels, son of a wealthy German manufacturer, in writing *The Communist Manifesto* (1848). This work, along with the later *Das Kapital* (the first volume of which appeared in 1867), contains the fundamentals of Marxism. Marx built his ideology on a basis of German philosophy (Hegelian idealism), French social thought (what he referred to as the Utopian Socialists), and British economics (particularly the economic liberalism of David Ricardo). The most salient points of Marx's ideology are summarized next.

Economic Interpretation of History Although people and history are complex, material economic considerations are most important. Economic interests and motivations underlie the most critical actions of human beings, just as the dominant characteristic of a historical epoch is its prevailing system of economic production. Societies are formed around the means of production, around the principal ways that human beings make a living. The political, religious, and cultural systems that develop must conform to the necessities of the economic and social systems, which form around the economic realities of life.

Class Struggle Societies are broadly divided into the haves and the have-nots. The haves are the owners of the means of economic production; the have-nots are the exploited laborers for these haves. The haves and have-nots are opposing classes with opposing interests. Above all, the haves are interested in maintaining a fundamental status quo, while the have-nots have much to gain from fundamental change. Thus, "the history of all hitherto existing society is the history of class struggle": in ancient times freeman versus slave; in medieval times landlord versus serf; in modern times capitalist versus proletarian. The bourgeoisie (the capitalists), having overcome the aristocracy (the feudal landlords) in a revolutionary struggle (such as the French Revolution), will in time be displaced by the proletariat (the industrial working class) in a new revolutionary struggle.

Surplus Value In the capitalistic industrial economy, the law of surplus value prevails. According to this law, workers, who are paid only subsistence wages, create, by their work, value in excess of their wages. This excess, surplus value, is the illegitimate source of profit for the capitalist.

Inevitable Destruction of Capitalism Capitalists are locked into a competitive struggle with one another. This struggle forces them to continually introduce new, costly machines while keeping wages to a minimum. Larger factories must be built, fewer and fewer capitalists succeed in the competitive struggle, and greater and greater quantities of goods are produced in a system running out of control. Correspondingly, the capitalist system is characterized by alternating periods of prosperity and depression. Under capitalism, then, the law of surplus value plus the increasingly more frequent and deep periods of depression will finally produce such misery that the working class will revolt, seize the means of production from the capitalists, destroy the capitalist system, and ultimately establish a classless socialist society.

Internationalism Workers in all countries have more in common with one another than they have with capitalists of their own country. Therefore workers should unite across national boundaries in their struggle against the common enemy—the capitalist bourgeoisie.

When *The Communist Manifesto* first appeared in 1848, it had little impact on the already developing revolutionary events of that year. It reflected, however, the intellectual and social turmoil being produced by the Industrial Revolution. In the following decades, Marxian socialism would grow to become a major theoretical and ideological force in the West (see Chapter 45).

6. THE ARRIVAL OF INDUSTRIAL SOCIETY

The industrialization of Western societies during the nineteenth century was of tremendous significance. Indeed, industrialization has become a measure of whether a society is considered "modern" or "traditional." Industrialization carried in its wake fundamental changes in literally all aspects of life, from the concrete reality of an individual's everyday life to the arrangement of classes in society. Conflict wrought by these changes was inevitable and widespread, whether in an intellectual realm, at the work site, or on the barricades. Generally, it was the industrial bourgeoisie that emerged victorious in these struggles, establishing its control over the economies and governments of the industrialized countries. It is the story of these struggles, combined with the political changes stemming from the French Revolution, that constitutes much of the meat of nineteenth-century history.

SUGGESTED READING

Economic Aspects

P. Deane, *The First Industrial Revolution* (1975). A balanced brief analysis.

E. L. Jones, *The European Miracle* (1987). Compares economic development in Europe and Asia.

D. S. Landes, *The Unbound Prometheus: Technological Change and Industrial Development in Western Europe from 1750 to the Present* (1969). A thorough, insightful description and analysis of the developing technology of the Industrial Revolution.

P. Mathias, *The First Industrial Nation* (1983). A useful survey of British industrialization.

S. Pollard, *Peaceful Conquest: The Industrialization of Europe* (1981). A general survey with a regional perspective.

Social Changes

R. Bridenthal and C. Koonz, eds., *Becoming Visible: Women in European History* (1976). Contains chapters on the significance of the Industrial Revolution for women.

C. Morazé, *The Triumph of the Middle Classes* (1968). A sympathetic survey.

P. N. Stearns, *European Society in Upheaval* (1967). A general survey of social classes and social history during the nineteenth century.

A. Sutcliffe, *Towards the Planned City: Germany, Britain, the United States and France, 1780–1914* (1981). Covers urbanization well.

P. Taylor, ed., *The Industrial Revolution: Triumph or Disaster?* (1970). Samples a variety of views on the benefits and burdens of industrialization.

E. P. Thompson, *The Making of the English Working Class* (1963). Challenging interpretation stressing the culture and activities of the working class.

L. Tilly and J. Scott, *Women, Work and Family* (1978). A highly respected work.

E. A. Wrigley, *Population and History* (1969). Introduction to demographic changes during the Industrial Revolution.

Economic and Social Thought

R. Heilbroner, *The Worldly Philosophers* (1972). A well-written history of economists and their ideas.

A. S. Lindemann, *A History of European Socialism* (1984). A good modern treatment.

F. Manuel, *The Prophets of Paris* (1962). A study of the French Utopian Socialists.

D. McLellan, *Karl Marx: His Life and Thought* (1977). An excellent biography and introduction.

CHAPTER 41
Romanticism in Philosophy, Literature, and the Arts

FIGURE 41.1 **Karl Friedrich Schinkel,** *Medieval Town on a River,* **1815** This painting by the German romantic artist Schinkel contains many of the key elements of romanticism: glorification of nature, religious mysticism, adoration of the medieval, and concern with the emotional. With these characteristics, romanticism stood in contrast to many of the industrial, secular, and rationalistic trends of the period. (Neue Pinakothek, Munich)

Thought and art generally reflect the societies in which they arise—sometimes in support of the dominant historical trends of an era, sometimes in reaction to those trends. In the final decades of the eighteenth century, romanticism began to replace classicism as the prevailing cultural style in the West. During the first half of the nineteenth century romanticism became the dominant spirit in thought and art. It had competitors and would decline in the second half of the nineteenth century, but it remains popular to this day. What was romanticism, and how was it connected to the societies in which it flourished?

1. THE NATURE OF ROMANTICISM

The romantic spirit had many facets, but essentially it was a reaction against the rationalism and formalism of the classic spirit that had been so powerful in the eighteenth century. Whereas classicism extolled reason and perfection of form, romanticism appealed to the emotions, to feeling, and to freedom and spontaneity of expression. Whereas the classicist was interested in the natural order and the laws of human beings and the universe, the romanticist loved to sing of woods and lakes and lovers' lanes and to dream of faraway or imaginary times and places.

Romanticism was associated with and was in part a product of the French Revolution and Napoleon. Many classicists had been interested in peacefully reforming society in accordance with the natural law. They did not anticipate the violent upheaval that came, although many of the radical revolutionary leaders and Napoleon believed themselves to be in the tradition of classical Greece and Rome. It was the romanticists, breaking sharply with past forms and traditions and with bold abandon trying the new, who reflected the revolutionary spirit. This does not mean that all romanticists were political radicals or even liberals. Some, like Shelley and Heine, were. Others, like Edmund Burke and Sir Walter Scott, were conservatives representing a reaction against the excesses of the Revolution.

Nationalism was another facet of romanticism. Whether liberal or conservative, the romanticist was likely to be an ardent nationalist. The romantic poet Lord Byron lost his life fighting for Greek national independence against the Turks. The dreamer and orator Giuseppe Mazzini was called the soul of Italian nationalism. He spent most of his adult life in exile because of his labors for a free and united Italy. Johann Gottfried von Herder, as early as the eighteenth century, had pleaded eloquently for a German national culture. The fraternity and freedom so common to the national movements before 1850, no less than pride in real or imagined national achievements, gave outlet to the emotions of the romanticist.

Romanticism also represented a reaction against the rationalistic deism of the eighteenth century and a return to mystic religion. In literature and art, romantics stressed the emotion of Christianity and the presence of God in nature. Romantic theologians such as Friedrich Schleiermacher (1768–1834) emphasized that the important part of religion was emotional—the feeling of dependence on an infinite God—not religious dogma or institutions. The revival of religion as part of the romanticism of the early nineteenth century brought about a renewed interest in the Middle Ages. The classicists had drawn their inspiration from pagan Greece and Rome. Now in the early nineteenth century the Knights of the Round Table and Siegfried and Brunhild came back into style once more. No more perfect example of the romantic spirit can be cited than the novels and verse of Sir Walter Scott, whose subject matter was primarily medieval. Gothic architecture enjoyed a revival. The "Dark Ages" were transformed into the "Age of Faith."

Finally, the interest in the Middle Ages and in nationalism reflected another aspect of romanticism: its passionate concern with history. History, written by people such as Thomas B. Macaulay (1800–1859) in Great Britain and Jules Michelet (1798–1874) in France, was literary, exciting, and dramatic—a story of heroic individuals, national struggles, and great accomplishments. It became a subject of great interest among scholars as well as the reading public.

2. THE PHILOSOPHY OF IDEALISM

Any discussion of romantic thought should begin with Jean-Jacques Rousseau (1712–1778), even though this French genius lived during the heyday of rationalistic classicism and before romanticism came into full flower. Rousseau, like most of his fellow philosophers of the Enlightenment such as Voltaire, Diderot, and Montesquieu, was a deist, believing in the mechanical universe of natural laws. However, he differed sharply with them over the place of reason. Far from believing that a person can know only what is perceived through the five senses and interpreted by reason, Rousseau stressed feeling, instinct, and emotions. He also anticipated the romantic movement in his inordinate love of nature. He would stretch himself out on the ground, dig his fingers and toes into the dirt, kiss the earth, and weep for joy. This emotional genius was a true romanticist in his revolt against the rules of formal society. Free love, undisciplined childhood and education, the noble savage—all were features of Rousseau's revolt. His influence on later generations was enormous.

It seems a far cry from the rough genius of Rousseau to the exquisitely ordered thought of Immanuel Kant (1724–1804), but the German philosopher was admittedly indebted to Rousseau. Kant, who was partly of Scottish ancestry, was a native of Königsberg in East Prussia. A frail and insignificant-looking man who never traveled more than fifty miles from the place of his birth, he slowly developed into one of the most powerful and influential thinkers of modern times. He was often in difficulty with the Prussian government because of his liberal and unorthodox views. Kant started out as a scientist and always respected the methods of natural science. He was also steeped in the philosophy of the Enlightenment. However, he was not satisfied with the conclusions of the eighteenth-century materialistic rationalists, and eventually he thought on beyond them. Kant came to believe that there are in reality not one but two worlds— the physical realm and the spiritual realm, or the realm of ultimate reality. The first he called the realm of phenomena; the second the realm of noumena. In the physical realm of phenomena the approach to truth of Descartes, Locke, and Voltaire—sense perception and reason—suffices. But in the spiritual realm of noumena, these methods fail. Ultimate spiritual truth may be attained only by faith, conviction, and feeling. Truths in the realm of the noumena, such as the existence of God, the immortality of the soul, or the existence of good and evil, cannot be proved by reason. And yet we are justified in believing them because they reinforce our moral sense of right and wrong. His principal work, *Critique of Pure Reason,* was a metaphysical answer of the highest intellectual order to the philosophers of the Enlightenment. These ideas came to be called the philosophy of idealism. Kant and his early-nineteenth-century followers represented a sharp reversal in the philosophical trend toward rationalism and materialism, which in a sense began in the thirteenth century with the efforts of Albertus Magnus and Thomas Aquinas to rationalize Christian doctrines.

The most influential of Kant's disciples was Georg Wilhelm Hegel (1770–1831). Hegel's chief interest was the philosophy of history. Like his master, he rejected the mechanistic amoral universe of the Enlightenment. He believed, rather, that a benevolent but impersonal God created and runs the universe, making human society better by a process of purposeful evolution. This evolution is achieved by a dialectical system of thesis, antithesis, and synthesis. Any given system or civilization (thesis) is challenged by its opposite (antithesis). From the struggle emerges a new system containing the best elements of both (synthesis). This synthesis then becomes a new thesis, which when it has served its purpose is challenged by a new antithesis, and so on. Hegel believed that every historical epoch is dominated by a *zeitgeist* (spirit of the time). The zeitgeist of the nineteenth century was German civilization, whose greatest contribution was freedom through disciplined order. Hegel exalted the state. Only in and through the state, he felt, can the individual find meaning and be free. Hegel's influence on romanticism and on the early nineteenth century in general was substantial.

3. ROMANTIC LITERATURE

The spirit of romanticism can be made to come alive in no better way than by a study of the British romantic poets. A number of British writers began to break with classicism during the course of the eighteenth century. The best-known and probably most representative of these writers was Robert Burns (1759–1796). Born in a humble clay cottage, the Scottish poet lived an undisciplined life as if he had been reared in accordance with Rousseau's *Émile*. Burns idealized nature and the rustic rural life with which he was intimately acquainted. In spontaneous verse written in his native Scottish dialect, he wrote an ode to a field mouse, "Wee, sleekit, cow'rin', tim'rous beastie," which he had turned up with his plow. In "The Cotter's Saturday Night" we are given a charming and sympathetic picture of village life among the poor of Scotland. "Auld Lang Syne" is sung with nostalgia every New Year's Eve by millions throughout the English-speaking world. "John Anderson, My Jo," a touching tribute to love in old age, could never have been written by Racine or Alexander Pope.

The romantic spirit, early reflected in the poetry of Robert Burns, reached maturity with William Wordsworth (1770–1850) and Samuel Taylor Coleridge (1772–1834). The two were warm friends. Both were closely associated with the beautiful lake country of northwest England, Wordsworth by birth and Coleridge by adoption. Together they took a trip to Germany, where they fell under the influence of Kant. Both, as young men, were ardent social reformers. The two collaborated on *Lyrical Ballads*, which appeared in 1798. *Lyrical Ballads* contains some of the best work of these gifted poets, such as Wordsworth's "Lines Composed a Few Miles above Tintern Abbey" (see Figure 41.2) and Coleridge's "Rime of the Ancient Mariner." Both men were masters of versification and poetic expression. They were also lovers and students of nature, and both of them, particularly Wordsworth, sensed a brooding, mystical presence of the divine. Wordsworth's "Intimations of Immortality" is sublime in its spiritual depth and insight. In their ardent love of nature, their introspective concern for the individual, their preoccupation with the spiritual rather than the material, and their greater attention to substance than to form, Wordsworth and Coleridge broke distinctly with the spirit of classicism.

Once the vogue of romanticism was dignified and popularized in Great Britain by Wordsworth and Coleridge, a host of romantic writers appeared. A younger trio of poetic geniuses of the highest order, Lord Byron, Percy Bysshe Shelley, and John Keats (all of whom lived briefly and died between the years 1788 and 1824), are well

FIGURE 41.2 J. M. W. Turner, *Tintern Abbey* Tintern Abbey, a twelfth-century Gothic ruin in Wales, was the object of both literary and artistic romanticism. Here Turner, the leading English romantic artist, evokes the power of nature, religion, and the medieval past. (The British Museum)

known and loved. All three gave spontaneous and unrestrained vent to their emotions. Byron and Shelley combined an exquisite esthetic sense with irrepressible revolutionary zeal, defying the forms and customs of society. Keats was a gentler soul, who after a lifelong quest for the beautiful died at the age of twenty-five.

Meanwhile, Sir Walter Scott in novel and verse was devoting his longer life (1771–1832) to glorifying the Middle Ages and his native Scotland. Scott, unlike Byron and Shelley but like Wordsworth and Coleridge in their mature and mellow later years, was conservative in his attitude toward public affairs.

On the other side of the Atlantic, Henry

Wadsworth Longfellow, James Fenimore Cooper, and Washington Irving were founding an American national literature. In their subject matter, their style, and their attitudes, they reflected the European romantic spirit. Many other American writers in the early nineteenth century also wrote in the romantic vein. Ralph Waldo Emerson (1803–1882) was considered a religious radical and skeptic in his day. He gave up his Puritan (by then Unitarian) pastorate at Boston's Old North Church because of his heterodoxy. However, in his essays and poems it was the romantic philosophy of Kantian idealism, not the rationalism of the Enlightenment, that he introduced into America. Edgar Allan Poe (1809–1849), short story writer, literary critic, and romantic poet of a high order, was in a sense an American Shelley, though less ethereal and more morbid. Henry David Thoreau (1817–1862) took Rousseau's back-to-nature idea more seriously than did its author. Rousseau, for all his passion for nature, would never have withdrawn from society for two years to live by Walden Pond in introspective solitude. Emerson, Poe, and Thoreau were all individualists to the point of being mild social revolutionaries. Thoreau preached civil disobedience and allowed himself to be put in jail rather than pay taxes for what he considered to be unworthy causes. The sensitive Poe, enduring oblivion and poverty, turned to drink and an early grave. Emerson weathered a storm of hostility from organized religion and society for his nonconformist views.

Romanticism came to German literature in the latter half of the eighteenth century, partly under the influence of the early British romanticists and partly as a result of the conscious effort of the Germans, led by Herder, to free themselves from bondage to French classical culture. Foremost among all German writers is Johann Wolfgang von Goethe (1749–1832). Like Shakespeare, Leonardo da Vinci, and Beethoven, Goethe is a genius of such proportions that he cannot be confined to any single cultural school or movement. However, insofar as it is possible to classify him, he belongs more nearly to the romantic tradition than to any other, both in time and in spirit. His prodigious energies were devoted essentially to a lifelong (eighty-three years) search for the secrets of happiness and wisdom. His encyclopedic mind delved fruitfully into literature, philosophy, science, and public affairs. His novels, lyrics, essays, scientific and philosophical treatises, and dramas fill 132 volumes. No writer except Shakespeare has had so many of his lyrics set to music. Goethe's masterpiece is *Faust*, a philosophical drama written in exquisite verse. It is about a medieval scholar who, dissatisfied with the fruits of knowledge, sells his soul to the Devil in return for earthly pleasure and wisdom. Goethe explores the depths of human experience and aspiration. *Faust* was sixty years in the making. In his medieval interests, his fresh, emotional spontaneity, his love of nature and of individual personality, and his courageous, robust, pioneering spirit, Goethe was a romanticist.

Goethe's friend and protégé, Friedrich Schiller (1759–1805), was more popular in his own day than the master himself. Schiller drew heavily on the Middle Ages and on nationalism (at a time when national aspirations were associated with freedom) for his dramas, histories, and lyrics. *William Tell,* a drama based upon the Swiss struggle for freedom from Hapsburg tyranny, is probably Schiller's best-known work. Neither Goethe nor Schiller can be considered a German nationalist in the narrow sense; both were universal in their interests and their appeal.

Heinrich Heine (1797–1856) was considered to be Goethe's successor as a writer of German lyrics, though not of Goethe's stature. Most of Heine's voluminous writing was in the field of romantic lyrical poetry. One of his most representative works was an ode to the Silesian weavers who rose up against the hardships caused by the Industrial Revolution, which was just coming to Germany, and were shot down by Prussian troops. Because of the hostility of the various German governments in the age of Metternich to his radical political ideas, Heine exiled himself from Germany. The last twenty-five years of his life were spent in Paris. Many of his later lyrics show a touch of the light gaiety of the French.

Literary romanticism flowered later in France than England or Germany. François-René de Chateaubriand (1768–1848), a disillusioned nobleman who began writing during the reign of Napoleon I, was one of the first French writers of influence to react against the rationalism of the Enlightenment. His *Genius of Christianity* is a return to mystic religion. He also dreamed and wrote of glorified Indians in faraway tropical

America. At almost the same time, Madame de Staël (1766–1817) analyzed and helped popularize romanticism. Alexander Dumas the elder (1802–1870) continues to delight young and old alike with his romantic and melodramatic *Three Musketeers* and *Count of Monte Cristo*, painting the haunting afterglow of medieval chivalry. George Sand (1804–1876), an unconventional woman and gifted author, wrote numerous popular novels filled with romantic passion and idealism. Victor Hugo (1802–1885) in his long and tumultuous life wrote a vast quantity of exquisite lyrics, dramas, essays, and fiction in the romantic tradition. His *Hunchback of Notre Dame* is medieval in setting. In *Les Misérables* he immortalizes and idealizes the masses of underprivileged humanity, preaching redemption and purification not by planned social reform but through suffering. Jules Michelet crossed historical and literary lines in his seventeen-volume *History of France*. He tells the thrilling story of France's long and glorious achievements, usually with skillful historical craftsmanship and always with matchless grace.

The first great figure in Russian literature was the romantic poet Alexander Pushkin (1799–1837). The chief inspiration for his great lyrics, dramas, histories, novels, essays, and tales came from French and British writers, particularly Byron. Because of his revolutionary radicalism (of the French variety), he was for a while exiled to southern Russia by the Russian government. Later he became a Russian nationalist and took many of his themes from Russian history. His tragic drama *Boris Godunov* (patterned after Shakespeare) is considered to be his masterpiece.

4. THE ROMANTIC SPIRIT IN THE ARTS

Words fail to convey the messages and meanings expressed in the visual and musical arts. This is particularly true of art, whose appeal is primarily to the emotions.

The leading painters glorified nature, religion, and nationalism (see Figure 41.1). John Constable (1776–1837) in Great Britain, Camille Corot (1796–1875) in France, and George Inness the elder (1825–1894) in the United States painted landscapes fit to have illustrated the moods of Wordsworth or Thoreau (see Color Plate 19 and Figure 41.2). Their idealizations of nature and the rural life would have delighted Rousseau and Burns. J. M. W. Turner (1775–1851) in England caught the romantic mood in his eerie, misty impressions of seascapes and mythological subjects (see Color Plate 20). Jean-François Millet (1814–1875) idealized both the French rural life (*The Sower* and *The Gleaners*) and mystic religion (*The Angelus*) (see Figure 41.3). His compatriot Eugène Delacroix (1798–1863) depicted on canvas Byron's *Prisoner of Chillon*. On great murals in the Louvre, the library of the Chamber of Deputies, and the Hôtel de Ville he portrayed glorious scenes from history (see Color Plate 21).

In the field of architecture the romantic movement was less pronounced. Its chief manifestation was a revived interest in the Gothic style. The French, after several centuries of apathy about if not scorn for anything associated with medievalism, suddenly showed a renewed interest in their magnificent Gothic monuments. The Houses of Parliament, constructed in London in the early nineteenth century when England was rapidly becoming industrialized, were built in the Gothic style.

The romantic spirit was caught and expressed by a host of great musicians. They went beyond the controlled classical music, trying to translate emotions into sound. First and foremost was Beethoven (1770–1827), who was not only one of the greatest of classic composers but also the first of the romanticists. His earlier work was in the spirit of his idol, Mozart. In maturity his originality overflowed the bounds of classic forms, becoming freer, more individualistic, and emotional. Beethoven lived through the upheavals of the French Revolution and Napoleon, and his keen interest in these dramatic events is reflected in his music. His Symphony no. 3 (*Eroica*) was dedicated to Napoleon, whom Beethoven at first regarded as the embodiment of the democratic ideals of the French Revolution. His Fifth and Seventh symphonies were inspired by the German nationalistic upsurge, which helped to overthrow Napoleon. Carl Maria von Weber (1786–1826), Franz Schubert (1797–1828), Felix Mendelssohn (1809–1847), and Robert Schumann (1810–1856) carried on in the spirit of the great Beethoven.

These gifted and youthful Germans ex-

FIGURE 41.3 Jean-François Millet, *The Angelus* The spirit of romanticism that dominated art during the first half of the nineteenth century was marked by a religious revival and by an admiration for the simple, rural life, which Millet effectively captures in painting. (Giraudon)

pressed in their melodic music the same spontaneous and emotional spirit that their contemporaries Byron, Shelley, and Keats were expressing in English verse. A German by adoption was the colorful Hungarian-born Franz Liszt (1811–1886) (see Figure 41.4). Liszt is believed to be the greatest concert pianist of his time. His glamorous personality and sensational, emotional compositions greatly popularized romantic music. Although Liszt was an international

figure, his Hungarian folk music was characteristic of the growing national sentiment of the time. He befriended the youthful Richard Wagner, who later married one of Liszt's illegitimate daughters.

The romantic spirit is nowhere better illustrated than in the work of the Polish-French pianist-composer Frédéric Chopin (1810–1849). Chopin could express his sweet sorrows in lilting nocturnes, his sunny gaiety in bright waltzes and

FIGURE 41.4 Josef Danhauser, *Liszt at the Piano*, 1840 This romantic painting brings together key figures of romanticism. At the center, Franz Liszt plays the piano for his friends. Standing, from left to right, are Victor Hugo, Niccolò Paganini, and Gioacchino Rossini. Sitting are Alexandre Dumas, George Sand (in men's clothes), and Marie d'Agoult. Above them is a portrait of Lord Byron and a bust of Ludwig van Beethoven. (Bildarchiv Preussischer Kulturbesitz, Berlin)

mazurkas, his national patriotism in stirring polonaises, or his deeper, dramatic moods in more formal ballades and concertos—all with equal skill and all in the romantic tradition. Meanwhile, other notable Frenchmen were writing romantic symphonies and operas. Charles-François Gounod's *Faust* is an operatic version of Goethe's great theme. The haunting melodies of Georges Bizet's (1838–1875) *Carmen* are widely known and sung. The greatest Italian romantic composer was Giuseppe Verdi (1813–1901). His operas *Aïda*, *La Traviata*, *Il Trovatore*, and *Rigoletto* are still sung every season in opera houses all over the world. Verdi was Italy's national cultural hero during the long, uphill fight for freedom and unity.

Richard Wagner (1813–1883) brought the romantic era in music to a dramatic climax. Wagner's tempestuous life, like his music, illustrates and marks the transition from the romantic, moderately liberal and nationalistic early nineteenth century to the more violent and restless spirit of the late nineteenth and early twentieth centuries. In his youth Wagner was a radical and

was exiled from Saxony in 1849 for his revolutionary activities. Later he became an extreme German nationalist—even a German "master racist" of the type that has brought so much violence to the twentieth-century world. His operas, though containing some of the world's greatest music, are also grandiloquent and often stridently nationalistic. *Tannhäuser*, *The Meistersingers*, *Siegfried*, *Götterdämmerung*, *Lohengrin*, and *Das Rheingold* are an important part of the opera repertory today.

Romanticism in the arts, as in literature and philosophy, reflected a new recognition that human beings are complex, emotional, and only sometimes rational creatures. In a civilization that was becoming more scientific, materialistic, industrial, and urban, romanticism was a counterweight for the human experience. Although new cultural trends such as realism would appear during the middle of the nineteenth century (see Color Plate 22), romanticism would remain a strong current in Western civilization well into the twentieth century.

SUGGESTED READING

General

K. Clark, *The Romantic Rebellion* (1973). Clearly written and useful.

M. LeBris, *Romantics and Romanticism* (1981). A well-illustrated survey of romanticism in its political context.

S. Prawer, ed., *The Romantic Period in Germany* (1970). A good collection of essays.

H. B. Schenk, *The Mind of the European Romantics* (1966). A solid survey.

J. L. Talmon, *Romanticism and Revolt: Europe, 1815–1848* (1967). A survey of romanticism in its broad historical context.

The Philosophy of Idealism

E. Cassirer, *Kant's Life and Thought* (1981). Excellent, though difficult.

R. Stromberg, *European Intellectual History since 1789* (1975). Surveys the topic well.

C. Taylor, *Hegel* (1975). Excellent introduction.

Romantic Literature

M. H. Abrams, *Natural Supernaturalism: Tradition and Revolution in Romantic Literature* (1971). A good survey of romantic literature.

J. S. Allen, *Popular French Romanticism* (1981). Relates literary romanticism and popular culture.

J. Wordsworth, *William Wordsworth and the Age of English Romanticism* (1987). Covers English romanticism well.

Romanticism in the Arts

A. Hauser, *Social History of Art* (1958). Relates artistic trends to social developments.

H. W. Janson, *History of Art* (1977). The standard survey with a section on romanticism.

CHAPTER 42

Conservatism, Restoration, and Reaction, 1815–1830

FIGURE 42.1 George Cruikshank, *The Peterloo Massacre,* 1819 This painting by Cruikshank depicts the troops of the conservative British government breaking up a rally for liberal political reform, including demands for universal suffrage and religious freedoms. During the restoration, many European governments attempted to repress liberal movements. (The Mansell Collection)

The overthrow of Napoleon in 1815 brought to an end, in Europe at least, the heroic and tumultuous epoch that had begun in 1789 with the meeting of the Estates General. The intervening twenty-six years had been filled with great expectation, experimentation, turmoil, and war. Now there were disillusionment and weariness. The European royalty and aristocracy, at long last triumphant over revolutionary France, were determined to put an end not only to the Mirabeaus, Robespierres, and Napoleons but also to the ideas of the Enlightenment.

The returning holders of power—the monarchs, the aristocrats, the established Christian churches, and the elite of the governmental and military bureaucracies—generally subscribed to a conservatism that was dominant between 1815 and 1830 and that would remain a powerful force throughout the nineteenth century. Conservatives tended to believe that a hierarchical Christian society authoritatively guided by traditional monarchs, aristocrats, and clergy was time tested and best. Edmund Burke (1729–1797), Great Britain's most influential conservative thinker, and conservatives in general rejected the abstract rationalism of the Enlightenment and the reforms of the French Revolution. Any rapid change was suspect, and the attempt by the middle class to grasp political power had been a presumptuous act by individuals who simply did not know how to rule. For conservatives the experience of the French Revolution was a lesson in what to avoid.

In order to achieve their conservative goals, to redraw territorial boundaries, and to establish lasting stability in Europe, the leaders of the victorious powers gathered at the Austrian capital of Vienna in the autumn of 1814. To this conference also flocked representatives of every state in Europe, hundreds of dispossessed princes, agents of every conceivable interest, and adventurers.

1. THE CONGRESS OF VIENNA, 1814–1815

The Congress of Vienna was dominated by the four major victors over Napoleon (see Figure 42.2). Great Britain was represented by her able foreign minister, Lord Castlereagh. Prussia's mediocre king, Frederick William III, headed his own delegation, as did Russia's tsar, the idealistic young Alexander I. Austria's emperor, Francis I, played host to the assembled great. However, the real leader of the Austrian delegation—and, indeed, the dominant figure of the whole congress—was the Austrian chancellor, Prince Klemens von Metternich. As guiding principles on which to base their decisions, the conferees decided on "legitimacy" and "stability." By *legitimacy* they meant that in the redistribution of various territories, attention would be paid not to the desires or interests of the people concerned but to the claims of the victorious—the former and future sovereigns. By *stability* they meant establishing and maintaining a balance of power within Europe, with particular focus on restraining France. Many of the decisions formalized at Vienna had already been made by the four major powers shortly before and after Napoleon's overthrow in April 1814 (see Map 42.1).

Thanks in no small measure to the presence of the clever and able Talleyrand, France, the cause of all the turmoil, got off lightly. Prussia would have severely punished and weakened France, but her three major colleagues were fearful of upsetting the balance of power. Already saddled with the restored Bourbons, France was merely reduced to almost the same boundaries it had had before the wars of the revolutionary era. The Congress of Vienna had originally imposed no indemnity on France. But because of Napoleon's return from Elba in the midst of the congress and his hundred-day fling that ended at Waterloo, the four great powers compelled France to cede the Saar Basin to Prussia, to pay an indemnity of 700 million francs, and to return the art treasures stolen by Napoleon from the various galleries of Europe. Allied forces were to occupy France until the indemnity was paid. To contain France within its frontiers and to discourage future French aggression, Prussia was given a sizable block of territory along the Rhine, the Austrian Netherlands (Belgium) was annexed to the Dutch Netherlands, and Piedmont was enlarged by the annexation of the city-state of Genoa.

The main powers, taking advantage of political changes that had occurred over the previous twenty-six years and trading among themselves, received new territories. Great Britain gained several strategic islands and colonies, increasing

FIGURE 42.2 Jean-Baptiste Isabey, *Congress of Vienna* The principal figures of the Congress of Vienna are portrayed by Isabey. From left to right: Metternich is standing before a chair, Castlereagh is sitting with crossed legs, and Talleyrand is sitting with his right arm on the table. (Culver Pictures)

her sea power and overseas dominance. Prussia added some areas in central Europe that made it more homogeneously German and Western. However, the Rhineland territory was not contiguous to the Prussian homeland—a situation that invited further aggression. Russia's acquisition of Polish territory made the great majority of the Polish-speaking people subjects of Russia and brought Russia farther into the heart of central Europe. Austria, in exchange for the Belgian Netherlands, took the two rich Italian provinces of Lombardy and Venetia. Its preeminence in Italy, together with its presidency over the German Confederation, made Austria the dominant power in central Europe. The Holy Roman Empire, which Napoleon had destroyed, was not restored, but in its place was erected the weak German Confederation under the permanent presidency of Austria. Napoleon's consolidation of the more than three hundred German states into thirty-nine was allowed to stand, bringing

the German people that much more political unity.

The Congress of Vienna has been both admired and criticized by observers ever since 1815. Critics point out that the peoples and territories of Europe were moved about by the great powers at Vienna like pawns on a chessboard, in complete disregard for the wishes of the people or for the spirit of nationalism that was now an increasingly virile force. Instead of trying to deal constructively with the budding forces of liberalism and nationalism, the great powers tried to ignore or repress them. Admirers point out that the Vienna settlement was not vindictive toward France and did establish a reasonable balance of power, both of which contributed to a century of freedom from Europe-wide war. While one may not agree with the conservative goals of the conferees, a settlement was achieved at Vienna and at least temporarily maintained in succeeding years.

Map 42.1 EUROPE, 1815 As this map indicates, the settlement at the Congress of Vienna left France with its lands little changed from 1789, but now France was bordered by strengthened states: the Kingdom of the Netherlands, Prussia, and the Kingdom of Sardinia. The victorious powers gained territories, but a balance of power was maintained.

2. THE CONCERT OF EUROPE

Metternich and his colleagues, pleased with their work, set up machinery for perpetuating it. Conveniently at hand was the Holy Alliance, conceived by Alexander to establish and safeguard the principles of the Christian religion. Russia (Orthodox), Austria (Roman Catholic), and Prussia (Protestant), the three bastions of conservatism, were to form the nucleus of the alliance. All the Christian states of Europe were invited to join, and only Great Britain and the Papal States did not. Metternich considered the Holy Alliance a "sonorous nothing" but saw in it an opportunity for influencing the tsar. Intended by Alexander I as a bulwark of Christianity, the Holy Alliance became a symbol of reaction and repression.

Much more earthly an agency for perpetuating the Vienna settlements was the Quadruple Alliance. This was a military alliance of Austria, Russia, Prussia, and Great Britain created in November 1815 for the purpose of guaranteeing for twenty years the territorial boundaries established by the Vienna settlement. Metternich was determined to make of the alliance an international military police force that would suppress any liberal or national movements. It was arranged that the four member powers should hold periodic congresses to carry out the purposes of the alliance.

The first congress was held at Aix-la-Chapelle in northwest Germany in 1818. The purpose was to arrange the withdrawal of occupying forces from French soil. Since France had demonstrated good behavior under the restored Bourbon king, Louis XVIII, it was not only freed of occupying forces but was admitted to the Quadruple Alliance. Congresses at Troppau in 1820 and at Laibach in 1821, both on Austrian soil, concerned themselves with an insurrection that had broken out in Naples against the tyrannical Bourbon king, Ferdinand I. An Austrian army was authorized to put down the insurrection and reestablish the hated Ferdinand I on his throne. The Neapolitan liberal volunteers, no match for the Austrian regulars, were soon defeated and their leaders executed, imprisoned, or exiled. What turned out to be the last of the congresses met in 1822 at Verona to deal with a liberal revolt in Spain against the reactionary Ferdinand VII. With the sanction of the Congress of Verona a French army crossed the Pyrenees and easily put down the rebellion.

The first of the alliance powers to repudiate the Metternich system was Great Britain. At the Troppau congress, the British clearly indicated their opposition to interfering in the internal affairs of other states. When the Verona congress decided, over British protest, on intervention in Spain, Britain's representative withdrew.

The Metternich system soon received further blows, some from unexpected quarters. At the Congress of Verona, the like-minded Austrians,

Russians, and Prussians had been alarmed not only by the rebellion in the Spanish homeland but also by the revolt of Spain's New World colonies. When the corrupt government of Ferdinand VII proved incapable of putting down the revolt, Alexander I, with Metternich's blessing, proposed to send a Russian fleet to help coerce the colonies. Great Britain, enjoying a lucrative trade with the rebellious colonies, did not wish to see them restored to Spanish dominion and commercial monopoly. The British minister, George Canning, who had succeeded Castlereagh in 1822, proposed to the government of the United States that Great Britain and the United States issue a joint statement against interference by the "Holy Alliance" in the affairs of the Western Hemisphere. However, Secretary of State John Quincy Adams foresaw that the time might come when the United States would wish to invoke such a policy alone, perhaps even against Great Britain. In 1823, President Monroe announced what has come to be called the Monroe Doctrine: The United States would regard any interference on the part of European powers in the affairs of the Western Hemisphere as an "unfriendly act." The United States was at the time, of course, a new and relatively weak nation, but Canning's immediate support of the American policy killed any further thought of "Holy Alliance" intervention in the New World, for Great Britain had unchallenged dominance of the seas. The Monroe Doctrine marked the beginning of active participation by the United States in affairs beyond its own immediate shores.

The next blow to Metternich's concert of Europe came when the Greeks turned against their Moslem Turkish overlords in the revolt of 1821–1829. The valiant efforts of the Greeks were not sufficient, however, to resist the power of the Ottoman Empire. By 1827 they were on the point of being hopelessly crushed. However, the sympathies of the great powers were being aroused for the courageous Greeks. Russia, Great Britain, and France in particular displayed a growing concern over the events in Greece. Russia's Orthodox Christian religion was the same as that of the Greeks. Furthermore, the Russians had long desired Constantinople, which controlled Russia's natural strategic and commercial outlet to the Mediterranean. Great Britain was concerned over the possibility of Russia's dominance in the Near East. In addition, the ruling classes in Great Britain and France were steeped in the classical culture of ancient Greece. Lord Byron, the most popular literary figure in Europe, lost his life fighting as a volunteer for Greece. In 1827 these three powers, over Metternich's protest, intervened in the Greek revolt and defeated the Turks on land and sea. The Treaty of Adrianople in 1829 granted independence to most of the Greeks on the home peninsula and local autonomy to the Serbs and Rumanians. The successful revolt of the Greeks was a victory for the resurging revolutionary principles of liberalism and nationalism. The intervention of Russia, Great Britain, and France further weakened the already battered Concert of Europe.

3. THE BOURBON RESTORATION IN FRANCE

When the victorious armies of the coalition powers entered France and deposed Napoleon in the spring of 1814, they brought "in their baggage" the members of the Bourbon royal family who had fled the Revolution. In their wake trooped the émigré nobility. A younger brother of the guillotined Louis XVI was placed on the throne as Louis XVIII. (The son of Louis XVI, who had died in prison in 1795, without having ruled, was considered to be Louis XVII.) The "restored" Bourbon king was now fifty-nine and too fat and gouty to walk unassisted. He had traveled much and unwillingly during the long, lean years of his exile. When Napoleon returned from Elba in 1815, Louis XVIII had to flee once more. After Waterloo he returned to his throne, which he considered "the most comfortable of armchairs," determined to do nothing that might force him to leave it again.

Upon assuming the throne, Louis XVIII issued a charter, or constitution, that retained Napoleon's administrative and legal system and civil and religious liberty. Lawmaking was placed into the hands of a two-chamber legislature. The upper house was made an aristocratic stronghold, and the lower house was elected by a highly restricted electorate. Only those who paid direct annual taxes of three hundred francs could vote; this limited the suffrage to about one hundred thousand out of a total population of nearly 30 million. The lower house could be dis-

solved by the king. Since the king also appointed and controlled his own ministers and the host of civilian and military officials, carried on foreign relations, controlled the military forces, and enforced the laws, his power was only somewhat limited by the charter.

Louis XVIII set out to use his powers with moderation so that tranquillity might be restored. There was no wholesale punishment of revolutionary leaders. The peasant and bourgeois purchasers of church and noble lands were not dispossessed. However, most of the returned émigrés—largely from the highest ranks of the clergy and the nobility—were of a different spirit. They came back from their unhappy exile angry and vengeful, demanding their old privileges and indemnification for their lands. Their leader was the king's younger brother, the Comte d'Artois—a typical Bourbon who had "never learned anything and never forgotten anything." The reactionaries controlled both houses of the national legislature, since even in the lower elected house, suffrage restrictions heavily favored the aristocracy and the *nouveaux riches* bourgeoisie. Louis XVIII found it increasingly difficult to hold these fire-eating reactionaries in check. Shortly before he died in 1824, he warned his incorrigible brother of the danger to the Bourbon dynasty if he did not adopt a more moderate attitude.

Unfortunately, Charles X, as the Comte d'Artois now styled himself, was a stranger to moderation. He quickly aroused animosity against his regime to an explosive pitch. The Napoleonic generals who had brought so much glory to France were immediately retired from duty. An indemnity was voted the émigrés for their confiscated lands, the money to be raised by reducing the interest on government bonds from 5 percent to 3 percent. This angered the upper bourgeoisie, who were the chief bondholders. The peasants were alarmed by a proposed establishment of primogeniture, which seemed to endanger the principle of equality and the security of land titles. The Jesuits were brought back to France, and favors were bestowed on the Catholic church. Opposition mounted rapidly. By 1827 Charles X had lost his majority in both houses of the national legislature. Totally blind to the political realities of the day, he twice dissolved the lower chamber and attempted to force the election of a friendly majority by censoring the press and using official pressure on the electorate. The hostile majorities only increased in number. Finally, in July 1830, the king dissolved the newly elected chamber, called for new elections, restricted the suffrage so drastically that only about twenty-five thousand very rich citizens could vote, and completely abolished the freedom of the press. These measures set off an uprising in Paris. The Parisian proletariat erected barricades in the streets that the disaffected rank and file of the army were "unable" to break. After three days of desultory fighting, the insurgents had the upper hand, and the last Bourbon king of France was on his way to exile in England.

4. RESTORATION AND REPRESSION IN THE GERMANIES

In central and eastern Europe, particularly in the Germanies, Italy, and Russia, the conservatives and the Metternich system were more secure. The Germanies in 1815 consisted of thirty-seven little states and two large ones—Prussia and Austria. In all of them the influence of Metternich was strong. The German Confederation was an improvement over the old Holy Roman Empire, which Napoleon had destroyed, only in the sense that Napoleon's consolidation of the more than three hundred states down to thirty-nine was allowed to stand. The Diet was only a gathering and debating place for the representatives of the rulers of the thirty-nine states. The confederation had no treasury and no army at its command. There was not even a flag to symbolize its German national character. Reactionary Austria enjoyed a permanent presidency over it.

The German nationalism and liberalism that existed in 1815 centered primarily in the little states, some of whose rulers defied Metternich by granting liberal constitutions. The national and liberal activities here were largely the work of university students and professors, who shortly after 1815 began to form *Burschenschaften*, or brotherhoods, for the purpose of promoting German nationalism, liberalism, and the Christian religion. In 1817, in commemoration of the three hundredth anniversary of Luther's publication of his Ninety-five Theses, the Burschen-

schaften staged a giant festival at Wartburg, where Luther had hidden and had begun his translation of the Bible. Although the festivities were primarily religious in character, enough enthusiasm for German nationalism and liberalism was displayed to fill Metternich with anxiety. The murder two years later of a reactionary propagandist by a fanatical student gave Metternich his opportunity to strike. Calling together the princes of the leading German states at Carlsbad, he joined them in drawing up a set of harsh decrees designed to crush the embryonic national and liberal movements. The Burschenschaften were outlawed. Strict censorship was established. Classrooms and libraries were supervised. Liberal students and professors were terrorized by spies and police. The Carlsbad Decrees succeeded in suppressing for a number of years this first outcropping of the revolutionary spirit in Germany since the overthrow of Napoleon.

In Prussia the militaristic, paternalistic, despotic Hohenzollerns reigned. Behind them stood the equally reactionary landed aristocracy, the *Junkers*. The Junkers served as officers in the Prussian army and filled the key posts in the civil service and administration. These military lords hated not only liberalism in any form but also German nationalism. They did not wish to see virile, martial Prussia contaminated by association with the lesser German states, which were now infected with the French disease of liberalism. It was only in the economic field that German unity received any encouragement from Prussia. Because its territory was separated into two noncontiguous segments, Prussia in 1819 began making commercial treaties with its smaller German neighbors, providing for the free flow of trade among them. By 1834 nearly all the states of the German Confederation except Austria had joined the Prussian-sponsored *Zollverein* (customs union). Though it was not so intended, the Zollverein proved to be a forerunner of German political unity under Prussian leadership.

As was to be expected, conservatism reached its height in Austria. The spirit of the French Revolution and Napoleon, with the one exception of nationalism, had hardly touched the Hapsburg state and its feudal society. In addition to the natural conservatism of the Hapsburgs and their chief minister, Austria had a language problem that caused its rulers to fear liberalism and nationalism like the plague. Austria proper is German-speaking, but during the sixteenth, seventeenth, and eighteenth centuries the Hapsburgs had annexed territories inhabited by Hungarian (Magyar), Czech, Slovak, Ruthenian, Polish, Rumanian, Serb, Croat, and Slovene language groups. In 1815 two Italian-speaking provinces were added. Before 1789 these various language groups had remained relatively quiet under their feudal lords, the Hapsburg dynasty, and the Roman Catholic church, but in the wake of the French Revolution, they began to stir with national consciousness.

Metternich saw clearly that if this new force were not suppressed, the Hapsburg state would fall apart. Furthermore, nationalism unchecked would cause Austria to lose its dominance over Germany and Italy. The various German and Italian states would be drawn together into powerful national states from which Austria would be excluded, for most of the people in the Hapsburg state were neither German- nor Italian-speaking. When these facts are considered, it is not surprising that Austria in 1815 was the most reactionary state in Europe save Russia. In the Hapsburg provinces Metternich's police and spies were everywhere. Permission to enter or to leave the country was made very difficult, lest dangerous ideas be brought in from the West. Classrooms, libraries, bookstores, and organizations of all kinds were considered suspicious and closely supervised. Even music (in the country of Mozart and Beethoven) was censored for fear that musical notes would be used as a cryptic code for conveying revolutionary ideas. On the surface, these policies appeared for some time to succeed. Nevertheless, Metternich was aware that the Hapsburg state stood on shaky ground.

5. RESTORATION AND REPRESSION IN ITALY

Austria dominated Italy even more completely than Germany. Lombardy and Venetia were annexed outright. Modena, Parma, and Tuscany were ruled by Austrian princes. The Papal States and Naples were under Austria's protection and guidance in both domestic and foreign affairs. In all these states the deposed aristocracy and clericals trooped back, full of hatred for French institutions and for the Italian liberals who had cooperated with Napoleon (see Figure 42.3). Nearly all the Italian intelligentsia were soon in prison or in exile. In the Papal States the Inquisition and the Index were restored, and such Napoleonic innovations as street lighting were done away with. Of all the Italian states, only Piedmont in the extreme northwest was free of Austrian control, but even here the restored heads of the House of Savoy were so reactionary as to cause Metternich only joy.

6. CONSERVATISM IN GREAT BRITAIN

Although Great Britain had been for years a home of representative government, its government in 1815 was far from democratic. The suffrage was so severely restricted by property qualifications that only about 5 percent of the adult males could vote. Furthermore, the industrial cities of the north, which had emerged since the last distribution of seats in Parliament, were not represented at all. Both houses of Parliament were therefore monopolized by the landed aristocracy. It must be remembered, however, that the cleavage between the middle class and the aristocracy was not so sharp in Great Britain as on the Continent. The law of primogeniture in Great Britain granted the eldest son the entire landed estate and permitted him alone to assume the title. Younger sons sought careers in the church, in the military, or in business. This process brought about much intermingling between the upper and the middle classes. The long-sustained prosperity of British commerce had produced a merchant class wealthy enough to purchase respectability, lands, and sometimes titles. The aristocracy frequently invested in commercial enterprises and later in industry. These facts help to explain why the great political and social struggles in nineteenth-century Britain, though sometimes bitter, lacked the violence of those on the Continent.

A period of economic depression and unrest in Great Britain followed the ending of the Napoleonic wars in 1815. For twenty-two years, with only one brief interruption, Britain had been engaged in a desperate struggle with France, a struggle that was economic as well as military. Meanwhile, British industrial expansion had gone on apace. The war's end found British

FIGURE 42.3 Repression in Italy This illustration shows Italians being shot as suspected revolutionaries; it epitomizes the spirit of reaction and repression as the great powers of Europe tried to restore the old order and stifle the new currents of liberalism and nationalism. (Historical Pictures Service, Chicago)

warehouses piled high with unsold goods. Thousands of returning veterans found no jobs. Strikes and riots, which had begun during Napoleon's blockade, increased. The conservative Tory party, which had seen the country through the war, was strongly entrenched in power. Both the Tories and the slightly more liberal Whigs were still badly frightened by the specter of French revolutionary Jacobinism. The government therefore took strong measures against the restless workers. Writs of habeas corpus were suspended. The climax came in 1819 when troops fired on a crowd that had assembled outside Manchester to listen to reform speeches. A number were killed and hundreds injured in this ''Peterloo Massacre'' (see Figure 42.1).

Within a few years, however, as the postwar crisis of depression and unrest eased, the Tory government yielded slightly to the pressure for reform. We have already seen how Foreign Secretary Canning by 1822 had deserted Metternich's reactionary Concert of Europe and aided independence movements in Latin America and Greece. During the 1820s the navigation laws were somewhat relaxed and the tariff slightly lowered. The Combination Laws were partially repealed, permitting laborers to organize unions, though not to strike. The civil disabilities against nonconforming Protestants and Roman Catholics were removed, permitting them to participate in political life on an equal basis with Anglicans. These measures, however, welcome as they were, did not get at the fundamental issue: a broadening of popular participation in the government. The pressure for suffrage reform would continue to mount, particularly from the industrial bourgeoisie, which was rapidly gaining in wealth.

7. REACTION AND REPRESSION IN RUSSIA

Even Russia had not escaped the influence of the French Revolution and Napoleon. Russia had joined in the second, third, fourth, and fifth coalitions against France, had been invaded and ravaged as far as Moscow in 1812, and had played a major role in the wars of liberation against Napoleon in 1813–1814. Meanwhile, the young tsar, Alexander I, and many of his aristocratic young army officers had picked up romantic and liberal ideas from the West. But Russia was not yet ripe for Western liberalism. It was a vast agricultural nation with a feudal social structure and a very small urban bourgeoisie that could serve as a liberal base. The Orthodox Christian church, dominated by an upper clergy drawn from the aristocracy, was a handy governmental agency for controlling the masses. The unstable Alexander I soon fell under the influence of Metternich and of his own reactionary boyar magnates and repented of his liberalism.

There was no trace of romanticism whatever in Nicholas I, Alexander's younger brother, who succeeded him in 1825. Nicholas was a handsome, austere autocrat whose military career wedded him to the concepts of discipline and authority. A quixotic revolt by a group of young liberal officers on the occasion of his ascension to the throne and a full-scale revolt by his Polish subjects in 1831 further embittered him against liberalism in any form. Both revolts were crushed with an iron hand. For thirty years (1825–1855) Nicholas I was to stand as the perfect symbol of absolute reaction and the armed guardian of the Metternich system. When at the end of the nineteenth century Russia did begin to yield to liberal and revolutionary forces, it was with disorder and violence.

8. CONSERVATISM AND THE CHALLENGE OF LIBERALISM

Between 1815 and 1830 the forces of conservatism were dominant. They acted both in reaction to the events of the French Revolution and the era of Napoleon and in accordance with their own ideology—a set of beliefs and policies in support of a traditional Christian, ranked, aristocratic society wedded to old institutions and suspicious of change. In the international field this conservatism was epitomized by Metternich's policies, the Holy Alliance, and the concert of Europe. In domestic politics, this conservatism was characterized by the restoration of power to the traditional monarchs and aristocrats, the renewed influence of Christianity, and the suppression of liberal and nationalistic movements. Yet conservatives were faced with formidable opponents even during the early years after the fall of Napoleon. The struggle between conservatism and liberalism, which would last into the twentieth century, had just begun.

SUGGESTED READING

General

F. Artz, *Reaction and Revolution, 1814–1832* (1968). The standard survey of the period.

R. Gildea, *Barricades and Borders: Europe 1800–1914* (1987). A good recent survey covering this period.

J. Weiss, *Conservatism in Europe, 1770–1945* (1977). A good analysis of conservatism in its broad context.

The Congress of Vienna

F. Bridge, *The Great Powers and the European States System, 1815–1914* (1980). Covers international developments of the whole period.

H. Nicolson, *The Congress of Vienna: A Study in Allied Unity 1812–22* (1970). An excellent volume on the subject.

The Bourbon Restoration in France

A. Jardin and A. J. Tudesq, *Restoration and Reaction* (1984). Covers France well.

P. Mansel, *Louis XVIII* (1981). A good biography.

Reaction in Central Europe

T. Hamerow, *Restoration, Revolution, and Reaction: Economics and Politics in Germany, 1815–1871* (1958). A respected, difficult analysis encompassing the period.

A. Sked, *The Decline and Fall of the Habsburg Empire, 1815–1918* (1989). A new interpretation stressing Habsburg strengths.

Conservatism in Great Britain

N. Gash, *Aristocracy and People. Britain, 1815–1867* (1979). A balanced coverage.

Reaction and Repression in Russia

A. Palmer, *Alexander I: Tsar of War and Peace* (1974). A thorough biography.

A. Ulam, *Russia's Failed Revolutionaries* (1981). Contains a good analysis of the Decembrists.

CHAPTER 43
Liberalism and Revolution, 1830–1850

FIGURE 43.1 The Reform Bill of 1832 This engraving from the April 15, 1832, issue of *Bell's Weekly Messenger* depicts the successful struggle to enact the liberal Reform Bill of 1832 in Great Britain. At the top, under the banner of reform, Whig leaders unite with the king to pass the bill. At the bottom, the British lion uses reform to defeat the fleeing Tories and the dragon representing the rotten borough system. (The Mansell Collection)

During the Restoration years following the defeat of Napoleon, liberalism was suppressed by the conservatives who came back into power. Between 1830 and 1850 liberals gained a series of victories, often by way of revolutions or threatened revolutions, marking this period as a heyday for liberalism (see Map 43.1). By the early 1830s Greece, Belgium, and most of Spain's New World colonies had gained their freedom. The restored French Bourbons had been overthrown in a liberal revolt. In Great Britain the Reform Bill of 1832 marked a new liberal era. A new constitution in 1834 brought liberal institutions to Spain. Liberal revolts and movements had at least raised their heads in Poland, Italy, and parts of Germany. By 1850 liberal institutions had spread and revolutions, almost all of which included strong liberal elements, had occurred in nearly every country of continental Europe.

1. THE GENERAL NATURE OF NINETEENTH-CENTURY LIBERALISM

Liberalism is a difficult term to define. It has various shades and from time to time changes its complexion. During the nineteenth century, liberalism had developed into an ideology—a loose set of beliefs about the world and how it should be.

The roots of liberalism stretch back through the French Revolution and the Enlightenment to the seventeenth-century political thoughts of John Locke and others. At the base of liberalism was a belief in individualism. Liberals optimistically believed that individuals, unaided and free from outside forces or institutions, should pursue their own interests. Individuals deserved equality before the law and the right to embark on careers open to talent. Government should be constitutional and based on popular sovereignty. The people should be represented by an elected legislature to which government ministers would be responsible. Government should be limited in its powers, with such individual freedoms as freedom of the press, of speech, and of assembly guaranteed. The role of the government should be that of a passive police officer, enforcing laws and contracts. Government should interfere in economic life as little as pos-

sible, leaving that realm to private enterprise. Liberals were also anticlerical; that is, they opposed interference in government by organized religion. During the first half of the nineteenth century, liberals were usually nationalists, since nationalism at that time was primarily concerned with freeing peoples from alien rule and uniting them under one flag, and nationalism seemed consistent with popular sovereignty, constitutional government, and people's rights. Liberals, particularly during the first half of the nineteenth century, were not democrats; liberals wanted to limit the right to vote to those holding wealth and the educated. Only later in the nineteenth century did liberals begin to favor universal male suffrage.

Liberals typically came from the middle class—the commercial and industrial bourgeoisie, the professionals, and the intellectuals. Their chief opponents were the vested interests of traditional society—the aristocracy, the clergy, and the military—seeking to retain their favored positions. The peasantry was still generally conservative, strongly influenced by the clergy and sometimes by the aristocracy, and not very active in politics. Liberals were sometimes contemptuous of the propertyless masses below, forming alliances with them against conservatives only so far as necessary. Middle-class liberals' contempt for those below them was often a mask for fear; their contempt of the aristocrats above them was tinged with envy.

Liberals stood in contrast to conservatives. Liberals were optimistic about the individual; conservatives were pessimistic. Liberals had great faith in reason; conservatives argued that reason was too abstract. Liberals favored many of the ideas and reforms of the Enlightenment and French Revolution; conservatives attacked them. Liberals valued the individual over society; conservatives felt the individual was secondary. For liberals the state was an agent of the people; for conservatives the state was a growing organism not to be tampered with.

After 1850 the nature of liberalism would change. The outcomes of the revolutions occurring between 1848 and 1850 were a blow to liberals. As commerce and industry spread, the bourgeoisie acquired wealth and power, and soon the vested interests of this class made it more hostile to rapid political and social changes.

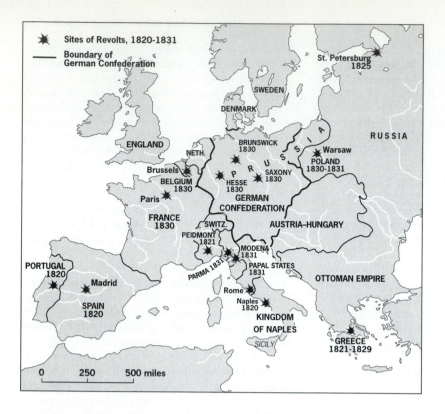

Sites of Revolts, 1820-1831

— **Boundary of German Confederation**

St. Petersburg 1825

SWEDEN

DENMARK

RUSSIA

ENGLAND

NETH.

BRUNSWICK 1830

P R U S S I A

Warsaw

Brussels

BELGIUM 1830

HESSE 1830

SAXONY 1830

POLAND 1830-1831

Paris

GERMAN CONFEDERATION

FRANCE 1830

SWITZ.

AUSTRIA-HUNGARY

PEIDMONT 1821

MODENA 1831

PORTUGAL 1820

Madrid

PARMA 1831

PAPAL STATES 1831

OTTOMAN EMPIRE

SPAIN 1820

Rome

Naples 1820

KINGDOM OF NAPLES

SICILY

GREECE 1821-1829

0   250   500 miles

Sites of Revolts, 1848-1849

— **Boundary of German Confederation**

SWEDEN

DENMARK

RUSSIA

ENGLAND

NETH.

Berlin

P R U S S I A

BELGIUM

Frankfurt

SAXONY

GERMAN CONFEDERATION

Prague

Paris

FRANCE

Vienna

Budapest

SWITZ.

Milan

AUSTRIA-HUNGARY

Novara

Venice

Turin

Custozza

PORTUGAL

Florence

PAPAL STATES

SPAIN

Rome

OTTOMAN EMPIRE

Naples

KINGDOM OF NAPLES

Palermo

SICILY

0   250   500 miles

Map 43.1 EUROPEAN REVOLTS, 1820–1831 AND 1848–1849 The first map indicates the location and dates of revolts, both major and minor, taking place between 1820 and 1831. The second map indicates the location of revolutions between 1848 and 1849. While the specifics of each outburst differed, most involved demands for liberal reform. Together, these maps reveal the geographical breadth of revolutionary activity during this period.

Its place in movements for political and social change was taken by the industrial working class, which was slowly becoming politically active. Groups deriving from the working classes, lower middle classes, and intelligentsia began to advocate greatly increased government intervention in economic affairs on behalf of the masses as well as the participation of the masses in political life. More progressive advocates of liberalism joined these groups in arguing for greater democratization of political life and government intervention in economic and social affairs. This, however, takes us beyond the primary concerns of this chapter. Liberalism flowered between 1830 and 1850, and this story needs to be told.

2. POLITICAL AND SOCIAL REFORM IN GREAT BRITAIN

During the 1820s Great Britain had already taken some moderate steps on the road to liberal reform (see pp. 546–547), but these steps did not go to the heart of the matter—broadening the franchise. Pressures mounted on the conservative Tories to effect electoral reform, but they were unwilling or unable to do it. Finally in 1830 the aristocratic but more liberal Whigs, long out of power, drove the Tory government from office.

The new prime minister, Earl Grey, immediately introduced and forced through Parliament the Reform Bill of 1832 (see Figure 43.1). This bill redistributed the seats of the House of Commons, taking many away from the "rotten boroughs" (once-important towns that had dwindled in population or even disappeared) and giving them to the industrial cities of the north. The suffrage was extended to all those who owned or rented property with an annual value of ten pounds. It is estimated that the number of eligible voters was thereby increased from approximately four hundred fifty thousand to eight hundred thousand out of a total population of some 16 million. Although on the surface the Reform Bill of 1832 appears innocuous, it represents a great turning point in British history. The long era of dominance of the conservative landed aristocracy was ending, and that of more liberal property owners, including the commercial and industrial bourgeoisie, had begun. The supremacy of the House of Commons over the House of

Lords, which had opposed the Reform Bill, was established. A new period of political and social reform had opened.

Both political parties recognized the new era. The Whig party, supported by the industrial bourgeoisie but containing a right wing of liberal aristocrats and left wing of intellectual radicals, changed its name to the Liberal party. For the next half century the Liberals were often in power, under the leadership of such personalities as Lord Grey, Lord John Russell, Viscount Palmerston, and eventually William E. Gladstone. The Tory party was still predominantly the party of the landed aristocracy, but it contained some bourgeois elements, and its more liberal wing, led first by Sir Robert Peel and later by Benjamin Disraeli, was now in ascendancy. The somewhat discredited "Tory" designation was changed to "Conservative."

Both parties, conscious of the rising importance of public opinion, supported a series of reforms. In 1833 slavery was abolished in the British Empire with compensation for slave owners. The Municipal Corporations Act applied the principles of the Reform Bill of 1832 to local government. The old penal code was reformed, reducing the number of capital offenses and generally softening the punishment of criminals. The penny post increased the circulation of mail and literature. Parliament granted small but gradually increasing subsidies to the schools, most of which were run by the Anglican church. Between 1833 and 1847 Parliament passed a series of laws that prohibited the employment in textile mills of children under nine and limited the hours of older children and women to ten hours a day. The employment of women and children in underground mines was prohibited. In 1846 the Corn Laws (the import tariff on grain), long opposed by liberals and the object of a major reform movement, were repealed, reducing the price of bread.

These reforms were the work not of the masses but of wealthy middle-class and aristocratic liberals along with a few intellectual radicals. The only reform movement initiated by the laboring classes in this period was the Chartist movement (see Figure 43.2). The hard-pressed urban workers, bitterly aware that they had been bypassed by the Reform Bill of 1832 and that they were not sharing in the unprecedented national prosperity, were dissatisfied with the reforms of

FIGURE 43.2 Chartist Print This print shows Chartists in a powerful but peaceful procession in London. (The Mansell Collection)

the bourgeois liberals. In 1838 working-class leaders drew up a People's Charter, which demanded (1) universal male suffrage, (2) the secret ballot, (3) removal of property qualifications for members of Parliament, (4) pay for members of Parliament, (5) annual elections, and (6) equal electoral districts. The charter was twice presented to Parliament and twice summarily rejected. In 1848, the Chartists planned a huge petition and demonstration in London. The frightened government prepared to use force. However, only a few mild disorders followed the third rejection, and the movement came to an end. Nevertheless, the Chartist movement had its influence. The most immediate result of the movement was to make both political parties aware of the growing influence of the working classes and the advisability of winning their favor. In the following decades, all the demands in the charter were enacted into law.

3. LIBERAL REVOLUTIONS IN BELGIUM AND FRANCE

The year 1830 was a bad one for conservatives in Belgium and France. The union forced upon Belgium and the Netherlands at Vienna had never been a happy one, and Belgian discontent with Dutch rule had been mounting for fifteen years. In addition to differences in language, the Belgians were Roman Catholic, whereas the Dutch were predominantly Calvinist. The Belgian economy was based on industry, the Dutch on commerce. Belgium, more populous than the Netherlands, was not given its fair share of representation in the government. When the halfhearted efforts of the Dutch failed to suppress the revolt, Austria and Russia threatened to intervene in the interests of legitimacy and tranquillity. They were deterred by British and French support of Belgian independence, which

FIGURE 43.3 Honoré Daumier, *The Chamber of Deputies* This print by the French artist Daumier presents a satirical view of the French Chamber of Deputies during Louis-Philippe's July Monarchy. This governmental body, though clearly more liberal than its predecessor under Charles X, was dominated by the relatively wealthy, satisfied upper classes. (The Art Institute of Chicago)

was thus achieved. Belgium soon adopted a liberal constitution and would remain a liberal nation throughout the nineteenth century.

The July Revolution in France was an even more serious blow to conservatism. Liberals and the people of Paris had toppled the reactionary regime of Charles X, the last of the Bourbons. There was strong sentiment to form a republic, but a coalition of liberal legislators and leaders of the wealthy bourgeoisie wanted only a constitutional monarchy. They set themselves up as a provisional government and named a new king: Louis-Philippe (1830–1848), head of the house of Orléans and a cousin of the departed Bourbon.

Louis-Philippe, recognizing that a new era had come to France, catered to the rich. He assumed the role of Citizen King, casting aside the trappings of royalty and donning those of the Parisian upper middle class. His eighteen-year reign came to be called the bourgeois monarchy (see Figure 43.3). His twofold policy, from which he never veered, was order and prosperity at home and peace abroad. One of his first acts was to lower the taxpaying requirements for voting from three hundred francs to two hundred francs per year. This act raised the electorate from approximately one hundred thousand to two hundred fifty thousand in a nation of some 32 million people and placed political control into the hands of the wealthy. Louis-Philippe's chief minister during the 1840s was the historian François Guizot, a thoroughgoing liberal who believed in government by the property-owning classes, particularly the bourgeoisie, and therefore opposed any further extension of the suffrage, even to members of the intelligentsia like himself.

Beneath the surface, problems simmered. The national prosperity was not shared by the working class, who suffered the usual hardships, insecurity, and maladjustments that accompanied the advent of industrialization. Slums mushroomed in Paris and the industrial cities of the northeast. Workers clamored for the right to vote and the right to organize unions but got neither. Poor harvests, financial crises, and growing unemployment in 1846 and 1847 heightened the frustration.

4. THE REVOLUTION OF 1848 IN FRANCE

The mounting discontent came to a climax in February 1848 when the government prohibited the holding of a reform banquet. Street brawling broke out in Paris. Louis-Philippe attempted to quiet people by dismissing Guizot, but the appeasement failed. A shot fired during a brawl between a mob and the troops guarding the residence of Guizot unnerved the troops, who fired a murderous volley into the mob and set off a full-scale insurrection. Barricades flew up all over Paris, and when the disaffected national guardsmen began going over to the rebels, Louis-Philippe followed Guizot into exile in Great Britain.

The working classes of Paris had triumphed, but only for a fleeting moment. A group of bourgeois liberals led by Alphonse de Lamartine hastily set up a provisional government that was republican in sentiment but in which the only prominent radical member was the socialist Louis Blanc. The provisional government immediately called for the election by universal male suffrage of an assembly to draw up a new constitution. Under the pressure of the Paris populace, the provisional government admitted the workingmen to the national guard, thereby arming them, and set up national workshops for emergency relief. The workshops, however, were a parody of those outlined by Louis Blanc, who cried that they were deliberately planned so as to ensure their failure. Workers of all kinds were assigned to hastily arranged projects, and when more workers enrolled than could be used, the

surplus workers were paid almost as much to remain idle. Tens of thousands rushed to Paris to join the workshops. The resulting demoralization of labor and the cost to the taxpayers thoroughly frightened all property owners, the peasants as well as the bourgeoisie. The elections held in April 1848 resulted in an overwhelming victory for the conservative republicans and limited monarchists, in part thanks to the conservatism of the landowning peasants, who constituted the great majority of the French population. The socialists were crushed. Even in Paris, their only real stronghold, they won a mere handful of seats.

One of the first acts of the newly elected Constitutional Assembly was to abolish the national workshops. The workers were told either to join the army or to go look for work in the provinces. The desperate Paris working class resorted to arms and the barricades: "Better to die from bullets than from starvation!" For four days all-out war raged in the streets of Paris between the working class, armed with national guard rifles, and the regular army of the conservative constitutional assembly, using artillery in addition to small arms. When the last barricade had been destroyed, some fifteen hundred, mostly workingmen, had been killed. Several hundred were sent overseas to French colonial prisons. Louis Blanc fled to Great Britain. The bloody "June Days" widened the cleavage between radical urban Paris and conservative rural France—a cleavage that has long complicated France's public life.

The inexperienced constitutional assembly hurriedly drew up a constitution establishing the Second French Republic. (The First French Republic had been declared by the revolutionists in 1792 and had been overthrown by Napoleon in 1804.) Legislative power was given to a single-chamber legislature elected by universal male suffrage. All executive and administrative powers were placed in the hands of a president, also elected by universal male suffrage. The first presidential election, in December 1848, resulted in a sweeping victory for Louis-Napoleon Bonaparte, nephew of Napoleon Bonaparte, as president. It took this ambitious and clever politician only three years to destroy the weak constitution and to take power in a coup d'état.

The Revolution of 1848 in France involved the first violent reaction of the urban working class

FIGURE 43.4 Revolution in Germany In central Europe in 1848, liberal sentiment emerged in the form of public demonstrations by the intelligentsia—particularly the university students. Here, in June 1848, German students convene at Wartburg, the castle that had once served as a refuge for Martin Luther. (Copyright Staatsbibliothek, Berlin)

against bourgeois liberalism. The working class was too small as yet to make any headway outside Paris. The revolution shattered against the solid mass of landowning peasantry allied with the propertied bourgeoisie. Its bloody suppression left a heritage of bitterness that would cloud the future of France.

5. THE REVOLUTION OF 1848 IN CENTRAL EUROPE

The February explosion in Paris set central Europe aflame with revolt (see Figure 43.4). However, the Revolution of 1848 in central Europe was a rising of the intelligentsia and the middle classes with a little support from the working class. Furthermore, in 1848 the cause of liberalism in central Europe was entwined with that of nationalism. The two forces frequently conflicted with each other, nationalism proving to be the more virile of the two.

The most crucial center of revolution was Vienna. This beautiful metropolis was the seat of the Hapsburg government, which not only ruled over the various language groups of the Austrian Empire but also dominated both the German Confederation and Italy. When early in March 1848 news of the events in Paris arrived in Vienna, the long-repressed student liberals began rioting in the streets and clamoring for an end to the Metternich system. As the uprising gained in momentum, Metternich was forced to flee for his life. The Hapsburg emperor, Ferdinand I, hastily abolished the repressive laws, ended serfdom, and promised constitutional representative government. However, he too was soon forced to flee his own capital. Meanwhile, the Magyars in Hungary, under the leadership of the eloquent Louis Kossuth, set up a liberal autonomous Hungary. The Czechs did the same in Bohemia and called for a Pan-Slavic congress to meet at Prague. In Austria's Italian provinces of Lombardy and Venetia the rebellious populace drove the Austrian garrisons into defensive fortresses and declared their independence. By June 1848 it appeared that the Hapsburg Empire would become liberalized, fall apart along national (language group) lines, or both.

In Berlin, the capital of Prussia, the news from Paris and Vienna set liberals demonstrating in the streets. The vacillating Hohenzollern king, Frederick William IV, promised a liberal constitution and support for German national unity. As in Paris, an unauthorized volley into the mob set off bloody street fighting, which the king ended by making further concessions to the liberals. Hohenzollern Prussia, like Hapsburg Austria, appeared for the moment to be on the road to liberal government.

Meanwhile, in the rest of the German states a group of self-appointed liberals called for a popularly elected assembly to meet at Frankfurt to construct a liberal German nation. The two questions confronting the Frankfurt Assembly were whether the German-speaking portions of the multilingual Hapsburg Empire should be included in the projected German nation and who should head the new nation. Tied in with the Austrian question was that of religion. With Austria (and Bohemia, which was alleged to be predominantly German), the Roman Catholics would predominate, and without Austria and Bohemia, the Protestants. For eleven precious months these knotty problems were debated. Eventually Austria virtually excluded itself by refusing to consider coming into the new German nation without its non-German provinces. By a narrow margin it was decided to offer the emperorship to the king of Prussia. But now it was too late, for the situation in Vienna and Berlin had changed drastically.

In Austria the inexperience and weakness of the liberals and the rivalries and conflicts among the various language groups played into the hands of the Hapsburgs. Skillfully playing off one group against another, the Austrian rulers beat down the liberal and national revolts one after the other. In Hungary they had the help of the reactionary Nicholas I of Russia, whose army crushed the rebels.

In Prussia, too, the liberals were weak and inexperienced. The unstable Frederick William IV, after his first uncertainty, gradually fell under the influence of his militaristic and reactionary Junker advisers. Further stiffened by the news from Vienna that the Hapsburgs had regained their autocratic position, he spurned the German crown offered him by the Frankfurt Assembly and replaced the constitution drawn up by Prussian liberals with one that was a travesty of liberalism.

The Hohenzollerns' rejection of the crown of a united liberal Germany blasted the hopes of the Frankfurt Assembly. When a few of the most determined attempted to continue their efforts, they were dispersed by Prussian troops.

6. REVOLUTION IN ITALY

On the Italian peninsula 1848 was a year of revolution. These revolts reflected an already long history of liberal and nationalistic movements in Italy. Soon after 1815 Italian nationalists began to form secret societies called *Carbonari* (charcoal burners), which met at night around charcoal fires to plot freedom from Austrian and local tyranny and to plan for national unification. In 1821 revolts erupted in Naples, Sicily, and Piedmont, but all were short-lived. In the early 1830s a romantic young intellectual, Giuseppe Mazzini (1805–1872), organized the Young Italy society, which was dedicated to the task of achieving a free, united Italian nation. Although the first uprisings inspired by the Carbonari and Young Italy were crushed by Austrian arms, the Italian national movement, once aroused, could not so easily be suppressed.

In 1848 revolutions occurred in Sicily, Naples, Piedmont, and Tuscany. By 1849 republics had been established in Rome and Venice, and other Italian states had adopted liberal constitutions. Yet the time for the permanent overthrow of

Austrian rule and the unification of Italy had not yet arrived. Austrian arms (and, in Rome, French arms) prevailed. It would be another ten years before liberalism and nationalism, under the leadership of Piedmont, would gain a more lasting victory in Italy.

7. AN ASSESSMENT

The struggles between liberals and conservatives, which had resulted in several liberal victories since 1830, came to a climax with the revolutions of 1848. Economic turmoil, demands for liberal reform, nationalistic sentiments, and ineptitude by frightened governments combined to spell a series of stunning victories for revolutionaries in almost every major country in Europe. The major exceptions were England, which had compromised in response to demands for liberal reform, and Russia, which remained the bastion of reaction. Once in power, the revolutionaries initiated major reforms, most of which fit well with the recognized canons of liberalism.

Nevertheless, the revolutionaries' victories were short-lived. By 1850 the conservative forces of order had regained control. Louis-Napoleon, soon to be Napoleon III, sat as president in France. The Prussian king regained control over his lands and ended hopes for a liberal unified German nation. In Austria and Hungary the Hapsburgs were again in power, just as they were in their Italian lands. Liberalism and nationalism were not yet strong enough to form new, lasting governments in these areas.

Several factors account for the defeat of liberal and nationalist forces, though the situation differed in each case. First, the alliance among middle-class liberals, radicals, socialists, artisans, and workers was one of convenience. Once revolutionary forces were in power, the interests of the various groups were too divergent for the alliance to hold. This division was most clearly evident in France, where the frightened middle class and conservative peasantry broke with the Parisian working classes, as revealed by the outcome of the elections and the bloody June Days. Second, liberalism and nationalism were forces that worked together when out of power; once in power they often were at cross-purposes. This lack of harmony between liberalism and nationalism was particularly pronounced in central Europe, where the aspirations of German, Polish, Magyar, Croatian, Serbian, and other nationalities conflicted with efforts to form new governments with liberal institutions. Third, the strength of conservatism and the forces of order should not be underestimated. With industrialization only beginning in central Europe, the main source of liberal strength, the industrial middle class, and an important source of revolutionary urban discontent, the working class, were weak. Revolutionary liberal leaders were inexperienced, particularly in central Europe and Italy. Once the shock of initial defeat was over, experienced conservatives marshaled their resources, and forces of order overcame the now divided revolutionary forces.

The reestablished governments had learned lessons from 1848 and maintained themselves with new vigor. In a few cases liberal reforms initiated between 1848 and 1850 were retained, and in other cases those reforms in modified form would be passed in succeeding years. But the great period of revolutionary liberalism ended in 1850.

SUGGESTED READING

General

C. Church, *Europe in 1830: Revolution and Political Change* (1983). A good starting point.

W. L. Langer, *Political Upheaval, 1832–1852* (1969). An excellent survey of the period.

Liberalism

A. Arblaster, *The Rise and Decline of Western Liberalism* (1986). A good recent account.

J. Gray, *Liberalism* (1986). An effective introduction.

Reform in Great Britain

D. Beales, *From Castlereagh to Gladstone, 1815–1885* (1969). A useful study of political history.

M. Brock, *The Great Reform Act* (1974). Solid, scholarly, respected.

D. Thompson, *The Chartists: Popular Politics in the Industrial Revolution* (1984). A thorough recent study.

The Bourgeois Monarchy in France

A. Jardin and A. Tudesq, *Restoration and Reaction, 1815–1848* (1984). A thorough coverage of France.

D. Pinkney, *The French Revolution of 1830* (1972). An excellent study of the topic.

Central Europe and Italy

I. Deak, *The Lawful Revolution: Louis Kossuth and the Hungarians, 1848–9* (1979). An excellent study of the individual and the revolution.

T. Hamerow, *Restoration, Revolution, Reaction 1815–1871* (1966). A highly respected analysis of Germany.

S. Wolf, *A History of Italy, 1700–1986* (1986). A good general account.

The Revolutions of 1848

M. Agulhon, *The Republican Experiment, 1848–1852* (1983). An excellent analysis of all aspects of the revolutions.

G. Duveau, *1848: The Making of a Revolution* (1967). An excellent study of the 1848 revolutions in France.

L. B. Namier, *1848: The Revolution of the Intellectuals* (1964). An eminent historian shows how nationalism wrecked the liberal movement.

P. Stearns, *1848: The Revolutionary Tide in Europe* (1974). A good summary.

CHAPTER 44

Nationalism and the Nation-State, 1850–1871

FIGURE 44.1 **Garibaldi Landing in Sicily** The period between 1850 and 1870 was marked by a strong growth of nationalism and the successful unification of Italy and Germany. Here the lifelong nationalist Garibaldi is heroically portrayed landing in Sicily in 1860 as part of the struggle for Italian unification. (Historical Pictures Service, Chicago)

By 1850 many of the revolutionaries' liberal and nationalistic aspirations were dashed as conservative, authoritarian rulers came to power. However, nationalism as a dynamic force remained powerful and would continue to increase in strength during the nineteenth and twentieth centuries. Between 1850 and 1871 almost all political leaders, whether liberal or conservative, recognized the strength of nationalism. Nationalism's political impact was manifested most dramatically in Louis-Napoleon's rise to power in France and in the successful struggles for national unification in Italy and Germany. More broadly, nationalism played a crucial role in the growing authority of the nation-state. Increasingly, central governments had to justify and bolster their authority by reference to a nation of citizens rather than dynastic links to the past. The period from 1850 to 1871, then, marks a time when nationalism grew from earlier roots to become a dominant force in Western political life and when the nation-state took on new authority and new functions.

1. THE NATURE OF NATIONALISM

Nationalism may be defined as feelings of common cultural identity and loyalty to one's country. What are the essential factors that contribute to these feelings? What makes a person a German or a Pole, even when there is no German or Polish national state?

The most important factor is language. Language brings people together in understanding and separates them from those they cannot understand. Probably second in importance is a historical tradition of unity. The Belgians with their two languages and the Swiss with their three languages and two religions illustrate the importance of this factor. Religion can be a powerful factor, too, though not so important as language. The German Empire with its common language came and held together in spite of a serious religious cleavage, and the Austrian Empire fell apart along language lines in spite of a common religion and a long tradition of unity under the Hapsburgs. Territorial compactness and natural boundaries frequently contribute to nationalism.

Until the French Revolution, national loyalty was chiefly centered on the ruling monarch or dynasty and was limited for the most part to the educated upper classes who participated in the government of the nation. The French Revolution gave birth to a new and more virile kind of nationalism. The establishment of equal rights and popular representative government, together with the abolition of old provincial boundary lines, brought the masses of people into direct partnership with the national government. Universal conscription into the revolutionary armies gave the people a sense of fraternity in a righteous cause—a crusade. Nationalism acquired the attributes of a religion. Such mass dynamism helped make the revolutionary and Napoleonic armies irresistible.

Nationalism soon spread to the other peoples of Europe. In the decades following the Napoleonic era industrialization and policies toward industrialization were becoming connected with nationalism. The revolutions of 1848 clearly demonstrated the revolutionary potential of nationalism. By midcentury nationalism had grown from its deeper roots to become entwined with the central political, economic, and social forces of modern times.

2. THE SECOND EMPIRE OF NAPOLEON III

In France, Louis-Napoleon Bonaparte blended support from below, reform, and authoritarian nationalism in his Second Empire, which was established in 1852 and lasted until 1870. Louis-Napoleon was originally elected president of France's Second Republic in 1848. He benefited from his illustrious name, his appeal to property owners longing for order, and his well-publicized promises to link democracy from below with reforming leadership from above. When the National Assembly refused to change the constitution so that he could run for a second term, he organized a coup d'état and seized power on December 2, 1851. Resistance was limited, though thousands were arrested and deported. He quickly granted universal male suffrage, and during the following year he held two plebiscites in which over 90 percent of the voters supported him and made him hereditary emperor—Napoleon III.

Under the new constitution, most power re-

FIGURE 44.2 Rebuilding Paris under Napoleon III Under Napoleon III, numerous slums and old, winding streets were torn down to make room for new, wide boulevards. The boulevards made it easier for authorities to maintain order and more difficult for revolutionaries to raise barricades. (The Mansell Collection)

sided in the emperor. Although there was an elected legislative body, it could not initiate legislation or exert control over Napoleon III's ministers. The emperor controlled elections by manipulating the electoral machinery, exerting official pressure, and supporting official candidates. He kept the press under scrutiny. Thus politically the Second Empire was clearly authoritarian, at least during the 1850s.

It was also during the 1850s that Napoleon III enjoyed his greatest successes. Economically France prospered, in part thanks to Napoleon III's policies. He encouraged industrialization and economic growth by promoting railroad construction, public works, and financial institutions. Two giant investment banking corporations, the Crédit Mobilier and the Crédit Foncier, mobilized huge amounts of capital for industry, railroads, and real estate. The Bank of France expanded until each of the country's eighty-six departments had at least one branch. Georges Haussmann, the prefect of Paris, had large parts of Paris torn down and rebuilt (see Figure 44.2). With a new sewer system, new parks, and new wide boulevards, Paris took on an envied image that would last well into the twentieth century.

Napoleon III also encouraged educational and social reforms, thereby increasing his popularity among a variety of groups. Hospitals, nurseries, and homes for the aged were built. Government subsidies kept the price of bread low. A system of voluntary social insurance for workers was instituted. Cooperatives were encouraged, and labor unions with limited rights to strike were partially legalized for the first time.

The peak of France's revived national prestige was reached during the Crimean War (1854–1856). Like his uncle, the second Napoleon was not satisfied with spectacular domestic achievements. His opportunity for glory in foreign affairs came when Tsar Nicholas I of Russia attempted to dismember the Ottoman Empire, "the sick man of Europe," and to achieve Russia's historic goal: Constantinople and access to the world through the Turkish Straits. France did not relish the prospect of an ambitious new rival in the Mediterranean. (Great Britain, with its vast holdings and interests in the Near and Far East, was even more sensitive to this threat than was France.) A second source of Franco-Russian conflict arose when the tsar, as the great champion of Orthodox Christianity, attempted to gain a protectorate over all Christians in the Ottoman Empire and over the Christian holy places in the Turkish province of Palestine. Since the Crusades France had been the leading champion of Catholic interests in the Near East, including the Christian shrines in the Holy Land. And Napoleon III's strongest ally in France was the Catholic church.

In 1853 the Russian army and navy suddenly attacked the Turks. Early the next year Great Britain and France sent their naval and military forces into the Black Sea and laid siege to Russia's naval base, Sebastopol, on the Crimean Peninsula. Sardinia came into the war to gain the friendship of France and Great Britain. Austria maintained a hostile and Prussia a friendly neutrality toward Russia. The war was fought with gross inefficiency on both sides. The only real hero was the British nurse Florence Nightingale, whose efforts helped to inspire the creation of the International Red Cross a few years later (1864).

Nicholas I died in 1855, humiliated by the knowledge that his creaking military machine was going to fail. The Peace of Paris in 1856 prohibited Russia's naval forces on the Black Sea and maintained the integrity of the Ottoman Empire. The autonomy of Serbia and the Rumanian provinces of Moldavia and Wallachia under the suzerainty of Turkey was guaranteed by the great powers. The Catholics were left in control of their shrines in the Holy Land. Great Britain at long last agreed to neutral rights on the high seas.

The chief loser of the Crimean War was Russia, whose massive military no longer looked so formidable. But more broadly a loss was suffered by the already crumbling Concert of Europe, which could no longer wield significant influence on behalf of a conservative international status quo. An immediate beneficiary of the Crimean War was Napoleon III. He played host to the peace conference and, of course, made it into a colorful spectacle. French nationalism and international prestige rose to new heights.

By 1859 Napoleon III had obtained not only the loyalty of the great majority of his own people but also some hegemony in the affairs of the European continent. France was prosperous and powerful. Then things began to go wrong. The dynamic force of nationalism, which he understood and used so well in France, he greatly underestimated abroad. In his efforts to control the Italian and German national movements he failed dismally—in the latter case fatally.

The first serious blunder came in 1859, when he made war on Austria in behalf of Italian freedom. The defeat of Austria set off a frenzy of Italian nationalism that threatened to dispossess all the rulers of the local states of Italy, including the pope. This situation alarmed and angered the French Roman Catholics, who blamed Napoleon. But when the French emperor deserted the Italian nationalists in the midst of the campaign, with the agreed-upon job only half done, he further alienated the French liberals, who were already unsympathetic to him.

Napoleon's efforts to create an overseas empire brought France little immediate profit and much trouble. The most ambitious and disastrous was his attempted conquest and control of Mexico. In 1862 he joined with Great Britain and Spain and seized several Mexican ports, ostensibly to collect debts owed by the revolutionary Juárez government. As soon as the British and Spaniards saw that Napoleon had more ambitious plans in mind, they withdrew. The French armies then marched on to Mexico City, drove the Juárez government into the hinterland, and set up a Hapsburg prince, Maximilian, as puppet emperor for France. The government of the United States protested vigorously in the name of the Monroe Doctrine, but embroiled in its own Civil War, it could do no more. As soon as the Civil War ended early in 1865, the American government dispatched victorious Union troops to the Mexican border. Napoleon III, now hard pressed at home, agreed to withdraw his troops. No sooner had the last French soldiers left Mexico City in 1867 than the Juárez forces captured and shot the well-meaning puppet emperor Maximilian. The Mexican fiasco added to the growing unpopularity of Napoleon III with the French people.

On the Continent, Napoleon III was attempting to slow the rapid growth of Prussia and to offset it by annexing territories on the left bank of the Rhine. His failures in this area of foreign policy would eventually prove fatal to his regime.

Meanwhile, the booming prosperity subsided after 1860. The Cobden Treaty, which lowered tariffs between Great Britain and France, flooded France with cheap British manufactured goods with which the less advanced French industries could not compete. The French textile industry also suffered heavily as a result of the American Civil War, which cut off its cotton supply. Both the industrial bourgeoisie and the proletariat were hard hit. Overexpansion and speculation began to take their toll.

The emperor attempted to allay the mounting discontent of liberals and workers. Beginning in 1859 he made one concession after another until by 1870 the Second Empire was, at least on paper, a limited constitutional monarchy with a liberal parliamentary government. But 1870 was too late. The showdown with Bismarck's rapidly forming German nation was at hand. The sick and discouraged Napoleon III blundered into a war with Germany for which his armies were woefully unprepared (see p. 571). He was defeated and captured, and his government was overthrown.

3. CAVOUR AND THE MAKING OF ITALIAN UNITY

For centuries Italy had been politically divided into various city-states, kingdoms, and provinces. After 1815 nationalistic sentiments and movements stirred throughout Italy. By 1848 three different plans for uniting Italy into a sovereign state had been developed; each had its own following. One plan was to make Italy a liberal democratic republic. This was the plan of Giuseppe Mazzini, an inspiring speaker and

writer but not a very practical organizer or man of action. His movement was called Young Italy. The second plan was to form an Italian confederacy under the leadership of the pope. The third plan was to make Italy a limited monarchy under the leadership of the House of Savoy, the ruling dynasty in Piedmont-Sardinia. During the Revolution of 1848, the first two plans were discredited. Mazzini's chaotic Roman Republic, which he set up after the rebellious populace had driven out the pope, outraged the Roman Catholic world and was overthrown by a French army of Louis-Napoleon. After this experience the pope bitterly opposed the unification of Italy, fearing that it would mean the loss of his political control over the Papal States.

At the same time, the heroic role played by Piedmont-Sardinia in battling the Austrians against hopeless odds won for the House of Savoy the devotion and confidence of Italian nationalists. However, the powerful Austrians were still in Lombardy and Venezia, the unsympathetic pope still ruled the Papal States, and the rest of the Italian states were weak and divided. Despite the new prestige of Sardinia, however, the task of uniting Italy required the work of a great political leader. He soon appeared: Camillo Benso, Count of Cavour (1810–1861).

Cavour was born into a well-to-do noble family of Piedmont. By the 1840s he was a successful businessman and had become enamored with moderate liberal ideas. Shortly before the Revolution of 1848, he founded a newspaper called *Il Risorgimento (The Resurgence)*, which never ceased to preach Italian unity. In 1850 Cavour was made minister of commerce and agriculture and two years later prime minister of Sardinia.

Cavour's goals were limited: to modernize Piedmont economically, to make Piedmont the center of the national unification movement, and to form a new Italian state as a constitutional monarchy rather than a democratic republic. To these ends, he worked to lower tariffs, build railroads, and balance Piedmont's budget. He supported the nationalistic Italian National Society, which worked toward national unification under Piedmont. Finally, he used diplomacy and Piedmont's relatively small army to gain international support and overcome the primary obstacle to unification—Austria.

Cavour sent Piedmont's army into the Crimean War in the hopes of winning French sympathy. The plan worked, and at the Paris Peace Conference in 1856 he was given an opportunity to state Italy's case against Austria impressively to the world. In 1858 Cavour and Napoleon met at Plombières, a French spa, and there Cavour persuaded Napoleon to fight Austria. Sardinia would provoke Austria into a declaration of war; France would help Sardinia drive the Austrians out of Lombardy and Venezia, which would then be annexed to the Kingdom of Sardinia. In payment Sardinia would cede the two little French-speaking provinces of Savoy and Nice to France.

When everything was in readiness in April 1859, Cavour easily provoked unsuspecting Austria into a declaration of war. To Austria's surprise, French armies poured across the Alps to fight alongside the Sardinians. In the two bloody battles of Magenta and Solferino, the Austrians were defeated and driven out of Lombardy. But to the dismay of Cavour, Napoleon suddenly made a separate peace with Austria (the Agreement of Villafranca) on condition that Sardinia receive Lombardy but not Venezia. Napoleon appears to have been motivated by the surprising bloodiness of the battles, the threatening attitude of Prussia, and the anger of the French Roman Catholics, who feared that the wild outburst of nationalism all over Italy following the victories over Austria threatened the independence of the Papal States. News of Magenta and Solferino set all Italy aflame with nationalistic fervor. Early in 1860, under Cavour's supporters, Tuscany, Modena, Parma, and Romagna (the northernmost of the Papal States) joined Piedmont, bringing together all of northern Italy except Venezia.

At this juncture, the rawboned Giuseppe Garibaldi, the most colorful of all the makers of the Italian nation, performed a daring exploit (see Figure 44.1). With a thousand civilian warriors dressed in red shirts and slouch hats, he sailed for southern Italy aboard two little Piedmontese ships. His goal was the conquest of the Kingdom of Naples, the largest and most populous of the Italian states, with a regular army of 124,000 men and a sizable navy. Cavour officially condemned the seemingly foolhardy expedition of the thousand but secretly aided it. Garibaldi's exploits read like a fairy story. He conquered the large island of Sicily, crossed the Strait of Messina, and entered triumphantly into Naples. The opposing troops had little heart for their cause and deserted to Garibaldi by the thousands after his first victories. Moving northward in the direction of Rome, Garibaldi defeated the last Neapolitan forces.

Not wanting to lose control of the situation and fearful that the daring but undiplomatic Garibaldi would march on Rome and bring down French armies, Cavour sent troops southward and seized all the pope's remaining territory except Rome and the territory immediately surrounding it. When Victor Emmanuel at the head of his army approached the forces of Garibaldi, the gallant warrior and patriot submitted to his king and retired to the rocky island of Caprera (see Figure 44.3). The Kingdom of Italy was formally declared in March 1861, with Victor Emmanuel II as king and the liberal Sardinian Constitution of 1848 as the national charter. The red, white, and green Sardinian flag now flew over all of Italy from the Alps to Sicily except Venezia and Rome (see Map 44.1). Those two provinces were not joined to the Italian state until 1866 and 1870, respectively, when, as we shall soon see, first Austria and then France were defeated by Prussia.

Cavour did not live to enjoy the fruits of his labors. Less than three months after the birth of his beloved Italian nation, he was dead. Paunchy, with ill-fitting glasses and a myopic stare, he was anything but impressive in appearance. Neither was he an orator. "I cannot make a speech," he once truthfully said, "but I can make Italy."

4. GERMAN UNIFICATION

During the 1850s both liberalism and nationalism began to make rapid headway in the German states. The area was industrialized rapidly. In Prussia the rise of a middle class, imbued with liberalism and German nationalism, challenged for the first time the dominance of the Junker aristocracy, who abhorred liberalism and whose national loyalty was limited to Prussia. The conversion of the Hohenzollerns and the Prussian Junkers to German nationalism was facilitated by the "Humiliation of Olmütz" in 1850. Shortly after the vacillating Frederick William IV had spurned the German national crown offered him by the Frankfurt Assembly in the spring of 1849,

FIGURE 44.3 Victor Emmanuel and Garibaldi This English engraving portrays King Victor Emmanuel and the heroic Garibaldi shaking hands in 1860, culminating the unification of Italy. (Culver Pictures)

he attempted to reorganize the German Confederation under Prussian leadership. The Hapsburg government of Austria, now completely recovered from its embarrassments of 1848–1849, mobilized its superior army and ordered him to cease. At the town of Olmütz in Austrian territory, the king of Prussia abjectly yielded. After this, the Hohenzollerns and more and more of the proud Junkers sought an opportunity to avenge the national insult to Prussia and replace Austria as leader of the Germanies (see Map 44.2).

In 1858 the unstable mind of Frederick William IV gave way, and his younger brother, who three years later became King William I, assumed leadership of the Prussian government as regent. Unlike his romantic, idealistic brother, William I was a militarist. His first move was to rejuvenate and greatly strengthen the Prussian military machine. The liberals, now strong in the Prussian Landtag, began to take alarm. Might not this all-powerful military machine be used to suppress liberalism? The liberals hoped that by holding up the military budget they might bargain for a stronger role for the legislature in the Prussian government. In 1862, after several years of haggling, the liberals finally defeated the military budget. Liberalism and nationalism had collided head-on. William I, unskilled in and unsympathetic with parliamentary government, threatened to resign. As a last resort, he called to the chancellorship Otto Eduard Leopold von Bismarck (see Figure 44.4).

Bismarck would remain chancellor for the next twenty-eight years. He stamped his iron will and his domineering personality not only on Prussia and Germany but also to a considerable degree on the rest of Europe. Upon assuming the chancellorship of Prussia in 1862, Bismarck, with the backing of the king and army, defied the liberal opposition in the Landtag, violated the constitution, and illegally collected the funds

Map 44.1 **THE UNIFICATION OF ITALY** This map shows the various stages of Italian unification after 1859. Most of Italy was unified under the leadership of Piedmont by 1860. The new Italian nation took advantage of international affairs to gain other territories after 1860.

Map 44.2 THE UNIFICATION OF GERMANY During the 1860s Prussia won its struggle with Austria for leadership in Germany. Through wars and diplomatic maneuvering, Bismarck welded numerous German states into a single nation by 1871.

necessary for the military program. "Not by speeches and majority resolutions," said Bismarck, "are the great questions of the time decided"—that was the mistake of 1848 and 1849—"but by blood and iron." He came to be known as the "Iron Chancellor." Prussian liberalism was crushed. Bismarck believed that military victories won on foreign soil would turn the Prussian

liberals into fervent German nationalists. This prediction soon came true.

Bismarck lost little time in putting his new military machine to work. An opportunity soon presented itself in the form of a dispute with Denmark over the long-standing and complex Schleswig-Holstein question. Schleswig and Holstein were two little provinces lying between

FIGURE 44.4 Bismarck Otto Von Bismarck had little faith in democratic processes for achieving purposes of state. Rather, he trusted "blood and iron." The German Empire bore in large measure the stamp of his personality and ideals. (The Granger Collection)

Prussia and Denmark. Their population was partly German speaking and partly Danish speaking. Since 1815 they had been ruled by the king of Denmark, though they had not been incorporated into Denmark. In 1863 the Danish king suddenly annexed Schleswig outright. Bismarck, seeing an opportunity to test the Prussian army, to annex some territory, and also to embroil Austria, declared war on Denmark in 1864. Since Holstein was a member of the German Confederation, Austria also entered the war against Denmark lest the leadership of the confederation pass to Prussia. Denmark sued for peace, and Bismarck made the peace settlement as complicated as possible. Schleswig and Holstein were to be ruled jointly by Prussia and Austria.

Bismarck soon used this unworkable arrangement to stir up trouble with Austria. His first task

was to obtain the support or neutrality of the other three continental powers, Italy, Russia, and France. Prussia had been the first great power to recognize the new Kingdom of Italy. Now, promising Venezia as a prize, Bismarck drew the new nation into an alliance against Austria. It was always a cardinal principle of Bismarck to maintain friendly relations with Russia (at Prussia's back door). When Russia's Polish subjects revolted once more in 1863, Prussia alone of the great powers supported Russia. Bismarck neutralized Napoleon III by personal persuasion and deception. By the spring of 1866, with everything in readiness, Bismarck created by threats and maneuvers a state of alarm in Austria, finally manipulating Austria into a declaration of war.

In the Austro-Prussian War most of the little German states supported Austria. Their military forces, however, were quickly crushed beneath the Prussian steamroller. Prussia's armies overwhelmed Austria, a nation of twice the size and population of Prussia and long the dominant power in central Europe. Bismarck saw that Austria was now harmless to Prussia and would make a valuable ally or at least friend in Prussia's future wars. Restraining his king and his generals, he made the terms of the Treaty of Prague extremely lenient. Austria was to pay no indemnity and to accept the rearrangement of Germany by Prussia. Austria was also forced to cede Venetia to Italy as Italy's reward for fighting on the side of Prussia.

Following the victory over Austria, Bismarck reorganized Germany. Hanover, Nassau, Frankfurt, and Hesse-Cassel were annexed to Prussia outright, bridging the gap between Prussia's Rhine province and the main body. The remaining twenty-one states north of the Main River were bound to Prussia in a North German Confederation. The confederation was completely dominated by Prussia, which alone constituted four-fifths of its area and population. Prussia's king and prime minister were made president and chancellor of the confederation, for which Bismarck drafted the constitution.

Its government was fundamentally autocratic, despite some democratic and liberal forms. The chief administrative officer was the chancellor (Bismarck), who was responsible only to the king of Prussia as president, by whom he was appointed. The legislative body was composed of the Bundesrat, whose members were really ambassadors of the twenty-two state governments, and the Reichstag, whose members were elected by universal male suffrage. All new laws required the approval of both bodies. The Reichstag had no control over the chancellor and his cabinet, as in Great Britain, and little control over the budget and the army and navy. If the Reichstag failed to vote a new budget, the old one automatically continued in force. This document later became the constitution of the German Empire.

Meanwhile, the former liberals in the Prussian Landtag, caught up in the nationalistic fervor following the victory over Austria, repented of their sin of having opposed Bismarck and voted him exoneration for having violated the constitution. The four predominantly Roman Catholic states south of the Main River (Bavaria, Württemberg, Baden, and part of Hesse-Darmstadt) were left out of the North German Confederation at the insistence of Napoleon III and because Bismarck preferred to have them come in later by their own choice. Bismarck recognized that the reluctant German states could be brought into the fold if German nationalism could be rallied against a foreign threat. France, itself stirred by nationalistic ambitions, provided that threat.

Bismarck's opportunity to confront France came in 1870, when the Spanish crown was offered to a Hohenzollern prince. Bismarck persuaded the reluctant prince to accept the Spanish offer, and the French immediately took alarm at the prospect of being surrounding by Hohenzollerns. Heavy French pressure was exerted on Prussia, to which both the prince and King William I yielded. However, the French ministers were still not satisfied and demanded more. After a meeting at Ems between the French ambassador and the Prussian king, the chancellor saw an opportunity to provoke the French into war. Cleverly editing the Ems dispatch so as to make it appear that the French ambassador and the Prussian king had insulted each other, he published it to the world. The French government, walking into Bismarck's trap, declared war.

The prevailing world military opinion was that this time Prussia had overreached herself and that Bismarck's work would be undone. But as in the case of the Austro-Prussian War, the military might of Prussia was grossly underestimated. The four predominantly Catholic south German states, far from joining Catholic France as Napoleon III had hoped, threw in their lot with Protestant, German-speaking Prussia as Bismarck had anticipated.

The issue of the war was decided in a matter of weeks. Count Helmuth von Moltke's superior hosts moved into France. The French were overwhelmed. One French army was surrounded at the fortress city of Metz, where it surrendered three months later. Another French army under Marshal MacMahon and Emperor Napoleon III was surrounded at Sedan and surrendered on September 2. Napoleon III himself was one of the captives. When this news reached Paris two days later, the liberals overthrew the government of the Second Empire and declared the Third French Republic. Within a matter of weeks Paris was surrounded by the Germans. For four months the great city held out; starvation forced it to surrender on January 28, 1871 (see Figure 44.5).

Bismarck forced stricken and helpless France to sign a treaty designed to cripple the nation beyond recovery. The Treaty of Frankfurt required France to pay an indemnity of 5 billion francs in gold. German troops would remain on French soil until this amount was paid in full (which Bismarck mistakenly hoped and expected would take a long time). The province of Alsace and the greater part of Lorraine were ceded to Germany. Since these provinces contained much of France's vital iron reserves, the seizure of Alsace and Lorraine long poisoned Franco-German relations.

On January 18, 1871, while the big German guns were still battering Paris, the heads of the twenty-five German states at war with France met on Bismarck's call at Versailles (behind the German lines) and in the Hall of Mirrors proclaimed William I emperor of the German Empire. The constitution that Bismarck had drafted for the North German Confederation became the constitution of the German Empire. Bismarck, of course, became its chancellor, and he lived to rule over his creation for the next nineteen years. The German Empire had now replaced France as the dominant power on the European continent and became a new rival of Great Britain for world hegemony.

FIGURE 44.5 **Victorious German Troops in Paris** Victorious German troops march down the Champs-Elysées (with the Arc de Triomphe in the background) at the end of the Franco-Prussian War. (Historical Pictures Service, Chicago)

In Germany, as in Italy, nationalism had succeeded. In the decades after 1871 the two new nation-states would join the competition in international affairs. And nationalism was strengthening the political institutions of other nation-states, furthering a trend that had already become apparent in France during the 1850s and 1860s. Nationalism would also contribute to the new imperialism of the late nineteenth century, which in turn would further increase the power of the nation-state and eventually help spread nationalism to the non-Western world.

SUGGESTED READING

General

W. E. Mosse, *Liberal Europe, 1848–1875* (1974). A useful comparative history.

N. Rich, *The Age of Nationalism and Reform* (1976). A solid survey.

The Nature of Nationalism

B. Shafer, *Faces of Nationalism* (1972). A good summary.

A. Smith, *Theories of Nationalism* (1983). A comparative approach.

The Second Empire of Napoleon III

A. Plessis, *The Rise and Fall of the Second Empire* (1985). A recent account.

N. Rich, *Why the Crimean War? A Cautionary Tale* (1985). A concise political and diplomatic interpretation.

T. Zeldin, *France, 1848–1945*, 4 vols. (1973–1980). Sophisticated, insightful, and thorough.

Cavour and the Making of Italian Unity

D. Beales, *The Risorgimento and the Unification of Italy* (1982). A brief survey with accompanying documents.

R. Grew, *A Sterner Plan for Italian Unity* (1963). An excellent analysis of the movement for Italian unification.

D. M. Smith, *Cavour* (1985). A highly respected work.

D. M. Smith, *Italy: A Modern History* (1969). A scholarly survey covering the period.

German Unification

E. Crankshaw, *Bismarck* (1981). A good biography that also covers unification.

T. S. Hamerow, *The Social Foundations of German Unification, 1858–1871* (1972). Relates the economic, social, and political factors behind German unification.

H. Holborn, *A History of Modern Germany*, 3 vols. (1959–1969). A detailed, scholarly survey.

M. Howard, *The Franco-Prussian War* (1969). An excellent analysis.

CHAPTER 45
Industrial Society, Social Classes, and Women

FIGURE 45.1 The Urban Classes This French cartoon of 1845 shows a typical Parisian apartment house in which the various social classes live in close proximity but different conditions. The bourgeoisie live on the first (American second) and second floors in wealth and prudent comfort. The lower classes, and aspiring artists, live on the bottom and upper floors in increasing poverty—thanks to their imprudence. (Bibliothèque Nationale, Paris)

Between 1850 and 1914 new areas in the West were industrializing, new industries were being developed, new methods of production were being used, and new business structures were emerging. The quantity and quality of industrial production underwent such a great change that historians have come to call these industrial developments the "second Industrial Revolution." During the same period social developments initiated during the earlier period of industrialization were maturing and evolving. Some, such as the rise of working-class organizations and ideologies, were directly connected to the industrial process. Others were more broadly based—the growth and movement of populations, the evolution of classes, and the developing experiences of women in an increasingly urbanized society. In short, mature, modern industrial economies and societies were becoming firmly established throughout the West.

1. THE SECOND INDUSTRIAL REVOLUTION

The first Industrial Revolution was initiated in Great Britain during the last decades of the eighteenth century. It spread to certain limited areas of western Europe and the United States during the first half of the nineteenth century. This early industrialization was based primarily on steam, iron, and textiles. During the 1850s and 1860s industrial production continued to expand, but mostly in the same areas and along the same lines as in earlier decades. In 1871 Great Britain was still the industrial leader, producing more industrial goods than the rest of the world combined. Besides Great Britain, only Belgium and parts of France, Germany, northern Italy, and the United States were industrially well developed.

The second Industrial Revolution was initiated in the last third of the nineteenth century. It was more widespread than the first Industrial Revolution and was based more on electricity, oil, steel, and chemicals. Great Britain, failing to invest sufficiently in new processes, falling behind in marketing techniques, and relying too heavily on old plants, lost its industrial leadership. Between 1871 and 1914 the United States and Germany surpassed Great Britain. By 1914

the Industrial Revolution had penetrated central and eastern Europe, Japan, Canada, Australia, and New Zealand; even India had a small textile industry. However, it was still in western Europe and the United States that most of the world's industry was to be found, and the greater part of Asia, Africa, and Latin America was still not industrialized. Moreover, it was in western Europe that both the prosperity and the uncertainties of economic life—exemplified by the industrial boom of 1850–1873 and the depression between 1873 and 1896—were experienced most.

New Products and Processes

Steel has been the mainstay of industry and transportation since the latter part of the nineteenth century. Until the mid–nineteenth century, steel was hard to make and very expensive. The discovery of the Bessemer process (1856) and the Thomas-Gilchrist process (1878) of removing impurities from molten iron greatly speeded up and cheapened the production of steel. In 1871 the total annual steel production of the entire world was approximately 1 million tons, of which about half was produced by Great Britain, a fourth by Germany, and an eighth by the United States. By 1914 the world's annual production had increased more than fiftyfold; the United States was producing approximately half the total, Germany a fourth, and Great Britain an eighth. Out of this steel were made tools and machines that constantly increased in numbers and efficiency. By 1914 in the industrialized countries, these increasingly automatic machines fabricated most metal, textile, leather, and wood products (see Figure 45.2).

The power to drive the steel machines was increasing in like proportion. In 1914 probably nine-tenths of the world's industrial power was still provided by the steam engine. Other and more efficient power generators, however, were rapidly coming to the fore. Between 1831 and 1882 the dynamo for generating electricity was developed by a number of inventors, the most important of whom were Michael Faraday (British), the Siemens brothers (German), and Thomas A. Edison (American). Sir Charles Parsons (British) patented the steam turbine in 1884. The turbine proved to be so efficient that it was soon used to drive the largest ships and even-

FIGURE 45.2 Krupp Works Germany industrialized rapidly during the last quarter of the nineteenth century. This photo shows the armaments factory at the Krupp works in Essen, Germany. (Culver Pictures)

tually to generate most of the world's electric power. In 1888 the electric motor was invented by Nikola Tesla, a naturalized American born in Croatia. The first practical internal combustion engine was invented by Gottlieb Daimler (German) in 1886. One year later he put it to work in the first automobile. In 1892 the diesel engine, which efficiently burned cheap crude oil, was invented by Rudolf Diesel (German). The invention of these two engines gave impetus to the oil industry.

In the last decades of the nineteenth century pure science was playing an increasingly vital role in industry, and both science and industry were being applied to agriculture. Physics contributed most heavily to the rapidly growing electrical industry. Chemistry made possible such important industries as synthetic dyes, wood pulp, paper, plastics, synthetic fibers, photography, and motion pictures. The electrical and chemical industries were most highly developed in Germany. The mechanization of agriculture made its first big advances in the great grain-growing areas of the United States, Canada, and Australia, although western Europe was also steadily increasing its agricultural yields through the use of farm machinery and scientific farming techniques.

Transport and Communications

Between 1850 and 1914 a large part of humanity became mobile. Whereas before 1850 relatively few people had ever seen more of the world than could be seen on journeys by foot or on horseback, by 1914 millions of people were traveling considerable distances, often by rapid conveyance. Even in places such as China, Turkey, and Brazil, trains chugged along, hauling people for distances and at speeds unknown before.

This was the greatest era of railroad building in history. There had been a rather lively building of railroads before 1850 in western Europe and the United States. However, between 1850 and 1914 the world's railway system was fundamentally completed. There has been relatively little railroad building since.

At the same time, the steamship was making comparable progress, although it had stiff competition from the sailing ship until near the end of the nineteenth century. Steel hulls of great size, turbine engines, and screw propellers were too much for the beautiful sails. The opening of the Suez Canal in 1869 and the Panama Canal in 1914, together with the increase in the size and speed of ships, brought the world and its peoples, commodities, and markets much closer together.

During the last three decades of the nineteenth century, the humble bicycle became a common and important means of locomotion, especially in Europe. But the bicycle was not fast enough for the industrial age. When Gottlieb Daimler attached his little combustion engine to a wagon in 1887, the automobile was born. It quickly captured the imagination of daring pioneers. Daimler sold his patent to a French company, and until the end of the century the French led the field in automobile development and production. Leadership passed to America with the founding of the Ford Motor Company in 1903. Henry Ford, who started out as a bicycle mechanic, applied the assembly-line method of mass production to the new automobile industry. The rapid spread of the automobile created vast new industrial empires in oil, rubber, and concrete.

After the turn of the century the airplane was invented. The first successful heavier-than-air flying machine was flown by Wilbur and Orville Wright in 1903 over the sand dunes at Kitty Hawk, North Carolina. Aviation was still in its infancy in 1914, but already its tremendous future was obvious.

Communications were developing faster yet. In 1844 Samuel F. B. Morse sent a message by wire forty miles from Baltimore to Washington. The telegraph, which transmitted messages almost instantaneously from one end of any length of wire to the other, caught on rapidly. In 1866 a telegraph cable was laid across the Atlantic, enabling news to travel from New York to London as quickly as from New York to Brooklyn. Ten years later Alexander Graham Bell, an American born in Scotland, invented the telephone, and in 1895 Guglielmo Marconi, an Italian, sent the first message by wireless telegraphy. Together with the revolution in transportation, these developments in communications accelerated the Industrial Revolution by greatly facilitating the large-scale mobilization of capital, raw materials, labor, and markets.

The Growth of Corporations and Monopolies

At the same time that industry was growing, individual companies were growing larger and combining to form monopolistic mergers or trusts. Such undertakings as railroads, shipping lines, and iron-and-steel mills were too large for all but a very few individuals to finance. As a rule, therefore, enterprises of this scope were carried on by joint stock companies. Entrepreneur capitalists would raise the necessary capital outlay by organizing a corporation and selling stock in it to other capitalists. All the industrialized countries encouraged the investment of capital in corporations by passing laws that limited the liability of stockholders to the amount of money invested (hence the "Ltd." usually seen after the name of a British corporation or combine). By 1914 most of the world's industry was controlled by large corporations and trusts. Although their stockholders were numbered by the thousands, they were really controlled by a relatively few banks and wealthy individuals. And between the owners of these corporations and the millions of workers lay a great gulf. The actual operation of the larger industries was carried on by hired managers, who hired, fired, and supervised the workers.

The giant corporations were ruthless in dealing with one another. In this era of unrestrained competition, the big and strong frequently destroyed the small and weak. The premium was on size and strength. The results were combines, mergers, and monopolistic trusts. The spectacular success of Rockefeller's Standard Oil Trust in the 1880s soon made it the model for many others, particularly in the United States, Germany, Japan, and to a lesser extent Great Britain. The German monopolistic combinations such as the giant I. G. Farben Industries (chemicals and dyes) were called *cartels.* They received government encouragement and support, particularly in their operations abroad. In Japan three-quarters of the nation's industry was controlled by five giant family corporations.

2. THE RISE OF WORKING-CLASS ORGANIZATIONS AND IDEOLOGIES

Labor Unions and Cooperatives

Wherever industrialization occurred, distressed laborers almost immediately attempted to protect themselves by banding together. However, until the 1870s inexperience, poverty, hostile governments, and unfavorable public opinion effectively hindered their efforts. Anti–labor union laws were not fully repealed in Great Britain until 1875 and in France until 1884. In Germany Bismarck persecuted labor unions until his dismissal in 1890. Until the 1880s the union movement in Europe was limited chiefly to skilled workers, organized by crafts, who were moderate in their aims and methods.

In the 1880s unionization spread rapidly to unskilled workers, cut across craft lines, and adopted socialistic programs (often Marxist) and more radical methods. In Great Britain the labor unions formed the national Trades Union Congress in 1868, and later they became identified with the Labour party, which was founded between 1881 and 1906. In Germany the individual unions in 1890 formed a national organization that was frankly Marxist. In France in 1895 the various unions banded together in the giant CGT

(Confédération Générale du Travail—General Confederation of Labor) with a radical program. By 1914 the working class in the industrialized countries was sufficiently large and organized (though only a minority was as yet unionized) to make itself a power to be reckoned with, both in the factories and mines and at the polls.

Meanwhile, a much bigger portion of the working class was participating in the milder cooperatives of various types. In 1910 in Great Britain membership in cooperative retail stores, fraternal insurance (friendly) societies, and credit associations is estimated to have been some 14 million, the great bulk of whom were wage earners. These organizations also provided much-needed social fellowship for workers. In the 1880s Denmark became the home of the agricultural cooperative movement. By 1914 nearly all of Denmark's agricultural commodities were cooperatively produced and marketed, and the movement had spread to most of northern Europe, to Italy, and to the United States.

Socialism

During the second half of the nineteenth century socialism became a major ideological force within the working class and came to influence the society and politics of the West in important ways. The most prominent source of socialism was Karl Marx, who, along with Friedrich Engels, had already produced *The Communist Manifesto* in 1848 (see Chapter 40). Marx argued that modern industrial society in the capitalist West was increasingly being split into two opposing classes: the capitalists (factory owners) and the workers. According to Marx, capitalism was doomed to be overthrown by a revolution of the working class and replaced by a socialist system.

Marx continued to write during the 1850s, 1860s, and 1870s, publishing his most important book, *Das Kapital,* in 1867. He played a key role in translating his ideas into actions by helping union organizers to form the International Working Men's Association (the First International) in 1864. The association was an amalgam of non-Marxian socialists (such as followers of Louis-Auguste Blanqui and Pierre-Joseph Proudhon), anarchists (such as Mikhail Bakunin), and Marxists, and it was divided at the start. Soon, however, Marx and his followers gained control. Although this organization proved to be fragile, falling apart in the 1870s after the Paris Commune, it helped spread Marx's socialism, particularly in Germany. The Second International was formed in 1889 and lasted until 1914. An international federation of socialist parties, it worked to spread socialism, maintain doctrinal purity, and develop socialist strategies.

After Marx's death in 1883, his followers split into various groups and often disagreed over the "correct" meaning of Marxism. The most important modification of Marxism was a moderate revisionism led by the German socialist Eduard Bernstein (1850–1932). Bernstein argued that Marx had made some errors and that a revolution would not be necessary. He advocated cooperation with the capitalistic classes to obtain all the immediate benefits possible for labor and a gradual approach to socialism. Others, such as the Polish-born socialist Rosa Luxemburg (1870–1919), attacked Bernstein's position as being too much of a compromise with bourgeois liberalism and nationalism. Active in Germany, Poland, and Russia, Rosa Luxemburg would later become a founding leader of the radical Spartacus League and the German Communist party.

In Germany, where socialism had its greatest success before 1914, the Social Democratic party formally rejected Bernstein's moderate revisionism but in practice often tended to follow it after the 1890s. By 1914 the party was able to poll some 4.5 million votes and had become the largest party in Germany. The French Socialists were more radical than the Germans. In 1905 the orthodox and revisionist wings of the French Socialists joined to form the United Socialist party under the leadership of the scholar-orator Jean Jaurès. By 1914 they numbered 1.5 million voters and had 110 seats in the Chamber of Deputies. Contrary to the expectations of Marx, socialism in Great Britain was weak and mild. Among the earliest British Socialists were George Bernard Shaw, H. G. Wells, and Sidney and Beatrice Webb. These intellectual radicals formed the Fabian Society, which was committed to moderation and gradualism. The Labour party, founded between 1881 and 1906, was also mild and grew slowly before 1914. Neither the Fabian Society nor the Labour party could be called Marxist, although both were influenced by Marx. In the United States, the socialist movement was rela-

tively weak and (in retrospect) mild. The first prominent American Socialist, Eugene V. Debs, did manage to poll nearly a million votes for president in 1912 and again in 1920.

Anarchism

Anarchism was an extremely radical movement that has often been confused with Marxism. While both were anticapitalist and gained most of their support from the working classes, anarchists stressed much more the elimination of the state and any authority that impinges on human freedom. Anarchists optimistically believed that human beings, once freed from the corrupting institutions that oppressed them, would naturally cooperate with one another. Anarchism's two most influential leaders were the Russian activist Mikhail Bakunin (1814–1876) and the exiled Russian theoretician Prince Pyoter Kropotkin (1842–1921). Anarchism became particularly influential in France, Spain, and Italy and among artists and intellectuals as well as members of the working classes. A relatively small wing of the anarchist movement turned to violent means to gain their ends. Among its victims were Tsar Alexander II of Russia in 1881, President Sadi Carnot of France in 1894, King Umberto I of Italy in 1900, and President William McKinley of the United States in 1901. This image of violence has tainted the general perception of anarchism ever since.

3. THE GROWTH AND MOVEMENT OF POPULATION

Since the eighteenth century, European population had been growing at a rapid pace. This growth continued as industrialization spread throughout Europe in the nineteenth century. Between 1850 and 1914 Europe's population expanded from 266 million to 450 million. However, there were important changes underlying this growth of population during the second half of the nineteenth century, particularly after 1870.

In many areas, particularly western Europe, increasing birthrates were no longer a prime generator of population growth; in fact, the birthrates were declining. A trend starting in the middle class and spreading to the working classes of marrying later and intentionally having fewer children was limiting the size of families. Because parents could rely more on infants surviving into adulthood, there was less need to have so many children. Moreover, parents who wanted to ensure their own and their children's rising economic well-being and social position elected to have smaller families, which were less expensive and required less division of assets. Despite the declining birthrate, population grew, fueled by an even greater decline in the death rate. This decrease was caused by a combination of improved public sanitation, economic growth, and medical advances.

This European population was not only growing but also moving in vast numbers in two main ways: from Europe to overseas areas, particularly the United States, and from the countryside to the city.

The overseas emigration of Europeans between 1850 and 1914 was phenomenal. Ever since the first settlements in the New World, there had been a sizable trickle of Europeans to the Americas. This trickle became a flowing stream in the mid–nineteenth century. Great numbers of British, Irish, and then German immigrants landed in the United States during the 1840s, 1850s, and 1860s. After 1870 the stream of Europeans emigrating overseas swelled into a rushing torrent as peoples from southern and eastern Europe joined the flow. In the brief span of forty-three years between 1871 and 1914, more than 30 million Europeans left their homelands and emigrated to the New World or to the British dominion territories. The great bulk of them came to the United States.

Several factors help explain this massive movement of Europeans overseas. Perhaps the greatest impetus was the growth of population. The growing numbers led to increasing competition for land in rural areas and for living space and jobs in urban areas. As different areas of Europe underwent the economic and social transformations connected with industrialization, people were uprooted from their traditional ways of life. When these upheavals were accompanied by political turmoil, many found additional reasons to emigrate. As these developments pushed Europeans from their homelands, opportunities in the New World, both real and imagined, pulled them across the Atlantic (see Figure 45.3). Land and economic opportunity

seemed abundant in such places as the United States, Canada, Argentina, and Brazil. Improvements in transportation—railroads and steamships—made travel to these faraway places easier. This combination of push from Europe and pull from the New World induced millions of relatively poor, young, and often unmarried Europeans to emigrate overseas. Although it is difficult to know how most of them experienced this change, clearly not all of them were satisfied. Approximately one-third of those emigrating overseas from Europe eventually returned.

Europeans were moving from the countryside to the city at an even faster pace than they were moving overseas. In 1850, despite a long process of urbanization, in no country did those in cities outnumber rural inhabitants. This picture changed rapidly during the second half of the nineteenth century. By the turn of the century more than half the population of western Europe lived in urban areas. Agriculture had become an occupation for the minority in Great Britain, Belgium, the Netherlands, Germany, and France.

The movement to the city was brought about by the opportunities in industry and commerce, the growing attractiveness of urban life, and the application of mechanization and science to agriculture, which now required far fewer workers to produce greater yields. The social problems of the cities were being recognized and attacked. A public health movement to improve water supplies and public sanitation by introducing piped water and sewer systems was initiated in England during the 1840s. Urban areas in other countries followed England's lead in the succeeding decades. Urban life was altered by the introduction of mechanized, regular, and reliable means of public transportation, particularly electric streetcars in the 1890s. This development widened opportunities for better housing, since people no longer had to live so close to work. The central areas, which had housed people of all social classes together, were becoming dominated by public buildings, retail outlets, businesses, and theaters (see Figure 45.1). Around the central areas new residential districts and suburbs formed, often separated into working-class and middle-class sections. Some limited private and public programs were initiated to facilitate the construction of cheap housing.

Cities were thus becoming more attractive. Urban planning spread throughout Europe in

FIGURE 45.3 *Welcome to the Land of Freedom* In this romanticized painting a variety of emotions is displayed on the faces of immigrants as they pass the Statue of Liberty in New York Harbor on their way to a new life. Between 1871 and 1914, more than 30 million Europeans emigrated overseas, most of them to the United States. (The Granger Collection)

the second half of the nineteenth century. The general pattern was initiated in Paris during the 1850s and 1860s, when the government tore down old, overcrowded, and almost inaccessible areas of the city, built large boulevards and parks, and provided for more open spaces. Other cities, such as Vienna and Cologne, followed the example of Paris. Together the spread of sanitation facilities, public transportation, urban planning, and new housing in Europe's cities was making life in the urban areas relatively safe and appealing compared to life in the countryside.

4. SOCIAL CLASSES

The class divisions of industrial society continued to develop along the lines already estab-

lished during the first half of the nineteenth century. The aristocracy continued to shrink in size and significance, yet it still retained some vestiges of wealth, prestige, and position. In part, it was supported by the increasingly conservative elite of the upper middle class. These families, who had gained great wealth from industry, commerce, and banking, mingled with the old aristocracy and copied much of its exclusive and expensive lifestyle. Numerous servants, at least one country house surrounded by an estate, membership in exclusive clubs, extensive travel, major contributions to good causes, and support of culture were almost requirements for full membership in this elite, which constituted less than 5 percent of the population.

The bulk of the middle class, ranging from small factory owners, shopowners, schoolteachers, and professionals to clerks and minor officials, continued to benefit from industrial expansion and urbanization. During the second half of the nineteenth century, however, there were some important changes in the outlook and composition of this class. Before 1848, the middle class was often revolutionary and certainly at the forefront of progressive political change. After 1848, the middle class ceased to be revolutionary and more often fought to retain the status quo rather than promote progressive reform. For the most part, the middle class was gaining what it wanted and was achieving dominance in Western society. In composition, the middle class was not only growing (to some 20 percent of the population) but also adding new groups to its numbers. The two most important of these new groups were professionals and white-collar employees. The professionals included people such as engineers, chemists, accountants, and architects as well as public and private managers. These people utilized their education and expertise to carry out the specialized tasks created by industrialization. In wealth, attitudes, and style of life they resembled the traditional middle-class entrepreneurs, merchants, and bankers they served. The white-collar employees were placed toward the bottom of the middle classes. They included the growing numbers of clerks, secretaries, bureaucrats, and salesmen who usually worked for large firms and earned little more than members of the skilled working class. But they self-consciously considered themselves apart from the working classes below them, subscribed to middle-class attitudes, and tried their best to follow a middle-class style of life—at least in appearances.

Generally, members of the middle class copied as much of the envied lifestyle of the wealthier upper middle class as they could. With care, most could afford one domestic, good food, a well-furnished apartment or house, schooling and perhaps music lessons for the children, attendance at cultural events, fashionable clothes, and travel. The middle-class home became a symbol of accomplishment and status, displaying wealth in a bounty of utensils, pictures, furnishings, and knickknacks. Magazines and stores appeared that both appealed to and channeled middle-class tastes. New department stores, such as the Bon Marché in Paris, offered to fulfill the desire for goods easily.

In values and beliefs, middle-class people thought that they represented what was correct and best in Western society. They believed that prudence, control, rationality, and hard work were the keys to success. They respected traditional Christian morality, sexual purity, and marital fidelity, while they denounced drinking, crime, excesses, and even poverty as vices. They felt they should be able to live up to these standards, at least in appearances if not always in practice. Money remained an important consideration for marriage, but a union was supposed to be centered on sentiment. While this was the period of Victorian sexual propriety for the middle class, it now appears that there was increasing acceptance and expectation of sexual enjoyment within the marriage. Children were at the center of the family and fewer in number; they remained at home through the adolescent years and were more extensively educated.

The working classes—the wage laborers with little if any capital—were headed by an elite of workers whose skills as artisans, machinists, foremen, or specialists were in great demand. Often they struggled to distinguish themselves from the bulk of the working classes below them by adopting a stern, moralistic attitude, copying the appearance of the middle class, and striving to ensure that their children would maintain or surpass their own position in the social hierarchy. The bulk of the working classes were factory laborers, construction workers, transport workers, unskilled or semiskilled day workers, and domestics.

Clearly, the working classes were benefiting from industrialization during the second half of the nineteenth century. Real wages were on the rise, perhaps doubling in Great Britain between 1850 and 1914. The working classes engaged in the proliferating leisure-time activities, which included public drinking and socializing in cafés and pubs, watching organized sports such as soccer, boxing, and racing, and attending music halls, vaudeville theaters, and amusement parks. Nevertheless, the working classes were still located toward the bottom of the social and economic scale, continually experiencing or being threatened by poverty, unemployment, poor housing, and insecurity. They may have been participating in an expanding industrial society, but that expansion did not benefit all equally. The gap between rich and poor remained wide;

FIGURE 45.4 Jules Adler, *An Atelier for the Cutting of False Diamonds at Pré-Saint-Gervais* Working-class women often took jobs in certain kinds of small factories and workshops for relatively poor pay. This painting shows the interior of a late-nineteenth-century Parisian workshop where women are making costume jewelry. (Musée Baron-Gérard, Bayeux)

the upper 20 percent of the population usually received more national income than the combined total of the remaining 80 percent.

This society of the late nineteenth and early twentieth centuries had acquired some permanence that reflected its mature industrial base. It was a society that was more affluent than ever but was still divided into classes of greatly differing status and wealth. Tensions ran through this society, as did great movements of people and ideas. Nevertheless, when the generations after World War I looked back to this society, it seemed enviable despite its faults.

5. WOMEN'S ROLES AND EXPERIENCES

It is difficult to summarize the situation of women between 1850 and 1914. Women's roles and experiences differed sharply according to class lines, and even within classes many of the relevant developments were contradictory. What generally unified women's experiences during this period, as before, was their legal inequality with men, their lack of political rights, their eco-nomic dependence and inferiority, and their social restrictions. In an age in which liberal values—stressing individualism, political rights, and equality before the law—were becoming firmly established, women were still relegated to a secondary position or actually excluded from most aspects of public life.

For middle-class women, the contradictions were greatest. The sexual division of labor, which separated the woman's sphere from the man's sphere, was rigidified by the growing cult of domesticity. Accordingly, women were glorified as caring mothers, supportive wives, and religious beings. Their place was in the home, where they were in charge of the domestic scene. The wife was supposed to defer and cater to her husband and take personal responsibility for nursing and rearing the children. The children's education and the religious well-being of the family were her realm. As domestic manager, she was supposed to have expertise as a consumer, and in turn she was the object of consumer advertising. She was also assumed to be interested in charity and willing to donate time for worthy causes. The middle-class wife was not expected to engage in paid occupations outside the home.

The more successfully middle class the family was, the less likely it was that the wife engaged in paid work. Nevertheless, toward the end of the nineteenth century some professions such as schoolteaching, social work, and nursing were expanding and opening to even married middle-class women. Still, most of these occupations were associated with women's domestic roles, were relatively low paying, and were considered most appropriate for unmarried women.

Within the working class, middle-class views about the separate spheres of women and men and the particular domestic nature of women hovered and had some important effects, but the actual experience of women differed. In general working-class women were much more likely to work for wages than middle-class women (see Figure 45.4). A common pattern was for young women to take jobs as domestics before they were married—often moving to cities for this purpose. In addition to the more traditional jobs for women in textiles, food processing, and retail outlets, some of the newer occupations in nursing and secretarial work were opening to women. When jobs were unavailable, prostitution (generally legal and regulated) remained at least a temporary alternative for some. After marriage, women were effectively excluded from several of the options they had when single. One of the main ways for working-class women to earn money was in "sweated industries," where they worked in small factories or at home, usually in textiles or decorating, and were paid by the piece. In all these occupations women continued to be discriminated against; they received lower pay than men for the same work and were excluded from many jobs open to working-class men. Often middle-class notions of domesticity were used to justify the lower pay and status of women's work, employers arguing that women's primary role was not in paid labor. Women were the first to be affected by new legislation controlling the hours and conditions under which workers could be employed, although these laws were often poorly enforced.

The image of domesticity was often in contrast to the realities of life for women. Venereal diseases rose to the point where they were a major cause of death. Illegitimacy was widespread, particularly in urban areas. Many more women were working for wages and in "inappropriate"

FIGURE 45.5 Emmeline Pankhurst Women led numerous demonstrations in their struggle to gain the vote, particularly in Great Britain. Here a policeman is arresting a leading suffragette, Emmeline Pankhurst. (Culver Pictures)

jobs than accepted notions of morality dictated. While working-class women may have suffered most from these realities, they affected women of all classes.

During this period some organized efforts to challenge the role and status assigned to women arose. The strongest feminist movements, particularly movements to extend voting rights to women, arose in Great Britain and the United States. In Great Britain organizations such as the National Union of Women's Suffrage Societies, led by Millicent Fawcett (1847–1929), and the more radical Women's Social and Political Union, led by Emmeline Pankhurst (1858–1928), petitioned, lobbied, and marched for the franchise (see Figure 45.5). Increasingly, women's organizations publicized their positions and used rallies to further their causes. Mass demonstrations occurred more often in the years before World War I. In 1908 a rally for female suffrage drew some 250,000 women to Hyde Park in London. Some women used more violent means to bring attention to their cause. But the government resisted, and success was achieved only at the end of World War I.

In other countries, women's organizations argued for the right to vote and for changes in women's social and economic position, but these organizations were often splintered and rarely achieved their goals. Many continental feminist leaders such as Louise Michel in France, Clara Zetkin in Germany, and Anna Kuliscioff in Italy associated themselves with socialist or radical movements. Only in Norway did women gain the right to vote in national elections before World War I. However, the issues of feminism were now being raised publicly as never before and would become more powerful during the twentieth century.

SUGGESTED READING

General

E. J. Hobsbawm, *The Age of Capital* (1975). Examines middle-class life during the second half of the nineteenth century.

N. Stone, *Europe Transformed, 1878–1919* (1984). A broad survey.

E. R. Tannenbaum, *1900: The Generation Before the Great War* (1976). Good essays on social history.

The Second Industrial Revolution

F. Crouzet, *The Victorian Economy* (1982). Good sections on this period.

D. S. Landes, *The Unbound Prometheus: Technological Change and Industrial Development in Western Europe from 1750 to the Present* (1969). An excellent survey emphasizing technological change.

A. S. Milward and S. B. Saul, *The Development of the Economies of Continental Europe, 1850–1914* (1977). A good treatment of the second Industrial Revolution.

The Rise of Working-Class Organizations and Ideologies

L. R. Berlanstein, *The Working People of Paris, 1871–1914* (1985). A comprehensive study.

J. Joll, *The Anarchists* (1964). A good examination of anarchism and anarchists.

G. Lichtheim, *Marxism* (1971). A highly respected treatment.

A. Lindemann, *A History of European Socialism* (1983). Connects thought and practice.

W. Sewell, Jr., *Work and Revolution in France* (1980). A good treatment of French socialism.

The Growth and Movement of Population

A. Briggs, *Victorian Cities* (1970). A good examination of Britain's industrial cities.

T. McKeown, *The Modern Rise of Population* (1976). A good introduction.

J. Merriman, ed., *French Cities in the Nineteenth Century: Class, Power, and Urbanization* (1982). A good selection of recent essays.

Social Classes

J. Donzelot, *The Policing of Families* (1979). An important interpretation stressing governmental interference with family life.

P. Gay, *The Bourgeois Experience: Victoria to Freud,* 2 vols. (1984–1986). An excellent study of sexuality and the middle class.

P. Joyce, *Visions of the People: Industrial England and the Question of Class, c. 1848–1914* (1991). An excellent recent interpretation.

Women

M. Boxer and J. Quataert, eds., *Connecting Spheres: Women in the Western World, 1500 to Present* (1987). Fine chapters covering the period.

P. Branca, *Women in Europe since 1750* (1978). A useful study.

R. Bridenthal and C. Koonz, *Becoming Visible: Women in European History* (1987). Contains good chapters covering the period.

M. Vicinus, *Suffer and Be Still: Women in the Victorian Age* (1972). Good essays on Victorian women.

CHAPTER 46
Science and the Challenge to Christianity

FIGURE 46.1 Thomas Eakins, *The Gross Clinic,* 1875 This realistic painting by Eakins of an operation in progress conveys the sense of power of modern science and the optimism with which science was viewed in the nineteenth century. The lack of religious references in this medical scene indicates some of the potential challenge of secular science to Christianity. (Jefferson Medical College, Thomas Jefferson University, Philadelphia)

By the middle of the nineteenth century, science had gained much prestige. It was increasingly connected with the inventions and technology of industrialization, which provided wealth and power. It seemed to go hand in hand with the rationalism and prevailing bourgeois liberalism of the period. Over the course of the nineteenth century, people assumed that scientists had, or soon would have, a firm understanding of the physical world. They were optimistic that scientific methods would provide a similar understanding of human society. Although this sense of certainty and optimism would be somewhat undermined in the decades surrounding the turn of the century, the period between 1850 and 1914 must be considered one of great progress in the sciences.

At the same time Christianity faced serious and fundamental challenges. It was attacked from several quarters, but at the base of the many challenges were the successes and increasing prestige of science. Christian leaders often had difficulty adjusting their theology and institutions to the scientific, liberal, and secular assumptions of the period.

1. THE PHYSICAL, BIOLOGICAL, AND MEDICAL SCIENCES

The greatest advances in the field of the physical sciences in the nineteenth and early twentieth centuries centered on discovering the nature of matter, energy, and electricity. John Dalton (1766–1844), a gifted British scientist and teacher, started a fruitful line of inquiry by reviving the theory that all matter is composed of atoms. Dalton eventually concluded that what distinguishes the various chemical elements is the weight of the atoms of which each element is composed. Building on Dalton's theories, the Russian chemist Dmitri Mendeléev (1834–1907) in 1870 worked out a periodic chart showing the atomic weight of all the known elements and indicating by gaps in the chart that others remained to be discovered. Both Dalton and Mendeléev thought that the atom was an indivisible solid. But in the 1890s the British physicist Joseph Thomson (1856–1940) and the Dutch physicist Hendrik Lorentz (1853–1928) independently discovered that atoms are composed of small particles, which Lorentz named electrons. Shortly thereafter another British physicist, Sir Ernest Rutherford (1871–1937), further developed Thomson's theories. Rutherford conceived of each atom as a miniature solar system, the nucleus being the sun and the electrons the planets. Furthermore—and this was most startling—Thomson and Rutherford suggested that the protons and electrons might not be matter at all but merely positive and negative charges of electricity.

Meanwhile in the 1890s the German physicist Wilhelm von Roentgen (1845–1923) discovered X rays, and the French physicist Pierre Curie (1859–1906) and his Polish wife Marie Curie (1867–1935) discovered radium and added to what was known about radioactivity.

During this same period, Albert Einstein (1879–1955), a German physicist who later fled to America, was assailing time-honored concepts not only about the stability of matter but also about time, space, and motion (see Figure 46.2). Einstein derived a formula equating mass and energy: $E = mc^2$ (E = energy in ergs; m = mass in grams; c = speed of light in centimeters per second). According to this formula, the atomic energy in a lump of coal is some three billion times as great as the energy obtained by burning the coal—a truth that was proved several decades later with the development of the atomic bomb. In 1905 Einstein proposed his theory of relativity, which made time, space, and motion relative to one another and to the observer, not the absolutes they had always been conceived to be.

These stunning discoveries in physics and chemistry were triumphs, reflecting a new sophistication in scientific theory and experimentation. But by the turn of the century a sense of uncertainty was creeping into elite scientific circles—a sense that the more we learn, the less solid and reliable the material world seems. This sense of uncertainty, particularly in physics, would spread in the early decades of the twentieth century.

The intellectual world was even more interested in and influenced by developments in the biological sciences. Evolution, like the atomic theory, had been suggested by the ancient Greeks and from time to time afterward. With the revival of scientific interests and attitudes in

FIGURE 46.2 Einstein Albert Einstein (1879–1955) became one of the most recognized figures of the twentieth century. His theory of relativity, first proposed in 1905, undermined the concept of a stable material universe that Newton had so beautifully formalized early in the eighteenth century. (Karsh, Ottawa/Woodfin Camp & Associates)

the seventeenth and eighteenth centuries, the thoughts of a number of scientists turned to the problem of the origin of the present world and its phenomena. By the mid–nineteenth century, the concept of a slow and gradual development of the earth's crust and its inhabitants was not at all uncommon among intellectuals. The time was ripe for a first-rate scientist to supply the evidence. That man was Charles Darwin (1809–1882).

Darwin was of a distinguished British family. His study of medicine at Edinburgh and theology at Cambridge failed to challenge him. The world of plants and, to a somewhat lesser extent, animals was his first love—or rather, his consuming passion. In spite of frail health, he turned his powers of observation and reflection to the amassing of biological knowledge. Gradually he developed his concept of evolution. Of great influence on his thinking was Malthus' *Essay on Population* (1798), which described the struggle

of human beings for food and survival, and Sir Charles Lyell's *Principles of Geology* (1830–1833), which was the first truly scientific treatise on geology. Lyell demonstrated by the study of fossils the likelihood of a gradual evolution of the earth's crust and of plant and animal forms over eons of time. Darwin published *On the Origin of Species by Natural Selection* in 1859. In this historic work he described, with an impressive array of factual data, convincing reasoning, and lucid prose, the long, slow evolution of present plant and animal species from simpler forms through a process of natural selection. In the struggle for survival in nature's jungle, the fittest survived. Those specimens that possessed the more useful characteristics—for instance, the horse with the longer legs—survived to produce more offspring and to transmit their superior qualities, both inherited and acquired, to future generations. Twelve years later (1871) in his *Descent of Man*, he undertook to show how humans had evolved from more primitive species by the same process. Although Darwin's work left many fundamental questions unanswered, his main thesis quickly gained general acceptance in the scientific world.

Few books in history have had so much influence as *On the Origin of Species*. The industrial bourgeoisie seized upon Darwin's theory as an explanation of and justification for its own success. Rulers and dominant groups everywhere derived comfort from it. Philosophers, notably Herbert Spencer, undertook to broaden the principle of evolution to make it the key to all truth. Meanwhile, Darwin's brilliant work not only popularized but also significantly contributed to the advancement of the biological sciences.

Medical science lagged far behind the physical and biological sciences at the opening of the nineteenth century. The seventeenth- and eighteenth-century scientists had made great progress in discovering the secrets of the stars, of the elements, and of plants and animals, but where the ailments of the human body were concerned, most were still holding to the theories of Galen, a Greek physician of the second century A.D. George Washington was bled to death in 1799 by a physician who was following the standard practice of the time.

Much groundwork had been laid, however, for medical progress. In the sixteenth century Andreas Vesalius made great advances in the study of human anatomy. In the seventeenth century William Harvey discovered the circulatory system and Antoni van Leeuwenhoek and Marcello Malpighi were using the newly invented microscope to explore the structure of human tissue and to discover the existence of microbes. By the late eighteenth century the British physician Edward Jenner was successfully inoculating against smallpox, though he did not understand the secret of its success. During the 1840s anesthesia was discovered and used successfully. But the whole field of germ diseases and infections was still a mystery.

The secrets of bacteria, their nature and their control, were first explored by the French chemist Louis Pasteur (1822–1895). During the 1860s Pasteur, after intensive and imaginative research, discovered that fermentation is caused by airborne bacteria that can be destroyed by boiling (or "pasteurization"). Later he discovered that many diseases of humans and animals are also caused by bacteria and that some of them can be prevented by vaccination. His spectacular services to French agriculture and to humankind made him the most honored man in France. Robert Koch (1843–1910), a country doctor in eastern Germany, hearing of Pasteur's first discoveries, picked up the trail and discovered the germs causing anthrax (a deadly disease of cattle), tuberculosis, sleeping sickness, and many other diseases. He became a professor at the University of Berlin and was awarded the Nobel Prize.

Also building on Pasteur's foundations was the renowned British surgeon Joseph Lister (1827–1912), who applied the new knowledge of bacteria to the use of antiseptics and disinfectants in surgery. His amazing success in controlling infection opened a new era in surgery, and Lister was raised to the peerage by the British government. The honors bestowed on Pasteur, Koch, and Lister, in contrast with the persecutions suffered by many of the sixteenth- and seventeenth-century scientists, are striking evidence of the triumph of science and the scientific spirit in the nineteenth century.

New discoveries in the physical, biological, and medical sciences did not, however, mean that women gained stature in the eyes of scientists. Darwin believed his findings showed men to be superior to women. Men in the sciences generally found support for their views that women were inferior to men and were appropriately dependent upon men. As with attitudes toward race, science was often used to justify assumptions about women and their proper domestic roles in a male-dominated family. Most universities, in fact, remained closed to women, though some separate women's colleges were starting to open in the last decades of the nineteenth century.

2. THE RISE OF SOCIAL SCIENCE

The spectacular successes of the natural sciences in the nineteenth century encouraged scholars to apply the techniques and principles of natural science to the study of the human mind and society. The result was the birth of modern psychology and sociology, both of which soon became popular.

Until the middle of the nineteenth century the mechanistic and associational approach to psychology stemming from the theories of John Locke (1632–1704) still prevailed. In the second half of the nineteenth century a number of psychologists began to systematically apply an empirical approach to the study of human behavior. One of the first to bring psychology into the laboratory was Wilhelm Wundt (1832–1920). In his famous laboratory at Leipzig he and his enthusiastic students tested human reactions and tried all sorts of carefully controlled and measured experiments on cats and dogs, assuming that the findings would also be applicable to human beings.

The Russian scientist Ivan Pavlov (1849–1936), pursuing Wundt's line of attack, excited the intellectual world with the discovery of the conditioned reflex. Pavlov showed meat to a hungry dog, and the dog's mouth watered. Then Pavlov rang a bell while showing the meat. Eventually the dog's mouth watered when only the bell was rung. The implication was that many of our human responses are purely mechanical reflexes produced by stimuli of which we are often unaware.

Sigmund Freud (1856–1939) created the greatest stir of all in the rapidly growing field of psychology. Freud was a Viennese neurologist who became the father of psychoanalysis. Freud concluded that much of human behavior is irrational, unconscious, and instinctual. He argued that conflict is a basic condition of life, particularly conflict between our innate biological drives (such as sex or aggression) and our social selves. These conflicts are worked out on a mostly unconscious level and in stages during childhood. These conflicts invariably cause frustration. Freud believed that much neurosis and psychosis stemmed from the suppressed and frustrated drives of early life—frustrations that then festered in the subconscious. He concluded that the correct therapy for such neuroses was to make the sufferer conscious of the facts and circumstances of the original frustration. He stressed the interpretation of dreams as a key tool for revealing the unconscious. Freud and his followers developed psychoanalysis into an influential theory of human behavior, an insightful method of psychological investigation, and a useful therapy for certain problems.

During the second half of the nineteenth century sociology acquired status as a social science. This new discipline was founded and named by Auguste Comte (1798–1857), an eccentric Frenchman of great energy and imagination. The history of humankind, said Comte, can be divided into three epochs. The first was religious, when mystical or supernatural explanations were assigned to all phenomena. The second was metaphysical, when general laws and abstract principles were taken as explanatory principles. The third, which humankind was on the point of entering, was the specific or positive, when the truth would be discovered by the scientific gathering of factual data. Comte had utter scorn for the first and little respect for the second epochs. He believed that humans and society are as susceptible to scientific investigation as minerals, plants, and the lower animals. His religion was the worship of humanity, and he had great faith in its future. These ideas were called *positivism*. Comte's followers, eager and numerous, placed great faith in statistics. They amassed vast arrays of statistical data on every conceivable social problem.

Second only to Comte in importance in the founding and promotion of sociology was the Englishman Herbert Spencer (1820–1903). Spencer shared Comte's scorn for mystical religion and denied that morals should be based on religion. He also shared Comte's faith in the progress of humanity. In his ten-volume *System of Synthetic Philosophy*, Spencer undertook to synthesize all human and social phenomena into one grand evolutionary system.

People's interest in themselves and in human society, together with the scientific spirit of the times, guaranteed great popularity for the social sciences. Anthropologists and archaeologists dug feverishly into the physical and cultural past of the human race. Political scientists and economists tended to forsake theory for the statistical and "practical." Strenuous efforts were made to make history a social science. Leopold von Ranke (1795–1886) strove to make history coldly scientific and morally neutral. History, he insisted, should be based on an exhaustive accumulation and analysis of documentary evidence. Ranke's historical attitude and methodology were imported from Germany into the United States, becoming the standard in both countries.

Between 1850 and 1914 natural scientists appeared to be solving the last mysteries of the material universe. Medical scientists appeared to be banishing pain and disease from the earth. Social scientists were amassing voluminous knowledge about the human mind and social relationships. Science had become one of the mainstays of the widely popular belief in progress.

3. CHALLENGES TO CHRISTIANITY

The rapid growth of science was just one of several challenges faced by organized religion in the West. Christianity also seemed to be threatened by most of the other major forces of modernization.

Industrialization was in many ways inimical to Christian faith and practices. Industrialization contributed to the mass migration of people from farm to city and from country to country, tearing them loose from old social patterns and institutions, of which the Church had long been one of the most important. Members of the flocks became separated from their pastors. Once in the active and exciting industrial cities, many of the newcomers seemed no longer to need the Church for their social life and entertainment.

The liberal and radical political movements of the late nineteenth century were for the most part anticlerical. The established churches in Europe, particularly the Catholic church, had long been allied with the conservative aristocracy and royalty. Liberals, when they came to power, often attacked the powers, the privileges, and the property of the established Church. France is a good example. After the revolutionary era ended with the overthrow of Napoleon, the Catholic church made a comeback. It allied itself with the Bourbon regime and with Napoleon III's Second Empire, and it opposed liberal movements, including the setting up of the Third French Republic. The liberal leaders of the Third Republic soon adopted anticlerical policies. During the 1880s the Ferry Laws loosened the hold of the Church on education by setting up a rival and favored system of public secular schools, in which the teaching of religion was banned. In 1901 the Associations Law virtually destroyed the Church's schools by outlawing the Catholic teaching orders or associations. In 1905 church and state were completely separated. In all the industrialized countries in this period, public secular education made great strides, usually under the sponsorship of liberal parties.

Another factor inimical to organized religion during the second half of the nineteenth century was the growth of nationalism, which afflicted all the great industrialized powers. International Catholicism and international Judaism were seen as competitors for nationalistic allegiance. Between 1872 and 1878 Bismarck waged *Kulturkampf* (battle for civilization) against the Catholic church in Germany (see p. 610). Bismarck regarded as intolerable the allegiance of millions of German citizens to a non-German pope and the formation of a Catholic political party in Germany. The anti-Semitism that arose in many countries at this time may be attributed in part to the resentment against the international character of Judaism and also to racism, which was often connected to strong nationalism. The Dreyfus case in France is an example (see p. 608). Bloody pogroms in Russia drove tens of thousands of Russian and Polish Jews to America. Many Jews themselves, after centuries of dispersion, became nationalistic and started a movement (Zionism) to set up a Jewish national state in Palestine.

In most of these challenges to Christianity, science—whether through use or abuse—was used to bolster or lend some credibility to the attack. During the twentieth century Christianity would learn to coexist with science, but in the nineteenth century the two were at odds with each other.

With the exception of the evolutionary hypothesis, the challenge to Christianity by natural science was more indirect than direct. The discovery of more and more of the secrets of the material world allowed people to attribute to natural causes many phenomena that previously had been attributed to divine intervention. Disease germs, for instance, now appeared to be doing things that had long been ascribed to God (see Figure 46.1).

The greatest conflicts between natural science and the Christian religion to emerge in the nineteenth century grew out of Darwin's evolutionary hypothesis. The publication of *On the Origin of Species* created an immediate religious storm. The proposal of a long, gradual, and seemingly mechanistic evolution of all present species from simpler forms appeared to contradict the account of divine creation given in the first chapter of Genesis. The whole process of evolution as suggested by Darwin appeared to leave God entirely out of the affairs of the universe. Any doubt concerning Darwin's place for human beings in his evolutionary hypothesis was removed when he published *The Descent of Man.* Human beings, he theorized, like all other living things, evolved from more primitive species. According to Darwin's hypothesis, in the view of many readers, a human being seemed to be just another animal, albeit the highest.

Clerics raged against Darwin and his hypothesis. Efforts were made, sometimes successfully, to suppress the reading of Darwin's books and the teaching of the evolutionary hypothesis in the schools. Darwin was not lacking in champions able and willing to assail the forces of religion. Thomas Huxley (1825–1895), a biologist, surgeon in the British navy, and president of the Royal Society, popularized Darwin's work in dozens of vigorous and lucid books and pamphlets and heaped withering scorn upon the clergy. He called himself "Darwin's bull-dog." Herbert Spencer was carried away with Darwin's thesis and built a whole system of philosophy around the idea of evolution. Spencer considered evolution the key to all truth and all progress. Ernst

Haeckel (1834–1919), a prolific German scientist and popularizer, made great claims for evolution and for science. He proclaimed that scientists would very soon be solving all the remaining mysteries of life and even creating life. The conflict between the evolutionists and the Christian clergy that raged in western Europe in the last four decades of the nineteenth century did not reach its climax in the United States until the 1920s.

The assault of social science upon Christianity was much more direct and severe than that of natural science. Anthropologists dug into the human race's distant past to unearth the primitive origins of its culture, of which religion is always an important part. Nearly all of them concluded that religion is based on primitive superstition. In 1890 Sir James Frazer (1854–1941) published *The Golden Bough,* a vast and fascinating history of early myths, superstitions, and cults from which he believed that modern religions, including Christianity, were derived.

Psychologists often viewed religion as a fantasy or illusion created by human beings. God, they felt, serves as a powerful parental figure to turn to when difficult problems drive human beings into a more childlike psychological state—someone who can be relied on to deal with a threatening world. Religion also provides psychological ecstasy as well as ways of enforcing constraint and control.

But it was the sociologists who were the most persistently and pointedly hostile to religion. Supernatural religion had no place whatever in Comte's positivism, humanity itself being the object of worship. Through volume after volume of Herbert Spencer's sociological writings ran a vein of hostility to mystic religion in general and to Christianity in particular. Mechanical evolution became, for Spencer, the key to all social progress; even morals evolved. Religious faith, said Spencer, retarded social progress and obscured human vision of the evolutionary social process.

Finally, the scientific spirit brought forth a number of biblical scholars who subjected the Bible to searching scrutiny and analysis—some for the purpose of establishing its exact meaning, others for the purpose of detecting error or fraud. This type of scholarship is called "higher criticism."

The first prominent nineteenth-century "higher critic" of the Bible was David Strauss (1808–1874), a Lutheran theologian at the University of Tübingen in Germany. After long years of laborious work, Strauss brought out a *Life of Jesus* in two volumes that stripped Christ of his divinity and undertook to explain in natural terms the miracles and prophecies recorded in the New Testament. Strauss asserted that the New Testament was a very unreliable document, that the authorship of the four Gospels could not be proved, and that the four accounts of the life of Jesus were contradictory.

Much more popular and influential was the charming one-volume *La Vie de Jésus* by Ernest Renan (1823–1892), a French scholar and a Catholic. Renan pictured Christ in solely human and natural terms. Renan attributed Christ's belief in his own divinity to hallucinations. But it was these psychological aberrations, Renan said, that gave him his power and drive and much of his appeal. The work of Strauss, Renan, and the numerous other "higher critics" appeared to many to bring religion within the compass of onrushing science.

4. THE CHRISTIAN RESPONSE

The first reaction of Christianity to the new challenges was angry rejection of the new ideas and forces. In 1864 Pope Pius IX (1846–1878) issued a *Syllabus of Errors,* errors that Roman Catholics were to avoid. These errors, eighty in all, included separation of church and state, civil marriage, secular education, freedom of speech and press, religious toleration, liberty of conscience, liberalism, and materialism. In 1870 Pius IX called a Vatican council (the first general council since that at Trent in the sixteenth century), which pronounced the doctrine of papal infallibility. According to this doctrine, the pope, when speaking *ex cathedra* (that is, officially *from the chair* of St. Peter) on a matter of faith or morals, is not subject to error. This was the most authoritarian position that the Church and the pope had ever taken, and it came at a time when the intellectual, political, and religious trends seemed to be in the opposite direction. In the late nineteenth and early twentieth centuries, the Catholic hierarchy excommunicated numerous members and several priests who had compromised the official doctrines of the Church.

Many Protestants also rejected the new ideas and forces, particularly fundamentalist sects that interpreted the Bible literally. More established churches, such as the Anglicans in Great Britain and Lutherans in Germany, resisted but had to contend with undisciplined dissent within their ranks and secular authorities that supported the new developments.

The second reaction of Christianity to the nineteenth-century challenges and assaults was to surrender to them. Many Christians, Catholics and Protestants alike, lost their faith and left their church. But many more who lost the traditional faith remained in their church and attempted to change its doctrines. They granted the claims of science and the "higher criticism," and they sympathized with the materialism, liberalism, and nationalism of the day. They continued to go to church, to sing the hymns, to say the prayers, and to recite the creeds, but they did not believe what they sang, said, and recited. They would reject the supernatural and deny the divinity of Christ. They would make the Bible a book of good literature and high ethical ideals; Christ, a great social reformer; and the Church, an instrument for the promotion of good will, wholesome fellowship, racial tolerance, temperance, charity, patriotism, and so on. These Christians came to be called *modernists*. The Catholic church declared officially against modernism in 1907, and by 1914 it appeared to have either suppressed the modernists in its ranks or driven them under cover. In the various Protestant churches in Europe modernism competed with fundamentalism, both extreme and moderate, and by 1914 modernism had tended to gain the upper hand. In the United States modernism in the Protestant churches did not reach its peak until the 1920s and 1930s.

The third reaction of Christianity was moderate compromise: an acceptance of proved scientific facts and reasonable deductions therefrom together with attempts to harmonize the findings of science with the fundamentals of the Christian faith. This attitude involved interpreting certain passages in the Bible figuratively, particularly the first chapter of Genesis, and admitting to a few errors in various versions of the Bible. This harmonizing Christian reaction led to an in-

FIGURE 46.3 Pope Leo XIII Leo XIII (1878–1903) was the first pope to face up to issues raised by science and modernization. While clinging to the traditional doctrines of the Church, he accepted new scientific discoveries and supported some liberal reform movements. (UPI/Bettmann Newsphotos)

creased awareness of the responsibility of the Christian churches to participate actively in the social and political problems of the day.

The Catholics were the first to reach this middle position. Leo XIII (see Figure 46.3), pope from 1878 to 1903, promoted the theology of Thomas Aquinas, which stressed the compatibility of faith and reason. He welcomed new scientific beliefs on condition that they be proved. He and his successors gradually took the position that natural science was not the province of the Church; that evolution could be taught in the Church's schools as a hypothesis; that the first chapter of Genesis should be taken figuratively; and that within these premises belief in evolution was a private and individual matter.

Leo XIII also faced up to some of the economic and social challenges of industrialization. In 1891, in the most famous of all his encyclicals, *Rerum Novarum* ("of new things"), he denounced materialism and Marxian socialism and proclaimed the sanctity of private property. He did, however, declare limits to the use of private property. Labor must not be treated as a commodity; workers must be paid a fair living wage and protected against too long hours, injury, and disease. Leo XIII advocated a wider distribution of property, labor unions for collective bargaining, and farming cooperatives. Roman Catholic labor unions were soon organized to challenge the socialist-dominated unions.

Christianity, so beset on its home grounds by challenges, assaults, and internal divisions during the late nineteenth century, was never more zealous in sending out missionaries to propagate the faith abroad. Roman Catholic, Protestant, and Eastern Orthodox missionaries vied with one another in Asia and Africa. By 1914 more than 40 million people outside western Christendom professed the Christian faith. But since the Christian missionaries in Asia and Africa were often associated with Western imperialism and exploitation, they frequently aroused resentment. In 1914 Christianity in the West was still on the defensive.

SUGGESTED READING

General

O. Chadwick, *The Secularization of the European Mind in the Nineteenth Century* (1975). A useful, well-written study.

P. A. Dale, *In Pursuit of a Scientific Culture: Science, Art, and Society in the Victorian Age* (1990). A thoughtful recent study.

The Physical, Biological, and Medical Sciences

E. Mayr, *The Growth of Biological Thought* (1982). A good recent survey.

M. Ruse, *The Darwinian Revolution* (1979). An excellent introduction.

The Rise of Social Science

R. Aron, *Main Currents in Sociological Thought*, 2 vols. (1965, 1967). An excellent survey of the founders of modern sociology.

P. Gay, *Freud: A Life for Our Time* (1988). A well-regarded study.

Challenges to Christianity

J. L. Altholz, *The Churches in the Nineteenth Century* (1967). A solid survey.

H. McLeod, *Religion and the People of Western Europe, 1789–1970* (1981). Useful chapters on the period.

J. McManners, *Church and State in France, 1870–1914* (1972). Solid and scholarly.

J. Moore, *The Post-Darwinian Controversies: A Study of the Protestant Struggle to Come to Terms with Darwin in Great Britain and America, 1870–1900* (1979). A respected analysis.

CHAPTER 47

Thought and Culture in an Age of Nationalism and Industrialization

FIGURE 47.1 Pablo Picasso, *Les Demoiselles d'Avignon*, 1906–1907 Between 1850 and 1914 artistic styles evolved rapidly, moving from realism to the beginnings of modernism. Picasso (1881–1973) was one of the most influential artists during the latter part of this period and throughout the twentieth century. This painting reflects the sense of revolt, the rapidly changing values, and the tendency to turn inward that characterized many cultural products of the late nineteenth and early twentieth centuries. (Oil on canvas, 8′ × 7′8″. Collection, The Museum of Modern Art, New York. Acquired through the Lillie P. Bliss Bequest)

The nationalism of the increasingly powerful Western nation-states, the challenges to established religious and moral values, and the tensions of industrial society are reflected in the thought and art of the period between 1850 and 1914. There was no sudden or drastic break with the spirit of idealism and romanticism that prevailed in the thought and art of the first half of the nineteenth century. Both idealism and romanticism continued throughout the nineteenth century and beyond. Nevertheless, after midcentury, realism tended to replace the romanticism of the early nineteenth century. As the bourgeoisie played a more dominant role in the culture of the period, artists, writers, and intellectuals became more of an avant-garde—increasingly critical of bourgeois values and tastes. By the end of the nineteenth century and the beginning of the twentieth, these artists, writers, and intellectuals were injecting a theme of pessimism and painful introspection into Western culture.

The nationalism that was such an important component of political and social developments during the period was reflected in a growing body of thought. Nationalism was also one of the elements behind the spread of state-sponsored educational reforms, which led toward expanded literacy and the growth of popular journalism.

In literature a stream of realism and naturalism, characterized by an almost scientific examination of life, seemed to focus on individual and social failings. Art tended to slip away from the grasp of the ordinary viewer as photography displaced traditional representational art and impressionists applied a new understanding of the physical world and optics to their paintings. Post-impressionists veered into even more disturbing styles as art, like the new scientific disciplines, became more specialized.

1. POPULAR EDUCATION, JOURNALISM, AND CULTURE

During this era of nationalism and spreading industrialization, and particularly after 1871, there were great advances in popular education. In 1871 northern Germany and Scandinavia were the only places in the world where practically everyone could read and write. In the United States most of the states had free public elementary schools, but a fifth of the total population was still illiterate. In Great Britain a third of the people were still illiterate, in France and Belgium a half, in Spain and Italy three-fourths, in Russia and the Balkans nine-tenths. Between 1868 and 1881 national systems of free and compulsory public education were established in nearly all the nations of western and central Europe and the United States. There was a variety of reasons for this growing commitment to public education. Public schooling was seen as a way to create more patriotic, nationalistic citizens. At the same time schools could help provide workers with the skills and discipline that modernizing economies and military establishments demanded. For the most part, the compulsory public school systems were limited to elementary education. While the core of the curriculum was generally the same for boys and girls—reading, writing, history, mathematics, and a few other subjects—boys were usually taught more science and skills such as carpentry while girls were taught domestic skills. By 1914 illiteracy had practically ceased to exist in Scandinavia, Germany, Great Britain, and the Netherlands. The illiteracy rate was less than 10 percent in the United States, Canada, France, and Belgium. In Italy it had been reduced to 50 percent and in Spain, Russia, and the Balkans to a little more than 50 percent. Literacy, of course, is only the first step toward education.

The rise in literacy was reflected in a growth of popular journalism. In 1850 newspapers were relatively few, small, expensive, and written for a limited educated clientele. The London *Times,* probably the world's most influential newspaper, had a daily circulation of less than fifty thousand. During the second half of the nineteenth century, nationalism and industrialization were accompanied by a new kind of newspaper, one that was cheap, sensational, and popular in its appeal. One of the pioneer popular journalists was Joseph Pulitzer (1847–1911), a Hungarian immigrant to the United States. Pulitzer founded the St. Louis *Post Dispatch.* He bought and built up the New York *World* until it became the country's biggest newspaper. With screaming headlines, flag-waving patriotism, an easy, catchy style, sensational news, popular causes and features, and above all comics, he made a fortune and became influential in politics. In the 1890s William Randolph Hearst built a great newspaper empire patterned after Pulitzer's. In Great Britain Alfred Harmsworth founded the halfpenny popular *Daily Mail,* made a fortune, and then bought the London *Times.* Before the end of the century five newspapers—two in London, two in Paris, and one in Berlin—had a daily circulation of more than a million each. *Le Petit Journal* in Paris had a circulation of more than two and a quarter million. This type of newspaper not only catered to the masses but also became a powerful molder of public opinion. Hearst boasted, with a modicum of truth, that he had manufactured the Spanish-American War. Since the popular newspapers made their money chiefly from advertising rather than from sales, they came increasingly to reflect the viewpoints of their chief advertisers, the great corporations. The big newspapers were themselves, of course, big business. Although they catered to the masses, they generally did not represent the interests of the masses.

Newspapers were part of the literature of popular culture. Pulp fiction was also spreading rapidly, as were other cultural outlets of the masses. The phonograph increased the demand for popular music, as did the growing number of urban music and dance halls. After the 1890s commercial films were produced. By 1914 millions of people were watching movies every week. New public libraries and museums were institutions that could serve all classes and blur the lines between popular and elite culture. Nevertheless, divisions between the classes were strong, and this was reflected in the differences between popular and elite culture.

2. CURRENTS OF THOUGHT: NATIONALISM, RACISM, AND DISENCHANTMENT

During the nineteenth century a strong current of thought reflected and supported the growing nationalism of that era. German thinkers in particular contributed to the intellectual foundations of nationalism. In the first half of the century, Georg Wilhelm Hegel (1770–1831) was most influential. Among other things, he argued that individual freedom depends on ordered discipline under a strong state and that the zeitgeist (spirit of the time) of the nineteenth century was the spirit of German civilization.

Even more directly supportive of nationalism were the ideas of people such as Heinrich von Treitschke, probably the most influential German historian of the decades surrounding the turn of the century, who proclaimed that Germany's victory over France demonstrated the superiority of military autocracy over liberalism. Only strong states ought to exist, he felt; dissident minorities, individualism, and parliamentary inefficiency must not be tolerated.

German thinkers were not the only ones to reflect the nationalism of the period in their ideas. The French historian Hippolyte Taine blamed France's defeat in 1870–1871 on the corrupting influence of liberalism born in the French Revolution and bred during the nineteenth century. He wanted to take France back to the days of the Old Regime. In Great Britain, Thomas Carlyle exalted heroes and hero worship, specifically the Prussian variety, in thunderous prose. Rudyard Kipling put his poetic gifts to use to sing of the glorious British Empire and the "white man's burden" of ruling and civilizing "backward" peoples.

The most extreme set of ideas underlying nationalism during the second half of the nineteenth century was racism (see p. 615). People of every nation began to think and talk of themselves as a distinct and superior breed. Language was more than ever confused with race. Thus one spoke of the various "races" in the Austro-Hungarian Empire. By far the most popular and serious of all the racial cults was the Aryan myth. The term *Aryan,* which was originally a linguistic term referring to the ancient Persians (Iranians) and later to all peoples speaking Indo-European languages, was now applied to the Germanic- or Teutonic-speaking peoples or to the Nordic (tall blond) type of northern European. After Germany's spectacular military triumphs and economic developments under Bismarck, the term *Aryan* came to be applied more specifically to Germans and to the energetic, aggressive, military qualities they were supposed to possess. Oddly, the two chief formulators of the Aryan myth were a Frenchman, Comte de Gobineau, and the renegade Englishman Houston Stewart Chamberlain, who left his homeland and became a German citizen. Their ideas, however, were taken much more seriously in Germany than in France or Great Britain. They argued that race was the key determinant of history. Chamberlain's racist ideas veered off into anti-Semitism, as did the ideas of other racist writers such as Richard Wagner. Wagner wrote violent propaganda tracts and composed grandiose operas that stridently extolled the virtues of the early Nordic (German) supermen—Siegfried and the Nibelungs.

Although many philosophers of Social Darwinism and liberalism remained optimistic about the evolution of human beings and human society ever onward and upward, a new, strong strain of disenchantment surfaced in late-nineteenth-century philosophy. A forerunner of these pessimistic philosophers who were to have so much influence on the twentieth century was Arthur Schopenhauer (1788–1860). In *The World as Will and Idea*, published in 1819, forty years before *On the Origin of Species*, this German thinker set forth the idea that one force governs and motivates the whole world of animate life, and that force is will—the will to survive. The world, therefore, is a cruel and heartless place full of struggling and competing creatures, a place where the strong and fierce devour the weak and gentle. The only possible happiness to be found in it is by ascetic denial and withdrawal. They suffer least who participate least in the hard, competitive world.

This line of thinking (at least a variation of it) was carried to its ultimate by an admirer of Schopenhauer, Friedrich Nietzsche (1844–1900). Nietzsche was a disillusioned German theological student turned philosopher. He was a pain- and nerve-racked genius. Two of his most influential works are *Thus Spake Zarathustra* and *Beyond Good and Evil*. Like Schopenhauer, he believed that the greatest force in the animate world is will. However, this will is not only to survive but also, in the strong at least, to achieve power. "The will to power" was Nietzsche's key phrase. If a superior society is to emerge, it will have to come about through the efforts of strong and gifted individuals who will rise to power because of their superior strength, will, and intelligence. Anything that contributes to power is good, be it strength of will, boldness, cunning, or intelligence. Whatever leads to weakness is

bad, be it gentleness, modesty, generosity, or compassion. The two greatest enemies of the good society are democracy and Christianity. Democracy is the rule by mediocre masses, cattle. But it was against Christianity that Nietzsche hurled his sharpest invective; he believed Christianity to be the greatest curse of Western civilization: a religion that extols the vices of slavery, such as meekness, compassion, sacrifice, and charity to compensate for actual weakness. He went on to attack many other accepted foundations of nineteenth-century civilization, including liberalism, rationalism, and science. Although not a nationalist or racist himself, his ideas would later be used by others to support militant nationalism and even racism.

Less caustic and far more popular was the French philosopher Henri Bergson (1859–1941). Like Nietzsche, he attacked bourgeois liberalism and extolled the instincts and the subjective will. His sense of the world as an evolving, vital, spontaneous place fit well with other trends in thought and the arts during the early decades of the twentieth century.

Also popular was the philosophy of pragmatism. The chief expounder of this school of thought, which has been so potent and widespread in the twentieth century, was William James (1842–1910), a professor of psychology and philosophy at Harvard University. Pragmatism reflected the uncertainties aroused by atomic physicists around the turn of the century. James rejected all absolutes of logic and religion. Truth, he stated, is relative, depending on the individual and the circumstances. A thing is true if it works and is useful. We cannot know ultimate religious or moral truths, for instance, but if a particular religious faith gives an individual confidence and peace of mind, then it is practical and therefore true for that person. Thus spiritual, moral, and human values became as relative in the minds of William James and the pragmatists as the physical world in the mind of Albert Einstein.

3. REALISTIC LITERATURE

Much of the literature of the second half of the nineteenth century, like the philosophy, reflected the materialism, the cynicism, and the pessimism of the age. However, there was a strong carryover of romanticism beyond 1850 and into the twentieth century. The romantic Victorian poets Victor Hugo, Robert Browning, and Alfred Tennyson lived on until 1885, 1889, and 1892, respectively. Although Browning was a rugged, analytical realist when probing the depths of human psychology and emotions, he tended at times to be an idealist and optimist, believing that "God's in his heaven, all's right with the world." And although in 1850 the young Tennyson in his *In Memoriam* revealed a religious skepticism bold for the time, in 1889 he hoped to see his "Pilot face to face" when he had "crossed the bar." Nevertheless, the prevailing and most significant trend in literature was realism. It was expressed most generally in the novel and drama rather than poetry. Realism tended to depict the seamy, sordid side of human nature and society. It villainized the *nouveau riche* industrial bourgeoisie and its religious and moral hypocrisy without idealizing the uprooted and distressed working class.

France took the lead in realistic literature. Honoré de Balzac (1799–1850) foreshadowed realism. In his scores of novels and tales he subjected the dominant middle class to increasingly exact and severe scrutiny. The first French novelist to catch the full flavor of realism was Gustave Flaubert (1821–1880). His *Madame Bovary* related the illicit sex life of the wife of a small-town French physician in such full and unblushing detail that it scandalized a public not yet accustomed to such unrestrained "realism." *Madame Bovary* became a model for other novelists.

Émile Zola (1840–1902), though like Flaubert interested in individual personality, was more concerned with social problems, particularly those created by industrialization. Zola was a bold and radical republican who played a major role in finally securing justice for Alfred Dreyfus (see p. 608). In twenty penetrating but sometimes tedious novels he depicted and analyzed the problems of a changing society. His sympathy was with the industrial working class, but he suffered from no illusions as to the natural goodness of people, including the distressed lower classes.

Charles Dickens (1812–1870) in Great Britain combined romanticism and realism. In his sentimentality, his moralizing, his optimism, and his spontaneous gush of words, he was a romantic. In his zeal for social reform, his pillorying of bourgeois arrogance and corrupt bourgeois institutions, and his graphic and often sordid detailing of the life of the urban working class, he was the first of the British realists. In *David Copperfield*, *Oliver Twist*, and *The Pickwick Papers*, three of the best known of his numerous and lengthy novels, a galaxy of characters of the middle and lower walks of life in industrial Britain parade realistically before us.

Mary Ann Evans (1819–1880), writing under the pen name George Eliot, wrote popular novels depicting the realities of British social life. In *Middlemarch: A Study of Provincial Life,* she sensitively related psychological conflicts to the determining social realities that surround her characters.

Thomas Hardy (1840–1928), unlike Dickens, had a pessimistic view of the universe. His vivid characters—ordinary English countryside folk—struggle Darwin-like against fate, environment, and their own frail natures without any help from God or Hardy. *The Return of the Native*, *The Mayor of Casterbridge*, and *Tess of the D'Urbervilles* are some of the best examples of the realistic novel in any language.

Probably the most typical of all the British realists was George Bernard Shaw (1856–1950). Of Irish birth, Shaw early crossed over to London, where he long remained the gadfly of bourgeois society. In scores of urbane and sophisticated novels, essays, and plays, he charmingly but caustically taunted Christianity, capitalism, and democracy. Shaw was a cynic, a socialist, and a stark materialist. He was the epitome of late-nineteenth-century and early-twentieth-century realism.

In the United States, the era of the realistic novel began with the works of Theodore Dreiser (1871–1945). Dreiser's novels depicted in hard, rough detail the life and the philosophy of the disenchanted, uprooted proletariat living in a materialistic, industrial world of changing values. His first novel, *Sister Carrie,* which appeared in 1900, was an American industrial version of *Madame Bovary* told with raw unrestraint. To escape poverty, Carrie became the mistress of a succession of men. The progressive degeneration of the characters constitutes the theme of the novel. Editors were so shocked at the frank and open presentation of lurid details that Dreiser had great difficulty getting the book published. The success of *Sister Carrie* was immediate, and other novels in a like vein followed.

One of the most influential of the realists was the Norwegian playwright Henrik Ibsen (1828–1906). A frustrated artist embittered by youthful poverty, Ibsen ridiculed bourgeois society in his popular dramas. In what is probably his best-known play, *A Doll's House*, one of his heroines rebels against the ''doll's house'' that her stodgy, hypocritical, middle-class husband has created for her. In *An Enemy of the People*, Ibsen reveals the fickleness of the masses and their unfitness for democratic government. *Ghosts* deals with the social and personal problems of syphilis.

In Russia, Ivan Sergeyevich Turgenev (1818–1883) and Fyodor Dostoyevski (1821–1881) combined realism with romanticism in much the same manner as did Dickens in Great Britain. In his masterpiece, *Fathers and Sons*, Turgenev grapples powerfully with the problems of the older, conservative Russian generation versus the modern, sophisticated, and radical younger generation. Dostoyevski's two greatest novels are *Crime and Punishment* and *The Brothers Karamazov*. In them he delves psychologically and mystically into the problems of evil and purification through suffering. He was deeply religious, but not in any formal or orthodox sense. Leo Tolstoy (1828–1910) was more completely dedicated to realism and devoted his life and writing almost exclusively to social reform. His masterpiece is *War and Peace*. In this gigantic novel, scores of personalities along with more impersonal social forces so interlace with and influence one another that not even the strongest individual—not even Napoleon—can work his will alone. In his later years Tolstoy sought to combine Christianity with socialism, giving up his great inherited wealth to set a good example. Anton Chekhov (1860–1904) wrote polished but realistic and pessimistic plays about Russian life. Maxim Gorky (1868–1936), up from the proletarian ranks, analyzed the social problems of the Russian masses in his dramas and novels.

The various veins of realistic literature, with all their variety, had many things in common. The literature almost invariably reflected the social dislocation brought about by the Industrial Revolution, particularly in its more advanced second phase. It reflected the materialism of an age of science and technology. It displayed over and over again the influence of Darwin and, later, of Freud. It was increasingly concerned with the disillusionment and cynicism brought about by changing religious and moral values.

4. IMPRESSIONIST AND MODERN PAINTING AND SCULPTURE

France, the birthplace of realistic literature, was also the chief seat of the impressionistic and modern painting and sculpture that predominated during the second half of the nineteenth century. Impressionism was a mild, sophisticated revolt against the artistic standards that had prevailed since the late fifteenth century. It reflected the intellectual challenge to traditional values and institutions that arose after midcentury. It took its chief inspiration from the seventeenth-century Spanish painters Velásquez and El Greco, from Japanese art, which was rediscovered after 1853, and from new scientific knowledge concerning the nature of color and light. Impressionistic painting was informal, unposed, and random-angled. It sought to convey by studied casualness the impression of a view one gets at a glance. The chief founder of the impressionistic style of painting was the Frenchman Édouard Manet (1832–1883). Among his more illustrious disciples were Claude Monet (1840–1926), Auguste Renoir (1841–1919), and Camille Pissarro (1830–1903) (see Color Plate 23 and Figure 47.2). These artists painted sunlit parks and landscapes, shimmering lakes and rivers, and subtle, sophisticated portraits. They omitted much detail, painting in only suggestive shapes, forms, and colors as first impressions and leaving the rest to the imagination. Their work was sensuous, decorative, and mildly iconoclastic.

The breach the impressionists made with long-established traditions was greatly widened near the end of the nineteenth century and early in the twentieth by more radical modern painters. The new trend was led by Paul Cézanne (1839–1906), a lifelong friend of Émile Zola (see Color Plate 25). Cézanne distorted freely in order to achieve a more powerful effect and applied thick paint to attain the appearance of solidity and roundness. Going far beyond Cézanne, the gifted but eccentric Frenchman Paul Gauguin

FIGURE 47.2 Claude Monet, *La Grenouillère,* **1869** Monet was a leading French impressionist. His bold use of color, his emphasis on the play of light, and his focus on the appearance of things were typical of impressionist painters. (The Metropolitan Museum of Art, Bequest of Mrs. H. O. Havemeyer, 1929. The Havemeyer Collection)

(1848–1903) and the Dutchman Vincent van Gogh (1853–1890) broke openly with the artistic standards of the past. Gauguin was interested in painting not the literal document of his subject but only what the subject meant to him. He painted the patterns formed in his mind by objects rather than the objects themselves, using violent reds, yellows, and greens. He finally became primitive, deserting Western civilization for the South Sea Islands. Gauguin's friend, van Gogh, would squeeze paint directly from the tube onto the canvas to achieve striking effects (see Color Plate 26). Like Gauguin, van Gogh was an expressionist, freely distorting the images of nature to make them express his own feelings. Cézanne, Gauguin, and van Gogh were the forerunners of many iconoclastic schools, such as cubism and futurism, that marked twentieth-century painting.

Two of the most influential of the revolutionary modern painters were the Frenchman Henri Matisse (1869–1954) and the Spanish-born (French by adoption) Pablo Picasso (1881–1973), both of whom received their chief inspiration from Cézanne. In some of their work they carried distortion to great extremes. Matisse became enamored with primitive culture. Picasso's figures

during one phase of his long career became geometric (hence cubism) and disjointed (see Figure 47.1). He occasionally gave up color entirely for black and white.

It is characteristic of an age of intellectual revolt and changing values that artists turn inward (see Color Plates 27 and 28). During the late nineteenth and early twentieth centuries, painting became highly individualistic. Artists tended to paint such objects as fruit, still life, and mandolins. Furthermore, they turned to figures on the periphery of a disintegrating society, such as prostitutes, solitary drinkers, blind beggars, and circus performers. The figures were separate from one another. This disjointedness and the symbols of science, machinery, and speed, which were so prominent in this painting, represented an age of intellectual revolt against traditional values, of materialistic science and technology, and of social tension. Unfortunately, much of this painting was so technical and highly specialized that it could be appreciated only by a relative few at a time when many were seeking enlightenment.

The rapid growth of cities and wealth during the second Industrial Revolution was responsible for the production of a large quantity of sculp-

FIGURE 47.3 **Auguste Rodin,** *Heroic Head* **(Pierre de Weissart), 1889, bronze** Rodin's powerful figures represent both a new departure in sculpture and a bridge from the nineteenth century to the twentieth. He brought the impressionist spirit to his work, and he was a forerunner of much of the abstract and symbolist sculpture of the twentieth century. (Norweb Collection, The Cleveland Museum of Art)

ture to decorate the new public buildings, squares, and parks. Most of it was patterned after the styles of the past, either classical or baroque, more often the latter. Probably the two sculptors of the period who most truly reflected the spirit of their own time and of future trends were Constantin Meunier (1831–1905) in Belgium and Auguste Rodin (1840–1917) in France. Meunier was the first great sculptor to recognize the importance of the industrial proletariat. Among his rugged and realistic statues are "The Hammersmith," "The Puddler," "The Mine Girl," and

"The Old Mine Horse." Rodin introduced impressionism into sculpture (see Figure 47.3). His most famous statue, "The Thinker," illustrates not only impressionistic art but also the influence of the classical, Renaissance, baroque, and romantic styles. Rodin was the forerunner of much of the modern, abstract, and symbolist sculpture of the twentieth century.

5. FUNCTIONAL ARCHITECTURE

The architecture of the period 1850–1914, like the sculpture, combined the old with the new. The prevailing style in the numerous and increasingly large public buildings continued to be classical or baroque. Gothic architecture, which had enjoyed a revival in the early part of the nineteenth century, was now limited primarily to university buildings and to churches. Even Byzantine, Moorish, and Oriental models appeared here and there throughout the West as the world was brought closer together by rapid communications.

The first great architect to develop a style appropriate to an age of steel, science, and speed was the American Louis Henry Sullivan (1856–1924). Sullivan argued that "form follows function"; that is to say, the style of buildings should be determined by their intended use and by the materials used in their construction (see Figure 47.4). The architectural devices of the past had lost their utility, were purely decorative. And in fast-moving, crowded, and growing New York and Chicago, what sense did horizontal Greek or Moorish lines make? Sullivan designed the first steel-supported skyscraper.

But Sullivan and his followers were not satisfied with the principle "form follows function." They decided that function is the prime purpose of architecture. The application of this principle came to be known as "functional architecture." Structural steel, reinforced concrete, and glass brick made it possible for the functional architects to achieve unbroken horizontal lines impossible for the Greeks and towering heights combined with gracefulness and light that the medieval Gothic builders could not have contemplated. Furthermore, the spirit of intellectual revolt against the standards and values of the past gave architects a freedom to experiment never before enjoyed. Finally, unprecedented wealth and technological advances provided them with the means to execute their ideas. Some of the massive utilitarian structures of this and later periods are creditable monuments to an age of materialism.

6. MUSIC OLD AND NEW

Of all the arts, music showed the least responsiveness to the economic and social trends between 1850 and 1914. Some of the greatest romantic composers lived well on into the second half of the nineteenth century. Wagner lived until 1883, Verdi until 1901. Their ranks were joined in the late nineteenth century by such great romanticists as Camille Saint-Saëns (1835–1921) in France and Peter Tchaikovsky (1840–1893) in Russia. Nor was there any lessening in the spirit of nationalism in music, which was such an important ingredient of romanticism. Wagner's nationalism became more militant after 1870. Tchaikovsky combined Russian nationalism with his romanticism. More strictly nationalist in their themes and folk tunes were the Russian Nikolai Rimsky-Korsakov (1844–1908), the Czech Antonín Dvořák (1841–1904), the Norwegian Edvard Grieg (1843–1907), and the Finn Jean Sibelius (1865–1957).

Not only romanticism but also classicism was carried over into the late nineteenth century by the great German composer Johannes Brahms (1833–1897). Spending the last thirty-five years of his life in the Hapsburg capital of Vienna, Brahms became an ardent Hungarian nationalist without giving up his loyalty to his native Germany. Probably more than any other musician, Brahms resembles Beethoven in style. Like Beethoven, he combined the classical spirit with the romantic.

One of the most important innovators in music of the period was the French composer Claude Debussy (1862–1918). Debussy was the father of impressionistic music. Experimenting with subtle and sophisticated dissonances, he was to music what Manet and Renoir were to painting. Meanwhile, in Germany Richard Strauss (1864–1949) was startling and scandaliz-

FIGURE 47.4 Louis Sullivan's Carson-Pirie-Scott Department Store The Carson-Pirie-Scott Department Store in Chicago was designed by the American architect Louis Henry Sullivan (1856–1924), who was the first to determine that function is the sole purpose of the style of a building. Sullivan designed the world's first steel-supported skyscraper. (Hedrich Blessing)

ing his pre–World War I audiences with his complex and sometimes harshly dissonant "realistic" tone poems. He is often said to have ushered in the "modern" period in music. In Russia, Igor Stravinsky (1882–1971) was beginning his long career of composing music that was still more iconoclastic and abstract. He is called the father of the expressionist school. Stravinsky, with his more violent and impetuous dissonances, bears somewhat the same relationship to Debussy as Picasso does to Monet in painting.

SUGGESTED READING

General

F. L. Baumer, *Modern European Thought* (1977). A good general introduction.

H. S. Hughes, *Consciousness and Society* (1979). A superb study of intellectual history during the period.

S. Kern, *The Culture of Time and Space, 1880–1918* (1983). An important, interpretive work.

P. Monaco, *Modern European Culture and Consciousness, 1870–1980* (1983). The early chapters cover the period well.

C. E. Schorske, *Fin-de-Siècle Vienna: Politics and Culture* (1980). An excellent study of one of Europe's cultural centers.

R. Shattuck, *The Banquet Years* (1968). A well-written account of the social and cultural life of late-nineteenth-century Paris.

Popular Education, Journalism, and Culture

C. M. Cipolla, *Literacy and Development in the West* (1969). Covers the rise in literacy during the period.

C. Cross, *A Social History of Leisure since 1600* (1990). A recent history that covers the period.

A. J. Lee, *The Origins of the Popular Press in Britain, 1855–1914* (1978). Covers aspects of popular culture and journalism.

M. Maynes, *Schooling in Western Europe: A Social History* (1985). Covers popular education well.

Currents of Thought

W. Kaufmann, *Nietzsche: Philosopher, Psychologist, Anti-Christ* (1974). A highly respected analysis of Nietzsche and his thought.

K. Löwith, *From Hegel to Nietzsche: The Revolution in Nineteenth-Century Thought* (1964). A good analysis.

L. Poliakov, *The Aryan Myth: A History of Racist and Nationalist Ideas in Europe* (1971). An excellent introduction.

Realistic Literature

R. Pascal, *From Naturalism to Expressionism: German Literature and Society, 1880–1918* (1973). A good survey.

Art, Architecture, and Music

P. Collaer, *A History of Modern Music* (1961). A well-written survey.

R. Herbert, *Impressionism: Art, Leisure, and Parisian Society* (1988). An insightful cultural history.

H. R. Hitchcock, *Architecture: 19th and 20th Centuries* (1958). A good survey.

R. Hughes, *The Shock of the New: Art and the Century of Change* (1981). Extremely well written.

J. Rewald, *Post Impressionism: From van Gogh to Gauguin* (1979). A respected study.

CHAPTER 48

Politics, Democracy, and Nationalism, 1871–1914

KEEPING IT DOWN!

FIGURE 48.1 Bismarck and the Socialists This satirical illustration from the September 28, 1878, edition of the British magazine *Punch* shows German Chancellor Bismarck in military dress vainly struggling to keep down the socialist "Jack in the Box." Although Bismarck banned the Social Democratic party in 1878, it would not die. In the years just prior to World War I it became Germany's largest single party. Other socialist parties grew throughout Europe during the same period. (*Punch,* September 28, 1878)

From the end of the Franco-Prussian War in 1871 until the outbreak of World War I in 1914, the West was free from major wars. Despite some changes and shaky beginnings, European nations survived the period with their governments intact. When the considerable economic expansion, cultural production, and imperial success are added to this political picture, the years between 1871 and 1914 may be viewed as a time of great progress for Europe.

Nevertheless, some disturbing trends were evident. The freedom from war was accompanied by a growing militarism in several nations and a new precarious complexity in international affairs. Moreover, governmental survival did not mean political peace; political unrest and even some revolutionary activity threatened many European nations. Imperial success was purchased at a price of heightened international rivalries. These disturbing trends would bear bitter fruit with the outbreak of World War I in 1914.

The strongest political forces of the period were the spread of democratic institutions and nationalism. Both forces had been under way since the first half of the nineteenth century. However, the spread of democratic institutions occurred quite unevenly. And nationalism, while it differed according to the conditions in each country, took on more conservative, aggressive, militaristic, and even racist overtones. The political developments between 1871 and 1914 can be well expressed by stressing the themes of democracy and nationalism and dividing our examination of European nations roughly between western and eastern Europe.

1. WESTERN EUROPE: THE SPREAD AND REFORM OF DEMOCRATIC INSTITUTIONS

Most of the western European countries had formed a national identity and initiated democratic reforms before the eastern European countries did. Between 1871 and 1914 democratic institutions continued to spread in western Europe and, in general, encountered fewer problems than in eastern Europe.

Great Britain

During the second half of the nineteenth century Great Britain was in a strong position. The country had avoided the revolutionary turmoil that struck the European continent between 1848 and 1850, largely due to the government's ability to reform and adapt just enough to contain the pressures for radical change. Liberalism seemed to be working well. The British economy was the most modern in the world, and the British people were relatively wealthy (although the condition of the working class was still unenviable). Yet Great Britain was not immune to the forces of nationalism that were growing everywhere in the West. In the decades following 1850 British nationalism grew, and liberal and conservative British politicians increasingly used it to gain support, increase the responsibilities of the national government, and justify foreign policy.

For most of the 1850s and 1860s liberals controlled the government. Lord Palmerston, a liberal Whig, was prime minister and leader of the Whigs for much of the period between 1855 and 1865. While modest domestic reforms to modernize government and increase the allegiance of the people to the government were instituted under his ministry, he relied on nationalistic sentiment for support. He willingly paraded British naval might whenever possible and sympathetically supported movements for national liberation abroad. But he did not bend to those who demanded greater inclusion in the political system by increasing suffrage.

By 1865 William E. Gladstone had risen to leadership within the Whig party and was transforming it into the more modern Liberal party. In 1866 he and the Liberal prime minister, Lord Russell, introduced a suffrage reform bill. Although the bill was defeated and the Liberal ministry was forced to resign, the narrowness of the defeat plus the popular demand for suffrage reform convinced the rising young leader of the Conservatives, Benjamin Disraeli (1804–1881), that reform was inevitable. The shrewd Disraeli decided to seize credit for the inevitable by introducing his own reform bill. The result was the Reform Bill of 1867, which, as amended by the Liberals, doubled the electorate and gave the vote to males in the lower middle class and upper working class for the first time. William E. Gladstone's Reform Bill of 1884 enfranchised most of the rural males. After 1884 virtually every male householder or renter in Great Britain could vote. Restricted woman's suffrage would come in 1918 and full suffrage in 1928.

Several liberal reforms were enacted during the 1850s, 1860s, and 1870s, making government responsible for primary schools, requiring competitive examinations for civil service, and removing some religious restrictions on non-Anglicans. Yet, until the end of the nineteenth century, both the Conservative and Liberal parties were still controlled by the aristocracy and the wealthy bourgeoisie. Although both parties were fairly benevolent toward the working classes, the large and discontented industrial proletariat wanted its fair share in the government. Between 1881 and 1906 its leaders turned to a program of moderate socialism, and with the aid of a number of intellectual radicals, notably George Bernard Shaw, H. G. Wells, and Sidney and Beatrice Webb, the Labour party was formed.

In 1906 the rejuvenated Liberal party came to power under the actual, if not official, leadership of the fiery young Welshman David Lloyd George, who also had the backing of the Labour party. Between 1906 and 1911 Lloyd George put through Parliament a revolutionary program of accident, sickness, old-age, and unemployment insurance. To meet this and other increased costs to the government, he forced through the reluctant House of Lords his famous budget of 1909, which shifted the "heaviest burden [of taxation] to the broadest backs." A steeply graduated income tax and high taxes on unearned income, inheritances, the idle parks of the landed aristocracy, and mining royalties struck heavily at the rich. The Parliamentary Reform Act of 1911 stripped the House of Lords of most of its former power and made the popularly elected House of Commons supreme. In 1914 the long-festering Irish question was resolved by granting self-government to Ireland, although the outbreak of World War I in that year delayed its implementation. And conflict between Protestants and Catholics in northern Ireland promised to persist. However, by 1914 Great Britain was on the road to greater social, economic, and political democracy.

Between 1871 and 1914 Britain increased its imperial holdings (see Chapter 50) and joined other nations in a dangerous international rivalry that combined nationalism and militarism. In the face of Germany's swift rise to power and prestige, the British took renewed pride in their dominant navy and in their empire, which contained one-fourth of all the earth's territory and people. Many well-to-do Britishers thought themselves to be so superior to the other peoples in Europe that they became the most unpopular of all travelers on the Continent. To some observers, it appeared that Great Britain was as big a bully on the seas and overseas as Germany was on the continent of Europe.

France

With the end of the Second Empire of Napoleon III during the Franco-German War of 1870–1871, the Third French Republic was proclaimed. However, the first elections, held in February 1871 after the surrender of Paris, resulted in a sweeping victory for the monarchists. This somewhat surprising result may be explained by the fact that the republican leaders wanted to continue the hopeless war with Germany. The city of Paris, made up largely of the liberal bourgeoisie and the radical proletariat, was unwilling to submit to the domination of conservative rural France. It declared its independence from the rest of France and set up its own city government, or commune. The Paris Commune gained a reputation as an experiment in Marxist socialism. In reality the Commune was dominated by a mix of different socialist and republican groups and was more radically democratic than anything else. Two months (April–May 1871) of fighting, culminating in a week of all-out warfare in the streets of Paris, were required for the rest of the French nation (with the regular army) to subdue the Commune (see Figure 48.2). Some twenty thousand Parisians were executed after they had surrendered, and seventy-five hundred were deported. The fall of the Paris Commune ended a threat to the integrity of France, heartened conservatives, and created martyrs for socialism.

The royalists, though in the majority, were split into a Bourbon faction and an Orléanist faction, neither of which was willing to yield to the other. Meanwhile, as this stalemate dragged on for several years, the liberals grew in strength. Finally, in 1875, the frustrated and frightened monarchists consented (by a single vote) to the adoption of a republican constitution. The constitution provided for a Chamber of Deputies elected by universal male suffrage, a Senate elected by a complicated indirect method, and a rather powerless president to be elected by the

FIGURE 48.2 Executions During the Paris Commune Bloodshed and bitter reprisals were common on both sides during the Paris Commune. Here, in 1871, Communards (including women) execute hostages in response to a previous execution of Communard leaders. (BBC Hulton/The Bettman Archive)

two legislative bodies. Most of the executive functions of the republic were to be carried on by a cabinet of ministers dependent on the Chamber of Deputies. It was not until four years later, however, that the liberal republicans under the leadership of the eloquent Léon Gambetta gained actual control of the republic.

But the Third French Republic, so furtively born, was still not safe. Powerful groups were hostile to it. The chief of these were the various factions of monarchists (Bourbons, Orléanists, and Bonapartists), the professional military, the Roman Catholic hierarchy, and large numbers of peasant proprietors. In the late 1880s these factions rallied around a handsome man on horseback, General Boulanger, who became so popular that he might have overthrown the republic had he been bolder and more skillful or had the republican leaders been less courageous. As it turned out, when he was summoned to answer charges of treason against the republic, he fled the country and eventually committed suicide.

In the 1890s the antirepublican forces rallied again around a group of army officers who had falsely accused a Jewish army captain, Alfred Dreyfus, and sent him to prison on Devil's Is-

land. This time the enemies of the republic were aided by a rising militant nationalism and anti-Semitism. It required twelve years for the republicans, inspired by the novelist Émile Zola, to get Dreyfus acquitted and the army officers who had imprisoned him punished. The Dreyfus case strengthened the republic and discredited its enemies.

Democratic government did not work as smoothly in France as in Great Britain. The tradition of extreme individualism, the animosity between clericalist and anticlericalist, the sharp cleavage between radical urban Paris and conservative rural France, lingering provincial loyalty, and a historic suspicion of strong government and high taxes—all contributed to the formation of a multiplicity of political parties. Thus the cabinet was forced to rely on the support of a precarious combination of parties (a *bloc*) in order to carry on the executive functions of government. In France the Chamber of Deputies could overthrow a cabinet without having to risk an immediate national election, as was the case in Great Britain. As a result, there was a rapid turnover of French ministries. During the forty-three years from 1871 to 1914, no fewer than fifty-one ministries attempted to govern France. Nevertheless, the French government was not as unstable as it might appear. The same groups of ministers often rotated in and out of office, sometimes simply exchanging one ministry for another. Moreover, the actual details of administration were carried on with relatively little interruption by a stable civil service, firmly built on the tradition of Richelieu and Napoleon I.

As the twentieth century opened, democratic government in France appeared to be firmly established and increasingly responsive to the will of the masses. Trade unions had been legalized, a modern system of public education that bolstered support for the republic was well established, and in 1905 all formal ties between the state and the Catholic church were broken. Factory laws were giving the workers increased protection. Between 1905 and 1910 a limited program of unemployment, old-age, accident, and sickness insurance was inaugurated. This program of social legislation, however, was only a modest beginning. The French masses, becoming more politically conscious and active, expressed their discontent in strikes and more votes for the Socialists.

France, like Great Britain, was subject to the growing nationalism of the period, which was related to international rivalries, imperial expansion, and military buildup. The already strong French pride had only been intensified by France's defeat at the hands of Germany in 1870–1871. The statue dedicated to the city of Strasbourg in the Place de la Concorde in Paris was draped in perpetual mourning as a constant reminder of the day of revenge. France greatly speeded up its overseas empire building and increased the size of its armed forces until they were larger in proportion to the population than those of the German Empire. France sought and found military allies. When a general strike in 1910 threatened the nation's military security and war preparations, Aristide Briand, himself a radical and former Socialist, did not hesitate to use the armed forces to break it up.

Italy

Italy entered the 1870s in a much weaker position than France or Great Britain. Italy had only just become a nation-state, and even that status was weakened by strong regional differences, partic-

ularly between the more economically developed north and the poorer south. Italy's new government was liberal, but the right to vote was limited to the middle and upper classes, who constituted a small minority of the nation's population.

Between the 1870s and World War I Italian governments weathered various political crises that sometimes reached revolutionary proportions. The nation was painfully modernizing and entering into the international arena. Italian governments became involved in the shifting international alliances of the period and the nationalistic race for colonial possessions. Toward the end of the period there were signs that Italy would follow the democratic pattern set by other Western nations. Economic and social reforms to benefit the working classes were enacted under the government of Giovanni Giolitti, and in 1911 universal male suffrage was enacted.

The Smaller Countries of Northern Europe

The people of the smaller countries of northern Europe also witnessed the triumph of democratic government during this period. Belgium adopted universal male suffrage in 1893. Here the weighted vote was established, men of wealth and education getting two or three additional votes. The Dutch Netherlands extended the suffrage in 1887 and again in 1896; in 1917 all adult men and women were given the right to vote. Norway adopted universal male suffrage in 1898, Sweden in 1909, and Denmark in 1914. In 1913 Norway became the first European country to grant the vote to women. In these five nations the traditional respect for government and the relatively high degree of literacy made democracy a vigorous reality.

2. EASTERN EUROPE: CONSERVATISM, MILITARISM, AND NATIONALISM

The democratic trends characteristic of western Europe were also occurring in eastern Europe, but they were longer in arriving, less firmly established, and not as complete as in western Europe. Moreover, nationalism, which was a general phenomenon, took on more strident, aggressive tones in eastern Europe, where national identity was less comfortably fixed. Most of eastern Europe remained in the control of conservative groups. The governments were autocratic in nature and more dependent on the military for support.

The German Empire under Bismarck and Kaiser Wilhelm II

The center of these trends in eastern Europe was the German Empire. Its creation by the blood-and-iron method, its autocratic constitution (despite the establishment of universal male suffrage), and its strong-handed leadership, first by the Iron Chancellor and then by Kaiser Wilhelm II, guaranteed that the German Empire would be an enlarged Prussia. The German Empire possessed a powerful army, a large, energetic, and disciplined population, a rapidly growing industrial machine, a fervent and restless national spirit. Bismarck ruled over his creation as chancellor for almost twenty years.

His first concern after the defeat of France and the declaration of the empire in 1870–1871 was to complete the consolidation and nationalization of the German states and people. The law codes, currencies, and military forces of the twenty-five lesser states were brought into conformity with those of Prussia. Banking and railroads were placed under control of the national government. The empire's spawning industry was protected against British competition by a high tariff. The French in Alsace-Lorraine, the Danes in Schleswig, and the more than 3 million Poles in the eastern districts were pressured to give up their language and traditions.

Two other groups in Germany excited Bismarck's suspicion and wrath: the Roman Catholics and the Socialists. Any German who had a foreign loyalty was intolerable to Bismarck. From 1872 to 1878, Bismarck waged a political power struggle with the Roman Catholics that came to be called the *Kulturkampf* (battle for civilization). The Jesuits were expelled, civil marriage was made compulsory, and all education, including that of Roman Catholic priests, was brought under state control and largely secularized. When the Roman Catholic clergy and most of the laity, which constituted approximately one-third of the total German population, resisted and rallied

to the pope, hundreds of priests and six bishops were arrested. But it was all to no avail. The Roman Catholic Center party in the Reichstag became stronger, and by 1878 Bismarck wanted its support for what he considered to be a struggle of greater importance—that against the Socialists. In 1878, upon the accession of a more conciliatory pope, Leo XIII, Bismarck "went to Canossa" and had the most severe of the anti-Catholic laws repealed.

In the same year he began a twelve-year crusade against the internationally minded Socialists (see Figure 48.1). He outlawed their publications, their organizations, and their meetings, and set the German police force upon them. But he only drove them underground. Throughout the decade of the 1880s, Bismarck sought to undercut the Socialists' appeal to the working class by setting up a comprehensive system of social insurance. Accident, sickness, and old-age insurance was provided for the industrial proletariat, the funds being raised by compulsory contributions from the workers, the employers, and the state. Although Bismarck's motives were not benevolent or humanitarian, his measures gave impetus to a trend toward state responsibility for social security. Nevertheless, the Socialists were not appeased, and Bismarck continued to fight them as long as he remained chancellor.

Bismarck's foreign policy after 1871 was one of security and retrenchment. He knew that France would be unforgiving and revengeful, forever seeking an opportunity to regain Alsace and Lorraine. Of France alone he had little fear, but France in league with other powers, particularly Russia and Great Britain, would be formidable. Therefore, his consistent policy was to maintain a close military alliance with Austria-Hungary and cordial relations with Russia and Great Britain. In 1873 Bismarck formed the Three Emperors' League among Germany, Austria-Hungary, and Russia. When the interests of Austria-Hungary and Russia proved to be incompatible, this league was replaced in 1879–1882 by the Triple Alliance among Germany, Austria-Hungary, and Italy. A separate "reinsurance treaty" of friendship and neutrality was made with Russia. Of course, Bismarck did not depend wholly on diplomacy. Throughout this period, the German military machine was made even more powerful.

In 1888 Wilhelm II (1888–1918) became kaiser. Wilhelm II was twenty-nine years of age when he ascended the throne. He had been brought up in the army, which was his first love. Egotistical and bombastic by nature, he was a dabbler in theology, history, and the arts and freely gave advice and instructions to the leading figures in those fields. He was also an eloquent, willing speaker and had his generous and humanitarian moments.

The young kaiser's personality and policies soon clashed with those of Bismarck. In 1890, just two years after he became emperor, Wilhelm II accepted Bismarck's reluctant resignation as chancellor. The immediate cause of the break was a disagreement over the control of the ministry and the repeal of the anti-Socialist laws, which Bismarck wished to be continued. The real reason, however, was that there was simply not room enough in Germany for two such prima donnas.

Bismarck's foreign policy was quickly reversed. The reinsurance treaty with Russia was immediately allowed to lapse, as the kaiser assumed a keen interest in extending German hegemony over the Balkans and the Ottoman Empire, areas the Russians considered to be vital to their own interests and ambitions. In 1894 Russia formed an alliance with France, the very thing that Bismarck had worked so hard to prevent. Wilhelm II also soon alienated Great Britain. His extension of German influence in the Near East, particularly his Berlin-to-Baghdad railroad project (see pp. 631–632), threatened an area in which Great Britain had many vital interests and through which ran its "lifeline" to India and the Far East. In China, too, German interests began to rival those of the British.

It was the kaiser's naval policy, however, that alarmed the British the most. Wilhelm was an ardent and lifelong navalist. "The waves beat powerfully at our national gates," he cried, "and call us as a great nation to maintain our place in the world. . . ." Germany's "place in the sun" was a favorite phrase of the Hohenzollern emperor. The Reichstag voted an enormous naval building program that was steadily increased until in 1908 it called for twenty-eight new battleships of the biggest and latest design. The purpose of this program was to give Germany a battle fleet so great that "a war against the mightiest naval power would endanger the supremacy of that power."

Great Britain, whose food supply as well as her empire depended on naval supremacy, took utmost alarm. Failing in efforts to reach an understanding with the kaiser's government, Britain launched a huge and costly naval building program of its own. In 1904 Britain joined France, and in 1907 Russia, in the Triple Entente, which was in reality a defensive military alliance. The interests and policies of Great Britain, France, and Russia had long been so discordant that nothing less than maximum alarm could have brought them together. Thus in seventeen years Wilhelm had undone Bismarck's work and brought about the "encirclement" of the fatherland by three of the world's greatest powers.

Germany's economic exploits under Bismarck and Wilhelm II were no less phenomenal than those in the military realm. In 1871 Great Britain was the world's leading nation in manufacturing and commerce; the Industrial Revolution was still in its early stages in Germany. By 1914 Germany was a close second to Great Britain in industry and commerce; in many areas, such as the production of steel and machinery, Germany had far outstripped Britain. In the up-and-coming chemical and electrical industries and in scientific agriculture and forestry, Germany was far in advance of all other nations. Germany was also first in the application of science to industry and in industrial and scientific research. By 1914 the German merchant marine had captured the lion's share of the lucrative transatlantic passenger traffic.

At a time when other industrial nations, particularly the United States, were beginning to restrict the giant monopolistic trusts, the German imperial government was encouraging and subsidizing its cartels in order that they might compete with foreign companies more effectively. More and more of the world's market was captured by German business. "Made in Germany" became a familiar mark from the Andean plateau to the Congo jungles. Germany's population, keeping pace with its economy, increased from 41 million in 1871 to 65 million in 1914. Meanwhile, heavy emigration (which had reached a peak in the 1880s of some two hundred fifty thousand a year, most of it to the United States) dwindled to a mere trickle. In 1914 the number of German emigrants was less than the number of workers coming into Germany from neighboring countries. Only the United States was keeping pace with Germany in overall economic advancement.

The industrialization of Germany, although accompanied by the growth of a large and prosperous bourgeoisie, did not produce a tide of liberalism as it had in the other Western industrialized nations. The middle classes allied themselves with the conservative government. Only the Social Democratic party (working class) and the small and weak Progressive party (intellectuals, professionals, and small-business people) advocated liberal or radical reforms. But even the Social Democratic party, by 1914 the largest party in the empire, was inundated by the flood of nationalism that welled up during the international crises that preceded World War I.

Russia

Until the 1850s Russia had remained relatively untouched by the Industrial Revolution and liberalism. Russia's government was autocratic under the tsar, its society was still feudalistic with serfs bound to the land and their lords, and its large army enjoyed an aura of near-invincibility. Russia had earned the reputation of being the most conservative and unreforming of the European powers. After the Crimean War of 1853–1856, it was clear that things would have to change soon.

Russia's army was humiliated in the war. Its leaders quickly realized that Russia was being left behind by the other powers, that the country lacked the economic and social foundations for a modern war—the railroads, the armaments industry, the social support. The new tsar, Alexander II (1855–1881), announced a series of reforms. The most important was the freeing of the serfs in 1861. While the measure put an end to that form of human bondage and did transfer land to the freed peasantry, it did not make the peasants fully independent and self-sufficient. In general they received only the poorest land, they remained burdened by payments owed to the state, and they were tied by collective ownership to their village commune (the *mir*). Other reforms

made the local judicial system more independent, created local political institutions with elected officials, encouraged primary and secondary education, relaxed censorship, and modernized the military. At the same time, the government initiated a program of railway construction, which stimulated related industries. In Russia's cities a still-small middle and working class began to grow.

A strong wave of dissatisfaction arose during the later years of Alexander II's rule. The former serfs had been cruelly disappointed by the fruits of emancipation. Another revolt of Russia's Polish subjects in 1863 made Alexander II more reactionary. His failure to follow through with more sweeping reforms after the emancipation of the serfs disappointed liberals, populists, and others, who were mostly intellectual young aristocrats. In despair over the possibility of reforming the huge Russian Empire by orderly methods, these young intellectuals became radical. They set out to undermine Russia's society, government, and church in order to build a new and modern Russia from the ruins. When their efforts were spurned by the masses whom they were seeking to uplift, a more violent wing of the revolutionaries turned to terror and assassination to achieve their ends. Numerous bureaucrats and police officials were slain by terrorists, and Tsar Alexander II himself was killed by a bomb.

The new tsar, Alexander III (1881–1894), was a harsh, reactionary autocrat. Blaming his father's death on softness, he set out to exterminate all liberalism in Russia. The ruthless Vyacheslav Plehve was made head of the secret police, and its agents were soon everywhere. Thousands of suspects were arrested. Some were shot or exiled to Siberia. Alexander initiated a sweeping reactionary program of Russianization. The censored press, the closely supervised schools, the secret police, and above all the clergy of the Orthodox church became potent agencies for Russianization. Non-Orthodox religions were persecuted. Language minority groups—the Poles, the Baltic peoples, the Finns, even the Ukrainians—were forced to use the Russian language. The Jews suffered the harshest persecution. They were subject to such abuse, including bloody pogroms, that more than a quarter million of them fled, mostly to the United States.

Alexander III was succeeded by Nicholas II (1894–1917), who was also reactionary but was less effective. Although Nicholas attempted to continue the policies of his father, he was unable to make them work. During the 1890s, Russia experienced a new surge of industrialization stimulated by the aggressive policies of Sergei Witte, the finance minister, and an infusion of foreign capital into Russia. A larger industrial bourgeoisie and proletariat emerged and with them movements for liberal and radical reform. Of the various liberal and radical parties that emerged, the one of greatest significance for the future was the Social Democratic party. This was a Marxist party whose leadership was made up almost entirely of intellectual radicals. Their chief concern was for the industrial proletariat. In 1903 the Social Democrats split into a moderate, gradualist wing called the Mensheviks (minority) and a violent revolutionary wing called the Bolsheviks (majority). The Bolsheviks were led by the brilliant, dynamic Vladimir Lenin, who was living in exile in Switzerland.

Taking advantage of the embarrassment of the tsar's government because of Russia's defeat by Japan in 1904–1905 (see p. 000), the various liberal and radical groups clamored for reform. In July 1904 the hated Plehve was assassinated. In January 1905 hundreds of peaceful demonstrators were shot down in front of the royal palace in St. Petersburg by the tsar's guard. This bloody event, known as "Red Sunday," fanned the flames of discontent (see Figure 48.3). In October 1905 a general strike completely paralyzed the country for ten days. Nicholas II, yielding at last, issued a manifesto that promised civil liberties and a popularly elected Duma. However, before the Duma could be elected, the return of the Russian troops from the Far East and a huge loan from Russia's ally, France, strengthened the hand of the tsar. During the next two years he and his advisers succeeded in reducing the Duma to a non–democratically elected body that had little real control over the government. Nevertheless, a break had been made in Russia's autocratic system. Russia's rural society had broken from its feudal bonds, its economy was industrializing, and its political system included parliamentary institutions that promised to gain authority in the future.

FIGURE 48.3 Red Sunday In January 1905 the tsar's guards shot down hundreds of peaceful demonstrators in front of the royal palace in St. Petersburg. This event, known as "Red Sunday," left a bitter memory with Russia's liberals and radicals. (The Granger Collection)

National Movements in Southeast Europe

While nationalism between 1871 and 1914 was crushing minority language groups in the German and the Russian empires, it was pulling the Austrian and Ottoman empires apart along language lines. After Austria's defeat by Prussia in 1866, the dominant German minority in Austria felt obliged to take the aggressive and restless Magyars of Hungary into partnership. The *Ausgleich* (compromise) of 1867 set up the Dual Monarchy of Austria-Hungary. Each country had its own separate parliament. But the two were united under a common ruler, the head of the House of Hapsburg; common ministries of war, finance, and foreign affairs; and joint delegations from the two parliaments, whose duty was to coordinate policies wherever possible. This arrangement was essentially an alliance between the Germans of Austria and the Magyars of Hun-

Map 48.1 LANGUAGE GROUPS, AUSTRIA-HUNGARY This map indicates the difficulties facing the Austro-Hungarian Empire in an age of growing nationalism. Satisfaction of demands for independence by the various ethnic or language groups would spell dismemberment of the empire.

gary against the Slavic, Rumanian, and Italian language groups, which constituted a majority of the total population of the Dual Monarchy. In effect, the Germans said to the Magyars: "You take care of your subject language groups [mostly Slavs], and we will take care of ours" (see Map 48.1).

Austria followed a relatively moderate policy in dealing with its subject language groups. Cultural autonomy was granted, and the suffrage was gradually extended until in 1907 all adult males were given the vote. However, the subject peoples were more interested in nationalism than in democracy. The various language groups developed images of a glorious cultural and political past. The prosperous Czechs of Bohemia were especially adamant. The problem was confounded by the fact that many of the language groups had kinspeople outside the Dual Monarchy whom they wished to join and who deliberately stirred up their disloyalty. Such groups were the Italians, the Poles, the Ruthenians

(Ukrainians), the Serbs, and the Rumanians. Parliamentary sessions in Austria frequently degenerated into shouting, inkstand-throwing melees among the various language groups. Moreover anti-Semitism in Austria was growing, a development not unrelated to these problems among different ethnic groups.

Hungary made no pretense of conciliation. The Magyar aristocracy ruled over the Slovak, Rumanian, Serb, and Croat minorities with an iron hand. The aristocracy also refused to permit its own Magyar masses to participate in the government. The nationalist discontent in Hungary was even greater than it was in Austria; the Yugo (southern) Slavs (Croats and Serbs) were particularly troublesome. This explosive nationalism threatened to blow the Austro-Hungarian monarchy apart and, because of the network of entangling alliances, to draw the other major powers into a world conflict.

Between 1871 and 1914 the Balkan portion of the Ottoman Empire was a hornets' nest of nationalism (see Map 48.1). The hatred of the Christian Balkan language groups for their Islamic Turkish masters was equaled only by their distrust for each other. The once-potent Ottoman Empire crumbled throughout the course of the nineteenth century, and one Balkan language group after another, now aflame with national pride and ambition, emerged as an independent nation. Meanwhile, all the great powers of Europe became involved in the strategic and troubled area of the Near East. Russia, Austria-Hungary, Great Britain, France, Germany, and Italy had important imperial, economic, and military interests in the Balkans. In addition, Russia and Austria-Hungary had serious nationalistic interests there. Russia considered itself the big brother and protector of the Slavic-speaking Serbs and Bulgarians. Austria-Hungary's large Rumanian and Yugoslav populations desired union with their free kinspeople in Rumania and Serbia. Between 1829 and 1913 first the Greeks, then the Serbs, Rumanians, and Bulgarians, and finally the Albanians gained their independence from the Ottoman Empire. In each case a major crisis occurred among the great powers. These Balkan crises became progressively more severe, until finally one crisis got out of control and exploded into World War I.

Nationalism and Anti-Semitism

Jews had long suffered from anti-Semitism, but between 1789 and 1871 there were signs of change. The ideals of the Enlightenment, the French Revolution, and liberalism worked against anti-Semitism. In several countries Jews gained new rights and legal equality, though rarely full acceptance.

During the second half of the nineteenth century, particularly after the 1880s, anti-Semitism was on the rise. The situation was worst in central and eastern Europe, where most Jews lived and where conservative, militant, aggressive nationalism was thriving. Right-wing anti-Semitic organizations, such as the Pan-German Association and the Christian Social Workers' party, formed and grew in Germany. In Austria the leaders of the Christian Socialist party and the German National party became openly anti-Semitic. In Rumania Jews were not allowed to vote. Some of the most violent anti-Semitic acts in the decades before 1914 occurred in Russia, where legal restrictions, persecutions, and pogroms caused much displacement, suffering, and loss of life among Jews.

One result of this mixture of liberation for Jews in some cases and increasing anti-Semitism in others was the growth of Zionism, a Jewish nationalist movement to create an independent state for Jews in Palestine. Theodor Herzl (1860–1904) became the leading figure in the Zionist movement. He gained financial support from the French banker Baron de Rothschild and others. By the turn of the century an international Zionist organization was formed and efforts were being made to establish a Jewish homeland in Palestine. It would be several decades before these efforts would bear fruit.

Of greater immediate consequence was migration. Between 1871 and 1914 some two million eastern European Jews moved westward, many crossing the Atlantic to the United States. Certainly there were also other reasons for this migration (see p. 580), but the anti-Semitism that accompanied right-wing nationalism in eastern Europe helped push Jews from their homes in search of better lives elsewhere.

SUGGESTED READING

General

A. J. Mayer, *The Persistence of the Old Regime in Europe to the Great War* (1981). A controversial interpretation.

N. Stone, *Europe Transformed, 1878–1919* (1984). A fine recent survey.

A. J. P. Taylor, *The Struggle for Mastery in Europe, 1848–1918* (1971). A good, interpretive study of international politics.

Great Britain

M. Bentley, *Politics Without Democracy, 1815–1914* (1984). Good political coverage.

D. Read, *England, 1868–1914. The Age of Urban Democracy* (1979). Relates politics and socioeconomic developments.

France

D. Johnson, *France and the Dreyfus Affair* (1967). Excellent study.

J. M. Mayeur and M. Rebérioux, *The Third Republic from Its Origins to the Great War, 1871–1914* (1984). A thorough synthesis.

R. Tombs, *The War Against Paris, 1871* (1981). A good analysis of the Paris Commune.

Italy

D. M. Smith, *Italy: A Modern History* (1969). A good survey.

J. A. Thayer, *Italy and the Great War: Politics and Culture, 1870–1915* (1964). A solid analysis of Italian political history.

Germany

G. Craig, *Germany, 1866–1945* (1980). Particularly good on German political history during this period.

H. U. Wehler, *The German Empire, 1871–1918* (1985). A recent interpretive study.

Russia

W. Blackwell, *The Industrialization of Russia* (1982). Good on this important topic.

H. Rogger, *Russia in the Age of Modernization and Revolution, 1881–1917* (1983). An excellent synthesis.

A. B. Ulam, *Russia's Failed Revolutionaries* (1981). A good study of Russia's revolutionary groups prior to 1917.

Southeast Europe

B. Jelavich, *History of the Balkans* (1983). A useful survey.

A. Sked, *The Decline and Fall of the Habsburg Empire, 1815–1918* (1989). Some good coverage of this area.

Nationalism and Anti-Semitism

G. L. Mosse, *Toward the Final Solution: A History of European Racism* (1978). A useful introduction.

P. Pulzer, *The Rise of Political Anti-Semitism in Germany and Austria* (1988). A respected analysis.

D. Vital, *The Origins of Zionism* (1975). The standard introduction.

CHAPTER 49

Democracy, Expansion, Civil War, and Reform in the United States, 1800–1920

FIGURE 49.1 John Gast, *Manifest Destiny* This painting reveals the idealized myth of westward expansion. Moving from the Atlantic coast cities of the East across the plains and mountains toward the Pacific, the goddess of Destiny carries a schoolbook in one hand and a telegraph wire in the other. Below her come white male hunters and settlers, pushing Indians and buffalo further west in retreat. In her wake follows the railroad. (Library of Congress)

By the end of the eighteenth century the United States was experiencing many of the same trends and developments as other nations of Western civilization. As we saw in Chapter 37, the United States was influenced by Enlightenment ideas, experienced a revolution, and established liberal political institutions—a pattern familiar to France and some other European nations. With the exception of the African slaves, almost all citizens of the new nation were of European stock. Most people worked the land, but there were some growing cities and early industrial establishments—again a pattern not too different from that of many areas in Europe.

There were some important differences between the United States and other Western nations in 1800. It had only recently emerged from colonial status and remained separated from Europe by the Atlantic Ocean. Politically and socially, the United States did not carry a strong legacy of monarchical rule or aristocratic distinctions. There was a surplus of land, thanks to the willingness of American citizens to take from the Indians, and a supply of cheap, noncompetitive labor, thanks to slavery.

During the nineteenth century the United States again shared in trends sweeping through the West while remaining strikingly distinct in some important ways. In this chapter we will emphasize the pattern of shared trends and distinctions as we trace major elements of U.S. history in rough chronological order. By the end of the second decade of the twentieth century, the United States will have reached a point where its development can be better viewed as integrated with that of other Western nations.

1. DEMOCRACY AND GEOGRAPHIC EXPANSION, 1800–1861

Democracy in the young American republic received a boost with the election of Thomas Jefferson as president in 1800. Jefferson represented the ideals of a nation of small farmers and the realities of a political democracy with a party system. The coming to power of this liberal theorist—the author of the Declaration of Independence—was a shock to the more elitist Federalists, who had flourished under presidents Washington and Adams. The conservative Founding Fathers had felt that the capable elite should rule and that political parties, or "factions," would undermine the new political system. Although the rich and well-born raised a cry of anguish at the triumph of Jefferson, he was a moderate individual who in fact did little that was radical as president. Although he was supported in the election by the yeoman farmers, he was an elegant Virginian and scholarly philosopher rather than a man of the masses.

The War of 1812 with Great Britain resulted in an upsurge of American nationalism, which helped mold America's evolving political institutions. A new crop of nationally minded statesmen appeared, the ablest of whom were Henry Clay, John C. Calhoun, and Daniel Webster. The war itself ended indecisively, yet the United States emerged with a stronger national economy and a greater sense of being a nation with its own character and institutions rather than a former British colony.

The War of 1812 also produced a hero, Andrew Jackson. His rise to the presidency signaled a new stage in the development of America's democratic institutions. Not only did it represent the rise of a common man to the presidency—he defeated formidable, established, sophisticated political giants—it also marked the rise of the western frontier states to national political importance and the early development of modern, mass-based political parties. During the Jacksonian era, which extended for some two decades after his election in 1828, democracy advanced as new states without property qualifications for voting were rapidly admitted to the Union and as the older states eliminated property qualifications from their voting requirements. Artisans and small farmers used the egalitarian rhetoric of the Jacksonian era to assert their own interests and power. Yet much of the so-called Jacksonian "revolution" was more superficial than substantial. American Indians fared worse during the Jacksonian era than before, and, like Jefferson, Jackson as president did little that was radical.

Meanwhile, the United States was expanding (see Map 49.1). Between 1800 and 1861 the United States was the most rapidly growing nation in the world, both in area and in population. The purchase of the Louisiana Territory by

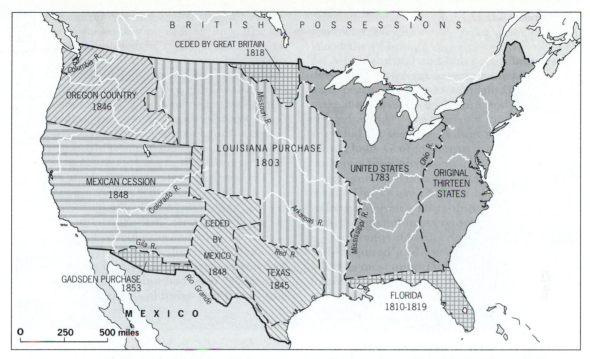

Map 49.1 **TERRITORIAL EXPANSION OF THE UNITED STATES, 1783–1853** Through a variety of means, including wars, purchases, treaties, and expropriation, the United States more than trebled its territory between 1800 and 1861. This territorial expansion kept land in surplus despite an unprecedented rate of population growth.

Thomas Jefferson from Napoleon in 1803 for some $16 million doubled the original area of the United States. In 1819 Florida was purchased from Spain for $5 million. Texas, which was even bigger than now, was annexed in 1845. The next year the Oregon Country was annexed after the settlement of a long-standing dispute with Great Britain. The annexation of Texas resulted in a war with Mexico (1846–1848). After a quick and easy victory, the United States took a huge block of Mexican territory, comprising the present states of California, Arizona, New Mexico, Nevada, Utah, and parts of Colorado and Wyoming. This territory was enlarged to the south in 1853 by the Gadsden Purchase from Mexico ($10 million). These additions within a period of fifty years more than trebled the original territory of the young American nation. Yet the cost was higher than the money paid for some of the territory. Indians had to be slaughtered and dispossessed.

Wars of conquest had to be fought (Mexico), and other wars had to be risked (Great Britain). Westward expansion was not simply a sanitary, heroic struggle to a predestined end (see Figure 49.1).

The growth in population was keeping pace with the increase in area. Between 1800 and 1861 the population of the United States increased from approximately 5 million to 32 million. Adding to the high rate of natural increase was an ever-increasing tide of immigration from Europe. After 1840 the largest immigrant groups were the Irish, most of whom settled in the cities of the Northeast, and the Germans, most of whom pushed on to the fertile lands of the Middle West.

Between 1800 and 1861, then, American political institutions had evolved along democratic and nationalistic lines. Voting rights had been extended to essentially all adult white males. Po-

FIGURE 49.2 A Northern Factory This lithograph of the Stillman, Allen & Co. Novelty Iron Works of New York City shows the more industrial, urban nature of the North in the middle decades just prior to the Civil War. (Museum of the City of New York)

litical power had been wrested from the elite circles of the old colonial well-to-do. A modern political party system had been developed. Americans pridefully thought of themselves and their institutions as distinct within Western civilization. The United States had expanded westward to the Pacific Ocean. The western frontier itself was one of the greatest of nationalizing influences. To it came people from all the seaboard states and from abroad who looked to the national government for protection, for roads and canals, and for land titles. It was in this period that American culture began to free itself from strictly European influence. The American Indian was idealized by Henry Wadsworth Longfellow and James Fenimore Cooper. Washington Irving's pen made the legends of American colonial days enchanting. Gilbert Stuart and Charles Willson Peale painted idealized portraits of American heroes. American schools and universities were teaching a particularly American version of civilization and world affairs.

2. SLAVERY, CIVIL WAR, AND RECONSTRUCTION, 1861–1877

The central event for American history during the nineteenth century was the Civil War, which broke out in 1861 and lasted until 1865. The nature of the Civil War has been debated endlessly, but certain features stand out. The North was increasingly a growing, urban, industrial society based on free labor (see Figure 49.2). The South remained agricultural, dependent on large plantation crops such as cotton, and based on slave labor (see Figure 49.3). The North was enjoying an increasing influence over national policies and generally favored federal over state power. The South saw its influence over national policies slipping and increasingly favored states' rights over federal power. The North seemed to represent a modernizing, democratic, nationalistic society; the South a traditional, unegalitarian, regional society. In great part, the Civil War was a clash between these increasingly different socie-

FIGURE 49.3 A Southern Plantation This picture, Charles Giroux's "Cotton Plantation," shows the contrasting rural society with a large population of slaves typical of the South. (Courtesy, Museum of Fine Arts, Boston, M. and M. Karolik Collection)

ties with different interests. But the issue that provided much of the emotional energy to this clash and that prior to 1861 tied together the issues dividing North and South was slavery.

The first boatload of slaves was brought to Virginia in 1619, one year before the Pilgrims landed at Plymouth Rock. Because of the tremendous amount of labor required to clear the American wilderness, the African slave trade flourished throughout the colonial period. By the time of the American Revolution, slaves constituted approximately one-fifth of the total population of the thirteen colonies. Slavery was recognized and protected by the national constitution. Because of the climate and the diversified economy, however, slavery proved to be unprofitable in the Northern states, and between 1777 and 1804 all the states north of Maryland passed emancipation laws. South of the Mason and Dixon line (the boundary between Maryland and Pennsylvania), where agriculture reigned supreme, slavery continued to be profitable and prevalent. But

by 1789 many Americans, in the South as well as in the North, disliked the institution. After the Revolution scores of antislavery societies were founded. It appeared possible that slavery in America was on its way to an early and peaceful end.

Some unforeseen developments, however, changed the attitude of the South toward emancipation, and a sharp line was drawn between the North and South over the slavery issue. The first of these developments was Whitney's invention of the cotton gin in 1793. This machine made the raising of cotton so profitable that soon large cotton plantations worked by slaves grew up throughout the South. The American South became the chief supplier of Britain's textile mills. By the mid–nineteenth century, slaves outnumbered whites in South Carolina and Mississippi, and in the rest of the Deep South slaves were about equal in number to whites. The Southern economy had become so wedded to cotton and to slavery that the Southern antislavery movement had faltered and the defense of slavery had gained momentum. Even more important than economic considerations in the development of proslavery sentiment in the South was the social problem. Slaves were seen not only as the basis of wealth but also as the basis of power and status by southern slaveholders. Slaveholders accepted as given the inferiority of African Americans. Southern whites did not believe that they could absorb into their society or even live alongside so many free African Americans under any circumstances. Meanwhile, in the free-labor North, antislavery sentiments were growing. Movements for the abolition of slavery became more prominent and forceful.

The critical issue became the extension of slavery to the western territories. The population of the northern states, with their growing industry, was rapidly outstripping that of the South. As the northwestern territories clamored for statehood without slavery, the Southerners took alarm. Already they were hopelessly outnumbered in the House of Representatives, whose membership is based on population. Their only security in the national government lay in the Senate, where each state has two members. The Southerners did everything in their power to slow down the settlement of the West and insisted that the admission of every free state must be accompanied by the admission of a slave state in order that equality in the Senate be maintained. But time and tide were on the side of the North. Geography, population, the growth of industrialization, and the march of liberalism in the Western world were irresistible.

In 1854 the Republican party was founded as a strictly Northern party committed to the restriction and, seemingly, ultimate extinction of slavery. In 1860, with Abraham Lincoln as its candidate, it won a sweeping victory over the Democrats, now split between North and South over the question of slavery. Rather than accept an inferior position in the nation and face the prospect of eventually having their power and status destroyed by some 4 million slaves forcibly freed in their midst, eleven southern states (about half the territory of the Union and a third of its population) seceded and set up an independent government.

The North had an overwhelming preponderance in population, wealth, industry, transpor-tation, and naval power. But the South enjoyed brilliant military leadership and the further advantage of fighting on its own soil for what it believed to be the survival of white civilization. The war lasted four bloody years. For three of the four years it looked as if the Union could not be restored. But after numerous discordant elements in the North were brought together, Great Britain and France tactfully neutralized, and, the winning commanders and strategy found, the southern armies were finally crushed.

Slavery was abolished and the authority of the national government restored, never to be seriously threatened again. However, the war left a legacy of sectional bitterness. The conciliatory Lincoln was assassinated just five days after the war ended. The radical Republican congressional leaders, who now gained control of the government, treated the defeated and devastated South as a conquered province. They sought to achieve basic reforms and to ensure political and civil rights for the freed slaves. The effort ended by 1877, when the last federal troops were finally withdrawn from the South. Over the course of the next twenty years many of the gains made by African Americans were lost. By this time a different dynamic was taking hold of American life and changing it in unprecedented ways: industrialization.

3. INDUSTRIALIZATION AND URBANIZATION, 1865–1901

Although the earliest factories were already present in the United States by the end of the eighteenth century, the growth of industrialization during the nineteenth century was at first quite slow. The French and British blockades during the Napoleonic wars and the War of 1812 with Britain cut the United States off from British manufacturers and caused much American commercial capital to be diverted to manufacturing. By the middle decades of the nineteenth century, industrialization was spreading, particularly in the Northeast. However, it was not until the years immediately following the Civil War that the United States joined other Western nations as a leading industrial power.

In most ways industrialization in the United States proceeded much as it did in other Western countries. New machines and sources of power were applied to the manufacturing process. Large factories sprang up in the East and Midwest, turning raw materials into finished products in great quantities. Working-class and urban populations connected with industrialization grew, fed both by migration from rural areas and by massive immigration from Europe. The United States proved to be subject to the same problems that plagued other industrializing nations: poor working conditions, low pay, child labor, urban slums, inadequate sanitation, and few social services.

However, there were a few elements that seemed to characterize the United States' growing industrialization between 1865 and 1901. Above all, the degree to which business became concentrated in the hands of a few individuals and corporations was striking. Industrial capitalists such as Andrew Carnegie (steel), John D. Rockefeller (oil), Cornelius Vanderbilt (railroads), and J. P. Morgan (finance) amassed unbelievable fortunes and power (see Figure 49.4). The corporations they founded, such as U.S. Steel and Standard Oil, soon gained monopolistic control over vast resources.

More than in most other nations, governmental policies during this period favored business in general and these huge industrial firms in particular. Not surprisingly, then, in the United States the unionization of labor was relatively slow to emerge. In part this was due to the continued abundance of cheap land and the influx of cheap, mobile labor from Europe. But unionization was also deterred by the determined resistance of industrial capitalists backed by private and public police power and by governmental policies and officials unsympathetic to unionization. Despite some earlier beginnings in various trades (such as the Knights of Labor), it was not until 1886 that Samuel Gompers, an immigrant from Great Britain, organized the American Federation of Labor—the first successful national labor organization in America.

By the end of the nineteenth century the United States not only was a major industrial power but also had outstripped the world in industrial production. The government and the economy of the country were still dominated by big-business interests that controlled the dominant "Old Guard" wing of the Republican party.

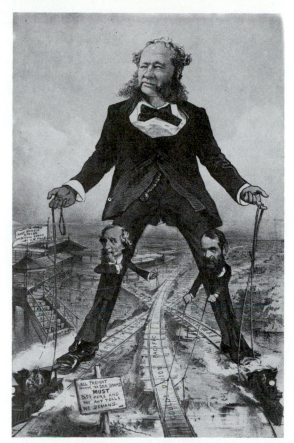

FIGURE 49.4 Cornelius Vanderbilt This cartoon attacks Cornelius Vanderbilt, who in the 1860s gained control over several railroads and amassed a great fortune. He is portrayed exercising monopolistic corporate power over the nation's railroads. (Culver Pictures)

Although the United States enjoyed enormous overall economic development, wealth was very unequally distributed, causing widespread discontent. Western and southern farmers had been clamoring for public regulation of the railroads, on which they were dependent. Small business, labor, and consumers demanded protection against the monopolistic practices and prices of the great trusts and corporations, which were protected by a prohibitively high tariff. The U.S. government remained behind almost that of all other industrial nations in its willingness to deal with social abuses stemming from industrialization. Millions deplored the city slums, the corrupt spoils system in the civil service, and the squandering of natural resources by private interests. The forces of reform were growing and would break out in the two decades following the turn of the century.

4. REFORM AND PROGRESSIVISM, 1901–1920

The great reforms of the progressive era are usually dated from 1901, when Theodore Roosevelt assumed the presidency. Roosevelt firmly believed in the capitalist system, but he was convinced that the time had come when the superiority of the government over private business must be asserted. After assuming the presidency in 1901 upon the assassination of William McKinley, "T.R.," as he was popularly known, immediately launched a vigorous program of reform. The Interstate Commerce Act of 1887 and the Sherman Antitrust Act of 1890, which had lain dormant, were activated. Organized labor was given a little support in its unequal fight with organized capital. Pure food and drug acts were designed to restrict the corporations and safeguard the public health. More than 200 million acres of forest and mineral lands and water power sites were withheld from private exploitation. He strengthened the merit system in the federal civil service. Many of his reform efforts were blocked by Congress and the federal courts, which were still controlled by the Republican Old Guard.

In 1912 the Democrats, under the leadership of Woodrow Wilson (1856–1924), gained their first clear-cut victory since the Civil War. Wilson proved to be more liberal than Roosevelt. With the Democrats in control of both houses of Congress, Wilson's administration sharply lowered the tariff, passed the Clayton Antitrust Act (more specific than the Sherman Act), gave further encouragement to organized labor, and set up the Federal Reserve Banking System, which removed control of the nation's financial policies from the hands of private interests on Wall Street and placed them in the hands of the federal government.

The passage of the long-struggled-for women's suffrage act in 1920 was the last reform of the progressive era. The return to power of the conservative Republicans under Warren Harding in 1920 brought the progressive period to a close. However, in those two decades American institutions and policies had adjusted to at least some of the social and economic realities of a modern democratic industrial society. At the same time the United States had joined other imperial powers with its acquisition of territories in Latin America, the Pacific, and Asia. Finally, the United States had become embroiled in World War I. From this point on, the United States would be too integrally connected to worldwide economic and political affairs to act in isolation.

SUGGESTED READING

General

R. Current et al., *American History: A Survey* (1987). A balanced, solid text.

Democracy and Geographic Expansion, 1800–1861

R. Billington, *Westward Expansion: A History of the American Frontier* (1974). An excellent survey.

J. Ellis, *After the Revolution: Profiles of Early American Culture* (1979). A useful survey of culture.

J. R. Howe, *From the Revolution Through the Age of Jackson: Innocence and Empire in the Young Republic* (1973). A good study of political development.

E. Spicer, *A Short History of the Indians of the United States* (1969). A useful introduction to the topic.

Slavery, Civil War, and Reconstruction, 1861–1877

M. Berry and J. Blassingame, *Long Memory: The Black Experience in America* (1982). A good survey.

E. Foner, *Reconstruction: America's Unfinished Revolution, 1863–1877* (1988). By a leading historian of the period.

E. D. Genovese, *Roll, Jordan, Roll: The World Slaves Made* (1974). A scholarly study of slave society.

J. M. McPherson, *Battle Cry of Freedom: The Civil War Era* (1988). Extremely well written.

Industrialization and Urbanization, 1865–1901

D. J. Boorstin, *The Americans: The National Experience* (1965). Useful sections on the impact of modernization.

D. Cashman, *America in the Gilded Age: From the Death of Lincoln to the Rise of Theodore Roosevelt* (1984). A well-written survey.

T. C. Cochran and W. Miller, *The Age of Enterprise* (1968). A broad, scholarly study covering the period.

Reform and Progressivism, 1901–1920

J. M. Cooper, Jr., *The Warrior and the Priest: Woodrow Wilson and Theodore Roosevelt* (1983). A comparative biography.

R. Hofstadter, *The Age of Reform: From Bryan to FDR* (1955). A classic.

A. Link and R. McCormick, *Progressivism* (1983). A succinct modern review.

S. M. Rothman, *Woman's Proper Place* (1978). Focuses on women's changing roles.

R. H. Wiebe, *The Search for Order, 1877–1920* (1968). Contains good material on reform and progressivism.

CHAPTER 50
Imperialism

FIGURE 50.1 Imperial Glory This picture of colonial troops parading in London in celebration of Queen Victoria's Diamond Jubilee in 1897 reveals some of the forces behind late-nineteenth-century imperialism: nationalistic pride, military power, social cohesion, and romantic sentiment. (Culver Pictures)

626

Between the fifteenth and eighteenth centuries European nations gained control over most of the Western Hemisphere, the west coast of Africa, and Southern Asia. Then, from the 1760s to the 1870s, there was a relative lull in expansion. Imperial powers such as Spain, Portugal, and France lost many of their overseas holdings during this period; even some of Britain's holdings in North America had been lost during the American Revolution. In the period between 1880 and 1914, however, there was a new burst of imperial expansion, the "new imperialism." Western powers engaged in a sudden quest for control over new territories in Asia, Africa, and the Pacific. Rapidly the West greatly increased its dominance over much of the rest of the world, taking Western culture and institutions to indigeous societies whether they wanted them or not.

1. CAUSES OF THE NEW IMPERIALISM

One of the chief impulses behind the new imperialism was economic. The rapid expansion of industry in Europe and the United States created a demand for greater markets, new sources of raw materials, and investment outlets for surplus capital. Many people in Western nations pushed for imperial expansion, optimistically assuming that the new markets, new sources of raw materials, and new investment outlets could be found. These advocates of imperialism were primarily those most directly in a position to profit from it—certain financiers, merchants, shippers, settlers, and colonial officials as well as industrialists with specific economic interests in non-Western lands.

Probably a greater impulse to the new imperialism was nationalism (see Figure 50.1). The outbreak of the new imperialism occurred shortly after the unification of Italy and Germany and during a period in which nationalism was on the rise throughout Europe. This nationalism turned into a new competitive struggle for international prestige among Western nations that spilled over into non-Western areas after 1880. Whether it was economically profitable or not, the national ego was flattered to see its colors spread over the map. Imperial conquest became

a measure of status, proof that a nation had become first rate. To be left behind in the imperial race was to be marked as a second-class nation. National egotism also gave the citizens of the great Western powers a sense of mission: They were bringing the blessings of their civilization to backward peoples. Rudyard Kipling expressed the belief of many Westerners when he sang in rhyme of the "white man's burden" to hold in tutelage and to civilize the "lesser breeds" of the earth.

Another motivating factor in the new imperialism was the evangelizing zeal of the Christian religion. Christianity had long taken to heart the command "Go ye into all the world and preach the gospel to every creature." At the very time that Christianity was wavering under attack in its homeland in the West, it was carrying on foreign missionary activity of unprecedented scope and intensity. More often than not, where the missionaries went, there went Western explorers, traders, troops, and officials.

In addition, political and diplomatic developments became intertwined after the 1880s to make colonial claims increasingly valuable assets. Here Bismarck set a pattern of making claims to colonial territories and using those claims as bargaining chips against other powers. His tactics forced other nations to make their own claims. Soon these claims were being used by Western nations to forge alliances or bargain with competitors in the growing international disputes of the period. The result was the virtual partition of Africa.

Finally, the processes involved in imperial expansion and the circumstances of the West help explain the new imperialism. Science and technology gave industrialized nations such a military advantage that they could easily conquer and control the nonindustrialized lands. Almost any penetration into such areas as Africa, southern Asia, or the Pacific quickly led to greater involvement and eventual control. Once missionaries or traders established their presence in a new area, their home governments were called on to provide support, enforce contracts, and protect private interests. To provide that support and protection, they had to create new facilities in the new lands, thus increasing the Western presence. The governments soon requested the cooperation of the native political leaders, and

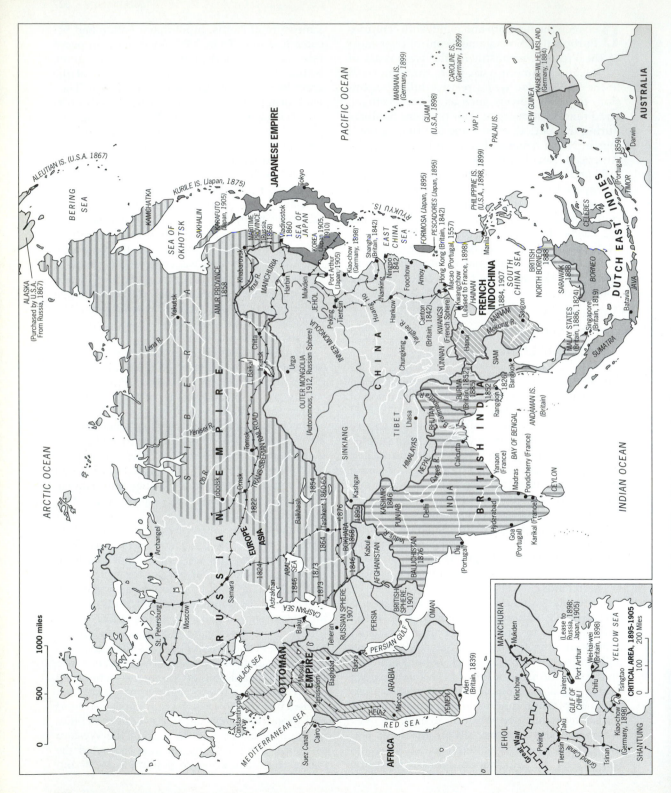

when it was not forthcoming, they used force. Indirect control could quickly turn into direct control as problems arose and then into expanding control as neighboring areas became of interest. Thus, the initial contacts by Western explorers, missionaries, or traders blossomed into full imperial control by Western nations.

2. THE EXPLOITATION AND AWAKENING OF CHINA

One of the most important scenes of European imperialism during the nineteenth century was China. This huge, populous country was the seat of the oldest continuous civilization in the world. For over three thousand years China had been a vast melting pot, absorbing invading peoples and cultures and welding them into a tough but resilient civilization. The military conquerors had always been swallowed up or conquered by Chinese culture.

Over time, the Chinese chose to isolate themselves from the outside world. A great wall (never completed), originally constructed to defend China's northern border, later symbolized its effort to retain the old and keep out the new. Although they admitted some European traders and Christian missionaries in the sixteenth and seventeenth centuries, they closed their doors rather tightly thereafter. By the mid–nineteenth century their society, weakened by internal problems under the declining Manchu dynasty, constituted a power vacuum that tempted exploitation by the West.

The first Europeans to force themselves upon the Chinese were the British. Going to war in 1839, when Chinese officials interfered with their sale of opium in China, the British, with their modern weapons, easily defeated the Chinese. By the terms of the Treaty of Nanking (1842), the Chinese ceded Hong Kong to the British, opened many of their ports to foreign trade free of restricting tariffs, and granted the foreigners extraterritorial rights. This was the first of a series of unequal treaties and the signal for all the great Western powers to rush into China and seize what they could. In the ensuing scramble it was the rivalry among the great powers themselves as much as Chinese resistance that saved China from complete loss of independence.

The British got the lion's share. In addition to Hong Kong and concessions in the Canton area of the southeast, they gained a virtual trading monopoly in the Yangtze Valley, which was the richest and most populous part of China. In the north they gained footholds in the capital city of Peking and its port city of Tientsin, in the Shantung peninsula, and in Manchuria. They gained dominion over Tibet. In the 1880s they seized control of Burma, which owed a tenuous allegiance to China. The French took large areas in southeast China and Hainan Island as their sphere. In the 1880s they completed the detachment of Indochina from Chinese sovereignty. The Russians took Manchuria as their sphere, annexed a large strip of China's northeast coast, including the port of Vladivostok, and became active in Korea. The Germans carved out for themselves much of the strategically located Shantung peninsula and built a powerful naval base at Kiaochow. In 1894 the rejuvenated and modernized Japanese went to war with China. They easily defeated China and not only took away Formosa and Korea but also forced China to pay a huge indemnity. Even the United States got into the act. The United States had launched an imperialist program in the Far East in 1898 by seizing the Philippine Islands and Guam from Spain. Now, fearful for its growing trade with China, the United States attempted to gain a sphere of influence in Fukien Province and demanded an Open Door policy in China with equal trading opportunities for all.

Meanwhile, Chinese nationalism was being aroused by the Western and Japanese aggressions against the "Celestial Empire." In 1899–1900 a serious uprising against the foreign exploiters, known as the Boxer Rebellion, took place. Thousands of Chinese Christians and a

---

Map 50.1 IMPERIALISM IN ASIA, 1840–1914 As the map on opposite page indicates, almost all the Western powers participated in the imperial expansion into Asia. Once Japan westernized, it too joined the imperial race.

number of foreigners were slain. This liberation movement was put down by British, French, German, Russian, Italian, Japanese, and American troops. The nationalist leaders were severely punished, and China was forced to pay the foreign governments a large indemnity.

A more far-reaching revolutionary movement, aimed not only at freeing China from foreign exploitation but also at modernizing and democratizing its society and government, was being organized by Dr. Sun Yat-sen (1866–1925). Sun, the son of a poor Chinese farmer, studied in a British mission school in Hawaii, became a Christian, and later graduated from the British medical school at Hong Kong. Eloquent and dynamic, he organized his followers into the Kuomintang party, which was committed to a three-point program: (1) national independence, (2) democratic government, (3) social justice. In 1911 the reformers launched a revolution against the Manchu dynasty, declared a republic, and elected Sun as provisional president. The revolution swept most of China. The Manchu officials in Peking, their power having evaporated, declared China a republic and abdicated in favor of General Yuan Shi-kai, organizer of the New Army of North China. Early in 1912 the idealistic Sun, in behalf of national unity and fearful of rising anarchy and warlords within and the possibility of Japanese and Russian intervention from without, yielded to General Yuan. Yuan, however, soon proved to be more interested in power than in liberal reform. When the Kuomintang party won the elections of 1913, he suppressed the party and had its most promising young leader assassinated. Sun disassociated himself from Yuan's dictatorship and resumed his liberal activities in South China. When World War I opened a new era in 1914, China was torn with revolution and division.

3. THE EMERGENCE OF JAPAN

Japan's reaction to Western intrusion was quite different from that of China. The Japanese people inhabit four large islands and some three thousand small ones stretching along the eastern coast of Asia for a distance of about two thousand miles. Like China, Japan had admitted the sixteenth- and seventeenth-century European traders and Christian missionaries but had evicted them and closed its doors after observing what was happening everywhere in Asia where Europeans were admitted. At mid–nineteenth century the Japanese were living in isolation.

In 1853, eleven years after the Treaty of Nanking opened up China, an American fleet commanded by Commodore Matthew C. Perry steamed into Tokyo Bay and pressured the Japanese to open their ports to American trade. The Japanese were much impressed by the technological superiority of the Americans. In 1868, just fifteen years later, a group of young Japanese overthrew the existing government and began reorganizing the Japanese government and society along modern Western lines (the Meiji Restoration). Taking what they considered to be the best from the various Western nations, they patterned their business methods after those of the United States, their legal system after the French, and their navy after the British. But it was Bismarck's Germany that impressed the Japanese the most. They built a military machine and an authoritarian governmental and educational system on the model of the German Empire.

In an incredibly short time Japan became a modern, industrialized, military, and, on the surface at least, westernized power (see Figure 50.2). In 1894 Japan attacked China, defeated it with ease, and forced it to pay a large indemnity and to give up Korea (which Japan annexed in 1910) and the island of Formosa. In 1902 Great Britain became the first Western power to treat an Asian nation as an equal by entering into a military alliance with Japan. Thus strengthened and reassured, Japan attacked Russia in 1904 and, to everyone's surprise, defeated Russia both on land and at sea. As a reward, Japan took the southern half of Sakhalin Island and Russia's railroad and port concessions in southern Manchuria, thereby becoming the dominant power in that large and valuable section of China. By 1914 Japan was a first-rate westernized power—industrialized, militaristic, and imperialistic.

4. COMPETITION FOR THE STRATEGIC NEAR AND MIDDLE EAST

The term *Near East* usually refers to the area at the eastern end of the Mediterranean: Egypt, the old Ottoman Empire, and the Balkan peninsula.

FIGURE 50.2 Japanese Silk Factory, 1905 By the early twentieth century Japan had successfully adopted Western industrial methods. In this 1905 photograph of a silk-weaving factory, supervising men are in formal Western attire and women work on the machines. (California Museum of Photography, University of California, Riverside)

In the nineteenth century the term *Middle East* usually meant the area of the Persian Gulf, the territory northwest of India, and sometimes Tibet. (By the middle of the twentieth century the term *Middle East* was generally used to designate the whole area from and including Egypt and Turkey to the western borders of India.) Before the development of its oil resources after World War I, this area (with the exception of the Balkan peninsula) was relatively poor. It was inhabited chiefly by Moslems, who were hostile to Europeans. The main importance of the area, therefore, was strategic. It is the land bridge between the world's two largest land masses—the continents of Eurasia and Africa. The opening in 1869 of the Suez Canal, which shortened the sailing distance between western Europe and the Far East by five thousand miles, doubled the strategic value of the Near and Middle East. Indeed,

Suez quickly became one of the most vital single commercial and military focal points in the world.

The Suez Canal was built by a French company between 1859 and 1869. However, in 1875 Great Britain, taking advantage of the Egyptian government's financial distress, purchased the khedive's controlling portion of the canal stock. Seven years later, to quell an anti-European insurrection, the British occupied Egypt with their military forces. The French acquiesced in the establishment of Britain's control over Egypt and the Suez Canal in return for British support of French dominance in Morocco.

Serious competition for the British in the Near East soon came from an unexpected source. Wilhelm II, upon becoming kaiser of the German Empire in 1888, immediately began to show a keen interest in the Ottoman Empire. In 1889

Wilhelm II visited Constantinople and declared himself to be the friend and benefactor not only of the Turks but also of all Moslems. Friendship was followed by economic concessions and German investments in the Ottoman Empire. A second visit by the kaiser in 1898 led to a concession to Germany to build a railroad from the Bosporus to the Persian Gulf. This, with its European connection, was the famous Berlin-to-Baghdad railroad. The British took alarm. The Baghdad Railroad, with a fortified terminus on the Persian Gulf, would undercut Britain's longer water route to the East and threaten India, Britain's richest colonial prize. A projected branch running down through Syria and Palestine to Hedjaz would menace the Suez Canal itself.

Russia was equally concerned. Since the days of Ivan III in the fifteenth century, one of Russia's major ambitions has been to gain a warm water outlet to the world through the Turkish Strait at Constantinople. Russia had long looked to Constantinople as the seat and legitimate capital of its Orthodox religion and Byzantine culture. The decay of the Ottoman Empire in the nineteenth century encouraged Russia to try for Constantinople, and only the intervention of Great Britain and France in the Crimean War (1854–1856) prevented Russia from attaining its goal. In 1877–1878 Russia defeated Turkey and threatened to dominate the whole Balkan peninsula. This time Great Britain and Austria-Hungary forced Russia to submit to a general settlement by the European powers. At the Congress of Berlin, 1878, Russian ambitions in the Near East were once more thwarted. Bismarck's support of Austria-Hungary and Great Britain at the Congress of Berlin marked the beginning of German-Russian estrangement. Russia's defeat by Japan in 1904–1905 caused Russia to intensify its pressure toward the Middle and Near East. Russia's southward expansion so menaced India that Great Britain extended the northwest Indian frontier to the Khyber Pass and crossed over the Himalayas to checkmate Russian influence in Tibet, Afghanistan, and Persia.

The new German threat in the Near and Middle East, however, caused the British and the Russians to settle their long-standing differences. In 1907 they neutralized Tibet and Afghanistan and divided Persia into three spheres of influence—a Russian sphere in the north, a British sphere in the south, and an "independent" sphere in the center. Great Britain, Russia, and France, now diplomatic allies, prevented the sale of Baghdad Railroad bonds in their respective countries in an effort to embarrass the financing of the costly undertaking. Germany went right ahead, however, with the extension of its influence in the Balkans and the Ottoman Empire. In 1913 Germany dispatched a military mission to Constantinople to reorganize and instruct the Turkish army. The Ottoman Empire's friendship and eventual alliance with Germany was undoubtedly motivated by a greater fear of Russia. By 1914 the area of the Near and Middle East was a giant powder keg with fuses leading to St. Petersburg, Berlin, and London.

5. THE SCRAMBLE FOR AFRICA

At the opening of the nineteenth century, Africa was the seat of several civilizations. In the north the long-established Islamic societies continued to evolve, though at a slow pace. In sub-Saharan Africa, particularly in the western and central Sudan where the Sahara Desert gave way to grasslands and trade flourished, many societies and states had developed over the centuries. Africa was affected by trade and contact with Europeans, but except for coastal and certain other limited areas, such as South Africa, most of Africa was generally free from western European control. The Portuguese, Spanish, British, and French had trading posts on the west coast, while the Dutch and Portuguese had posts and settlements around the southern cape.

By the middle decades of the nineteenth century the French had conquered Algeria and made it a part of France and had pushed up the Senegal River in the west. The British had taken the Cape Colony from the Dutch during the Napoleonic wars, and the Dutch settlers had moved northward into the interior.

After 1880, however, the tempo of European activity changed drastically. Such a mad scramble for Africa took place among the powers of western Europe that by 1914 the only independent areas left were Ethiopia in the east and Liberia in the west. Ethiopia, with French aid, had

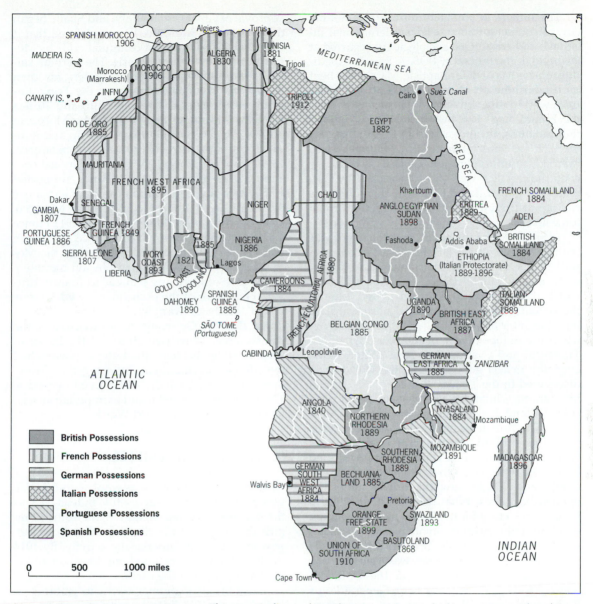

Map 50.2 IMPERIALISM IN AFRICA, 1914 This map indicates how the vast majority of Africa was carved up by European nations in the two decades of the 1880s and 1890s.

repulsed an invading Italian army, and Liberia had been sponsored by the United States as a hoped-for receptacle for liberated slaves. The rest of the huge continent had been seized by France, Great Britain, Germany, Portugal, Belgium, Italy, and Spain (listed in the approximate order of size of territory held) (see Map 50.2). The treatment of Africans was often similar to that accorded the native Americans in the sixteenth and seventeenth centuries.

The seizure of so much territory did not occur, of course, without serious international incidents and crises. One such incident occurred at Fashoda in the Sudan in 1898. A French expedition under Major Jean-Baptiste Marchand, bent on establishing an all-French axis across Africa from west to east, arrived at Fashoda and hoisted the French flag. The British, however, claimed the Sudan as an appendage of Egypt. Furthermore, they were interested in a Cape-to-Cairo railroad running through all British territory, even though they were already blocked by German East Africa. Lord Kitchener therefore hurried down from the north with a superior British force and compelled the French to withdraw.

In South Africa the British fought a major war with the Dutch settlers (1899–1902). When British settlers began to move into the Cape Colony early in the nineteenth century, the Calvinist Dutch Boers (farmers) who had settled there in the seventeenth century trekked northward far into the interior. Eventually the British recognized the independence of the two Boer states, Transvaal and Orange Free State. When, however, the richest gold mines in the world were discovered in the Transvaal in the 1880s, British immigrants (Uitlanders) flooded in. The unwelcome Uitlanders were badly treated by the Dutch Boers. The British empire builder Cecil Rhodes, with the support of powerful interests back home, was determined to brush aside the two little Boer republics. When the able Boer president, Paul Kruger, saw the British intent, he opened hostilities. What the world expected to be an easy victory for the British took three years of all-out military effort involving severe casualties and enormous costs. Britain's treatment of the defeated Boers, however, was lenient. They were taken into partnership in the Union of South Africa, and their war hero, General Louis Botha, was elected the Union's first prime minister. During the course of the struggle, a telegram of congratulation from the German kaiser to President Kruger and the British seizure of a German ship attempting to violate the British blockade caused great tension between Great Britain and Germany. As the kaiser admitted, only the superiority of the British navy prevented him from going to war.

The British navy also proved decisive in two crises over Morocco. In 1905 France, with the approval of Great Britain, Italy, and Spain, began the conquest of Morocco. France claimed that it was necessary because of continual raids by Moroccan tribes on French Algeria. The German kaiser, seeing an opportunity to assert his own power and possibly to break up the Triple Entente, which France, Great Britain, and Russia were then forming, appeared at the Moroccan port of Tangier on a German warship and indicated his support of Moroccan independence. Great tension followed. At an international conference at Algeciras in Spain, France, supported by her own ally, Great Britain, and by Germany's ally, Italy, won limited control over Morocco. Disorder continued, however, and in 1911 France sent a conquering army into Morocco, at which point Germany dispatched a cruiser to the Moroccan port of Agadir. Again tension mounted. In the face of Germany's threat to France, Britain's chancellor of the exchequer, Lloyd George, talked loudly of war. Again Germany backed down. Between Germany and Morocco stood the British navy. These two efforts of the kaiser to drive a wedge between the Entente powers had the effect of driving them closer together. Moreover, his own ally, Italy, had proved uncertain. These two crises growing out of imperialism hastened the coming of World War I.

6. THE BRITISH EMPIRE

Of all the European overseas empires, the British was by far the most successful. Indeed, it was the dazzling size and wealth of the British Empire that helped to excite the other European powers to greater imperialistic activity. By 1914 the British Empire included one-fourth of all the land and people of the earth.

Great Britain's commerce with its empire was enormous. In 1914 Britain's foreign investments, most of which were in the empire, totaled $20 billion—one-fourth of the total wealth of the homeland. (By comparison, France had $9 billion invested abroad; Germany, $6 billion. The United States was a debtor nation.) The empire, furthermore, provided lucrative and often glamorous careers for thousands of British governors, army and navy officers, diplomats, and civil servants of every description.

In the latter part of the nineteenth century,

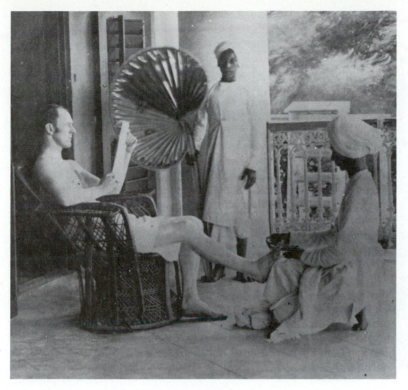

Figure 50.3 The British in India This photo of Indian servants catering to a British gentleman indicates the gulf between the British ruling class and the Indians they governed. It also reveals the appeal to Britishers of the foreign service. (BBC Hulton/The Bettmann Archive)

Great Britain adopted the policy of granting self-government to the English-speaking portions of its empire. Canada, which had gained self-government in 1849, was granted dominion status in 1867. With dominion status, the only remaining effective bond was allegiance to the British crown. The British governor-general was only a figurehead like the king at home. Australia was made a self-governing dominion in 1901, New Zealand in 1907, and the Union of South Africa in 1910. The policy was successful. All the dominions rallied to the mother country in both world wars.

Great Britain's richest imperial prize was India (see Figure 50.3). India's more than 300 million inhabitants accounted for at least three-fourths of the total population of the whole empire. India was nearly twenty times as large as Great Britain and more than seven times as populous. It was the mother country's best customer and supplied many minerals and raw materials.

Until 1858 India was governed by the British East India Company, a private stock company. However, the great Sepoy Mutiny of 1857, the first large-scale uprising of the Indians against British rule, caused the British government to take over the government of India from the company. Between 1858 and 1914 Great Britain spent millions of dollars in India on railroads, industries, education, and public health. The enormous growth of India's population, which more than doubled during the period, is testimony to some improvement in the conditions of life under British rule. But the British took out of India more than they brought in, and they showed no inclination to grant self-government. Indian dissatisfaction with British rule mounted steadily. In the late nineteenth century, nationalism, which had provided so much aggressive energy for Europe, was coming to Asia—to India as well as to Japan and China. In 1885 the All India Congress party was formed for the purpose of achieving Indian

FIGURE 50.4 Imperialism Satirized This cartoon, which appeared in 1899, satirizes the attitudes of smug righteousness and superiority with which the Americans, the British, and the European nations extended their dominance over the rest of the world. The United States was dominant in the Western Hemisphere, the European imperialist powers in the Eastern Hemisphere. (New York Public Library Picture Collection)

independence. By 1914 it was becoming obvious that India would not remain a placid, profitable colony much longer.

7. THE LEGACY OF IMPERIALISM

The Western world's technology, its dynamic capitalism, and above all its aggressive nationalism had enabled it between 1880 and 1914 to subject most of the rest of the world to its domination (see Figure 50.4). Western peoples and their economies became entwined in large parts of Africa and Asia as never before (see Maps 50.1 and 50.2). Rather than striving for a better understanding of these non-Western societies, Westerners were usually encouraged to view others in condescending, arrogant, or racist terms.

In the process of dominating the non-Western world, Western nations not only exploited the natural and human resources of conquered lands but also profoundly undermined the cultures, societies, and political organizations of native peoples. Economies that had been balanced and well-functioning in the environment were distorted and ruined as they were transformed to serve the demands of Western commerce. New activities, such as mining and railroad building, often employed native laborers in inhumane ways and at great cost to lives. Political structures that had long functioned effectively were distorted or destroyed in just a few years. New social and political divisions were created as Western administrators favored certain groups to pass on their orders to others.

Few in the West were able or willing to recognize how destructive the policies of imperialism could be. By 1914 most people in the Western world had come to view imperialism as a normal and permanent state. In the course of the twentieth century, however, some of the very forces that had accounted for the new imperialism would lead to its demise. The non-Western world was irreversibly changed by Western imperialism, but it would not remain under the thumb of Western nations for long.

SUGGESTED READING

General and Causes

M. Doyle, *Empires* (1986). Imperialism in a comparative context.

D. K. Fieldhouse, *The Colonial Experience: A Comparative Study from the Eighteenth Century* (1982). A good introduction.

D. Headrick, *Tools of Empire* (1981). Examines what made imperial expansion relatively easy.

T. Smith, *The Patterns of Imperialism* (1981). A good survey.

The Exploitation and Awakening of China

J. K. Fairbank, *The United States and China* (1979). A scholarly, lucid history of China by a leading expert.

I. Hsu, *The Rise of Modern China* (1975). A useful survey.

The Emergence of Japan

W. Beasley, *The Meiji Restoration* (1972). A good analysis of this crucial development.

R. Storry, *A History of Modern Japan* (1982). Good on the period.

Competition for the Near and Middle East

S. N. Fisher, *The Middle East: A History*, 2nd ed. (1969). A reliable text.

The Scramble for Africa

A. Christopher, *Colonial Africa* (1984). A useful introduction.

J. Gallegher, R. Robinson, and A. Danny, *Africa and the Victorians: The Climax of Imperialism* (1961). A good, controversial analysis.

The British Empire

W. Baumgart, *Imperialism: The Idea and Reality of British and French Colonial Expansion* (1982). An up-to-date study.

P. Moon, *The British Conquest and Domination of India* (1989). Good chapters on the period.

B. Porter, *The Lion's Share, A Short History of British Imperialism, 1850–1970* (1975). A solid survey.

The Legacy of Imperialism

D. Headrick, *The Tentacles of Progress: Technology Transfer in the Age of Imperialism, 1850–1940* (1988). Focuses on the economic disruption caused by Western technology.

D. Mannoni, *Prospero and Caliban: The Psychology of Colonization* (1964). An excellent analysis from a psychological perspective.

RETROSPECT

The first half of the era between 1776 and 1914 was a period of great political, economic, and social upheaval. Politically and socially, it was a time of high expectation and excitement. In a matter of weeks—and sometimes days—the kind of fundamental changes that usually require decades took place. Time-honored institutions, privileges, and customs toppled. Wealth, power, and rights were redistributed. Economically, changes came somewhat slower but were even more fundamental. Goods and services were produced in different ways and in different places. Where people lived, how they made a living, and how they related to one another were changing in irreversible, revolutionary ways.

The Western Hemisphere was the stage for

the first of these revolutions. The American Revolution was primarily a matter of the thirteen English colonies winning their independence from the mother country. As a result of the Revolution, loyalist lands were redistributed and the royal governors and their aristocratic councils gave way to the more democratic legislatures. The Declaration of Independence and the new Constitution were filled with the ideas of the Enlightenment.

The changes brought about by the French Revolution were more dramatic and significant for Western civilization. French society on the eve of the Revolution was still essentially feudal, with its privileged clergy and nobility. Government was in the hands of a monarch. Within a few months of the outbreak of the Revolution in 1789, a series of sweeping reforms had occurred—the end of feudalism, the Declaration of the Rights of Man, and the drawing up of a liberal but moderate constituion.

But the nobility and clergy were not willing to see their privileges so easily lost. Nor were the radical Jacobins convinced that the Revolution had gone far enough. They wished to see the principles of ''Liberty, Equality, Fraternity'' extended beyond France's borders. When Austria and Prussia intervened in behalf of the French royalty and nobility, the radicals deposed and beheaded Louis XVI. All the great powers of Europe except Russia formed a coalition for the purpose of ending this threat to the established order. The revolutionary radicals, now in control, inaugurated a Reign of Terror for the purpose of uniting and mobilizing the nation. It was remarkably successful; the internal enemies of the Revolution were terrorized into silence or support, and the foreign enemies were defeated and driven back beyond the frontiers. But no one seemed able to consummate the Revolution and restore peace. The radical Jacobins were overthrown by the bourgeois moderates, and the Terror ended; but the moderates, too, proved unable to bring peace at home and abroad.

In 1799 a coup d'état brought Napoleon Bonaparte to power. Over the next few years he instituted stabilizing reforms that affirmed some of the changes wrought by the French Revolution and destroyed others. His fifteen-year rule was marked by almost continual warfare.

Meanwhile, another kind of revolution was taking place in western Europe—the Industrial Revolution. By the end of the eighteenth century new factories, using new sources of power, new machines, and new methods of production, were sprouting up in Great Britain in great numbers. Great Britain's economy was experiencing unprecedented, sustained growth. The Industrial Revolution had begun. Over the course of the nineteenth century it spread to continental Europe and other parts of the world. Great social changes followed in the wake of industrialization. Cities grew, the class structure changed, new social institutions developed, and even the function of the family and the role of women evolved. The first beneficiaries of the Industrial Revolution were the industial bourgeoisie—the factory owners. Whether the industrial proletariat benefited during the early period of industrialization is questionable. While their wages may have risen, they lost skills and security and became the virtual slaves of factory owners. These radical changes in production and distribution and the ensuing stresses prompted new economic and social thought—economic liberalism, Utopian Socialism, and Marxism.

Both an affirmation of and a reaction to the revolutionary spirit that engulfed the Western world between 1776 and 1850 were reflected in the romanticism that characterized the philosophy, literature, and arts of the period. For liberals, romanticism affirmed the optimism, individualism, and heroism epitomized by the French Revolution, Napoleon, and the revolutions of the first half of the nineteenth century. For conservatives, romanticism rejected the rationalism of the Enlightenment and affirmed the glories of the prerevolutionary and preindustrial world, where the mysteries of nature and religion dominated. Although romanticism would remain an influential and popular cultural style after midcentury, the ensuing period would be more accurately reflected by realism.

At the Congress of Vienna in 1814–1815, the major powers structured a peace settlement at the end of the Napoleonic wars in accordance with the principles of conservatism. In many ways the ensuing decades between 1815 and 1850 were a struggle between these forces of conservatism and the newer forces of liberalism. Despite various revolutionary rumblings, the forces of conservatism generally remained in control until 1830. After 1830 reform and revolution in the name of liberalism started to wrestle control from the conservatives, culminating in the great liberal and nationalistic revolutions of 1848. Yet this great defeat for the conservative forces of order was short-lived. By 1850 most were back in power again and the great period of liberal revolution was over.

Between 1850 and 1914 developments in Western civilization were dominated by the spread of nationalism and industrialization. Both had their roots in the preceding decades, but until the middle of the nineteenth century they were relatively limited in scope and intensity. During the second half of the century nationalism spread to new areas, achieved new successes, and took on a more pragmatic, aggressive quality. At the same time, industrialization matured in Western societies and spread into the non-Western world.

Between 1850 and 1871 nationalism was used to strengthen the political institutions of the nation-state. The Second Empire of Napoleon III provides an outstanding example of nationalistic state building during this period. Domestically, Napoleon III involved the government in a series of new economic and social programs; in foreign affairs he intervened in areas stretching from Russia to Mexico. However, the fruits of nationalism were even more significant in Italy and Germany. First Italy, under the guidance of Piedmont and its prime minister, Cavour, unified most of the diverse states of the Italian peninsula into a single nation in 1860. Then Prussia, under the leadership of Bismarck, used war and diplomacy to unify Germany into a powerful new nation in 1871.

Meanwhile, the second Industrial Revolution was taking place in the West. Steel, chemicals, and electricity were replacing iron, textiles, and steam as the basis of new industrial development. Countries such as Germany and the United States successfully challenged the long leadership of Great Britain in industrial production. The industrial societies became much more urbanized and were dominated by the middle class, but the working classes were now rising to the fore with their own organizations and ideologies. Most significant was the rise of Marxist socialism, a powerful ideology that won many adherents and that was thrust into public life by socialist unions and socialist political parties.

Thought and culture between 1850 and 1914 reflected the influence of nationalism and industrialism. Both stressed secular beliefs and a certain pragmatic scientific approach. Both contributed to the growing problems facing Christianity during the period. The spread and prestige of the natural and social sciences were particularly strong and were reflected in some of the literary and artistic trends of the period. Toward the end of the nineteenth century and the beginning of the twentieth century, however, a new strain of disillusionment, uncertainty, and even pessimism was appearing in philosophy, literature, art, and even science. This disturbing cultural trend foreshadowed the devastating turmoil of the decades following the outbreak of World War I in 1914.

Between 1871 and 1914 Europe was characterized politically by the spread of democratic institutions and the growth of a more militant nationalism. While the spread of democracy occurred in some form throughout Europe, it was more complete and more closely associated with liberalism in western Europe. In eastern Europe the spread of democracy was much less complete and, in some cases, more a matter of form than substance. There, governments such as those under Kaiser Wilhelm II in Germany, the tsars in Russia, and the emperor in Austria-Hungary tended to be conservative and authoritarian.

Meanwhile, in the United States many of the main developments occurring during the nineteenth century roughly paralleled European developments. Democratic institutions, along with a growing sense of nationalism, were spreading as the country expanded. At the same time that the Industrial Revolution was spreading from Great Britain to other areas of Europe, the United States was industrializing its economy—particularly after the Civil War ended in 1865. And like other Western governments, the American government attempted to adjust to the pressures of a mature industrial society by instituting political reforms toward the end of the nineteenth and the beginning of the twentieth centuries.

After 1880 nationalism and industrialization combined to thrust the leading nation-states of the West into a new imperial race. Within two decades the Western powers carved vast areas of Africa, Asia, and the Pacific into colonies and territories of imperial interest. As a result of this imperial expansion, non-Western societies were undermined and irreversibly changed, and the Western powers became locked into added rivalries that would bear the fruits of war in 1914.

PART SEVEN

WAR AND GLOBAL INTERDEPENDENCE, 1914–PRESENT

The outbreak of total war in 1914 initiated a new era of destruction, upheaval, and revolutionary change in the West. At great cost, liberal democratic powers won the war, but the developments that followed were not encouraging. Revolutions in Russia had not only brought down the tsarist government but also brought the Bolsheviks to power. The Bolsheviks transformed Russia into the Communist Soviet Union, which by the 1930s was a totalitarian nation pursuing policies in fundamental opposition to those of the capitalistic West. Fascism, which directly and violently identified liberalism and democracy as enemies, arose in Europe, first in Italy and later in Nazi Germany. Meanwhile, hopes for the spread of liberal democracy in southern and eastern Europe, and Japan were dashed as these areas turned to authoritarian forms of government. The Great Depression of the 1930s increased strains in this already tense environment. World War II, which broke out in 1939, seemed to many to be a destructive continuation of the violence unleashed by World War I.

For most of the period after 1945 the basic trends were toward recovery, growth, and relative stability. Two competing superpowers, the United States and the Soviet Union, were the dominating nations in the West and, to a considerable extent, the world. Colonies controlled by the old imperial powers gained their freedom. Rather than by direct control, the West became tied to the non-Western world by expanding communications, economic interdependence, international organizations, systems of alliances, ideological competition, and cultural exchange.

In recent years stunning new developments seem to have altered the course of history. In the Soviet Union and Eastern Europe, communism has collapsed. In western Europe, new steps toward greater union have been taken. Along the rim of the Pacific Ocean, economic development has shifted the economic balance of power in the world toward Asia.

CHAPTER 51
World War I, 1914–1918

FIGURE 51.1 Trench Warfare This photo of French troops on the western front in World War I illustrates the type of war it was: fought in deep, barbed-wire-covered trenches by foot soldiers wearing masks against poison gas. Despite the assumptions to the contrary by offense-minded generals, the advantage was with the defense. (Roger-Viollet)

The first blow that rocked the twentieth-century world was World War I. To most people, busy with their daily tasks, it seemed to be a sudden and unforeseen disaster. To statesmen and informed students of world affairs, it was the snapping of long-developing tensions.

1. ORIGINS OF THE WAR

National, imperial, and economic rivalry underlay the developments that led to the outbreak of World War I (see p. 644). The increasingly militant nationalism that had been growing since the mid–nineteenth century encouraged nations to view one another as dangerous rivals in the struggle for national power and prestige. The outburst of imperialism in the decades before 1914 pitted these nationalistic rivals against one another in the race to acquire colonies and expand their international influence. The growth of industrial and financial capitalism created a context of competitive economic struggle.

These rivalries were reflected in international affairs, particularly in the system of alliances among the European states. During the last decades of the nineteenth century, the various powers bound themselves into alliances based on shared interests with an eye toward maintaining a balance of power in the potentially dangerous international arena (see pp. 610–611). Although the alliances were not always steady, they may have helped maintain a sense that major wars could be avoided. By 1904, ten years before the outbreak of World War I, Europe was divided into two powerful alliance systems: the Triple Alliance, composed of Germany, Austria-Hungary, and Italy, and the Triple Entente, composed of France, Russia, and Great Britain.

Suspicion and fear between the two power combinations mounted steadily. A ruinous armaments race ensued; the powers of the Triple Entente strove desperately to overcome Germany's long lead in land forces, while Germany sought to erase Great Britain's naval advantage. Rivalries and conflicts among the various members of the two alliances cropped up all over the world, threatening to embroil all the other members. In 1905–1906 and again in 1911 two such clashes occurred in Morocco between France and Germany (see p. 634).

It was in the Balkans that these rivalries and conflicts entwined into a series of crises after 1908 that would result in a fatal explosion. Austria-Hungary had vital interests in the Balkans that grew out of the history and polyglot nature of its empire. It was composed of numerous language groups, some of which, particularly the Serbs, Croats, Slovenes, and Rumanians, had linguistic kin in the Balkans. As the Ottoman Empire in the Balkan peninsula disintegrated in the nineteenth and early twentieth centuries, the various Balkan language groups emerged as independent nations. These free peoples constituted a strong attraction for the members of their language groups in Austria-Hungary, who wished to break loose and join them. This was particularly true of Serbia, which attracted the Hapsburg's Yugoslav subjects (the Serbs, Croats, and Slovenes). But if the Yugoslavs should join Serbia, Austria-Hungary's other language minorities—Italians, Czechs, Slovaks, Poles, Rumanians, and Ruthenians—would also demand their freedom from Austrian and Hungarian rule and the Dual Monarchy would fall apart. Austria-Hungary therefore felt it must control the Balkan peninsula in self-defense. It was also the only direction in which it could expand, particularly after its exclusion from Germany in 1866.

Overlying the interests of Austria-Hungary in the Balkans were those of Russia and Germany. Russia had long pursued ambitions for influence and expansion in the Balkans. Germany, which also had its own interests in the area (see p. 611), felt it must support Austria-Hungary, its most effective and reliable ally. Italy, Great Britain, and France also had interests in the Balkans and in the Near and Middle East, although their primary concern was their commitments to their respective allies.

The first Balkan crisis occurred in 1908, when Austria-Hungary suddenly annexed two provinces, Bosnia and Herzegovina, which were inhabited by Serbs and Croats. Serbia had planned to annex these territories, peopled by its own linguistic kin. Serbia appealed to Russia, and Russia threatened Austria-Hungary, whereupon Germany rattled its mighty sword and forced Russia to back down.

A second Balkan crisis occurred in 1912–1913. The various Balkan states defeated Turkey and then fought among themselves over the spoils.

WHERE HISTORIANS DISAGREE

Causes of World War I

World War I shattered the world of 1914 and nearly destroyed a whole civilization. It is natural, then, that many historians and others should spend a great deal of time and thought trying to assess the causes of and assign responsibility for such a disaster.

Initially, people had great difficulty distinguishing causes from responsibility. Most nations were allies or supporters of the victors, and they held Germany responsible for the war. To them, that was little different than concluding that Germany had caused the war. This view was formalized in Article 231 of the Treaty of Versailles.

During the 1920s a reaction against this harsh judgment set in. Several historians offered "revised" analyses of responsibility for World War I. Harry Elmer Barnes concluded that primary blame rested not with Germany but rather with Russia, France, and Serbia. Sidney Bradshaw Fay argued that World War I was a war that no one had really wanted, and that if blame must be assigned, it should go to Russia, France, and England as much as anyone.

Responses to these "revisionist" judgments soon appeared. Since then the scholarly and ideological struggle has continued, some historians pointing to Germany, others to the Allies, still others to Austria-Hungary.

In recent decades scholars have tended to avoid assigning responsibility or blame for the war and instead to focus on what were the crucial causes of the war. Many historians point to the system of alliances that developed in the decades prior to 1914. These alliances divided nations into hostile, distrustful camps. In this system of alliances the acts of one nation became tied to the acts of others. Increasingly, each nation lost its ability to be flexible. Thus, when a relatively local problem between Serbia and Austria-Hungary got out of control, other nations were sucked into a conflict they did not want by the terms of the alliances they had formed and feared to violate.

Other historians focus on nationalism as the real underlying cause of the war. They argue that it was nationalism that caused nations to view everything in terms of rivalry. It was nationalism that spurred the imperial struggle, the buildup of arms, the willingness to fight, the refusal to compromise, and the underestimation of war costs.

More recently, some historians have emphasized the social tensions of European nations as the more profound underlying cause for the war. They point to growing social unrest in almost all European nations and the revolutionary threat in some. These social tensions made governments and people unusually willing to go to war as a means of letting off social pressure and bringing internal unity in the face of an external threat. The near-collapse of all opposition to war once war was declared (even among committed socialists) seems to support this view.

Finally, there are those, particularly Marxist scholars, who argue that World War I stemmed from economic rivalries. They emphasize that as industrial and financial capitalism developed, so did the international interests of influential economic groups. Economic rivalry led to imperial rivalry and eventually to military rivalry. It was these economic factors that set the stage for the particular events leading to the outbreak of World War I.

Ultimately, there are always individuals who make the decisions leading to war. The deeper question is what forces create a situation in which such decisions occur and result in a major war such as World War I.

Victorious Serbia threatened to expand. Austria-Hungary not only thwarted Serbia's expansion to the Adriatic Sea but also threatened to annihilate Serbia. Again Serbia appealed to Russia, and again Germany forced Russia to back down. Each of these crises brought the world close to war, increased international tension, and speeded up preparations for a final showdown.

When a third crisis occurred in the Balkans in the summer of 1914, all the great powers of Europe were bound by their alliances to become involved. This time, all it seemed to take was an incident.

On June 28, 1914, Austrian Archduke Franz Ferdinand was shot by Gavrilo Princip, a Bosnian Serb, in Sarajevo, the capital of the Austro-Hungarian province of Bosnia. The assassination was a deliberate plot involving numerous Serbian army officers. Franz Ferdinand, heir to the Austro-Hungarian throne, was singled out because the Serbs feared that his liberal policy toward the Yugoslavs in Austria-Hungary would allay their discontent, thereby lessening their desire to break away and join Serbia. After the assassination, the government of Austria-Hungary decided to crush Serbia and establish its own dominance in the Balkans once and for all. This tactic would require the backing of Germany, for clearly Russia would not stand aside and allow its Serbian kin and allies to be so treated or its own national interests to be thus violated. At a fateful conference in Berlin eight days after the shooting, the German government gave Austria-Hungary a "blank check." The Germans urged Austria-Hungary to act quickly while world opinion was still outraged by the assassination and promised support in any emergency.

Armed with Germany's blank check, Austria-Hungary presented Serbia with an impossible ultimatum. When Serbia failed to yield to all of its terms, Austria-Hungary declared war and invaded Serbia. Russia mobilized its forces in anticipation of becoming involved in the war. Given the nature of current military strategies, the demands of military timetables, and in particular the circumstances of Russia's clumsy military establishment, Russia's military mobilization was understood to require Germany's military mobilization. In turn, such general mobilization on both sides made it extremely difficult to prevent the outbreak of war. Germany sent harsh ultimatums to both Russia and France. When Russia failed to reply and France gave an unsatisfactory reply, Germany declared war on Russia on August 1 and on France two days later. The next day, August 4, when German troops violated Belgian neutrality on their way to attack France, Great Britain declared war on Germany. Thus, by August 4, 1914, all the great powers of Europe except Italy were at war (see Map 51.1). Italy claimed that it was not obligated to aid its allies, Germany and Austria-Hungary, since they were the aggressors. The following year, after receiving promises from France and Great Britain that it would reap the spoils of victory, Italy entered the war on the side of the Entente powers. To the side of Germany and Austria-Hungary came Turkey and Bulgaria; these were referred to as the Central Powers. To the side of the Entente powers, which came to be called the Allies, eventually came much of the rest of the world—some thirty-two nations in all. This was truly a world war.

2. THE WESTERN FRONT

Almost everywhere the unwanted war was nevertheless greeted with expressions of nationalistic joy. Most expected the war to be short and easy, perhaps like the Franco-Prussian War of 1871. All expected to win.

The German high command had long anticipated the situation that confronted it in August 1914 and had developed a plan of operation known as the Schlieffen plan. This plan called for a holding action against the slow-moving Russians while the main German forces thrust through neutral Belgium to quickly knock out France, which possessed the only army in the world that gave the Germans any real concern. Then the Germans would concentrate on and destroy Russia with relative ease. Great Britain, her allies gone, would sue for peace.

The Schlieffen plan nearly succeeded. Four weeks after the beginning of hostilities, the German forces were outside Paris ahead of schedule. Nevertheless, the Germans were increasingly vulnerable. Stubborn Belgian resistance had held up the Germans long enough for the French to

Map 51.1 WORLD WAR I This map indicates the surrounded position of the Central Powers and the areas of greatest fighting (and greatest destruction) during World War I.

redeploy their forces to the north and for the British to throw their small army across the Channel. Germans were suffering unanticipated casualties along the western front. Transportation and logistics were difficult. At a critical moment, some one hundred thousand of their best troops under generals von Hindenburg and Lu-

dendorff were detached and sent east for use against the Russians, who had invaded Germany with unexpected speed. Nearing Paris, there was a gap in the German First Army's eastern flank and its western flank lay exposed. At this juncture, the desperate French and British armies turned on the Germans and in the bloody seven-day Battle of the Marne not only halted the Germans but drove them back several miles. Both sides extended their lines from the Swiss border to the North Sea and entrenched.

This was the beginning of a war of attrition. Generals and military strategists had anticipated a short war dominated by rapid movements of men and arms and dramatic offensive thrusts. The reality was a long war dominated by fixed positions and defensive forces. Generals failed to realize that the machine gun, modern artillery, mass mobilization, and trenches were changing the nature of warfare (see Figure 51.1). Acting on old assumptions and flying in the face of these new military realities, generals on both sides ordered offensive thrusts again and again over the next three years. Each time the results moved lines only yards or a few miles, and each time the human costs were staggering. In the nine-month Battle of Verdun, the French held the Germans back; some 700,000 lives were lost. The four-month Battle of the Somme between the British and Germans was even bloodier. Like Verdun, it ended in a stalemate. In the indecisive Passchendaele offensive, the British alone lost some 400,000 soldiers.

Battles were also fought in the air and on the seas. The British navy set up a blockade of Germany. However, the Germans soon overcame Britain's Achilles' heel with a new weapon: the submarine. Eventually the Allies developed mines, depth charges, and tactics to counter German submarines. In the Battle of Jutland, the only major naval battle of the war, the British fleet thwarted the effort of the German fleet to break the blockade but suffered serious losses. But it was on the ground that most of the massive struggle was taking place. After three years of fighting, neither side could break through on the western front.

3. THE EASTERN FRONT

On the eastern front the war was not the immobile defensive struggle that characterized that on the western front. Initially Russia, with its huge but inadequately supplied army, pushed into German and Austro-Hungarian lands. But by the end of August the German armies, reinforced by troops from the western front, trapped the Russians at Tannenberg and administered a crushing defeat that sent them reeling back into Russia.

Further south, however, the Russians were victorious at Lemberg against the Austro-Hungarian army. This victory was only temporary. In 1915 the Germans delivered a series of hammer blows on the Russians, driving deep into Russia and inflicting immense casualties. Disertions, lack of effective leadership, and insufficient supplies plagued Russian efforts. That same year the Serbs were defeated by German, Austrian, and Bulgarian forces and eliminated from the war. An Anglo-French effort to come to the aid of the hard-pressed Russians by breaking through Turkish defenses at the Dardanelles was beaten back with heavy losses.

In 1916 Russia made one more great effort against the Austro-Hungarian forces in the south. Under General Aleksei Brusilov, Russian armies almost forced the Austro-Hungarians to withdraw from the war. A year later, overwhelmed by German forces and a revolution of its own, Russia withdrew from the war. Under the harsh Treaty of Brest-Litovsk Germany gained much territory from Russia, as well as the ability to transfer more of its forces to fight against the weary French and British troops on the western front.

Meanwhile, in northeastern Italy, Austrian and German troops won some battles that were costly on both sides, but their advances were limited and not decisive for the war as a whole. Further south and east, Allied and Arab forces were gaining the upper hand against the Ottoman Turks. In addition to their own importance, these battles drew men and materials from the western front, all of which added to the burdens being carried on the home fronts.

4. THE HOME FRONT

As the months dragged on and the toll of lives and material spent on the war rose, it became apparent that whole societies would have to be mobilized to support the war effort. World War I would be a total war that blurred distinctions between combatants and civilians, between the battle lines and the home front.

FIGURE 51.2 Women War Workers During World War I the British created large armaments plants under the Ministry of Munitions. Under the wartime pressure women replaced men in numerous occupations usually reserved for men. (Imperial War Museum, Great Britain)

The most pressing need was to organize the economy to produce the materials consumed by modern warfare—most obviously the high quantities of bullets, shells, guns, and armaments of all types (see Figure 51.2). But a vast array of other materials were also necessary—everything from food and uniforms to trucks and railway cars. Over the long haul, the war demanded both an advanced industrial capability and efficient organization of that capability to produce what was needed and get it where it could be used. To varying degrees, the governments of the major powers, particularly Germany, Great Britain, and France, took control of their economies. Production, consumption, wages, and prices were determined by governmental agencies rather than the free marketplace.

The mobilization of resources included human resources. Not only were men drafted into the armed services, but women and men on the home front were often required to work in accord with priorities determined by the government. Labor unions were brought into partnership with the government. Class distinctions blurred as more and more members of society were included in the war effort.

Women's roles changed as they assumed jobs previously reserved for men. They took over jobs ranging from work in munitions industries to clerical positions in the armed services. In Great Britain alone the number of women working outside the home increased twentyfold to some 5 million by 1918. Similar patterns held in other countries. Although these new patterns of work for women would not last beyond the war's end, they were a crucial part of the massive mobilization necessary to support total war.

Politically, governments became intolerant of dissent. Constitutional and democratic processes were often ignored in the name of authority and efficiency. Propaganda was used to create support for the government and hatred for the enemy.

Those nations less able to organize and maintain this vast effort—such as the Austro-Hungarian and Russian empires—faltered first. They lacked the strong industrial base and organizational strength of Germany, France, and

Great Britain. But over time, even the strongest nations weakened under the strain. By 1917 the threat of mutiny by the troops was accompanied by political and social protests against the war. It had become clear that the war would be won or lost on the home front as much as on the battle lines.

5. THE ENTRY OF THE UNITED STATES AND THE VICTORY OF THE ALLIES

When the war began in 1914, President Woodrow Wilson admonished the American people to remain neutral in thought as well as in deed. However, from the beginning, the great majority of public opinion in the United States was that Germany and its allies were the aggressors. During the course of the war, the United States increasingly became economically tied to the Allied cause. The sinking of American ships by German submarines, however, provided the immediate impetus for the entry of the United States into the war. When the Germans first began large-scale sinkings of merchant and passenger ships in 1915, President Wilson protested so vigorously that the Germans finally agreed to desist. Great Britain and France, it is true, had seized some American ships attempting to evade the blockade of Germany, but no lives had been lost and damages had been paid. Early in 1917 the German high command decided to launch an unlimited submarine campaign against enemy and neutral shipping alike. At about the same time, British intelligence turned over to the United States the Zimmermann note, in which Germany offered U.S. territory to Mexico as a reward for attacking the United States.

German leaders fully expected that these policies would bring the United States into the war, but they also believed that Great Britain and France would be crushed before any appreciable American weight could be brought to bear in Europe. The American government immediately broke off diplomatic relations with Germany. After several American ships had been sunk, Congress, on April 6, 1917, at the request of President Wilson, declared war on the German imperial government.

Although a full year elapsed before American troops were able to play an important role at the front, the boost in Allied morale was immediate, and the Americans lost no time supplying financial, material, and naval aid. The total contribution of the United States to the Allied victory was relatively small compared with that of France and Great Britain, but America's role, coming as it did when both sides were approaching exhaustion, was probably decisive. At the beginning of 1918 the race was between Germany and the United States. Germany transferred troops from the Russian front to overwhelm Great Britain and France before large numbers of American troops could arrive, while the United States strove to raise, train, and transport sufficient forces to France to stem the German tide.

In March 1918 Field Marshall Erich Ludendorff, now in command of the German armies, launched the first of a series of massive blows on the western front designed to end the war. The British and French were driven back with heavy losses. In desperation, they at long last agreed to a unified command under France's General Ferdinand Foch. The Americans, under General John J. Pershing, also accepted his command. By the middle of June, Ludendorff had launched four great drives, and the Allied lines had been battered so thin that when the climactic fifth drive began along the Marne River in mid-July 1918, Ludendorff wired the kaiser: "If the attack succeeds, the war will be over and we will have won it." When Foch heard the opening German barrage, he wired his government: "If the present German attack succeeds, the war is over and we have lost it." The Germans were stopped by a narrow margin. Foch, now receiving a swelling stream of fresh American troops and armaments, immediately ordered a counterattack. In the Allied counterattack, the tank, developed by the British, proved to be the breakthrough weapon. German strength and morale waned rapidly; the war was lost.

The first of the Central Powers to go out of the war was Bulgaria, which at the end of September 1918 surrendered to French, British, and Serbian forces operating from the Greek port of Salonika. A month later Turkey surrendered to British imperial forces in the Near East. Austria-Hungary, its various language groups in revolt,

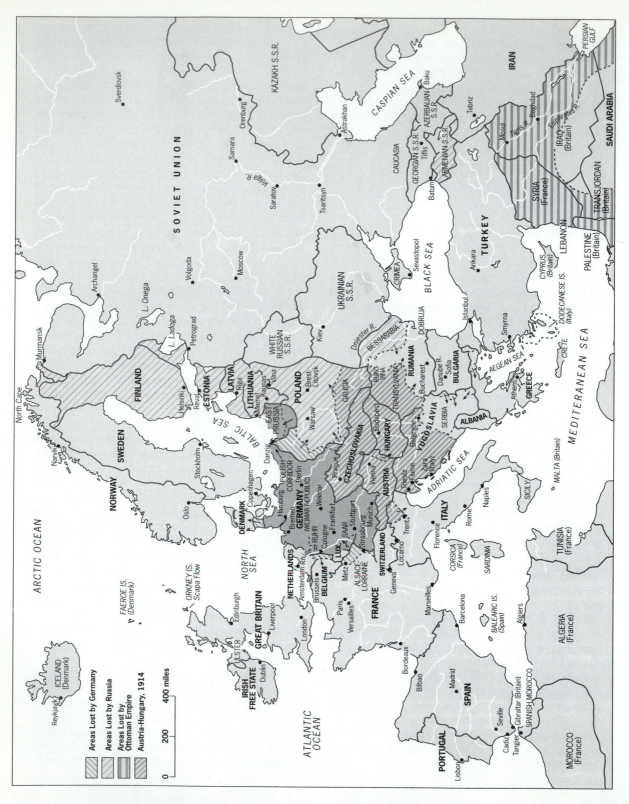

ARCTIC OCEAN

North Cape

Murmansk

Narvik

SWEDEN

NORWAY

Oslo

Stockholm

Reykjavik

ICELAND
(Denmark)

FAEROE IS.
(Denmark)

ORKNEY IS.;
Scapa Flow

Edinburgh

GREAT BRITAIN

Liverpool

London

ULSTER

IRISH
FREE STATE

Dublin

ATLANTIC
OCEAN

NORTH
SEA

NETHERLANDS

BELGIUM

Amsterdam

Brussels

Paris

Versailles

FRANCE

Bordeaux

SPAIN

Madrid

Bilbao

Barcelona

Seville

Cadiz

Lisbon

PORTUGAL

Gibraltar (Britain)

Tangier

SPANISH MOROCCO

MOROCCO
(France)

ALGERIA
(France)

Algiers

BALEARIC IS.
(Spain)

Marseilles

CORSICA
(France)

SARDINIA

TUNISIA
(France)

Sverdlovsk

S O V I E T   U N I O N

Orenburg

Samara

Saratov

Volgoda

Moscow

Archangel

L. Onega

L. Ladoga

Petrograd

Murmansk

FINLAND

Helsinki

Revel

ESTONIA

LATVIA

Riga

LITHUANIA

Kovno

Kaunas

Memel

Vilna

EAST
PRUSSIA

Danzig

POLISH
CORRIDOR

POLAND

Warsaw

Brest-
Litovsk

WHITE
RUSSIAN
S.S.R.

Kiev

UKRAINIAN
S.S.R.

KAZAKH S.S.R.

CASPIAN SEA

Astrakhan

Volga R.

Tsaritsyn

BALTIC SEA

Copenhagen

DENMARK

Hamburg

Bremen

Berlin

GERMANY
(WEIMAR REPUBLIC)

Weimar

RUHR

Cologne

Frankfurt

LUX.

SAAR

Metz

ALSACE-
LORRAINE

Strasbourg

Stuttgart

Munich

SWITZERLAND

Geneva

Locarno

Trent

Prague

CZECHOSLOVAKIA

Vienna

AUSTRIA

Budapest

HUNGARY

GALICIA

Dniester R.

BESSARABIA

BUKO-
VINA

TRANSYLVANIA

RUMANIA

Bucharest

DOBRUJA

Danube R.

Sofia

BULGARIA

YUGOSLAVIA

SERBIA

Belgrade

Zara
(Italy)

Fiume

Trieste

ALBANIA

ADRIATIC SEA

ITALY

Rome

Naples

Florence

Trent

SICILY

MEDITERRANEAN SEA

MALTA (Britain)

AEGEAN SEA

GREECE

Athens

CRETE

DODECANESE IS.
(Italy)

BLACK SEA

Sevastopol

CRIMEA

Istanbul

Smyrna

Ankara

TURKEY

CAUCASIA

Batum

Tiflis

GEORGIAN S.S.R.

AZERBAIJAN S.S.R.

Baku

ARMENIAN S.S.R.

Tabriz

IRAN

Mosul

Baghdad

Tigris R.

Euphrates R.

IRAQ
(Britain)

PERSIAN
GULF

SAUDI ARABIA

SYRIA
(France)

LEBANON

TRANSJORDAN
(Britain)

PALESTINE
(Britain)

CYPRUS
(Britain)

Areas Lost by Germany

Areas Lost by Russia

Areas Lost by
Ottoman Empire

Austria-Hungary, 1914

0   200   400 miles

650

surrendered on November 3 to Italian, British, and French forces driving in from Italy. The following day a full-fledged mutiny that had been brewing for several days broke out in the German navy and quickly spread throughout Germany. Popular uprisings brought down the kaiser's government. On November 11 the German commanders, their armies hopelessly beaten and in full retreat from France and Belgium, accepted Foch's armistice terms, which amounted to outright surrender. However, the German commanders manipulated events so that most of Germany's population was unaware of the extent of Germany's military collapse (no foreign soldiers were yet on German soil), and a new civilian government of republicans and socialists had to accept responsibility for the surrender. This tactic set the stage for future charges that Germany had not really been beaten but had been "stabbed in the back" by the political forces that would rule Germany during the 1920s.

6. THE PEACE SETTLEMENT

The Allied statesmen who gathered in Paris in January 1919 to try to make a lasting peace were confronted with a formidable task. Hate and disillusionment poisoned the atmosphere. Although all thirty-two of the victorious Allies were represented at the Paris Peace Conference, the great decisions were really made by the leaders of France, Great Britain, and the United States (see Figure 51.3). The French delegation was headed by Premier Georges Clemenceau, the aged "Tiger of France." As host of the conference and head of the nation that had done the most to defeat Germany and that had suffered greatly, he expected to dominate the decisions. Leading the British delegation was the eloquent and fiery "Little Welsh Attorney," Prime Minister David Lloyd George. As spokesman for the British Empire, which comprised one-fourth of all the land and people in the world, he also expected to

dominate the conference. At the head of the American delegation was the idealistic President Woodrow Wilson.

A fundamental and bitter clash immediately developed between Clemenceau, who wanted a hard peace that would mutilate Germany and make it harmless in the future, and Wilson, who wanted a "just" peace free of vindictiveness of any kind. In the end Wilson received support from Lloyd George. Great Britain needed the trade of a recovered Germany and did not wish to see France become too dominant on the Continent. The Treaty of Versailles with Germany reflected Wilson's ideas in fundamental principles, though not in every detail.

Six months of hard work and bitter wrangling were required to draw up the treaty (see Map 51.2). Its most important terms were, in brief, as follows: Germany and its allies were forced to accept full responsibility for the war. Germany was compelled to give up all its overseas colonies and concessions. Alsace and Lorraine were returned to France. The Polish-speaking areas of eastern Germany were ceded to the resurrected Polish state. With one exception, wherever doubt existed as to the wishes of the people in the affected areas, plebiscites were held to determine their desires. The exception was the "Polish corridor," which was cut along the Vistula River to give Poland an outlet to the sea. Germany's armed forces were severely cut down and saddled with permanent limitations. Its general staff was to be dismantled and its top war leaders tried for violations of the rules and customs of war and, if found guilty, punished. (The kaiser fled to the Netherlands just before Germany collapsed, and the Netherlands refused to give him up.) Finally, Germany was held liable for an indemnity that in 1921 was set by an Allied reparations commission at approximately $33 billion. Wilson and Lloyd George believed these terms to be just. Clemenceau considered them to be suicidally lenient.

The treaties with Germany's allies were ac-

Map 51.2 EUROPE, 1923 As a result of World War I the Austro-Hungarian and Ottoman empires were dismembered and both Germany and Russia suffered important losses of territory. However, the newly established states of eastern Europe were vulnerable and cut off from their strongest potential support: France and Great Britain.

FIGURE 51.3 The Big Four
The "Big Four" as they posed for newsreels at Versailles in 1919. Left to right, David Lloyd George, Vittorio Orlando, Georges Clemenceau, Woodrow Wilson. The biggest controversy that developed at the peace conference was between Clemenceau, who demanded a harsh treaty with Germany, and Wilson, who insisted upon a "just" treaty. (UPI/Bettmann Newsphotos)

tually more severe than the Treaty of Versailles because the principle followed in territorial rearrangements was freedom or union of all national language groups, and Germany was more homogeneous linguistically than were its allies. The polyglot Austro-Hungarian Empire was split up along language lines. The Czechs and Slovaks were formed into the new state of Czechoslovakia, which unfortunately also included sizable German and other minorities. The Poles were joined to Poland, the Rumanians to Rumania, the Italians to Italy, and the Serbs, Croats, and Slovenes to Serbia, which now became Yugoslavia. Thus the Dual Monarchy was cut down from a nation of 50 million, second in area only to Russia among the nations of Europe, to an Austria of 6.5 million German-speaking Austrians and a Hungary of 8 million Magyars. Turkey was shorn of its far-flung non-Turkish territories. The new national boundaries, in spite of the painstaking care with which they were drawn, left many pockets of discontent to breed future conflicts.

Wilson placed his chief hopes for peace in an association of nations that would peaceably settle the tensions and conflicts that were certain to arise in the future. He insisted that its framework be incorporated in the treaty with Germany. The first twenty-six articles of the Treaty of Versailles therefore constitute the covenant of the League of Nations.

The League of Nations had no military forces at its command. Its only teeth, so to speak, were Article X and Article XVI. Article X stated that every member undertook to guarantee the territorial integrity of every other member. In other words, if one member was attacked, all the other members were morally obligated to come to its aid. However, there was no way to compel them to do so. Article XVI stated that if a nation went to war in violation of a decision of the League, all the members of the League were to boycott the aggressor. This weapon (economic sanctions) could have been a potent deterrent if faithfully applied.

In the last analysis, however, the success of the League of Nations depended primarily upon the support of the Big Three victorious democracies—the United States, Great Britain, and France. The refusal of the United States to join the League (see pp. 681–682) was a body blow. Great Britain and France immediately lost faith in it and began to pursue their traditional nationalistic aims. Moreover, a defensive alliance among France, Great Britain, and the United States, desperately wanted by France and agreed to at the conference, was not ratified by the governments of Great Britain or the United States. France felt betrayed and left alone to face a resentful Germany.

7. THE EFFECTS OF WORLD WAR I AND THE PEACE SETTLEMENT

World War I profoundly affected the West. Much of Europe was shattered by this war of unprecedented scope and destructiveness. Over 10 million people had been killed, some 3 million of them civilians. Even more had died of diseases or hardships traceable to the war. More than 20 million had been wounded. The cream of a generation of Europe's future leaders had been lost, a reality that helps account for the poor quality of leadership during the 1920s and 1930s. The financial and material losses were incalculable. A tenth of the richest part of France had been laid waste. The most developed part of Russia was devastated. The European nations were saddled with heavy debts. The German, Austro-Hungarian, Ottoman, and Russian empires had collapsed. The British and French empires were seriously weakened. The economic system of capitalism, based on a relative lack of governmental control over economic and social affairs, was undermined during the war as central governments mobilized and managed their nations' economies as never before. Propaganda was unleashed on a massive scale and would thereafter become an important fixture of twentieth-century life.

The peace settlement negotiated in Paris left no one satisfied and many deeply resentful. Russia, which had suffered great losses, was not even invited to the conference. Germany, which would have to play an important role in postwar Europe, was not allowed to participate in the talks—rather, its representatives were presented with a treaty and offered little choice but to sign a humiliating and weakening settlement. The U.S. government refused to sign the treaty. France's thirst for revenge was not satisfied, and France soon felt itself isolated. The settlement left the newly established nations in eastern Europe in a weak position. Certainly, the task facing the negotiators was difficult and perhaps overwhelming. The passions and destruction unleashed by the war may have been so great that no settlement would have been satisfactory. However, the Treaty of Versailles left a legacy of disappointment and resentment to be built upon during the two decades separating World Wars I and II.

SUGGESTED READING

Origins of World War I

F. Fischer, *Germany's Aims in the First World War* (1967). A controversial account stressing Germany's responsibility for the war.

J. Joll, *The Origins of the First World War* (1984). An excellent analysis.

L. Lafore, *The Long Fuse* (1971). A good analysis of the causes of the war.

The War

G. Hardach, *The First World War: 1914–1918* (1977). A useful, broad survey.

K. Robbins, *The First World War* (1984). Covers all aspects of the war.

A. Solzhenitsyn, *August 1914*. An inspired, detailed account of the Tannenberg campaign, which virtually knocked Russia out of the war.

B. Tuchman, *The Guns of August* (1963). A well-written account of the immediate background to and opening campaigns of World War I.

The Home Front

F. L. Carsten, *War Against War* (1982). A good study of radical movements in Great Britain and Germany.

J. Williams, *The Home Fronts: Britain, France, and Germany, 1914–1918* (1972). A comparative study of the domestic impact of the war.

J. Winter and R. Wall, eds., *The Upheaval of War: Family, Work and Welfare in Europe, 1914–1918* (1988). Covers economic and social developments.

The Peace Settlement

H. Nicolson, *Peacemaking 1919* (1965). A good examination of the Versailles process and settlement.

D. Stevenson, *The First World War and International Politics* (1988). Good on the difficulties of the peace.

The Effects of World War I

R. Albrecht-Carrie, ed., *The Meaning of the First World War* (1965). Stresses international affairs.

P. Fussell, *The Great War and Modern Memory* (1975). Stresses the psychological significance of the war.

J. Roth, ed., *World War I* (1967). An excellent collection of essays analyzing the significance of the war.

B. Schmitt and H. Vedeler, *The World in a Crucible, 1914–1919* (1984). Includes an analysis of the consequences.

Historical Fiction

E. Hemingway, *A Farewell to Arms*. A famous novel based on the author's experiences on the Italian front.

E. M. Remarque, *All Quiet on the Western Front*. Has brought home to millions the horrors of trench warfare in World War I.

CHAPTER 52
Revolution and Communism in Russia

FIGURE 52.1 Serov, *Lenin Proclaiming Soviet Power* This painting shows Lenin, with Stalin and other Bolshevik leaders, proclaiming to the revolutionary forces the Bolsheviks' assumption of power in 1917. The style of the painting, social realism, is typical of Soviet art during the 1920s and 1930s. (Sovfoto)

World War I not only was militarily devastating for Russia but also was something the centuries-old tsarist government could not survive. In March 1917 the government of Nicholas II was swept from power by a revolution. This was the beginning of an extended period of revolutionary events in Russia that eventually resulted in the rise to power of the Bolsheviks, who in turn attempted to establish their vision of a Communist society in Russia. By the 1930s Russia was ruled by a totalitarian government that was effecting a massive economic, social, and cultural transformation of the nation and that was seen as a threat by most nations of the West.

1. THE RUSSIAN REVOLUTION OF 1917

Without the strain of World War I, revolution might not have occurred as and when it did, but that a revolution occurred should not be surprising. The violent Russian upheaval of 1917 was the result of maladjustments and discontent that had long been developing. Russia, except for a handful of intelligentsia, had been virtually bypassed by the great liberalizing movements, such as the Enlightenment and the French Revolution, that had influenced western Europe. The Industrial Revolution, which brought in its wake liberalism and radicalism, reached Russia only in the 1890s. While western Europe and parts of central Europe and the United States were becoming politically, economically, and socially modernized, Russia remained a land of peasantry, feudal aristocracy, and tsarist autocracy. In the latter half of the nineteenth century many of the frustrated Russian intelligentsia turned to revolutionary doctrines and even terrorism in an effort to effect rapid change. Others, including elements from the small but growing middle class, hoped for more moderate liberal reforms. But the tsarist government, particularly under Nicholas II (1894–1917), was generally reactionary and unbending.

The growing pressures for change exploded in the revolution of 1905. With little support and faced with dissension and revolt on all sides, Nicholas II was forced to grant some liberal reforms and promised to give the elected Duma some real powers. But as soon as the crisis passed, Nicholas II returned to his old policies and rejected the substance of the liberal reforms.

The outbreak of the war in 1914 brought some temporary national unity as most factions rallied to the support of the nation. Soon, however, the strains of war proved too much for the inept Russian government. Russia suffered staggering losses at the hands of the German armies. Behind the lines the suffering of the civilian population, much of which could be attributed to the corrupt bureaucracy of the tsar, was acute. Members of the Duma and others increasingly demanded liberal reform, but the tsar and his ministers refused to share power. The disintegration of Russia's military forces was reflected in the disintegration of Russia's government. The tsar increasingly fell under the influence of his unbending wife, Alexandra. She in turn fell under the influence of Grigori Efimovich Rasputin (1871?–1916), an uneducated Siberian monk who claimed to have the power to heal the tsar's hemophilic son. Even the tsar's aristocratic supporters, a group of whom murdered Rasputin late in 1916, were demanding fundamental change.

In early March 1917, the dam broke. Demands for bread in Petrograd quickly turned into riots and strikes. The tsar's troops were unable to restore order, often refusing to fire on the rioters—many of them led by women—or actually joining them. On March 12 the Duma organized a Provisional Government and three days later Nicholas II resigned. The new Provisional Government was dominated by liberals and moderate socialists. The leading figures of this government were Pavel Milyukov and Prince Georgi Lvov, both relatively moderate liberals. The Provisional Government enacted into law civil liberties, religious freedom, equality before the law, union rights, and other typical liberal reforms. Its more moderate faction promised to turn Russia into a Western-style political democracy and enact fundamental social reforms; others demanded more radical change. However, in addition to its inexperience, its differing factions, and the pressures for change, the Provisional Government labored under two burdens. First, it had to share power with the newly organized soviets—political organizations of workers, soldiers, and radical intellectuals—particularly the powerful Petrograd soviet. Second, it chose to continue the war that was draining Russia. Some of the crucial connections between these two burdens are indicated by the Petrograd Soviet's issuance of Order Number 1, which declared that military officers would be democratically elected by soldiers and military decisions would be democratically made. Order Number 1 contributed to the continuing disintegration of the Russian forces.

In May the liberal leaders of the Provisional Government resigned and the socialist Alexander Kerensky (1881–1970) became the leading figure in the government. By this time, however, the Bolshevik wing of the Marxist Social Democratic party was starting to play an important role in Russian affairs.

2. THE RISE OF THE BOLSHEVIKS

Marxism became influential among some intellectuals toward the end of the nineteenth century. In 1898 Russian Marxists formed the Social Democratic party, whose principal leaders were Gregory Plekhanov (1857–1918) and his disciple Vladimir Ilich Ulyanov (Lenin) (1870–1924). Repression by the tsar's government forced the Social Democrats into exile. At a London conference in 1903 the radical Bolshevik wing under Lenin split from the more moderate Mensheviks.

Until 1917, Lenin's Bolsheviks remained only a minor party. Its leaders were hunted down by the state police and shot, imprisoned, or exiled. For some seventeen years Lenin remained in exile in Switzerland, keeping his party alive and plotting the eventual overthrow of the tsar's government. During that time he developed theoretical and tactical principles for the successes the Bolsheviks would enjoy in 1917. Three of these principles were crucial. The first was that the party should not be open and democratic but rather should be an elite, highly trained, and constantly purged group of dedicated Marxist revolutionaries. The second was that the socialist revolution need not be a revolution of only the industrial working class; in Russia it could also be a dual revolution of workers and peasants— all part of an even broader socialist revolution that would sweep other countries of Europe. The third was a continuing opposition to World War I.

Lenin and the Bolsheviks' chance came in the months after the fall of the tsar's government in March 1917. In April 1917 the German government transported Lenin from his place of exile in Switzerland to the Russian border in an effort to increase the chaos and remove Russia from the war. Lenin refused to cooperate with the Provisional Government and instead unleashed a barrage of appealing slogans such as "peace to the army, land to the peasants, ownership of the factories to the workers." Meanwhile, the Socialist Kerensky came to power, but he was unable to extract Russia from the war. Bolshevik influence was growing, particularly among the Petrograd workers and soldiers. In July the Bolsheviks decided the time was ripe to seize power, but the effort failed. The Bolsheviks were not yet a dominant force, and the Kerensky government arrested many Bolsheviks and forced others, including Lenin, to flee to exile in Finland. The Kerensky government was further weakened by the failure of a new Russian offensive in the war and a threatened coup d'état by General Lavr Kornilov. This threat led Kerensky to release the Bolsheviks and rely on the soviets to defend the capital in September. By October the Bolsheviks, under the leadership of Lenin and the brilliant Leon Trotsky (1877–1940), gained control over the Petrograd and Moscow soviets. Lenin again judged the time was ripe for revolution, and this time he was right. On November 6 Trotsky conducted a well-organized revolution, seizing the crucial centers of power and arranging for the transfer of power to the soviets and Lenin. On November 7 the Bolshevik majority elected Lenin the head of the new government (see Figure 52.1).

3. THE BOLSHEVIKS IN POWER, 1917–1927

The Bolsheviks immediately moved to fulfill their promises and consolidate their power. In place of the old tsarist hierarchy, a pyramid of people's councils, or soviets, was set up. These councils were elected by universal suffrage but were actually dominated by a relatively few Communist party members. When national elections failed to return a Bolshevik majority to a Constituent Assembly, Lenin had the Red Army disperse it. Capitalism was abolished. A barter system of exchange replaced money, the value of the ruble having been destroyed by inflation and devaluation. All industry and commerce were placed under the management of committees of workers responsible to party commissars. The land was nationalized and its management turned over to local peasant committees. They in turn distributed it to individual peasants to be worked by their own labor. All crop surpluses were turned over to the state. Church lands were expropriated by the state.

In order to free the new regime for the enormous task of refashioning Russian society, Lenin immediately opened peace negotiations with the Germans. The Germans, realizing Russia's helplessness (Russian troops were deserting in droves), demanded the harshest of terms. Lenin attempted to stall them off, but when the Germans threatened to march on Petrograd and Moscow, he was forced to sign the Treaty of Brest-Litovsk in March 1918. Russia lost Finland, Estonia, Latvia, Lithuania, the Ukraine, Bessarabia, its Polish provinces, and some of its Trans-Caucasian territory. These lands contained one-third of Russia's European population, three-fourths of its iron, and nine-tenths of its coal. In addition, Russia was compelled to pay a heavy indemnity.

But these hard terms were not the end, nor the worst, of Lenin's woes. Two years of bitter civil war followed the peace with Germany. The aristocracy, including most of the higher army officers, launched a counterrevolution against the Bolshevik regime. These "White" forces were aided by various other disaffected groups and by French, British, Polish, Japanese, Czech, and U.S. troops. It was with the greatest of difficulty that the "Red" armies, hastily organized by Trotsky, finally defeated the "Whites." In doing so, the Bolsheviks regained the Ukraine. However, a large additional strip of territory was lost to Poland, thanks largely to French armed intervention on the side of the Poles. Moreover, military and civilian deaths stemming from the civil war and the accompanying disease and starvation probably approached some 4 to 6 million people.

Russia's war-torn economy was a shambles. The civil war compounded the destruction already suffered in World War I. Indeed, part of the reason for the Bolshevik victory in the civil war was their policy of "war communism," which succeeded in mobilizing Russia's economy and society for the war effort but also further disrupted normal economic activities. Lack of experience and some unpopular policies added to the economic difficulties. Often workers did not know how to run factories and trains. The distribution of goods was in inexperienced hands. When peasants saw that their surpluses would be seized by the government, they often resisted or refused to raise more than they needed for themselves. By 1921 some 30 million Russians were threatened with starvation, and in spite of considerable foreign relief, particularly from the United States, many did starve.

Lenin, a realist, saw the necessity for retreat. In 1921 he launched the NEP (New Economic Policy), which was a temporary compromise with capitalism. The popular Nikolai Bukharin (1888–1938) was chosen to carry out the new policy. In order to provide incentive, industries employing fewer than twenty workers were permitted to operate under private ownership. These little industrial capitalists were called *nepmen*. Enterprising peasants, called *kulaks*, were permitted to own and rent land and hire laborers. Money and credit were restored. This small-scale capitalistic activity was closely supervised and regulated by the state. However, the NEP provided enough incentive to pull the Russian economy out of chaos. In 1923, just as the new policy was beginning to function, Lenin suffered a paralytic stroke. He died the following year.

Lenin's death precipitated a power struggle among his chief associates (see Figure 52.2). Most assumed that his successor would be Leon Trotsky, who had been the chief organizer of the Red Army and had planned its victory over the Whites. A brilliant, eloquent Communist theorist, he was an apostle of world revolution. Trotsky, however, underestimated Joseph Stalin, executive secretary of the Communist party. This unobtrusive, taciturn man was an unscrupulous behind-the-scenes operator. Stalin was the son of poverty-stricken ex-serfs. Expelled from an Orthodox seminary because of his Marxist views and activities, he became a professional revolutionist and terrorist. (*Stalin* is a pseudonym meaning "man of steel.") He was repeatedly arrested and imprisoned and repeatedly escaped. World War I found him in exile in Siberia. Taking

FIGURE 52.2 Trotsky and Stalin This rare photograph, taken in 1923 at a party meeting, shows the feud between Stalin (seated, at right) and Trotsky (standing, at left) that ended with Trotsky's murder in Mexico in 1940. As the brilliant, eloquent Trotsky speaks, the taciturn Stalin, son of ex-serfs, eyes him coldly. (UPI/ Bettmann Newsphotos)

advantage of the amnesty granted to all political prisoners by the Kerensky regime in 1917, Stalin hastened to Petrograd, where he became a devoted associate of Lenin. He played a prominent role in the civil war against the Whites and became executive secretary of the Communist party. In this key position he made himself master of the all-important party machinery.

In this struggle for leadership, Trotsky took the position that all efforts must be made to bring the socialist revolution to other parts of Europe, and that without support from other, more advanced socialist nations, socialism in Russia would fail. Trotsky also favored ending the NEP and immediately launching a policy of massive industrialization. Stalin took a more moderate stand, arguing that socialism in one country (Russia) was possible and therefore all efforts should be pointed toward securing what had already been gained in Russia. Trotsky was the more compelling speaker and accomplished theorist, but he also conveyed an element of arro-

FIGURE 52.3 *The Five-Year Plan in Four Years* In this 1930s Soviet propaganda poster, *The Five-Year Plan in Four Years,* Stalin is portrayed leading industrial development against the reactionary forces of capitalism and religion. (The Fotomas Index, London)

gance. Stalin was more adept at political in-fighting. By conspiring with prominent groups of Bolsheviks and playing one faction against another, Stalin isolated Trotsky and had him expelled from the party and exiled from Russia. By the end of 1927 Stalin had maneuvered himself into a position of dominance over the Communist party and dictatorship over the Soviet Union.

4. THE FIVE-YEAR PLANS AND THE PURGES

In 1928 Stalin launched the first of a series of five-year plans (see Figure 52.3). They were units of planned economy with certain specific goals or objectives to be achieved every five years. They marked the end of the NEP, which had served its purpose of pulling the Communist economy through its first major crises. The objectives of the First Five-Year Plan were (1) the elimination of the last remnants of capitalism, (2) the industrialization of the Soviet Union, (3) the collectivization and mechanization of agriculture, and (4) national defense. However, underlying these objectives were even more fundamental goals: transforming the economy and

society of the Soviet Union into a Communist economy and society and training and socializing Soviet citizens to be adaptive participants in this Communist system. Rarely has such an ambitious program been undertaken.

Achievement of the first goal meant the liquidation of the *nepmen* and the *kulaks*. When tens of thousands of the independent peasant-proprietor *kulaks* resisted, Stalin simply eliminated them. The consolidation of their farms into mechanized collectives and the organization of giant state farms went on apace. The state farms were huge areas of up to three hundred thousand acres in size run by party managers and hired laborers. Every effort was made to mechanize them. Vast tracts of land in southeast Russia and Siberia were brought under cultivation for the first time. The collective farms were of various types. In the most common type independent farmers surrendered their lands and horses but retained their houses, gardens, cattle, pigs, and chickens for their own private use. The collective farm was run by elected managers who were instructed and supervised by party officials. Elimination of the tiny individual tracts, each one of which had been surrounded by ditches or hedgerows, made mechanization possible. A certain amount of the harvest was set aside for taxes, insurance, improvements, and feed. A large part had to be sold to the state at a fixed price. The rest was distributed to the peasant members in proportion to the amount of their original contribution to the collective in land and horses and to the amount and quality of their work. The mechanization of Russia's agriculture required the construction of huge quantities of tractors and farm machinery.

Since the Industrial Revolution was still in its infancy in Russia in 1928, industrialization meant building almost from the ground up and concentrating on producer rather than consumer goods. Western engineers and technicians were lured to Russia with high salaries. Capital was obtained by exporting scarce supplies of wheat, often at ruinously low prices. At the cost of much privation, enormous strides were made. Steel mills, power plants, foundries, mines, refineries, and railroads were built all over the Soviet Union. At Dnepropetrovsk on the Dnieper River, the world's largest dam and hydroelectric power plant were constructed. At the end of 1932 it was announced that all the goals of the First Five-Year Plan had been reached several months ahead of time.

During the 1930s the Second and Third Five-Year Plans were launched. In general, the stress remained on collectivization and mechanization of agriculture and on heavy industrialization. However, there was a new emphasis on the production of consumer goods that enabled the masses to enjoy a slowly rising standard of living.

The results of the five-year plans are difficult to evaluate accurately. What might have happened if the policy choices had been different is unknown. The results in agriculture were most questionable. Clearly millions of people suffered as Stalin tried to make the peasantry pay for industrialization one way or another. Rural families, communities, and established ways of life were torn apart. There was tremendous resistance to collectivization as well as mismanagement and drought. At times famine became a reality, as did a state of near civil war in the countryside. At one point Stalin admitted that problems with collectivization had claimed some 10 million human victims and brought about the destruction of half of the nation's draft and farm

animals. Yet by 1939 over 90 percent of Soviet agriculture was collectivized and much of it was mechanized.

The results of the five-year plans in industry and defense were more gratifying and, in many ways, phenomenal. In 1928, at the beginning of the First Five-Year Plan, the Soviet Union was far behind other nations in industrial production. During the First Five-Year Plan industrial production doubled, a record equaled again in the Second Five-Year Plan. During this period the Soviet Union managed to achieve an unprecedented rate of growth in industrial output, but at great human cost. By 1941, when the Germans invaded the Soviet Union, it had become the fourth greatest industrial power in the world. In a number of categories it had surpassed both Great Britain and Germany and was second only to the United States. The Soviet Union could never have withstood the German assault had this not been true.

The 1930s were also the time of the Great Purges. In 1934 Sergei Kirov (1888–1934), a high Soviet official, was assassinated. It is unclear whether Stalin's enemies were responsible or whether Stalin himself ordered the assassination only to use it as an excuse to eliminate potential rivals. However, a long period of party purges, arrests, trials, imprisonments, and executions soon followed. Eventually almost all the original Bolshevik leaders were removed from power and from the party, as were most of the Red Army's top officer corps. By the end of the Great Purges in 1939, hundreds of thousands—perhaps millions—of people had been affected. The government, the Communist party, and the military were now staffed by new, generally younger figures all beholden to Stalin.

Stalin's motives for the Great Purges are a matter of debate. Some argue that the purges were a manifestation of his paranoia; others argue that they were a logical step in the process of moving the Soviet Union from a revolution in 1917 to a totalitarian Communist state in the 1930s. In any case, they did consolidate Stalin's power and eliminate all potential pockets of resistance to him. But the price was high. The purges were part of a pattern of repression that Stalin used during his five-year plans and would continue to use until his death in 1953. Some scholars estimate that in all, the starvation, the executions, and the force-labor camps may have caused the deaths of up to 40 million Soviet citizens.

5. TOTALITARIAN CONTROL

Between 1917 and 1939 the government effected totalitarian rule in the Soviet Union. The government was dominated by the Communist party, and the party head served as virtual dictator. Not only did the party enjoy a monopoly over political affairs and the armed forces, it also controlled the economic, social, religious, and cultural life of the nation to an unprecedented degree.

The Soviet Political System

On coming to power, the Bolsheviks divided the Russian Empire into eleven socialist republics—Russia proper and ten other language or dialect areas. In 1939–1940 five more were added from territories seized by Russia at the outbreak of World War II. The Soviet Union was in theory a union of autonomous republics. (U.S.S.R. stands for "Union of Soviet Socialist Republics.") Actually, however, Russia itself constituted at least four-fifths of the total area and population and dominated the Union.

The Soviet system of government as originally set up consisted of a pyramid of elected councils—village, district, county, and provincial—culminating in the Union Congress of Soviets, which met once every two years and chose executive and administrative boards. Voting was by show of hands in mass meetings. The urban vote was given more than double the weight of the rural vote, since bolshevism's chief concern was the industrial proletariat. In 1936 Stalin promulgated a new constitution, which appeared to be more democratic. Voting was to be by secret ballot, the differential between the urban and the rural vote was abolished, and the members of the various soviets in the pyramid were to be elected directly by the local districts. The member republics in the Union were allegedly granted complete autonomy.

Only the Communist party was permitted to engage in organized political activity. It named the official candidates, made all political policies and platforms, and conducted all election promotion and propaganda. Opposition to the party's official candidates and program was considered to be disloyal and was ferreted out and crushed by the state police, both secret and regular. The all-powerful Communist party was organized on an authoritarian basis. The Politburo, sixteen men meeting in secret and responsible only to the secretariat of the party, made all decisions, which were transmitted without question down through the chain of command to the local cells. The real center of power in the Soviet system was the secretariat of the Communist party, and the first (or general) secretary of the party was the most powerful figure in the Soviet Union. Obedience to superiors was demanded of all party members. Party members were carefully selected and trained. As set up by Lenin, the total number was kept relatively small.

Soviet Culture and Society

In 1917 more than 60 percent of the Russian people were illiterate. It was Lenin's belief that a Communist state required an educated populace in order to succeed. Nearly all the top Bolsheviks themselves were educated—in fact, they would be considered members of the intelligentsia in almost any time or place. Little could be done in the educational field in the first turbulent years of the Communist regime, but education received major attention in Stalin's five-year plans. In 1928 the Communists launched a vast program of free compulsory secular education. The program covered all levels—elementary, secondary, and higher—for both young and adults. It included a comprehensive system of technical and on-the-job training. Science and engineering were particularly stressed. Of course, Soviet education was interlarded with Communist propaganda, but its standards were high, and it turned out the trained people who were needed.

Advanced scholarship and the arts were not neglected. An extensive program of scholarships, prizes, and institutes was inaugurated for the purpose of encouraging and subsidizing superior talent. Soviet musicians, architects, painters, and dancers more than held their own in international competition. Yet the arts were subject to official Communist ideology. All liberal, bourgeois, or capitalistic literature (which was most

FIGURE 52.4 Women Workers and Architects Conferring The Soviet government promoted social realism to make art relevant to the working masses and carry explicit messages. Here the sun streams in on women workers and architects conferring over plans for a new factory. On the left a bust of Stalin looks on. (Tass from Sovfoto)

of it) was heavily censored. Such world-renowned composers as Prokofiev and Shostakovich occasionally fell into official disfavor because of their modern "bourgeois" music. When some powerful commissar decided that the Mendelian law of genetics, which is generally accepted in the world of science, ran counter to the party line, Soviet geneticists were forced to disclaim it.

Soviet society was made more egalitarian. Although the party, governmental, military, and cultural elite enjoyed some advantages, most class distinctions were eliminated. Women particularly benefited, because all formal discrimination against them was eliminated (see Figure 52.4). In the years just after the revolution, women gained the right to vote as well as legal

equality within marriage. Abortion was legalized and the right to divorce established. Thanks to the views of Bolshevik leaders and the demand for workers, Soviet women probably gained unparalleled economic equality with men. They received equal pay and were offered equal educational and professional opportunities. However, not all of these gains for women lasted. New policies in the 1930s made abortion illegal. Women rarely moved into the highest economic or political positions. Strong patterns of discrimination left Soviet women with the burdens of household management along with work outside of the home and some of the realities of inequality that generally prevailed elsewhere in the West.

In many ways Soviet society displayed the

marks of totalitarian control. Most social organizations were saturated with official Communist ideology. The Communist party and the state took direct control when any social organization showed signs of gaining significant influence. Agents of the state, ranging from minor bureaucrats to members of the secret police, pervaded Soviet society. Terror, most evident during Stalin's Great Purges, was an ever-present weapon.

Religious Policy

The religious policy of the Bolsheviks upon gaining power in Russia was quite similar to that of the French revolutionists in 1789–1794. All church property was confiscated. The churches themselves were turned into museums or clubs of various kinds, although they were sometimes leased to religious congregations for purposes of worship. No religious instruction whatever was permitted in the schools, which were all public and secular. The churches were forbidden to give organized religious instruction and even to maintain seminaries for the training of their own clergy. At the same time, the schools were flooded with Communist propaganda.

The Communist leaders claimed that their harsh treatment of the churches was necessitated by the active opposition of the churches to the Communist government. They claimed that when they had first come to power, they had granted religious freedom for the first time in Russian history, but that the churches had immediately used this freedom to advocate the overthrow of the very government that had granted it. They further claimed that churches had always been the tools and agents of capitalistic governments and interests. Whatever truth there may be in these claims, it would appear that religion was perceived as a problem and danger to the Soviet regime.

6. THE SOVIET UNION AND THE WORLD

When the Bolsheviks first took over in 1917, they confidently expected some of the capitalistic governments in the war-weary world to collapse and follow Russia along the path to communism. To encourage them to do so and to avoid fulfillment of the harsh terms of the Treaty of Brest-Litovsk, the Communist leaders began an active campaign of revolutionary infiltration and subversion abroad, particularly in Germany. Although some headway was made in Germany, Bavaria falling under Communist control for a brief time, the only country to embrace communism was Hungary, where in 1919 Béla Kun set up a Communist dictatorship that lasted four months. To guide and aid the Communist parties in other countries in the common cause of world revolution, the Bolsheviks set up the Comintern (Communist International), with headquarters in Moscow.

The Western capitalistic powers were antagonistic to the Soviet Union. Thinking that the Bolshevik regime would soon collapse, France, Great Britain, Japan, and the United States landed troops on Russian soil in 1918 and aided the counterrevolutionary White forces. France helped the Poles to seize a large strip of Russian-speaking territory. Great Britain and France organized the anti-Soviet regimes in the countries of eastern Europe bordering the Soviet Union into a *cordon sanitaire* (health or quarantine belt). For several years, no Western power would recognize the Bolshevik regime. The Soviet Union was refused admission to the League of Nations until 1934, eight years after Germany had been admitted and one year after it had withdrawn under the guidance of Hitler. Even then the Western powers steadfastly refused to cooperate with the Soviet Union in any collective action against the rising Fascist menace.

Nonetheless, the failure of the Communist movements abroad and of the Bolsheviks' early efforts to communize Russia overnight caused the Soviet leaders to adopt a more conciliatory attitude toward the capitalist powers. The NEP needed foreign commerce and foreign capital in order to function. Eventually, the Soviet Union gained official recognition abroad. In 1922 Germany established official relations with the Soviet Union. Great Britain and France recognized the Soviet Union in 1924. The last capitalist state of the West to recognize the Soviet Union was the United States, which held off until 1933.

The five-year plans, which began in 1928, required much Western capital and technical assistance. Therefore, the next ten years represented the high tide of Soviet tractability toward the capitalist Western democracies. Stalin, unlike Trotsky, was more interested in "socialism in one country" than in world revolution, which he believed would come later. The Comintern was allowed to languish. Of course, the Soviet Union's fear of the growing Nazi German menace after 1933 was a significant factor in its conciliatory attitude toward the capitalistic democracies. This honeymoon ended in 1938 with the Munich crisis (see p. 686). From that time on, Stalin was apparently convinced that real cooperation with the Western democracies was impossible. The cooperation forced upon the Soviet Union and most of the capitalist world by the menace of the Axis during World War II lasted only until victory was assured. Meanwhile, after Hitler came to power in 1933, the greatest threat to both the Soviet Union and the capitalist democracies was Nazi Germany.

SUGGESTED READING

General

E. H. Carr, *A History of Soviet Russia*, 7 vols. (1951–1964). Scholarly and highly respected.

R. W. Clark, *Lenin* (1988). A good recent study.

I. Deutscher, *Stalin: A Political Biography* (1967). Not only a scholarly biography of Stalin but also a good history of the whole Communist movement in Russia.

The Russian Revolution and the Rise of the Bolsheviks

R. Daniels, *Red October* (1969). A well-written account of the Bolshevik revolution.

W. Lincoln, *Red Victory: A History of the Russian Civil War* (1989). Recent and comprehensive.

A. Ulam, *The Bolsheviks* (1968). A good introduction stressing Lenin's doctrines.

The Bolsheviks in Power, the Five-Year Plans, and the Purges

R. Conquest, *The Great Terror* (1968). An excellent study of Stalin's purges.

S. Fitzpatrick. *The Russian Revolution*. 1982. A brief, analytical treatment of the period.

G. Leggett, *The Cheka: Lenin's Secret Police* (1981). A good study of this topic.

J. P. Nettl, *The Soviet Achievement* (1967). A good analysis of economic development in the Soviet Union.

Totalitarian Control

S. Fitzpatrick, *Cultural Revolution in Russia, 1928–1931* (1978). A good analysis.

K. Geiger, *The Family in Soviet Russia* (1968). Well written.

R. Marshall, *Aspects of Religion in the Soviet Union, 1917–1967* (1971). A good book on this difficult subject.

R. Pipes, *The Formation of the Soviet Union* (1964). Stresses the problem of Soviet minorities.

The Soviet Union and the World

G. Kennan, *Russia and the West Under Lenin and Stalin*. By a former American ambassador to the Soviet Union; a harsh perspective.

A. Ulam, *Expansion and Coexistence: Soviet Foreign Policy* (1974). Scholarly, by a respected expert.

Historical Fiction

A. Koestler, *Darkness at Noon* (1956). A classic novel of bolshevism and the purges.

B. Pasternak, *Doctor Zhivago* (1974). Nobel Prize winner's novel depicting life in the Soviet Union by a man who experienced it.

A. Solzhenitsyn, *The Gulag Archipelago* (1974). A vivid account of terror.

CHAPTER 53
The Rise of Fascism and Authoritarianism

FIGURE 53.1 Mussolini Addresses the Masses
This photo of Mussolini addressing a huge crowd in Rome after a victory of the Italian forces in Ethiopia shows some of the typical traits of fascism and authoritarianism during the 1920s and 1930s: nationalism (the flag), militarism (the uniform), and mass politics (the cheering crowd). (UPI/Bettmann Newsphotos)

During World War I many hoped that victory against the Central Powers would be a blow to authoritarianism and a triumph for liberal democracy. By the time of the Paris Peace Conference in 1919, a shadow was already being cast on these hopes by the triumph of the Bolsheviks in Russia. Nevertheless, the arrangements made at Paris seemed to establish parliamentary democracy in the states of eastern Europe and affirm it in western Europe. But in only a few years these optimistic hopes were dashed by the rise of authoritarian governments in southern, eastern, and central Europe and by the growth of authoritarian political movements within several Western democracies.

1. TOTALITARIANISM, FASCISM, AND AUTHORITARIANISM

The 1920s and 1930s witnessed a great growth of totalitarianism, fascism, and right-wing authoritarianism. Of these political systems, totalitarianism was the most revolutionary and rigorous. In a totalitarian system, a single political party with a revolutionary ideology controls the government. It appeals for active support from the masses and is dominated by a dictatorial leader. No opposition is tolerated. Propaganda, force, and terror are openly used to ensure control and further the goals of the government. Modern communications, technology, and organization are used to control the economic, social, religious, and cultural life of the nation as much as possible. The liberal ideology of limited government and individual rights is formally rejected in a totalitarian system.

As we have already seen in Chapter 52, totalitarianism had its beginnings in the Soviet Union under Lenin and came to full flower under Stalin during the 1930s. Since this totalitarianism was based on Communist ideology, it is often called totalitarianism of the Left. Totalitarianism arose in a mild form in Italy during the 1920s and in a virulent form in Germany during the 1930s. Since this totalitarianism was based on Fascist ideology, it is often called totalitarianism of the Right.

Both fascism and communism were ideologies—sets of ideas and values—that were gaining strength in the West throughout the 1920s and 1930s, but fascism proved to be the greater immediate threat to liberal democracy. Generally, fascism was antiliberal, antidemocratic, anti-individualistic, and anti-Communist. It was ultranationalistic and militaristic. It was tied to somewhat mystical ideas of the all-powerful expansive state, of race, and of will. Fascism was initiated by Mussolini during the 1920s. During the 1920s and 1930s Fascist parties spread throughout Europe. The greatest triumph of fascism came with the rise to power of Hitler and nazism in Germany during the 1930s. Some other governments in southern, central, and eastern Europe were influenced by fascism and had some of its trappings, but for the most part they were right-wing authoritarian regimes.

Right-wing authoritarian regimes were less ideologically based than Fascist regimes, and they controlled life in their nations to a much lesser degree than totalitarian systems did. Usually they amounted to a dictatorship backed by the military and conservative forces of the nation. They tended to be most concerned with preserving order and protecting the established status quo against perceived threats from liberal democracy, socialism, or communism.

Together totalitarianism, fascism, and right-wing authoritarianism posed a serious threat to the advocates of liberal democracy in the West. Indeed, the hoped-for triumph of liberal democracy after World War I seemed to be turning into a triumph for its enemies—a triumph that would lead to growing conflict and a renewal of war in 1939. The story of the rise of fascism and authoritarianism begins with Italy, where Mussolini set up the first Fascist dictatorship (see Figure 53.1).

2. MUSSOLINI CREATES THE FIRST FASCIST STATE

Italy emerged from World War I battered and humiliated. Although it was one of the victorious Allies, Italy's armies had made a poor showing, and Italy had realized few of the grandiose ambitions for which it had entered the war. In the Paris peace settlements Italy had been awarded the adjacent Italian-speaking areas of Austria-Hungary but had been denied further acquisitions east of the Adriatic and in Asia and Africa, some of which it ardently desired. These frustrations were severe blows to Italian national pride.

Italy's weak economy emerged from the war acutely maladjusted. The national debt was huge and the treasury empty. The inflated currency, together with a shortage of goods, raised prices ruinously. Hundreds of thousands of demobilized veterans could find no jobs. In the summer of 1919, there was widespread disorder. Veterans began seizing and squatting on idle, and sometimes cultivated, lands. Sit-down strikes developed in the factories. During the winter of 1920–1921, several hundred factories were seized by the workers, and Marxism seemed to be gaining strength. The Italian government, torn by factions, seemed too weak to prevent the disorder and protect private property. Although the strife diminished and the Marxist threat waned before the end of 1921, landlords and factory owners were thoroughly frightened. Many of them, and indeed many small-business and professional people, longed for vigorous leadership and a strong government. The vigorous leader who stepped forward was Benito Mussolini. The strong government was his Fascist dictatorship.

Mussolini was a dynamic organizer and leader. The son of a blacksmith, he became first a teacher and later a radical journalist and agitator. Before World War I he was a pacifistic socialist, but during the war he became a violent nationalist. After the war he began organizing unemployed veterans into a political action group with a socialist and extremely nationalistic program. During the labor disturbances of 1919–1921, Mussolini stood aside until it became apparent that the radical workers' cause would lose; then he threw his support to the capitalists and the landlords. Crying that he was saving Italy from communism and waving the flag of nationalism, Mussolini organized his veterans into terror squads of blackshirted "Fascisti," who beat up the leaderless radical workers and their liberal supporters. He thereby gained the support of the frightened capitalists and landed aristocracy. By 1922 Mussolini's Fascist party was strong enough to "march on Rome" and seize control of the faction-paralyzed government. Appointed premier by the weak and distraught King Victor Emmanuel III, Mussolini acquired extraordinary powers. Between 1924 and 1926

Mussolini turned his premiership into a dictatorship. All opposition was silenced. Only the Fascist party could engage in organized political activity. The press and the schools were turned into propaganda agencies. The secret police were everywhere. Eventually, the Chamber of Deputies itself was replaced by Mussolini's hand-picked Fascist political and economic councils.

Italy's economic life was strictly regimented, but in such a way as to favor the capitalistic classes. Private property and profits were carefully protected. All labor unions were abolished except those controlled by the Fascist party. Strikes and lockouts were forbidden. Wages, working conditions, and labor-management disputes were settled by compulsory arbitration under party direction. An elaborate system of planned economy was set up to modernize, coordinate, and increase Italy's production of both industrial and agricultural goods. The complicated economic and political machinery that Mussolini created for these purposes was called the corporate state. On the whole there was probably a small decline in per capita income under Italian fascism despite some superficial gains. The budget was balanced and the currency stabilized. But Italy's taxes were the highest in the world, and labor's share of economic production was small.

Fascism, however, was primarily political, not economic, in character. The essence of its ideology was nationalism run wild. Although Italy never became such a full-blown, viciously anti-Semitic police state as Germany, Mussolini understood the dynamic, energizing quality of militant nationalism. His writings and speeches rang with such words as *will, discipline, sacrifice, decision,* and *conquest.* "The goal," he cried, "is always—Empire! To build a city, to found a colony, to establish an empire, these are the prodigies of the human spirit. . . . We must resolutely abandon the whole liberal phraseology and way of thinking. . . . Discipline. Discipline at home in order that we may present the granite block of a single national will. . . . War alone brings up the highest tension, all human energy, and puts the stamp of nobility upon the people who have the courage to meet it." This grandiose vision was reflected in Fascist trappings and symbols, which were adopted from ancient Rome.

Fascism clashed head-on with Christianity

**FIGURE 53.2 Max Beckmann,
The Night, 1918–1919**
Beckmann, a German artist,
reflects the sense of violence
and disillusionment stem-
ming from World War I in
this scene of overwhelming,
absurd torture. (Kunstsam-
mlung Nordrhein-Westfalen,
Düsseldorf)

both in spirit and in deeds. Nevertheless, Mussolini realized the advantage of coming to terms
with the powerful Catholic church and made a
treaty with Pope Pius XI—the Lateran Treaty of
1929. The pope recognized Mussolini's regime.
(Since the pope had been despoiled of his territories [1860–1870], he had refused to recognize
the Italian government.) In return, Mussolini
paid him nearly $100 million in cash and govern-
ment bonds from a hard-pressed national treasury and allowed the teaching of religion by
Catholic clergy in the public schools. This seeming accord, however, was uneasy and quarrelsome from the start.

The building of a powerful army and navy
and the recovery of Italy's national prestige were
always uppermost in Mussolini's thoughts. Fascist Italy's militarism, self-assertiveness, and expansive ambitions played an important part in
the breakdown of the peace settlement and the
return to war. But before we examine these activities, we must examine the rise of fascism in
Germany and authoritarianism elsewhere, which
contributed to the outbreak of World War II.

3. THE WEIMAR REPUBLIC IN GERMANY

Germany emerged from World War I defeated,
humiliated, and angry. As late as July 1918 the
nation had seemed to be close to victory; four
months later it had been forced to surrender,
hopelessly beaten. Then it was compelled to sign
a dictated peace treaty, the terms of which it considered unjust. The Weimar Republic (so called
from the city famous for Goethe and Schiller,
where its constitution was drawn up), which the
Germans set up in 1919, was structured to be a
model liberal democracy. Politically divided and
inexperienced, it inherited the taint of defeat
from World War I and had to face tremendous
postwar problems (see Figure 53.2).

Almost as soon as the Social Democrats, led
by Friedrich Ebert, came to power, they were
challenged, first by an uprising of radical Marxists (Spartacists), then by right-wing nationalists
(under Wolfgang Kapp). Both of these challenges
were met, but then economic problems threatened the new government. In the early 1920s in-

flation grew at an alarming rate. In January 1923, after the German government chose to default on its first payment of the huge reparations bill, French and Belgian troops occupied the Ruhr Valley, Germany's richest industrial area. The Germans fought back sullenly with passive resistance. The French countered by trying to stir up a secession movement from Germany in the Rhineland. Bloodshed between the occupying troops and the civilian population was frequent. Although the occupying forces were unable to collect any reparations, Germany's economy was paralyzed and a wild inflation swept the country. Thus more seeds of bitterness were sown.

In August 1923 Gustav Stresemann became head of the German government and offered conciliation. An international commission headed by Charles G. Dawes of the United States drew up a plan for the withdrawal of the occupying forces, for an international loan to Germany, and for the orderly payment of Germany's reparations installments. The German economy quickly recovered. From 1924 to 1929 Germany was the most prosperous nation in Europe and made its reparations payments as scheduled, mostly with loans from the United States. Under Stresemann's leadership Germany sought a *rapprochement* with its former enemies. In 1925 it signed the Treaty of Locarno with France, Great Britain, Italy, and Belgium, guaranteeing Germany's existing frontiers with France and Belgium. In 1926 Germany was admitted to the League of Nations, and Stresemann was elected president of the League. However, at home power was slipping from the moderate political parties toward the extremes, reflecting Germany's underlying economic and social maladjustments. One of the growing extremes was National Socialism, organized and led by Adolf Hitler.

4. THE RISE OF HITLER AND NATIONAL SOCIALISM

Adolf Hitler was the son of a middle-aged Austrian customs official and a young, sensitive, unhappily married mother. Of an artistic temperament, he went off to Vienna at an early age to seek an artist's career. Denied admission to the art academies for lack of training and too proud

to work as a laborer, he lived for years in poverty and sometimes in squalor. He fed his ego with German master-race theories and filled his heart with hatred of the Jews. At the outbreak of World War I Hitler was in Munich, Germany, eking out a living at crude artwork such as making posters. The ardent young German nationalist threw himself eagerly into the war, which he considered to be a righteous crusade for the beloved fatherland. Attaining the rank of corporal, he got his first taste of command. The experience of war—the sense of mission and unified struggle—would stay with Hitler and prove to be a source of appeal to many in future years. When the war ended, he was in a hospital, a victim of poison gas.

After the war Hitler frequented beer cellars, haranguing demobilized and unemployed troops and organizing them into violent political action groups. He soon discovered his magnetic powers of oratory and leadership. The disgruntled and the disenchanted, particularly the frustrated university students and demobilized lesser army officers, began attaching themselves to Hitler in increasing numbers. He organized them into the National Socialist (Nazi) party. Among his most important early followers were Hermann Göring, who became second in command; Rudolf Hess, who became head of the political section of the party; and Paul Joseph Goebbels, who became the chief Nazi propagandist. As early as 1923 Hitler, in league with the popular war hero Field Marshal Ludendorff, made his first grab for power (the famous Beer Hall Putsch). It was premature, however, and Hitler was jailed for nearly a year. While in jail he wrote *Mein Kampf* (*My Struggle*), which became the Nazi bible.

National Socialism, as outlined in *Mein Kampf,* was the German brand of fascism. In fact, the Nazis were heavily indebted to Mussolini for both ideology and methodology. At the center of its basic philosophy is the German master-race concept. The old Nordic myth of Gobineau and Chamberlain was revived. The terms *German, Nordic,* and *Aryan* were used interchangeably without regard to scientific fact. It was held that the Germans, the only pure representatives of the tall, blond Nordic "race," are superior to and destined to conquer and rule all other peoples. Militarism, indomitable will, pride, aggressiveness, and brute strength were held to be virtues; gentleness, peacefulness, tolerance, pity, and modesty, vices.

As a specific program of action, National Socialism was primarily concerned with foreign affairs. It called for repudiation of the Treaty of Versailles; all-out rearmament; the recovery of all territories, including colonies, lost at the end of World War I; and the annexation of all neighboring German-speaking territories such as Austria, the Netherlands, and most of Switzerland. Then the master race must have *Lebensraum* (living space), which was to be obtained by driving to the east (*Drang nach Osten*), particularly by conquering and enslaving the Soviet Union. There is little doubt that in the Nazi mind world domination was the ultimate goal.

The domestic program was vague and contradictory. Trusts and department stores were to be nationalized. Unearned income was to be abolished. Communism was to be destroyed and labor unions rigidly controlled. Finally, persecution of the Jews was part of the Nazi program. Over time, persecution escalated from legal discrimination to economic exploitation to violence and, finally, to literal extermination. The capitalist classes never took the socialist aspects of Hitler's program seriously. As in Italy, they looked to the Fascists to provide strong government, protect property, and control the working classes.

Hitler copied many of Mussolini's techniques. The rank and file of Nazi party members, wearing brown shirts, were organized along military lines as storm troopers. They marched, sang, and intimidated and beat up the opposition. An elite corps of black-shirted "SS" troops supervised and policed the brown shirts. Pagan symbolism, such as the swastika, was adopted. All party members swore unquestioning and undying allegiance to Hitler.

5. THE TRIUMPH OF HITLER

At first National Socialism grew slowly but steadily. National Socialism appealed particularly to youth, displaced veterans, and people from many classes who felt insecure and threatened by change. It promised much, seemed to provide membership in a movement with a clear

cause and direction, and offered simple solutions to difficult problems. From 1925 to 1929, when Germany under Stresemann's leadership was the most prosperous nation in Europe and was being wooed by her former enemies, Nazi party membership grew from 27,000 to 178,000.

After the Great Depression of 1929, which struck Germany along with the rest of the capitalistic world, the Nazis gained rapidly. In the parliamentary elections of 1930 they obtained several million votes and increased their seats in the Reichstag from 12 to 107. They appealed to a broad spectrum of disaffected workers, members of the middle and lower middle classes, veterans, and particularly the young. They were now strong enough to disrupt the orderly functioning of parliamentary government, and President Paul von Hindenburg resorted to ruling by presidential decree. In the presidential election of 1932 Hitler ran as the Nazi candidate. The moderate and liberal parties, which in 1925 had feared and opposed Hindenburg, now persuaded him to run again as the only man who could stop Hitler (Hindenburg was now eighty-five years old). Hitler got enough votes to force a runoff election against the popular and venerable idol. In the runoff election Hindenburg was elected, but Hitler received more than 13 million votes. In parliamentary elections a few months later, the Nazis obtained 230 out of 608 seats in the Reichstag, the largest number ever held by any party under the Weimar Republic. Hindenburg now offered to make Hitler vice-chancellor, but Hitler, sensing complete dictatorship in the offing, refused.

Meanwhile, the Nazis, under Hitler's instructions, paralyzed Germany's political life with terror. When chaos threatened to play into the hands of the Communists, in January 1933, Hindenburg offered and Hitler accepted the chancellorship. Franz von Papen, head of the militaristic Nationalist party, was made vice-chancellor. It was the great industrialists who finally gave the Nazis the necessary support to come to power. Hitler, determined to have nothing less than complete dictatorship, immediately called for parliamentary elections. Now in official control of the state police and the agencies of information in addition to their own highly disciplined party machinery, the Nazis skillfully used every device of propaganda to frighten and con-

WHERE HISTORIANS DISAGREE

What Caused Nazism?

The rise of nazism in Germany was so dramatic and of such consequence that it demands explanation. Yet perhaps no other development has remained more difficult to explain.

Perhaps the simplest explanation for the rise of nazism focuses on the politics of Hitler's rise in the 1920s and 1930s—that the political parties of the Weimar Republic were disorganized, that political leaders were weak, that there was so much political struggle and intrigue going on that Hitler did not even need to seize power. This interpretation stresses the political failure of the Social Democrats and Communists to unify against the Nazi threat and the political blindness of those conservatives who offered him the chancellorship even though they opposed him, believing that they could gain power themselves while controlling Hitler.

The economic interpretation, favored by many Marxists, holds that nazism was a logical consequence of the last, monopoly stage of capitalism—that large landowners and industrialists resorted to nazism in a period of economic crisis in order to prevent the collapse of capitalism and the spread of socialism. This interpretation stresses the growing strength of the Communist party and the restlessness of the working class. Thus Germany's real power holders tried to use Hitler and his nazism to control the threatening masses and maintain the endangered economic system that served the Junkers and industrialists.

A third interpretation holds that nazism was a logical continuation of German history itself. It stresses that the German people had long displayed tendencies favoring the authoritarianism, militarism, and racism that came to characterize nazism. This interpretation argues that in retrospect it is no surprise that Prussia had always been militaristic, that the liberal revolutions of 1848 failed in Germany, that Bismarck united the nation by blood and iron, that the leading philosophers of racism were German, and that the democratic Weimar Republic was never very popular or effective.

More recently, psychosocial interpretations have been proposed to explain the rise of nazism in Germany. According to these interpretations, nazism both reflected and responded to the desires of certain large groups of Germans—people traumatized by the war such as the veterans and the young who suffered hunger and loss of their fathers, people disoriented by the political and economic upheavals immediately following the war, and people weakened and immobilized by the Great Depression. Nazism seemed to promise a sense of direction, action, purpose, power, and pride to these people.

An underlying controversy among historians is whether nazism should be viewed as an aberration of Western history. Many historians stress that nazism should be viewed as limited in time and place, that it was an unlikely product of circumstances. They stress the extraordinary character and role of Hitler, the peculiar circumstances of Germany after World War I, and the extreme qualities of nazism.

Others argue that there were many points of continuity between nazism and Western history. They stress the growth of fascism and totalitarianism in the West, the widespread nationalism and racism, and the general appeal of authoritarian practices in times of war or socioeconomic crises.

These and other interpretations are evolving as historians gain distance from the 1920s, 1930s, and 1940s. The topic remains controversial, and the debates over the causes of nazism are likely to continue for some time.

FIGURE 53.3 Adolf Hitler at Buckeberg Walking between two lines of Nazi banners, Adolf Hitler makes a carefully staged, dramatic entrance to a mass meeting at Buckeberg, Germany, in 1934. (Heinrich Hoffman, *Life* Magazine © 1945 Time, Inc.)

fuse the people. Like the Fascists in Italy, they exaggerated and exploited the Communist threat. Five days before the elections, they made use of the burning of the Reichstag building, blaming the Communists. The elections themselves, however, were by secret ballot and were relatively free. The Communists polled 4.8 million votes, the Center (Roman Catholic) party 5.5 million, the Social Democrats (workers and small-business and professional people's party) 7.2 million, the Nazis 17 million, and von Papen's Nationalists 3 million. The Nazi and Nationalist votes combined gave Hitler 52 percent of the seats in the Reichstag. A few days later Hitler, wearing his Nazi party uniform, appeared before the newly elected Reichstag, from which the

every device of propaganda to frighten and con-Communists were excluded, and demanded dictatorial powers for four years. They were granted with only 94 opposing (Social Democratic) votes. Long before the four years had expired, the moderate parties had been destroyed, and the Nazi dictatorship was complete (see Figure 53.3).

6. NAZI GERMANY

The Reichstag, having voted Hitler dictatorial powers, adjourned, to meet henceforth only on the call of the *Führer* (leader) for the purpose of voting approval of his acts. Hitler disbanded all political parties except the National Socialist party. Freedom of speech, press, and assembly was abolished. An elaborate and all-powerful secret police, the Gestapo, was established under the direction of Heinrich Himmler to spy out and destroy opposition. Political opponents, homosexuals, and gypsies, among others, were made objects of persecution. Hitler's most intense hatred was vented on the Jews, who were subjected to every conceivable humiliation. As fast as their services could be dispensed with, they were driven out of public and professional life. Eventually the Nazis embarked on a program to exterminate all the Jews under their control. It is estimated that by the end of World War II the Nazis had murdered 6 million Jews out of a world total of 15 million.

The control and molding of thought always held high priority in Nazi activities. Indeed, this control appears to be an absolute necessity for any totalitarian dictatorship. Under the direction of Goebbels, minister of propaganda, the German press and radio spewed forth a constant stream of false or distorted information. To read or listen to foreign newspapers or broadcasts was made a crime. An incessant hate campaign was waged against the liberal democratic world. The schools were, of course, nazified. Only Nazi party members could be school administrators. Unsympathetic teachers were dismissed and punished. Members of Nazi youth organizations were set to spy on their teachers and parents. Textbooks were rewritten to conform to German master-race theories. The burning of liberal books, sometimes even those of Germany's greatest literary figures, such as Goethe and Schiller, became a national fad. The Nazi minister of education admitted that the sole function of education was the creation of Nazis. Hitler wrote in *Mein Kampf* that the German youth's "entire education and development has to be directed at giving him the conviction of being absolutely superior to the others . . . the belief in the invincibility of his entire nationality." The arts were nazified, and only party members or sympathizers were permitted to publish, exhibit, or perform.

Since National Socialism was essentially an anti-Christian ideology, the Nazis realized the necessity of controlling the religious establishment. Much of the Lutheran church, which was the official state church and included more than half the German people in its membership, was brought under Nazi domination. Nazi officials attempted to turn it into a propaganda agency. The few Lutheran pastors who resisted, like Martin Niemöller, were thrown into concentration camps. The smaller Protestant denominations met the same fate. Hitler found it much more difficult to deal with the Catholic church, whose higher authority lay outside Germany. Although he soon signed a concordat with the pope, the terms proved to be unworkable. Catholic clergy, churches, and schools were subjected to constantly increasing pressures, indignities, and physical abuse.

The Nazis rejuvenated and regimented Germany's economic life. The property and the profits of the capitalist classes were given special consideration. Labor unions were brought under Nazi control, and a system of enforced arbitration of disputes between labor and management was set up along the lines that Mussolini had established in Italy. Strikes and lockouts were forbidden. The entire German economy was forced into the overall pattern and policies of the Nazi government. The vast rearmament program gave employment to millions. Superhighways, airfields, hospitals, and apartment houses were built all over Germany. The most intricate financial trickery was resorted to, but the Nazis expected eventually to finance their huge undertakings out of the spoils of victorious war.

Even family life came under Nazi control. Until they were needed for the war effort, women were encouraged to fulfill their primary duties as homemakers subordinate to their husbands and as producers of Aryan children. Children were encouraged to join Nazi youth organizations, which expanded rapidly to encompass the majority of boys and girls by the late 1930s.

All other activities were subordinated to the prime purpose of making a military comeback. Shortly after assuming power, Hitler took Germany out of the League of Nations and out of the disarmament conference that was in progress in Geneva. Rearmament was pushed as rapidly as possible, and in 1935 Hitler openly repudiated the disarmament clauses of the Treaty of Versailles. In 1936 Hitler remilitarized the Rhineland and sent decisive aid to General Franco's Fascist rebels in Spain (see Chapter 54). The following year he made an alliance with Italy and Japan. This Berlin-Rome-Tokyo Axis was aimed specifically at the Soviet Union. More broadly, it was an aggressive antiliberal alliance for military expansion. Meanwhile, other events taking place elsewhere in Europe also threw liberal democracy into retreat.

7. AUTHORITARIAN REGIMES IN EASTERN AND SOUTHERN EUROPE

Beginning in the 1920s, hopes for permanently establishing parliamentary regimes in eastern and southern Europe were dashed by the rise of right-wing authoritarian governments. Some of them had elements of Fascist ideology and policy, but most were dictatorships by royal or military figures and individuals backed by the military and conservative powers of the nation.

The rise of right-wing authoritarian regimes in eastern and southeastern Europe was initiated in Hungary under the regency of Admiral Miklós Horthy and the rules of Count Stephen Bethlen during the 1920s and General Julius Gömbös during the 1930s. In 1926 General Josef Pilsudaski set up a military dictatorship in Poland. In 1929 a royal dictatorship was established in Yugoslavia under King Alexander I; after his assassination in 1934 an authoritarian regime was set up under the regent, Prince Paul. During the 1930s royal dictatorships were established in Rumania and Bulgaria. After 1934 Austria succumbed to authoritarian rule under Engelbert Dollfuss and then Kurt von Schuschnigg until its annexation by Hitler in 1938. In 1936 Greece's shaky parliamentary regime fell to the dictatorship of General Ioannes Metaxas. Czechoslovakia was an exception. There parliamentary democracy survived until the nation fell to Hitler in 1938.

The Iberian peninsula, a scene of considerable turmoil, was an area where fascism became attractive to many. In Portugal authoritarianism and political instability were the rule rather than the exception during the 1920s and eventually led to the establishment of a strong dictatorship under Antonio de Oliveira Salazar in 1932. In Spain General Miguel Primo de Rivera ruled as de facto dictator between 1923 and 1930. After a democratic interlude between 1930 and 1936, the rise of the Fascist Falange and the revolt of Span-

ish generals led to a civil war and the triumph of General Francisco Franco as dictator in 1939.

Almost all these authoritarian regimes emphasized nationalism and militarism. They were bolstered by a fundamental fear of change, particularly the kind of change liberal democracy and socialism represented. Many regimes provided fertile ground for the growth of Fascist organizations and the enactment of Fascist policies, but with the possible exception of Franco's Spain, these governments were not Fascist in the same sense as Italy under Mussolini and Germany under Hitler. This description of Europe's authoritarian regimes also describes Japan's government during the 1930s, which would become one of the Axis powers in 1937.

8. THE TRIUMPH OF AUTHORITARIANISM IN JAPAN

Three divergent groups competed for the leadership of postwar Japan. The dominant group was made up of the great industrialists. Seventy-five percent of Japan's industry and capital was concentrated in the hands of five great families, called the *zaibatsu*. This handful of industrial giants had such a stranglehold on the Japanese economy that it was also able to control the highly restricted government. The *zaibatsu*, enjoying this economic and political monopoly, wished to see no fundamental change in Japan's undemocratic society; it advocated instead the peaceful economic penetration of Asia.

The liberals constituted the second group. This faction, with university professors and students providing much of the leadership, set out to broaden the suffrage, which was restricted to the well-to-do, to encourage the more effective unionization of labor, and to diminish the power of the military. Because of the political inexperience and the long tradition of passive submission to authority on the part of the Japanese masses, these were difficult undertakings. They were made more difficult by the activities of Marxists, who confused liberal reform movements and tainted them with the suspicion of treason. Nevertheless, Japan made encouraging progress toward liberal democracy. In 1925 the suffrage was broadened. Soon afterward, two liberal political

FIGURE 53.4 Japan Invades China Here Japanese soldiers are celebrating victory after a new assault on China in 1937. This photograph, showing armed Japanese troops on Chinese soil under the Japanese flag, symbolizes key elements of Japanese policy during the 1930s: nationalism, militarism, and expansionism. (Ullstein Bilderdienst, West Berlin)

parties appeared. The military budget was reduced. The prestige of the professional military declined to such an extent that many officers ceased wearing their uniforms in public.

The professional military, however, was determined to strengthen and exploit its own traditional power. In the late 1920s a group of restless, ambitious young army officers began to accuse their leaders of softness and plotted to seize control of both the armed forces and the government. When a coup planned for early 1931 was exposed and blocked, the conspirators decided on a bold move to throw the country into such hysteria and confusion that they could seize power. In October 1931 the Japanese army stationed in Manchuria made an unauthorized attack on the Chinese forces and began the conquest of all Manchuria. The next year Japanese forces attacked Shanghai, the chief port of China (see Figure 53.4). Once the fighting with huge and potentially dangerous China began, war fever and patriotic hysteria swept Japan, just as the army plotters had foreseen. They then assassinated the premier and numerous other government officials and civilian leaders and cowed the rest into submission. Once in control, the military turned to the destruction of the liberals. Liberal university professors were accused of disloyalty and silenced, dismissed, or imprisoned. The schools and the press and radio were made organs of propaganda. All democratic processes of government and civil rights were destroyed. The military and state police were given unlimited authority. The *zaibatsu* were corrupted and won over with lush military contracts.

Meanwhile, Japanese overran all Manchuria, which was made into a puppet state of Manchu-kuo. When the League of Nations declared Japan an aggressor and ordered its withdrawal from Manchuria, Japan defied the League and instead withdrew from the organization. In 1937 Japan joined the Berlin-Rome Axis. That same year, Japan began an all-out assault on China proper. The Axis powers were on the march.

SUGGESTED READING

Totalitarianism, Fascism, and Authoritarianism

H. Arendt, *The Origins of Totalitarianism* (1951). A brilliant but difficult analysis.

F. L. Carsten, *The Rise of Fascism* (1982). A good, scholarly analysis.

E. Nolte, *The Three Faces of Fascism* (1963). A respected but difficult intellectual history of fascism in Italy, Germany, and France.

S. Payne, *Fascism: Comparison and Definition* (1980). A respected general interpretation.

H. A. Turner, Jr., ed., *Reappraisals of Fascism* (1975). A good collection of articles.

Mussolini and Italian Fascism

A. Lyttleton, *The Seizure of Power: Fascism in Italy, 1919–1929* (1973). An excellent analysis of the rise of fascism in Italy.

D. M. Smith, *Mussolini* (1982). An excellent biography.

E. R. Tannenbaum, *The Fascist Experience: Italian Society and Culture, 1922–1945* (1972). A fine examination of life in Fascist Italy.

The Weimar Republic

P. Gay, *Weimar Culture: The Outsider as Insider* (1968). An excellent examination of Weimar Germany.

E. Kolb, *The Weimar Republic* (1988). A useful recent introduction with bibliography.

Hitler and Nazi Germany

J. Bendersky, *A History of Nazi Germany* (1985). A useful brief survey.

A. Bullock, *Hitler: A Study in Tyranny* (1971). A classic biography of Hitler.

I. Kershaw, *The Nazi Dictatorship* (1985). A broad interpretation of policy and ideology.

J. Stephenson, *The Nazi Organization of Women* (1980). A useful study of women in Nazi Germany.

Authoritarian Regimes in Eastern and Southern Europe

B. Jelavich, *History of the Balkans,* vol. 2 (1983). A good survey.

J. Rothschild, *East Central Europe Between the Two World Wars* (1973). A useful general account.

The Triumph of Authoritarianism in Japan

R. Benedict, *The Chrysanthemum and the Sword* (1967). Examines the role of the professional military in Japan.

E. O. Reischauer, *The Japanese* (1977). A highly respected survey.

CHAPTER 54
Paralysis of the Democratic West

FIGURE 54.1 The Great Depression in New York Jobless and homeless men wait in line for a free meal in New York in 1930. These Depression breadlines are part of the reason for the seeming impotence of the democratic nations in the face of the growing Fascist menace. The Great Depression, which began in 1929, did not end until 1942, when World War II pumped billions of dollars into the American economy. (UPI/Bettmann Newsphotos)

The Western democracies emerged from World War I victorious. In many ways, each hoped to return to the way things had been before the war, to quickly get back to "normal." But instead of the hoped-for smooth sailing, the Western democracies were faced with a series of challenges in the two decades following the war.

1. CHALLENGES OF THE 1920s AND 1930s

The first challenge was the immediate problem of postwar dislocation and recovery. The human, material, and economic losses were unprecedented and unequally borne—France and Belgium suffered most among the Western democracies. Soldiers had to be reintegrated into civilian life, economies had to be shifted from wartime production, and trade patterns had to be reestablished.

The second challenge was the roller-coaster ride of tension, optimism, and disillusionment that characterized international affairs in the 1920s and 1930s. The Treaty of Versailles left few happy and many resentful. The payment of reparations and wartime debts threatened the international order during the years immediately following the war. Then from 1925 to 1929, a period known as the Locarno Era, international tensions diminished and progress was made toward peace and disarmament. The Locarno Pact in 1925 (guaranteeing international boundaries in Europe), the admission of Germany to the League of Nations in 1926, the Kellogg-Briand Pact of 1928 (proclaiming a commitment to international friendship), and the earlier Washington Conference of 1921–1922 (limiting naval strength) seemed to establish a basis for optimism in international affairs. After 1930, however, this optimism gave way to disillusionment as discord, rearmament, and aggression marked international affairs.

The third challenge was the Great Depression. Economic depressions were not new to the West, but one of this magnitude and duration was unprecedented. In October 1929 the American stock market, bloated by speculation and borrowed money, crashed. Since the end of World War I, the international economic order had become dependent on the United States, par-

ticularly to keep up the flow of loans, debt payments, and trade. The U.S. financial crisis quickly spread to Europe. Stocks lost their value, banks failed, and confidence collapsed. This sudden financial crisis reflected the fragility of the postwar economic order, and between 1929 and 1933 economies almost everywhere were in a tailspin. World industrial production fell by more than 33 percent. Unemployment grew to massive proportions. Policies adopted to deal with the crisis probably made things worse—trade barriers rather than cooperation typified international economic policy, and cuts in spending instead of deficit spending marked domestic economic policy. Some countries started to recover after 1933, but in other cases the Great Depression extended until World War II.

The final challenge was the threat from the political extremes—communism on the left, fascism on the right. The most obvious threats were international, since communism was growing stronger in the Soviet Union and fascism was spreading in central and southern Europe. But the threats were internal as well, for both Communist and Fascist political organizations were growing within the Western democracies, particularly during the 1930s.

The political and social development of each of the Western democracies greatly depended on how they met these four challenges. In retrospect it is easy to be harsh on the leaders of these societies, for in the end the world was immersed in another war even more destructive than World War I. However, these challenges were extraordinary, and the leaders trying to deal with them often labored under overwhelming difficulties.

2. THE HARASSED BRITISH EMPIRE

At the end of World War I the British Empire still included one-fourth of all the land and people on the globe. Nevertheless, Britain's economy, empire, and world position were shaken beyond recovery. Britain's far-flung possessions in Asia and Africa were beginning to stir restlessly as the spirit of nationalism, which had long provided the European world with so much of its expansive energy, spread eastward. Great Britain found it advisable to grant freedom to its already self-governing dominions in the hope of retaining their loyalty. In 1931 the Statute of Westminster gave complete independence and equality with the mother country to Canada, Australia, New Zealand, the Union of South Africa, Newfoundland, and the Irish Free State (free since 1922). Great Britain could no longer count on their material support in world policies, nor could it count on its restless colonies. Furthermore, Britain was now clearly second to the United States as an industrial and financial power. (It would require many years, however, for the British to readjust their thinking to the reality of their country's reduced position.)

At home, postwar Britain was harassed by acute economic problems. The national debt had quintupled during the war. Britain owed the United States a heavy war debt. German submarines had taken a toll of 9 million tons of British ships with their cargoes. British exports met sharply increased competition in the world markets, particularly from the United States. Rising protective tariffs all over the world hindered its commerce. Mines and industrial plants were antiquated and in disrepair. Returning servicemen found few jobs. Unemployment hovered around 3 million, a figure that came to be accepted as normal. Government support for the unemployed, sick, aged, and destitute increased Britain's financial problems.

These chronic economic ills were reflected in Great Britain's troubled postwar policies. In 1922 the Conservatives broke up Lloyd George's wartime coalition government of Liberals and Conservatives and won the ensuing parliamentary elections. They sought to restore classical nineteenth-century capitalism by means of rigid entrenchment of government spending, particularly on social services. This policy was so hard on the distressed masses that in 1924 a Labour-Liberal coalition headed by the Labour party leader, Ramsay MacDonald, ousted the Conservatives. The Labour party was now stronger than the Liberal party, and as times grew harder and feelings more bitter, the once-great Liberal party was virtually crushed between the more extreme parties—Labour on the left and Conservative on the right.

But the majority of the British people were not yet ready to accept the mildly socialistic program the Labour party advocated. MacDonald's ministry lasted less than a year. Dependent on the Liberals for his majority, he was forced to follow a moderate course. When he recognized the Soviet Union and made a commercial treaty with it, the Conservatives were able to capitalize on public suspicion and drive him from power. From 1925 to 1929 the Conservatives wrestled with rising discontent, strikes, and the steady growth of the Labour party. In 1929 a Labour victory, supported by the much-dwindled Liberals, again brought Ramsay MacDonald to the head of the government. His moderation in the face of the deepening economic depression, however, caused the majority of his Labour followers to repudiate him two years later. But MacDonald was unwilling to give up the honors of office. In 1931 he therefore formed a national coalition of right-wing Labourites, Liberals, and Conservatives to deal with the mounting domestic and foreign crises. This national coalition was dominated by the Conservatives, and MacDonald was really a captive of the Conservatives until he resigned in 1935. The Conservative-dominated coalition ruled Great Britain until the end of World War II. Although Great Britain was recovering from the Great Depression, the government was on the whole ineffective in dealing with social maladjustment at home and Fascist aggression abroad. The Conservative prime ministers Stanley Baldwin and Neville Chamberlain, who followed Ramsay MacDonald as head of the national government, were unimaginative and unprepared for the challenges that would face them.

3. FRUSTRATED FRANCE

Although France enjoyed the advantage of being economically more self-sufficient than Great Britain, France had suffered greater wounds in World War I than had its island neighbor. Most of the fighting had taken place on French soil. A tenth—the most productive tenth—of its land area had been devastated. The retreating Germans had laid waste much of what had not been destroyed in battle. Orchards had been chopped down and mines wrecked, many beyond repair. Even more tragic was the loss of life. France, with the lowest birthrate of any major nation in the world, suffered by far the heaviest casualties per capita of any of the combatants. Out of a population of less than 40 million, it suffered almost 1.4 million battle deaths and 1.7 million wounded. The civilian death rate from direct and indirect causes had also been high. France had fewer people in 1918 than in 1914, even after the return of Alsace and Lorraine.

Postwar France was confronted with a staggering job of economic reconstruction and an equally staggering war debt. To meet these obligations and to finance the reconstruction, the French government counted on German reparations, but little was forthcoming. Inflation became a chronic headache. A more basic and long-range problem was French industry, which was rapidly falling behind that of its competitors. The highly individualistic French had not gone in for large-scale corporate industry to the same extent as the Americans, British, and Germans. The little French family industries had difficulty competing with mass production. A like situation prevailed in French agriculture, most of which took place on thousands of little family farms too tiny to use machinery profitably. Industrial and agricultural production per worker was lower in France than in most other major Western nations.

Considering the serious plight of France's postwar economy and the habitual disorderliness with which its multiparty democracy traditionally functioned, one is impressed by the remarkable stability of the French government during the decade of the 1920s. From 1919 to 1924, a bloc of conservative parties was in power. It followed an antilabor, probusiness policy. It also favored the Roman Catholic church and pressed hard for collection of German reparations. Meanwhile, discontent among the laboring classes was mounting. In 1924, the year of MacDonald's first Labour ministry in Great Britain, the parties of the Left under the leadership of Edouard Herriot were victorious. Like MacDonald, Herriot pursued a prolabor policy, advocating an increase in social services and soft money. He was also conciliatory toward Russia and Germany. But, also like MacDonald, he lasted less than a year.

From 1926 to 1929, a strong right-of-center national bloc under the leadership of Raymond Poincaré was in power. Poincaré checked the inflation by rigid retrenchment. Upon his retirement in 1929, however, the increasing pressure of discontent threw the country into political turmoil. No leader or political combination seemed to be capable of dealing with the economic crisis brought on by the world depression, the growing menace of fascism, or the unrest in the French colonies. Ministry followed ministry in rapid succession. Scandals and riots occurred, and Fascist groups appeared. In 1936 the Popular Front, consisting of left-wing parties under the leadership of the mild Socialist Léon Blum, came to power (see Figure 54.2). The Blum ministry obtained a forty-hour week and two weeks' annual vacation with pay for the workers. It also nationalized the Bank of France and the great munitions industries. This was too much for the powerful propertied interests, who drove Blum from office the following year. But the conservative parties that regained control were unable to agree upon firm policies, whether domestic or foreign.

Thus France, like Great Britain, in the face of resurgent Nazi Germany, swashbuckling Mussolini, and militaristic Japan, could summon little strength or unity. The propertied classes were unwilling to share their wealth or privileges or to change their nineteenth-century practices. They feared and hated Léon Blum. The Great Depression persisted and fueled political turmoil. The army was basking in past glory. Seeking to maintain the status quo, the French were defense-minded. They constructed the Maginot line fortifications along the German border and formed defensive alliances with Poland, Czechoslovakia, Yugoslavia, and Rumania. These alliances, however, were no stronger than the faith those small countries had in France's ability to defend them, which by the late 1930s was very little.

4. THE UNITED STATES AND THE GREAT DEPRESSION

The United States emerged from World War I the world's richest nation. Although its entry into the war at its most critical phase was probably decisive in determining the outcome, the United

FIGURE 54.2 The Popular Front In 1935 Socialists, Communists, and others on the French Left united for the first time as the Popular Front. In 1936 the Popular Front came to power under the leadership of the Socialist premier, Léon Blum. This photo shows Blum (on the left) and Maurice Thorez, secretary of the French Communist party, at a 1937 Bastille Day rally in Paris. (Photo Trends)

States suffered far less war damage than any of the other major participants. President Wilson assumed a leading role in the making of the peace settlements and in the creation of the League of Nations.

When President Wilson returned from Paris in the summer of 1919 and sought to persuade his country to join the League of Nations, he faced a strong challenge from his political enemies, led by Henry Cabot Lodge. Wilson's opponents refused to accept the treaty, and particularly the League of Nations, as proposed by Wilson. Wilson, seeing the treaty and the League as a matter of principle, refused to compromise. In his struggle to rally support, Wilson suffered a paralytic stroke. Since he was unable thereafter to lead the fight for the treaty and was unwilling to give the leadership to others, his opponents easily defeated ratification in the Senate.

The League was not an issue in the presidential election of 1920. However, the victor, Warren G. Harding, announced that the League was now a dead issue. And during the cynical and disillusioned decade of the 1920s American public opinion became overwhelmingly isolationist. When, during the international crises of the 1930s, the League and the harassed British and French governments sought the support of the United States against the Fascist aggressors, they sought in vain.

The decade following World War I was a period of relative but uneven prosperity in the United States. The all-out war effort had brought about a great expansion of American industry and unleashed huge quantities of money and credit. In 1914 the United States had been a debtor nation. It emerged from the war a creditor to most of Europe to the amount of $10 billion, a figure that doubled during the next ten years. Its chief economic competitors came out of the war battered and shaken. Production, profits, and purchasing power reached new heights. However, it was an uneven and unsound prosperity. Agriculture was depressed by surplus commod-

FIGURE 54.3 Food-lines in Paris While the Great Depression was initiated in the United States, it soon spread to most of Europe. Some of the consequences were unemployment and long lines of people waiting for free food, as indicated by this 1931 photograph of Parisians near a food distribution center. (Harlingue/Roger-Viollet)

ities and low prices, which meant low purchasing power for the farm population of the South and the Middle West. Nor did wages climb as rapidly as profits and prices in the industrial Northeast. Production was growing faster than consumer demand, which meant growing unemployment and industrial surpluses. Foreign markets were diminished by a policy of higher and higher tariffs designed to protect American industry from foreign competition. The government's philosophy of noninterference with free enterprise (except for tariffs) permitted unlimited speculation in the soaring stock market, often with other people's money and with unrestrained use of credit.

The stock market crashed in October 1929. Stock values tumbled. Thousands of banks and businesses failed. The crisis soon spread to Europe, where nations were dependent on American credit and commerce that rapidly dried up. The economic depression extended over the entire capitalist world. Millions were thrown out of work in country after country (see Figure 54.1). In 1932 unemployment in the West rose to 22 percent, leaving some 30 million out of work. Some nations—the United States, Germany, and Britain—were hit early and hard. Others—France, Italy, and states in eastern Europe where the economies were more self-sufficient or agricultural—were hit later and more softly (see Figure 54.3). A few others—the Scandinavian democracies with their Social Democratic governments, their welfare policies, and their economic cooperatives—managed to get through the Great Depression with relative ease. Most often, governmental policies in the United States and other leading states, such as raising tariffs, increasing currency controls, and otherwise relying on laissez-faire economics, probably made matters worse. The depression deepened.

In the presidential election of 1932 the Democratic candidate, Franklin D. Roosevelt, defeated Hoover, ending twelve years of Republican rule. The Roosevelt administration immediately launched a series of sweeping economic and social reforms that came to be called the New Deal. The New Deal was not a radical, new departure but, rather, a further advance along the progressive lines established by Theodore Roosevelt and Woodrow Wilson and during World War I, when the government had engaged in economic planning and control. First, emergency measures were taken to relieve the suffering of the 12 million unemployed and their families. The chief of these was the setting up of the huge Works Progress Administration, which provided a large number of jobs. The Wagner Act strengthened the position of the labor unions by guaranteeing the right of collective bargaining. Old-age and unemployment insurance were inaugurated. For the desperate farmers, measures were passed that granted debt relief, commodity loans, price supports, and payments for acreage reduction. Deflation was checked by a devaluation of the dollar. Investments and deposits were protected by strict government supervision. Steps were taken to conserve the nation's natural resources against wasteful private exploitation. Gradually, some popular confidence was restored and the nation's economy began to recover. However, economic problems persisted and full recovery was not achieved until World War II, which forced the government to finance the war with greater deficit spending.

5. DISILLUSIONMENT AND UNCERTAINTY IN THOUGHT AND CULTURE

The war, the movements of international and domestic politics, and the Great Depression affected all aspects of life during the 1920s and 1930s. The growing sense of disillusionment, uncertainty, and turning inward that marked political and social life was reflected in some of the most important cultural trends of the period.

In philosophy there was a wave of attacks on nineteenth-century optimism and rationalism that expanded the ideas set forth earlier by philosophers such as Friedrich Nietzsche in Germany and Henri Bergson in France (see p. 598). The most widely read of these post–World War I philosophers was Oswald Spengler. In his *Decline of the West* (1918), Spengler argued that the West was in decline, that World War I was the beginning of the end. This sense of decay and crisis appeared in many other works, most notably in José Ortega y Gasset's *Revolt of the Masses* (1930), which lamented the decline of liberal civilization and the rise of ''mass man'' in the West.

Sigmund Freud's ideas (see pp. 589–590), which emphasized the irrational, unconscious, and instinctual aspects of human thought and behavior, also stemmed from the period just before World War I, but during the 1920s and 1930s they gained wide acceptance. The unconscious and the irrational were also present in the best literature of the period. The Irish writer James Joyce (1882–1914) and German authors Franz

Kafka (1883–1924) and Hermann Hesse (1877–1962) (see pp. 729–730) wrote disquieting, introspective fiction. These same themes can be seen in artistic styles, such as the Dada movement, which stressed the purposelessness of life, and surrealism, with its exploration of dreams and the unconscious (see p. 731 and Color Plate 39).

Certainly there was a variety of cultural trends during the period, many of them far more traditional than these (see pp. 729–732). But it was the books and paintings and thoughts that emphasized uncertainty, doubt, and turning inward that best reflected experience in the Western democracies after World War I and that anticipated the violence that was to come.

6. THE ROAD TO WAR

Early in the 1930s, international affairs started slipping out of control. The League of Nations was challenged, rearmament spread, and aggression became the order of the day. Efforts to appease the aggressors and prevent the dreaded return to total war failed. By the end of the decade a new world war had broken out.

Breakdown of the League of Nations

The only international agency that existed for the maintenance of the peace was the League of Nations, which after the defection of the United States was largely dependent on Great Britain and France for support. For twelve years the League supervised the implementation of the peace treaties, administered relief to tens of thousands of war victims, promoted international goodwill, and settled numerous international disputes. None of these settlements, however, involved the disciplining of a major power, and thoughtful observers dreaded the time when the League would be called on to do so.

When in 1931 Japan began the conquest of Manchuria, China appealed to the League for protection. The League appointed a commission headed by Britain's Earl of Lytton to make an on-the-spot investigation. The Lytton Commission reported that Japan was guilty of aggression, having violated its solemn obligations both as a League member and as a signatory of the Kellogg-Briand Pact of Paris (1928), which outlawed war as an instrument of national policy. Forceful League action, however, would be largely dependent on Great Britain and France, which were unwilling to act without American support. President Herbert Hoover, reflecting the isolationist sentiment of American public opinion, would not consent to the use of force, the threat of force, or even economic pressure by the United States. The British and French governments, harassed by their own domestic economic and political problems and the rising menace of fascism in Europe, could not bring themselves to act alone. The League, without their backing, did nothing. It had failed its first major test and was on the way out as a potent force for peace. Japan's successful defiance of the League of Nations helped convince Mussolini and Hitler that they could safely launch aggressions of their own.

The death blow was struck by Mussolini. Late in 1935 the Italian dictator invaded Ethiopia in East Africa. Ethiopia was a member of the League and appealed to it for protection. Great Britain, concerned for its numerous interests in the Near and Middle East and for its lifeline to the Far East, now became greatly agitated. Under the leadership of Great Britain and France, the League declared Mussolini to be the aggressor and invoked economic sanctions (Article XVI) against him. A list of commodities that League members were not to sell Mussolini was drawn up. However, the list did not include oil, and it soon became obvious that this was the commodity upon which the success of his aggression depended. But it quickly became apparent that, to be effective, an embargo on oil would require the cooperation of the United States. American exports of oil to Mussolini had trebled since the beginning of his campaign against Ethiopia. When the British and French governments requested the cooperation of the United States in withholding excess oil from Mussolini, Secretary of State Cordell Hull and President Roosevelt were sympathetic but were unable to get the oil companies to comply or to get Congress to force compliance. The press and public opinion were overwhelmingly isolationist, and Congress reflected that view. Mussolini got his oil. Britain and France, unwilling to resort to the only other means of stopping him, a shooting war, gave up

the League struggle. Mussolini conquered Ethiopia. The League of Nations, for all practical purposes, was dead.

Appeasement

Since the triumph of the Nazis in 1933 Germany had been preparing for a military comeback. In March 1936 Hitler ordered his armed forces into the Rhineland, which, according to the Treaty of Versailles, was to be permanently demilitarized. France, recognizing this move as the gravest threat and challenge to itself, called for Great Britain's support. The British offered none. The French fretted and fumed but in the end did nothing. Hitler had won his gamble.

Fascism's next triumph was in Spain. Until 1931, it was dominated by the landed aristocracy, a few rich capitalists, aristocratic army officers, and the Catholic church. Most people were poor, landless peasants. Since the turn of the century and particularly since 1918, the pressure of discontent had been rising. In 1931 the king yielded, restored the constitution, and granted elections. The liberal and radical groups won such a sweeping victory that the king fled the country. The reformers then proceeded to make over the Spanish nation. They drew up a democratic constitution, granted local autonomy to Catalonia (the northeasternmost section of Spain, including Barcelona), began a sweeping program of public education, started to modernize the army by placing promotions on a merit basis, granted religious freedom, seized the lands and schools of the Catholic church, and planned to break up the great estates into peasant-owned farms.

There was much violence—riots and attacks on priests, nuns, and private property. After two years the conservative propertied interests, with the vigorous support of the pope, won the elections by a narrow margin and began to undo the reforms. Early in 1936, however, the liberal and radical parties won again and resumed their drastic reform program. The privileged classes were now desperate. In July 1936 a group of generals led by General Francisco Franco launched an armed rebellion against the government. Although the rebels enjoyed the advantage of professional military leadership, the regular army, and most of the country's wealth, they were unable to make headway against the Loyalists, who enjoyed the support of the majority of the rank and file of the people.

The Spanish Civil War soon became a battle-field in the world struggle of fascism, liberalism, and communism. Hitler and Mussolini, seeing in it an opportunity to advance the cause of fascism, gain a like-minded ally and a strategic military position, and test their new weapons, sent abundant arms and troops to aid Franco. The Loyalists appealed to the democracies for aid but received none, although a few volunteers from the democracies fought as individuals in the Loyalist cause. The only nation that supported the Loyalists was the Soviet Union, but the amount of aid it could send was quite small and tainted the Loyalist cause with the suspicion of communism. After three years of slaughter, Franco and his German and Italian allies beat down the last organized Loyalist resistance. A dictatorship was established over Spain. Liberalism was shattered. The world prestige of Fascist Germany and Italy rose while that of the democracies declined further.

The year 1937 was the year of decision—the point of no return on the road to war. In that year the three great Fascist powers formed the Berlin-Rome-Tokyo Axis, which was aimed specifically at the Soviet Union but was in reality an alliance of these aggressor nations for expansion. In that year the military strength of the Axis powers—their war plants running day and night—forged ahead of that of the rest of the world. In that year the Nazis blueprinted their timetable of conquests, and Japan began its all-out assault on China.

Early in 1938 the Nazis' timetable began to function. In March they overran Austria without opposition, annexing the 6.5 million Austrians to the German Reich (Empire). Great Britain and France denounced this open aggression and violation of the Treaty of Versailles but did nothing.

Almost immediately Hitler turned his big propaganda guns on his next victim, Czechoslovakia. In constructing this little country out of Austro-Hungarian territory at the end of World War I, the Allied peacemakers had left 3.5 million German-speaking people on the Czech side of the border. Although these Sudeten Germans had never been a part of Germany and were separated from Germany by the Sudeten Moun-

tain Wall, Hitler now claimed them. The Czech republic was allied with France and Russia, and in the coming war that Hitler was planning against those two countries, Czechoslovakia could be a threat to the German flank.

As early as May 1938 Hitler threatened Czechoslovakia. The Czechs, however, surprised him by rushing to their defenses. Hitler spent the next four months arousing his people to readiness for war and softening up the democracies by keeping them in a constant state of tension and alarm. This psychological warfare culminated in a giant Nazi rally at Nuremberg in mid-September. There Hitler screamed to his frenzied followers that if the Sudeten areas were not surrendered to him by October 1, he would march. With France and the Soviet Union standing firm in their alliance with Czechoslovakia, the world anxiously awaited the beginning of a major conflict that was likely to become World War II.

At this juncture, British Prime Minister Neville Chamberlain took it upon himself to fly to Hitler's retreat at Berchtesgaden and plead for a compromise. The upshot was a conference at Munich on September 29, 1938 (see Figure 54.4). The participants were Hitler, Mussolini, Chamberlain, and Premier Édouard Daladier of France. Chamberlain persuaded Daladier to yield to Hitler's demands for the Sudeten areas of Czechoslovakia. Czechoslovakia and its ally, the Soviet Union, were not consulted. This was one of Hitler's greatest triumphs.

The Outbreak of War

Although the four participating powers at Munich had agreed to become joint protectors of what remained of Czechoslovakia, in March 1939 Hitler overran the remainder of the stricken little republic without warning. This crass act of betrayal opened the eyes of even Neville Chamberlain to the fact that Hitler could not be appeased. When Hitler threatened Poland, Great Britain and France decided to draw a line. In April 1939 they made a guarantee to Poland that they would come to its aid if it were attacked and resisted the attack. Hitler, however, was not deterred. He was demanding, among other things, the return to Germany of the Polish Corridor, which separated East Prussia from the rest of Germany, and the city of Danzig, which was

FIGURE 54.4 The Munich Conference The chief participants at the Munich Conference pose for the photographer in September 1938. Left to right: Chamberlain, Daladier, Hitler, and Mussolini. The sellout of Czechoslovakia and the Soviet Union at Munich by Chamberlain and Daladier, in an attempt to appease Hitler, destroyed any hope of maintaining a unified front in Europe against Nazi Germany. (UPI/Bettmann Newsphotos)

governed by the League of Nations. But by now it was apparent to almost everybody that specific Nazi demands were tied to unlimited aggression. Throughout the summer of 1939 the Germans made feverish preparations for war and kept up a drumfire of vilification of Poland and the democracies. Meanwhile, both sides were bidding for the support of the Soviet Union. But after Munich, Stalin had no confidence in the integrity of the capitalistic democracies. He decided to try to make his own peace with Hitler.

On August 23, 1939, the world was stunned by the signing of a ten-year peace pact by Hitler and Stalin. In return for the Soviet Union's neu-

trality while Germany conquered Poland, Hitler gave Stalin a free hand to reannex the territories in eastern Europe, including eastern Poland, that Russia had lost at the end of World War I.

With the Soviet Union safely neutralized, Hitler readied the attack on Poland as quickly as possible. At the last moment the British government instructed its ambassador in Berlin to ask Hitler what concessions by Poland he would accept to refrain from war. Hitler informed the ambassador that he was not interested in concessions, that his army and his people were ready and eager for war, and that he could not disappoint them now. The wires between Warsaw and

Berlin were cut, lest the Poles make a last-minute peaceable surrender to Hitler's demands. At dawn on September 1 the Germans launched an all-out attack on Poland by land, sea, and air.

Two days later Great Britain and France declared war on Germany, Hitler having ignored their ultimatum to desist. World War II had begun.

SUGGESTED READING

General

D. Silverman, *Reconstructing Europe after the Great War* (1982). A good analysis.

R. J. Sontag, *A Broken World, 1919–1939* (1971). An excellent survey of the period.

R. Wohl, *The Generation of 1914* (1979). A creative interpretation of the impact of World War I in the postwar years.

The Harassed British Empire

N. Branson and M. Heinemann, *Britain in the Nineteen Thirties* (1971). A social and economic perspective.

R. Graves and A. Hodge, *The Long Weekend: A Social History of Great Britain, 1918–1939* (1963). A vivid and witty picture of the British ruling classes between the wars.

J. Stevenson, *British Society 1914–1945* (1984). An important new analysis.

D. Thomson, *England in the Twentieth Century, 1914–1963* (1965). A good survey.

Frustrated France

J. Colton, *Léon Blum, Humanist in Politics* (1966). An excellent biography of Blum.

N. Greene, *From Versailles to Vichy: The Third Republic, 1919–1940* (1970). A good survey of France during the period.

The United States and the Great Depression

D. Aldcroft, *From Versailles to Wall Street, 1919–1929* (1977). An excellent economic analysis of the period.

C. Kindleberger, *The World in Depression, 1929–1939* (1986). A good comparative analysis.

G. Perrett, *America in the Twenties* (1982). A good general account.

Disillusionment and Uncertainty in Thought and Culture

J. Willett, *Art and Politics in the Weimar Period: The New Sobriety, 1917–1933* (1978). A broad analysis, well illustrated.

The Road to War

H. Browne, *Spain's Civil War* (1983). A useful analysis.

G. A. Craig and F. Gilbert, eds., *The Diplomats, 1919–1939* (1965). A good collection of essays on international relations.

W. Neuman, *The Balance of Power in the Interwar Years, 1919–1939* (1968). A good study of international relations.

A. Rowse, *Appeasement* (1961). By a bitter eyewitness of British appeasement efforts.

CHAPTER 55
World War II, 1939–1945

FIGURE 55.1 A German Concentration Camp World War II was the most destructive war in history. Of particular brutality were the genocidal programs of Nazi Germany, which resulted in scenes like this one from the Landsberg concentration camp. (AP/Wide World Photos)

To much of the disillusioned and paralyzed democratic world, the outbreak of World War II seemed the beginning of the end of liberal Western civilization. For over two years these dire fears appeared to be justified. The seemingly invincible German and Japanese military machines swept on to victory after victory. Although liberal Western civilization would survive, World War II was by far the most destructive conflict in history. It served as a capstone to the period of unmatched death, loss, disruption, and terror begun by World War I.

1. TWO YEARS OF AXIS TRIUMPH

Striking without official warning at dawn on September 1, 1939, the German air force caught the Polish air force on its various airfields and destroyed it on the ground. Thereafter the German *Luftwaffe*, by ravaging Polish cities and communications centers and harassing troop movements, prevented the complete mobilization of the Polish army. Meanwhile, Nazi tanks and infantry poured into Poland from the north, west, and south. The Poles cried for help from France and Great Britain. The French and the British mobilized their armies along the German West Wall fortifications, and the British fleet blockaded Germany by sea. But that was all. The mechanized might of Nazi Germany overwhelmed Poland in a matter of days.

The Soviet Union, in accordance with its agreement with Hitler, proceeded to reannex territories in Poland and Eastern Europe that it had lost at the end of World War I. Estonia, Latvia, and Lithuania were absorbed politically into the Soviet Union. In October 1939 the Soviet Union demanded three strategic little strips of Finnish territory. When the Finnish government refused, the Soviet Union attacked Finland and took these territories by force. In June 1940, while Hitler was busy in Western Europe, the Soviet Union demanded and procured from Rumania the return of Bessarabia.

Early in April 1940 the Germans suddenly overran Denmark and Norway. The British fleet, attempting to intercept the invasion of Norway, was beaten off with heavy losses by the German air force. Denmark and Norway provided the Nazis with important food, timber, and mineral resources, sea and air bases, and a safe route for vital iron ore coming from Sweden.

On May 10, 1940, the German armies assaulted Luxembourg, the Netherlands, Belgium, and France. Luxembourg offered no resistance. The Netherlands fought heroically but was overwhelmed in six days. Trusting to the Maginot line to hold along the German border, the British army and a large part of the French army moved into Belgium to support the hard-pressed Belgian forces. In a surprise move through the Ardennes forest, powerful German mechanized forces on May 14 smashed through the French defenses at Sedan and drove quickly to the English Channel, cutting off the Belgian, British, and French armies in Belgium. Again the German ''blitzkrieg''—a combination of highly coordinated air strikes and rapid deployment of tanks and motorized columns—proved overwhelming. Although some 300,000 British and a few French troops escaped by sea from Dunkirk, all the Belgian troops, the bulk of the French troops together with their weapons and supplies, and the British weapons and supplies were captured.

Only five more days of fighting, June 5–10, were required for the Germans to crush the remaining organized French resistance and turn the French retreat into a disorderly rout. On June 10 Paris was declared an open city (see Figure 55.2). And on that day Mussolini, thinking it safe, declared war on France and Great Britain. On June 16 Marshal Philippe Pétain became premier of France and the following day dispatched a surrender team to Hitler. On June 25 the ''fighting'' ceased. The collapse of the French military machine after five days of fighting was a colossal military debacle. Hitler forced a harsh treaty on the helpless French. The northern half of France and all the Atlantic coastal area were placed under German occupation. The unoccupied portion was compelled to disarm and cooperate with Germany. Some 2 million French prisoners were held as hostages to ensure French good behavior. In unoccupied France, Marshal Pétain and Pierre Laval set up a semi-Fascist regime, with headquarters at Vichy, and undertook to cooperate with Hitler.

Not all of the French accepted defeat. Many resisted the German army of occupation courageously throughout the war, suffering heavy casualties in doing so. General Charles de Gaulle,

Figure 55.2 Hitler at the Eiffel Tower, Paris, June 1940
The first year of World War II was marked by a series of stunning German victories. In June 1940 Hitler was in Paris. The Eiffel Tower, a symbol of French independence and power, is behind him. (Brown Brothers)

having unsuccessfully attempted to warn his superiors of the unreadiness of the French army, escaped to Great Britain and declared himself leader of the Free French. With energy and skill he strove to rally the French both inside and outside the homeland to resist the Germans and the Vichy collaborators and to restore the dignity and honor of France.

The collapse of France left Great Britain to face the German fury alone. Hitler now demanded that Britain surrender or suffer annihilation. The situation was desperate. Nearly all of Britain's land armaments had been lost at Dunkirk. Against the nearly one hundred fifty battle-tried Nazi divisions, Britain had only one fully equipped division. And although Great Britain did have the English Channel and the world's greatest navy, the fighting around Norway had demonstrated that navies could no longer control narrow waters dominated by a hostile air force. Britain's chief weapon of defense was its relatively small but efficient air force. Not the least of its assets was Winston Churchill, who, on May 10, 1940, had at last replaced Neville Chamberlain as prime minister. The dynamic and eloquent Churchill defied Hitler: "We shall fight on the beaches; we shall fight on the landing grounds; we shall fight in the fields and in the streets; we shall fight in the hills; we shall never surrender."

Throughout the month of July 1940 Nazi invasion forces gathered along the French coast opposite Britain, twenty-four miles away. To make the crossing, however, absolute control of the air over the Channel was required. Early in August, therefore, swarms of German bombers and fighter escorts flew over the Channel, seeking to destroy the British air force and its landing fields. In the ensuing air battles, the British pilots in their swift Spitfires and heavily armed and manueverable Hurricanes knocked down German planes at the ratio of two or three to one. Nevertheless, by the end of August the British air forces were facing annihilation by sheer weight of numbers. At this critical juncture the Nazis suddenly shifted to massive daylight attacks on London, the world's largest city. The destruction and the suffering were immense, but the British defenses were improving, thanks to the use of radar, the total mobilization of the economy, the breaking of the German secret code (project Ultra), and the high morale of the people. The loss of German planes was so great that early in October the Nazis once more shifted their tactics to night attacks, which were more terrifying but less effective. Although the destructive air raids on Great Britain's cities, together with the even more menacing submarine attacks on British shipping, continued until the end of the war, the immediate threat of invasion had now passed (a winter crossing of the Channel would be too risky); the Battle of Britain had been won.

While the Battle of Britain was at its height, Mussolini set into operation his grandiose schemes for conquering an empire. Upon entering the war in June 1940 he had closed the Mediterranean to British shipping. In September his armies moved on Egypt and the Suez Canal from Libya to the west and from Ethiopia to the south. In October his armies attacked Greece from Albania. To meet this threat, Churchill made a daring and farsighted military move. Believing Suez to be the most strategic spot in the world in a global war, he sent half of Britain's scarce supply of tanks and artillery around Africa to Egypt while the Nazis stood poised across the Channel for the invasion of Great Britain. Mussolini's forces met disaster everywhere. The Greeks defeated them and drove them back into Albania. A squadron of British torpedo planes delivered a lethal blow to the Italian fleet at its base in southern Italy. During the winter of 1940–1941 the Fascist armies moving on Egypt were completely destroyed by light, mobile British forces; Mussolini's bubble had burst with a feeble pop; henceforth he was hardly more than a prisoner of the German forces that were sent to save him.

When in October 1940 it became evident that Great Britain could not be invaded that year, Hitler ordered his planners to complete blueprints for the earliest possible invasion of the Soviet Union. The conquest of the Soviet Union had always been uppermost in Hitler's thoughts, but he had hoped first to dispose of the French and British threat to his rear. The plans called for an assault date not later than May 15, 1941. But first the Balkan flank was to be secured. Hungary and Rumania yielded to Hitler's threats and joined the Axis alliance in November 1940; Bulgaria, in March 1941. Immediately Nazi forces poured into those countries. Yugoslavia and Greece, however, refused to yield, and the Germans attacked them in April 1941. Yugoslavia was overrun in eleven days, Greece in three weeks. The British forces that Churchill had dispatched to Greece were driven out of the peninsula and also off the island of Crete. Suez now appeared to be

doomed. It was open to attack from the north; to the west Germany's Afrika Korps, which had been sent to replace the defeated Italians, had driven the British back to the border of Egypt; pro-Nazi movements had broken out in Iraq, Iran, and French Syria. At this point, however, Hitler hurled his main forces against the Soviet Union, giving the British a breathing spell to recoup their strength in the Near and Middle East.

On June 22, 1941, the Germans launched, against the Soviet Union, the most massive assault in history. They were joined by the Hungarians, Rumanians, and Finns. Although Stalin was able to throw an equal number of divisions against the invaders, his troops were not so well trained, led, or equipped. Hitler expected to crush Soviet resistance in six weeks; the top British and American military leaders were of the same opinion. The Russians fought with determination, but the Nazi war machine crunched ever forward until by December 1 it was within sight of Moscow. Leningrad was surrounded, and Rostov, the gateway to the Caucasus oil fields, was captured. The richest and most productive part of the Soviet Union was in German hands. The Russians had suffered such staggering casualties that Hitler announced that the Soviet Union was destroyed and would never rise again. At this point the Japanese entered the war by attacking the United States on December 7, 1941. By that time, however, the Arctic winter, the lack of adequate supplies, and the Soviet counterattacks had forced the Germans to halt and in some places retreat. The Soviet Union was still alive, and the United States was now in the war.

2. THE NAZI EMPIRE

By 1942 Hitler ruled most of continental Europe from the English Channel to Moscow. He had initiated his "New Order"—basically a program of racial imperialism—in the lands he controlled. The conquered peoples were used according to their ranking in Hitler's racial hierarchy. Those most directly related to the Nazi conception of the "Aryan race," such as the Scandinavians, the Anglo-Saxons, and the Dutch, were treated well and would supposedly be absorbed into the Nazi Empire as partners with the Germans. The "Latin races," such as the French, were considered clearly inferior but tolerable as supportive cogs in the New Order. Slavs were toward the bottom of Hitler's ranking; they were to be isolated, shoved aside, and treated like slaves. Large numbers of Russians, Poles, and others were removed from their lands and turned into slave laborers, more often than not perishing under the harsh conditions of their new existence.

Lowest on Hitler's scale were the Jews and such other groups as socialists, gypsies, intellectuals, Jehovah's Witnesses, and the mentally ill. These people were systematically hunted, rounded up, transported to concentration camps, and exterminated. This process was the "Final Solution to the Jewish Problem," and the SS, under Heinrich Himmler, was given the special duty of carrying it out. The quantity and quality of programmed inhumanity, torture, and death were so unprecedented that they could not be believed or understood. While some resistance did take place, Jews were trapped in an extraordinarily powerful system that was thoroughly organized against them. Rebellions within the camps were almost always in vain. Those on the outside who might have done something—the British and Americans who knew and might have bombed gas chambers or railway lines to the camps—did nothing. In the end some 6 million Jews were killed in that systematic, bureaucratized horror along with perhaps another 6 million victims of other groups (see Figure 55.1).

This massive effort to racially reorganize Europe and perpetuate genocidal policies took priority over even the war effort—continuing until the last days of the war and using up needed troops and materials. Indeed, Nazi Germany itself was only partially organized for the military effort in the early years of the war, finally turning to full mobilization after 1942. Under the leadership of Albert Speer, German production multiplied in 1943 and 1944 despite Allied bombing.

The resources and treasures of conquered lands were taken or put under the control of the Nazis and used to further the Nazi war effort and implement the New Order. The Nazis attempted to gain the submission and cooperation of conquered peoples through the use of force and terror. While the Nazis always managed to find collaborators in occupied lands, they were never able to stamp out persistent resistance.

Such resistance movements grew in France, Poland, Denmark, Greece, Yugoslavia—indeed, in almost every occupied territory. They established underground networks, provided intelligence to the Allied forces, conducted guerrilla actions, aided escaping prisoners or Jews, sabotaged military installations, and generally tied down Nazi forces that might have been used on the war fronts.

3. THE UNITED STATES' ENTRY INTO THE WAR

The outbreak of the war in Europe caused hardly a ripple in the isolationist sentiment of the American public and Congress. Most isolationists believed that the French army and Maginot line, together with the British navy, were capable of containing the Nazis.

But suddenly, in May–June 1940, the picture drastically changed. The French army and Maginot line ceased to exist, and the British navy was in grave danger. Much of it would be used up in the defense of Britain in case of invasion. Roosevelt promptly came forward with a three-point program: (1) all-out rearmament, (2) bipartisanship in foreign affairs, (3) all aid short of war to those fighting the Axis (which at the moment meant Great Britain). There was little opposition to the first two points, and Roosevelt managed to overcome objections to aiding the British. American involvement grew from the supply of arms to the convoying of ships across the Atlantic by the American navy. Aid was extended to the Soviet Union, and in June 1941 Axis consulates were closed.

In August 1941 Roosevelt and Churchill met at sea and drawn up the Atlantic Charter, a joint statement of ideals and war purposes. In it appeared such pregnant phrases as "their countries seek no aggrandizement, territorial or other; . . . they respect the right of all peoples to choose the form of government under which they will live; . . . after the final destruction of the Nazi tyranny, . . . the establishment of a wider and permanent system of general security. . . ." The Soviet Union subscribed to the Atlantic Charter shortly afterward. Thus, by October 1941 the United States was engaged in a shooting—but not yet official—war with Germany and was in a virtual alliance

FIGURE 55.3 Pearl Harbor
On December 7, 1941, the Japanese attacked Pearl Harbor, Hawaii, and destroyed the Pacific fleet in the harbor and the air force on the ground. The attack brought the United States into the war. This photo shows the USS *California* as it went down. (UPI/Bettmann Newsphotos)

with Great Britain, one of the belligerents. The American people's eyes were on the Atlantic, where at any moment some new German act of aggression might make war official and total.

It was not in the Atlantic, however, but in the Pacific that the history-changing blow was struck; and not by Germany, but by Japan. Early in 1939 the Japanese, having conquered all the populous coastal areas of China and having driven Chiang Kai-shek's forces far into the Chinese interior, turned southward toward the territories of Southeast Asia and the southwest Pacific. These territories, rich in rubber, tin, rice, copra, and oil, belonged (with the exception of independent Thailand) to France, the Netherlands, Great Britain, and the United States. Since the French, Dutch, and British had their hands full in Europe with the growing Nazi menace, President Roosevelt transferred the American fleet from the Atlantic to Pearl Harbor in Hawaii as a deterrent to further Japanese aggression. He also gave the Japanese the required six months' notice of the termination of the commercial treaty

of 1911. These moves appear to have given the Japanese pause.

In 1940, however, after Hitler's conquest of France and the Netherlands and threatened conquest of Great Britain, the Japanese became much bolder. They took advantage of France's helplessness to occupy northern French Indochina and threatened the Dutch East Indies. But in the following year, 1941, when the Germans overran the Balkans and launched what promised to be a lethal attack on the Soviet Union, the Japanese leaders decided that the day of Axis world triumph was at hand.

Tensions rose between Japan and the United States. Finally, on December 7, 1941, a large squadron of Japanese bombers and torpedo planes took off from carriers in a position north of Hawaii and caught the American fleet anchored in Pearl Harbor by surprise (see Figure 55.3). With little loss to themselves, the Japanese planes crippled the American navy in the Pacific and destroyed the air force in Hawaii on the ground. In rapid succession Japan and the

United States declared war on each other, and within four days the United States was at war with the other Axis powers.

4. THE HOME FRONT

As in World War I, it became necessary to mobilize not only the armed forces of a nation but the society as a whole for the war effort. Governments took greater control over their economies than in peacetime. Civilians had to live with hardship so that supplies could be produced for the armed forces. As labor shortages arose, women were asked to assume jobs normally reserved for men. Political executives assumed more powers than they usually held, political dissent was discouraged, and propaganda was used to support the efforts on the home front as well as the battlefield.

Not all the nations involved mobilized their home fronts to the same degree. Great Britain and the Soviet Union did the most, reflecting the fact that these two nations were most threatened in the early years of the war. Germany was slower to mobilize its home front fully, in the early years relying on quick victories and spoils from conquered lands to support its needs. The United States, less threatened by the war, mobilized more slowly and unevenly.

The circumstances of World War II made the home front experience different than in World War I in some important, frightening ways. New military technologies and strategies made civilians targets as never before. This was demonstrated most clearly in the German bombing of British cities and the Allied bombing of German cities. In Dresden alone, three days of Allied bombing in 1945 resulted in some one hundred thousand deaths, most of them civilians. Even worse were the civilian deaths caused by the atomic bombs dropped on Hiroshima and Nagasaki (see Figure 55.4). Internally, certain groups of civilians were made to suffer far more than others. The Nazis followed a policy of racial imperialism and extermination in their lands (see pp. 692–693). In the United States, Japanese Americans on the West Coast were removed from their homes and businesses and placed into camps. In various occupied areas of Europe, re-

sistance movements blurred the lines between the military and civilian spheres (see p. 693).

5. THE CLIMAX AND TURNING POINT OF THE WAR, JUNE–AUGUST 1942

The entry of the United States, with its enormous resources and industrial potential, changed the whole complexion of the war. Together with the totally mobilized British economy and the massive economic and military resources of the Soviet Union, the long-term advantage was now clearly on the side of the Allies. However, many months would be required to mobilize America's resources, and the Axis was determined to win decisively before that mobilization could be achieved (see Map 55.1). To bring about Allied solidarity, Churchill hastened to Washington, where, on January 1, 1942, he and Roosevelt launched the United Nations Alliance. Twenty-six nations, of which the United States, Great Britain, and the Soviet Union were the Big Three, promised to give their all to the common effort, to make no separate peace, and to abide by the principles of the Atlantic Charter. By the end of the war, the number of member nations had risen to forty-seven.

The now-global war was fought in three major theaters: (1) the Soviet Union, (2) the Mediterranean and western Europe, and (3) the Pacific. The Axis powers made their climactic bid for victory on all three fronts between June and August 1942. The biggest front in terms of numbers of troops, weapons, and casualties involved was that in the Soviet Union. Despite frightful losses, the Soviets had managed to keep their army intact and to relocate or rebuild their wartime factories. The Soviet people were unified against the foreign aggressors in what they called the "Great Patriotic War of the Fatherland." The Germans, after having been stopped in December 1941 by the Russian winter and the counterattacks, resumed their forward thrust in June 1942, this time in the southern sector. Refreshed and reequipped, they seemed irresistible. By August they had reached the outskirts of Stalingrad on the Volga. Here Stalin ordered a stand; the battle of Stalingrad raged for six months. In Feb-

FIGURE 55.4 Hiroshima after A-Bomb This photo of Hiroshima, taken shortly after the first atom bomb was dropped, shows the incredible destructive power of atomic weapons. (Sygma)

ruary 1943, the Russians, having closed a pincer behind the Germans in Stalingrad, captured all who had not been killed of an army of almost three hundred thousand men. This action was the turning point; the Germans began a slow but general retreat.

The crucial battle on the Mediterranean and Western European front was fought in Egypt. General Rommel's tough Afrika Korps in its first drive on Suez in 1941 had been stopped and pushed back into Libya by the British. In June 1942 Rommel's forces, greatly strengthened, struck the British desert forces a shattering blow and chased them in near rout to El Alamein, only sixty-five miles from Alexandria. Suez seemed doomed, and the British fleet prepared to evacuate the Mediterranean before it could be bottled up. Churchill rushed to the scene and put in a

team of winning commanders: Sir Harold Alexander in overall command and General Bernard Montgomery as field commander. In August Rommel's forces assaulted the British positions at El Alamein and were stopped. A race to build up men and supplies ensued; the British, with massive aid from the United States, won. Late in October 1942 Montgomery's superior Eighth Army attacked Rommel's forces and, after a desperate battle, drove them back across the desert in defeat. Suez and the Middle East were now saved from the Axis, and for the first time Great Britain and the United States were in a position to assume the offensive.

President Roosevelt had agreed with Churchill that the first priority should be defeating Germany, which represented the gravest threat. Therefore the United States concentrated most of

Sequence of German Expansion to 1942
1. Austria, Czechoslovakia, Poland, 1939
2. 1940, Denmark, Norway
3. 1940, Low Countries, France
4. 1940-1941, Balkans
5. 1942-1943, Russian Front
6. 1942, Vichy

Axis Powers, 1939

Greater Germany, 1942

Areas of Axis Control, 1942

German Allies

Neutral Countries

Areas Annexed by Russia, 1939-1940

Pre-1939 Political Boundaries

0   200   400 miles

ICELAND

SWEDEN

NORWAY 2
Oslo
Stockholm

FINLAND
(June 1941)
Helsinki

Leningrad

SOVIET UNION

NORTH SEA

ESTONIA
Riga LATVIA
LITHUANIA

Moscow

Glasgow
Edinburgh
Belfast
IRELAND
Dublin
GREAT BRITAIN
Coventry
London
Amsterdam

DENMARK 2
Copenhagen
DANZIG
EAST PRUSSIA

Smolensk

INVASION OF LOW COUNTRIES
(May 29–June 2, 1940)
NETHERLANDS
Brussels 3
BELGIUM
DUNKIRK EVACUATION
(May 29–June 2, 1940)
Paris

GERMANY
Berlin
Warsaw
POLAND
(September 1939)

Kiev

Stalingrad

ATLANTIC OCEAN

LUX.
Maginot Line
3
FRANCE
(June 1940)
Vichy
6

Nuremberg
Munich
SWITZ.
Bern
Milan

CZECHOSLOVAKIA
(To Germany 1938)
AUSTRIA
(To Germany 1938)
HUNGARY
Budapest

RUMANIA
(November 1940)

BESSARABIA

5

CASPIAN SEA

Marseilles

Belgrade
YUGOSLAVIA

Bucharest

BLACK SEA

Sevastopol

PORTUGAL
Lisbon
SPAIN
Madrid
NATIONALIST VICTORY
(April 1939)

CORSICA
Rome
ITALY
Naples
SARDINIA

ALBANIA
(To Italy 1939)
GREECE
Athens

BULGARIA
Sofia

Istanbul
Ankara

TURKEY

IRAN
(To Great Britain and Russia 1941)

SPANISH MOROCCO
Casablanca
Oran
MOROCCO
(France)

Algiers
Tunis
SICILY

MALTA
(Great Britain)

CRETE
(May 1941)

CYPRUS
(Great Britain)

LEBANON
(France)
PALESTINE
(Great Britain)

SYRIA
(To Great Britain 1941)

IRAQ
(To Great Britain 1941)

TRANSJORDAN
(Great Britain)

TUNISIA
(France)
Tripoli

MEDITERRANEAN SEA

Benghazi
Tobruk
El Alamein
Cairo

ALGERIA
(France)

LIBYA (Italy)

EGYPT

SAUDI ARABIA

Map 55.1 EUROPE, 1942 This map shows the furthest extent of Axis power during World War II. By the end of the year German expansion had been stopped at Stalingrad in the east and Egypt in North Africa.

its efforts toward Europe, which made the war in the Pacific more difficult and predominantly naval in character.

Three days after Pearl Harbor, Japanese carrier-based torpedo planes struck the British Asiatic fleet a crippling blow in the Gulf of Siam. Now, with unchallenged mastery of the Pacific, the Japanese within the space of a few months were able to conquer a vast area in the Southwest Pacific and Southeast Asia with relative ease. The American islands of Wake, Guam, and the Philippines; British Hong Kong, Malaya, Singapore, and Burma; and the Dutch East Indies were overrun. In May 1942 Japanese naval forces were turned back by the Americans in the Battle of the Coral Sea, northeast of Australia. However, the main Japanese fleet was preparing a major thrust at Hawaii, which it could easily have made immediately after Pearl Harbor. The U.S. navy, which had broken the Japanese code, massed for an all-out battle. Early in June 1942, just as the Stalingrad and El Alamein campaigns were beginning, the two powerful naval forces came within carrier plane range of each other off Midway Island, a thousand miles west of Hawaii. The climactic Battle of Midway was fought at long range entirely by aircraft and submarines. American planes sank all four of the Japanese carriers, while the Japanese were able to destroy only one of three American carriers. Pounded from the air and without air cover, the Japanese commander ordered a retreat, never to become so bold again. In August 1942 the Americans assumed the offensive by attacking Guadalcanal in the Solomon Islands northeast of Australia. By that time, it was evident that the tide was beginning to turn on all three fronts.

6. VICTORY

Although the greatest crises had passed by the end of 1942, two and a half more years of bloody fighting were required to subdue the Axis. In fact, the defeat of the Axis could not have been achieved at all without a high degree of cooperation among the Big Three allies. President Roosevelt, with his winsome personality, played an important part in maintaining mutual confidence and cooperation among the Allied powers, which were so divergent in their ideologies and specific interests. The chief planners of the coordinated global strategy were Churchill for Great Britain, Stalin for the Soviet Union, and Army Chief of Staff George Marshall for the United States.

The Russian Front

The Battle of Russia was the greatest and most destructive battle in history. Some 9 million men (five hundred divisions) were engaged. For two and a half years after Stalingrad, the Germans were slowly beaten back, doggedly contesting every foot of ground. At last, in April 1945, the Russians entered Berlin. Along the fifteen hundred miles between Stalingrad and Berlin lay the wreckage of the greater part of Hitler's war machine. But the richest and most productive part of the Soviet Union lay devastated. At least 20 million Russians had been killed—possibly many more.

The Mediterranean and Western European Front

In November 1942, just as the Germans were beginning to retreat from El Alamein, a combined Anglo-American force under the command of General Dwight D. Eisenhower landed in French North Africa. Early in 1943, the converging forces of Eisenhower and Montgomery cornered the Afrika Korps in Tunisia, where it surrendered in May.

Meanwhile, most of the threats from German submarines and planes were being eliminated as the British and Americans gained in the air and on the seas. Massive bombing raids pounded Germany. The distinction between strategic military targets and civilian populations blurred as Germany's cities were leveled.

In July 1943 the Anglo-American forces conquered the island of Sicily, which they used as a base for the invasion of southern Italy. Mussolini was forced to resign on July 25, and Italy surrendered. However, the peninsula was held by strong German forces. By the end of 1943 the Allies had reached Cassino Pass, about seventy-five miles south of Rome. At this point, the major objectives in the Mediterranean area had been achieved, and Eisenhower, along with most of his forces, was transferred to Great Britain to

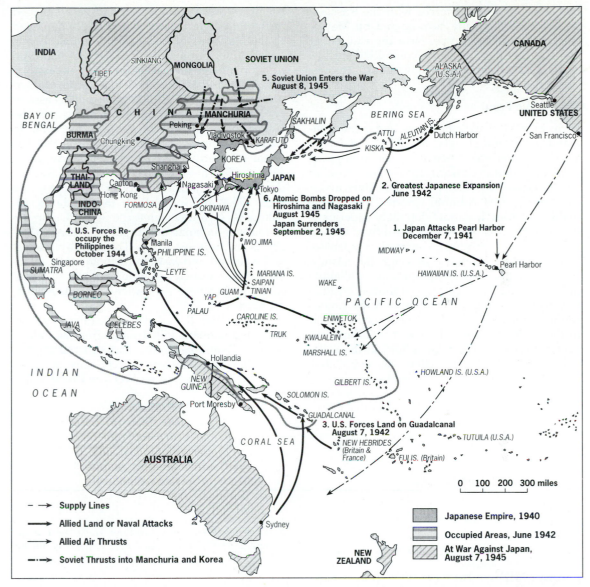

INDIA

SINKIANG **MONGOLIA** **SOVIET UNION**

TIBET

5. Soviet Union Enters the War August 8, 1945

C H I N A **MANCHURIA** SAKHALIN

BAY OF BENGAL Peking KARAFUTO

BURMA Chungking Vladivostok

Shanghai **KOREA**

THAI-LAND Canton Nagasaki Hiroshima **JAPAN**

Hong Kong Tokyo

INDO-CHINA *FORMOSA* OKINAWA

4. U.S. Forces Re-occupy the Philippines October 1944 Manila *PHILIPPINE IS.*

Singapore

SUMATRA LEYTE

BORNEO YAP *GUAM TINIAN* *WAKE*

PALAU *MARIANA IS.* *SAIPAN*

JAVA *CELEBES* CAROLINE IS. *ENIWETOK*

TRUK KWAJALEIN

Hollandia *MARSHALL IS.*

NEW GUINEA *GILBERT IS.*

INDIAN OCEAN

Port Moresby *SOLOMON IS.*

CORAL SEA GUADALCANAL

3. U.S. Forces Land on Guadalcanal August 7, 1942

NEW HEBRIDES (Britain & France)

AUSTRALIA *FIJI IS. (Britain)*

Sydney

CANADA

ALASKA (U.S.A.)

BERING SEA Seattle **UNITED STATES**

ATTU *ALEUTIAN IS.* Dutch Harbor San Francisco

KISKA

2. Greatest Japanese Expansion June 1942

6. Atomic Bombs Dropped on Hiroshima and Nagasaki August 1945

Japan Surrenders September 2, 1945

1. Japan Attacks Pearl Harbor December 7, 1941

MIDWAY Pearl Harbor

HAWAIIAN IS. (U.S.A.)

P A C I F I C   O C E A N

HOWLAND IS. (U.S.A.)

TUTUILA (U.S.A.)

NEW ZEALAND

- - → Supply Lines
⟶ Allied Land or Naval Attacks
→ Allied Air Thrusts
- ·→ Soviet Thrusts into Manchuria and Korea

0 100 200 300 miles

Japanese Empire, 1940
Occupied Areas, June 1942
At War Against Japan, August 7, 1945

Map 55.2 THE PACIFIC WAR This map shows the furthest extent of Japanese expansion, attained in June 1942, and the course of the American counterattack across the Pacific islands toward the Japanese mainland between 1942 and 1945.

---

command the main Anglo-American thrust across the Channel.

This thrust came on June 6, 1944. Thanks in large measure to complete Allied mastery of the skies, successful landings were made on the Normandy coast. After a rapid buildup, the Anglo-

American forces broke out of the beachhead and before the end of the year cleared practically all of France. Germany, meanwhile, was being pulverized from the air. Early in 1945, the American and British forces, now joined by French units, broke through the German West Wall, crossed the Rhine, and joined forces with the Russians on the Elbe. Germany surrendered on May 8, ending the war in Europe. Near the end, Hitler and several other top Nazis committed suicide, and Mussolini was shot by Italian partisans.

The Pacific Front

Early in 1943, American forces under the command of General Douglas MacArthur and with a strong naval escort began an island-hopping campaign northwestward from their base in Australia (see Map 55.2). At the same time, under the command of Admiral Chester Nimitz, the main American fleet, now definitely superior to the Japanese fleet, thrust westward from Hawaii toward Japan, capturing the numerous Japanese-held islands in its path. Although the islands, many of them covered by jungles, were bloodily defended, the American forces moved steadily toward Japan itself. In October 1944 the American forces made a bold landing on Leyte Island in the Philippines, which brought the Japanese fleet out for a last desperate effort. In the Battle of Leyte Gulf, the Japanese fleet was annihilated. Cut off, uncovered, and subjected to ceaseless air and sea attacks, Japan was doomed. After Germany surrendered in May 1945, American, Brit-

ish, and Russian troops that had been engaged in the European theater were rapidly deployed to the Far East. In mid-July the atomic bomb, which American and British scientists had been developing for several years, was successfully completed and tested. The United States wanted to avoid the heavy casualties that a direct assault on the Japanese home islands would cause. The United States thus decided to use the bomb to shock Japan into surrender, a decision that has remained controversial ever since. On August 6, 1945, the first atomic bomb to be used in warfare destroyed the Japanese city of Hiroshima (see Figure 55.4) and some eighty thousand of its inhabitants. Two days later, the Soviet Union declared war on Japan and began to overrun Manchuria and northern Korea. The next day, August 9, the second and last atomic bomb then in existence demolished the industrial city of Nagasaki. The Japanese surrendered five days later, on August 14, 1945.

World War II had ended. Estimates of soldiers and civilians killed range from 30 million to 50 million; even more had suffered injuries from the war. Western society now faced an overwhelming task of recovery and reorganization.

SUGGESTED READING

General

B. Liddell Hart, *History of the Second World War* (1980). A good military history.

J. Keegan, *The Second World War* (1990). A lively recent survey.

D. Watt, *How War Came: The Immediate Origins of the Second World War* (1989). A step-by-step account.

G. Wright, *The Ordeal of Total War, 1939–1945* (1968). A thoughtful analysis; goes far beyond the military aspects.

Two Years of Axis Triumph

W. Churchill, *Their Finest Hour* (1949). The second and best of Churchill's great six-volume history of the war. Covers the defeat of France and the Battle of Britain.

M. Dziewanowski, *War at Any Price: World War II in Europe, 1939–1945* (1987). Has good chapters on the period.

The Nazi Empire

A. Dallin, *German Rule in Russia, 1941–1945* (1957). A good analysis.

L. Dawidowicz, *The War Against the Jews, 1933–1945* (1976). A thorough study.

T. Des Pres, *The Survivors* (1976). A good analysis of life in Hitler's concentration camps.

J. Haestrup, *Europe Ablaze* (1978). A thorough study of the resistance movements.

R. Hilberg, *The Destruction of the European Jews*, 3 vols. (1985). An exhaustive account.

M. Marrus, *The Holocaust in History* (1987). Covers all aspects.

The Entry of the United States

A. R. Buchanan, *The United States and World War II*, 2 vols. (1964). A good survey.

J. Campbell, ed., *The Experience of World War II* (1989). Good sections on this topic.

A. Iriye, *The Origins of the Second World War in Asia and the Pacific* (1987). An in-depth analysis.

Allied Victory

M. Sherwin, *A World Destroyed: The Atomic Bomb and the Grand Alliance* (1975). Analyzes the final years of the war and the role of the atomic bomb.

J. Toland, *The Last Hundred Days* (1966). A fine account of the end.

CHAPTER 56
The Recovery of Europe and the Superpowers, 1945–1980s

FIGURE 56.1 The Division Between East and West The post–World War II division between East and West in Europe is symbolized by the Berlin Wall and the Brandenburg Gate in Berlin, blocked by barbed wire and troops in 1961. (AP/Wide World Photos)

In 1945 much of Europe was in ashes. Disorganization was the rule, and effective governments were often virtually nonexistent. The economic destruction was so great that the immediate problem was not so much how to rebuild factories and initiate economic growth but how to minimize the starvation that faced millions and create shelter for the dislocated. The European nations would revive with amazing speed and go on to establish new patterns of relative political stability and economic growth. However, before that could happen, Europeans had to deal with the immediate problems of the settlement of World War II and the beginnings of the Cold War.

1. THE SETTLEMENT AND THE COLD WAR

In 1945 the leaders of the victorious nations were confronted with the tasks of making a lasting peace and restoring a shattered world. From the beginning these tasks were hampered by hostility between the United States and the Soviet Union. This hostility, which came to be called the "Cold War," pervaded and poisoned every area of postwar international relations. To understand the nature of the peace settlement and the origins of the Cold War, one must go back to the conferences held by the Allies during the war and to the legacy of assumptions held by participants in those conferences.

Legacy of Assumptions

Although Great Britain, the United States, and the Soviet Union had been cooperating allies during most of World War II, they approached one another with differing perceptions and a history of distrust. Since the Communists had come to power in Russia in 1917, the leaders of the Soviet Union and the capitalist democracies had viewed each other as opponents. As ideologies, communism and capitalism had always been in direct opposition. As practiced in the Soviet Union under Lenin and Stalin, communism took a totalitarian form, in sharp contrast to the democracies of Great Britain and the United States. Specific developments between the Russian Revolution of 1917 and World War II added to the hostility between the Soviet Union and the capitalist democracies. During the Russian civil war, the Western nations had supported anti-Bolshevik forces with materials and some troops. The United States had not recognized the Bolshevik government until 1933. The Soviet Union had not even been invited to the Munich Conference of 1938. In viewing the rise of Fascist and authoritarian governments during the 1920s and 1930s, many in the Western democracies found consolation in the opposition of these governments to communism. In the 1930s, the Western democracies failed to ally with the Soviet Union against the growing threat of Nazi Germany. In 1939 Stalin entered into an astonishing pact with Hitler, enabling Nazi forces to concentrate on western Europe during the first years of World War II.

Hitler's invasion of the Soviet Union and the entry of the United States into the war united Great Britain, the United States, and the Soviet Union as allies more in opposition to Nazi Germany than in agreement over principles or goals. When concrete negotiations for war aims and terms of a settlement took place, the history of hostility, distrust, and fear between the capitalist and Communist powers caused problems. These problems would increase after the war, when the threat of Nazi Germany would no longer hold the Allies together.

The Conferences and the Settlement

The decisions that led to the peace settlements, that helped shape Europe in the immediate postwar years, and that laid the groundwork for the Cold War were made in a series of conferences held by the leaders of Great Britain, the United States, and the Soviet Union. The first conference took place in December 1943 at Teheran. There, Churchill's plan to open a front in Eastern Europe, which would have given Great Britain and the United States more influence there, was rejected. Eastern Europe was open to the advancing Soviet troops.

The next meeting of the three heads of state was in February 1945 at Yalta. They agreed to divide Germany into four occupation zones and to occupy Germany for a long time. Concerning

FIGURE 56.2 Allied Leaders at Yalta With victory over the Axis in sight, the terms of the settlement were negotiated at the Yalta Conference, February 1945. Churchill, Roosevelt, and Stalin, representing the Big Three Allied powers, made a series of agreements concerning the major postwar problems. (UPI/Bettmann Newsphotos)

Eastern Europe, Stalin argued that the area was already behind Soviet lines and was vital to his nation's security: The Soviet Union had been invaded through these countries in both world wars, and many of them had been Hitler's allies. Therefore, he asserted, the Soviet Union should maintain a measure of control over these countries. Roosevelt and Churchill insisted that these countries must be given complete independence. These disagreements were not resolved at Yalta nor at the last meeting, held in July 1945 at Potsdam (see Figure 56.2).

While the war ended in 1945 with a complete victory for the Allies, the basis of postwar problems was already present. The legacy of distrust and hostility between Communist Russia and the capitalist West had not been eradicated by the temporary period of cooperation during the war years. Decisions and disagreements at the wartime conferences had resulted in resentments and accusations on both sides, particularly over Eastern Europe. Faced with the reality of Eastern Europe's being behind Soviet lines, Great Britain and the United States were at a disadvantage. Europe, though struggling to recover, was already politically divided. Political divisions would merge into Cold War divisions in the years following 1945.

The Cold War

The Cold War was the struggle between the United States and the Soviet Union, each supported by its respective non-Communist and Communist allies, that colored international relations during the four decades following World War II (see Map 56.1). On the one side the Soviet Union strove to secure itself from external threats and to spread its version of communism to the border states and elsewhere in the world. On the other side the United States strove to contain Soviet influence and to counter Communist threats wherever they were perceived throughout the world. It was a war fought in almost all ways except open military conflict, and the threat of military force was always present. At times, the Cold War became violent, but the two superpowers never came together in direct armed combat.

For the most part, the fragile spirit of cooperation between the Western democracies and the Soviet Union was broken by developments

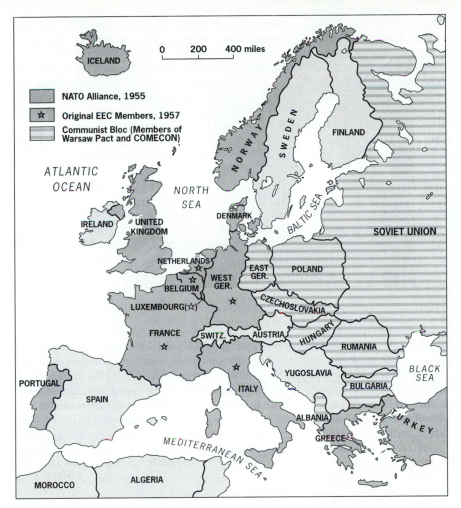

Map 56.1 EUROPE DURING THE COLD WAR This map indicates the Cold War divisions in Europe during the 1950s. With some exceptions, the nations of Western Europe joined NATO, a non-Communist military organization headed by the United States. Also with a few exceptions, nations in Eastern Europe joined the Warsaw Pact, a Communist military organization headed by the Soviet Union.

in Eastern Europe. The United States and its allies felt that wartime agreements and a sense of justice should compel the Soviet Union to allow free elections in Eastern European states, all of which should be independent of Soviet control. The Soviet Union felt that these same wartime agreements and a higher sense of justice recognized the overriding need for the Soviet Union to make sure the Eastern European states remained friendly and under Soviet influence. The United States became increasingly outraged when developments in Eastern Europe went Stalin's way. By 1950 all the states of Eastern Europe were controlled by Communists and, with the

exception of Yugoslavia under Josip Broz Tito, were dominated by the Soviet Union.

The struggles over Eastern Europe spread to Western Europe, where strong Communist parties in France and Italy pursued policies approved by Moscow. The United States and its allies feared that these parties would subvert non-Communist governments and help spread Soviet control further south and west.

The verbal denunciations and discord over events in Europe were accompanied by a breakdown of cooperation between the United States and the Soviet Union. President Truman, who succeeded Roosevelt on April 12, 1945, was in favor of a tougher policy toward the Soviet Union. In May he cut off aid to the Soviet Union. When the possibility of international control of atomic weapons arose, the Americans and Russians could not agree. This led to the nuclear weapons race, which has flourished ever since.

The breakdown of cooperation was most striking in Germany. In accordance with the Potsdam agreements, most of Germany was divided into four occupation zones: American, Russian, British, and French. Berlin, which was in the Russian zone, was divided into four sectors and made the headquarters of a four-power coordinating commission. Sharp cleavages soon developed among the occupying powers, particularly between the United States and the Soviet Union. The Soviet Union, having suffered more at the hands of Germany during World Wars I and II than any other major nation, was determined to keep Germany permanently weak and as much as possible under Soviet domination. The United States, on the other hand, having little fear of Germany and seeing it as a valuable potential ally against the Soviet Union, set out to restore and rearm the nation. Matters came to a head in 1948–1949. In March 1948 the United States, having succeeded in merging the three western zones and stepping up their economy to a level much higher than that agreed upon at Potsdam, announced plans for the creation of an independent West German state. To the Soviet leaders, this was the last straw. They attempted to dissuade the Western powers from going ahead with the project by blockading the three western zones of Berlin in the hope of starving them out. For eleven months, from June 1948 to May 1949, the Soviets stopped all land traffic across their zone from the West to Berlin. The Western powers defeated the blockade through a giant airlift. The United States proceeded to set up the German Federal Republic, which began to function in September 1949. One month later the Soviet Union set up the German Democratic Republic in its zone.

Meanwhile, new policies were raising the Cold War to a higher level. In 1947 President Truman initiated a policy of military containment called the Truman Doctrine, which meant that the United States would draw a military ring around the Soviet Union and its satellites. His secretary of state, George Marshall, supplemented the Truman Doctrine with the Marshall Plan, a package of economic aid to European nations designed to strengthen them and tie them to American influence. Two years later the United States organized the North Atlantic Treaty Organization (NATO), which was a military alliance among the United States, Canada, and most of the nations of Western Europe against the Soviet Union (see p. 717).

The Soviet Union responded by establishing the Council for Mutual Economic Assistance (COMECON), a Soviet "Marshall Plan" for Eastern Europe. In the following years the Soviet Union continued to strengthen its military ties with its allies, eventually countering NATO by establishing the Warsaw Pact organization.

By 1950 one stage of the Cold War was completed. Europe was clearly divided into a Communist camp in the east under the control of the Soviet Union and a non-Communist camp in the west under the leadership of the United States. The Cold War would continue in different ways and with varying intensity over the next four decades. Both sides were pitted against each other in a worldwide war of propaganda. Political struggles almost anywhere, whether purely internal matters or not, became potential fields for a victory or defeat in a Cold War competition. This competition expanded to the non-Western world and to a variety of fields not usually thought of as political, from the exploration of space to the Olympic games.

In 1950 the Korean War shifted the focus of the Cold War from Europe to the non-Western world. It also revealed how real the risk of military combat was in the struggle between Communist and non-Communist forces. In the mid-1950s there were some signs of a relaxation in the Cold War. Stalin died in 1953, and later that year an armistice was signed in Korea. The Soviet government made overtures to the United States to end the Cold War. In 1955 Soviet troops left Austria, which became an independent, neutral state. That same year a conference was held in Geneva among the leaders of Great Britain, France, the United States, and the Soviet Union. Little of substance was accomplished, but at least it symbolized an effort to solve problems peacefully. Talk of "peaceful coexistence" between the superpowers became popular and seemed confirmed when the two powers agreed to talks for a nuclear test ban treaty in 1958.

This apparent thaw in the Cold War was mitigated by some chilling developments. In the same year that Stalin died, John Foster Dulles became U.S. secretary of state in the new Eisenhower administration. It was his belief that all communism was a Moscow-directed conspiracy bent upon world conquest. The time had come, he proclaimed, to pass over from containment to liberation. The United States tried to apply the lessons learned in the struggles over Eastern Europe and Korea to Southeast Asia, where the French had lost to Communist-led insurgents in Vietnam. Efforts to hold a meeting between the American and Soviet heads of state in 1960 broke down amid Cold War accusations. In 1961 irritations over Germany were exacerbated by the construction of the Berlin Wall, which sealed off democratic West Berlin from East Berlin and the rest of Communist East Germany (see Figure 56.1). In 1962 the Cuban missile crisis, a Cold War confrontation over the placement of Russian missiles in Cuba, came close to erupting into a real war.

Nevertheless, the 1960s and most of the 1970s witnessed a general lessening of tensions in the Cold War. A nuclear test ban treaty between the two powers was signed in 1963, and strategic arms limitation talks were initiated in 1969. After 1969 relations between the United States and the Soviet Union were often described by the word *détente*, which emphasized cooperation rather than confrontation.

In the later 1970s and early 1980s events proved that the Cold War was not over. The increasing ties between Communist China and the United States were perceived as a threat by the Soviet Union. When Jimmy Carter became president in 1977, the Soviet leaders quickly took offense at his insistence on the granting of human rights throughout the world, including the Soviet Union, and they were uncomfortable with his more open style of diplomacy. A Soviet invasion of Afghanistan in 1979 led to an American boycott of the Olympic Games in 1980 and an embargo on grain shipments to the Soviet Union. The Reagan administration took a much tougher stand toward the Soviet Union and communism

in general, reviving Cold War rhetoric and dramatically increasing arms production. In the 1980s the Polish crisis, American attempts to limit exportation of certain technology and materials by Western nations to the Soviet Union, the deployment of new American missiles in Europe, the American Strategic Defense Initiative, and the rejection of the 1979 Strategic Arms Limitation Treaty heightened the tensions between the two powers.

2. REVIVAL OF A DIVIDED EUROPE AND THE WEST

Within the context of the Cold War struggle, Europe survived the difficult years immediately following World War II, recovered by the 1950s, and grew in new directions in the following decades. Yet there was a fundamental division between west and east in Europe, with Western Europe turning toward parliamentary democracy and support from the United States and Eastern Europe turning toward communism and support from the Soviet Union.

Western Europe

After World War II the nations of Western Europe returned to liberal democratic forms of government. The political parties of the center generally came to power. On the Continent the Christian Democratic parties were particularly strong in France, West Germany, and Italy. They had ties to traditional prewar conservative parties but became more progressive after World War II. They stood for democracy, economic growth, moderate social reform, antifascism, and anticommunism. Their main competitors were a variety of moderate, democratic Socialist parties with ties to traditional prewar Socialist parties. With the exception of Great Britain, where the Labour party came to power in 1945, these Socialist parties usually found themselves in opposition rather than in power. Initially, Communist parties were also strong, but after 1947, when the Cold War heated up, these parties were systematically excluded from participation in national governments.

While the United States emerged from World

War II economically strong, the postwar European governments were faced with the tremendous task of leading their countries to economic and social recovery. After the first few very difficult years, when hunger and dislocation were more a rule than an exception, Western Europe entered into a period of strong economic recovery lasting well into the 1960s. The economic recovery was fueled by money from the American Marshall Plan, pent-up demand since the beginning of the war for goods and services, cheap skilled labor, and a surprisingly high birthrate. Different mixtures of national planning and free enterprise were used to direct the recovery. International cooperation, such as the Organization of European Economic Cooperation (OEEC) and the European Coal and Steel Community, and the already high level of industrial and technological sophistication attained by Western Europeans, facilitated the recovery. Accompanying economic growth were government social policies providing for health care, unemployment relief, old-age benefits, and family support.

In the late 1960s and 1970s new problems appeared. The economic growth of the 1950s and early 1960s leveled off. Inflation became widespread, particularly after 1973, when oil prices started a dramatic rise. At the same time, growth rates started to decline and unemployment began to rise. This "stagflation"—economic stagnation coupled with sharp inflation—persisted into the 1980s. Partial recovery in the mid-1980s, led by the United States, was uneven and purchased at a high price. Governmental deficits and problems with trade balances became common in the West. Nevertheless, a huge amount and array of new goods and services were produced and consumed in the decades after World War II. Far greater access to and use of consumer debt, particularly charge cards, enabled consumers to buy quickly and try to pay for it later. Electric household appliances, home entertainment equipment, and, more recently, computer and home office machines spread into homes throughout the West. Far more tourists than ever vacationed in foreign lands.

Social dissatisfaction was evidenced in a variety of movements, from the student protests of the late 1960s to the radical separatist movements of the 1970s and 1980s. Most dramatic was the increase of terrorism, which was used as a political tactic by desperate groups such as the Provisional Wing of the Irish Republican Army (IRA), the West German Baader-Meinhof gang, the Italian Red Brigades, and the Palestine Liberation Organization (PLO). While the period cannot be called one of political instability, voters often turned out incumbent parties in hopes that the opposition parties could solve problems. Socialist parties that came to power seemed to have as much trouble dealing with apparently intractable problems as their conservative counterparts.

These general trends and variations of them can best be understood by examining developments in some individual countries between 1945 and the present.

Great Britain

In Great Britain the Labour party swept to victory in elections held in July 1945, just as the war was coming to an end. Clement Attlee succeeded Churchill as prime minister. The problems confronting Britain and the Labour government were indeed formidable. More than half of Great Britain's merchant marine had been sunk; a third of its buildings had been destroyed or damaged; its foreign investments had been liquidated and used up; Great Britain owed the United States a huge debt; and its empire was tottering. The Labour government strictly rationed the short supplies, raised taxes on the rich, and lowered taxes on the poor. It nationalized the Bank of England, the coal mines, the electrical and gas industries, inland transportation, and the steel industry. Altogether, some 20 percent of Britain's economy was socialized. A vast program of social security, public education, public housing, and national health insurance was launched. The dismantling of the British Empire was begun—India, the biggest of all of Britain's colonial prizes, was given its independence in 1947 (see Chapter 58). The six years of Labour rule were years of austerity for the middle and upper classes. However, the general morale of the people was high, and Britain recovered.

Unfortunately, Great Britain's economic condition was fundamentally unsound. The loss of its overseas investments and resources and of the income from most of its prewar shipping, together with the antiquated state of most of its mines and factories, left Britain far short of the funds needed for war repair, debt repayment, and social services. By 1949 the serious deficit in the balance of trade had become apparent, followed by a weakening of the pound and mounting inflation. Rising discontent enabled Churchill and the Conservatives to return to power in 1951. With the exception of denationalizing the steel and trucking industries, they tampered little with the Labour party's program, most of which the great majority of the British people now clearly favored.

But neither the Conservatives, who governed Britain from 1951 to 1964 and again from 1970 to 1974, nor the Labourites, who governed from 1964 to 1970 and again from 1974 to 1979, were able to strengthen Britain's deteriorating economy, which was not yet socialistic but was too restricted to allow free competitive capitalism to function as it had in the nineteenth century. Furthermore, it was difficult for many Britishers to adjust to their greatly diminished place in the world. Many could still remember the glamorous days when Britain ruled the seas and an empire over which the sun never set. But increasing numbers of the young and the poor knew and cared little about past glories. Lawlessness and violence escalated, reaching its peak of intensity in Ulster. There the Roman Catholic minority struggled fiercely to gain equality with the Protestant majority; many of the Roman Catholics demanded separation from Britain and union with Ireland. The Protestants fought equally fiercely to maintain their supremacy. Violence begat violence. Hundreds on both sides were killed, and hopes for a harmonious society were destroyed for the foreseeable future.

Widespread dissatisfaction with the inability of the Labour party to discipline its own trade unions and to lessen the rate of inflation resulted in a sweeping victory for the Conservatives in 1979. Margaret Thatcher became Britain's first female prime minister. The coming into production of the North Sea oil discoveries of several years earlier promised to strengthen Britain's economy, which had been in decline since World War I. Nevertheless, during the early 1980s Britain's economy remained troubled. With unemployment at more than 12 percent year after year and economic growth modest, Britain was burdened with one of the poorest-performing economies in Western Europe. Urban riots reflected growing dissatisfaction. Yet thanks to the nationalistic unity fostered by the brief Falklands War with Argentina in the spring of 1982, the divisions within the Labour party (which led to the creation of a new party, the Social Democrats), and a moderately improving economy, Thatcher's Conservatives managed to maintain control over the government.

France

France emerged from the war not only ravaged but also, unlike Britain, defeated and demoralized. General Charles de Gaulle returned to France in 1944 with the American and British liberators, who gave official recognition to the government he set up in Paris. However, the first postwar elections, held in October 1945, resulted in a sweeping victory for the parties of the Left, with which the authoritarian de Gaulle could not cooperate. Early in 1946 he went into temporary retirement. The leftist coalition, suspicious of authority, drew up a constitution very similar to that of the Third Republic, with its weak executive. The one noteworthy advance made by the new constitution was the granting, at long last, of female suffrage. The Fourth Republic, like the Third, was plagued by a multiplicity of parties and political instability.

Despite these difficulties the Fourth French Republic made some noteworthy changes in French economic and social life. Under the Monnet Plan, free enterprise was combined with economic planning. Major banking and insurance facilities, coal mines, and gas and electrical utilities were nationalized. Social services, somewhat less comprehensive than those of the British Labour government, were inaugurated. A strong if uneasy economic recovery was achieved. By 1958 the output of goods and services was far in excess of that before World War II. These accomplishments of the Fourth Republic, however, were offset by its unsuccessful effort to hold on to the French Empire. A costly attempt to put down a war for independence in Indochina, which had broken out in 1942, resulted in humiliating defeat for the French (see p. 741). In 1954 France was forced to grant independence to Indochina. An even costlier war to try to save Algeria, in 1954–1962, also ended in failure (see pp. 746–747). Inability to solve the Algerian prob-

FIGURE 56.3 Charles de Gaulle After the French army in Algeria revolted against the French government in 1958, de Gaulle was recalled by popular acclaim and given an overwhelming mandate to rewrite the constitution. With dispatch he set up the Fifth French Republic and was elected its first president. This photo shows de Gaulle on tour of the French provinces. (Henri Cartier-Bresson/Magnum)

lem led to the mutiny of the French army in Algeria in May 1958, which brought down the government. Charles de Gaulle was recalled from his twelve-year retirement. The problems confronting him were formidable—a mutinous army, a disintegrating empire, a seemingly endless war in Algeria, a disgruntled working class, an inflated currency, governmental weakness amounting to anarchy, widespread cynicism.

De Gaulle was probably the only person in France who could have reestablished civilian control over the mutinous army, which he deftly proceeded to do. He drew up a new constitution that greatly strengthened the executive branch of the government, and in December 1958 he was elected first president of the Fifth French Republic by an overwhelming majority (see Figure 56.3). He immediately granted independence to all of France's colonies except Algeria, which had a large French population. Algerian independence was granted four years later. He undertook to strengthen France's capitalistic economy by means of an austerity program. In spite of widespread strikes, France's economy was soon operating at its highest level in history, and the French masses were enjoying new prosperity.

In foreign affairs, de Gaulle set out to restore France's "greatness"—its prestige in world affairs and its hegemony in Western Europe. He also sought to make Western Europe a "third force" independent of both American and Soviet domination. To achieve these ends, he created at great cost an independent nuclear strike force, cultivated cordial relations with Germany, withdrew France's military forces from NATO because of its domination by the United States, and vetoed Great Britain's entry into the European Common Market because of its close ties to its Commonwealth associates and to the United States.

For eleven years these policies worked with remarkable success. France regained much of the stability and prestige it had lost in 1940. De Gaulle's strong role, of course, encountered much opposition, mostly from the extreme Right and extreme Left. His position and that of France's economy were weakened by massive student and labor union strikes and riots in 1968. When, in early 1969, de Gaulle asked for a vote of confidence from the French people and lost by a narrow margin, he resigned.

During the early 1970s Gaullists remained in power under the more moderate leadership of Georges Pompidou. In 1974 the elegant, urbane Valéry Giscard d'Estaing, a moderate conservative, defeated his Communist- and Socialist-backed opponent by the narrowest of margins. Giscard d'Estaing represented France's technocratic Right and pursued a policy of slow modernization and social conservatism. Stunning change came in the elections of 1981, which brought the Socialists, under the leadership of François Mitterrand, into power. Immediately, policies stressing nationalization of industries and banks, shorter hours and increased pay for workers, and progressive social programs were enacted. Yet several years of persistent economic problems, particularly inflation and high unemployment, dampened the reforming zeal of the Socialists and led them to reverse some of their policies.

West Germany

The German Federal Republic was formally established in September 1949. It had a liberal democratic government similar to that of the Weimar Republic. The Christian Democratic party, a slightly right-of-center party with Roman Catholic leanings, won the first election, and its leader, the elderly and pro-Western Dr. Konrad Adenauer, became the first chancellor. The Western powers replaced their military governors with civilian commissioners and relaxed their control over Germany.

West Germany's industrial economy recovered rapidly, in part thanks to American assistance in replacing wrecked industrial plants with the most modern equipment and to American military protection, which relieved West Germany of the enormous military costs that burdened the economies of the United States, Great Britain, and France. By 1957 West Germany had regained its former industrial supremacy in Western Europe.

In 1963 Adenauer finally stepped down (at eighty-seven) as chancellor. His Christian Democratic successors vigorously pursued his policies of strengthening West Germany's military ties with the United States, demanding the reunification of Germany and the recovery of lost territories in Eastern Europe, and establishing a place in the family of nuclear nations.

In 1969 Willy Brandt, a Social Democrat, became chancellor and launched Germany on a new course. His government quickly signed a nuclear nonproliferation treaty that had been long pending and entered into bilateral talks with East Germany and the Soviet Union. In Au-

gust 1970 Chancellor Brandt and Soviet Premier Kosygin signed a treaty renouncing force or the threat of force in international relations and accepting the existing boundary lines of Eastern Europe, including the Oder-Neisse line between East Germany and Poland. An official accompanying letter specified that the treaty left open the possibility of the future reunion of the two Germanies. This possibly momentous treaty was accompanied by trade agreements that promised a greatly stepped-up commerce between West Germany and the Soviet Union. The Social Democrats instituted and implemented many social programs, such as a comprehensive system of national health insurance and government ownership of public utilities. In economic policy, the German Social Democrats, unlike the French and British Socialists, who advocated government ownership or control, followed a policy of codetermination between labor and management—*mitbestimmung*. West Germany's industrial economy had become the most prosperous in the Western world.

The economic problems plaguing other Western nations finally caught up with West Germany in the early 1980s. In 1982 Helmut Schmidt and his Social Democratic party fell from power and were replaced by the more conservative Christian Democratic party, led by the new chancellor Helmut Kohl. The rise to power of Kohl and the Christian Democrats was affirmed by elections in 1983, which also witnessed the first substantial entry into national politics of the environmentalist Green party.

Southern Europe

Italy After the end of World War II Italy abolished the monarchy and established itself as a republic. The Christian Democrats under the leadership of Alcide de Gasperi emerged as the dominant political party. The Italian Communist party also came out of World War II in a strong position, initially sharing power with the Christian Democrats in a coalition government. After 1947 the Communists, although continuing to command 25 to 35 percent of the vote and winning control of local elections throughout Italy, were excluded from national government. For the next three decades the Christian Democrats dominated the Italian government, although almost always in shaky alliances with other parties. Even though governments did not last long, the government bureaucracy was resistant to change and the same group of high governmental officials continued in office in succeeding governments.

Italy, and particularly northern Italy, enjoyed rapid economic growth and modernization in the 1950s and 1960s, for the first time becoming a leading industrial power in Europe. After the late 1960s Italy experienced greater economic, social, and political instability. Inflation became a perennial problem. Industrial growth slowed. The government, with its entrenched and sometimes corrupt bureaucracy, became less able to react to problems. In the mid-1970s voters turned increasingly to the Italian Communist party, which under Enrico Berlinguer was adopting more moderate policies. Radical groups, such as the Red Brigades, resorted to terrorism. By the 1980s the dominant Christian Democratic party was losing control of the government for the first time. In August 1983 Bettino Craxi was named the first Socialist premier of Italy, but his coalition government was only moderately different from preceding governments. A decade later massive dissatisfaction with Italian politics would undermine Italy's post-war political system.

Spain, Portugal, and Greece The three southern European nations of Spain, Portugal, and Greece did not enter the mainstream of European developments until the 1970s. Both Spain, under Francisco Franco, and Portugal, under Antonio Salazar, remained out of World War II and retained their prewar authoritarian governments. Compared with the economies of other nations of Western Europe, their economies were less modernized and their people had a lower standard of living. Major political change came for both in the mid-1970s. In Portugal in 1974 General Antonio de Spinola headed a revolt that removed Marcelo Caetano, Salazar's authoritarian successor, from power. A year later Portugal held its first elections, and the Socialists, led by Mario Soares, gained control of the government. Spain underwent similar changes after the death of Franco in 1975. With the support of King Juan Carlos, a democratic constitution was approved in 1976. In 1982 the Socialists, under the popular Felipe Gonzáles, were elected to power for the

first time. Both nations went on to enjoy relative political stability and, particularly in Spain, economic growth.

Greece, which suffered greatly during World War II, emerged from it in chaos and civil war. The Greek Royalists, with the help of first the British and then the Americans, were victorious. Greece became politically stable and remained so until the mid-1960s, when threats from both the Left and Right led to the fall of the monarchy and, in 1967, a coup by conservative army officers. Their strong, authoritarian grip on Greek life was broken in 1974, when a confrontation with Turkey over Cyprus proved too difficult to handle. After 1975 Greece was governed by democratic rule, culminating in the election of the Socialists under Andreas Papandreou in 1981.

All three countries have followed a similar pattern: They broke from authoritarian rule in the mid-1970s, established a democratic form of government, and eventually elected a Socialist government. All three governments have had to deal with economies less modern than those in Western Europe and with societies that have had a lower standard of living. Yet events have pulled these southern European countries into the mainstream of Western European affairs; in the 1980s all three gained membership in the Common Market.

The United States

Of the Western powers, only the United States emerged from World War II virtually unscathed materially. The war had forced billions of dollars into circulation, ended the long depression, and destroyed much of the nation's foreign competition. The end of the war found big business and a high-spending military machine in close alliance and firmly entrenched. For most of the three decades following 1945, the United States enjoyed great economic prosperity. The pinnacle of prosperity came in the early and mid-sixties. Under presidents Kennedy and Johnson, the government pursued liberal policies of social reform, which included attacks on poverty, new educational programs, low-income housing projects, and governmental support of medical services. These policies put the United States more into line with other Western nations that had already established these social and "welfare state" institutions. However, the expansion of new social programs and unquestioned prosperity would come to an end in the 1970s and 1980s. Indeed, underlying the prosperity and confidence of the decades after World War II was a series of problems, which often resulted in anxiety, unrest, fear, and violence.

The first was the Soviet Union and communism. From the very beginning of the postwar era, Americans feared the Soviet Union and communism. Many journalists, military leaders, politicians, and business and professional people exploited this fear. During the early 1950s Senator Joseph McCarthy of Wisconsin fanned this fear into hysteria. In the eyes of McCarthy and his millions of followers, the American government, defense industries, armed forces, and educational system were honeycombed with Communists and fellow travelers.

In 1957, just as McCarthyism was subsiding, the American people were shocked by the news that the Soviet Union had orbited a satellite— Sputnik. The implication was that the lean and eager Russians had forged ahead in nuclear weapons and delivery systems while the soft, contented Americans had slept. The United States had, of course, been working on a satellite of its own for some time and in 1958 successfully orbited one. In 1961 the Soviet Union and the United States sent men into space and began to race each other to the moon. This race was won by the United States in 1969 at a cost of some $40 billion.

Americans were greatly concerned over repeated Communist successes in Asia (see Chapter 58), and closer to home a Communist takeover in Cuba in 1959 caused grave anxiety. The Cuban rebel leader, Fidel Castro, overthrew an American-supported rightist dictatorship. In 1961 the American government encouraged and aided an unsuccessful attempt by Cuban refugees to overthrow the Castro regime and the following year, by heavy threats, forced the Soviet Union to dismantle the missile bases it had constructed in Cuba. This was the most frightening of all the confrontations between the two nuclear powers, both of which had the nuclear capacity to destroy all the people on the earth.

America's next problem was its long-festering failure to integrate its large African-American population. By 1945 African Americans numbered some 20 million—about a tenth of the total population—and although some advancement in material well-being and social equality had been made, the gains fell far short of the promises. African-American veterans returning from World War II were particularly frustrated. In 1954 the Supreme Court outlawed segregation in the public schools and later mandated forced busing as a means of implementing the decision. In the following years the civil rights movement was born, as African Americans struggled for greater equality within American society. White resistance flared up first in the Deep South and later in the large industrial cities of the North. Federal troops and marshals were used to overcome white resistance in the South. Millions of whites in the large northern industrial cities fled to the suburbs. In 1964 Congress passed civil rights acts that guaranteed voting rights and broadly outlawed racial discrimination. Nevertheless, this legislation did not end the turmoil that had been unleashed. Riots occurred in major cities during the 1960s, reaching a climax in 1968 following the murder of Dr. Martin Luther King, Jr., the most prominent of the African-American leaders. During the 1970s and 1980s, the position of blacks in American society evolved, but the record has been mixed. On the one hand, the elevation of many African Americans to positions of political leadership and the growing numbers of African Americans in middle-class jobs and residential areas indicate important change. On the other hand, African Americans remain overrepresented in the growing core of inner-city unemployed who live below the poverty line.

Several other problems created social unrest during the 1960s. College students staged protests over a variety of issues including racial inequality, poverty, destruction of natural resources, and American involvement in the Vietnam War (see pp. 741–743). Women organized and demanded equal rights. Radical organizations, particularly on the political Left, grew and were unusually active.

While some of these problems became less immediate in the 1970s, new problems arose. In 1974, confidence in the American political system was shaken by the Watergate scandal, which revealed widespread misconduct and crimes within the highest levels of President Nixon's administration. Numerous high officials in the Nixon administration were forced to resign and were convicted and imprisoned. In August 1974, after it had become obvious that the president would be impeached by the full House and convicted by the Senate, Nixon resigned. He was succeeded by Gerald Ford, the conservative Republican leader who granted Nixon full pardon for all crimes he "may have committed while in office."

At almost the same time, economic problems stemming from the cost of the Vietnam War, an unfavorable balance of trade, growing inflation, and the fourfold increase in oil prices between 1973 and 1974 started catching up with the United States. The country was entering a new period of declining growth rates, increasing unemployment, and rising prices. In the world marketplace, it was losing its dominance.

In 1976 Ford was narrowly defeated by Jimmy Carter. The Carter administration was confronted by spiraling inflation, a threatened fuel shortage, a high rate of unemployment (particularly among African Americans and youths), a sense of disillusionment over the Vietnam War and its end, and widespread distrust of government at all levels—difficult problems that were not solved. The Carter administration was further burdened with trying to free American hostages from a hostile Iran and a new rise in oil prices.

In 1980 Ronald Reagan and the Republican party were elected to power and initiated a series of conservative policies in an attempt to undo several of the liberal reforms of the previous decades. Defense spending increased; a harsher line was taken toward communism; American arms and forces were sent to several areas throughout the world; programs to protect the environment, the worker, and the unemployed were attacked; and tax reforms that benefited mainly the corporations, the wealthy, and the middle class were enacted. The recession that began in the late 1970s deepened, with unemployment figures higher than in any years since the Great Depression of the 1930s. After 1983 the economy was in recovery, but the relative prosperity had been purchased by a series of huge governmental deficits.

Eastern Europe and the Soviet Union

The Soviet Union and Eastern Europe participated in the general European recovery from World War II, but their recovery was slower and not nearly as spectacular as in Western Europe. Certainly the economies of Eastern Europe started from a lower base and had to overcome greater difficulties. During the 1950s and 1960s the Soviet and Eastern European economies modernized and people enjoyed a rising standard of living. Soviet and Eastern European citizens did not participate nearly as fully in the consumerism experienced in the West, but they were assured of steady employment, inexpensive housing, and access to health and educational facilities. The basic social services were extensive. With the exception of the elite of the Communist party and certain professionals, the gap between the rich and poor classes narrowed. The Soviet Union initially set the pattern of economic and political development, but over time the various nations within the Soviet sphere of dominance moved in their own directions.

The Soviet Union The Soviet Union emerged victorious from World War II, but the social and economic costs were high. Few changes from prewar policies were evident. Stalin continued to assert totalitarian rule with a tightly planned economy stressing heavy industrialization. Political dissent was not allowed, and purges removed those perceived as potential threats. Prisons and forced-labor camps remained a feature of Stalin's rule. Despite the heavy expenditures required to maintain the Red Army, the Soviet Union recovered.

The death of Stalin in 1953 led to a liberalization of policies within the Soviet Union. Initially, Georgi Malenkov and Nikita Khrushchev struggled for power, but by 1955 Khrushchev had emerged as Stalin's successor. The most dramatic indication of changes from the Stalin era came in a 1956 speech in which Khrushchev denounced the crimes of Stalin before startled Communist leaders in Moscow. Khrushchev removed many of the conservative Stalinists within the party hierarchy but avoided the use of harsh Stalinist purges. Controls over cultural life were slightly loosened, as evidenced by the publication of novels by Boris Pasternak. Economically, there was a new stress on consumer goods and an attempt was made to reform agricultural policy. Khrushchev also embarked on an ambitious foreign policy. But he may have tried to do too much at once, for domestic and international difficulties began to undermine his position. The gravest problems occurred in foreign affairs. The Soviet Union became involved in a growing ideological dispute with the Chinese Communists, who were younger and more evangelical in the Marxist faith than the Russians (see p. 738). The split between the Soviet Union and China was intensified by boundary disputes. Then, in 1962, Khrushchev blundered into a showdown with the United States by trying to set up Soviet nuclear missiles in Cuba and was forced to make a humiliating retreat.

In October 1964 Khrushchev was suddenly ousted from power by his colleagues in the party's Central Committee. Leonid Brezhnev replaced him as party secretary, eventually emerging as the actual head of government by the late 1960s. Brezhnev reversed some of the liberalization of the Khrushchev years but did not fully return to Stalinist policies or practices. The Brezhnev era was marked by relative stability within the Soviet Union. The Soviet economy has continued to expand, but unevenly and not as rapidly as expected—in part thanks to the drain of military and administrative expenditures. By the 1980s the Soviet Union was a world leader in the production of steel, oil, and coal. Soviet agriculture was less successful. Although mechanization constantly increased, periodic droughts, poor management, and lack of incentive forced the government to make repeated and expensive grain purchases from the United States and Canada. The standard of living rose, but it still trailed that of the West and even that of some of the satellite countries in Eastern Europe. Soviet citizens did, however, enjoy free education and medical services and relative job security. The Soviet Union continued to assert itself internationally as a world power, as indicated by its involvement and intervention in Czechoslovakia in 1968, Africa in the 1970s, Afghanistan in 1979, and Poland during the 1980s.

Eastern Europe The governments and economies of Eastern Europe were brought under Stalin's control and set up in imitation of the Soviet model during the late 1940s. Initially the Soviet Union drained off economic resources from these countries to strengthen its own economy. Soon single-party "people's democracies" were estab-

lished in Poland, East Germany, Czechoslovakia, Hungary, Rumania, Yugoslavia, and Albania. Each of these governments was dominated by the head of its Communist party, who usually ruled in Stalinist fashion. Each country developed a planned economy stressing industrialization and collectivization of agriculture, and generally a high rate of economic growth was achieved. Each was required to cooperate politically, economically, and militarily with the Soviet Union. All major policies were tightly coordinated with the wishes of Moscow. Contact with the West was strictly limited. The one exception was Yugoslavia, where in 1948 Tito managed to break from the rest of the Communist bloc and take an independent course. Tito initiated a more decentralized form of communism stressing increased local control and worker participation in management.

Nevertheless, Eastern Europe was not a mere appendage to the Soviet Union, even during the Stalinist period. Each state had its own sense of nationalism, each had its own particular ethnic mix, and each had its own history. The Soviet Union did not find it easy to gain or maintain control.

The first stirrings of revolt against Soviet control followed Stalin's death. In 1953 East Berliners rose but were quickly crushed by force. Following Khrushchev's 1956 speech denouncing Stalin and some of his policies, Poland rose in revolt and asserted some independence from Moscow. A compromise left Poland within the Soviet sphere of control while avoiding the use of Soviet troops in Poland. Poland would enjoy a mild liberalization of its intellectual life and greater independence in determining its economic policies. Shortly thereafter, a more violent armed revolt took place in Hungary. This more challenging demand for independence was met by an invasion of troops and the ouster of the new government. Nevertheless, under the Moscow-approved but moderate János Kádár, Hungarians were allowed increased individual freedom and greater national self-determination.

These revolts revealed some of the discontent and hopes for greater independence within the Eastern European nations, but the Soviet response also indicated the allowable limits to any deviance from the Soviet line. National differences between the various Eastern European

FIGURE 56.4 Soviet Tanks in Prague Efforts by Czechoslovakia to reform its socialist system and gain greater independence from Moscow were brought to an end in August 1968 by a Soviet invasion. Here Soviet tanks overwhelm any potential resistance in the streets of Prague. (Josef Koudelka/Magnum)

states and the Soviet Union were recognized. Contact with the West would be allowed. Cultural activities might be less restricted than in the Soviet Union. But the fundamental political, economic, and military cooperation with Moscow was not to be violated.

After the late 1950s the various Eastern European nations pursued separate courses within the limits set by the Soviet Union. East Germany, Hungary, and Rumania remained relatively tranquil during the 1960s, 1970s, and early 1980s. East Germany has closely followed the Soviet line while developing its industrial capacity. Hungary managed to orient its economy toward consumer goods, due to a loosening of state control and the introduction of limited capitalistic practices at the local level. Rumania took a more politically independent and conservative course

under the leadership of president Nicolae Ceauşescu.

Albania, Czechoslovakia, and Poland were more of a problem to Moscow. In 1961 Albania, under Enver Hoxha, broke from Moscow and took the side of the Chinese in the Sino-Soviet split. Since Albania was surrounded by the already independent Yugoslavia and Greece, there was little the Soviet Union could do. In 1968 the Alexander Dubček government in Czechoslovakia went too far in allowing intellectual freedom and some democratization. The Soviet Union mobilized the troops of the Warsaw Pact nations and occupied Czechoslovakia (see Figure 56.4). Dubĉek and his supporters, along with their liberalizing policies, were removed from power. In 1980 the Polish government began to have difficulty maintaining its control over the nation.

Mainly protesting the continuing economic mismanagement and corruption within the government, Polish workers struck and organized a union, Solidarity, under the leadership of Lech Wałesa. Solidarity became increasingly powerful and was succeeding in forcing the government to grant concessions. When the union seemed to be going too far, pressure from Moscow and resistance from conservative elements in the Polish government stiffened. In December 1981 martial law was declared by the new leader of the Polish Communist party, General Wojciech Jaruzelski. After a series of governmental crackdowns, Solidarity was outlawed in October 1982.

In the mid-1980s, most of the Eastern European nations remained Communist and under the shadow of the Soviet Union. This, as we shall see in a later chapter, would soon change.

3. INTEGRATION AND INTERNATIONAL ORGANIZATIONS

In the years following World War II it became evident that there were advantages to dealing with problems cooperatively and through international organizations. The European nations had long suffered from competitive nationalistic rivalries. The world in 1945 was no longer a place where a country such as Great Britain or France was strong enough to get its own way. The developing Cold War was forcing countries to take sides whether or not they wanted to. After the destruction of World War II and particularly under the new threat of atomic weapons, the international pursuit of peace seemed even more pressing.

During the 1940s and 1950s a number of cooperative international organizations were formed. Some were military, such as NATO (an alliance of the United States, Canada, and the non-Communist nations of Europe) and its counterpart, the Warsaw Pact (an alliance of the Soviet Union and the Communist nations it dominated in Eastern Europe). Others were economic, such as the Organization for European Economic Cooperation (for coordination among the recipients of Marshall Plan funds) and the Council for Mutual Economic Assistance, or COMECON (the Soviet response to the Marshall Plan). The most important of these organizations were the efforts toward the integration of Western Europe and the United Nations.

European Integration

In 1949 several nations in Western Europe took an initial step toward political integration by setting up the Council of Europe. Many hoped that this organization would develop into a parliament of Europe with real political power. However, the major European nations were unwilling to give the council significant power, and it remained an organization of potential.

Western Europe was more successful in taking steps toward economic integration. In 1950 France and Germany created the French-German Coal and Steel Authority. In 1952 it was expanded into the European Coal and Steel Community with the addition of Italy, Belgium, Luxembourg, and the Netherlands. In 1957 these same six nations signed the Treaty of Rome establishing the European Economic Community (the Common Market). Its purpose was to eliminate tariff barriers, cut restrictions on the flow of labor and capital, and generally integrate the economies of the member nations. The organization was a surprising success in the 1960s, eliminating tariff and immigration barriers ahead of schedule while its member nations enjoyed relative prosperity. During the 1970s and 1980s other nations joined the Common Market: Great Britain, Ireland, and Denmark in 1973; Greece in 1981; Portugal and Spain in 1986.

The United Nations

In 1945 the world's leaders set up the United Nations to provide for international cooperation and act as a watchdog over peace. It did an enormous amount of work in economic, cultural, and humanitarian fields, most of which did not make headlines. It assisted in arranging cease-fires in several conflicts between Israel and the Arab states and helped stop wars between India and Pakistan, and the Netherlands and Indonesia. Under the leadership of the United States, it fought in the Korean War, 1950–1953 (see pp. 739–740). In recent years the United Nations has won prestige for its effective role in areas of conflict such as the Middle East (particularly in facilitating the cease-fire between Iran and Iraq in 1988), southern Africa, and the western Sahara. Yet from the beginning the United Nations has been hampered by the unwillingness of the major powers to submit to its authority, embodied formally in the right of the permanent members of the Security Council to veto any action involving the use of force or the threat of force. Often it has proven unable to prevent wars or assert its will over defiant nations. The United Nations has reflected more than controlled the domestic and international problems of its member nations over the past forty years.

SUGGESTED READING

General

W. Laqueur, *Europe since Hitler* (1982). A scholarly, respected survey.

D. Urwin, *Western Europe since 1945: A Political History* (1989). A full political survey.

J. R. Wegs, *Europe since 1945* (1983). A concise survey.

The Settlement and the Cold War

W. Lafeber, *America, Russia, and the Cold War, 1945–1966* (1978). A revisionist interpretation.

B. Weisberger, *Cold War, Cold Peace: The United States and Russia since 1945* (1984). A good general account.

D. Yergin, *The Shattered Peace* (1977). A balanced, well-written study of the Cold War.

Revival of a Divided Europe and the West

R. Aron, *The Imperial Republic: The United States and the World, 1945–1973* (1974). A sophisticated analysis of American dominance.

T. Ash, *The Polish Revolution: Solidarity* (1984). A full account.

S. Cohen, *Rethinking the Soviet Experience: Politics and History Since 1917* (1985). Analyzes the debates in Soviet studies.

W. Connor, *Socialism, Politics and Equality: Hierarchy and Change in Eastern Europe and the USSR* (1979). A good account.

A. W. De Porte, *Europe Between the Superpowers: The Enduring Balance* (1979). A good analysis of Europe in the context of the superpowers.

A. H. Halsey, *Change in British Society* (1981). A solid study.

D. L. Hanley et al., eds., *France: Politics and Society Since 1945* (1979). A good collection of essays.

J. Hough and M. Fainsod, *How the Soviet Union Is Governed* (1978). A useful general study.

W. Leonhard, *Three Faces of Communism* (1974). Analyzes the ideological divisions of the Communist world.

A. Marwick, *British Society Since 1945* (1982). A good survey.

A. Milward, *The Reconstruction of Western Europe, 1945–1951* (1984). A fine study.

T. Rakowska-Harmstone and A. Gyorgy, eds., *Communism in Eastern Europe* (1984). Covers each country.

H. Turner, Jr., *The Two Germanies since 1945* (1987). A good political history.

Integration and International Organizations

R. Mowat, *Creating the European Community* (1973). A study of European integration.

C. Tugenhat, *Making Sense of Europe* (1986). An evaluation of the Common Market.

CHAPTER 57

Society and Culture in the Twentieth Century

719

Social, intellectual, and cultural trends have followed two broad patterns since World War I. Until 1945, there was a widespread sense of anxiety, disillusionment, and uncertainty in the West. In part, these feelings were an extension of a trend already developing in the two or three decades prior to World War I, but after World War I they were no longer confined to elite intellectual and cultural circles. They were also a reflection of the social turmoil and sense of decay that spread and deepened in frightening ways after 1914. Much of the art, literature, philosophy, and even science of the 1920s and 1930s reflected this insecurity, this doubting of established values, this questioning of the future.

Since 1945 social, intellectual, and cultural trends have been marked by a complex mixture of continuity and change. There is still much of the disillusionment and anxiety that characterized the earlier decades of the twentieth century. At the same time, there has developed a new sense of experimentation and productivity, which reflects the lessening of social turmoil and a greater sense of stability compared with the difficult decades prior to World War II.

With these two broad patterns in mind, let us attempt to identify and explore some of the social, religious, intellectual, and cultural developments of Western civilization in the twentieth century.

1. WESTERN SOCIETY IN THE TWENTIETH CENTURY

Demographic and Social Changes

Population in the West has been growing since World War I, but at varying rates. The broad pattern shows a slowing down of population growth as societies became more fully modernized, a pattern that has been evident in some countries since the end of the nineteenth century. During the 1940s and 1950s birthrates in most Western countries were relatively high (the "baby boom"), leading to an increase in the population. During the 1960s birthrates started to decline and reverse, to the point in the 1970s, 1980s, and 1990s where several countries have birthrates that are sufficient only to maintain the population or that will result in a declining population. Some governments, such as that of France, have encouraged larger families with financial aid. This encouragement of larger families probably came more from cultural and racial concerns than economic need, for immigrants were available and used to expand the labor pool. Changes in the makeup of the population are also evident. As a result of improved life expectancy, populations in the West have been growing older on the average, giving elderly persons' groups more potential political power and making the social needs of the elderly more pressing.

Perhaps more important than population changes have been changes in where and how people live. Urbanization has increased in recent decades. Large cities have been swollen by migration from rural areas and immigration from southern areas. Northern European cities have absorbed large numbers of people from southern Italy, Greece, Turkey, and Africa, just as cities in North America have been expanded by people from Latin America and Asia. With the people have come the traditional urban problems: congestion, overburdened transportation systems, insufficient social services, pollution, crime, and inadequate housing. At times the inner core of great cities has deteriorated and even suffered a decline in population, but this has usually been more than matched by the growth of surrounding suburbs. New shopping and industrial centers have grown up in the periphery of the older cities and even on the fringes of older suburbs. In reference to cities such as Paris, London, New York, and Moscow, it has become more accurate to include the metropolitan areas around them rather than merely the city itself.

In recent decades the most modern societies in the West have been termed "postindustrial," to emphasize the declining importance of traditional manufacturing industries and the growing importance of providing services—often through the use of high technology. The key figures in this postindustrial society are financiers, technicians, managers, and professionals rather than industrial entrepreneurs.

There have also been some broad shifts in the social classes that make up Western society. Generally, the shift has been away from rural classes to urban classes, away from traditional industrial jobs to service and white-collar jobs, and away from small firms toward corporate and governmental organizations. Class distinctions remain but are less clear than before. Society has become generally more mobile, both geographically and socially. While birth into wealth and position remains a great advantage, education or technical skill has increasingly become a relatively democratic avenue for social mobility.

In Western Europe and the United States the very wealthy have generally managed to retain or even improve their position at the top of society despite the growth of social welfare programs and efforts in some countries to lessen the gap between rich and poor. Most of the remnants of the traditional aristocracy have disappeared or merged with the wealthy upper middle class. While this elite class retains some protective barriers against intrusion from below and maintains itself through the aid of inheritance, it is increasingly being joined by a newer elite of corporate and governmental managers, successful professionals, and those with high scientific or technological expertise. These people tend to be highly educated, pragmatic, with a stake in the status quo, and yet always threatened by their younger, more recently educated competitors in the corporate or bureaucratic hierarchy.

Just below these elites is the bulk of the middle class. Made up primarily of middle- and lower-level managers in corporate and governmental bureaucracies, those who hold salaried white-collar jobs in services, and professionals in a growing number of fields, this class has grown substantially. Entrance into this class is gained primarily through education, specialization, and technical expertise.

Since the end of World War II the industrial working class has generally seen an improvement in its standard of living and, at least until the 1960s, relative job security. Yet its ranks were thinning as the traditional industrial base eroded, forcing many to become service workers or enter the bottom level of white-collar employment. As economic problems became more acute in the 1970s, the early 1980s, and again in the 1990s, industrial workers faced unemployment matched only by pre–World War II statistics and declines in real income that had to be compensated for by more married women entering the paid work force. As they have grown more affluent, the distinction between them and the lower

middle class has lessened: The incomes, diets, housing, leisure-time activities, and often even political affiliations of the two classes are becoming similar. Yet the working class has remained distinct in many ways; it has fewer opportunities for social mobility and greater frustrations at the workplace.

Some of the problems faced by workers has been brought into focus by the influx of immigrants. After the 1950s, many of Western Europe's laborers were immigrants drawn by the lure of jobs from southern Europe and other places such as Turkey, North Africa, and former colonies where economic circumstances were often desperate. They filled the lowest-paid and least desirable jobs. Women were particularly vulnerable to exploitation. Often immigrants were not encouraged to put down roots and become assimilated. Rising unemployment in the recessionary years of the 1970s, 1980s, and 1990s created new pressures on this pool of immigrant workers. Laws were passed to restrict further immigration. The millions who remained or managed to get in anyway increasingly suffered racial and anti-immigrant attacks and became the victims of right-wing political movements such as France's National Front.

In many countries there remained a core of inner-city slum dwellers. They were usually without regular jobs, often marked by race or ethnic origin, and subject to the worst problems of urban life. In recent years there have been disturbing signs that this core of often homeless urban poor is growing.

The decline of rural populations has continued, with variations in each country. Generally, agricultural productivity has been increasing, lessening the need for people on the farms. Many rural people have moved into the cities, leaving a small percentage of the population to grow food for the rest and for export. Those who have adjusted to the changing rural life—by mechanizing, enlarging their land holdings, joining cooperatives, and specializing—have enjoyed an uneven but generally rising standard of living. But there remains a core of rural poor who have not adjusted to the agricultural changes since World War II or who have fallen victim to economic forces beyond their control. Rural life has also become less isolated with the spread of highways, cars, telephones, radio, and television.

In Eastern Europe social changes followed the model established in Russia after the revolution in 1917. The traditional landed aristocracy disappeared rapidly as their lands were taken away and redistributed or nationalized. Large collectivized farms arose. The Eastern European states nationalized the factories, the banks, the commercial houses, and the large retail outlets of the middle class. The distinctions between urban classes were lessened as the state standardized basic housing, social services, consumption, and even leisure activities. Nevertheless, a new privileged order arose. High-level party and governmental leaders, certain professionals, and the cultural elite enjoyed more access to consumer goods, improved housing, better educational opportunities, and greater political influence than the rest of the population. This social inequality within these Eastern European socialist societies has been a source of discontent and turmoil in recent years.

The Family

Since World War I, and in particular over the past few decades, the family in the West has become smaller, more mobile, and less stable. Although people still tend to marry within their social, religious, and ethnic groups and with an eye toward economic considerations, emotional attraction continues to grow as the primary consideration in mate selection. In the past few decades sexual fulfillment has been added as an increasingly important condition for marriage and its continuation. The development of new methods of contraception, particularly the contraceptive pill in the 1960s, and the accompanying acceptance of the idea of contraception (and, to a lesser extent, abortion) have given women and men greater sexual freedom and choice over marriage and childbearing. Since the baby boom of the immediate post–World War II years, married couples have had fewer children on average. The nuclear family—the couple and its children—has become more geographically mobile, and ties to extended family members such as grandparents, uncles, aunts, and cousins have become more distant. Other institutions, such as the school, the university, peer groups, family courts, family therapists, child psychologists, and day care centers, have grown to take over functions that the family used to perform more exclusively.

The increase in premarital sex, cohabitation, gay lifestyles, divorce, and nontraditional family arrangements, as well as a recent trend toward declining marriage rates and postponing marriage and childbearing have led many to question the viability of the modern family. The single-parent household and the childless household are gaining acceptance. The rate of divorce has risen sharply since World War II, particularly since the 1960s. Yet the family is not disappearing, as some critics have argued. Rather, its form and its functions are evolving, as are the roles its members, particularly women, are expected to play.

Women

Some of the most important social changes have involved the role of women within the family and in society as a whole. In both World War I and World War II women assumed jobs and responsibilities previously thought beyond their "legitimate sphere," but with the return of the soldiers they were pressured to return to their more traditional domestic roles. However, the long-run trend in the twentieth century, and particularly since the 1950s, has been for women to enter the paid work force in a greater variety of jobs. In particular, married women have been moving out of their middle-class roles as housekeepers, child rearers, and supporters of their income-producing husbands. The female wage-earning work force is no longer dominated by the young and single, as it was earlier in the twentieth century. With a growing life expectancy (now over seventy-five years in most Western countries), more women have been turning to "second careers" at middle age, often involving a return to school to acquire new skills. Well over 50 percent of all married women in the United States now work outside the home, a dramatic increase from pre–World War II levels and a pattern that has generally prevailed in the West. Women, both married and unmarried, are moving into jobs that were once the almost exclusive domain of men, from the legal and medical professions to all varieties of blue-collar work. However, discrimination based on gender is far from over. Women remain underrepre-

FIGURE 57.2 French Women's Movement The women's movement since the 1960s has been international. Here French women demonstrate for equal pay with men for equal work. (Martine Franck/Magnum)

sented in most higher-paying, higher-status occupations and still earn only between 60 and 80 percent of men's salaries. And more often than not, women who work outside the home still remain responsible for most of the domestic work at home.

The women's liberation movement, gaining force since the 1960s, has made many women more conscious of their common concerns (see Figure 57.2). Generally, this movement demands that women no longer be oppressed or considered second-class citizens, whether in their political rights, the wages they earn, the positions they hold, or the attitudes they or their society share. This movement has struggled not only to open political, economic, and social life to all, regardless of sex, but also to change stereotypical portrayals of femininity and common assumptions about differences between the sexes that contribute to barriers facing women. Feminists have led the struggles to liberalize divorce laws and to legalize contraception and abortion and have pushed for changes in scholarship to reflect women's concerns and perspectives.

In some ways women's circumstances differed in the Soviet Union and Eastern Europe, while in some ways they were the same. More Soviet women worked, sometimes in traditionally elite occupations such as medicine, and held

political positions than in the West. Nevertheless, they usually received lower pay than men and were expected to maintain their traditional roles at home. For the most part they were kept out of higher political positions. Feminism as a political or social movement scarcely touched them.

These changes are of great potential significance to women and, by necessity, to men. As with most fundamental historical changes, they will take a long time to have full effect. The changes women are initiating will require numerous subtle changes in the way we raise our children and the messages our culture transmits about gender and sex roles.

Youth and Education

One of the institutions most affected by social changes, and in particular changes in the family, has been education. Schools have been expected to adapt to social and economic changes and take up functions that were once handled by parents as part of child rearing. Schools are expected to assist children who have emotional, social, and family problems as well as purely academic problems.

With the growing demands for democratization of educational opportunities, universities have had to open their doors to more than the traditional elite. The number of students attending college and going on for advanced degrees has increased dramatically since World War II. Universities have had to change their curricula to fit the new demands of a mobile society and a modern economy. The strains on universities were particularly great in the 1960s, when students in many Western nations combined discontent with the university with attitudes critical of the values and behavior of their parents' generation. Students attacked the lack of humaneness, the restrictive behavior and values, the social inequities, and the competitive impersonality of the traditional adult world of their parents as represented by the large, bureaucratized, impersonal university. They criticized governmental policies and rallied around issues such as opposition to the Vietnam War and support for national liberation movements in the non-Western world. The numerous demonstrations and disruptions of university life often spread into the surrounding communities, involving clashes with police and other public authorities. The most dramatic confrontations took place in 1968 in France, where a student revolt threatened to overturn the government, particularly when students gained the sympathetic, if temporary, support of workers. The government eventually retained control, but numerous reforms of universities in France and elsewhere were instituted in the late 1960s and early 1970s. Since then student activism has diminished. Students have veered away from the traditional liberal arts curriculum and have become more concerned with preparing for careers in an increasingly competitive economic environment. Programs and majors in fields such as business administration, computer science, and the professions have proliferated.

Social Welfare

After World War I and particularly after World War II, trends toward increased governmental responsibility for social welfare accelerated. Most countries increased their traditional social security benefits for unemployment, retirement, sickness, and old age. Government expenditures for education expanded. In some countries, particularly Great Britain, steps were taken to ensure that medical services were available to all. New governmental programs were established to provide family allowances, maternity grants, and low-income housing.

In general, governments began to be held responsible for providing a floor of social and economic well-being below which their citizens should not be allowed to fall. The expanded role of the state in providing a large array of social services within an economic system that still remained substantially capitalistic has been termed the creation of the "welfare state." The degree of involvement varied in each country. The governments of the Communist nations in Eastern Europe assumed the most control over social and economic matters, but the services they could provide were limited by the economic well-being of the nation. Among the nations of Western Europe the Scandinavian countries generally went the furthest in providing social services for their citizens. The United States, with its own particular problems and aversion to programs that hint of socialism, lagged behind in governmental provision of social services.

Of course, these services came at a price. Taxes rose to pay for them. Governmental bureaucracies grew to administer them. Moreover, critics question the quality of some of the services provided, particularly medical services. Yet once established, such social programs were rarely reversed—although the Reagan administration in the United States during the 1980s made efforts to do just that.

However, efforts by governments to promote social welfare did not end the persistant social problems. In addition to poverty, the high rate of crime and the proliferation of drug abuse in recent decades attest to the sense of alienation and dissatisfaction in many Western societies. In the 1980s and 1990s the spread of AIDS has challenged the ability of government and science to solve difficult new problems.

2. RELIGION AND THEOLOGY IN THE TWENTIETH CENTURY

Christianity remained an important religious force in Western civilization despite the secularization that took place during the twentieth century. However, in the long run, Christian churches as institutions have continued to suffer

FIGURE 57.3 Areas such as Africa and Latin America have gained increasing attention within the Catholic church in recent decades. Here, in one of his many trips outside of Europe, John Paul II rides in a motorcade in Zaire. (UPI/Bettmann Newsphotos)

a decline in influence in the West, particularly since World War II. Strenuous efforts were made to restore some of the lost unity of Christendom to enable the Christian church to face its problems with a united front. In 1948 leaders of hundreds of Protestant and Orthodox denominations met in Geneva and set up the World Council of Churches. The most spectacular step in this direction was taken by Pope John XXIII (1958–1963), who called the Second Vatican Council (1962–1965) in the spirit of Christian tolerance and unity. Although John XXIII died during the first year of the council and was succeeded by Paul VI (1963–1978), who was a less vigorous innovator, the Second Vatican Council introduced an ecumenical spirit into the Catholic church and showed a willingness to modernize the ritual and discipline that had been formalized by the Council of Trent in the sixteenth century. When Paul VI died in 1978, the College of Cardinals elected John Paul I, a man of great personal charm, who lived less than a month. The new pope, John Paul II, a Pole, was the first non-Italian pope since the early sixteenth century. Relatively young, forceful, and knowledgeable, John Paul II has traveled extensively, particularly to politically controversial areas such as Africa,

Central America, and Poland (see Figure 57.3). He has managed to convey an image of renewed dynamism and activism in the Catholic church. Nevertheless, he has been conservative in matters of faith and morals, refusing to liberalize Church policy toward theological doctrines, the priesthood, the family, and sex.

Theology in the Western world during the twentieth century for the most part reflected the materialism of the age and the influence of existentialist philosophy. Strong efforts were made to update Christian theology by making it a more secular philosophy. Paul Tillich (1886–1965), a German Protestant who spent his later years in the United States, conceived of God as "ultimate truth" and "inner reality." Such traditional terms as *original sin, salvation, forgiveness, immortality,* and *atonement* were useful symbols under his pen, actually referring to personal and social ethics. Harvey Cox (1929–) of Harvard University, in his widely read *The Secular City* (1965), defined Christianity as a continuing social revolution. During the 1960s numerous religious cults, some of them quite wealthy and some violent, sprang up to offer companionship and certainty in this materialistic, competitive, perplexing world.

On the other hand, a few powerful voices

FIGURE 57.4 Moon Walk In July 1969 human beings walked on the moon. The United States' Apollo 11 moon mission is an example of the powerful combination of government and science. (NASA)

called for a return to an enlightened orthodox Christianity, notably the neo-Calvinists Karl Barth (1886–1968) in Switzerland and Reinhold Niebuhr (1892–1971) in the United States. God, they said, created the universe and runs it for his holy purpose, but selfish pride separates human beings from God. Only the Christian religion can remove that pride and bring men and women into God's purpose. Jacques Maritain (1882–1973) in France called for a return to the teachings of St. Thomas Aquinas. These learned theologians contributed dignity to the continuing claims of traditional Christianity.

3. TWENTIETH-CENTURY SCIENCE

After World War I most scientific research was still carried out by individuals or small groups of scientists in a university setting. There was a sense of separation between the theoretical and applied sciences, between the research carried out by the best scientific minds and the later application of their discoveries by engineers or technicians. After World War II, that pattern would be modified by closer ties between science and technology and by a new infusion of funds for scientific research by government and big business (see Figure 57.4). Scientists tended to work in organized teams, in larger research laboratories with extremely expensive and sophisticated equipment, and with specific goals in mind. These trends are most clear in the physical sciences, particularly physics.

In the two decades after World War I, the main thrust in physics was to continue the probing of the atom, which was begun in the nineteenth century, to discover the truths concerning the nature of matter. The results tended to be disillusioning. Albert Einstein had undermined the Newtonian world of physical stability with his relativity theory (see p. 587). A more shattering blow was delivered by Max Planck (1858–1947). Although he published his quantum theory in 1900, its full impact was not realized until the decades following World War I. According to this theory, energy is transmitted not in a steady, measurable stream, as had long been supposed, but in little leaps or packets (quanta), and the behavior of subatomic particles is so irregular and complex that the ultimate secrets of nature can never be fathomed by objective observation. In 1919 Ernest Rutherford (1871–1937) opened the world of subatomic particles and the possibility of changing the structure of atoms by bombarding them with subatomic particles. The sense of relativity and uncertainty in physics was furthered by Werner Heisenberg (1901–1976), who in 1927 formulated the "principle of uncertainty." He argued that any model or measurement of atoms was inherently approximate and relative.

Since World War II, teams of physicists have used huge, powerful, expensive accelerators to explore the subatomic world to a far greater degree than was possible before the war. Astrophysicists combined computer and radio telescope technology to expand our understanding of the universe. At the same time, many of these scientists were employed by government and industry to create new, more destructive weapons of war or products, such as computer chips and superconductors, that are of economic importance to our consumer society.

The most exciting discoveries in the biological sciences were in the field of genetics. In 1953 the nature of the complicated DNA molecule, which controls the pattern of all living things, was discovered. It is assumed that by tampering with this molecule new forms of life may be created, and that given characteristics in all living things, including humans, can be controlled. Recent research into gene splitting and genetic engineering gives truth to this assumption.

The most beneficial discoveries in the field of biological science during the twentieth century have been those that prevent and cure human ailments. Viruses were isolated, and their role in causing many diseases, including infantile paralysis, influenza, and the common cold, was recognized. Vaccines were developed to combat the infantile paralysis virus and a number of others

successfully—but the common cold still plagues most of humanity. During the late 1920s and the 1930s penicillin and sulfa drugs were discovered. These "miracle drugs" kill or control the bacteria causing many human infections. Since World War II drugs have been found useful in treating mental illness, and artificial and transplanted kidneys and hearts have saved or lengthened many lives.

The chief drawback in the application of these wonderful discoveries has been their high and continually soaring cost and the shortage of trained personnel to administer them. Many nations, Great Britain and Sweden among the first, recognized the enormous importance of public health by developing comprehensive programs of national health insurance. Communist regimes, of course, always made the practice of medicine a public rather than a private matter.

The social sciences have continued to emphasize the application of the methods being used so successfully in the natural sciences—rigorous empirical research, inductive and deductive reasoning, conclusions couched in the value-free language of relativism and probabilities. In recent decades, three new approaches have been used in several of the social sciences. The first is an extension of previous methods—quantitative research aided by computers and newly developed statistical tools. Computers have enabled researchers to work with massive quantities of materials and factors. Statistical tools have sharpened the probability or predictability of their conclusions. The second is structuralism, which stresses the rules or the forms of behavior rather than the specific content. The third is relativism, which rejects universal values and assumes that societies and cultures should be viewed within their own time, place, and context.

Of all the social scientists, the sociologists and anthropologists have been the most optimistic and energetic. Like other social scientists, they attempted to apply the scientific method to the study of human behavior. Max Weber (1864–1920) of Germany set up ideal types or models as a method of scientifically analyzing various sociological problems—a method that has been widely used ever since. Émile Durkheim (1858–1917) established a sociological tradition emphasizing the use of statistics for analyzing social behavior. Karl Mannheim (1893–1947), a refugee from Nazi Germany to Great Britain, developed a sociology of knowledge. He argued that ideas are related to and influenced by social forces to a much greater degree than had been suspected. Anthropologists tended to move from their earlier measurements of skulls and other physical features to the concept that differing cultures are based essentially on differing ways of interpreting experience and adapting to the environment. Claude Lévi-Strauss, perhaps the most influential anthropologist of recent decades, used a structuralist perspective to analyze the forms and rules of culture.

Between World War I and the 1950s psychology continued to be strongly influenced by Freudian theory and practice, which emphasized the irrational, unconscious, sexual, and aggressive elements in human thought and behavior. Behaviorism was also growing, and by the 1960s it overshadowed Freudianism. In the past two decades so many theories, approaches, therapies, and subdisciplines have proliferated within psychology that no single trend can be identified as dominant. Perhaps the most promising discoveries in recent years have been in physiological psychology. With so many people turning inward for answers and with secular explanations for human behavior deemed so important, psychology remains a field of growing influence.

Of all the social sciences, economics has taken most advantage of computer-aided quantitative research and sophisticated statistical tools. It is also the social science that most directly influences policy. Both governmental and private institutions rely on economists for the decisions they make. Underlying the quantitative research and statistical tools used by economists are more fundamental economic theories. Since the 1930s Keynesian economic thought has been most influential in countries with capitalistic or mixed economies. In 1936, in the midst of the Great Depression, John Maynard Keynes (1883–1946) published *The General Theory of Employment, Interest and Money,* advocating government regulation of the capitalistic system. He claimed that in times of recession the government should increase the supply of money in circulation by lowering interest rates and by deficit spending on public works. In times of inflationary boom it

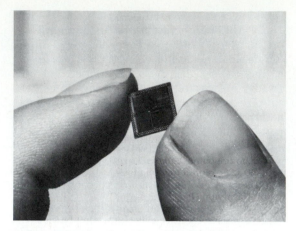

FIGURE 57.5 The Computer The development of tiny computer chips such as this has resulted in vast changes in science, business, and industry. (Charles Feil/Stock, Boston)

should restrict the money supply by raising interest rates and by other means. Liberals, not only in Keynes' native Britain but throughout the capitalistic world, accepted his theories, as indeed did many conservatives. But by the late 1970s and early 1980s it appeared that Keynesian theory could not account for many economic problems, particularly the combination of inflation and economic stagnation (with accompanying unemployment) that many termed "stagflation." Some theorists have called for greater governmental controls over wages and prices as well as general economic planning; others have attacked governmental involvement in the economy as doing more harm than good.

Probably the most important new tool for both the natural and social sciences is the computer (see Figure 57.5). The computer first became a tool of significance in the 1940s. By the 1950s and 1960s it was becoming linked with modern technology in a variety of ways, with a strong impact on the sciences and in the economy. With the new developments in computer technology, particularly miniaturization, the use of computers proliferated in almost all fields of science during the 1970s, 1980s, and 1990s. Its ability to store and manipulate information has made the computer a necessity rather than a luxury for most scientists. Yet it is still no more than a tool. The scientist must feed the computer the right information, ask useful questions, and interpret the answers.

4. TWENTIETH-CENTURY CULTURE

Philosophy

Philosophical thought in the twentieth century has been dominated by three trends, all of which can be traced back to the period just before World War I (see pp. 597–598 and 684). The first trend, which has clearly prevailed in Great Britain and the United States, is a combination of analytical philosophy and logical positivism. Analytical philosophy was first developed by Alfred North Whitehead (1861–1947) and Bertrand Russell (1872–1970) of Great Britain on the eve of World War I. The outstanding philosopher of logical positivism (or logical empiricism) was Ludwig Wittgenstein (1889–1951). Both analytical philosophy and logical positivism spurned any concept that could not be rationally and mathematically expressed. Under the influence of these doctrines, philosophy became highly technical, focusing on the exact meaning of words and logical relationships rather than the broad and ethical questions that traditionally concerned philosophers.

The second trend, which became more dominant on the European continent, is existentialism. Existentialism has its roots in the disenchantment of the late nineteenth century and the environment of anxiety resulting from the two world wars, the Great Depression, and the tensions of the Cold War. Existentialism drew heavily from Friedrich Nietzsche, who argued that there were no absolutes when he said "God is dead." Existential philosophy was also influenced by the mid–nineteenth-century Danish theologian Søren Kierkegaard, who rejected systematized and institutionalized Christianity in favor of personal inspiration and individual commitment. In Germany during the 1920s Martin Heidegger and Karl Jaspers developed aspects of existentialist philosophy. Thereafter, the center of existentialist thought shifted to France.

The most influential existentialist philosopher has been Jean-Paul Sartre (1905–1980). He argued that ultimately there is no meaning to existence and no final rights or wrongs. Individuals are born and simply exist. Individuals are free and responsible for the decisions and actions they take in life. Individuals must establish their own standards and their own rules, and each must take responsibility for living up to them. In the end, one simply dies.

The third trend, which has been a school of philosophy of varying strength, is Marxism (see pp. 527–528). Marxism emphasized historical determinism, ethical relativism, and social meaning behind philosophical concepts. During the 1920s and 1930s, it grew in influence in several academic circles and disciplines. Since World War II its influence has waxed and waned, and its doctrines have been modified in several ways. But on the whole, it has remained influential as a philosophical and historical perspective in a variety of disciplines.

Literature

The literature of the twentieth century, like the philosophy, is essentially an outgrowth and continuation of the literature of the late nineteenth century. A number of the great realistic writers of the early twentieth century lived and wrote until the middle of the century. The realism that had shocked many Victorians was succeeded by the more starkly naked naturalism. The focus tended to shift to a more subjective point of view and to the feelings, uncertainties, and unconscious motives of individuals.

In English-speaking Europe, James Joyce (1882–1941), an Irish expatriate in Paris, Virginia Woolf (1882–1941), an English novelist and critic, and T. S. Eliot (1888–1965), an American expatriate in London, developed the stream-of-consciousness technique. They placed words and thoughts out of sequence, providing new insights into the psyche with dramatic effect. This method clearly reflected the introspection of Freudian psychology.

In Germany, Franz Kafka (1883–1924) depicted the alienation and frustrations of an intellectual in the World War I era. The haunting, ambiguous quality of his fiction symbolizes the uncertainties and fears of his age. Most of his work was published after his death, and he enjoyed wide popularity only after World War II. Hermann Hesse (1877–1962) also reflected the uncertainty and sense of alienation in Germany during the World War I era in his novels. His writings, particularly those stressing a youthful and psychologically insightful search for meaning in a life always threatened by despair, became particularly popular after World War II. Perhaps the towering figure of twentieth-century German literature was Thomas Mann (1875–1955). His style and content were more traditional than that of Kafka or Hesse, always stressing a reverence for human beings in the often distressing environment of Mann's lifetime.

In France, Marcel Proust (1871–1922) developed introspective writing to new depths in his influential *Remembrance of Things Past*. In seven volumes of exquisitely polished prose he subjects to withering psychological analysis the remnants of French noble society and the vulgar social-climbing *nouveau riche* bourgeoisie who were trying to imitate the nobility. During the 1940s and 1950s, Albert Camus (1913–1960) popularized existentialism in his novels and plays, stressing the plight of the individual seeking understanding and identity in an amoral and purposeless universe. One of the leading playwrites of the era, the Irishman Samuel Beckett (1906–1990), also lived in France. He helped develop perhaps the most important trend in plays written since World War II—the "Theater of the Absurd." In works such as *Waiting for Godot* (1952), Beckett used unconventional staging and writing to break from traditionally realistic action. Audiences were forced to focus on what might be happening and how it might relate to human feelings and problems of existence. In this sense, the "Theater of the Absurd" reflected similar concerns expressed by existentialists. During the 1960s writers such as Alain Robbe-Grillet and film directors such as François Truffaut and Jean-Luc Godard made France the center of the *nouvelle vague* (new wave) in literature and film, stressing experimentation and imaginative techniques.

In the Soviet Union, Boris Pasternak (1890–1960) wrote in the grand manner of Tolstoy and Dostoyevski. His most well-known novel is *Doc-*tor Zhivago, which traces life in Russia before, during, and after the Bolshevik Revolution in 1917. More recently, Alexander Solzhenitsyn (1919–), who has lived in the United States since his expulsion from the Soviet Union in 1974, has written novels critically depicting life in the Soviet Union during the Stalinist era.

In the United States Sinclair Lewis (1885–1951), much like Theodore Dreiser, ridiculed both the hypocritical and "puritanical" bourgeoisie and the stupid, vulgar masses. Babbitt, Elmer Gantry, and Arrowsmith, the deflated heroes of Sinclair Lewis' novels by those titles, became stereotypes of typical Americans in the minds of thousands of atypical American readers of books. Eugene O'Neill (1888–1953) wrote plays in which the dramatic tension was maintained by psychological conflict (like those of Anton Chekhov—see p. 600) rather than development of plot and action. Ernest Hemingway (1898–1961) was an existentialist, entertaining his readers with his crisp, sophisticated prose. William Faulkner (1897–1962), with great depth and artistry, tore away the veil woven by civilization to conceal the violent and animallike nature of ordinary people. He extended the complex stream-of-consciousness technique.

The Fine Arts

The fine arts of the Western world in the twentieth century, like the philosophy and the literature, have generally proceeded along the guidelines laid down by the artists and writers of the late nineteenth century—disenchantment, rejection of tradition, a search for new values, and experimentation. These characteristics have become intensified by the materialism and the uncertainties of the twentieth century.

Without a doubt, the most gifted and influential painter of the twentieth century was Pablo Picasso (1881–1973) (see Figure 57.6). A Spaniard, he emigrated to Paris as a young man. There he was influenced by the French postimpressionists (see pp. 600–601). In order to penetrate the surface and reveal the inner reality of things, Picasso would take his subjects apart—arms, heads, violin parts—and rearrange and distort them for maximum effect. Early in the century,

FIGURE 57.6 Picasso's *Guernica* This large mural in black and white by one of the greatest artists of the twentieth century captures some of the worst features of the century—war, terror, brutality, disjointedness, lack of direction, and despair. Guernica was a small Spanish town destroyed by the German air force during the Spanish Civil War. (Museo Nacional del Prado)

at about the same time that young Whitehead and Russell were proclaiming their analytic philosophy based on mathematics, Picasso introduced cubism into the world of painting (see Figure 52.1). This technique was an effort, suggested by Cézanne, to demonstrate the solidity of the material universe by portraying the geometric composition of objects—spheres, cones, and cylinders. Cubism suggests the twentieth century's obsession with science.

Another prominent style of twentieth-century painting came to be called surrealism, whose chief proponents were Max Ernst (1891–1976) (see Color Plate 29), a German who later moved to the United States, and Salvador Dali (1904–1989) (see Color Plate 30), a Spaniard who lived many years in the United States. The surrealists, under the influence of Freud and his psychoanalytical techniques, attempted to express their imagination uncontrolled by reason and to suggest the activities of the subconscious mind, whether dreaming or awake. Picasso and Matisse, who were really laws unto themselves, painted many canvases in the surrealist style.

A third popular twentieth-century style of painting was expressionism, which had its origin in northern Europe, particularly Germany (see Figure 53.2). Its chief proponent was Vasili Kandinsky (1866–1944), a Russian who came to live in Germany. The expressionists, motivated by inner necessity, attempted to express freely their emotional reactions rather than the representation of the natural appearance of objects, resorting to abstraction and to violent distortion of color and form.

In recent decades, artistic styles such as pop art, op art, photo-realism (see Figure 57.1), and postmodernism have proliferated, often crossing boundaries between commercial and high art, between representational and abstract art (see Color Plate 31), and between traditional and nontraditional mediums (see Color Plate 32). All these styles reflect the artistic and the speculative mind of the Western world in the twentieth century—disenchantment, rejection of tradition, search for new values, and a turning inward for inspiration.

Twentieth-century architecture has been

FIGURE 57.7 Pompidou Center of Art and Culture, Paris The controversial Pompidou Center of Art and Culture, built in the center of Paris during the 1970s, carries the idea of functionalism in architecture to an aesthetic extreme. Structural and functional elements of the building show prominently on the outside, creating a vast open space on the inside. (B. Annebicque/Sygma)

dominated by the functional style (see Figure 57.7), developed in Germany by Walter Gropius' Bauhaus school, in France by architects such as Le Corbusier, and in the United States by Louis Henry Sullivan (see pp. 602–603). Sullivan's most illustrious student, and perhaps the best-known architect of the twentieth century, was Frank Lloyd Wright (1869–1959). Like his teacher, Wright believed that function is the sole purpose of architecture. He further insisted that form should conform to the materials used and to the setting. He made brilliant use of the cantilever (a projecting member supported at only one end) to achieve striking horizontal lines and an unobstructed spaciousness. These effects were made possible by the tensile strength of steel. Wright combined artistic skill with a Shavian scorn for traditional values and institutions. The most spectacular monuments of functional architecture are, of course, the great bridges and skyscrapers, most of them in the United States.

Twentieth-century music, too, is for the most part a continuation and development of styles formulated during the period 1871–1914. Richard Strauss (1864–1949) and Igor Stravinsky (1882–1971), two of the originators of modern music, lived far into the twentieth century. During the course of the century, Western music became increasingly dissonant, atonal, and experimental. These qualities probably found their ultimate composer in the Viennese Arnold Schoenberg (1874–1951), who abolished key, revolutionized the conception of melody, and replaced the seven-tone scale with one of twelve tones. Recent decades have witnessed the introduction of a universe of everyday and electronically produced sounds into music.

Popular Culture

The twentieth century has witnessed an explosion of popular culture. Several developments account for the huge variety and availability of popular literature, art, and music. There has been a tremendous expansion of communications—from cheap newspapers and paperback novels to radio, cinema, and television. Numerous large public facilities—from museums and concert halls to stadiums—have been built. The rising level of education has stimulated greater interest in cultural activities. Increasing affluence and leisure time among the urban classes have enabled more people to take advantage of cultural offerings.

FIGURE 57.8 Fritz Lang's *Metropolis* This eerie, futuristic scene from Fritz Lang's film *Metropolis* (1925) illustrates the overwhelming power of urban architecture and technology as well as the potential of the cinema as an artistic medium. (National Film Archive, London)

The products of popular culture are usually distinct from those of elite culture, but there has been some blurring of the lines between the two in recent decades. In cinema, an almost endless stream of what critics consider undistinguished but popular films are produced year after year. Yet cinema is perhaps the most original art form produced during the twentieth century (see Figure 57.8). The works of filmmakers such as Ingmar Bergman in Sweden and Federico Fellini in Italy reveal the potential of cinema as a sophisticated, creative, artistic medium. In music there is much that distinguishes the dissonant, atonal music of Arnold Schoenberg from rock and roll performed by groups such as the Beatles, but the distinction blurs with jazz, a development of America's black culture emphasizing sophisticated improvisation and rhythm. In art, most of the abstract or expressionistic paintings of the twentieth century remain outside popular taste, but what was once elite art, such as the romantic or realistic paintings of the nineteenth century, or even avant-garde, such as impressionism, is now extremely popular.

SUGGESTED READING

General

M. Crouzet, *The European Renaissance since 1945* (1971). A balanced account emphasizing society and culture.

S. Hoffmann and P. Kitromilides, *Culture and Society in Contemporary Europe* (1981). A good collection of essays.

Western Society in the Twentieth Century

S. de Beauvoir, *The Second Sex* (1962). A classic, crucial analysis of women.

C. Bouchier, *The Feminist Challenge: The Movement for Women's Liberation in Britain and the United States* (1983). A useful study.

D. Caute, *The Year of the Barricades: A Journey Through 1968* (1988). A study of youth culture since World War II.

A. Cherlin, *Marriage, Divorce, Remarriage* (1981). An interpretive analysis of the American family.

J. Lovenduski, *Women and European Politics: Contemporary Feminism and Public Policy* (1986). A good recent analysis.

R. Rubinstein, *Alchemists of Revolution: Terrorism in the Modern World* (1987). A comparative study.

E. Shorter, *The Making of the Modern Family* (1978). Well written, controversial.

Religion and Theology in the Twentieth Century

S. P. Schilling, *Contemporary Continental Theologians* (1966). A good survey of modern theology.

Twentieth-Century Science

J. Galbraith, *Age of Uncertainty* (1978). Writing lucidly for the nonspecialist, Galbraith argues for tight economic controls.

J. Ziman, *The Force of Knowledge: The Scientific Dimension of Society* (1976). An excellent analysis and bibliography.

Twentieth-Century Culture

W. Barrett, *Irrational Man* (1962). A good treatment of existentialism.

M. Biddiss, *Age of the Masses: Ideas and Society since 1870* (1977). A fine intellectual history.

R. Maltby, ed., *Passing Parade: A History of Popular Culture in the Twentieth Century* (1989). An excellent survey.

M. Marrus, ed., *Emergence of Leisure* (1974). An important collection.

A. Neumeyer, *The Search for Meaning in Modern Art*. A useful guide for the nonspecialist.

J. Passmore, *A Hundred Years of Philosophy* (1968). A good, concise survey.

H. Read, *A Concise History of Modern Painting* (1974). An excellent brief survey.

E. Salzman, *Twentieth Century Music: An Introduction*. A good survey.

R. Stromberg, *European Intellectual History since 1789* (1986). Chapters survey the period.

R. Williams, *Communications* (1976). Analyzes the media.

CHAPTER 58

Decolonization and the Non-Western World, 1945–Present

FIGURE 58.1 Victory Parade in China, 1970 An imposing ninety-foot statue of Chairman Mao Tse-tung towers over marchers celebrating the twenty-first anniversary of the Communist victory in China. The rise of China as a world power in recent decades exemplifies the growing importance of connections between the Western and non-Western worlds. (Sipahioglu/Sipa/Special Features)

The devastation of two world wars and the rising movements for independence within their colonies were too much for the European imperial powers to handle. Sometimes gracefully and sometimes only after protracted violence, Europe lost almost all its colonies in the two decades following World War II. As the formerly colonized peoples acquired their independence, they began to assert their power in many areas of the non-Western world. It soon became clear that neither Europe nor the superpowers could act without taking into account the concerns, power, and problems of the non-Western world.

1. JAPAN BETWEEN EAST AND WEST

Japan emerged from World War II defeated on sea and land, the shocked victim of history's first two atomic bombs used for military purposes. Since the United States had played by far the major role in the defeat of Japan, the United States refused to share the occupation and governing of the Japanese islands with its former allies. President Truman appointed General Douglas MacArthur supreme commander of the Allied powers in Japan and gave him absolute authority.

During the first year and a half of MacArthur's command a democratic constitution similar to that of Great Britain was drawn up and put into effect. In the first elections under the new constitution, which gave women the right to vote and guaranteed civil liberties, the Social Democrats, who were somewhat similar to the British Labourites, won the largest number of seats in the national legislature. The activities of Japanese labor unions were encouraged, and they became effective for the first time. The five great families (the *zaibatsu*) who had monopolized Japan's industry and finance disbanded their great business combinations under pressure from the occupation authorities. Demilitarization was carried out, and a number of top Japanese war leaders were tried and executed or imprisoned.

Of greatest significance was MacArthur's land-reform program. The great mass of Japanese farmers were poverty-stricken, landless sharecroppers, giving up from 50 to 70 percent

of their yield to absentee landlords. Laws sponsored by MacArthur forced the landlords to sell the government all land in excess of seven and a half acres (more in less fertile areas). The government, in turn, sold the land in plots of seven and a half acres to the tenant farmers, who were given thirty years to pay for them. By the end of 1946 Japan appeared to be on the way to becoming a liberal democracy.

Early in 1947, when the Cold War was being stepped up in intensity, General MacArthur suddenly reversed his liberal policy. He first cracked down on the newly formed labor unions. Industrial decentralization ceased, and land redistribution slowed down. Obviously, the United States was now interested in making Japan, like Germany, a link in the containment chain that it was forging around the Soviet Union. By 1949 the more conservative Liberal party, which later became the Liberal Democratic party, gained power and would hold it in elections through the following four decades.

During the 1950s and 1960s Japan made an astounding economic recovery that surpassed even that of West Germany. Like West Germany, Japan received massive American aid. In rebuilding its ruined industries, Japan adopted the most modern and scientific labor-saving devices (see Figure 58.2). It benefited from the rapid expansion of higher education and readily available, high-quality labor. By the mid-1960s Japan was the third greatest industrial power in the world, outranked only by the United States and the Soviet Union, and the Japanese people were enjoying a standard of living and social peace such as they had never known before. The Japanese, like the Germans, benefited greatly from American military protection, which relieved them of the enormous cost of maintaining a big military establishment. They also sold large quantities of industrial products, particularly electronics and automobiles, to the United States and bought relatively few American goods in return. Furthermore, the Japanese labor unions, like the German unions, but unlike the American, British, and French unions, have followed a policy of cooperation—codetermination—with their corporate managers.

Political stability and economic prosperity continued through the 1970s. In 1978 Japan signed a treaty of friendship and commerce with

FIGURE 58.2 Matsushita Electrical Industrial Company By the 1970s Japan was a leading industrial power, particularly in electronics. Plants such as this Matsushita Electrical Industrial Company (producing VCRs) used technology and disciplined labor to manufacture products for the home and foreign markets. (Courtesy Matsushita)

the People's Republic of China. During the 1980s Japan managed to maintain a striking degree of economic health with a comparatively high growth rate and lower rates of unemployment and inflation than any industrial power of the West.

2. THE RISE OF COMMUNIST CHINA

Across the Sea of Japan a very different and even more exciting drama was being enacted in China. Here, a massive upheaval involving one-fourth of the world's population took place. Sun Yat-sen, after launching his revolution against both China's foreign exploiters and its own reactionary and conniving government (see p. 630), died in 1925, in the midst of the struggle. His place at the head of the revolutionary Chinese government was taken by his young, vigorous supporter, General Chiang Kai-shek, who soon gained control of all China. Chiang, a professional soldier, was much more interested in making China a powerful and independent nation than in liberalizing its government and society. Under him, the revolutionary Kuomintang party, then dominant in China, swung definitely to the right. When the Chinese Nationalist armies were

defeated by the Japanese in 1937–1938 and driven deep into the interior, Chiang and the Kuomintang were cut off from the chief bases of their liberal support, which were the great coastal cities. Heavily dependent then on the warlords and landlords of the interior, they moved still further to the right.

Meanwhile, as China's Confucian civilization was crumbling faster than Sun's Western liberalism could replace it, another Western influence moved into the vacuum: Marxism. The hostility that the Western democracies showed to Sun's revolutionary liberal movement encouraged the Chinese Communists. In 1927 the Communists found an able leader in the scholarly and shrewd Mao Tse-tung (see Figure 58.3). This dedicated revolutionary from well-to-do peasant stock had risen to leadership by sheer force of intellect, personality, and energy. Chiang exerted every effort to crush the Chinese Communists—much more, in fact, than he spent to drive out the Japanese invaders. During the years 1939–1945, when the Kuomintang forces were getting further and further out of touch with the Chinese masses, Mao's Communists were waging incessant guerrilla warfare against the Japanese and gaining a greater following among the Chinese people.

Following the surrender of Japan in August 1945, a bitter struggle for the control of China

FIGURE 58.3 Mao Tse-tung and Ho Chi Minh These men were two of East Asia's most dynamic leaders since World War II. The North Vietnamese, though eager to get aid from China, were always suspicious and fearful of their big neighbor to the north. (Brian Brake/Rapho/Photo Researchers)

ensued between Chiang's Kuomintang forces, now known as the Chinese Nationalists, and the Chinese Communists. In this struggle the United States supported the Nationalists. However, the Communists won the support of ever-increasing numbers of the Chinese people. Morale in the long inactive and graft-ridden Nationalist armies was low, while that in the Communist armies, toughened by the continuous fighting against the Japanese, was high. During 1949 the victorious Communists swept over the entire Chinese mainland. Chiang, with a remnant of his Nationalist forces, mostly officers, fled to the island of Formosa (Taiwan), where after June 1950 they were protected by the U.S. navy.

In 1949 Mao proclaimed the People's Republic of China, and the following year he formed an alliance with the Soviet Union. With Soviet aid, he began the enormous task of industrializing and communizing the world's most populous nation. In 1953, after a delay caused by China's involvement in the Korean War (see the following section), Mao launched his First Five-Year Plan, which was similar to Stalin's First Five-Year Plan of twenty-five years earlier. The Chinese Communists, however, were starting from a much lower base than the Russians. Industry and agriculture were both collectivized, and the emphasis was on building heavy industry. In 1957 the government announced that the First Five-Year Plan had been a great success.

The following year it launched its Second Five-Year Plan. The vast new goals in industry and agriculture were to be achieved by communizing Chinese society more completely than had ever been attempted in the Soviet Union. The entire population was organized into strictly regimented communes. China's huge and rapidly growing population was set to building irrigation dams and ditches, steel mills, factories, railroads, schools, and hospitals in a frenzied hurry. This plan was called the "Great Leap Forward." But the plan was too ambitious. In 1959 a series of droughts and floods produced near-famine conditions in many areas. Overzealous local party officials provoked resentment and resistance among the harried populace. The realistic Red leaders slackened the pace and eased the regimentation.

The failure of the Great Leap Forward gave rise to ideological differences and set off a power struggle within the Communist party hierarchy. A moderate group led by Liu Shao-chi, president of the republic and second in command to Party Chairman Mao, wished to slow down the pace of communization, produce more consumer goods, and encourage, at least temporarily, individual initiative. Mao took a different line. He believed that many dangerous remnants of pre-revolutionary capitalistic China and the newly bloated bureaucracy had to be destroyed. In 1966 he unleashed tens of thousands of Red Guards—fanatical Communist youths—upon the moderate element in what he called a "cultural revolution" and with the support of the regular army succeeded, after three years of turmoil, in crushing the moderates.

Meanwhile, China and the Soviet Union were drifting apart. In 1956 an ideological dispute had begun when Khrushchev denounced Stalin. Peking accused Moscow of becoming soft toward the capitalistic, imperialist West. In 1960 the Soviet Union began to withhold promised economic and technological aid from China. In 1964 Red China exploded its first nuclear device. The Soviets moved many of their best mechanized divisions to the Far East, where in 1968 they clashed with Chinese units along their disputed border—the longest international border in the world. Both Red giants, fearful of each other, sought a détente with the United States. In 1971 the United States ceased to block the admission of Red China to the United Nations, making it possible for the United Nations to admit the People's Republic of China (1971) and expel the Republic of China on Taiwan. Emissaries were exchanged between Peking and Washington.

In a power struggle following Mao's death in 1976, more moderate officials led by Deng Xiaoping came to power. In 1978 they initiated the policy of the "Four Modernizations." The policy was a dramatic departure from many elements of Mao's economic policies in favor of more pragmatic methods. To foster rapid economic development and greater productivity, there was a new emphasis on economic decentralization. A more market-oriented economy was introduced into the countryside and, later, some urban areas. By the mid-1980s these policies were resulting in new relations with Japan and the United States, more foreign loans, the opening of China to tourism and foreign investment, new economic growth, and greater economic freedom (see p. 762).

3. THE KOREAN WAR

The bitter Left-Right conflict among the Asiatic peoples and the global Cold War struggle between the United States and the Soviet Union merged in Korea to produce a shooting war of major proportions. In August 1945, in accordance with the Yalta Agreements, the forces of the Soviet Union overran Japanese-held Korea north of the thirty-eighth parallel, and the forces of the United States began to occupy Korea south of the thirty-eighth parallel. These moves were supposed to be for the purpose of setting up a free and united Korean nation. However, the Soviet Union immediately proceeded to set up a Communist dictatorship in North Korea under Kim Il-sung. The land was distributed to the peasants, and industry was nationalized. In South Korea the United States authorities sponsored a right-wing government under the leadership of the aged and reactionary Korean patriot Syngman Rhee. Late in 1948 the Soviet forces withdrew from North Korea, leaving behind an energetic Communist regime well armed with the latest Soviet weapons. Six months later the American forces withdrew from South Korea, leaving behind the Syngman Rhee landlord regime armed mostly with the weapons that had been captured from the Japanese. Both the North and South Korean governments talked loudly of conquering each other.

On June 25, 1950, North Korea suddenly attacked South Korea. The high-spirited, well-armed North Korean Communists easily defeated the South Koreans. The United States persuaded the United Nations to take drastic action. Taking advantage of the absence of the Soviet Union's representative, the Security Council called upon all the members of the United Nations to furnish military forces to repel the North Korean aggression and asked President Truman to name the commander of the U.N. forces. Truman named General MacArthur to command them. Truman also announced that he had already ordered American forces into the Korean War, that the American navy would protect Chiang's Chinese Nationalists on Taiwan against the Chinese Communists, and that American aid to the French fighting the native Communists in Indochina would be greatly increased.

The forces of the United Nations, mostly Americans, quickly defeated the North Koreans. By late November 1950 MacArthur's forces were approaching the Yalu River, which forms the Korean-Chinese border. At this point Red China entered the war and severely defeated MacArthur's forces, driving them in headlong retreat back down the peninsula. Eventually the battle line became stabilized roughly along the thirty-eighth parallel. Two years of negotiations brought an armistice in 1953. Total casualties—dead, wounded, and missing—are estimated to have been approximately a million and a half on each side. The war ended just about where it had started. However, Communist military aggression had been checked with severe punishment. The United Nations had functioned effectively and increased its prestige. Probably of equal significance is the fact that a revolutionary new Asiatic power, Red China, had fought the greatest Western power, the United States, to a standstill.

Since the end of the war, North and South Korea have gone their separate ways. North Korea has remained a tightly controlled Communist state under the long rule of Kim Il-sung. South Korea has remained under the control of right-wing authoritarian leaders, but its society is more open and more economically dynamic than that of the North. During the 1970s and 1980s it became one of the most rapidly growing and industrializing economies in the world, and recently it has shown signs of broadening political participation.

4. THE REVOLT OF SOUTHERN ASIA

The end of World War II found the huge British, Dutch, and French empires in southern Asia aflame with the spirit of nationalism and revolt. Of the Western imperial powers, only the United States escaped direct embroilment in this revolt by granting independence to the Philippines in 1946.

In India, the world's second most populous country, the leader of the independence movement was Mohandas K. Gandhi (1869–1948), one of the most dynamic personalities of the twentieth century. This middle-class Hindu, educated in Great Britain, was a master of the psychology of the Indian masses. His chief tactics were passive resistance and civil disobedience. The British were unable to cope with him.

Indian nationalism reached its peak during World War II, but Churchill would not hear of Indian independence. "I did not become the king's first minister," said the doughty warrior, "in order to preside over the liquidation of the British Empire." The British Labour party, however, upon coming to power in 1945 immediately announced its determination to grant India independence. In 1947 independence was granted to India, containing some 350 million people, and Pakistan, with more than 70 million people.

Religious and national strife soon broke out between Hindu India and Moslem Pakistan. Gandhi tried to quell the strife, but he was assassinated in 1948 by a fanatical Hindu nationalist. Open war between the two states began in 1948 over possession of the disputed state of Kashmir. The United Nations was able to end the shooting but not the dispute.

One of Gandhi's most devoted followers, Jawaharlal Nehru, a charming, wealthy British-educated Hindu of the highest (Brahmin) caste, became the first prime minister of India (see Figure 58.4). The problems confronting him were staggering. Most of India's millions were poverty-stricken and illiterate. They spoke more than eight hundred languages and dialects (fewer than 50 percent spoke the official Hindi). Some 100 million Indians were of the untouchable class. Nehru inaugurated a liberal and mildly socialistic program somewhat similar to that of the British Labour government. Border clashes with Pakistan and Red China pushed India into accepting military aid from both the United States and the Soviet Union.

When Nehru died in 1964, his successors were confronted by rising discontent. In 1966 Nehru's daughter, Indira Gandhi, became prime minister. Many Indians felt that the economic and social reform program of the Nehrus was not drastic enough. In spite of sizable loans and much technical assistance from the United States, Great Britain, and the Soviet Union, India's standard of living was not keeping abreast of its ever-mounting population. In 1974, while millions of its people stood on the brink of starvation, India exploded its first nuclear device. In 1975 the opposition to Prime Minister Gandhi's administration became so disruptive that she invoked constitutional emergency decrees that amounted to dictatorship. But the opposition only increased. In 1977 Mrs. Gandhi granted national elections and was driven from power. However, her successors had little success in dealing with the overwhelming problems facing India. Indira Gandhi returned to power as prime minister in 1980, but she was assassinated by Sikh extremists in 1984. She was succeeded by her son, Rajiv Gandhi, who held office until 1989 and who was assassinated during the 1991 elections. India still struggles with the problems of religious differences (particularly with the Sikhs of Punjab) and linguistic differences (as with the Tamils in the

FIGURE 58.4 Nehru and Gandhi Two great charismatic leaders of Asian independence, India's Jawaharlal Nehru and Mahatma Gandhi, are shown during a meeting of the All India Congress in Bombay in 1946. (UPI/Bettmann Newsphotos)

south) in a difficult environment of uneven economic development, overpopulation, and poverty.

Pakistan, divided into two states more than a thousand miles apart (see Map 58.1) and with a fragile constitutional government, soon became a military dictatorship closely aligned with the United States. In 1971 East Pakistan rebelled against the less populous but dominant West Pakistan and, with the help of India, gained its independence as the Republic of Bangladesh—but not before some 3 million of its helpless citizens had been slaughtered by the West Pakistani army. From 1977 to his death in 1988, Muhammad Zia ul-Haq held power and remained an important if difficult ally of the United States.

The British Labour government also granted independence to Ceylon, Burma, and Malaya. This left only Hong Kong as a reminder of British imperialism in Asia.

The rich and populous Dutch East Indies declared independence at the end of World War II. The Dutch resisted fiercely for four years but yielded to pressure from the United Nations. In 1949 the Republic of Indonesia was recognized as an independent nation—a nation of approximately 125 million people, mostly Moslems, living on several thousand tropical islands rich in tin, rubber, oil, and many other valuable products.

Of all the European colonial regimes in Asia, that of the French in Indochina was probably the most predatory and the most hated. Immediately after the surrender of Japan in August 1945, the Indochinese nationalists, under the leadership of Ho Chi Minh, a Russian-trained Communist, proclaimed the independent "democratic" Republic of Vietnam. The returning French imperialists were fiercely resisted by the native Communist nationalists. Heavy fighting ensued, in which the French were aided by American Marshall Plan money. The majority of the Vietnamese people apparently preferred the Communists to the French, and the forces of Ho Chi Minh won victory after victory despite American aid to the French.

In 1954 the French government admitted defeat and ceded the northern half of Vietnam to the Communists. Although South Vietnam technically remained a part of the French Union, French influence quickly vanished. The United States, in accordance with its policy of military containment of communism—both Russian and Chinese—undertook to establish its power not only in South Vietnam but also in Laos and Cambodia, which the French had also freed. Vigorous military and financial aid was given to the conservative Ngo Dinh Diem regime in South Vietnam. Fearful of a Communist victory at the polls, American authorities refused to permit the hold-

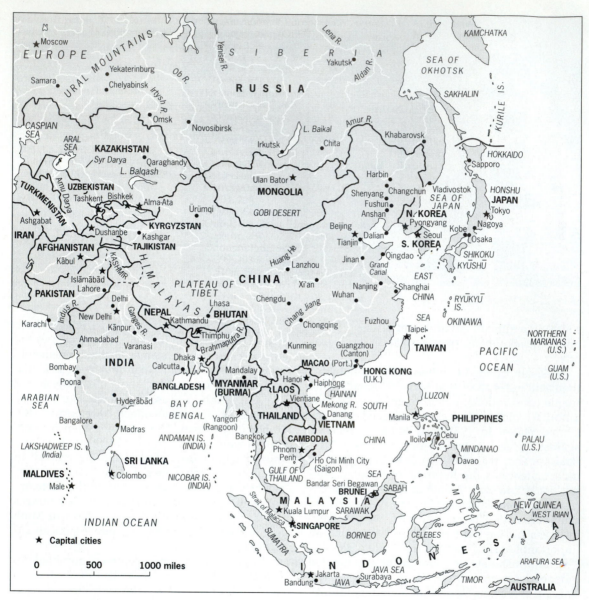

Map 58.1 ASIA, 1993 Containing more than one-half of the world's population, Asia has been of growing concern to the Western nations since 1945. Two wars (the Korean and Vietnamese) have directly involved Western nations, while the economic might of Japan and the potential power of China are seen as threatening to many Western interests.

Figure 58.5 Vietnam, 1969
The intervention of the United States in Vietnam for the purpose of containing communism (Russian and Chinese, it was believed) resulted in greater bombing and destruction than in World War II. Millions of Vietnamese were killed, maimed, and made homeless. (Philip Jones Griffiths/Magnum)

ing of national elections, which had been promised by an international commission when the French withdrew. Diem became increasingly unpopular. Almost immediately, he was faced with a rebellion of his own people supported and soon led by the Communists in both South and North Vietnam. In 1963 Diem, having lost the confidence and support of his American protectors, was overthrown and assassinated by a group of his own officers, who set up a harsh military dictatorship of their own. Early in 1965 the Vietnamese Communists, with significant material aid from both the Soviet Union and Red China, greatly stepped up their war against the American-supported but weakening South Vietnamese forces. The United States retaliated with heavy bombing of North Vietnam and increased its armed forces to over 500,000 troops. Vietnam was rapidly being devastated (see Figure 58.5).

Meanwhile, public opinion all over the world, including the United States, was becoming incensed at the wanton destruction. In 1968 a massive North Vietnamese surprise offensive convinced the American government that victory could not be won, and the United States began long, dreary peace talks with the North Vietnamese in Paris. In 1969 Ho Chi Minh died, but the war and new massive bombings (the United States dropped more explosives on Vietnam than were used by all combatants during World War

II) dragged on until 1973, when peace agreements were finally signed and the United States withdrew its armed forces, leaving behind huge stores of war matériel for the South Vietnamese.

The civil war in Vietnam, however, continued as both sides refused to abide by the terms of the peace agreements. As in China and Korea, the graft-ridden armed forces of a corrupt government trying to maintain the old aristocratic society of a bygone era were no match for the high-spirited Communist forces. In 1975 the Communists swept to victory over all Vietnam and shortly thereafter over the rest of Indochina—Cambodia and Laos. Even then the violence did not end. In Cambodia the Communist Pol Pot regime devastated that society, resulting in the death of over a million people and ending in an invasion and occupation of Cambodia by Vietnam. Relations between Vietnam and China remain shaky, with violence having broken out along their border more than once in recent years.

5. THE EMBATTLED MIDDLE EAST

One of the most explosive areas in the world of the latter half of the twentieth century was the Middle East—that area between and including Egypt and Iran, where East meets West (see Map

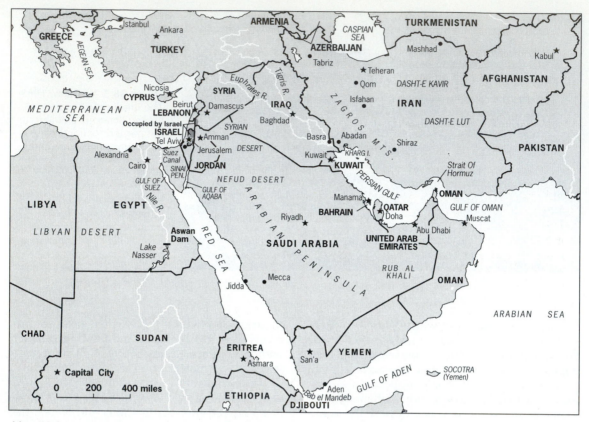

Map 58.2 **THE MIDDLE EAST, 1993** Since 1945 the Middle East has been wracked by several outbreaks of war involving Israel and its neighbors. Cold War involvements, the growing strength of Arab nationalism, and OPEC control over oil production have made this part of the world of crucial concern to the West.

58.2). It is probably the most strategic area in the world. It forms the bridge between the world's two greatest land masses, Eurasia and Africa, and through it pass the chief communication lines between the East and the West. The Middle East is the heart of the Islamic world, which stretches from Morocco to Indonesia and contains over 500 million followers of the Prophet. It is also the heart of the tumultuous Arab world. Moreover, the area contains more than half the world's known oil reserves.

During the early part of the century, while the great European powers competed for control of the Middle East, Arab nationalism was rising. This nationalism was vented first against the British, who were the dominant power in that

area. As anti-British hostility mounted in the years between the two world wars, Great Britain began to relax its control. By the end of World War II only Cyprus, Palestine, and the Suez Canal remained in Britain's possession, and the British were bidding strongly for Arab friendship. But continued British possession of the Suez Canal and the admission of tens of thousands of Jews into Palestine under the Balfour Declaration of 1917 proved to be effective barriers to Anglo-Arab accord.

Palestine was the ancient home of the Jews. However, in A.D. 70 they were dispersed by the government of the Roman Empire. In the seventh century the Islamic Arabs conquered Palestine and lived there until the twentieth century—thirteen hundred years. In the late nineteenth century, the Zionist movement began—a movement to restore Palestine as a national home for the Jews. During the anti-Semitic persecutions of the Hitler era, thousands of European Jewish refugees, many of them wealthy, poured into Palestine, buying up the land and dispossessing the Arabs. The whole Arab and Islamic world became incensed.

In 1948 the British Labour government turned Palestine over to the United Nations. The Jews immediately proclaimed the State of Israel and accepted the boundary lines the United Nations had drawn to divide Palestine between the Jews and the Arabs. The Arab League refused to accept this arrangement and began hostilities with a view to eliminating the Jewish state. Tiny Israel, however, well armed and well financed, was more than a match for the Arabs. After a year of fighting, the United Nations succeeded in bringing about a truce. Israel had somewhat expanded its original borders, and it had expelled nearly half a million Arabs who had fought to destroy the State of Israel. Arab nationalism was thoroughly aroused, and border raids recurred as the Arabs armed for a renewal of the struggle. Israel, in the meantime, receiving financial aid from Jews abroad, prospered, built modern cities, introduced irrigation and scientific agriculture, and became a vigorous, democratic, cooperative Western society.

The Arabs found a vigorous leader when in 1952 a military coup in Egypt brought Gamel Abdul Nasser to power. Nasser set out to unite the Arab world and inflame it against the West. When he threatened Israel, seized the Suez Canal, and aided France's rebellious subjects in North Africa, he was attacked by Israel, Great Britain, and France in 1956. He was saved only by the threatened intervention of the Soviet Union, which caused the United States to exert sufficient pressure on the three invading powers to force them to give up their assault. But nothing had been settled. Nasser continued to arouse Arab nationalism against Israel, and the Arab states received a swelling stream of arms from the Soviet Union.

In 1967 Nasser again brought on a showdown. He had prohibited the use of the Suez Canal by the Israelis since the 1956 war. When he blockaded Israel's only port on the Red Sea and Egyptian, Syrian, and Jordanian armies massed along the Israeli borders, the Israelis suddenly attacked them and crushed them in six days' time. The Israelis then occupied Egyptian territory east of the Suez Canal, Syria's Golan Heights, and Jordanian territory west of the Jordan—territories the Israelis claimed were necessary for their security.

The six-day 1967 war humiliated not only the Arab world but also the Soviet Union, which rushed billions of dollars' worth of arms, including deadly surface-to-air missiles (SAMs), together with thousands of military "advisers," to Egypt and Syria. Nasser died in 1970 and was succeeded as president of Egypt by Anwar Sadat.

As the Israelis were celebrating their Yom Kippur holidays in October 1973, Egypt and Syria, supported by the rest of the Arab states (except Morocco), suddenly attacked them. This time the Arabs, much better armed and trained than before, inflicted serious casualties on the Israelis and pushed them back on all fronts. Several weeks were required for the heavily outnumbered Israelis to recover from their initial shock, receive massive fresh supplies from the United States, and mount offensives of their own. They then crossed the Suez Canal, surrounded an entire Egyptian army, and began advancing on Cairo to the west and Damascus, the Syrian capital, to the east. At this juncture the Soviet Union threatened to intervene. The United States alerted its armed forces and forced the Israelis to halt their advance. The United Nations helped to arrange a cease-fire.

The Arabs now made full use of their oil weapon; they quadrupled the price of their oil, curtailed production, and placed a complete embargo on its shipment to the United States and the Netherlands. These measures added greatly to the strain of inflation that had long gripped the capitalistic world. The poorer nations of Asia and Africa were particularly distressed.

In November 1977 Egyptian President Sadat surprised the world by going to Jerusalem and beginning negotiations with Israeli Premier Menachem Begin for a peace settlement. Sadat was denounced by all his Arab neighbors for breaking the solid Arab front against Israel. Negotiations soon broke down, but in 1978 U.S. President Carter persuaded Sadat and Begin to sign the first draft to a peace treaty, which was finalized in 1979 and led to an Israeli withdrawal from the Sinai and open borders between the two nations.

The Palestinian refugees were one of the most tumultuous elements in the whole Middle Eastern complex. Fleeing Palestine after the 1948 war, they first attempted to overthrow the government of Jordan. Failing there, they took refuge in Lebanon, which was too weak to expel them. Their numbers grew constantly until by 1975 there were between 2 million and 3 million of them. In that year they joined the Islamic Lebanese majority in attempting to overthrow the Christian-dominated government. In the civil war that followed, Beirut, the capital city and one of the most prosperous banking and commercial centers in the Middle East, was wrecked. Syria took advantage of the turmoil to move in and gain military control over most of the country. In 1982 Israel invaded Lebanon and occupied the southern half of the country. In vain, troops from Western nations, including Italy, France, Great Britain, and the United States, were stationed in Beirut by 1983, only to be withdrawn in 1984. Lebanon would continue to be wracked by civil war and international animosities, and the Palestinian's struggles with Israel seem far from over. Under the leadership of the Palestine Liberation Organization and other radical groups, Palestinians continued to resist Israeli troops from within Israeli-occupied territories and resort to guerrilla and terrorist tactics almost everywhere. Israel responded with intransigence. Recently, however, the Palestine Liberation Organization, under the leadership of Yasir Arafat, gained increased international stature. By admitting Israel's right to exist and rejecting terrorism, the Palestine Liberation Organization convinced the United States to open negotiations with it for the first time. In 1991, 1992, and 1993 new Middle East talks and the election of the more flexible Labour party to power in Israel brought more hope for peace between Israel and its neighbors, culminating in September 1993 with a treaty of mutual recognition between Israel and the Palestine Liberation Organization and the promise of new agreements in the Middle East.

The enormous oil wealth pouring into the Middle East accelerated the demands for change. Countries such as Saudi Arabia and Kuwait suddenly became wealthy, commanding strategic oil reserves and great financial muscle. But in other countries, problems arose. In 1978 Iran, second only to Saudi Arabia in the production of oil and precariously situated between the Soviet Union and the Persian Gulf, was the scene of massive uprisings. The shah's government was strongly supported by the United States as a military strong point on the border of the Soviet Union. Though modernizing the country, the shah's government was a military dictatorship. Now it was beset on the one hand by young liberals who wanted to democratize and further modernize Iran and on the other by the masses led by Islamic fundamentalists who rejected the West and secularism in favor of old Islamic values. Early in 1979 the shah was forced to flee, and the reins of government were seized by the seventy-nine-year-old popular Islamic mystic Ayatollah Khomeini, who set up an Islamic republic (see Figure 58.6). The nationalistic Khomeini was strongly anti-American, anti-Soviet, and anti-Israeli. The violence and instability continued and indeed was increased in 1980 by the outbreak of a costly war between Iran and Iraq that lasted until 1988. More violence was to come. In 1979 the Soviet Union invaded Afghanistan, sparking strong Islamic resistance that continued after the Soviet withdrawal in 1989. In 1990 Iraq invaded and overwhelmed Kuwait. The next year an American-led and United Nations-sanctioned coalition massively bombed Iraq and threw Iraqi troops out of Kuwait. These events indicate that the turmoil that has marked the Middle East has few boundaries.

6. THE EMANCIPATION OF AFRICA

Africa was the last of the continents to rise against European imperialism (see Map 58.3). France and Great Britain, which held the most territory in Africa, were the first to begin to dismantle their vast empires there.

The end of World War II found France's huge North African empire seething with unrest. Its population, largely Islamic, was agitated by the rampaging Arab nationalism in the Middle East. In 1956, France granted independence to Morocco and Tunisia. The problem of independence or autonomy for Algeria was much more complex because of the presence there of more than

FIGURE 58.6 Khomeini In 1979 the Shiites' leader, Ayatollah Khomeini, gained power in Iran. As spiritual head of an Islamic fundamentalist movement, Khomeini commanded the passionate allegiance of masses of followers. (UPI/Bettmann Newsphotos)

Africa, and invited them to form a voluntary union with France. All but one, French Guinea, did so.

Great Britain's experiences in Africa following World War II were quite similar to those of France. All the native populations caught the spirit of nationalism and turned in resentment against their white masters. Native terror bands, notably the Mau Mau in Kenya, made British life and property increasingly unsafe. In 1957 Great Britain granted independence to its Gold Coast colony, which became the Republic of Ghana. This proved to be the first step in the eventual freeing of Britain's remaining African colonies. During the next few years one after another of Britain's African territories was freed. By 1965 all of Britain's African empire had been dismantled.

In two of the former British African colonies sizable white minorities attempted to continue their domination over the black majorities and in so doing created tensions that became global in scope. In Rhodesia approximately a quarter million whites ruled 6 million blacks. When in 1965 the British government pressed the all-white government of Rhodesia to grant suffrage to blacks, that government declared its independence from Great Britain. Almost immediately the black majority demanded suffrage and civil equality; when it was refused, many of them resorted to guerrilla warfare, aided by neighboring black nations and by the Soviet Union. In 1980 freedom was gained. Zimbabwe acquired full independence from Great Britain, and Robert Mugabe, one of the principal black guerrilla leaders, was named prime minister.

South Africa was the scene of a bigger and potentially even more dangerous racial conflict. The Dominion of South Africa had since 1931 (by the Statute of Westminster) been completely free. There the prosperous white minority of 4 million whites clung desperately to its superiority over 18 million blacks and other nonwhites. In 1948 and thereafter, the white minority took severe measures to suppress the increasingly restless black majority and to enforce *apartheid* (racial segregation). When in 1961 several fellow members of the British Commonwealth censured South Africa because of its racial policies, South Africa withdrew from the Commonwealth, taking its large mandate, South-West Africa (Namibia), with it. Under pressure from the angry

a million French settlers who feared reprisals from the 8 million Islamic Algerians. Efforts to hold back independence resulted in open revolt by Algerians that France could not handle and that helped bring de Gaulle back to power in France. In 1962, bowing to the force of Arab nationalism, he granted Algeria independence. Meanwhile, he had granted independence to all the other French colonies, most of which were in

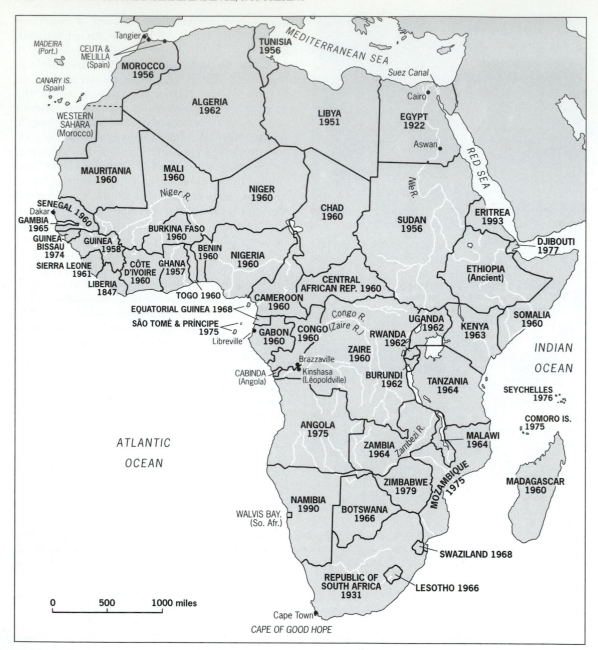

Map 58.3 AFRICA, 1993 As this map indicates, the vast majority of African nations gained their independence during the 1950s and 1960s. Instability, often stemming from the legacy of Western colonialism, has plagued much of the continent.

black majority and from the Organization of African Unity (set up in 1963 by the completely freed African nations), the United Nations, and world opinion, the all-white government of the Republic of South Africa from time to time made token concessions to apartheid but steadfastly refused to grant majority rule. During the 1970s and 1980s the situation became increasingly polarized and explosive. White South Africa remained almost completely isolated in the world, censured because of its racism, a place where massive violence was expected to break out as peaceful alternatives for change were rejected. In 1989 F. W. de Klerk was elected prime minister, and he initiated policies that promised real change for South Africa. Over the next few years relations were established with the African National Congress, much of apartheid was abolished, negotiations to share political power with South African blacks were initiated, and South Africa withdrew from Namibia.

The decision of the World War II Allies to free oil-rich Libya from Italian control was consummated in 1951. In 1960 Italy granted independence to Somalia in East Africa, and Belgium gave up the Congo. Finally, Portugal freed her large African colonies in 1975, bringing to an end (with the exception of a few bits of territory here and there) the era of European domination of Africa that had begun in the fifteenth century.

The granting of independence, of course, did not bring peace and prosperity to the African people. The boundaries of the African states had been drawn in many cases quite arbitrarily by nineteenth-century European imperialists sitting around plush green-topped tables in London or Brussels dividing up the spoils. In the Congo, for instance, tribal warfare flamed up immediately after independence. Russian and Chinese Communist agents moved in to exploit the chaos. U.N. Secretary-General Dag Hammarskjöld lost his life there in a plane accident while trying to mediate the differences. In Nigeria, the Ibos in the eastern region attempted to secede and set up the independent Republic of Biafra. Thousands died in the futile struggle, and tens of thousands died by starvation. Since the newly freed African people were left without political experience and with few, if any, self-generated political institutions, instability, bloodshed, and rule by military strongmen were often the result. Charismatic liberation leaders such as Kwame Nkrumah in Ghana and Jomo Kenyatta in Kenya (where a relatively stable parliamentary system was established) were more the exception than the rule.

Economically the European colonial powers did not leave African countries with a firm basis for balanced prosperity or self-sufficiency. In the early 1990s Africa's economy was still primarily agricultural, despite a large development of oil and gas production in Libya, Algeria, and Nigeria and a beginning of industrialization (mostly foreign) in certain areas such as the Ivory Coast. Of course, gold and diamond mining in South Africa was still a source of great wealth. Africa's rapidly growing population, dependent for the most part on agriculture, was faced with an increasing threat of hunger and starvation. An unprecedented drought in the huge sub-Saharan region of northern Africa during the 1970s, 1980s, and 1990s brought death by starvation to tens of thousands (see Figure 58.7).

7. LATIN AMERICA

Finally, there remains to be examined a large and populous area of the world which is, in a sense, neither East nor West—Latin America (see Map 58.4). Just as Japan is a highly industrialized nation located in the East, Latin America is *in* but, in many respects, not *of* the West. Its religion and languages are, of course, Western. But the poverty and illiteracy of the masses, the underdeveloped economies, and the unstable political institutions more closely resemble those of southern Asia and Africa than Western Europe and the United States.

At the end of World War II the governments of the twenty independent Latin American states were all republics in name. In reality, however, most of them were rightist dictatorships, representing the interests of the well-to-do bourgeoisie, the landowning classes, and the professional military. The Roman Catholic church, which during the nineteenth century had been one of the most powerful rightist forces, had during the twentieth century tended to become much more liberal. In some of the Latin American republics,

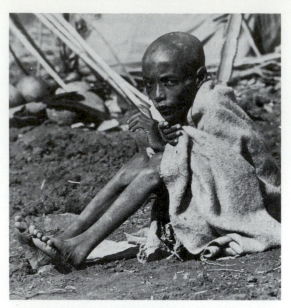

FIGURE 58.7 Ethiopian Refugee In recent decades, large areas of Africa have suffered from war, drought, and overpopulation. The results have been malnutrition, disease, starvation, and death. This photo of a starving child at a refugee camp in Ethiopia is all too common. (Michel Philippot/Sygma)

notably Chile, the Church was now actively engaged in liberal social and economic reform movements. Costa Rica was the most democratic of the republics. In Mexico a stable (though primarily one-party) democratic regime had since 1934 been pursuing a liberal program of economic, social, and educational reforms.

Throughout most of Latin America the poor, illiterate, and ever more numerous masses became increasingly restive after World War II. Many of them turned to communism and were encouraged and supported by the Soviet Union. The United States, on the other hand, supported the rightist governments. In 1954 a military force armed by the United States invaded and overthrew the leftist government of Guatemala. Ten years later a rightist military takeover in Brazil was encouraged and applauded by the United States. In 1948 the twenty Latin American "republics" were persuaded to join the United States in an Organization of American States

(OAS) for the purpose of resisting outside (Communist) interference. The Latin Americans were primarily interested in economic aid from the United States and were generally disappointed.

In Cuba the policy of the United States backfired. In 1959 the rightist dictator, Fulgencio Batista, long supported by the United States, was overthrown by the leftist revolutionary Fidel Castro. Castro began a sweeping program of social and economic reforms including the seizure of property owned by citizens and corporations of the United States. The fumbling efforts of the United States to overthrow the Castro regime drove it into the arms of the Soviet Union. Cuba became a Communist beachhead in the Western Hemisphere.

In 1970 Chile became the first nation in the world to vote a Marxist regime into power. As a result of a split between the conservatives and the moderate liberals, Salvador Allende was elected president (with 36 percent of the vote) and immediately launched a Marxist program. All industrial properties, the biggest of which were owned by U.S. corporations, were nationalized. The U.S. government determined to destroy the Allende regime. In 1974 the Central Intelligence Agency admitted that it had spent $11 million bribing Chilean legislators, stirring up labor strife, and supporting right-wing elements. In 1973 the Allende regime was overthrown by the professional military, which set up a rightist military dictatorship. Allende and thousands of his followers were executed.

In 1979 the Sandinistas, a leftist revolutionary force, overthrew the Somoza dictatorship in Nicaragua. During the 1980s, the new government pursued policies of radical social and economic reform, but it was weakened by pressure from the United States and the American-backed contra guerrillas.

In the 1990s Latin America, like much of the non-Western world, remains an area of sharp and dangerous contrasts. Its rich natural resources are not being developed and used for the benefit of the rapidly increasing population, which for the most part is poor and illiterate. Increases in productivity seem more than matched by a rapid inflation of prices for goods and services. Great modern cities such as Mexico City and São Paulo, which rival New York and Chicago in size and modernity, stand sur-

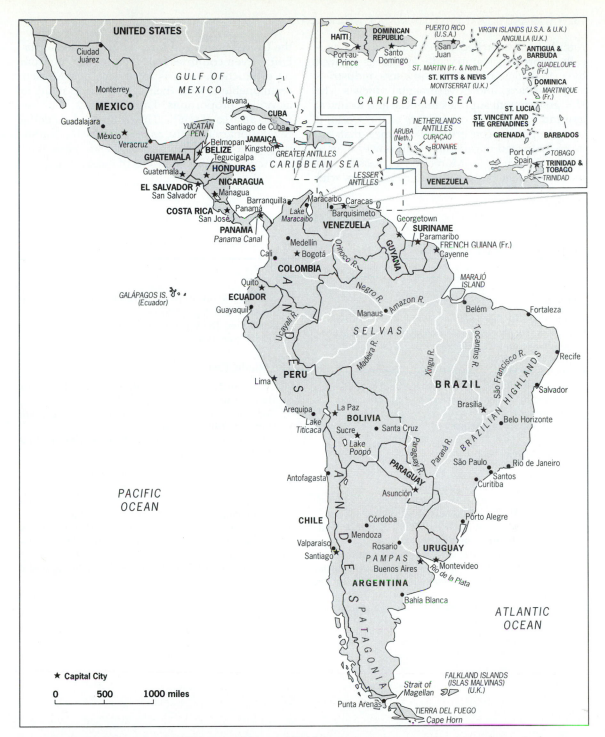

Map 58.4 LATIN AMERICA, 1993 With one of the world's highest population growth rates and seemingly unbridgeable gaps between the rich few and the poor masses, Latin America has become an area of great political, economic, and social instability. This instability has drawn the Western powers, particularly the United States, into Latin American affairs.

rounded by wretched hovels and an economically depressed countryside. Wealth is enjoyed by a small class of large landowners, industrialists, financiers, and governmental officials. The U.S. government supplies financial and technical assistance, but as in other parts of the world, it often supports conservative regimes that are more interested in retaining their power than in aiding their people. Moreover, a massive and mounting debt burden threatens relations with the United States and international financial stability. Even countries bolstered by income from oil production, such as Venezuela and Mexico, seem unable to keep their debts from growing to alarming proportions. Latin America thus remains an area of political instability and potential revolutionary activity, as revealed by the continuing guerrilla activity, coups d'état, mass demonstrations, and revolutions of recent years.

SUGGESTED READING

General

R. von Albertini, *Decolonization* (1971). A good survey.

C. E. Black, *The Dynamics of Modernization: A Study in Comparative History* (1966). Spans the Western and non-Western worlds.

R. Critchfield, *Villages* (1980). Focuses on rural life in non-Western nations.

T. Von Laue, *The World Revolution of Modernization: The Twentieth Century in Global Perspective* (1987). Good on the impact of modernization.

Asia and Africa

F. Ansprenger, *The Dissolution of the Colonial Empires* (1989). A full historical analysis.

W. Brown, *The United States and India, Pakistan, and Bangladesh* (1972). An excellent brief survey.

F. Butterfield, *China, Alive in the Bitter Sea* (1982). Well-written observations by a journalist.

P. Caputo, *A Rumor of War* (1977). Fine book on the Vietnam War, by a Marine officer who served in Vietnam.

C. Fitzgerald, *The Birth of Communist China*. By a leading expert.

I. K. Y. Hsu, *China Without Mao: The Search for a New Order* (1982). A highly respected work.

A. Mazrui and M. Tidy, *Nationalism and New States in Africa* (1984). A good survey.

E. Reischauer, *The Japanese* (1977). A brilliant and highly readable analysis.

The Middle East

A. Goldschmidt, Jr., *A Concise History of the Middle East* (1987). A useful overview.

W. Polk, *The Elusive Peace: The Middle East in the Twentieth Century* (1980). A fine survey.

J. Voll, *Islam: Continuity and Change in the Modern World* (1982). A brief survey.

Latin America

D. Collier, ed., *The New Authoritarianism in Latin America* (1979). Points to political problems in Latin America.

W. La Faber, *Inevitable Revolutions: The United States in Central America* (1984). A good background to this tension-filled area.

R. J. Shafer, *A History of Latin America* (1978). A useful survey.

CHAPTER 59
The Collapse of Communism and New Realities

Historians rely on time to gain a historical perspective on events. Therefore, it is difficult to evaluate the importance of very recent events. Nevertheless, it appears that three developments over the past few years mark an end of an era stretching back to World War II or even World War I and the beginning of a new period. The first of these is the collapse of communism in the Soviet Union and Eastern Europe. The second is a series of steps that have changed international relations and the positions of the principal powers in the West, most notably the movement toward economic integration in Western Europe, the growing power of the newly unified Germany, and the changing position of the United States. The third is the increasing economic strength of areas rimming the Pacific Ocean, particularly in East Asia.

All of these developments have roots going back into the 1970s if not earlier, but it was after the mid-1980s that these developments appeared or acquired new significance. As a beginning date, 1985 might be chosen, for it marked the coming to power of reformers led by Mikhail Gorbachev in the Soviet Union; or 1989, when the nations of Eastern Europe broke from their Soviet ties and communism; or 1991, when the Soviet Union itself fell apart.

1. THE COLLAPSE OF COMMUNISM

Certainly the collapse of communism in the years between 1985 and 1991 is the most dramatic and far-reaching development of recent years, for it marks an end to the Cold War era, which began just after World War II, and to Soviet communism, which stretches back to World War I. In this sense, the collapse of communism may signal the end of the twentieth century as a historical period and the beginning of the twenty-first century.

Origins

Long-term economic problems underlay the collapse of communism in the Soviet Union and Eastern Europe. The Soviet Union and Eastern Europe experienced economic growth in the years after World War II and enjoyed relative prosperity during the 1960s. But it may be that the Soviet brand of state socialism was effective only for initial industrialization, such as the creation of large textile and steel factories, and for certain focused projects, such as the construction of large dams, military hardware, or manned rockets. It was not well adapted to the more complex, rapidly changing, technologically sophisticated economy of the 1970s and 1980s.

During the 1970s, central planning and collectivization, the hallmarks of the Soviet economic system, caused growing problems. Central planning created a large bureaucracy that discouraged economic efficiency and reduced productivity. Planners ordered factories to produce goods that did not meet more rapidly changing producers' or consumers' demands. Plant managers were often unable to get needed materials or labor without long delays while distant officials made decisions. Workers had guaranteed employment and few incentives, which encouraged poor work, low productivity, and absenteeism. Similar problems arose in agriculture, where collectivization discouraged effective decision making, hard work, and productivity. The rates of economic growth were declining, the Soviet Union had to import grain from the capitalist West (in part due to unusually poor weather conditions), and there was a growing sense that the Soviet economy would not catch up with the more rapidly moving economies of the West.

By the 1980s, the Soviet economy was characterized by more and more inefficiency, the decline of old industries and factories built decades earlier, an inability to incorporate new technological innovations into production rapidly, labor imbalances, the production of low-quality goods, and shortages of food, raw materials, and consumer goods. Workers had money but not the selection or quality of goods they wanted and knew were available in the West. Well-educated urban professionals, managers, and technicians—wealthier and by then constituting some 20 to 25 percent of the population—were experiencing similar frustrations with the economy. Commonly, the only way to get many desired goods was through the expensive and illegal black market—which was of growing importance—or through corruption. It was increasingly apparent that only a small elite, mostly made up of Communist party and government officials, had real access to desired goods and services. It was this elite, which clung to its power and privilege, that enjoyed the higher standard of living available to the middle and upper classes in the West.

Three developments occurring during the decade between 1975 and 1985 exacerbated these fundamental economic problems undermining Soviet communism. The first was the decline of the Soviet leadership. After 1975 Brezhnev weakened noticeably and was probably often ill in the seven years before his death in 1982. Most of the Soviet leadership was made up of old men in long-established offices; the immediate successors to Brezhnev, Yuri Andropov (1982–1984) and Konstantin Chernenko (1984–1985), died shortly after assuming office. These leaders were reluctant to alter course or make way for a new generation of leaders who might try out new ideas to meet the problems that were undermining the Communist economy.

The second was the spread of modern communications and the growing dissident movement within the Soviet Union. Everything from television to tourism was making censorship more difficult and allowing images of life in the wealthier West to spread in Soviet society. Computers and photocopiers further facilitated the spread of uncontrolled information in the Soviet Union and aided the growing dissident movement, whose most notable leader was the Nobel Prize–winning physicist Andrei Sakharov (1921–1989). It was becoming more difficult to hide the economic as well as the political and human rights problems of the Soviet Union.

The third was the Soviet invasion of Afghanistan in 1979, which turned into a costly military quagmire. The Soviet economy was already burdened by large annual expenditures for the military, in part associated with the Cold War arms race (which the United States under Reagan in the 1980s vigorously pursued) and with the Brezhnev doctrine of willingness to intervene when nations threatened to drop out of the Communist fold. The conflict in Afghanistan stretched on for years, putting new strains on the Soviet economy and increasing the unpopularity of the Soviet leadership, which was unable or unwilling to extract itself from this widely condemned war.

Gorbachev and New Leadership: *Perestroika, Glasnost,* and Disarmament

From a peasant background, Mikhail Gorbachev (1931–) received a strong university education and rose rapidly through the Communist party ranks. In 1985, Gorbachev, at the relatively young age of 54, was appointed leader of the Soviet Union. He reflected the views of reformers within and outside the party who had recognized the fundamental economic problems plaguing the Soviet Union and who were willing to initiate change. Over the next few years he embarked on a three-pronged policy of reform in hopes of transforming the Soviet economy and bringing it up to the standard of Western capitalist economies: *perestroika, glasnost,* and disarmament.

Perestroika constituted Gorbachev's policy for fundamental economic reform. The goal of *perestroika* was to decentralize planning, to allow prices to be influenced by market forces rather than be set by the government, and to remove some of the control over land and agricultural practices exercised by large state farms and place it into the hands of families and cooperatives. In short, *perestroika* constituted a transition to a mixed socialist-capitalist economy, with both socialist planning and a capitalist free market. The process would take time and would be painful, for in the short run it would cause further shortages of consumer goods, inflation of prices, and unemployment. In part to get the strength and resources to carry out *perestroika*, Gorbachev embarked on the policies of *glasnost* and arms reduction.

Glasnost curtailed censorship, encouraged more open discussion of everything from culture to politics, and opened the doors to democratization of the Communist party and the Soviet political system. Dissidents such as Andrei Sakharov were freed. Governmental proceedings were made more public, even televised. In the spring of 1989 the first open elections since 1917 were held, resulting in the defeat of numerous Communist dignitaries. As a logical extension of *glasnost*, Gorbachev indicated that the Brezhnev doctrine of intervention in Eastern Europe, where there were renewed demands for change, had ended. Gorbachev hoped the policies of *glasnost* would elevate his prestige internationally, win foreign political and financial support, and provide cultural and political acceptance at home for his bold restructuring of the Soviet economy.

In 1985 Gorbachev initiated a series of steps to limit and reduce the Soviet military forces. He recognized that the arms race with the United States and the war in Afghanistan were great burdens on the already strained Soviet economy. In meetings with U.S. presidents almost every year between 1985 and 1991, Gorbachev pushed for more and more dramatic arms reductions. These meetings resulted in agreements for important reductions in nuclear weapons and conventional forces in the Soviet Union, the United States, and Europe. At the same time, Gorbachev pursued policies to extract Soviet forces from the war in Afghanistan. These efforts were completed in 1989, when the Soviet Union withdrew its last troops. These dramatic acts elevated Gorbachev's stature both abroad and at home and promised to lighten the burden of military expenditures.

By 1989 the policies of *glasnost* and arms reduction were well under way. However, *perestroika* was proving more difficult and creating much resistance. Only halting steps were made toward fundamental restructuring of the Soviet economy. At this point, events in Eastern Europe took a dramatic turn.

Revolution in Eastern Europe

In 1989 the Communist regimes of Eastern Europe fell one after another. In a series of mostly "velvet," or nonviolent, revolutions, the Eastern European nations cut the ties binding them to the Soviet Union, enacted democratic political reforms, and introduced capitalism into their economies (see Map 59.1). These revolutions had roots in the past but in the short run were made possible by the example of the reforms being instituted by Gorbachev in the USSR and his stated willingness to let events in Eastern Europe unfold without fear of Soviet intervention.

Poland led the movement early in 1989 when negotiations between Communist leader Wojciech Jaruzelski and the outlawed opposition union Solidarity resulted in the legalization of Solidarity and, in June, elections. Solidarity's stunning victory caused Jaruzelski to ask Solidarity to form a new government. By the end of the year Jaruzelski had stepped down, and new elections were called for. Communist rule in Poland was over.

Hungary and Czechoslovakia quickly followed. In the summer and fall of 1989 Hungary, which already had a more mixed economy than the Soviet Union and had experienced some hints of reform in 1988, called for elections, established a multiparty political system, and initiated economic reforms to open the country to private enterprise. By the end of 1989 Hungary's Communist party had reorganized itself into the Hungarian Socialist party. Czechoslovakia was hit with nationwide demonstrations for political reform in the fall of 1989. These soon resulted in the resignation of the hard-line Communist government and the rise to power of Vaclav Havel, a playwright who had recently been imprisoned for his views, and Alexander Dubček, the leader who had tried to liberalize Czechoslovakia in 1968.

The Communist regime in East Germany was the most powerful in Eastern Europe. In the fall of 1989 antigovernment demonstrations spread in East Germany. The hard-line Communist leader Erich Honecker was soon ousted from office. East Germans were increasingly able to cross borders to the West. Finally, in November 1989, the Berlin Wall, erected in 1948 and the most powerful symbol of the Cold War, was torn down and the border to West Germany was opened (see Figure 59.1). In a few months the Communists were ousted from power, and within a year East and West Germany were reunified.

The old Communist regimes in the rest of Eastern Europe were also soon toppled. In Bulgaria an internal coup deposed the Stalinist ruler, Todor Zivkov. In Rumania, the relatively independent but dictatorial Communist leader Nicolae Ceaușescu was overthrown in the most violent of the Eastern Europe revolutions. The follwing year witnessed the collapse of Albania's independent but highly Stalinist regime.

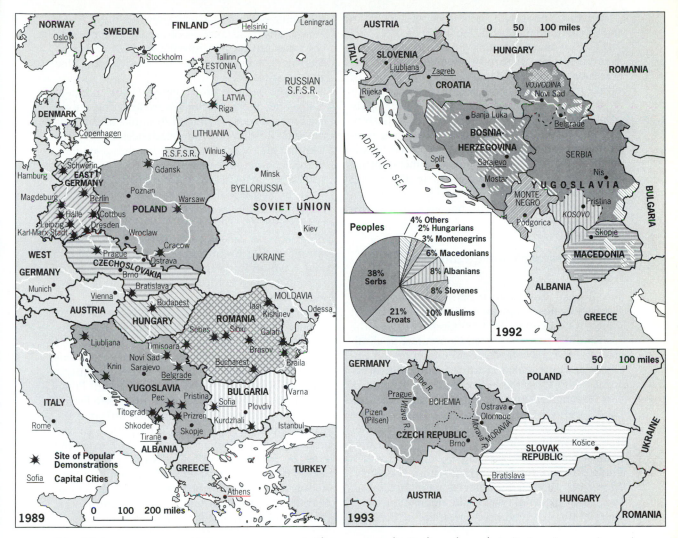

Map 59.1 UPHEAVAL IN EASTERN EUROPE SINCE 1989 These maps indicate the upheavals in Eastern Europe since 1989. The first shows the sites of popular demonstrations during 1989, which led to the fall of communist regimes there. The next two reveal continuing problems with ethnic and religious divisions in the region causing Yugoslavia to disintegrate and Czechoslovakia to divide.

Finally Yugoslavia, long independent from the Soviet Union, was falling apart. In 1991 and 1992, Slovenia, Croatia, Bosnia-Herzegovina, and Macedonia declared their independence as what was once Yugoslavia sank into the chaos of ethnic and religious civil war (see Map 59.1).

In less than a year the old Communist regimes had been removed from power in Eastern Europe, generally being replaced by new governments supporting independence, democratic institutions, and fundamental economic reforms. These events had repercussions in the Soviet Union, where developments were moving beyond the control of Gorbachev and the reformers.

The Collapse and Disintegration of the Soviet Union

In a logical extension of his policy of *glasnost*, Gorbachev pushed through political reforms that called for elections. In 1990 Gorbachev got the Communist party's Central Committee to eliminate the party's constitutional monopoly on political power. He also instituted new political reforms calling for more elections and creating a new, strong presidency—an office separate from the Communist party hierarchy. These policies had the effect of democratizing Soviet politics and undermining the political power of the Communist party. They also had the effect of weakening support for Gorbachev within the party. Moreover, these same policies were facilitating the rise of his chief rival in the opposition, Boris Yeltsin, the newly elected president of the Russian Republic.

Meanwhile, Gorbachev was making only halting steps in his effort to restructure the Soviet economy—*perestroika*. Plans were announced to move the economy away from central planning and then delayed or withdrawn, perhaps in anticipation of the difficulties (unemployment, inflation, and dislocation) the transition would cause. Some steps were taken, but these steps were often theoretical and difficult to put into practice. Uncertainty grew as economic decision makers and the populace did not know what to expect. The reformers, who wanted to move faster, grew frustrated, and the old Communist guard grew more and more alienated. As the economic pain grew, Gorbachev's popularity declined, and resistance—both from Communists who thought he was moving too fast and from reformers who thought he was moving too slowly—grew.

At the same time movements for independence and ethnic tensions were growing within the Soviet Union. Estonia, Lithuania, and Latvia pressed Moscow for independence. In 1991 the Ukraine also voiced a desire for independence. Ethnic conflict and nationalistic demands were spreading in Armenia, Azerbaijan, Moldavia, Georgia, and elsewhere. Gorbachev resisted the demands for independence and tried to quell the ethnic conflicts, but he was losing control of the situation. As a compromise solution, in the spring of 1991 he proposed a "treaty of union," which would have granted independence to the republics while holding them together as a confederation.

In August 1991, as the treaty of union was about to take effect, Communist hard-liners from inside the government and the KGB seized power from Gorbachev. Within three days this coup failed, thanks to the hard-liners' ineptitude and the opposition marshaled by Russian President Boris Yeltsin and his supporters (see Figure 59.2). Gorbachev and Yeltsin then stripped the Communist party of much of its power. By the end of the year, Gorbachev resigned, much of the former Soviet Union was reorganized into a loose confederation called the Commonwealth of Independent States, and several chunks of the former Soviet Union had acquired complete or partial independence (see Map 59.2).

Summary: Collapse and Conflict

In 1985, Mikhail Gorbachev came to power in the Soviet Union. Attempting to deal with growing problems that his predecessors refused to acknowledge, he and the reformers who supported him pursued the risky policies of *perestroika, glasnost,* and arms reductions. The course of history in the Soviet Union, Eastern Europe, and the West changed. In 1989 most of the Communist regimes of Eastern Europe fell, ties to the Soviet Union were severed, and political and economic reforms were initiated. Soviet support for Marxist regimes in the rest of the world was also end-

FIGURE 59.2 Mikhail S. Gorbachev and Boris Yeltsin were the two central figures in the collapse of Communism in the Soviet Union. Here Gorbachev is interrupted by Yeltsin while speaking before the Russian parliament just after the failed August 1991 coup. (Agence France-Presse)

ing. In 1991 the Communist party fell from power in the Soviet Union and the union itself fell apart.

The years after 1991 indicate that this period remains one of transition, with the results still unclear. In the former Soviet Union, Boris Yeltsin retains a very precarious hold on power as President of Russia, but his efforts at reform have been met with resistance and few positive results. Nationalistic, ethnic, religious, and cultural conflict rage in several republics of the former Soviet Union. Disappointment and pessimism probably outweigh relief and optimism for most people. There are signs that things are likely to get even worse before they get better. In Eastern Europe, the economic transition is going at varying rates—more quickly in Poland and Hungary, more slowly in Bulgaria, Rumania, and Albania—but almost everywhere painfully and with still-disappointed expectations. In some areas nationalistic, ethnic, and religious rivalries have created divisions, most dramatically in Yugoslavia, where civil wars have marked the collapse of that country, more peacefully in Czechoslovakia, which reluctantly agreed to divide itself into the Czech Republic and Slovakia.

Finally, it should be stressed that a few nations in the world remain Communist, though they are now more isolated and their commitment to communism seems more fragile. Moreover, while the collapse of communism has weakened Communist beliefs and movements in Europe and elsewhere, the Soviet model of communism should not be confused with the socialist policies adopted quite successfully in the Scandinavian nations in particular and many Western nations in general. While many analysts herald events in this period as the triumph of capitalism, others argue that in the long run the collapse of Soviet communism could facilitate the adoption of moderate policies associated with democratic socialism.

2. INTEGRATION, THE RISE OF GERMANY, AND CONSERVATISM IN EUROPE

During the late 1980s and early 1990s, Europe's international system was being restructured by new impulses toward integration. European integration took root in the late 1950s, when six

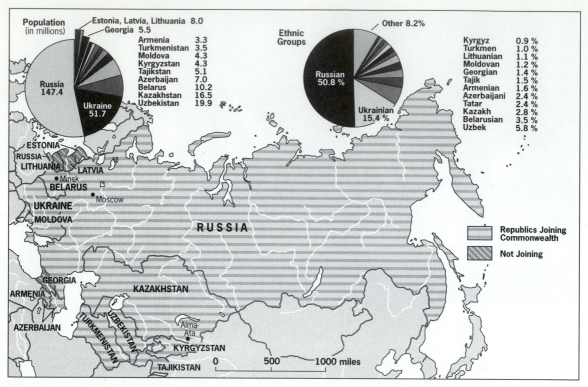

Map 59.2 THE NEW COMMONWEALTH In 1991 the Soviet Union dissolved. Most of the republics within that union joined the new Commonwealth of Independent States, a loose confederation, while some republics, such as Lithuania, Latvia, and Estonia, broke away.

Western European nations established the European Economic Community (Common Market). In slow, uneven steps, the European Community grew during the 1960s and 1970s (see pp. 717–718).

During the 1980s and early 1990s, new steps were taken to broaden and deepen its importance. In 1981 a European Parliament at Strasbourg was elected; while not yet politically strong, it was a significant step that signaled the possibility of greater political and military integration. In 1986 Portugal and Spain joined the European Community. In 1990 the former East Germany, thanks to its unification with West Germany, became part of the community. In 1992 the twelve members of the European Community eliminated all major internal barriers to trade, the flow of capital, and the movement of people. That same year the European Community agreed with the seven-member European Free Trade Association to form the European Economic Area, creating the world's largest trading bloc and paving the way for several new countries to seek full membership. A number of Eastern European nations are also anxious to join. Also in 1992, France and Germany agreed to form a joint army corps, the European Corps, open to other members of the Western European Union. With the Maastricht Treaty, the European Community made plans to establish a common currency and a central bank by 1999. However, growing opposition to the Maastricht Treaty casts doubt on whether those plans will be carried out.

The potential of the European Community is tremendous. The present twelve members have more than 340 million inhabitants and a combined gross national product approximately

equal to that of the United States. Its people are relatively wealthy and enjoy free access to an immense single market. Despite some strong resistance to further integration and disagreement on common policies such as what to do about the conflicts in Yugoslavia, there are signs that a more collective European identity is forming and that the European Community may be willing to start acting in common both politically and militarily.

Two other trends of considerable importance arose in Europe during the late 1980s and early 1990s. The first was the new importance of Germany. During the decades after World War II West Germany successfully rebuilt its economy to the point where it enjoyed even greater prosperity than the other large states of Europe such as France, Great Britain, and Italy. With communism collapsing in the late 1980s and early 1990s, Germany acted early, sending far more aid and investing far more extensively in Eastern Europe and the former Soviet Union than any other nation did. These costly efforts may bear the fruits of new economic and political influence in the future. Meanwhile, German unification in 1990 gave Germany new recognition as a European power and confirmed Germany as a world economic leader—first in exports, second in favorable balance of trade, and third in gross domestic product. West German Chancellor Helmut Kohl and his conservative Christian Democrats emerged victorious from reunified Germany's first national elections.

This victory of the conservative Christian Democrats in Germany was part of the second trend sweeping most of Europe since the mid-1980s: a general political shift toward the right. The traditional strength of Communist parties in Western Europe was waning, and socialists were being converted, at least in part, to capitalism. In general, political parties of the Left, whether in power as they were in France under François Mitterrand and Spain under Felipe González Marquez or not, were moderating their policies. Nationalized industries were being privatized—sold to private investors—under the conservatives in Great Britain and the socialists in France. Economic planning and state regulation of economic affairs were broadly under attack. The cost of social programs was being questioned. Even the Scandinavian nations, long the bastions of social democracy, were taking steps toward the right.

It is too early to tell if this trend toward the right will be fundamental and lasting or whether it is part of a cycle of swings between Left and Right that has been going on since World War II. However, when coupled with the fall of communism and the political conservatism of the United States, this trend seems to take on an added significance for the future.

3. THE UNITED STATES: MILITARY ASCENDANCY AND ECONOMIC PROBLEMS

The collapse of communism and disturbing economic trends left the United States in a mixed and unfamiliar position in the late 1980s and early 1990s.

With the former Soviet forces in decline and the dissolution of the Warsaw Pact in 1991, the United States emerged as the world's only military superpower. Some of that military dominance was demonstrated when, in 1991, the United States led a United Nations–authorized coalition to repel Iraq's invasion of Kuwait. In a six-week war the U.S.-dominated coalition was easily victorious.

At almost the same time, there were more indications that the United States, while still wealthy and with the world's largest gross domestic product, was a declining economic power. By the mid-1980s, years of budget deficits, in part fueled by high military spending and tax cuts, created a massive, growing national debt. In 1985 the United States, long a creditor nation, became the world's largest debtor nation, and almost every year since 1985 the debt has grown at an increasing rate. Meanwhile, the United States has been suffering in the economic competition with its Asian and European rivals. Large trade imbalances and major losses in manufacturing to overseas competitors have become common. One response to this economic competition, particularly in light of the European Community's moves to create a single European market, has been the effort to create a free trade zone among Mexico, the United States, and Canada—the North American Free Trade Agreement.

Debate has grown in the United States over

the significance of the convergence of military dominance and relative economic decline. Some argue that there is no longer a need for such costly military expenditures and that money saved from military expenditures should be used for domestic programs or to lower the public debt. Others worry that the United States will be more tempted to use military might to disguise economic problems or pursue economic goals; they point to the role that U.S. interests in Middle East oil played in the U.S.-led war with Iraq.

4. THE PACIFIC RIM, JAPAN, AND CHINA

The recent steps toward economic integration in Europe and the economic problems experienced by the United States are related to economic developments in the lands along the rim of the Pacific Ocean, particularly in East Asia.

Countries enjoying relative political stability, offering cheap and disciplined labor, and open to capitalism—such as Hong Kong, Taiwan, South Korea, and Singapore—have attracted investment (particularly from large multinational corporations) and experienced strong economic growth. Over the last decade these countries have competed successfully with the United States and Europe, particularly in electronics, textiles, plastics, and heavy manufacturing.

Japan has enjoyed economic leadership in Asia for decades (see pp. 736–737) and has become more of a world economic power. Year after year this relatively small country has led the world in enjoying a large favorable balance of trade and now has the world's second largest gross domestic product. By the mid-1980s Japan was a world leader in automobile production and electronics. The country has made numerous foreign investments and become a major worldwide creditor, in recent years acquiring a dominant position in international banking. It has a growing opportunity to translate that economic position into political power.

China has had a great economic potential for a long time. By the mid-1980s the new economic policies initiated by Deng Xiaoping in 1978 (see p. 739) that relaxed state controls over the economy were bearing fruit. Trade agreements with Japan and the United States increased foreign investment in China and rapidly expanded trade. By the mid-1980s Chinese farmers were producing a surplus of food for export. In certain areas of the country, particularly the "New Economic Zones" in the southeast, new capitalistic investments and manufacturing created large growth rates. As opposed to the Soviet Union, China's economic reforms were made without corresponding political reforms. China attempted to embrace capitalism while retaining its Communist political structure. Whether that can continue was called into question in 1989, when massive demonstrations, organized by students and intellectuals and calling for political reform, were held in Beijing. Supported by China's rural population and most of the army, the government used violence to end the demonstrations. Nevertheless, many analysts expect change in the upcoming years as China's leadership ages and new pressures for political reform increase.

These developments in East Asia challenge some of the economic dominance enjoyed by the West for so long. They are another sign that the West has become deeply tied to other areas of the world and that we need to view recent history from a global as well as a Western perspective.

5. PROBLEMS OF THE PRESENT AND FUTURE

Along with the hopes engendered by the collapse of communism, the promises of integration in Europe, and the realities of economic growth in East Asia, there are several growing and persisting problems in Western civilization.

In the wake of communism's collapse, division and ethnic conflict have arisen in several areas of Eastern Europe and the former Soviet Union. The most costly armed conflict in Europe since World War II broke out in Yugoslavia in the early 1990s. Continued conflict in the Middle East, where Europeans and Americans have important interests, again drew Western forces into combat. Though the threat that the Cold War would turn into a world war has diminished, the large-scale arms trade continues and the worldwide spread of nuclear weapons remains out of control.

Experience in the 1970s, 1980s, and again in the 1990s shows us that economic growth cannot be taken for granted. Unemployment, inflation,

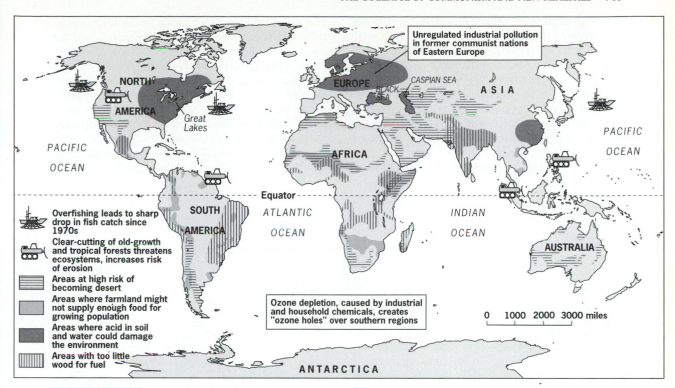

Map 59.3 GLOBAL ENVIRONMENTAL PROBLEMS This map indicates some widespread environmental problems, most of which stem from population increases, industrial production, and exploitation of natural resources. Other problems could be added to this list, such as the emissions of "greenhouse gases" by industry believed to be causing a rise in global temperature, with uncertain consequences for coastal areas, agriculture, and wildlife, and the depletion of species as thousands of plant and animal species become extinct each year. While this map reveals how some areas of the world are affected more than others, it also shows how global and interconnected these environmental problems are.

and declining personal incomes have created social discontent that governments seem impotent to master. Moreover, the price we pay for economic growth and modernization seems to have been rising in recent years. Industrialization, urbanization, and affluence have strained our natural resources (see Map 59.3). Our air, our fresh water, even our seas are becoming more polluted. Depletion of the protective ozone layer and a heating up of the atmosphere, hastened by deforestation, threaten us. Our land is becoming blighted by concrete, tasteless commercial development, and poisonous wastes. Our cities have become sources of poverty, crime, and drug addiction as much as wealth and hope. The relentless march of technology, with its accompanying urbanization, has brought many creature comforts to the masses, but it has robbed millions of their manual skills, social contacts, and sense of community. Government has expanded the social services it provides, but that has not created a greater sense of inclusion in modern society; rather, a sense of alienation seems to persist and new conflicts arise as immigrants, minorities, and women assert themselves. Science and government, so successful in creating new military weapons and certain large projects such as space exploration, have been unable to halt the deadly worldwide AIDS epidemic.

There is a growing awareness that the relatively affluent West cannot ignore the non-Western areas of the world—some in East Asia with a new competitive edge, far more with crushing debts, pressing needs, and unmet demands. Indeed, the gap between the affluent, industrialized nations of the north and the poor, developing nations of the south has been growing rather than narrowing. Worse, it is in the south that the burden of population growth is by far the heaviest.

All these problems now weigh upon the West and are not likely to go away in the foreseeable future. In some ways Western civilization and its institutions, which have been so long in developing—the family, governments, courts of law, churches, traditions of social and moral behavior—are being severely tested. While problems of the present usually seem more difficult than those of the past, the consequences of not dealing with today's problems are likely to be catastrophic. Whether and how Western civilization handles these challenges remains to be seen.

SUGGESTED READING

The Collapse of Communism

T. G. Ash, *The Magic Lantern: The Revolution of '89 Witnessed in Warsaw, Budapest, Berlin and Prague* (1990). A fine account of events by a knowledgeable observer.

J. F. Brown, *Surge to Freedom: The End of Communist Rule in Eastern Europe* (1991). A useful summary.

R. Dahrendorf, *Reflections on the Revolution in Europe* (1991). A careful analysis of political and economic prospects in Eastern Europe.

G. Hosking, *The Awakening of the Soviet Union* (1990). Focuses on the social changes underlying reform in the Soviet Union.

R. J. Kaiser, *Why Gorbachev Happened: His Triumphs and His Failures* (1991). Stresses the difficulties facing Gorbachev.

B. Nahaylo and V. Swoboda, *Soviet Disunion: A History of the Nationalities Problem in the USSR* (1990). Reveals the problems facing Gorbachev and the republics of the former Soviet Union.

Integration, Germany, and European Politics

N. Colchester and D. Buchan, *Europower: The Essential Guide to Europe's Economic Transformation in 1992* (1990). Historical analysis of and speculations on the future of the European Community.

J. W. Friend, *Seven Years in France: François Mitterrand and the Unintended Revolution, 1981–1988* (1989). Emphasizes how adaptable Mitterrand and the French Socialists have been.

P. Jenkins, *Mrs. Thatcher's Revolution: The Ending of a Socialist Era* (1988). A study of Europe's leading conservative politician.

D. Marsh, *The Germans: Rich, Bothered and Divided* (1990). A good recent analysis prior to unification.

The United States

David Halberstam, *The Next Century* (1991). A well-written analysis and speculations.

P. Kennedy, *The Rise and Fall of the Great Powers: Economic Change and Military Conflict from 1500 to 2000* (1987). Sections focus on connections between economic and military power in the United States.

J. R. Schlesinger, *America at Century's End* (1989). A good recent analysis.

The Pacific Rim, Japan, and China

D. Aikman, *Pacific Rim: Area of Change, Area of Opportunity* (1986). Emphasizes the significance of economic changes.

D. W. W. Chang, *China under Deng Xiaoping: Political and Economic Reform* (1991). An optimistic analysis.

M. Fathers and A. Higgins, *Tiananmen: The Rape of Peking* (1990). A study of the Democracy Movement and demonstrations in Beijing in 1989.

C. V. Prestowitz, Jr., *Trading Places: How We Allowed Japan to Take the Lead* (1988). Analyzes Japan's economic challenge to the United States.

Problems of the Present and Future

D. B. King, *The Crisis of Our Time: Reflections on the Course of Western Civilization, Past, Present, and Future* (1988). An interesting, speculative account.

State of the World. A Worldwatch Institute Report on Progress Toward a Sustainable Society (1984 to present). An annual report emphasizing environmental conditions.

RETROSPECT

A long period of relative peace, growing prosperity, and sense of progress ended in August 1914. World War I initiated a three-decade period in which Europe would be shattered politically, economically, and socially by war, revolution, and depression.

The European nations were plunged into World War I by an entangling alliance system that enhanced economic and nationalistic rivalries and by persistent domestic tensions that encouraged national governments searching for unity to adopt belligerent policies. The hoped-for short war turned into a nightmarish struggle between the Central Powers and the Allies. The destruction went beyond the massive human and material toll to the political entities themselves. The German, Austro-Hungarian, Russian, and Ottoman empires did not survive the war. The British and French empires were both weakened, as indeed were Britain and France themselves. Efforts to make a durable peace and to set up an international organization, the League of Nations, to keep the peace foundered on the rocks of national self-interest. Instead, the peace settlements left a legacy of resentment that would haunt the West during the following two decades.

The victors in World War I were the liberal democratic nations, and it was hoped that this victory would be turned into a permanent gain for liberal democracy. The trend toward totalitarianism, fascism, and authoritarianism during the 1920s and 1930s dashed these hopes. The first blow to liberalism and capitalism came during the final stages of World War I, when revolution brought a Communist regime to power in Russia. Lenin led the revolutionary Bolsheviks to victory in November 1917 and over the next few years extracted the Soviet Union from World War I, defeated rivals in a bloody civil war, and established the foundations of a totalitarian state. By the end of the 1920s Lenin's successor, Stalin, had initiated the five-year plans that would collectivize Soviet agriculture and industrialize the nation. His Great Purges in the 1930s eliminated all resistance, completing the transformation of the Soviet Union into a totalitarian state.

The next blow to liberalism came with the rise of fascism in Italy under Mussolini during the early 1920s. Over the next few years Mussolini took steps to turn his Fascist regime into a totalitarian state, but these steps were always incomplete. Full-blown totalitarian fascism was established during the 1930s in Nazi Germany under Hitler. Much more than the Italian variety, German fascism was tinged with violence and racism. Both regimes denounced liberal democracy and, indeed, most of the developments since the French Revolution that Western liberals had pointed to with pride. With their emphasis on nationalism, militarism, and expansion, these Fascist regimes represented a direct threat to peace and the democratic West.

Two more blows to liberalism seriously undermined the position of the democratic West. The first was the rise of authoritarian regimes in southern Europe, eastern Europe, and Japan—almost all replacing governments that had more liberal leanings. The second was the Great Depression, which encouraged authoritarian movements everywhere and caused the Western democracies to turn inward. Thus, during the 1930s, when the threat from Fascist and authoritarian nations was growing, the Western democracies were increasingly paralyzed by their own domestic problems.

Neither the foundering League of Nations nor a policy of appeasement could restrain Germany, Italy, and Japan from pursuing their policies of expansion. In 1939 World War II broke out. For over two years the Axis powers seemed unstoppable, gaining victory after victory. By the end of 1942, however, overexpansion by the Axis forces, the stiff resistance by Soviet troops, the heroic struggle by the British, and the entrance of the United States into the war had started to turn the tide. Almost three years of struggle on a world-wide basis were necessary to end the war in 1945. By that time the Nazis had carried out a policy of genocide and enslavement as part of Hitler's racist "New Order," and war had claimed some 40 million lives.

At the end of World War II devastation and disorganization were the rule rather than the exception. Most nations of Europe were so weakened that they had to rely on one of the two new superpowers that had emerged from World War II: the United States and the Soviet Union. Soon, even the unity of the victorious allies, which included the United States and the Soviet Union, proved too fragile to last. Deep-seated discord between these respective leaders of the non-Communist and Communist worlds broke out into the Cold War. Europe became divided into two camps—one of democratic capitalism (though often with elements of socialism mixed in) led by the United States, the other of communism modeled and led by the Soviet Union. This division of Europe and the broader Cold War struggle would dominate international policies for decades to come. Yet, despite the destruction of World War II, the emergence of the dominating superpowers, and the disunity brought about by the Cold War, European nations recovered, expanded their economies, and enjoyed relative political stability during the following decades. Problems in the 1970s and 1980s did not diminish from that record; rather, they indicated that Western civilization had to face and deal with new and previoulsy ignored difficulties. One way that nations attempted to solve common problems was through regional integration and internationalism, but the results were mixed.

The most significant social, intellectual, and cultural changes in Western civilization during the twentieth century are more difficult to pinpoint than the concrete political and economic developments. For the most part, the social, intellectual, and cultural developments have been a continuation of trends already under way by the end of the nineteenth century. Western society became more urbanized as it adjusted to the demands of continuing economic modernization. Women changed their roles and their perception of themselves, a reflection of some of the changes occurring within the basic unit of Western society: the family. The Christian churches continued to have difficulty adjusting to a changing, secularizing, scientific world. Intellectual and cultural trends reflected the richness of Western life as well as the often discouraging problems encountered by the West since the end of the ninetenth century.

In the decades following World War II, France, England, Belgium, the Netherlands, and other Western nations lost most of their colonial empires. The new and old nations of the non-Western world struggled to get onto their feet and assert themselves in an environment marked by Cold War rivalries, deep-rooted internal discord, and the disruption caused by the incomplete spread of Western values and institutions to their lands. In different ways, Japan and China emerged as leading economic and political powers in the Far East. The struggle between Hindus and Moslems in India, Pakistan, and Bangladesh and the wars in Southeast Asia made the British and French (and, later, American) withdrawals from southern Asia problematic. The Middle East has been marked by a series of wars and disruptions as well as the emergence of a new power bloc based on wealth from oil production. The long-lasting lack of peace between Israel and most of its neighbors, violence in divided Lebanon, and the war between Iran and Iraq suggest that this area of the world will remain explosive for the foreseeable future. Africans face tremendous difficulties in creating unity in nations artificially created by colonial powers and burdened by harsh economic conditions. The political instability of most African nations attests to these difficulties. Most Latin American nations have for decades been dominated by a wealthy elite and often right-wing authoritarian governments (supported, and usually staffed, by the military). As the area's population grows, so does the contrast between the few haves and the mass of have-nots. Revolutions, guerrilla activities, and political upheavals indicate that stability may be the exception rather than the rule in Latin America.

In recent years, new developments have marked the end of a period that stretches back to World War II or even World War I and the beginning of what may be a new historical era. The most dramatic and significant change is the collapse of communism in the Soviet Union and Eastern Europe. The roots of the collapse stretch back to economic and political problems that were growing in the 1970s and 1980s. Trying to deal with these problems, Gorbachev initiated policies of *perestroika, glasnost,* and disarmament in the Soviet Union and gave the Eastern European nations more of a free hand in determining their own destinies. In 1989 revolutions toppled Communist regimes through Eastern Europe. By 1991 the Communists were also out of power in the Soviet Union, which itself disintegrated.

Less dramatic but important developments were occurring elsewhere. Europe was taking new, if halting, steps toward full economic integration and even some political and social integration. Germany, newly unified, was gaining strength and stature. The United States found itself in the position of being an uncontested mil-

itary superpower but facing more and increasingly successful economic competition. Much of that economic competition came from the East Asian nations along the Pacific Rim, to which economic development was shifting the world's economic balance of power.

At the same time, new and persistent social and environmental problems are facing the West and the world. These problems promise to test both our spirit and our abilities in disturbing ways.

INDEX

Note: Page numbers followed by the letter *f* or *m* indicate figures or maps, respectively.